THE OXFORD HANDBOOK OF

LAND POLITICS

THE OXFORD HANDBOOK OF

LAND POLITICS

Edited by

SATURNINO M. BORRAS JR.

and

JENNIFER C. FRANCO

OXFORD
UNIVERSITY PRESS

OXFORD
UNIVERSITY PRESS

Oxford University Press is a department of the University of Oxford.
It furthers the University's objective of excellence in research, scholarship,
and education by publishing worldwide. Oxford is a registered trade mark of
Oxford University Press in the UK and certain other countries.

Published in the United States of America by Oxford University Press
198 Madison Avenue, New York, NY 10016, United States of America.

Library of Congress Cataloging-in-Publication Data
Names: Borras Jr., Saturnino M., 1965– editor. | Franco, Jennifer C., 1947– editor.
Title: The Oxford handbook of land politics / [edited by] Saturnino M.
Borras Jr. and Jennifer C. Franco.
Other titles: Handbook of land politics
Description: New York, NY : Oxford University Press, [2025] |
Series: Oxford handbooks series | Includes bibliographical references and index. |
Identifiers: LCCN 2025006522 (print) | LCCN 2025006523 (ebook) |
ISBN 9780197618646 (hardback) | ISBN 9780197618653 (epub) |
ISBN 9780197618677 (online)
Subjects: LCSH: Land use—Political aspects. | Land use—Social aspects.
Classification: LCC HD1251 .O94 2025(print) | LCC HD1251 (ebook) |
DDC 333.73—dc23/eng/20250331
LC record available at https://lccn.loc.gov/2025006522
LC ebook record available at https://lccn.loc.gov/2025006523

ISBN 978–0–19–761864–6

DOI: 10.1093/oxfordhb/9780197618646.001.0001

Printed by Marquis Book Printing, Canada

MIX
Paper | Supporting responsible forestry
FSC® C103567
FSC www.fsc.org

Contents

Foreword

The Politics of Land

IAN SCOONES

LAND is central to contemporary debates about politics. Land sustains the livelihoods of millions through farming, livestock keeping, hunting, and collecting. Such livelihoods are intimately bound up with nature and the complex and diverse ecosystems that thrive on land. Land creates a sense of identity refracted through gender, race, class, and other axes of difference. Through diverse institutions and forms of authority, land connects citizens and states, corporations and capital, and is the locus of accumulation, extraction, and control. Access to land is thus contested, negotiated, and claimed through multiple, competing actors, linked to a myriad of struggles. Land, in other words, connects us all through its politics.

Across thirty-eight chapters, this extraordinary handbook offers an invaluable guide to these debates. There are diverse contributions coming from very different locations, backgrounds, and positions. The debates in these pages are located in the broad and inclusive field of critical agrarian studies, allowing for both the theoretical eclecticism shown in the opening chapters and a commitment to change offered in some of other contributions. The authors are a veritable who's who of this now expansive field, and the *Handbook* is edited by two of the leading lights—Jun Borras and Jenny Franco—who bring both intellectual rigor and practical experience founded in a scholar-activist tradition.

The editors suggest that there are many ways of reading the *Handbook*. It is long and there is lots of fascinating material, so take your time. It is not organized into any demarcated sections, although there are clear clusters, as the editors outline in their extended introduction (Borras and Franco). The introduction provides a route map to the rich contents, while offering new, synthetic interpretations and frameworks that allow any reader to make the most of the different chapters.

Diverse Theoretical Traditions

The opening chapters provide a taste of a whole array of theoretical traditions. Even if they refer to different literatures and use different terminologies, they all have connections, illuminating the diverse politics of land. These connections between theoretical frames often go unnoticed given the way academic debates are siloed, so collecting them in one place is a real service. Reading them together, you will get a sense of how a diverse, heterodox perspective emerges—yes, with contradictions and disconnects, but also suggesting very productive questions and new lines of thinking.

These chapters move from classic Marxist perspectives, which come in many forms (Bernstein), to World Systems theory (Ajl), to World Ecology (Patel), to Ecosocialism (Holleman), to Chayanovian perspectives on peasant politics (van der Ploeg), to post-structural/post-developmental theories (Gutierrez-Escobar), and to anarchist positions (Grubačić et al.). Other chapters, later in the book, bring in feminist perspectives (Ojeda), political ecology (Cavanagh and Benjaminsen), and more.

All have different angles, and so different implications for how land is seen and its politics constructed, but all add up to a firm belief that the politics of land is central to how we must understand and, in turn, act in our world. Celebrating the conceptual diversity and avoiding sectarian, doctrinaire, and introspective debates is a hallmark of the new brand of critical agrarian studies, drawing on the Marxist tradition but going beyond it in new and interesting ways. All readers will find fascinating insights in these chapters, and hopefully novel ways of connecting ideas and generating new questions.

The many chapters range from big-picture, longue durée historical perspectives to more micro, located studies on national or local dynamics. Moving across scales—of space and time—is another important characteristic of critical agrarian studies, generating the ability to connect the wider story with local action and practical change. So, for example, there is an excellent chapter on food regimes and so, by implication, land regimes (McMichael), where key moments in a longer history generate a temporarily stable relationship between states, capital, and diverse institutions. There are also macro-scale analyses of contemporary geopolitics (Dwyer), reflections on national development in the Cold War era (Kay), and analyses of land in conditions of conflict and violence (Grajales and Chauveau).

These wider perspectives in turn need to be read alongside more focused and located contributions around particular places and contexts, including sub-Saharan Africa (Peters) and China (Ye; Xu and Borras). Not getting constrained by scale-based analysis or sectoral foci but always moving between and across scales is an important feature of critical agrarian studies and a great strength of the *Handbook*. Having one foot on the ground, linked to immediate, local issues and a wider sense of the bigger story over time, is always essential for effective engagement.

Taking inspiration from the more classic theoretical traditions, a number of important contributions develop newer angles. The argument, elaborated at length in the introduction, that when thinking about land, we must go beyond a sole focus on production to think about the role land plays in social reproduction too is vital. This requires a focus on hidden labor and practices of care, which are often carried out by women and all connected to the land (Cousins). Equally, a concern with the wider ecological processes that sustain life and the environment, and climate more generally, means that the growing field of political ecology becomes core to an expanded field of critical agrarian studies. This requires attention to the politics of environmental management, conservation, and human–nature entanglements (Cavanagh and Benjaminsen), highlighting questions of agrarian and environmental justice (Martinez-Alier) and socioecological relations (Montefrio).

Land and Livelihoods

The connections between land and diverse, complex livelihoods in (mostly) rural settings is central to any study of land politics. The chapters emphasize that we must go beyond the classic vision of the rural smallholder, petty commodity producer, or subsistence peasant. Instead, rural people connected to the land combine different sources of livelihood. They are semi-proletarians who link farming with wage-work, migrants, part-time urbanites, traders, entrepreneurs, and so on. They are, in other words, diverse "classes of labor" or "working people," not just farmers (Franco and Borras). This means that a focus on mobility and migration (Otsuki and Zoomers) and connections to urban life (Jacobs) are essential, as well as wider considerations of labor relations in agrarian change (Chambati).

Within this fast-changing context, how land is used for production of course still remains significant. What form agricultural production takes is the concern of a number of chapters, highlighting the contrasts between the damaging effects of large-scale, intensive systems that are connected through global markets and transport networks across the world (Weis) and more place-based agroecological alternatives (Vandermeer and Perfecto). Questions of how production is organized, by whom, and in relation to what land resources result, in turn, in very different patterns of accumulation and differentiation, and thus the trajectory of livelihoods and the use and care of land in any place.

The politics of land access and control is a central theme running throughout the *Handbook*. With land as a site of contestation, contributions highlight how such struggles are refracted through questions of race (Mollet), ethnicity (Dang et al.; Moreda), and struggles around dispossession (Adnan). And access to land and resources is in turn deeply affected by the climate crisis, as the social relations around land shift under climate change (Ribot).

Land is, of course, implicated in wider circuits of capital and market relations, especially as processes of commodification and financialization occur apace. The financial and contractual dimensions of land and its use are thus emphasized in important chapters on financialization (Isakson) and contract farming (Amanor). Land relations are being further influenced by the expansion of digitalized control, allowing demarcation and registration, as well as appropriation and extraction (Fraser). All these processes define how livelihoods are played out in any given setting and, in the words of the introduction, the questions of "Who gets what land, how, how much, for how long, for what purposes, who doesn't get any, and who gets to decide?" (Borras and Franco).

Land and Authority

Land is central to much wider political processes and deeply implicated in forms of authority and control through a range of institutions, as many chapters confirm. Land is thus central to understanding how states are formed (Sud), societies are ordered, citizens are constructed, social movements are mobilized, and notions of property are defined and created (Ofstehage and Wolford).

Instead of the mechanistic, legalistic approaches to land that so dominate policy discourses around land "regularization," land tenure "security," and so on, there needs to be an appreciation that land relations are continuously in-the-making, with boundaries that are always negotiated and fuzzy. This means that conventional, fixed notions of "property" are inadequate, as are stable ideas of land units, such as delineated plots or farms. Land is constituted in a mosaic, with hybrid relations and no standard version of private, state, or even communal property systems (Borras and Franco). Land is not just a "thing" defined in law through formalized property rights; land relations emerge through an ongoing process of assemblage, which is always social and political (Ojeda).

And it is this process that constitutes land politics, as the powers to rule and to access land for livelihoods are relationally constructed through institutionalized patterns of land control (Lund). Very often, scientific discourses are deployed to define why certain types of land use and user are deemed acceptable, while others are not; and why certain areas are defined as "idle" or "wasteland" and others are demarcated for productive use or created as off-bounds for conservation. Thus, from the relationship between slave and plantation owner to colonial subject and settler state to forest dweller and a government agency implementing its climate commitments through carbon offset schemes, the way people, states, and land interact is governed by a particular politics that is always imbued with assumptions about the role of land and who should have rights over it.

Citizens may confront the formal, legalized definitions of land use through informal claims and improvised acts of possession and occupation, combined with pleas for recognition that emerge via attempts to make such claims visible to authorities through various means (Lund). A feminist perspective, in turn, upsets any conventional understanding of land as individualized (male-owned) property because the process of property-making is replete with gendered exclusions and masculine constructions (Ojeda). In this way, the "seduction of formalization," so prevalent in mainstream land policy, is challenged (Borras and Franco). As many chapters argue, we must see land as politics and politics as land, with struggles across both local and global spheres always centering on people, land, and territory.

Emerging Themes

What, then, are the new axes of debate, transforming our understandings of agrarian change and politics of land offered in the pages of the *Handbook*? There are many, but here I will highlight just four that struck me.

- First is the move from seeing land as only a site of production and accumulation, to also seeing it as a site of social reproduction and the locus of highly gendered social and cultural relations. This suggests a much more diverse land politics going beyond class to gender, race, identity, and so on. It, in turn, suggests a renewed focus on labor, with complex livelihoods generated from multiple sources beyond the fixed plot of land, through migration, trade, and so on. The classic categories of land-based classes centered only on production are thus unsettled as new forms of livelihood are created. As a result, the dynamics of differentiation and accumulation shift, and land politics change as a wider appreciation emerges of Henry Bernstein's classic questions of agrarian political economy—who owns what, who does what, who gets what, and what they do with it?
- Second, the centering of nature, environment, and climate in relation to land is a theme that resonates across many chapters. Humans and nature (and so, land) are inseparable yet have often become disconnected by the forces of capitalist modernity. The importance of reconnecting is central, requiring a new political ecology/economy of land. This has deep implications for how we see land, again not just as a demarcated plot but as part of a wider living landscape and territory within a broader planetary system. This highlights the crucial connection between land and the climate crisis. Changing land use, whether through deforestation, intensive agriculture, and the extraction of water or minerals is a major contributor to climate change. As the regimes of extraction evolve under new frontiers of capitalism, land is central. Such regimes of food, water, and energy are constituted through a contested politics, and as the imperative to switch from fossil fuel dependence and intensive, polluting systems of agriculture accelerates, new challenges emerge. In the rush to "net zero," for example, alternative energy, climate adaptation, and nature-based "solutions" are offered, yet all these have implications for who controls the land. For example, land grabs are increasingly justified in the name of green and climate "transitions," which, in turn, create new land-based politics across the world.
- Third, many chapters argue for going beyond a narrow, individualized approach to land rights, tenure security, and land governance. This managerial, administrative, and technocratic frame dominates policy thinking but is incompatible with the realities on the ground. As the introduction points out, such efforts to provide "security" for women, Indigenous peoples, and others can paradoxically lead to opportunities for dispossession as speculation, appropriation, and extraction increase in areas where "regularization" has generated legibility through demarcation and delimitation (Borras and Franco). Instead, there is a need to think about land as constituted through hybrid, mosaic forms of property relations, with property-making as a continuous, contested, and negotiated process. Land is always embedded in power relations, and so thinking about how authority over land is generated—through interactions between citizens, states, corporations, and other actors—can help us elaborate more appropriate democratic institutions for land control and a more innovative, grounded approach to "land governance."
- Finally, the *Handbook* points to the importance of understanding land as a "regime" situated in a wider historical political economy context. As the introduction

highlights, a land regime—just as a food regime—is stabilized, perhaps only tentatively and temporarily, by a set of political-economic forces that operate within a particular phase of capitalism. But regimes change due to the intersection of local struggles and wider political forces and interests (Borras and Franco). Today, these are influenced by new frontiers of extraction and accumulation, linked to globalized economic relations, changing food systems, and heightening climate-environment imperatives. Meanwhile, authoritarian, populist regimes define the nation in terms of the relationship between "the people" and their mother- or fatherland, always in ways that act to exclude some, while incorporating others in a populist politics of land and belonging. Until we understand this wider historically situated, structural context, the attempts to address the pressing challenges of land and its use at more local levels—whether through moves to agroecology or food sovereignty, for example—will remain elusive.

A Rich Resource

This is a rich, diverse, and deeply informed collection, mixing theoretical perspectives and grounded reflections. By going beyond a narrow Marxist canon to encompass a wide array of perspectives, it takes no particular line. The introduction encourages readers to find their own way, to read across conceptual framings and reflect on different dimensions—in other words, to generate a critical sensibility to agrarian studies and land politics. For any student of land or, indeed, politics more generally, as well as activists and practitioners grappling with the challenges of land politics, this *Handbook* is an enormously valuable and vital resource.

About the Volume Editors

Saturnino M. Borras Jr. is Professor of Agrarian Studies at the International Institute of Social Studies of Erasmus University Rotterdam (EUR). He is a member of the distinguished Erasmus Professor Program at EUR, Distinguished Professor at China Agricultural University in Beijing, and an associate of the Transnational Institute. He was Editor-in-Chief of the *Journal of Peasant Studies* for fifteen years, until 2023. He coordinates the international network Initiatives in Critical Agrarian Studies and is a coeditor of its Peasant Studies and Agrarian Change book series.

Jennifer C. Franco is a researcher at the Transnational Institute, especially in the Agrarian and Environmental Justice Program and the Myanmar-in-Focus Program. She is Adjunct Professor at the College of Humanities and Development Studies of China Agricultural University in Beijing. She does extensive work on land issues using a scholar-activist method both in her research and social justice advocacy work.

Foreword Contributor

Ian Scoones is a Professor at the Institute of Development Studies at the University of Sussex in the UK. Taking an interdisciplinary perspective to land, agriculture, and livelihoods, he has worked on issues of agrarian change over forty years, mostly in eastern and southern Africa, and helped found the Land Deal Politics Initiative in 2011. He was the Co-director of the ESRC STEPS Centre focusing on the politics of sustainability (steps-centre.org) and was principal investigator of the ERC Advanced Grant funded PASTRES project, which explored pastoralism and uncertainty across three continents (pastres.org). His most recent book is *Navigating Uncertainty: Radical Rethinking for a Turbulent World* (Polity Books, 2024) and his on-going work on land issues in Zimbabwe can be found in the blog, zimbabweland.wordpress.com.

Contributors

Shapan Adnan is a Visiting Professor at the London School of Economics and Political Science, based in the Department of Geography and Environment. Formerly, he was a Professorial Research Associate at the Department of Development Studies of the School of Oriental and African Studies, University of London, and a Visiting Research Fellow at the Contemporary South Asian Studies Programme of the University of Oxford. Adnan holds a PhD in social and political sciences from the University of Cambridge. He has taught at the National University of Singapore, the University of Dhaka, and the University of Chittagong. His teaching, research, and publications are in the fields of political economy, sociology, politics, and demography.

Max Ajl is a Senior Fellow at in the Department of Conflict and Development Studies at Ghent University and a researcher with the Tunisian Observatory for Food Sovereignty and the Environment. He is an editor at *Agrarian South* and *Journal of Labor and Society*, and has written for *Agrarian South*, *The Journal of Peasant Studies*, *Globalizations*, *Review of African Political Economy*, *Middle East Report*, and many other scholarly and popular journals. He researches climate politics, Tunisian national liberation, agrarian politics in the Arab region, and Arab intellectual history. He is the author of *A People's Green New Deal* (Pluto).

Kojo S. Amanor is a Research Professor at the Institute of African Studies, University of Ghana. His main research areas are in land relations, agricultural commercialization, the expansion of agribusiness and agribusiness relations, smallholder farming systems, natural resource management, and the history of development within Africa.

Lorenza Arango completed her PhD study at the International Institute of Social Studies of Erasmus University Rotterdam, Netherlands.

Moges Belay is a PhD researcher at the International Institute of Social Studies of Erasmus University Rotterdam, Netherlands, and a lecturer at Addis Ababa University in Ethiopia.

Tor A. Benjaminsen is a Human Geographer and Professor at the Norwegian University of Life Sciences, where he studies and teaches political ecology, in particular related to issues of climate justice, land-use conflicts, and pastoral development. He is a lead author of the Sixth Assessment Report of the IPCC and Associate Editor of *Political Geography*.

Zeynep Ceren Eren Benlisoy is an independent researcher based in Turkey. She was a postdoctoral research at the International Institute of Social Studies in The Hague in 2022–2023.

Henry Bernstein is Professor Emeritus of Development Studies at the School of Oriental and African Studies, University of London, and Adjunct Professor, China Agriculture University, Beijing. He was formerly editor, with T. J. Byres, of the *Journal of Peasant Studies*, and founding editor, again with Byres, of the *Journal of Agrarian Change*.

Connor Cavanagh is Associate Professor in the Department of Geography, University of Bergen, Norway. His current research examines trade-offs, inequalities, and unanticipated outcomes resulting from landscape-scale conservation and environmental change mitigation schemes. He is a lead author of the IPBES Nexus Assessment and a contributing author to the IPCC Sixth Assessment Report. Recent publications include articles in *Energy Research & Social Science*, *Annals of the American Association of Geographers*, *Political Geography*, and *The Journal of Peasant Studies*.

Walter Chambati is Executive Director, Sam Moyo African Institute for Agrarian Studies, Harare, Zimbabwe, and Research Fellow, College of Graduate Studies, University of South Africa. He obtained a PhD in Public Administration from University of South Africa. Earlier degrees, a BSc. (Hon) in Agriculture (Economics) and Master of Management were awarded by the Universities of Zimbabwe and Witwatersrand. His research mainly examines agrarian transformation in Africa. Recent publications include *Labour Questions in Global South* (Springer Press, 2021) and *Farming and Working under Contract: Peasants and Workers in Global Agricultural Value Systems* (Tulika Press, 2022).

Jean-Pierre Chauveau, a socio-anthropologist, is senior researcher emeritus at the IRD (French Institute for Development Research). His research, which began in the 1970s, has focused on the long-term interrelationships between development mechanisms and policies and the processes of social change in rural West Africa. His recent research focuses on the role of land tenure and political violence in these dynamics in Côte d'Ivoire. He is a member of the Technical Committee on Land Tenure and Development, which operates under the authority of the Agence Française de Développement and the French Ministry of Foreign Affairs.

Priscilla Claeys is Associate Professor in Food Sovereignty, Human Rights and Resilience at the Centre for Agroecology, Water and Resilience, Coventry University (UK). She received her PhD in political and social sciences from the University of Louvain in 2013. From 2008 to 2014, she worked as a Special Advisor to Olivier De Schutter, the UN Special Rapporteur on the right to food. Her research areas include the right to food and food sovereignty, agrarian movements, global food governance, legal mobilization, and the creation of new human rights. She has published *Human Rights and the Food Sovereignty Movement: Reclaiming Control* (Routledge, 2015) and coedited two books. Her research has notably featured in *The Journal of Peasant Studies*, *Sociology*, and *Globalizations*.

Lorenzo Cotula is in the Natural Resources research group at the International Institute for Environment and Development.

Ben Cousins, Professor Emeritus, is affiliated with the Institute for Poverty, Land and Agrarian Studies at the University of the Western Cape, which he founded in 1995 and directed until 2010. His research focuses on land and agrarian reform, land tenure, common property, rural class dynamics, small-scale agriculture, and livestock production.

Bao-Nguyet Dang is a PhD researcher at the International Institute of Social Studies of Erasmus University Rotterdam, Netherlands.

Michael B. Dwyer is a political geographer whose research examines the intersection of land governance and international development. He is the author of *Upland Geopolitics: Postwar Laos and the Global Land Rush* and coeditor of *Turning Land into Capital: Development and Dispossession in the Mekong Region*, both published in 2022. He is Assistant Professor of Geography at Indiana University Bloomington and an Associated Senior Research Scientist with the University of Bern's Center for Development and Environment.

Alistair Fraser has held the position of Lecturer in the Department of Geography, Maynooth University, since 2007. He is the author of *Global Foodscapes: Oppression and Resistance in the Life of Food* (Routledge, 2016), the coauthor with Rob Kitchin of *Slow Computing: Why We Need Balanced Digital Lives* (Bristol University Press, 2020), and the sole author of articles in journals such as *Journal of Peasant Studies*, *Annals of the American Association of Geographers*, *Journal of Rural Studies*, and *Human Geography*.

Julien-François Gerber teaches at the International Institute of Social Studies in The Hague. Prior to that, he lived in Bhutan, India, the United States, and Catalonia. He is interested in the political economy of flourishing and alienation, and has published on capitalism, degrowth, agrarian change, and psychoanalysis. He coedited *Post-Growth Thinking in India* (2018).

Jérémie Gilbert is Professor of Human Rights Law, Centre for Equality, Justice and Social Change.

Christophe Golay is Visiting Professor of International and Development Studies, Geneva Graduate Institute.

Jacobo Grajales is Professor of Political Science at the University of Lille, France, and fellow of the Institut Universitaire de France. Having previously conducted research on the relationships between the state and armed groups in Colombia, he is now harnessing a comparative perspective to examine the ties between postconflict politics and land policies through field research in Colombia, Côte d'Ivoire, and Liberia. He is coeditor of the *Journal of Peasant Studies*. His past and current research projects and publications can be found at www.jacobo-grajales.net.

Andrej Grubačić is a world historian, Balkan federalist, and professor of anthropology and social change at the California Institute of Integral Studies. He is the editor of the *Journal of World-Systems Research* and has coauthored, among others, *Wobblies and Zapatistas* (2008) and *Living at the Edges of Capitalism: Adventures in Exile and Mutual Aid* (2016).

Laura Gutiérrez-Escobar was born in Bogotá, Colombia. Gutiérrez-Escobar holds a BA in History (Universidad Nacional de Colombia), a Master in Latin American Studies (University of Texas, Austin), and a PhD in Anthropology (University of North Carolina, Chapel Hill) and is now Assistant Professor at the Instituto de Bioética, Pontificia Universidad Javeriana (Bogotá).

Hannah Holleman is Associate Professor of Sociology and Environmental Studies at Amherst College in Amherst, Massachusetts, and author of *Dust Bowls of Empire: Imperialism, Environmental Politics, and the Injustice of "Green" Capitalism* (Yale University Press, 2018).

S. Ryan Isakson is Associate Professor of Global Development Studies and Geography at the University of Toronto. Broadly, his research focuses upon the political economy of food systems and agrarian change. Along with Jennifer Clapp, he is a co-author of *Speculative Harvests: Financialization, Food, and Agriculture* (Fernwood Press, 2018).

Ricardo Jacobs is Assistant Professor in the Department of Global Studies, University of California, Santa Barbara.

Cristóbal Kay is Emeritus Professor in the International Institute of Social Studies (ISS) of Erasmus University Rotterdam having joined ISS in 1989. He received his first degree from the University of Chile in Santiago and his D.Phil from the University of Sussex. Before joining the ISS, he was a lecturer at the University of Chile and the University of Glasgow. He has for many years been a visiting professor at the Facultad Latinoamericana de Ciencias Sociales in Ecuador and a Professorial Research Associate of the Department of Development Studies at the School of Oriental and African Studies, University of London. His research has been and is on the genealogy of theories of development and on agrarian change from a comparative perspective largely centered on Latin America. He has been the editor of *The European Journal of Development Research*, a coeditor of the *European Review of Latin American and Caribbean Studies* and, more recently, of the *Journal of Agrarian Change*.

Sai Sam Kham is a PhD researcher at the International Institute of Social Studies of Erasmus University Rotterdam, Netherlands.

Miloon Kothari is a leading voice on human rights, especially economic, social, and cultural rights. An architect by training, Mr. Kothari has extensive experience in the area of housing and land rights. He graduated from the Pratt Institute and Columbia University in New York City and Maharaja Sayajirao University. Mr. Kothari has been a Guest Professor at many universities and institutions. He is the coordinator of the South Asian Regional Programme of the Habitat International Coalition's Housing and

Land Rights Network and is founding member of the International NGO Committee on Human Rights in Trade and Investment. Mr. Kothari is also a member of the Leadership Council of the Global Women and AIDS Coalition, UNAIDS. In September 2000, the UN Commission on Human Rights appointed Mr. Kothari as the Special Rapporteur on Adequate Housing. In his work as Rapporteur he focused on strategies to ensure respect for human rights in postconflict and postdisaster situations. He actively contributed to the standard-setting process as part of his rapporteur work, including the preparation of Principles and Guidelines on Development-Based Evictions and Displacement, in his 2007 report to the UN Human Rights Council. And in recent years, he has been particularly active on issues such as women's rights to land, inheritance, property, housing and globalization, and trade liberalization and their impact on the right to adequate housing and other related rights. He currently serves as Convenor of the Working Group on Human Rights in India and the UN.

Christian Lund is Professor at the University of Copenhagen. He is the author of *Law, Power, and Politics in Niger* (Lit Verlag and Transaction Publishers), *Local Politics and the Dynamics of Property in Africa* (Cambridge University Press), and *Nine-Tenths of the Law: Enduring Dispossession in Indonesia* (Yale University Press).

Joan Martínez-Alier is Emeritus Professor at ICTA-Universitat Autònoma de Barcelona. A leading scholar in the fields of ecological economics, political ecology, and environmental justice, as recognized by his receipt of the Balzan prize in 2020 and the Holberg prize in 2023, he is Co-director of the Atlas of Environmental Justice, which has nearly 4,000 entries.

Philip McMichael is Professor Emeritus of the Department of Global Development at Cornell University.

Sharlene Mollett is Associate Professor in the Department of Human Geography and Global Development Studies at University of Toronto Scarborough, Canada.

Marvin Joseph F. Montefrio is Associate Professor in the Department of Environmental Studies at Yale-NUS College.

Tsegaye Moreda is an Assistant Professor of Critical Agrarian Studies at the International Institute of Social Studies (The Hague) of Erasmus University Rotterdam, Netherlands. He is a member of the research team of the European Research Council Advanced Grant [grant number 834006]–awarded project "Commodity & Land Rushes and Regimes: Reshaping Five Spheres of Global Social Life (RRUSHES-5)." He is coeditor of *The Routledge Handbook of Global Land and Resource Grabbing* (Routledge, 2023). He is an Associate Editor of *World Development*.

Andrew Ofstehage began his studies in agronomy before taking an interest in how commodity booms depend on, exploit, and transform land. In Bolivia, he saw how a rising global interest in quinoa led to conflicts over land, the radical intensification of farming practices, and eventually (in some places) a return to a more balanced land use strategy. While these changes and conflicts took place on the ground, they connected to community-led fights with transnational mining corporations over water and land use rights and with the plurinational state's interest in gaining sovereignty over the natural resources within its borders and selling them. Later, in his comparative ethnography of two communities of American farmers in the Brazilian Cerrado, he observed the fungibility of citizenship in the face of rural crisis, if only for those privileged enough to make selectively porous borders work to their benefit.

Diana Ojeda is a feminist geographer working on issues of dispossession and land grabbing from a perspective that bridges feminist political ecology and critical agrarian studies. She is a Professor in the Department of Geography and the Department of International Studies and Director of the Commons Program at the Ostrom Workshop, Indiana University Bloomington.

Kei Otsuki is Professor of International Development Studies at Utrecht University. Her research projects focus on translocal development in the process of energy transitions and urbanization in various geographical settings across the Global North and South.

Raj Patel is Research Professor in the LBJ School of Public Affairs at The University of Texas at Austin.

Ivette Perfecto is the Bunyan Bryant Collegiate Professor of Environmental Justice in the School for Environment and Sustainability at the University of Michigan, Ann Arbor.

Pauline E. Peters is a social anthropologist, retired from the faculties of the Department of Anthropology and the Kennedy School, Harvard University. She continues as a Fellow of the Center for African Studies and of the Center for International Development at Harvard. Her research concentrates on countries in southern Africa, including Malawi and Botswana, with publications on land, rural economy, kinship, and gender.

Jan Douwe van der Ploeg is Emeritus Professor of Wageningen University in the Netherlands. He is Adjunct Professor of the College of Humanities and Development Studies of China Agricultural University in Beijing. Among his books are *Peasants and the Art of Farming: A Chayanovian Manifesto* (Fernwood, 2013) and *The New Peasantries: Rural Development in Times of Globalization*, 2nd edition (Earthscan/Routledge, 2018).

Doi Ra completed her PhD study at the International Institute of Social Studies of Erasmus University Rotterdam, Netherlands. She is a researcher at the Transnational Institute (TNI).

Jesse Ribot studies local democracy, resource access, and climate-related vulnerabilities in West Africa. He teaches environmental politics at American University, taught in Geography and Anthropology at University of Illinois, was a senior associate at the World Resources Institute, and taught in Urban Studies and Planning at MIT. He has held fellowships, makes films, blows glass, pots, and sculpts. See www.jesseribot.com.

Andro Rilović is a radical economist, lecturer in degrowth and European economics at the University of Amsterdam, and one of the editors of the Degrowth.info web-portal.

He is interested in degrowth and anarchism, and how these two movements can, together, create new community development models.

Nikita Sud is Professor of the Politics of Development at the University of Oxford and a Fellow of Wolfson College. Her research interests center on states, space, and nature in the Global South, especially Asia. Her most recent monograph is *The Making of Land and the Making of India* (Oxford University Press, 2021).

Verónica Torres-Marenco received her PhD in Law at the University of Greenwich.

John Vandermeer is the Asa Gray Distinguished University Professor of Ecology and Evolutionary Biology and the Arthur F. Thurnau Professor at the University of Michigan, Ann Arbor.

Tony Weis is Professor in the Department of Geography and Environment at Western University.

Wendy Wolford began with an interest in how unequal land ownership generated long-term underdevelopment in Latin America. She spent time with the Movement of Landless Workers (MST) in Brazil and saw both the power of the state in establishing settlement and ownership policies and the power of organizations in fighting back against unequal and unfair land settlement policies. At the same time, watching the MST and the Brazilian state interact made it clear that defining social movements and the state as either clearly distinct or antagonistic is misleading. In Brazil, the social movements fighting for land and the state often work in tandem, whether because the state supports a limited set of distribution goals or because there are actors within the state who agree with the movements' goals. Recognition of the porousness of the borders between civil society and the state help to provide a more nuanced view of the way in which mobilization has long constituted the state.

Yunan Xu is an Assistant Professor of China and Global Studies, University of Cambridge, UK. She was previously a postdoctoral researcher at the International Institute of Social Studies of Erasmus University Rotterdam, Netherlands. She is a section coeditor of *The Journal of Peasant Studies*.

Jingzhong Ye is a Professor of Development Studies and Dean at the College of Humanities and Development Studies, China Agricultural University. His research interests include development intervention and rural transformation, rural society and agrarian change, rural–urban migration and the left-behind population, agrarian sociology and land politics, rural education and social problems. He is a coeditor of the *Journal of Peasant Studies*.

Annelies Zoomers is Professor of International Development Studies at Utrecht University and a member of the Advisory Council on International Affairs for the Dutch Government. She was the Chair of the Netherlands Land Academy between 2009 and 2019.

CHAPTER 1

LAND AND SOCIAL LIFE

SATURNINO M. BORRAS JR. AND
JENNIFER C. FRANCO

Introducing the Handbook: Framing Land Politics

THE climate crisis has resulted in serious academic research and public and political debates about "just transition" in human-nature and human-nonhuman relations (Newell and Mulvaney 2013; Tsing, Mathews, and Bubandt 2019). The alarming depletion of biodiversity to a critical level has prompted a push for international conventions to address biodiversity issues (Corson and MacDonald 2012). The rise of right-wing authoritarianism and populism worldwide has been recasting the discussion about "big politics," which usually centers on megacities, toward a better understanding of its roots in the countryside (Scoones et al. 2018; Mamonova and Franquesa 2020). The global economy has generated unprecedented levels of wealth amid the joblessness and precarity of at least a billion working people (Davis 2006). The global food system represents a similar contradiction: it produces so much food that, if it were evenly distributed, would be enough to feed everyone, yet nearly a billion people are chronically hungry. And yet the supposed solution to hunger is to produce more food through the same system. The search for sources of renewable energy, sites for food production expansion, the expanded scope of conservation for carbon-offset projects—and, most importantly, the promise of windfall profits through these frontiers of capital—have played a major role in the global land rush (White et al. 2012; Dell'Angelo et al. 2017; Levien 2018; Grajales 2021; Neef et al. 2023; Borras and Franco 2024; Wolford et al. 2024). Extreme violence inflicted on peoples, some of it with genocidal characteristics, has been a part of the territory grabbing that accompanied the rise of global capitalism, colonialism, and imperialism (Van Leeuwen and Van der Haar 2016). These violent practices have not completely disappeared in the twenty-first century, as the cases of the Rohingya in Myanmar and the conflicts in Ukraine and Palestine have reminded us (Hall 2023; Prasse-Freeman 2023; Tramel 2024). Rising geopolitical tension is partly linked to increasing competition over resources, such as raw materials needed for the expanded reproduction of capital and for opening new markets for commodities, alongside strategic shifts toward a multipolar world (McMichael 2020). All these era-defining social phenomena facing humanity have connections with the politics of land. Making sense of these phenomena, therefore, requires a fundamental understanding of the politics of land, and vice versa. This handbook offers a set of analytical tools for understanding the relationship between land politics and broader social life.

Land has multiple meanings: the soil with its organic matter, a plot for farming or a range for animal grazing, a housing space, a landscape, a socio-agroecological zone for human-nonhuman coexistence, a territory, a homeland. As a shorthand, we use the umbrella concept of "land in production and social reproduction." The term *social reproduction* is used here broadly and will be explained in more detail below. This overarching conceptual handle will help us to highlight the connections between the individual contributions to the handbook. All the contributors take political economy as a starting point, but they take off from different intellectual traditions, and have different approaches, areas of interest, and thematic emphases.

This handbook brings together key perspectives in terms of theoretical traditions and themes in land politics and social life—namely, food, labor, climate change, citizenship, and geopolitics. It is neither a collection of random perspectives nor an all-inclusive compendium. Despite the breadth of its coverage, its scope is nevertheless limited, and this can be seen in two ways. First, it is a collection of perspectives that locate the politics of land in relation to societal transformations in the context of contemporary global capitalism. All the contributions are critical of capitalism, and of theories that justify and celebrate it. Second, most of the contributions are focused on political dynamics of social change in, and in relation to, the rural world. But if the scope of the collection is limited in some ways, it is extensive in other ways. First, it demonstrates why and how it is not possible to understand big politics centered around megacities or the global workings of capitalism without having a systematic understanding of the politics of land that is focused on, but not confined to, the countryside and of how this shapes spheres of social life. Second, most of the contributions to this handbook are conceptually broad and sweeping, rather than narrowly empirical. The collection is framed to offer a conceptual and methodological guide, a set of heterodox tools for analysis, which will not become outdated. The handbook has been compiled for academics, development practitioners, and social justice activists alike.

We understand the politics of land as the relatively stable pattern of who gets to have access to land, why, how, what kind of land and how much, where and for how long, for what purposes, and with what implications for who wins and who loses? These are questions based on social relations that are in turn rooted in class and other social group formations enacted within the inseparable spheres of state and society. Framed this way, our treatment of land politics comes from a broad tradition of political economy, the fundamental basis of the much broader and looser field of critical agrarian studies. We draw our understanding of agrarian political economy from a heterodox tradition that brings into dialogue Marxist and Marxist-informed traditions and those that are provoked by Marxist traditions yet have overlapping views. Henry Bernstein's interpretation of political economy fits easily into these various currents; he describes political economy as "the social relations and dynamics of production and social reproduction, property and power in agrarian formations and their processes of change, both historical and contemporary" (2010a, 1). For Bernstein, this kind of political economy rests on four fundamental co-constitutive questions—namely, who owns what (social relations of property), who does what (social relations of labor), who gets what (social relations of remuneration, income, profit, rent), and what do they do with it (social relations of consumption and social reproduction)? The contributions to this handbook come from critical perspectives of social relations around land in the context of contemporary global capitalism, and from theoretical perspectives that are Marxist, strongly influenced by Marxist ideas, or based in radical ideas provoked by Marxist views. With these diverse interpretations of the field as its starting point, the collection is firmly located in the broad, newly emerged field of critical agrarian studies. It is important to note that, though there are many overlapping and unified views among the handbook contributors, there are also some competing and contradictory positions. Where and how they diverge and disagree can be significant. As Bernstein (2010a, 11) reminds us, "The strongest arena of disagreement about Marx's ideas and how to interpret and apply them, is among Marxists, or those strongly influenced by Marx." There are ample illustrations of this in this handbook.

Although the collection covers extensive ground, it is not all-encompassing. For example, there are eight chapters dedicated to big-picture theoretical traditions, which cover much of the scholarly tradition that looks critically at land in the context of capitalism and alternatives to capitalism. We are able to cover clashing positions, for example, between Bernstein's (this volume) orthodox Marxist view on the superiority of large farms over small farms in terms of efficiency and productivity, and Jan Douwe van der Ploeg's opposing position in favor of small-scale farms (this volume). But the collection is not able to engage with all the currents within and between such traditions. On the issue of agrarian questions or land questions, for instance, there are more than enough distinct currents within Marxism to fill a handbook solely dedicated to this themed cluster.

There are similarly competing positions on how to interpret what the "development of productive forces" could mean in the era of climate change. Some Marxist scholars, especially those from ecological Marxism, such as John Bellamy Foster (2000) and James O'Connor (1998), have different views from orthodox Marxists (see Bernstein 2010b; Holleman this volume). There are equally compelling views that are hybrid versions, sitting between iconic poles, such as those that fuse some elements of Chayanovian perspectives with Marxist fundamentals (see, e.g., White 2018), or present a reinterpretation of Chayanovian or Marxist perspectives, as in the classic works of Teodor Shanin (1983) and as argued recently by Jan Douwe van der Ploeg (this volume, and 2024) and Shanin et al. (2024). Other contributions are heterodox and draw from important traditions (see the chapters by Patel, Martinez-Alier and Ajl, and Ojeda, this volume).

This method of combining elements from iconic traditions has been done before: earlier classic works have also adapted relatively eclectic approaches, such as those of Karl Polanyi ([1944] 2001), Barrington Moore Jr. (1967) and Eric Wolf (1969), although they are all firmly within a radical political economy tradition.

Who gets what land, how, how much, for how long, for what purposes, who doesn't get any, and who gets to decide? These are some of the most basic and inherently inseparable questions that define the politics of land. The "what" is not only a plot of land but could be a landscape, an agroecological zone, a territory, a homeland. The "who" is not random individuals but refers to groups of people who interact with each other through interlocking class and nonclass relations of race, ethnicity, caste, gender, generation, citizenship, and religion, among others. The "how" is both political and institutional, and it is not only about a particular class or group having a land monopoly through the institution of an individual private property system. Rather, it is about effective control through a variety of mechanisms in which an actor (an individual or a group, a natural person or an entity, or the state or nonstate) is able to make claims, exercise control, and extract benefit from having a claim or access to particular demarcated land plots, landscapes or territories (Vandergeest and Peluso 1995; Ribot and Peluso 2003; Peluso and Lund 2011).

A basic starting point for us is that it is not natural that a class or group of people gets to control most of the land, leaving others with little or none or with ample land but of poor quality and in isolated geographic locations. Where this happens, we assume it is because of the conditions shaped by existing social structures and institutions, resulting in land-based exploitation and oppression. We understand land access and land relations to be organically embedded in society—aligning in some ways with Polanyi's argument ([1944] 2001). We thus see land access not in a minimalist way as a farm plot or home lot, but rather, as parts of a broader whole. We understand access to land as something diverse, multiple, and multisited to the point that plotting and connecting the dots will yield a graphic image of a spider's web, rather than just one or two lines of connections (a home lot to farm plot, for example). Rather than a vertical hierarchy of importance (which is more important: access to farmland or a home lot?), we see a nonhierarchical, horizontal plurality of land access for production and social reproduction to produce exchange value and use value. Thus, farmland, home lots, playgrounds for children, landing access to a riverbank to fetch water for laundry, access to a local community forest, and so on, are all part of this plurality.

Given this view of land access, the institutional question of property is less about either-or, dichotomous choices, such as private freehold versus private usufruct, private freehold versus state, privatization versus commoning.[1] It is about the structures and institutions that connect different types of land access through different types of institutional mechanisms.[2] It is a mosaic. Boundaries are an intrinsic part of land politics, but not necessarily or always in the way neoclassical economics would suggest—that is, solid, legal, and private property boundaries, often secured with material fences and protected and enforced through the coercive apparatus of the state (police, military, judiciary, and prison). Rather, if land access is inherently plural and diverse in most societies, then boundaries are equally diverse, ranging from solid to fluid, impermeable to porous, long-term to transient. What stabilizes the social relations around land access in and through the landscape, socio-agroecological zone, or territory is the fluidity, malleability, and porosity of boundaries that are dynamically negotiated, contested, and transformed within these spaces. In any landscape and at any conjuncture, a relatively stable combination of these types of boundaries coexist. Once this pattern is challenged, however, with the aim of replacing it with a new combination, the political contest has the potential to be fierce and could unfold simultaneously in ways described by Kerkvliet (2009) as "official politics," "advocacy politics," and "everyday politics." This mosaic necessarily includes human and nonhuman relations. When a farmland is degraded because of sustained chemical use, it impacts the organic matter in the soil, pollinator bees, and so forth: this in turn impacts the ability of a farming household to progress or even survive. When a community forest is destroyed in favor of an open pit mine, the space is laid waste and all nonhuman species disappear. Thus, the mosaic of land access is necessarily and always an interspecies mosaic, a concept that is central to understanding land in production and social reproduction (see Weis, this volume; Montefrio, this volume; Tsing, Mathews, and Bubandt 2019). Ultimately, we believe that politics of land is, immutably, an issue of the relationship between the parts and the whole, and vice versa. These are important conceptual building blocks that we will come back to later when we discuss land in production and social reproduction and the concept of land regime.

Our ordering of the chapters starts with a set of contributions on broad theoretical traditions and their understanding of the politics of land in relation to capitalism and alternatives within and beyond capitalism, all of which are either Marxist or influenced or provoked by Marxist ideas. These are the chapters on orthodox Marxist tradition by Henry Bernstein world ecology by Raj Patel; ecosocialism by Hannah Holleman; dependency and world systems theory by Max Ajl; the anarchist tradition by Andrej Grubačić, Julien-François Gerber, and Andro Rilović; the Chayanovian tradition by Jan Douwe van der Ploeg; a postdevelopment and poststructuralist perspective from Laura Gutierrez-Escobar; and a feminist perspective from Diana Ojeda. Part of the rationale for this choice is that these are among the most popular currents in radical political economy that investigate capitalism and social life. Bringing these chapters together allows us to explore whether they all have a systematic view of land politics, and if so, what it is. By opening the collection this way, we hope to shed light, for those working on the broad theme of political economy of development and capitalism, on how and why land is a key element in understanding global capitalism and the alternatives to it; and, conversely, to make it easier for those working on the relatively narrower parameters of land politics to connect with broader themes of capitalism and alternatives.

This set of theoretical approaches is followed by four chapters that look into the political economy of food and agriculture, starting with Philip McMichael's land in food regimes and followed by Tony Weis's chapter on industrial livestock and interspecies relations. The set is completed with two other chapters that focus on the defining features of contemporary global capitalism: financialization (Ryan Isakson) and digitalization (Alistair Fraser) of land, agriculture, and food (see also Visser, Sippel, and Thiemann

2021). After this group of four chapters comes another cluster of four contributions that directly engage with climate and environmental politics and situate land politics in these. This cluster begins with Jesse Ribot's chapter on climate change and ends with John Vandermeer and Ivette Perfecto's chapter on agroecology. In between are chapters on agrarian justice and environmental justice, by Joan Martinez-Alier, and socioecological relations in land politics by Marvin Joseph F. Montefrio. Together, these four chapters address some of the most important themes of our time and pinpoint the key role land politics plays in these.

Global capitalism has generated vast wealth since the 1980s, and yet it has also resulted in unprecedented levels of inequality, exploitation, and extraction in various forms. That the profit-making machine of global capitalism can continue to churn is partly because working people subsidize it, effectively forced to take care of the cost of social reproduction. The next set of six chapters looks at land from the perspective of a matrix of land and labor and production and social reproduction in the rural-urban continuum. Kojo Amanor's chapter on contract farming accompanies chapters on social reproduction by Ben Cousins, semi-proletarianization by Walter Chambati, human mobilities and migration by Kei Otsuki and Annelies Zoomers, and urban agriculture by Ricardo Jacobs. Land, migration, and social reproduction as a thematic cluster is a set of some the oldest issues addressed in political economy, but contemporary scholarship has generated a considerable degree of excitement about new ways of understanding these phenomena (Cousins, this volume; Bhattacharya 2017; O'Laughlin 2022; Ossome 2022).

The next cluster of chapters contains nine contributions on the state, authority, and citizenship that cover issues of indigeneity, race, and ethnicity. It opens with some fundamental questions, considered in very engaging manner by Christian Lund, who asks: What do we talk about when we talk about land? He then navigates the complex theories on public authority, property, and citizenship in which land is central. Lund's chapter overlaps with and speaks to related framings on the state and citizenship by Andrew Ofstehage and Wendy Wolford and Nikita Sud's notion of "land-making as state-making." These are followed by chapters on land in violent conflict by Jacobo Grajales and Jean-Pierre Chauveau, and on the fiercely contested nature and future of customary land tenure in Sub-Saharan Africa by Pauline Peters. The last three chapters in this set are on the politics of indigeneity, race, and ethnicity layered in class and gender politics by Sharlene Mollett; Tsegaye Moreda; and Bao-Nguyet Dang, Doi Ra, Lorenza Arango, Moges Belay, Sai Sam Kham, and Zeynep Ceren Eren Benlisoy. They are the very heart and soul of the handbook. Individually and together they offer a clear and nuanced guide to help readers navigate the complicated maze of the politics of land.

Four chapters are then grouped together in a thematic cluster on geopolitics, beginning with Cristóbal Kay's historical account of the centrality of land in geopolitics and the debates about development, capitalism, and socialism during the Cold War era. The next three chapters in this cluster are more contemporary, starting with Jingzhong Ye's contextual chapter focused on the role land politics has played since 1949 in the internal transformation of China, which has partly led to its becoming a key geopolitical actor today (Ye 2015). Michael B. Dwyer's chapter illustrates the way big historical geopolitical dynamics actually unfold at a local level, while the chapter by Yunan Xu and Jun Borras offers a supplementary way of looking at land politics, focusing on land use dynamics in the context of international political economy, in what others call "telecoupling" or land systems (Liu et al. 2013; Meyfroidt et al. 2022).

The final thematic cluster of the collection looks at resistance to dispossession and alienation and the contexts, institutional instruments, and strategies used to frame resistance. It starts with a chapter by Priscilla Claeys, Lorenzo Cotula, Jérémie Gilbert, Christophe Golay, Miloon Kothari, and Veronica Torres-Marenco about popular institutional instruments that are used in land claim-making and invoked as a right to resist—namely, land as a human right. The next chapter tackles one of the contemporary axes of land conflicts today, which is between working people and big conservation organizations in alliance with the state: Connor Cavanagh and Tor Benjaminsen take on this topic with a focus on Africa. Shapan Adnan maps various contexts, strategies, and goals of resistance to land alienation in a global context. Finally, this thematic cluster—and indeed the collection as a whole—ends with a chapter by Jennifer Franco and Jun Borras on the contemporary land struggles by working people.

Land in Production and Social Reproduction

In classical agrarian studies and development studies, the dominant treatment of land is in the context of agriculture, which is, in turn, to a large extent examined in the context of the contribution of agriculture to the development of capitalism or, in some cases, the construction socialism (Kautsky [1899] 1988; Lenin [1899] 2004; for an overview, see Akram-Lodhi and Kay 2010a, 2010b; for a recent take, see Shattuck et al. 2023). In this light, land is almost always taken to mean farmland (or grazing land, commercial forest land, and so on) in relationship to wider processes of industrialization and urbanization (Kay 2009). The main concern is the contribution of land to the development of productive forces and to producing commodities for exchange, or to the process of generalized commodification. In other words, land in the sphere of production. This is not to say that the treatment does not include the dimension of social reproduction—it does. However, the focus is on how farmland, or pasture or commercial forest land, can be used to produce exchange value and use value, and how exchange value can be used in a subsistence-oriented manner, especially in the condition of generalized commodification of social reproduction (purchasing food, paying for care services, and so on). In this collection, we build on this classic formulation and take a wider view on land—namely, land in production and social reproduction, wherein social reproduction is taken in a much broader sense. Land is seen as a means of production and social reproduction, taking a unitary view of the production and social reproduction sphere, building on the discussion by O'Laughlin (2022) that itself takes off from Marx:

> Whatever the social form of the production process, it has to be continuous, it must periodically repeat the same phases. A society can no more cease to produce than it can cease to consume. When viewed, therefore, as a connected whole, and in the constant flux of its incessant renewal, every social process of production is at the same time a process of reproduction. The conditions of production are at the same time the conditions of reproduction.
>
> (Marx [1867] 1976, 711)

With this as a broad reference point, we apply the lens of land politics, an angle that is more fully engaged by Cousins (this volume) and Ojeda (this volume). Land in the production sphere—that is, land in the production of exchange value—is often expressed through formal census data on land property and land use that are key to understanding the formal capitalist economy. Yet land is also a means of social reproduction. Access to land—or to various aspects of nature at large, such as farmland, food gardens, grazing areas, forest, water, public space, and so on, usually primarily for use value—is important to the ability of working people (Shivji 2017) or classes of labor (Bernstein 2010a) to reproduce their labor—that is, to secure their basic needs for food, clothing, shelter, and general care (Pattenden 2018; Shah and Lerche 2020; Ossome 2022). This land access can be big in scale and easy to spot; it can be access to a community forest, not only for nontimber forest products but also for the protection the forest offers to the community, for example, against storm surges or landslides. But land access can also be low key and invisibilized in everyday life, as in a small pond where a water buffalo can take a regular bath to cool off, or a public space for a children's playground or for religious infrastructure. A right-of-way may be a nonissue for many, but when you live in a *resguardo* (a Colombian Indigenous people's settlement) that is completely surrounded by private *fincas* and agribusiness plantations, then land access in the form of a right-of-way becomes an essential resource that is fiercely contested between those who feel trapped inside the *resguardo* and those who live on its perimeter.

Working classes often sell their labor power cheaply, at below survival levels: they are able to do this because a large part of the social reproduction cost—healthcare, care of children and the elderly, daily subsistence, etc.—is shouldered by the family of the worker (Burawoy 1976). Having access to a small plot of farmland, a food garden, a housing lot, or access to forest, water, rangeland for livestock, and a community and public health system allows them to survive, and for a few, even to accumulate (Pattenden 2018; Shah and Lerche 2020; Borras et al. 2022). Although this is more obvious for rurally rooted workers, even those who are largely or completely urban-based find themselves in a similar situation. Access to space that is close to sources of livelihoods, whether wage work or street peddling, is key for the urban working classes; it draws people to towns and cities and has led to a mushrooming of slums worldwide. An important aspect of urban agriculture and animal husbandry is linked to working people's survival strategy, where land as urban space proves to be important (Jacobs this volume; McClintock 2014; Siebert 2020).

If we take a simple, classic formulation of land in the productive sphere for a rural working household (in societies with a significant agrarian sector), a number of images come to mind, such as farming (farmland, farm plot), pastoralist activities (grazing land), and rustic housing (see Figure 1.1).

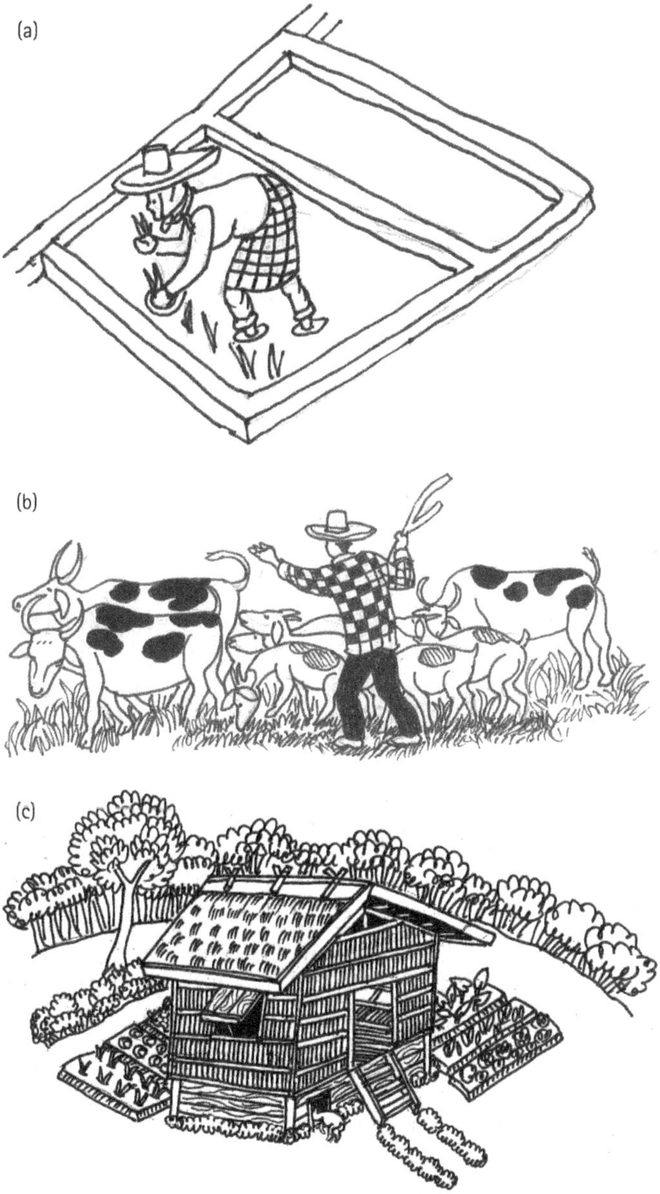

FIGURE 1.1. A plot, a pasture, or a home lot.

Source: Artwork by Filipino activist artist Boy Dominguez (2024).

However, when we adopt the formulation proposed in this handbook—namely, land in production and social reproduction, a markedly different set of images appears. Rather than simple, individual pictures, this formulation conjures a more complex, mosaic-like image, as shown in Figure 1.2. And if we construct imaginary connecting lines from the homes to places of productive and social reproductive activities, an interlaced structure, a mesh, emerges (Figure 1.3). Many of the everyday activities are (literally, figuratively, and politically) difficult to see from the outside; one has to search and look closely. In this context, it becomes clear that the activities illustrated by the images in Figure 1.1 (a plot, a pasture, and a home lot) are not sufficient to ensure the continuous renewal of life and society. That cycle of renewal requires the range of activities portrayed in Figure 1.2. It is not the plot of farmland, disembedded from its socio-ecological zone, that matters most, but the whole landscape, zone, or territory—and its integrity. This view does not deny the importance of the farm plot; it only emphasizes the point that its importance is enacted through its embeddedness in the social relations and interspecies relations in the landscape, zone, or territory. A household not only has plural and diverse land access needs if it is to sustain life, but it also interacts with other households in the landscape. The result is a mesh of land access. The criss-crossing routes and side-by-side sites of land access from two households shown in Figure 1.3 look complex and messy. Imagine what it will look like when we plot the routes and sites of all the households in a landscape, and those of other actors, such as the village government.

Moreover, the landscape, or socio-agroecological zone, though key, must in turn be seen in its embeddedness in wider systems (the subnational state or the nation-state, for example, or, indeed, global capitalism). Otherwise, it can be reduced to a mere "enclave" with all the weaknesses and problems that go with that (Li 2014), which resonates with Nancy Fraser's concern about the "merely environmental" in her critique of environmental-justice movements that are not embedded in system-wide struggles (Fraser 2021). We can illustrate our point with a negative hypothetical example: A community made up of a landscape, socio-agroecological zone, or territory is abandoned by its people because of violent conflict and militarization, and the community members become internally displaced people (IDP) living in distant refugee camps. While they are away, various elite groups carry out extractive activities in the original community: mining, deforestation, and new plantations. Later, the government passes a law on land restitution based on individual claims. Some of the people successfully clear the administrative hurdles and are awarded an individual plot in their original community. They return to claim it, only to find out that the community—the landscape, zone, territory—in which the original farm plot had been embedded was gone; it had been destroyed and replaced by a completely different one in which any possible reconstruction of the farm plot would not make sense and almost certainly fail. In such cases, land restitution is unlikely to achieve its goal of restorative justice. What was destroyed was the community, the landscape, socio-agroecological zone, territory, or homeland; what is being restituted is a farm plot. The mosaic has been destroyed; what is being restituted is partial, small fragments of that mosaic. This hypothetical example highlights the strategic

FIGURE 1.2. Landscape.

Source: Artwork by Filipino activist artist Boy Dominguez (2024).

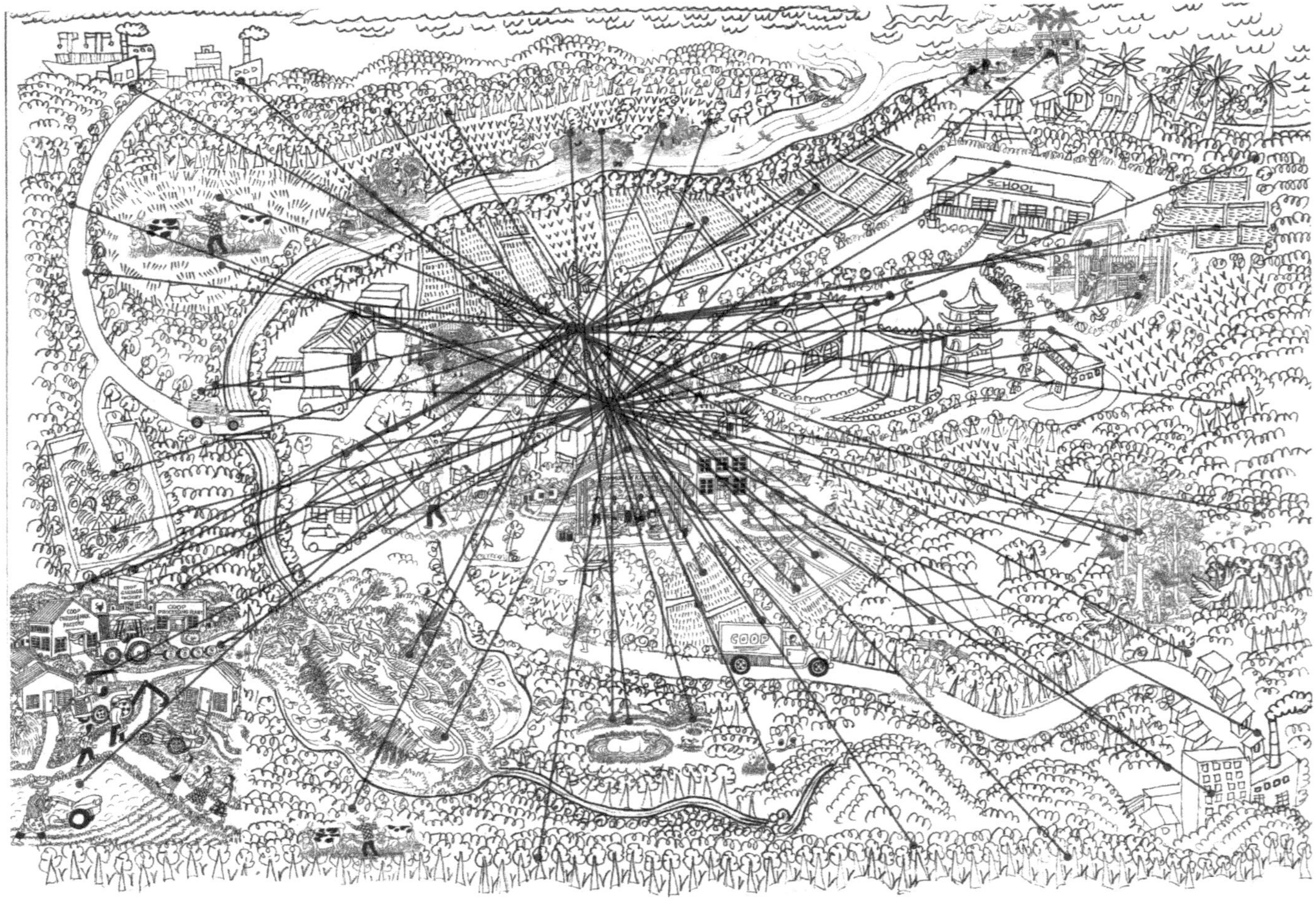

FIGURE 1.3. A mesh of land access in a landscape.

Source: Original artwork by Boy Dominguez. Digital line graphics by John B. Tan.

importance of maintaining or reconstructing the integrity of a landscape, zone, or territory in relation to an individual farm plot to serve as material basis for the repeated renewal of life and society.

This notion of *the continuous renewal of life and society* is a key point of interest for us, suggesting that social reproduction ought, beyond labor reproduction, to include as broad a range of life activities as possible—namely, socioecological, sociocultural, and sociopolitical reproduction. When seen from this perspective, land and land politics acquire a more complex meaning. Socioecological reproduction is based on the fundamental premise that social life cannot be sustained if ecological reproduction is not also sustained. When a paddy field is poisoned by the tailings of a nearby gold mine, the peasants or pastoralists who rely on that land and water as a means of production and social reproduction may no longer be able to pursue accumulation prospects, and those who are involved in a simpler reproduction mode of living are likely to face a reproduction squeeze. The destruction of ecology might not only mean the disruption of livelihoods; it could very well mean the destruction of the material basis for sustaining life in particular landscapes or socio-agroecological zones. Wiping out natural pollinators through the widespread use of pesticides impacts production in that socio-agroecological zone (Weis, this volume). The arguments for the indivisibility of "human–nature relations," as Patel (this volume) explains from the world-ecological perspective and Martinez-Alier (this volume) explains from an "environmental justice" perspective, extended to "human–nonhuman relations" as both Weis and Montefrio (this volume) elaborate, represent a fundamental assumption in which land is a significant element that informs most of the contributions to this collection, as well as our own reading of what land is and why it is such an important aspect of social life in general and social reproduction in particular.

Moreover, in many societies, especially racialized and multiethnic ones, land as a means of social reproduction takes on a sociocultural relevance. In such cases, the renewal of life and society depends in part on the ability of groups of people to reproduce as distinct ethnic or Indigenous peoples—an ability that depends, in turn, on having access to land as a territory or "homeland" despite all the complexities and contradictions that this entails (Mamdani 1996, 2020). This sense of having a territory—a homeland—is a key aspect of autonomy and the capacity to reproduce as a people, even when, at particular moments in their histories, the members of these societies do not live in the physical space of their territory or homeland. This handbook underscores not only this sense of identity politics based on relations to land but also the interlocking class relations and other axes of social difference, such as race and ethnicity, as in the cases elaborated by Moreda (this volume) and Bao et al. (this volume). Research has shown how such interlocking axes of social relations shape gender and generational relations, and vice versa (Park and White 2017; White 2020; Dieng 2024), as discussed here in the chapters by Mollett (this volume) and Ojeda (this volume). Others look at land from a sociopolitical perspective in which a territory or homeland is seen in political terms, whether in the context of a nation-state or nation more broadly, and associated with the notions of the autonomy and sovereignty of particular people that allows them to reproduce as a people. Many geopolitical tensions and wars in the past and today are linked to the sociopolitical dimension of land as territory and homeland.

In short, formulating land as a means of production and social reproduction is another way of saying that land has multiple meanings that emerge out of social relations in economic, ecological, social, cultural, and political spheres and that these are co-constitutive processes. This fundamental assumption about what land means lies at the heart of this handbook.

Land in Critical Agrarian Studies

Although this handbook takes a broad perspective on land politics and aims to generate a wide conversation and scholarship, it remains rooted in the field of critical agrarian studies. We understand critical agrarian studies as a field that "enquires into the causes, conditions and consequences of societal transformations by focusing its analysis on the interaction between social structures, institutions and actors that shape the processes of change in, and in relation to, the rural world" (Borras 2023, 449–450). It is founded in political economy and takes social relations as a unit of inquiry, paying "attention to questions of agency of the exploited, oppressed and marginalized groups in the rural–urban and agriculture–industry entanglement, particularly their autonomy and capacity to interpret—and change—their conditions" (450). The term "critical" is based on three defining characteristics of this field— (a) it "interrogates . . . neoliberal theories"; (b) it is "sympathetic to radical social movements and their proposed alternatives, but is vigilant in scrutinizing these in theory and practice"; and (c) it "questions, and works to transform, the very institutions of the global circuits of knowledge" (450). Logically, we take this field to be inherently interdisciplinary and broad, drawing its theoretical traditions and methodological preferences from critical currents in associated disciplines and fields, including anthropology, sociology, political science, economics, geography, international relations, and political economy, and from studies in gender, environment, climate, food, migration, social movements, and so on (Edelman and Wolford 2017; Akram-Lodhi et al. 2021). Finally, following Borras (2023), we take this field to be "politically engaged," trying to interpret the world in order to change it into something better and more just; "pluralist" ideologically and politically, allowing various radical (that is, anticapitalist) ideas to blossom while avoiding sectarianism; and "internationalist," based on the assumption that capitalism has global roots even when it spreads unevenly in the social structures and institutions in and across nationally bounded societies.

The foundations of critical agrarian studies are firmly located in classical agrarian studies, which have been primarily engaged in problematizing the location of agriculture and peasants in the transition to capitalism—and, for that matter, socialism (Byres 2009; Akram-Lodhi and Kay 2010a, 2010b). Classical agrarian studies, in turn, overlap with development studies, both fields having gained ground around the same time, in the middle of the twentieth century. In its most basic interpretation, the field of development studies problematizes questions of how to achieve some improvement in the well-being of humanity or, indeed, to escape poverty. At its inception as a field, it focused on the social conditions of poorer Third World countries, which often roughly translated to the development of capitalism (or socialism) in these societies (Kay [1989] 2010). Key to the problematics of both classical agrarian studies and development studies is the role played by, and the fate of, agriculture and the peasantry in the transition to either capitalism or socialism. This puts land front and center. The dominant convention in classical agrarian studies and development studies in valorizing the land issue has been land reform (Kay 2002). There are three key currents of land reform in this tradition—namely, redistributing land to individual peasants to create a sector of smallholder peasant producers that can transition into productive capitalist farmers; expropriating large landholdings from landed classes and creating state or cooperative farms (or both) in which peasants can transition to become agricultural workers; and reallocating economically inefficient lands (large and small properties) to more efficient land users (farmers or big capital) through the market.

The first current includes a mixture of radical agrarian populist, moral economist, heterodox Marxist, sustainable livelihoods, and progressive liberal perspectives. The second current combines different strands within Marxism. It is important to point out that the first and second currents have generated significant overlaps, for instance, in their interpretations of land policy questions (e.g., Moyo 2011; Moyo and Yeros 2005; Cousins and Scoones 2010; Scoones et al. 2010), but also polarized positions, as Griffin, Khan, and Ickowitz (2002) and Byres (2004) have shown. The fault-lines in the theoretical traditions cut into thematic fields of inquiry, such as gender studies (Agarwal 1994; Meinzen-Dick et al. 1997; Deere and Leon 2003; Razavi 2009; Tsikata 2016). Yet despite the major disagreements about the what, why, and how of land reform among scholars in the first and second currents, there is a consensus that land monopoly is the basis of exploitation and oppression, especially in agrarian societies, and a barrier to the development of productive forces. The major divergence on the issue of land monopoly is over what should replace the land monopoly of the landed classes—small-scale family farms or state and collective farms. The third current originates in the neoclassical economics and New Institutional Economics perspective (Harriss, Hunter, and Lewis 1995). In terms of land, a key tenet of this tradition is that the formalization of private property rights facilitates land sales and rental markets, which are assumed to be the best way of reallocating land to the most efficient land uses and land users. Among the policies that are proposed to achieve this is to formalize land titles, on either an individual or a group basis, but with a preference for the individual (Deininger and Binswanger 1999; de Soto 2000). In societies characterized by land-based inequality, this might mean simply ratifying what exists. But neoliberal thinkers see land monopoly as inhibiting the realization of the free markets, and in societies where land monopolies exist, they also call for land reform. In the era of neoliberalism, variations of the "willing seller–willing buyer" arrangements have been promoted, with generally dismal outcomes, especially when measured from a redistributive justice perspective (Deininger 1999; for a critique, see Lahiff, Borras, and Kay 2007).

All three currents are generally focused on finding the most efficient way of mobilizing agriculture and the peasantry—thus, land—to attain a certain degree of improvement in the well-being of humanity, albeit with competing interpretations of what efficiency means. Our view is that land in agriculture and the peasantry are fundamental to the context of transitions to capitalism or socialism. But this does not give us a full understanding of the politics of land—that is, of why access to and control over land are so fiercely contested in so many locations for so much of the time, or why most land redistribution programs that have been attempted in contemporary capitalism have failed to result in a robust middle-farmer sector. This is partly because the conventional and dominant view on land in agriculture and the peasantry is too centered on production. This illuminates many important social phenomena and the competing interpretations of these, but not fully. We believe it is critical to see land as fundamental in not only production but also in the connected production and social reproduction whole.

Land Regime, Land Grabs, and Land Rush

Three overlapping concepts are key to understanding land politics today in the context of the conversation in this handbook—namely, land regime, land grabbing, and land rush.[3] The first, *land regime*, is the routinized, relatively stable pattern of social structures, ideology, and state and nonstate, formal and informal, institutional rules that govern the claims over ownership, control, access, distribution, valorization, and use of land—rural and urban, agricultural and nonagricultural—in relation to capitalism. We say that land regimes exist in relation to capitalism because, though the latter is not the only global variable that shapes land politics, it is certainly the most crucial one today (Bernstein 2010a; Moore 2015). The concept of land regime builds on scholarship that broadly advocates the study of coexisting land-based social relations, or "landscapes," "land tenure systems," or "land tenure regimes," usually in relation to something wider.[4] Using the concept of land regime allows us to avoid localist and sectoralist views on land that pertain only to a village land politics or refer only to patterns of land use and land users. Our point is that even when one is focusing an analysis on a local or sectoral case, it is impossible to understand that case without linking the land issue to a broader, systemwide land regime. The land regime perspective thus allows us to discern the patterns in aggregate structural, institutional, and political shifts in social relations around land. It removes blinkers that might limit our inquiry to a specific plot of land, landscape, or sector. For example, if we were to examine land politics in Colombia only through the lens of peasants or *campesinos* or just from the perspective of Indigenous peoples or of Afro-Colombians, we would miss the relational nature of land politics across these three sectors (not to mention other sectors beyond these three): they are co-constitutive. Sectoral approaches, or what Rojas (2024) calls "merely sectoral" approaches, to land in Colombia have inadvertently played into the divide-and-rule strategy of the ruling classes acting through the central state, for example, Indigenous versus peasants.

Capitalism has a long history of cycles of land grabbing, beginning with the English land enclosures of the sixteenth century (Marx [1867] 1976, pt. 8). We define contemporary *land grabs* as "the capturing of control of relatively vast tracts of land and other natural resources through a variety of mechanisms and forms that involve large-scale capital that often shifts resource use orientation into extractive character" (Borras et al. 2012, 851; see also Peluso and Lund 2011; Li 2014). This may be "for international or domestic purposes, as capital's response to the convergence of food, energy and financial crises, climate change mitigation imperatives, and demands for resources from newer hubs of global capital" (Borras et al. 2012, 851). Based on this "control grabbing" definition, we see land grabbing as an element of the everyday workings of global capitalism, echoing Harvey's point about the relations between accumulation and dispossession (Harvey 2003). This definition allows us to capture varieties of land grabbing that use different institutional mechanisms, operate at different scales, and whose outcomes are varied. Land grabbing can be corporate-led, or not, or large-scale in terms of the amount of land and capital involved, or not. But the general effect is "control grabbing" of land and resources that, when aggregated at the landscape level or societywide, has a significant impact, causing shifts in social structures, institutions, and the politics around land relations. Large-scale land grabs by corporate capital and the state, as well as "pin prick" land grabs and various forms of extra-economic coercion (Hall, Hirsch, and Li 2011; Alonso-Fradejas 2012; White et al. 2012; Dell'Angelo et al. 2017; Grajales 2021; Ouma 2020; Neef et al. 2023; Wolford et al. 2024) are components of the dynamics of a generalized commodification. However, at certain historical moments land grabbing acquires a particular tempo, gains momentum, and develops into a full-scale frenzy and a spectacle. These are moments of a land rush.

The term *land rush* denotes a chaotic, relatively short-lived, historical juncture marked by a sudden surge in the demand for land, accompanied by an extremely speculative and competitive, often violent and convulsive, transition from one set of rules on commodity and land politics to another. More narrowly, it refers to that insurgent moment when the prevailing "land regime" is seriously challenged but has not yet been fully replaced by a new regime. Land rush encompasses various elements: land enclosures, land grabs, land deals, land acquisitions, commodity booms—small, medium, and large—and multiple actors (state, nonstate, corporate, and noncorporate). It has distinctive sociopolitical features—namely, wild speculations, hyperbolic claims, fantastic spectacles, and a convulsive atmosphere, very much aligning with Anna Tsing's (2000) notion of spectacle and spectacular accumulation.

Land rush can emerge from any one or a combination of three broad possibilities: (a) there is sudden massive speculative demand for land but no clear set of rules on how to effectively respond to such a demand; (b) there is a clear existing set of rules on (re) allocating land control and use, but it does not allow the surging speculative demand for land to be met; or (c) there is a new set of rules on land (re)allocation and land use and a push by some to get ahead of the rest by taking advantage of such the changes. In all cases, a land rush has the element of extreme urgency and is relational. The sense of urgency owes to the desire to be ahead of others; a land rush is thus extremely time-sensitive. A land rush is centrally about changes over a timeline: whether land prospectors and investment prospectors are able to take advantage of new rules in investing in land, or are able to push for changes from old rules to new rules. It is about the changing correlation of the state and social forces that are drawn to the land rush, and the shifting structure of political opportunities available to them. Its relational character can be seen in at least two ways. First, the actions of any one player can only be calculated in relation to those of others, whether one is offering land or wanting to grab land. Second, the rush is inherently multisited geographically, spurred on by wild projections about how much land is required by land prospectors and the desire of investment prospectors to offer as much land as possible, where comparative features of these offerings can make a huge difference in the outcomes of the land rush. Here, the geographical spread in land rushes is understood in relative terms: the land rush can be bounded within a national territory, a transnational regional area, or global. This geographically multisited characteristic also contributes to a temporal unevenness, and the combination of the two means that any major land rush is plural and diverse, and more accurately referred to as "land rushes" (Messerli et al. 2014). Moreover, the term *land control* has multiple meanings: land control to shape food and agricultural production systems, land control to capture carbon in forestry conservation projects, land control to allow for the capture of hydropower in mega dam projects, land control to capture subsoil minerals, and so on. This allows for broader meanings of land control and land grabbing that include "green grabbing" and "water grabbing" (Fairhead, Leach, and Scoones 2012; Mehta, Veldwisch, and Franco 2012; Ojeda 2012; Franco and Borras 2019; Bruna 2022), or land politics as water politics or river politics (Cortesi 2021; Suhardiman, Giordano, and Molle 2012; Boelens et al. 2023). Holliday (1999) used the term "(world) contagion" in his description of the California gold rushes in the second half of the nineteenth century. This has resonance with the recent global land rush which spread globally in two ways: first, geographically, as it gained ground in all corners of the world (Desmarais et al. 2015; Roman-Alcala 2015; Van der Ploeg, Franco, and Borras 2015; Kay, Peuch, and Franco 2015); second, in and through spheres of social life, as it reshaped and was shaped by food politics, climate change politics, labor regimes and migration, nation-building and citizenship, and geopolitics.

These three concepts are at the heart of what we are arguing here. Land grabbing is an inherent element of everyday capitalism and the dynamics of land politics within it. The best way to understand its impact is to see land from the perspective of the connected production–social reproduction whole. Land rush is a short-lived insurgent moment that occurs when land grabbing escalates into a generalized frenzy. Combining these two concepts can help us grapple with the events since 2000s that have partly defined the international political economy. But to understand the relevance of land grabbing and land rush in global capitalism, it is important to view them through a land regime (or systemwide) lens.

Land and Social Life

Land politics shapes various spheres of social life—namely, food politics, climate change politics, labor and migration, nation-building and citizenship, and geopolitics. At the same time, these spheres of social life shape land politics. The meaning and importance of land and how the politics around it emerge and evolve under contemporary global capitalism vary, partly because of the uneven development of capitalism geographically and over time within and across the spheres of social life. We now turn to a highly abbreviated introduction to each of the spheres of social life that are relevant to this handbook.

Land and Food Politics

Land and food are organically linked, and the politics around them are intimately entwined. Food production, circulation, exchange, and consumption, as well as food loss and waste, will be linked to questions of land for as long as food production requires natural inputs and human labor. This relationship has taken the "metabolic rift" path under capitalism (Foster 1999). Disruption in commodity and land politics can trigger far-reaching effects in food politics, and vice versa. When soil is degraded, food production is impacted; when human–nonhuman relations are disrupted, for example, chemical agriculture against natural pollinators, food production is affected (see Weis this volume; Montefrio this volume). When households that rely on access to land as their means of production and social reproduction to produce exchange value and use value lose such access, fully or partially, their capacity for food provisioning is undermined. When a territory of a people is violently occupied by an external force, their short-term and long-term autonomy and ability to pursue food sovereignty are compromised. When extreme disruptions occur, the ability of people to produce and consume food in and near their territory is radically reduced and food access becomes dependent on supply chains traversing long geographical distances, accelerating the metabolic rift.

The chemicalization and industrialization of food and agriculture in the "Age of Capital" means that fossil capital has become central, cutting across spheres of commodity production, circulation, and consumption, from food politics to transportation infrastructure (Friedmann and McMichael 1989; Malm 2016). In contemporary capitalism, this has been further consolidated and expanded by the financialization of agriculture, food, and land (Isakson 2014; Ouma 2014, 2020; Sommerville and Magnan 2015; Visser 2017; Clapp and Isakson 2018; Fairbairn 2020). The intertwined digitalization and financialization of land and food reminds us again of the intimate linkages between the politics of land and food, which have changed some notions in land politics. It is now quite reasonable to ask the strange-sounding question, "What owns the land?" (Ashwood et al. 2022). These issues are elaborated in the chapter by Fraser, Isakson, and McMichael (this volume). That land and food politics are intertwined can be seen in the historical evolution of food regimes, as examined by Friedmann and McMichael (1989) and McMichael (2012), as well as in McMichael's chapter in this volume. The first food regime (1870s–1920s) was anchored by the British Empire, while the second food regime (1930s–1970s) was dominated by the United States (Friedmann and McMichael 1989). There is no consensus about what kind of global food regime there is at present, in the early twenty-first century, although McMichael's (2013) notion of a "corporate food regime" (anchored principally by transnational corporations) seems to be widely endorsed. His recent analysis of the rising role of China in the global food regime is now a key reference point in this inquiry (McMichael 2020), even while the role of transnational companies remains central (Canfield, Anderson, and McMichael 2021; Clapp 2023). The current food regime is polycentric institutionally, geopolitically, and substantively: institutionally because both the state and corporations have the power, albeit in tension with each other, to shape and maintain the food regime; geopolitically because a plurality of regional power blocs have leverage in shaping and maintaining the food regime in their geopolitical spheres of influence (noting particularly the role of the BRICS countries, especially China); and substantively because the food regime that we know today may no longer be a specifically food-centered regime, given the rise of the "global flex agro-commodity complex" (Borras et al. 2016), the emergence of which was facilitated by and resulted in contemporary commodity and land regime transitions.

Breaking out from capitalist global food systems through a radically different system of food production, circulation, exchange, consumption, and waste, specifically through agroecological transition (Rosset and Altieri, 2017), requires a fundamental democratization of the politics of land that would allow for the emergence of appropriate agroecological zones as the material basis for agroecological transition. It also requires addressing the question of "distancing" caused by the metabolic rift through a complex notion of "localization" as argued by Robbins (2015), which, though not limited to land as space, deals primarily with land politics.

This is the main message in the chapter by Vandermeer and Perfecto (this volume). Without a prior or accompanying—and very specific type of—democratization of land politics, it is not possible to even begin to think about agroecological transition. The first step in any agroecological transition is ensuring that those who work the land have the autonomy and capacity to break away from a chemical-based industrial agriculture way of farming. If they do not have control over the land, this first step will never happen. If young people want to start farming using agroecological methods (and it may be that young people are more open to new ways of sustainable farming), the first requirement would be to secure access to land, but this may not be possible for generational reasons (White 2020).

Land and Climate Politics

Land and land politics are front and center when it comes to the causes of and remedies for climate change. The agrofood system contributes up to 40 percent of greenhouse gas (GHG) emissions, and this has largely to do with land politics. According to the 2019 Intergovernmental Panel on Climate Change (IPCC) report, *Climate Change and Land*, changes in land cover has accounted for nearly a quarter of total GHG emissions since the 1960s (IPCC 2019; see also Cavanagh and Benjaminsen this volume; Ribot this volume). Yet the general discussion about the role of agriculture and livestock in climate change is too muddled. Consciously or not, the tendency in the mainstream narrative is to treat agriculture and the livestock sector as homogeneous. One strand of the debate advocates for a sustainable intensification in agriculture and livestock production to cater to ever-increasing consumption requirements. This almost always means privileging hyper-capital-intensive production systems that already exist, such as modern mechanized, monoculture plantations and intensive livestock production (Weis this handbook, and 2013; Hall et al. 2017; Li and Semedi 2021; Wolford 2021; León Araya 2023; Wang and Xu 2024). The flipside of this argument is the insinuation that particular types of production systems, such as swidden agriculture, mobile pastoralism, and artisanal fishing, are economically inefficient and ecologically destructive (Mertz et al. 2009; Dressler et al. 2017; Franco and Borras 2019; Scoones 2021). This, in turn, justifies reallocating access to the means of production and social reproduction (mainly land) away from ordinary working people, which is often achieved by criminalizing swidden agriculture, land grabbing via extra-economic coercion, or soliciting consent with the seductive offers of formalized individual private property land titles, which leads ultimately to sedentarization and the release of larger swathes of land for takeover by big capital.

If this narrative is to be challenged, an important starting point is to treat agriculture and livestock as internally heterogeneous, based on existing social relations around property, labor, remuneration, and reproduction, and to demonstrate that GHG emission levels differ markedly among social classes and production systems within these sectors. It is the chemical-based, industrial monoculture models of capitalist agriculture and intensive livestock that have contributed massively to GHG emissions. There are huge differences between a large-scale oil palm plantation that has emerged from a natural forest or peatland and small-scale swidden agriculture in Indonesia; or between intensive meat and dairy production in Europe, which relies on soya imports from countries in the Amazon, and small-scale mobile cattle pastoralism in Gambella, Ethiopia. Scoones (2021) shows how significant these differences are in the livestock sector, and the implications for climate change and the politics of resources. On a bigger scale and wider horizon, this brings us back to the "Age of Capital"—the "Capitalocene"—as the cause of the current climate crisis (Moore 2017). And it ultimately brings us back to the politics of land. When cattle ranchers in Colombia continue to expand by clearing the Amazon rainforest, their actions are directly facilitated by the politics around land.

When intensive livestock producers in Europe continue to enjoy a stable supply chain of feed, especially soya, this is directly facilitated and maintained by land policies and politics. The network of connections involved in land use change is often long-distance and indirect, highlighting the importance of the notion of ILUC (indirect land use change) and why it is fiercely contested in policy processes (Liu et al. 2013; Xu and Borras this handbook).

Furthermore, many elements of climate change mitigation and adaptation are land-based, under a broad umbrella of "nature-based solutions." The emerging dominant global strategy is veering toward GHG emission offset strategies, which essentially allows "business as usual" in fossil-based corporate profit-making as long as GHG emissions are offset somewhere else. This strategy has led to the 'global green carbon rush', with market-based mitigation and adaptation initiatives launched in the form of nature conservation and programs such as Reducing Emissions from Deforestation and Forest Degradation (REDD+) and Clean Development Mechanism (CDM; Corbera and Schroeder 2011). The axes of power relations are between the centers of capital wanting to continue the expanded reproduction of capital, and those in the periphery that have vast spaces for conservation and carbon sequestration. Some call this "green colonialism" (Hamouchene and Sandwell 2023). Many of these initiatives have resulted in resource grabbing along the lines of green grabbing. Classic examples include a case in Cambodia, when a natural forest was grabbed from villagers, and all the trees cleared and the fields burned and then replanted with a fast-growing tree used to construct an industrial tree plantation for a carbon sequestration investment (Scheidel and Work 2018). What we have in this case is a net emissions gain, not carbon saving, and extraction, not sustainability, despite claims to the contrary by the corporate interests that were behind the industrial tree plantation (Kröger 2014; Xu 2020). There are far too many examples of this, from large-scale conservation projects, the fortress conservation type or otherwise (Cavanagh and Benjaminsen this volume; Brockington 2002; Arsel and Büscher 2012) to creating renewable sources of energy that is principally about relocating land access, taking it from the hands of ordinary working people and putting it under the control of states and big capital in solar-, wind-, and hydropower projects (Dunlap 2018; Stock and Birkenholtz 2021; Torres Contreras 2022). Not only are such projects questionable solutions to the climate crisis: they themselves become frontiers of expanded reproduction of capital. The central concern of purported mitigation and adaptation strategies has much more to do with making a profit than genuinely addressing the climate crisis (Paprocki 2019).

Land and Labor

Land and labor are intertwined: land is transformed and reproduced through labor and human intervention, and labor is reproduced through land. A landscape or socio-agroecological zone is constructed by the social relations underlying it even when these are not immediately apparent or have become invisibilized (Mitchell 1996).

To continue our discussion of land in production and social reproduction, all working people have issues related to land, even if they are varied, concerns about whether and how farmland enables peasants to pursue productive and social reproductive activities or how access to a space in a slum dwelling enables some stevedores to access wage work. Therefore, the ways in which land politics shapes the ability of working people to pursue productive and social reproductive activities in order to live or even accumulate is far more wide-ranging than the dominant treatment in classic agrarian studies—or, for that matter, in the narratives of some peasant movements—which privileges production-centric views on land, such as farmland or grazing land, inadvertently narrowing the focus on land questions to the rural and agricultural settings of the global South and global North. This category is important, but is just one of the broad categories of land politics in relation to labor and human-nature interactions. There are three other categories that are also relevant: global South–global North/rural/nonagricultural; global South–global North/urban/agricultural, and global South–global North/urban/nonagricultural (Borras and Franco 2023). Typologizing the land question in this way, which is firmly anchored in the perspective of land in production and social reproduction, helps us to organize our analysis of how land shapes labor and human-nature relations. This means that we can begin to fully engage with the question raised by Levien, Watts, and Yan (2018) about how political struggles over the means of production and social reproduction, specifically land, unfold in today's global capitalism. Jacobs (this volume) explores this question in the context of how land politics shapes working people's autonomy and capacity to survive in the city through livelihood activities with agrarian characteristics. How ordinary people decide to pursue what livelihoods, and where, depends in part on how the politics of land shapes and limits the possibilities that are available. For example, Indigenous peoples in Altillanura and the Amazon regions were given demarcated and formally constituted *resguardos* that are geographically isolated with land that is too marginal agro-economically to be the basis for reproducing life. One group decided to swallow the bitter pill of going to work in the oil palm plantation that they accused of having grabbed their ancestral land; another group resettled informally in a slum dwelling on the outskirts of a medium-sized town far away from their *resguardos*, where they sought jobs in hydrocarbon mining extraction and any other odd jobs they could find (Arango 2023). Having farmland or grazing land is not a guarantee for simple reproduction of life and society. Many peasants in Myanmar work their farmland from May to October, and take jobs as sugarcane cutters in Yunnan, China, from November to April. The socioeconomic and socioecological quality of their farmland and the broader agroecological zone is not sufficient to guarantee simple reproduction, much less to achieve any of their lofty dreams of modest accumulation (Borras et al. 2022).

The making of land into farmland, landscape, agroecological zone, territory, or homeland comes about through labor. Labor, specifically migrant labor from Vietnan, has transformed the landscape of Guangxi (China) into a patchwork of eucalyptus tree plantations, interwoven with sugarcane farms (Xu 2020). The labor of swidden farmers transforms and maintains a landscape, just as small-scale mobile pastoralists transform and maintain a grazing range. The labor of intensive livestock and dairy farmers in Europe, along with that of their hired (usually migrant) workers transforms their local landscape. But this is not the only transformation that takes place. The labor-landscape interaction in European intensive livestock and dairy farming, in turn, shapes and is shaped by the labor-landscape interaction in distant places where soya, a key feedstuff for European livestock, is produced, such as the Americas. The social relations behind the kind of commodity produced, how it is produced, and for what purposes do matter in terms of how we understand the way labor and human intervention transform land and land politics. The role labor plays in the transformation of a swidden agriculture landscape is significantly different from the way labor is mobilized in intensive capitalist agriculture, which transforms its respective landscape very differently.

Land and labor are inseparable, and many of the big issues that carry the banner of either land issues or labor issues are in fact land *and* labor issues (Amanor this volume; Chambati this volume; Oya 2013; Watts [1983] 2013; Pye 2017; Gyapong 2021; Illien, Perez, and Bieri 2022; Ra 2022; Serrano 2023; Shah 2023). It is likely that the recent global land rush and land grabbing may have contributed to expanding the size of, and worsening the conditions for, the "relative surplus population" (Marx [1867] 1976; Li 2010). This population lives and works in precarious conditions, without stable jobs or livelihoods, social security and healthcare, or adequate housing. Nearly two decades ago, Davis (2006, 178) estimated their number to be one billion. The highly mechanized nature of many of the enterprises that have emerged out of recent commodity and land rushes, including industrial monoculture plantations, may have aggravated this labor situation, and it is possible that widespread land grabbing might have significantly contributed to the recent unprecedented levels of rural-urban and cross-country migration (Sassen 2014). Otsuki and Zoomers (this volume) address this issue from the broader context of human mobility.

Land and Citizenship

In societies where the agrarian sector remains important, land, political power, and democracy are inseparable: the landed classes tend to monopolize political power, acting inside, through, and outside the state (Moore 1967; Harvey 1998; Sikor and Lund 2009; Wittman 2009). Those who have no land, or whose land is too insignificant in size, quality, and location, tend to have less political power. This brings us to the issue of citizenship rights. In this context, democratizing land politics is a fundamental element in the transition from clients to citizens (Fox 1994). Many twentieth-century land reforms, though mostly oriented to economic production, were also concerned with democratizing political power. Land reform has been a key issue in democratization debates, notably in the 1980s and 1990s, and especially with regard to "rural democratization" (Fox 1990; Lara and Morales 1990; Putzel 1992). When share tenants are instructed by their landlord to vote for the latter's candidate during an election, there is little that the tenants can do other than obey (Franco and Borras 2005). In many societies, the struggle for land entails navigating a legal institutional maze, which requires citizenship rights. This becomes a chicken-and-egg situation of democratizing land and democratizing broader politics and the legal complex more generally (see Franco 2008; Lund 2021; Coronado 2022).

The history of haciendas and plantations worldwide provides one of the most brutal illustrations of the relationship between land and citizenship. Plantation owners owned land and slaves, owners of haciendas owned land and bonded labor and subordinated peasants. Citizenship rights were for the ruling landed classes, and not for the slaves and other subordinated classes (Mintz 1986). Grabbing lands from Indigenous people and turning some of them who survived the genocide into cheap labor was part of the genesis of the California capitalist agriculture that emerged in the mid-nineteenth century. These Indigenous workers would be joined and replaced, in waves over time, by batches of migrant workers—Chinese, Japanese, Filipinos, Indians, Mexicans. From the 1850s to the Great Depression of the 1930s, the history of California's agriculture was one of land, migrant labor, and the denial of citizenship rights. Migrant workers were, by design, illegalized, informalized, denied the right to access land and most civil and political rights, and the objects of racist attacks and periodic forced deportations (Mitchell 1996; McWilliams [1935] 2000; Ngai 2021). These political dynamics did not disappear with the end of the Great Depression; they continue to this day. Nor is this phenomenon confined to California. We see similar patterns of the relationship between land, migrant labor, and citizenship today in the Syrian and Kurdish farmworkers in Turkey, Myanmar farmworkers in Thailand and China, Central American migrant workers in Canada, Nicaraguan migrants in Costa Rica, Zimbabwean farmworkers in South Africa, South Sudanese farmworkers in Ethiopia, Venezuelan farmworkers in Colombia, to name just a few.

Furthermore, as discussed earlier, land means territory and homeland. When people are displaced, expelled, uprooted from their territory and homeland, or when their homeland is violently destroyed through bombing or mass ecological plunder and destruction, it is hard to envisage how they can ensure the continued renewal of life and society. Such horrendous phenomena are among the defining characteristics of contemporary global capitalism. Where such events occur, they often have a material basis in the politics of class and interlocking axes of difference, especially race and ethnicity. When Rohingya villages were burned down by the Myanmar military and the villagers driven out of the country, it was justified by the fact that they were not citizens of Myanmar in the first place. Around the world, the rise of the far right is intimately linked to ethno-nationalist and racist narratives (Scoones et al. 2018; Edelman 2021). Indeed, as Sud (this volume, and 2020) frames it: land-making is state-making.

A useful analytical approach to situating land and citizenship dynamics is James O'Connor's argument that modern capitalist states, especially those faced with fiscal pressures, must pursue two permanent but contradictory tasks, namely, to facilitate capitalist accumulation while trying to maintain a historically determined minimum level of political legitimacy (O'Connor [1973] 2017; see also Fox 1993). For societies outside the centers of advanced capitalism, the ability of their central states to intervene by kickstarting, expanding, or sustaining economic growth is usually constrained, forcing many of them to rely on extractive industries (Burchardt and Dietz 2014; Arsel, Hogenboom, and Pelligrini 2016; McKay 2017; Ye et al. 2020; McKay et al. 2021; Chagnon et al. 2022). Whether this involves oil and gas extraction, rare earth mining, or the expansion of agribusiness plantations, for extractive industries to emerge and be sustained relies on land policy and politics that are favorable for the owners of big capital. The central state plays a critical role in enabling extraction in its various forms. Yet it does so while trying to maintain political legitimacy. Many Latin American governments that have experienced cycles of left-wing victories have performed a delicate balancing act between pursuing capitalist accumulation and political legitimacy. Many have implemented policies that redistribute a significant portion of the income from extractive industry to working people through populist programs, such as providing guaranteed basic income for sections of working people. Others have combined this with stricter environmental regulations in the extractive sector, and so on. When villagers protested widespread land grabbing through land concessions for corporate capital in Cambodia between 2008 and 2012, the government imposed a limit of 10,000 hectares per company (in fact, this is easily circumvented by the owner, who simply register multiple companies, getting 10,000 hectares of land for each). But perhaps the most important political-legitimacy-seeking act of the Cambodian government in attempting to smooth its concession-driven commercialization of land was its 2012–2013 land titling program that benefited a substantial number of small farmers. The flipside of this is that most lands outside the scope of the program are there for the taking for land concessions and extractive industries (Dwyer 2015; Beban 2021).

Land and Geopolitics

Land—as a scarce resource; as key to accessing and extracting raw materials and cheap labor; as space; as territory and homeland in the context of uneven capitalist development; and as a key element in capitalist efforts to address recurring crises of overaccumulation—is a strategic object of geopolitics.

Control grabbing as the main defining element of land grabbing occurs in historical and contemporary geopolitics in various ways, including in the brutal method of direct colonial territory grabbing and settler colonialism. There are fewer recent examples in this category, except for the Russian invasion of Ukraine (Hall 2023), although past cases cannot necessarily be consigned to the history books (on the case of Palestine, see Tramel 2024), nor can their colonial legacies be completely expurgated in the postcolonial nation-states. Below this scale of sovereign territory and homeland grabbing, however, we find subnational control grabbing of territory, landscapes, agroecological zones, and plots of land as a means of production in the context of capitalism's never-ending search for ways to expand profits. One way to do this is to grab the means of production at the cheapest cost possible, which usually entails land and cheap labor. Land here is both a means of production and an entry point for accessing other resources, whether physically through mining or the siting of pipelines or waste dumps, or through creative accounting such as in carbon sequestration and trade. It is no coincidence that powerful states can be found transacting different types of land deals in distant countries. It is also not uncommon to see countries hurriedly passing laws to regulate, if not altogether prohibit, the foreignization of land (Zoomers 2010; Sauer and Leite 2012; Fairbairn 2020). Finally, land plays a role in geopolitical dynamics through ILUC, as mentioned earlier. A classic example is the enormous power that China exerts upon the global soya trade—and consequently on land use politics within the soya sector—by being the single biggest soya commodity buyer (Oliveira and Hecht 2016; Oliveira and Schneider 2016). In effect, China controls the equivalent of more than 30 million hectares of land in the Americas without having made any direct investment in land for soya production (Xu and Borras, this volume).

Geopolitical dynamics are also enacted through land and land politics. The Cold War offers a useful illustration of this: while much of the socialist bloc was sponsoring radical, socialist-oriented land reforms, the United States took an active role, largely through the Alliance for Progress, on behalf of the advanced capitalist world, in sponsoring preemptive limited liberal land reforms to counter the radicalization of the world's countryside (Putzel 1992). The immediate post–Cold War 1990s witnessed the United States taking the lead, through various institutions funded by the US Agency for International Development USAID and the World Bank, in rushing into the former socialist countries to quickly privatize land property (Spoor 2008). Kay's chapter (this volume) gives us a tour of the second half of the twentieth century, navigating us through this critical historical period when land reform was a key issue in geopolitical maneuvering. Dwyer's chapter (this volume) picks up where Kay leaves off, providing a bridge to contemporary global land politics, especially in the period of the global land rush (see also Dwyer 2022).

The recent commodity and land rushes have occurred within a changing geopolitical configuration as the rise of the BRICS countries, especially China, nudges us toward a multipolar world (Bräutigam 2011; Scoones et al. 2016). Thus, the rushes are both part of the process, and initial outcomes, of radically changing geopolitics. It is very likely, as McMichael (2020) suggests, that regime transitions in the food and flex crops complex and the shifts in climate change politics have become intertwined with the most recent geopolitical dynamics, coinciding with this move toward a polycentric world politics. We see China, through its "Going Out" policy, aggressively investing in multiple countries around the world, including in the land sector in developing countries in Africa, Asia, and Latin America (Bräutigam 2011; Scoones et al. 2016), although it is not possible to have a good understanding of China's "Going Out" policy without a having a grasp of the agrarian transformations happening inside China itself (Zhang and Donaldson 2008; Yan and Chen 2015; Ye 2015; Zhan 2019; Andreas et al. 2020).

The Asian, European, and African portions of Chinese investment initiatives have been consolidated in megaprojects around the Belt and Road Initiative, a modern-day revival of the ancient China-led initiative to build the Silk Road. The other BRICS countries have pursued similar policies, although on a much smaller scale than China—for example, Brazil's investments in Mozambique (Wolford and Nehring 2015; Monjane and Bruna 2020) and South Africa (Hall 2011). The Gulf States have also participated in this process to a significant extent (Henderson 2022).

Nevertheless, we should be mindful of the important reminder from Dywer (this volume and 2022) and Lu (2021) that the macropolitics of geopolitics encounters micropolitics on the ground, producing a much more complex set of political dynamics. The lessons from the geopolitical shaping of local land politics are a reaffirmation of the nuanced global and local dialectical processes of transformation that Harriet Friedmann and Philip McMichael (Friedmann and McMichael 1989; McMichael 2013), the original theorists of the food regime, have identified as a cornerstone in such an inherently multiscalar perspective.

Conclusion

A key assumption in this volume, which forms the basis of various issues for discussion, is that land must be seen in and through the connected whole of production and social reproduction, and through various spheres of social life. This is not something new. The classic book by Michael Watts ([1983] 2013) explores these interconnections. What we have done is to update and broaden such discussions in the contemporary context. It is only by clarifying this fundamental assumption about the meaning of land that we can explore other social science inquiries and make sense of competing interpretations of contemporary land struggles such as Bernstein's position, which regards them as less significant than the twentieth-century land struggles (Bernstein, this volume, and 2018), and the argument of Levien, Watts, and Yan (2018, 876):

> Struggles over means of both production and social reproduction remain as important as ever but are not playing out in remotely the same way as Marx predicted. Land remains an important focus of such struggles, even if its precise significance remains fiercely debated. Such struggles are also, Marxists increasingly recognize, inextricably bound up with non-class forms of power and domination, whether patriarchy, racism, casteism, or anti-immigrant nativism. Keeping in mind the extreme geographical variation in these trends, these are roughly the coordinates that define agrarian change and politics in the early twenty-first century.

We close our introductory discussion with the issue of land struggles, reflecting the way that we have organized the sequence of chapters. The last four chapters of this handbook are all related to political struggles around land. The chapter by Claeys et al. is on human rights as a framework for understanding land. The human-rights-based framing of land struggles has gained traction since the 1980s (Monsalve 2013; Sandwell et al. 2019). Various international conventions have contributed to this rising political currency, including the UN Declaration on the Rights of Indigenous Peoples (UNDRIP) in 2007, the UN Declaration on the Rights of Peasants and Other Working Peoples in the Rural Areas (UNDROP) of 2018 (Claeys and Edelman 2020), and around a dozen other treaties and international agreements related to global land governance (Margulis, McKeon, and Borras 2013; Seufert 2013). These are important reference points in contemporary land struggles that contain elements of their classic counterparts, especially those in the twentieth century. Today's struggles are rooted in class politics by poor peasants, farmworkers, and small pastoralists and by competing and counter movements among rich peasants, as seen, for example, in the great 2019–2021 Indian farmers' protest (Baviskar and Levien 2021; Lerche 2021), and the 2020–2023 Dutch farmers' protests (Van der Ploeg 2020). But the twenty-first-century agrarian movements combine class politics with non-class-oriented struggles (anti-ecological plunder, antipatriarchy, antiracism), which were less significant features of great peasant movements and peasant wars of the twentieth century (Wolf 1969; Edelman and Borras 2016; Edelman 2024). Everyday forms of peasant resistance (Scott 1985) have also been revalued during the past two decades with more compelling studies published (O'Brien and Li 2006; Moreda 2015). Adnan (this volume) has provided an excellent mapping of the literature on resistance to land enclosures, historical and contemporary (see also Hall et al. 2015).

One set of social movements that has emerged quite significantly since the 1980s are the environmental movements, and more recently, climate justice movements. Our interest in this volume is whether and how these social movements speak to or overlap with agrarian issues and movements. Land is a common reference point for the environmental, climate, and agrarian movements, and it is central in environmental struggles, especially in conservation issues (Cavanagh and Benjaminsen, this volume). Yaşın (2022) talks about the environmentalization of agrarian questions and the agrarianization of climate justice movements, and others argue that anti-extractivism is often expressed in land struggles (Nygren, Kröger, and Gills 2022). There is growing agreement on this point (Gerber 2011; Claeys and Delgado Pugley 2017; Calmon, Jacovetti, and Koné 2021; Sekine 2021; Shah 2023). While, objectively speaking, it is increasingly obvious that the land issue is an environmental issue, and vice versa, the extent to which political struggles have been able to catch up with this reality remains limited. This partly affirms Fraser's (2021) critique of environmental justice movements as "merely environmental." But there is also much room for improvement on the side of the land and agrarian movements in how to reframe their struggles to organically embed them in environmental issues (although agrarian platforms such as agroecology are deeply environmental). These are some of the issues explored in the final chapter by Franco and Borras, which provides a typology of global land struggles. This is a useful heuristic tool in pursuing further analytical exploration of these issues, and inquiring into the dynamic historical continuum of what was, what is, and what ought to be in relation to these land movements, given the changed and changing global political economy and political ecological context of such struggles.

Notes

1. See Agrawal, Erbaugh, and Pradhan (2023) for a state of the art perspective on the commons that is relevant to our discussion here.
2. For a broadly relevant discussion in the context of China, see Ho (2001) and Ye (2015).
3. Our discussion in this section draws on Borras and Franco (2024).
4. There are several excellent studies on which we build our understanding of the concept of land regime, including Mitchell (1996), Ribot and Peluso (2003), Lund (2006), Boone (2013), Li (2014), and German (2022).

References

Agarwal, Bina. 1994. *A Field of One's Own: Gender and Land Rights in South Asia*. Cambridge, UK: Cambridge University Press.

Agrawal, Arun, James Erbaugh, and Nabin Pradhan. 2023. "The Commons." *Annual Review of Environment and Resources* 48:31–558.

Akram-Lodhi, A. Haroon, and Cristóbal Kay. 2010a. "Surveying the Agrarian Question (Part 1): Unearthing Foundations, Exploring Diversity." *Journal of Peasant Studies* 37 (1): 177–202.

Akram-Lodhi, A. Haroon, and Cristóbal Kay. 2010b. "Surveying the Agrarian Question (Part 2): Current Debates and Beyond." *Journal of Peasant Studies* 37 (2): 255–284.

Akram-Lodhi, A. Haroon, Kristina Dietz, Bettina Engels, and Ben M. McKay, eds. 2021. *Handbook of Critical Agrarian Studies*. Cheltenham, UK: Edward Elgar.

Alonso-Fradejas, Alberto. 2012. "Anything but a Story Foretold: Multiple Politics of Resistance to the Agrarian Extractivist Project in Guatemala." *Journal of Peasant Studies* 42 (3–4): 489–515.

Andreas, Joel, Sunila S. Kale, Michael Levien, and Qian Forrest Zhang. 2020. "Rural Land Dispossession in China and India." *Journal of Peasant Studies* 47 (6): 1109–1142.

Arango, Lorenza. 2023. "Indigenous Peoples, Commons and the Challenge of Sustaining Life amid Capitalist Land Grabs." Land Rush Working Papers and Notes Series No. 4. International Institute of Social Studies. https://www.iss.nl/en/research/research-projects/commodity-land-rushes-and-regimes/land-rush-working-paper-notes-series.

Arsel, Murat, and Bram Büscher. 2012. "Nature™ Inc.: Changes and Continuities in Neoliberal Conservation and Market-Based Environmental Policy." *Development and Change* 43 (1): 53–78.

Arsel, Murat, Barbara Hogenboom, and Lorenzo Pellegrini. 2016. "The Extractive Imperative in Latin America." *Extractive Industries and Society* 3 (4): 880–887.

Ashwood, Loka, Matthew Canfield, Madeleine Fairbairn, and Kathryn De Master. 2022. "What Owns the Land: The Corporate Organization of Farmland Investment." *Journal of Peasant Studies* 49 (2): 233–262.

Baviskar, Amita, and Michael Levien. 2021. "Farmers' Protests in India: Introduction to the JPS Forum." *Journal of Peasant Studies* 48 (7): 1341–1355.

Beban, Alice. 2021. *Unwritten Rule: State-Making through Land Reform in Cambodia*. Ithaca, NY: Cornell University Press.

Bernstein, Henry. 2010a. *Class Dynamics of Agrarian Change*. Halifax, CAN: Fernwood.

Bernstein, Henry. 2010b. "Introduction: Some Questions concerning the Productive Forces." *Journal of Agrarian Change* 10 (3): 300–314.

Bhattacharya, Tithi. 2017. *Social Reproduction Theory: Remapping Class, Recentering Oppression*. London: Pluto.

Boelens, Rutgerd, Arturo Escobar, Karen Bakker, Lena Hommes, Erik Swyngedouw, Barbara Hogenboom, et al. 2023. "Riverhood: Political Ecologies of Socionature Commoning and Translocal Struggles for Water Justice." *Journal of Peasant Studies* 50 (3): 1125–1156.

Boone, Catherine. 2013. "Land Regimes and the Structure of Politics: Patterns of Land-Related Conflict." *Africa* 83 (1): 188–203.

Borras, Saturnino M., Jr. 2023. "Politically Engaged, Pluralist and Internationalist: Critical Agrarian Studies Today." *Journal of Peasant Studies* 50 (2): 449–489.

Borras, Saturnino M., Jr., and Jennifer C. Franco. 2023. *Scholar-Activism and Land Struggles*. Rugby, UK: Practical Action Publishing.

Borras, Saturnino M., Jr., and Jennifer C. Franco. 2024. "Land Rush." *Journal of Peasant Studies* (March): 1–16. Online. https://doi.org/10.1080/03066150.2024.2317961

Borras, Saturnino M., Jr., Jennifer C. Franco, S. Gomez, Cristóbal Kay, and M. Spoor. 2012. "Land Grabbing in Latin America and the Caribbean." *Journal of Peasant Studies* 39 (3–4): 845–872.

Borras, Saturnino M., Jr., Jennifer C. Franco, S. R. Isakson, L. Levidow, and P. Vervest. 2016. "The Rise of Flex Crops and Commodities: Implications for Research." *Journal of Peasant Studies* 43 (1): 93–115.

Borras, Saturnino M., Jr., Jennifer C. Franco, D. Ra, T. Kramer, M. Kamoon, P. Phyu, et al. 2022. "Rurally Rooted Cross-Border Migrant Workers from Myanmar, Covid-19, and Agrarian Movements." *Agriculture and Human Values* 39 (March): 315–338.

Bräutigam, Deborah. 2011. *The Dragon's Gift: The Real Story of China in Africa*. Oxford: Oxford University Press.

Brockington, Daniel. 2002. *Fortress Conservation: The Preservation of the Mkomazi Game Reserve, Tanzania*. Bloomington: Indiana University Press.

Bruna, Natacha. 2022. "A Climate-Smart World and the Rise of Green Extractivism." *Journal of Peasant Studies* 49 (4): 839–864.

Burawoy, Michael. 1976. "The Functions and Reproduction of Migrant Labor: Comparative Material from Southern Africa and the United States." *American Journal of Sociology* 81 (5): 1050–1087.

Burchardt, Hans-Jürgen, and Kristina Dietz. 2014. "(Neo-)extractivism—a New Challenge for Development Theory from Latin America." *Third World Quarterly* 35 (3): 468–486.

Byres, Terence J. 2004. "Neo-Classical Neo-Populism 25 Years On: *Déjà Vu* and *Déjà Passé*. Towards a Critique. " *Journal of Agrarian Change* 4 (1–2): 17–44.

Byres, Terence J. 2009. "The Landlord Class, Peasant Differentiation, Class Struggle and the Transition to Capitalism: England, France and Prussia Compared." *Journal of Peasant Studies* 36 (1): 33–54.

Calmon, Daniela, Chantal Jacovetti, and Massa Koné. 2021. "Agrarian Climate Justice as a Progressive Alternative to Climate Security: Mali at the Intersection of Natural Resource Conflicts." *Third World Quarterly* 42 (12): 2785–2803.

Canfield, Matthew, Molly D. Anderson, and Philip McMichael. 2021. "UN Food Systems Summit 2021: Dismantling Democracy and Resetting Corporate Control of Food Systems." *Frontiers in Sustainable Food Systems* 5: Article 661552. doi:10.3389/fsufs.

Chagnon, Christopher W., Francesco Durante, Barry K. Gills, Sophia E. Hagolani-Albov, Saana Hokkanen, Sohvi M. Kangasluoma, et al. 2022. "From Extractivism to Global Extractivism: The Evolution of an Organizing Concept." *Journal of Peasant Studies* 49 (4): 760–792.

Clapp, Jennifer 2023. "Concentration and Crises: Exploring the Deep Roots of Vulnerability in the Global Industrial Food System." *Journal of Peasant Studies* 50 (1): 1–25.
Clapp, Jennifer, and S. R. Isakson. 2018. *Speculative Harvests: Financialization, Food, and Agriculture.* Rugby, UK: Practical Action Publishing.
Claeys, Priscilla, and Deborah Delgado Pugley. 2017. "Peasant and Indigenous Transnational Social Movements Engaging with Climate Justice." *Canadian Journal of Development Studies* 38 (3): 325–340.
Claeys, Priscilla, and Marc Edelman. 2020. "The United Nations Declaration on the Rights of Peasants and Other People Working in Rural Areas." *Journal of Peasant Studies* 47 (1): 1–68.
Corbera, Esteve, and Heike Schroeder. 2011. "Governing and Implementing REDD+." *Environmental Science & Policy* 14 (2): 89–99.
Coronado Delgado, Sergio A. 2022. "Peasants, Protests and Litigation: Struggles over Land and Institutions in Colombia." Doctoral diss., International Institute of Social Studies.
Cortesi, Luisa. 2021. "An Ontology of Water and Land in North Bihar, India." *Journal of the Royal Anthropological Institute* 27 (4): 870–889.
Corson, Catherine, and Ken I. MacDonald. 2012. "Enclosing the Global Commons: The Convention on Biological Diversity and Green Grabbing." *Journal of Peasant Studies* 39 (2): 263–283.
Cousins, Ben, and Ian Scoones. 2010. "Contested Paradigms of 'Viability' in Redistributive Land Reform: Perspectives from Southern Africa." *Journal of Peasant Studies* 37 (1): 31–66.
Davis, Mike. 2006. *The Planet of Slums.* New York: Verso.
Deere, Carmen Diana, and Magdalena León. 2003. "The Gender Asset Gap: Land in Latin America." *World Development* 31 (6): 925–947.
de Soto, Hernando. 2000. *The Mystery of Capital: Why Capitalism Triumphs in the West and Fails Everywhere Else.* New York: Basic Books.
Dell'Angelo, Jampel, Paolo D'odorico, Maria Cristina Rulli, and P. Marchand. 2017. "The Tragedy of the Grabbed Commons: Coercion and Dispossession in the Global Land Rush." *World Development* 92:1–12.
Deininger, Klaus. 1999. "Making Negotiated Land Reform Work: Initial Experience from Colombia, Brazil and South Africa." *World Development* 27 (4): 651–672.
Deininger, Klaus, and Hans Binswanger. 1999. "The Evolution of the World Bank's Land Policy: Principles, Experience, and Future Challenges." *World Bank Research Observer* 14 (2): 247–276.
Desmarais, Annette A., Darrin Qualman, Andre Magnan, and Nettie Wiebe. 2015. "Land Grabbing and Land Concentration: Mapping Changing Patterns of Farmland Ownership in Three Rural Municipalities in Saskatchewan, Canada." *Canadian Food Studies* 2 (1): 16–47.
Dieng, Rama Salla. 2024. "Racial Capitalism and Women's Horticultural Labour in Senegal: Neo-Housewifisation and the Micro-Politics of Paternalism." *Journal of Peasant Studies* (May): 1–27. Online. https://doi.org/10.1080/03066150.2024.2343332.
Dressler, Wolfram H., David Wilson, Jessica Clendenning, Rob Cramb, Rodney Keenan, Sango Mahanty, et al. 2017. "The Impact of Swidden Decline on Livelihoods and Ecosystem Services in Southeast Asia: A Review of the Evidence from 1990 to 2015." *Ambio* 46: 291–310.
Dunlap, Alexander. 2018. "Counterinsurgency for Wind Energy: The Bíi Hioxo Wind Park in Juchitán, Mexico." *Journal of Peasant Studies* 45 (3): 630–652.
Dwyer, Michael B. 2015. "The Formalization Fix? Land Titling, Land Concessions and the Politics of Spatial Transparency in Cambodia." *Journal of Peasant Studies* 42 (5): 903–928.

Dwyer, Michael B. 2022. *Upland Geopolitics: Postwar Laos and the Global Land Rush*. Seattle: University of Washington Press.

Edelman, Marc. 2021. "Hollowed-Out Heartland, USA: How Capital Sacrificed Communities and Paved the Way for Authoritarian Populism." *Journal of Rural Studies* 82:505–517.

Edelman, Marc. 2024. *Peasant Politics of the Twenty-First Century: Transnational Social Movements and Agrarian Change*. Ithaca, NY: Cornell University Press.

Edelman, Marc, and Saturnino M. Borras Jr. 2016. *Political Dynamics of Transnational Agrarian Movements*. Rugby, UK: Practical Action Publishing.

Edelman, Marc, and Wendy Wolford. 2017. "Introduction: Critical Agrarian Studies in Theory and Practice. Symposium: Agrarianism in Theory and Practice." *Antipode* 49 (4): 959–976.

Fairbairn, Madeleine. 2020. *Fields of Gold: Financing the Global Land Rush*. Ithaca, NY: Cornell University Press.

Fairhead, James, Melissa Leach, and Ian Scoones. 2012. "Green Grabbing: A New Appropriation of Nature?" *Journal of Peasant Studies* 39 (2): 237–261.

Foster, John Bellamy. 1999. "Marx's Theory of Metabolic Rift: Classical Foundations for Environmental Sociology." *American Journal of Sociology* 105 (2): 366–405.

Foster, John Bellamy. 2000. *Marx's Ecology: Materialism and Nature*. New York: Monthly Review Press.

Fox, Jonathan, ed. 1990. "The Challenge of Rural Democratisation: Perspectives from Latin America and the Philippines." Special Issue. *Journal of Development Studies* 26 (4): 1–18.

Fox, Jonathan. 1993. *The Politics of Food in Mexico: State Power and Social Mobilization*. Ithaca, NY: Cornell University Press.

Fox, Jonathan. 1994. "The Difficult Transition from Clientelism to Citizenship: Lessons from Mexico." *World Politics* 46 (2): 151–184.

Franco, Jennifer C. 2008. "Making Land Rights Accessible: Social Movements and Political-Legal Innovation in the Rural Philippines." *Journal of Development Studies* 44 (7): 991–1022.

Franco, Jennifer C., and Saturnino M. Borras Jr., eds. 2005. *On Just Grounds: Struggling for Agrarian Justice and Citizenship Rights in the Rural Philippines*. Quezon City: Institute for Popular Democracy.

Franco, Jennifer C., and Saturnino M. Borras Jr. 2019. "Grey Areas in Green Grabbing: Subtle and Indirect Interconnections between Climate Change Politics and Land Grabs and Their Implications for Research." *Land Use Policy* 84:92–199.

Fraser, Nancy. 2021. "Climates of Capital for a Trans-environmental Eco-Socialism." *New Left Review* 127(January–February): 94–127.

Friedmann, Harriet, and Philip McMichael. 1989. "Agriculture and the State System: The Rise and Decline of National Agricultures, 1870 to the Present." *Sociologia Ruralis* 29 (2): 93–117.

Gerber, Julien-Francois. 2011. "Conflicts over Industrial Tree Plantations in the South: Who, How and Why?" *Global Environmental Change* 21 (1): 165–176.

German, Laura. 2022. *Power/Knowledge/Land: Contested Ontologies of Land and Its Governance in Africa*. Ann Arbor: University of Michigan Press.

Grajales, Jacobo. 2021. *Agrarian Capitalism, War and Peace in Colombia: Beyond Dispossession*. New York: Routledge.

Griffin, Keith, Azizur R. Khan, and Amy Ickowitz. 2002. "Poverty and the Distribution of Land." *Journal of Agrarian Change* 2 (3): 279–330.

Gyapong, Adwoa Y. 2021. "Land Grabs, Farmworkers, and Rural Livelihoods in West Africa: Some Silences in the Food Sovereignty Discourse." *Globalizations* 18 (3): 339–354.

Hall, Derek. 2023. "Russia's Invasion of Ukraine and Critical Agrarian Studies." *Journal of Peasant Studies* 50 (1): 26–46.

Hall, Derek, Phil Hirsch, and Tania M. Li. 2011. *Powers of Exclusion: Land Dilemmas in Southeast Asia*. Singapore: National University of Singapore Press.

Hall, Ruth. 2011. "Land Grabbing in Southern Africa: The Many Faces of the Investor Rush." *Review of African Political Economy* 38 (128): 193–214.

Hall, Ruth, Marc Edelman, Saturnino M. Borras Jr., Ian Scoones, Ben White, and Wendy. Wolford. 2015. "Resistance, Acquiescence or Incorporation? An Introduction to Land Grabbing and Political Reactions 'from Below.'" *Journal of Peasant Studies* 42 (3–4): 467–488.

Hall, Ruth, Ian Scoones, and Dzodzi Tsikata. 2017. "Plantations, Outgrowers and Commercial Farming in Africa: Agricultural Commercialisation and Implications for Agrarian Change." *Journal of Peasant Studies* 44 (3): 515–537.

Hamouchene, Hamza, and Katie Sandwell. 2023. *Dismantling Green Colonialism: Energy and Climate Justice in the Arab Region*. London: Pluto Press.

Harriss, John, Janet Hunter, and Colin Lewis, eds. 1995. *The New Institutional Economics and Third World Development*. London: Routledge.

Harvey, David. 2003. *The New Imperialism*. Oxford: Oxford University Press.

Harvey, Neil. 1998. *The Chiapas Rebellion: The Struggle for Land and Democracy*. Durham, NC: Duke University Press.

Henderson, Christian. 2022. "The Rise of Arab Gulf Agro-capital: Continuity and Change in the Corporate Food Regime." *Journal of Peasant Studies* 49 (5): 1079–1100.

Ho, Peter. 2001. "Who Owns China's Land? Policies, Property Rights and Deliberate Institutional Ambiguity." *China Quarterly* 166:394–421.

Holliday, James S. 1999. *Rush for Riches: Gold Fever and the Making of California*. Berkeley: University of California Press.

IPCC. 2019. *Climate Change and Land. An IPCC Special Report on Climate Change, Desertification, Land Degradation, Sustainable Land Management, Food Security, and Greenhouse Gas Fluxes in Terrestrial Ecosystems*. International Panel on Climate Change. Accessed May 17, 2020. https://www.ipcc.ch/srccl/.

Illien, Patrick, Helena Pérez Niño, and Sabin Bieri. 2022. "Agrarian Class Relations in Rwanda: A Labour-Centred Perspective." *Journal of Peasant Studies* 49 (6): 1181–1206.

Isakson, S. Ryan. 2014. "Food and Finance: The Financial Transformation of Agro-Food Supply Chains." *Journal of Peasant Studies* 41 (5): 749–775.

Kautsky, Karl. (1899) 1988. *The Agrarian Question*. 2 Vols. London: Zwan Publications.

Kay, Cristóbal. 2002. "Why East Asia Overtook Latin America: Agrarian Reform, Industrialisation and Development." *Third World Quarterly* 23 (6): 1073–1102.

Kay, Cristóbal. 2009. "Development Strategies and Rural Development: Exploring Synergies, Eradicating Poverty." *Journal of Peasant Studies* 36 (1): 103–137.

Kay, Cristóbal. (1989) 2010. *Latin American Theories of Development and Underdevelopment*. London: Routledge.

Kay, Sylvia, Jonathan Peuch, and Jennifer C. Franco. 2015. *Extent of Farmland Grabbing in the EU: A Study*. Policy Department B: Structural and Cohesion Policies. European Parliament, Brussels.

Kerkvliet, Benedict J. T. 2009. "Everyday Politics in Peasant Societies (and Ours)." *Journal of Peasant* Studies 36 (1): 227–243.

Kröger, Markus. 2014. "The Political Economy of Global Tree Plantation Expansion: A Review." *Journal of Peasant Studies* 41 (2): 235–261.

Lahiff, Edward, Saturnino M. Borras Jr., and Cristóbal Kay. 2007. "Market-Led Agrarian Reform: Policies, Performance and Prospects." *Third World Quarterly* 28 (8): 1417–1436.
Lara, Francisco, Jr., and Horacio R. Morales Jr. 1990. "The Peasant Movement and the Challenge of Rural Democratisation in the Philippines." *Journal of Development Studies* 26 (4): 143–162.
Lenin, Vladimir I. (1899) 2004. *The Development of Capitalism in Russia*. Honolulu, HI: University Press of the Pacific.
León Araya, Andres. 2023. "Monocrops." *Journal of Peasant Studies* 50 (3): 797–808.
Lerche, Jens. 2021. "The Farm Laws Struggle 2020–2021: Class-Caste Alliances and Bypassed Agrarian Transition in Neoliberal India." *Journal of Peasant Studies* 48 (7): 1380–1396.
Levien, Michael. 2018. *Dispossession without Development: Land Grabs in Neoliberal India*. New York: Oxford University Press.
Levien, Michael, Michael Watts, and Hairong Yan. 2018. "Agrarian Marxism." *Journal of Peasant Studies* 45 (5–6): 853–883.
Li, Tania M. 2010. "To Make Live or Let Die? Rural Dispossession and the Protection of Surplus Populations." *Antipode* 41:66–93.
Li, Tania M. 2014. "What Is Land? Assembling a Resource for Global Investment." *Transactions of the Institute of British Geographers* 39 (4): 589–602.
Li, Tania M., and P. Semedi. 2021. *Plantation Life: Corporate Occupation in Indonesia's Oil Palm Zone*. Durham, NC: Duke University Press.
Liu, Jianguo, Vanessa Hull, Mateus Batistella, Ruth DeFries, Thomas Dietz, et al. 2013. "Framing Sustainability in a Telecoupled World." *Ecology and Society* 18 (2): 26.
Lu, Juan. 2021. "Grounding Chinese Investment: Encounters between Chinese Capital and Local Land Politics in Laos." *Globalizations* 18 (3): 422–440.
Lund, Christian. 2006. "Twilight Institutions: Public Authority and Local Politics in Africa." *Development and Change* 37 (4): 685–705.
Lund, Christian. 2021. *Nine-Tenths of the Law: Enduring Dispossession in Indonesia*. New Haven, CT: Yale University Press.
Malm, Andreas. 2016. *Fossil Capital: The Rise of Steam Power and the Roots of Global Warming*. New York: Verso Books.
Mamdani, Mahmood. 1996. *Citizen and Subject: Contemporary Africa and the Legacy of Late Colonialism*. Princeton, NJ: Princeton University Press.
Mamdani, Mahmood. 2020. *Neither Settler nor Native: The Making and Unmaking of Permanent Minorities*. Cambridge, MA: The Belknap Press of Harvard University Press.
Mamonova, Natalia, and Jaume Franquesa. 2020. "Populism, Neoliberalism and Agrarian Movements in Europe: Understanding Rural Support for Right-Wing Politics and Looking for Progressive Solutions." *Sociologia Ruralis* 60 (4): 710–731.
Margulis, Matias E., Nora McKeon, and Saturnino M. Borras Jr. 2013. "Land Grabbing and Global Governance: Critical Perspectives." *Globalizations* 10 (1): 1–23.
Marx, Karl. (1867) 1976. *Capital*. Vol. 1. London: Penguin.
McClintock, Nathan. 2014. "Radical, Reformist, and Garden-Variety Neoliberal: Coming to Terms with Urban Agriculture's Contradictions." *Local Environment* 19 (2): 147–171.
McKay, Ben M. 2017. "Agrarian Extractivism in Bolivia." *World Development* 97: 199–211.
McKay, Ben M., Alberto Alonso-Fradejas, and Arturo Ezquerro-Cañete, eds. 2021. *Agrarian Extractivism in Latin America*. London: Routledge.
McMichael, Philip. 2012. "The Land Grab and Corporate Food Regime Restructuring." *Journal of Peasant Studies* 39 (3–4): 681–701.

McMichael, Philip. 2013. *Food Regimes and Agrarian Questions*. Rugby, UK: Practical Action Publishing.
McMichael, Philip. 2020. "Does China's 'Going Out' Strategy Prefigure a New Food Regime?" *Journal of Peasant Studies* 47 (1): 116–154.
McWilliams, Carey. (1935) 2000. *Factories in the Field: The Story of Migratory Farm Labor in California*. Berkeley: University of California Press.
Mehta, Lyla, Gert Jan A. Veldwisch, and Jennifer Franco. 2012. "Introduction to the Special Issue: Water Grabbing? Focus on the (Re)Appropriation of Finite Water Resources." *Water Alternatives* 5 (2): 193–207.
Meinzen-Dick, Ruth, Lynn R. Brown, Hilary S. Feldstein, and Agnes R. Quisumbing. 1997. "Gender, Property Rights, and Natural Resources." *World Development* 25 (8): 1303–1315.
Mertz, Ole, Christine Padoch, Jefferson Fox, Rob A. Cramb, Stephen J. Leisz, et al. 2009. "Swidden Change in Southeast Asia: Understanding Causes and Consequences." *Human Ecology* 37: 259–264.
Messerli, Peter, Markus Giger, Michael B. Dwyer, Thomas Breu, and Sandra Eckert. 2014. "The Geography of Large-Scale Land Acquisitions: Analysing Socio-ecological Patterns of Target Contexts in the Global South." *Applied Geography* 53: 449–459.
Meyfroidt, Patrick, Ariane De Bremond, Casey M. Ryan, Emma Archer, Richard Aspinall, Abha Chhabra, Gilberto Camara et al. 2022. "Ten Facts About Land Systems for Sustainability." *Proceedings of the National Academy of Sciences* 119 (7): e2109217118.
Mintz, Sidney W. 1986. *Sweetness and Power: The Place of Sugar in Modern History*. London: Penguin.
Mitchell, Don. 1996. *The Lie of the Land: Migrant Workers and the California Landscape*. Minneapolis: University of Minnesota Press.
Monjane, Boaventura, and Natacha Bruna. 2020. "Confronting Agrarian Authoritarianism: Dynamics of Resistance to PROSAVANA in Mozambique." *Journal of Peasant Studies* 47 (1): 69–94.
Monsalve, Sofia S. 2013. "The Human Rights Framework in Contemporary Agrarian Struggles." *Journal of Peasant Studies* 40 (1): 239–290.
Moore, Barrington, Jr. 1967. *Social Origins of Dictatorship and Democracy: Lord and Peasant in the Making of the Modern World*. Boston, MA: Beacon Press.
Moore, Jason W. 2015. *Capitalism in the Web of Life: Ecology and the Accumulation of Capital*. New York: Verso Books.
Moore, Jason W. 2017. "The Capitalocene, Part I: On the Nature and Origins of Our Ecological Crisis." *Journal of Peasant Studies* 44 (3): 594–630.
Moreda, T. 2015. "Listening to Their Silence? The Political Reaction of Affected Communities to Large-Scale Land Acquisitions: Insights from Ethiopia." *Journal of Peasant Studies* 42 (3–4): 517–539.
Moyo, Sam. 2011. "Three Decades of Agrarian Reform in Zimbabwe." *Journal of Peasant Studies* 38 (3): 493–531.
Moyo, Sam, and Paris Yeros, eds. 2005. *Reclaiming the land: The Resurgence of Rural Movements in Africa, Asia and Latin America*. London: Zed Books.
Neef, Andreas, Chanrith Ngin, Tsegaye Moreda, and Sharlene Mollett. 2023. *Routledge Handbook of Global Land and Resource Grabbing*. New York: Routledge.
Newell, Peter, and Dustin Mulvaney. 2013. "The Political Economy of the 'Just Transition.'" *The Geographical Journal* 179 (2): 132–140.

Ngai, Mae. 2021. *The Chinese Question: The Gold Rushes, Chinese Migration, and global Politics*. New York: W. W. Norton.

Nygren, Anja, Markus Kröger, and Barry Gills. 2022. "Global Extractivisms and Transformative Alternatives." *Journal of Peasant Studies* 49 (4): 734–759.

O'Brien, Kevin J., and L. Li. 2006. *Rightful Resistance in Rural China*. Cambridge, UK: Cambridge University Press.

O'Connor, James R., ed. 1998. *Natural Causes: Essays in Ecological Marxism*. New York: Guilford Press.

O'Connor, James. (1973) 2017. *The Fiscal Crisis of the State*. London: Routledge.

Ojeda, Diana. 2012. "Green Pretexts: Ecotourism, Neoliberal Conservation and Land Grabbing in Tayrona National Natural Park, Colombia." *Journal of Peasant Studies* 39 (2): 357–375.

O'Laughlin, Bridget. 2022. "No Separate Spheres: The Contingent Reproduction of Living Labor in Southern Africa." *Review of International Political Economy* 29 (6): 1827–1846.

Oliveira, Gustavo, and Susanna B. Hecht. 2016. "Sacred Groves, Sacrifice Zones and Soy Production: Globalization, Intensification and Neo-nature in South America." *Journal of Peasant Studies* 43 (2): 251–285.

Oliveira, Gustavo D. L., and Mindi Schneider. 2016. "The Politics of Flexing Soybeans: China, Brazil and Global Agroindustrial Restructuring." *Journal of Peasant Studies* 43 (1): 167–194.

Ossome, Lyn. 2022. "Introduction: The Social Reproductive Question of Land Contestations in Africa." *African Affairs* 121 (484): e9–e24.

Ouma, Stefan. 2014. "Situating Global Finance in the Land Rush Debate: A Critical Review." *Geoforum* 57:162–166.

Ouma, Stefan. 2020. *Farming as Financial Asset: Global Finance and the Making of Institutional Landscapes*. Newcastle upon Tyne, UK: Agenda Publishing.

Oya, Carlos. 2013. "The Land Rush and Classic Agrarian Questions of Capital and Labour: A Systematic Scoping Review of the Socioeconomic Impact of Land Grabs in Africa." *Third World Quarterly* 34 (9): 1532–1557.

Paprocki, Kasia. 2019. "All That Is Solid Melts into the Bay: Anticipatory Ruination and Climate Change Adaptation." *Antipode* 51 (1): 295–315.

Park, Clara. M. Y., and Ben White. 2017. "Gender and Generation in Southeast Asian Agro-commodity Booms." *Journal of Peasant Studies* 44 (6): 1103–1110.

Pattenden, Jonathan. 2018. "The Politics of Classes of Labour: Fragmentation, Reproduction Zones and Collective Action in Karnataka, India." *Journal of Peasant Studies* 45 (5–6): 1039–1059.

Peluso, Nancy L., and Christian Lund. 2011. "Introduction: New Frontiers of Land Control." *Journal of Peasant Studies* 38 (4): 667–681.

Polanyi, Karl. (1944) 2001. *The Great Transformation: The Political and Economic Origins of our time*. Boston, MA: Beacon Press.

Prasse-Freeman, Elliott. 2023. "Refusing Rohingya: Reformulating Ethnicity amid Blunt Biopolitics." *Current Anthropology* 64 (4): 432–453.

Putzel, James. 1992. *A Captive Land: The Politics of Agrarian Reform in the Philippines*. New York: Monthly Review Press.

Pye, Oliver. 2017. "A Plantation Precariat: Fragmentation and Organizing Potential in the Palm Oil Global Production Network." *Development and Change* 48 (5): 942–964.

Ra, Doi. 2022. "Land, Labour, Social Reproduction and the Global Land Rush: Insights from Myanmar (Burma)." Land Rush Working Paper & Notes No. 3. https://www.iss.nl/en/resea

rch/research-projects/commodity-land-rushes-and-regimes/land-rush-working-paper-notes-series.

Razavi, Shahra. 2009. "Engendering the Political Economy of Agrarian Change." *Journal of Peasant Studies* 36 (1): 197–226.

Ribot, Jesse, and Nancy L. Peluso. 2003. "A Theory of Access." *Rural Sociology* 68 (2): 153–181.

Robbins, Martha Jane. 2015. "Exploring the 'Localisation' Dimension of Food Sovereignty." *Third World Quarterly* 36 (3): 449–468.

Rojas, Itayosara H. 2024. "Limits and Possibilities of Contemporary Land Struggles by Indigenous Peoples, Black Communities and Campesinos in the Colombian Amazon." Land Rush Working Paper & Notes No. 7. https://www.iss.nl/en/research/research-projects/commodity-land-rushes-and-regimes/land-rush-working-paper-notes-series.

Roman-Alcalá, Antonio. 2015. "Broadening the Land Question in Food Sovereignty to Northern Settings: A Case Study of Occupy the Farm." *Globalizations* 12 (4): 545–558.

Rosset, Peter M., and Miguel A. Altieri. 2017. *Agroecology: Science and Politics*. Rugby, UK: Practical Action Publishing.

Sandwell, Katie, A. Castañeda Flores, Lyda Fernanda Forero, Jennifer Franco, S. Monsalve Suárez, Andrea Nuila, and Philip Seufert. 2019. *A View from the Countryside: Contesting and Constructing Human Rights in an Age of Converging Crises*. Amsterdam: Transnational Institute; The Hague: Emancipatory Rural Politics; Heidelberg: FIAN International.

Sassen, Saskia. 2014. *Expulsions: Brutality and Complexity in the Global Economy*. Cambridge, MA: Harvard University Press.

Sauer, Sergio, and Sergio Pereira Leite. 2012. "Agrarian Structure, Foreign Investment in Land, and Land Prices in Brazil." *Journal of Peasant Studies* 39 (3–4): 873–898.

Scheidel, Arnim, and Courtney Work. 2018. "Forest Plantations and Climate Change Discourses: New Powers of 'Green' Grabbing in Cambodia." *Land Use Policy* 77: 9–18.

Scoones, Ian. 2021. "Pastoralists and Peasants: Perspectives on Agrarian Change." *Journal of Peasant Studies* 48 (1): 1–47.

Scoones, Ian, Nelson Marongwe, Blasio Mavedzenge, Felix Murimbarimba, Jacob Mahenehene, and Chrispen Sukume. 2010. *Zimbabwe's Land Reform: Myths and Realities*. London: James Currey.

Scoones, Ian, Kojo Amanor, Arilson Favareto, and Gubo Qi. 2016. "A New Politics of Development Cooperation? Chinese and Brazilian Engagements in African Agriculture." *World Development* 81: 1–12.

Scoones, Ian, Marc Edelman, Saturnino M. Borras Jr., Ruth Hall, Wendy Wolford, and Ben White. 2018. "Emancipatory Rural Politics: Confronting Authoritarian Populism." *Journal of Peasant Studies* 45 (1): 1–20.

Scott, James C. 1985. *Weapons of the Weak: Everyday Forms of Peasant Resistance*. New Haven, CT: Yale University Press.

Sekine, Yukari. 2021. "Emerging 'Agrarian Climate Justice' Struggles in Myanmar." *Journal of Peasant Studies* 48 (3): 517–540.

Serrano, Angela. 2023. "Restructuring Palm Oil Value Chain Governance in Colombia through Long-Term Labour Control." *Journal of Agrarian Change* 23 (3): 547–567.

Seufert, Philip. 2013. "The FAO Voluntary Guidelines on the Responsible Governance of Tenure of Land, Fisheries and Forests." *Globalizations* 10 (1): 181–186.

Shah, Amod. 2023. "Rethinking 'Just Transitions' from Coal: The Dynamics of Land and Labour in Anti-coal Struggles." *Journal of Peasant Studies* 50 (6): 2145–2164.

Shah, Alpa, and Jens Lerche. 2020. "Migration and the Invisible Economies of Care: Production, Social Reproduction and Seasonal Migrant Labour in India." *Transactions of the Institute of British Geographers* 45 (4): 719–734.

Shanin, Teodor, ed. 1983. *Late Marx and the Russian Road: Marx and the Peripheries of Capitalism*. New York: New York University Press.

Shanin, Teodor, Alexander Nikulin, Irina Trotsuk, and Jan Douwe van der Ploeg, eds. 2024. *Peasants: Chayanov's Recovered Essays*. Rugby, UK: Practical Action Publishing.

Shattuck, Annie, Jacobo Grajales, Ricardo Jacobs, Sergio Sauer, Shaila S. Galvin, and Ruth Hall. 2023. "Life on the Land: New Lives for Agrarian Questions." *Journal of Peasant Studies* 50 (2): 490–518.

Shivji, Issa G. 2017. "The Concept of 'Working People.'" *Agrarian South: Journal of Political Economy* 6 (1): 1–13.

Siebert, Anne. 2020. "Transforming Urban Food Systems in South Africa: Unfolding Food Sovereignty in the City." *Journal of Peasant Studies* 47 (2): 401–419.

Sikor, Thomas, and Christian Lund. 2009. "Access and Property: A Question of Power and Authority." *Development and Change* 40 (1): 1–22.

Sommerville, Melanie, and Andre Magnan. 2015. "'Pinstripes on the Prairies': Examining the financialization of Farming Systems in the Canadian Prairie Provinces." *Journal of Peasant Studies* 42 (1): 119–144.

Spoor, Max, ed. 2008. *The Political Economy of Rural Livelihoods in Transition Economies*. London: Routledge.

Stock, Ryan, and Trevor Birkenholtz. 2021. "The Sun and the Scythe: Energy Dispossessions and the Agrarian Question of Labor in Solar Parks." *Journal of Peasant Studies* 48 (5): 984–1007.

Sud, Nikita. 2020. *The Making of Land and the Making of India*. New Delhi: Oxford University Press.

Suhardiman, Diana, Mark Giordano, and François Molle. 2012. "Scalar Disconnect: The Logic of Transboundary Water Governance in the Mekong." *Society & Natural Resources* 25 (6): 572–586.

Torres Contreras, Gerardo A. 2022. "Twenty-Five Years under the Wind Turbines in La Venta, Mexico: Social Difference, Land Control and Agrarian Change." *Journal of Peasant Studies* 49 (4): 865–883.

Tramel, Salena. 2024. "Territory Grabbing and the Undermining of Palestinian Food Sovereignty." Land Deal Politics Initiative (LDPI) 2024 Working paper Series No. 12. https://peasantjournal.org/news/working-paper-series-international-conference-on-global-land-grabbing-bogota-colombia/.

Tsikata, Dzodzi. 2016. "Gender, Land Tenure and Agrarian Production Systems in Sub-Saharan Africa." *Agrarian South: Journal of Political Economy* 5 (1): 1–19.

Tsing, Anna L. 2000. "Inside the Economy of Appearances." *Public Culture* 12 (1): 115–144.

Tsing, Anna L., A. S. Mathews, and N. Bubandt. 2019. "Patchy Anthropocene: Landscape Structure, Multispecies History, and the Retooling of Anthropology. An Introduction to Supplement 20." *Current Anthropology* 60 (20): S186–S197.

van der Ploeg, Jan Douwe. 2020. "Farmers' Upheaval, Climate Crisis and Populism." *Journal of Peasant Studies* 47 (3): 589–605.

van der Ploeg, Jan Douwe. 2024. "On Interpretation and Relevance: An Introduction to 6 Recovered Essays." In *Peasants: Chayanov's Recovered Essays*, edited by Teodor Shanin,

Alexander Nikulin, Irina Trotsuk, and Jan Douwe van der Ploeg, xxvii–xxxv. Rugby, UK: Practical Action.

van der Ploeg, Jan Douwe, Jennifer C. Franco, and Saturnino M. Borras Jr. 2015. "Land Concentration and Land Grabbing in Europe: A Preliminary Analysis." *Canadian Journal of Development Studies* 36 (2): 147–162.

van Leeuwen, Mathijs, and Gemma van der Haar. 2016. "Theorizing the Land–Violent Conflict Nexus." *World Development* 78:94–104.

Vandergeest, Peter, and Nancy L. Peluso. 1995. "Territorialization and State Power in Thailand." *Theory and Society* 24 (3): 385–426.

Visser, Oane. 2017. "Running Out of Farmland? Investment Discourses, Unstable Land Values and the Sluggishness of Asset Making." *Agriculture and Human Values* 34:185–198.

Visser, Oane, Sarah R. Sippel, and Louis Thiemann. 2021. "Imprecision Farming? Examining the (In) Accuracy and Risks of Digital Agriculture." *Journal of Rural Studies* 86:623–632.

Wang, Chunyu, and Yunan Xu. 2024. "Reflecting on the Plantationocene: The Political Economy of Sugarcane Plantations in Guangxi, China." *Journal of Peasant Studies* 51 (3): 564–585.

Watts, Michael J. (1983) 2013. *Silent Violence: Food, famine, and Peasantry in Northern Nigeria.* Athens, GA: University of Georgia Press.

Weis, Tony. 2013. *The Ecological Hoofprint: The Global Burden of Industrial Livestock.* London: Zed.

White, Ben. 2018. "Marx and Chayanov at the Margins: Understanding Agrarian Change in Java." *Journal of Peasant Studies* 45 (5–6): 1108–1126.

White, Ben. 2020. *Agriculture and the Generation Problem*. Rugby, UK: Practical Action Publishing.

White, Ben, Saturnino M. Borras Jr., Ruth Hall, Ian Scoones, and Wendy Wolford. 2012. "The New Enclosures: Critical Perspectives on Corporate Land Deals." *Journal of Peasant Studies* 39 (3–4): 619–647.

Wittman, Hannah. 2009. "Reworking the Metabolic Rift: La Vía Campesina, Agrarian Citizenship, and Food Sovereignty." *Journal of Peasant Studies* 36 (4): 805–826.

Wolf, Eric R. 1969. *Peasant Wars of the Twentieth Century*. Norman: University of Oklahoma Press.

Wolford, Wendy. 2021. "The Plantationocene: A Lusotropical Contribution to the Theory." *Annals of the American Association of Geographers* 111 (6): 1622–1639.

Wolford, Wendy, and R. Nehring. 2015. "Constructing Parallels: Brazilian Expertise and the Commodification of Land, Labour and Money in Mozambique." *Canadian Journal of Development Studies* 36 (2): 208–223.

Wolford, Wendy W., Ben White, Ian Scoones, Ruth. Hall, Marc Edelman, and Saturnino M. Borras Jr. 2024. "Global Land Deals: What Has Been Done, What Has Changed, and What's Next?" *Journal of Peasant Studies*. https://doi.org/10.1080/03066150.2024.2325685.

Xu, Yunan. 2020. *Industrial Tree Plantations and the Land Rush in China: Implications for Global Land Grabbing*. London: Routledge.

Yan, Hairong, and Yituan Chen. 2015. "Agrarian Capitalization without Capitalism? Capitalist Dynamics from Above and Below in China." *Journal of Agrarian Change* 15 (3): 366–391.

Yaşın, Zehra Taşdemir. 2022. "The Environmentalization of the Agrarian Question and the Agrarianization of the Climate Justice Movement." *Journal of Peasant Studies* 49 (7): 1355–1386.

Ye, Jingzhong. 2015. "Land Transfer and the Pursuit of Agricultural Modernization in China." *Journal of Agrarian Change* 15 (3): 314–337.
Ye, Jingzhong, Jan Douwe van der Ploeg, Sergio Schneider, and Teodor Shanin. 2020. "The Incursions of Extractivism: Moving from Dispersed Places to Global Capitalism." *Journal of Peasant Studies* 47 (1): 155–183.
Zhan, Shaohua. 2019. "Accumulation by and without Dispossession: Rural Land Use, Land Expropriation, and Livelihood Implications in China." *Journal of Agrarian Change* 19 (3): 447–464.
Zhang, Qian Forrest, and John A. Donaldson. 2008. "The Rise of Agrarian Capitalism with Chinese Characteristics: Agricultural Modernization, Agribusiness and Collective Land Rights." *China Journal* 60: 25–47.
Zoomers, Annelies. 2010. "Globalisation and the Foreignisation of Space: Seven Processes Driving the Current Global Land Grab." *Journal of Peasant Studies* 37 (2): 429–447.

CHAPTER 2

MARXISM(S) AND THE POLITICS OF LAND

HENRY BERNSTEIN

Introduction

Several challenges immediately confront any consideration of the topic of Marxism(s) and the politics of land. One is the fractured histories of Marx interpretation and the clashes of the thinkers and movements claiming the authority of his ideas: "if a Marxist, what kind of Marxist?" (Vanaik 2017, 19). A second is that the Marxisms of different regimes were once applied in the most momentous attempts in modern history to change the social relations of land and of production from it, notably, following the Russian and Chinese revolutions. A third challenge is presented by the gaps, and tensions, between Marxist analyses of capitalist economy, which its adherents consider the best available, and the fortunes of political projects pursued by Marxist parties and movements that have lost so much ground in recent decades. Related to the last challenge is that some of the social science analysis of land and agrarian issues today is influenced by Marxist ideas without identifying fully with Marxism. This is reflected in a notion of "critical agrarian studies," which can draw on Marxism but also seeks to distance itself from some Marxist positions (e.g., Akram Lodhi et al. 2021). In any case, to understand both the histories of Marxism and attempts to formulate and implement policies on land that claim its inspiration requires keen attention to specific contexts and conjunctures.

This article proceeds via a sequence of themes: Marx on landed property and rent in capitalism; transitions to capitalism in Marx, Lenin, and subsequent Marxism; developments of capitalism; transitions to socialism in the USSR and China; and Marxism(s) and politics of land. A significant dimension of the last, beginning with (the late) Marx, are the relations between Marxism(s) and the arguments and programs of agrarian populism. The latter are centered on advocacy of the "peasant way" as the resolution of central issues of farming, not least food production, intensified today in the context of global ecological crises.

Landed Property and Rent in Capitalism

The most prominent of Marx's theories about land concerned the categories of rent he described in his critique of "classical" political economy, which was a key step in formulating his own (uncompleted) theorization of the capitalist mode of production and its "laws of motion." The main discussions of rent are in part 6 of volume 3 of *Capital* (Marx 1981) and in part 2 of *Theories of Surplus Value* (Marx 1968). The reason Marx devoted so much attention to rent is that it was key to the political economy of Smith, Malthus, and Ricardo that he studied intensively, at a time when landed property loomed large in a British economy that was still in the early stages of industrialization.

For our present purposes, suffice it to say, first, that previous political economists saw rent as an economic category given, and differentiated, by the nature of the commodity being rented, which in their context was agricultural land. For Marx, as for his predecessors, rent is one of the three main sources of revenue in capitalist society, the others being profits and wages. Second, however, Marx understood rent as constituted by class relations in capitalism rather than given by the intrinsic qualities of different kinds of land, although the productivities of different types of land provided one element of his theory of rent: the first type of differential rent. Accordingly, and third, Marx distinguished rent in capitalism from the rents of landed property of a precapitalist kind (e.g., feudal rents). Fourth, Marx sought to integrate landed property and rent in his complex theorization of the capitalist mode of production and its circuits of production, realization, and distribution of value, which is where the main difficulties and disputes are located (Fine 2019). These arise from Marx's attempts to integrate types of rent with his considerations of value, including the "transformation problem" of the relations between values and prices. Fifth, his primarily social (class) view of rent meant that Marx saw capitalist landed property as a "third class" of capitalism, along with the bourgeoisie (capital) and proletariat (labor), as argued in a sophisticated analysis by Neocosmos (1986), albeit a typically parasitic class because rent is a deduction from total surplus value in circulation that would otherwise be available for productive investment.

Finally, the components and steps of Marx's abstract theory of rent do not translate simply into empirical indicators of levels of rent as revenue and of different patterns of landed property in the varied times and places of capitalism. Indeed, de jure rights in land as private property, the basis of rent revenue (visible and invisible), remain incomplete and contested in much of the world today—notably, in the South (Hall 2013). In sub-Saharan Africa, for example, de jure land rights are not fully established, although there is much evidence of de facto land markets and conflicts over land (Chimowhu and

Woodhouse 2007; Peters 2004), as well as of an increasing concentration of land ownership (Jayne et al. 2016); and in China, the legal status of rights to land is often deeply ambiguous (Ho 2001).

A particular instance of landed property and rent are the widespread practices of sharecropping. This has attracted much attention from both conventional (neoclassical) economics and Marxist scholars, among whom T. J. Byres's (1983) edited collection was a landmark.

More widely, Marx's views have been followed up by others writing in the Marxist tradition, who have used his theory of rent (or differing interpretations of it) to investigate issues outside agriculture, such as urban land markets (Harvey 1985) and mining (Fine 1994). Capps (2016) introduced the innovative category of "tribal landed property" in the context of South Africa and other colonial formations in sub-Saharan Africa. There are also notions of "ecological rents" generated by "cheap nature" (land, water, minerals, energy) in capital's endless drive to exploit and accumulate (Moore 2015), and of "institutional rents"—that is, the benefits accruing from holding political and bureaucratic office in land and agricultural policymaking and delivery (de Janvry 1983).

Finally, a more expansive, if looser, conception of rent centers on ownership and acquisition of land and other assets and the revenue derived from them rather than on investing capital in developing production and the productive force. One recent example is Christophers (2020), who argues that the prevalence of revenue from capital's ownership of assets, including land, instead of productive investment, makes the United Kingdom's economy a case of "rentier capitalism," a term typically applied to states with major oil revenues.

In sum, concepts of rent, and the specific conditions, dynamics, forms, and effects of landownership, point to the profound inequalities in capitalism in agriculture and beyond, both historically and today.

Transitions to Capitalism

Marx also wrote about the creation and consolidation of landed property as a commodity in transitions to capitalism, with the consequent dispossession of those working the land as small producers or peasants of different kinds. They then became available as workers "freed" from access to land as the basis of their reproduction, hence "free" to sell their labor power to capital (Bernstein 2010, chaps 1 and 2). This was presented historically in the famous final part of volume 1 of *Capital* on primitive accumulation (Marx 1976), which proposed in effect an "enclosure" model of transitions to capitalist farming, the basis of capitalism more widely, including industrialization.

Lenin's (1973a) *The Development of Capitalism in Russia*, published in 1899, is the most comprehensive investigation of the transition to capitalism in a single (and "backward") country in the canon of classic Marxism. Lenin advanced the work of Marx and Engels in two ways. Much cited, however brief a statement it is, was Lenin's suggestion that there are two principal paths to agrarian capitalism: "from above" (the "Prussian path") in which landed property of precapitalist provenance converts itself into capitalist landed property and farming, and "from below" (the "American path") via the development of commodity production among (initially) small farmers. The second path occurs through the class differentiation of the farmers who are subject to the disciplines of commodity production, producing three classes of peasants: "rich," "middle," and "poor," respectively, those able to accumulate land and other means of farming to become capitalist farmers; those able to reproduce themselves as agricultural petty commodity producers based on access to small property and family labor; and who are those unable to do so and become increasingly dependent on selling their labor power to reproduce themselves. Lenin envisaged that the dynamics of commodification would increasingly squeeze the middle peasants, forcing most of them into the ranks of "poor peasants" (and landless proletarians). In effect, then, his schema of peasant class differentiation and rural class formation added a second "model" of transition to agrarian capitalism to Marx's enclosure "model."

Lenin's analysis of peasant class differentiation in late nineteenth-century Russia has been vastly influential and also strongly contested—methodologically, for example, because of his use of (official) surveys at single points in time to deduce trends, and empirically, for exaggerating the extent of peasant class differentiation (Shanin 1972). There is, nonetheless, a powerful analytical core in Lenin's account, which had been indicated by Marx—namely, that "middle peasant" (or "family" or "peasant") farming, like other petty commodity production in transitions to and mutations of capitalism, represents an unstable combination of class places and dynamics of both capital (possession of means of production, including land) and labor. At the same time, investigation of the tendency to class formation in the countryside is always likely to reveal a great diversity of forms, degrees, and outcomes across specific instances.

Subsequently, T. J. Byres extended Lenin's brief sketch of the two "paths." In research on the "substantive diversity" of paths of agrarian transition in different times and places of the capitalist world economy, Byres (1991) brought important Asian examples into the frame of analysis. Byres (1996) also wrote a detailed analytical and historical account of Germany and the United States, the two "paths" noted by Lenin.

The "models" of capitalist agrarian transition left by Marx and Lenin have been extensively investigated in subsequent Marxist research on processes of class struggle and class formation in the countryside, and have also been considerably elaborated (Bernstein and Byres 2001). The elaborations can be indicated by a series of questions (drawing on Bernstein 2015b), and applied to issues of developments within capitalism (see the section "Developments of Capitalism" below). A first cluster of questions can be framed as (I) *internal to the countryside*, addressing the following:

1. The "commodification of subsistence" (Brenner 2001) and of the means of subsistence of ("peasant") farmers: Are they able to reproduce themselves outside a (competitive) market exchange of what they produce (sale of "output") and how they produce it (purchase of "inputs," often, in fact, including labor)?

This connects with a second theme:

2. The commodification of land: Does agrarian transition necessarily involve dispossession of "peasant," small, or "family" farmers, whether by direct means (expropriation through enclosure) or indirect means (crises of reproduction exerted by market pressures)?
3. How are new classes of capitalist landed property, agrarian capital, and wage labor formed? By what means and with what effects?
4. How, in what forms, and how far does the accumulation and concentration of capital in the means of agricultural production (land and instruments of labor) proceed?
5. Is there accumulation "from above" and/or "from below," the latter through the class differentiation of farmers, as highlighted by Lenin?
6. What are the effects for production growth in farming, realized through the development of the productive forces, especially, growth in labor productivity?

Two further themes push against limiting such processes of change to social forces in the countryside, thereby bringing in (II) *rural-urban interconnections*:

7. On the side of capital, what is the significance, and the effects, of "capital beyond the countryside" that invests in farm production directly or indirectly (the latter, for example, through contract farming) and/or invests in, and possibly dominates, circuits of finance, marketing, processing, and distribution that integrate farming within a capitalist "agricultural sector"?
8. On the labor side, what is the significance of "rural labor beyond the farm" involving rural industrialization (from older to more contemporary forms of nonagricultural wage employment) or regular rural labor migration, as vital elements of the incomes and reproduction of classes of labor in the countryside (which may also engage in some limited "own account" farming)?

Questions 7 and 8 (together with 6) point toward (III) the place of agriculture within larger *"national" economies*, which becomes more explicit with a further theme:

9. What are the contributions of agriculture to industrialization? Do (particular) states facilitate, hinder, or "block" (i) the transfer of agricultural surpluses to industrial accumulation directly through the taxation of the agrarian classes or indirectly through the terms of exchange between agriculture and industry or (ii) the development of a home market integrating exchange between agriculture and industry? How? And how much? (The subtitle of Lenin's study of Russia in 1899 was *The Process of the Formation of a Home Market for Large-Scale Industry*.)

A final theme concerns the character and effects of (IV) the capitalist *world economy*:

10. What are the effects for agrarian change at particular places and times during the formation and interactions of (i) international divisions of labor in agricultural production, (ii) international trade in agricultural commodities, (iii) how trade is organized and financed, (iv) international investment in agriculture and (v) the international state system?

Table 2.1 summarizes these questions.

These questions can also inform the investigation of the processes of dispossession of land and their main class agents, illustrated in Table 2.2.

The listing of such questions and the themes they highlight is unavoidably general. These questions and themes contain, or indeed conceal, much dispute within Marxism, and in any case, they can only sketch an initial agenda. Beyond that, the specificities, modalities, complexities, durations, and contradictions of agrarian transitions in the different places and times of capitalism—the "substantive diversity" of paths of agrarian transition (Byres, above)—require detailed investigation.

Questions 1 to 6 about commodification, class formation, accumulation, and growth of agricultural productivity traverse the histories of capitalism, from the original

Table 2.1. Key Questions in the Political Economy of Agrarian Change

Themes	Locus	Questions
I Agrarian class formation	Countryside	1–5
Growth of production and productivity		6
II Rural-urban interconnections:	"National" [and international → IV]	7
• "capital beyond the countryside"	"National" [and international → IV]	8
• "rural labour beyond the farm"		
III Agrarian basis of industrialization	"National"	9
IV International divisions of agrarian labour, trade etc.	Capitalist world economy	10

Table 2.2. Types of Land Dispossession in Capitalism

Type	Main class agents	From "above"	From "below"	"Internal" to countryside	"External"
1	Landed property, agrarian capital	✓		✓	
2	Rich peasants, emergent capitalist farmers		✓	✓	
3	Urban classes of capital, political elites	✓			✓
4	International (+ Indigenous) capitals and states	✓			✓

Source: Adapted from Bernstein (2015a).

English agrarian transition of the fifteenth or sixteenth century to considerations of change in the countrysides of the global South today. Accounts that do not specify international determinations (in Marx's term) tend to resonate an "internalist" problematic—"internal" to the countryside or to countries (or both)—reflecting the conditions of the original English transition and also evident in Lenin (1973a), which contains virtually no reference to the capitalist world economy of his time. This is common to such Marxist scholars (despite other differences between them) as Brenner (1976) and Byres (1996) for whom, first, the emergence of agrarian capitalism is explicable principally, or exclusively, by the formation of classes of capitalist landed property, agrarian capital, and wage labor through social struggle internal to the countryside (Questions 2–5). Second, agriculture must contribute a surplus available to fund industrialization (Questions 6 and 9, emphasized by Byres). Third, the development of a home market integrates exchange between agriculture and industry as the basis of "national" development (Question 9).

The "internalist" problematic features in historical comparisons between the English transition and other European cases—France, Prussia/Germany, the Netherlands, the "second serfdom" of Eastern Europe—from the late medieval or early modern period onward (inter alios Brenner 1976; Byres 1996, 2003; Wood 2002; Heller 2011), and to other cases elsewhere (Isett and Miller 2016). A striking finding of Byres's studies is that the contributions of agriculture to industrialization—"agrarian transition" in his sense of the term—did not always require the (prior) development of capitalist farming, conceived as the formation of capitalist landed property, agrarian capital, and wage labor combined in large-scale production (Questions 1–6). In the East Asian cases, the accumulation fund for industrialization was secured by taxing peasant farming (and peasant farming with growing productivity); and in the United States, through the terms of trade between industry and agriculture, the latter characterized by "petty commodity production from below" (Byres 2003).

Several further questions, then, arise. First: Is a transition to capitalist agriculture, in the sense of large-scale farming employing wage labor, a *necessary* condition of industrialization? Byres's comparative studies suggest that the answer is no in the East Asian cases.

Second, and following: Is the formation of capitalist landed property, agrarian capital, and agricultural wage labor combined in large farms—derived from the original English transition—the *only* form the development of capitalist agriculture can take? Few Marxist scholars today would subscribe to this position.

And third: How well does an "internalist" approach travel across the different places and times of capitalism, from the original English transition to explorations of agrarian change in the world today? Is the first set of questions and themes, though still relevant, sufficient to explore agrarian transitions across the past five centuries or so of capitalism on a world scale? What other determinations might the histories of capitalism require? This connects with Questions 7 and 8, and with Question 10, discussed further below.

Rural-urban interconnections—signaled by Questions 7 and 8—start to stretch any framework that limits the class dynamics of transition to the countryside, and to indicate a need for extensive attention to the (changing) relations between agriculture and industry in the histories of capitalism, especially, I suggest, from the nineteenth century because the debates of the sixteenth to eighteenth centuries in Europe and elsewhere address agrarian transitions before the emergence and rise to dominance of capitalist industry.

In Question 10, the "internalist" problematic in both senses is challenged most strongly by insistence on the global character of capitalism from its origins, as fundamental to its emergence as to its subsequent development (below).

The list of questions summarized in Table 2.1 and the schema of land dispossession in Table 2.2 should be seen as heuristic. They cannot provide substantive accounts of the diversity of paths of agrarian transition and drivers of land dispossession in the histories of capitalism, and do not pretend to. Accounts of that diversity start to add complications that point to some vexed issues in Marxist debate of land and agrarian change:

- What is considered "capitalist" and why (hence by implication "pre-" or "noncapitalist")?
- What forms of capitalist development of agriculture might there be other than the archetypal large-scale farm employing wage labor?
- What is the relative weight of, and the interactions between, determinations internal to the countryside and to the "national," and the latter to "external" determinations that derive from the dynamics of the capitalist world economy?

The aspiration to clarify, through simplification, some of the key analytical elements in the study of agrarian change across centuries of capitalism (inevitably) transgresses aspects of those histories. For example, there were important instances of seasonal wage employment and labor migration by peasants at various times and places of early capitalism; hence it is not exclusively a "new" question or theme. And, as indicated, there are various important arguments about the significance of colonial agrarian change in Asia and Africa, and about the effects of state formation in Europe at different moments of its agrarian transitions and subsequent industrialization Also, it could be argued that just as Table 2.1 signals a (historical) movement of "capital beyond the countryside," from the "national" to the international plane, the same can apply to "rural labor beyond the farm" given the importance of international migrant labor, involuntary (e.g., slavery) or "voluntary," in capitalist farming both historically and today.

However, the primary note of caution here concerns the formulation of "capital beyond the countryside." What it aims to signify is capital of nonagrarian, nonrural provenance and character that enters, directly or indirectly, into agricultural commodity production and shapes it to a greater or lesser extent through specific, and varying, forms of integration with markets. In turn, this affects the conditions of reproduction and hence the relative fortunes of different classes of agricultural producers. In earlier histories of capitalism, the types of "capital beyond the countryside" were mostly money-lending capital and merchant capital, both indicated by Marx. Today, the canvas of "capital beyond the countryside" is greatly expanded with internationalized agribusiness upstream and downstream of farming. Upstream, "agri-input" corporations are typically industrial, especially chemical, conglomerates. Downstream, they comprise industrial corporations that are sourcing and processing feedstuffs for the "global meat complex" and manufacturing "durable foods" and other "agri-food" capitals in global circuits of distribution (e.g., the contemporary "supermarket revolution" (Reardon et al. 2003). Moreover, within current dynamics of globalization are new frontiers that are of interest to finance capital, as is speculation in futures markets for land, and for food and feed (and biofuel stocks), as discussed further below.

Developments of Capitalism

Among Marxists, major contentions persist about "national" paths of capitalist development and the question of whether capitalism was international from its beginnings or has become so in the context of modern imperialism (from the 1870s, according to Lenin 1973b) and contemporary globalization. The former ("internalist" problematic) runs the danger of "methodological nationalism"; the latter, the danger of "world system determinism," relegating the importance of class formation in particular countrysides and countries. In fact, the theme "developments of capitalism" brings international dynamics into the framework, increasingly so as the history of capitalism advances.

Of course, international trade, along with the spread of European colonialism and its institutions, such as plantation slavery in the Americas, played a key role in the emergence and early development of capitalism on a world scale, as Marx noted. And since Marx, much attention has been given to the formation and mutations of capitalist world economy, whether directly inspired by Marx or otherwise influenced by Marxist ideas. For example, Wallerstein's world-system analysis emphasizes the interconnections between the international state system and patterns of international trade, investment, and finance in the formation and functioning of the capitalist world economy (and its mutations). The title of its first volume on this theme is *Capitalist Agriculture and the Origins of the European World-Economy in the Sixteenth Century* (Wallerstein 1974). A seminal work by Mintz (1985) traced the interconnections of plantation slavery in the Americas, early industrialization in Europe, and the contributions of sugar to the diets of the new European working class.

Indeed, sugar was the first bulk commodity of transoceanic trade in the modern world, followed by wheat from the United States and Canada, which is at the center of the innovative analysis of international food regimes by Friedmann and McMichael (1989). The notion of a food regime "links international relations of food production and consumption to forms of accumulation broadly distinguishing periods of capitalist transformation" (95)—that is, accompanying or following capitalist industrialization. The first food regime identified was from 1870 to 1914, during the (final) period of British hegemony in the world economy. This established an international division of labor between North America (predominance in world markets in grain that was produced mostly by "family" farmers), Europe (more diversified commercial farming, large and small in scale), and the South, mostly colonial in Africa and Asia (exports of tropical commodities produced by both plantations and peasant farmers). A second international food regime (1945–1973) was constructed under US hegemony in the has post-1945 world economy and centered on US grain exports; and McMichael (2013) elaborated a third "corporate food regime" since the 1980s in the period of (neoliberal) globalization. For this approach (as for Wallerstein), the formation and shifts of the international state system are central to world markets in agricultural commodities, and their consequences for the organization of farming, how it changes, and how this affects how land is owned and used. Most importantly, analysis of the third food regime suggests the transnationalization or globalization of some of the dynamics noted so far, especially regarding "capital beyond the countryside." The modalities of (financialized) corporate agribusiness include both "new" themes—global sourcing of raw materials for processing (biofuels, as well as foods and feeds for the "global meat complex"), international market liberalization, and the ever-intensifying industrialization (mechanization and "chemicalization") of both crop and livestock production and its ecological consequences (Weis 2010)—and "old" themes in new historical conditions, such as land grabbing, and the accelerated dispossession of small farmers/"peasants" (Araghi 2009).

Notions of enclosure and of primitive accumulation (Marx) have also (re)surfaced in major ways in recent decades to explain practices that are widespread in contemporary capitalism, for example, "land grabbing" in the global South. This sometimes deploys and extends the notion of "enclosure" that was familiar to Marx—the conversion to private property of commons used by peasants for grazing livestock, collecting wood and wild plants, fishing, and hunting game, as well as of farmland—to all forms of "commons," material and social, that capital seeks to enclose and the various forms of resistance to this dynamic (De Angelis 2007).

Much recent analysis of "ongoing" or "continuous" primitive accumulation derives, directly or indirectly, from the perspective of Rosa Luxemburg, who proposed that

> real life has never known a self-sufficient capitalist society under the exclusive domination of the capitalist mode of production . . . the realisation of the surplus value for the purposes of accumulation is an impossible task for a society which consists solely of workers and capitalists . . . Realisation of the surplus value . . . requires as its prime condition . . . that there should be strata of buyers outside capitalist society . . . such social organisations or strata whose own mode of production is not capitalistic.
>
> (Luxemburg 1951, 348)

In an influential approach inspired by Luxemburg, Maria Mies (2014) emphasized plunder from "outside" capitalist social relations that is vital to their reproduction, especially those of patriarchy, colonies (in the formation and functioning of imperialism), and nature-ecology, to which "peasants" are sometimes added. In all these instances she saw control over land and its enclosures as central. Probably the best-known shorthand formula of continuing primitive accumulation is David Harvey's (2003) (contentious) notion of "accumulation by dispossession," including of land—that is, instead of principally by the accumulation of productive capital. This can further contribute to the position that advanced capitalism continues to require primitive accumulation beyond its conventional (internal) mechanisms of expanded reproduction and through its exactions of surplus value from peasantries and the "semi-proletariat" (informally employed workers) in the South. This is seen by some as the definitive feature of modern imperialism (e.g., Moyo et al. 2013), in which the principal political thrust of anti-imperialism centers on the "national question" in the South, to which the agrarian question is pivotal (Shivji 2019).

In effect, this means that much of the attention to issues of land today is on the contradictions and struggles between all noncorporate farmers—"people of the land" (Desmarais 2007)—and corporate agribusiness, which is a shift from the initial Marxist focus on class struggle between ("peasant") farmers and landed property, evident in the Russian and Chinese revolutions, and also on struggle generated by peasant class differentiation.

Transitions to Socialism? The USSR and China

A third area in the interpretation and contestation of Lenin's analysis of peasant class differentiation, the political, is of even greater significance in Russian and early Soviet history and beyond. It centers on any expectation that peasant class differentiation generates "class struggle in the village" to the benefit of the projects of revolutionary politics based in the (urban) proletariat—an expression of "the peasant problem" that was to haunt the political ideas and practices of Russian Marxists from the Russian revolution of 1905–1907 to the revolution of 1917 and the Bolshevik regimes that followed (Bernstein 2018). The massive role played by the peasantry in 1905–1907, especially in actions against the landlords, sparked reconsideration by some Russians at the time of its political role in any future Russian revolution, not least by Lenin (in the interpretation of Shanin 1986). There were rich and complex Bolshevik debates in the 1920s that placed issues of the "agrarian question" and peasantry at the center of the ideas and practices in the transitions to socialism. The centrality of the "worker-peasant alliance" to the Russian revolution was symbolized by the hammer and sickle of the Soviet flag. Among the early moments of the Soviet debates were various pronouncements by Lenin in his final years, which recommended taking a cautious and gradual approach toward the peasantry and how it could be integrated with plans for socialist transition.

All that, and so much else, was cut short by the victory of Stalin(ism), and the landmark moment of the drastic collectivization of agriculture he decreed in 1929. Although it is often argued that Stalin's forced collectivization of land and agriculture had little to do with the ideas of Marx and Lenin, there was nonetheless a ("rational") kernel in the notion that collective and planned large-scale farming was the necessary pathway, or at least goal, of socialist construction. This view was shared by, among others, the leading Russian historian of the 1920s and critic of Stalin's policies, Viktor Danilov (1988). That this goal fell victim to the savagery of Stalin's collectivization, and to the subsequent contradictions of Soviet agriculture until the end of the USSR, was a question of how it could be pursued—a matter, as always, of politics.

The second great socialist revolution of the twentieth century happened in China, in circumstances that were considerably different from those in Russia. The long course of the Chinese revolution, from the 1920s to the 1940s, took place in a society that was even more "peasant," as it were, than Russia and that was, indeed, the last of the great agrarian civilizations established before the modern period of world history. Interestingly, one of Mao's earliest analyses, written in 1927, was the "Report of an Investigation of the Peasant Movement in Hunan," his home province (Mao 1967).

China experienced what is probably the greatest of the "peasant wars of the twentieth century" (Wolf 1969). Moreover, in 1927 the Chinese Communist Party (CCP) had lost its principal proletarian base in the working class of Shanghai with the massacres unleashed by Chiang Kai-shek's Kuomintang. Subsequently, following its "Long March," and by establishing liberated zones in Yan'an and elsewhere, the CCP was able to experiment with policies to reduce the burdens on peasants of rent and debt.

The main policies under the early communist regime were land reform, in the sense of redistributing proprietary rights to land, to destroy the basis of ("feudal") landlordism (1949–1953); measures to encourage rural cooperatives (1953–1958); and then the more radical push to form rural communes (from 1958 on). Each step, from the "land to the tiller"-style redistribution of land rights to "lower stage" and "higher stage" cooperatives to the formation of communes, entailed increasing the scale of land area covered and membership. Communes were meant to act not only as organizers of (collective) agricultural production, but also as political units, providers of services, and sites of "backyard" industry. The rationale was that the socialist transformation of the Chinese countryside would initially proceed by substituting plentiful labor for scarce capital—that is, by mobilizing commune members for the construction of infrastructure, such as irrigation works, roads, and other building, as well as for labor-intensive farming and industry. The ambitions for the communes were accelerated during the Great Leap Forward of 1958–1962. It is widely held that the diversion of energies in the communes from farming to "backyard" industry, together with natural disasters and the range of different responses by local cadres (Bramall 2011), resulted in serious shortfalls in food production and were a major contribution to widespread famine in 1959–1961.

From the 1950s, following several decades of tortuous division within the CCP leadership and social turmoil (Lin 2021)—as in the Soviet 1920s—and which included the "Great Proletarian Cultural Revolution" from 1966 to Mao Zedong's death in 1976, the end of the communes as the basis of landholding and collective production was announced with the establishment of the Household Responsibility System (HRS) in 1978 and its completion in 1984. The HRS returned land and other means of farming to individual peasant households, which now had fixed-term contracts with state agencies, creating a very different basis for pursuing agricultural "modernization" that was also supported by further market-oriented reforms (Ye 2015). Agricultural production in China underwent significant growth for a time. Many commentators argued that the return to the individualization of household farming was the principal reason for that growth. However, some scholars (e.g., Bramall 1993) dissented from views that the HRS was a necessary recognition of market-led development and its incentives for farmers (mainstream development theory) or a restoration of "autonomy" to peasant households and, indeed, one that had been triggered by peasant actions—a populist view advanced by van der Ploeg and Ye (2016).

There is no doubt, however, that the end of the communes and the introduction of the HRS was one significant moment, among others, in establishing China's "capitalist road" initiated under the leadership of Deng Xiaoping. Subsequent developments bring China's agrarian dynamics and peasant experiences into line with those of other countrysides in the global South in recent decades: land dispossession and the loss of farmland to industrial and infrastructure construction and real estate development; the development of agribusiness and corporate farming; foreign trade liberalization, and outward Chinese investment in land and agribusiness in other countries; the use of foreign migrant labor in commercial agriculture, both large and smaller in scale; and, not least, the massive migration of Chinese rural people to work in urban construction, industries, and services.

Several brief observations conclude this section.

First, one should note other attempts to forge a socialist system of agriculture, both in mostly peasant societies (e.g., Vietnam) and in countries where large-scale capitalist agricultural enterprises offered opportunities for nationalization (Cuba, Nicaragua).

Second, the Russian and Chinese revolutions and the land reforms they initially instituted (or, in the Bolshevik case, accepted) occurred in the context of massive upheavals that undermined old regimes and the places within them of classes of (precapitalist) landed property. In Russia, this included the weakening of Tsarist autocracy accelerated by the country's growing defeat in World War I; in China, a long disintegration of the central state was compounded by regional warlordism and the Japanese occupation. In both countries, the revolutions were able to mobilize the energies of peasant anti-landlordism, China's revolution being the most massive and radical instance of anti-imperialist "national liberation" in the twentieth century.

Third, even though Russia's Marxists were much closer intellectually, and geographically, to Marx than were Mao Zedong and other CCP leaders, by 1949 the CCP had established a strong base in many of China's rural areas, in contrast with the virtually complete absence of the Bolsheviks in the Russian countryside.

Finally, the failures or reversals of socialist construction in agriculture in both Russia and China, and elsewhere, has left a vacuum in Marxist thinking. There is no viable model of socialist transition in agriculture today, any more than there was in Marx's day.

This means that other, mostly populist, ideas and interventions have been able to occupy the spaces left by Marxism.

Marxism(s) and Politics of Land

To begin the discussion of Marxism(s) and the politics of land, it is worth noting the major contributions of Alexander V. Chayanov (1888–1937), the great Russian agricultural economist, who died in one of Stalin's prison camps. First, Chayanov developed a theory of peasantry as a particular type of economy based in "family farming." This entails a distinct form of economic calculation, aimed at achieving simple reproduction (albeit with enhanced standards of living). Most of the differentiation that can be observed among peasants, for example, in areas of land farmed, is "demographic"—that is, tied to the different stages of the household generational or domestic cycle—rather than the class differentiation Lenin highlighted (Chayanov 1966). Second, Chayanov analyzed the agricultural sector as a whole, of which farming was one component in the circuits of finance, marketing, processing, regulation, and so on, that integrate agriculture (Banaji 2021, 12–13, 99). Capitalist development of agriculture means that farmers are increasingly exposed to exploitation and domination by banks and merchant capital, a dynamic best exemplified by the United States at that time, the 1920s (Chayanov 1966, 262–263). Chayanov did not accept that there are key economies of scale in farming as there are in the other aspects of integration of the agricultural sector just indicated. Third, then, Chayanov believed that given peasant cooperation and state support for other economies of scale in integration (finance, technical innovation, input supply, marketing, processing), along with the appropriate regulation of agriculture, the peasant farm could, and should, be the basis of future agricultural development, given peasants' intimate knowledge of their land and its specific environments, which they farm through their own organization of ("family") labor (Chayanov 1991).

Chayanov was the most important theorist available to contemporary and subsequent agrarian populism (see van der Ploeg 2013; and this volume). Indeed, much of the history of modern "peasant studies" can be written in terms of the opposed legacies of Marx/Lenin and Chayanov, if sometimes simplistically so (Bernstein 2009).

Another set of issues, of wide and intense interest, takes off from the brief but vivid observations of Marx and Engels about the peasantries and peasant politics of their time. Marx and Engels assumed that there was no longer any peasantry left in Britain after it had "completed" the transition to capitalism, which happened at a time when most of the rest of Europe and the colonial world had not yet done so and still had sizeable peasantries. In 1894, Engels addressed the issue in "The Peasant Question in France and Germany," writing that in those countries, as elsewhere, "the peasant is a very essential factor of the population, production and political power" (Engels 1970, 457) with strategic implications for the programs of socialist parties based in the urban working class, of which the German Social Democratic Party (SDP) was the leading exemplar of the time. This was also the concern of the SDP's leading theorist, Kautsky (1988), in his 1899 work *The Agrarian Question*, which included a consideration of the various ways peasant farmers can be integrated in the course of capitalist development, instead of "disappearing" abruptly or comprehensively.

Most famous, or infamous, was Marx's earlier description of the French peasantry of the mid-nineteenth century as resembling "a sack of potatoes" in its inability to constitute itself as a collective political actor, a class able to act in its own interest. (Marx 1973, 239). This metaphor appeared in a section of Marx's *Eighteenth Brumaire of Louis Bonaparte* (Marx 1973, 238–245), which gives a more substantial, and nuanced, explanation of his position, embracing the material (smallholding as the basis of peasant production and reproduction), cultural (religion, for example), and political effects of both.

> In so far as millions of families live under economic conditions of existence that separate their mode of life, their interests and their cultural formation from those of the other classes and bring them into conflict with those classes, they form a class. In so far as these small peasant proprietors are merely connected on a local basis, and the identity of their interest fails to produce a feeling of community, national links, or a political organization, they do not form a class.
>
> (Marx 1973, 239)

Marx went on to distinguish

> the (conservative) peasant who wants to consolidate the condition of his social existence, the smallholding . . . [and] the (revolutionary) peasant who strikes out beyond it . . . the country people who want to overthrow the old order by their own energies, in alliance with the towns.
>
> (Marx 1973, 240)

In such pregnant if schematic observations, Marx pointed ahead to some of the massive political upheavals that were to follow in predominantly peasant societies, with critical consequences for land and the stances taken by Marxists. Some decades later, toward the end of his life, and with another Russian reference point, Marx sought to develop his understanding of precapitalist formations and their institutions, not least, the forms of communal land tenure and governance. He learned Russian so that he could follow the intense debates in Russia about land, including the arguments of more, and less, revolutionary populism. Many of the Russian Populists followed Marx's analysis of capitalism but argued that a future Russian socialism should, and could, build on the *mir*—that is, the peasant landholding commune. A much discussed, if very brief, commentary on this by Marx in 1881 included responses to questions posed to him in a letter by the Russian revolutionary Vera Zasulich (Shanin 1983).

Marx's attention was mostly on Europe, including Russia, although his journalism took in momentous events in other parts of the world, including China and India; he followed the Civil War in the United States closely and was resolutely opposed to the capitalist slavery of the American South. This meant that he did not systematically consider the immense part played by peasant rebellion and revolution in the making of the modern world and in transitions to modernity (Moore 1966), which continued after his death. Interest in, and sympathy, for uprisings—in which loss of land, threats to landholding, and demands for land were until the 1970s major features of much Marxist and other radical writing in and on the Third World; for example, in India, where the rural uprising in Telangana in the years immediately after independence from colonial rule was subject to massive military suppression (Sundarayya 1972), and in Latin America (Huizer 1973). It can be proposed, however, that the period of both the incidence of and hopes for "peasant war" as a decisive political form was largely finished by the 1970s. The victory of the Vietnamese in their struggle for national liberation in 1975 (the same year Portugal's African colonies gained independence) marked the end of the great era of the "peasant wars of the twentieth century"—indeed, it was the Vietnamese struggle that inspired Eric Wolf's (1969) seminal work. Since then, armed peasant "resistance" on any similarly large scale has been absent, marked by the failure of Guevarist guerrilla efforts in Latin America and of Sendero Luminoso (Shining Path) in Peru, which claimed "Maoist" credentials, as did the more successful movement in Nepal and the struggling "Naxalite" guerrilla groups in India's northern hills (Shah 2018).

Marx's formulation of the peasant who is unable to produce "a feeling of community, national links, or a political organization" has been overtaken by subsequent events. Although the peasant actions against landlordism in the Russian revolution of 1917 were self-organized at local levels (or "spontaneous"), and those of China were aggregated and led by the CCP, a variety of national political bodies representing peasant or, at least, agrarian interests were important politically in different places and at different moments of the twentieth century, for example, the "Green" or peasant parties of Central and Eastern Europe in the 1920s and 1930s (Mitrany 1961). And today, many national or regional peasant and (small) farmer political formations are member organizations of the international La Vía Campesina with its strongly populist imprint (Edelman 2003; Desmarais 2007). One of the best known of those formations is the Brazil's Movimento dos Trabalhadores Rurais Sem Terra (MST), the "Landless Workers Movement" (Wolford 2010). Some leading ideologues and activists of La Via Campesina are or were Marxists of various stripes (Jun Borras, pers. comm.), as are some founding members and key figures in the MST. India's leading communist writer on agrarian issues, Utsa Patnaik, who once wrote a notable Marxist critique of Chayanov (Patnaik 1979) and has made major contributions to the methodology of peasant class differentiation (Patnaik 1987), now downplays class divisions in the Indian countryside in the interests of a broad "anti-imperialism" (Patnaik 2012).

In short, people can change their minds; some distinctions are not categorical and can shift with the historical context. Moreover, it is impossible to generalize adequately about movements and organizations claiming to represent peasant interests. Their composition, goals, and leadership span a wide range, from those that serve the interests of rich peasant or commercial farmers to those that appear more radical. Rather similarly to the Russian Populists of the late nineteenth century, some of today's supporters of La

Vía Campesina subscribe to much of the Marxist analysis of modern capitalism, especially in its international dimensions, and some favor the group's more radical member organizations (e.g., Borras 2020). Moreover, many Marxists support the actions heralded by more radical agrarian populism, for example, resisting corporate agribusiness land grabbing, mining, and other energy capitals and measures taken to liberalize domestic and international agricultural trade in commodities. A recent, and highly publicized, instance of such resistance, was the Indian "farmers' revolt" against the 2020 laws of the Modi government intended to further liberalize agricultural markets and to support agribusiness capital, which in November 2021, the government said would be withdrawn. The "farmers' revolt" was supported by populists and Marxists alike, if not for the same reasons. Moreover, it rested on a class alliance that was most unusual in India and unlikely to endure (Lerche 2021).

Nonetheless, the sticking point between Marxist and agrarian populist ideas and politics remains the latter's insistence on the "peasant way" as the basis for any socially and ecologically progressive farming. One of the intellectual foundations of this position is Chayanov's theorization of the peasant household, along with notions of the virtues and capacities of peasant "community" (less pronounced in Chayanov), which Marxists see as both essentialist in intellectual terms and prey to a romantic utopianism. Perhaps the most startling expression of an agrarian populist worldview is the position that peasants today are the potential gravediggers of present-day capitalism, replacing the proletariat of Marxist tradition (McMichael 2006).

Reasons for skepticism are, first, the "orthodox" Marxist view that (small) farming in capitalism is based in and reinforces private property. This view was articulated by Rosa Luxemburg in 1918 in her notes on the Russian revolution: "an enormous, newly developed and powerful mass of owning peasants who will defend their newly won property with tooth and nail against every attack" (Luxemburg 1918, chap. 2). Second is the Marxist view (following Lenin) that "peasants" today are constituted within capitalist social relations (commodification) and differentiated by them, in short, that "peasants" are not a (single) class, nor can their places within capitalist production and reproduction enable them to act like one. Third is an often-overlooked dimension of the second point, that the fates of rural areas, and their distributions and uses of land, are increasingly interconnected with urban and nonagricultural dynamics, affecting all rural classes, if in markedly different ways. Fourth, is the view of some, if not all, Marxists that "big is beautiful": large-scale farming enjoys economies of scale, and with them productivities of labor, that small-scale farming cannot hope to attain.

Conclusion

The current state of Marxist ideas and the politics on land issues within the wider political economy of agrarian change displays the syndrome outlined here. Marxism remains intellectually vibrant and continues to make major contributions to both historical scholarship and accounts of contemporary change within capitalism, but the presence and significance of fewer or less potent Marxist political parties and movements are overshadowed by those flying various agrarian populist banners. At the same time, more radical populisms take much from Marxist analysis of capitalism while adhering to variants of "the peasant way" as the path beyond capitalism.

Among the developments in Marxist thinking is the "ecological Marxist" (or Red-Green) project to construct an explanation of ecological crisis that results from capital's relentless drive to exploit nature, not least because it affects land, undermining the reproduction of its qualities hence what and how much can be produced from it: soil fertility, water supply, (adverse) climate change, biodiversity, and so on. New readings of Marx are a notable feature of this project, arguing that a materialist ecology was present, if not explicitly or systematically elaborated, in his writings, including his observations about developments in the capitalist agriculture of his time (Foster 2000; Moore 2015; Saito 2017).

A second major development is the growth and influence of materialist-feminist work on social reproduction (Bhattacharya 2017; and this volume). Gender relations and dynamics were marginal to the classic works of Marxism and, indeed surprisingly so, in the household-centered theories of Chayanov and his followers. Building on several generations of previous feminist scholarship that explored the gendered foundations of rural household functioning, its divisions of labor, claims on land and the products of labor, strong gender inequalities in land reform programs, and so on, innovative materialist-feminist research and debate open up the "hidden abode" of social reproduction and its various dimensions and sites. As with "ecological Marxism," this entails complementing, expanding, and sometimes revising basic tenets of Marx's theorization of the capitalist mode of production, the multiple social differences and divisions within capitalist societies and capitalism globally, and the concrete conditions and effects of capitalist dynamics.

Among all of these in a world of triumphant, and triumphalist, capitalism, there is little evidence of "the (revolutionary) peasant who strikes out beyond [the smallholding] . . . the country people who want to overthrow the old order by their own energies, in alliance with the towns" (Marx, cited above). The latter part of that judgment, updated to overthrowing the order of capitalism, is also much debated regarding the world's proletarians or "classes of labor."

Acknowledgments

The author is grateful for comments on earlier drafts by Jairus Banaji, Ben Cousins, Cristobal Kay, and the editors of this Handbook. Given the limited length of this entry in relation to the scale of the subject and the radical abbreviation of its observations on theory, history, and politics, the usual disclaimer—that the author must bear full responsibility for its content—applies even more forcefully.

References

Akram-Lodhi, A. Haroom, K. Dietz, B. Engels, and B. M. McKay, eds. 2021. *Handbook of Critical Agrarian Studies*. Cheltenham, UK: Edward Elgar.

Araghi, F. 2009. "Accumulation by Displacement, Global Enclosures, Food Crisis, and the Ecological Contradictions of Capitalism." *Review* 32 (1): 113–146.

Banaji, J. 2021. *A Brief History of Commercial Capitalism*. Chicago: Haymarket Books.

Bernstein, Henry. 2009. "V. I. Lenin and A. V. Chayanov: Looking Back, Looking Forward." *Journal of Peasant Studies* 36 (1): 55–81.

Bernstein, Henry. 2010. *Class Dynamics of Agrarian Change*. Halifax, CAN: Fernwood.

Bernstein, Henry. 2015a. "Land Relations in Sub-Saharan Africa and China: Preliminary Notes for Comparison and Contrast." In *The Land Question: Socialism, Capitalism and the Market*, edited by Mahmood Mamdani, 17–76. Kampala, Uganda: Makerere Institute of Social Research.

Bernstein, Henry. 2015b. "Some Reflections on Agrarian Change in China." *Journal of Agrarian Change* 15 (4): 454–477.

Bernstein, Henry. 2018. "The 'Peasant Problem' in the Russian Revolution(s), 1905–1929." *Journal of Peasant Studies* 45 (5–6): 1127–1150.

Bernstein, Henry, and T. J. Byres. 2001. "From Peasant Studies to Agrarian Change." *Journal of Agrarian Change* 1 (1): 1–56.

Bhattacharya, T., ed. 2017. *Social Reproduction Theory: Remapping Class, Recentering Oppression*. London: Pluto Press.

Borras, Saturnino M., Jr. 2020. "Agrarian Social Movements: The Absurdly Difficult but Not Impossible Agenda of Defeating Right-Wing Populism and Exploring a Socialist Future." *Journal of Agrarian Change* 20 (3): 3–36.

Bramall, Chris. 1993. "The Role of Decollectivisation in China's Agricultural Miracle, 1978–90." *Journal of Peasant Studies* 20 (2): 271–295.

Bramall, Chris. 2011. "Agency and Famine in China's Sichuan Province, 1958–1962." *China Quarterly* 208: 990–1008.

Brenner, R. 1976, "Agrarian Class Structure and Economic Development in Pre-industrial Europe." *Past and Present* 70: 30–75.

Brenner, R. 2001, "The Low Countries in the Transition to Capitalism." *Journal of Agrarian Change* 1 (2): 169–241.

Byres, T. J., ed. 1983. "Sharecropping and Sharecroppers." Special issue. Journal of Peasant Studies 10 (2–3).

Byres, T. J. 1991. "The Agrarian Question and Differing Forms of Capitalist Agrarian Transition: An Essay with Reference to Asia." In *Rural Transformation in Asia*, edited by J. Breman and S. Mundle, 3–76. Delhi: Oxford University Press.

Byres, T. J. 1996. *Capitalism from Above and Capitalism from Below: An Essay in Comparative Political Economy*. London: Macmillan.

Byres, T. J. 2003. "Structural Change, the Agrarian Question and the Possible Impact of Globalization." In *Work and Well-Being in the Age of Finance*, edited by J. Ghosh and C. P. Chandrasekhar, 171–211. New Delhi: Tulika Books.

Capps, G. 2016. "Tribal Landed Property: The Value of the Chieftaincy in Contemporary Africa." *Journal of Agrarian Change* 16 (3): 452–477.

Chayanov, A. V. 1966. *The Theory of Peasant Economy*. Edited by D. Thorner, B. Kerblay, and R. E. F. Smith. Homewood, IL: Richard Irwin for the American Economic Association. (Original work published 1925).

Chayanov, A. V. 1991. *The Theory of Peasant Co-operatives*. London: I. B. Tauris.

Chimhowu, A., and P. Woodhouse. 2007. "Customary vs Private Property Rights? Dynamics and Trajectories of Vernacular Land Markets in Sub-Saharan Africa." *Journal of Agrarian Change* 6: 3.

Christophers, B. 2020. *Rentier Capitalism: Who Owns the Economy and Who Pays for It?* London: Verso Books.

Danilov, V. P. 1988. *Rural Russia under the New Regime*. London: Hutchinson.

De Angelis, M. 2007. *The Beginning of History: Value Struggles and Global Capital*. London: Pluto.

de Janvry, A. 1983. "Why Do Governments Do What They Do?" In *The Role of Markets in the World Food Economy*, edited by D. G. Johnson and G. E. Schuh. Boulder, CO: Westview Press.

Desmarais, A.-A. 2007. *La Via Campesina: Globalization and the Power of Peasants*. Halifax, CAN: Fernwood.

Edelman, M. 2003. "Transnational Peasant and Farmer Movements and Networks." In *Global Civil Society Yearbook 2003*, edited by M. Kaldor, H. Anheier, and M. Glasius, 185–220. London: SAGE.

Engels, Friedrich. 1970. "The Peasant Question in France and Germany." In *Karl Marx and Friedrich Engels: Selected Works*. Moscow: Progress Publishers.

Fine, B. 1994. "Coal, Diamonds and Oil: Towards a Comparative Theory of Mining." *Review of Political Economy* 6 (3): 279–302.

Fine, B. 2019. "Marx's Rent Theory Revisited? Landed Property, Nature and Value." *Economy and Society* 48 (3): 450–461.

Foster, J. Bellamy. 2000. *Marx's Ecology: Materialism and Nature*. New York: Monthly Review Press.

Friedmann, Harriet, and Philipe McMichael. 1989. "Agriculture and the State System: The Rise and Decline of National Agricultures, 1870 to the Present." *Sociologica Ruralis* 29 (2): 93–117.

Hall, D. 2013. *Land*. Cambridge, UK: Polity Press.

Harvey, D. 1985. *The Urbanization of Capital: Studies in the Theory and History of Capitalist Urbanization*. Oxford: Blackwell.

Harvey, D. 2003. *The New Imperialism*. Oxford: Oxford University Press.

Heller, H. 2011. *The Birth of Capitalism: A Twenty-First Century Perspective*. London: Pluto.

Ho, P. 2001. "Who Owns China's Land? Policies, Property Rights and Deliberate Institutional Ambiguity." *China Quarterly* 166: 394–421.

Huizer, G. 1973. *Peasant Rebellion in Latin America*. Harmondsworth, UK: Penguin.

Isett, Christopher, and Stephen Miller. 2016. *The Social History of Agriculture: From the Origins to the Current Crisis*. Lanham, MD: Rowan and Littlefield.

Jayne, T. S., J. Chamberlin, L. Traub, N. Sitko, M. Muyanga, F. K. Yeboah, et al. 2016. "Africa's Changing Farm Size Distribution Patterns: The Rise of Medium-Scale Farms." *Agricultural Economics* 47 (S1): 197–214.

Kautsky, Karl. 1988. *The Agrarian Question*. 2 vols. Translated by Peter Burgess. London: Zwan. (Original published in 1899).

Lenin, Vladimir I. 1973a. *The Development of Capitalism in Russia: The Process of the Formation of a Home Market for Large-Scale Industry*. In *Collected Works*, vol. 3., Moscow: Progress Publishers.

Lenin, Vladimir I. 1973b. *Imperialism, The Highest Stage of Capitalism*. In *Collected Works*, vol. 22. Moscow: Progress Publishers. (Original work published 1916.)
Lerche, J. 2021. "The Farm Laws Struggle 2020–2021: Class-Caste Alliances and Bypassed Agrarian Transition in Neoliberal India." *Journal of Peasant Studies*. doi:10.1080/03066150.2021.1986013.
Lin Chun. 2021. *Revolution and Counterrevolution in China*. London: Verso Books.
Luxemburg, Rosa. 1918. *The Russian Revolution*. Marxist Internet Archive. https://www.marxists.org/archive/luxemburg/1918/russian-revolution/.
Luxemburg. Rosa. 1951. *The Accumulation of Capital*. London: Routledge and Kegan Paul.
Mao Zedong. 1967. "Report of an Investigation of the Peasant Movement in Hunan." In *Selected Works*, vol. 1. Beijing: Foreign Languages Press.
Marx, Karl. 1968. *Theories of Surplus Value*. Moscow: Progress Publishers.
Marx, Karl. 1973. "The Eighteenth Brumaire of Louis Bonaparte." In *Karl Marx: Surveys from Exile: Political Writings*, vol. 2, edited by David Fernbach. Harmondsworth, UK: Penguin Books.
Marx, Karl. 1976. *Capital*. Vol. 1. Harmondsworth, UK: Penguin Books.
Marx, Karl. 1981. *Capital*. Vol. 3. Harmondsworth, UK: Penguin Books.
McMichael, Philip. 2006. "Reframing Development: Global Peasant Movements and the New Agrarian Question." *Canadian Journal of Development Studies* 27: 471–483.
McMichael, Philip. 2013. *Food Regimes and Agrarian Questions*. Halifax, CAN: Fernwood.
Mies, M. 2014. *Patriarchy and Accumulation on a World Scale: Women in the International Division of Labour*. London: Bloomsbury.
Mintz, Sidney. 1985. *Sweetness and Power: The Place of Sugar in Modern History*. New York: Viking.
Mitrany, D. 1961. *Marx against the Peasant: A Study in Social Dogmatism*. New York: Collier Books. (Original work published in 1951).
Moore, Barrington, Jr. 1966. *Social Origins of Dictatorship and Democracy: Lord and Peasant in the Making of the Modern World*. Boston: Beacon Press.
Moore, J. W. 2015. *Capitalism in the Web of Life: Ecology and the Accumulation of Capital*. London: Verso.
Moyo, S., P. Jha, and P. Yeros. 2013. "The Classical Agrarian Question: Myth, Reality and Relevance Today." *Agrarian South* 2 (1): 93–119.
Neocosmos, M. 1986. "Marx's Third Class: Capitalist Landed Property and Capitalist Development." *Journal of Peasant Studies* 13 (3): 5–44.
Patnaik, Utsa. 1979. "Neo-populism and Marxism: The Chayanovian View of the Agrarian Question and Its Fundamental Fallacy." *Journal of Peasant Studies* 6 (4): 375–420.
Patnaik, Utsa. 1987. *Peasant Class Differentiation: A Study in Method with Reference to Haryana*. New Delhi: Oxford University Press.
Patnaik, Utsa. 2012. "Some Aspects of the Contemporary Agrarian Question." *Agrarian South* 1 (3): 233–254.
Peters, Pauline E. 2004. "Inequality and Social Conflict over Land in Africa." *Journal of Agrarian Change* 4 (3): 269–314.
Reardon, T., C. Timmer, C. Barret, and J. Berdegué. 2003. "The Rise of Supermarkets in Africa, Asia and Latin America." *American Journal of Agricultural Economics* 85 (5).
Saito, K. 2017. *Karl Marx's Ecosocialism: Capital, Nature, and the Unfinished Critique of Political Economy*. New York: Monthly Review Press.
Shah, A. 2018. *Nightmarch: Among India's Revolutionary Guerrillas*. London: C Hurst & Co.

Shanin, T. 1972. *The Awkward Class: Political Sociology of Peasantry in a Developing Society; Russia 1910–1925*. Oxford: Clarendon Press.
Shanin, T., ed. 1983. *Late Marx and the Russian Road: Marx and the "Peripheries" of Capitalism*. London: Routledge and Kegan Paul.
Shanin, T. 1986. *Russia 1905–7: Revolution as a Moment of Truth*. Vol. 2 of *The Roots of Otherness: Russia's Turn of Century*. London: Macmillan.
Shivji, I. 2019. "Sam Moyo and Samir Amin on the Peasant Question." *Agrarian South* 8 (1–2): 287–302.
Sundarayya, Puccalapalli. 1972. *Telangana People's Struggle and Its Lessons*. Calcutta: Desraj Chadha for the Communist Party of India (Marxist).
Vanaik, A. 2017. *The Rise of Hindu Authoritarianism: Secular Claims, Communal Realities*. 2nd ed. London: Verso Books.
van der Ploeg, J. D. 2013. *Peasants and the Art of Farming: A Chayanovian Manifesto*. Halifax, CAN: Fernwood.
van der Ploeg, J. D., and J. Ye, eds. 2016. *China's Peasant Agriculture and Rural Society: Changing Paradigms of Farming*. London: Routledge.
Wallerstein, I. 1974. *The Modern World-System I: Capitalist Agriculture and the Origins of the European World-Economy in the Sixteenth Century*. New York: Academic Press.
Weis, T. 2010. "The Accelerating Biophysical Contradictions of Industrial Capitalist Agriculture." *Journal of Agrarian Change* 10 (3): 315–341.
Wolf, Eric. 1969. *Peasant Wars of the Twentieth Century*. London: Faber and Faber.
Wolford, Wendy. 2010. *This Land Is Ours Now: Social Mobilization and the Meanings of Land in Brazil*. Durham, NC: Duke University Press.
Wood, E. M. 2002. *The Origin of Capitalism: A Longer View*. London: Verso.
Ye Jingzhong. 2015. "Land Transfer and the Pursuit of Agricultural Modernization in China." *Journal of Agrarian Change* 15 (3): 314–337.

CHAPTER 3

LAND IN WORLD-ECOLOGY PERSPECTIVES

RAJ PATEL

Introduction to World-Ecology

Every political economist needs a theory of action at a distance. Whether land is enclosed and transformed because of supply and demand, by wars among great powers, in the *Sturm und Drang* of imperial terraforming, or simply from the exigencies of "globalization," there is always a story that connects land in one place to decisions made by humans elsewhere. This chapter examines a relatively new theory: world-ecology. Before we situate a world-ecological view of land in a broader context, a word about terms. *World-ecology* needs its hyphen. Without it, unsuspecting readers might imagine that "world ecology" refers to the study of the relationship between species and abiotic habitats, on a planetary scale. While the earth's ecology is certainly grist for scholars of world-ecology, the intellectual lineage that matters most is that in which "ecology" comes to substitute for "system": world-systems theory. For the unfamiliar, world-systems theory isn't just the operating "system of the world" (Stephenson 2005). It is, rather, the tradition that drew on the Annales school of world history, principally through Fernand Braudel's work, which took a particular structural and sociological bent through Immanuel Wallerstein's world-systems theory (Wallerstein 1974; Braudel 1972).

The first volume of Wallerstein's analysis of the modern world-system has a subtitle that provides a helpful point of departure: "Capitalist Agriculture and the Origins of the European World-Economy in the Sixteenth Century." Finding the origins of a world-system in the 1500s, at the dawn of capitalism, fits well with the temporal concerns of the Annales school, and its interest in the backdrop of events within the structures and conjunctures of the longue durée (Braudel 1972, 16; Forster 1978). So, too, does the analysis of the forces that implicated peasantries and workers in the grand arcs of history. The Annales school had little use for transcripts of diplomatic history between great powers. The full title of the Annales journal—*Annales: Economies, sociétés, civilizations*—signaled the ambition. Far more interesting to this journal's contributors were the temporal cycles of commodities, flows of people and ideas, and long-term ecological shifts that provided the material backdrop for the courtroom dramas with which other historians preoccupied themselves. The same interests are the grist for both world history and world-ecology.

Across the vast canvas of exchanges and transformations that took place in the early modern era, Wallerstein (1979) identified an analytical relationship that could weave those relationships together in a dramatically new way: "the defining characteristic of a social system [is] the existence within it of the division of labour" (5). Centering the question of work allows for a supple reading of history and the present. When the task of analysis is to investigate the geography produced through the division of labor instead of comparing divisions of labor within spatial units defined *a priori*, vital connections emerge across, as Braudel (1972) originally offered, the Mediterranean world. Here, at the heart of world-system analysis, lie the entwined questions: "Who does the work, where are they doing it, and for whom?" (See, similarly, Bernstein 2006.)

Dialectic analysis of the division of labor offers rich rewards. In her overview of world-systems theory, Harriet Friedmann helpfully summarizes three linked outcomes that become far easier to see through a world-systems lens. When looking at capitalism's development, the world-system approach foregrounds, first, the development of an international system of prices. Unlike the ancient trade routes, these patterns allow the simultaneous transmission of the same price to producers that might be continents apart. Second, the international division of labor fosters "a larger-than-local pattern of specialized production and interdependence" (Friedmann 2000, 501). In the discipline of international relations, this is sometimes understood as the ongoing ledger of "uneven and combined development" (Rioux 2015). Finally, a system of states that recognized each other, and whose practices involved safeguarding and expanding the property rights of its dominant actors, was a third component outcome.

Using world-systems analysis, units of political geography emerge from the processes of capitalist accumulation and crisis. World-systems thinking can be understood as a rejoinder to methodological approaches in liberalism, in which units of comparison such as nation-states are assumed to be natural and independent, operating in the universe of liberal political economy, whose hidden laws of motion might be discerned with sufficiently elegant comparative experiments (Hollis and Smith 1990). Yet this understanding of "globalization" generally fails to account for the processes that produced it. In response, theorists keen to stretch the liberal field have supplemented it with approaches that take the international, not as a given, but as a product of a process of a spatially connected and crisis-ridden expansion of capitalism. As Justin Rosenberg explains, "The significance of 'uneven and combined development' lies in its utility for exactly the opposite exercise: namely, for reintegrating 'the international' within the remit of 'the social.'" (Callinicos and Rosenberg 2008, 86).

Sociologists have been engaged in this project this for some time. World-systems theory encourages a less black-box approach to international relations, asking questions of incorporated comparison (McMichael 1990). So, for instance, instead of asking what the trade in enslaved people did to Martinique, a world-systems approach would locate flows of people, capital, and commodities through Martinique to Europe, the Americas, and beyond, and ask how flows made places, and vice versa, rather than assume the ontological stability of either capital flows or nation-states (Tomich 1990; Ferdinand and Smith 2021).

A world-systems approach also offers the chance to investigate other moments in the division of labor across the world-system before European hegemony. Although Wallerstein was interested in the rise of Europe, that was not the only or the first such system. There is an ongoing project to recuperate the origins of the European world-system in previous world-systems in Africa and Asia (Abu-Lughod 1989).

This analytical depth comes, however, with new sets of problems. If the units of analysis themselves are a product of capitalism's own dialectics, then world-systems theory must answer an additional question that liberal political economy need never confront: How does the world-system change over time? For historians of an older school, the answer obviously lies in the jostling of nation-states and their prosecutions of wars for dominions that ultimately became independent and formed the system of nation-states we find today. For world-systems theorists, nation-states emerge in the flux of relations of power that extend between the core of the world- system, and its peripheries and semi-peripheries. The nation-state is merely an outcome of a greater and more relevant set of forces operating at the level of the world-system. States, therefore, receive comparatively little analysis in Wallerstein's work (Navarro 1982).

A position of comparative disinterest in states is, at least, sustained by argument. The real engine for change in the world-system is systemic crisis. Every world-system has a beginning and an end, brought about by the impossibility of managing the contradictions internal to it (Wallerstein 1988). Not all contradictions are fatal in the short run—within the modern world-system, the process of resolving contradictions brought about the rearrangement of financial hegemons, with the most important flows of finance shifting from the Netherlands to the United Kingdom to the United States (Arrighi 1994). Crisis can make itself felt across a society, but in the modern world-system, it is precipitated by the consequences of the capitalist division of labor.

The story Wallerstein (1988) offers is that the bourgeoisie

> sporadically accede to some redistribution of surplus value to working strata in order to recreate and expand effective demand, thus permitting renewed expansion. This solves the middle-run problem. However, over the long run, it means a "freeing" of the factors of production, which means a reduction in long-run profit margins. . . . As time goes on, oppressed strata are more and more able to rebel, and more and more ready to do so. By the nineteenth century, the level of possibility and will had reached the point that we began to see the emergence of antisystemic movements in their two classical forms (the socialist movements and the nationalist movements). This political development threatened the logic of the system—endless accumulation of capital—in two ways. First, it strengthened the hands of the world's working strata in the constant battle over the division of surplus-value, and therefore threatened

> long-run profit margins. Secondly, in order to counter the working strata politically, the accumulators of capital have been forced to turn over an ever-greater share of surplus-value to their agents and defenders . . . The only thing the accumulators of capital can really do is more of the same. They can treat these rebellions as part of the short-run problems to which there are middle-run solutions, solutions of "cooptation" . . . But this "cooptation" is a process that, in the long run, attacks both the economic and the political underpinnings of the system. (586–587)

An analysis that centers a falling rate of profit is certainly helpful in understanding the upheavals of the modern economy (Kliman 2012). It does appear, however, to be a story in which labor and capital matter most centrally, and land appears only as a place of postponement of the central dynamic of crisis. Absent from the dialectical analysis of the division of labor is a discussion of what is transformed by that labor. Particularly in a time where the word *crisis* is increasingly autocompleted as "climate crisis," this agnosticism about the relationships beyond labor and capital seems a particularly profound oversight.

Frontiers in World-Ecology

World-ecology draws both on Marx and a Marxist tradition to enrich the analysis. An important point of departure is the work of British cultural theorist Raymond Williams. In *Keywords*, he observes: "Nature is perhaps the most complex word in the language" (Williams 1976, 219). The division between nature and society, between the thinking and unthinking world, is one that is sometimes attributed to Descartes. World-ecology suggests, however, that Descartes was less a philosopher than a stenographer of already-existing imperatives of capitalist expansion, with precedents had been set long before he was born, and ideas that were coming to him from as far away as New Spain (Dussel 2008).

The transmuting of nature into commodities is a central concern of world-systems theory and world-ecology, and both are concerned with the boundary conditions of the circulation of capital. That boundary is the site of a great deal of analytical work. Rather than see labor being applied at the frontier, as Moore (2015) notes,

> abstract social labor does not *create* frontiers so much as it *is* [original emphasis] a frontier process itself. That frontier is the boundary between commodified and uncommodified life, and capital moves across that boundary through the mapping and quantifying technics of abstract social nature. For all the "self-contained" character of *Capital*, the production of surplus value is not only the proletarianization of labor and the accumulation of capital, but the production of global spaces of capitalization and appropriation. (138)

It's hardly surprising that "the frontier" is the focus of many attempts at conceptual clarification (Beckert et al. 2021a, 2021b; Mostern 2021; Berg 2021). Under world-ecology, capitalism is understood to operate through the creation and "cheapening" of, inter alia, food, energy, work, care, money, nature, and lives (Patel and Moore 2017). Thus, as Moore (2014) observes:

> While all civilizations had frontiers of a sort, capitalism was a frontier. The extension of capitalist power to new spaces that were uncommodified became the lifeblood of capitalism. . . . I wish to highlight two relational axes of these frontiers. First, commodity frontier movements were not merely about the extension of commodity relations, although this was indeed central. Commodity frontier movements were also, crucially, about the extension of territorial and symbolic forms that appropriated unpaid work in service to commodity production." (288)

Capitalism's boundaries do not mere merely move through a space that capital itself creates and maps. Frontiers endure. Capitalism quickly exhausts the web of life's "free gifts," but the violent smoothing of territory, time, and space that is necessary to engage in appropriation and commodification leaves traces, remains, debris, and detritus (Chari 2013; Stoler 2013). Within the refuse of the first wave of appropriative colonial encounter lie the *matériel* and culture to fix the crises that will inevitably attend cycles of accumulation. Consider, for instance, the fate of an early outpost in the Portuguese empire, Madeira, so called because it was "an island of wood," *ilha da madeira*:

In 1455, the Venetian traveler and slaver Alvise da Ca'da Mosto observed that "there was not a foot of ground [on the island] that was not entirely covered with great trees." He continued, with a developer's eye for improvement:

> It was therefore first of all necessary, when it was desired to people it, to set fire to them, and for a long while this fire swept fiercely over the island. So great was the first conflagration, that [I was told] this Zuanconzales, who was then on the island, was forced, with all the men, women, and children, to flee its fury and to take refuge in the sea, where they remained, up to their necks in water, and without food or drink, for two days and two nights or thereabouts, to escape destruction. By this means they razed a great part of this forest, and cleared the ground for cultivation.
>
> (Cadamosto [1455] 1937, 9)

In an era when raging forest fires augur planetary destruction, it is jarring to read a description in which an uncontrolled inferno heralds not the end of civilization, but its arrival. In Cadamosto's description, the condition of being a climate refugee is temporary. Although the settlers are escaping the flames in the sea, they are secure in their knowledge that after the fire clears, they will be able to cultivate the land and improve it (Li 2007). Astute observers will note the continuity today with Brazilian president Jair Bolsonaro's approval of the Amazon in flames (Hope 2019).

When he visited Madeira, Cadamosto reported on the booming trade in wheat that fed the burgeoning archipelago of Portuguese colonial conquests (Serrao 1954). Madeira's wood was initially used for lumber in shipbuilding and construction; that was before entrepreneurs recruited the world's leading hydrological engineers to terraform the island, so that flows of water could be channeled to the soil, where a thirsty sugarcane crop could reliably be cultivated (Patel and Moore 2017). With the crop environment suitably altered, trees became sources not of construction material, but fuel. Through the frontier, the trees were transformed in their social relations from free gift of construction material to "cheap energy," firewood for a newly refashioned island geared to sugar production (Ghosh 2021; Moore 2009; Greenfield 1977; Vieira 1996a, 2004; Schwartz 2004). The opportunity cost of growing sugar rose so high that it no longer made sense to grow the wheat that had once been the island's principal export. The webs of trade that took cones of sugar off the island were tasked with bringing back food from other outposts of the Portuguese empire. By 1508, it was the Azores that fed Madeira because, as Serrao observed "sugar killed wheat" (Serrao 1954, 339, 40).

The sugar boom had burned through the island by the 1530s, and where no commercially useful trees remained, a crisis ensued, and the frontier was recursively shaped: Madeira became an outpost for ships carrying enslaved Africans across the Atlantic. Today, the constellation of forces that give Europeans cheap air travel, disposable income, visa-free access to a colonial island in the sun, and political formations that depend on low-wage service work in the Portuguese periphery have enabled savvy entrepreneurs to reconfigure the architecture of Madeira's ghastly past. The plantations where hundreds of enslaved people lived and died harvesting and grinding sugar cane next to the cane mill in Carheta is now a site of thanatourism (Vieira 1996b; Dann and Seaton 2001).

In one of the oldest examples of the permanence of a frontier, Madeira's key commodity has shifted over capitalism's crisis-punctuated arc, from shipbuilding planks, to sugar, to services for traders of enslaved people destined for sugar plantations in Brazil, to services for tourists curious about the conditions of those enslaved people. World-ecology understands a frontier not as a thing but as a dynamic field of power relations operating in the web of life, an always-unstable hegemonic process in which the capitalist imperative to secure profit creates and recreates governing institutions to order humans, and more-than-humans, in ways that will perpetuate cycles of dispossession and exploitation. In Madeira's case, though the commodity has changed, the frontier as a field of power remains. The configurations of local action on the land arise through factors that range from the availability of cheap money—understood as low-interest-rate loans successively borrowed from the fifteenth-century banks in Genoa, the Portuguese tourist board, and the European Union's Regional Development Funds—for commercial development to the existence of affordable air travel and cheap fuel. This constellation of forces involves flows of capital through Brussels, Riyadh, and London, before it reconfigures Funchal.

Capitalism is forever moving through new frontiers. In world-ecology "frontier" is a pivotal concept. As Moore (2015) notes, "New frontiers of appropriation have been central to launching, and sustaining, long waves of accumulation" (88). Early modern capitalism's expansion and success lay in the extent to which the frontiers of commodification outpaced the demand for products drawn from those frontiers. In the measurement and government of those zones of accumulation (and frontiers of disposal, understanding nature as a frontier into which waste is dumped freely), new forms of space, time, and social relations between humans and the web of life have been fashioned and maintained.

Understanding the successive constructions and reconstructions of frontier processes on Madeira is helpful both in illustrating how capitalism might be understood as a frontier, but also in understanding what happens when capitalism transforms the planet. With each successive wave of destruction and reconstruction, Madeira is actively remade. It's not the same Madeira as before, but it's still Madeira. There is a sedimented history (Hall 2005), not just in the vestige of the name "island of trees" for an island without them, but in the biophysical and social relations that attend the conditions of the possibility of change on the island at any given time.

The conditions on Madeira are shaped by, and shape, relations beyond the island. Here, we turn to a kind of crisis that world-ecology explores in ways that world history finds secondary: the metabolic rift. As John Bellamy Foster and Hannah Holleman note (Foster and Holleman 2014), the idea of a metabolic rift comes from Marx's *Grundrisse*:

> It is not the *unity* [orig. emphasis] of living and active humanity with the natural, inorganic conditions of their metabolic exchange with nature, and hence their appropriation of nature, which requires explanation or is the result of a historic process, but rather the *separation* [orig. emphasis] between these [natural,] inorganic conditions of human existence and this active existence, a separation which is completely posited only in the relation of wage labor and capital.
>
> (Marx 1973, 489)

In the first volume of *Capital*, in the discussion of modern industry and agriculture, Marx (1978) makes this a little clearer.

> In modern agriculture, as in urban industry, the increase in the productivity and the mobility of labor is purchased at the cost of laying waste and debilitating labor-power itself. Moreover, all progress in capitalist agriculture is a progress in the art, not only of robbing the worker, but of robbing the soil; all progress in increasing the fertility of the soil for a given time is a progress towards ruining the more long-lasting sources of that fertility. The more a country proceeds from large-scale industry as the background of its development, as in the case of the United States, the more rapid is this process of destruction. Capitalist production, therefore, only develops the techniques and the degree of combination of the social process of production by simultaneously undermining the original sources of all wealth—the soil and the worker. (638)

There are two key features to note here. First, the spatial rift between country and city creates an opportunity for capitalist agriculture to degrade the land in one place to feed the people in another. Soil nutrients don't return to country loam from city plates. Under capitalist cycles, nutrients flow from country to city and then out to sea. The physical metabolic process here is, to use the modern word, unsustainable. That tendency to destroy the basis of profit is a central crisis tendency (Foster and Magdoff 2000). It is a source of value that is unseen by world-historical analysis (Salleh 2010), much less the broader world of international relations theory that offers its own take on globalization (Rosenberg 2005).

Land played a central role in Marx's understanding. Soil fertility through the 1820s and 1830s declined, and this spawned the emergence of modern soil science as a technology for fixing what capitalism had broken in the earth. The boom in the global fertilizer industry, with guano shipped from Peru to the United Kingdom at quantities that rose a hundredfold from 1841 to 1847, serves as a marker for the capitalist recognition of soil fertility (Foster and Magdoff 2000), and for the imperial politics that fixed a problem in domestic soil through imperial conquest (Cushman 2013).

The second key idea in Marx's observations about industrial agriculture lie in the relation of the soil to the worker. Second, Marx is explicit in understanding that the soil and the laborer are separate, but that both are "original sources for all wealth." There are crisis tendencies in what we have come to call both "social" and "natural" metabolic orders: cities chew up and spit out soil nutrients and capitalism does the same to workers. Separating "nature" and "society" is, however, an error of thinking that itself emerges in capitalism, from the world-ordering that happens through frontiers. Luckily, Marx has a method for what good analysis should do here: think dialectically.

In cracking open the question of how, when, and where "work" happens and opening the question about the beings that do it, world-ecology is able to augment world-historical approaches to combined and uneven development (Löwy 2010; Harvey 2001). Crises met with a spatial fix (Harvey 1981) can be ones occasioned not by a crisis of accumulation as traditionally conceived (Foster 1999), but biophysical crises that are *simultaneously* crises occasioned by capitalism's crises of labor-power and profit (Moore 2011b).

Marx's metabolic rift is a theoretical approach that explores how the transformation of matter in one place is related to the operations of capital in another. The rift can span not only the divide between country and city, where the profit motive organizes interventions into the life cycles in the soil to send food to new classes of urban consumers, but can also reach from one corner of the planet to another.[1] McMichael (2012, 146) observes that "the metabolic rift is not only about a material transformation of production, with spatial consequences; it is also about an epistemological break."

Thus, capitalism is only able to understand and meet the climate crisis through the development of markets for ecosystems as a service. Developing this idea further, Schneider and McMichael note, it is hard under capitalism to diagnose a crisis of accumulation as embedded in the biophysical world and its "environmental" crises, precisely because of the enforcement of an "epistemic rift," one that sequesters knowledge about interruptions in flows of capital away from the destruction of the web of life that makes such flows profitable (Schneider and McMichael 2010).

Understanding capitalism's aporias helps return us with a fresh view on what labor might be. Work in world-ecology is differentiated. There is no labor-power without reproductive labor, and that uncounted work is central to the feminist politics of world-ecology, through "the subordination of women, nature and colonies" (Mies 1986, 77; Federici 2014). "Cheap care," "cheap nature," and "cheap work" are, however, different under world-ecology (Patel and Moore 2017; Ivancheva and Keating 2021). Although they share the same characteristics of "free gifts" (Moore 2015), they are appropriated, extracted, commanded, and governed differently. Through hegemonic processes of domination and consent, each is corralled into modern forms of care, space, and time. The "underground of capitalist patriarchy" as Mies puts it (1986, 77), is both a suppressed and vital force for the circulation of capital: the care within the web of life that allows for productive labor is unacknowledged and essential. Pari passu, so are the production of the substance of abstract labor-power and of abstract nature, of *time* and *space,* through which relations of domination can be rendered legible by capitalism (Moore 2018). Capitalism, in other words, produces a ledger of when, where, and with whom it operates. Although reproductive labor and the sustenance of the web of life require work, capitalism requires that work largely to be free. The operations of power that sustain such legibility are, in turn, grist for analysis.

The ledger is never stable, however, because humans and the more-than-human world buck back. Fixing the meaning of words requires institutional mediation, as Lund (this volume) points out. A central institution in this process of capitalist instruction is the modern police force. Without the threat of state-sanctioned violence to those who traduce private property arrangements, the modern technology of the fence would be meaningless. The meaning of a hedge around enclosed private property comes from the violence that attends its unauthorized crossing by commoners (Blomley 2007). States and their institutions create and attempt to maintain hegemony over time, space, and social relations, productive and reproductive (Cousins, this volume). Standardized work time (Thompson 1967; Martineau 2017) and map-making (Akerman 2017) have, increasingly, become the purview of central government. The processes and projects of the regulation of capitalist space and time are, as McMichael notes (this volume), intrinsic to the development project.

As with all policing, states' policing of time and space involves arts of recognition and diagnosis (Montague 2022). Recognizably foreign bodies—human or more-than-human—are occasion for the state to act. As Sagoff observes in his discussion of invasive species (2009), action by the state always requires a narrative. To police boundaries of species purity with chemicals, the state narrates a time of national purity before the colonial transfer of species, in which natives (not humans, but other beings) didn't have to suffer foreign pests. These hegemonies are socioecological projects in themselves, as well as means of interpolating and governing nature and society (Moore 2011a, 125).

As with any hegemony, the state's attempts to maintain its powers are always resisted. As a range of commentators have noted, the impositions of capitalist time (Rifkin 1987, 2017), space (Williams 2003; Craib 2017), and relationality (Youatt 2017) have all been—and continue to be (Estes 2019)—contested. Through these conflicts, capitalism's frontiers shift. When enslaved human labor ceased to be conscionably cheap—and it is worth observing that human trafficking today occurs at levels comparable to the transatlantic slave trade (International Labour Organization 2017)—capitalists found new sources of cheap *matériel* in order to make profit (Moore 2010a; Patel and Moore 2017).

Frontiers aren't linear progressions from one kind of extraction to another, generating and responding to a network of crises, on the same bit of land. Tourism is, after all, just the latest in a series of fixes to capitalist crises (Fletcher 2011). A set of geographical co-ordinates can, however, contemporaneously host multiple frontiers, and resistances to capitalist expansion. Tourism need never feature. As Cons and Eilenberg (2018) observe, frontiers can be seen as assemblages, spaces that are simultaneously economic boundary activity, lawlessness, wilderness. Within that field of possibility—Deleuze and Guattari (1983) call it a "hodgepodge" (7)—the process of capitalist recognition of value, articulated by metabolic crisis and active resistance by those from whom work is conscripted, can happen on the same piece of land simultaneously. With the crafting of new kinds of property relations, as well as the deployment of national narratives and police, land can become a quizzical thing, and subject to richer analysis. To see this, consider the commodity that came to define "the frontier," at least in large parts of the Americas: gold.

Three Vignettes from Yanomami Territory

Gold

Gold was mined in Brazil almost from the first moment of colonialism. An early wave of mining ran from 1553 to 1597 (Pérez-Aguilar et al. 2013), though the most significant colonial boom and bust ran through the long eighteenth century, 1690 to 1750 (Russell-Wood 1984), with particularly fierce bursts of extractive activity in Minas Gerais and Mato Grosso. The gold boom involved its own circuits of ecological destruction. Mercury was an essential part of the gold refining process, combined and processed with the ore to produce a gold-mercury amalgam that continues to pollute the waterways of the original gold rush (Costa 2011). Those toxic remains are the modern trace of nineteenth-century Portuguese trade patterns.

The Portuguese Empire's commercial and military decline was postponed and then fixed with Brazilian exports and concessions to British capital in Brazil (Inikori 2020). Gold flowed out of Brazil to the British to pay for keeping the Spanish at bay. To do that, capitalist orders pushed families of slavers and enslaved people through the *cerrado* in Minas Gerais, bringing with them regimes to discipline household, race, and class divisions. Always, with the arrival of oppression, capitalism's least willing participants created spaces of fugitivity and subversion (Higgins 1999; Harmey and Moten 2013). Indeed, farther north in Maranhão and Pará, communities of fugitive formerly enslaved people, quilombos, exploited the divisions between domestic and international bourgeois interests, and funded their autonomy through their knowledge of the geography and geology of the Gurupí River (Abreu 2018). Quilombo communities sold gold to stay free (Cleary 1990, 29–31). Capitalist demands for *specie*, money in coin rather than paper (Maurer 2006), in Europe made possible the existence of autonomous groups in Brazil.

The gold rush has returned, and it is sometimes forgotten that the twentieth-century Brazilian gold rush outproduced those on the more famous frontiers of California and the Klondike (Cleary 1990). Gold remains a billion-dollar annual business, though the zones of exploitation have since moved. Today, one of the most ruthlessly exploited areas is in Yanomami territory (Figure 3.1).

Indigenous people came to govern their own land through broader geopolitical forces: the Brazilian military in the 1940s was concerned to occupy the sparsely inhabited northern Amazonian region lest it fall to incursions by foreigners. In the process, infrastructure and matériel needed to be built and placed, and Indigenous communities, contained (Schwartzman 1996). Brazil followed the containment strategies developed in the nineteenth century by the US government to manage its own Indigenous populations, which were subsequently used by settler governments worldwide (Marya and Patel 2021). In 1967, the Brazilian government created the Fundação Nacional do Índio (FUNAI; National Indian Foundation), a successor agency to the Serviço de Proteção ao Índio (Indian Protection Service) founded in 1910. FUNAI is management agency with the authority to govern Indigenous people and to parcel and delimit private property in and around Indigenous territory.

Yanomami territory itself has largely been observed in the breech. Indigenous territory is akin to a semiporous membrane. Indigenous claims outside it are proscribed, but settler incursions inside are open to judicial confusion, ambiguity, and lengthy legal processes that allow a de facto redrawing of boundaries while the de jure discussions

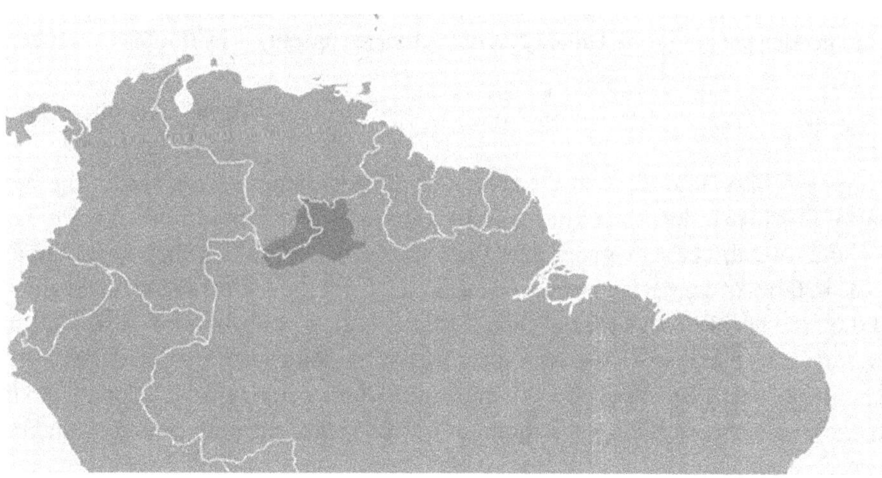

FIGURE 3.1. Yanomami Territory straddles the border of what is currently northern Brazil and southern Venezuela. cc-by-sa-3.0 Javierfv1212.

plod on for decades. Indeed, as Holston has suggested, the history of Brazilian land law is not one of deficit but, rather, of overwhelming surfeit. In the strategic ambiguities and confusions that emerge from this overdetermination of property, the landed elite's access to the best lawyers allows them to prevail while preserving the appearance of rule of law (Holston 2008, chap. 4). Through such tactics, the Brazilian government had long encouraged incursions into Indigenous territory. Before its recent status as a gold frontier, Yanomami territory was a site of cassiterite tin ore, opened by the Brazilian government of the 1980s and 1990s (Gibbons 1991).

Today, Yanomami territory is pockmarked with artisanal gold-mining operations. A recent investigation by the Associated Press found that in the state of Roraima, which is partially covered by Yanomami territory, and where all gold mining is illegal, the state has been implicated in providing cheap fuel for light aircraft supply lines to service the estimated 20,000 miners in the territory (Cowie and Biller 2022). For ten grams of gold, a pilot and jet fuel can be purchased to take food to and return gold from Indigenous land.

Prospectors have been implicated in a series of massacres of Indigenous people, most horrifically in 1993 (Weiss and Weiss 1993). The Federal Police and FUNAI dissembled around that event, and though some of the perpetrators have been caught, justice remains elusive. Recently, artisanal miners protested their treatment by some of the Brazilian federal forces, who have made a few efforts to stop the illegal mining. Despite the illegality of all gold prospecting by *garimpeiros* (small-scale miners) in the state, there is an Association of Independent Prospectors of Roraima, whose members at a recent protest wore shirts proclaiming their status as legitimate workers "Garimpeiro, Trabaljador!" Given the license traditionally afforded such incursions into Indigenous territory, the workers may quite reasonably feel the sting of betrayal. As the Associated Press reported:

> "We are the founders of the state," said Isa Carine Farias, the association's president, and who told the AP she previously worked with illegal mining. "They take an Indigenous person to the United Nations (climate summit); why not take a miner, too?"
>
> (Cowie and Biller 2022)

Garimpeiros have a notion that the land, and the gold beneath it, is part of the patrimony of Brazilian citizenship. They identify as the source of labor in the trinity of land, labor, and capital. The state guarantees their access to land, so that their labor can participate in flows of capital from the gold reclaimed from the subterranean world and out into the markets of Boa Vista, and thence to the trading desks London, Shanghai, and New York. This happens *because* the apparatus of the state has vouchsafed this activity as a quintessentially Brazilian one, as workers turn debt, personal and national, into foreign exchange as part of a great national mission. This is the petit bourgeois national dream, gold-plated.

The Brazilian national story isn't the only one about Yanomami territory. Although the state guards its borders, compassing it in latitude, longitude, depth, and airspace, there are other ways to see and narrate the land (Scott 1998). As Rosset observes, there's a tension between the idea of land, understood as that fungible and contested national patrimony demanded by movements for agrarian reform, and the notion that every individual place is unique, narrated into relations of reciprocity that predate the nation-state (2013). The difference between fungible parcels of land, and anchored Indigenous territory, is a difference of narrative regime. While many stories of gold lead to riches under capitalism, Yanomami traditions offer different narratives both about how humans are bound to particular geographies, and even around the relations between humans and gold. Ramos (2010) observes that there is a legend among the Sanumá communities in the Auaris River valley that the gold is guarded by a spirit who commands, "Take only a little or I'll kill your children!" (127).

Land is the complex of territory understood as falling within the jurisdiction of the state, and the complex of territory understood as that nonfungible commodity belonging to Yanomami traditions of place and identity. In either case, the narrative is central to the constitution of the frontier. The Brazilian constitution doesn't come by its name accidentally (Chamber of Deputies Directing Board 2010). It is that nexus of laws that comes to constitute the land in particular ways, licensing it as a frontier for new capitalist enterprise. It is not possible, in other words, to stabilize the "land" part of "land, labor, and capital" without the nation-state, in which the term "nation" is a central feature.

The narratives by and about the Brazilian nation, on the one hand, and the Yanomami one, on the other, are contested terrains of knowledge, produced through processes of colonial capitalism (Long and Long 1992). In this, social scientists are far from innocent. Colonial academic knowledge of Yanomami ethnohistory is part of the problem (Coello de la Rosa 2018). Anthropological representations of Yanomami communities have cast them as citizens in waiting, whose congenital violence disqualifies them from current membership of the polity (Chagnon 1997)—though such conservative tendencies have had countervailing forces within anthropology (Turner 1993). Indeed, that ineradicable cultural propensity for violence licenses not just the state's use of force, but that of the prospectors, who continue to kill Indigenous people under cover of national destiny. It is through academic representations of Yanomami people that "Indigenous" becomes a synonym for "violent," allowing "Brazilian" to mean "civilized."

If narration is central to the rendering of land as a legible frontier, into which capital may safely flow, it is important to recognize the importance of the ways that material transformations can, in turn, affect narratives, which, in turn, inflect flows of capital. Global warming is not just a discursive phenomenon—it is a material one (Fox and Alldred 2020). The political discourses that constitute political responses to this zenith of capitalist crisis are shaped by capital itself, and reflect the different interests of capitalists at given moments of hegemony. Capitalists are interested in creating new stabilities to encourage investment in land; those investments are also strategic interventions in the normalizing of understandings about what land is, and what it might be. Frontier land can always be a site of competing interests between different kinds of capitalists and those who resist incorporation into the capitalist world-ecology, like the Yanomami. The next section discusses how Yanomami territory has come to be in the sights of "green finance."

Green Carbon Capital

There is no reason why the same land cannot be a site of multiple flows of capital from within different members of a given hegemonic bloc. Indeed, hegemonic blocs form and reform precisely through shifts in the primacy of forms of capital. Arrighi (1994) observes, for instance, the shift in hegemonic predominance from manufacturing toward finance capital over the long twentieth century. In the subterranean land of Yanomami territory, one can observe two frontiers supervenient upon each another, with the power of extractive capital constituting and possibly ceding to that of financial capital.

Land is already an asset class. That is, it can be a frontier for physical extraction and also a fungible part of a portfolio in which it is, to use Fairbairn's exquisite phrase, "like gold with yield" (Fairbairn 2014, 2020). America's largest farmland owner, Bill Gates, with his fellow investors in farmland, enjoys the security of an asset that is fairly liquid, appreciates steadily in value, and also offers revenue from the rent paid on it by rentier farmers (O'Keefe 2021). Gates abets and profits from the power shift within the dominant hegemonic bloc from productive capital to financial capital.

Financial capital is never, itself, a stable category. It, too, is constantly in the process of reinvention, in search of new frontiers. The climate crisis offers an opportunity to create another stream of financial benefit from any given area of land, for example, through the REDD Reducing Emissions from Deforestation and Forest Degradation (REDD) effort and the issuing of carbon credits where the sequestering of carbon is provided as a service (Sullivan 2009; Beymer-Farris and Bassett 2012; Tni 2016). REDD revenue streams have in some cases been created the expense of small-scale agricultural producers (Kansanga and Luginaah 2019). Increasingly, it is becoming clear that the greatest repository of carbon in terrestrial forest systems lies not in the trees, but in the soil, where most terrestrial carbon is locked. Soil is capable of sequestering a great deal of carbon, and it is already being reviewed as a possible addition to REDD+ (Strey et al. 2017).

Given the vigor with which capitalism has deforested the planet, it should surprise no one that some of the land with the most biodiversity and richest soil is land that has managed to resist the incursions of capitalist forces. Indigenous communities are just 5 percent of the world's population, yet occupy 25 percent of its land and live with 80 percent of its biodiversity (Sobrevila 2008, xii). This is not, however, to present some automatically romantic purity of ecological praxis. In *Land's End*, Tania Li offers a rebuke to those who would ascribe to Indigenous communities an unimpeachable subjectivity or imperviousness to capitalism. On the contrary, she notes, the Indigenous highlanders whom she studied in Indonesia, though they were

> imagined by activists of the global indigenous and peasant movements to be securely attached to their land and communities, joined the ranks of people unable to sustain themselves. Surely, if anyone could continue to live in the countryside on the old terms, it should be them. . . . The process that dislodged them from their land wasn't initiated by land-grabbing corporations or state agencies. There was no "primitive accumulation" of the kind Marx described, "written in the annals of mankind in letters of blood and fire." The process through which they lost control over their collectively owned land was far less dramatic, even mundane. It was the highlanders themselves who took the initiative to plant tree crops, which had the effect of individualizing their land rights and led to the formation of capitalist relations in which their capacity to survive was governed by rules of competition and profit.
>
> (Li 2014, 3–4)

In the state of Acre, in Brazil's northwest, the quantification of ecosystem services has produced a regime that both identifies and rewards labor that will build the soil's carbon stores. It is, as Greenleaf (2020) observes, an ambivalent outcome, allowing peasants and low-income land-workers to supplement their incomes enough to survive, but not enough to enjoy autonomy. Indigenous communities have created REDD projects to benefit from these flows of capital and to defend against logging (Vitel et al. 2013), and are caught in matrices of power that make it particularly important to avoid romanticizing Indigenous communities (Shah 2012).

The carbon sequestered above and beneath the soil is increasingly valuable. In California, for instance, recent attempts to create a pool of new forest growth against which pollution might be traded has been undone by wildfires that have burned through 95 percent of that buffer meant to ensure the permanence of carbon sequestration (Badgley et al. 2022). As the hunt continues in the United States for alternative buffers that will allow the ongoing licensing of pollution, the pool of potential additive projects might be widened by looking internationally. The subterranean carbon in Yanomami territory is a green goldmine that solves the liquidity crisis in carbon credits. The green money, the possibility of microbial carbon sequestration in the Amazon, recapitulates the high colonial mission for silver in South America (Moore 2010b) as part of a hunt for cheap money (Patel and Moore 2017). The analogy holds, with the search for cheap money animated by the potentially deflationary constraints on industrial capital, and the need for profit from finance capital, as Arrighi (1994) observed in the successive waves of financial hegemony in Europe and, eventually, America in the twentieth century. In the twenty-first century, instead of mining specie, the biology of sequestered carbon is rendered tradable through digital distributed ledgers (Woo et al. 2021), blockchains of green gold, from which Indigenous communities may receive a sliver if they're lucky.

It is possible to avoid romanticization and still observe that the land has value for finance capital in large part because Indigenous communities have not reduced the land to a smoldering wreck. As Davi Kopenawa, a Yanomami shaman and educator has pointed out, there is a clear reason why forest carbon has not been commodified. It is, literally unthinkable to do so, because "Since the beginning of time, *Omama* has been the center of what the white people call ecology" (Kopenawa, Albert, and Dundy 2013, 393; emphasis in original). Kopenawa is clear that there are battle lines. "The forest is alive. It can only die if the white people persist in destroying it. If they succeed, the rivers will disappear underground, the soil will crumble, the trees will shrivel up, and the stones will crack in the heat. The dried-up earth will become empty and silent" (2013, vii).

The macrobiome of the Amazon is being commodified to fix the climate crisis. Jair Bolsonaro, the patriarch of national patrimony, understands this well. He points out that the Amazon is "like a virgin that every pervert from the outside lusts for" (Globo G1 2019). In his role as gatekeeper to this sexualized prize, he proclaims himself the pimp in chief.

Feces

There is another crisis in which Yanomami territory is summoned as a fix for a literal human metabolic crisis, prompted by critical approaches to urbanization (Lefebvre 2003; Roy 2016; Brenner and Schmid 2015) and by the need for specificity in understanding the dialectics of frontiers with other zones of capital flow. The metabolic rift points to the processes by which capitalism alienates human social relationships from those of the rest of the web of life (Foster 2000; Moore 2015). Perhaps the maximum *reductio* of this alienation comes from the compounding of capitalist development with the misrecognition of what humans are. Although it serves capital to enumerate and discipline unitary human bodies, humans aren't singular beings. We are holobionts, systems of different species that live within still larger ecosystems (Gilbert, Sapp, and Tauber 2012; Baedke, Fábregas-Tejeda, and Nieves Delgado 2020; Marya and Patel 2021). Humans are and contain multitudes, but many civilizations—not just modern capitalist colonial ones—have disciplined humans into modes of singular and individual recognition. Capitalists have a particular interest in individuation, from the selling of individual humans into slavery to the calculations of units of labor-power to the disciplining of a racialized and gendered workforce (Hall 1980). That process of straightening queer beings is of more than metaphorical concern (Griffiths 2015).

Ignoring the more-than-human beings that allow us to be human has made it easy to kill them. Modern capitalist planetary transformations have resulted in systematic differences between the gut microbiomes of city-dwellers in the global North and those of people living in rural areas in the global South (Conteville, Oliveira-Ferreira, and Vicente 2019). Although there is evidence that capitalism's food system is central to the denuding of the microbiome (Segata 2015), it is not the only cause. There are, for instance differences in skin microbiomes within cities (Kim et al. 2018). Class is also a factor, though not in the way one might presume: in one study, wealth was a proxy for less robust microbiomes, possibly because of higher exposure to household disinfectants (Mello et al. 2016).

The consequences of denuded microbiomes range from asthma to depression. Conversely, Vunk and Burkholder (2017) note, therapies have already been trialed or are under development for augmenting human microbiomes in order to treat colorectal cancer, obesity, allergies, asthma, anxiety, obsessive-compulsive disorder, osteoporosis, and *Clostridium difficile* infection. The discovery of such therapies points, Vunk and Berkholder argue, to "the benefits of mining Indigenous microbiota" (94).

"Mining" is the tempting word here because it allows the reification of bacteria in the microbiome into a commodity, like coal or oil. As such, this grammatical action recalls the words of Christopher Columbus (2003) upon seeing the land of the new world, when he observed that there were therapies in this frontier waiting to be brought home:

> I can never tire my eyes in looking at such lovely vegetation, so different from ours. I believe that there are many herbs and many trees that are worth much in Europe for dyes and medicines but I do not know them, and this causes me great sorrow. (123)

The value of the Yanomami microbiome is a new frontier, even if the anxieties it treats about modernity might be a little older (Hobart and Maroney 2019). A small industry exploring the virtues of their microbiome, as evinced through the analysis of feces, has seized the scientific imagination and print space in a range of scientific journals (Clemente et al. 2015; Conteville, Oliveira-Ferreira, and Vicente 2019; Knight 2015). Most of the papers so far restrict themselves to analyses or animal model transplants. As a recent *New York Times* article observes, modern Columbuses have sought El Dorado in Indigenous fecal transplants, administering them to themselves without government approval (Kolata 2021).

This final vignette points not to a problem of commodification but to one of labor. Land is always made valuable by work. The monetizable benefits of Indigenous microbiota comes from their interaction with the microbiomes of humans in the global North. It is hard in modern English to use pronouns other than "it" for microbes, but the difficulty in seeing personhood in these beings is a sign of the nature–society divide (Williams 1976). For those less willing to entertain personhood to read the medical interest in microbiomes as an attempt to put "nature to work," there is another concealed source of labor here. Insofar as the microbiota are the result of sophisticated practices of human ecological interaction, and insofar as those practices involve both cooking and the dissemination of repositories of knowledge around how to live with flora and fauna, and insofar as both these activities are predominantly led by women in Yanomami communities (Ramos 1996), then the theft of Indigenous shit is the appropriation of reproductive labor.

We have written elsewhere about how capitalism needs "cheap care" (Patel and Moore 2017). Every world factory has its mine, its farm, and its household. Every moment of capitalist profit is supported by a necessarily uncounted but valuable hinterland of unpaid and appropriated work. In this way, it is possible to see the thriving microbiome of Yanomami people as the product of women's work, and the work of generations of experiments of being consonant with the sustaining of the Amazonian macrobiome.

Of course, humans' first inoculation with a rich microbiome happens, literally, during reproductive labor: vaginal birth sets humans up with a, hopefully, rich and functional microbiome. It is every capitalist's first free gift (Lokugamage and Pathberiya 2019). For many in the global North, that biome is then denuded by exposure to the dysfunctions of the wider capitalist biome. In Yanomami territory, gut microbial diversity remains through childhood, tended through women's labor in diet and agriculture. This is the labor that is stolen when the night soil on the land is appropriated in the attempt to "re-wild" the denuded microbiome of those in the global North. That history can readily be taken and used to colonize the guts of colonists, in a bitter twist on Nick Estes's (2019) observation that "our history is the future." Such a theft, already reportedly underway (Kolata 2021), falls into old patterns in which the embodied work and knowledge of Indigenous communities is part of a frontier of colonial expansion (Isla 2007; Brockway 1979).

Conclusion

Land is a living palimpsest in which capital's attempts at creating and manifesting certain relations over others become both project and process (McMichael and Weber 2022). World-ecology offers an approach to decoding it that ought, if conducted properly, also offer a key to decolonizing it (Coulthard 2014).

These three vignettes have pointed out that the categories of land, labor, and capital are dynamic material entities, seething with internal dynamics. The stability of land as a factor of production, where labor might be applied and profits drawn, is much better read as the process and product of complex dynamics of crisis and appropriation. World-ecological ideas of "frontier" help to show how vital the idea of land is and the multidimensional palimpsest of projects that might be written upon it historically and simultaneously through the appropriation of new kinds of work in response to new kinds of crisis. Such an analysis specifically encourages a reconsideration of the agents of labor, the appropriation of their work through capitalism's expanding crises, and the new optics and sciences developed to fix and attend to a series of metabolic rifts. Just as the original metabolic rift spawned a science to amend soil, today's crises in human metabolism have spawned sciences that are scouring the world for new human inoculants, and finding them "free," a product of labor that is ready to be alienated. Whether the narratives that facilitate that alienation are about the march toward national greatness or "for all mankind," the application of state force is an important part of the process by which such new property will be claimed and the crisis policed (Hall et al. 2013).

Ultimately, then, world-ecology points analysts toward the deep narrative questions of "who does the work." It may be that "frontier" is not the right term to describe the process of constituting place, fixing workers, denoting those whose work is to be free, and stabilizing social relationships sufficiently for profit to be extracted from them. When a better analysis comes along, world-ecology will have done its part. For now, though, a world-ecological approach queers the ideas of "land" and "labor" in the "land, labor, capital" trinity to keep scholars busy for a little while yet.

Acknowledgments

The author is grateful to Gonçalo Santos, Debjani Bhattacharyya, Nitin Batla, Christian Schmid, Milica Topalovic, Hans Hortig, Nazli Tumerdem, Jun Borras, Jennifer Franco, Neil Brenner, Phil McMichael, Jason Cons, Olaf Corry, Jason Moore, and the participants of the Sessions on Territory—Urbanism and the Countryside seminar at the ETH Zurich Department of Architecture.

Note

1. There is a vigorous ontological debate over whether labor and nature can be said to be distinct, or whether terminological transformation is needed to recognize the fact that labor is itself made possible by the web of life. For those curious about the discussion, see Moore (2017); White, Gareau, and Rudy (2017); Foster and Clark (2016); Malm (2018, chap. 6); and Gellert (2019). Participants in this debate, while disagreeing in theory and in precise terminology, appear to agree that in practice, a reasonable response to the climate catastrophe is vigorous resistance from movements of the working class in defense of a livable planet and for ecologically enlightened socialism.

References

Abreu, Johnathan A. 2018. "Fugitive Slave Communities in Northern Brazil between 1880 and 1900: Territoriality, Resistance, and the Struggle for Autonomy." *Journal of Latin American Geography* 17 (1): 195–221. doi:10.1353/lag.2018.0008.

Abu-Lughod, Janet L. 1989. *Before European Hegemony: The World System A.D. 1250–1350*. New York: Oxford University Press.

Akerman, James R. 2017. *Decolonizing the Map: Cartography from Colony to Nation*. Chicago: University of Chicago Press.

Globo G1. 2019. "'Brasil É Uma Virgem Que Todo Tarado De Fora Quer', Diz Bolsonaro Ao Falar Sobre Amazônia." https://g1.globo.com/politica/noticia/2019/07/06/brasil-e-uma-virgem-que-todo-tarado-de-fora-quer-diz-bolsonaro-ao-falar-sobre-amazonia.ghtml.

Arrighi, Giovanni. 1994. *The Long Twentieth Century: Money, Power and the Origins of Our Times*. London: Verso.

Badgley, Grayson, Freya Chay, Oriana S. Chegwidden, Joseph J. Hamman, Jeremy Freeman, and Danny Cullenward. 2022. "California's Forest Carbon Offsets Buffer Pool Is Severely Undercapitalized." *Frontiers in Forests and Global Change*. doi:10.3389/ffgc.2022.930426.

Baedke, Jan, Alejandro Fábregas-Tejeda, and Abigail Nieves Delgado. 2020. "The Holobiont Concept before Margulis." *Journal of Experimental Zoology Part B: Molecular and Developmental Evolution* 334 (3): 149–155. doi:10.1002/jez.b.22931.

Beckert, Sven, Ulbe Bosma, Mindi Schneider, and Eric Vanhaute. 2021a. "Commodity Frontiers and Global Histories: The Tasks Ahead." *Journal of Global History* 1–4. doi:10.1017/s1740022820000431.

Beckert, Sven, Ulbe Bosma, Mindi Schneider, and Eric Vanhaute. 2021b. "Commodity Frontiers and the Transformation of the Global Countryside: A Research Agenda." *Journal of Global History* 16 (3): 435–450. doi:10.1017/s1740022820000455.

Berg, Maxine. 2021. "Commodity Frontiers: Concepts and History." *Journal of Global History* 16 (3): 451–455. doi:10.1017/s1740022821000036.

Bernstein, Henry. 2006. "Is There an Agrarian Question in the 21st Century?" *Canadian Journal of Development Studies / Revue canadienne d'études du développement* 27 (4): 449–460. doi:10.1080/02255189.2006.9669166.

Beymer-Farris, Betsy A., and Thomas J. Bassett. 2012. "The Redd Menace: Resurgent Protectionism in Tanzania's Mangrove Forests." *Global Environmental Change* 22 (2): 332–341. http://dx.doi.org/10.1016/j.gloenvcha.2011.11.006.

Blomley, Nicholas. 2007. "Making Private Property: Enclosure, Common Right and the Work of Hedges." *Rural History* 18 (01): 1–21.

Braudel, Fernand. 1972. *The Mediterranean and the Mediterranean World in the Age of Philip II*. Translated by Sîan Reynolds. Vol. 1. New York: Harper & Row.

Brenner, Neil, and Christian Schmid. 2015. "Towards a New Epistemology of the Urban?" *City* 19 (2–3): 151–182. doi:10.1080/13604813.2015.1014712.

Brockway, Lucile H. 1979. "Science and Colonial Expansion: The Role of the British Royal Botanic Gardens." *American Ethnologist* 6 (3): 449–465. doi:10.1525/ae.1979.6.3.02a00030.

Cadamosto (Alviseda Ca' da Mosto). (1455) 1937. *The Voyages of Cadamosto and Other Documents on Western Africa in the Second Half of the Fifteenth Century*. London: Hakluyt Society Publications.

Callinicos, Alex, and Justin Rosenberg. 2008. "Uneven and Combined Development: The Social-Relational Substratum of 'the International'? An Exchange of Letters." *Cambridge Review of International Affairs* 21 (1): 77–112. doi:10.1080/09557570701828600.

Chagnon, Napoleon A. 1997. *Yanomamö*. 5th ed. Case Studies in Cultural Anthropology. Fort Worth, TX: Harcourt Brace College.

Chamber of Deputies Directing Board. 2010. "Constitution of the Federative Republic of Brazil. Constitutional Text of October 5, 1988, with the Alterations Introduced by Constitutional Amendments No. 1/1992 through 64/2010 and by Revision Constitutional Amendments No. 1/1994 through 6/1994." Government of Brazil's Documentation and information Center Publishing Coordination in Brasília.

Chari, Sharad. 2013. "Detritus in Durban: Polluted Environs and the Biopolitics of Refusal." In *Imperial Debris*, edited by Ann Laura Stoler, 131–161. Durham, NC: Duke University Press.

Cleary, David. 1990. *Anatomy of the Amazon Gold Rush*. 1st ed. Iowa City: University of Iowa Press.

Clemente, Jose C., Erica C. Pehrsson, Martin J. Blaser, Kuldip Sandhu, Zhan Gao, Bin Wang, Magda Magris, et al. 2015. "The Microbiome of Uncontacted Amerindians." *Science Advances* 1 (3): e1500183. doi:10.1126/sciadv.1500183.

Coello de la Rosa, Alexandre. 2018. "The 'Fierce People' in the Context of Us Foreign Politics: A Historical Anthropology Approach to Napoleon Chagnon's Interpretation of the Yanomami." *Social Anthropology* 26 (4): 519–534. doi:10.1111/1469-8676.12544.

Columbus, Christopher. 2003. "Journal of the First Voyage of Columbus." Doc. No. AJ-062. American Journeys Collection. Wisconsin Historical Society Digital Library and Archives.

Cons, Jason, and Michael Eilenberg. 2018. "Introduction: On the New Politics of Margins in Asia." In, *Frontier Assemblages* 1–18. Oxford: John Wiley & Sons, Ltd.

Conteville, Liliane Costa, Joseli Oliveira-Ferreira, and Ana Carolina Paulo Vicente. 2019. "Gut Microbiome Biomarkers and Functional Diversity within an Amazonian Semi-nomadic Hunter-Gatherer Group." *Frontiers in Microbiology* 10: 1743. doi:10.3389/fmicb.2019.01743.

Costa, Diogo M. 2011. "Archaeo-Environmental Study of the Almas River: Mining Pollution and the Cerrado Biome in the End of the Nineteenth Century in Mid-western, Brazil." *Journal of Archaeological Science* 38 (12): 3497–3504. doi:10.1016/j.jas.2011.08.012.

Coulthard, Glen Sean. 2014. *Red Skin, White Masks: Rejecting the Colonial Politics of Recognition*. Minneapolis: Minnesota University Press.

Cowie, Sam, and David Biller. 2022. "Tarnished Gold: Aircraft, Fuel Key to Illegal Amazon Mining." *Associated Press*, 11 January 2022. https://apnews.com/article/amazon-mining-indigenous-gold-environment-brazil-c30953daa8482e42288ba509fe2e256a...

Craib, Raymond B. 2017. "Cartography and Decolonization." In *Decolonizing the Map: Cartography from Colony to Nation*, edited by James R. Akerman. pp. 11–71 Chicago: University of Chicago Press.

Cushman, Gregory T. 2013. *Guano and the Opening of the Pacific World: A Global Ecological History, Studies in Environment and History*. New York: Cambridge University Press.

Dann, Graham M. S., and A. V. Seaton. 2001. "Slavery, Contested Heritage and Thanatourism." *International Journal of Hospitality & Tourism Administration* 2 (3–4): 1–29. doi:10.1300/J149v02n03_01.

Deleuze, Gilles, and Félix Guattari. 1983. *Anti-Oedipus: Capitalism and Schizophrenia*. Minneapolis: University of Minnesota Press.

Dussel, Enrique. 2008. "Meditaciones Anti-Cartesianas: Sobre el Origen del Anti-Discurso Filosófico de la Modernidad." *Tabula Rasa* 9: 153–198.

Estes, Nick. 2019. *Our History Is the Future: Standing Rock versus the Dakota Access Pipeline, and the Long Tradition of Indigenous Resistance*. London: Verso.

Fairbairn, Madeleine. 2014. "'Like Gold with Yield': Evolving Intersections between Farmland and Finance." *Journal of Peasant Studies* 41 (5): 777–795. doi:10.1080/03066150.2013.873977.

Fairbairn, Madeleine. 2020. *Fields of Gold: Financing the Global Land Rush*. Ithaca, NY: Cornell University Press.

Federici, Silvia. 2014. "The Reproduction of Labour Power in the Global Economy and the Unfinished Feminist Revolution." In *Workers and Labour in a Globalised Capitalism: Contemporary Themes and Theoretical Issues*, edited by Maurizio Atzeni, 85–107. New York: Palgrave Macmillan.

Ferdinand, Malcom, and Anthony Paul Smith. 2021. *Decolonial Ecology: Thinking from the Caribbean World, Critical South*. Medford, MA: Polity Press.

Fletcher, Robert. 2011. "Sustaining Tourism, Sustaining Capitalism? The Tourism Industry's Role in Global Capitalist Expansion." *Tourism Geographies* 13 (3): 443–461. doi:10.1080/14616688.2011.570372.

Forster, Robert. 1978. "Achievements of the Annales School." *Journal of Economic History* 38 (1): 58–76. doi:10.2307/2119315.

Foster, John Bellamy. 1999. "Marx's Theory of Metabolic Rift: Classical Foundations for Environmental Sociology." *American Journal of Sociology* 105 (2): 366–405.

Foster, John Bellamy. 2000. *Marx's Ecology: Materialism and Nature*. New York: Monthly Review Press.

Foster, John Bellamy, and Brett Clark. 2016. "Marx's Ecology and the Left." *Monthly Review* 68 (2): 1–25.

Foster, John Bellamy, and Hannah Holleman. 2014. "The Theory of Unequal Ecological Exchange: A Marx-Odum Dialectic." *Journal of Peasant Studies* 41 (2): 199–233. doi:10.1080/03066150.2014.889687.

Foster, John Bellamy, and Fred Magdoff. 2000. "Liebig, Marx and the Depletion of Soil Fertility: Relevance for Today's Agriculture." In *Hungry for Profit: The Agribusiness Threat to Farmers, Food and the Environment*, edited by Fred Magdoff, John Bellamy Foster, and Frederick H. Buttel, 43–60. New York: Monthly Review Press.

Fox, Nick J., and Pam Alldred. 2020. "Re-assembling Climate Change Policy: Materialism, Posthumanism, and the Policy Assemblage." *British Journal of Sociology* 71 (2): 269–283. doi:10.1111/1468-4446.12734.

Friedmann, Harriet. 2000. "What on Earth Is the Modern World-System? Foodgetting and Territory in the Modern Era and Beyond." *Journal of World-Systems Research* 6 (2): 480–515. doi:10.5195/jwsr.2000.214.

Gellert, Paul K. 2019. "Bunker's Ecologically Unequal Exchange, Foster's Metabolic Rift, and Moore's World-Ecology: Distinctions with or without a Difference?" In *Ecologically Unequal Exchange: Environmental Injustice in Comparative and Historical Perspective*, edited by R. Scott Frey, Paul K. Gellert, and Harry F. Dahms, 107–140. Cham, Switzerland: Springer International.

Ghosh, Amitav. 2021. *The Nutmeg's Curse: Parables for a Planet in Crisis*. Chicago: University of Chicago Press.

Gibbons, Ann. 1991. "Yanomami People Threatened." *Science* 252 (5013): 1616.

Gilbert, Scott F., Jan Sapp, and Alfred I. Tauber. 2012. "A Symbiotic View of Life: We Have Never Been Individuals." *Quarterly Review of Biology* 87 (4): 325–341. doi:10.1086/668166.

Greenfield, Sidney M. 1977. "Madeira and the Beginnings of New World Sugar Cane Cultivation and Plantation Slavery: A Study in Institution Building." *Annals of the New York Academy of Sciences* 292 (1): 536–552. doi:10.1111/j.1749-6632.1977.tb47771.x.

Greenleaf, Maron. 2020. "The Value of the Untenured Forest: Land Rights, Green Labor, and Forest Carbon in the Brazilian Amazon." *Journal of Peasant Studies* 47 (2): 286–305. doi:10.1080/03066150.2019.1579197.

Griffiths, David. 2015. "Queer Theory for Lichens." *UnderCurrents: Journal of Critical Environmental Studies* 19: 36–45.

Hall, Stuart. 1980. "Cultural Studies: Two Paradigms." *Media, Culture & Society* 2 (1): 57–72.

Hall, Stuart. 2005. "The Rediscovery of 'Ideology': Return of the Repressed in Media Studies." In *Culture, Society and the Media*, edited by Tony Bennett, James Curran, Michael Gurevitch, and Janet Wollacott, 61–95. London: Routledge.

Hall, Stuart, C. Critcher, Tony Jefferson, John Clarke, and Brian Roberts. 2013. *Policing the Crisis: Mugging, the State and Law and Order*. Basingstoke, UK: Palgrave Macmillan.

Harmey, Stefano, and Fred Moten. 2013. *The Undercommons: Fugitive Planning* and *Black Study*. New York: Minor Compositions.

Harvey, David. 1981. "The Spatial Fix—Hegel, Von Thunen and Marx." *Antipode* 13 (3): 1–12. doi:10.1111/j.1467-8330.1981.tb00312.x.

Harvey, David. 2001. *Spaces of Capital: Towards a Critical Geography*. Edinburgh: Edinburgh University Press.

Higgins, Kathleen J. 1999. *"Licentious Liberty" in a Brazilian Gold-Mining Region: Slavery, Gender, and Social Control in Eighteenth-Century Sabará, Minas Gerais*. University Park: Pennsylvania State University Press.

Hobart, Hi'Ilei Julia, and Stephanie Maroney. 2019. "On Racial Constitutions and Digestive Therapeutics." *Food, Culture & Society* 22 (5): 576–594. doi:10.1080/15528014.2019.1638120.
Hollis, Martin, and Steve Smith. 1990. *Explaining and Understanding International Relations*. Oxford: Clarendon Press.
Holston, James. 2008. *Insurgent Citizenship: Disjunctions of Democracy and Modernity in Brazil*. In-Formation Series. Princeton, NJ: Princeton University Press.
Hope, Mat. 2019. "The Brazilian Development Agenda Driving Amazon Devastation." *Lancet Planetary Health* 3 (10): e409–e411. doi:10.1016/s2542-5196(19)30195-0.
International Labour Organization. 2017. *Global Estimates of Modern Slavery: Forced Labour and Forced Marriage*. International Labour Organization (Geneva). http://www.alliance87.org/global_estimates_of_modern_slavery-forced_labour_and_forced_marriage.pdf.
Inikori, Joseph E. 2020. "Atlantic Slavery and the Rise of the Capitalist Global Economy." *Current Anthropology* 61 (S22): S159–S71. doi:10.1086/709818.
Isla, Ana. 2007. "An Ecofeminist Perspective on Biopiracy in Latin America." *Signs: Journal of Women in Culture and Society* 32 (2): 323–332. doi:10.1086/508378.
Ivancheva, Mariya, and Kathryn Keating. 2021. "Revisiting Precarity, with Care: Productive and Reproductive Labour in the Era of Flexible Capitalism." *Ephemera: Critical Dialogues on Organization* 20 (4): 251–282.
Kansanga, Moses Mosonsieyiri, and Isaac Luginaah. 2019. "Agrarian Livelihoods under Siege: Carbon Forestry, Tenure Constraints and the Rise of Capitalist Forest Enclosures in Ghana." *World Development* 113: 131–142. doi:10.1016/j.worlddev.2018.09.002.
Kim, Hye-Jin, Hanbyul Kim, Jin Ju Kim, Nu Ri Myeong, Taeyune Kim, Taehun Park, et al. 2018. "Fragile Skin Microbiomes in Megacities Are Assembled by a Predominantly Niche-Based Process." *Science Advances* 4 (3): e1701581. doi:10.1126/sciadv.1701581.
Kliman, Andrew. 2012. *The Failure of Capitalist Production Underlying Causes of the Great Recession*. London: Pluto Press.
Knight, Rob. 2015. "Why Microbiome Treatments Could Pay Off Soon." *Nature* 518 (7540): S5–S. doi:10.1038/518s5a.
Kolata, Gina. 2021. "You're Missing Microbes. But Is 'Rewilding' the Way to Get Them Back?" *New York Times*, 20. https://www.nytimes.com/2021/07/19/health/human-microbiome-hadza-rewilding.html.
Kopenawa, Davi, and Bruce Albert. 2013. *The Falling Sky: Words of a Yanomami Shaman*. Translated by Nicholas Elliott and Alison Dundy. Cambridge, MA: The Belknap Press of Harvard University Press.
Lefebvre, Henri. 2003. *The Urban Revolution*. Minneapolis: University of Minnesota Press.
Li, Tania. 2007. *The Will to Improve: Governmentality, Development, and the Practice of Politics*. Durham, NC: Duke University Press.
Li, Tania. 2014. *Land's End: Capitalist Relations on an Indigenous Frontier*. Durham, NC: Duke University Press.
Lokugamage, A. U., and S. D. C. Pathberiya. 2019. "The Microbiome Seeding Debate—Let's Frame It around Women-Centred Care." *Reproductive Health* 16 (1). doi:10.1186/s12978-019-0747-0.
Long, Norman, and Ann Long. 1992. *Battlefields of Knowledge: The Interlocking of Theory and Practice in Social Research and Development*. London and New York: Routledge.
Löwy, Michael. 2010. *The Politics of Combined and Uneven Development: The Theory of Permanent Revolution*. Chicago: Haymarket Books.

Malm, Andreas. 2018. *The Progress of This Storm: Nature and Society in a Warming World.* London: Verso.

Martineau, Jonathan. 2017. "Making Sense of the History of Clock-Time, Reflections on Glennie and Thrift's Shaping the Day." *Time & Society* 26 (3): 305–320. doi:10.1177/0961463x15577281.

Marx, Karl. 1973. *Grundrisse: Foundations of the Critique of Political Economy.* New York: Vintage Books.

Marx, Karl. 1978. *Capital: A Critique of Political Economy.* Translated by Ben Fowkes. Harmondsworth, UK: Penguin Books in association with New Left Review.

Marya, Rupa, and Raj Patel. 2021. *Inflamed: Deep Medicine and the Anatomy of Injustice.* New York: Farrar, Straus and Giroux.

Maurer, Bill. 2006. "The Anthropology of Money." *Annual Review of Anthropology* 35 (1): 15–36. https://doi.org/10.1146/annurev.anthro.35.081705.123127.

McMichael, Philip. 1990. "Incorporating Comparison within a World-Historical Perspective: An Alternative Comparative Method." *American Sociological Review* 55 (3): 385–397.

McMichael, Philip. 2012. "In the Short Run Are We All Dead?" In *The Longue Durée and World-Systems Analysis*, edited by Richard E. Lee, 137–160. Albany: State University of New York Press.

McMichael, Philip, and Heloise Weber. 2022. *Development and Social Change: A Global Perspective.* 7th ed. Thousand Oaks, CA: SAGE.

Mello, Carolina S., Mirian S. Carmo-Rodrigues, Humberto B. A. Filho, Lígia C. F. L. Melli, Soraia Tahan, Antônio C. C. Pignatari, et al. 2016. "Gut Microbiota Differences in Children from Distinct Socioeconomic Levels Living in the Same Urban Area in Brazil." *Journal of Pediatric Gastroenterology and Nutrition* 63 (5): 460–465. https://journals.lww.com/jpgn/Fulltext/2016/11000/Gut_Microbiota_Differences_in_Children_From.4.aspx.

Mies, Maria. 1986. *Patriarchy and Accumulation on a World Scale: Women in the International Division of Labour.* London: Zed.

Montague, Jules. 2022. *The Imaginary Patient: How Diagnosis Gets Us Wrong.* London: Granta.

Moore, Jason W. 2009. "Madeira, Sugar, and the Conquest of Nature in the 'First' Sixteenth Century: Part I: From 'Island of Timber' to Sugar Revolution, 1420–1506." *Review (Fernand Braudel Center)* 32 (4): 345–390. http://www.jstor.org/stable/41427474.

Moore, Jason W. 2010a. "Cheap Food and Bad Money: Food, Frontiers, and Financialization in the Rise and Demise of Neoliberalism." *Review (Fernand Braudel Center)* 33 (2/3): 225–261. http://www.jstor.org/stable/23346883.

Moore, Jason W. 2010b. "'This Lofty Mountain of Silver Could Conquer the Whole World': Potosí and the Political Ecology of Underdevelopment, 1545–1800." *Journal of Philosophical Economics* 4 (1): 58–103.

Moore, Jason W. 2011a. "Ecology, Capital, and the Nature of Our Times: Accumulation and Crisis in the Capitalist World-Ecology." *Journal of World-Systems Research* 17 (1): 107–146. https://doi.org/10.5195/jwsr.2011.432.

Moore, Jason W. 2011b. "Transcending the Metabolic Rift: A Theory of Crises in the Capitalist World-Ecology." *Journal of Peasant Studies* 38 (1): 1–46. https://doi.org/10.1080/03066150.2010.538579.

Moore, Jason W. 2014. "The End of Cheap Nature; or, How I Learned to Stop Worrying About 'the' Environment and Love the Crisis of Capitalism." In *Structures of the World Political Economy and the Future of Global Conflict and Cooperation*, edited by Christopher Chase-Dunn and Christian Suter, 285–314. Berlin: Lit Verlag.

Moore, Jason W. 2015. *Captialism in the Web of Life: Ecology and the Accumulation of Capital.* London: Verso.
Moore, Jason W. 2017. "Metabolic Rift or Metabolic Shift? Dialectics, Nature, and the World-Historical Method." *Theory and Society* 46 (4): 285–318. https://doi.org/10.1007/s11186-017-9290-6.
Moore, Jason W. 2018. "The Capitalocene Part II: Accumulation by Appropriation and the Centrality of Unpaid Work/Energy." *Journal of Peasant Studies* 45 (2): 237–279. https://doi.org/10.1080/03066150.2016.1272587.
Mostern, Ruth. 2021. "Comments on Time, Space and Method for the Study of Commodity Frontiers and the Transformation of the Global Countryside." *Journal of Global History* 16 (3): 456–461. doi:10.1017/s1740022820000443.
Navarro, Vicente. 1982. "The Limits of the World Systems Theory in Defining Capitalist and Socialist Formations." *Science & Society* 46 (1): 77–90. http://www.jstor.org/stable/40402376.
O'Keefe, Eric. 2021. "Bill Gates: America's Top Farmland Owner." *The Land Report*, January 11. https://landreport.com/2021/01/bill-gates-americas-top-farmland-owner/.
Patel, Raj, and Jason W. Moore. 2017. *A History of the World in Seven Cheap Things: A Guide to Capitalism, Nature, and the Future of the Planet.* Berkeley: University of California Press.
Pérez-Aguilar, Annabel, Caetano Juliani, Edson José de Barros, Márcio Roberto Magalhães de Andrade, Elton Soares de Oliveira, D. de A. Braga, et al. 2013. "Archaeological Gold Mining Structures from Colonial Period Present in Guarulhos and Mairiporã, São Paulo State, Brazil." *Geoheritage* 5 (2): 87–105. https://doi.org/10.1007/s12371-013-0074-8.
Ramos, Alcida Rita. 1996. *Yanomami and Gender: Toward a Sanumá Theory of Knowledge.* Departamento de Antropologia, Universidade de Brasília.
Ramos, Alcida Rita. 2010. "A Tale of Gold and Tears: The El Dorado of the Yanomami." *Indiana* 27: 125–139. doi:10.18441/ind.v27i0.125-139.
Rifkin, Jeremy. 1987. *Time Wars: The Primary Conflict in Human History.* New York: Henry Holt.
Rifkin, Mark. 2017. *Beyond Settler Time: Temporal Sovereignty and Indigenous Self-Determination.* Durham, NC: Duke University Press.
Rioux, Sébastien. 2015. "Mind the (Theoretical) Gap: On the Poverty of International Relations Theorising of Uneven and Combined Development." *Global Society* 29 (4): 481–509. https://doi.org/10.1080/13600826.2014.983047.
Rosenberg, Justin. 2005. "Globalization Theory: A Post Mortem." *International Politics* 42 (1): 2–74. https://doi.org/10.1057/palgrave.ip.8800098.
Rosset, Peter. 2013. "Re-thinking Agrarian Reform, Land and Territory in La Via Campesina." *Journal of Peasant Studies* 40 (4): 721–775. https://doi.org/10.1080/03066150.2013.826654.
Roy, Ananya. 2016. "What Is Urban about Critical Urban Theory?" *Urban Geography* 37 (6): 810–823. https://doi.org/10.1080/02723638.2015.1105485.
Russell-Wood, A. J. R. 1984. "Colonial Brazil: The Gold Cycle, C. 1690–1750." In *The Cambridge History of Latin America*, vol. 2: *Colonial Latin America*, edited by Leslie Bethell, 547–600. Cambridge, UK: Cambridge University Press.
Sagoff, Mark. 2009. "Who Is the Invader? Alien Species, Property Rights, and the Police Power." *Social Philosophy and Policy* 26 (2): 26–52. https://doi.org/10.1017/S0265052509090165.
Salleh, Ariel. 2010. "From Metabolic Rift to 'Metabolic Value': Reflections on Environmental Sociology and the Alternative Globalization Movement." *Organization & Environment* 23 (2): 205–219. https://doi.org/10.1177%2F1086026610372134.
Schneider, Mindi, and Philip McMichael. 2010. "Deepening, and Repairing, the Metabolic Rift." *Journal of Peasant Studies* 37 (3): 461–484. https://doi.org/10.1080/03066150.2010.494371.

Schwartz, Stuart B. 2004. *Tropical Babylons: Sugar and the Making of the Atlantic World, 1450–1680*. Chapel Hill: University of North Carolina Press.

Schwartzman, Stephan. 1996. "Brazil the Legal Battle over Indigenous Land Rights." *NACLA Report on the Americas* 29 (5): 36–43. https://doi.org/10.1080/10714839.1996.11725759.

Scott, James C. 1998. *Seeing like a State: How Certain Schemes to Improve the Human Condition Have Failed*. Yale Agrarian Studies. New Haven, CT: Yale University Press.

Segata, N. 2015. "Gut Microbiome: Westernization and the Disappearance of Intestinal Diversity." *Current Biology* 25 (14): R611–613. https://doi.org/10.1016/j.cub.2015.05.040.

Serrao, Joël. 1954. "Le Blé des Îles Atlantiques: Madère et Açores aux Xve et Xvie Siècles." *Annales. Economies, sociétés, civilisations* 9 (3): 337–541. https://doi.org/10.3406/ahess.1954.2292.

Shah, Alpa. 2012. "Eco-Incarceration? 'Walking with the Comrades.'" Review of *Broken Republic: Three Essays, Arundhati Roy. Economic and Political Weekly* 47 (21): 32–34. http://www.jstor.org/stable/23214868.

Sobrevila, Claudia. 2008. "*The Role of Indigenous Peoples in Biodiversity Conservation: The Natural but Often Forgotten Partners*." The World Bank (Washington D.C.: The World Bank Group). http://documents1.worldbank.org/curated/en/995271468177530126/pdf/443000WP0BOX321onservation01PUBLIC1.pdf.

Stephenson, Neal. 2005. *The System of the World*. London: Arrow.

Stoler, Ann Laura. 2013. *Imperial Debris: On Ruins and Ruination*. Durham, NC: Duke University Press.

Strey, Simone, Jens Boy, Robert Strey, Anna Welpelo, Regine Schönenberg, Charlotte Schumann, and Georg Guggenberger. 2017. "Digging Deeper: The Value of Deep Soil Carbon for Potential Redd+ Projects in Tropical Forest Communities in Amazonia." *Erdkunde* 71 (3): 231–239. http://www.jstor.org/stable/26380275.

Sullivan, Sian. 2009. "Green Capitalism, and the Cultural Poverty of Constructing Nature as Service-Provider." *Radical Anthropology* 3: 18–27.

Thompson, E. P. 1967. "Time, Work-Discipline, and Industrial Capitalism." *Past & Present* 38: 56–97. http://www.jstor.org/stable/649749.

Transnational Institute. 2016. "Our Land Is Worth More Than Carbon." Amsterdam: TNI. Accessed November 17. https://www.tni.org/en/article/our-land-is-worth-more-than-carbon.

Tomich, Dale W. 1990. *Slavery in the Circuit of Sugar: Martinique and the World Economy, 1830–1848*. Johns Hopkins Studies in Atlantic History and Culture. Baltimore, MD: Johns Hopkins University Press.

Turner, Terence. 1993. "The Role of Indigenous Peoples in the Environmental Crisis: The Example of the Kayapo of the Brazilian Amazon." *Perspectives in Biology and Medicine* 36 (3): 526–545. https://doi.org/10.1353/pbm.1993.0027.

Vieira, Alberto. 1996a. "A Escravatura Na Madeira Nos Séculos Xv a Xvii: O Ponto Da Situação." Centro Estudos História Atlântico (Madeira: 1996). http://www.ceha-madeira.net/escravos/escravo3.htm.http://www.ceha-madeira.net/escravos/escravo3.htm.

Vieira, Alberto. 1996b. *Escravos Com E Sem Açúcar*. Região autónoma de Madeira: Centro de Estudos de História do Atlântico.

Vieira, Alberto. 2004. "Sugar Islands. The Sugar Economy of Madeira and the Canaries, 1450–1650." In *Tropical Babylons: Sugar and the Making of the Atlantic World*, edited by Stuart B. Schwartz, 42–84. Chapel Hill: University of North Carolina Press.

Vitel, Claudia Suzanne Marie Nathalie, Gabriel Cardoso Carrero, Mariano Colini Cenamo, Maya Leroy, Paulo Mauricio Lima A. Graça, and Philip Martin Fearnside. 2013. "Land-Use Change Modeling in a Brazilian Indigenous Reserve: Construction of a Reference Scenario for the Suruí Redd Project." *Human Ecology* 41 (6): 807–826. https://doi.org/10.1007/s10745-013-9613-9.

Vunk, Tyler, and Kristin M. Burkholder. 2017. "The Role of the Indigenous Gut Microbiota in Human Health and Disease." In, *Modeling the Transmission and Prevention of Infectious Disease*, edited by Christen J. Hurst. Advances in Environmental Microbiology, 75–104. Cham, Switzerland. Springer International Publishing.

Wallerstein, Immanuel Maurice. 1974. *The Modern World-System*. Vol. 1: *Capitalist Agriculture and the Origins of the European World-Economy in the Sixteenth Century*. New York: Academic Press.

Wallerstein, Immanuel Maurice. 1979. *The Capitalist World-Economy: Essays, Studies in Modern Capitalism*. Cambridge, UK: Cambridge University Press.

Wallerstein, Immanuel. 1988. "Typology of Crises in the World-System." *Review (Fernand Braudel Center)* 11 (4): 581–598. http://www.jstor.org/stable/40241112.

Weiss, Zezé, and Martin D. Weiss. 1993. *The Yanomami Massacres and the Role of a Powerful Anti-Native Alliance*. New York: Amanaka'a Amazon Network.

White, Damian F., Brian J. Gareau, and Alan P. Rudy. 2017. "Ecosocialisms, Past, Present and Future: From the Metabolic Rift to a Reconstructive, Dynamic and Hybrid Ecosocialism." *Capitalism Nature Socialism* 28 (2): 22–40. doi:10.1080/10455752.2017.1296479.

Williams, Randall. 2003. "A State of Permanent Exception: The Birth of Modern Policing in Colonial Capitalism." *Interventions* 5 (3): 322–344. https://doi.org/10.1080/1369801032000135602.

Williams, Raymond. 1976. *Keywords: A Vocabulary of Culture and Society*. New York: Oxford University Press.

Woo, Junghoon, Ridah Fatima, Charles J. Kibert, Richard E. Newman, Yifeng Tian, and Ravi S. Srinivasan. 2021. "Applying Blockchain Technology for Building Energy Performance Measurement, Reporting, and Verification (MRV) and the Carbon Credit Market: A Review of the Literature." *Building and Environment* 205. https://doi.org/10.1016/j.buildenv.2021.108199.

Youatt, Rafi. 2017. "Personhood and the Rights of Nature: The New Subjects of Contemporary Earth Politics." *International Political Sociology* 11 (1): 39–54. https://doi.org/10.1093/ips/olw032.

CHAPTER 4

TRACING THE LAND IN DEPENDENCY AND WORLD-SYSTEMS THEORIES

MAX AJL

Introduction

Land, agriculture, and peasants have been central to dependency and world-systems analyses. They revised "modernization" theories that had understood land primarily through an industrial teleology, seeing land as a source for inputs into industry. They also saw land as the social-geographical-spatial basis for backward agricultural production based on inefficiently allocated labor, with low or zero marginal productivity, and therefore the home of a population to be shifted into a growing industrial sector (Rostow 1990). These ideas generally developed within states and institutions that had been the historical beneficiaries of development and colonialism. They could not see land as the fulcrum for a transformation in the world-system, or those living on the land as those having had their hands on that fulcrum.

Those who did not benefit from this history came to see things differently. They put land, agrarian reform, the small peasantry, and the landless front and center in theories of underdevelopment, dependency, colonialism, neocolonialism, national liberation, and postcolonial planning (Amin 1990; Cabral 1979; Moyo, Jha, and Yeros 2013). Their challenge was epistemological, methodological, and programmatic: to the Eurocentrism of dubious inferences about developmental processes blind to constitutive elements of world history and accumulation, to the single-unit-nation-state focus of Western approaches to development. To theories of development that have not dealt adequately with enduring agrarian questions of land, nation, ecology, and gender. And to the role of smallholders in national-popular development.

What do macrostructural contributions from the South and informed by the thinking of the South teach us about land that theories born in northern cloisters do not? And what ideas do those contributions offer contemporary thinking about popular development? For one, land is a global relationship. "Canonical" agrarian questions of labor, politics, and industrialization, and "later" agrarian questions of national liberation, ecology, and gender/social reproduction, have always "been a national interpretation of a global process" (McMichael 1997, 632–633)—that is, "a great overriding cultural phenomenon, the world-wide spread and diffusion of a particular cultural system, that of North Atlantic capitalism," which set in motion accumulation on world scale (Wolf 1969, 276). And two, they have clarified its polarizing, hierarchical, and exploitative nature. Whether through direct colonial control leading to surplus extraction; indirect neocolonial extraction based on uneven exchange and political engineering via military intervention, coup d'etat, and sanctions; settler expansion and land alienation via primitive accumulation, or otherwise, the key contribution of these theories has been to clarify that land and agrarian issues are central to imperialism. Three, they show that land is not merely a space for a social or economic history of production. Land is geographically and geopolitically significant: it is where national liberation struggles occur. A corollary: land as territory is interlocked spatially and politically with other liberated zones (Nabolsy 2021). Capitalism and national liberation have been equally global, their achievements and advances interlocked. Land is therefore essential to imperialism, national domination, and the struggles that seek to end them.

This chapter considers land within a broad understanding of dependency and world-systems over time and space. It takes the core-periphery dyad as constitutive of the modern world system. Debates over modes of production, patterns of labor exploitation, and their relationship to the worldwide expansion of capitalism, including through imperialism and colonialism have been central to the peripheral historiography of peripheral capitalism. Likewise, such discussion, including the transition to capitalism, has been central to a certain sector of world-systems and dependency theories. In particular, this debate was central in rupturing the "feudal" thesis of Latin American and other peripheral agricultures, a conception which supported Communist parties' alliances with their national bourgeoisies (Bambirra 1978, 26–44).

Yet it is undernoted that the origins of dependency did not lie in a detached search for knowledge, but in applied development planning, which continued to be a central incubator, especially for Arab world-systems and dependency approaches. Accordingly, the chapter focuses on literatures that have been neglected in the disciplinary formation and intellectual history of dependency and world-systems theory: those concerned with planning to break from underdevelopment, and the wide range of peripheral literatures and practices that worked explicitly within a dependency framework yet are essentially absent from the historiography. In that sense, the chapter is a corrective, putting national liberation through smallholder agrarian development at the center of dependency/world-systems thinking. In so doing, it does not attempt a genealogical reconstruction or conceptual survey of the central contributions of dependency or world-systems thinking. Rather, the focus is diagnostic and pedagogical: one, to understand the sources of underdevelopment within the world system, and two, to survey, over time and space, peripheral thinkers who sought to directly address those patterns of underdevelopment through a variety of nonorthodox developmental options. And as a subset of two, to show how they converged on models based on shielding and nurturing postcolonial agrarian South peasant technological, ingenuity, political mobilization, and developmental contributions as part of a holistic peasant-centered development path. It selects central figures from peripheral regions for their account of historically specific mechanisms or models of underdevelopment and the relationship of underdevelopment with land. Because the historical formation of peripheries is socially and politically uneven—ranging from mercantilist imperialism and the slave trade and a mix of franchise and settler colonialism in Africa, to franchise colonialism in South Asia linked with drain, to settler and franchise colonialism in the Arab-African region, neocolonialism succeeding all phases with the advent of formal independence, to the structural subordination in the international division of labor amidst politically independent states in Latin America—a selection of prominent theorists allows for a selective but representative presentation of the landscape. Throughout, land and peasants are central; in particular, their products are central to northern accumulation and their peripheral populations play a central role in suppressing wages on a world scale, thereby stabilizing capitalism.

The chapter begins by introducing initial mechanisms of underdevelopment as they were placed on the table by Raul Prebisch: *deteriorating terms of trade*. It pairs those insights with the similar South Asian notion of *drain*. It then considers the contributions of the central theorists of dependency and world systems and their theoretical fellow-travelers—Samir Amin, Walter Rodney, and Utsa and Prabhat Patnaik—and how land threads through their accounts. It centers on the role of land as resistance: the broad sweep of thinking focused on land as a locus for the production of socially necessary use values. This approach first reconsiders national liberation as the central problematic. It then moves on to the antidependency modeling for self-reliant national development.

Initial Conceptions of Unequal Exchange

Poverty in the periphery initially presented itself alongside sharp disparities in levels of industrialization between the colonizing and colonized or formerly colonized world. As developmental divergence became ever clearer, southern economists sought ways to break from "backwardness."

A central diagnosis was the deteriorating terms of trade, the taproot to Arab-African and Latin American conceptions of dependency, and the varied Euro-American unequal exchange and world-systems theorists (Amin 1994, 51–52; Brolin 2007; Raffer 1987). From the late 1940s, the Economic Commission for Latin America, or CEPAL, and the Argentinian economist and planner Prebisch, its chief, sought to understand why the economies of Latin America had failed to industrialize in ways that mimicked the core, and the persistent declines in the terms of trade for their products: coffee, copper (Love 1980). Prebisch saw that the international division of labor was failing to disburse the benefits of productivity increases in the industrial sector, primarily concentrated in the northern countries (Love 1990; Prebisch 1950; Toye and Toye 2003). They thought that because of the industrial revolution, the core, which controlled capital goods, could integrate technical progress, spread improved technology, and ensure that some of the gains from productivity went to their working classes. The rigidity of northern wages protected them from downturns, whereas the disorganization of primary-sector workers in the periphery pushed against any such rigidity. Furthermore, in the periphery, technologies were primarily imported and used in the export sector. Finally, many argued that the periphery was dualist: one portion was locked into low-productivity subsistence agriculture; the other, an export enclave, and unarticulated, since it relied on technology from the core. The large labor surplus of the periphery, in turn, further depressed peripheral wages, and trade, vampire-like, sucked the lifeblood of productivity increases from the export sector. The periphery remained poor, unable to satisfy the basic needs of its people and with penurious current account imbalances (Kay 1991).

Since, as these scholars saw it, the periphery was the zone of extraction and agriculture, where wealth seemed to come from the land, and as those goods would receive ever-fewer-batches of northern manufactures, requiring ever-growing mounds of coffee to pay for the same car from a US factory, they saw development as a question of carrying out a sharp rupture with primary export dependence, and a move to rapidly industrialize (Prebisch 1950, 8–9). This was the theoretical basis for the policy of import-substitution industrialization, which sought to produce at home what Latin America had been importing. As the policy evolved, it looked to regionwide markets to break from the straightjacket of constrained domestic demand.

Bourgeois South Asian theories of drain likewise emphasized flows over classes: the colonial-inflicted drain of the surplus, what nationalist writers called the "bleeding" of India. Through the colonial administration, with its "unrequited exports," its land taxes, and the home charges spent to keep colonial administrators fed and housed, India suffered, and was not able to accumulate enough locally to industrialize (Bach 2019, 127–128). To put a stop to the drain, therefore, the solution was national sovereignty. Likewise, the equation of industrialization with development was central in W. A. Lewis's dualist economics. He thought that agricultural labor often had no marginal productivity, justifying its shift from agriculture to a potentially burgeoning manufacturing sector (Lewis 1954). This line of thought, "industrialization by invitation," essentially sought to build up an industrial plant by "inviting" foreign capital to supply local needs (Girvan 2006; Girvan and Girvan 1973; Levitt 2004; Witter 2021).

Land in the geopolitical sense was critical in shaping the birth of these theories. Latin America incubated a notion of deteriorating terms of trade born within sovereign nation-states, even if their sovereignty was the fruit of criollo-settler decolonization and enduring White capitalist power structures. Prebisch's focus on long-term and deteriorating trade terms went with relative lack of focus on the nature and class basis of the Latin American states. Accordingly, the policy foundered on insufficient attention to the role of land, peasants, and agriculture in underdevelopment. The problem was not just more industry, but the need to summon an internal market that would be wide enough for industrialization to benefit from economies of scale; this implied large-scale agrarian reform, which was absent from the agenda of the developmentalist Latin American states supporting CEPAL. The innovation and sociology of CEPAL was its Achilles Heel: precisely because it was not merely a sociology of underdevelopment but a schematic for development, early iterations of CEPAL's thinking could not bring about a rupture with the structuralism and sidestepping of class that was constitutive of developmentalist thinking on the whole. Similarly, industrialization by invitation was the child of demographically tiny potential Caribbean markets, which justified using the already-technically sophisticated foreign capital to develop. Similarly, the political inheritors of drain theory viewed development as achievable without a rupture with capitalism. Only later would foundational structuralist thinkers move to progressively sharper ruptures with the myth of economic development (Furtado 1976, 2020).

Marxist Dependencies

With the lighting of the communist beacon in Cuba, and the outbreak of the peasant war of national liberation in China, peasants were putting land, sovereign national development, and land-to-the-tiller agrarian reform on the agenda. If this had originally been the work of organic theorists like Mao Zedong, Fidel Castro, and Che Guevara, others the world over responded to what had been done and sought to craft their own theories to suit the moment. They went beyond structuralism's inattention to class, the assumption of the neutrality of the state, and their consequent inability to theorize a domestic basis of specific peripheral patterns of development; instead they began to interweave internal and external class structures and the resultant flows to try to interpret patterns of development. If such thinking was concentrated in the South, it also provoked a northern critique of modernization theory and an associated rethinking of global history: world-systems theory.

Latin America

In Latin America, many Brazilian-born thinkers, including Theotonio dos Santos, Vania Bambirra, and Ruy Mauro Marini, fled to Chile in the wake of Brazil's essentially anti-agrarian-reform military coup. Inspired by Cuba's revolution, they crafted theories that sought a break with *desarrollismo* and to situate the popular classes at the center of revolutionary theory and practice, and in so doing, to reanalyze imperialism as it manifested in the peripheries of the world system (Bambirra 1978, 17–18). Santos defined dependency as "the economy of certain countries . . . conditioned by the development and expansion of another economy to which the former is subjected" (Dos Santos 1970, 231; 2003). Others worked similar furrows. Bambirra, for example, wrote of the major insurrectionary processes in Latin America, and typologized dependent social formations. Both were organically linked with an agrarian through line: she emphasized the revolutionary role of immiserated rural classes, in particular, through guerrilla warfare, and their role in concrete situations of underdevelopment (Bambirra 1999). Marini focused on internal class relationships and their relationship with imperialism, as he tried to expand beyond a pure focus on the terms of trade to understand how the surplus value lost by national capital in international trade could be regained domestically—how one dominant economy could affect the development pattern of a subordinate economy.[1]

Criticisms of dependency, in particular, those heavily focused on "internalist" explanations, have claimed that it ignores domestic class structures.[2] Yet Marini argued that unequal exchange and domestic relative surplus value and absolute surplus value extraction worked in concert. Latin America had been and remains a land of only partial industrialization, and now premature industrialization. Nevertheless, the wealth secured from the land, whether from mining pits or agricultural plots, has remained important. Because capital moves from arenas of lower profit rates to those of higher ones, the deteriorating terms of trade for commodity exports would logically, absent a compensatory mechanism, lead to disinvestment in those sectors. Why would capital invest where returns are low? Marini deduced that a reaction of the Latin American ruling class invested in those sectors was to super-exploit their work force, paying workers so little that salaries fell below the cost of social reproduction, as wage cuts ate into the consumption fund, and domestic capital, unable to find its sustenance through international trade, gorged on domestic labor.[3] This was equally seen in the industrial sector, where emerging Brazilian industrial capital, which was often tied into transnational subcontracting chains, would suppress wages below the level needed for social reproduction— hence *super-exploitation*, Marini's central contribution to dependency theory, and deeply connected to his global and world-systemic analysis of how cheapened goods as inputs into northern food baskets were central to northern industrial take-off (Marini 1973).

Land and the types of social formations that exist on certain land masses did not merely enter at the level of economics, but were central to dependency's political vision. Marini and his co-thinkers, alongside fellow-travelers like the North American–German dependency and world systems theorist Andre Gunder Frank, considered the Latin American revolution a necessarily continental affair (Marini 1969, 20).

South Asia

Cousins of dependency/world-systems analysis also emerged from the South Asian subcontinent, where Indian Marxists scrutinized the focus on international value flows and the polarized nature of global accumulation. Utsa and Prabhat Patnaik, Indian economists and professors at Jawarhlul Nehru University, have most clearly developed the mechanics of drain. They start with the axial factor of production: the land and what is produced on it. They argue that imperialism is based on a specific kind of domination that core imperialist and temperate states exert over peripheral, subjugated, and semitropical or tropical states: the dominant states obtain the products needed by the core, including its consumers and the monopoly commodity chains that are sources of profit, provisioning, and reproduction, and ensure that those products arrive at the core at nonincreasing supply prices. The Patnaiks argue that global imperialism is intertwined with the need to defend the dollar as a store of value—the sovereign currency of a specific and leading nation within the world system. Sustained inflation and the undermining of the leading currency as a store of value would encourage wealth hoarders to rush to gold or any other perceived-to-be-stable commodity. This process is to be avoided at all costs. The patterns of power and production therefore need to uphold the social and political structures that suppress inflation.

These three themes structure the Patnaiks' intervention in the role of land and agricultural production in imperialism and global accumulation. The first is drain and its effects. They argue that the British colonial endeavor in South Asia was essentially a suction-like removal of physical commodities from India, which had tremendous social effects. In India it occurred via tax extraction from peasants and artisans, essentially by paying them for their goods with the money they had paid in taxes, as it switched from one hand to the other in the colonial administration. Peasants were taxed in cash and therefore had to sell something that would secure them cash, which was a time-tested mechanism for leveraging subsistence or petty-commodity producers into capitalist market dependence. It also altered the structural composition of what these producers grew on their land. In effect, the British colonialists obtained these goods for free, and the price of the colonial administration was borne by the colonized. Furthermore, as demand for tropical goods that could not be grown in the cold British climate, such as spices and coffee, increased in the United Kingdom and in other temperate settler-colonies where land had been seized through settler genocides, the metropolis agitated to extract ever more of them, which meant suppressing domestic demand. South Asia thus served as a keystone of the entire European imperial apparatus—and not merely South Asia, but the South Asian land and peasantry, were the foundation stones of original accumulation and British capitalism and imperialism: "A cold temperate country which acquired political control over a tropical region, in effect sat on a gold mine: it not only got goods it could never produce, completely free for its own use, it also got such goods free to exchange against imports from sovereign temperate lands" (Patnaik and Patnaik 2016, 35). The ripping open of the South Asian social formation also led to deindustrialization as British exports replaced homespun manufactures. The result was the creation of massive labor reserves.

These "drains" and disarticulations had social corollaries. First, diverting domestic fertile land away from domestic food production to sow crops for export was not only about shifting, in a kind of fluid model, the production structure. It was about politically engineering the reduction of the social power that economists call "demand." Reductions in social power are registered in the social well-being of poor people. This was a central mechanism of colonial drain. The consequences in South and Southeast Asia were tremendous, above all, for those who lived off the land. Under the Dutch colonial imposition, per capita food-grains output in Java dropped from 199 kilograms (about 438 pounds) annually in 1885 to 162 kilograms (about 357 pounds) annually in 1940, while sugarcane production rose 762 percent, and rubber production increased 332 percent. The nineteenth century saw famine blight the subcontinent as colonial chicanery desiccated food-grain provision, and export crops—needed for specie—replaced consumption goods. As a result, food-grain availability decreased sharply. Colonized India in the fifty years before Independence saw the growth rate of commercial commodity exports increase at ten times the pace of food-grains. In Eastern India, food production fell by 38 percent (Patnaik 2007, 27–30).

Indeed, these processes have neoliberal corollaries: the lands of the North remain unable to produce tropical foodstuffs, and the lands of the South have, in effect, been partially reconquered by the technocrats of monopoly finance—the World Bank, the International Monetary Fund, and the associated "sound money" provisions and prescriptions. The collapse of the USSR accelerated this process (Banerjee 2020). As a result, people are again going hungry worldwide, and it is a hunger that is often directly linked to the richly fertile land they inhabit.

Finally, all of this was done, in part, to preserve the value of northern money through diversion of land to export commodities and destruction of demand. This meant that there was no price-push inflation in the costs of those commodities, and thus no endogenous threat to the stability of imperial currencies. Land is therefore tied tightly to northern reliance on the South to protect its currency, as well as capitalism and imperialism. Furthermore, as with theories of deteriorating terms of trade, the political relationship with land conditioned the "economic" relationship of value extraction, therefore demanding a certain political solution. Unequal exchange concerns accumulation through unequal power dynamics in market exchange under conditions of sovereignty (Dussel 1988). In contrast, drain concerned direct political control over surplus value, which could be addressed using either national-bourgeois or revolutionary solutions.

The Indian "school" likewise took a world-systemic turn, going beyond relations between nations to a holistic assessment of the role of distinct, interlocking historical patterns in accumulation: during the monopoly capital-imperialist stage, capital exports from Britain worked in tandem with population exports through settler-colonialism for the dual ends of capital accumulation and resolving social pressure; and this was enabled by the drain coming into Britain through its extraction from the subcontinent, a strategy also used by other European colonial powers (Bagchi 2008).

Arab Dependency

Dependency also had an African-Arab birth, technically in Paris, but by way of a young Egyptian economist, Samir Amin.[4] Amin had been a communist from a young age, and his ideas had formed and hardened in the crucible of the major nationalist and national liberation struggles of the 1950s: he had lived through the Asian and African movements for national liberation, reading Mao Zedong, and watching with intrigue and admiration the Chinese national revolution—the work of peasants—and political struggles with Maghrebi and sub-Saharan African students, as they struggled to shatter the grip of colonialism in their homelands (Amin 1994, 2006).

Amin's 1957 doctoral dissertation, published first in French, and later in English, in 1974, by Monthly Review Press, sought to understand, untangle, and undo mainstream theories of development—the theories of modernization positing the replicability of the core and the Western path to development—which suppressed how the wealth of those nation-states rested on their domination of other lands and transmuted the historically forged underdevelopment of the peripheries into a kind of lack, one that could be then alchemized into development by the proper application of technical knowledge and planning. In Amin's dissertation, he built on the Prebisch thesis of the worsening terms of trade for the primary products of the periphery (Amin 1957, 94–125; 1970; 1974b). He argued that landowners would generally spend their rents on imports rather any kind of local investment, importing few capital goods and thus slowing the rate of domestic capital accumulation, and thereby linking widespread and grievous agrarian inequality of large portions of the periphery to underdevelopment. Furthermore, Amin argued that there was an in-built tendency toward labor surpluses and the build-up of massive labor reservoirs. Other land-based activity suffered, too, because colonialism advanced, and partially articulated, precolonial economies, with interactions between artisanry and small-scale manufacturing. Farming gave way to dissolution of domestic primary processing—woodworking, cotton-spinning, jute weaving—faced with competition from the core as colonial control collapsed any political measures to protect national production.

Amin argued that international circulation realized value in trade, and that this process was connected with domestic class structures in the periphery: a substantial subsistence sector in the countryside; widespread marginalization; primary commodity export sectors, whether of raw material or food products; and industrialization producing only for export or for a narrow domestic market. Such products were important insofar as return to labors, or the wage share of the product price, was less than it would be in the center. In essence, the shapes and sizes of these gears could vary, within limits, but the machine was oriented to wage compression to maintain a low price for everything produced and traded on international exchanges.

Amin noted that capitalism, accumulation on a world scale, created two interlocking, mutually constituting poles of production, two interwoven social formations connected by the threads of military aggression, unequal trade, finance, and debt: cores and peripheries. Cores were, above all, characterized by autocentric logics of accumulation: their dynamic, the pulsing engine that paced and powered the accumulation process, was endogenous. Cores had five central traits that marked them out as distinct formations: *one*, the ability, more or less, to reproduce and provision their work force, meaning having national agricultures for food and national industries for consumption goods; *two*, a centralized surplus and financial institutions capable of administering it, along with the political capacity to mobilize and if necessary direct surplus through state spending; *three*, control over a domestic market largely reserved for local production and a system of production competitive enough to produce goods, usually, but not solely manufactures, which would be competitive on foreign markets; *four*, formal national ownership over natural resources, and freedom of choice as to how to make use of them; and *five*, local control over technology. Relations with other markets and producers were subordinated to the domestic formation's needs, and the "logic of internal accumulation" (Amin 1990, 11). Finally, cores were characterized by the central logic governing accumulation: the relationship between a domestic capital-goods sector and a domestic consumer-goods sector that were producing for local consumption, and an articulation of domestic manufacturing and agricultural sectors, thereby ensuring that some of the benefits of productivity increases would fall to the hands of the local working class, enlisting them in a social compact.

Amin defined peripheries as almost the shadow cast by the core: they lacked a local bourgeoisie; there was no local state control over accumulation. The systemic coding, the key logic of local accumulation, was very different: exports in the technologically advanced enclave export sector worked in tandem with a constrained internal market (the child of aborted or stillborn agrarian reform) and luxury consumption. Low wages implied low buying power and depended on mammoth labor reservoirs. This was the combination that conjured dwarf markets—with so little land and so little power and a surfeit of landless people removed from the land via historical primitive accumulation, it followed that few could afford what was produced. Such low wages, in turn, worked, much as Marini argued, as a sop for the capitalists suffering from the cuts of unequal exchange. They could compensate for their losses in international markets with gains won from bereft domestic laborers (Amin 1974a).

African World-Systems Theory

Walter Rodney was a major popularizer of dependency thinking in the African continent. A preeminent Caribbean-born pan-Africanist, he was central to the debates at Dar es Salaam, where he wrote most of his best-known study *How Europe Underdeveloped Africa* (Rodney 2012). Rodney's world-systems and dependency analysis embraced a non-Eurocentric vision of popular development and "control of the economy on behalf of the working classes" (14). He understood gaining such control to be the way to resolve the systemic program and trap of underdevelopment imposed by imperialism and neocolonialism. Rodney made clear that underdevelopment had been historically imposed by forcing countries away from any unfolding of their own processes of development, and vampirically draining their "surplus" to the dominant nations. Africa was enfolded in capitalist domination through commodity trade and the slave trade long before formal colonization.[5]

With the advent of formal colonization, which came at a decisive moment for Africa's possible development, the situation worsened. The colonizers installed infrastructure, especially transport, simply to facilitate the export of the basic commodities it needed from the continent for their own production and profit. Whereas before colonization, most of the people in Africa could make a living from the land, colonization changed all that: it was a process of primitive accumulation without full proletarianization. Africa was, instead, marked by a kind of semi-proletarianization, wherein wages were set so low that most workers effectively had to work on miniplots in addition to working on colonial farms, plantations, or mines in order to secure their needed daily bread. The official wages were "usually insufficient to keep the worker physically alive," allowing for a massive extraction for surplus value (Rodney 2012, 176). Europe was able to keep wages low by simply setting them low and them setting force upon workers who agitated for higher wages. Furthermore, Rodney argued, the colonial state encountered a small and fragmented proletariat, which was easier to keep disorganized and to exploit. Racial justifications emerged to justify these super-low wages. And even when Africans tried to organize in trade unions, the regimes disorganized or blocked them. As a result, from cacao to gold, Africa was a figurative and literal mine for European colonial capital, exporting massive amounts of wealth during the period of formal colonization: "because of the super-profits created by non-European peoples ever since slavery, the net flow was from colony to metropole. What was called 'profits' in one year came back as 'capital' the next" (Rodney 2012, 255).

To effect a rupture in this imposed stagnation, Rodney openly advocated for state socialist planning of production, consumption, and development. He also advocated for the development of socialist thinking by the "African Revolution," and for it to come "from those who have had the historical experience of, and socialisation under, slavery, colonialism, de-culturalization, racism and super-exploitation which has been the peculiar lot of Africans" (1972, 75). Such thinking emerged against a broader tableau wherein many were thinking about the trials and tribulations of postcolonial socialist construction against imperialist headwinds.

The Critique of Modernization Theory

In the North, the critique of modernization theory started with Paul Baran's *The Political Economy of Growth* in which he pointed out that northern "modernization rested on a 'transfusion' from non-European countries, 'boost[ing]' the former while causing a 'serious setback to . . . [the] primary accumulation of capital'" in the latter (1957, 276). Baran was a major spur to Latin American dependency, which was, in turn, a major contributor, alongside Frantz Fanon and the African liberation movements, to world-systems theory in general, and to the analysis of Immanuel Wallerstein (1970, 2000) in particular. Carrying forward the insights of Latin American structuralism and dependency, Wallerstein elaborated the ideas of the core and the periphery to create a tripartite model, with the semiperiphery in between (1974, 2011). These elaborations attacked the idea that one could understand development primarily through bundles of causes interacting within national bounds. Instead, the unit of analysis had to be the world system, including modes of labor exploitation, state strength, and decisions about the former so as to maximize profit on the world market.[6] Later, Wallerstein became identified, alongside Frank, Giovanni Arrighi, and Amin, in debates on the world system as the "Gang of Four." These thinkers deployed a range of approaches, but shared a common taproot in their critique of modernization; they embraced a global and world-systemic holistic approach,[7] and three of the four traced their empirical formation to Africa, where the mercantilist slave trade and national liberation movements had birthed radical thinking about the impacts of colonial disarticulation, neocolonial depredation, and the efforts to rupture neocolonialism—the topic to which we now turn (Arrighi 1979; Nkrumah 1974).

Land as Resistance

Land threads throughout dependency theories and their cousins as a central locus of oppression, exploitation, primitive accumulation, and spoliation: land as the source of tropical commodities, of minerals, of super-exploited labor, and as the geographical home base of the social formations that are subject to national domination at the hands of the core. Yet these theories and their cognates also offer a basis for thinking about land as a basis of resistance, not simply through critical withdrawal from or fierce defense of subsistence in the face of predatory colonial, neocolonial, or capitalist aggression, but for thinking through and achieving resistance. They focused on national-level planning, the role of peasants, and the agricultural surplus; and tended to converge on the need for rupture, for a break with the prevailing world economic order to undertake a process of development based on the essentially untried "peasant path."

We may start with Amilcar Cabral, whose work on neocolonialism and national liberation put the problematic most clearly. Cabral had forged and sharpened his thinking while waging a people's war against a colonial intruder. For Cabral (1979), colonialism and neocolonialism were based on "the negation of the historical process of the dominated people by means of violent usurpation of the freedom of development of the national productive forces." He presciently understood that under extant African realities, a national capitalism, reflecting any kind of endogenous social patterning, was impossible. It would lead to the continued subjugation of the national productive forces—for example, the land, nascent industrial plant, labor, natural resources—to imperialist control and profit. In a neocolonial situation, which usually followed or existed alongside a nationalist or national revolution but did not have to, a "national solution" would not resolve the problem of the lack of domestic control over the productive forces. The post-colonial political forces controlling the country would generally lack the capacity and any vested interest in suppressing the imperialist negation of the freedom of development of the territorial productive forces. Therefore, neocolonialism, based on particular patterns of extraction and exploitation—mostly primary-commodity export in the African context—demanded "a profound mutation in the process of development of the productive forces"; and furthermore, "the destruction of the capitalist structure implanted in the national territory by imperialism," which there put on the table "a socialist solution." Still, putting the domestic productive forces under national control could only be the beginning. From the late 1960s onward, as the North Star of China rose over the postcolonial world, it produced a set of theories, organically linked to Arab dependency, which crystallized, in model and thought, a conception of what had occurred in China and sought to cast it as a model for postcolonial and anti-neocolonial development.

After a short period of Soviet-inspired development, China had carried out a program of development aimed at maximizing self-reliance. By the 1960s, this strategy had become a watchword in eastern Africa, its influence seen in the Arusha Declaration; the revolutionary surge in Zanzibar, for which the Chinese were close consultants; and then the dependency thinking that grew in the womb of the debates at Dar es Salaam University (Babu 2002; Lal 2015; Shivji 2008; Wilson 2014). By the early 1970s, the Egyptian economists Mohamed Dowidar and Fawzy Mansour, among others, were teaching this model at African Institute for Economic Development and Planning, which Amin had founded to train planning cadres across the African continent. At a series of meetings and in a series of manifestoes and documents, from the Cocoyoc Declaration to the meetings in Latin America that eventually produced a "Latin American world model," self-reliance or autocentered development was in the air ("Cocoyoc Declaration" 1975; Herrera 1971).[8]

Amin developed the model most clearly. Yet similar modeling can be found in the works of those Egyptian scholars and is the background against which a remarkably wide range of thinking (becoming a virtual *lingua franca* across southern heterodox and communist planning circles), including on the Caribbean, Central America, and South America, developed concerning how to apply thinking around dependency to the problems of peripheral development (Thomas 1974; Thompson 1987). Delinking meant shattering a set of dynamics and value flows that were largely bound up with unequal agrarian structures, labor reservoirs, super-exploitation, unequal exchange, and tropical and mineral commodity exports, but also subcontracting in industrial and service-value chains. These mechanisms of accumulation were also chains controlling the direction of development of peripheral productive forces. Delinking and autocentered development meant a move toward a self-reliant, inward-facing, and popular strategy of "endogenous development" (Kenrick, Oteiza, and Zammit 1983; Mansour 1979). Following a certain understanding of what had happened in China, a national "popular alliance" of peasants and workers would set in place a set of choices according to its own law of value (Amin 1990, 18–19).[9]

If the dominant prices were the quantitative expression of a social engineering project, a project of class warfare from above, then different prices were needed to carry out a popular development pattern. This alliance rested on three legs: first, renouncing the "capitalist rationality" and making all external relations subject, not to exploitative "comparative advantage" choices, but to national (and implicitly peasant-worker) values. Second, gathering the political strength to do so, meaning, somehow, the mass mobilization of peasants and proletarians—or, in the modern age, semi proletarians, slum dwellers, the rural proletariat, and others. Third, "technological absorption and ingenuity" (Amin 1990b, 60). Amin and others abstracted their model from their understanding of price setting in China. Wages were to reflect labor inputs, and prices would be gauged to ensure that rural and urban workers would receive rewards commensurate with their labor inputs. Rising urban productivity would, therefore, not necessarily translate into equally rising urban wages.[10] For Amin, the urban industrial sector would partially feed the rural sector, through the technical upgrading of agriculture, while rural producers would grow food for people in the cities (Ajl 2014; Chachra 2020; Moyo, Jha, and Yeros 2013). In agriculture, this would often rest on the "renovation and improvement of traditional technologies," alongside the modulated adoption and adaptation of imported technology (Amin 1990, 64–67).

From Egypt to Tunisia, scholars explored the social role and prospects for technology as a central mechanism when diagnosing, reproducing, or challenging dependency. This focus on technology has several nested aspects. First, rather than assuming a technological choice would produce development, through the outwards irradiation of technical progress, a kind of crystallization of rationality in the form of efficiency and productivity, they wished to first ask: which technologies for what kind of development (Mahjoub 1982)? Technological choices had to be nested within and could only be selected against the background of a specific development goal. Industrialization and agriculture alike would orient primarily to satisfying basic needs, which would be a massive improvement for most of the population. All of this would occur within the framework of self-reliant, autocentered, or independent development—three phrases that were largely interchangeable in Arab dependency thinking (Fergany 1987). For Ismail-Sabri Abdallah, Egypt's Vice-Minister of Planning under Gamal Abdel Nasser and then Anwar Sadat, this entailed a rural industrialization strategy that would place light and medium industries around the countryside. Intellectually, and in terms of technological research and development, this meant studying "traditional" industries and handicrafts, as mechanisms for producing basic consumption goods and in terms of the technical upgrading of agriculture. Some technologies might be discarded; some might be adapted and improved; and some could be used as is (Abdallah 1980; Abdel-Fadil 1982; Ajl 2021a; Dowidar 1979, 1984; Naṣṣār 1982). Abdallah was especially concerned with the damage large plans could inflict on the physical environment, which was a broader concern among Arab dependency planners (Abdalla 1977; Naṣṣār 1982). Most especially, the planners perceptively saw the damage large hydraulic installations were wreaking on the landscape, the water cycle, and underground reservoirs.

Mahjoub, and alongside him the prescient Tunisian agroecologist Slaheddine el-Amami, were in conversation with Abdallah, who was particularly central in pushing Mahjoub to see the centrality of the ecology. They focused on an antidependency form of agricultural research and development that would applying all the hard-earned techniques of scientific, lab-based experiments and documentation to substantiate, defend, and if possible improve upon North Africa's "traditional" farming systems.[11] The focus would be on the latent promise of "native" seeds or the efficiency and logic of using "traditional" hydraulics to harvest rainwater to make sedentary agriculture possible in bands of land "conventionally" considered too dry to farm (El-Amami 1982, 1983, 1984). Such mechanisms, based on decentralized labor and decentralized and popularly held repositories of knowledge, had an elective affinity with an anti-neocolonial and antidependency, pro-popular, and pro-peasant development strategy. As Amami wrote,

> The Arab countries must encourage the promotion of a socio-economic ecology which analyzes the "rationality" of local populations with a view towards injecting technological improvements corresponding to the aspirations and mutations of these populations and not to the sophisticated and very expensive technology giving the illusion of "miracle" solutions.
>
> (el-Amami 1976)

Here was an artisanal epistemological bridge between the methodology of the laboratory and that of the ethnographer and ethno-agronomist (Ajl 2019). It valued the kinds of knowledge belonging to the direct producers and their capacity to think, and called for an interplay of knowledges that rested directly on the acknowledgment of the rationality of those practices. These ideas were not quite discarded. Rather, they were depoliticized and implemented in narrowly technical ways, often with European foundation funding. Their harvest was not, then, liberation, but a new kind of chain. Elsewhere in the agrarian south, in Nicaragua, a focus on endogenous resource mobilization through land-based industries and energy sources and an attempt to shift to proto-agroecological practices were another living approach to antidependent autonomous development: in this case, one put to an end by US neocolonial violence (Faber 1999).

Conclusion

This chapter has considered the role of land and the bundle of social forces, categories, positions, and processes bound up with land in the making and unmaking of dependency. These include the role of colonial invasion, imperial drain, and neocolonial unequal exchange in accumulation on a world scale. They further include the role of large-scale agrarian inequality; massive peasant, formerly peasant, or semi-proletarianized labor reserves; and tropical commodity-crop export in reproducing underdevelopment, and the northern reliance on southern commodity crops for social reproduction of their workforce. It has considered how these distinct understandings of land interlocked with different territorial forms of colonial and neocolonial domination, in turn yielding spatially and geographically particular ways of understanding these situations of oppression: sovereign states facing unequal exchange produced the theory of the declining terms of trade. Colonialism produced diagnoses of value-flow focused, as with Rodney, on commodity export and the slave trade; and for the Patnaiks, direct colonial drain and demand deflation—less bread in peoples' mouths. They and Amin and the Marxist current of Latin American dependency zeroed in on the role of super-exploitation and unequal exchange—interwoven in the fabric of a hierarchical and polarized land-ownership pattern—in stabilizing global value flows, uneven accumulation, and the reconstruction and re-forging of cores and peripheries.

The chapter then considered the role of land and peasants in national liberation and patterns of popular and national development that sought to shatter dependency and neocolonial relations—in particular, the cluster of thinking concentrated around the notion of self-reliance. In contrast to modernization theologies of development, this literature argues for putting the peasant in a lead position when it comes to the political mobilization, planning, and social reproduction strategies of nationalist development. It collected thinkers like Amami, Mahjoub, and Abdallah, who showed that the peasantry were not merely potential political actors or the foundation stones of a potential development path. They were, further, the guardians of a trove of knowledge, which could be a bequest from the past to a self-reliant future, a decentralized utopian pattern of planning.

Yet the horizon sketched out by these thinkers was unreachable, for the ideology of developmentalism and its heterodox and ecological elements often grew up in state institutions that were both shield and cage. On the one hand, the legitimacy of the Arab nationalist states was based on their serving the popular well-being, which meant embracing an associated developmentalist ideology. Hence, the National Planning Institute of Kuwait, Amami's Centre de Recherche en Génie Rurale, and the Institute for National Planning in Cairo were homes for linkages between the South and the Eastern Bloc, seminaries for Arab dependency, and open to ecological critique (Ajl 2021b). They were nodal points in a broader network of tricontinental thought, wherein concern for ecology was inseparable from a popular development project. On the other hand, these states had military origins and were hostile to internal democracy, which became their weakness (Kanafani n.d.; Megahed and Ghannam 2022). They could not politically mobilize the peasantry, and they lacked a sufficiently class-conscious developmentalism that would even plan *for* the peasantry, even if not *with* the peasantry. Even prescient programs like Amami's could not effectively distribute power to a class whose exclusion was the basis of postcolonial state formation.

Finally, the chapter argued for the role of land and territory in understanding the political struggles around and against colonialism and neocolonialism, around and against dependency. Just as accumulation on a world scale has been organized spatially on colonial and then neocolonial lines—now understood as the North-South conflict—resistance, from national liberation movements to socialist construction, have been interlinked and grounded spatially and vis-à-vis territory, as a means of offering refuge, materiel, planning counsel, solidarity, and of holding open the space for development itself. The thinkers thus argue compellingly that national liberation, guarded by the keepers of the keys of landscape knowledges—namely, those living on or tied to the land—remains the untried land-based path to liberation in the twenty-first century.

Acknowledgments

Thanks to Phil McMichael for discussion.

Notes

1. This is the argument of Smith (2016); also see Higginbottom (2010) and Latimer (2021).
2. E.g., the work of Agustin Cueva, to which Bambirra (1978) responds.
3. See this work, which presents an analogous argument related to the British colonization of South Asia: Patnaik (2018).
4. Amin is seldom included in discussions of dependency theory and often excluded from discussions on world-systems theory as well.
5. See Depelchin (1992) on the necessity of including the slave trade era in the period of colonialism.
6. For critiques, see Friedmann and Wayne (1977); McMichael (1990); and Skocpol (1977).
7. For discussion, see Valiani (2021).
8. The Cocoyoc Declaration was adapted by those attending in a UNCTAD.UNEP symposium on "Patterns of Resource Use, Environment and Development Strategies," which was held in Cocoyoc, Mexico, October 8–12, 1974.
9. Amin overstated the degree to which the Chinese model successfully broke with urban bias (a bias inseparable from the need for heavy industrialization in the face of NATO aggression in Korea and elsewhere). See Bramall (2008).
10. These were only rough approximations of the Chinese model, as there was some disparity between urban and rural consumption, although not nearly so wide as in other Third World countries. Figures on per capita food absorption and overall income are contested. See Bramall (2008, 291–310).
11. Thanks to Habib Ayeb for suggesting this interpretation to me.

References

Abdalla, Ismaïl-Sabri. 1977. *Development and the International Order Selected Papers*, INP, Cairo.

Abdallah, Ismaïl-Sabri. 1980. "Arab Industrialization Strategy Based on Self-Reliance and Satisfaction of Basic Needs." In *IFDA Dossier 16*, 1–12. International Foundation for Development Alternatives.

Abdel-Fadil, M. 1982. *Al-Fikr al-iqtiṣādī al-ʿarabī wa-qaḍāyā at-taḥarrur wa-ăt-tanmiyah wa-ăl-waḥdah*. Beirut, Center for Arab Unity Studies.

Ajl, Max. 2014. "The Hypertrophic City versus the Planet of Fields." In *Implosions/Explosions*, edited by Neil Brenner, 533–550. Berlin: Jovis.

Ajl, Max. 2019. "Auto-Centered Development and Indigenous Technics: Slaheddine el-Amami and Tunisian Delinking." *Journal of Peasant Studies* 46 (6): 1240–1263.

Ajl, Max. 2021a. "The Arab Nation, The Chinese Model, and Theories of Self-Reliant Development." In *Beyond Nationalism and the Nation-State: Radical Approaches to Nation*, edited by İlker Corut and Joost Jongerden, 139–157. Abingdon, UK: Routledge.

Ajl, Max. 2021b. "The Hidden Legacy of Samir Amin: Delinking's Ecological Turn." In "Samir Amin and Beyond: Development, Dependence and Delinking in the Contemporary World." Special issue, *Review of African Political Economy* 48 (167): 82–101.

Amin, Samir. 1957. "Les effets structurels de l'intégration internatioale des économies précapitalistes: Une étude théorique du mécanisme qui a engendré les économies dites sous-développées." Thesis, Université de Paris.

Amin, Samir. 1970. *L'accumulation à l'échelle mondiale*. Paris: Anthropos.

Amin, Samir. 1974a. "Accumulation and Development: A Theoretical Model." *Review of African Political Economy* 1:9–26. https://doi.org/10.1080/03056247408703234.

Amin, Samir. 1974b. *Accumulation on a World Scale: A Critique of the Theory of Underdevelopment*. New York: Monthly Review Press.

Amin, Samir. 1990. *Delinking: Towards a Polycentric World*. London: Zed Books.

Amin, Samir. 1994. *Re-reading the Postwar Period*. New York: Monthly Review Press.

Amin, Samir. 2006. *A Life Looking Forward: Memoirs of an Independent Marxist*. London: Zed Books.

Arrighi, G. 1979. "Peripheralization of Southern Africa, I: Changes in Production Processes." *Review (Fernand Braudel Center)* 3 (2): 161. https://www.jstor.org/stable/40240833.

Babu, A. R. M. 2002. *The Future That Works: Selected Writings of A.M. Babu*. Eds. Salma Babu and Amrit Wilson. Trenton, NJ: Africa World Press.

Bach, Maria V. S. B. 2019. "Redefining Universal Development from and at the Margins—Research Portal, King's College, London." PhD thesis, King's College London. https://kclpure.kcl.ac.uk/portal/en/theses/redefining-universal-development-from-and-at-the-margins(e6154c5d-9962-4721-bc3d-a141ec2f9682).html.

Bagchi, A. K. 2008. *Perilous Passage: Mankind and the Global Ascendancy of Capital*. Lanham, MD: Rowman and Littlefield.

Bambirra, Venia. 1978. *Teoría de la dependencia: Una anticrítica*. Mexico City: Ediciones Era.

Bambirra, Venia. 1999. *El capitalismo dependiente latinoamericano*. Mexico City: Siglo XXI.

Banerjee, A. 2020. "The Longer 'Food Crisis' and Consequences for Economic Theory and Policy in the South." In *Rethinking the Social Sciences with Sam Moyo*, edited by Praveen Jha, Paris Yeros, and Walter Chambati, 152–179. New Delhi: Tulika Books.

Baran, A. 1957. *The Political Economy of Growth*. New York: Monthly Review Press.

Bramall, C. 2008. *Chinese Economic Development*. New York: Routledge.

Brolin, John. 2007. "The Bias of the World: Theories of Unequal Exchange in History." PhD, Lund University.

Cabral, A. 1979. *Unity and Struggle: Speeches and Writings of Amilcar Cabral*. New York: Monthly Review Press.

Chachra, S. 2020. "A Future of Urbanity: Cities and Countrysides for All." In *Rethinking the Social Sciences with Sam Moyo*, edited by Praveen Jha, Paris Yeros, and Walter Chambati, 215–223. New Delhi: Tulika Books.

"The Cocoyoc Declaration." 1975. *International Organization* 29 (3): 893–901.

Depelchin, J. 1992. *From Congo Free State to Zaire: How Belgium Privitized the Economy*. Dakar: Codesria.

Dos Santos, Theotonio. 1970. "The Structure of Dependence." *American Economic Review* 60 (2): 231–236. https://www.jstor.org/stable/1815811.

Dos Santos, Theotonio. 2003. *La teoría de la dependencia: Balance y perspectivas*. Buenos Aires: Plaza y Janes.

Dowidar, Mohamed. 1979. "The Self-Reliance Strategy of Development and the New International Economic Order." *Mondes en Développement* 26: 249–254.

Dowidar, Mohamed. 1984. "National Development Strategy and Long Term Solutions to the Balance of Payment Problems in African Economies." *L'Égypte Contemporaine* 75 (398): 295–332. https://www.africabib.org/rec.php?RID=192855638.

Dussel, Enrique D. 1988. *Hacia un Marx desconocido: Un comentario de los manuscritos del 61–63*. Mexico City: Siglo XXI.

El-Amami, Slaheddine. 1976. *Projets de Coopération Régionale en Matière de Recherche Scientifique et Technologiques, Conférence Des Ministères des États Arabes Charges de l'Application de la Science et de la Technologie au Développement, UNESCO, Rabat, 16–25 August 1976*. Les Cahiers du CRGR. CRGR; MoA, 76/37.

El-Amami, Slaheddine. 1982. "Pour une recherche agronomique au service d'une technologie nationale intégrée." In *Tunisie: Quelles Technologies? Quel Développement?* edited by Azzam Mahjoub, 15–20. Tunis: GREDET.

El-Amami, Slaheddine. 1983. "Changing Concepts of Water Management in Tunisia." *Impact of Science on Society* 33 (1): 57–64.

El-Amami, Slaheddine. 1984. *Les aménagements hydrauliques traditionnels en Tunisie*. Tunis: Centre de Recherche en Génie Rural.

Faber, Daniel. 1999. "La liberación del medio ambiente: The rise and fall of revolutionary ecology in Nicaragua, 1979–1999." *Capitalism Nature Socialism* 10 (1): 45–80. https://doi.org/10.1080/10455759909358848.

Fergany, N., ed. 1987. *Al-tanmīyya al-mustaqila fi al-waṭan al-ʿarabī* [Independent development in the Arab nation]. Beirut: Center for Arab Unity Studies.

Friedmann, H., and J. Wayne. 1977. "Dependency Theory: A Critique." *Canadian Journal of Sociology / Cahiers Canadiens de Sociologie* 2 (4): 399–416. https://doi.org/10.2307/3340297.

Furtado, Celso. 1976. *Economic Development of Latin America: Historical Background and Contemporary Problems*, 2nd ed. Cambridge, UK: Cambridge University Press.

Furtado, Celso. 2020. *The Myth of Economic Development*. Translated by Jordan B. Jones Tosi. Cambridge, UK: Polity.

Girvan, N. 2006. "Caribbean Dependency Thought Revisited." *Canadian Journal of Development Studies/Revue Canadienne d'études du Développement* 27 (3): 328–352.

Girvan, N., and C. Girvan. 1973. "The Development of Dependency Economics in the Caribbean and Latin America: Review and Comparison." *Social and Economic Studies* 22 (1): 1–33.

Herrera, A. Oscar. 1971. *Un proyecto latinoamericano de modelo mundial*. Fundación Bariloche.

Higginbottom, Andrew. 2010,. "Underdevelopment as Super-Exploitation: Marini's Political-Economic Thought." Conference paper. Historical Materialism: Crisis and Critique, 7th Annual Conference, November 13, London. https://eprints.kingston.ac.uk/id/eprint/23279/.

Kanafani, Ghassan, n.d. "The Resistance and Its Problems: The View of the Popular Front for the Liberation of Palestine." In *Collected Works*, edited by L. Brehony.

Kay, Cristóbal. 1991. "Reflections on the Latin American Contribution to Development Theory." *Development and Change* 22 (1): 31–68. https://doi.org/10.1111/j.1467-7660.1991.tb00402.x.

Kenrick, C., E. Oteiza, and J. A. Zammit. 1983. *Autoafirmación colectiva: Una estrategia alternativa de desarrollo*. Mexico: Fondo de Cultura Económica.

Lal, P. 2015. *African Socialism in Postcolonial Tanzania*. Cambridge, UK: Cambridge University Press.

Latimer, Amanda. 2021. "Super-Exploitation, the Race to the Bottom, and the Missing International." In *The Palgrave Encyclopedia of Imperialism and Anti-imperialism*, edited by I. Ness and Z. Cope, 2546–2561. Cham: Palgrave Macmillan. https://doi.org/10.1007/978-3-030-29901-9_273.

Levitt, K. 2004. "Independent Thought and Caribbean Community." *Canadian Journal of Development Studies/Revue Canadienne d'études du Développement* 25 (2): 225–237.

Lewis, W. Arthur. 1954. "Economic Development with Unlimited Supplies of Labour." *Manchester School* 22 (2): 139–191. https://doi.org/10.1111/j.1467-9957.1954.tb00021.x.

Love, J. L. 1980. "Raul Prebisch and the Origins of the Doctrine of Unequal Exchange." *Latin American Research Review* 15 (3): 45–72.

Love, J. L. 1990. The Origins of Dependency Analysis. *Journal of Latin American Studies* 22 (1–2): 143–168.

Mahjoub, A. 1982. *Technologie et développement*. Thesis, Universite d'Aix-Marseille-II.

Mansour, Fawzy. 1979. *Operational Guidelines for Arab Collective Self-Reliance?* Dakar, IDEP, https://repository.uneca.org/handle/10855/42400.

Marini, Ruy Mauro. 1969. *Subdesarrollo y revolución*. Mexico: Siglo Veintiuno Editores.

Marini, Ruy Mauro. 1973. *Dialéctica de la dependencia*. Era México.

McMichael, Philip. 1990. "Incorporating Comparison within a World-Historical Perspective: An Alternative Comparative Method." *American Sociological Review* 55 (3): 385–397. https://doi.org/10.2307/2095763.

McMichael, Philip. 1997. "Rethinking Globalization: The Agrarian Question Revisited." *Review of International Political Economy* 4 (4): 630–662.

Megahed, K., and O. Ghannam. 2022. "The Rocket in the Haystack: Between Nasser's Developmental Vision and the Neo-imperialist Mission." *Africa Development / Afrique et Développement* 47 (1): 59–104. https://www.jstor.org/stable/48645754.

Moyo, Sam, Praveen Jha, and Paris Yeros. 2013. "The Classical Agrarian Question: Myth, Reality and Relevance Today." *Agrarian South: Journal of Political Economy* 2 (1): 93–119. https://ags.sagepub.com/content/2/1/93.short.

Nabolsy, Z. el. 2021. "Lotus and the Self-Representation of Afro-Asian Writers as the Vanguard of Modernity." *Interventions* 23 (4): 596–620. https://doi.org/10.1080/1369801X.2020.1784021.

Naṣṣār, ʿAlī. 1982. *Al- Imkānāt al-ʿarabīya: Iʿāda naẓar wa-taqwīm fī-ḍanʾ tanmiya badīla*. Beirut: Markaz Dirāsāt al-Waḥda al-ʿArabīya.

Nkrumah, K. 1974. *Neo-colonialism: The Last Stage of Imperialism*. Panaf.

Patnaik, Utsa. 2007. *The Republic of Hunger and Other Essays*. Merlin Press.

Patnaik, Utsa. 2018. "Profit Inflation, Keynes and the Holocaust in Bengal, 1943–44." *Economic & Political Weekly* 53 (42): 33.

Patnaik, Utsa, and Prabhat Patnaik. 2016. *A Theory of Imperialism*. New York: Columbia University Press.

Prebisch, Raul. 1950. *The Economic Development of Latin America and Its Principal Problems*. Report. United Nations Department of Economic Affairs.

Raffer, K. 1987. *Unequal Exchange and the Evolution of the World System*. New York: St. Martin's Press.

Rodney, Walter. 1972. "Tanzanian Ujamaa and Scientific Socialism." *African Review* 1 (4): 61–76.

Rodney, Walter. 2012. *How Europe Underdeveloped Africa.* Cape Town: Fahamu and Pambazuka Press.

Rostow, W. W. 1990. *The Stages of Economic Growth: A Non-communist Manifesto.* New York: Cambridge University Press.

Shivji, I. G. 2008. "Revisiting the Debate on National Autonomous Development." In *The African Union and New Strategies for Development in Africa*, edited by S. Adejumobi and A. Olukoshi, 177–206. Amherst, MA: Cambria Press.

Skocpol, Theda. 1977. "Wallerstein's World Capitalist System: A Theoretical and Historical Critique." *American Journal of Sociology* 82 (5): 1075–1090. https://www.jstor.org/stable/10.2307/2777814.

Smith, John. 2016. *Imperialism in the Twenty-First Century: Globalization, Super-Exploitation, and Capitalism's Final Crisis.* New York: Monthly Review Press.

Thomas, C. 1974. *Dependence and Transformation.* New York: Monthly Review Press.

Thompson, Robert. 1987. *Green Gold: Bananas and Dependency in the Eastern Caribbean.* London: Latin American Bureau.

Toye, J. F., and Richard Toye 2003. "The Origins and Interpretation of the Prebisch-Singer Thesis." *History of Political Economy* 35 (3): 437–467.

Valiani, S. 2021. "Onward To Liberation!—Samir Amin and the Study of World Historical Capitalism." *Journal of World-Systems Research* 27 (2): 566–585.

Wallerstein, Immanuel. 1970. "Frantz Fanon: Reason and Violence." *Berkeley Journal of Sociology* 15, 222–231.

Wallerstein, Immanuel. 1974. "The Rise and Future Demise of the World Capitalist System: Concepts for Comparative Analysis." *Comparative Studies in Society and History* 16 (4): 387–415. https://doi.org/10.1017/S0010417500007520.

Wallerstein, Immanuel. 2011. *The Modern World-System I: Capitalist Agriculture and the Origins of the European World-Economy in the Sixteenth Century.* Berkeley: University of California Press.

Wallerstein, Immanuel. 2000. *The Essential Wallerstein.* New York: New Press.

Wilson, Amrit. 2014. *The Threat of Liberation: Imperialism and Revolution in Zanzibar.* London: Pluto Press.

Witter, M. 2021. "Caribbean Economic Thought: Advances, Retreat, Current Challenges." *Agrarian South: Journal of Political Economy* 10 (3): 463–491. https://doi.org/10.1177/22779760211053083.

Wolf, Eric R. 1969. *Peasant Wars of the Twentieth Century.* Norman: University of Oklahoma Press.

CHAPTER 5

LAND IN THE CHAYANOVIAN TRADITION

JAN DOUWE VAN DER PLOEG

Introduction

The work and life of Alexander Chayanov are narrowly interwoven with both the Russian peasantry of the early twentieth century and the October Revolution of 1917. He was, in fact, one of the main connections between the two. He helped to organize the Russian peasantry into a dense web of cooperatives that spanned the country, and was active in outlining the land reform. He was convinced that Russian peasant communities (and their cooperatives) could operate as important drivers of the transition toward socialism. As a critically engaged scholar, Chayanov also developed a theory on the organization and development of peasant agriculture. He considered this theory, grounded on the specificity of the peasant farm, to be in line with (if not a further unfolding of) Marxist theory. Leninists of that time (and later the followers of Stalin) considered this to be *not* the case. For them the Chayanovian approach was an expression of repudiable "populism." Today, though, its value and relevance are widely recognized, and the approach itself has been enriched, not only through research, but also, and especially, by new achievements created by peasant movements all over the world.

The Development of Productive Forces

> The land itself is of little interest to us. When we talk about land, we mean work on the land.
>
> —Chayanov, "On the Agrarian Question" (1917)

The Chayanovian approach to the agrarian question puts the question of what is done with land center stage. The organization and development of agricultural production create the framework in which the issue of land is discussed and played out. The ownership of land is secondary, only entering the analysis insofar as it favors or blocks the development of agricultural production. This does not mean that Chayanov perceived class relations in the countryside, town-countryside relations, or the role of the state as irrelevant. On the contrary, he wrote: "The first condition of the farmer's work is certainly land [and] the first step in agrarian reorganization must be land reform" (Chayanov 1917).[1] The point, though, is that the meaning, impact, and historical role of class and property relations etc., are assessed through the effects that they exert on the organization and development of agricultural production.

Within this framework, the "development of the productive forces" was the guiding principle. Not one "single *desjatína* of land" may be left uncultivated (1.0 *destajína* equals 1.09 hectare) and everything should be done to "make two ears [of grain] grow upon a spot of ground where only one grew before" (Chayanov 1917). Chayanov understood land as a source of wealth—wealth that is represented by, and embodied in, the harvests obtained. Land is the resource that, through human labor, converts seeds and solar energy into food and other agricultural products. Thus, land generates productive employment, livelihoods, and prospects for the future for the many millions of people who live and work in the countryside. Consequently, the rural economy (and, more generally, town-countryside relations) need to be structured to allow for "the fullest possible use of its means of production and work force" (Chayanov 1917).

Land also literally provided *space* to Russian peasant families to expand or reduce their productive activities according to the demographic cycle of the family. With more mouths to feed and more hands to do the job, the amount of cultivated land was expanded, while intragenerational succession sparked a return to smaller farms, which, over time, and according to the demographic cycle, were enlarged again. Thus, the stratification of the (Russian) peasantry into large, medium, and small farmers (using more or less land) was basically, at least in the Chayanovian analysis, a demographic and therefore a cyclical phenomenon. In the contrasting Leninist position the same stratification was understood as *class* differentiation (into rich, poor, and in-between farmers), assumedly an irreversible phenomenon (see Bernstein, this volume). It is to be noted that the seemingly infinite amount of land in Russia at that time, as well as the role of peasant communities (the *Mir*) in its (re)distribution were important boundary conditions that strongly conditioned the varying amounts of land being used by different peasant families.[2]

In his work, Chayanov strongly focused on *how* agricultural production was organized and developed; this orientation toward *the use of land* has subsequently been shown to be a very powerful approach—both scientifically and politically. On a scientific level, it allows us to organically interlink three analytical levels. First, the microlevel of farm and family, where the search for a satisfactory *labor income*[3] spurs the actors involved to consider their levels of input and labor use and the techniques they employ to make all kinds of improvements that, together, flow into a process of ongoing intensification (which shows up in steadily rising yields and a shift toward cropping schemes with more high-value products). Second, the mesolevel of rural communities and cooperatives, where we encounter cultural repertoires that are favorable (or not) to such (labor-driven) intensification, and which bring about (or hinder) much-needed agricultural improvements. And third, the macrolevel of society as a whole, where enough food and raw materials for further industrial processing are needed, as is a strong internal market (to a large degree consisting of the purchasing power of the many millions of people in the countryside) that will spur industrial development centered on the production of consumption goods (Akram-Lohdi and Kay 2010a, 2010b). The Chayanovian approach helps to align and integrate these three levels—at least potentially—and once such an alignment is successfully realized in practice it can generate considerable cohesion.

From a political point of view, the focus on production and the associated development of productive forces has proven to be powerful insofar as it introduces peasantries and peasant agriculture into the debates on revolution, transformation, and political struggle as progressive forces. It aligns the emancipation of the peasantry (the improvement of their living and working conditions) with broader societal needs and priorities. The current struggles for food sovereignty (in a world where far too many people still experience hunger, poverty, food scares and scarcities, lack of employment opportunities etc.) are clear expressions of the mobilizing power of an orientation on the ways in which land is *used*.

The focus on land use (and the need and possibility to significantly improve it) is complemented by two additional lines of reasoning. First, it introduces *agency*: the "will and knowledge" (Chayanov 1917)[4] of the many who work and live in the countryside. It is through the agency of peasants that agriculture is developed and food sovereignty (as we say today) can be secured. In this respect peasants come to the fore, together with others, as "builders of real life," the "social builders of today" (Chayanov 1917). By building on the design and promise entailed in peasant agriculture, rural people have the potential to be a strong driving force for a new society. By improving *land use* (i.e., the organization and development of agricultural production), peasants can simultaneously be the architects, agents, and beneficiaries of agrarian reform. Thus the Chayanovian approach not only ties these different levels together; it also aligns different roles, just as it (potentially) makes the past, present, and future flow together into one strong stream, capable of transforming society.

Second is the notion of coproduction. In Chayanov's works land definitely is not a static, or an indifferent, category (Chayanov 1924). When the land is worked, it is "reproduced," or it is not, in which case one is talking about extractivist agriculture (Ye et al. 2019) that basically plunders and destroys the land. "Reproduction of the land" means maintaining or even enhancing soil fertility (through a range of interconnected practices, including fertilizing, ploughing, edging, and multiple cropping). It also includes the construction, maintenance, and improvement of fences, access roads, terraces, infrastructure for irrigation or drainage, and so on. Land is actively improved (or not), and this is part of a strategy that is intrinsic to farming as coproduction—that is, the ongoing interaction, and mutual transformation, of man and living nature (Toledo 1990). Without such reproduction, production will, sooner or later, come to an end. And through the slow, but stubborn and persistent, improvements of land (and other resources) continuous growth and development become possible.

In practice the development of land, and the agricultural production that follows, is driven forward by the search for a labor income that meets the needs and expectations of the farming family while also reflecting the drudgery of tilling the land.[5] The search for a well-equilibrated labor income, which is far more complex than might appear at first sight (High Level Panel of Experts 2013), is central to peasant agriculture and makes for an agriculture, provided that the politico-economic space to do so exists (Halamska 2004) that is more productive (in terms of realized yields) than capitalist agriculture. (This is shown with mathematical precision, in Chayanov 1917 and [1925] 1966.)

Once Again: The Meaning of Land

The very process of working the land gives meaning to the land for those who work it, especially those who do so autonomously. The land provides them with their identity as peasants (an identity that is also often related to the *domus*, the unity of land and family (Le Roy Ladurie 1980), just as it provides them (at least partially) with the material means for existence and survival. In some conditions it is their last resort (i.e., when hunger, marginalization, or violence, or all of these, ravage the countryside); in others, it represents a promise (albeit often a meager one) for the future. People relate to each other through the land (Arensberg and Kimbal 1948; van der Ploeg, Ye, and Lu 2014); this is especially true for gender and intragenerational links. Throughout all this there is constant striving to achieve a balance between utility and drudgery. What, and how much, does the land render us?[6] And, what are the requirements for making her do so?

Utility and drudgery are far from ahistorical categories. They are socially defined and, consequently, manifest in different and sometimes contrasting ways. In an impressive study by Catherine Laurent and Jacques Remy (1998) identified eleven institutional patterns[7] that link land and the people who work it in different ways. These are (the percentages in parentheses show their presence in French agriculture at the end of the 1990s):

1. employee-run companies (1%);
2. capitalist agriculture (3%);
3. agriculture as a structural profession (20%);
4. agriculture based on a traditional farming logic (21%);
5. rural enterprises (8%);
6. non-integrated multi-activity (7%);
7. subsistence farming for retired farmers (13%);
8. qualifying for social welfare coverage/pension payments (9%);
9. agricultural production for home consumption and barter (2%);
10. luxury agriculture (4%); and
11. small-scale recreational agriculture (12%).

Each category works according to a specific set of objectives that imbue the land with a specific meaning. Land can be for rendering profits (category 2 and probably 1), a labor income (3, 4, and sometimes 1), a lifestyle (5, 10, and 11), new ways of personal unfolding (6), a complement to other sources of income (7 and partly 8), and a last resort (9 and partly 8). Formulated more generally, people's positions within the wider society strongly contribute to the concrete, time-and-space-bounded meaning attached to the land. And this concrete meaning is, of course, historically contingent.

Throughout history the land often has been, for many millions of people, a last resort. It was, and is, a means for surviving, for generating at least a bare minimum existence. It was a fallback position. For others, it was, and is, an aspiration: a desperately aspired to goal—sometimes against all odds.

In *Apostles of Inequality*, Jim Handy (2022) convincingly retells the story of enclosures, the making of the English working class and the emergence of politico-economic theories (including those of Ricardo, Smith, Malthus, and Young) that addressed dispossession, starvation, and despair as the logical consequences of market dynamics. Handy refers to the demands for, and dreams of having, a rural cottage or—at least—a cottage garden.[8] The dispossessed countered the humiliation and hopelessness they experienced with an outcry for some land—land to protect them, at least a little, from the vagaries of the untrammeled capitalism of those days. He masterfully shows how this outcry translated into social struggle, arson, and the menacing presence of the mysterious "Captain Swing."[9]

On the Enigmatic Nature of Social Reproduction

Captain Swing is long forgotten today. Nonetheless, in our contemporary world there are, once again, many millions of people for whom the land is their last resort. Globally, there are some 500 million small farms of less than 2 hectares (High Level Panel of Experts 2013), and many of them are, indeed, nothing more than a last resort: a place for obtaining, at least, the minimum required for survival. But even this last resort is permanently threatened. In this respect, it is telling that some 70% of all poor people (those living on less than the proverbial one dollar a day) live in the countryside and depend, directly or indirectly, on farming. For most of them their small farm is like a *trench* (a metaphor derived from the work of Frei Sérgio Görgen (2017), the Brazilian priest and leader of the peasant movement Movimento dos Pequenos Agricultores (Movement of Small Farmers), who wrote *Trincheiras da Resistência Camponesa* (Trenches of peasant resistance). The small farm is a (self-constructed) refuge but, at the same time, a place that allows for moving forward, inspired by the dream of developing it into a place of relative autonomy and prosperity.

The planet is at present immensely "overpopulated," at least with respect to global capitalism's need for an industrial reserve army. This "surplus" (relative to the needs of capitalism) is scattered throughout the countryside or living a marginal existence in towns, cities, and metropolises. Wherever they may be, there are people for whom global capitalism has no role. They are marginal to the dynamics of capital: dispensable as pawns, downtrodden, and mostly made invisible. They are *The Wretched of the Earth* of Franz Fanon (1995).[10] In other words, they, at least when they have maintained their rural roots, are the very people who are looking for, constructing, and taking refuge in their "trenches," their little farms. By having, working, and stubbornly defending their farms (often using remittances rendered through labor migration), they (often barely) produce and reproduce their own living.

From a theoretical perspective their existence as small farmers might be understood as being an intrinsic part of "social reproduction" (see Ben Cousins in this volume). Through their misery and poverty, they do surely contribute to keeping the wages paid in the capitalist segments of the economy to extremely low levels (just as occurred in the times described by Jim Handy). They also provide a permanent, seemingly never-ending, flow of cheap labor to factories, plantations, construction sites and to perform many urban services. They reproduce themselves on their small farms (through cheap, underpaid labor) in the same way that small farms as a whole contribute to the social reproduction of capital and capitalism.

What does this imply? Taking a merely functionalist approach, it could be argued that the existence of an extended small-farm sector is *functional* to capitalism, or parts of it, such as large-scale plantation agriculture (Boltvinik and Mann 2016). It helps to "reproduce" capitalism—it is part and parcel of its "social reproduction." This may partly be the case.[11] But in real life it is also significant whether the poor depend on terrible workhouses (see Handy 2022; Polanyi 1957) organized by the state (and meant to cower the working class into docility) or in their *own* cottages and cottage gardens.

Interestingly, cottage gardens (or vegetable gardens, as they are called today) abound throughout Europe, but their "biography" has highly divergent historical roots. Some stem from ancient times; others are rooted in the social struggles of the recent past; and yet others were created by industrial conglomerates. In the 1930s the infamous Krupp war industry built many cottages and associated gardens for its workers—they were meant to simultaneously discipline and demobilize the labor force because being fired meant losing one's house and garden.

Here, precisely, lies the decisive difference. Having *one's own* house and garden (a self-organized last resort) means, in real life, that one can better face (and eventually fight) the bosses. A house and garden that the boss provides implies the opposite. It is *relations* that matter, not the "things" as such. Thus, when it comes to social reproduction, specific questions need to be asked. What are the main institutions that secure social reproduction? Who constructed them? By whom or what are they governed? Who reaps the benefits? And what difference do they make within the framework of sociopolitical struggles?

There are many oil-producing countries in the world. Most of them harbor impoverished populations ruled in authoritarian ways by enriched elites. One of the few exceptions is Norway. It is a democratic society. Wealth is fairly equally distributed, and there are extensive welfare safety nets. Much of the oil wealth is accumulated in a huge state fund that invests in pensions and sustainability. According to Ottar Brox (2006), this deviation from the rule owes to Norway's early industrial workers being labor migrants from the countryside. Their fallback position (owning their own farms) allowed them to create strong labor unions and engage in militant social struggles—all of which contributed to Norway becoming a democratic society and having a relatively equal distribution of social wealth.

An example of "without oil" can be found in Italian history. The many sons of landless peasant families who fought in World War I (many in the terrifying war theater in the Dolomite mountains) were promised their own piece of land as "payment" for their war service. Those promises were never fulfilled, however, provoking a widespread bitterness (reflected in some of the beautiful songs of *Mistero Buffo*, the opera by Dario Fo)[12] that was, in turn, a fertile breeding ground for Mussolini's fascism—especially when the Duce started to distribute newly colonized land to rural families (Pennacchi 2010).

Having access to and being able to work the land can make a considerable difference. This applies to single families and, sometimes, to entire nations, depending on the concrete circumstances. Understanding the role and meaning of land thus requires a thorough empirical study, which must include the particularities of society and history. As Chayanov (1917) put it, very much as Marx had argued before, the analysis needs "to move from the world of abstract ideas and conflicting principles to the field of specific, organizational, economic work" (intro.). If not, any understanding of the agrarian question will remain myopic.

The Agrarian Question and Land Reform

In the Chayanovian approach land is perceived as a (potential) source of wealth. If the full potential of this resource is blocked, there evidently is an agrarian question, which needs to be remedied by agrarian reform. Chayanovians see peasant agriculture as the best possible mechanism to optimally unlock the potentials entailed in the countryside. It should be noted that Chayanov conceptualized the agrarian question in a fundamentally different way from Lenin. From the Chayanovian perspective, the agrarian question exists, and it shows up as a permanent slowdown of agrarian growth and rural development, which hinders or even completely blocks the broader development of productive forces. The agrarian question is, in other words, the underdevelopment of the rural. It is about agriculture and the countryside not being able to meet societal needs and expectations, which coincides with the suppression of peasant agriculture and the subordination of peasants. This broad conception (that is also more than valid and relevant under current conditions) differs considerably from the (narrower) Leninist definition, where the agrarian question figures as agriculture making an insufficient (or even zero) contribution to the process of capital accumulation (Lenin [1914] 1972). Associated with these contrasting views is the radically different position vis-à-vis the peasantry. From a Leninist viewpoint (and, later, in nearly all modernization theories), peasant agriculture is seen as an obstacle to progress; the main factor to be eradicated (Lenin [1899] 1964). By contrast, in the Chayanovian view it is to be nurtured as the main lever for forging progress.

The view of peasant agriculture as (potentially) highly productive has been affirmed and reaffirmed in an impressive body of literature (exemplified in, e.g., CIDA 1966; Feder 1973; Netting 1993). From a comparative point of view, peasant agriculture excels in generating the highest yields, employment levels, and levels of income per unit of land. Maybe surprisingly, it also shows the highest levels of investment per unit of land (CIDA 1966; High Level Panel of Experts 2013). Recent studies also show that peasant agriculture contributes positively to biodiversity, landscape maintenance, and a reduced use of fossil fuels and chemical inputs (see van der Ploeg and Ventura 2014). Yet such benefits are still often contested, sometimes with theoretical arguments, sometimes by referring to situations of marginalization. When peasant agriculture is blocked, it is difficult, indeed, for it to render positive outcomes.

In the Chayanovian approach, marginalized peasant agriculture represents an expression of the agrarian crisis—or as he put it, the blocking of the "fullest use of the means of production and work force." This generates the need for land reform. "The first condition of the farmer's work is certainly land; therefore, the first step of our agrarian reorganization must be land reform. All the lands of our homeland should be given to free labour. However, we frankly admit that the land reform alone cannot help our village" (Chayanov 1917). Consequently, Chayanov distanced himself from "the simple way to expropriate private property" and from "seizing private estates by following the principle of 'grab what you can.'" This approach, he argued, would "confuse and complicate the agrarian question rather than solve it." In the end a "socialization" was needed, for "according to this idea, land is a public domain . . . and not a property. It belongs equally to everyone, like light and air. The peasant labour economy is [to be] only a user of this free element" (Chayanov 1917). Therefore, the issue of land would not be resolved, once and for all, with its redistribution. During and after agrarian reform, it is necessary to ensure "that the usable land of each family does not exceed the labour standard [i.e., availability of labor]." Agrarian reform might well require moving people from densely populated areas to areas where there is a shortage of labor.

Apart from (re)distributing the land, a truly *agrarian* reform must meet three criteria (Chayanov 1917; 1988).[13] First, the productive forces need to be developed. Potential productive power needs to be unleashed and the contribution to the national income "progressively" enlarged. Second, the living and working conditions of the people who work on the land must be improved. Third, the distribution of the national income needs to be democratized. Inequalities between the town and the countryside need to be eliminated; agrarian reform should secure the "most uniform distribution [of national income] among all people contributing to its creation" (1988, 141). Here, agrarian reform clearly goes beyond the boundaries of the rural. It also implies major transitions in society as a whole. This is the clear line of demarcation between the Chayanovian approach and land reform as it has been implemented in the Western Hemisphere since World War II.

In summary: "We must facilitate work on the land, multiply its power, improve all its conditions, double and triple its productivity" (Chayanov 1988). Views like these have been repeated many times by other notable Marxists. Emilio Sereni (1979), the great Italian intellectual, peasant leader, and (communist) politician wrote about "the struggle of [rural] workers and peasants for the improvement of their livelihoods *and the progressive development of our agriculture*" (439; my translation, italics added).

In the Chayanovian approach, agrarian reform embraces a wide and ambitious program; and more so because it not only includes, from a political point of view, "a liberation from the arbitrariness of the old authorities and police surveillance, but also the free creation of the democratic state." This point of view is typically reflected in, for example, Latin America in the critique on *gamonalismo*, the social formation centered around the figure of the *gamonal*, the dictatorial landowner who was able to control nearly all public life. See for example, Jose Carlos Mariategui (1925) and Hildebrando Castro Pozo (1936).

In the Meantime: Land and Land-Use under Capitalist Conditions

Wherever a needed agrarian reform is lacking, land use is, and necessarily will be, at the heart of several main contradictions. Under capitalist conditions land is a confusing and contested issue. It is several things at the same time and these different meanings struggle, as it were, for dominance. Land is longed for by many (although they are increasingly distributed in an uneven way over the globe), as a main lever for constructing a farm, an associated livelihood, some autonomy, the prospect of improvement and emancipation, as well as contributing to the well-being of the next generation. At the same time, land is an object of speculation, a resource allowing for private wealth and accumulation, and frequently a source of considerable power. Land is "a right to life" (Chayanov 1988; see also United Nations 2019) as much as it is a commodity. It is being "grabbed" as much as it is "re-conquered" through for example, *tomas de tierra* (land occupations in Latin America). Land often shows high levels of underutilization (as in Brazil, for example) and this has provoked *campamentos* and, later, the surge of *asentamentos* and tens of thousands of new small farms (Cassel 2022).

Peasant agriculture operates within the many contradictions of capitalism. The peasantry is a noncapitalist segment of the wider capitalist economy (Chayanov [1924] 1966). Internally there is no capital-wage labor contradiction. There is no wage labor, or capital (as understood in the Marxist tradition). Peasant agriculture is subordinated to another set of contradictions that emerge at the interfaces between peasant farms, on the one hand, and the capital invested in trading, banking, food processing, the provisioning of inputs and technologies etc., on the other (see also McMichael, this volume). To grasp this contradictory constellation, Teodor Shanin (1990), who builds strongly on previous work of Chayanov, introduced the concepts of "economic logic" and "social logic." The combination of these two powerful concepts reflects the typical location of the peasantry within the wider capitalist context and is very useful in helping us unravel the heterogeneity of peasant agriculture. Whereas economic logic follows the "dull compulsion" of the markets (reflected in, among other things, the squeeze on agriculture), social logic represents a counterpoint and is able to trigger countertendencies. Social logic refers to, and is derived from, forces external to the markets. These might be the balances entailed within the farming family (e.g., the demographic balance, the balance of drudgery and utility), it might also be farmers' emancipatory aspiration to have their own farm and autonomy and the prospect of developing a "beautiful farm" where the work can be done "gently" (Zuiderwijk 1998).

The contradictions between economic logic and social logic (contradictions that evolve in many different ways) turn the peasant farm into a site of struggle (indeed, into a *trench*) where subordination to capital and opposition to it come together and enter into an ongoing struggle that sometimes seems to be dormant but which, at other moments, might explode. It is a struggle that also often divides the farming population, and some opt for incorporation into the dynamics and mechanisms of capital ("the entrepreneurial farmers" as signaled in Chayanov 1927b; see also Shanin 1990, 234–242, who builds on Nemchinov 1926), while others opt for opposition.

Such fights "from the trenches" abound in contemporary history. They were widespread in Peru before, during, and after the agrarian reform of 1969, and they basically centered around the question, "What was to be *done* with the land" (Diez Hurtado and Burneo 2022). Create more productive employment? Enlarge production beyond the boundaries imposed by capital and the state? Construct autonomy? Strengthen peasant movements? The same questions have reappeared, albeit in different circumstances and answered in different ways, in Europe over the past thirty years. Can the land be turned to meet new societal demands through (new forms of) multifunctionality? (Schneider and Niederle 2010; Oostindie 2015). Probably the most telling expression today is the worldwide drive toward agroecology (Rosset and Altieri 2017).

Rural Communities and Cultural Repertoire

It is important to note that Chayanovian theory does *not* conceptualize peasants as atomized elements. Instead, they are perceived as belonging to wider rural communities (i.e., the Russian *Mir*), which, though they may be divided into different strata, are also the social carriers of a jointly shared cultural repertoire that shapes how farming should be organized and how peasant farmers should relate to one another, their land, and their animals.

Cultural repertoire has a central place in Chayanovian analysis of peasant realities, although it is a term he would not have been familiar with. The idea is implicit in Chayanov's original works (notably, in *Theory of the Peasant Economy* (1927a)), and was made explicit later on in an extended body of literature that builds on the original work of Chayanov (see, e.g., Long 1984). The different balances identified in the *Theory of the Peasant Economy* definitely refer to the *farming family* as the main decisional center, and the categories that are used for reasoning and calculating (notions such as "drudgery," "utility," and "consumer needs") cannot be but *socially defined*. The way the relevant markets are read and translated into an organizational plan (with, and through, notions such as "labor income" or "net product") and local town-countryside relations (as reflected in the multifunctionality of farms—that is, in trading, processing, weaving, and other forms of handicraft) equally refer to cultural repertoire. Peasants' modus operandi is by no means determined by prevailing commodity prices, as economists would have us believe. This is reflected in the statement that "there are millions of economic agents with their own skills and ideas about agriculture, who will not obey any orders; [instead] they will do everything on their own and according to their own understanding" (Chayanov 1917). *Local* parameters (the family, the region, local scarcity, and kinship relations) equally impact on farming and clearly condition the way in which peasants read, interpret, and translate market signals into actions that the economist understands as guided solely by "economic logic."[14]

Local cultural repertoires (or the "moral economy" as James Scott 1976, calls it) entail, and offer peasant families, the concepts to be used in their economic reasoning. "Labour income" (or net product as it also is called in Chayanovian writings) guides and governs the "reading of the market." It can be equated to a strategic folk concept encountered in many peasant societies: "the clean part" (Slicher van Bath 1956; Zhao and van der Ploeg 2014). This, basically, is the difference between the amount of money coming in and the amount going out. This rubric is used to monitor and control the commodity relations in which the farm is embedded and, particularly, to keep monetary expenditure at a low level (thus generating and reproducing a style of farming economically, i.e., a low external input agriculture, as specified in Reijntjes, Haverkort, and Waters-Bayer 1992).

Cultural repertoire is not just subjective, nor is it an individual attribute. It is jointly shared by larger groups of, in this case, agricultural producers. It is what ties them together. It allows for communication and the sharing of experiences. It ties collective (and historically delivered) knowledge and practical experience together, just as it offers a framework for assessing the value of novel experiences and insights. It is what Jean-Pierre Darré (1984) conceptualized many decades later as *un groupement professionel local*, "a group of local professionals": it shapes and reproduces agricultural practices, just as it helps to modify them. In short, *cultural repertoire co-defines how the land is worked*. The unity of cultural repertoire and work implies that working the land is very much value laden. Consequently, the values central to the rural community are conferred to, and embodied in, the land itself. In this respect Julio Valladolid Rivera (1998), a gifted Peruvian agronomist tellingly talks of *nurturing*: "The nurturing of the *chacra* [the field] is the heart of Andean culture which, if not the only activity carried out by the peasants, is the one around which all aspects of life revolve" (51). If well-nurtured, the *chacra* in turn renders those who are working it a range of benefits (in a way this very much reflects the balance of drudgery[15] and utility). The relation between the two, between man and land, is reciprocal. As the more profane Chinese peasants say: "[If you work hard], the land will not be lazy" (Arkush 1984),[16] just as, in the Andean mountains, "Mother Earth might be generous," and "peasants will feel joy and gratitude [as well as] profound feelings of affection and respect" (Vallodolid Rivera 1998, 51). Exotic as this may appear to some readers today, we should not forget that, until recently, similar relations existed in European agriculture (Mendras 1970). Neither should we neglect serious endeavors to rethink farming and ground it again in a "cosmo-vision" that looks for a well-equilibrated balance between men and living nature (Haverkort and Reijntjes 2010; Toledo and Barrera-Bassols 2008; Barkin, forthcoming; Wright 2021).

With cultural repertoire, the rural community enters the scene as well—and like local culture it takes a central position in the theater where farming takes place. The rural community is not just the carrier of cultural repertoire (each defining the other), it also specifies the rules that govern access to, and use of, the land. Thus, the community strongly influences *how the land is worked.*

Acknowledgments

I am grateful to Ye Jingzhong, Sergio Schneider, Jun Borras, and Jenny Franco for their stimulating comments. I thank Nick Parrott for having corrected my use of the English language.

Notes

1. Apart from the Russian text written and published in 1917, only an Italian translation by Fiorenzo Sperotto (Chayanov 1988) is available. The Russian text has recently been translated into English and will be published by Practical Action Books. See Chayanov (forthcoming) in References. Unless otherwise noted, the English translations in the chapter are from this work (of which I have seen an advance copy)—as yet it is not possible to offer page numbers.
2. As Chayanov himself indicated, this was in strong contrast with the situation in, for example, Western Europe of that time. Here, facing a scarcity of land, the demographic cycle spurred an intensification of land use.
3. Labor income is a key concept in the Chayanovian tradition. This is calculated as the sum of the value of production (marketed and/or partly consumed in the family) minus any monetary costs incurred.
4. Throughout his different texts Chayanov also refers to the "resistance" of peasants and their "understandings and desires."

5. Agricultural production is taken to the point where utility (i.e., meeting needs and expectations) and drudgery meet. The balance of the two is one of the mechanisms that govern agricultural production at the microlevel. This is extensively explained in Chayanov ([1925] 1966).
6. Not only in terms of gross production, but equally in terms of employment, income, food, livelihood, quality of labor, autonomy, pride etc.
7. In a historical perspective we should probably follow Andrew Pearse (1975), who wrote about "land-labour institutions." Laurent and Remy use a slightly different wording: "land-based activity systems" (note that the term "activity" again refers to what is done with the land). In another contribution Laurent et al. (1998) showed that the (relative) presence of these categories has varied throughout recent history.
8. Such demands represented the mirror side of the enclosures. The latter showed up, according to Arthur Young, as "an open war against cottages" (quoted in Handy 2022, 42).
9. Social struggles at that time (acted out in setting farms ablaze and destroying labor-replacing machinery) were said to have been organized by "Captain Swing." Such mythical constructs abound in many episodes of peasant (and industrial) struggle and warfare.
10. Some 150 years before, Belfast newspapers (those aligned with the British) had described starving Irish peasants as "wretched idiots" (see Handy 2022, 174–175).
11. Although one may wonder how the presence of large masses of impoverished peasants in, say, Latin America helps to reproduce the industrial and service sectors that mainly, or exclusively, rely on a highly educated and well-trained labor force.
12. With lyrics that include, among others, "but the bosses for whose money I was fighting did not give me anything when I asked for it."
13. For this section I used the Italian translation (*Che cos'è la questione agraria*) of the original Russian language manuscript from 1917 (*Čto takoe agrarnij vopros*). The Italian translation is included in Sperotto (1988).
14. In fact, economists often talk about "maximizing utility," which is what peasants try to do, except that their perception of "utility" is more broadly defined and socially contextualized than that of an economist.
15. The notion of drudgery is also nicely reflected in the title of van den Berg (1990): *La tierra no da así nomás* (The land will not give anything for nothing).
16. The saying literally goes as follows: "If man [*sic*] works hard, etc." However, it is evident that "man" here refers to both women and men (see, e.g., Meng 2014).

References

Akram-Lodhi, A. Haroon, and Cristóbal Kay. 2010a. "Surveying the Agrarian Question (Part 1): Unearthing Foundations, Exploring Diversity." *Journal of Peasant Studies* 37 (1): 177–202.

Akram-Lodhi, A. Haroon, and Cristóbal Kay. 2010b. "Surveying the Agrarian Question (Part 2): Current Debates and Beyond." *Journal of Peasant Studies* 37 (2): 255–284. https://doi.org/10.1080/03066151003594906.

Arensberg, C. M., and S. T. Kimball. 1948. *Family and Community in Ireland*. 2nd ed. Cambridge, MA: Harvard University Press.

Arkush, D. 1984. "If Man Works Hard the Land Will Not Be Lazy: Entrepreneurial Values in North Chinese Peasant Proverbs." *Modern China* 10 (4): 461–479.

Barkin, David. Forthcoming. *Porque Economía Ecológica Radical?* Mexico City: n.p.

Berg, Hans van den. 1990. *La Tierra no da asi Nomas: Los ritos agricolas en la religion de los Aymara-Cristianos*. La Paz: Instituto de Historia Social Boliviana.
Boltvinik, J., and S. A. Mann. 2016. *Peasant Poverty and Persistence in the Twenty-First Century: Theories, Debates, Realities and Policies*. London: Zed Books.
Brox, Ottar. 2006. *The Political Economy of Rural Development: Modernisation without* Centralization? Edited by and introduced by John Bryden and R. Storey. Delft, Netherlands: Eburon.
Cassel, Guilherme. 2022. "Family Agriculture and Rural Development in Brazil (2003–2010)." In *Rural Vitalization: Comparative Analysis of Rural Development Policies in Different Countries*, edited by Ye Jingzhong, Wu Huifang, and Jan Douwe van der Ploeg, 23–46. Beijing: Social Sciences Academic Press.
Castro Pozo, Hildebrando. (1936) 1973. *Del Ayllu al Cooperativismo Socialista*. Lima: PEISA.
Chayanov, Alexander V. 1917. *What Is the Agrarian Question?* [in Russian]. Moscow: Joint-Stock Company Universal Library. Published in Italian by Franco Angeli in Chayanov 1988; to be published in English as "On the Agrarian Question," in Chayanov (forthcoming).
Chayanov, Alexander V. 1924. *Die Sozial Agronomie, ihre Grundgedanken und ihre Arbeitsmetoden*. Berlin: Verlagsbuchhandlung Paul Parey.
Chayanov, Alexander V. (1924) 1966. "On the Theory of Non-capitalist Economic Systems." In *The Theory of Peasant Economy*, by A. V. Chayanov, edited by Daniel Thorner, Basile Kerblay, and R. E. F. Smith, 1–28. Manchester, UK: Manchester University Press.
Chayanov, Alexander V. (1925) 1966. *The Theory of Peasant Economy*. Edited by Daniel Thorner, Basile Kerblay, and R. E. F. Smith. Manchester, UK: Manchester University Press.
Chayanov, Alexander V. (1927a) 1991. *The Theory of Peasant Co-operatives*. Columbus: Ohio State University Press.
Chayanov, Alexander V. (1927b) Forthcoming. "Letter to V. M. Molotov on the Current State of Agriculture in the USSR Compared with Its Pre-War State and the Situation of Agriculture of Capitalist Countries." In *Peasants: Chayanov's Recovered Essays* by A. V. Chayanov. Halifax, CAN: Fernwood Publishing.
Chayanov, Alexander V. (Čajanov, Aleksandr Vasil'evč). 1988. *L'economia di Lavoro: Scritti Scelti*. A Cura di Fiorenzo Sperotto. Istituto nazionale di sociologia rurale 19. Milan: Franco Angeli.
Chayanov, Alexander V. Forthcoming. *Peasants: Chayanov's Recovered Essays*. Halifax, CAN: Fernwood Publishing.
CIDA (Comite Interamericano de Desarrollo Agricola). 1966. *Tenencia de la Tierra y Desarrollo Socio-Economico del Sector Agricola: Peru*. Washington, DC: Unión Panamericana.
Darré, Jean-Pierre. 1984. "La production des normes au sein d'un réseau professionnel. L'exemple d'un groupe d'éleveurs." *Sociologie du Travail* 26 (2): 141–156.
Diez Hurtado, Alejandro, and Maria Luisa Burneo, eds. 2022. *Nuevas Miradas sobre la Reforma Agraria Peruana*. Lima: Cisepa-PUCP.
Fanon, Frantz. 1995. *The Wretched of the Earth*. London: Penguin Books.
Feder, Ernest. 1973. "Bodennützung und Betriebsführung in einder Latifundio-landwirtschaft." In *Gewalt un Ausbeutung: Lateinamerikas landwirtschaft*, edited by Ernest Feder, 185–208. Hamburg: Hoffmann und Campe Verlag.
Görgen, Frei Sergio A. 2017. *Trincheiras da Resistência Camponesa: Sob o pacto de poder do agronegócio*. Candiota, Brazil: Instituto Cultural Padre Josimo.
Halamska, Maria. 2004. "A Different End of the Peasants." *Polish Sociological Review* 3 (147): 205–268.

Handy, Jim. 2022. *Apostles of Inequality*. Halifax, CAN: Fernwood Publishing.

Haverkort, Bertus, and Coen Reijntjes. 2010. "Diversities of Knowledge Communities, Their Worldviews and Sciences: On the Challenges of Their Co-evolution." In *Traditional Knowledge in Policy and Practice: Approaches to Development and Human Well-Being*, edited by Suneetha M. Subramanian and Balakrishna Pisupati, 12–30. Tokyo: United Nations University Press.

High Level Panel of Experts. 2013. *Investing in Smallholder Agriculture for Food Security: A Report by the High Level Panel of Experts on Food Security and Nutrition of the Committee on World Food Security*. HLPE Report 6, June. Rome: Food and Agriculture Organization of the United Nations.

Laurent, Catherine, and Jacques Remy. 1998. "Agricultural Holdings: Hindsight and Foresight." *Etudes et Recherches des Systemes Agraires et Developpement* 31: 415–430.

Laurent, Catherine, S. Cartier, C. Fabre, P. Mundler, D. Ponchelet, and Jacques Remy. 1998. "L'activité agricole des ménages ruraux et la cohesion économique et sociale." *Économie Rurale* 224: 12–21.

Lenin, Vladimir I. (1914) 1972. "The Agrarian Question in Russia," In *Collected Works*, vol. 20, 375–377. Moscow: Progress Publishers.

Lenin, Vladimir I. (1899) 1964. "The Development of Capitalism in Russia," 4th ed., *Collected Works*, vol. 3. Moscow: Progress Publishers.

Le Roy Ladurie, Emmanuel. 1980. *Montaillou: Cathars and Catholics in a French* Village, *1294–1324*. Harmondsworth, UK: Penguin.

Long, Norman. 1984. *Family and Work in Rural Societies: Perspectives on Non-wage Labour*. London: Tavistock.

Mariátegui, José Carlos. 1925. *Siete Ensayos de Interpretación de la Realidad Peruana*. Amauta, Lima.

Mendras, Henri. 1970. *The Vanishing Peasant: Innovation and Change in French Agriculture*. Cambridge, UK: Cambridge University Press.

Meng, Xiangdan. 2014. "Feminization of Agricultural Production in Rural China: A Socio-economic Analysis." PhD thesis, Wageningen University.

Nemchinov, V. S. 1926. *Izbrannye Proizvedeniya*. Vol. 1. Moscow.

Netting, R. Mc. 1993. *Smallholders, Householders: Farm Families and the Ecology of Intensive, Sustainable Agriculture*. Stanford, CA: Stanford University Press.

Oostindie, Henk. 2015. "Family Farming Futures: Agrarian Pathways to Multifunctionality: Flows of Resistance, Redesign and Resilience." PhD thesis, Wageningen University.

Pearse, Andrew. 1975. *The Latin American Peasant*. London: Frank Cass.

Pennacchi, Antonio. 2010. *Canale Mussolini*. Milano: Mondadori.

Polanyi, Karl. 1957. *The Great Transformation: The Political and Economic Origins of Our Time*. Boston: Beacon Press.

Reijntjes, Coen, Bertus Haverkort, and Ann Waters-Bayer. 1992. *Farming for the Future: An Introduction to Low-External-Input and Sustainable Agriculture*. London and Leusden, Netherlands: Macmillan and ILEIA.

Rosset, Peter M., and Miguel A. Altieri. 2017. *Agroecology: Science and Politics*. Agrarian Change and Peasant Studies Series 7. Halifax, CAN: Fernwood Publishing.

Schneider, Sergio, and Paulo A. Niederle. 2010. "Resistance Strategies and Diversification of Rural Livelihoods: The Construction of Autonomy among Brazilian Family Farmers." *Journal of Peasant Studies* 37 (2): 379–405.

Scott, James. 1976. *The Moral Economy of the Peasant*. New Haven, CT: Yale University Press.

Sereni, Emilio. 1979. *Storia del Paesaggio Agraria Italiano*. Rome: Editore Laterza.

Shanin, Teodor. 1990. *Defining Peasants, Essays concerning Rural Societies, Expolary Economies, and Learning from Them in the Contemporary World*. Oxford: Basil Blackwell.

Slicher van Bath, Bernard H. 1956. "Een Fries landbouwbedrijf in de tweede helft van de zestiende eeuw." In *Agronomisch-Historische Bijdragen* 4, 11–180. Wageningen, Netherlands: Veenman en Zonen.

Sperotto, Fiorenzo. 1988. *L'economia di lavoro, scritti scelti*. Milan: Franco Angeli/INSOR.

Toledo, Victor M. 1990. "The Ecological Rationality of Peasant Production." In *Agroecology and Small Farm Development*, edited by Miguel Altieri and S. Hecht, 53–60. Ann Arbor, MI: CRC Press. Published Spanish in 1992 as "La racionalidad ecologica de la produccion campesina." In *Campesinado e Historia*, edited by E. Sevilla Guzman and M. Gonzalez de Molina, 197–218. Madrid, Spain: La Piqueta.

Toledo, Victor M., and N. Barrera-Bassols. 2008. *La Memoria Biocultural: La importancia ecológica de las sabidurías tradicionales*. Barcelona: Icaria Editorial.

United Nations. 2019. United Nations Declaration on the Rights of Peasants and Other People Working in Rural Areas. Resolution adopted by the General Assembly on 17 December 17, 2018. United Nations. New York.

Valladolid Rivera, Julio. 1998. "Andean Peasant Agriculture: Nurturing a Diversity of Life in the *Chacra*." In *The Spirit of Regeneration: Andean Culture Confronting Western Notions of Development*, edited by F. Apfel-Marglin and PRATEC, 51–80. London: Zed Books.

van der Ploeg, Jan Douwe, Ye Jingzhong, and Pan Lu. 2014. "Peasants, Time and the Land: The Social Organization of Farming in China." *Journal of Rural Studies* 36: 172–181.

van der Ploeg, Jan Douwe, and Flaminia Ventura. 2014. "Heterogeneity Reconsidered." "Sustainability Governance and Transformation." Special Issue, *Current Opinion in Environmental Sustainability* 8: 23–28. http://dx.doi.org/10.1016/j.cosust.2014.07.001.

Wright, Julia, ed. 2021. *Subtle Agroecologies: Farming with the Hidden Half of Nature*. Routledge Kegan Paul.

Ye Jingzhong, Jan Douwe van der Ploeg, Sergio Schneider, and Teodor Shanin. 2019. "The Incursions of Extractivism: Moving from Dispersed Places to Global Capitalism." *Journal of Peasant Studies* 47 (1): 155–183.

Zhao, Yong, and Jan Douwe van der Ploeg. 2014. "Telling Data: The Accountancy Record of a Chinese Farmer." *NJAS (Wageningen Journal of Life Sciences)* 6: 21–28.

Zuiderwijk, Adri. 1998. "Farming Gently, Farming Fast: Migration, Incorporation and Agricultural Change in the Mandara Mountains of Northern Cameroon." PhD thesis, Centrum voor Milieustudies, Rijksuniversiteit, Leiden.

CHAPTER 6

LAND AND ECOSOCIALISM

In Defense of the Commons

HANNAH HOLLEMAN

Introduction

At the heart of ecosocialist perspectives and struggles with respect to land is a deep theoretical and practical engagement with the historic necessity of healing the ecological and social rifts that have been generated throughout the long history of capitalist-colonial development and beyond. A commitment to historical materialist analyses distinguishes the ecosocialist approaches to this project. Therefore, questions of land are treated, not in terms of abstract ethics or principles, but in terms of real struggles for a world of substantive equality and sustainable ecology, against the patriarchal capitalist-imperialist juggernaut that is threatening much of life on the planet.

This chapter begins with a brief introduction to ecosocialism before tracing the roots of contemporary ecosocialist thinking about the land back to the rich classical formulations articulated by Karl Marx and others who followed. Marx and other early socialists saw the ongoing expropriation of land and the enclosure of the commons as defining the reorganization of global agriculture and society and as a precondition and persistent requirement of capitalism's system of exploitation. Like ecosocialists today, they were often inspired by, and saw their work as extending for a new era, the revolts of populations all over the world in defense of their "natural economies." The remnants of communal forms in Europe, Asia, Africa, the Americas, and Australia, together with the resistance to capitalism and colonialism that they engendered, represented for early socialists like Marx, Frederick Engels, and Rosa Luxemburg genuine human-material needs, pointing in the end not to the past but to the future in the higher society of socialism (Foster, Clark, and Holleman 2021).

The emancipatory potential of ecosocialism today, as I discuss in the final sections of the chapter, lies in the recognition—already present in early socialist thought and movements—that the struggles against the expropriation of land, labor, and corporeal life and those against the exploitation of rural and urban labor are inherently interconnected and must be seen as equally integral to the movement for a better world. Recognizing these interconnections is itself a challenge under capitalism, for many reasons, including for the Left. However, building a praxis based on this recognition is the real and urgent necessity for us all.

Therefore, instead of providing a genealogy of ecosocialist approaches to land over time, I draw explicit connections between classical articulations of ecosocialism and the movements of our era that reveal a living tradition and path forward, in theory and practice, for a world that is in crisis. I focus on intersectional ecosocialist perspectives with respect to the land, wherein links between diverse struggles are forged and recognized as a basis for the broad socioecological solidarity we need to work toward a society "in which the free development of each is the condition for the free development of all," and wherein we may "govern the human metabolism with nature in a rational way' " (Marx and Engels [1872] 1978, 49; Marx [1894] 1991, 959). Such organized efforts to put theory into practice on the land and to practically inform new theoretical development represent the forward movement of ecosocialism today.

What Is Ecosocialism?

The traditions informing ecosocialist thought are quite varied, extending far back in time and spanning diverse cultures and contexts around the world. However, the contemporary emergence of ecosocialism as a distinct perspective can be traced to the 1960s. In the context of the global revolts of that period was the beginning of a process of recovering and elaborating upon "the ecological aspects of socialism that had been buried in much of the institutional Left" (Brownhill et al. 2022, 3).

The first known pamphlet dedicated to defining ecosocialism was published in 1980 by the Writers and Readers Cooperative in London, at the commission of members of the Socialist Environment and Resource Association (SERA), founded in 1973 (Angus 2013; SERA, n.d.). As expressed in this pamphlet, the goal of ecosocialism was to forge an environmental socialism and a working-class, socialist environmentalism focused on democratizing, socializing, greening, and planning production to meet social needs. This was an important response to the disempowering emphasis on consumption by middle-class environmentalists in wealthier countries, as well as to the "jobs versus the environment" trope that was undermining movement solidarity, especially in rural extractive areas (Foster 1993). It was also an important response to the anti-ecological and anti-democratic betrayals of socialism in countries like the USSR, where pathbreaking contributions to ecological and social thought, produced in the cauldron of revolution, were repressed.

Among other concerns, the pamphlet's authors emphasized the need for socially useful, safe, and ecological technology and infrastructure, and to stop the destruction of farmland by agribusiness. However, the pamphlet was clear that the final goal wasn't simply alternative production and a democratically planned economy, but that these were preconditions for broader social change. The struggle they envisioned was a coordinated democratic movement that would, following Marx, "humanise nature and naturise humans." Against the goal of economic growth, achieved at great ecological and social cost, that funnels outsized benefits to the already affluent, SERA activists emphasized "selective growth" to meet human needs. The goal was a "pragmatic, ecology-conscious, anti-imperialist socialist society fully confident in its technological capacity but not obsessed with advanced technology" (Croall and Sempler [1980] 2013). Many elements of this perspective are carried forward in ecosocialist and broader green-left politics today.

Since this articulation of ecosocialism as a distinct perspective—which emerged from activists at the nexus of the labor, socialist, ecology, antiwar, and antinuclear movements in the United Kingdom—ecosocialism has, over several decades, broadened, deepened, and been reformulated globally from the ground up. Importantly, urban ecosocialists, especially from the North, have been challenged to recognize ecosocialism's deeper roots in anticolonial and anticapitalist Indigenous and peasant struggles, and in the historic struggles for freedom and in defense of the commons that go back millennia. As ecosocialist Hugo Blanco (2009) emphasized, ecosocialism is only new for the urban population. Indigenous people of Latin America, for example, have "been struggling for 5 centuries for ecosocialist principles"—namely, for collectivism (another word for socialism) and for love of Mother Earth/Nature (another expression for ecology).

Today, ecosocialism has developed with the input of many tributaries. Reflecting this, a group of ecosocialist collaborators recently defined ecosocialism for our era as

> a movement, a perspective, a practice, and in some cases an institutional politics that gathers together socialist and ecological principles and objectives. It is socialist in the sense of identifying capitalist relations as the ultimate and systemic cause of structural inequalities and environmental destruction. Politically, this means struggling for social equality by establishing social control over the means of life and ending all forms of exploitation of nature, which includes people. This struggle embraces decolonization and cross generational justice as well as overcoming the gendered and racialized class hierarchies that capitalism depends on for the exploitation of the unwaged majority of the world's people, notably women. It means developing respect for differing knowledge systems, striving to combine them to the benefit of all. Ecosocialism is environmentalist in calling attention to the biophysically destructive character of currently conventional power relations and their imposed ways of living. Ecosocialism premises the understanding of biophysical processes on diverse forms of systematic knowledge and inquiry, institutional and otherwise. Ecosocialism, in other words, stands for the development of ecologically sane egalitarian communities worldwide.
>
> (Brownhill et al. 2022, 3)

Because ecosocialists today are concerned with the systemic transformation of society and ecological restoration but positioned differently in the world system and embedded in diverse communities, politics, and cultural and local economic contexts, they are engaged in political projects that take a variety of forms and emphasize different immediate priorities. However, there is a broad understanding across ecosocialist traditions that capitalism systematically undermines the ecological basis of all life on earth, including human life, by subordinating use-values—including real social and ecological reproductive needs—to exchange values in the service of capital accumulation (Kovel and Löwy 2001; Foster and Clark 2009; Bellofiore 2018; Satgar 2018; Satgar 2022). And that the expropriation of land and the violent enclosure of the commons are both necessary preconditions and an ongoing requirement of this imperialistic process, and at the core of the existential socioecological crises we face today.

Several contemporary modes of thought see these conditions as inevitable or natural—the result of human nature and/or supposedly natural hierarchies—or mere externalities to internalize within an otherwise desirable or, at least, unbeatable system. However, ecosocialists take an historical materialist approach. This means understanding the specificity of current developments and the possibility, necessity, and, indeed, the reality—as reflected in the longer history of human development and struggle—of socioecological relations and systems of provisioning geared toward use-values and based on reciprocity instead of expropriation, justice and liberation instead of oppression; the democratic distribution of power and decision-making throughout society; common enrichment instead of private riches for a few; and creative, intergenerational caretaking of one another and the land. The work of Marx has been of particular importance in contemporary ecosocialist conceptions that center land in broader visions of social change, past, present, and future. And it is his foundational work that we turn to next.

In Defense of the Commons: Marx and Classical Ecosocialism

Among Marx's prodigious contribution to our understanding of the transformation, across time and space, of the human relationship to the land and the rest of nature, I emphasize only a subsection here that informs both ecosocialist understandings of the goals of socialism and critiques of the existing social order.

Marx's significant insights about land and the human relation to it, emerge in part as a consequence of his early development of an ontology that positioned humans as nothing, if not part of nature. One of the only universal, transhistorical realities of the human condition, as he succinctly put it, is that "man *lives* from nature, i.e., nature is his *body*, and he must maintain a continuing dialogue with it if he is not to die. To say that man's physical and mental life is linked to nature simply means that nature is linked to itself, for man is a part of nature" (Marx 1974a, 328; Foster 1999, 381).

Central to this dialogue is the labor process, which is "first of all, a process between man and nature, a process by which man, through his own actions, mediates, regulates and controls the metabolism between himself and nature" (Marx [1867] 1990, 283). It is through our labor that we transform nature for our sustenance and desires. Therefore, labor "as the creator of use-values, as useful labor, is a condition of human existence which is independent of all forms of society; it is an eternal and natural necessity which mediates the metabolism between man and nature, and therefore human life itself" (Marx [1867] 1990, 133).

Every society develops its own social metabolism, its own way of organizing labor and production and, therefore, of interacting with the rest of nature. How it manages this interaction reflects the broader social relations and, in turn, shapes them (Mészáros 2000). Marx understood that the human relationship to the land was central to this process, and that therefore studying changes to this relationship under different social orders was the key to understanding whether a society, in ecological and social terms, is sustainable, healthy, and just—whether humans and the rest of nature might flourish under its social order, or perish.

Marx was raised in Prussia/Germany at a time when vestiges of communal or indeterminate property relations remained. Although access to the commons was critical to the survival of many people, the poor, especially, were increasingly criminalized as thieves when, for example, they were found gathering firewood or berries, or fishing and hunting for sustenance (Marx 1842; Linebaugh 2014; Foster, Clark, and Holleman 2021). As a young man he was outraged by the criminalization of poverty; the denial of the very right to existence implied by the enclosure of the commons and the privatization of land. The real theft, as he saw it, was in the usurpation of the commons for the benefit of a few, at the expense of the many (Marx 1842). He came to understand that capitalism was predicated on the destruction of the "natural economy"—or noncommodity and communal systems of provisioning—via the expropriation (or appropriation without reciprocity) of the very basis of life itself (Foster and Clark 2018).

Marx did not romanticize communal systems, and indeed, he was critical of them, especially where patriarchal or other nonegalitarian, oppressive social relations prevailed (Anderson 2016; Foster, Clark, and Holleman 2021). However, he saw the communal control of land, the labor process, and production as an essential precondition for the development of a society in which humans and the broader natural world of which we are a part would not only survive but thrive freely for generations to come.

At odds with these priorities, bourgeois property relations, enforced by the capitalist state, allow for the exclusion of entire sections of society "from the very earth itself as their habitat" and the extreme degradation and despoliation of the land in the pursuit of profit. As capitalism advances, Marx ([1894] 1991) wrote, "One section of society here demands a tribute from the other for the very right to live on earth, just as landed property in general involves the right of the proprietors to exploit the earth's surface, the bowels of the earth, the air and thereby the maintenance and development of life" (908–909). He determined that

> from the standpoint of a higher socioeconomic formation, the private property of individuals in the earth will appear just as absurd as the private property of one man in other men. Even an entire society, or all simultaneously existing societies, taken together, are not the owners of the earth. They are simply its possessors, its beneficiaries, and have to bequeath it in an improved state to succeeding generations as boni patres familias [good heads of household]. (911)

This was not simply a moral statement; it was based on Marx's intensive investigations into the origins, ongoing requirements, and consequences of capitalist development, wherein the brutal commodification of life itself was predicated on the violent expropriation of land, labor, and bodies around the world. He documented, perhaps more fully than anyone in his time, how the enclosure of the commons and the privatization and commodification of land went hand in hand with the commodification of people in the slave trade; the brutal exploitation of landless peasant populations turned into workers and forced to labor under inhumane conditions; the creation of unfavorable economic conditions for the peasants who remained on the land; murder and genocide, especially in the capitalist-colonial quest for land and the development of plantation agriculture and other extractive pursuits; a reinscription of the patriarchal family and gendered labor; and the despoliation of the land.

The political economists and elites of Marx's era (like those of ours) attempted to naturalize colonialism, slavery, enclosure/private property, patriarchy, and the concentration of wealth at the top of society. Marx decried their use of distorted concepts of human nature and every form of prejudice—racism, classism, misogyny, nationalism, and xenophobia—as well as religion, to justify a whole host of deplorable antisocial and anti-ecological practices. He also exposed the myth of what he called "so-called primary accumulation," which was deployed to suggest that the source of the concentration of capital and ownership in the leading capitalist nations was the outcome of hard work and savings. Wealth and power, in this fairy tale, were the inherent rights of the possessors of capital and the owners, of both land and the other means of production, such as the factories.

Through an extraordinary commitment to historical research across multiple languages, and by learning from the movements and revolts of his period and earlier, Marx showed that there was nothing less natural than this state of affairs. Rather, "the expropriation of the direct producers was accomplished by the means of the most merciless barbarism, and under the stimulus of the most infamous, the most sordid, the most petty and the most odious of passions" (Marx [1867] 1990, 928).

In England and Europe, "the expropriation of the agricultural producer, of the peasant, from the soil is the basis of the whole process," though "the history of expropriation assumes different aspects in different countries, and runs through its various phases in different orders of succession, and at different historical epochs" (Marx [1867] 1990, 876). Indeed, the modern worker was a consequence of this process: "The immediate producer, the worker, could dispose of his own person only after he had ceased to be bound to the soil" (875).

Alongside dispossession and the creation of the landless working (or jobless) poor in Europe, colonialism "was the 'strange God' who perched himself side by side with the old deities of Europe on the altar, and one fine day threw them all overboard with a shove and a kick. It proclaimed the making of profit as the ultimate and sole purpose of mankind" (Marx [1867] 1990, 918). As Marx wrote, "The discovery of gold and silver in America, the extirpation, enslavement and entombment in mines of the Indigenous population of that continent, the beginnings of the conquest and plunder of India, and the conversion of Africa into a preserve for the commercial hunting of blackskins, are all things that characterize the dawn of the era of capitalist production. These idyllic proceedings are the chief moments of primitive accumulation" (915).

Capitalist agriculture—or agriculture reoriented to facilitate the accumulation of capital—which reflected all of these pathologies, was bound up with industrial development. So, for example, "the cotton industry introduced child-slavery into England" in the manufactures, where they were seen to have nimble fingers, and in the "United States it gave the impulse for the transformation of the earlier, more patriarchal forms of slavery into a system of commercial exploitation" (Marx [1867] 1990, 925). In the most industrialized capitalist agriculture of his era, Marx saw that the concentration of land ownership, the increasingly large scale and industrialization of operations, and the application of science and industrial technique had numerous critical consequences, including the following.

First, it was based on "large landed property," which "reduces the agricultural population to an ever decreasing minimum and confronts it with an ever growing industrial population crammed together in large towns," thus driving urbanization and landlessness (Marx [1894] 1991, 949). Industrial capitalist agriculture then, "annihilates the bulwark of the old society, the 'peasant,' and substitutes for him the wage-labourer" (Marx [1867] 1990, 637).

Second, it destroys traditional methods of cultivation so that "in agriculture, as in manufacture . . . the process of production also appears as a martyrology for the producer; the instrument of labour appears as a means of enslaving, exploiting, and impoverishing the worker; the social combination of labour processes appears as an organized suppression of his individual vitality, freedom, and autonomy" (Marx [1867] 1990, 638).

Finally, ecologically, the removal of the rural population, urbanization, and industrial methods of cultivation to produce goods for sale on the increasingly international market created "conditions that provoke an irreparable rift in the interdependent process of social metabolism, a metabolism prescribed by the very laws of life itself. The result of this is the squandering of the vitality of the soil, which is carried by trade far beyond the bounds of a single country" (Marx [1894] 1991, 949). Whereas before, the wastes of the peasant producers were recycled back into the land, creating the conditions for long-term soil fertility, now the wastes were concentrated in urban areas, to where food and fiber were shipped—and where sanitation was criminally neglected by the elites in power—creating stench, disease, and death. The loss of the natural fertility of the soil also stimulated further colonial catastrophes as the capitalist powers scoured the globe, went to war, and enslaved new populations in their quest to find alternative fertilizers to address a growing crisis of soil exhaustion (Marx [1867] 1990, 38; Foster 1999; Angus 2018). The guano trade and wars illustrate the horror of this process (Foster and Clark 2009).

Marx wrote then:

> In modern agriculture, as in urban industry, the increase in productivity and mobility of labour is purchased at the cost of laying waste and debilitating labour-power itself. Moreover, all progress in capitalist agriculture is a progress in the art, not only of robbing the worker, but of robbing the soil; all progress in increasing fertility of the soil for a given time is a progress towards ruining the more long-lasting the sources of that fertility. The more a country proceeds from large-scale industry as the background of its development, as in the case of the United States, the more rapid is the process of destruction. Capitalist production, therefore, only develops the techniques and the degree of combination of the social process of production by simultaneously undermining the original sources of all wealth—the soil and the worker.
>
> (Marx [1867] 1990, 638)

Capitalist agriculture, "by destroying the circumstances surrounding that metabolism, which originated in a merely natural and spontaneous fashion . . . compels its systematic restoration as a regulative law of social production, and in a form adequate to the full development of the human race" (Marx [1867] 1990, 638).

Marx's [1894] 1991) analyses of capitalist-colonial developments progressed alongside his investigation into a wide variety of other social and economic systems, which he saw as pointing toward future possibilities for "a conscious and rational treatment of the land as permanent communal property, as the inalienable condition for the existence and reproduction of the chain of human generations" (948–949). In particular, his "studies into communal property led him far beyond the European past (and present) to investigations of societies in pre-Columbian America, Asia, Africa, and Australia" (Foster, Clark, and Holleman 2021, 16–17). Much of this work is found in his *Ethnological Notebooks* and letters to Vera Zasulich (Shanin 1983; Marx 1974).

Altogether, Marx's analysis led him over time to adopt a revolutionary, anticolonial, abolitionist, antipatriarchal, and open-ended politics. While he saw in the urban working classes in Europe a concentrated, "historical motive power of society" against capitalism (Marx [1867] 1990, 637), he also saw in other contexts, Russia, for example, that the peasant commune "was the fulcrum for social regeneration" (Marx, letter to Vera Zasulich, quoted in Shanin 1983, 124). And he became a major exponent of anticolonial revolt throughout the world and of abolition, and worked to build working-class support for ending slavery and colonialism. He did not advocate a return to the past, which was, besides, impossible, but for a future, higher form of society—socialism—built on diverse struggles for liberation and the defense of the commons.

While ecosocialists today have developed new lines of thinking and new perspectives on revolutionary struggle and aims, we have inherited from Marx an integrated approach that can generate abundant insights into new and developing conditions as the struggle against the destructive forces of capital continues in our era. Importantly, Marx's approach meant that his perspective changed as conditions changed, as his understanding developed, and as he faced challenges to his existing knowledge. This open-endedness is critical and is, in part, why his work has remained relevant today, providing a basis for understanding the need for solidarity in the face of seemingly diverse struggles that are, in fact, joined in the historical process of capitalism's development. Finally, Marx's theorization of the metabolic rift of capitalism, which compels systemic restoration of the conditions of sustainability, and his conception of the commons as a future-oriented project—with deep roots in diverse cultures—points toward possibilities for future socialisms where relations between peoples, and between peoples and the land, may be imagined for anew (Foster 1999; Wittman 2009; Löwy 2017; Kerr et al. 2019; Saito 2020).

Although ecosocialists today draw on many sources, past and present, Marx's "ecosocialism," as Kohei Saito (2017) calls it, has become an increasingly important resource in our time, not only for insights into the developments of his time, but into possibilities for ours. In particular, Marx's understanding that we belong to the land, it does not belong to us, remains a radical proposition.

Ecosocialism and the Land Today

Both during Marx's lifetime and since his death, socialists have played a significant role in the development of ecological thinking (see Foster 2020) and liberatory socioecological practice with respect to the land. This is perhaps most pronounced in the waves of anticolonial, socialist struggles that have attempted to redefine both the relations between peoples and the relations between people and the land. The links between movements and academia in the development of intellectual traditions have meant that ecosocialist perspectives on land have developed from several directions at once, though there is room for more cross-fertilization. Bringing ecosocialists together across languages and cultures is particularly fruitful when it happens.

Ecosocialists straddling movements and academia have developed lines of inquiry focused on land that inform our thinking on agroecology, agroforestry, and food sovereignty; peasant, Indigenous, and women's land struggles; democratic planning and agricultural production; soil ecology and soil science; the land-water nexus; heteropatriarchy and capitalist agriculture; demilitarization and land restoration; land-use change and land tenure; urbanization and the countryside; the role of capitalist agriculture in the rise of zoonotic infectious disease (such as Covid-19); and much more.

Indigenous socialists have contributed prominently to ecosocialist thinking, articulating the necessary preconditions for, and paths toward, revolutionary change with respect to the land in documents such as the "People's Agreement on Climate Change and the Rights of Mother Earth" (see Cochabamba Protocol 2010; Turner 2010). More recently, in the settler-colonial context of Turtle Island (a.k.a. the United

States of America), the Red Nation has put Indigenous land sovereignty and Native women's leadership at the center of the revolutionary socialist agenda (Red Nation 2021). They have also made important connections linking abolitionist work and the struggle against racial capitalism with the struggles for Indigenous sovereignty and against bourgeois property relations in general. As they put it: "Black and Indigenous liberation struggles are abolitionist and, when attached to socialist projects toward full communism, seek the end of all logics of carcerality, including private property that warehouse people, cage animals, and enclose lands within borders."(Red Nation 2020, 24).

Peasant feminist socialists, too, have informed ecosocialist visions of the transformation of society along socialist and ecological lines. For example, the 2019 Declaration of CLOC–La Vía Campesina (CLOC = Coordinadora Latinoamericana de Organizaciones del Campo), shared with the world, stated:

> As women of the countryside, we struggle for an equitable and egalitarian society; a society that transforms the power relations that have meant the subordination of women, particularly those of us who live in rural areas, in conditions of poverty and discriminations; those of us who have been oppressed under patriarchal policies, to agri-business systems of exploitation through transnational companies, to displacements, forced migration and violence....
>
> ... In this process of feminist construction that emerges from the rural territories and peoples, the debate goes hand in hand with action and the struggle in Stop Violence Against Rural Women, against agri-business and toxic agrochemicals. It is the struggle for life, for the defense of Seeds which are Heritage of our Peoples in the Service of Humanity; for the equal right to land ownership, against exploitations, violence and abuse in the workplace; for fair and equal pay. Agroecology as an ancestral system of production that ensures Food Sovereignty is an important contribution from the women of CLOC/LVC made with the aim of moving forward in the transformation of society; it is a struggle of the entire peasant movement at a global scale. That is why it is also part of popular and peasant feminism.
>
> (León 2019; also La Vía Campesina 2019)

Ecofeminist ecosocialists have emphasized that "indigenous women's stewardship of the commons and re-invention of subsistence livelihoods across the world are at the core of 'ecosocialist ecofeminism'" (Brownhill and Turner 2020).

Ecosocialists have, in some of the work described above, directly extended Marx's conception of the metabolic rift into a body of work on the "ecological rift of capitalism" and what healing and restoration might look like given where we are today. A bibliography containing many of these works in English is available at MROnline, https://mronline.org/2013/10/16/metabolic-rift/. However, it is easy to search across languages to find a significant international body of ecosocialist work on questions related to land and social transformation.

While varying strands of ecosocialist writing now circulate in public debates and through movements that both define themselves in relation to ecosocialism and many that do not, ecosocialism comes to life on the land today in movements that are giving birth to new futures on diverse soils.

Ecosocialist Action on the Ground: For Land and Sovereignty

The First Ecosocialist International: Answering the Cry of Mother Earth

Land was at the center of the First Ecosocialist International in 2017, a gathering in Yaracuy, Venezuela—near the birthplace of maroon liberation struggles in the country—of representatives from "19 countries and five continents, 12 original peoples from Our America, and ecosocialist activists from 14 states of Venezuela," to develop a collaborative, decolonial program drawing on rich and varied global traditions "to reverse the destructive process of capitalism; to return to our origins and recuperate the ancestral spirituality of humanity; to live in peace, and end war" (First Socialist International 2017). This built on efforts going back several decades to develop ecosocialist theory and practice, drawing on many tributary movements.

Participants in the gathering, which was organized by and for activists on the ground, working across a range of contexts, committed "first of all to weave ourselves into the diverse struggles of the original peoples of the five continents to reclaim and demarcate their lands and territories." They created the "Combined Strategy and Plan of Action," calling attention to the interrelationship between cosmovisions and the land, and the necessity of ending the destruction of languages and thereby critical ways of knowing. To guarantee Indigenous sovereignty and get land back, the plan called for "the expulsion of transnational corporations, paramilitary groups and landowning mafias." These goals were connected to protecting food, seed, and medicinal sovereignty, expanding Indigenous ecological methods of cultivation, andmaintaining a transnational alliance against agribusiness and further attempts to patent and commodify life.

In this ecosocialist vision, which includes specific strategies for change, the emphasis is on the collective knowledge and practices toward transformation that already exist in diverse cultural traditions. It is hopeful in that it identifies how much we have to build on in responding to "the cry of Mother Earth." The vision emphasizes the interrelated, shared practices of healing, for both the land and people:

> We will strengthen and continue to promote the experiences we have consolidated... which inspire autonomous practices based on ancestral cultures, and which have a positive influence on individual and collective mental health. These practices are healing because they promote more healthy relationships between human beings and Mother Earth; based on the reality of what we are; generating solutions from the

> micro to the macro; reconstructing a great transformative and pluricosmovisionary quilt. Thus we shall transform ourselves and our world through concrete and interconnected examples, which will open cracks in the great fraud of the disassociating capitalist society in which we are submerged.
>
> (First Ecosocalist International 2017)

Activists who participated in this gathering of rural and urban socialists took their work back home. The goal was to build a global network of solidarity in struggle—uniting urban, rural, and broader movements, as well as movements in the global South and global North.

Cooperation Jackson: Ecosocialism and Land in the City

One of the participating organizations at the First Ecosocialist International was Cooperation Jackson, founded in 2014 in Jackson, Mississippi. This organization is working toward an important vision for ecosocialist organizing in the "South of the North" that is both internationalist and place-based—grounded in the local land, community, and traditions of Black liberation (Cooperation Jackson and Center for Grassroots Organizing 2021). It is a vehicle for "sustainable community development, economic democracy, and community ownership" (Cooperation Jackson n.d.). The "broad mission of Cooperation Jackson is

> to advance the development of a regenerative economy in Jackson, MS based on a program centered around food sovereignty, which is rooted in the practices of agroecology, combined with local resourcing provisioning to build a locally grounded supply chain production that is rooted in the practices of working class self-organization and economic democracy to create a sustainable future.
>
> (Cooperation Jackson 2021)

The organization describes its grassroots efforts as follows:

- Develop concrete strategies to rapidly address the advancing climate catastrophe
- Initiate just transition plans from the bottom up that lead to a regenerative, ecosocialist future based on non-extractive and non-exploitative systems of production and reproduction where the means of production are democratically owned and controlled by communities of associated producers
- Coherently plan for the coming waves of climate migration within the context of fighting for decolonization, in the form of land back transfers to Indigenous nations and land steward agreements for Blacks and Latinos based on these land grant transfers. (Cooperation Jackson 2021)

Cooperation Jackson is building a network of cooperatives and land trusts to move land and production in Jackson and beyond into communal ownership and control—while working toward transformative social change. In addition to supporting the real needs of the community and ecological restoration, this work begins the process of removing provisioning systems from corporate control. So far, the group has built the Freedom Farms Cooperative, the Green Teams Landscaping Coop, and the Community Production Cooperative, and at the same time, it has engaged in a wide range of community organizing, outreach and education, and transnational solidarity-building efforts (Cooperative Jackson 2019).

Indeed, Cooperation Jackson is a beacon of anti-imperialist, transnational solidarity, desperately needed in a country that has played an outsized role in perpetuating global violence and standing in the way of a "just transition" around the world. They regularly organize meetings with grassroots movements—for example, in 2021 they brought together activists from the MST in Brazil and the Palestinian Union of Agricultural Workers Committees to discuss "Food Sovereignty and People's Struggles for Liberation" (Saul 2018; Cooperation Jackson 2021). Their participation in the First Ecosocialist International also speaks to their commitment to coordinate movement efforts between the North and South. The organizers have been important voices urging climate action at the global and national level (such as the Green New Deal in the United States) that is shaped directly by input from frontline ommunities in the global South and Indigenous communities(Akuno 2019).

Importantly, Cooperation Jackson is re-envisioning relationships between peoples and between people and the land in urban spaces to provide for the needs of both humans and other species. Cooperation Jackson's director Kali Akuno (2019) highlights that

> a significant part of the sixth extinction event is the rapid loss of habitat and corresponding ecological destruction that countless species have suffered the past two hundred years. We have to, and I stress have to, figure out a way to severely restrict our habitat (i.e. land) use and engage in some major ecological restoration.
>
> The challenge is how to produce more food, on smaller plots of land, without resorting to genetic modification. We haven't figured this out, to my mind. Not even close. I think permaculture points us in the right direction, as does some degree of small-scale agriculture to at least break the stranglehold the monopolies currently have. I also think we will need to maximize urban density, fairly significantly, to enable more habitats to be recuperated for other species and to restore ecological balance and the replenishment of the soil, which are major carbon sinks. In doing this we will have to turn our urban spaces into "living farms" to address many of our caloric needs.

In the United States, where 83 percent of the population lives in urban areas, and with 68 percent of the global population expected to live in cities by 2050, it is critical to the future of the land and of ecosocialism that urban-based organizations understand their relationship to the land and to rural struggles, across national boundaries (O'Neill 2022; United Nations 2018).

Ecosocialist Education and Multiscalar Solidarity

In addition to the international and very local ecosocialist organizations just described, ecosocialists around the world have built several forms of transnational, national, and regional solidarities that are impacting land politics and advancing ecosocialist thought.

For example, the anti-imperialist and ecosocialist organization in Mauritius, Rezistans ek Alternativ, has helped organize a national movement that includes "left trade unionists, activists of social movements, fishermen, small planters, environmentalist activists, women's movements, and particularly youth movements." This movement has fought for more than a decade for "participatory democracy, the socialization of the economy, the protection of public goods, the protection of common goods, such as agricultural land, biodiversity and marine resources, as well as the law of nature" (Subron 2013).

The organization has identified and fought against new forms of land- and ocean-grabbing and enclosure, especially by foreign capital, and it has advocated for communal land control and protection, as well as for rights for agricultural workers and peasants. It has also fought for the demilitarization of the land, decolonization, removal of the notorious US military base—Diego Garcia—from the Chagos Islands, and for the right of return of the Chagossians, who were forcibly removed from their lands between 1968 and 1973 (Twyman-Ghoshal 2022). Mauritius won a recent victory when the International Court of Justice in the Hague issued an advisory ruling that during decolonization, the United Kingdom acted unlawfully when it separated the Chagos from Mauritius in a backroom deal granting the United States exclusive control of the islands (Wilkins 2019). Now, activists are fighting for the dismantling of the base and the right of return of the people who belong there.

Importantly, Rezistans ek Alternativ has organized the School of Ecology in Mauritius (https://soe.caresmauritius.org/) to build a regional movement—bringing together activists from nations in Eastern Africa all the way to South Africa and from the islands of the Western Indian Ocean (Madagascar, Seychelles, Réunion Rodrique, Comores)—along ecosocialist lines. The school's objectives include:

> Linking and articulating the multi-dimensional crisis—financial/economic, ecological and social—affecting humankind and its habitat, with a special focus on the Ocean. Introducing the concept of Nature as a subject and not as an object, natural resources as commons and a source of sustainable livelihoods and biodiversity to be nurtured, not a private or state property. Promoting the laws of nature in opposition to the law of capitalism. Building capacity and generates knowledge for the development of political people's power for policy and structural change in society to address the looming ecological disasters.
>
> ("Background," "Aims and Objectives," School of Ecology Mauritius website, https://soe.caresmauritius.org/spip.php?article12)

Participants in the school are representatives from regional movement organizations, including farmers, fishers, trade unionists, environmentalists, and many more. Their work is facilitated by sophisticated translation across numerous languages (e.g., Morisien, or Mauritian Creole; French; English; and more, depending on the participants' needs). The organizers learn from one another's struggles, study and work together, and develop shared perspectives and goals.

The School of Ecology also helps link this network in the Indian Ocean region with international movements. Members of the MST (Movimento dos Trabalhadores Rurais Sem Terra) from Brazil and La Vía Campesina have participated, and the organizations have given mutual support.

A shared sense of urgency exists as never before for solidarity-building in the region in the face of climate change and sea-level rise. Therefore, the organization has also worked to lay the foundations for an Indian Ocean People's Movement to address:

- The rising impact of the climate and ecological crisis on the Indian Ocean and its People
- The plundering, capture, and extractivism of the ocean commons and wealth
- The increasing militarism/nuclearisation of the Ocean
- Failure of institutional power, economic-social systems in protecting the Ocean and its people ("About: Indian Ocean People's Conference," School of Ecology Mauritius, https://soe.caresmauritius.org/spip.php?article21)

In addition to this important project in the Indian Ocean region, organizations around the world have been building movement capacity, fostering community empowerment, and developing new forms of ecosocialist organizing and thinking. More well-known examples of movements incorporating ecosocialism into some strands of their work include the MST in Brazil (Sales Diniz and Gilbert 2013; Meek and Tarlau 2020) and the transnational movement La Vía Campesina (Capire 2021). The work of these two organizations has also been a source of inspiration for ecosocialist theory and practice. Some perhaps less-familiar examples (for some readers) of explicitly ecosocialist networks include the International Institute for Research and Education based in Amsterdam, Islamabad, and Manila (https://www.iire.org) and the Global Ecosocialist Network (http://www.globalecosocialistnetwork.net/)—both of which are building spaces of solidarity and education across borders and addressing land questions specific to the needs of their participating organizations and communities.

Ecosocialism and a Future on the Land

In April 2022, the IPCC (Intergovernmental Panel on Climate Change 2022) released another damning report on global failures to mitigate climate change, At the press conference announcing the report's release, United Nations secretary-general António Guterres blasted government and business leaders who have lied to cover up their inaction. Guterres also, following the report's implications, was clear that our best hope is to look for change from the ground up rather than the top down, and to build on global movements, in particular, the struggles of Indigenous communities and our youth (United Nations 2022).

We are living in a time when the system, driven by the same forces socialists identified more than a century ago, is rapidly and radically altering the human relation to land in ways that are both qualitatively and quantitively different than in earlier eras. Much of the land on which we, and our more-than-human relatives, depend is becoming less habitable. The IPCC report released in April 2022 is too long and complex to summarize here, but four points stand out (1) It is clear that incremental change is insufficient. We need transformative, or systemic, change and we need it fast. (2) The only barrier to change is political. We have the resources, technology, finances, and knowledge to change the situation. We need the politics. (3) Collective action underpins systemic change. (4) The richest 10 percent are the most responsible for the catastrophe that is upon us; it is with the rest of us that hope for the future lies.

It is striking that in this most mainstream and hallowed of scientific bodies, the IPCC, the message now is that radical change is happening one way or another. So the question we confront is, What kind of change—catastrophic or socially and ecologically transformative? As the Red Nation (2020) recently stated, this is "a time of extreme clarification" (1).

To draw on the words Marx used to describe the real question of "land and existence" raised by the destruction of the soil and the decimation of the population in Ireland under British capitalism-colonialism—today, too, "ruin or revolution is the watchword" (Marx 1867; Foster 2022). The meaning of all of this, as ecosocialists have understood, is that "the movement toward socialism, that is, toward a society of ecological sustainability and substantive equality, will have to proceed much faster: by big steps, if not leaps. We can no longer depend—if we ever could—on a process of gradual evolution" (Magdoff and Williams 2017).

Ecosocialists around the world have long helped clear a path toward the kind of transformative change we need in the human relation to land and the rest of nature—providing a countermovement to capital to go directions that are clearly necessary and urgent. Now, what would this look like with more people walking down it?

Acknowledgments

I appreciate the thoughtful comments of the editors and reviewers of this chapter. Each suggestion was very helpful.

References

Akuno, Kali. 2019. "It's Eco-Socialism or Death." *Jacobin*, February 15. https://jacobinmag.com/2019/02/kali-akuno-interview-climate-change-cooperation-jackson.

Anderson, Kevin. 2016. *Marx at the Margins: On Nationalism, Ethnicity, and Non-Western Societies*. Expanded ed. Chicago: University of Chicago Press.

Angus, Ian. 2013. "Recovering Our History: 'Eco-Socialism in a Nutshell.'" *Climate and Capitalism*, November 13. https://climateandcapitalism.com/2013/11/13/recovering-history-eco-socialism-nutshell/.

Angus, Ian. 2018. "Cesspools, Sewage, and Social Murder: Environmental Crisis and Metabolic Rift in Nineteenth-Century London." *Monthly Review*, July 1. https://monthlyreview.org/2018/07/01/cesspools-sewage-and-social-murder/.

Bellofiore, Riccardo. 2018. "The Multiple Meanings of Marx's Value Theory." *Monthly Review*, April 1. https://monthlyreview.org/2018/04/01/the-multiple-meanings-of-marxs-value-theory/.

Blanco, Hugo. 2009. "Hugo Blanco on 'Ecosocialism' and Indigenous Struggles." *Climate and Capitalism*, February 16. https://climateandcapitalism.com/2009/02/16/hugo-blanco-on-ecosocialism-and-indigenous-struggles/.

Brownhill, Leigh, Salvatore Engel-Di Mauro, Terran Giacomini, Ana Isla, Michael Löwy, and Terisa E. Turner, eds. 2022. Preface to *The Routledge Handbook on Ecosocialism*, 1–12. New York: Routledge.

Brownhill, Leigh, and Terisa E. Turner. 2020. "Ecofeminist Ways, Ecosocialist Means: Life in the Post-capitalist Future." *Capitalism Nature Socialism* 31 (1): 1–14.

Capire. 2021. "Pancha Rodríguez: Food Sovereignty Is About Deciding To Change the World: Via Campesina." La Vía Campesina, 27 April 27. https://viacampesina.org/en/pancha-rodriguez-food-sovereignty-is-about-deciding-to-change-the-world/. (First published by Capire on April 16, 2021).

Clark, Brett, and John Bellamy Foster. 2009. "Ecological Imperialism and the Global Metabolic Rift: Unequal Exchange and the Guano/Nitrates Trade." *International Journal of Comparative Sociology* 50 (3–4): 311–334.

"Cochabamba Protocol: People's Agreement on Climate Change and the Rights of Mother Earth." 2010. Madre (website), April 22, 2010. https://www.madre.org/press-publications/statement/cochabamba-protocol-peoples-agreement-climate-change-and-rights-mother.

Saul, Quincy. 2018. "Jackson Convergence Report: The First Ecosocialist International Takes Root and Makes Routes on Turtle Island." Cooperation Jackson. June 4. https://cooperationjackson.org/blog/2018/7/13/jackson-convergence-report-the-first-ecosocialist-international-takes-root-and-makes-routes-on-turtle-island.

Cooperation Jackson. 2019. "Building a Solidarity Economy in Jackson, Mississippi." October 10. https://cooperationjackson.org/blog/2019/10/10/building-a-solidarity-economy-in-jackson-mississippi.

Cooperation Jackson. 2021. "A Sustainable Economy Is a Cooperative Economy." https://cooperationjackson.org/events-calendar/2021/12/8/a-sustainable-economy-is-a-cooperative-economy.

Cooperation Jackson and the Center for Grassroots Organizing. 2021. "Decolonization, Reparations, and Climate Emergency Preparedness: Clarifying the CJ and CGO Collaboration." Cooperation Jackson, July 29. https://cooperationjackson.org/announcementsblog/2021/7/29/y9nfneov5wswdx9elieav6cwoz4tnj.

Croall, Stephen, and Kaianders Sempler. (1980) 2013. "Ecosocialism in the Nutshell." Updated with a new introduction by Ian Angus. *Climate and Capitalism* (online). https://climateandcapitalism.com/wp-content/uploads/2013/11/Ecosocialism-in-a-Nutshell.pdf. (Original work published in London by the Writers and Readers Publishing Cooperative.)

First Ecosocialist International. 2017. "The First Ecosocialist International: Combined Strategy and Plan of Action." Ecosocialist Horizons (website), December 19. http://ecosocialisth

orizons.com/2017/12/the-first-ecosocialist-international-combined-strategy-and-plan-of-action/.
Foster, John Bellamy. 1993. "The Limits of Environmentalism without Class: Lessons from the Ancient Forest Struggle of the Pacific Northwest." *Capitalism Nature Socialism* 4 (1): 11–41.
Foster, John Bellamy. 1999. "Marx's Theory of Metabolic Rift: Classical Foundations for Environmental Sociology." *American Journal of Sociology* 105 (2): 366–405.
Foster, John Bellamy. 2020. *The Return of Nature: Socialism and Ecology*. New York: Monthly Review Press.
Foster, John Bellamy. 2022. *Capitalism in the Anthropocene: Ecological Ruin or Ecological Revolution*. New York: Monthly Review Press.
Foster, John Bellamy, and Brett Clark. 2009. "The Paradox of Wealth: Capitalism and Ecological Destruction." *Monthly Review*, November https://monthlyreview.org/2009/11/01/the-paradox-of-wealth-capitalism-and-ecological-destruction/.
Foster, John Bellamy, and Brett Clark. 2018. "The Expropriation of Nature." *Monthly Review*, March. https://monthlyreview.org/2018/03/01/the-expropriation-of-nature/.
Foster, John Bellamy, Brett Clark, and Hannah Holleman. 2021. "Marx and the Commons." *Social Research: An International Quarterly* 88 (1): 1–30.
Intergovernmental Panel on Climate Change. 2022. *Climate Change 2022: Mitigation of Climate Change*. Working Group III Contribution to the IPCC Sixth Assessment Report (AR6). Climate Change 2022: Mitigation of Climate Change. https://www.ipcc.ch/report/ar6/wg3/.
Kerr, Rachel Bezner, Catherine Hickey, Esther Lupafya, and Laifolo Dakishoni. 2019. "Repairing Rifts or Reproducing Inequalities? Agroecology, Food Sovereignty, and Gender Justice in Malawi." *Journal of Peasant Studies* 46 (7): 1499–1518.
Kovel, Joel, and Michael Lowy. 2001. "An Ecosocialist Manifesto." Environment and Ecology, September. http://environment-ecology.com/political-ecology/436-an-ecosocialist-manifesto.html.
La Vía Campesina. 2019. "VI Women Assembly of the CLOC-LVC: Declaration." July 24. https://viacampesina.org/en/vi-women-assembly-of-the-cloc-lvc-declaration/.
León, Osvaldo. 2019. "The Latin American Coordination of Rural Organizations (CLOC) at 25 Years: Via Campesina." La Vía Campesina, June 19. https://viacampesina.org/en/the-cloc-at-25-years/.
Linebaugh, Peter. 2014. "Karl Marx, the Theft of Wood, and Working-Class Composition: A Contribution to the Current Debate." In "Legacies of Radical Criminology in the United States." Special issue, *Social Justice* 40 (1–2): 131–132.
Löwy, Michael. 2017. "Marx, Engels and Ecology." *Capitalism Nature Socialism* 28 (2): 10–21.
Magdoff, Fred, and Chris Williams. 2017. *Creating an Ecological Society: Toward a Revolutionary Transformation*. New York: Monthly Review Press.
Marx, Karl. 1842. "Proceedings of the Sixth Rhine Province Assembly. Third Article: Debates on the Law on Thefts of Wood." Supplement to the *Rheinishche Zeitung*, nos. 298, 300, 303, 305 and 307. October 25, 27 and 30, November 1 and 3, 1842.
Marx, Karl. (1894)1991. *Capital: A Critique of Political Economy*. Vol. 3. New York: Penguin Classics.
Marx, Karl. (1867) 1990. *Capital: A Critique of Political Economy*. Vol. 1. New York: Penguin Classics.
Marx, Karl. 1867. "On the Irish Question." Speech. Marxist Internet Archive. https://www.marxists.org/archive/marx/iwma/documents/1867/irish-speech.htm.

Marx, Karl, and Friedrich Engels. (1872) 1978. *Manifesto of the Communist Party*, 2nd ed. In *The Marx-Engels Reader*, edited by Robert C. Tucker, 469–500. New York: W. W. Norton.
Marx, Karl. 1974. *The Ethnological Notebooks of Karl Marx: Studies of Morgan, Phear, Maine, Lubbock*. 2nd ed. Assen, Netherlands: Van Gorcum & Comp.
Marx, Karl. 1974a. *Early Writings*. New York: Vintage.
Meek David, and Rebecca Tarlau. 2020. "Educating for Ecosocialism." *NACLA Report on the Americas* 52 (2): 206–213.
Mészáros, Istvan. 2000. *Beyond Capital: Toward a Theory of Transition*. New York: Monthly Review Press.
O'Neill, Aaron. 2022. "Urbanization in the United States 1970–2020." Statista, February 2. https://www.statista.com/statistics/269967/urbanization-in-the-united-states/.
Red Nation. 2020. *Communism Is the Horizon: Queer Indigenous Feminism Is the Way*. TheRedNation.org. http://therednation.org/wp-content/uploads/2020/09/TRN-pamphlet-final.pdf.
Red Nation. 2021. *The Red Deal: Indigenous Action to Save Our Earth*. New York: Common Notions.
Saito, Kohei. 2017. *Karl Marx's Ecosocialism: Capital, Nature, and the Unfinished Critique of Political Economy*. New York: Monthly Review Press.
Saito, Kohei. 2020. *Marx's Theory of Metabolism the in the Age of Global Ecological Crisis*. Leiden: Brill.
Sales Diniz, Aldiva, and Bruce Gilbert. 2013. "Socialist Values and Cooperation in Brazil's Landless Rural Workers' Movement." *Latin American Perspectives* 40 (4): 19–34.
Satgar, Vishwas, ed. 2018. *The Climate Crisis: South African and Global Democratic Eco-Socialist Alternatives*. Johannesburg: Wits University Press.
Satgar, Vishwas. 2022. "Marx, the Commons and Democratic Eco-Socialism." In David Fasenfest (ed) *Marx Matters*, 181–197. Leiden: Brill.
Shanin, Teodor, ed. 1983. *Late Marx and the Russian Road: Marx and "The Peripheries of Capitalism."* New York: Monthly Review Press.
Socialist Environment and Resource Association (SERA). n.d. *Labour's Environment Campaign*. https://www.sera.org.uk/about. Accessed December 19, 2022.
Subron, Ashok. 2013. "The Dynamic of the Victorious Struggle of the Workers in the Sugar Industry has Spread to other Areas." By Jean Nanga. *International Viewpoint*. January 10. https://internationalviewpoint.org/spip.php?article2858
Turner, Terisa E. 2010. "From Cochabamba, a New Internationale and Manifesto for Mother Earth." *Capitalism Nature Socialism* 21 (3) (August): 56–74.
Twyman-Ghoshal, Anamika. 2022. "How the US and UK Worked Together to Recolonise the Chagos Islands and Evict Chagossians." The Conversation, February 24. https://theconversation.com/how-the-us-and-uk-worked-together-to-recolonise-the-chagos-islands-and-evict-chagossians-177636.
United Nations. 2018. "68% of World's Population Projected to Live in Urban Areas by 2050, Says UN." May 16. https://www.un.org/development/desa/en/news/population/2018-revision-of-world-urbanization-prospects.html.
United Nations. 2022. "Secretary-General Warns of Climate Emergency, Calling Intergovernmental Panel's Report 'a File of Shame', While Saying Leaders 'Are Lying', Fuelling Flames." Press Release. April 4. https://press.un.org/en/2022/sgsm21228.doc.htm.

Wilkins, Brett. 2019. "Diego Garcia: UN Court Calls on Britain to 'Decolonize' Chagos Islands." Common Dreams, February 25. https://www.commondreams.org/views/2019/02/25/diego-garcia-un-court-calls-britain-decolonize-chagos-islands.

Wittman, Hannah. 2009. "Reworking the Metabolic Rift: La Vía Campesina, Agrarian Citizenship, and Food Sovereignty." *Journal of Peasant Studies* 36 (4): 805–826.

CHAPTER 7

LAND IN THE ANARCHIST TRADITION

ANDREJ GRUBAČIĆ, JULIEN-FRANÇOIS GERBER, AND ANDRO RILOVIĆ

Introduction

> For we must begin with the land if only because the basic materials for life are acquired from the land. This is not only an ecological truth but a social one as well.
>
> —Murray Bookchin

THIS chapter explores how the anarchist tradition relates to land. "Land and Liberty" is a slogan that is often used to encapsulate the relationship anarchism has had to the land question. First used by the Narodniks in the 1870s, and then by Mexican revolutionaries in the 1910s, Spanish anarchists in the 1930s, and many others since, this slogan captures much of the essence of anarchist or anarchistic thinking on land—namely, that direct democratic control over land is a necessary condition for the construction of a free society (Seaweed 2013). In the most direct way, the possession of land by the producers means freedom from the landowner and, by extension, from state structures.

Many anarchists would agree that the main problem with capitalism is that it allows for nonuser ownership—that is, it enables people who do not actually use resources in a socially beneficial way to still own them. In response to this, anarchism has promoted institutional arrangements based on usufruct and democratic self-management. These two notions can be seen as key anarchist contributions to the land question. *Usufruct* refers to the freedom of individuals in a community of producers to enjoy the fruits of a resource, such as land, merely by virtue of the fact that they are using or working on it to meet their needs. A plot of land under usufruct cannot be sold or leased. Usufruct is thus based on the ethical principle that genuine needs and labor generate entitlements to the fruits of a given resource. But this is not all. In the anarchist sense, usufruct implies a reunification of ownership and political deliberation (Blaufarb 2016), as we will see. Thus the socialization of power abolishes "the economy" as a separate domain of existence.

In this chapter, we use the term *anarchistic* to describe the broad family of social formations and movements practicing usufructuary and antiauthoritarian self-management because obviously not all of them are or were claiming the anarchist tradition (Roman-Alcalá 2021). These institutional principles have old roots indeed, and usufruct might well be humanity's main historical way of "appropriating" resources. The idea that needs and work create certain entitlements was common in precapitalist economies, where the usufruct of land could typically start with the clearing of a field; but after some time, when the cycle of rotating agriculture leaves no visible trace of labor, the possessor's entitlement disappears and the plot is again available for other community members (e.g., Gerber and Veuthey 2011). These principles are still in practice today in some regions of the world. They are, of course, completely at odds with capitalist principles, where rights have to be recognized by the state—"formalized"—and where assets can be accumulated ad infinitum, largely disconnected from human and nonhuman needs.

As we will see, building on the fundamental principles of self-management and usufruct, the anarchist lens offers insights into the land question and extends it to community and ecology. The chapter is divided into three parts covering theoretical roots, historical examples, and contemporary green anarchism, with special reference to the emerging degrowth movement.

Anarchist Perspectives on Land

Anarchism has always been keenly interested in the land question and in the consequences of different land regimes for the possibility of organizing a free society (Roman-Alcalá 2021). This concern is visible in several of the seminal texts in the Western anarchist tradition, which began in the nineteenth century, such as the works of Pierre-Joseph Proudhon, Pyotr Kropotkin, Mikhail Bakunin, or Élisée Reclus.

Before turning to these authors, we would like to point out that anarchistic concerns with land are at least as old as agriculture itself if we consider all the doctrines that opposed institutionalized hierarchical rule over societies and favored instead mutual aid and voluntary association. Demands for land redistribution along autonomist and usufructuary lines have been theorized and put into practice by a variety of proto-anarchist or anarchistic movements, ranging from Daoist dissidents in sixth-century BCE China (Rapp 2012) to the contemporary militants of the Autonomous Administration of North and East Syria, widely known as Rojava, a territory based on the principles of grassroots democracy, women's liberation, and ecology (Öcalan 2011). Finley (1983) noted that in countless agrarian societies since antiquity, the perennial revolutionary program of the peasantry can be summarized as "cancel the debts and redistribute the land" (108).

Enough land and revenue are indeed fundamental to the simple reproduction of poor and middle peasants' households, and they remain therefore also the key assets to defend in order not to become landless and fully subjugated. There is thus a deep history of constant struggle against, and flight from, large landowners and state structures by those who have opposed hierarchical organizations of societies (Thompson 1966; Scott 2009; Graeber and Wengrow 2021).

The first person to call himself an "anarchist" was also the first radical thinker to offer an elaboration of self-management—"le père de l'autogestion," Pierre-Joseph Proudhon. In 1840, in his famous essay "What Is Property?" Proudhon (1994) contested the absoluteness of the right to property. He did not refute the right to possession, but he linked it to usufruct: the occupant is a "possessor or usufructuary, a condition that excludes proprietorship" (66). According to him, these alternative possession-based relations must be regulated by use and need to enable material reproduction (Gerber and Steppacher 2017). It is important to note here a clear distinction between socialization (self-management) and nationalization (state management), an option advocated by state socialists of the nineteenth and early twentieth centuries. If nationalization suggests a transfer of property from individual to the state, socialization suggests abolishing this modern concept altogether. Instead, Proudhon's concept of socialized possession is thus defined by *usufruct*, or the right to use *(ius utendi)*.

According to Daniel Guérin (2017), one of the most competent historians of anarchism, self-management was "without any doubt the most original creation of anarchism, and goes right to the heart of contemporary realities" (81). As Guérin put it: "Who should manage the economy? Private capitalism? The state? Workers' organisations? In other words, there were—and still are—three options: free enterprise, nationalisation, or socialisation (i.e., self-management)" (82). The ideas of usufruct and self-management militate against the "great demarcation" between public power and private property—namely, against this great divide of modernity from which flowed the critical distinctions between "the political" and "the social," "state" and "society," and "sovereignty" and "ownership." As Blaufarb (2016) so perceptively notes, the great demarcation not only destroyed the conceptual basis of the Old Regime, but it also laid the foundation of capitalist modernity.

Proudhon's conception of self-management and usufruct had inspired the Communards of Paris, who in 1871 proclaimed that they "want land, which is not the product of any human labor, but only the raw material given freely to everyone by nature, to not be the property of any individuals, but to become the inalienable dominion of humanity" (quoted in Tomba 2019, 106). With this proclamation, the Communards had not only announced the beginning of an anarchistic politics of agrarian self-management; they had also signaled a profound reconfiguration of property relations that were, and still are, predicated on the great demarcation between sovereignty and ownership that lies at the very core of the modern conception of politics. But the Communards also rejected nationalization, seeing it as just another form of property, and made the land a communally regulated dominion of humanity, the use of which was usufructuary. This was true of factories and abandoned houses, as well as of the land, as estates were taken and placed under the control of associated workers (Edwards 1973). The Paris Commune was finally drowned in blood, but this particular conception of ownership, as a different configuration of communal freedom and possession, defined in opposition to the modern logic of property, has made anarchistic politics of agrarian self-management distinct from Marxism and other political movements that promote the expropriation of the land in favor of the state (see Bernstein, this volume).

Along similar lines, other theorists and practitioners in the Western anarchist tradition have also argued that access to land is a necessary condition for freedom, if not always a sufficient one. The deprivation of land, they argued, almost certainly results in some form of enslavement, whether it is tenancy, sharecropping, wage-labor, or slavery itself. But the land question couldn't be understood without taking into account all the other key societal institutions. Kropotkin (2011) argued that to secure any gains from an incipient social revolution, the issue of food provisioning was of paramount importance—"it is bread that the Revolution needs" (74). This was to be achieved by abolishing private property and establishing a system of farming collectives around major population centers—in other words, by a wide-ranging program of land redistribution and an entirely new land regime. Bakunin (1972), similarly, was a firm believer in a possible alliance of workers and peasants in a revolutionary movement. Like workers, peasants have the potential, he thought, to become revolutionary when they choose to "take the land and throw out those landlords who live by the labor of others" (204). Reclus (2013), for his part, spent less time discussing land in its productive sense and was more concerned with "land as nature" and the need to conserve it as such. He can thus be considered a direct precursor of the environmental justice movement that began in the 1960s and, in particular, the green current of anarchist thought (more about this below). Within this framework, Reclus also clearly stressed the importance of land redistribution according to the principles of usufruct (113–119).

The Agrarian Communes of Makhnovshchina

After the Paris Commune, the next practical chapter in the anarchist project of agrarian self-management is the fascinating historical episode of Makhnovshchina. Despite its authoritarian outcome, the long history of the Russian Revolution (1905–1921) reveals other, defeated possibilities and submerged concepts of politics and property beyond private or state ownership.

In the summer of 1919, Nikolai Rogdaev, an anarchist organizer among both workers and peasants, known as "Uncle Vanya," had moved from Moscow east to the city of Samara to assist with the project of organizing the Samara federation of anarchist communists. In Alexandre Skirda's (2002) illuminating account, the Bolshevik administration was removed from Samara and replaced with the democratic Provincial

Soviet Congress. The members of the congress were involved in extensive communication with a prominent anarchist organizer in Ukraine by the name of Nestor Makhno. Rogdaev has long been impressed with Makhno's great ability and passionate belief in the democratic potential of peasant politics. Makhno was a soldier of great ability. As Paul Avrich describes Makhno, "[He] was the very incarnation of peasant anarchism, the partisan leader in closest touch with the most cherished hopes and feelings of the village" (quoted in Smolski et al. 2018, 480). As the leader of the insurgent anarchist army he fought alongside the Red Army against the forces of Generals Denikin and Wrangel. With the slogan "Land and Liberty," Makhno's army went to create communes in Gulyai Polye and Yeklaterinoslav. Large landholdings were socialized, and the local administration was organized around communal principles (Guérin 2017). The slogan Land and Liberty was not exclusive: workers were invited to "join the hands with the peasants." At the Second Regional Congress in Gulyai Polye, the social revolution was defined as a multiplication of libertarian soviets and socialization of land (Makhno 1934; Skirda 2002; Smolski et al. 2018). Lenin was not in agreement. When Makhno himself visited Vladimir Ilich, he reports that that obstinate Bolshevik comrade could never accept the role of the peasants in establishing an emancipated society in the "here-and-now" (Makhno [1918] 2005, 511–512). Both Lenin and Trotsky were deeply skeptical of any potential connection between the insurgent peasantry and proletariat, and fearful of the profoundly libertarian trajectories within the Socialist Revolution. Makhno tried to bring Rogdaev to Ukraine, but the Bolsheviks intercepted the courier. Uncle Vanya was held in Moscow under Lenin's watchful eye, and Trotsky advised that Makhnovshchina, regardless of its inestimable contribution to the struggle against the White reaction, had to be suppressed (Avrich 1970). The moment Wrangel was defeated, the Bolsheviks turned against the Makhnovists, criminalizing "banditry," and banned the planned 1920 pan-Russian anarchist congress in Kharkov and ordered Makhno's arrest. Makhno's escape to France signaled a sad ending to an ambitious federalist experiment of agrarian self-management in Ukraine (Avrich 1970; Skirda 2002).

Land during the 1936 Spanish Revolution

Usufruct and self-management appeared again only a decade later in Republican Spain. In the wake of the Spanish Revolution of July 19, 1936, large landowners abandoned their property and took refuge abroad (Leval 2018; Mintz 2013; Guérin 2017). What is surprising and unique about this experience is a sudden and spontaneous emergence of the agrarian "collectives." The agricultural workers and day laborers socialized property and instituted agrarian self-management. The Spanish anarchist confederation of labor, or CNT, called a regional congress of Catalonian peasants on September 5 and agreed to the socialization of land under libertarian self-management. Although the larger estates were socialized, the small landowners had a choice between individual property and collective property (Leval 2018). The peasants, however, had socialized the property without waiting for legal decrees. What is so remarkable in the case of Spanish agricultural socialism is the extent of the anarchist education and a collectivist tradition. In a certain sense, social consciousness was higher in the country than in the cities. A vast majority—perhaps as high as 90 percent—of agricultural workers chose to join collectives. This decision created a close alliance between the peasants and the city workers, along the lines the Ukrainian anarchists had dreamed about a decade before. Everything was socialized and used in common, with the exception of clothing, furniture, personal savings, small domestic animals, garden plots, and poultry that was kept for family use. The sheep belonging to the community were divided into flocks of several hundred and put in the charge of shepherds.

The self-managed collectives had two components, economic and geographical. What this meant in practice is that a general assembly of peasants in each village elected a management committee that was responsible for economic administration. The only permanent position was the one of the secretaries, while all the assembly members continued doing their manual labor. Membership was entirely voluntary, and the heart of the system, just as in the case of the Paris Commune, was the imperative mandate: the peasants were divided into groups of ten or more, each of which was given an area to cultivate and was led by one recallable delegate. The management committee received the delegates every day. Regarding the communal administration, the general assembly convened at least once a week. Village artisans of different kinds were also grouped in collectives (Leval 2018).

Collectives were experimenting with different forms of product distribution. Monetary compensation was based on need, and the daily wage could only be exchanged for consumer goods in the communal shops. Services such as electricity or medical care were all free, as was education. Private property was allowed and tolerated, and those who had opted to remain private producers were even admitted to general assemblies. They were able to use most of the collective benefits. As the time went on, in most villages the individual peasants or traders, feeling isolated, decreased in number.

The communes were united into cantonal federations, above which were regional federations. Solidarity between villages was encouraged, and tools, raw materials, and surplus labor were all made available to communities in need (Guérin 2017). The extent of rural socialization was not uniform. In Aragon, for example, more than three-quarters of the land was socialized, a much smaller percentage than in Catalonia. In the rich Levante region, some 900 collectives were established, covering 43 percent of the geographical area; and in Castile, about 300 collectives were organized by 100,000 members (Leval 2018; Mintz 2013; Guérin 2017). In the southern areas, which were not controlled by the anarchists, there were no examples of rural self-management.

Agrarian self-management was an indisputable success (Mintz 2013). Socialized agriculture showed itself to be superior both to private ownership and to small farms cultivated with poor seed and without fertilizers. Self-management showed its remarkable organizational ability and capacity for coordination in the Levante, where modern commercial techniques were successfully employed. Crops were diversified, irrigation extended, reforestation initiated, and tree nurseries started. Rural technical schools were built, and demonstration farms set up; selective cattle breeding was developed, and auxiliary agricultural industries were put into operation (Mintz 2013; Guérin 2017). This success should not be seen as separate from educational efforts: an enormous literacy campaign was undertaken, and regional federations offered a program of lectures, films, and theater performances in all the villages (Leval 2018; Mintz 2013; Guérin 2017).

The Agrarian Economy of Zapatismo

Self-management and usufruct are at the heart of modern Zapatismo. After the Mexican Revolution of 1910–1920, the peasants received not "land and freedom" but land and the state. Land reform, through the establishment of the communally owned ejido, was an important link between the state and the people in Chiapas. Its promise and shortcomings gave rise to conditions that were favorable to exilic formation: the perception of the state was an unreliable provider of public goods, resentment of and wariness toward state institutions, and a growing conception of the state as "bad government." Land reform in Chiapas was substantial, but it did not instigate profound sociopolitical transformation or even end the primacy of the finca (large estate) as a key productive unit. Furthermore, the relationship between the *ejidatarios* (farmers working on communal land) and the state bureaucratic agencies had a formative influence on self-governance and the possibility of "delinking" from state structures in many localities.

The Zapatista rebellion in Chiapas began on January 1, 1994, the day that the North American Free Trade Agreement (NAFTA) went into effect. At the national level, the Institutional Revolutionary Party, the Partido Revolucionario Institucional, subsequently lost the presidential elections of July 2000 to the National Action Party, the PAN (Partido Acción Nacional), ending more than seventy years of one-party rule. From the very beginning, the rebellion emphasized the priority of territory and usufruct. The Zapatista conception of governance is distinguished by common possession democratically regulated in the forms of local self-government.

The rebel territory was enacted through the creation of thirty-eight autonomous municipalities (MAREZ) in December 1995 (Grubačić and O'Hearn 2016; Hesketh 2010). Two years later, the terms *Indigenous* and *autonomous* were linked to rebellion in the Zapatista descriptions of these municipalities (Mora 2008). During the first months of the rebellion, the Zapatistas "recuperated" between 500,000 and 700,000 hectares of land (about 1.2 to 1.7 million acres, or 4900 to 6900 square kilometers) from latifundists, which provided a material base for the construction of the rebel territory (Harvey 1998; Kaufman 2010; Grubačić and O'Hearn 2016). As Lieutenant Coronel Moisés, an officer in the Zapatista Army of National Liberation (Ejército Zapatista de Liberación Nacional, EZLN), explained,

> The land where the [Zapatista] compañeros and compañeras are now is their own property, land we recuperated. We discovered . . . that what [capitalism] does is make us prisoners of where we work. That's how capitalism functions: you work on ranches, or work in factories, and the profit is not for the people who work. Without this, we wouldn't be where we are today. It is clear to us as Zapatistas that since we became owners of these lands, as they are our means of production, this is the base from which to attack capitalism.
>
> (quoted in Kaufman 2010, 150)

The municipalities were, in turn, organized into five autonomous zones, or *aguascalientes* (zones of encounter, later renamed *caracoles*); these opened relationships with national and international civil society, and were primarily under the control of EZLN commanders.

Since at least 1996, the Zapatistas have faced major problems in establishing sovereignty in their territory. First, Zapatista municipalities are "alliances of villages with a variety of historical backgrounds" (Barmeyer 2009, 61). Many of the Zapatista-dominated communities border villages that are loyal to the PRI. In some villages and towns, there are separate administrative structures for the Zapatistas and the national parties (Grubačić and O'Hearn 2016). The problem of divided and shifting loyalties was especially painful from 1997 to 2004 (Barmeyer 2009). The exception were the *nuevos centros de populacion*, new communities established on recovered land, where support for Zapatismo was almost unanimous. These new communities are obliged to support the EZLN. To leave the movement, they would also have to leave the homestead.

Sovereignty in the rebel territory was consolidated in three phases: 1994–1997, 1997–2003, and 2003–present. During the second period, especially after the government's betrayal of the San Andrés peace accords in 2001, a comprehensive political restructuring took place. In August 2003, the Zapatistas announced the creation of the Juntas de Buen Gobierno (Good Government Councils) to govern the five autonomous spaces, now called *caracoles*, and especially to coordinate activities regarding health, education, and agriculture.

The Zapatista economy developed in two distinct periods: 1994–1998, and then *la resistencia*, which began in 1998. The primary economic goal is self-sufficiency—that is, active independence from the state and its social programs. The primary method was growing and selling agricultural produce. This was arrested, however, by emerging communal conflicts and as large numbers of villages began leaving the organization. From 1998, there was considerable effort to boost (autonomous) production. In 2001, a program for production and commercialization was initiated to improve living conditions by promoting cooperation, democracy, and communal organization. It included many microprojects and a schooling farm in Zona Selva Tojolabal that was focused on sustainable management, cattle vaccination, and basic agricultural training (Barmeyer 2009, 159; Grubačić and O'Hearn 2016). The agricultural projects include the development and use of bioinsecticides and composting and organic fertilizer, the rejection of genetically modified seed and chemical treatments, and the preservation of soil and conservation of native seeds (Earl and Simonelli 2005; Barmeyer 2009; Kaufman 2010; Grubačić and O'Hearn 2016). The products are sold to local, national, and international customers, and the financial management remains in the hands of community members. One example of this is the women's collective from the village of Oventik, Mujeres por la Dignidad (Women for Dignity). The cooperative was formed in 1997 and now has more than 700 members from four municipalities. Products from Zapatista communities, including clothing, artwork, and coffee are sold at a solidarity café in San Cristóbal (Hesketh 2010; Kaufman 2010). This strategy ensures that the primary producers, not middlemen, receive the full benefit of their labor.

In many villages, usufruct coexists with individual entrepreneurship. Communal projects often compete against the desire for individual profit, and private enterprise can stand in the way of a self-managed economy. In one village, people worked their milpas and cultivated maize during the week. On Saturday, the whole village assembled to accomplish a collective task that benefited the whole community. Participation was obligatory and regulated by a rotation system (Barmeyer 2009, 74; Grubačić and O'Hearn 2016). Most Zapatistas see no contradiction in participating in the collective project and increasing the profitability of their land (Earl and Simonelli 2005; Barmeyer 2009; Mora 2008; Grubačić and O'Hearn 2016). Small-scale production and commerce include cooperatives, coffee shops, artisan shops, bakeries, and various cooperative ventures. A bank in La Realidad provides loans at 2 percent interest (Hesketh 2010, 257).

Statistics are hard to come by, but the socialized surplus is used in two principal ways: to acquire products that the autonomous communities cannot produce themselves and to reinvest in other community projects (Earl and Simonelli 2005; Barmeyer 2009; Kaufman 2010). According to Kaufman (2010, 184), there is a third form of surplus distribution that goes into national and international solidarity projects: in 2005, corn was sent to Cuba; and in 2006, to Oaxaca and San Salvador Atenco.

The Zapatistas display considerable ingenuity in meeting multiple obstacles. For example, they created a system of collective warehouses in the jungle zone to avoid market fluctuations; dependency on "coyotesm," or intermediaries; and prohibitive transportation costs (Earl and Simonelli 2005; Barmeyer 2009; Kaufman 2010; Mora 2008). Flexibility was important: when the members of one association of Zapatista producers failed to raise enough money to build a community warehouse, they bought a communal truck instead and used it to take their produce to the local market and bring back essential goods like soap, sugar, and tools they bought at wholesale prices (Barmeyer 2009, 159). Some large collective purchases are made to alleviate intensive, usually gendered labor (e.g., corn-grinding machines) or to get a better price (livestock). Ad hoc committees operate during situations of communal emergency, for example, to obtain food or to raise cash by harvesting rare timber (Kaufman 2010, 183; Barmeyer 2009, 80). Finally, new population centers have an important economic role because recovered land is often ideal for cattle pastures or coffee plantations. New communities provide a crucial resource for the survival and economic autonomy of the whole Zapatista territory. Zapatistas communities live beyond minimum subsistence, and hunger has been almost eradicated.

Some autonomous production, such as the production of organic food, is done on a smaller scale and the surplus is (for the most part) retained locally. Some Zapatista products, however, are exported to capitalist markets, primarily niche solidarity markets. Coffee earnings are linked to the world market, and the territory is also increasingly dependent on seasonal work, migration, and remittances.

It is important to note that the Zapatista project very closely resembles those of the French, Russian, and Spanish anarchists. The emphasis is placed on usufruct, not private or state ownership. Autonomy in practice, as understood by the Zapatistas, implies self-management as a socialized process of active care of both the people and the land.

Land in Eco-Anarchism

Since the 1960s, anarchist thinking has become more attuned to ecological questions. Two main branches of eco-anarchism have emerged: one is the bioregional and deep ecology constellation (e.g., Sale 2000), and the other is the current of "social ecology" (e.g., Bookchin 1982). We focus here on the second one, mostly because of its clear continuity with the older anarchistic traditions discussed above. Our main reference is the work of Murray Bookchin, probably the most influential author in eco-anarchism, and also one of the first anarchists to address environmental questions in decentralist and anticapitalist terms.

Bookchin's "anarchist ecology" has its roots in the soil. Since he saw every plot of land as a complex and dynamic living entity composed of dead matter and organisms, his approach to agriculture is literally ecological: "Land is neither a 'resource' nor a 'tool,' but the *oikos* [the home] of myriad kinds of bacteria, fungi, insects, earthworms, and small mammals" (Bookchin 1976, 6). On the one hand, the soil is influenced by humans because agriculture directly intervenes in its biogeochemical cycles; on the other hand, "it becomes very difficult to understand human social institutions without referring to the prevailing agricultural practices of a historical period and, ultimately, to the soil situation to which they apply" (6). Accordingly, recognizing a nonhierarchical intertwining of ecological systems and social systems becomes fundamental to Bookchin's conception of land, of anarchism, and of what he calls "radical agriculture." Essentially, "radical agriculture seeks to restore humanity's sense of community: first, by giving full recognition to the soil as an ecosystem, a biotic community; and second, by viewing agriculture as . . . the practical, day-to-day interface of soil and human communities, the means by which both meet and blend" (7). In this framework, humanity is part of the natural world, and is in no way above it.

In this sense, Bookchin's (1976) radical agriculture is obviously a form of agroecology: "The radical agriculturist . . . must live on intimate terms with a given area of land and develop a sensitivity for its special needs—needs that no textbook approach can possibly encompass" (8). His critique of organic agriculture is explicit: "To be a technical connoisseur of an 'organic' approach to agriculture is no better than to be a mere practitioner of a chemical approach. We do not become 'organic farmers' merely by culling the latest magazines and manuals in this area, any more than we become healthy by consuming 'organic' foods acquired from the newest suburban supermarket. . . . Radical agriculture, in short, implies not merely new techniques in food cultivation, but a new non-Promethean sensibility toward land and society as a whole" (8). Yet Bookchin was by no means antitechnology. Like Kropotkin, he knew that there are limits to traditional forms of agriculture, especially when it relies on the back-breaking work of families, particularly the women in those families (Morris 2021).

Following the footsteps of Kropotkin and Mumford, Bookchin ([1995] 2021) proposed to extend this blending of ecological and social communities across urban and rural lands as well. He advocated for a regeneration of cities that would be scaled down to human needs and political maneuverability. He envisaged a future use of the land in terms of decentralized, moderately sized towns that would bring the countryside into the city, and the city into the countryside. The culturally diverse and genuinely social aspects of city life must be allowed to shape rural communities; and a stronger sense of community and a more direct relationship with nonhuman nature must shape urban communities. In his eco-municipalist model, not unlike the historical examples we saw earlier, Bookchin defended a multilevel confederation of egalitarian and sustainable communal entities governed by direct democracy while being connected to the land and its ecology.

Land in the Degrowth Movement

Many of Bookchin's ideas are very much alive today, not only in social ecology, but also in the degrowth movement or, at least, in an important portion of the movement. In fact, the similarities between degrowth and eco-anarchism are striking, and sometimes unknown to the participants of both communities. As an anticapitalist project and a research field, degrowth aims at stabilizing economies at a sustainable level of resource throughput while radically reorganizing societies around human and nonhuman flourishing (e.g., Latouche 2009; Gerber 2020). Degrowthers posit that the world's colossal and unequal metabolism requires a drastic resizing and reorganization. They call for the "overdeveloped" regions to initiate a democratic process of equitable contraction of their energy and material demands. But the critique of growthism and of industrial productivism, and the promotion of alternatives, also concern "underdeveloped" regions, as many authors from the global South have argued (see also Gutiérrez Escobar, this volume).

So far, degrowthers have mainly written about land to make explicit how the Capitalocene is associated with unsustainable land uses (e.g., Haberl et al. 2011). They have advocated for a "great transformation" in socioecological regimes, away from the land-use patterns and metabolic profiles of industrial economies, and toward sustainable alternatives. Scheidel and Sorman (2012), for example, show that eco-modernist approaches to solving the question of "sustainable energy"—such as biofuels, dams, wind farms, and big solar installations—cannot be the solution. Everything else remaining the same, a large-scale transition away from fossil fuels would drive a massive demand for land and more land grabbing. It would be so as long as current levels of production and consumption are not also problematized, which means, in short: as long as industrialized regions do not also degrow their use of energy and materials.

How to move toward degrowth alternatives, then? There is no single degrowth transition theory. Some of the most vocal degrowthers focus on policy actions within the nation-state, whereas a good proportion of the movement shows anarchistic sympathies and would support the view that alternatives can only be built here and now, "in the shell of the old." The reason is straightforward: no government has shown serious interest in leading a postgrowth transition, and little indicates that this will change anytime soon.

Returning to land, Baumann et al. (2020) convincingly argue that the degrowth movement has given insufficient attention to the centrality of land in a postgrowth transition. These authors elaborate on the basic fact that access to land creates a massive barrier—so big that it sometimes passes unnoticed!—to any kind of degrowth transition. Indeed, the cost of land (rents or mortgages) forces people to engage in wage labor, which immediately thwarts any possibility of pursuing degrowth in their lives and communities. "Meeting this obligation [to pay for one's land plot] is no small matter and has a range of knock-on implications: affecting what a person does for work, how much they work, their need for a car, what they wear, where they source their food, and a range of other consumer habits" (388).

From a degrowth perspective, Baumann et al. (2020) propose a reformist strategy to address this barrier. It involves an important state intervention in (a) decommodifying land to make available public housing, and (b) providing a living wage for anyone helping build local, self-managed, ecologically viable, and socially just communities and economies. "Such an opportunity, if properly supported, could show that access to land plus a participation income could help build new forms of genuinely sustainable development 'beyond the market.' . . . Progressively, as new skills are found, this group [of state-supported community builders] could begin to demonstrate a new type of productive and political agency that is consistent with the degrowth imaginary" (396). The authors see this land-based step toward a degrowth society as being politically more realistic than a universal basic income.

From an anarchist perspective, there is no doubt that degrowth needs to put the decommodification of land and labor at the center, and the "first step" proposal by Baumann et al. has the advantage of being electorally thinkable in today's world. But anarchists are often suspicious of "transitions," "stages," or "steps," since the work of building alternatives has already been going on for some time, in many different forms. Instead of "anticipatory politics" looking for a future "transition," it is prefigurative politics in the full sense that many anarchists would advocate. This implies that anarchism claims an *anachronistic* temporality—namely, a temporality "ahead of our time" and antagonistic to the dominant one. The work of confronting structures and building alternatives has, in effect, "anachronistically" already started, as exemplified by the European Action Coalition for the Right to Housing and to the City (2016), which includes a variety of grassroots movements fighting against the commodification of land and housing. It includes squatters, tenants, slum and self-built neighborhood dwellers, victims of inadequate housing, and victims of eviction and debt. The viability of Baumann et al.'s proposal is likely to depend on similar movements, and even more crucially, on the possibility that it can be sustained by the communities rather than by the state. Here again, the usufructuary socialization of land and housing seems more promising than a nationalization that isn't controlled by the communities themselves.

Conclusion

We showed in this chapter that the promotion of usufruct and democratic self-management is a distinctively anarchist contribution to the land question. These notions are central not only to Proudhon's mutualism but also to many historical experiences of agrarian autonomy that are like those we briefly presented here; it also became a cornerstone of Bookchin's social ecology and eco-anarchism in general.

Socializing usufruct through direct democracy eliminates exclusive nonuser ownership of the means of production and, by extension, the class of capitalist owners. Workers and peasants become the direct organizers of the process of their labor, which enables them to work and produce freely and retain the full value of whatever they sell. It is therefore not surprising, as we saw, that demands for ownership systems based on self-management and usufruct have been a defining feature of revolutionary movements throughout history (Grubačić and Graeber 2004).

Everywhere around the world, often for more than two centuries, old usufruct systems are being transformed under the influence of capitalism and nation-states (see also Peters, this volume). But there are also resurgences of new usufructuary socialization principles in multiple contemporary grassroots initiatives, especially in the global South. Most anarchists do not advocate a return to the past. They argue that a reconstruction of communal usufructuary systems based on direct democracy may represent the best institutional option for a sustainable degrowth future (Gerber 2020). On this, much is to be learned from Indigenous societies (Barker and Pickerill 2012). As we have seen here, anarchists advocate for an "anachronistic temporality" that is prefiguratively ahead of our time even as it draws on ancestral ecological values. It should be clear by now that anarchism and agrarian and indigenous movements may have a lot in common. Anarchism can translate between struggles in the global North and South, and this was, in fact, the most important quality of anarchism between 1870 and 1936 (Anderson 2005; Konishi 2013; Khuri-Makdisi 2010). Today, anarchism is possibly in a position to assume this role again (Grubačić 2013).

Acknowledgments

We'd like to express our gratitude to Jun Borras, Jenny Franco, Shivani Kaul, and Antonio Roman-Alcalá for their encouragement and constructive comments. All errors and shortcomings remain, of course, ours.

References

Anderson, Benedict. 2005. *Under Three Flags: Anarchism and the Anti-colonial Imagination*. London: Verso.

Avrich, Paul. 1970. *Kronstadt 1921*. Princeton, NJ: Princeton University Press.

Bakunin, Mikhail. (1870) 1972. "Letters to a Frenchman on the Present Crisis." In *Bakunin on Anarchy*, edited by Sam Dolgoff, 183–217. New York: Vintage Books.

Barker, Adam J., and Jenny Pickerill. 2012. "Radicalizing Relationships to and through Shared Geographies: Why Anarchists Need to Understand Indigenous Connections to Land and Place." *Antipode* 44 (5): 1705–1725.

Barmeyer, Niels. 2009. *Developing Zapatista Autonomy: Conflict and NGO Involvement in Rebel Chiapas*. Mexico City: University of Mexico Press.

Baumann, Alex, Samuel Alexander, and Peter Burdon. 2020. "Land Commodification as a Barrier to Political and Economic Agency: A Degrowth Perspective." *Journal of Australian Political Economy* 86: 379–405.

Blaufarb, Rafe. 2016. *The Great Demarcation: The French Revolution and the Invention of Modern Property*. Oxford: Oxford University Press.

Bookchin, Murray. 1976. "Radical Agriculture." In *Radical Agriculture*, edited by Richard Merrill, 3–13. New York: Harper and Row. (Original essay published in 1972.)

Bookchin, Murray. 1982. *The Ecology of Freedom: The Emergence and Dissolution of Hierarchy*. Palo Alto, CA: Cheshire Books.

Bookchin, Murray. (1995) 2021. *From Urbanization to Cities: The Politics of Democratic Municipalism*. Chico, CA: AK Press.

Earle Duncan, and Jeanne Simonelli. 2005. *Uprising of Hope: Sharing the Zapatista Journey to Alternative Development*. Walnut Creek, CA: Altamira Press.

Edwards, Stewart. 1973. *The Paris Commune, 1871*. Chicago: Quadrangle.

European Action Coalition for the Right to Housing and to the City. 2016. *Resisting Evictions across Europe*. Accessed October 19, 2021. https://zwangsraeumungverhindern.nostate.net/images/Resisting-Evictions-Across-Europe.pdf.

Finley, Moses. 1983. *Politics in the Ancient World*. Cambridge, UK: Cambridge University Press.

Gerber, Julien-François. 2020. "Degrowth and Critical Agrarian Studies." *Journal of Peasant Studies* 47 (2): 235–264.

Gerber, Julien-François, and Rolf Steppacher. 2017. "Basic Principles of Possession-Based Economies." *Anthropological Theory* 17 (2): 217–238.

Gerber, Julien-François, and Sandra Veuthey. 2011. "Possession *versus* Property in a Tree Plantation Socio-Environmental Conflict in Southern Cameroon." *Society and Natural Resources* 24 (8): 831–848.

Graeber, David, and David Wengrow. 2021. *The Dawn of Everything: A New History of Humanity*. New York: Farrar, Straus and Giroux.

Grubačić, Andrej. 2013. "The Anarchist Turn." In *The Anarchist Turn*, edited by Jacob Blumendfeld, Chiara Bottici, and Simon Critchley, 187–201. London: Pluto Press.

Grubačić, Andrej, and David Graeber. 2004. "Anarchism, or the Revolutionary Movement of the Twenty-First Century." ZNet. January. Accessed October 31, 2022. https://theanarchistlibrary.org/library/andrej-grubacic-david-graeber-anarchism-or-the-revolutionary-movement-of-the-twenty-first-centu

Grubačić, Andrej, and Denis O'Hearn. 2016. *Living at the Edges of Capitalism: Adventures in Exile and Mutual Aid*. Oakland: University of California Press.

Guérin, Daniel. 2017. *For a Libertarian Communism*. Oakland, CA: PM Press.

Haberl, Helmut, Marina Fischer-Kowalski, Fridolin Krausmann, Joan Martínez-Alier, and Verena Winiwarter. 2011. "A Socio-Metabolic Transition Towards Sustainability? Challenges for Another Great Transformation." *Sustainable Development* 19: 1–14.

Harvey, Niel. 1998. *The Chiapas Rebellion: The Struggle for Land and Democracy*. Durham, NC: Duke University Press.

Hesketh, Chris. 2010. "Clash of Spatializations." Unpublished PhD diss., University of Nottingham.

Kaufman, Mara. 2010. "We Are from Before, Yes, but We Are New: Autonomy, Territory, and the Production of New Subjects of Self-Government in Zapatismo." Unpublished PhD diss., Duke University.

Konishi, Sho. 2013. *Anarchist Modernity: Cooperatism and Japanese-Russian Intellectual Relations in Modern Japan*. Cambridge, MA: Harvard University Press.

Kropotkin, Peter. (1906) 2011. *The Conquest of Bread*. Mineola, NY: Dover.

Khuri-Makdisi, Ilham. 2010. *The Eastern Mediterranean and the Making of Global Radicalism, 1860–1914*. Berkeley: University of California Press.

Latouche, Serge. 2009. *Farewell to Growth*. Cambridge, UK: Polity.

Leval, Gaston. 2018. *Collectives in the Spanish Revolution*. Oakland, CA: AK Press.

Makhno, Nestor. (1918) 2005. "Visit to the Kremlin." In *No Gods, No Masters: An Anthology of Anarchism*, edited by Daniel Guérin, 501–514. Oakland, CA: AK Press.

Makhno, Nestor. 1934. "Over the Fresh Grave of Comrade N. Rogdaev." *Probuzhdeniye* 52–53. Accessed December 10, 2021. https://libcom.org/library/over-fresh-grave-comrade-n-rogdaev.

Mintz, Frank. 2013. *Anarchism and Workers' Self-Management in Revolutionary Spain*. Oakland, CA: AK Press.

Mora, Mariana. 2008. "Decolonizing Politics: Zapatista Indigenous Autonomy in an Era of Neoliberal Governance and Low Intensity Warfare." Unpublished PhD diss., University of Texas at Austin.

Morris, Brian. 2021. "Murray Bookchin and Radical Agriculture." In *Enlightenment and Ecology: The Legacy of Murray Bookchin in the 21st Century*, edited by Yavor Tarinski, 29–40. Montreal: Black Rose Books.

Öcalan, Abdullah. 2011. *Democratic Confederalism*. London: Transmedia Publishing.

Proudhon, Pierre-Joseph. (1840) 1994. *What Is Property?* Cambridge, UK: Cambridge University Press.

Rapp, John A. 2012. *Daoism and Anarchism: Critiques of State Autonomy in Ancient and Modern China*. New York: Bloomsbury.

Reclus, Élisée. 2013. *Anarchy, Geography, Modernity: Selected Writings of Élisée Reclus*. Edited and translated by John Clark and Camille Martin. Oakland, CA: PM Press.

Roman-Alcalá, Antonio. 2021. "Agrarian Anarchism and Authoritarian Populism: Towards a More (State-)Critical 'Critical Agrarian Studies.'" *Journal of Peasant Studies* 48 (2): 298–328.

Sale, Kirkpatrick. 2000. *Dwellers in the Land: The Bioregional Vision*. London: University of Georgia Press.

Scheidel, Arnim, and Alevgul H. Sorman. 2012. "Energy Transitions and the Global Land Rush: Ultimate Drivers and Persistent Consequences." *Global Environmental Change* 22: 588–595.

Scott, James C. 2009. *The Art of Not Being Governed: An Anarchist History of Upland Southeast Asia*. New Haven, CT: Yale University Press.

Seaweed. 2013. *Land and Freedom: An Open Invitation*. Accessed October 19, 2021. https://theanarchistlibrary.org/library/seaweed-land-and-freedom.

Skirda, Alexandre. 2002. *Facing the Enemy: A History of Anarchist Organization from Proudhon to May 1968*. Oakland, CA: AK Press.

Smolski, Andrew, Javier Sethnes Castro, and Alexander Reid Ross. 2018. "Lessons from Exits Foreclosed: An Exilic Interpretation of the Mexican and Russian Revolutions, 1910–1924. *Capital & Class* 42 (3): 453–488.

Thompson, Edward P. 1966. *The Making of the English Working Class*. New York: Vintage Books.

Tomba, Massimiliano. 2019. *Insurgent Universality: An Alternative Legacy of Modernity*. Oxford: Oxford University Press.

CHAPTER 8

LAND FROM POSTSTRUCTURALIST/ POSTDEVELOPMENT PERSPECTIVES

LAURA GUTIÉRREZ-ESCOBAR

Land: A Polysemic Concept

According to the *Oxford English Dictionary*, land is "the surface of the earth that is not sea." However, land is a polysemic concept, possessed of a myriad of sociopolitical and cultural meanings that extend beyond this definition. By "land" one can refer to a certain terrestrial environment and the associated biological community, to a term synonymous with a country or ancestral place of origin, or to an economic or a financial asset, an object of taxation, a source of social distinction and political power, a category of identity, or a means of production, among others (Li 2014; Manley, Foot, and Davis 2019; Stringer 2017).

Despite its internal differences, liberal and orthodox Marxist political economy conceptualized land mainly as a resource, a means of production, and a source of rent; an important commodity, whose circuits of investment and circulation, as well as ownership structure—were fundamental to developing agrarian capitalism (see Bernstein, this volume). Poststructuralist and postdevelopment studies complicate and destabilize—"deconstruct" in Jacques Derrida's words—the meaning of land. This chapter argues that these two theoretical frameworks contribute to a series of conceptual and political shifts and displacements in the understanding of land established in the strands of liberal and orthodox Marxist political economy. I focus on three pivotal concepts: territory, the "more than human," and sovereignty.

A rather elusive term, *poststructuralism* refers to "a more or less loosely grouped collection of texts and philosophers which came to prominence in France during the

1960s," particularly Michel Foucault, Jacques Derrida, Gilles Deleuze, and Félix Guattari (Harrison 2006, 122). Poststructuralism critiques orthodox Marxist and liberal political economy in seeking to overcome explanations of social phenomena based on "grand" theories—teleological and transcendental conceptual structures such as modes of production, the free market, or the self-interested individual—that are seen to erase difference and historicity (Harrison 2006, 125).[1] Poststructuralism focuses its analysis of social phenomena on the issues of difference, power, discourse, and representation, destabilizing modern authoritative claims to truth and certainty (Wylie 2006, 288–289).

One current powerful grand narrative is that of *development*. Emerging after World War II, but grounded in long-term historical processes of modernity and capitalism, the goal of development was to help nonindustrialized societies to become like Euro-American ones through economic growth (Rostow 1959). Rural development was marked by the Green Revolution oriented by a partial modernization of agriculture that included limited land reform, mechanization, subsidized credit, access to markets, irrigation channels, and other infrastructure, as well as the extensive use of agrochemicals and certified seeds. The Green Revolution aimed to provide cheap food for the growing urban and industrial working classes and raw materials for the nascent industries in the underdeveloped countries. Likewise, it sought to (a) solve the problem of food surpluses in industrial societies by exporting them as food aid to "feed the hungry" in the so-called Third World; (b) to prevent "Red Revolutions"—socialist, peasant-based revolutions that demanded land reform—in the context of the Cold War; and (c) to partially dismantle the semifeudal rent-seeking landowning class that continued to hold power in many countries (Patel 2013; Perkins 1997).

Since the 1980s, postdevelopment studies have advanced a critique of development as a dominant discourse in Foucault's terms—a particular configuration of knowledge and power established by expert knowledges and practices (Escobar 1994). This discourse invented Latin America, Africa, and parts of Asia as "underdeveloped" or "the Third World"—undermining other ways of defining their realities—by stressing the precarious achievement of the main features of modernity: scientific thought, urbanization, industrialization, liberal democracy, and so on (Escobar 1994).

Postdevelopment studies, on the one hand, question the central tenets of development: economic growth, progress, modernization, industrialization, the exploitation of nature, and the Green Revolution (Gudynas 2011, 21–25). On the other hand, they emphasize the importance of devising alternatives to development and new civilizatory models that are rooted in the knowledge and practices of grassroots social movements and marginalized communities (Acosta 2012; Escobar 2014; Gudynas 2011; Mignolo 2011).

First, following Tania Li, I illustrate how poststructuralism and postdevelopment studies deconstruct the notion of land as a pure, natural, "inert" resource; means of production; and commodity to be exploited. I focus on the "territorial turn" in Latin America and the displacements it enacts on the conceptualization of land from a postdevelopment perspective. Second, I analyze how postdevelopment and poststructuralism challenge anthropocentric notions of land to conceive "more-than-human" territories. Third, I discuss some essential questions and issues related to land, focusing on land reform and land sovereignty. I end by suggesting poststructuralist and postdevelopment theories need to envision future trajectories and research agendas toward further understanding how the socioecological crisis and the current shifting geopolitical order emerging from the rise of China are transforming the way we understand land.

Deconstructing Land beyond Capitalism

Poststructuralism and postdevelopment studies share a critique of political economy and put forward alternative notions of economy and politics. They deconstruct what poststructuralist feminist geographers J. K. Gibson-Graham (2006) call "capitalocentric" discourse, or the modern economic narratives that naturalize capitalism as an all embracing, progressive, rational, and self-producing system that becomes the standard from which to judge all other economic and noneconomic practices as being the opposite, the complement, or a deficient imitation of capitalism. They also emphasize the necessity of theorizing and supporting economic and political diversity and difference around notions of community and the commons, mutual aid and care, and well-being, among others (Gibson-Graham 2006).

Deconstructing the concept of "land," then, implies destabilizing or unfixing it from the narratives of capitalism to reveal its difference and surplus meaning. Instead of mainly defining land as an "inert" natural resource, means of production, or commodity to be exploited, such deconstruction reframes land in terms of the culturally mediated articulations of biology and sociopolitical history (Escobar 1999).

An illustrative example of deconstructing land arises from Tania Li's question, What is land? This ontological interrogation of land in itself disputes any stable and naturalized definition of land, including the most common, that land is a "natural resource." As she writes, land "uses and meanings are not stable and can be disputed . . . [Land] has an especially rich and diverse array of "affordances"— uses and values it affords to us, including the capacity to sustain human life" (Li 2014, 589).

Li (2014) deconstructs land by reframing it as a "provisional assemblage of heterogenous elements including material substances, technologies, discourses and practices" (589). Based on her fieldwork in Indonesia, Li argues that a different array of actors from villagers to scientists, investors, or government officials "have distinct views on what land is (its ontology), what it can or should do (its affordances) and how humans should interact with it" (590). She contrasts the definition of land from a governmental rationality in Foucault's terms, or a "concern to secure 'the right manner of disposing things' to optimise the health and wealth of populations at large" (590), with the fact that there is no word for land in the language of Indigenous highlanders in Sulawesi,

Indonesia. These highlanders instead have words for other assemblages of specific material qualities and conditions of what we call "land" and the social and spiritual relations associated with them, such as "soil (petu), primary forest (do'at), secondary forest (ulat), fallowed garden (abo), active garden (jo'ong), grassy patch (gio), barren zone (doilas), the head of a watershed (ompogan) which is the home of spirit owners of the earth and water (togu petu, togu ogo), and so on." However, when these Indonesian farmers started growing cacao, a new crop, for external markets, and thus conceiving land as a commodity and a site of investment, they invented the word *Lokasi* to name this new resource assemblage: "a plot of land that was detached from neighbouring plots, and detached from the sweat of the person who first cleared the do'at and transformed its status" (600).

Li's poststructuralist account of land as an arrangement of closely related social, spiritual, technological, and ecological relations resonates with the more complex and holistic notions of land emerging from postdevelopment thinkers in Latin America, to which I now turn.

From Land to Territory: A Latin American Perspective

In Latin America, the concept of "territory" does not necessarily equate with, and often interpellates, the nation-state. During colonial times, enslaved Black peoples escaped and occupied land in remote areas, where they constituted communities with various degrees of autonomy and freedom, known, for instance, as *quilombos* in Brazil and *palenques* in Colombia. Indigenous people also struggled to maintain their economic and political autonomy, knowledge systems, and ways of life in the *resguardos,* collective lands granted by the Spanish Crown, and to protect themselves from abuses by the local elite landowners and the church.

After independence, Indigenous and Afro-descendant—as well as ethnically mixed peasants—continued to struggle over collective and individual rights to land, as well as to maintain autonomy and their ways of life, in the context of the new nation-states. With the emergence and consolidation of communist and socialist parties, as well as rural unions and organizations, across Latin America during the twentieth century, these struggles revolved around the demand for land reform and were often framed in class-based discourses and practices. Moreover, since the 1960s, rural social relations and struggles have been reconfigured around the policies, institutions, and discourses associated with a development paradigm that stressed individual rights, economic growth and productivity, market integration, and modernization. In this context, Indigenous, Afro-descendant, and peasant traditions of struggle and demands that differed from or challenged the development paradigm were marginalized, but never lost.

Since the 1980s, Latin American social movements and communities have brought to the fore the concept of territory to reclaim and visibilize their historical epistemic and political struggles in the defense of their ways of life, autonomy and self-governance, ethnic-based and collective rights (Porto-Gonçalves 2009), and the refunding of the nation-state as plurinational in dispute with the hegemonic project of neoliberal multiculturalism (Cusicanqui 2012; Hale 2005; Restrepo 2008).

Examples include the Zapatista in Chiapas, Mexico (Reyes and Kaufman 2011); the coca-growing peasant movement and the Aymara Indigenous movement in Bolivia (Gutiérrez Aguilar 2005; Mamani 2004), the Black Communities' Process in the Colombian and Ecuadorian Pacific Coast (Escobar 2014), and the Mapuche in Chile (Tricot 2009). Some peasant movements are also claiming rights in the language of difference and demands for not only land, but also for territory—many of them are associated with La Via Campesina (Rosset 2013)—such as the Movimento dos Trabalhadores Rurais Sem Terra (MST; "Movement of Landless Rural Workers") in Brazil (Wolford 2010).

These movements are all diverse, and it is beyond the scope of this chapter to explain each of them. However, they all reveal, in different ways, that agrarian-based and rural ethnic and peasant communities have long conceptualized land as more than a resource, private property, or commodity; and in relation to territory, the communal and the collective, and interculturality. For instance, Black communities on Colombia's Pacific coast define their territories as "ancestral," establishing a continuity with the struggles and cosmovisions of enslaved Black people they descend from (Escobar 2014, 80). Their organization, the Black Communities' Process, struggles for the "Right to a space to be (Right to territory)," which they explain as follows:

> The development and recreation of our cultural vision requires the territory as a vital space. We cannot be if we do not have the space to live according to what we think and want as a way of life. Hence, our vision of territory is the vision of the habitat; that is, of the space where the black man and the black woman collectively develop their being, in harmony with nature.
>
> (quoted in Escobar 2014, 85–86)

Their notion of territory is constituted by practices of territoriality or the collective appropriation of a space in which to live that guarantees their ethnic, historic, and cultural survival (Escobar 2014, 88). Their territory includes not only land but also water, as the Pacific Ocean and multiple rivers provide spaces in which to recreate their culture and lives. Furthermore, the Black Communities' Process speaks of a "territory-region of the Pacific" that is intercultural—including Indigenous communities—and extends beyond the borders of Colombia to encompass Black communities in Ecuador.

Thus the concept not only of land but also of territory has been expanded to recognize there are multiple territorialities that do not conform with the Cartesian cartography of the nation-states (Escobar 2008, 90–91; Porto-Gonçalves 2009). Rather, territorialities are based on subaltern notions that form a network of bodies, places, practices, identities, and knowledges with no fixed borders. Further examples are feminist territorialities (Ulloa 2016) developed by decolonial, Indigenous, and communitarian feminist scholars who seek to decenter the notion of territory to include different scales and spaces, particularly to advance the notion of the body as territory (Zaragocin and Caretta 2021). There are also new forms of urban territorialities designed by social movements such as the *piquetero* (unemployed workers) and the squatters from the poor neighborhoods of Buenos Aires, Argentina, or El Alto, Bolivia, who engage in *trabajo territorial* (territorial work) and form *microgobiernos barriales* (Mamani 2005) to reclaim urban land for political mobilization and protests, housing, local forms of food provisioning in popular kitchens and urban agriculture, and the takeover of abandoned factories and business (Halvorsen 2019; Massida 2018; Torres 2011).

In dialogue with these social movements and community-based mobilizations, Latin America postdevelopment thinkers have reconceptualized land in relation to territory based on multiple alternative paradigms, such as *buen vivir* and rights of nature (Acosta 2012; Gudynas 2009), *comunalidad* (Esteva 2015; Gutiérrez Aguilar 2018; Mamani 2004), non-state-based politics and autonomy (Zibechi 2010), postpatriarchal and feminist economies (Quiroga Díaz 2019; Ulloa 2016), and transitions to postextractivism (Gudynas 2013; Vittor et al. 2012). I expand on one of these alternative paradigms—the commons—as an example of how the "territorial turn" challenged hegemonic conceptions on land, particularly those that stress land value is based on private property and commodification.

Drawing from Marx's analysis of land enclosures as primitive accumulation, studies on the commons define them as anything material and immaterial that is indispensable for collective wellbeing as humans and with other species (Bollier 2002)—or what Stephen Gudeman (2001, 30) has called the sacra—and, as such, cannot be enclosed and privatized (Bollier 2002, 2014).

The commons emphasize the importance of stewardship and common access to resources that are linked to shared identities and history, place-based economies, and social relationships and institutions grounded on reciprocity and solidarity, as well as on coercive means of social control and discrimination (Bollier 2002, 2014). Radical perspectives on the commons critique standard views of the commons as an issue of proper management of common resources to avoid their depletion (Ostrom 1990), to define them as a site of struggle against capitalist enclosures and the commodification of life. Geoger Caffentzis and Silvia Federici (2014) refer to these anticapitalist commons not as a thing, but as a process of "common-ing" (see also Bollier 2014).

Bollier (2014) defines commons as "a resource + a community + a set of social protocols" (15). However, he has also emphasized a relational and interepistemic approach to commons that dissolves the opposition between nature and society/culture (147) and honors "the new and diverse types of knowledges that are collectively constructed by commoners themselves" (154). Based on Bollier's initial definition, but integrating the relational perspective, a commons, such as land, may be defined as "an interspecies assemblage + a set of practices + a cosmovision / way of worlding." In other words, a community, composed of both humans (i.e., farmers) and nonhumans (i.e., land, water, seeds) that live and subsist together according to their distinctive socionatural practices, knowledges, and ways of inhabiting the world (Gutierrez Escobar 2016, 219).

On the other hand, from the Latin American perspective, the commons are conceived in terms of the heterogeneous forms of communal existence throughout the region. Commons depend upon a *trama comunitaria* or a weaved set of social relationships where knowledge, practices, labor, and social agreements converge to support the care of these commons and generate usufruct rights among the people of the community (Composto and Navarro 2014). For instance, the *cargo* system (Mexico) or the *minga* (Andes)—a baroque hybridization of the colonial and the Indigenous social institutions—as well as the localized markets where common goods are traded rather than abstract Wall Street markets; (Gutiérrez Aguilar 2018).

Studies on commons, then, question the value of land as mainly a means of production and a privately owned commodity for capital accumulation. Land, like water or seeds, is valued as communal and life-giving, and therefore, its full commodification, which results in the exclusion of some people and communities from having access to it and subsisting on it, is unacceptable and rejected by many because its leads to severe dispossession and human suffering. These studies also show how social movements and ethnic and peasant communities and peoples are now in dispute with capital and the state not only over their lands, but also over their commons such as seeds, rivers, forests, mountains or minerals (Porto-Gonçalves 2006, 167) reflecting a more relational view of territory as an unbroken continuity between humans and nonhumans.

In other words, there are peoples' struggles for the defense of land and territory; a space and community to live—and not only to produce—against development/extractivist projects of large-scale mining, corporate agriculture, resort tourism, hydroelectric dams, etc. (Alimonda et al. 2017). Also these social movements have to compete and negotiate their rights to land with armed and illegal actors such as drug traffickers, paramilitaries, and guerrillas (Ballvé 2012; Courtheyn 2018; Ojeda and Berman-Arévalo 2020), as well as other powerful actors including international NGOs and among ethnic and peasant communities that partially or completely share the same territory (Bocarejo 2011; Ojeda and González 2018; Ulloa 2010, 2011).

I end this section by briefly mentioning two critiques of postdevelopment thinking. Colombian anthropologists Eduardo Restrepo and Axel Rojas identify three shortcomings of postdevelopment thinking: the marginal presence of specific in-depth ethnographic analysis, the need to more deeply historicize race and modernity, and the erasure of class as a analytical and political category (Restrepo and Rojas 2010, 214–223). Bolivian anthropologist Silvia Rivera Cusicanqui (2012) has also questioned the cryptic language and overtheorization of postdevelopment thinkers, which restricts the dialogue and coproduction of knowledge with social movements and activists in Latin America, and strengthens their academic privileges, particularly among those who are located in universities in the global North.[2]

From Anthropocentric to "More-Than-Human" Notions of Land

In orthodox Marxism and structuralist anthropology, cultural ecology and other strands of social sciences considered "nature" as ontologically fixed and universal to all cultures. Instead, poststructuralist approaches argue that "conceptions of nature are socially constructed, that they vary according to cultural and historical determinations, and that, therefore, our own dualistic view of the universe should not be projected as an ontological paradigm onto the many cultures where it does not apply" (Descola 1996, 82). Accordingly, poststructuralist scholars emphasize the existence of many different social constructions of nature. There are many ethnographic examples of how non-western peoples in the Amazon (Descola 1994; Kohn 2013), Indonesia (Tsing 2005), Colombia (Gudeman and Rivera 1990) or the Artic (Ingold 1980) do not place humans and nonhumans in different ontological realms. In contrast, these peoples consider that humans belong to a wider community of living and nonliving beings where plants, animals, land, rivers, or mountains, along with spirits, are conceived and treated as persons. As such, land signaled profound connections between humans and other living beings, including wild and cultivated plants or water.

An example of a poststructuralist analysis of land in connection to more-than-human relations comes from an emerging literature on posthuman ecologies that is focused on soils. Drawing on feminist approaches to care, Puig de la Bellacasa (2017) speaks of "embodied caring human-soil relationalities" where humans are members of soil communities. For Puig de la Bellacasa, conceiving the soil as a "living multispecies world" allows us to slow down our productivist pace and "dominant futuristic drive" in order to value other forms of ecological temporalities and "make time for soil" as a practice of human care and responsibility that confront exploitative practices. These different temporalities extend from geological processes to ecological cycles of the multispecies community and food webs that make soil—and are vital for maintaining its fertility—including the different ways humans grow food (Puig de la Bellacasa 2017, 188–215). Caring for soil is also a practice of mainly nonindustrial and agroecological farmers who are "acutely protective of their soil, treating it with the commitment, concern and empathy normally reserved for close family members" (Guy Watson, quoted in Puig de la Bellacasa 2017, 197).

Kristina Lyons (2016) looks at soil politics in the context of the war on drugs and the aerial fumigation of coca plants by the military in southern Colombia. Lyons shows that Amazonian soils do not conform with the expectations of the soil scientists, state development planners, and agribusiness companies that regard "good" soils as those designed for endless productivity, growth, and market-oriented agriculture. Rather, the ecology and regeneration of Amazonian soils depend on farmers' practices that allow for organic decay, decomposition, and fragility. These human-soil relations have become a form of resistance against the criminalization of small farmers who grow illicit (mostly coca) and commercial crops, and home gardens while also conserving patches of the Amazon rainforest in their farms and communities (Lyons 2016).

These relational approaches to soil contribute to shifting the vision of land away from being an "inert" resource to be exploited to one that recognizes that land is an ecosystem, with a multiplicity of life forms, socioecological relations, and political agency that we need to care for.

Within postdevelopment studies, the territorial turn has also contributed to the more recent emergence of a body of scholarship on the political ontology of territory (Blaser 2013; De la Cadena 2015; Escobar 2014). This political ontology goes beyond the conception of socially constructed nature to acknowledge that ethnic communities, together with multiple "earth-beings," produce territory, such as mountains or rivers, that are endowed with agency (De la Cadena 2015). In the process, each enacts different ways of knowing and being in the world, showing the existence of a pluriverse (Escobar 2008).

Struggles for Land Sovereignty and Land Reform

Struggles over land property, access and use have characterized all societies. The question of who can own, access, and use land is extremely complex and controversial because of how valuable land is. It entails defining which individuals and groups in society, both citizens and foreigners, have (and do not have) rights to buy, sell, inherit, rent, transfer or expropriate land. Further, a) what are the conditions under which all of these land deals are carried out in terms of prices, time frames, credit mechanisms (loans, interests), or compensations; b) which kinds of land are involved, regarding its geographical location, fertility, access to water or markets, and so on; and c) who (and who does not) gets to define all of these questions and by which means (law, violence, and so forth).

The complexity of land issues has resulted in a multiplicity of systems of land tenure (private, communal, open-access, state-owned), use (agriculture, grazing, hunting-gathering, recreation, mining, urban development), and management (soil conservation, flood mitigation; Manley, Foot, and Davis 2019). These different systems of land tenure, use, and management mirror the broad legal property systems and the political and moral conceptions of property of each society.

Land property and distribution are crucial in defining inequality because land is not only a factor of production, but also a form of rent-seeking, financial speculation, and money laundering that confers social distinction (Bourdieu 1984) and economic, political, and military power (UNCCD 2017, 191). For instance, there is evidence of the strong relationship between land concentration processes and armed conflict and war across the global South in Colombia (Courtheyn 2018), South East Asia (Chao 2013), and Africa (Thaler 2013). Furthermore, land inequality is not only structured around class relations but also race and gender relations. For instance, the multiple forms of discrimination and violence of patriarchal relations influence women's ability to access, legally own, and inherit land, which in turn, impacts their opportunities to access credit, participate in the market, increase their incomes, make decisions within the family and community, or flee contexts of domestic violence (Deere and León 2000; UNCCD 2017, 208–211).

Food Regimes and the Global Land Grab

The corporate (McMichael 2009) or neoliberal food regime (Otero 2012) has led to the consolidation of all these trends in land inequality. The food regimes framework analyses agriculture's and food's role—as well as the agency of agrarian social movements—in the historical process of capital accumulation and the formation of a global food system (McMichael 2009, 140). It identifies three main regimes in the twentieth century, characterized by historical contradictions that produce crises and transitions from one food regime to the other. The current corporate food regime emerged around the 1980s with the globalization project that was based on the "free" market model and dominated by the interests of transnational corporations and the World Trade Organization, which control the food system from production to consumption. The central contradiction is between the agri-food corporate establishment and the global and local food sovereignty movements represented, for example, by La Vía Campesina (McMichael 2009, 151). Mexican sociologist Gerardo Otero (2012) refers to the neoliberal food regime to emphasize that its hegemonic feature is neoliberalism rather than corporations. Otero identifies three interconnected characteristics of this food regime: the role of the state and a new form of regulation, transnational agri-food corporations, and agricultural biotechnology (Otero 2012).

The current food regime exacerbates the global land grab, or the massive appropriation of land by governments and corporations in less powerful regions and countries, particularly but not only in Sub-Saharan Africa, South East Asia, and Latin America. Against the backdrop of a financial, ecological, and energy crisis, corporations and governments are acquiring land as an investment to secure food and energy security or increase profits, or both, from financial speculation and from the global boom in biofuel and agricultural commodities markets (Borras et al. 2012; Borras et al. 2011; De Schutter 2011; Wolford et al. 2013). Due to rising of finance and corporate power that characterizes the neoliberal food systems, the struggle for land has taken on new meanings and actors, such as "capitalized land owners, financial capital and transnational corporations" (Rosset 2017, 389).

Land grabbing may be associated with the expansion of genetically modified seeds, as the in the case of Argentina, Brazil, and Paraguay (Domínguez and Sabatino 2017; Fernandes et al. 2010; Palau 2004); water grabbing (Kay and Franco 2019; Mehta et al. 2012); or green grabbing resulting from payments for environmental services, carbon markets, or sources of "clean" energy such as wind power or lithium (Argento et al. 2017; Buscher et al. 2012; Cárdenas 2012; Fairhead Leach, and Scoones 2012; Fletcher and Büscher 2017). However, the grabbing of commons can also happen without the control and grabbing of land (Dell'Angelo et al. 2017). For instance, biotechnology corporations promote the enclosure of seeds through intellectual property rights or genetic contamination—along with the knowledges connected to the conservation of those seeds—without necessarily land grabbing (Fitting 2011; Hernández Vidal 2019; Kloppenburg 2004; Shiva 1997; Silva Garzón and Gutiérrez Escobar 2020).

New Perspectives on Land Reform and Land Sovereignty

The transnational movement La Vía Campesina (LVC), supported by the NGO Food and Information Network (FIAN) and the Land Research Actor Network, launched the "Global Campaign for Land Reform." The centerpiece of the campaign is the demand for what LVC calls an "integral and popular land reform" that is not limited to redistributing land and access to productive resources, but is also about the defense of territory within the framework of food sovereignty and agroecology (La Vía Campesina 2017; Rosset 2013). This integral and popular land reform aims to be part of the solution to the environmental crisis through some combination of traditional farming and agroecology, the fight against the global land grab, the protection of other commons, such as water and biodiversity, the production of healthy and nutritious food, and the provision of dignified living conditions for small-scale food producers from peasants to fishermen and pastoralist peoples (Rosset 2013, 726).

In connection, "land sovereignty" is the right of peoples to control land use, access, and benefits. "Land sovereignty embraces plural understanding of property rights—encompassing communal, community, state, and/or private property rights—privileging the commons without romanticizing it; recognising the importance of state property while confronting the contradictory role of state in land conflicts" (Borras and Franco 2012, 1).

One of the debates within LVC is over the social actor that should implement the land reform. Until 2000, LVC pressured democratically elected governments to undertake land reform. However, in light of the disenchantment with progressive governments and the increasing alliance between transnational capital and national elites, there is a call for social movements to pursue agrarian reform from below via public policy interventions and forms of civil disobedience, such as land occupations and protests; through the democratization of knowledge and exchange (*diálogo de saberes*) and social relations free of racist, class, and patriarchal forms of oppression (Borras 2009; La Vía Campesina 2017; Rosset 2013).

Similarly, the Brazil-based Movimento dos Trabalhadores Rurais Sem Terra ("Movement of Landless Rural Workers") advocates for a new kind of agrarian reform that has several important characteristics. First, its aim is to provide land to landless people in their regions of origin rather than using land distribution as a colonization strategy, particularly of the Amazon (Wolford 2010, 218–219). Second, the MST's call for agrarian reform aims to reverse the migration from the countryside to the slums in the cities of Brazil—a migration pattern that affects peasants around the world. Third, the agrarian reform is connected to the provision of stable markets, such as the Brazilian government's program Zero Hunger, and to the demand for agricultural credit, extension assistance, and infrastructure in the settlements (Wolford 2010, 216–217) Fourth, in dispute with the Brazilian state and the agribusiness and financial elites that conceptualize agrarian reform as a development tool, the MST envisions reform as a site to defend and boost small-farm production and food sovereignty. In sum, MST's agrarian reform is not limited to the right to land—for instance, gaining land titles—but to the " 'right to have rights,' a dignified living, and substantive citizenship" (Wolford 2010, 222).

In summary, land reform and land sovereignty from a territorial perspective[3] include thinking about land as a commons; granting communities rights to forms of living off the land other than agriculture, such as fishing areas to traditional fishermen or forests to forest-based people; to reimagine land tenure to include cooperatives or urban agriculture; and to recognize the ecologically or spiritually and ancestral territories of nomadic and Indigenous peoples beyond the notion of productive land.

There are several challenges associated with this agenda. The first concerns the questions, How can different peoples peacefully coexist and share one territory (Bocarejo 2011)? And how can new alliances be created among the urban poor, who are also being displaced from their land and territory by urban real estate speculation?

The second asks, How can land and territorial struggles be articulated from different rural communities and social movements across regions, respecting their cosmovisions and sustaining truly democratic forms of collaboration, knowledge production, and political mobilization among them. Furthermore, how can people's rights to land be articulated with the rights of nature and, particularly, the rights to other commons such as water or seeds?

Third is the issue of gender inequality in access to land, especially within the framework of neoliberal market-led reforms. On one hand, these reforms expand land titling for women as a strategy to dismantle communal land tenure systems. On the other hand, there is a question of how to implement communal land tenure in ways that grant women equality. At the same time, communal land titling may become useful for land grabbing by making it easier for land speculators and transnational companies to negotiate and to bribe community leaders (La Vía Campesina 2017; Rosset 2017) As Li (2014) argues, the recognition of communal land may become a "means of dispossession, when a 'customary chief' who claims to have jurisdiction over communal land signs off on a land deal without consulting the people affected. Instead of protecting landholders from land alienation (often the goal of the collective tenure regimes, both colonial and contemporary), communal tenure can provide a convenient 'one-stop-shop' for large-scale investors" (598).

Possible Future Trajectories and Research Agendas

To ensure the continuing relevance of poststructuralist and postdevelopment approaches, I suggest two important issues to be further integrated in future trajectories and research agendas. First, it is important to design transitions to agrifood systems that can truly adapt and reverse the socioecological crisis (the impacts of climate change, biodiversity loss, and contamination) for all people, particularly those who have been historically marginalized, enacting environmental justice. The urgency of the need to do this cannot be understated. We are crossing planetary boundaries that will make climate change, the collapse of biodiversity and ecosystems, ocean acidification, the alteration of water and nutrient cycles, and chemical pollution irreversible. There are many calls from academics and activists to address the current food crisis—which has been exacerbated by the Covid-19 pandemic—by embracing agroecology and supporting peasants and urban farmers instead of the chains in the capitalist market (Altieri and Nicholls 2020; Clapp and Moseley 2020; Gliessman 2020; Montenegro de Wit 2021; van der Ploeg 2020). For Altieri and Nicholls, for instance, post-Covid public policies need to promote redistributive land reform to "directly impact on the underlying inequalities of the dominant global agrifood system" (Altieri and Nicholls 2020, 893).

Postdevelopment and poststructuralist studies may need to politically and epistemologically reconceptualize the issue of class and inequality to help bring justice to the fore in transitions to sustainable food systems and land reform. In other words, how does class—and class relations with respect to land—look from a poststructuralist and a postdevelopment perspective? This endeavor may benefit from revisiting Marx and Marxist theory—for instance, the Frankfurt School and the Cultural Marxists—and establishing more profound dialogues with the contemporary wave of Marxisms.

Second, what will rural development look like under a China-dominated global geopolitical order—or at least a multipolar world in which China, India, and Russia dispute US leadership? Certainly, in the twenty-first century, the rapid industrialization of China and the growth of its middle class generated a commodity boom—what Svampa and Slipak (2015) call the "Beijing Consensus." This commodity boom allowed for a cycle of extractivism that in Latin America provided agricultural inputs (particularly, genetically modified soy and maize) or lithium and other minerals, that lead to land grabbing or to reconfigurations of land use and property (Otero 2021, 18). Much has been said about the influence of Confucian traditions on capitalist development China—akin to Max Weber's theory about the influence of Protestantism in the birth of industrial capitalism in Europe. How will the growing influence of China's capitalism and one-party state reconfigure the values, practices, and discourses on land, as well as the processes of resistance and emancipation around land reform and land sovereignty?

Acknowledgments

I am very grateful to the reviewers—Astrid Ulloa (Universidad Nacional de Colombia) and Diana Ojeda (Universidad de los Andes at Bogotá)—as well as to professors Elizabeth Fitting, Jun Borras, and Arturo Escobar for their careful reading and comments that greatly improved this article. All shortcomings are my own.

Notes

1. Of course, Marxism itself has diverse "orthodox" traditions, some of them more sensitive to integrating cultural perspectives and challenging teleological structural explanations such as the Cultural Marxists (E. P. Thompson, Stuart Hall). Moreover, certain Marxists, such as Gramsci, are an inspiration for both orthodox Marxists and other thinkers who are outside this tradition, including poststructuralists. For instance, Gramsci's concept of hegemony is central for Ernesto Laclau and Chantal Mouffe, among others. I thank Jun Borras for this observation.
2. In addition, a well-known debate took place after a series of polemic articles by *Le Monde Diplomatique*'s editor for Bolivia Pablo Stefanoni (Stefanoni 2010, 2011) and subsequent replies by Arturo Escobar (Escobar, 2011) among others.
3. Not all of these movements necessarily identify with the tenets of post-structuralism and/or post-development, and some of them may be even closer to Marxist-Leninists. I thank Jun Borras for this clarification.

References

Acosta, Alberto. 2012. *Buen Vivir. Sumak Kawsay. Una Oportunidad Para Imaginar Otros Mundos*. Quito: Abya-Yala.

Alimonda, Héctor, Catalina Toro Pérez, and Facundo Martín. 2017. *Ecologia Politica Latinoamericana. Pensamiento Critico, Diferencia Latinoamericana y Rearticulación Epistémica*. Buenos Aires y Ciudad de México: Clacso y Universidad Autónoma Metropolitana.

Altieri, Miguel A., and Clara I. Nicholls. 2020. "Agroecology and the Reconstruction of a Post-COVID-19 Agriculture." *Journal of Peasant Studies* 47 (5): 881–898. https://doi.org/10.1080/03066150.2020.1782891.

Argento, Melisa, Florencia Puente, and Ariel Slipak. 2017. "¿Qué Debates Esconde La Explotación Del Litio En El Noroeste Argentino? Perspectivas y Proyecciones Sobre La Dinámica Empresas-Estado-Comunidad." In *Ecología Política Latinoamericana. Pensamiento Crítico, Diferencia Latinoamericana y Rearticulación Epistémica*, edited by Héctor Alimonda, Catalina Toro Pérez, and Facundo Martín, 403–429. Buenos Aires: CLACSO.

Ballvé, Teo. 2012. "Everyday State Formation: Territory, Decentralization, and the Narco Landgrab in Colombia." *Environment and Planning D: Society and Space* 30 (4): 603–622. https://doi.org/10.1068/d4611.

Blaser, Mario. 2013. "Ontological Conflicts and the Stories of Peoples in Spite of Europe: Toward a Conversation on Political Ontology." *Current Anthropology* 54 (5): 547–568. https://doi.org/10.1086/672270.

Bocarejo, Diana. 2011. "Dos Paradojas Del Multiculturalismo Colombiano." *Revista Colombiana de Antropología* 47 (2): 97–121.

Bollier, David. 2002. "Silent Theft: The Private Plunder of Our Common Wealth." New York: Routledge.

Bollier, David. 2014. "Think Like a Commoner: A Short Introduction to the Life of the Commons." British Columbia: New Society Publishers.

Borras Jr., Saturnino M., Jennifer C. Franco, Sergio Gómez, Cristobal Kay, and Max Spoor. 2012. "Land Grabbing in Latin America and the Caribbean." *Journal of Peasant Studies* 39 (3–4): 845–872. https://doi.org/10.1080/03066150.2012.679931.

Borras, Jun. 2009. "La Vía Campesina and Its Global Campaign for Agrarian Reform." In *Transnational Agrarian Movements Confronting Globalization*, edited by Jun Borras, Marc Edelman, and Cristobal Kay, 91–122. Chichester: Wiley-Blackwell.

Borras, Saturnino M., and Jennifer C. Franco. 2012. "A 'Land Sovereignty' Alternative: Towards a Peoples (Counter)-Enclosure." *Transnational Institute*, 1–12. https://www.tni.org/files/a_land_sovereignty_alternative_.pdf.

Borras, Saturnino M., Ruth Hall, Ian Scoones, Ben White, and Wendy Wolford. 2011. "Towards a Better Understanding of Global Land Grabbing: An Editorial Introduction." *Journal of Peasant Studies* 38 (2): 209–216. https://doi.org/10.1080/03066150.2011.559005.

Bourdieu, Pierre. 1984. *Distinction: A Social Critique of the Judgement of Taste*. Cambridge: Harvard University Press.

Buscher, Bram, Sian Sullivan, Katja Neves, Jim Igoe, and Dan Brockington. 2012. "Towards a Synthesized Critique of Neoliberal Biodiversity Conservation." *Capitalism, Nature, Socialism* 23 (2): 4–30. https://doi.org/10.1080/10455752.2012.674149.

Caffentzis, George, and Silvia Federici. 2014. "Commons against and beyond Capitalism." *Community Development Journal* 49 (SUPPL.1): i92–i105. https://doi.org/10.1093/cdj/bsu006.

Cárdenas, Roosbelinda. 2012. "Green Multiculturalism: Articulations of Ethnic and Environmental Politics in a Colombian 'Black Community.'" *Journal of Peasant Studies* 39 (2): 309–333. https://doi.org/10.1080/03066150.2012.665892.

Chao, Sophie. 2013. "Agribusiness Large: Scale Land Acquisitions and Human Rights in Southeast Asia." Moreton-in-Marsh. http://www.forestpeoples.org/sites/fpp/files/publication/2013/08/lsla-studies.pdf.

Clapp, Jennifer, and William G. Moseley. 2020. "This Food Crisis Is Different: COVID-19 and the Fragility of the Neoliberal Food Security Order." *Journal of Peasant Studies* 47 (7): 1393–1417. https://doi.org/10.1080/03066150.2020.1823838.

Composto, Claudia, and Mina Lorena Navarro. 2014. *Territorios En Disputa. Despojo Capitalista, Luchas En Defensa de Los Bienes Comunes Naturales y Alternativas Emancipatorias Para América Latina*. Mexico: Bajo Tierra Ediciones.

Courtheyn, Christopher. 2018. "Territories of Peace: Alter-Territorialities in Colombia's San José de Apartadó Peace Community." *The Journal of Peasant Studies* 45 (7): 1432–1459. https://doi.org/10.1080/03066150.2017.1312353.

De la Cadena, Marisol. 2015. *Earth Beings. Ecologies of Practice Across Andean Worlds*. Durham: Duke University Press.

Deere, Carmen, and Magdalena León. 2000. *Género, Propiedad y Empoderamiento: Tierra, Estado y Mercado En América Latina*. Bogota: Universidad Nacional de Colombia.

Dell'Angelo, Jampel., D'odorico, Paolo., Rulli, Maria Cristina, & Marchand, Philippe. 2017. "The Tragedy of the Grabbed Commons: Coercion and Dispossession in the Global Land Rush." *World Development* 92: 1–12.

Descola, Philippe. 1994. *In the Society of Nature: A Native Ecology in Amazonia*. Cambridge: University of Cambridge Press.

Descola, Philippe. 1996. "Constructing Natures." In *Nature and Society. Anthropological Perspectives*, edited by Philippe Descola and Gísli Pálsson, 82–102. New York: Routledge.

Domínguez, Diego, and Pablo Sabatino. 2017. "Acaparamiento de Tierras y Agronegocios En Argentina." In *Concentración, Acaparamiento de Tierras, Desarrollo Rural y Derecho a La Alimentación*, edited by Flavio Bladimir Rodríguez, Juana Camacho Segura, and Juan Carlos Morales, 177–206. Bogotá: Universidad Externado de Colombia, ICANH, FIAN Colombia.

Escobar, Arturo. 1994. *Encountering Development: The Making and Unmaking of the Third World*. Princeton University Press.

Escobar, Arturo. 1999. "After Nature. Steps to an Antiessentialist Political-Ecology." *Current Anthropology* 40 (1): 1–30.

Escobar, Arturo. 2008. *Territories of Difference Place, Movements, Life, Redes*. Durham: Duke University Press.

Escobar, Arturo. 2011. "¿"Pachamámicos" versus 'Modérnicos'?" *Tabula Rasa* 15 (julio-diciembre): 265–273. https://www.redalyc.org/pdf/396/39622587015.pdf.

Escobar, Arturo. 2014. *Sentipensar Con La Tierra. Nuevas Lecturas Sobre Desarrollo, Territorio y Diferencia*. Medellín: Ediciones UNAULA.

Esteva, Gustavo. 2015. "Para Sentipensar La Comunalidad." *Bajo El Volcán* 15 (23): 171–186.

Fairhead, James, Melissa Leach, and Ian Scoones. 2012. "Green Grabbing: A New Appropriation of Nature?" *Journal of Peasant Studies* 39 (2): 237–261. https://doi.org/10.1080/03066150.2012.671770.

Fernandes, Bernardo Mançano, Clifford Andrew Welch, and Elienaí Constantino Gonçalves. 2010. "Agrofuel Policies in Brazil: Paradigmatic and Territorial Disputes." *The Journal of Peasant Studies* 37 (4): 793–819. https://doi.org/10.1080/03066150.2010.512459.

Fitting, Elizabeth M. 2011. *The Struggle for Maize Campesinos, Workers, and Transgenic Corn in the Mexican Countryside/Elizabeth Fitting*. Durham and London: Duke University Press.

Fletcher, Robert, and Bram Büscher. 2017. "The PES Conceit: Revisiting the Relationship between Payments for Environmental Services and Neoliberal Conservation." *Ecological Economics* 132: 224–231. https://doi.org/10.1016/j.ecolecon.2016.11.002.

Gibson-Graham, J. K. 2006. *Postcapitalist Politics*. University of Minnesota Press.

Gliessman, Steve. 2020. "Confronting Covid-19 with Agroecology." *Agroecology and Sustainable Food Systems* 44 (9): 1115–1117. https://doi.org/10.1080/21683565.2020.1791489.

Gudeman, Stephen. 2001. *The Anthropology of Economy: Community, Market, and Culture*. New Jersey: Wiley-Blackwell.

Gudeman, Stephen, and Alberto Rivera. 1990. *Conversations in Colombia. The Domestic Economy in Life and Text*. Cambridge: Cambridge University Press. https://doi.org/10.1017/CBO9780511558009.

Gudynas, Eduardo. 2009. "Entre El Fantasma De La Modernidad Y El Desafío Biocéntrico." *Revista Obets* 4: 49–53.

Gudynas, Eduardo. 2011. "Debates Sobre El Desarrollo y Sus Alternativas En América Latina: Una Breve Guía Heterodoxa." In *Más Allá Del Desarrollo*, edited by Miriam Lang and Dunia Mokrani, 21–53. Quito: Ediciones Abya Yala and Fundación Rosa Luxemburg.

Gudynas, Eduardo. 2013. "Extracciones, Extractivismos y Extrahecciones. Un Marco Conceptual Sobre La Apropiación de Recursos Naturales." *Observatorio Del Desarrollo*, no. 18: 1–18.

Gutiérrez Aguilar, Raquel. 2005. *Los Ritmos Del Pachakuti Movilización y Levantamiento Popular-Indígena En Bolivia (2000-2005)*. Buenos Aires: Tinta Limón.

Gutiérrez Aguilar, Raquel. 2018. *Comunalidad, Tramas Comunitarias y Producción de Lo Común. Debates Contemporáneos Desde América Latina*. Oaxaca: Colectivo Editorial Pez en el Árbol- Casa de las preguntas.

Gutierrez Escobar, Laura. 2016. "The Political Ontology of Seeds: Seed Sovereignty Strunggles in An Indigenous Resguardo in Colombia." University of North Carolina at Chapel Hill.

Hale, Charles R. 2005. "Neoliberal Multiculturalism: The Remaking of Cultural Rights and Racial Dominance in Central America." *Political and Legal Anthropology Review* 28 (1): 10–28. http://www.jstor.org/stable/24497680.

Halvorsen, Sam. 2019. "Decolonising Territory: Dialogues with Latin American Knowledges and Grassroots Strategies." *Progress in Human Geography* 43 (5): 790–814. https://doi.org/10.1177/0309132518777623.

Harrison, Paul. 2006. "Poststructuralist Theories." In *Approaches to Human Geography*, edited by Stuart Aitken and Gill Valentine, 122–135. London: SAGE Publications Ltd.

Hernández Vidal, Nathalia. 2019. "La Cosecha Epistémica: Un Análisis de La Praxis Epistémica de Los Guardianes de Semillas En Colombia." In *Ciencia, Tecnología y Sociedad En América Latina. La Mirada de Las Nuevas Generaciones*, edited by Rosalba Casas and Tania Pérez, 41–63. Buenos Aires: CLACSO.

Ingold, Tim. 1980. *Hunters, Pastoralists and Ranchers*. Cambridge University Press.

Kay, Sylvia, and Jenny Franco. 2019. "The Global Water Grab: A Primer." In *Green Planet Blues. Critical Perspectives on Global Environmental Politics*, edited by Geoffrey Dabelko and Ken Conca, 6th ed., 342–356. New York: Routledge. https://doi.org/10.4324/9780429322204-34.

Kloppenburg, J. R. 2004. *First the Seed: The Political Economy of Plant Biotechnology, 1492-2000*. Second. Wisconsin: The University of Wisconsin Press.

Kohn, Eduardo. 2013. *How Forests Think: Toward an Anthropology Beyond the Human*. Berkeley: University of California Press.

Li, Tania Murray. 2014. "What Is Land? Assembling a Resource for Global Investment." *Transactions of the Institute of British Geographers* 39 (4): 589.

Lyons, Kristina. 2016. "Decomposition as Life Politics: Soils, Selva, and Small Farmers under the Gun of the U.S.-Colombian War on Drugs." *Cultural Anthropology* 31 (1): 56–81. https://doi.org/10.14506/ca31.1.04.

Mamani, Pablo. 2004. *El Rugir de Las Multitudes. La Fuerza de Los Levantamientos Indígenas En Bolivia/Qullasuyu*. La Paz: Aruwiriyi y Yachaywasi.

Mamani, Pablo. 2005. *Microgobiernos Barriales. Levantamiento de La Ciudad de El Alto (Octubre de 2003)*. El Alto and La Paz: CADES/IDIS-UMSA.

Manley, Will, Katharine Foot, and Andrew Davis. 2019. "A." In *Dictionary of Agriculture and Land Management*. Oxford University Press.

Massida, Adriana. 2018. "Utopian Visions for Buenos Aires Shantytowns: Collective Imaginaries of Housing Rights, Upgrading and Eviction (1956–2013)." *Bulletin of Latin American Research* 37 (2): 144–159. https://doi.org/https://doi.org/10.1111/blar.12559.

McMichael, Philip. 2009. "A Food Regime Genealogy." *Journal of Peasant Studies* 36 (1): 139–169. https://doi.org/10.1080/03066150902820354.

Mehta, L., G. J. Veldwisch, and J. Franco. 2012. "Introduction to the Special Issue: Water Grabbing? Focus on the (Re)Appropriation of Finite Water Resources." *Water Alternatives* 5 (2): 193–207.

Mignolo, Walter. 2011. *The Darker Side of Western Modernity: Global Futures, Decolonial Options*. Durham and London: Duke University Press.

Montenegro de Wit, Maywa. 2021. "What Grows from a Pandemic? Toward an Abolitionist Agroecology." *Journal of Peasant Studies* 48 (1): 99–136. https://doi.org/10.1080/03066150.2020.1854741.

Ojeda, Diana, and Eloisa Berman-Arévalo. 2020. "Ordinary Geographies: Care, Violence, and Agrarian Extractivism in "Post-Conflict" Colombia." *Antipode* 52 (6): 1583–1602.

Ojeda, Diana, and María Camila González. 2018. "Elusive Space: Peasants and Resource Politics in the Colombian Caribbean." In *Land Rights, Biodiversity Conservation and Justice: Rethinking Parks and People*, edited by Sharlene Mollett and Thembela Kepe, 89–106. Routledge.

Ostrom, Elinor. 1990. *Governing the Commons: The Evolution of Institutions for Collective Action*. Cambridge: Cambridge University Press.

Otero, Gerardo. 2012. "The Neoliberal Food Regime in Latin America: State, Agribusiness Transnational Corporations and Biotechnology." *Canadian Journal of Development Studies/ Revue Canadienne d'études Du Développement* 3: 282–294.

Otero, Gerardo. 2021. "Dependent Development and Beyond: Can Latin America Transcend Extractivism ?" *Lasa Forum* 52 (4): 15–20.

Palau, Tomas. 2004. *Capitalismo Agrario y Expulsión Campesina : Avance Del Monocultivo de Soja Transgénica En El Paraguay*. Universidad Católica Nuestra Señora de la Asunción, Intermon Oxfam and Unión Europe.

Patel, Raj. 2013. "The Long Green Revolution." *Journal of Peasant Studies* 40 (1): 1–63. https://doi.org/10.1080/03066150.2012.719224.

Perkins, John H. 1997. *Geopolitics and the Green Revolution : Wheat, Genes, and the Cold War*. Oxford: Oxford University Press.

Ploeg, Jan Douwe van der. 2020. "From Biomedical to Politico-Economic Crisis: The Food System in Times of Covid-19." *Journal of Peasant Studies* 47 (5): 944–972. https://doi.org/10.1080/03066150.2020.1794843.

Porto-Gonçalves, Carlos Walter. 2006. "A Reinvenção Dos Territórios: A Experiência Latino-Americana e Caribenha." In *Los Desafíos de Las Emancipaciones En Un Contexto Militarizado*, edited by Ana Esther Ceceña, 151–197. Buenos Aires: Clacso.

Porto-Gonçalves, Carlos Walter. 2009. "De Saberes y de Territorios-Diversidad y Emancipación a Partir de La Experiencia Latino-Americana." *Polis Revista Latinoamericana* 22: 37–52.

Puig de la Bellacasa, María. 2017. *Matters of Care: Speculative Ethics in More than Human Worlds*. Minneapolis: University of Minnesota Press.

Quiroga Díaz, Natalia. 2019. *Economía Pospatriarcal. Neoliberalismo y Después*. Buenos Aires: Editorial Lavaca.

Restrepo, Eduardo. 2008. "Multiculturalismo, Gubernamentalidad y Resistencia." In *El Giro Hermenéutico de Las Ciencias Sociales y Humanas. Diálogo Con La Sociología*, edited by Oscar Almario and Miguel Ruiz, III:1–13. Medelin: Universidad Nacional de Colombia.

Restrepo, Eduardo, and Axel Rojas. 2010. *Inflexión Decolonial: Fuentes, Conceptos y Cuestionamientos*. Popayán: Universidad Javeriana y Universidad del Cauca.

Reyes, Alvaro, and Mara Kaufman. 2011. "Sovereignty, Indigeneity, Territory: Zapatista Autonomy and the New Practices of Decolonization." *South Atlantic Quarterly* 110 (April): 505–25. https://doi.org/10.1215/00382876-1162561.

Rivera Cusicanqui, Silvia. 2012. "Ch'ixinakax Utxiwa: A Reflection on the Practices and Discourses of Decolonization." *South Atlantic Quarterly* 111 (1): 95–109. https://doi.org/10.1215/00382876-1472612.

Rosset, Peter. 2013. "Re-Thinking Agrarian Reform, Land and Territory in La Via Campesina." *Journal of Peasant Studies* 40 (4): 721–775. https://doi.org/10.1080/03066150.2013.826654.

Rosset, Peter. 2017. "Evolución En La Forma de Pensar Un Movimiento Social Acerca de La Reforma Agraria, La Tierra y El Territorio: El Caso de La Vía Campesina." In *Concentración, Acaparamiento de Tierras, Desarrollo Rural y Derecho a La Alimentación*, edited by Flavio Bladimir Rodríguez, Juana Camacho Segura, and Juan Carlos Morales, 387–419. Bogota: Universidad Externado de Colombia, ICANH, FIAN Colombia.

Rostow, W. W. 1959. "The Stages of Economic Growth." *The Economic History Review* 12 (1): 1–16. https://doi.org/10.2307/2591077.

Schutter, Olivier de. 2011. "How Not to Think of Land-Grabbing: Three Critiques of Large-Scale Investments in Farmland." *Journal of Peasant Studies* 38 (2): 249–279. https://doi.org/10.1080/03066150.2011.559008.

Shiva, Vandana. 1997. *Biopiracy the Plunder of Nature and Knowledge*. Boston: South End Press.

Silva Garzón, Diego, and Laura Gutiérrez Escobar. 2020. "Revolturas: Resisting Multinational Seed Corporations and Legal Seed Regimes through Seed-Saving Practices and Activism in Colombia." *Journal of Peasant Studies* 47 (4): 674–699. https://doi.org/10.1080/03066150.2019.1668780.

Stefanoni, Pablo. 2010. "Pachamamismo Ventrílocuo." *Rebelión*. https://rebelion.org/pachamamismo-ventrilocuo/.

Stefanoni, Pablo. 2011. "¿A dónde Nos Lleva El Pachamamismo?" *Tábula Rasa*, 15: 261–264.

Stringer, Lindsay. 2017. "Land Degradation." In *International Encyclopedia of Geography: People, the Earth, Environment and Technology*, edited by Douglas Richardson, 3956–3961. Wiley and American Association of Geographers. https://doi.org/10.1002/9781118786352.wbieg0159.

Svampa, Maristella Noemí, and Ariel Slipak. 2015. "China En América Latina: Del Consenso de Los Commodities Al Consenso de Beijing." *Revista Ensambles* 0(3): 34–63.

Thaler, Kai. 2013. "Large-Scale Land Acquisitions and Social Conflict in Africa." In *Food Sovereignty: A Critical Dialogue*, 1–15. Program in Agrarian Studies, Yale University, and The Journal of Peasant Studies.

Torres, Fernanda. 2011. "Territorio y Lugar: Potencialidades Para El Análisis de La Constitución de Sujetos Políticos: El Caso de Un Movimiento de Desocupados En Argentina." *Geograficando* 7 (7): 209–238.

Tricot, Tito. 2009. "El Nuevo Movimiento Mapuche: Hacia La (Re)Construcción Del Mundo y País Mapuche." *Polis (Santiago)* 8 (24): 175–196. https://doi.org/10.4067/s0718-65682009000300010.

Tsing, Anna Lowenhaupt. 2005. *Friction an Ethnography of Global Connection*. New Jersey: Princeton University Press.

Ulloa, Astrid. 2010. *The Ecological Native Indigenous Peoples' Movements and Eco-Governmentality in Colombia*. New York: Routledge.

Ulloa, Astrid. 2011. "The Politics of Autonomy of Indigenous Peoples of the Sierra Nevada de Santa Marta, Colombia: A Process of Relational Indigenous Autonomy." *Latin American and Caribbean Ethnic Studies* 6 (March): 79–107. https://doi.org/10.1080/17442222.2011.543874.

Ulloa, Astrid. 2016. "Feminismos Territoriales En América Latina: Defensas de La Vida Frente a Los Extractivismos." *Nómadas*, no. 45: 123–139. https://doi.org/10.30578/nomadas.n45a8.

UNCCD. 2017. "Global Land Outlook." https://knowledge.unccd.int/glo/GLO_first_edition.

Vía Campesina, La. 2017. *Struggles of La Vía Campesina for Agrarian Reform and the Defense of Life, Land, and Territories.* Harare: La Vía Campesina.

Vittor, Luis, Hoinathy Remadji, and Alberto Acosta. 2012. "Postextractivismo: Alternativas a Un Modelo Agotado." Madrid: Fuhem Ecosocial.

Wolford, Wendy. 2010. *This Land Is Ours Now. Social Mobilization and the Meanings of Land in Brazil.* Durham: Duke University Press.

Wolford, Wendy, Saturnino M. Borras, Ruth Hall, Ian Scoones, and Ben White. 2013. "Governing Global Land Deals: The Role of the State in the Rush for Land." *Development and Change* 44 (2): 189–210. https://doi.org/10.1111/dech.12017.

Wylie, John W. 2006. "Poststructuralist Theories, Critical Methods, and Experimentation." In *Approaches to Human Geography*, edited by Stuart Aitken and Gill Valentine, 298–310. London: SAGE Publications Ltd.

Zaragocin, Sofia, and Martina Angela Caretta. 2021. "Cuerpo-Territorio: A Decolonial Feminist Geographical Method for the Study of Embodiment." *Annals of the American Association of Geographers* 111 (5): 1503–1518. https://doi.org/10.1080/24694452.2020.1812370.

Zibechi, Raul. 2010. *Dispersing Power. Social Movements as Anti-State Forces.* Oakland: AK Press.

CHAPTER 9

LAND IN FOOD REGIMES

PHILIP MCMICHAEL

INTRODUCTION

> The story of our relationship to the earth is written more truthfully on the land than on the page.
>
> —Kimmerer (2013, 341)

LAND has multiple meanings in food-regime histories. These range from land as sacred territory converted into frontiers of capital accumulation for commodity crops, to land as a site of agro-chemical experimentation, to land an increasingly valuable source of data as the new "digital frontier." Here we examine these wellsprings of value, marked by shifting tensions across time and space, where food regimes are contested fields of power, shaping key geopolitical conjunctures.

The "food regime" concept examines the provisioning of food on a world, or imperial, scale. Thus, in the nineteenth century, British outsourcing of its staple food supplies (grains and meat) to imperial frontiers in New World settlements established the first food regime. And Britain's late nineteenth-century "free trade" empire *prefigured* the United States' Cold War empire in the mid-twentieth century, which, in turn, foreshadowed a corporate empire at the turn of the twenty-first century.

Regime succession involved the restructuring of the interstate system. In this way, twentieth-century decolonization and nationalism reworked the classical era of imperialism. This defined the US-centered food regime, which deployed food aid and Green Revolution technologies to reconstruct a First World–Third World neocolonial transnational complex, foreshadowing late twentieth-century corporate transnationalism enabled by neoliberal states. The long-term global consequence has been to enclose land for industrial agriculture at the expense of—and generating forms of resistance by—small-scale producers, farmworkers, fisherfolk, pastoralists, and Indigenous peoples.

The original conceptualization focused on the first two regimes (Friedmann and McMichael 1989), and the concept kept evolving through critical reformulations (eg., Araghi 2003). While Campbell (2009, 2020) emphasizes food-regime political-ecological dimensions, foreshadowing reflexive environmental and Indigenous relations that are prominent today, the questions of whether and to *what* extent a third regime is identifiable have framed most of the debate (Friedmann 2005; Pritchard 2009), alongside some antipathy to world-historical analysis in the interest of addressing "subjectivities" (e.g., LeHeron and Lewis 2009, 164), which can be done by looking at situated case studies (e.g., Akram-Lodhi 2013; McMichael 2010; Trauger 2015; Lapegna 2016; Campbell 2020). In the first instance, food-regime analysis serves to underscore *the mutual conditioning of food provisioning and modern geopolitical power in shaping* interstate, and landed, relations.

I argue that a third, "corporate" food regime emerged in the late twentieth century, instituted in 1995 by the World Trade Organization (McMichael 2005, 2009, 2013a). For Burch and Lawrence, financialization is the leading edge of a third food regime (2009), which Otero (2012) calls the "neoliberal" food regime, to emphasize state agency. However, neoliberal states necessarily serve market rule, as exhibited in the attempt at corporate capture of the UN Food System Summit of 2021 (Canfield et al. 2021; McMichael 2021; but see Fakhri 2022).

Friedmann's (2005) claim that a third food regime has yet to materialize invokes the original conception of a food regime as a contested field of power. Following environmentalists' critiques of industrial agri-food systems, she envisions a potential "corporate-environmental" food regime developing as firms appropriate such values (if not practices). There is substantial evidence that agri-food conglomerates exert downward pressure on socioecological standards, often through acquisition, such as Amazon's absorption of Whole Foods (Mooney 2017, 59–61; Matthews 2018), and ravage environments in the global South. Bernstein (2016) and Friedmann (2016) contest my emphasis on the global peasant countermovement as the key political tension in the corporate food regime. Although the transcendence of "agriculture without farmers" cannot simply be a "peasant solution," the international "peasant" coalition has been the key prophetic voice calling the corporate takeover for what it is: a worldwide enclosure of lands (White et al. 2012), large-scale undermining of ecological integrity,[1] and an assault on human rights. This is a powerful critique of the direction of capitalist modernity from rural producers.

Because contemporary small-scale farming conditions are symptomatic of the regime, this critique is not a blast from the past invoking traditional producers. It reflects a politics of the present, addressing the threat to all landed farming cultures (shared seeds and local knowledges), which account for two-thirds of the world's food (GRAIN 2022a), and are facing elimination (Calo et al. 2021). Covid-19 and Russia's military violence in Ukraine have revealed the fragility of the global food trade (McMichael 2022). And the steady undermining of soil health across the world portends a seriously challenged future.

While each regime is historically distinctive, successively they have extended the reach of capitalism, *annihilating space by time* via rising velocities of commodity circulation premised on an advancing land frontier. The enclosure and disruption of these ecosystems has simultaneously advanced the *annihilation of time by space*, as the future closes in on a planet seriously compromised by long-term terrestrial and atmospheric degradation.

Food Regime Ecological Override

Historically, food-regime transitions have presided over a cumulative conversion, from thinking about land ecologies as "an integral spiritual dimension of human life" to viewing them as "an objectified source of power and profit."

The colonization of the New World was premised on dispossessing native peoples of their habitats. In Australia, Sydney's first governor, following imperial orders, proclaimed immediate sovereignty over all lands in 1788. This proclamation took its justification from British philosopher John Locke's doctrine of natural law, which grounded the rights to landed property in the application of labor to the land. As a *Sydney Morning Herald* editorial observed of Aboriginals in 1838:

> This vast land was to them a common—they bestowed no labour upon the land—their ownership, their right, was nothing more than that of the Emu or the Kangaroo . . . The British people . . . took possession . . . and they had a perfect right to do so, under the Divine authority, by which man was commanded to go forth and people, and till the land.
>
> (cited in McMichael 1984, 41)

The basis of this (terra nullius) claim to sovereign territory as landed property was the cornerstone of European imperialism via the commercial exploitation of colonial and New World "frontiers." It was premised on the claim that non-European lands embodied an "unproductive wilderness," thereby racializing capitalism in the making of the modern world. In the formal colonization of Northern America, "the idea of improving the *land* became a metonym for a racial project carried out by a population of 'improved' *people*: an ontological claim linking whiteness and settler sovereignty." Territorial claims were justified by Virginia's governor Thomas Jefferson, who noted that Indians lived off nature's "spontaneous production," so that "no society with systemic government had arisen among the Indians, and thus no nation or national territory." Accordingly, once dispossessed, Indians "were 'free' to sell their labor on the market" (Palmer 2020, 796–797)—similarly for Black Americans since emancipation (Holloway 2021). Such dispossession continues today, for example, with Brazilian president Jair Bolsonaro's opening of Amazonian Indigenous reserves in 2019, declaring: "Indigenous people want to work, they want to produce, and they can't. They live isolated in their areas like cavemen" (quoted in Phillips 2019).

Physical and ontological violence against Indigenous peoples defined settler farming in "invisible worlds," where the ontology of the farm as a bounded "unnatural" unit of commodity production overrode landscape ecosystems and Maori/Aotearoan gardens in colonial New Zealand (Campbell 2020). Such invisibilization informs the recovery of the sophistication of Aboriginal people's socioeconomic practices across the Tasman Sea in Pascoe's *Dark Emu Black Seeds: Agriculture or Accident*? Here, a civilization based in landscape and soil management defined the ecological rationality of so-called prehistoric people: "Aboriginal people are born of the earth and individuals within the clan had responsibilities for particular streams, grasslands, trees, crops, animals and even seasons. The life of the clan was devoted to continuance" (Pascoe 2014, 145; cf. Gammage 2012).

*Dis*continuance characterizes the food regime: deepening land alienation across earthly space and time. For many non-Western cultures, nature is intrinsic to ways of living and socioecological reproduction (Toledo 2022). The continuing elimination of Indigenous food cultures erodes lifeworlds and the resilience of land—invoking the aphorism: "Just as people have a right to their land, so land has a right to its people" (Grey and Patel 2015, 436).

The contemporary intensification of recognition and activism for Indigenous (food) sovereignty claims, foreshadowed in the UN Declaration of the Rights of Indigenous Peoples (2007),[2] underscores the ongoing contention over land enclosure (e.g., Matties 2016; Mayes 2018; Estes 2019; Ferrando et al. 2020). Recent mobilization against the construction of oil pipelines through ancestral territories in the United States had a double purpose: to protect Indigenous lands[3] and the planet from fossil fuels—representing full circle activism[4] on the part of so-called prehistoric people challenging dispossession by accumulation (Kapoor 2021).

Land and the Metabolic Rift

Coinciding with processes of displacement is the intensifying "metabolic rift," Marx's (1973, 489) term for the decline of soil fertility, caused by the break in the human recycling of nutrients to the soil caused by the separation of town and country (see also Foster 1999; Moore 2000). While Foster (1999) locates the rift in the urban-industrialization of the mid-nineteenth century, a richer version is that the rift is a long-term consequence of historical capitalism's exhaustion of local ecologies by intensive mining and of the plantation systems imposed during the colonial era (Moore 2000), and of course, continuing today.

The metabolic rift in the separation of countryside and city is fundamental to food-regime dynamics, beginning with settler colonization of Indigenous habitats and the food provisioning of late nineteenth-century European urban-industrial centers. And though the Native Americans managed their ecosystems and the "interactions among people, plants, animals, and climate left behind a majestic store of loamy, fertile topsoil . . . just 0.1 percent of Iowa's tallgrass prairie remains today," and 50 percent of the topsoil has been lost "since being subjected to the plow" (Philpott 2020a, 74).

The metabolic rift intensified as agrochemicals supplemented the plow. Successive food regimes extended agroindustrial frontiers worldwide, privileging agroexporting. Destruction of the *Cerrado*, the richest savanna in the world and Brazil's largest biome, is exemplary. Because of its use of lime treatments complemented by heavy doses of phosphorus fertilizer, the Green revolutionary Norman Borlaug extolled this agroindustrial frontier in 1997 as the new "bread basket," in a "messianic belief in the gospel of better living through chemistry" (Philpott 2020a, 99–100), expressing the "epistemic rift" that accompanied the metabolic rift (McMichael 2009; Schneider and McMichael 2010). Thus, alienation from ecosystems engenders techno-fetishism, undermining common-pool resources and representing land acquisitions as "unquestioned conditions for proper development" (Gerber and Haller 2020, 18).[5]

The *Cerrado*'s native vegetation, home to traditional communities who were cultivating crops and raising cattle, once covered an area larger than Great Britain, France, and Germany combined. Less than half of it remains:

> The fruits of converting the *Cerrado* are fed into the maw of the global commodity market—soybeans to feed livestock in China, sugar cane to make ethanol to meet U.S. biofuel mandates, beef to feed the world's growing middle classes . . . In a bet that these global appetites will keep expanding, the retirement investment giant TIAA-CREF has spent hundreds of millions to purchase *Cerrado* farmland.[6]

This contemporary commodification of land overrides its capacity as a species-and-human habitat and carbon sink, so that landscape ecologies and rural working families become abstractions and victims in an agrochemical regime. The current Argentinian soy boom exemplifies this, where *pampas* are "farmed from a distance, with aid of satellites and high-tech instruments, by professionals and entrepreneurs who 'farm' from the comfort of urban settings and IT offices [in] transcendence of the urban/rural divide by modernization of the countryside." Mothers mobilize around the risks to child health from agrochemicals, evoking "a way of 'knowing' risk that is different from modern, corporate-sponsored science . . . [emerging] from felt, lived experience of taking care of loved ones, of gathering data constantly on their children" (Leguizamón 2020, 146–147).

Commandeering twenty-first century "frontiers" includes the conversion of degraded or prior use lands,[7] using public agronomic research and chemical-intensive agroindustrial practices.[8] In South America such conversions have enabled the recolonization of the Brazilian Cerrado and Argentinian and Uruguayan Pampas as newly capitalized frontiers of soybean production.[9]

Accordingly, if the British-centered food regime depended on *extensive* accumulation, cheapening wage foods with offshore wheat and meats, and the US-centered industrial food regime produced durable foods, such as green revolution staples and animal protein via *intensive* accumulation, then the corporate-centered food regime's global food supply chains includes *convertive* accumulation based on "biophysical override" via evolving agrotechnologies (Weis 2010).

Landed Relations

"Frontier" settlement in the British-centered food regime embodied distinctive patterns of land use. Friedmann's essential distinction between settler "household" and "capitalist" farmers clarified the market (and state) forces that were at work constructing a world wheat market during the last quarter of the nineteenth century. Absent a frontier labor market, settler household farmers, with combine harvesters but no need for profit, produced wheat at competitive prices, surviving world price depressions from 1882 to 1896 and 1925 to 1935 (cf. European capitalist farmers). "Open" land was the key and the object of soil mining: "Colonists brought forth crops from the fertile virgin soil without replenishing it, and then moved on to new homesteads . . . [and] once capitalist production had been undermined by household competition, reproduction through reduction of personal and productive consumption could proceed still further, resulting in the combined economic and ecological crisis of the Dustbowl in the 1930s" (Friedmann 1978, 566–568).

With wheat and meat as threads, the initial food regime bound settler farmers in North America, as well as the Antipodes, to industrial consumers (firms and wage laborers) across the Atlantic. In the United States and Australia in particular, these commercial frontiers sustained a purposeful national articulation of agricultural and manufacturing sectors in the late nineteenth century (Friedmann 1978; McMichael 1984). This process prefigured the postimperial norm that informed the US-centered food regime as it projected its hegemonic model of "economic nationalism" via the postcolonial "development project" in the Cold War era (McMichael 1996).

The US-centered regime was premised on food surpluses that originated in the rehabilitation of US agriculture after the Dust Bowl collapse, using supply-management policies, price supports, and production controls to regulate markets and the Commodity Credit Corporation to purchase surplus grain (Winders 2009, 329–330). In the postwar period grain surpluses were recycled to strategic Third World states as concessional food aid to support industrial development with cheap 'wage foods,' sometimes at the expense of the domesic farming systems (Friedmann 1982).

Meanwhile, the United States' public intervention in the 1940s extended to experimenting with engineered hybrid seeds in Mexico. Here, the mode of food-regime succession can be represented by distinguishing settler frontiers, understood as the offshore expansion of the *nation* via the migration of displaced "Old World" farmers, from Green Revolution agricultural technopolitics as a global expansion of the *state* (Arrighi 1978; cf. Patel 2013). If the former involved frontiers of White settlement, the latter involved capitalist farming methods' metastasizing to select states depending on the US Cold War security concerns. Here public-philanthropic partnerships in Mexico, India, and other postcolonial states, incorporated territorial lands into global food-regime relations.

Green Revolution

The Green Revolution was the principal medium through which the US model of chemical agriculture was introduced into the postcolonial world—it was a transfer of technology with specific political choices, and consequences (Patel 2013). It appealed to the "economic nationalism" that was central to "developmentalism" at the time. In the 1960s, India's prime minister, Jawaharlal Nehru, blocked by landlord-dominated state governments that were unfavorable to land reform, settled for accepting US help in encouraging India to embrace Green Revolution technology, at the expense of promoting extant ecological alternatives (Ajl and Sharma 2022).

Hybrid seeds were designed to overcome indigenous land-race limits on chemicalization. Invoking metabolic rift outcomes, an Indian farmer noted: "Chemical fertilizer makes the crop shoot up . . . whereas organic manure makes for strength. Without strength, no matter how much fertilizer you put, the field won't give output" (quoted in Gupta 1998, 4). Hybrid seeds rupture natural cycles, substituting linear flows of commodified inputs and outputs, exposing farmers to a land-based "chemical treadmill."

The expansion of Green Revolution agriculture reflected the competing organizing principles in the US-centered food regime: the national and the international. Nationally, postcolonial governments sought to improve agricultural productivity and the delivery of rice, maize, and wheat to urban centers. This import-substitution strategy supplemented their food aid. Internationally, the US food aid encouraged the adoption of Green Revolution technology, providing counterpart funds and loans from institutions such as the US Agency for International Development (USAID) and the World Bank (George 1977, 174–175), laying the foundation for farm land deterritorialization.

Second Green Revolution and Market-Led Agrarian Reform

Development of the "world steer" heralded the Second Green Revolution, as feed crops were needed to supply an international animal protein industry (Sanderson 1986; DeWalt 1985).[10] Meanwhile, horticultural products augmented the international division of labor as "new agricultural countries" grew fruit and vegetable exports (Friedmann 1991).[11] This new global agribusiness involved specialized, high-input agriculture servicing high-value markets and food-processing and agrochemical firms. Whereas the first Green Revolution was a public initiative geared to national markets (for staples), its successor has been a private initiative geared to global markets (for higher-value foods). This switch launched the corporate food regime, characterized by intensifying land enclosure across the global South for export agriculture that would "feed the world."

Integral to this shift in the early 1990s was the World Bank's market-led agrarian reform (MLAR) policy, designed to replace state-led land reform with land markets orchestrated by local elite classes. Building on 1980s neoliberal structural adjustment programs (SAPs), debt repayment under MLAR required shrinking the public sector across the global South and Fpromoting agroexport revenue. Land privatization encouraged foreign investment, producing a "bifurcated agrarian structure" of outward-looking corporate green revolution agriculture and localized peasant-style farming (Akram-Lodhi 2007). A withdrawal of farm subsidies and rural infrastructural supports accompanied the MLAR treatment of land as a market rather than according to socioecological logic (Lahiff, Borras, and Kay 2007, 1430–1431).[12]

Markets being "gendered institutions," MLAR generally excluded women smallholders from land and from gainful off-farm labor relations, as corporate agriculture created "a gender-segregated workforce, within which women are overwhelmingly employed in more insecure, less well paid and lower-skilled activities" (Razavi 2007, 1494–1495).[13] This is illustrated by the impact of land reform in Mexico in the 1990s that privatized its historic *ejido* system of collective land ownership. Women were displaced from traditional *milpa* farming into "mobile maquiladoras" producing "corporate tomatoes":

> The only Mexican inputs are the land, the sun, and the workers . . . The South has been the source of the seeds, while the North has the biotechnology to alter them . . . The workers who produce the tomatoes do not benefit . . . They now travel most of the year—with little time to grow food on their own plots in their home communities . . . With this loss of control comes a spiritual loss, and a loss of a knowledge of seeds, of organic fertilizers . . . of sustainable practices such as crop rotation or leaving the land fallow for a year—practices that had maintained the land for millennia.
>
> (Barndt 1997, 59–62)

The enclosure of land and traditional practices via the market logic deepen processes of "de-agrarianization," reordering rural life access to off-farm labor sources (Bryceson 2004; Kabeer and Tran Thi van Anh 2002; Bezner Kerr 2005; Scoones 2009).

Just as food regimes evolve and are modified, so too, have green revolution meanings and practices evolved. By the early 2000s, rural poverty and food insecurity had come into development agency view, and African governments were subsidizing the Gates and Rockefeller Foundations' Alliance for a Green Revolution in Africa (AGRA) to the tune of $1 billion a year (Malkan 2021). AGRA expected to address food insecurity by increasing land productivity. The tag line for AGRA on the Rockefeller Foundation webpage is "working along the agricultural supply chain to catalyze a uniquely African green revolution."[14] Since AGRA focuses on staple foods for African consumption, as in the first Green Revolution, the "*agricultural* supply chain" refers to the upstream delivery of imported fertilizers, agrochemicals, and purchased (sometimes biotech-fortified) seeds. In other words, even as it has been unsuccessful in reducing food insecurity,[15]

AGRA has performed as a pioneering conduit for foreign agrotechnologies, to the detriment of African farming and lands.

The AGRA experiment foreshadowed a general resolve on the part of development agencies to embrace a new initiative advocated in the 2008 *World Development Report*, placing "agriculture afresh at the center of the development agenda" (World Bank 2007, 1). This initiative, with public support, would be "led by private entrepreneurs linking producers to consumers" organizing "value chains that bring the market to smallholders and commercial farms" (World Bank 2007, 7–8; cf. Deininger and Byerlee et al. 2011). As a new model of agriculture for development, value-chains are premised on displacing local markets and deskilling and indebting farmers to secure their labor on land converted to extractive monocultures to supply distant markets, shifting the value to the agro-input suppliers and processors (McMichael 2013c). Increased debt can lead to "land mobility," as anticipated by AGRA,[16] contributing to the so-called twenty-first-century land grab that includes "control grabbing," enclosing not just land parcels but future possibilities *on* the land (Kerssen 2013; Transnational Institute 2013; Peluso and Lund 2011; McKay 2018).[17]

Land Grabbing and Food Regime

Twenty-first-century enclosure for industrial food and feed production increasingly threatens the lifeworlds of so-called unproductive populations.[18] Foreign investors and development agencies partner with domestic political-economic elites, exercising capital sovereignty (cf. Halperin 2013). This, in turn, has precipitated mobilizations for "food sovereignty" (Desmarais 2007).

In 2000, in the wake of the World Trade Organization (WTO) liberalization rules, La Vía Campesina proclaimed: "The massive movement of food around the world is forcing the increased movement of people." But as the new-century financial era loomed, the massive movement of money around the world was forcing the increased movement of people in an investment-centered assault on land users everywhere via land and green grabs in which institutions and states were complicit (Fairhead, Leach, and Scoones 2012; Sikor and Newell 2014; McMichael 2015). Global production networks and supply chains have formed a "transnational land investment web" (Borras et al. 2020).

This twenty-first-century "land rush" coincided with a conjunction of food, financial, and energy crises.[19] In this moment, portfolio investors began seeing land investment (especially in the global South) as "good as gold," a key source of future income, whereas for the agrarian classes, "land [remained] a crucially important source of food and livelihoods" (Fairbairn 2020, 12). Such portfolio ownership disdains responsibility, encouraging investment intermediaries to consolidate landed property and augment its value by pushing "agriculture toward large-scale and more capital-intensive production" (Fairbairn 2020, 135; Larder, Sippel, and Lawrence 2015).

After a short-term surge between 2007 and 2010, land acquisitions since 2013 had totaled about 30 million hectares by 2020, of which between 9 million and 22 million hectares were put into production (Land Matrix 2021, 9, 11, 12).[20] Community exclusion from land puts "enormous strain on land rights and governance systems. In many countries in Africa, for example, customary rights [have been] lost permanently, often leaving institutional voids" (Land Matrix 2021, 12; Global Witness 2017; cf. Wily 2011, 751). Such land acquisitions are "a core driver of land-use change, contribute substantially to deforestation, habitat destruction, and land degradation, and, consequently, are associated with massive losses of biodiversity and high carbon emissions, particularly when tropical rainforests are affected" (Land Matrix 2021, 14).

In response to this threat numerous, and ongoing, instances of local resistance emerged across the global South (e.g., Borras and Franco 2013; Liberti 2014; Vergara-Camus 2014; Hall et al. 2015; McKeon 2015; Claeys 2015; Wise 2018; Gyapong 2021).[21] The resistances registered the deepening of the corporate food regime, given the widening gap between land costs in North and South—encouraging "world farm" proliferation via a global conversion of farmland to a source of food, feed, agrofuels, and general biomass as a new accumulation frontier. Speculative financial investment in land renders crops increasingly fungible to enhance portfolio flexibility (McMichael 2012, 684). More recently, "well-balanced" financial portfolios include farmland as a low-risk "asset class," cashing in on two long-term trends: rising middle-class consumption of "high-protein, high-status foods like meat and nuts . . . [and] the steady shrinkage of arable land" (Philpott 2020b, 3). Such speculative investment underscores fundamental food-regime tensions "between visions of agriculture, food systems, territory and society" (Cotula 2021).

The 2008 food crisis also intensified development-agency-abetted land grabbing around the world as a response to rising hunger and cascading food riots (Patel and McMichael 2009). The High-Level Conference on World Food Security in 2008, hosted by the Food and Agriculture Organization (FAO) of the United Nations, recommended: "Governments, supported by their international partners, must now undertake the necessary public investment and provide a favourable environment for private investments" (quoted in Urquhart 2008, 2). In response, the Terra Preta Forum, organized by civil society organizations to parallel the FAO's World Food Summit, released a statement: "The serious and urgent food and climate crises are being used by political and economic elites as opportunities to entrench corporate control of world agriculture and the ecological commons" (La Vía Campesina 2008).

In the fallout from the "food crisis," in 2010 the International Planning Committee for Food Sovereignty (IPC) gained a foothold in the UN's Committee on World Food Security (CFS), in the form of the Civil Society Mechanism (CSM),[22] which represented small-scale producers across the world's lands, forests, and waters. The CSM had an early success in the FAO with passage of "The Voluntary Guidelines on the Responsible Governance of Tenure of Land, Fisheries and Forests," which covered "all forms of tenure: public, private, communal, indigenous, customary, and informal."[23]

Since then, food sovereignty possibilities have been jeopardized by parastatal land concessions, accompanied by "insulated contractual regimes" (Cotula 2021). These reposition "state-controlled territories" by offshore investor-state alliances engaging in food regime "deterritorialization" (cf. Ong 2006),[24] assisted by the World Bank's Foreign Advisory Service (FIAS) initiative: Investing Across Borders (Daniel 2010 15, 17–18; cf. Narula 2013).

In 2012, such patterning informed the New Alliance for Food Security and Nutrition made up of the G8, the African Union, the New Partnership for Africa's Development (NEPAD), nine African governments, and over a hundred private corporations. This "multistakeholder" public-private partnership reframed government land and food policy to promote cross-border "agricultural growth corridors." This entailed enclosing land for large-scale industrial agriculture and incorporating small producers into corporate value chains by having them grow foodstuffs primarily for export (Paul and Steinbrecher 2013; McKeon 2014).[25] Proliferation of global supply chains, via deterritorialization,[26] confirms the food sovereignty movement's critique that the food regime is disabling both territorial sovereignty and producer sovereignty.[27]

Food Sovereignty Countermovement

In this moment of direct and indirect land grabbing, the food sovereignty movement, as the central oppositional reflex *within* the food regime, focuses on producer rights, to be protected by states. Central to this outcome is land reform, as Nyéléni, the movement newsletter, claims:

> In the context of food sovereignty, agrarian reform benefits all of society, providing healthy, accessible and culturally appropriate food, and social justice. Agrarian reform can put an end to the massive and forced rural exodus from the countryside to the city, which has made cities grow at unsustainable rates and under inhuman conditions.
>
> (Nyéléni, 2006)

The complement to this vision is agroecology, which is reportedly achieving "productivity increases more impressive than those achieved by Green Revolution programs. One University of Essex study surveyed nearly 300 large ecological agriculture projects across more than 50 poor countries and documented an average 79% increase in productivity with decreasing costs and rising incomes" (Wise 2020). This trajectory needs scaling up and out to address the climate-intensifying degradation of soil and water cycles.

Mobilization of multiclass alliances against capital sovereignty[28] has the potential to reform states from within and from the bottom up (IPES Food and ETC Group 2021). One recent dramatic alliance stemmed from Prime Minister Modi's attempt in 2020 to dismantle the legal and social protections for India's stratified farm sector, encouraging agroexport investments to, benefit its wealthy class of farmers and threatening the livelihoods of two-thirds of India's 1.3 billion people (Dhar 2021; Ghosh 2020). This attempt to implement market rule was interrupted by a substantial multiclass push-back led by northern Indian farmers, supported by emergent lower-class farmer and farm-laborer solidarities across caste lines and impressive urban civil alliances against the Bharatiya Janata Party government's procorporate position (Pattenden and Bansal 2021; Aga 2021; Narayan 2020).[29]

Meanwhile, in the south of India the Zero Budget Natural Farming (ZBNF) program multiplies peasant-based agroecological farming, with state support. La Vía Campesina reported: "The ZBNF movement has achieved massive scale not only because of effective farming practices, but because of a social movement dynamic" (La Vía Campesina 2018). It was initially led by the Karnataka Rajya Raitha Sangha, a wealthy and conservative chapter of La Vía Campesina, but nevertheless has historically been opposed to the WTO and the entrance of transnational seed and food-processing corporations into Indian markets (Baviskar and Levien 2021, 1344). Originating in Karnataka state with 100,000 farms, it has been supported in Andhra Pradesh, Tamil Nadu, and Kerala states by millions of farmers (Rosset and Altieri 2017, 75; Khadse et al. 2018).[30]

However, the situation in Andhra Pradesh illustrates the dangers of capital-state co-optation. This is seen in the discrepancy between nominal "zero budgets" and the substantial financialization of its Climate Resilience ZBNF (CRZBNF) program by the French Bank BNP Paribus, a global supporter of the coal industry (including in Gujarat), and the World Bank's International Finance Corporation (IFC). CRZBNF claims that with "the UN Sustainable Development Goals' global corporate plan, we strive to engage in partnerships and opportunities that *do not only consider financial performance*, but also positive impacts on environment and society" (Saldanha 2018, 9). Direct Benefit Transfer of patented biodigital information to individual farmers, assisted by the state, enables a corporate intellectual-property-rights override of farmers' rights: "CRZBNF appears to be governed in a manner that is quite opposed to the principles of ZBNF, and the broader agro-ecological systems of farming" (Saldanha 2018, 56). Similarly, the agroecological System of Rice Intensification developed in India has been adopted by 20 million farmers in sixty-one countries, including Vietnam, Cambodia, Nepal, the Philippines (Vidal 2019), and West Africa (Styger and Traoré 2018). The agribusiness colossus, Olam, has established a Sustainable Rice Platform, declaring: "Companies must change and reduce their resource intensity" (Vidal 2019).

Here, countermovement success depends on consolidating grassroots mobilizations and civil pressure and monitoring regulatory frameworks in a "Long Food Movement" (IPES Food and ETC Group 2021), in addition to modeling the effects of agroecological transition across diverse regions (Gliessman 2018).

The Digital Frontier

Food regime frontiers mutate. The contemporary digital frontier continues capital's *revaluation of its landed relations* across space and time. Processes of confiscation (colonization), conversion (agrotechnologies), and cyberization (digital technologies) distinguish successive regimes, in combined and uneven forms. Thus, whereas the Green Revolution was selective, treating technification as a "side project" for wealthier farmers in a peasant world, surveillance agriculture is designed to appropriate, individuate, and technify *all* "farming decision processes at the expense of group dynamics" (Stone 2022, 17).

Biodigitalization is represented as ultimately sanitizing agri-food systems by creating sterile high-tech environments, such as vertical farming and the robotization of agricultural labor (Reisman 2021). Here, "advances in digitalization, automation, synthetic biology, and molecular technologies promise to take the risks—and the people—out of food systems. New players argue that producing protein in petri-dishes, letting artificial intelligence manage the farm or invisibly nudge consumer behaviour . . . are the route to resilience" (IPES Food and ETC Group 2021, 5).

Besides rendering the social content of farming cultures redundant, digitalization "could mean the mass abandonment of 300 million farms, the forced migration of well over 1 billion people, the dismantling of diversified food webs that sustain 70% of the world's population, surrendering the food security of billions of people to untested technologies managed by for-profit companies with no serious skin in the game" (IPES Food and ETC Group 2021, 16).

The succession of food regime "frontiers" replaces public commons (territories, knowledges, sociality) with an increasingly global land space subject to control, and now to be governed by technology that combines Big Ag and Big Data (e.g., Google, Microsoft, Amazon, Alibaba), financed by asset managers such as BlackRock, Vanguard, Capital Group, Fidelity, and the Carlyle Group. While the digital frontier presents itself as "climate-smart" and sanitizing, it is dominated by most of the world's biggest agrochemical firms (Stone 2022, 8).

Food-regime dynamics stem from regime structuring and restructuring and transition across time and space. Land (re)colonization is already underway via extensive digital mapping technologies in the form of a "data grab" (Fraser 2019). Each square kilometer, every square centimeter, of farmland is being mapped "for soil, nutrients, moisture, and sunshine." This is being combined "with massive genomic data sets to suggest AI-designed 'climate-smart' agroecosystems building from DNA upwards, [and] ecosystems [that] will be engineered for optimal performance" (IPES Food and ETC Group 2021, 63).

In South America, for example, "digital fencing" enables the financial enclosure of ranch and crop land from a distance. Land is confiscated from collective territories via the cadastral registration of individual titles sponsored by the World Bank and justified in the name of market rule (GRAIN 2022b). In Africa, the Zambian government partners with Medici Land Governance, "a blockchain company and subsidiary of the US-based online retailer Overstock, to assist with land registration and titling" for "citizen-centric land administration" and, potentially, enhancing women's access (Hughes et al. 2022; Hughes 2020). The goal of the National Land Titling Program is to register "all property in the country in order to provide security of tenure to property owners" (Mousseau et al. 2020; Mandhu et al. 2019, 20). In 2018, Medici Land partnered with the World Bank to extend blockchain technology for land-titling registration globally (World Bank 2019).

Accordingly, biodigital technologies in northern large-scale industrial agricultural regions[31] are now selecting converted land in the global South as a new data frontier. These interventions introduce "precision agriculture," where sensors can generate remote information for managing machinery and applying fertilizer and chemicals to targeted units of land for efficiency and yield increase, with data blockchain consolidation providing "value for seed and chemical firms, agronomists, co-operatives, farm insurance providers, and machinery firms" (Fraser 2019, 899). Infrastructures to enable the spread of digital surveillance techniques in the South are in their infancy; however, "new soil" (data) "from new parts of the world and different types of cultivation systems are crucial to the development of digital technologies and algorithms" (Stone 2022, 5, 9). And insofar as the "precision" concept invokes environmentalism, linked to "climate-smart agriculture," it serves to legitimize financial and policy support for the biodigitalization of agriculture (Newell and Taylor 2018, 17),[32] discounting agroecological methods and La Vía Campesina claims to "cool the planet" (La Vía Campesina 2009).

Meanwhile, for degraded "old soil," the UN projects the world has about sixty years of food harvests left (Monbiot 2015), and in 2020, a report on global soils warned of soil sterility for one third of agricultural soils, with a third of farmland worldwide significantly degraded (IPES Food and ETC Group 2021, 25). This scenario is as devastating as it is grotesque—revealing the longue durée effects of intensive soil mining from the early plantation era through the recent time span of capital's food regime, widening the historic rift in human and land relations.[33] Displacing humans from food landscapes via biodigitalization intensifies, in a "trade-off" between reductions in energy and chemical use and human touch and learning. Aerial drones spot and target-spray weeds, monitoring crops, forests, and workers. Such "precision farming" perpetuates agroindustrialization,[34] fetishizing information technology and transforming "agriculture without farmers" into "agriculture without humans."

The International Panel of Experts on Sustainable Food Systems and ETC Group (IPES Food and ETC Group 2021) have said: "There is no such thing as (agri)business-as-usual over the next quarter century. Some of our basic assumptions about food systems—that food is produced from soil and sunlight, that food supply chains require farmers and food companies—will be upended by these developments" (55). The question arises of whether data can be used collectively or only by large agribusiness and digital corporations, reinforcing a digital divide, if not wholesale dispossession by digital accumulation.

Whether "data sovereignty" is possible is perhaps anticipated by the United States' grower-run data cooperative, the Grower Information Services Cooperative, joining with the Agricultural Data Coalition of farmers, lawyers, engineers, and businesses (Fraser 2019, 907; 2020). And, with agroecological transitions across the world accounting for 30 percent of farms (Biovision Foundation for Ecological Development & IPES-Food 2020, 4), companies such as East Africa's We-Farm provide farmer-to-farmer digital networks for over a million small farmers in Kenya and Uganda, a program that is being replicated elsewhere by open-source access data firms and network platforms that are enabling farmers' independence from corporate management to share local knowledges (Prause, Hackfort, and Lindgren 2021; Wittman et al. 2020).

At present, precision-agriculture equipment and farm-management platforms constitute the principal digital relations, and farmers are required to provide soil-related details to access the technology—realizing "data grab." Such farm-management services can be linked to sales of seeds and pesticides, as in Syngenta's operations in the world's "top four agriculture markets: the US, Brazil, China and Europe" (Prause, Hackfort, and Lindgren 2021). Accordingly, digital power portends substantial change in the structure and operations of the economic, genomic/Crispr, and informational dimensions of corporate power. The long-standing division between (a) agrochemical and fertilizer firms, (b) grain traders and plant breeders, and (c) retailers and farm-machinery firms no longer exists; "the new Big Data platform invites—almost requires—cross-sectoral convergence, and those who control the platform can literally regroup the industrial landscape" (Mooney 2018, 5). The potential enclosure of small-scale and peasant farmlands en masse may ensue, insofar as a "capital logic" overrides the "territorial logic" of food sovereignty (cf. Arrighi 1990).

This may be foreshadowed in the recent consolidation of the fifteen CGIAR Research Centers into a single administrative unit, co-chaired by the senior program officer of the Gates Foundation, fulfilling its website claim that "a key trigger of agricultural transformation is a conducive policy environment" (Navdanya 2020, 67, 70), which will oversee 50 percent of the world's plant-breeding germplasm and supervise nine crops and select fish and livestock species (ETC Group 2021, 25). As addressed below, the consolidation of private governance (via private-public partnerships) stems from the inordinate power of corporate finance in industrializing and digitalizing a global agri-food system (vs. territorial food cultures), exploiting the climate and environmental crisis to justify private control, especially where "only a handful of donors— including France, Switzerland, Germany, the Food and Agriculture Organisation of the United Nations (FAO) and the International Fund for Agricultural Development—have explicitly recognised agroecology as a key solution for building sustainable food systems" (Pavageau et al. 2020 3).[35]

Corporate governance of the food regime was the eventual goal of the World Economic Forum (WEF) when it partnered with the UN to stage the 2021 Food Systems Summit. It enabled the elevation of private interests in WEF founding chair Klaus Schwab's proposed "Great Reset," having characterized corporations as "the trustees of society" (Schwab 2019). Allied development of an International Platform for Digital Food and Agriculture (resembling the IPCC) suggests a consolidation of digital governance, informed by the recently formed Science Policy Interface (SPI), in service of private interests (Clapp et al. 2021). This was anticipated by the United Nations Food Systems Summit (UNFSS) Scientific Group, which advocated bankrupt Green Revolution–type solutions in an age of melting glaciers, hunger, and biodiversity loss, and overstepped its scientific bounds by entering "into governance realms it doesn't know much about—while it continues to erect boundaries against those who do," such as the UN Committee on World Food Security (CFS), and its High-Level Panel of Experts (HLPE), who investigate issues of food security, nutrition, and human rights (Montenegro de Wit and Illes 2021; Fakhri 2021).

While digitalization and financialization may deepen the monopoly of the material dimensions, as well as strategic knowledge and informational dimensions, of the food regime, gene drives anticipate a brave new world. The application of gene drives as sexual reproduction vectors altering the genetic make-up of insects on the order of a whole species, across generations are likely to target flour beetles, rodents, planthoppers, fruit flies, aphids, expanding "the technosphere at the expense of the biosphere" (Pimbert and Anderson 2018). No matter that agroecology practices reduce pest impacts naturally, preserving insect and plant species alien to farming but part of biodiversity maintenance (ETC Group 2018).

Conclusion

This chapter describes the changing meanings of land from the long industrial era to the present. The rich soils that nurtured frontier settler farming in the New World incubated agroindustrial technologies as the Green Revolution redefined modern agriculture. Now, with "data as the new soil," land is subject to financial management by distant "agricultural technology providers" in the new age of biodigitalization and "precision agriculture" (Fraser 2019). This long-term trajectory defines capital's food regime as one of land occupation and commodification. This has been enabled by the progressive removal of landscape knowledges from the human tillers of soil.

Land is the ultimate lens through which the political history of capital's food regime may be examined and assessed. Land's civilizational value has been transformed by the rupturing of Indigenous lifeworlds and the ongoing attempt by capital to deepen agrifood commodity relations and manage the material and reputational damage associated with an intensifying metabolic rift. This trajectory has been engineered by changing geopolitical relations across the three food regimes. Whether a new food regime emerges in the restructuring of agrotechnologies by digital capitalism may depend on the course of the 2030 Sustainable Development Goals, as well as geopolitical reconfiguration.

The World Economic Forum's partnership with the United Nations for the 2021 Food Systems Summit, which was geared to the SDGs 2030, attempted to consolidate global food governance by the corporate sector under the pretext that it would prevent multilateral chaos, expressed in rising citizen disaffection with public and environmental disorder, and in the name of a self-serving "multistakeholderism" (McMichael 2021; Schwab and Malleret 2020). Here, "'multi-stakeholderism' is everywhere as corporations—sensing the social and environmental tipping points ahead—seek to draw governments, scientists, and a handful of civil society organizations into an artificial new multilateralism" (IPES Food and ETC Group 2021, 4). The global resistance by civil society was fortified by the UNFSS's hollow gesture, strengthening the foundation for a Long Food Movement—which rehearses the principal tension in the corporate food regime, centered on the question of "food sovereignty" (McMichael 2013a; Shattuck Schiavoni, and VanGelder 2019).

Unlike the previous two food regimes, the corporate variant has not been governed by a hegemonic state. Rather, with the formation of the WTO rules, member states signed on to a general agreement to internalize the principle of comparative advantage, compromising their agri-food sovereignty. Although the United States and the European Union continued their "breadbasket" role into the early twenty-first century, new agroexport powers, such as Brazil, China, and India, emerged. Such "multipolarity" has nurtured an emergent development, in which geoeconomic processes are restructuring the food regime via supply chains organized by corporate and financial deals *with, within,* and *across* states, creating a "multiplex" world. "The nature of economic interdependence today is denser, consisting of trade, finance, and global production networks and supply chains, whereas . . . multipolarity is mainly trade-based" (Acharya 2017, 11). In lieu of a hegemonic state, states broker the recomposition of market relations, reconfiguring food regime "territoriality" (McMichael 2020). In other words, unlike previous free trade agreements, those that are emerging "serve primarily to secure access to resources, protect rights to corporate data exploitation, and put unfavourable regulations into the deep freeze" (IPES Food and ETC Group 2021, 5).

This invokes the geopolitical question of China's escalating position within and against the corporate food regime as its agroexport power and agro-import needs deepen (McMichael 2020). In replacing the United States as the dominant exporter of cheap (subsidized) foods, depressing world food prices,[36] China has jeopardized trade rules governance (Hopewell 2020). Alongside this geopolitical tension, China's state-centered development and exceptional agrarian protectionism suggest an alternative model for stabilizing landed relations and rehabilitating ecosystems (van der Ploeg and Ye 2016).

As rule-governed WTO mechanisms are experiencing paralysis, corporate governance via recent WEF and UN dictates is positioning itself to assume power. The digital frontier beckons, and in this transitional vortex, "food regime" structuring may lose coherence, insofar as "a system of proprietary markets and the commodification of data . . . is about to replace the neoliberal free market paradigm" (Staab 2019, 43; quote translated from the German in Prause, Hackfort, and Lindgren 2021). In this scenario, the concept of "techno-feudalism" resonates (with data sovereignty), where "the global economy is powered by the constant generation of central bank money, not by private profit. Meanwhile, value extraction has increasingly shifted away from markets and onto digital platforms, like Facebook and Amazon, which no longer operate like oligopolistic firms, but rather like private fiefdoms or estates" (Varoufakis 2021; cf. Dean 2022). In this rearticulation of space land remains the object, but its biophysical health may be incidental to data concerns, with estates prospering only to the extent that a "space of flows," expressing the sovereignty of movement, exists. If not, they lose their purpose. And this is the ultimate paradox of landed space, possibly and hopefully invoking a substantive multiperspectival outcome in the form of "global ecology" (Ruggie 1993) as the recognition of collective existence on planet Earth.

Acknowledgments

The author is grateful for the very helpful assistance from Marvin Joseph Montefrio and Jun Borras in revising this chapter.

Notes

1. See Monbiot, George. 2022. "Salt of the earth." *The Guardian Weekly*, 13 May, 40–44. https://www.scribd.com/article/574262899/Salt-Of-The-Earth
2. The declaration was initially opposed by the original Anglophile settler states (Canada, United States, Australia, and New Zealand) and was reversed a decade later. Interestingly, the Inuit in northern Canada connect their sovereignty to Canadian sovereignty in the Artic region (Nunavut), contributing to a mutual recognition that each depends on the other (Hall 2013, 76–79).
3. Such lands nurture growing Indigenous farming and ranching (Montalvo 2021; McNulty 2022). See also Rights and Resources Initiative (2015).
4. Regarding "the environment and our long-term well-being. Canada sure hasn't done that" (Glenn Coulthard of the Yellowknives Dene First Nation, quoted in Lindeman 2020).
5. Cf. "The epistemic character of Westernized property regimes may be at an inflection point" (Calo et al. 2021, 6).
6. Conant (2018). https://medium.com/@foe_us/is-land-speculation-helping-destroy-brazils-birthplace-of-waters-be9b0d2ea572.
7. Goldstein (2014) notes the Indonesian government's expansion of oil palm plantations onto degraded land (for rehabilitation) to avoid further deforestation (131)—palm oil is the world's most versatile vegetable oil; two-thirds of it is used in food production, and the plantations account for 10% of global crop land (Tullis 2019).
8. To reformulate "conversion," it is worth noting that some commercial land could be rehabilitated for healthy use, insofar as meat substitutes are now produced in labs (Mann 2021), and palm oil (Dineen 2022).
9. As China's soy importing has intensified (Peine 2010; Oliveira and Hecht 2016).
10. Aquaculture (Blue Revolution) is part of this Second Green Revolution (Islam 2014).
11. In North Africa: "Input subsidies decreased, and states withdrew tenancy protection. Land theretofore devoted to food-grain production increasingly went to export-oriented agriculture: flowers, fruits, and vegetables ungrowable in northern winters" (Ajl 2020, 13).
12. "Structural adjustment in the 1980s dismantled the elaborate system of public agencies that provided farmers with access to land, credit, insurance inputs, and cooperative organization. The expectation was that removing the state would free the market for private actors to take over these functions . . . Too often that didn't happen" (World Bank 2007, 138).
13. Cf. Levien (2017); Valencia et al. (2021).
14. The Rockefeller Foundation. Alliance for a Green Revolution in Africa. https://www.rockefellerfoundation.org/initiative/alliance-for-a-green-revolution-in-africa/.

15. See, for example, https://www.iatp.org/africas-choice. And see Kirubel (2021; Wise 2020; and Malkan 2021).
16. AGRA predicted that such "agricultural transition" would involve "market-oriented farmers operating profitable farms that generate enough income to sustain their rise out of poverty. Over time, this will require some degree of *land mobility* and a lower percentage of total employment involved in direct agricultural production" (quoted in Community Alliance for Global Justice 2011; italics added).
17. "A single case of land grabbing can involve some people experiencing expulsion, while others are incorporated into the new economic enterprise as contract growers, and still others as wage laborers. This diversity of experience largely shapes the political reactions to land grabbing" (Transnational Institute 2013, 15). See also Chung 2015 for analysis of liminal conditions of incomplete enclosure, in Tanzania.
18. For example, the *IFC Performance Standards on Social and Environmental Sustainability* of World Bank's International Finance Corporation suggested: "Private sector projects may create opportunities for Indigenous Peoples to participate in, and benefit from, project-related activities that may help them fulfill the aspiration for economic and social development" (quoted in Daniel 2010, 50).
19. Financial capital shifted significantly into speculative ventures in land, food, and biofuels; the 800% increase in investment agrofuels between 2004 and 2007 contributed substantially to the food price inflation crisis of 2007–2008 (Holt-Giménez 2007, 10) and an intensification of land grabbing (McMichael 2012).
20. Departing from, or complementing, previous patterns of investment in high-value export crops, the new investment patterns in the global South favor bulk commodities—thus, for Southeast Asia, "83% of the farmland being acquired or leased on a long-term basis is dedicated to the production of major row crops (soft oilseeds, corn, wheat and feed grains)" (Borras and Franco 2010, 31). Henriques (2011) noted that a Bank report on land acquisitions showed that only 37% of the land grew food crops.
21. There are few analyses of (variable) activist *impact on investors* in land (but see Borras, Franco, and Wang 2013; Mamonova 2015; and Salverda 2019).
22. Now the Civil Society and Indigenous Peoples' Mechanism (CSIPM).
23. FAO (2022): https://www.fao.org/3/i2801e/i2801e.pdf.

    The Tenure Guidelines informed land struggles in India, Mali, Uganda, Argentina, and Italy (McKeon, 2013), though recent assessments suggest quite uneven implementations. See also a recent complementary update on feminist activism via La Vía Campesina and the Civil Society and Indigenous Peoples' Mechanism (CSIPM) in the CFS regarding new Voluntary Guidelines on Gender Equality and Women's Empowerment: https://www.tandfonline.com/eprint/ZNIJAUNSRFXP9QMGQG2V/full?target=10.1080/21683565.2022.2091717.
24. Deterritorialization extends to "agro-security mercantilism" (McMichael 2013b), led by Saudi Arabia and South Korea but extending to other Gulf and East Asian states, involving the state-led securing of land offshore in Africa, Southeast Asia, and Latin America (Makki 2013; Cochrane and Amery 2017; Belesky and Lawrence 2018; Townsend 2020; Henderson 2021).
25. France withdrew from the project, on the grounds that it undermines producers' farming livelihoods. And the World Bank (2014), in context of the rising controversy over enclosure and resettlement stalemates, shifted course, claiming that "contract farming operations allow farmers to remain in control of their most important asset, their land, thus avoiding disputes over access to resources and community displacement. Outgrower

schemes also support far more jobs than estate farms" (26). I attended this policy announcement at the FAO in 2014.

26. "Since 2008, leading farm management companies, including Cresud/Brasilagro, Adecoagro, SLC Agrícola, El Tejar, TIAA-CREF, Multigrain/Xingu Agro, and V-Agro, acquired collectively over 750,000 hectares in Brazil, drawing venture capital from multiple financial partners in Brazil, EU, and especially US and Japan" (Oliveira 2018, 118).
27. This intervention anticipated Franco and Borras's (2012) concept of "land sovereignty."
28. Cf. Harvey (2017), pointing out that Marx's complete analysis of the movement of capital, invading all lifeworlds with commodification, broadens conditions for anticapitalist alliance-building.
29. See *The Journal of Peasant Studies* special forum, for in-depth analysis of the class, caste, and gender dimensions of the uprising: https://www.tandfonline.com/toc/fjps20/48/7?nav=tocList.
30. Meanwhile, industrial rice yields are plateauing in California and Europe, as well as in China and Indonesia (De Schutter and Frison, 2017).
31. Where they are used on "over 75% of corn acres in the United States, 80% of grain farms in Australia and two-thirds of all arable land in the Netherlands" (Stone 2022, 2).
32. Meanwhile, the biotech industry is looking to avoid consumer resistance to its association with GMOs, in labeling and oversight: "Expect to see major flows of investment into biotech strategies that do not modify the DNA of the food product itself, but instead modify elements of the agroecosystems like the soil ecosystem, the insects, or the weeds" (IPES Food and ETC Group 2021, 66; see also Taylor 2018).
33. Note that a third of Latin America's lands no longer have speakers of the Indigenous languages that once described them (IPES and ETC Group 2021, 28).
34. Termed the "Fourth Industrial Revolution," especially in WEF circles.
35. This is consistent with the titling of the recent HLPE/CFS Report, *Agroecological and Other Innovative Approaches* (FAO 2019).
36. Until the onset of Covid-19 (McMichael 2022).

References

Acharya, Amitav. 2017. "After Liberal Hegemony: The Advent of a Multiplex World Order." *Ethics & International Affairs*, September 8. https://www.ethicsandinternationalaffairs.org/2017/multiplex-world-order/

Aga, Aniket. 2021. "Farm Protests in India Are Writing the Green Revolution's Obituary." *Scientific American*, January 24. https://www.scientificamerican.com/article/farm-protests-in-india-are-writing-the-green-revolutions-obituary/.

Ajl, Max. 2020. "Does the Arab Region Have an Agrarian Question?" *Journal of Peasant Studies* 48 (5): 955–983.

Ajl, Max, and Divya Sharma. 2022. "The Green Revolution and Transversal Countermovements: Recovering Alternative Agronomic Imaginaries in Tunisia and India." *Canadian Journal of Development Studies*. https://doi.org/10.1080/02255189.2022.2052028.

Akram-Lodhi, Haroon. 2007. "Land, Markets, and Neoliberal Enclosure: An Agrarian Political Economy Perspective." *Journal of Peasant Studies* 28 (8): 1437–1456.

Akram-Lodhi, Haroon. 2013. *Hungry for Change. Farmers, Food Justice and the Agrarian Question*. Halifax & Winnipeg: Fernwood Publishing.

Araghi, Farshad. 2003. "Food Regimes and the Production of Value: Some Methodological Issues." *Journal of Peasant Studies* 30 (2): 337–368.
Arrighi, Giovanni. 1978. *The Geometry of Imperialism*. London: Verso Books.
Arrighi, Giovanni. 1990. "The Three Hegemonies of Historical Capitalism." *Review (Fernand Braudel Center)* 13 (3): 365–408.
Barndt, Deborah. 1997. "Bio/Cultural Diversity and Equity in Post-NAFTA Mexico." In *Global Justice, Global Democracy*, edited by Jay Drydyk and Peter Penz, 55–69. Winnipeg, CAN: Fernwood Press.
Baviskar, Amita, and Michael Levien. 2021. "Farmers' Protests in India: Introduction to the JPS Forum." *Journal of Peasant Studies* 48 (7): 1341–1355.
Belesky, Paul, and Geoffrey Lawrence. 2018. "Chinese State Capitalism and Neomercantilism in the Contemporary Food Regime: Contradictions, Continuity and Change." *Journal of Peasant Studies* 46 (6): 1119–1141.
Bernstein, Henry. 2016. "Agrarian political economy and modern world capitalism: The contributions of food regime analysis." *Journal of Peasant Studies* 43 (3): 611–647.
Bezner Kerr, Rachel. 2005. "Informal Labor and Social Relations in Northern Malawi: The Theoretical Challenges and Implications of *Ganyu* Labor for Food Security." *Rural Sociology* 70: 167–187.
Biovision Foundation for Ecological Development & IPES-Food. 2020. Money Flows: What is holding back investment in agroecological research for Africa? Biovision Foundation for Ecological Development & International Panel of Experts on Sustainable Food Systems. https://www.ipes-food.org/_img/upload/files/Money%20Flows_Full%20report.pdf
Borras, Saturnino M. Jr., and Jennifer C. Franco. 2010. "From threat to opportunity? Problems with the idea of a 'code of conduct' for land-grabbing." *Yale Human Rights & Development L.J.* 13: 507–523.
Borras, Saturnino M., Jr., and Jennifer C. Franco. 2012. "A 'Land Sovereignty' Alternative? Towards a Peoples' Counter-Enclosure." TNI Agrarian Justice Programme Discussion Paper. Transnational Institute, Amsterdam. https://www.tni.org/en/publication/a-land-sovereignty-alternative-0.
Borras, Saturnino M., Jr., and Jennifer C. Franco. 2013. "Global Land Grabbing and Political Reactions 'from Below.'" *Third World Quarterly* 34 (9): 1723–1747.
Borras, Saturnino M., Jr., Jennifer C. Franco, and Chunyu Wang. 2013. "The Challenge of Global Governance and Land Grabbing: Changing International Agricultural Context and Competing Political Views and Strategies." *Globalizations* 10 (1): 161–179.
Borras, Saturnino M. Jr., Elyse N. Mills, Philip Seufert, Stephan Backes, Daniel Fyfe, Roman Herre, and Laura Michele. 2020. "Transnational Land Investment Web: Land Grabs, TMCs, and the Challenge of Global Governance." *Globalizations* 17 (4): 608–628.
Burch, David, and Geoffrey Lawrence. 2009. "Towards a Third Food Regime: Behind the Transformation." *Agriculture and Human Values* 26 (4): 267–279.
Bryceson, Deborah. 2004. "Agrarian Vista or Vortex: African Rural Livelihood Policies." *Review of African Political Economy* 31 (102): 617–629.
Calo, Adam, Annie McKee, Coline Perrin, Pierre Gasselin, Steven McGreevy, Sarah Ruth Sippe et al. 2021. "Achieving Food System Resilience Requires Challenging Dominant Land Property Regimes." *Frontiers in Sustainable Food Systems* 5 (1): 6835–6844. https://www.frontiersin.org/articles/10.3389/fsufs.2021.683544/full.
Campbell, Hugh. 2009. "Breaking New Ground in Food Regime Theory: Corporate Environmentalism, Ecological Feedbacks and the 'Food from Somewhere' Regime?" *Agriculture and Human Values* 26 (4): 309–319.

Campbell, Hugh. 2020. *Farming inside Invisible Worlds: Modernist Agriculture and Its Consequences*. New York: Bloomsbury Academic.
Canfield, Matt, Molly D. Anderson, and Philip McMichael. 2021. "UN Food Systems Summit 2021: Dismantling Democracy and Resetting Corporate Control of Food Systems." *Frontiers in Sustainable Systems* 5: 661552. doi: 10.3389/fsufs.2021.661552
Chung, Youjin B. 2015. "Engendering the New Enclosures: Development, Involuntary Resettlement and the Struggles for Social Reproduction in Coastal Tanzania." *Development and Change* 48 (1): 98–120.
Claeys, Priscilla. 2015. *Human Rights and the Food Sovereignty Movement*. London: Routledge.
Clapp, Jennifer, Molly Anderson, Maryam Rahmanian, and Sofia Monsalve Suarez. 2021. "An 'IPCC for Food'? How the UN Food Systems Summit Is Being Used to Advance a Problematic New Science-Policy Agenda." IPES Food, July. http://www.ipes-food.org/_img/upload/files/GovBrief.pdf.
Cochrane, Logan, and Hussein A. Amery. 2017. "Gulf Cooperation Council Countries and the Global Land Grab." *Arab World Geographer* 20 (1): 17–41.
Community Alliance for Global Justice. 2011. "Footloose Farmers," AGRA Watch, August 19. https://agrawatch.wordpress.com/tag/land-mobility/.
Conant, Jeff. 2018. "Is land speculation helping destroy Brazil's 'birthplace of waters?' *Friends of the Earth*. https://medium.com/@foe_us/is-land-speculation-helping-destroy-brazils-birthplace-of-waters-be9bod2ea572.
Cotula, Lorenzo. 2021. "The Global Land Rush Revisited." Farmlandgrab.org, November 17. https://www.farmlandgrab.org/post/view/30657.
Daniel, Shepard. 2010. *(Mis)Investment in Agriculture: The Role of the International finance Corporation in Global Land Grabs*. Oakland, CA: Oakland Institute.
Dean, Jodi. 2022. "Same as it ever was?" *New Left Review* May 6. https://newleftreview.org/sidecar/posts/same-as-it-ever-was?pc=1440.
Deininger, Klaus, and Derek Byerlee. 2011. *Rising Global Interest in Farmland: Can It Yield Sustainable and Equitable Benefits?* Washington, DC: World Bank.
De Schutter, Olivier, and Emile Frison. 2017. "Modern Agriculture Cultivates Climate Change: We Must Nurture Biodiversity." *Guardian*, January 9. https://www.theguardian.com/global-development/2017/jan/09/modern-agriculture-cultivates-climate-change-nurture-biodiversity-olivier-de-schutter-emile-frison.
Desmarais, Annette Aurelias. 2007. *La Via Campesina: Globalization and the Power of Peasants*. London: Pluto Press.
Dhar, Sushovan. 2021. "Farmers' Mobilisation in the Backdrop of an Agrarian Crisis." Committee for the Abolition of Illegitimate Debt (CADTM), May 21. https://www.cadtm.org/Peasant-mobilisation-in-the-backdrop-of-an-agrarian-crisis.
DeWalt, Billie. 1985. "Mexico's Second Green Revolution: Food for Feed." *Mexican Studies/Estudios Mexicanos* 1: 29–60.
Dineen, James. 2022. "Can Lab-Grown Palm Oil Save the World's Tropical Forests?" *Mother Jones*, January 9. https://www.motherjones.com/environment/2022/01/synthetic-palm-oil-save-tropical-forests-deforestation/?utm_source=mj-newsletters&utm_medium=email&utm_campaign=daily-newsletter-01-10-2022.
Estes, Nick. 2019. *Our History is the Future*. London & New York: Verso.
ETC Group. 2018. Forcing the Farm. How Gene Drive Organisms Could Entrench Industrial Agriculture and Threaten Food Sovereignty.

ETC Group. 2021. Hijacking Food Systems: Techno-Fix Takeover at the FSS. *Communique* #118, July. https://etcgroup.org/sites/www.etcgroup.org/files/files/final_fss_en_for_web_revised_130821.pdf.

Fairbairn, Madeleine. 2020. *Fields of Gold. Financing the Global Land Rush*. Ithaca and London: Cornell University Press.

Fairhead, James, Melissa Leach, and Ian Scoones. 2012. "Green Grabbing: A New Appropriation of Nature?" *Journal of Peasant Studies* 29 (2): 237–261.

Fakhri, Michael. 2021. "A Trade Agenda for the Right to Food." *Development* 64: 212–219.

Fakhri, Michael 2022. "The Food System Summit's Disconnection from People's Real Needs." *Journal of Agricultural and Environmental* Ethics 35 (3): 1–9.

FAO. 2022. *Voluntary Guidelines on the Responsible Governance of Tenure of Land, Fisheries and Forests in the Context of National Food Security*. First revision. Rome. https://doi.org/10.4060/i2801e

Ferrando, Tomaso, Isabel Álvarez Vispo, Molly Anderson, Sophie Dowllar, Harriet Friedmann, Antonio Gonzalez, et al. 2020. "Land, Territory and Commons: Voices and Visions from the Struggles." *Globalizations* 17 (7): 1276–1290.

Foster, John Bellamy. 1999. "Marx's Theory of the Metabolic Rift: Classical Foundations for Environmental Sociology." *American Journal of Sociology* 105 (2): 366–405.

Fraser, Alistair. 2019. "Land Grab/Data Grab: Precision Agriculture and Its New Horizons." *Journal of Peasant Studies* 46 (5): 839–912.

Fraser, Alistair. 2020. "The Digital Revolution, Data Curation, and the New Dynamics of Food Sovereignty Construction." *Journal of Peasant Studies* 47 (1): 208–226.

Friedmann, Harriet. 1978. "World Market, State, and Family Farm: Social Bases of Household Production in the Era of Wage-Labor." *Comparative Studies in Society and History* 20 (4): 545–586.

Friedmann, Harriet. 1982. "The Political Economy of Food: The Rise and Fall of the Postwar International Food Order." *American Journal of Sociology* 88S: 248–286.

Friedmann, Harriet. 1991. "Changes in the International Division of Labor: Agri-Food Complexes and Export Agriculture." In *Towards a New Political Economy of Agriculture*, edited by W. Friedland, L. Busch, F.H. Buttel, and A. Rudy, 65–93. Boulder, CO: Westview.

Friedmann, Harriet. 2005. "From Colonialism to Green Capitalism: Social Movements and the Emergence of Food Regimes." In *New Directions in the Sociology of Global Development*, 11, edited by Frederick Buttel and Philip McMichael, 229–267. Oxford: Elsevier.

Friedmann, Harriet. 2016. "Commentary: Food regime analysis and agrarian questions: Widening the conversation, *Journal of Peasant Studies*, 43 (3): 671–692.

Friedmann, Harriet, and Philip McMichael. 1989. "Agriculture and the State System: The Rise and Fall of National Agricultures, 1870 to the Present." Sociologia Ruralis 29 (2): 93–117.

Gammage, Bill. 2012. *The Biggest Estate on Earth*. Sydney: Allen & Unwin.

George, Susan. 1977. *How the Other Half Dies: The Real Reasons for World Hunger*. Harmondsworth, UK: Penguin Books.

Gerber, Jean-David, and Tobias Haller. 2020. "The Drama of the Grabbed Commons: Anti-politics Machine and Local Responses." *Journal of Peasant Studies* 48 (6): 1304–1327.

Ghosh, Jayati. 2020. "Farmers vs. the Indian State." Project Syndicate, December 11. https://www.project-syndicate.org/commentary/india-farmer-protests-government-reaction-by-jayati-ghosh-2020-12?barrier=accesspaylog.

Gliessman, Stephen. 2018. *Breaking Away from Industrial Food and Farming Systems: Seven Case Studies of Agroecological Transitions*. IPES Food. https://www.ipes-food.org/_img/upload/files/CS2_web.pdf.

Global Witness. 2017. *At What Cost?* Report, July 24. https://www.globalwitness.org/en/campaigns/environmental-activists/at-what-cost/.

Goldstein, Jenny. 2014. "The Afterlives of Degraded Tropical Forests New Value for Conservation and Development." *Environment and Society* 5 (1): 124–140.

GRAIN. 2022a. Peasants Still Feed the World, Even if the FAO Claims Oherwise. February 2. https://grain.org/en/article/6790-peasants-still-feed-the-world-even-if-fao-claims-otherwise.

GRAIN. 2022b. The Digitalization of Land: More Data, Less Land. April 15. https://grain.org/en/article/6832-the-digitalisation-of-land-more-data-less-land.

Grey, Sam, and Raj Patel. 2015. "Food Sovereignty as Decolonization: Some Contributions from Indigenous Movements to Food System and Development Politics." *Agriculture and Human Values* 32 (3): 431–444.

Gupta, Akhil. 1998. *Postcolonial Developments: Agriculture in the Making of Modern India*. Durham, NC: Duke University Press.

Gyapong, Adwoa Yeboah. 2021. "Land Grabs, Farmworkers, and Rural Livelihoods in West Africa: Some Silences in the Food Sovereignty Discourse." *Globalizations* 18 (3): 339–354.

Hall, Derek. 2013. *Land*. London: Polity Press.

Hall, Ruth, Marc Edelman, Saturnino M. Borras Jr., Ian Scoones, Ben White, and Wendy Wolford. 2015. "Resistance, Acquiescence or Incorporation? An Introduction to Land Grabbing and Political Reactions 'from Below.' " *Journal of Peasant Studies* 42 (3–4): 467–488.

Halperin, Sandra. 2013. *Re-envisioning Global Development: A Horizontal Perspective*. London: Routledge.

Harvey, David. 2017. *Marx, Capital and the Madness of Economic Reason*. Oxford: Oxford University Press.

Henderson, Christian. 2021. "The Rise of Arab Gulf Agro-Capital: Continuity and Change in the Corporate Food Regime." *Journal of Peasant Studies* 4 (162): 599–614.

Henriques, Gisele. 2011. "Stop the Land Grab." *The Guardian*, February 12. https://www.theguardian.com/commentisfree/2011/feb/12/global-land-grab-farmers.

High Level Panel of Experts. 2019. *Agroecological and Other Innovative Approaches for sustainable agriculture and food systems that enhance food security and nutrition*. HLPE Report 14. Rome: Food and Agriculture Organization of the United Nations.

Holloway, Kali. 2021. "Forced off Their Land." *The Nation*, November 15. https://www.thenation.com/article/society/black-farmers-pigford-debt/.

Holt-Giménez, Eric. 2007. "Exploding the Biofuel Myths." *Le Monde diplomatique*, July, 10–11.

Hopewell, Kristen. 2020. *Clash of Powers: US-China Rivalry in Global Trade Governance*. Cambridge, UK: Cambridge University Press.

Hughes, Ailey Kaiser. 2020. "Technology for Land Governance: Ensuring That Women Benefit from the Revolution." *African Journal on Land Policy and Geospatial Sciences* 3 (2): 21–28.

Hughes, Ailey Kaiser, Marie Grace Nishimwe, Dr. Said Ngoga Rutabayiro, Roger Mizero, Athanase Akumuntu, Sylvain Muyombano, et al. 2022. "Harnessing Technology to Advance Citizen-Centric Land Administration in Rwanda." *African Journal on Land Policy and Geospatial Sciences* 5 (2): 344–354. https://revues.imist.ma/index.php/AJLP-GS/article/view/31345/16434.

IPES Food and ETC Group. 2021. A *Long Food Movement: Transforming Food Systems by 2045*.

Islam, Saidul. 2014. *Confronting the Blue Revolution: Industrial Aquaculture and Sustainability in the Global South*. Toronto: University of Toronto Press.

Kabeer, Naila, and Tran Thi van Anh. 2002. "Leaving the Rice Fields, but Not the Countryside." In *Shifting Burdens: Gender and Agrarian Change under Neoliberalism*, edited by Shahra Razav, 109–150. Bloomfield, CT: Kumarian Press.

Kapoor, Dip. 2021. "Rural Dispossession and Resistance in Asia and Africa." In *The Essential Guide to Development Studies*, edited by Henry Veltmeyer and Paul Bowles, 2nd ed., 341–349. London: Routledge. https://www.farmlandgrab.org/uploads/attachment/10.4324_9781003037187-51_chapterpdf.pdf.

Kerssen, Tanya. 2013. *Grabbing Power: The New Struggles for Land, Food and Democracy in Northern Honduras*. Oakland, CA: Food First Books.

Khadse, Ashlesha, Peter Rosset, Helda Morales, and Bruce G. Ferguson. 2018. "Taking Agroecology to Scale: The Zero Budget Natural Farming Peasant Movement in Karnataka, India." *Journal of Peasant Studies* 45 (1): 192–219.

Kimmerer, Robin Wall. 2013. *Braiding Sweetgrass, Indigenous Wisdom, Scientific Knowledge and the Teachings of Plants*. Minneapolis, MN: Milkweed.

Lahiff, Edward, Saturnino M. Borras Jr., and Cristobal Kay. 2007. "Market-Led Agrarian Reform: Trajectories and Contestations." *Third World Quarterly* 28 (8): 1417–1436.

Lindeman, Tracey. 2020. "'Revolution Is Alive': Canadian Pipeline Protests Spawn Climate and Indigenous Rights Movement." *The Guardian*, February 28. https://www.theguardian.com/world/2020/feb/28/canada-pipeline-protests-climate-indigenous-rights.

Land Matrix. 2021. *Taking Stock of the Global Land Rush*. Analytical Report 3. Center for Development and Environment, University of Bern. https://doi.org/10.48350/156861.

Lapegna, Pablo. 2016. *Soybeans and Power. Genetically Modified Crops, Environmental Politics, and Social Movements in Argentina*. New York: Oxford University Press.

Larder, Nicolette, Sarah Ruth Sippel, and Geoffrey Lawrence. 2015. "Finance Capital, Food Security Narratives and Australian Agricultural Land." *Journal of Agrarian Change* 15 (4): 592. https://doi.org/10.1111/joac.12108.

La Vía Campesina. 2008. https://viacampesina.org/en/civil-society-declaration-of-the-terra-preta-forum/.

La Vía Campesina. 2009. "Feeding the world and cooling the planet": La Vía Campesina's Fifth International Conference, 15 October. https://viacampesina.org/en/feeding-the-world-and-cooling-the-planet-la-vcampesinas-fifth-international-conference/

La Vía Campesina. 2018. "A Major Breakthrough in Scaling Up Agroecological Farming in Karnataka, India." June 26. https://viacampesina.org/en/a-major-breakthrough-in-scaling-up-agroecological-farming-in-karnataka-india/.

Leguizamón, Amalia. 2020. *Seeds of Power: Environmental Injustice and Genetically Modified Seeds in Argentina*. Durham, NC: Duke University Press.

LeHeron, Richard, and Nick Lewis. 2009. "Discussion: Theorising food regimes: Intervention as politics." *Agriculture and Human Values* 26, 345–349.

Levien, Michael. 2017. "Gender and Land Dispossession: A Comparative Perspective." *Journal of Peasant Studies* 44 (6): 1111–1134.

Liberti, Stefano. 2014. *Land Grabbing: Journeys in the New Colonialism*. London: Verso Books.

Makki, Fouad. 2013. "Development by Dispossession: *Terra Nullius* and the Social-Ecology of New Enclosures in Ethiopia." *Rural Sociology* 79 (1): 79–105.

Malkan, Stacey. 2021. "African Groups Want Gates Foundation, USAID, to Shift Agricultural Funding as Hunger Crisis Worsens." US Right to Know (USRTK), September 8. https://usrtk.org/tag/alliance-for-a-green-revolution-in-africa/.

Mamonova, Natalia. 2015. "Resistance or Adaptation? Ukrainian Peasants' Responses to Large-Scale Land Acquisitions." *Journal of Peasant Studies* 42 (3–4): 607–634.
Mandhu, Fatima, Anthony Mushinge, and Christopher Mulenga. 2019. *Land Governance in Zambia: Synthesis Report*. Land Governance in Southern Africa Symposium. The NUST-NELGA Hub. Windhoek, Namibia, September 3–4.
Mann, Alana. 2021. *Food in a Changing Climate*. Bingley, UK: Emerald Publishing.
Marx, Karl. 1973. *Grundrisse*. New York: Penguin.
Matthews, Kayla. 2018. "Why It Matters That Amazon Bought Whole Foods." Blue and Green, October 15. https://blueandgreentomorrow.com/news/why-matters-that-amazon-bought-whole-foods/.
Matties, Zoe. 2016. "Unsettling Settler Food Movements: Food Sovereignty and Decolonization in Canada." *Cuizine: Journal of Canadian Food Cultures* 7 (2): n.p. https://doi.org/10.7202/1038478ar.
Mayes, Christopher. 2018. *Unsettling Food Politics: Agriculture, Dispossession and Sovereignty in Australia*. London & New York: Rowman & Littlefield.
McKay, Ben. 2018. "Control Grabbing and Value-Chain Agriculture: BRICS, MICs and Bolivia's Soy Complex." *Globalizations* 15 (1): 74–91. https://doi.org/10.1080/14747731.2017.1374563.
McKeon, Nora. 2013. "'One Does Not Sell the Land Upon Which the People Walk': Land Grabbing, Transnational Rural Social Movements, and Global Governance." *Globalizations* 10 (1): 105–122.
McKeon, Nora. 2014. *The New Alliance for Food Security and Nutrition: A Coup for Corporate Capital?* Amsterdam: Transnational Institute.
McKeon, Nora. 2015. *Food Security Governance: Empowering Communities, Regulating Corporations*. London: Routledge.
McMichael, Philip. 1984. *Settlers and the Agrarian Question: Foundations of Capitalism in Colonial Australia*. Cambridge UK: Cambridge University Press.
McMichael, Philip. 1996. *Development and Social Change: A Global Perspective*. Thousand Oaks, CA: Pine Forge Press.
McMichael, Philip. 2005. "Global Development and the Corporate Food Regime." In *New Directions in the Sociology of Global Development*, 11, edited by Frederick H. Buttel and Philip McMichael, 229–267. Oxford: Elsevier.
McMichael, Philip. 2009. "A Food Regime Genealogy." *Journal of Peasant Studies* 36 (1): 139–139.
McMichael, Philip, Ed. 2010. *Contesting Development. Critical Struggles for Social Change*. New York: Routledge.
McMichael, Philip. 2012. "The 'Land Grab' and Corporate Food Regime Restructuring." *Journal of Peasant Studies* 39 (3/4): 681–701.
McMichael, Philip. 2013a. *Food Regimes and Agrarian Questions*. Halifax, CAN: Fernwood Press.
McMichael, Philip. 2013b. "Land Grabbing as Security Mercantilism in International Relations." *Globalizations* 10 (1): 47–64.
McMichael, Philip. 2013c. "Value-Chain Agriculture and Debt Relations: Contradictory Outcomes." *Third World Quarterly* 34 (4): 671–690.
McMichael, Philip. 2015. "The Land Question and the Food Sovereignty Project." *Globalizations* 12 (4): 434–451.

McMichael, Philip. 2020. "Does China's 'Going Out' Strategy Prefigure a New Food Regime?" *The Journal of Peasant Studies* 47 (1): 116–154.

McMichael, Philip. 2021. "Shock and Awe in the UNFSS." *Development* 64 (3–4): 162–171. https://doi.org/10.1057/s41301-021-00304-1.

McMichael, Philip. 2022. "Covid-19 and the Future of Food." In *Covid-19 and the Future of the Global Political Economy: Crises in the 21st Century*, edited by Tim Di Muzio and Matt Dow, 204–219. London: Routledge.

McNulty, Anna. 2022. "A Return to Native Agriculture." Civil Eats, January 21. https://civileats.com/2022/01/21/a-return-to-native-agriculture/.

Monbiot. 2015. "We're Treating Soil like Dirt: It's a Fatal Mistake, as Our Lives Depend on It." *The Guardian*, March 25. https://www.theguardian.com/commentisfree/2015/mar/25/treating-soil-like-dirt-fatal-mistake-human-life.

Montalvo, Melissa. 2021. "Indigenous Food Sovereignty Movements Are Taking Back Ancestral Land." Civil Eats, March 31. https://civileats.com/2021/03/31/indigenous-food-sovereignty-movements-are-taking-back-ancestral-land/.

Montenegro de Wit, Maywa, and Alistair Illes. 2021. "Woke Science and the 4th Industrial Revolution: Inside the Making of UNFSS Knowledge." *Development* 64 (3–4): 151–163.

Mooney, Pat. 2017. *Too Big to Feed: Exploring the Impacts of Mega-Mergers, Consolidation and Concentration of Power in the Agri-Food Sector*. IPES Food Report 03, October. International Panel of Experts on Sustainable Food Systems. www.ipes-food.org.

Mooney, Pat. 2018. *Blocking the Chain*. Report. ETC Group, Global Change–Local Conflict? (GLOCON), INKOTA, and Rosa Luxemburg Stiftung, Val David, CAN, and Berlin.

Moore, Jason. 2000. "Environmental Crises and the Metabolic Rift in World-Historical Perspective." *Organization & Environment* 13 (2): 123–157.

Mousseau, Frédéric, Andy Currier, Elizabeth Fraser, and Jessie Green. 2020. "Driving Dispossession. The Global Push to Unlock the 'Economic Potential' of Land." *Oakland Institute*. July. https://www.oaklandinstitute.org/sites/oaklandinstitute.org/files/driving-dispossession.pdf.

Narayan, 2020. "Farm Protests in India are Writing the Green Revolution's Obituary." *Scientific American*, January 24. https://www.scientificamerican.com/article/farm-protests-in-india-are-writing-the-green-revolutions-obituary/

Navdanya. 2020. "Gates Ag-One and the Recolonisation of Agriculture." In *Gates to a Global Empire, over Seed, Food, Health, Knowledge . . . and the Earth: A Global Citizens' Report*, edited by Carla Ramos Cortés, 67–85. Rome: Navdanya International. https://navdanyainternational.org/wp-content/uploads/2020/10/GATES-AG-ONE.pdf.

Newell, Peter, and Olivia Taylor. 2018. "Contested Landscapes: The Global Political Economy of Climate Smart Agriculture." *Journal of Peasant Studies* 45 (1): 108–129.

Narula, Smita. 2013. "The Global Land Rush: Markets, Rights and the Politics of Food." *Stanford Journal of International Law* 49 (1): 103–175.

Nyéléni, 2006. First Manifesto/Call of Social Movements and Civil Society Toward the 'Land, Territory and Dignity' Forum, Porto Alegre, March 6–9. http://www.nyeleni.org/spip.php?article54.

Oliveira, Gustavo de L. T. 2018. "Chinese Land Grabs in Brazil? Sinophobia and Foreign Investments in Brazilian Soybean Agribusiness." *Globalizations* 15 (1): 114–133.

Oliveira, Gustavo, and Susanna Hecht. 2016. "Sacred Groves, Sacrifice Zones and Soy Production: Globalization, Intensification and Neo-nature in South America." *Journal of Peasant Studies* 43 (2): 253–285.
Ong, Aihwa. 2006. *Neoliberalism as Exception: Mutations in Citizenship and Sovereignty*. Durham, NC: Duke University Press.
Otero, Gerardo. 2012. "The Neoliberal Food Regime in Latin America: State, Agribusiness Transnational Corporations and Biotechnology." *Canadian Journal of Development Studies* 33 (3): 282–294.
Pattenden, Jonathan, and Gaurav Bansal. 2021. "New Class Alliance in the Indian Countryside? From New Farmers' Movements to the 2020 Protest Wave." *Economic and Political Weekly* 61 (26–27): 22–29.
Paul, Helena, and Ricarda Steinbrecher. 2013. "African Agricultural Growth Corridors and the New Alliance for Food Security and Nutrition: Who Benefits, Who Loses?" Report, June. EcoNexus. http://www.econexus.info/sites/econexus/files/African_Agricultural_Growth_Corridors_&_New_Alliance_-_EcoNexus_June_2013.pdf.
Palmer, Meredith Alberta. 2020. "Rendering Settler Sovereign Landscapes: Race and Property in the Empire State." *Environment and Planning D: Society and Space* 38 (5): 793–810. https://doi.org/10.1177%2F0263775820922233.
Pascoe, Bruce. 2014. *Dark Emu, Black Seeds: Agriculture or Accident?* Broome, WA: Magabala Books.
Patel, Raj. 2013. "The Long Green Revolution." *Journal of Peasant Studies* 40 (1): 1–65.
Patel, Raj, and Philip McMichael. 2009. "A Political-Economy of the Food Riot." *REVIEW (Fernand Braudel Center)* 32 (1): 9–35.
Pavageau, Charlotte, Stefanie Pondini, and Matthias Geck. 2020. *Money Flows: What Is Holding Back Investment in Agro-Ecological Research in Africa?* Report. Biovision Foundation for Ecological Development and International Panel of Experts on Sustainable Food Systems (IPES Food).
Peine, Emelie Kaye. 2010. "Corporate Mobilization on the Mato Grosso Soybean Frontier, Brazil." In *Contesting Development: Critical Struggles for Social Change*, edited by Philip McMichael, 132–146. London: Routledge.
Peluso, Nancy, and Christian Lund. 2011. "New Frontiers of Land Control: An Introduction." *Journal of Peasant Studies* 38 (4): 667–681.
Phillips, Dom. 2019. "Bolsonaro Declares 'the Amazon Is Ours' and Calls Deforestation Data 'Lies.'" *The Guardian*, July 19. https://www.theguardian.com/world/2019/jul/19/jair-bolsonaro-brazil-amazon-rainforest-deforestation.
Philpott, Tom. 2020a. *Precarious Bounty: The Looming Collapse of American Farming*. London: Bloomsbury.
Philpott, Tom. 2020b. "Rivers of Finance, but Not a Drop to Drink: Financialization, Power and Agriculture in California's Parched Central Valley." *Food First Backgrounder* 26 (4): 1–4.
Pimbert, Michel, and Colin Anderson. 2018. "The Battle for the Future of Farming." The Conversation, November 21. https://theconversation.com/the-battle-for-the-future-of-farming-what-you-need-to-know-106805.
Prause, Luisa, Sarah Hackfort, and Margit Lindgren. 2021. "Digitalization and the Third Regime." *Agriculture and Human Values* 38: 641–655.
Pritchard, Bill. 2009. "The Long Hangover from the Second Food Regime: A World-Historical Interpretation of the Collapse of the WTO Doha Round." *Agriculture and Human Values* 26 (4): 297–307.

Razavi, Shahra. 2007. "Liberalisation and the Debates on Women's Access to Land." *Third World Quarterly* 28 (8): 1479–1500.
Reisman, Emily. 2021. "Sanitizing Agri-Food Tech: COVID-19 and the Politics of Expectation." *Journal of Peasant Studies* 48 (4): 910–933.
Rights and Resources Initiative. 2015. *Who Owns the World's Land? A Global Baseline of Formally Recognized Indigenous and Community Land Rights*. Washington, DC. https://rightsandresources.org/wp-content/uploads/GlobalBaseline_web.pdf.
Rosset, Peter M., and Miguel A. Altieri. 2017. *Agroecology: Science and Politics*. Halifax, CAN: Fernwood Press.
Ruggie, John Gerard. 1993. "Territoriality and Beyond: Problematizing Modernity in International Relations." *International Organization* 47 (1): 139–174.
Saldanha, Leo F. 2018. A Review of Andhra Pradesh's Climate Resilient Zero Budget. https://www.readkong.com/page/a-review-of-andhra-pradesh-s-climate-resilient-zero-budget-7851491
Salverda, Tijo. 2019. "Facing Criticism: An Analysis of (Land-Based) Corporate Responses to the Large-Scale Land Acquisition Countermovement." *Journal of Peasant Studies* 46 (5): 1003–1020.
Sanderson, Steven. 1986. "The Emergence of the 'World Steer': Internationalization and Foreign Domination in Latin American Cattle Production." *In Food, the State, and International Political Economy*, edited by F. L. Tullis and W. L. Hollist. Lincoln: University of Nebraska Press.
Schneider, Mindi, and Philip McMichael. 2010. "Deepening, and Repairing, the Metabolic Rift." *Journal of Peasant Studies* 37 (3): 461–484.
Schwab, Klaus. 2019. Why we need the 'Davos Manifesto' for a better kind of capitalism. https://www.weforum.org/agenda/2019/12/why-we-need-the-davos-manifesto-for-better-kind-of-capitalism/.
Schwab, Klaus, and Thierry Malleret. 2020. *Covid-19: The Great Reset*. Los Angeles: Forum Publishing. http://reparti.free.fr/schwab2020.pdf.
Scoones, Ian. 2009. "Livelihoods Perspectives and Rural Development." *Journal of Peasant Studies* 36 (1): 171–196.
Shattuck, Annie, Christina Schiavoni, and Zoe VanGelder, eds. 2019. *The Politics of Food Sovereignty: Concept, Practice and Social Movements*. London: Routledge.
Sikor, Thomas, and Peter Newell. 2014. "Globalizing Environmental Justice?" *Geoforum* 54, 151 157.
Staab, Philipp. 2019. *Digitaler Kapitalismus: Markt und Herrschaft in der Okonomie der Unknappheit*. Berlin: Suhrkamp Verlag.
Stone, Glenn Davis. 2022. "Surveillance Agriculture and Peasant Autonomy." *Journal of Agrarian Change* 22 (3): 608–631. https://doi.org/10.1111/joac.12470.
Styger Erika, and Gaoussou Traoré. 2018. 50,000 Farmers in 13 Countries: Results from Scaling up the System of Rice Intensification in West Africa. https://sriwestafrica.files.wordpress.com/2018/04/sri-waapp-book-single-p-8mb.pdf.
Tadele, Kirubel. 2021. Independent expert evaluations confirm that the Alliance for a Green Revolution in Africa has failed. African Food Sovereignty Alliance (AFSA), July 23. https://afsafrica.org/a-sting-in-the-agra-tale-independent-expert-evaluations-confirm-that-the-alliance-for-a-green-revolution-has-failed/
Taylor, Marcus. 2018. "Climate-Smart Agriculture: What is it Good For?" *The Journal of Peasant Studies* 45 (1): 89–107.

Toledo, Victor M. 2022. "Agroecology and Spirituality: Reflections about an Unrecognized Link." *Agroecology and Sustainable Food Systems* 46 (4): 626–641. https://doi.org/10.1080/21683565.2022.2027842.

Townsend, Sarah. 2020. "Seeds of Gulf-Africa Agribusiness." *Cairo Review of Global Affairs* 44 (Winter). https://www.thecairoreview.com/essays/seeds-of-gulf-africa-agribusiness/.

Transnational Institute. 2013. *The Global Land Grab*. Amsterdam: TNI Agrarian Justice Program. https://www.tni.org/files/download/landgrabbingprimer-feb2013.pdf.

Trauger, Amy. 2015. *Putting Food Sovereignty in Place*. New York: Routledge.

Tullis, Paul. 2019. "How the World Got Hooked on Palm Oil." *The Guardian*, February 19. https://www.theguardian.com/news/2019/feb/19/palm-oil-ingredient-biscuits-shampoo-environmental.

Urquhart, Sam. 2008. "Food Crisis, Which Crisis? Our Crisis or Theirs? The Battle over the World's Food Supply Relocates to Rome." Guerrilla News Network, June 2. http://gnn.to/articles/3718/food_crisis_which_crisis.

Valencia, Vivian, Hannah Wittman, Andrew D. Jones, and Jennifer Blesh. 2021. "Public Policies for Agricultural Diversification: Implications for Gender Equality." Frontiers in Sustainable Food Systems, December 3. https://www.frontiersin.org/articles/10.3389/fsufs.2021.718449/full.

van der Ploeg, Jan Douwe, and Jingzhong Ye, eds. 2016. *China's Peasant Agriculture and Rural Society: Changing Paradigms of Farming*. London: Routledge.

Varoufakis, Yanis. 2021. "Techno-Feudalism Is Taking Over." Project Syndicate, June 28. https://www.project-syndicate.org/commentary/techno-feudalism-replacing-market-capitalism-by-yanis-varoufakis-2021-06.

Vergara-Camus, Leandro. 2014. *Land and Freedom: The MST, the Zapatistas, and Peasant Alternatives to Neoliberalism*. London: Zed Books.

Vidal, John. 2019. "We're Losing Species at Shocking Rates—So Why Is Conservation Failing?" *The Guardian*, September 18. https://www.theguardian.com/environment/2019/sep/18/losing-species-shocking-rates-why-conservation-failing.

Weis, Tony. 2010. "The Accelerating Biophysical Contradictions of Industrial Capitalist Agriculture." *Journal of Agrarian Change* 10 (3): 315–341.

White, Ben, Saturnino M. Borras Jr., Ian Scoones, and Wendy Wolford. 2012. "The New Enclosures: Critical Perspectives on Corporate Land Deals." *Journal of Peasant Studies* 39 (3-4): 619–647.

Wily, Liz Alden. 2011. "The Law Is to Blame: The Vulnerable Status of Common Property Rights in Sub-Saharan Africa." *Development and Change* 42 (3): 733–757.

Winders, Bill. 2009. "The Vanishing Free Market: The Formation and Spread of the British and US Food Regimes." *Journal of Agrarian Change* 9 (3): 315–344.

Wise, Tim. 2018. "Seeds of Resistance, Harvests of Hope: Farmers Halt a Land Grab in Mozambique." Food Tank, October. https://foodtank.com/news/2018/10/seeds-of-resistance-harvests-of-hope-farmers-halt-a-land-grab-in-mozambique/.

Wise, Tim. 2020. "Africa's Choice: Africa's Green Revolution Has Failed, Time to Change Course." Institute for Agriculture and Trade Policy, July 28. https://www.iatp.org/africas-choice.

Wittman, Hannah, Dana James, and Zia Mehrabi. 2020. "Advancing Food Sovereignty through Farmer-Driven Digital Agroecology." *International Journal of Agriculture and Natural Resources* 47 (3): 235–248. https://www.researchgate.net/publication/348052178_Advancing_food_sovereignty_through_farmer-driven_digital_agroecology.
World Bank. 2007. *World Development Report, 2008*. Washington, DC: World Bank.
World Bank. 2014. *Benchmarking the Business of Agriculture*. Washington, DC: World Bank. http://bba.worldbank.org/.
World Bank. 2019. *Enabling the Business of Agriculture*. Washington, DC: World Bank.

CHAPTER 10

A POLITICAL ECOLOGY OF FINANCIALIZATION AND FARMLAND CONTROL

S. RYAN ISAKSON

INTRODUCTION

WHILE mortgage lending has long given financial actors a certain degree of control over land, their influence in shaping how the resource is used and who benefits from its use has increased noticeably over the course of the twenty-first century. This is reflected in a growing array of financial products that are tied to land, an expanding cast of financial actors that are seeking profits in land markets, and the sheer quantity of financial funds that are invested in land. These dynamics are all indicators of how the control of land has been shaped by the financialization of capitalism, broadly, and land markets, in particular. In this chapter I draw on the existing literature to critically evaluate how the contemporary process of financialization is reconfiguring land markets and property relations, giving particular attention to the farmland sector.

Since the 2007–2009 Great Recession and the correlated spike in food prices, financial activity in the farmland sector has grown substantially. Between 2005 and 2022, the number of investment funds focused on farmland increased more than tenfold, from an almost negligible nineteen funds before the financial crisis to more than two hundred today (Garzon and Viton 2022). In the US market alone, forty funds raised nearly US$9 billion to invest in farmland between 2016 and 2021 (Darbyshire 2022).

A variety of novel investment vehicles have been introduced over the past two decades that go beyond the long-standing practice of mortgage lending, and instead focus on the direct acquisition of farmland. Flush with finance capital from deep-pocketed institutional investors, which are often the pension funds, hedge funds, and endowment funds that have developed a newfound interest in farmland, these investment vehicles have acquired significant quantities of farmland in prominent agricultural countries across the globe. In the Canadian prairie province of Saskatchewan, for instance, investor ownership of farmland increased eighteenfold in sixteen years, from 52,000 acres in 2002 to 945,000 acres in 2018, some 12 percent of that increase occurring during the four-year period from 2014 to 2018 (Desmarais et al. 2017; Magnan, Davidson, and Desmarais 2023). Farther south, in Brazil, two prominent US-based asset management firms, TIAA and Harvard Management Company, have amassed a combined total of some 750,000 hectares of farmland since 2008, making them the largest foreign landowners in the country (Mendonça 2023). Meanwhile, financialized agricorporate investors acquired nearly 200,000 hectares of farmland in the New England North West region of New South Wales, Australia, between 2004 and 2019 (Pritchard et al. 2023). These trends are mirrored in the investment activities of wealthy individuals, such as Microsoft founder Bill Gates, media mogul Ted Turner, and Amazon founder Jeff Bezos, who have all diversified their portfolios with farmland acquisitions. Over the past two decades, "Farmer Bill," as *The Land Report* dubbed Gates, has acquired some 242,000 hectares of prime farmland in eighteen US states, making him the largest owner of private agricultural land in the country (O'Keefe 2021).

These mounting financial investments in farmland are reflective of a broader process known as *financialization* that has been unfolding since the late 1970s. Generally understood as the increased influence of financial actors, logics, and institutions on the functioning of economies and their governing bodies, financialization has its origins in the decline of the US manufacturing sector since the 1970s and the associated demise of the Fordist social compact of paying industrial workers decent wages (Epstein 2005; Kotz 2019; Krippner 2011). The combination of growing international competition and declining consumer purchasing power undermined the profitability of US manufacturing, deterring further investment in the sector. Meanwhile, the so-called Volker Shock dramatically increased interest rates at a time when the liberalization of international and domestic financial markets was facilitating the development of new financial products and expanded investment opportunities. In this context, investing in financial markets emerged as a profitable outlet for overaccumulated capital. In the United States and other developed nations, the composition of profit-making activities shifted away from those of the "real" economy—that is, from producing and distributing goods and services—in favor of financial activities associated with generating dividends, interest, and capital gains (Krippner 2011; Epstein and Jayadev 2005). Of course, one should be careful not to engage in "anaemic geographies" that universalize the process and specificities of this financialization of accumulation in the Global North to other regions of the world (Christophers 2012, 271). Yet scholars have also observed that, as profit-making in core countries increasingly accrues through financial channels, financial flows from the North to the South have increased as well, albeit in ways that reinforce the subordinate position of emerging economies (Bonizzi et al. 2020).

After a series of financial bubbles, the fragility of the financial fix as a solution to overaccumulated capital came to the fore during the 2007–2009 Great Recession. As the financial sector collapsed, investors sought refuge in physical assets such as timberland and farmland. Indeed, such "flights to quality" are not unusual during economic downturns. Though the returns may not be spectacular, financial pundits praise the security of land investments. These pundits have long maintained that farmland provides a reliable hedge against inflation, meaning that it retains its value and delivers stable returns over time. Moreover, they note, the returns are negatively correlated with conventional financial assets (e.g. stocks and bonds), making acquiring farmland a desirable means of diversifying one's investment portfolio. Since the early 2000s, this traditional narrative has been augmented with new concerns about the growing scarcity of agricultural land and uncertainties about the global food supply, giving rise to promises of even stronger returns (Nuveen 2020; FarmTogether 2023; Schmidt 2023).

Drawing on the work of economic geographer David Harvey, many early scholars of the financial land rush likened it to his concept of the "spatial fix," since farmland has functioned as a sponge that absorbs overaccumulated capital (Sommerville 2013; Fairbairn 2014; Isakson 2014; Knuth 2015). According to Harvey (2001, 2003), economic crises can be attenuated by reorienting surplus capital into intensive investments in the built environment of a particular place, through its geographic expansion into new markets, or both. Ekers and Prudham (2017, 2018) build on Harvey's work to argue that such fixes increasingly unfold through human relations with nature and, ultimately, the production of nature. These "socio-ecological" fixes, as they call them, highlight how the processes of capital accumulation unfold through both social and socionatural relations, becoming inscribed on landscapes, including farmers' fields.

But if likening the financial land rush to a spatial fix provides a useful framework for describing the general dimensions of the phenomenon, Ouma (2014, 2016) has taken this scholarship to task for its deterministic portrayal of capitalism and an overly structuralist interpretation of financialization in the farmland sector (cf. Li 2015). Instead, he argues, more attention should be given to place-based particularities, including the agency of agricultural and financial actors and the on-the-ground practices of formatting farmland for financial purposes, including resistance to this. As we will see, Ouma's critique has helped to spur a rich and insightful literature about the practices, techniques, and challenges of transforming farmland into a financial asset. This scholarship highlights that farmland is not a ready-made asset class. Its enrollment into financial circuits is contingent upon its assetization, or the creation of specific socio-institutional configurations that enable the extraction of steady, reliable streams of financial income (Swyngedouw and Ward 2022; Haila 1988; Sippel and Visser 2021). Moreover, as I will argue, these challenges to assetization point to weaknesses that can be leveraged by actors seeking to halt or unravel the financial formatting of farmland.

I draw from this rich and expanding literature of financialization in agrarian contexts to argue that the financial assetization of farmland has exacerbated socioeconomic inequality and intensified environmental degradation in agrarian communities. My analysis is informed by Peluso and Lund's (2011) concept of land control, which I understand as the practices that shape how land is used, who is able to access the benefits from it, and who is excluded from those benefits (cf. Borras et al. 2012). This approach helps to highlight the political nature of financialization, which not only debundles and rebundles farmland in novel ways that unlock financial value (Isakson 2014), but also rebundles power relations in agrarian contexts (Ribot and Peluso 2003). Financial actors have been able to exercise their tremendous economic power vis-à-vis agricultural producers to institute new property relations that make it easier for them to extract value from agricultural production. This, in turn, has compelled the intensification of agro-extractive practices that undermine the ecological foundations of sustainable agriculture. To be sure, efforts to enlist farmland for financial purposes can take various forms and may or may not be successful; they can therefore be defeated. Defeating them, however, requires an understanding of how that process works. This chapter is a modest effort toward that end.

Context—the History, Geography, and Actors of the Financialized Land Rush

The links between finance and farmland are long-standing, dating back to at least the third century AD, when the Roman emperor Severus Alexander made no-interest loans available to the poor for the purchase of farmland (Turvey 2017). Some fifteen hundred years later, beginning around 1765, the state banks in many European countries adopted a similar model to help liberate farmers from feudal servitude and promote family farms; their efforts were complemented by the parallel development of cooperative farm-mortgage credit associations (Turvey 2017; Chang 2009; Guinnane 2011). As these examples suggest, entanglements between finance and farmland throughout history have generally—but not exclusively—centered on the provisioning of credit for land purchases. This relationship between the financial and farmland sectors has changed noticeably in recent decades. Although private financial actors continue to exercise *indirect* control over farmland through mortgage lending, they are now also exercising more *direct* control via their increasing ownership of farmland and influence over agricultural producers (Fairbairn 2020). Here, I provide a sketch of key historical moments in the financial sector's growing control of agricultural land, and provide an overview of the different types of financial actors involved. As with financialization generally, many of the early moments in this shift were rooted in changes in the US economy, but they have played a key role in reshaping farmland sectors across the globe, albeit unevenly and in different ways.

To understand the history and geography of financialization in farmland markets, it is helpful to understand the different types of financial actors involved. In the major grain-producing countries, commercial banks and life insurance companies have historically been the most prominent sources of private credit for farmland purchases (Fairbairn 2020; Sommerville and Magnan 2015; Guinanne 2011). Some readers might be surprised to read that life insurance companies played this role, but the relationship makes sense when one considers the long-term nature of life insurance policies. More important than immediate returns life insurance companies need secure investments that will pay out over time (Fairbairn 2020).

Insurance companies are one of many types of *institutional investors*. Institutional investors are professional companies or organizations that invest money on behalf of their clients or members. Other types of institutional investors include pension funds (which invest on behalf of employees), endowments (which invest on behalf of a non-profit), and sovereign wealth funds (which invest on behalf of nations), along with mutual funds, hedge funds, and commercial banks (which all pool and manage the funds of individual investors). Whereas institutional investors manage the funds of others, *retail investors* are individuals who invest their own money on their own behalf. If institutional and retail investors meet particular requirements (e.g., sufficient wealth, professional experience), they may qualify as *accredited investors*, a status that allows them to invest in risky, unregulated financial products. Much of the growing investment in farmland since the 2000s is associated with the entrance of pension funds, sovereign wealth funds, and other deep-pocketed institutional investors into the farmland marketplace, all seeking to profit from the agricultural sector. Nonetheless, all types of investors, including retail investors, have played a role. Indeed, it is not uncommon for different types of financial actors to work together in the assetization of farmland (Smith, Langford, and Lawrence 2023; Garcia-Arias et al. 2021; Mendonça 2023; Sosa Varrotti and Gras 2021).

The United States is home to most of the world's largest agricultural investment funds, and widely recognized as the epicenter of contemporary farmland financialization (Preqin 2016). As Madeleine Fairbairn (2020) has lucidly detailed, the architecture for the financial land rush emerged from a series of booms and busts in the country's agricultural sector during the twentieth century. Of note are the rising commodity prices in the 1970s that spurred demand for farmland among agricultural producers wishing to expand their operations. The associated rise in farmland prices, in turn, piqued the interest of institutional investors, who were facing growing risks and shrinking returns elsewhere during the years of general economic malaise. But after the US Federal Reserve jacked up interest rates in 1979 and commodity prices dropped in the 1980s, many farmers were unable to pay their mortgages on the high-priced farmland and defaulted. Life insurance enterprises, which were not only the dominant originators of farmland mortgages at the time but had also dramatically increased their own equity investments in farmland during the boom, suddenly found themselves the owners of significant quantities of prime agricultural land—albeit lower-valued.

Seeking to profit from their expanded landholdings, major US insurers created farmland-focused asset-management companies that, as the name suggests, managed the funds of other types of investors seeking to profit from their agricultural operations. The asset-management companies that emerged from this period—including Hancock Agricultural Investment Group, Prudential Global Investment Management, and UBS AgriVest—are widely recognized today as the progenitors of the farmland investment space (Fairbairn 2020). Pioneers they may have been, but neither the asset-management firms nor the funds they created garnered much interest from other institutional investors during the 1980s and '90s, when greater returns could be generated from investments outside the relatively staid agricultural sector.

Due to a confluence of factors, interest in the farmland-focused asset-management companies increased dramatically in the mid-2000s. As noted above in the introduction, farmland provided a secure place for investors to deposit surplus cash amid the growing risks and shrinking investment opportunities of the 2007–2009 financial crisis. At the same time, new biofuel mandates in the European Union and other countries and the attendant spike in food and commodity prices in 2008 gave rise to a new narrative that significant returns could also be earned from agricultural production (HighQuest Partners, United States 2010; Schmidt 2023). Indeed, the financial pundits likened farmland to "gold with yield" or "gold with a coupon," recognizing that, not only could farmland retain and possibly even appreciate in value, but it has the added benefit of being a productive asset that can generate returns in the forms of rent or agricultural output over time (Fairbairn 2014, 785). Seeking to tap into the new "black gold," deep-pocketed pension funds and other institutional investors channeled billions of dollars into the previously parched agricultural investment funds. The pioneers of farmland investment were suddenly awash with cash.

The flood of capital spurred a rapid proliferation of asset-management companies that offered a variety of agri-food investment products and was a major driver of a global land rush (Cotula 2012; Mechiche-Alami et al. 2019). The number of farmland-focused investment funds has increased more than 1,000 percent since 2002 (Garzaron and Viton 2022). Yet more important than the growth in the number of funds is the amount of capital being poured into them by institutional investors who were previously ambivalent about farmland. Pension funds, for instance, have some US$48 billion in assets under management, of which "other assets" such as farmland have captured a steadily growing share since 2002 (Willis Towers Watson 2023). Largely absent from the farmland investment space two decades ago, pension funds now account for nearly one-third of the institutional investments in farmland and agriculture (Preqin 2016). Sovereign wealth funds are another new player. Between 2005 and 2015, fourteen of the state-backed investors channeled more than US$11 billion into funds targeting farmland and agriculture from the Philippines and Mexico to Canada and Australia (Favas 2018). Other major institutional investors in the farmland investment space include endowments and foundations, which account for 14 percent and 12 percent, respectively, of institutional farmland investments (Preqin 2016).

According to the financial data management company Preqin, the value of assets under management by agricultural and farmland investment funds ballooned 43 percent, from US$22.2 billion in 2016 (Preqin 2016) to US$31.7 billion by 2018 (cited in Ouma 2020). A more recent estimate puts the market value of farmland investments at US$2.7 trillion (Kiernan-Stone 2023). These numbers may seem substantial, but they represent only a small fraction of the overall assets controlled by institutional investors—which, as Madeleine Fairbairn (2020) has astutely observed, is still enough money to purchase a lot of farmland, especially in poorer countries where prices are relatively lower.

Economists have celebrated the financial sector's newfound interest in farmland, proclaiming that the influx of capital will help to boost production and close the so-called yield gap between actual and potential agricultural output in the Global South (Deininger and Byerlee 2011; Luyt, Santos, and Carlta 2013). To be sure, it is possible to invest in farmland in poorer countries throughout the world, including in Africa (Ouma 2020; Ducastel and Anseeuw 2017; Bélair 2021; Cotula 2012); Latin America (Sosa Varrotti and Gras 2021; Mendonça and Pitta 2018; Garcia-Arias et al. 2021); Asia (Preqin 2016; Salerno 2017; Meyer 2016; Borras, Franco, and Nam 2020); and Eastern Europe (Visser and Spoor 2011; Kuns, Visser, and Wästfelt 2016; Luyt, Santos, and Carlta 2013). In actuality, however, the vast majority of investment funds and financial flows target the farmland in a select number of major grain-exporting countries. Luyt, Santos, and Carlta (2013, 32) report that just five countries—the United States, Canada, Brazil, Australia, and New Zealand—account for about two-thirds of the global "investible" farmland market. Within this select group, most investments target the United States and Canada. Drawing on a proprietary database, Ouma (2020) found that 54 percent of investment funds focus on the North American countries. Similarly, the investment data company Preqin (2016) reported that of the seventy-seven farmland-focused funds that closed between 2011 and 2016, one-third had a primary focus on North America, capturing US$5.7 billion, or 35 percent of the capital raised during the five-year period.

To date, there has been no systematic study of *why* financial investors primarily target the farmland in just a handful of countries and generally avoid those in the Global South. However, a casual review of reports in the financial press and existing literature suggests that farmland investors still seek security; correspondingly, they prefer countries with proven land markets characterized by secure property rights and established links to international commodity markets over potentially more transformative investments in riskier contexts. More research is needed on this topic. Of equal and related interest is how the financial assetization of farmland shapes the flow of capital between countries and whether, as scholars have argued regarding the broader process of financialization, it works to reinforce the subordinate position of economies in the Global South (Bonizzi et al. 2020; Garcia-Arias et al. 2021).

Investment Strategies and Products

As discussed in the previous section, many different types of financial actors are involved in the contemporary land rush. Though they may share a common interest in profiting from their farmland investments, there are also important differences within and among the groups of investors. An understanding of those differences can be instrumental in efforts to stall or unravel financialization in a given context. There are obvious and important variations, including the amount of capital each group has at its disposal. But even more subtle distinctions, such as appetites for risk, time horizons for realizing returns, investment styles, and motives to invest, can have important ramifications for the socioeconomic and environmental outcomes of financialization in the farmland sector. A frequent priority for sovereign wealth funds, for instance, is to ensure that the citizens of the investing nation will have access to food, particularly from water-intensive crops, helping to ensure political stability at home (Favas 2018; Sippel, Larder, and Lawrence 2017). Pension funds are generally more interested in low-risk but stable returns that will fund their beneficiaries' retirement plans over time. Meanwhile, more aggressive investors, such as hedge funds and private equity groups, are generally willing to take on riskier investments that have the potential to generate higher returns in a short amount of time.

As Knuth (2015) has observed, financial actors with a shorter time horizons and greater appetites for risk can typically be understood as "market-makers," who put their capital to work in the creation of farmland-based investment products. In other words, they perform the work of assetization (Birch and Ward 2022). More risk-averse investors with longer time horizons are more likely to channel their funds into these already-created investment vehicles or to purchase the farmland once it has been assetized by the market-makers. There is some evidence to suggest that land transactions among different types of investors have become more common in recent years in Canada (Magnan and Sunley 2017) and Australia (Pritchard et al. 2023). However, the underlying motives and dynamics of such investor-to-investor transactions are not well understood, nor are the implications for agricultural communities and land use practices.

In terms of investment strategies, Fairbairn has (2014) identified three general models, which she labels own lease-out, lease-operate, and own-operate. The relative risks and benefits of each model are largely determined by the extent to which they engage farmland as a store of value or a productive asset. The own-lease-out model is, arguably, the least risky of the three. As the name suggests, investors pursuing this strategy acquire farmland and then rent it out to agricultural producers, who are oftentimes the same farmers who were working the land before the change in ownership. In doing so, the investors procure an asset that is a renowned store of value; they are also entitled to the rental income from that land and, if they decide to the sell the land in the future, to any gains from appreciation. Meanwhile, they offload the risks associated with uncertain commodity prices and agricultural production onto their tenant farmers. At the other end of the spectrum, investors who seek to profit from agricultural production but have little interest in locking substantial sums of capital into farmland ownership can engage in the lease-operate model. This is arguably the riskiest of the three models, because in this arrangement investors rent farmland seek profits in the uncertain arena of agricultural production, often pinning their hopes on complementary investments in new technologies, higher-value crops, or both. Finally, own-operate investors combine the security of land ownership with the risks and potential rewards associated with agricultural production.

In practice, farmland investments can take numerous forms. Table 10.1 provides an overview of the best-known types of investment vehicles. Although a variety of qualities distinguish the different investment products from one another, here I briefly highlight three. The first is liquidity; some investments are more liquid than others, meaning that they can more easily be converted into ready cash than relatively "illiquid" investments can. Direct ownership of farmland, for instance, is notoriously illiquid. It can be difficult

Table 10.1. Types of Farmland Investment Vehicles

Investment Vehicle	Description	Degree of Liquidity	Wealth Requirements and Other Notes
Direct ownership	Investors acquire land and either directly manage the farm or hire an operator to do so. The high transaction costs of acquiring and then selling farmland encourages longer-term strategies.	Highly illiquid	Meaningful investment requires significant amounts of capital that tend to be "locked into" the farmland for extended periods of time. Direct ownership is typically an option only for wealthy individuals and institutional investors.
Private equity investment	Fund managers use the pooled capital from multiple investors to gain control over high-valued assets such as publicly listed companies or a portfolio of farmland properties. Private equity investment promises high returns within a medium-length time horizon, typically 5–10 years. Investors are entitled to a pro rata share of the fund's returns.	Illiquid	Due to high participation fees and investment minimums, private equity is only available to high-net-worth individuals and institutional investors.
Securities in agricultural corporations (i.e., stocks, bond, options)	Investors purchase securities in publicly listed agricultural operations companies that cultivate crops. Securities can take the form of stocks (shares in the ownership of the corporation), bonds (loans to the corporation), or options (rights to ownership). Securities are recognized for their fungibility, meaning that those associated with agricultural operations companies can be readily interchanged with securities in other types of corporations.	Highly liquid	Equities are available to investors of all sizes, from small retail investors to deep-pocketed institutional investors, who often include stocks in their portfolios. Although investing in agricultural operating corporations enables investors to profit from agricultural production, it does not usually provide direct exposure to the benefits associated with farmland ownership.
Real estate investment trusts (REITs)	Though they can focus on various types of properties, agricultural REITS acquire multiple farmland properties or the mortgages on them and compile them into a single holding. Investors can purchase tradable shares that entitle them to a portion of the associated returns or losses. Most farmland REITs generate income through the collection of rental or mortgage payments from farmers, but they occasionally realize capital gains by selling properties that have appreciated in value.	Publicly listed REITs are highly liquid; private REITs are much less so.	Shares in farmland-focused REITS can vary in size, making them available to small retail investors. Shares for publicly listed REITs can be traded on stock exchanges, making them highly liquid. Shares in private REITs have a higher investment minimum and cannot be redeemed for multiple years, making them less liquid.
Fractional investment (i.e., crowdfunding)	In fractional investing, companies purchase farmland through crowdfunding. They identify properties that they would like to purchase and divide them into fractional shares. The shares are typically expensive and available only to accredited investors. Shareholders receive regular dividends based on the rental payments received by the company. Holding periods are typically 5–10 years; upon sale of the land investors receive a pro rata share of any appreciation of the land.	Illiquid	By owning shares in an entity that legally owns the land, fractional investors own a portion of that land by proxy. To date, there is no secondary market for shareholders to exchange their shares during the holding period, though a prominent US-based firm, Acretrader, has plans to create a marketplace for doing so in the future.

and time-consuming for a landowner to find a buyer willing to pay the asking price just at the time that the owner would like to sell. Investment vehicles, such as private equity and fractional ownership arrangements, are also illiquid because they require investors to commit to multiyear ventures. In contrast, investment products such as securities (i.e., stocks and bonds) in publicly listed agricultural corporations can be readily sold on stock exchanges, making them highly liquid.

The other two important differences among investment products are the extent to which they expose investors to the benefits of farmland ownership and their availability to actors with varying levels of wealth. When investment opportunities elsewhere in the economy are limited, financial actors value farmland because it is a relatively secure place to park their capital, and they have come to expect that its value will appreciate over time. Direct ownership of farmland is the clearest means of accessing these benefits. But, in addition to tying up capital in a highly illiquid asset, direct ownership comes with the additional challenge that farmland is prohibitively expensive for most individual investors to purchase in meaningful quantities. Other products, such as shares in publicly listed agricultural operations corporations, are highly liquid and therefore available to less affluent investors, but the returns are generally limited to the profits from agricultural production, not farmland ownership per se. As I discuss in the following section, a relatively novel investment vehicle, *real estate investment trust* (REIT), overcomes these trade-offs, albeit in ways that transfer control of farmland away from those who work the land to an expanding class of financial landlords.

Financial Assetization

Despite the proliferation of land investment vehicles and the growing volume of capital that is poured into them, financial actors face numerous challenges when assembling farmland as a financial asset. Conventional assets, such as stocks, bonds, and currencies, have standardized qualities that render them interchangeable and easily tradable in financial markets. Farmland, in contrast, is characterized by an "inconvenient" and "stubborn" materiality that complicates its transformation into a financial asset (Fairbairn 2020, 81; Sippel 2023, 850). It is fixed in place, which contributes to its notorious illiquidity. Moreover, farmland plots come in various shapes and sizes that differ in an array of physical attributes, including soil type and fertility, topography, climatic conditions, slope, and access to water and relevant infrastructure. No two plots are alike, making it difficult for investors to compare one with another.

In addition to its "inconvenient materiality" (Fairbairn 2020, 81), the assetization of farmland is complicated by the unique role it plays in society. Unlike stocks and bonds, populations throughout the world have deep cultural connections to the lands that have sustained them, often for many generations. Similarly, land control is rooted in histories of place-based politics that have produced systems of rights that may or may not be conducive to financial operations and rationalities. For many, the cultural connection to land and the political privileges emanating from its control are considered priceless and elude market logics.

Few scholars have directly addressed the topic of private property rights in this arena, yet they are an important precondition to the financial assetization of land. Without secure property rights, the possibilities for generating financial returns are highly uncertain, and investments are extremely risky (Li 2015). Transforming land into property regimes that are legible to finance typically entails colonial enclosures of Indigenous land (Blomley 2003). Documenting how the Brookfield Asset Management Company and public pension plans came to acquire 800,000 hectares of Indigenous nations' land on Vancouver Island in Canada, Ekers (2019, 2023) is one of the few scholars to explicitly trace this connection, although Pritchard et al. (2023) and Sommerville (2018) have recognized similar dynamics of Indigenous dispossession and financialization elsewhere in Canada and Australia.

There is some evidence to suggest that financialization and land concentration are mutually reinforcing. Desmarais et al. (2017), Sommerville (2018), and Pritchard et al. (2023), for instance, observe that financial investors prefer large, aggregated farms that can absorb significant amounts of capital in a single purchase; that is, the existence of large agricultural holdings makes it easier for financiers to assemble an investment-worthy asset. Meanwhile, brokers and other entities have emerged that consolidate multiple farms with the sole intent of packaging them for financial acquisition (Sippel 2023; Pritchard et al. 2023; Knuth 2015). Indeed, financial analysts Wheaton and Kiernan (2012) celebrate the potential for well-heeled investors to acquire fragmented family farms and aggregate them into large holdings that are suitable for industrial forms of agriculture. Yet even without aggregation, predatory lending, throughout the Global South, including microlending, has been used as a mechanism to separate peasant and other small-scale agricultural producers from their land (Green 2019, 2022; Paprocki 2016; Casolo and Doshi 2013). The financial assetization of farmland can take many forms and sizes.

When acquiring farmland, financial investors often collaborate with different sets of powerful actors, including states, private companies, and multilateral development banks (Borras et al. 2020). Daniel (2012) documented various World Bank initiatives to mitigate many of the risks that might deter financial actors from investing in farmland in the Global South. Several scholars have also observed that states play a particularly important role in arbitrating whether and how financial actors can invest in farmland and other natural resources (Sippel and Weldon 2021; Kay and Tapp 2022). In many contexts, neoliberal policies have worked to create favorable socio-institutional environments. In 2003, for instance, the Canadian prairie province of Saskatchewan relaxed its ownership laws, allowing private equity firms, pension funds, and wealthy individuals to acquire some 850,000 acres of prime agricultural land over the ensuing decade (Desmarais et al. 2017; Magnan and Sunley 2017). Similarly, in the United States, tax exemptions have facilitated farmland investments for pension and endowment funds, and liberalized tax and security laws have enabled the creation of new products, including the aforementioned fractional investment funds (Fairbairn 2020; Ashwood et al. 2022; Shah 2023).

The rollback of state supports for agricultural producers in the major grain-producing countries, including Australia (Pritchard et al. 2023; Smith, Langford, and Lawrence 2023), Canada (Magnan and Sunley 2017; Desmarais et al. 2017), and the United States (Clapp and Isakson 2018; Fairbairn 2020), have left distressed farmers with little choice but to partner with eager financial investors. In the contemporary context of austerity governance, some of the governments that have been reluctant to directly support their farmers—for example, those of Tanzania (Ouma 2020; Belair 2021) and Australia (Larder et al. 2015)—actively encourage struggling agricultural producers to partner with private financial investors.

Yet even in accommodating policy contexts, success in the financial assetization of farmland is not a given. As many scholars have detailed, the developers of specialized financial products must put in a significant amount of work to garner social legitimacy for their activities and make the messy complexities of farmland legible to investors. Li (2014), Visser (2017), and Fairbairn (2020), for example, describe how financial market-makers simplify the social and physical heterogeneity of farmland to a limited number of abstract indicators that are of particular interest to investors, such as calculable risks and potential returns. This practice, they note, aims to standardize farmland in the same way that more conventional asset classes have been standardized. Securities and commodities futures, for example, have standard features that facilitate their market exchange and enhance their liquidity (cf. Cronon 1991; Clapp and Martin 2015). Building on this work, scholars Salerno (2014), Ducastel and Anseeuw (2017), Ouma (2020), and Sippel (2023) have detailed the challenges that intermediaries (e.g., land brokers and asset managers) encounter on the ground when trying to package plots of farmland for financial investment, including the valuing of agricultural assets, neutralizing protests from local actors, and massaging the complexities of agricultural production into financial metrics. To facilitate this process, brokers and other intermediaries generate "imaginaries" using story and other discursive approaches to convince potential investors that farmland is a reliable investment that is qualitatively similar to established asset classes (Sippel and Visser 2021, 272). The recent proliferation of digital agricultural technologies has helped to legitimate these narratives by generating numerical data that are widely recognized as proof in the financial sector (Sippel 2023; Duncan et al. 2022).

The potential of farmland investments to increase agricultural output is a dominant theme in financiers' stories, many of which tap into Malthusian concerns about food and resource scarcity (Visser 2017; Clapp and Isakson 2018; Fairbairn 2020). In recent promotional literature, for instance, the prominent asset-management company Nuveen, a subsidiary of the US pension fund TIAA, warns that feeding a growing world population amid urban development, water scarcity, and increasing protein consumption will necessitate a 60 percent increase in agricultural productivity by 2050, but sees this as an opportunity: "Together," Nuveen maintains, "these factors will drive increased value for agricultural land and create opportunities for early investors" (2020, 5). The implication is that land investors not only stand to profit, but by making farmland more productive, they are also doing their part to "feed the world."

As Kish and Fairbairn (2018) argue, the narratives that financial actors will increase agricultural output serve a dual purpose.: On the one hand, they help to recruit financial capital for the funds by promising high returns from a relatively novel and untapped investment frontier. But, they also help to win over policymakers and civil-society actors who are wary of land grabs and speculative financial activities. In other words, the discourse "doing the right thing is just good business" (Kish and Fairbairn 2018, 574) helps to ensure the profitability of farmland investment while also dissuading public disapproval. To bolster the social legitimacy of their activities, many investment funds say that they will contribute to local development by creating employment opportunities; supporting the construction of roads, schools, and other infrastructure; and partnering with NGOs on initiatives to improve nutrition and education (HighQuest Partners, United States 2010; Magnan 2012; Sommerville 2018; Kish and Fairbairn 2018). Despite such promises, the development outcomes of financial investments in farmland are questionable at best, a theme that I discuss in the next section (see "Socioecological Ramifications").

Market-makers, in addition to making farmland legible to investors and generating supporting narratives, have also contributed to the financial assetization of farmland by innovating new products that facilitate its exchange in financial markets. As noted earlier, the illiquidity of farmland is one of the greatest barriers to formatting it for financial purposes. Most of the vehicles for direct investment in farmland require a long-term commitment, are not easily transferable, and are only available to wealthier investors (Table 10.1). A relatively recent innovation, farmland-focused real estate investment trust (REIT), however, circumnavigates these challenges; REITs provide direct exposure to the benefits of farmland ownership with a liquid investment product that is accessible to investors of varying levels of wealth. Most REITs operate as holding companies, raising capital to acquire multiple properties, which they rent to land users. Through a process known as *securitization*, the REIT company then sells shares to investors, which entitles them to a portion of the associated revenues and losses. The shares for most REITs are treated like stocks, and are even traded on the same public exchanges, making them significantly more liquid than other land-investment vehicles and interchangeable with more conventional financial assets, such as corporate securities.

REITs themselves are not an especially novel financial product. REITs focused on commercial properties have been widely traded in the United States since the 1960s, and REITs specializing in timberland have been available since the 1990s. Not until the early 2000s were REITs deployed in the assetization of farmland. The first farmland REITs were introduced in Bulgaria around 2005, as investors sought to cash in on the rising land prices associated with the country's admission into the European Union (Fairbairn 2020). With financial interest in farmland growing, REITs were introduced in countries throughout Europe, North America, and Australia in the 2010s. Yet, despite being widely celebrated in the financial press (Whittaker 2024; Darbyshire 2022; Hall 2019), the actual number of farmland REITs is still relatively small. In the United States, for instance, there are just two publicly traded REITs. The larger of these, Farmland Partners, owns nearly 60,000 hectares of prime row-crop farmland in twenty US states (Farmland

Partners n.d.). Its major competitor, Glandstone Land, owns nearly 47,000 hectares of water-abundant fruit and vegetable cropland in fifteen US states (Gladstone Land, n.d.). At the time of this writing, the total market value of the shares of both companies exceeded US$500 billion. Nonetheless, shares in REITs are accessible to even the lowest-grade investors. Between 2019 and 2024, shares in Farmland Partners hovered around US$13 per share; those from Gladstone mostly traded below US$20 per share. Those looking for an even more affordable piece the farmland pie can invest in the Australian Rural Funds Management REIT or the Bulgarian Advance Terrfund REIT, whose shares have consistently traded below US$2 per share. REITs rent nearly all of the land that they control to farmers on a *triple-net* basis, which means that in addition to paying rent, the agricultural producers are responsible for paying all the property's operating expenses, including taxes, insurance, water fees, and maintenance costs (Robaton 2015; Gladstone Land, n.d.). Such arrangements help to ensure stable returns for investors while passing the risk of rising operating costs onto the renters.

Socioecological Ramifications

The financial assetization of farmland is not a simple process, and success is certainly not a given. When it is successful, however, assetization often institutes new property relations that enable the financial actors to profit from farmland without actually engaging in agricultural production (cf. Lapavitsas 2013; Gunnoe 2014). But these arrangements exacerbate socioeconomic inequality and shape how the agricultural producers relate to the land, inscribing financialization on the agrarian landscapes. In particular, the processes of financialization have constrained agricultural producers' access to and control of farmland, reduced their returns from farming, and compelled many to adopt more industrialized and less ecologically sustainable land use practices.

The most obvious way that financialization has shaped farmland access and control is through higher land prices. In 2002, for instance, the loosening of land ownership rules in Saskatchewan, Canada, unleashed a wave of financial acquisitions of the province's farmland and contributed to a 260 percent increase in farmland prices over the next thirteen years (Sommerville 2018; cf. Magnan and Sunley 2017; Desmarais et al. 2017). And in many other contexts, though the shift was less dramatic, the entrance of institutional investors was also linked to a significant increase in farmland prices, including in Australia, Argentina, Tanzania, and the United States (Sippel, Larder, and Lawrence 2017; Smith, Langford, and Lawrence 2023; Sosa Varrotti and Gras 2021; Darbyshire 2022; Ouma 2020). According to Savills, a real estate adviser company, between 2002 and 2021, average farmland prices in fifteen key agricultural countries increased at a compound annual rate of 11 percent. After a relatively flat period between 2014 and 2020, a rise in commodity prices in 2021 renewed financial actors' interest in farmland, and average prices appreciated an impressive 18 percent, the largest increase since the 2007–2012 food crisis (Buckingham 2022; Darbyshire 2022).

Financial actors claim that their farmland purchases allow older farmers to cash out their assets, contributing to their retirement security (Smith, Langford, and Lawrence 2023). To be sure, the entrance of financial actors and the associated rise in farmland prices have given a significant economic boost to those wishing to exit agriculture. But it has also proved to be a formidable barrier for those who do not—that is, aspiring farmers, who desire access to land, and established agricultural producers, who hope to expand their existing operations (Desmarais et al. 2017). Rising farmland prices are not only making it increasingly difficult for farmers to purchase land, but they have also translated into rising rental prices and higher fees that have made even leasing prohibitively expensive in many contexts (Sosa Varrotti and Gras 2021; Magnan, Davidson, and Desmarais 2023; Rotz, Fraser, and Martin 2019; Mendonça 2023; Sommerville 2018).

Increased farmland prices are reflective of the emergence of farmland as a "pure" financial asset, one whose market value exceeds its physical worth. Scholars have observed that in many of the key agricultural markets, including Australia (Smith, Langford, and Lawrence 2023), Brazil (Mendonça 2023), and Canada (Magnan, Davidson, and Desmarais 2023; Rotz, Fraser, and Martin 2019), these higher farmland prices are not justified by the productive potential of the land. The decoupling of prices from the productive value of farmland suggests that buyers are more interested in the contractual claim to land than the land itself. Such financial logics have become more common among established actors in the agricultural sector. In the Canadian prairies, for instance, farmers are increasingly buying land for speculative purposes (Magnan, Davidson, and Desmarais 2023; Aske 2022). Similarly, Smith, Langford, and Lawrence (2023) observe that in Australia, large corporate livestock companies engage in a form of speculative acquisition that entails buying and selling individual properties at strategic times in the property value cycle to realize capital gains (cf. Sippel, Larder, and Lawrence 2017). This practice has proven to be quite lucrative for the corporate speculators; however, the authors observe that it also contributes to increasingly high and volatile land prices, which creates uncertainty for agricultural producers. Meanwhile, in Argentina and Brazil, growing financial investments in farmland management companies have provided those enterprises with the means to speculate on farmland, again, helping to drive up farmland prices (Sosa Varrotti and Gras 2021; Mendonça 2023).

The means by which financial actors acquire farmland vary, but they often entail some form of compulsion, some sharper than others. Sometimes, agricultural producers are coerced into parting with their land. One of the largest financial investors in farmland, the US-based pension fund TIAA, for instance, was accused of acquiring a significant chunk of the Brazilian land in its portfolio from a notorious broker who had been linked to the falsification of land titles, intimidation using armed thugs, and setting fire to the homes of uncooperative landowners (Mendonça 2023; GRAIN 2015). Most land is acquired in more mundane transactions with purportedly "willing" sellers who confront less noticeable compulsions. In one of the few studies to investigate farmers' motivations, Sippel, Larder, and Lawrence (2017) explained why many agricultural producers in New South Wales, Australia, for example, accept and accommodate financial actors' acquisitions of land. They found that some of the farmers welcomed the "big money" the financiers paid for land that they had wanted to offload anyway, and that others appreciated that the financial intervention enabled investments in agricultural infrastructure and improve the viability of farming in a difficult economic context (cf. Smith, Langford, and Lawrence 2023). Similarly, Langford et al. (2021) studied the various strategies Indigenous landowners in northern Australia deploy to court financial investors. Yet, as both authors document in their respective studies, not all the rural actors were equally enthusiastic about the potential of financial investment, and some expressed considerable unease (cf. Sippel, Larder, and Lawrence 2017). Skepticism was particularly pronounced in the Canadian prairies (Magnan et al. 2023; Desmarais et al. 2017) and the Brazilian Cerrado (Mendonça 2023), where rural actors expressed concerns that the financial assetization of farmland was associated with fraying community trust and cohesion, reduced access to land, and degraded local soil and water resources.

Even when farmers accept and accommodate financial actors, it is important to consider the broader political and economic conditions that shape those sentiments and actions. What appears to be a willing transaction may, in fact, be a product of farmers' recognition of having limited alternatives. In the contemporary era of neoliberal austerity governance, many states are unwilling to invest in agriculture. Instead, they encourage producers to seek funding through partnerships with private finance and agrifood corporations (Larder et al. 2015; Ouma 2020; Borras et al. 2020). The aforementioned Indigenous farmers who courted investors in northern Australia were desperate for economic opportunities, yet the Commonwealth government limited its role to helping the landowners attract private investors to finance development initiatives. Meanwhile, in Sippel et al.'s (2017) study, Australian farmers understood financial intervention as a means of coping with various stressors, including excessive debt, high input costs, drought, and an inability to access affordable financing through other channels (cf. Smith, Langford, and Lawrence 2023). In other words, land sales are often a product of agrarian distress. If one considers the widespread economic hardship experienced by contemporary farmers, it is little wonder that many feel compelled to "willingly" part with their farmland (Clapp and Isakson 2018). Indeed, in 2015, the CEO of the US REIT Farmland Partners relished the low commodity prices farmers were being paid, noting, "A little bit of pain in farmland country makes our job easier" (Kesmodel and Newman 2015).

Investors, leveraging their control of financial resources, can persuade distressed agricultural producers to divest their farmland. In own-operate operations, the financial actors often sweeten the deal with promises to create meaningful employment for the local actors (HighQuest Partners, United States 2010; Magnan 2012). In actuality, the number of jobs created regularly falls far short of expectations, and the jobs that are offered tend to be poorly compensated, physically demanding, and limited to young, able-bodied males (Borras et al. 2020; Mendoça 2023; Belair 2021; Adams et al. 2019; Sommerville and Magnan 2015; Kuns, Visser, and Wästfelt 2016; Alhassan, Shaibu, and Kuwornu 2018). As noted earlier, in own-lease operations, it is not uncommon for financial landlords to lease the land back to the farmers who had previously owned it.

Although these arrangements may enable investments that improve the profitability and competitiveness of the agricultural operations on that land, they also introduce hierarchical social relations that institutionalize the transfer of value from the agricultural producers to their financial landlords, reducing the farmers' control over the land and land use practices. But as Olivier De Schutter, the former UN Special Rapporteur on the Right to Food, has argued, state investment could also improve the competitiveness of farmers and make is possible for them to retain the value from their productive activities without compromising their land rights (De Schutter 2011).

Just as financial accumulation reconfigures the power dynamics and distribution of value from agricultural production, it also shapes socioecological relations on the farm, inscribing the financialization of capitalism on agrarian landscapes. In the Canadian plains, Magnan, Davidson, and Desmarais (2023), found that, compared to other types of landlords, corporate lessors put relatively more stipulations in their contracts, requiring renters to follow to specific land use practices, particularly related to soil fertility and pest management. Such controls may be intended to maintain the ecological integrity of the farmland; however, the authors also found that financiers tend to be absentee landlords. As Clapp (2014, 798) has argued, such "distancing" limits financial owners' understanding of the particular environmental conditions on the farm and thus their ability to know which practices are best suited to the socioecological context. In fact, investors' demands for quick returns on overpriced land compel the agricultural producers to intensify their agro-extractive practices, accelerating the environmental degradation of the land. In the United States, for instance, the need to generate immediate returns, combined with the limited tenure security they receive from financial landlords, pressures farmers to increase short-term yields, necessitating excessive withdrawals of groundwater (Fairbairn et al. 2021). Similarly, the high rents charged by financial landowners have discouraged Canadian farmers from investing in long-term soil health and compelled them instead to intensify applications of agrichemicals and expand cultivation into wetlands and marginal environments (Rotz, Fraser, and Martin 2019).

Research in a variety of contexts—including Eastern Europe (Kuns, Visser, and Wästfelt 2016), Canada (Rotz, Fraser, and Martin 2019), Brazil (Mendonça 2023; Spadotto et al. 2021), Myanmar (Borras, Franco, and Nam 2020), Argentina (Garcia-Arias et al. 2021), and Cambodia (Hunsberger et al. 2017)—suggests that investors have a preference for the large-scale industrial cultivation of flex crops and cookie-cutter agricultural practices, which are ill-suited to local environmental contexts and are a major contributor to climate change (Clapp and Isakson 2023). In Brazil (Mendonça 2023; Spadotto et al. 2021), Argentina (Garcia-Arias et al. 2021), and Myanmar (Borras, Franco, and Nam 2020), these changes in land use practices have been linked to deforestation, the degradation of local soil and water resources, and the displacement of traditional food systems, which are not only the foundation of resilience-enhancing, culturally appropriate diets, but also help to conserve biodiversity, maintain soil quality, and sequester greenhouse gases. Given the gendered dimensions of procuring food, fuel, and water in many of these contexts, it is likely that rural women bear the brunt of the problems resulting from the degradation of food systems and the local environment (Deere 1995; Agarwal 1997; Razavi 2009).

Conclusion

Although the process of financialization has been unfolding since the 1970s, it did not directly impact farmland markets until the 2007–2009 Great Recession. As financial markets imploded and the "real" economy of goods and services stalled, investors sought refuge in tangible assets like land. Heretofore, investors had largely ignored farmland, seeking more profitable returns in one financial market after another, from speculative investment in corporate securities to the currencies of emerging market countries to dot-com stocks and mortgage-backed securities. But as the financial crisis unfolded, farmland's proven ability to retain its value over time became more appealing. What's more, with the attendant 2007–2012 food price crisis, expectations that farmland could, in fact, deliver spectacular returns grew. So, too, did financial investments. Pension funds and other heavyweight institutional investors began to fill previously parched land-based investment funds with cash, spurring the growth of asset-management companies specializing in the agricultural sector and the development of an array of investment products tied to farmland, including private equity investments, real estate investment trusts, fractional investment platforms, and a variety of investment products composed of related corporate securities.

Proponents maintain that financial interventions in the farmland sector will generate a host of social benefits, including the creation of rural employment, nest eggs for retiring farmers, rural infrastructure funding, and capital investments on farms, thereby improving agricultural productivity and contributing to food security. There is, however, little empirical support for these claims. On the contrary, the financial assetization of farmland has been linked to a host of socioeconomic and ecological problems in agrarian communities. Employment generation is consistently lower than promised, and the few jobs that are created are physically demanding and poorly compensated. Moreover, the financialization of farmland ownership in agrarian communities exacerbates the political and economic inequalities. The activities of financial actors are linked to rising land prices in a variety of contexts. Though increased land prices may benefit farmers seeking to exit agriculture, they also make it prohibitively expensive for aspiring farmers to enter the sector or existing producers to expand their operations. Farmers must pay increasingly high rents to financial landlords, who hope to recoup their investments by capturing the value that those who actually work the land produce, exacerbating economic inequality. As farmland prices rise and exceed the productive potential of the land, agricultural producers feel pressured to generate immediate returns through the application of inappropriate technologies and the intensification of agro-extractive practices, resulting in deforestation, degradation of soil health and water supplies, and increased greenhouse gas emissions, among other environmental problems.

Thus, despite the growing financial interest in farmland, transforming land into a financial asset is not a straightforward process. Farmland is not an asset in waiting; rather, it must be assembled as such (Li 2014). That is, it must be assetized. In part, this process is contingent on the presence of accommodating state policies and a favorable agricultural sector characterized by secure property rights and the existence of large chunks of land with the potential to absorb substantial quantities of financial capital. But assetization also requires significant work on the part of land brokers and other intermediaries, who, among other tasks, are enlisted to defuse public opposition and to present plots of land in ways that are appealing and legible to investors,—notably through measurements of anticipated risks and returns. Financial engineers have also struggled to overcome farmland's "stubborn materiality" by creating investment products that are liquid (meaning that they can be easily bought and sold) and standardized (meaning that they can be easily compared to other types of financial assets, including other farmland products; Fairbairn 2020, 81).

The challenges associated with assembling farmland as a financial asset point to weaknesses that can potentially be exploited by those who are interested in exorcizing financial capital from the agricultural sector and advancing more democratic forms of land control and ecologically sustainable land uses. Efforts to assetize farmland can fail. Studies report that some fund managers have struggled to attract sufficient capital and that a number have folded (Cotula 2012; Magnan 2015; Chung and Gagné 2021; Wolford et al. 2024). Though resistance is not always successful, opposition by local communities can stymie land grabbing initiatives (Blache 2020; Konforti 2022; Joshi 2023; Salverda 2022; Wolford et al. 2024). For example, protesters could strategically target land developers' limited understanding of local environmental contexts, especially concerning the availability of water resources (cf. Chung 2019; Adams et al. 2019; Franco, Mehta, and Veldwisch 2013). States could also play a role. To be sure, state efforts to prevent the further acquisition of farmland by financial actors in Brazil and Canada were only marginally successful because financial capital found creative ways around the legislative barriers (Fairbairn 2015; Mendonça 2023; Magnan, Davidson, and Desmarais 2023). Yet more meaningful state interventions could make a difference. Legislation that meaningfully improves the economic standing of agricultural producers would reduce their reliance on private finance (De Shutter 2011). Similarly, taxing capital gains on farmland investments or holdings could reduce their profitability for financial actors. More radical interventions, such as instituting alternative property regimes, could prevent the acquisition of farmland for speculative purposes. More targeted research and analysis of potential strategies to counter the financial assetization of farmland is needed. My hope is that this short chapter provides a basic understanding of its importance and inspires future action toward that end.

References

Adams, Ellis A., Elias D. Kuusaana, Abubakari Ahmed, and Benjamin B. Campion. 2019. "Land Dispossessions and Water Appropriations: Political Ecology of Land and Water Grabs in Ghana." *Land Use Policy* 87: 104068.

Agarwal, Bina. 1997. "'Bargaining' and Gender Relations: Within and Beyond the Household." *Feminist Economics* 3 (1): 1–51.

Alhassan, Suhiyini I., Mohammed T. Shaibu, and John K. M. Kuwornu. 2018. "Is Land Grabbing an Opportunity or a Menace to Development in Developing Countries? Evidence from Ghana." *Local Environment* 23 (12): 1121–1140.

Ashwood, Loka, John Canfield, Madeleine Fairbairn, and Kathryn De Master. 2022. "What Owns the Land: The Corporate Organization of Farmland Investment." *Journal of Peasant Studies* 49 (2): 233–262.

Aske, Katherine. 2022. *Finance in the Fields: Investors, Lenders, Farmers, and the Future of Farmland in Alberta*. Parkland Institute report, June 2022. Parkland Institute, Edmonton, CAN. https://assets.nationbuilder.com/parklandinstitute/pages/1979/attachments/original/1654755581/parkland-report-finance-in-the-fields.pdf?1654755581.

Bélair, Joanny. 2021. "Farmland Investments in Tanzania: The Impact of Protected Domestic Markets and Patronage Relations." *World Development* 139: 105298.

Birch, Kean, and Callum Ward. 2022. "Assetization and the 'New Asset Geographies.'" *Dialogues in Human Geography* 14 (1): 9–29. https://doi.org/10.1177/20438206221130807.

Blache, Adriana. 2020. "Conflict and Resistance Around a Rice Development Scheme in the SAGCOT Area of Tanzania." In *Land, Investment and Politics: Reconfiguring Eastern Africa's Pastoral Drylands*, edited by Jeremy Lind, Doris Okenwa, and Ian Scoones, 78–88. Suffolk, UK: James Currey.

Blomley, Nick. 2003. "Law, Property, and the Geography of Violence: The Frontier, the Survey, and the Grid." *Annals of the Association of American Geographers* 93 (1): 121–141.

Bonizzi, Bruno, Annina Kaltenbrunner, and Jeff Powell. 2020. "Subordinate Financialization in Emerging Capitalist Economies." In *The Routledge International Handbook of Financialization*, edited by Philip Mader, Daniel Mertens, and Natascha van der Zwan, 177–187. London: Routledge.

Borras, Saturnino M., Jr., Jennifer C. Franco, and Zau Nam. 2020. "Climate Change and Land: Insights from Myanmar." *World Development* 129: 104864.

Borras, Saturnino M., Jr., Cristóbal Kay, Sergio Gómez, and John Wilkinson. 2012. "Land Grabbing and Global Capitalist Accumulation: Key Features in Latin America." *Canadian Journal of Development Studies / Revue canadienne d'études du développement* 3 (4): 402–416.

Borras, Saturnino M., Jr., Elyse N. Mills, Philip Seufert, Stephan Backes, Daniel Fyfe, Roman Herre, et al. 2020. "Transnational Land Investment Web: Land Grabs, TNCs, and the Challenge of Global Governance." *Globalizations* 17 (4): 608–628.

Buckingham, Nicola. 2022. "Another Strong Year for Land as Commodity Prices Drive Activity." Savills (website), September 20. https://www.savills.co.uk/research_articles/229130/332444-0.

Casolo, Jennifer, and Sapana Doshi. 2013. "Domesticated Dispossessions? Towards a Transnational Feminist Geopolitics of Development." *Geopolitics* 18 (4): 800–834.

Chang, Ha-Joon. 2009. "Rethinking Public Policy in Agriculture: Lessons from History, Distant and Recent." *Journal of Peasant Studies* 36 (3): 477–515.

Christophers, Brett. 2012. "Anaemic Geographies of Financialisation." *New Political Economy* 17 (3): 271–291.
Chung, Youjin B. 2019. "The Grass Beneath: Conservation, Agro-Industrialization, and Land–Water Enclosures in Postcolonial Tanzania." *Annals of the American Association of Geographers* 109 (1): 1–17.
Chung, Youjin B., and Marie Gagné. 2021. "Understanding Land Deals in Limbo in Africa: A Focus on Actors, Processes, and Relationships." *African Studies Review* 64 (3): 595–604.
Clapp, Jennifer. 2014. "Financialization, Distance and Global Food Politics." *Journal of Peasant Studies* 41 (5): 797–814.
Clapp, Jennifer, and S. Ryan Isakson. 2018. *Speculative Harvests: Financialization, Food, and Agriculture*. Halifax, CAN: Fernwood Press.
Clapp, Jennifer, and S. Ryan Isakson. 2023. "Private Finance for Food System Climate Adaptation: Opportunity or Contradiction?" *Current Opinion in Environmental Sustainability* 61: 101273.
Cotula, Lorenzo. 2012. "The International Political Economy of the Global Land Rush: A Critical Appraisal of Trends, Scale, Geography, and Drivers." *Journal of Peasant Studies* 39 (3–4): 649–680.
Cronon, William. 1991. *Nature's Metropolis: Chicago and the Great West*. New York: W. W. Norton.
Daniel, Shepard. 2012. "Situating Private Equity Capital in the Land Grab Debate." *Journal of Peasant Studies* 39 (3–4): 703–729.
Darbyshire, Madison. 2022. "Investors Seeking Inflation Hedge Snap Up US Farmland." *Financial Times*, April.
Deere, Carmen Diana. 1995. "What Difference Does Gender Make? Rethinking Peasant Studies." *Feminist Economics* 1 (1): 53–72.
Deininger, Klaus, and Derek Byerlee. 2011. *Rising Global Interest in Farmland: Can It Yield Sustainable and Equitable Benefits?* Washington, DC: World Bank Publications. https://siteresources.worldbank.org/DEC/Resources/Rising-Global-Interest-in-Farmland.pdf.
De Schutter, Olivier. 2011. "How Not to Think About Land Grabbing: Three Critiques of Large-Scale Investments in Farmland." *Journal of Peasant Studies* 38 (2): 249–279.
Desmarais, Annette Aurélie, Darrin Qualman, André Magnan, and Nettie Wiebe. 2017. "Investor Ownership or Social Investment? Changing Farmland Ownership in Saskatchewan, Canada." *Agriculture and Human Values* 34 (1): 149–166.
Ducastel, Antoine, and Ward Anseeuw. 2017. "Agriculture as an Asset Class: Reshaping the South African Farming Sector." *Agriculture and Human Values* 34 (1): 199–209.
Duncan, Emily, Sarah Rotz, André Magnan, and Kelly Bronson. 2022. "Disciplining Land Through Data: The Role of Agricultural Technologies in Farmland Assetisation." *Sociologia Ruralis* 62 (2): 231–249.
Ekers, Michael. 2019."Financiers in the Forests on Vancouver Island, British Columbia: On Fixes and Colonial Enclosures." *Journal of Agrarian Change* 19 (2): 270–294.
Ekers, Michael. 2023. "Land Grabbing on the Edge of Empire: The Longue Durée of Fee-Simple Forest Lands and Indigenous Resistance in British Columbia." *Journal of Peasant Studies* 50 (7): 2799–2828.
Ekers, Michael, and Scott Prudham. 2017. "The Metabolism of Socioecological Fixes: Capital Switching, Spatial Fixes, and the Production of Nature." *Annals of the American Association of Geographers* 107 (6): 1370–1388.

Ekers, Michael, and Scott Prudham. 2018. "The Socioecological Fix: Fixed Capital, Metabolism, and Hegemony." *Annals of the American Association of Geographers 108* (1): 17–34.

Epstein, Gerald A. 2005. "Introduction: Financialization and the World Economy." In *Financialization and the World Economy*, edited by Gerald A. Epstein, 3–16. Cheltenham, UK: Edward Elgar.

Epstein, Gerald A., and Arjun Jayadev. 2005. "The Rise of Rentier Incomes in OECD Countries: Financialization, Central Bank Policy and Labor Solidarity." In Epstein, *Financialization and the World Economy*, 46–74.

Fairbairn, Madeleine. 2014. "'Like Gold with Yield': Evolving Intersections Between Farmland and Finance." *Journal of Peasant Studies 41* (5): 777–795.

Fairbairn, Madeleine. 2015. "Foreignization, Financialization, and Land Grab Regulation." *Journal of Agrarian Change* 15 (4): 581–591.

Fairbairn, Madeleine. 2020. *Fields of Gold: Financing the Global Land Rush*. Ithaca, NY: Cornell University Press.

Fairbairn, Madeleine, Jim LaChance, Kathryn Teigen De Master, and Loka Ashwood. 2021. "*In Vino Veritas, In Aqua Lucrum*: Farmland Investment, Environmental Uncertainty, and Groundwater Access in California's Cuyama Valley." *Agriculture and Human Values 38* (1): 285–299.

Farmland Partners. n.d. "Our Scale and Diversification Set Us Apart." Farmland Partners (website). https://www.farmlandpartners.com/.

Farmtogether. 2023. "Introduction to Farmland Investing." Farmtogether. https://farmtogether.com/learn.

Favas, Matthieu. 2018. "The Sovereign Wealth Fund Dilemma." Agri-Investor, January 31. https://www.agriinvestor.com/sovereign-wealth-fund-dilemma/.

Franco, Jennifer, Lyla Mehta, and Gert Jan Veldwisch. 2013. "The Global Politics of Water Grabbing." *Third World Quarterly 34* (9): 1651–1675.

Garcia-Arias, Jorge, Alan Cibils, Agostina Costantino, Vitor B. Fernandes, and Eduardo Fernández-Huerga. 2021. "When Land Meets Finance in Latin America: Some Intersections Between Financialization and Land Grabbing in Argentina and Brazil." *Sustainability 13* (14): 8084.

Garzaron, Lucia, and Roberto Viton. 2022. *Investing in the Pillars of Global Agriculture: Investment Opportunities in the Food and Agricultural Sector Through an Infrastructure and Real Estate Lens*. May. Bertrange, Luxembourg: Valoral Advisors.

Gladstone Land. n.d. "Farmland Portfolio." Gladstone Land (website). https://www.gladstonefarms.com/farmland-portfolio.

GRAIN. 2015. "Socially Responsible Farmland Investment: A Growing Trap." *Against the Grain* (website). October 14, 2015. https://grain.org/article/entries/5294-socially-responsible-farmland-investment-a-growing-trap.

Green, W. Nathan. 2019. "From Rice Fields to Financial Assets: Valuing Land for Microfinance in Cambodia." *Transactions of the Institute of British Geographers 44* (4): 749–762.

Green, W. Nathan. 2022. "Financing Agrarian Change: Geographies of Credit and Debt in the Global South." *Progress in Human Geography 46* (3): 849–869.

Guinnane, Timothy W. 2011. "The Early German Credit Cooperatives and Microfinance Organizations Today: Similarities and Differences." In *The Handbook of Microfinance*, edited by Beatriz Armendáriz and Marc Labie, 77–100. Singapore: World Scientific Publishing.

Gunnoe, Andrew. 2014. "The Political Economy of Institutional Landownership: Neorentier Society and the Financialization of Land." *Rural Sociology 79* (4): 478–504.

Haila, Anne. 1988. "Land as a Financial Asset: The Theory of Urban Rent as a Mirror of Economic Transformation." *Antipode* 20 (2): 79–101.

Hall, Archie. 2019. "Farmland-Focused Trust Launches $300m UK Float." *Financial Times*, December 19. https://www.ft.com/content/4f53823e-21c1-11ea-92da-f0c92e957a96.

Harvey, David. 2001. "Globalization and the 'Spatial Fix.'" *Geographische Revue: Zeitschrift für Literatur und Diskussion* 3 (2): 23–30.

Harvey, David. 2003. *The New Imperialism*. New York: Oxford University Press.

HighQuest Partners, United States. 2010. "Private Financial Sector Investment in Farmland and Agricultural Infrastructure." OECD Food, Agriculture, and Fisheries Papers, No. 33. Paris: OECD Publishing.

Hunsberger, Carol, Esteve Corbera, Saturnino M. Borras Jr., Jennifer C. Franco, Kevin Woods, Courtney Work, et al. 2017. "Climate Change Mitigation, Land Grabbing and Conflict: Towards a Landscape-Based and Collaborative Action Research Agenda." *Canadian Journal of Development Studies / Revue canadienne d'études du développement* 38 (3): 305–324.

Isakson, S. Ryan. 2014. "Food and Finance: The Financial Transformation of Agro-Food Supply Chains." *Journal of Peasant Studies* 41 (5): 749–775.

Joshi, Saba. 2023. "Gender and Land Dispossession in India: Dynamics of Women's Participation in Anti-Land Grabbing Struggles." In *The Routledge Handbook of Global Land and Resource Grabbing*, edited by Andreas Neef, Chanrith Ngin, Tsegaye Moreda, and Sharlene Molett, 177–187. London: Routledge.

Kay, Kelly, and Renee Tapp. 2022. "Un/Making Assets: The Institutional Limits to Financialization." *Annals of the American Association of Geographers* 112 (5): 1243–1259.

Kesmodel, David, and Jesse Newman. 2015. "Farmland Investments Take Root." *Wall Street Journal*, August 4.

Kiernan-Stone, Lynda. 2023. "Farmland: A Historically Stable Asset During Uncertain Times." Global AgInvesting, March 30. https://www.globalaginvesting.com/spotlight-farmland-a-historically-stable-asset-during-uncertain-times-a-new-study-released-by-farmtogether/.

Kish, Zenia, and Madeleine Fairbairn. 2018. "Investing for Profit, Investing for Impact: Moral Performances in Agricultural Investment Projects." *Environment and Planning A: Economy and Space* 50 (3): 569–588.

Knuth, Sarah Elisabeth. 2015. "Global Finance and the Land Grab: Mapping Twenty-First Century Strategies." *Canadian Journal of Development Studies / Revue canadienne d'études du développement* 36 (2): 163–178.

Konforti, Lazar. 2022. "The Moral Economy of Defence of Territory and the Political Economy of Extractivism in the Polochic Valley, Guatemala." *Journal of Agrarian Change* 22 (4): 740–765.

Kotz, David M. 2019. "Financialization and Neoliberalism." In *Relations of Global Power: Neoliberal Order and Disorder*, edited by Gary Teeple and Stephen McBride, 1–18. Toronto: University of Toronto Press.

Krippner, Greta. 2011. *Capitalizing on Crisis: The Political Origins of the Rise of Finance*. Cambridge, MA: Harvard University Press.

Kuns, Brian, Oane Visser, and Anders Wästfelt. 2016. "The Stock Market and the Steppe: The Challenges Faced by Stock-Market Financed, Nordic Farming Ventures in Russia and Ukraine." *Journal of Rural Studies* 45: 199–217.

Langford, Alexandra, Geoffrey Lawrence, and Kiah Smith. 2021. "Financialization for Development? Asset Making on Indigenous Land in Remote Northern Australia." *Development and Change* 52 (3): 574–597.

Lapavitsas, Costas. 2013. "The Financialization of Capitalism: Profiting without Producing." *City* 17 (6): 792–805.

Larder, Nicolette, Sarah Ruth Sippel, and Geoffrey Lawrence. 2015. "Finance Capital, Food Security Narratives and Australian Agricultural Land." *Journal of Agrarian Change* 15 (4): 592–603.

Li, Tania Murray. 2014. "What Is Land? Assembling a Resource for Global Investment." *Transactions of the Institute of British Geographers* 39 (4): 589–602.

Li, Tania Murray. 2015. "Transnational Farmland Investment: A Risky Business." *Journal of Agrarian Change* 15 (4): 560–568.

Luyt, Ian, Nuno Santos, and Arianna Carlta. 2013. *Emerging Investment Trends in Primary Agriculture: A Review of Equity Funds and Other Foreign-Led Investments in the CEE and CIS region*. Rome: Food and Agriculture Organization of the United Nations.

Magnan, André. 2012. "New Avenues of Farm Corporatization in the Prairie Grains Sector: Farm Family Entrepreneurs and the Case of One Earth Farms." *Agriculture and Human Values* 29 (2): 161–175.

Magnan, André. 2015. "The Financialization of Agri-Food in Canada and Australia: Corporate Farmland and Farm Ownership in the Grains and Oilseed Sector." *Journal of Rural Studies* 41: 1–12.

Magnan, André, Melissa Davidson, and Annette Aurélie Desmarais. 2023. "'They Call It Progress, but We Don't See It as Progress': Farm Consolidation and Land Concentration in Saskatchewan, Canada." *Agriculture and Human Values* 40 (1): 277–290.

Magnan, André, and Sean Sunley. 2017. "Farmland Investment and Financialization in Saskatchewan, 2003–2014: An Empirical Analysis of Farmland Transactions." *Journal of Rural Studies* 49: 92–103.

Martin, Sarah J., and Jennifer Clapp. 2015. "Finance for Agriculture or Agriculture for Finance?" *Journal of Agrarian Change* 15 (4): 549–559.

Mechiche-Alami, Altaaf, Carlo Piccardi, Kimberly A. Nicholas, and Jonathan W. Seaquist. 2019. "Transnational Land Acquisitions Beyond the Food and Financial Crises." *Environmental Research Letters* 14 (8): 1–13.

Mendonça, Maria Luisa. 2023. *The Political Economy of Agribusiness: A Critical Development Perspective*. Halifax, CAN: Fernwood Publishing.

Mendonça, Maria Luisa, and Fábio Teixeira Pitta. 2018. "International Financial Capital and the Brazilian Land Market." *Latin American Perspectives* 45 (5): 88–101.

Meyer, Gregory. 2016. "The Great Land Rush: Investors Face Conflict in Quest for Farms." *Financial Times*, March 2.

Nuveen. 2020. "Investing in Farmland." London: Nuveen Natural Capital.

O'Keefe, Eric. 2021. "Farmer Bill." Newsletter. *Land Report*, January 11. https://landreport.com/farmer-bill.

Ouma, Stefan. 2014. "Situating Global Finance in the Land Rush Debate: A Critical Review." *Geoforum* 57:162–166.

Ouma, Stefan. 2016. "From Financialization to Operations of Capital: Historicizing and Disentangling the Finance–Farmland-Nexus." *Geoforum* 72: 82–93.

Ouma, Stefan. 2020. *Farming as Financial Asset: Global Finance and the Making of Institutional Landscapes*. Newcastle upon Tyne, UK: Agenda Publishing.

Paprocki, Kasia. 2016. "'Selling Our Own Skin': Social Dispossession Through Microcredit in Rural Bangladesh." *Geoforum* 74: 29–38.

Peluso, Nancy Lee, and Christian Lund. 2011. "New Frontiers of Land Control: Introduction." *Journal of Peasant Studies 38* (4): 667–681.

Preqin. 2016. *Preqin Special Report: Agriculture*. New York: Preqin.

Pritchard, Bill, Elen Welch, Guillermo Umana Restrepo, and Lachlan Mitchell. 2023. "How Do Financialised Agri-Corporate Investors Acquire Farmland? Analysing Land Investment in an Australian Agricultural Region, 2004–2019." *Journal of Economic Geography 23* (5): 1037–1058.

Razavi, Shahra. 2009. *The Gendered Impacts of Liberalization: Towards "Embedded Liberalism"?* London: Routledge.

Ribot, Jesse C., and Nancy Lee Peluso. 2003. "A Theory of Access." *Rural Sociology 68* (2): 153–181.

Robaton, Anna. 2015. "Farming REITs: Farmland Partners Is Becoming a Player in the Agricultural Real Estate Business." *REIT Magazine*, January–February. https://www.reit.com/news/reit-magazine/january-february-2015/farming-reits.

Rotz, Sarah, Evan D. G. Fraser, and Ralph C. Martin. 2019. "Situating Tenure, Capital and Finance in Farmland Relations: Implications for Stewardship and Agroecological Health in Ontario, Canada." *Journal of Peasant Studies 46* (1): 142–164.

Salerno, Tania. 2014. "Capitalising on the Financialisation of Agriculture: Cargill's Land Investment Techniques in the Philippines." *Third World Quarterly 35* (9): 1709–1727.

Salerno, Tania. 2017. "Cargill's Corporate Growth in Times of Crises: How Agro-Commodity Traders Are Increasing Profits in the Midst of Volatility." *Agriculture and Human Values 34* (1): 211–222.

Salverda, Tijo. 2022. "Time Will Tell: Temporalities of a European Land Deal in Zambia and Its Critics." *Geoforum 137*: 126–134.

Schmidt, Dan. 2023. "How to Invest in Farmland: 7 Simple Ways." *Market Beat*, April. https://www.nasdaq.com/articles/how-to-invest-in-farmland:-7-simple-ways. Accessed October 1, 2023.

Shah, Nirav. 2023. "Investment in American Farmland Is Growing Across the Country by Leaps and Bounds. Why?" *Wisconsin State Farmer*, August 6. https://www.wisfarmer.com/story/news/2023/08/06/why-are-investors-rushing-to-grab-up-farmland/70540543007/.

Sippel, Sarah Ruth. 2023. "Tackling Land's 'Stubborn Materiality': The Interplay of Imaginaries, Data and Digital Technologies Within Farmland Assetization." *Agriculture and Human Values 1*: 849–863.

Sippel, Sarah Ruth, Nicolette Larder, and Geoffrey Lawrence. 2017. "Grounding the Financialization of Farmland: Perspectives on Financial Actors as New Land Owners in Rural Australia." *Agriculture and Human Values 34* (2): 251–265.

Sippel, Sarah Ruth, and Oane Visser. 2021. "Introduction to Symposium 'Reimagining Land: Materiality, Affect and the Uneven Trajectories of Land Transformation.'" *Agriculture and Human Values 38*: 271–282.

Sippel, Sarah Ruth, and Timothy Weldon. 2021. "Redefining Land's Investability: Towards a Neo-Nationalization of Resources in Australia?" *Territory, Politics, Governance 9* (2): 306–323.

Smith, Kiah, Alexandra Langford, and Geoffrey Lawrence. 2023. "Tracking Farmland Investment in Australia: Institutional Finance and the Politics of Data Mapping." *Journal of Agrarian Change 23* (3): 518–546.

Sommerville, Melanie. 2013. "Financializing Prairie Farmland: Farmland Investment and the Restructuring of Family Farming Systems in Central Canada." LDPI Working Paper 38. Land Deal Policies Initiative.

Sommerville, Melanie. 2018. "Old Roots, New Shoots: Thickening the Local Histories of Agri-Food Financialization." In *The Financialization of Agri-Food Systems*, edited by Hilde Bjorkhaug, André Magnan, and Geoffrey Lawrence, 223–243. London: Routledge.

Sommerville, Melanie, and André Magnan. 2015. " 'Pinstripes on the Prairies': Examining the Financialization of Farming Systems in the Canadian Prairie Provinces." *Journal of Peasant Studies* 42 (1): 119–144.

Sosa Varrotti, Andrea P., and Carla Gras. 2021. "Network Companies, Land Grabbing, and Financialization in South America." *Globalizations* 18 (3): 482–497.

Spadotto, Bruno Rezende, Yuri Martenauer Saweljew, Samuel Frederico, and Fabio Teixeira Pitta. 2021. "Unpacking the Finance-Farmland Nexus: Circles of Cooperation and Intermediaries in Brazil." *Globalizations* 18 (3): 461–481.

Swyngedouw, Erik, and Callum Ward. 2022. "Land as an Asset." In *Political Economy of Land*, edited by Mika Hyötyläinen and Robert Beauregard, 40–55. London: Routledge.

Turvey, Calum G. 2017. "Historical Developments in Agricultural Finance and the Genesis of America's Farm Credit System." *Agricultural Finance Review* 77 (1): 4–21.

Visser, Oane. 2017. "Running Out of Farmland? Investment Discourses, Unstable Land Values and the Sluggishness of Asset Making." *Agriculture and Human Values* 37:185–198.

Visser, Oane, and Max Spoor. 2011. "Land Grabbing in Post-Soviet Eurasia: The World's Largest Agricultural Land Reserves at Stake." *Journal of Peasant Studies* 38 (2): 299–323.

Wheaton, Bradley, and William J. Kiernan. 2012. "Farmland: An Untapped Asset Class? Quantifying the Opportunity to Invest in Agriculture." Global AgInvesting: Research and Insight, December.

Whittaker, Matt. 2024. "Seed Capital: How to Invest in Farmland as a Portfolio Diversifier." U.S. News and World Report, February 9. https://money.usnews.com/investing/articles/how-to-invest-in-farmland-as-alternative-investment.

Willis Towers Watson. 2023. *Thinking Ahead Institute: Global Pension Assets Study 2023*. Research study by TAI and Willis Towers Watson. https://www.thinkingaheadinstitute.org/research-papers/global-pension-assets-study-2023/.

Wolford, Wendy W., Ben White, Ian Scoones, Ruth Hall, Marc Edelman, and Saturnino M. Borras, Jr. 2024. "Global Land Deals: What Has Been Done, What Has Changed, and What's Next?" *Journal of Peasant Studies* 1-38. https://doi-org.myaccess.library.utoronto.ca/10.1080/03066150.2024.2325685.

CHAPTER 11

THE POLITICS OF LAND IN A DIGITAL WORLD

ALISTAIR FRASER

Introduction

Use of digital technologies is expanding. Capitalist enterprises have taken the lead in transforming the means of production. Round upon round of substantial investment in semiconductor production has created the conditions for waves of new firms to emerge by supplying services to consumers and generating valuable insights from analyzing their clicks, taps, and swipes. Activity in all economic sectors has become infused with pervasive and penetrating digital technologies, which yield an intense, fast-paced, connected, and yet problematic and, to a growing extent, inescapable *digital life* for billions of people.

My aim is to explain how all this action matters when we are thinking about the politics of land. My approach is to first provide an account of the wider context, the technological transformations shaping *all* aspects of society. Second, I zoom in on developments affecting the food system and agrarian sectors, focusing on precision agriculture, which involves the rollout of products intended to enable food producers to optimize resource use and maximize outputs. I ask: What happens to the politics of land when new technologies are deployed on capital-intensive farms in the global North, or when services are targeted at small-scale food producers and peasants in the global South? Finally, I examine how digitalization matters for those engaged in resistance and struggle against the dominant trends shaping the politics of land.

A Digital World Emergent

To suggest that a digital world is emerging requires highlighting four broad developments. First is the ongoing increase in computing power, which is led by semiconductor manufacturers that are creating new techniques to "print" transistors onto silicon wafers (Miller 2022). Global semiconductor sales have soared, from US$139 billion in 2001 to US$574 billion in 2022 (Semiconductor Industry Association 2023). A second development, downstream from semiconductor manufacturers, is the rollout by electronics manufacturers of trillions of digital devices, ranging from powerful smartphones and laptop computers to component parts such as cameras and other types of sensors. Firms and workers produce (or, in some cases, assemble) digital devices all over the world, albeit with major concentrations in Asian nodes of the trans-Pacific electronics-software industrial complex. Trade in information and communications technology goods rose from a value of US$873 billion in 2011 to US$2.7 trillion in 2021 (United Nations Conference on Trade and Development 2023). The third is the large and expanding network of software developers at tech firms who are creating services and apps (applications or programs) for use by firms, governments, and individuals across the planet. Some of the firms involved in these three developments (e.g., IBM, Intel) have been at work for decades; others (e.g., Facebook, ByteDance) are more recent creations. All are pushing to create "suites of technology" (Fraser 2007)—novel arrangements of services with consumer-facing and "back-end" devices—that will strike a chord with consumers (individuals, government, or other firms), gain market share, and generate profits. Finally, then, what brings things together is the fourth development: the geographically uneven but often rapid expansion in the availability of high-speed broadband (and mobile) Internet, whose use requires powerful chips running on a wide range of devices (laptops, phones, servers, routers) to process information streams according to the coded instructions inside digital services and apps.

Considerable current and signposted future investments point only toward the continued expansion of this digital world: semiconductor firms are building new chip manufacturing plants, often boosted by state subsidies via policies such as the US CHIPS and Science Act of 2022 (Swanson 2023); device industry leaders such as Samsung are expanding their capacity to produce screens for smartphones and other products (Reuters 2023); and there is considerable investment in software tools, including a surge of artificial intelligence (AI) applications that are trying to emulate the impact of flagship efforts such as DeepMind's AlphaFold (Varadi et al. 2022) and OpenAI's generative AI models. Around 3,200 AI start-ups received $US52 billion in venture capital investment in 2022 (GlobalData 2023). Consumers, meanwhile, drive demand for more powerful software and devices, integrating digital technologies into their personal lives when they track their health data and share videos of momentous and mundane activities, and because they are compelled to use smartphone apps or other devices in their working lives, in all types of jobs.

There is no shortage of scholarship on these developments, on what we might refer to as "the digitalization of everything." One body of work, known as "critical data studies," stands out for its alertness to processes of oppression that are yielding injustice and generating resistance (e.g., see Iliadis and Russo 2016; Kitchin and Lauriault 2018; Ettlinger 2018; Kitchin and Fraser 2020). A core concern is the way digitalization produces and generates a continuous and expanding demand for data. For some of the world's largest tech firms, as critics such as Shoshana Zuboff (2019) points out, user-generated data will be packaged for the sake of selling advertisements on websites or social media. Data also become a core product to be fed back into the system to guide investment and to reproduce on an expanding basis the conditions for accumulation: investment in plants, machinery, or skills cannot proceed without evidence, drawing upon data analysis. All new products and services reflect interpretations of data analysis enriched by insights drawn from the digital arena. Today's investments in data-hungry AI technologies bolster the drive to source data. Only by observing and analyzing action on the ground—in the city, at home, and on farms—will AI models (and parent firms) improve their predictions (Nost and Colven 2022). Digitalization enrolls all forms of life, because modeling experience (and working to anticipate a world of contingency) requires learning about—and gathering data about—every type of living entity, environment, and scene. It is, then, a straightforward move (but see Mumford 2022) to conceptualize the current structure and guiding ethos of our digital world as giving rise to and cementing the place of *data colonialism*, which entails dispossessing and alienating digital subjects of the data they generate (e.g., see Thatcher, O'Sullivan, and Mahmoudi 2016; see also Couldry and Mejias 2020). A digital world intrudes and extracts: everything must be scrutinized; data from all forms of action must be gathered, bundled, and analyzed. There is a rush to digitalize, to colonize. Crucially, data colonialism emerges from a research and development milieu in Silicon Valley, where the class, racial, and gender biases of software developers have gone unchallenged for decades (e.g., see Noble 2018; Noble and Roberts 2019), and where current practices, such as using low-wage Kenyan workers to train AI models (Dzieza 2023; see also Hao and Hernández 2022), build on racial capitalism and contribute to the creation of a frightening, destructive "world computer" (Beller 2021).

Even at this early stage of development, there is ample evidence that a digital world entails a troubling *digital life* for much of humanity. Firms and governments are embracing suites of digital technologies in efforts to increase automation, which has wide-ranging and worrying effects for employment prospects across all economic sectors, including in the advanced services sector, given some of the results of recent investments in AI (e.g., on the impact of robotic process automation in the call centers sector; see Peck 2017). Prospects of a peaceful life are also troubled by central aspects of digitalization, such as social media, the popularity of which can be manipulated, including by far-right actors, for the sake of sowing division and accumulating and deploying oppressive political power (e.g., see Ekman 2018; Lee [2019] emphasizes that state-run media is also used for these purposes). In more general terms, digitalization unravels elements of democratic life—including the essential need to speak up, protest, or organize for the sake of pursuing social change in workplaces and beyond—given the scope for firms, governments, and even individuals to use digital technologies as surveillance weapons to shut down alternative possibilities or otherwise undermine the basis for critical thought (e.g., see Ettlinger 2022).

Digital Technologies, Food, and the Agrarian Sector

The food system is digitalizing. Digital technologies pervade trade and logistics networks, as data points contribute to data streams that guide automated investment decisions and thereby prices (e.g., see Hayles [2017] on high-frequency financial trading systems). Food processing corporations take advantage of social media usage to observe and analyze consumers (e.g., see Martini, Massa, and Testa 2013), while crafting new flavors, adjusting taste, tweaking palates, and boosting sales across line extensions attuned to geographical difference in region-focused factories (e.g., see Nestlé India 2022; also Fraser 2021). Supermarkets construct novel mechanisms to conduct extensive, ongoing daily surveillance and manipulation of consumers in stores and online, including radical efforts to automate the groceries delivery market (e.g., on the British online supermarket Ocado, see Fraser 2020). An array of providers is developing food-delivery apps and other services for handling inventory control and payments, targeting the entire market, from the smallest restaurants to the largest fast-food chains (e.g., see Chandler 2023). Digital technologies even shape what happens in the final moments of the food system—at the ultimate point of consumption on dinner tables, streets, or in cars—when consumers use social media (or other apps) to share photos of (or upload to the cloud data or reviews about) their sandwich, noodle dish, or snack (Lupton and Feldman 2020). Reflecting wider societal transformations, the food system is now infused with digital technologies; novel practices and norms are now in play.

A similar set of developments is affecting agrarian actors and their practices. The central factor here is the expansion of so-called *precision agriculture*, which refers to a "data-driven production system in which a mix of environmental and on-field data (from sensors and the internet) drives agronomic decisions such as planting and pesticide application" (IPES-Food and ETC Group 2021, 152; see also Fraser 2019b; Miles 2019).[1] It involves "digital software tools for mapping and monitoring the farm . . . drones, 'ag robots,' sensors and other elements of on-farm automation networked together into an 'internet of farming things'" (ETC Group 2021, 152). The case for precision agriculture is based on the argument that

> food production is inefficient, unpredictable and imprecise and so we must leverage newly-available technologies to produce more food more reliably (i.e., increase yields) for a growing global population—without increasing the need for land and while reducing negative environmental impacts from agriculture. Data-driven decision-making, it is claimed, will allow farmers to increase yields even while reducing herbicide- and fertilizer-use because input-prescriptions will be meticulously accurate, down to the level of the field, the row, and even the individual plant (ETC Group 2022, 21).

Crop farmers can use technologies such as autonomous optical spot spraying, where a robot crosses a field, identifies weeds, and blasts them with a laser (e.g., see Gerety 2020). Drones now monitor soil conditions and create data in yield-mapping platforms (Klauser and Pauschinger 2021). In orchards, robots identify and pick ripe fruit at harvest time, having also cared for the crop during the growing season (Legun, Burch, and Klerkx 2023).

The development of precision agriculture technologies is led by agricultural technology providers (ATPs), which range from small start-ups to the world's largest farm machinery and agricultural chemical firms. Carbon Robotics is a typical small start-up: it was established in 2018 to produce "AI-powered robotic systems that precisely identify, weed and thin specialty vegetable crops using lasers with millimeter accuracy, while observing the conditions of the crop and soil in a field for later analysis" (Carbon Robotics 2023). Another is Plantix, acquired in 2023 by HELM, a German industrial firm (HELM 2023), which uses AI to drive a smartphone app that conducts plant-disease recognition, detection, symptom identification, and diagnosis. Indeed, reflecting a dynamic within the wider digital economy, the goal for many start-ups is to achieve scale via acquisition by larger firms. For example, in 2022, Deere & Company acquired AgriSync, Ag Systems, and SureFire Electronics (Deere & Company 2022); in 2021, it acquired Bear Flag Robotics for US$250 million (IPES-Food and ETC Group 2022). Deere & Company now has a Production and Precision Agriculture corporate segment (with US$22.5 billion in sales in 2022), which targets "production-scale growers of large grains, small grains, cotton, and sugarcane. Main products include large and certain mid-size tractors, combines, cotton pickers, sugarcane harvesters and loaders, and soil preparation, seeding, application and crop care equipment" (Deere & Company 2022, 72). The company also runs a digital platform, the John Deere Operations Center, which is in use across 143 million hectares of farmland. Bayer, another agricultural supplier, boasts that its Field View platform "extracts 87.5 billion datapoints from 180 million acres (78.2 million hectares) of farmland in 23 countries and funnels it into the cloud servers of Microsoft and Amazon" (Food Barons 2022, 9). Smaller firms such as Connecterra are also developing these types of platforms (Connecterra 2023).

If the bulk of precision agriculture products target large capital-intensive operations in the world's wealthiest economies, food producers operating at a small scale in many of the world's poorest countries are not out of the picture (Fairbairn and Kish 2022; Stone 2022). ATPs are keen to pitch their products as solutions that can be adopted by smallholders: IBM partners with Latin American nonprofits to provide climate data (Flavia 2023); Corteva, Syngenta, and others take part in initiatives such as "the Agriculture Innovation Mission for Climate" (led by fossil fuel giants the United Arab Emirates and the United States), which include digitalizing projects (AIM for Climate 2023); and Chinese ATPs use thirteen Precision Agricultural Demonstration Bases to show off their products to hosts from low-income countries (China Daily 2022). And national governments argue that digital technology can be deployed to develop their agricultural sectors. Thailand, for example, as part of a "Thailand 4.0" development strategy, hopes to use digital technologies in a drive to make its agricultural sector "smart" (Chiengkul 2019). Across global South contexts, development agencies, national governments, and ATPs coalesce around a vision of upgrading agrarian sectors via practices akin to precision agriculture. The prospect of delivering remote (privatized, automated, AI-led) agricultural extension (and, based on the model adopted by Plantix, links to seed and chemical suppliers) to pursue higher yields is now in view (Fairbairn and Kish 2022).[2]

Peasant Prospects in a Digital World

The promotion, insertion, and development of precision agriculture is bound up with a rush by the firms that are developing these new products to collect, analyze, and use data generated on the land. Users give these companies permission to transfer data when they sign end-user agreements or licenses; but they can never know, nor will they be told, what the firms will do with the data. One use is clear: the expanding stock of data will inform product development—for example, when a firm improves a tractor via a software update or when it draws on analysis of users' behavior to introduce the latest version of an app. Capitalists and states have always been interested in understanding action on the land: capitalists have collected data for the sake of creating products by observing how plants are cultivated or how the impact of pests can be reduced, while states have searched for mechanisms to achieve order and control (Scott 1998). The difference with the current situation is the scale, intensity, and breadth of the data-collection process. What digital life in general enables is an extensive and exhaustive "data grab," and specific arrays of digital devices and services are at work on the land that are capable of collecting trillions of data points about all forms of action (labor practices, energy use, animal-animal interactions, soil health, climate variability etc.) all day every day, every week, every year.

Peasants' prospects are undermined in the rush to embrace the crucial facets of the "agri-food tech solutionism" (Fairbairn and Guthman 2020) accompanying data colonialism. Digitalization increases the visibility of smallholders to agribusinesses (Fairbairn and Kish 2022). A fundamental element is "legibility"—that is,

> systems of governance that aim to control otherwise unruly situations . . . by making those situations "legible" to would-be managers, i.e., understandable enough to allow for the imposition of systems of control [and] processes of simplification, often accomplished through quantification and subsequent optimization. Legibility involves both ways of knowing or seeing in a limited sense, and acts of control and management that derive their logic from these ways of knowing.
>
> (Liu and Sengers 2021, 10)

To the extent that agricultural technologies are "based on simplified models and aim to eliminate human action and natural variability as sources of unpredictability in the management of land and labor" (11), precision agriculture mirrors and amplifies a broader process of normalizing large-scale industrial agriculture as "conventional"—a process that also ethnocentrically renders peasant or small-scale production as "deviant" (e.g., with reference to Canada, see Rotz and Kepkiewicz 2018). At issue are the biases underpinning digitalization. Class, racial, and gender biases of software developers in tech firms have played a part in the development of numerous high-profile abuses when new products encounter the real world (see Noble 2018). In agriculture, systems to create legibility reflect biases toward developing services and devices that will be sold for use in certain types of environments. For example, variable rate application techniques using the Normalized Difference Vegetation Index (NDVI) for vegetation health tend only to work "for crops that are replanted every year with the aid of GPS units or laser guidance systems [and are] more difficult for orchards or vineyards that are not replanted annually" (Liu and Sengers 2021, 14). Thus, as Bronson (2019) notes, "farmers working outside of the dominant industrial model" (3), have access to a limited range of digital products compared to farmers operating on larger standardized plots. Firms are creating models and maps that "are made meaningful only if one adheres to a rigid conventional farming strategy of seeding in neat rows separated by areas of soil free of weeds" (4).

Consider now the compounding effect of the biases embedded in the use of AI in agriculture, which creates models to guide action based on analyses of diverse datasets (e.g., see Kujawa and Niedbala 2021). The quality of AI outputs depends, in part, on the quality of data they can draw upon. There are already concerns that AI-generated outputs are "poisoning" datasets that future AI systems will need to draw upon (Giordani 2022). In agriculture, the centrality of "poisoning" raises the question of how firms creating AI products will cope with the existence of (from the perspective of AI producers, deviant) food producers who are, per Bronson (2019), "working outside of the dominant industrial model." Leading AI firms will be under intense pressure (from competitors or via economic relations with downstream firms such as processors and supermarkets) to ensure they input a certain type or quality of data. What will those firms do to ensure that their AI systems can draw from "unpoisoned" data? Will the use of AI in agriculture increase the pressure to standardize environments? Some AI researchers propose that "integrated prediction algorithms [can unravel] the complex interplay between genetics, nutrition, agronomy and the environment that influence on-farm performance" (Hayes et al. 2023). In one such scenario, AI might enable the introduction of seed or chemical products to support an expansion of genetic diversity in agriculture. But another scenario is that the firms bringing to market tomorrow's precision agriculture products—products that are infused with AI, targeted at standardized farming operations, and use a prediction- or model-friendly range of gene diversity—will further erode gene diversity and encourage the expansion of monocultures to satisfy food processors' demands for simplified diets. The latter scenario is more likely, so long as the economic basis for using AI in agriculture must fit within the tight parameters set by the "corporate food regime" (McMichael 2005).

Overall, then, I argue that a striking picture emerges when the data grab (the constant watching, scrutiny, surveillance, and ongoing analysis of agricultural, environmental, socioecological data) and the biases at work in the emergence of precision agriculture (the sense that only a certain type of agriculture, "industrial" agriculture, might have a future) are examined together. The digitalization of agriculture, especially as it moves into its AI epoch, raises the prospect of pressure building on "deviant" nonconforming farmers (and other food producers on adjacent or distant land). It exposes peasants to the market's latest biases and emphases, and introduces a scenario whereby technological advance will rely on nonconforming food producers, especially peasants and smallholders, getting out of the way of those using the dominant suites of agricultural technology. A crucial point here is that, although some precision agriculture firms are start-ups, the sector is driven forward by (and via the data grab it stands to give increased market power to) a small number of huge, powerful supplier corporations with a strong tradition of acquiring competitors to achieve scale. As has been documented across food systems research, lead agricultural supplier firms use their scale to mobilize financial and now digital services in efforts to outmaneuver farmers or stand up to other powerful agents in the food industry, such as food processors and supermarkets (e.g., see Clapp 2023). Capital-intensive farmers operating at scale and using precision agriculture are already under pressure. Caught in the middle between firms up- and downstream that are deploying digital technologies to reduce their operating costs and to model conditions, they stand a chance *only* if they consistently improve yields, make debt repayments, tap into state supports, and take advantage of price fluctuations. But digitalization yields a grimmer future for smaller-scale food producers, such as the peasants or petty commodity producers who exist in tension alongside the circuits of capital and data that define "conventional" agriculture. If precision agriculture technologies and practices can deliver higher yields per input for the producers operating at scale, pressure (not least regarding the sale price of agricultural commodities) will build on the excluded producers operating at a smaller-scale and/or in environmental contexts where digital supports might help but are unavailable. In short, precision agriculture amplifies the pressure on peasants, who are already squeezed by a food system dominated by the corporations upstream and downstream of the land. An embrace of precision agriculture reinforces biases and deepens the likelihood of reproducing capital-intensive food production systems, with concomitant effects on the types of environments that will be deemed acceptable in models of a digital-friendly world.

A point to dwell upon, then, and a starting place for further research, is to consider how precision agriculture has become imbricated with broader processes of digitalization, with the result that investors and speculators desire certain types of consolidated and rationalized landscapes. Precision agriculture tries to provide an array of new technical "solutions" to the persistent socioecological challenges encountered by food producers globally. It does so in a way that researchers of global land grabs will recognize insofar as digitalization and the data grab propels and amplifies the global rush to control land and eliminate forms of life and food production practices that do not fit within emerging technical models of agrarian life. Research on the global land rush is charting the dynamic processes that are shaping the land and communities across the world (e.g., see Borras et al. 2022b). Digitalization introduces new energy to debates about land grabs.

Digital Technologies and (the New Horizons of) Resistance

The process of fast-paced, far-reaching technical advance charted above generates profound consequences for the politics of land. Taking cues from Liu and Sengers (2021, 23), it is not only "important to reflect on the logics that are being built into digital agriculture systems, to identify places where systems built on those logics perpetuate harm," but it is also necessary to consider what it might mean to "develop design orientations for these systems based on alternative logics" (23). Digitalization has already provoked numerous novel responses that reflect wider societal shifts in resistance strategies and tactics; "alternative logics" have inspired alternative "design orientations." Countering the story of powerful digital firms expanding, transforming, and dominating all aspects of social life, there is evidence now of moves to exploit, manipulate, and subvert digital technologies for the sake of resisting and undermining oppressive processes (Ettlinger 2018, 2022). In short, digital technologies shape—and have a role to play in exploring—new horizons of resistance. Two connected issues demand attention here.

First, consider food sovereignty construction, which is a crucial, ongoing, and experimental process led by peasants and small-scale food producers, and their allies, with a view to remaking food systems at the local, regional, and global scale (e.g., see McMichael 2014; Schiavoni 2017). Digital technologies present opportunities to build networks (via websites), find allies (using social media), deepen bonds of solidarity (via blog posts to present testimony), and extend material or symbolic support (via crowdfunding). Video-sharing sites such as YouTube can facilitate peer-to-peer education, akin to the campesino-a-campesino techniques used in Cuban efforts to expand agroecological knowledge (e.g., see Rosset et al. 2011). Digital technologies can support efforts to connect rural and urban populations, for example, through the use of simple apps, such as WhatsApp, to help establish food-sovereignty alliances that match food producers in rural areas with urban dwellers, or more sophisticated protocols, such as those emerging via organizations such as the Open Food Network. Digital technologies alter the dynamics of food-sovereignty construction. What we cannot know today is how peasants and small-scale food producers will work in the coming years to develop strategies to contest, resist, and build alternative socioecological arrangements; but what we should expect, I argue, is that those arrangements will entail a digital practice, at a minimum to facilitate communication and, possibly, with a view to constructing radical suites of technology to enable inclusive, democratic decision-making and resource sharing. Food-sovereignty construction will involve "curating data," insofar as it will be a "practice that involves presenting, positioning, and translating data amidst an expanding constellation of contingencies" (Fraser 2020, 209). Curating effectively, by using digital tools in an astute manner, can amplify and propel acts of resistance, although such action will always be exposed to oppressive surveillance and cannot be idealized (Ettlinger 2018).

The second issue centers on the role of digital technologies in the development of a politics of land capable of responding to the effects of climate change in the twenty-first century. Greenhouse gas emissions are occurring at such high levels that global temperatures will increase in the next few decades. Questions arise now about how this development will impact on the politics of land (e.g., see Borras et al. 2022a). One response is to ask: What might be the lineaments of a politics of land oriented around withdrawing carbon from the atmosphere? How would such a politics be plugged into digital life? As was made clear in the previous points regarding food-sovereignty construction, digital technologies can amplify and propel acts of resistance. With regard to carbon removal, a planetary-scale politics is required to provide food, shelter, and care at the same time as environments such as croplands, grasslands, forests, and coastal or riverine wetlands are managed and governed to maximize their potential to capture and store carbon (Fraser 2023). It is possible to imagine how facets of digital life might play a supporting role. For example, lower-cost and hackable open-source technologies, including open-source intelligence, might help distant allies understand each other's actions and form crucial new bonds of solidarity. What seems obvious is that tomorrow's—or 2050s or 2100s—digital technologies and practices will also matter, which, in turn, means that the interest in owning and controlling land will expand. The trend since the 1980s has been for digital technologies to be adopted and used in ways that their designers and manufacturers never imagined. If there is a politics of land responding to climate change by removing carbon, there will be an ongoing, yet always urgent need to scrutinize and theorize how that moment's digital technologies are to be enrolled.

Conclusion

I have demonstrated how the politics of land is now a digital affair. Apps, platforms, swipes, and clicks are factors shaping what happens when food is produced in capital- and labor-intensive operations the world over. Protocols, standards, and other aspects of digital governance, such as laws about privacy and cybersecurity, come into play in new ways now that the land is exposed to incursions by autonomous drones and other robots or to surveillance from proliferating satellites. Analysts of the politics of land need to give digital life more attention. Power relations matter between food producers and food corporations; between people on the ground and distant or nebulous multilateral agencies; between local traditional practice and modernizing national governments; and between classes of agrarian workers and landowning capitalists. Today, these relations shape the politics of land in ways that reflect their entanglement with the processes and pressures emerging from far-reaching technological advances and ruthless competition for market share across digital networks. What digitalization means for the politics of land is that a tweak by Google or Meta—some novel lines of code written with the intent of altering a service or app that has no apparent relevance for the agrarian sector—can, by chance, spread throughout, or have a sudden impact on, a complex and fast-moving "planetary cognitive ecology" (Hayles 2017). Likewise, what digitalization means is that a protest on a farm in Kenya, or a tweet about a crop disease in Brazil, can have unanticipated cascading and multiplying effects in distant places. In a digital world, what human geographers have referred to as the "chance of space" (Massey 2005) *swells*, so that everyone now is exposed to the rapid unfolding of expanding "constellations of contingencies" wrought by proliferating digital devices and services that are being used in ways their designers and sellers did not anticipate (Fraser 2019a). We cannot examine the politics of land while ignoring digital life. Likewise, understanding the significance of digitalization is helped when we view it in relation to an unfolding and continuing corporate interest in owning and controlling land. It is necessary to realize that the people developing digital services and devices are going to shape rural areas and agrarian sectors. Critical agrarian studies will need to integrate insights from (seemingly) alien fields such as critical data studies. Analysis of the politics of land must grapple with the creation and contestation of new digital products and practices brought to life by obscure and well-known firms shaping how land will be used now and in the future.

Notes

1. There is a growing critical literature regarding developments that are akin to precision agriculture, whose authors use cognate terms such as "digital agriculture" (e.g., Klerkx, Jakkub, and Labarthec 2019; Prause, Hackfort, and Lindgren 2021), "surveillance agriculture" (Stone 2022), and "smart farming" (Fraser 2022).
2. Faxon (2023) points out a crucial additional consideration here: in places such as Myanmar, digital technology's presence is played out, not via apps or devices promoted by ATPs, but rather on platforms such as Facebook, which became "simultaneously a platform for selling seeds, seeking advice, and cultivating solidarity." A type of digital agriculture took shape that resembled "appropriated agritech, a generic technology repurposed for agrarian ends" (12).

References

Agriculture Innovation Mission for Climate. 2023. https://www.aimforclimate.org/innovation-sprints/.

Beller, Jonathan. 2021. *The World Computer: Derivative Conditions of Racial Capitalism*. Durham, NC: Duke University Press.

Borras, Saturnino M., Jr., Ian Scoones, Amita Baviskar, Marc Edelman, Nancy Lee Peluso, and Wendy Wolford. 2022a. "Climate Change and Agrarian Struggles: An Invitation to Contribute to a *JPS* Forum." *Journal of Peasant Studies* 49 (1): 1–28.

Borras, Saturnino M., Jr., Jennifer C. Franco, T. Moreda, Y. Xu, N. Bruna, and B. A. Demena. 2022b. "The Value of So-Called 'Failed' Large-Scale Land Acquisitions." *Land Use Policy* 119: 106199.

Bronson, K. 2019. "Looking through a responsible innovation lens at uneven engagements with digital farming". *NJAS - Wageningen Journal of Life Sciences* 90–91: 100294.

Carbon Robotics. 2023. "About the Company." https://carbonrobotics.com/company.

Chandler, Adam. 2023. "Delivery Apps Just Did the Impossible." *The Atlantic*, July 15. https://www.theatlantic.com/technology/archive/2023/07/dominos-deliver-uber-eats-app/674716/.

Chiengkul, Prapimphan. 2019. "Uneven Development, Inequality and Concentration of Power: A Critique of Thailand 4.0." *Third World Quarterly* 40 (9): 1689–1707.

China Daily. 2022. "Technology Improving Agriculture." *China Daily*, July 5. https://www.chinadaily.com.cn/a/202207/05/WS62c39225a310fd2b29e6a61c.html.

Clapp, Jennifer. 2023. "Concentration and Crises: Exploring the Deep Roots of Vulnerability in the Global Industrial Food System." *Journal of Peasant Studies* 50 (1): 1–25.

Connecterra. 2023. "About Us." https://connecterra.ai/company/about-us/.

Couldry, Nick, and Ulises A. Mejias. 2020. *The Costs of Connection: How Data Is Colonizing Human Life and Appropriating It for Capitalism*. Stanford, CA: Stanford University Press.

Deere & Company. 2022. *John Deere 2022 Annual Report*. https://s22.q4cdn.com/253594569/files/doc_financials/2022/ar/2022-John-Deere-Annual-Report.pdf.

Dzieza, Josh. 2023. "AI Is a Lot of Work." *The Verge*, June 20. https://www.theverge.com/features/23764584/ai-artificial-intelligence-data-notation-labor-scale-surge-remotasks-openai-chatbots.

Ekman, Mattias. 2018. "Anti-refugee Mobilization in Social Media: The Case of Soldiers of Odin." *Social Media and Society* 4 (1): Article 2056305118764431.

ETC Group. 2022. *Food Barons 2022*. https://www.etcgroup.org/files/files/food-barons-2022-full_sectors-final_16_sept.pdf.

Ettlinger, Nancy. 2018. "Algorithmic Affordances for Productive Resistance." *Big Data & Society* 5 (1): Article 2053951718771399.

Ettlinger, Nancy. 2022. *Algorithms and the Assault on Critical Thought: Digitalized Dilemmas of Automated Governance and Communitarian Practice*. London: Routledge.

Fairbairn, Madeleine, and Julie Guthman. 2020. "Agri-food Tech Discovers Silver Linings in the Pandemic." *Agriculture and Human Values* 37: 587–588.

Fairbairn, Madeleine, and Zenia Kish. 2022. "Exporting the Digital Revolution to Farmers in the Global South." In *The Nature of Data: Infrastructures, Environments, Politics*, edited by Jenny Goldstein and Eric Nost, 211–229. Lincoln: University of Nebraska Press.

Faxon, Hilary Olivia. 2023. "Small Farmers, Big Tech: Agrarian Commerce and Knowledge on Myanmar Facebook." *Agriculture and Human Values* 40: 897–911.

Fraser, Alistair. 2007. "Coded Spatialities of Fieldwork." *Area* 39 (2): 242–245.

Fraser, Alistair. 2019a. "Curating Digital Geographies in an Era of Data Colonialism." *Geoforum* 104:193–200.

Fraser, Alistair. 2019b. "Land Grab/Data Grab: Precision Agriculture and Its New Horizons." *Journal of Peasant Studies* 46 (5): 893–912.

Fraser, Alistair. 2020. "The Digital Revolution, Data Curation, and the New Dynamics of Food Sovereignty Construction." *Journal of Peasant Studies* 47 (1): 208–226.

Fraser, Alistair. 2021. "Food, Digital Life, and New Environment-Development Dynamics." *Routledge Handbook of Development and Environment*, edited by Brent McCusker, Waquar Ahmed, Maano Ramutsindela, and Patricia Solís, 79–89. London: Routledge.

Fraser, Alistair. 2022. "'You Can't Eat Data'? Moving beyond the Misconfigured Innovations of Smart Farming." *Journal of Rural Studies* 91:200–207.

Fraser, Alistair. 2023. "Up in the Air: The Challenge of Conceptualizing and Crafting a Post-carbon Planetary Politics to Confront Climate Change." *Journal of Peasant Studies* 50 (1): 96–113.

Flavia Roberta Freitas de Oliveira E Silva. 2023. The Fight for Food Security Must Empower Smallholder Farmers." IBM (*blog*). https://www.ibm.com/blog/food-security-smallholder-farmers/.

Gerety, Rowan Moore. 2020. "How Technology Might Finally Start Telling Farmers Things They Didn't Already Know." *MIT Technology Review*, December 18. https://www.technologyreview.com/2020/12/18/1013239/precision-agriculture-farmwise-remote-sensing-salinas/.

Giordani, John. 2022. "What You Need to Know about the New Threat: Poisoned AI." *Forbes*, May 23. https://www.forbes.com/sites/forbestechcouncil/2022/05/23/what-you-need-to-know-about-the-new-threat-poisoned-ai/.

GlobalData. 2023. "Artificial Intelligence Startups Raise over $50 Billion Venture Capital Funding in 2022, Reveals GlobalData." GlobalData, March 13. https://www.globaldata.com/media/business-fundamentals/artificial-intelligence-startups-raise-over-50-billion-venture-capital-funding-in-2022-reveals-globaldata/.

Hao, Karen, and Andrea Paola Hernández. 2022. "How the AI Industry Profits from Catastrophe." *MIT Technology Review*, April 20. https://www.technologyreview.com/2022/04/20/1050392/ai-industry-appen-scale-data-labels/.

Hayes, Ben J., Chensong Chen, Owen Powell, Eric Dinglasan, Kira Villiers, Kathryn E. Kemper, et al. 2023. "Advancing Artificial Intelligence to Help Feed the World." *Nature Biotechnology*, 41 (9): 1188–1189.

Hayles, N. Katherine. 2017. *Unthought: The Power of the Cognitive Nonconscious*. Chicago: University of Chicago Press.

HELM. 2023. "HELM Takes Majority of Shares in Agritech Startup Plantix." HELM, April 27. https://www.helmag.com/news-exhibitions/news/detail/helm-takes-majority-of-shares-in-agritech-startup-plantix.

Iliadis, Andrew, and Federica Russo. 2016. "Critical Data Studies: An Introduction." *Big Data and Society* 3 (2): Article 2053951716674238.

IPES-Food and ETC Group. 2021. *A Long Food Movement: Transforming Food Systems by 2045*. Report. IPES Food Panel. Brussels, Belgium. http://www.ipes-food.org/_img/upload/files/LongFoodMovementEN.pdf.

Kitchin, Rob, and Tracy Lauriault. 2018. "Towards Critical Data Studies. Charting and Unpacking Data Assemblages and Their Work." In *Thinking Big Data in Geography*, edited by Jim Thatcher, Josef Eckert, and Andrew Shears, 3–20. Lincoln: University of Nebraska Press.

Kitchin, Rob, and Alistair Fraser. 2020. *Slow Computing: Why We Need Balanced Digital Lives*. Bristo, UK: Bristol University Press.

Klauser, Francisco, and Dennis Pauschinger. 2021. "Entrepreneurs of the Air: Sprayer Drones as Mediators of Volumetric Agriculture." *Journal of Rural Studies* 84:55–62.

Klerkx, Laurens, Emma Jakkub, and Pierre Labarthec. 2019. "A Review of Social Science on Digital Agriculture, Smart Farming and Agriculture 4.0: New Contributions and a Future Research Agenda." *NJAS—Wageningen Journal of Life Sciences* 90 (1): Article 100315.

Kujawa, Sebastian, and Gniewko Niedbała. 2021. "Artificial Neural Networks in Agriculture." *Agriculture* 11 (6): 497.

Lee, Ronan. 2019. "Extreme Speech in Myanmar: The Role of State Media in the Rohingya Forced Migration Crisis." *International Journal of Communication* 13:3203–3224.

Legun, Katharine, Karly Ann Burch, and Laurens Klerkx. 2023. "Can a Robot Be an Expert? The Social Meaning of Skill and Its Expression through the Prospect of Autonomous AgTech." *Agriculture and Human Values* 40: 501–517.

Liu, Jen, and Phoebe Sengers. 2021. "Legibility and the Legacy of Racialized Dispossession in Digital Agriculture." *Proceedings of the ACM on Human-Computer Interaction* 5 (CSCW2 480): 1–21.

Lupton, Deborah, and Zeena Feldman, eds. 2020. *Digital Food Cultures*. London: Routledge.

McMichael, Philip. 2005. "Global Development and the Corporate Food Regime." In *New Directions in the Sociology of Global Development*, vol. 11, edited by Frederick H. Buttel and Philip McMichael, 265–299. Bingley, UK: Emerald Publishing.

McMichael, Philip. 2014. "Historicizing Food Sovereignty." *Journal of Peasant Studies* 41 (6): 933–957.

Martini, Antonella, Silvia Massa, and Stefania Testa. 2013. "The Firm, the Platform and the Customer: A 'Double Mangle' Interpretation of Social Media for Innovation." *Information and Organization* 23 (3): 198–213.

Massey, Doreen. 2005. *For Space*. London: SAGE.

Miller, Chris. 2022. *Chip War: The Fight for the World's Most Critical Technology*. New York: Simon and Schuster.

Miles, Christopher. 2019. "The Combine Will Tell the Truth: On Precision Agriculture and Algorithmic Rationality." *Big Data and Society* 6 (1): Article 2053951719849444.

Mumford, Densua. 2022. "Data Colonialism: Compelling and Useful, but Whither Epistemes?" Information, *Communication and Society* 25 (10): 1511–1516.

Nestlé India. 2022. *Annual Report 2022*. https://www.nestle.in/sites/g/files/pydnoa451/files/2023-03/17-3-Annual-Report-2022.pdf.

Noble, Safiya Umoja. 2018. *Algorithms of Oppression: How Search Engines Reinforce Racism*. New York: New York University Press.

Noble, Safiya Umoja, and Sarah Roberts. 2019. "Technological Elites, the Meritocracy, and Postracial Myths in Silicon Valley." In *RACISM POSTRACE: Report # 6*. University of California eScholarship, edited by Roopali Mukherjee, Sarah Banet-Weiser, and Herman Gray, 113–130. Duke University Press. https://escholarship.org/uc/item/7z3629nh.

Nost, Eric, and Emma Colven. 2022. "Earth for AI: A Political Ecology of Data-Driven Climate Initiatives." *Geoforum* 130 (March): 23–34.

Peck, Jamie. 2017. *Offshore: Exploring the Worlds of Global Outsourcing*. Oxford: Oxford University Press.

Prause, Louisa, Sarah Hackfort, and Margit Lindgren. 2021. "Digitalization and the Third Food Regime." *Agriculture and Human Values* 38: 614–655.

Reuters. 2023. "Samsung Display to Invest $3.1 Bln in OLED Production in South Korea." Reuters, April 4. https://www.reuters.com/technology/samsung-display-invest-31-bln-oled-production-south-korea-2023-04-04/.

Rosset, Peter Michael, Braulio Machín Sosa, Adilén María Roque Jaime, and Dana Rocío Ávila Lozano. 2011. "The Campesino-to-Campesino Agroecology Movement of ANAP in Cuba: Social Process Methodology in the Construction of Sustainable Peasant Agriculture and Food Sovereignty." *Journal of Peasant Studies* 38 (1): 161–191.

Rotz, Sarah, and Lauren Wood Kepkiewicz. 2018. "Settler Colonialism and the (Im)Possibilities of a National Food Policy." *Canadian Food Studies* 5 (3): 248–258. https://doi.org/10.15353/cfs-rcea.v5i3.275.

Schiavoni, Christina M. 2017. "The Contested Terrain of Food Sovereignty Construction: Toward a Historical, Relational and Interactive Approach." *Journal of Peasant Studies* 44 (1): 1–32.

Scott, James C. 1998. *Seeing like a State: How Certain Schemes to Improve the Human Condition Have Failed.* New Haven, CT: Yale University Press.

Semiconductor Industry Association. 2023. Semiconductor Association *Factbook 2023.* Washington, DC: Semiconductor Industry Association. https://www.semiconductors.org/wp-content/uploads/2023/05/SIA-2023-Factbook_1.pdf.

Stone, Glenn Davis. 2022. "Surveillance Agriculture and Peasant Autonomy." *Journal of Agrarian Change* 22 (3): 608–631.

Swanson, Ana. 2023. "The CHIPS Act Is about More Than Chips: Here's What's in It." *New York Times*, February 28. https://www.nytimes.com/2023/02/28/business/economy/chips-act-childcare.html.

Thatcher, Jim, David O'Sullivan, and Dillon Mahmoudi. 2016. "Data Colonialism through Accumulation by Dispossession: New Metaphors for Daily Data." *Environment and Planning D: Society and Space* 34 (6): 990–1006.

United Nations Conference on Trade and Development. 2023. *Bilateral Trade Flows by ICT Goods Categories, Annual.* UNCTAD, Geneva, Switzerland. https://unctadstat.unctad.org/wds/TableViewer/tableView.aspx?ReportId=15850.

Varadi, Mihaly, Stephen Anyango, Mandar Deshpande, Sreenath Nair, Cindy Natassia, Galabina Yordanova, et al. 2022. "AlphaFold Protein Structure Database: Massively Expanding the Structural Coverage of Protein-Sequence Space with High-Accuracy Models." *Nucleic Acids Research* 50, no. D1 (January): D439–D444. doi:10.1093/nar/gkab1061.

Zuboff, Shoshana. 2019. *The Age of Surveillance Capitalism: The Fight for a Human Future at the New Frontier of Power.* New York: Public Affairs.

CHAPTER 12

ACCESS FAILURE

Deep Explanation of Climate-Related Crises

JESSE RIBOT

The contention that famine results from a kind of natural law has no basis in scientific knowledge.

—Josué de Castro (1952, 12)

Access to the state is a precondition for membership in the African bourgeoisie with the state exploiting peasants through extra-economic coercion. In this context, democratization must remove the strait-jacket which stifles the peasantry, because any popular movement to transform political life must sever the hold that ruling classes exercise over rural producers.

—Michael J. Watts (1991, 25)

Introduction

Over forty years ago, Amartya Sen (1980, 620) observed that "food availability is certainly among the influences affecting starvation. But there are reasons for disquiet about this focus on food, and the importance attached to it to the exclusion of other variables." People who do not study food security often still believe that famines are caused by food shortages. Yet this belief has become even more implausible in the years since Sen (1980) demonstrated that modern-era food crises unfold where there is more than enough food for everyone.

Today, it seems to many that the disasters that follow climate events are caused by the weather—or by changing weather. As with famine, however, though climate is certainly associated with crises, there are many "reasons for disquiet" about the current focus on climate as the cause. Indeed, there is now an attention attached to climate change "to the exclusion of other variables" (Sen 1980). Even though many now recognize complex social and political-economic causalities, this myopic view of the causes of crises remains widespread—in climate-change-impact modeling, policy circles, and journalism (Cottier et al. 2022; Lahsen and Ribot 2021).

Shallow explanations of famine misguided and hindered famine prevention and response. Simplistic assumptions about crises that follow climate events have the same effect. They hide the many causes of, and, thus, potential protections against, crises. While de Castro (1952) had already observed the multiple social causes of famine and the ways that a narrow focus on food availability obscures other causes, Sen's (1980) work galvanized modern attention to other causes.

In more recent years, even the United Nations Office for Disaster Risk Reduction (UNDRR) has understood that disasters are not natural. They stem from preexisting vulnerabilities that enable a climate event to push people over the edge into crisis. So, this argument, made for environment-related crises in 1976 by O'Keefe, Westgate, and Wisner, appears to have gone mainstream—it is now integrated into the Sendai Framework for Disaster Risk Reduction[1] (United Nations Development Programme 2015).

Yet the analysis of root causes has not been widely used in climate change circles, and the response to disasters remains anodyne. In most instances "vulnerability" is being used only as an indicator of who is at risk, rather than an analytic of root causes of crisis (see IPCC 2014, 2012). So, how do we conduct a full, deep social analysis of the causes of climate-related disasters (a la Watts 1983a; Blaikie et al. 1994; Wisner et al. 2004)? We start with the disasters, by understanding the fragilities they reveal, and then trace out the causes of these fragilities.

Following Sen's (1984, 312), "consequentialist" view, unacceptable outcomes, such as famine, should move us to question even the institutions and arrangements that cause them—institutions and arrangements that society often assumes to be natural and efficient—such as free markets.[2] Indeed, Sen shows that markets that are operating efficiently cause famines by allocating food away from the poor and hungry—as they have no effective demand. To transform consequentialism into a method of analysis, following Sen, I take what I call a "problem-oriented" view by starting with unacceptable outcomes, the "problems," and asking about the chains of causality that produced them.

Framing causality as "entitlement failure," Sen (1981, 1984; also see Drèze and Sen 1989) laid the groundwork for analyzing the causes of vulnerability to hunger and famine. *Entitlements* are the total set of rights and opportunities with which a household can command—or through which it is legally "entitled" to obtain—different bundles of commodities. These are the legal means of accessing commodities. In short, a household's assets—stores of food or things they can trade for food or use to produce food—buffer its members against food shortage (Swift 1989, 11). Yet a person's entitlements can be inadequate or fail.[3] So that household does not have the legal means or, shall we say, the rights to attain sustenance.

The very fact that "entitlements" can fail—that people can go hungry or die in the context of legal and socially accepted market arrangements—led Sen to question free markets and moved him to push for regulation and intervention. Yet Sen's analysis of markets as cause of crisis does not go far enough. While trade can allocate food away from the hungry, we can't take the initial condition of household assets as a given. The position from which households trade also has causes. Long histories of exploitation and unequal exchange, as well as more recent land grabs (Borras et al. 2018, 2021), enabled and twisted by hierarchies of access to representation, rights, and resources, can shape the distribution of the assets people have before they even enter into an ostensibly "free" market. We must question not only the operation (and naturalized legitimacy) of markets, but also the origins of the distribution of access to land and other key complementary assets.

So, what causes the observed outcomes, the abhorrent events such as famine or displacement? Causal analysis can link the distributions and the security of held assets to human action and institutions, and can judge them to be responsible or change them to improve outcomes (or both). An empirical causal analysis extends the judgment from consequence to cause; making it possible to weigh and judge the causal chain behind the loss and damage. Causes of damage, pain, or suffering can be linked to social and political-economic structures, intentions, or negligence (Calabresi 1975; Hart and Honoré 1959), and with these insights, moral judgment of causality can then be a matter of public debate. Through understanding the deep root causes, the public debate can be extended to the weighing of the role of individual or public agency or interest behind the cause. In this manner we can identify the full range of causes that can be part of remedy and improvement, while also attributing blame and responsibility (see Ribot 2022).

The analysis of the causes of any depravation, such as hunger or loss, is the analysis of access to necessities—via access to resources, markets, authority, and political representation. This chapter turns to "access" analysis (à la Ribot 1998; Ribot and Peluso 2003) as a means of understanding the causes of vulnerabilities to hunger, famine, dislocation, economic loss, or any other damage in the face of climate variability or change. In this frame, hunger, famine, or dislocation in the face of a climate event or climate change is an "access failure"—failed access to land and failed access to many other complementary rights, institutions, infrastructures, and resources.

Entitlement Failure to Access Failure

> Access and negotiation over natural resources must be facilitated among many actors who compete for them, and local social and environmental problems must be seen in the context of broader patterns of influence and change.
>
> —Claude Raynaut (2001, 9)

The move toward access analysis is a shift from explaining only hunger and famine (the focus of entitlements analysis) to analyzing a broader set of losses and damages (or even of gains and benefits). That is, access analysis focuses on any chosen "problem," defined as a loss or a hindered attainment of something valued. It is also a shift from an obsessive focus on food availability decline (often referred to as "FAD") in the analysis of famine, or from the climate hazard in the case of current weather extremes, to an analysis that can overturn climate as the specious sole causal focus in the many current crises that are now being attributed to climate and climate change. Further, it moves us from a proximate or shallow individualized neoclassical analysis toward a broader and deeper structural and political-economic analysis (as has been practiced by de Castro 1946, 1952; Galtung 1969; Watts 1983b; Blaikie 1985; Fine 1997, 633; de Waal 1997; Devereux 2000, 27; Wisner et al. 2004; Somers 2008; Colette 2016, among others).

In the agrarian world, access to land is a key element of access to various assets and relations that could spell security. This access goes far beyond legal land title. En*title*ment is a concept based in notions of legal *right—the* right to have endowments and assets. It entitles one to various things. Access is broader than this because it is a descriptive or empirical notion of the *ability* to attain the benefits from things (Ribot and Peluso 2003). This "ability" is much broader than "rights." Rights claims are enforceable—by law, custom, or convention. They imply social contracts that underpin the plausible ability to have others support one's claims—to have or to be or to do—in the world. Ability is broader because it can also include attainment by force, violence, and stealth, in addition to law, custom, and convention, and all of the identities and structures that enable one to attain benefits—such as food, or protection from extreme weather or a virus. The boundaries of the legal are fluid; they can be reconfigured by political movements, social pressures, violence, or force—depending on social conditions that configure and reconfigure property relations (Watts 1991; Fine 1997; Lund 2020).[4] Assets—and the law—are not a fixed starting point. Indeed, such legalized concepts as "citizenship" can determine (via class, caste, ethnicity, religion, gender, age, history, place of origin etc.) who has and who does not have the rights that law affords (because even access to legal belongings, freedoms, rights and recourse matter, à la Somers 2008, 5; Agamben 1998).

In his work on "capabilities," Sen (1984) made a similar shift from a legalistic focus to a focus on outcomes. The focus on outcomes, the consequentialism noted above, enabled him to evaluate consequence in terms of human rights beyond mere legal rights—as the legal rights were systematically precluding these human rights. Without exploring the causes of these outcomes, beyond the proximate functioning of markets, Sen developed concept of capabilities—the valued doings and beings that entitlements enable—to critique the economic model without discarding it. He showed how markets can harm those in need, yet he did not call into question the origin of the distributions of endowments and assets that had created the initial conditions of inequality and were part of the precarity of some social strata. His micro focus enabled a detailed analysis of why some were capable of meeting their basic needs, and others were not. Entitlements could not, however, explain the origins of the initial distributions that had enabled skewed capability outcomes. He did add to his analysis the role of such institutions as elections and free media—as means by which people could shape the legal environment in which they lived. But he remained neutral on social movements and other forms of power outside of the vote. Watts (1991), however, modulated to a more-structural frame by introducing empowerment as the ability to influence the political economy that forms entitlements.

In his consequence-sensitive approach, the consequence Sen is most concerned with is "freedom"—freedom from and freedom to; in particular, the freedom from poverty and the freedom to "be" and "do," to "function" to achieve desirable outcomes (Sen 1984). These freedoms require food entitlements as a necessary condition—because, in his model, laws and markets shape access to these necessities. Broader desired outcomes, of course, also require freedom from oppressive regimes, social stigmas, skewed cultural norms, and petty theft, as well as state and structural violence. Thus, capabilities broaden attention beyond mere legal individual ownership and shift the moral obligation from the individual to society. The notion of "entitlements," if taken at face value (without consequence sensitivity), implicitly legitimizes, or at least accepts, any existing distribution of property while occluding nonlegal, extralegal, and illegal forces. Nevertheless, Sen's framing, his analysis of entitlement failure, gives us a strong basis for accounting for immediate micro determinants of hunger. Sen's approach is ultimately an individualist microeconomic frame. As Fine (1997), however, states, "The micro-foundations of the entitlement approach are to be rejected because of their inability to address satisfactorily the social relations and structures through which famines are fundamentally caused" (630). Capabilities get us part way to a broader multidimensional view. But because capabilities do not engender a causal analysis of initial distributions, since they are set up to justify a moral position, a deeper access analysis is needed to empirically interrogate *why* people do or do not achieve different desired outcomes—this is about why they have the endowments and assets that they have. This is partly due to previous "entitlements," but also partly due to a broad range of other factors—that include identities, belongings, extramarket social relations, violence, theft, and so forth.

A broader and deeper empirical view of the causes of hunger or of the damages that follow climate events, in contrast to entitlements and consistent with capabilities, would frame assets as depending on the "ability" (as supported by rights and other structures or powers), rather than just the "right," of the household to produce a surplus that it can store, invest in productive capacity and markets, and use in the maintenance of social relations (see Scott 1976; Berry 1993; Ribot 1998; Ribot and Peluso 2003). These assets and extended entitlements are the means of achieving capabilities. Rights-based, entitlement approaches and rule of law are not everything—they only include the enforceable claims. Access theory—explaining the *ability* of people to benefit from things—provides fuller empirical (rather than only legal-focused) analytic of what people are able to obtain and use via legal, illegal, and other relational means of obtaining things and benefits. Ability is also broader than capacity insofar as it is not merely about the innate characteristics of those at risk—ability is a manifest characteristic rather than a potential. Access analysis is about all observable and imputable factors that enable and disable benefit. Access theory focuses on the ability to benefit from tangible and intangible things, including material assets, knowledge, ideologies, discourses, doxas, habitus, social relations, social status, social structures, legal and political structures, stealth, and violence (see Ribot and Peluso 2003).

Vulnerability in an entitlement framework is the risk that a household's alternative commodity bundles will fail to buffer them against hunger, famine, dislocation, or other losses. This is not a risk of "entitlements failure" to Sen; but is a risk of "access failure" (failure to access or enjoy the benefits of these alternative commodity bundles) in an access framing. Vulnerability is a relative measure of the household's proneness to such failure (Downing 1991; also see Downing 1992; Watts and Bohle 1993, 46; Chambers 1989, 1). By starting with the components of an "entitlement" framing (that is, production, investments, stores, and claims) of what enables households to maintain food consumption, an access framework allows us to analyze the causes of food crises. Analyzing chains of the factors that produce household crises reveals a whole range of proximate and distal causes—hopefully, signaling potential policies to reduce vulnerability (Blaikie 1985; Turner, Matson et al. 2003; Turner, Kasperson et al. 2003). This social model applied to instances where climate events are associated with food crisis replaces ecocentric models of natural hazards and environmental change (Watts 1983a). By showing a range of causes, legal, illegal, or structural, environmental stresses are located among and their role explained within other material and social conditions that shape household well-being. For example, there may be hunger during a drought because of privatization policies that limit pastoral mobility, making pastoralists dependent on precarious rain-fed agriculture (Franke and Chasin 1980; Smucker and Wisner 2008; also see Leichenko and O' Brien 2008).

Household-based social models also illustrate how important it is that assets are sufficient to cope with or adjust to (as in buffer against) environmental variations and changes, so that land-based production activities are not undermined by and do not undermine the natural resources they depend on (Blaikie 1985). Household models, however, often fail to account for intrahousehold gender and age differences in production, consumption, and reproduction; so internal household struggles must be made an explicit part of any complete analysis. Gender-differentiated access to household food and assets, and to natural resources, jobs, markets, services, and representation, is foundational to household and individual well-being (see Guyer and Peters 1987; Vaughan 1987; Carney 1988; Drèze and Sen 1989; Hart 1992; Agarwal 1993; Schroeder 1999; Turner 2000). If the household models are not fully theorized, they may also miss broader structural relations of production and exchange within markets and a globalized system that shape broader-scale distributions (Polanyi [1944] 2001; Leichenko and O' Brien 2008; Butler 2009; Fraser 2011, 2021). But all of these should be linked into chains of causality by a full, deep, causal analysis of access and of access failures.

In a sense, the most fundamental limit to entitlements is the shallow neoclassical assumption that assets and rules are a given—as if they have no causality, no history. Cause is parked in the lack of assets—and/or lack of the ability to exchange them for food. This is complemented by extended entitlements whose cause can also be located in the failure of social reciprocities or state social protections—the moral and legal social contracts under which people live. Yet the existing distribution of assets and social protections that a storm or drought finds in place have historical antecedents—causes. Entitlements analysis starts with assets and protections. It does not explain them. Access analysis traces back the chains of causality to the structures and relations that produce unacceptable (in a consequentialist sense) distributions that result in hunger, famine, dislocation, and other damages that follow a drought or storm. The conditions of vulnerability—entitlement—are not taken as a given, but as a set of conditions of empowerment and disempowerment and of distributional inequity that have causes.

In this sense, it is important to place entitlement theory within a broader political economy and empowerment approach (Watts 1983b; Watts and Bohle 1993) and links it to Sen's (1984, 1999) capacities and capabilities thinking (also see Bebbington 1999; Yohe and Tol 2002). Bringing together various readings of causality, an access framing also outlines recursive elements of vulnerability analysis by exploring ways in which those at risk shape the political economy that shapes the entitlements behind precarity or security (Watts 1991; also see Ribot 1995, 2014). Emancipatory recursive elements, which are most in need of development, include representation (Sen 1981, 1999; Watts and Bohle 1993; Appadurai 1984; Lappé 2013), structural relations (Polanyi [1944] 2001; Scott 1976; Swift 1989; Watts 1991; Moore 1997; Pelling 2003; Fraser 2021), and discursive effects (à la Beck 1992; Rose 1996; Butler 1997, 2009; Fraser 2000; Luhmann 2002; Agrawal 2005; Wolford 2007; Wilkinson 2010; Connolly 2013). Causal chains (Blaikie 1985) and access theory (Ribot and Peluso 2003) frame the empirical starting point for explaining assets, social protections, and relations of emancipation.

Although they are *triggered*[5] by climate stress, the evidence is overwhelming that climate-related disasters must be understood in the context of historical, social, and political-economic arrangements that render people secure or vulnerable. This is evident, as the same magnitude environmental event causes quite different damages in the same place as circumstances on the ground improve. In Bangladesh, fatalities were reduced from more than 500,000 to 3,406 deaths between cyclones Bohla and Sidr, which hit the same coastline with a similar storm surge and intensity. The damages were not due to the cyclones, and the reductions were due to planning reforms (Batha 2007; Bern et al 1993; CEDMHA 2007; 7; Government of Bangladesh 2008; MFDMB 2008). There are many examples where the climate events of same magnitude cause very different damage in different places or at different times in the same place. In 1877–1878, more than 400,000 people perished in the Grande Seca, "great drought," in Northeast Brazil, but a drought of a similar magnitude in the southwest of the United States would not have killed anyone—perhaps some cattle. Damages follow from differences in the conditions on the ground—they do not fall from the sky. Droughts become deadly due to security and options on the ground. The 1943 West Bengal famine was caused by well-functioning markets, not drought or absolute shortage (Sen 1981). The 1959–1960 famine in China was produced by dysfunctional upwardly accountable administration, not drought (Jisheng 2012). The 2011 Somali famine was a product of "interplay of livelihoods, clan and politics," not drought (Majid and McDowell 2012, 37). The 1,300 fatalities in New Orleans in 2005 resulted from a long history of government negligence, not hurricane Katrina (White House 2006; Somers 2008; Hayes 2009; Bullard and Wright 2009).

Conducting a fully social analysis of the causes of loss or damage—and of crisis on a larger scale—requires tracing causality from that problematic outcome to the multiple factors that impinged upon its occurrence. This is an application of access analysis—an analysis of how a person or a group is deprived of some benefit that they need or desire, how they are deprived of security or made vulnerable.

Access Analysis of Trans-Saharan Migration

On April 19, 2015, a boat from Libya sank off the island of Lampedusa with 729 African migrants onboard; twenty-nine of them survived. Most were from the Sahel, and many came from the forest villages of Tambacounda (or Tamba), where I had worked for the past thirty years. The media immediately labeled them "climate refugees," as if they had made this risky trip to escape the stresses of climate change. They had not. They had many motivations for taking this journey. Climate was not one of them. The rains in the Sahel had been increasing, not decreasing, for more than twenty years (Biasutti and Giannini 2006).[6] Although the Sahel is a semiarid region,, there is no reason to believe it cannot easily support those who live there. Nonetheless, there is an annual hungry season—the growing season when stocks run low and the next crop is yet to be harvested. Indeed, this hungry season persists, through good and bad years. Sahelian farmers and pastoralists live in an economy that pushes their income down below subsistence—year after year.

In 2017, Papa Faye and I conducted field research in Tambacounda among the families of those who had perished on the trip (see Ribot, Faye, and Turner 2020). The twenty village-level authorities (Imams and chiefs) we interviewed told us that emigration had gone up significantly over the previous five years and was much higher than it had been ten or twenty years ago. Rising Europe-bound emigration has been reported elsewhere in the Sahel (e.g., Turner and Teague 2019; Turner et al. 2021). These rates of emigration cannot, however, be attributed to climate or climate change—notwithstanding those who label them climate migrants (Friedman 2016; Foote 2016; Rigaud et al. 2018); both journalists and climate scientists are engaged in such attributions (see Cottier et al. 2022; also see Lahsen and Ribot 2021 on attribution).

Indeed, there are widespread reports that the Sahelian ecology is "regreening" or, shall we say, improving rather than declining. We are not seeing desertification, but rather return of forests. Further, maps of food insecurity for Senegal show that food insecurity in the Casamance and Tambacounda regions is higher than other areas in the country where climate change has introduced more variability (Rioux 2011; VAM 2014). Climate change cannot explain the migration we observe. Indeed, Giannini et al. (2017) have shown a distinct mismatch between climate-stressed zones and food insecurity in other parts of the Sahel. In short, we must put the role of climate stress in its proper place and refocus on other causes of out-migration.

Starting from migrants' decisions to depart, we tried to understand why these young men (and they were all men)[7] in Tambacounda were choosing to make the perilous journey across the Sahara Desert and Mediterranean Sea. What did these young men have, what did they want, what did they need, what did they lack, and what moved them to go? What made them take this risk? The answers were many. First, we established that they were aware of some of the risks. Many had heard about extortion and theft en route; death in the desert (which is even more likely than at sea); ransoming by Al Qaeda, Boko Haram, Tuareg Rebels, or Libyan Army, who would capture them and call their parents to ask for payments. They knew of slave labor, death at sea, abuses in Europe, and the shame of being repatriated from Libya or Europe. They justified taking these risks by adopting the fatalist position that their fate was written, and God would protect them, despite the elders' insistence that God does not condone suicide.

We asked these young men about their lives and futures in Tambacounda. They felt a lack of respect, saying they had no role in the family or the community at home. They felt there was no future at in Tamba. They noted the ongoing subsistence crisis—the hungry season and their deep anxiety about feeding their children and parents. The young men told us that they could not marry since families wanted to marry their daughters to men who had migrated and could send remittances back home or men in families with migrants. The migration situation had created a class society of have migrants and have-not migrants. Those who received remittances were not as likely to suffer the hungry season. But the most striking thing was that these young men wanted to contribute to life at home and felt they did not have the means to do so. They wanted to be in and live in Tambacounda but to do so with dignity and respect. They could not find this. One aspiring migrant said, "Here there is no life." His statement was mirrored by others, who would say on departure "Barsa walla barsak," meaning "Barcelona [Europe] or death."[8] They were saying that they would risk dying in transit rather than living the social death they felt by staying at home.

The decision to migrate seems driven by these sentiments. But the situation would be quite different were it not for widespread material precarity. The youth attributed the hopelessness they felt to their economic conditions and prospects. Each sector—peanuts, millet, cotton, maize, charcoal, and labor—left most of them below subsistence. Interestingly enough, these people have assets. Land is not scarce in this rain-fed agricultural zone. The surrounding forests are hunting grounds, and stock many other products. These farmers have land, forests, and their own labor. They have some equipment. There are even formal social services in place. What they lack, however, is *fair access* to the surrounding forests, the markets, and to government services. Land rights in this region are not a key issue—as land is abundant (we will return to the topic of abundance and land development later.) Nor is it the poorest who emigrate. Those who depart are able to save enough to start the trip (Ribot, Faye, and Turner 2020; Bredeloup and Pliez 2005, 13). Many also had remunerative jobs (see Robin, Lalou, and Ndiaye

2000, xxiii). In short, the reasons for their departure seem to turn on long-term hopes and experiences rather than immediate deprivations.

Charcoal and cotton production and access to services (Ribot 1998; Faye 2017; Faye and Ribot 2017) provide good examples of socially stratified access to natural resources and other goods. Forest access is restricted by the forest service. A license is required for transporting forest goods to markets. These licenses are issued by the forest service to urban merchants, which enables the formation of a merchant oligopsony that sets prices and reaps virtually all the sector's profits. There are further layers on access to licenses, as this is a function of the merchant's ethnic identity and wealth, factors that shape their access to government. Indeed, there are many other ways, including permits for cutting and various credit arrangements that skew access to forest-sector profits (Ribot 1998; Faye 2017). In our study of Tambacounda (Ribot 1998; Ribot, Faye, and Turner 2020), we found that the cotton sector was under the control of one monopoly buyer. This buyer set the prices. Here, having to purchase cottonseed, fertilizer, and pesticides on credit left many farmers in debt after the production season. Further, when farmers and pastoralists need veterinarian and medical services from the government—which, ostensibly, are subsidized—they are made to pay full market price, which they cannot afford. Services are effectively denied.

Agricultural land comes into this picture as the basis of livelihoods, but also as an underdeveloped and abundant resource. The enormous agricultural potential of the Tambacounda Region, touted by the Statistical Bureau of the Government of Senegal (see Sane and Diallo 2019, 50), makes agricultural development attractive. Sane and Diallo cite the FAO's Global Environment Fund's focus on "integration of climate resilience in agropastoral production for food security in vulnerable rural zones" (51). But why is climate the issue only now? Why is it even necessary as a justification for long-needed investments? Water availability in the zone has been known to require infrastructure development for a very long time (Franke and Chasin 1980 and Raynaut 1998, who both remark that there has also long been famine in the region, yet vulnerability is not addressed). Further, climate change, as noted above, is not yet, even if it may soon be, a major issue in the Tambacounda region. The issue is not climate change but a long-standing failure to invest in developing the productivity of the land (that is, as Brottem and Brooks 2018, 124–125, note, "negligent government policies" and "a lack of externally supported infrastructure"). Tambacounda has not been given access to the kind of essential infrastructure that has long been developed in Senegal's northern Région du Fleuve along the Senegal River.

Land in the rain-fed drylands of Tambacounda is abundant. Without irrigation, however, the land remains unattractive to outside investors or for government infrastructure projects. Indeed, at the expense of regions like Tamba, there is a long history of development initiatives being "concentrated particularly in large zones devoted to commercial agriculture" (Raynaut 2001,16; 1998). Papa Faye, a fellow researcher in Senegal, notes that irrigation in Tamba is more expensive than in the North (pers. comm. 2022), and thus has a lower return on investment for government or for agrobusiness. Although the Falémé or Gambia Rivers run through Tambacounda, the topography does not allow for gravity-fed irrigation systems, so that pumping stations would be required. However, Senegal's North, along the Senegal River, is gravity irrigated, and so infrastructure is less costly. Cheap labor from Tamba now serves the North—as the lower productivity in Tamba has cheapened Tamba's labor. Investment has been in places where the returns are higher, rather than where needs are most acute.

Tamba is also farther than the Northern regions from Senegal's market center, Dakar, making Tambacounda less commercially competitive for agricultural development. The government made the choice to invest in the North in the 1960s, leaving Tamba behind. Big agrobusinesses can now be found in the North. So, the key land question is one of subnational regional investment politics. Investing in Tamba, we can hypothesize, could have a positive return but less than elsewhere in Senegal. Investing in Tamba would also give labor a reason to stay, reducing the supply of cheap labor to the North. Tamba, it seems, serves as a cheap labor reserve for other parts of Senegal and for Europe. The state has chosen—following either a strictly market logic or a skewed developmentalism—to leave Tamba behind. In this case, Tamba's land could have more value with higher productivity, but without access to infrastructure investments, the farmers of Tamba cannot benefit; they do not have access to the more-stable production that irrigation could provide. Young men see their families struggling, see little hope for the future, and leave.

These are just some of the factors that shape the assets, endowments, rights, and economic context in which youth in Tambacounda decide to depart. Figure 12.1 provides

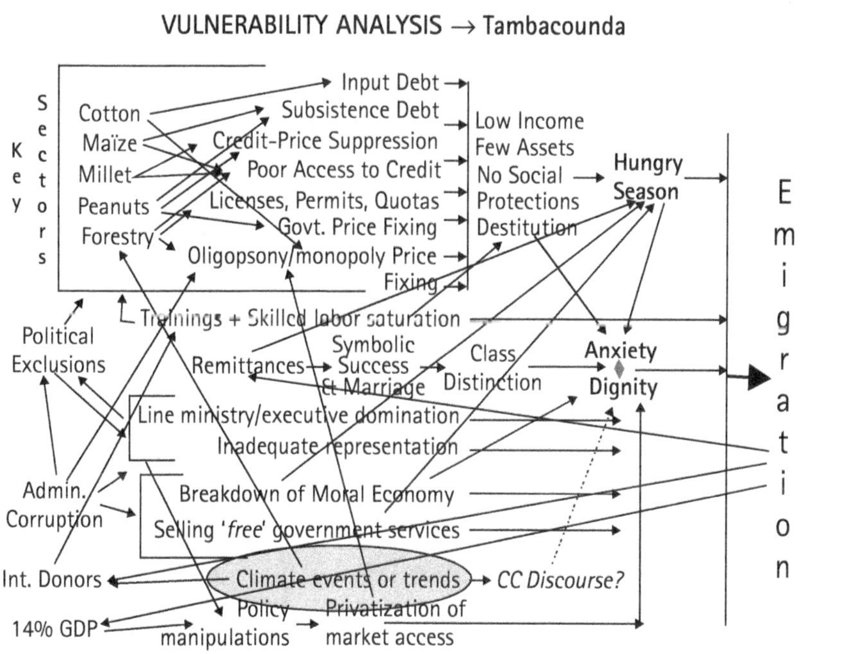

FIGURE 12.1. Schematic diagram of the many social and political-economic factors shaping young Sahelian farmers' and pastoralists' decision to take the risk to emigrate from Senegal across the Sahara and Mediterranean toward Europe.

a fuller picture of the factors at play. Their entitlements are clearly failing, caused by a broader access failure—made visible by a deeper analysis of access. They may have land and labor, but they cannot enjoy the profits from their own productivity. In addition, when asked what they can do, youth feel disenfranchised. They do not see any way to influence the political economy that shapes their precarity. Left feeling hopeless, they choose between *Barcelona* and *death*. The political economy of material deprivation and marginality shapes their expectations of marriage, jobs, and respect, and their feelings of exclusion or disenfranchisement. Farmers and pastoralists do not have access to resources, markets, development investments, representation, or any of the basic necessities that would make life in Tambacounda feel secure. So, while emigration is a decision, it is a decision made in the face of material deprivation. It is no surprise that none of those we interviewed mentioned climate or climate change as a cause of their emigration choice.

Conclusion

The ostensibly climate-related migration from the Sahel toward Europe starts at the confluence of access failures at home (Ribot, Faye, and Turner 2020).[9] The case study of Tambacounda progressively contextualizes the access failures that result in departures. Departure can be read as a moment of lost security because migration involves great risk. It is a moment when young men's vulnerabilities to hunger and hopelessness at home are transfigured into vulnerabilities to loss, insult, abuse, slavery, and death in the desert or at sea.

Departure can also be viewed as a means of access to a benefit because it involves a spark of hope and the promise of a potential role in family life via remittances, and the respect this brings—the need for hope and dignity is part of the cause of the vulnerabilities they take on as migrants. The Tambacounda case shows that material access failures at home, which date back to colonial and postcolonial failures to invest in Tembacounda's productivity and security, shape decisions that usher young men into new dangers in search of a future.

Access failure, illustrated in the Tambacounda case, is broader than entitlement failure. It can identify the social, political-economic, and institutional production of the precarity we hope to reduce. Access analysis can identify the proximate and distal, immediate and long-past, direct and structural, and shallow and deep, as well as legal, extralegal, and illegal causes of deprivations and attainments (see Ribot and Peluso 2003). Here I use the term "deep explanation," or "deep causality," simply to contrast it with the all-too-common "shallow" forms of causal analysis, which assume initial conditions (as in economics and in much climate 'impact' modeling) or focus on what's countable at the expense of the things that count (as with computational approaches, see Cottier et al. 2022). Causes of access failure must draw on many methods—from process tracing to statistics, focusing on everything from micro-decisions to macrostructures—to produce a fuller and deeper accounting.

The decision to depart is as an act of agency within structures. It is, ironically, a way for young men to take their fates into their own hands, in the name of a fatalism that relies on God's will and protection. This is also the moment of crisis at which vulnerability to death in the desert and at sea, and to insult and injury en route, are made materially likely, and risk is taken on by departing bodies. Here structure and agency work together via a set of discursive and recursive interactions between affect and materiality (Ribot 2014, 2022). The failed ability to access resources, markets, and the state is, among other causes, a product of failed rights to use resources (as allocated by the forest service), organization of the market (permits, oligopsony and monopsony, social ties), and relations to government (as those of the charcoal merchants versus peasant producers). Such failures fit into a long history of failed access to agricultural infrastructure investments because of the privileging of the most lucrative zones for development over human security in the more marginal zones, where the return on investments would still be positive. These failures are embedded in failed ability of peasant farmers and pastoralists to influence rights—that is, to shape the political economy that shapes their vulnerabilities—via emancipation or representation (see Watts 1991). Agency, nevertheless, takes place within and shapes these arrangements (viz Weheliye 2014). These arrangements shape the scope of agency.

Analysis of access failure involves tracing the causes of crises from the moment of loss (death at sea, slavery in Libya, the hungry season, lack of dignity, lack of hope) to the decision to depart, the social and political-economic roots of the material conditions at departure, to the multiscale causes of those conditions, and, ultimately, to what society can and should do to prevent losses and damages. Those include any arenas in which society can respond, could have responded, and thus should have acted to prevent crises (Ribot 2022)—such as infrastructural development, the restructuring of market access (permits and licenses), and price supports. These causal links can lead to biophysical-infrastructural phenomena that are within human ability to control, protections from the biophysical world that could have been implemented or developed, the building of buffering assets for those who are marginalized by social or economic systems, the reform of those systems, or any other social actions that society agrees should be in place. We learn what these are by tracing out, across space and back through time to the human actions and inactions that generate pain and suffering, and could also be turned toward well-being and security. The process does not stop at entitlements; it goes deeper to explain the accumulation and dispositions behind them.

Sen's (1984) capabilities approach provides us with a moral metric for achieving the minimum of what he calls "functionings," or the desired beings and doings that people *should* have access to via access to the means for achieving them.[10] Access analysis helps us understand why people do or do not achieve basic capabilities and greater aspirations. Ironically, while departure does, for those few who make it to Europe, fulfill some sense of hope for dignity and respect at home—a kind of coming of age, for having reached a seemingly promised land—the misery, disrespect, racism, menial work and, perhaps, disillusionment found on arrival, hardly reflects laudable capabilities or the achievement of the desired being or doing. The beings and doings this voyage does enable access to include a recognition that obviates the initial hope at the cost of great risks and hard labors in the desert, Libya, the sea, and in Europe (also see Turner, Ribot, and Moumouni 2022; Turner et al. 2022).

Indeed, following Nussbaum (2001), migrants' achievement can be viewed as preferences that reflects a derisively low expectation for self, in which they have "chosen," and are perhaps even "content" with, one set of sufferings over another. These low expectations also need explanation in a political-economic frame (such as the misrecognition addressed by affirmative action in the United States, à la Fraser (2000, 2007). Indeed, while neoclassical economists may shy away from accounting for taste, and the mere act of having made a "choice" might even feel just to old Pareto (and Bentham), the consequences are still "reprehensible" (Sen 1984). Sen's consequentialism brings us back to the basic question of the acceptability of initial conditions and why anyone tolerates them. Does tolerance reflect the false consciousness associated with Marx (Lukács 1923), Gramsci's (1971) hegemony, Bourdieu's (1972) habitus, Foucault's (1977) subjectivities, Nussbaum's (2001) entrenched preferences, Taylor's (1994) or Fraser's (2007) misrecognition? Is it simply resignation to Agamben's (1998) bare life, or is it Weheliye's (2014) more-affirming life within the margins of deprivation and oppression?

Osmani (2005) considers poverty to be a deprivation that is a human rights abuse. It seems the departure from the Sahel is driven by and arrives at other reprehensible conditions that must be viewed as abuses—as poverty is not the only driver. To trace causality, because we judge these outcomes to be unacceptable, leads us to responsibility and blame, and perhaps response in repairs or reparations. Asking where the initial distributions come from by interrogating the origins of accumulation and deprivation have always been contentious questions as they point fingers toward individuals and institutions that are or serve powerful beneficiaries. The vulnerabilities lived, the risks taken, and gains achieved reflect failed access to basic human rights. So, we still need to account for both what is found to be worth achieving and how access to the means of achieving it is either established or denied.

Concerning the deep causes of crisis, causes of climate-related disasters, we must still interrogate how and why broader understandings of causality—those pointing toward root causes—are continuously pushed aside. There is a politics of knowledge concerning what is in and out of public focus—how and why different analytics are chosen that frame in or out different causes (Cottier et al. 2022). Yet, no matter what, in a problem-oriented approach, we need to keep unacceptable pain and suffering at the center, and we need to ask the contentious question of what caused this and what could have and can be done—keeping consequentialism central. A deep analysis makes evident factors and processes that are not visible to the naked eye. What is apparent or seems obvious is not always true or right. Indeed, by focusing on "deep" analysis and explanation we can distinguish our work from the "shallow" analyses that are so common.

Acknowledgments

Thanks to Jun Borras, Jenny Franco, Christian Lund, and Sara Vigil for their deeply constructive guidance.

Notes

1. "Policies and practices for disaster risk management should be based on an understanding of disaster risk in all its dimensions of vulnerability, capacity, exposure of persons and assets, hazard characteristics and the environment" (United Nations Development Programme 2015, 23).
2. Sen (1984) notes, "Since it is implausible—indeed I believe incredible—to claim [by privileging 'just' acquisition] that consequences in the form of life or death, starvation or nourishment, indeed pleasure or pain, are intrinsically matters of moral indifference, or have only very weak intrinsic moral relevance, it is not easy to see why history-based rules of procedure should be so invulnerable to the facts of their consequences" (313).
3. Entitlement failure happens "either because of a fall in her endowment (e.g. alienation of land, or loss of labour power due to ill health), or because of an unfavorable shift in her exchange entitlement (e.g. loss of employment, fall in wages, rise in food prices, drop in the price of goods or services she sells, decline in self-employed production)" (Drèze and Sen 1989, 23).
4. As Fine (1997), points out, "A weapon, for example, is an endowment that has an exchange value with an equivalent in food; but it can also gain a purchase on access to food through (collective) violence as well as redefine property rights and ownership, but only depending upon the shifting social conditions in which it is wielded" (629).
5. Viewing hazards as "triggers" rather than causes makes it possible for analysts to include the causes of the fragilities that enable hazards to result in damages. "Climate, 'overpopulation' and war, while potentially significant as proximate or trigger factors, have been substantially discredited as primary factors" (Watts 1991, 15). "The challenge today is to integrate agency and structure in examinations of the production of vulnerability, in specific places, whilst also acknowledging the importance of physical systems in generating hazard that can trigger disaster" (Pelling 2003, 47). Wisner, Blaikie, and Cannon (2004) point to how "most government agencies charged with such responsibilities as 'environment,' 'health and welfare' and 'public safety' generally still deal with disasters as though they are *equivalent to* the hazards that trigger them" (61).
6. Although overall rainfall has increased, climate change is changing rainfall patterns and variability. Short periods of intense flooding with long periods of dry season can be devastating for farmers. The magnitude of these changes in variability are, however, not clear.
7. It is not a new phenomenon that migrants are largely men (Robin, Lalou, and Ndiaye 2000, 18).
8. "Barcelona" refers to Europe in general. It was an earlier destination for migrants, who are now, more often, heading to Italy and other destinations.
9. For the case of emigration from Niger toward Libya, see Turner, Ribot, and Moumouni (mimeo 2022); and Turner et al. (mimeo 2022).
10. Capability is a political goal, the actual functions (desired beings and doings) are the individual choice. The key for Sen (1984) is that people have the ability to make this choice.

Nussbaum (2001) asks a slightly different question, whether desires and preferences can really be "a guide to what is really just and good" (70). When people accept what others find to be unacceptable conditions, can we simply allow them this privilege—and refrain for accounting for taste?

References

Agamben, Giorgio. 1998. *Homo Sacer: Sovereign Power and Bare Life*. Stanford, CA: Stanford University Press.

Agarwal, Bina. 1993. "Social Security and the Family: Coping with Seasonality and Calamity in Rural India." *Agriculture and Human Values* 17 (3): 156–165.

Agrawal, Arun. 2005. *Environmentality: Technologies of Government and the Making of Subjects*. Durham, NC: Duke University Press.

Appadurai, Arjun. 1984. "How Moral Is South Asia's Economy? A Review Article." *Journal of Asian Studies* 43 (3): 481–497.

Batha, E. 2007. "Cyclone Sidr Would Have Killed 100,000 Not Long Ago." Alertnet [online], November 16. UNEP (United Nations Environment Program). 2009. New Science and Developments in our Changing Environment. Nairobi: UNEP.

Bebbington, A. 1999. "Capitals and Capabilities: A Framework for Analysing Peasant Viability, Rural Livelihoods and Poverty." *World Development* 27 (12): 2021–2044.

Beck, Ulrich. 1992. *Risk Society: Towards a New Modernity*. London: SAGE.

Bern, Caryn, J. Sniezek, G. M. Mathbor, M. S. Siddiqi, C. Ronsmans, A. M. Chowdhury, et al. 1993. "Risk Factors for Mortality in the Bangladesh Cyclone of 1991." *Bulletin of World Health Organization* 71 (1): 73–78.

Berry, Sara. 1993. *No Condition is Permanent: The Social Dynamics of Agrarian Change in Sub-Saharan Africa*. Madison: University of Wisconsin Press.

Biasutti, Michela, and Alessandra Giannini. 2006. "Robust Sahel Drying in Response to Late 20th Century Forcings." *Geophysical Research Letters* 33: L11706. doi:10.1029/2006GL026067.

Blaikie, Piers. 1985. *The Political Economy of Soil Erosion in Developing Countries*. London: Longman Press.

Blaikie, Piers, Terry Cannon, Ian Davis, and Ben Wisner. 1994. *At Risk: Natural Hazards, People's Vulnerability, and Disasters*. London: Routledge.

Borras, Saturnino M., Jr., Jennifer Franco, Clara Mi Young Park, Mads Barbesgaard, Yukari Sekine, Ye Lin Myint, Thant Zin. 2018. "The Twin Challenge of Agrarian and Climate Justice: Connections and Contradictions between Climate Change Mitigation Politics, Land Grabbing and Conflict in Myanmar." Transnational Institute (TNI) Working Paper Series, February 25.

Borras, Saturnino M., Jr., Ian Scoones, Amita Baviskar, Marc Edelman, Nancy Lee Peluso, and Wendy Wolford. 2021. "Climate Change and Agrarian Struggles: An Invitation to Contribute to a JPS Forum." *Journal of Peasant Studies*, 49(1): 1–28. doi:10.1080/03066150.2021.1956473.

Bourdieu, Pierre. 1972. *Outline of a Theory of Practice*. Cambridge, UK: Cambridge University Press.

Bredeloup, Sylvie, and Olivier Pliez. 2005. "Migrations entre les deux fleuves du Sénégal." *Autrepart* 36: 3–20.

Brottem, Leif, and Bonnie Brooks. 2018. "Crops and Livestock under the Sun: Obstacles to Rural Livelihood Adaptations to Hotter Twenty-First-Century Temperatures in Eastern Senegal." *Land Degradation & Development* 29 (1): 118–126.

Bullard, Robert D. and Beverly Wright, eds. 2009. *Race, Place, and Environmental Justice after Hurricane Katrina: Struggles to Reclaim, Rebuild, and Revitalize New Orleans and the Gulf Coast.* Boulder, CO: Westview Press.

Butler, Judith. 1997. *Excitable Speech: A Politics of the Performative.* London: Routledge.

Butler, Judith. 2009. *Frames of War: When Is Life Grievable?* New York: Verso.

Calabresi, Guido. 1975. "Concerning Cause and the Law of Torts: An Essay for Harry Kalven, Jr." *University of Chicago Law Review* 43 (1): 69–108.

Carney, Judith. 1988. "Struggles over Land and Crops in an Irrigated Rice Scheme: The Gambia." *Agriculture, Women and Land: The African Experience*, edited by Jean Davison, 59–78. Boulder, CO: Westview Press.

CEDMHA (Center for Excellence in Disaster Management and Humanitarian Assistance). 2007. "Cyclone Sidr Update." November 15.

Chambers, Robert. 1989. "Vulnerability, Coping and Policy." *IDS Bulletin* 20 (2): 1–7.

Lund, Christian. 2020. *Nine-Tenths of the Law: Enduring Dispossession in Indonesia.* New Haven: Yale University Press.

Colette, April L. 2016. "The Politics of Framing Risk: Minding the Vulnerability Gap in Climate Change Research." *World Development Perspectives* 1: 43–48.

Connolly, William E. 2013. *The Fragility of Things: Self-Organizing Processes, Neoliberal Fantasies, and Democratic Activism.* Durham, NC: Duke University Press.

Cottier, Fabien, Marie-Laurence Flahaux, Jesse Ribot, Richard Seager, and Godfreyb Ssekajja. 2022. "Re-framing the Frame: Cause and Effect in Climate-related Migration." *World Development.* Published online July 6, 2022. https://www.sciencedirect.com/science/article/pii/S0305750X22002066?dgcid=author.

de Castro, Josué. 1946. *La Alimentación en los Tropicos.* Mexico City: Fondo de Cultura Económica.

de Castro, Josué. 1952. *The Geography of Hunger.* Boston: Little, Brown and Company.

de Waal, Alex. 1997. *Famine Crimes: Politics and the Disaster Relief Industry in Africa.* Oxford: African Rights and International African Institute/James Currey.

Devereux, Stephen. 2000. "Famine in the Twentieth Century." IDS Working Paper 105. Brighton, UK: Institute for Development Studies.

Downing, Thomas E. 1991. "Assessing Socioeconomic Vulnerability to Famine: Frameworks, Concepts, and Applications." Final Report to the U.S. Agency for International Development, Famine Early Warning System Project, January 30.

Downing, Thomas E. 1992. "Vulnerability and Global Environmental Change in the Semi-Arid Tropics: Modeling Regional and Household Agricultural Impacts and Responses." Paper presented to the International Conference on Sustainable Development in the World's Drylands, Jan 27–Feb 1. Fortaleza-Ceará, Brazil.

Drèze, Jean, and Amartya Sen. 1989. *Hunger and Public Action.* Oxford: Clarendon Press.

Faye, Papa. 2017. "The Politics of Recognition, and the Manufacturing of Citizenship and Identity in Senegal's Decentralised Charcoal Market." *Review of African Political Economy* 44 (151): 66–84.

Faye, Papa, and Jesse Ribot. 2017. "Causes for Adaptation: Access to Forests, Markets, and Representation in Eastern Senegal." *Sustainability* 9 (2): 311. doi:org/10.3390/su9020311.

Fine, Ben. 1997. "Entitlement Failure." *Development and Change* 28: 617–647.

Foote, Willy. 2016. "Climate Refugees Are Leaving the Farm Behind." *Forbes*, July 20.

Foucault, Michel. 1977. *Discipline and Punish: The Birth of the Prison.* New York: Random House.

Franke, Richard W., and Barbara H. Chasin. 1980. *Seeds of Famine: Ecological Destruction and the Development Dilemma in the West African Sahel.* Montclair, NJ: Allanheld, Osmun.

Fraser, Nancy. 2000. "Rethinking Recognition." *New Left Review* 3 (3): 107–120.
Fraser, Nancy. 2007. "Re-framing Justice in a Globalizing World." In *(Mis)recognition, Social Inequality and Social Justice: Nancy Fraser and Pierre Bourdieu*, edited by Terry Lovell, 17–35. Abingdon, UK: Routledge.
Fraser, Nancy. 2011. "Marketization, Social Protection, Emancipation: Toward a Neo-Polanyian Conception of Capitalist Crisis." In *Business as Usual: The Roots of the Global Financial Meltdown*, edited by Craig J Calhoun and Georgi M. Derluguian, 137–158. New York: New York University Press.
Fraser, Nancy. 2021. "Climates of Capital: For a Trans-environmental Eco-socialism." *New Left Review* 127: 94–127.
Friedman, Thomas L. 2016. "Out of Africa." *New York Times*, April 13. www.nytimes.com/2016/04/13/opinion/out-of-africa.html?mcubz=0.
Galtung, Johan. 1969. "Violence, Peace, and Peace Research." *Journal of Peace Research* 6: 167–191.
Giannini, Alessandra, P. Krishna Krishnamurthy, Rémi Cousin, Naouar Labidi, and Richard J. Choularton. 2017. "Climate Risk and Food Security in Mali: A Historical Perspective on Adaptation." *Earth's Future* 5 (2): 144–157.
Government of Bangladesh. 2008. "Cyclone Sidr in Bangladesh: Damage, Loss, and Needs Assessment for Disaster Recovery and Reconstruction." Report prepared by the Government of Bangladesh Assisted by the International Development Community with Financial Support from the European Commission, April.
Gramsci, Antonio. 1971. *Selections from the Prison Notebooks of Antonio Gramsci*. New York: International Publishers.
Guyer, Jane, and Paulene Peters. 1987. "Conceptualizing the Household: Issues of Theory and Policy in Africa." *Development and Change* 18 (2): 197–327.
Hart, Gillian. 1992. "Household Production Reconsidered: Gender, Labor Conflict, and Technological Change in Malaysia's Muda region." *World Development* 20 (6): 809–823.
Hart, H. L. A., and A. M. Honoré. 1959. *Causation in the Law*. 2nd ed. Oxford: Oxford University Press.
Hayes, Ashley. 2009. "Army Corps of Engineers Liable for Katrina flooding." CNN, November 19. http://www.cnn.com/2009/US/11/18/louisiana.katrina.lawsuit/index.html.
IPCC (SREX). 2012. *Managing the Risks of Extreme Events and Disasters to Advance Climate Change Adaptation: A Special Report of Working Groups I and II of the Intergovernmental Panel on Climate Change*. Edited by C. B. Field, V. Barros, T. F. Stocker, D. Qin, D. J. Dokken, K. L. Ebi, et al. Cambridge, UK, and New York: Cambridge University Press. https://www.ipcc.ch/site/assets/uploads/2018/03/SREX_Full_Report-1.pdf.
IPCC. 2014. *Climate Change 2014: Impacts, Adaptation, and Vulnerability. Part A: Global and Sectoral Aspects. Contribution of Working Group II to the Fifth Assessment Report of the Intergovernmental Panel on Climate Change*. Edited by C. B. Field, V. R. Barros, D. J. Dokken, K. J. Mach, M. D. Mastrandrea, T. E. Bilir, et al. Cambridge, UK, and New York: Cambridge University Press.
Jisheng, Yang. 2012. *Tombstone: The Great Chinese Famine 1959–1962*. New York: Farrar, Straus and Giroux.
Lahsen, Myanna, and Jesse Ribot. 2021. "Politics of Attributing Extreme Events and Disasters to Climate Change." *WIREs Climate Change*. 13:e750. wires.wiley.com/climatechange1of11https://doi.org/10.1002/wcc.750.
Lappé, Francis Moore. 2013. "Beyond the Scarcity Scare: Reframing the Discourse of Hunger with an Eco-mind." *Journal of Peasant Studies* 40 (1): 219–238.

Leichenko, Robin M., and Karen L. O'Brien. 2008. *Environmental Change and Globalization: Double Exposures*. New York: Oxford University Press.
Luhmann, Niklas. 2002. *Risk: A Sociological Theory*. New Brunswick, NJ: Adeline Transaction.
Lukács, György. 1923. *History and Class Consciousness*. London: Pattern Books.
Majid, Nisar, and Stephen McDowell. 2012. "Hidden Dimensions of the Somalia Famine." *Global Food Security* 1: 36–42 http://dx.doi.org/10.1016/j.gfs.2012.07.003.
MFDMB (Ministry of Food and Disaster Management of Bangladesh). 2008. *Super Cyclone Sidr 2007: Impacts and Strategies for Interventions*. Bangladesh Secretariat, Dhaka. Available at: https://www.preventionweb.net/files/9470_cyclonebangladesh.pdf.
Moore, M. 1998. "Death without Taxes: Democracy, State Capacity, and Aid Dependence in the Fourth World." In *Towards a Democratic Developmental State*, edited by Gordon White and Mark Robinson, 86–111. Oxford: Oxford University Press.
Nussbaum, Martha C. 2001. "Adaptive Preferences and Women's Options." *Economics and Philosophy* 17: 67–88.
O'Keefe, Phil, Ken Westgate, and Ben Wisner. 1976. "Taking the Naturalness out of Natural Disasters." *Nature* 260: 566–567.
Osmani, S. R. 2005. "Poverty and Human Rights: Building on the Capability Approach." *Journal of Human Development* 6 (2): 205–219.
Pelling, M. 2003. *The Vulnerability of Cities: Natural Disasters and Social Resilience*. London: Earthscan.
Polanyi, Karl. (1944) 2001. *The Great Transformation*. 2nd ed. Boston: Beacon Press.
Raynaut, Claude. 1998. "Diversité et Dynamique des Relations Sociétés-Nature au Sahel." *Natures Sciences Sociétés* 6 (2): 59–62.
Raynaut, Claude. 2001. "Societies and Nature in the Sahel: Ecological Diversity and Social Dynamics." *Global Environmental Change* 11: 9–18.
Ribot, Jesse. 1995. "The Causal Structure of Vulnerability: Its Application to Climate Impact Analysis." *GeoJournal* 35 (2): 119–122.
Ribot, Jesse. 1998. "Theorizing Access: Forest Profits along Senegal's Charcoal Commodity Chain." *Development and Change* 29 (2): 307–341.
Ribot, Jesse. 2014. "Cause and Response: Climate Vulnerability in the Anthropocene." *Journal of Peasant Studies* 4 (5): 667–705.
Ribot, Jesse. 2022 "Framing Causality and Responsibility: Toward a Sociodicy of Climate-Related Crises." *Journal of Peasant Studies* 49 (4): 683–712.
Ribot, Jesse, Papa Faye, and Matthew Turner. 2020. "Climate of Anxiety in the Sahel: Emigration in Xenophobic Times." *Public Culture* 32 (1): 45–75.
Ribot, Jesse, and Nancy Lee Peluso. 2003. "A Theory of Access: Putting Property and Tenure in Place." *Rural Sociology* 68 (2): 153–181.
Rigaud, Kanta Kumari, Alex de Sherbinin, Bryan Jones, Jonas Bergmann, Viviane Clement, Kayly Ober, et al. 2018. *Groundswell: Preparing for Internal Climate Migration*. Report of the World Bank, Paris.
Rioux, Janie. 2011. *Analyse Globale de la Vulnérabilité, de la Sécurité Alimentaire et de la Nutrition. République du Sénégal 2010*. Rome: Food and Agricultural Organisation of the United Nations.
Robin, Nelly, Richard Lalou, and Mamadou Ndiaye. 2000. *Facteurs d'attraction et de répulsion à l'origine des flux migratoires internationaux*. Rapport National Sénégal. Dakar: IRD et Eurostat.
Rose, Nicolas. 1996. "The Death of the Social? Re-figuring the Territory of Government." *Economy and Society* 25 (3): 327–356.

Sane, Hamide, and Moussa Diallo. 2019. "Tambacounda 2019: Situation Economique et Sociale Regionale." République du Sénégal, Ministère de l' Économie, du Plan et de la Coopération, Agence Nationale de la Statistique et de la Démographie, September.

Schroeder, Richard. 1999. "Community Forestry and Conditionality in the Gambia." *Africa* 69 (1): 1–22.

Sen, Amartya. 1980. "Famines." *World Development* 8 (9): 613–621.

Sen, Amartya. 1981. *Poverty and Famines: An Essay on Entitlement and Deprivation*. Oxford: Oxford University Press.

Sen, Amartya. 1984. "Rights and Capabilities." In *Resources, Values and Development*, edited by Amartya Sen, 307–324. Oxford: Basil Blackwell.

Sen, Amartya. 1999. *Development as Freedom*. New York: A. A. Knopf.

Scott, James C. 1976. *The Moral Economy of the Peasant: Rebellion and Subsistence in Southeast Asia*. New Haven, CT: Yale University Press.

Smucker, Thomas A., and Ben Wisner. 2008. "Changing Household Responses to Drought in Tharaka, Kenya: Vulnerability Persistence and Challenge." In *Changing Household Responses to Drought in Tharaka, Kenya: Vulnerability, Persistence and Challenge*, edited by Ben Wisner. Journal Compilation of the Overseas Development Institute, 190–215. Oxford: Blackwell.

Somers, Margaret R. 2008. *Genealogies of Citizenship, Markets, Statelessness, and the Right to Have Rights*. Cambridge, UK: Cambridge University Press.

Swift, Jeremy. 1989. "Why Are Rural People Vulnerable to Famine?" *IDS Bulletin* 20 (2): 8–15. https://www.tandfonline.com/eprint/3ZVQ24AZRMFPSSER3IK4/full?target=10.1080/03066150.2021.1996355.

Taylor, Charles. 1994. "The Politics of Recognition"." In *Multiculturalism: Examining the Politics of Recognition*, edited by Amy Guttman, 25–74. Princeton, NJ: Princeton University Press.

Turner, Matthew D. 2000. "Drought, Domestic Budgeting and Wealth Distribution in Sahelian Households." Development and Change 3 (4): 1009–1035.

Turner, Billy L., II, Roger E. Kasperson, Pamela A. Matson, James J. McCarthy, Robert W. Corell, Lindsey Christensen, et al. 2003. "A Framework for Vulnerability Analysis in Sustainability Science." *Proceedings of the National Academy of Sciences of the United States of America* 100 (14): 8074–8079.

Turner, Billy L., II, Pamela A. Matson, James J. McCarthy, Robert W. Corell, Lindsey Christensen, Noelle Eckley, et al. 2003. "Illustrating the Coupled Human-Environment System for Vanalysis: Three Case Studies." *Proceedings of the National Academy of Sciences of the United States of America* 100 (14): 8080–8085.

Turner, Matthew, Jesse Ribot, and Oumarou Moumouni. 2022. "Suffering for Dignity and Hope: Young Nigeriens Choose Perilous Trans-Saharan Migration." *Journal of Peasant Studies*. Accepted August 2022. Published online 18 October 2022. https://www.tandfonline.com/eprint/DUCZWZNUYKNUNNAWETZZ/full?target=10.1080/03066150.2022.2121647.

Turner, Matthew, Soumaila Abdoulaye Sambo, Jesse Ribot, and Papa Faye. 2021. In Review [October]. "Climate Migrants? Identifying the Social Causes of Sahelian Trans-Saharan Migration." *Geoforum*.

Turner, Matthew D., and Molly S. Teague. 2019. "Trans-Saharan Labor Emigration from Niger: Local Governance as Mediator of Its Underlying Causes and Consequences." ILCD Working Document No 16. Visby, Sweden: Swedish International Centre for Local Democracy.

United Nations Development Programme. 2015. *Sendai Framework for Disaster Risk Reduction 2015-2030*. Report of Third United Nations World Conference on Disaster Risk Reduction, held from March 14 to 18, 2015 in Sendai, Miyagi, Japan.

VAM (Service de l'Analyse de la Sécurité Alimentaire). 2014. *Analyse de la vulnérabilité globale à la sécurité alimentaire et de la nutrition*. Sénégal, Rome: Programme Alimentaire Mondiale.

Vaughan, Megan. 1987. *The Story of an African Famine: Gender and Famine in Twentieth Century Malawi*. Cambridge, UK: Cambridge University Press.

Watts, Michael J. 1983a. "On the Poverty of Theory: Natural Hazards Research in Context." In *Interpretations of Calamity*, edited by Kenneth Hewitt, 231–261. London: Allen Unwin.

Watts, Michael J. 1983b. *Silent Violence: Food Famine and Peasantry in Northern Nigeria*. Berkeley: University of California Press.

Watts, Michael. 1991. "Entitlements or Empowerment? Famine and Starvation in Africa." *Review of African Political Economy* 51: 9–26.

Watts, Michael J., and Hans Bohle. 1993. "The Space of Vulnerability: The Causal Structure of Hunger and Famine." *Progress in Human Geography* 17 (1): 43–68.

Weheliye, Alexander G. 2014. *Habeas Viscus: Racializing Assemblages, Biopolitics, and Black Feminist Theories of the Human*. Durham, NC: Duke University Press.

White House. 2006. "The Federal Response to Hurricane Katrina." February. Accessed December 5, 2008. https://georgewbush-whitehouse.archives.gov/news/releases/2006/02/20060223.html.

Wilkinson, Iain. 2010. *Vulnerability in Everyday Life*. London: Routledge.

Wisner, Ben, Piers M. Blaikie, and Terrance Cannon. 2004. *At Risk: Natural Hazards, People's Vulnerability and Disasters*, 2nd ed. London: Routledge.

Wolford, Wendy. 2007. "Land Reform in the Time of Neoliberalism: A Many-Splendored Thing." *Antipode* 39 (3): 550–570.

Yohe, G. and R. S. J. Tol. 2002. "Indicators for Social and Economic Coping Capacity—Moving Toward a Working Definition of Adaptive Capacity." *Global Environmental Change* 12 (1): 25–40.

CHAPTER 13

AGRARIAN JUSTICE AND ENVIRONMENTAL JUSTICE

JOAN MARTÍNEZ-ALIER

Introduction: Social Metabolism and Agrarian Studies

THE "eco-modernists" argue that humans should protect nature and improve human well-being by developing technologies that decouple economic growth from environmental impacts. This is a mainstream position, recognized in United Nations Sustainable Development Goal 8, which calls for economic growth everywhere, as if this were a sustainable policy. *Eco-modernism* is similar to what, in 2002, I called "the gospel of eco-efficiency" to describe a political current that is indifferent to the value of "wilderness" and strongly opposed to "the environmentalism of the poor and the indigenous." "Eco-modernism" is successful in public relations, but it does not always work in practice.

Eco-modernism is not new to agrarian studies. Long before the term was invented, Liebig, in 1840, lamented that the large-scale commercial agriculture that was sending products to distant markets did not return the nutrients to the soil. Marx quoted him approvingly. Liebig was an "ecomodernist," in favor of adding fertilizers to the land to compensate for the lack of nutrients. He lamented the possible exhaustion of guano deposits in Peru (because of the high rate of extraction that took place in that commodity frontier from 1840 to 1880), and he proposed introducing factory-made chemical fertilizers to the fields of Europe. He had himself researched some of the biochemical cycles, and he knew what he was talking about (although it was Jean-Baptiste Boussingault who discovered the nitrogen cycle). Liebig signaled this "metabolic gap" (Foster 2000), and he proposed to correct it through the chemical fertilizer industry. We now know that the "metabolic rift"—or "circularity gap" or "entropy hole"—of modern industrial fossil-fuel-based economies is not easily mended (Georgescu-Roegen 1971).

Many years after the introduction of Chilean nitrates (until 1914) and manufactured chemical fertilizers to overcome Liebig's (and Marx's) "metabolic rift" in the nutrient inflow into agriculture, we now complain of excessive nitrogen (N) in water tables, the eutrophication of water bodies, and, at the same time, the gradual exhaustion of phosphorus (P) deposits. The technical remedies of eco-modernism caused new problems. We also learned that the increased reliance of modernized agriculture on fertilizers and other inputs of fossil fuel energy, meant a decrease in the energy return on investment (EROI) of agriculture (Odum 1971; Pimentel et al. 1973). EROI means the energy return on energy input; the acronym was used first by Charles Hall (Hall and Cleveland 1981; Hall, Cleveland, and Kaufmann 1986). Agriculture has always been a system of converting the energy of the sun, and other energy inputs, including from human work, into the kilocalorie (kcal) content of crops and other by-products such as milk, dung, and straw. In 1880, Sergei Podolinsky was one of the first to quantify the energetics of agriculture as a system that produces energy (by photosynthesis) and is open to the entry of sun energy and to energy inputs from human and animal work, gaining, forty years later, Vernadsky's admiration for it (Vernadsky 1924; Martinez-Alier 1990).

In the last decades, we have realized that the EROI—that is, the efficiency of this transformation of energy—declines the more capitalized agriculture becomes, which is an argument that the Via Campesina has made (Martinez-Alier 2011). This finding helps to throw doubt on what Giampietro and Mayumi (2009) have called the "biofuel delusion" or "the fallacy of large scale agro-biofuels production."

Thus, the metabolic view of the agricultural economy has finally become well known (González de Molina and Toledo 2014). It was absent for a long time from mainstream agricultural economics, which described agricultural economy in terms of economic concepts, and not in terms of metabolism. We can speculate on what Marx would have thought of the fantastic boom of the fertilizer industry in Germany and elsewhere in the early twentieth century and of the Haber-Bosch process, discovered in 1914. What would he have thought of "peak oil," the nuclear energy industry and nuclear arms, carbon dioxide emissions from fossil fuels and climate change, and declining EROIs and the increasing human appropriation of net primary production, or "HANPP" (Temper 2016)? It is impossible to say. What we do know is that some of the leading Marxist writers of the early twentieth century, such as Karl Kautsky (*The Agrarian Question* [1899]) and Rosa Luxemburg (*The Accumulation of Capital* [1913]), did not put the quantitative study of human ecology in terms of social metabolism at the center of their preoccupations. They were close to doing so. But, ultimately, they did not.

The Narodnik writers could have based their defense of the peasantry on the metabolic approach, because of the virtues of peasant agriculture from an ecological point of view (less use of fossil fuels, preservation, and the coevolution of seeds). It was, perhaps, still too early (Franco 2019). The opposition between, on the one side, the Chayanovian view of the persistence of the peasantry and, on the other side, the mainstream economic and Leninist views of the obsolescence of the peasantry cannot really be interpreted as an opposition between ecological thinking and economic thinking. Chayanov could have been but was not a proto-ecological economist; perhaps he had no time because of his early death (as a victim of Stalin) to study the energetic and material metabolism of agriculture, as we have done since. He could have made an ecological argument in defense of the peasantry as ecological anthropologists, as Netting, in his praise for smallholders, would do later (Martinez-Alier 1995). To my knowledge, neither did Teodor Shanin become an explicitly ecological pro-peasant writer. He was pro-peasant, but not based on ecological arguments.

To the old Narodnik slogan in Russian and other Slavic languages, *Zemlya i Volya*, "land and freedom" (*Tierra y libertad* in Spanish anarchism and in Zapata's Mexican Revolution of 1910) we should add water and air so that we can properly catalog the many historical and contemporary struggles of peasants and landless workers (and/or Indigenous peoples) to defend themselves against land grabbing, water grabbing, and air pollution. Zapata, whose opposition to the water-guzzling sugar mill industry in Morelos and defense of Indigenous land and water commons sparked the Mexican Revolution, could have used the slogan *Tierra, agua y libertad*. Neruda wrote the famous line "Agua no te vendas" (water do not sell yourself). We could now add "Aire no te vendas" thinking to so many of the conflicts over windmills because of their land and materials requirement (Avila 2018; Temper et al. 2020). Some of these wind- and land-grabbing conflicts take place in Mexico, particularly on the Tehuantepec Isthmus, not far from Morelos, with protagonists who are Indigenous local farmers.

I shall now empirically document some selected socio-environmental conflicts regarding rural land use, drawing mostly from the Environmental Justice Atlas ([EJAtlas]; www.ejatlas.org; Martinez-Alier 2021).

CAFOs in Europe and the United States

A CAFO, or a "concentrated animal feeding operation" (as these are called in the United States but also in China and elsewhere), refers to one that is sized at more than 1,000 animal units. An *animal unit* is the animal equivalent of 1,000 pounds live weight (e.g., 1,000 animal units equals 1,000 heads of beef cattle; 700 dairy cows; 2,500 swines, weighing more than 55 pounds each; 125,000 broiler chickens; or 82,000 laying hens). CAFOs are, in effect, excrement factories.

The opposition to CAFOs adds new issues to the agrarian question, which originally concerned questions of land ownership, forms of land tenure and land use and the exploitation of labor, the persistence or disappearance of the peasantry, and land reforms. The new questions are, Should we consume so much meat? Are we blind to animal suffering? Are we worried about the impact on human health from such concentrations of animals, for example resistance to antibiotics? How is the HANPP increased by the need to provide feedstuffs for so many animals? Is animal excrement being recycled? Here, we are more in the terrain of food regimes (McMichael 2013) than of the traditional agrarian question. Environmental and human health issues gain more relevance.

Some political ecologists study the socio-environmental conflicts that arise concerning CAFOs, and we have started to record some of these conflicts in the EJAtlas. These conflicts are not only NIMBY (not in my backyard) conflicts (i.e., no CAFO in my backyard); they also become NIABY (not in anyone's backyard) conflicts by focusing on land and water use and pollution over wide areas, air pollution, excessive antibiotics use, and possible sources of zoonotic viruses. I will briefly consider some of these conflicts, beginning in France, with *usine à mille vaches*, "the farm of a thousand cows" (Figure 13.1).

The French authorities approved the country's first hyper big cattle-farm project, to be established in the north of France, but the local population and some organizations were strongly against its development. The farm, located in Buigny-Saint-Maclou in the Somme, was the project of Michel Ramery, a local construction-industry mogul, who decided to combine several large-scale dairy farms into a single 1,000-cow, 750-calf unit, linked to the largest anaerobic digestion unit (methanation unit) in Europe. At the forefront of the opposition to the project was the ad hoc resistance group Novissen, made up of local residents and farmers (Novissen is an acronym for "Nos villages se soucient de leur environnement" [Our villages care about their environment), and the Confédération Paysanne (the French branch of the Via Campesina). The farm's importing of GMO soybeans for feed was a key factor in the opposition. In 2021 it was announced that "the farm of a thousand cows" was over. The cattle farm closed its doors on January 1, 2021, after ten years of heated conflict between the environmental activists and the dairy farm owner.

FIGURE 13.1. Members of Novissen protesting against the "usine à mille vaches." Source: EJAtlas.

The United States is a land of CAFOs. Among several cases included in the EJAtlas, I focus on one in rural Michigan, which has been polluted since the 1990s because of weak regulation and government subsidies. The case became well known when Lynn Henning exposed the socio-environmental injustice, and she was awarded the Goldman Environmental Prize in 2010 for her focus on water quality and for fighting the pollution from concentrated animal feeding facilities. The full story of Lynn Henning's efforts would fill several pages. Here is a brief summary.

In a CAFO, high-pressure sprayers remove waste from the floors using powerful chemical solvents. The runoff is channeled into huge open pits or vats on the CAFO's property. This toxic brew of feces and urine, chemical agents, pesticides, hormones, bacteria such as *E. coli*, antibiotics, blood, and even birth fluid and decaying carcass parts is left to ferment for weeks, emitting noxious fumes and dangerous chemical compounds, including methane, ammonia, and hydrogen sulfide. The fermented waste is then trucked or piped to nearby fields where, untreated, it is sprayed as fertilizer, seeping into groundwater supplies and running off into local streams and rivers. The CAFOs typically pay the family farmers, who are often economically stretched to the point of near collapse and need the money, for permission to spray their fields, creating toxic conditions on their property. Henning, a soy and corn farmer, began finding manure leaking into the water shortly after the CAFOs arrived in her rural community of Clayton, in Michigan's Lenawee County. Her mother and father-in-law, both in their eighties at the time and living within three hundred meters (less than a quarter mile) of a CAFO, were diagnosed with hydrogen sulfide poisoning, resulting in irreversible brain damage. There were twelve CAFOs within ten miles of Henning's home, which together housed about 20,000 dairy cattle. Henning and other concerned neighbors formed an environmental justice organization (EJO), the Environmentally Concerned Citizens of South Central Michigan, and brought CAFOs to justice.

The "eco-modernist" political ecologist Paul Robbins famously praised CAFOs as impressive milk- and meat-production enterprises. In a debate in the journal *Political Geography* between partisans of eco-modernism and partisans of degrowth (Robbins 2019; Gómez-Baggethun 2020), Robbins takes the side of the eco-modernists, and Gómez-Baggethun takes the side of the degrowthers. There is a third side to the debate. It is the side of environmental justice, which can go together with "degrowth in practice," as when activists blockade oil or gas pipelines, stop coal-fired power plants or uranium mining, or when CAFOs are stopped by activists for very material reasons.

Pesticides and Plantations

Modern plantation farming has meant the increased use of pesticides. Without pesticides and herbicides, it would be impossible to grow some crops or a much greater amount of human labor would be needed to grow them. The "slow murder" caused by the use of endosulfan on cashew plantations in Kerala, India, is a documented case. "Slow murder" is how Sunita Narain, director of the NGO Centre for Sciences and

Environment in Delhi, described endosulfan pollution (which only with time would show its murderous nature). The Kasargod District of Kerala is famous for its cashew plantations. The Plantation Corporation of Kerala, a state enterprise, cultivates vast areas of land to grow the cashew crop. To protect this crop, the pesticide endosulfan was used, causing significant harm to human health.

Another case in the United States involved César Chavez, founder of the United Farm Workers of California. Here, we see an overlap of working-class environmentalism, rural labor complaints, and human health issues. The first case of childhood cancer was reported in 1978, in the town of McFarland (population: 6,200) in Kern County, California. Over the next seven years, there were thirteen cases of childhood cancer, and in 1985, the county declared McFarland a cancer cluster site. The county's investigation into the possible causes of these cases of childhood cancer focused on exposure to pesticides, hazardous waste, and contaminated drinking water. In particular, the investigation looked at four pesticides used on the county's grape farms, which employed large numbers of migrant workers. In 1988, twelve million pounds of pesticides were used on grapes alone in California, some of which were known to cause cancer. The activist and labor leader César Chavez went on a water-only "fast for life" hunger strike in 1988, partly motivated by the cluster of cancer cases in McFarland, and started a campaign to urge growers to stop using those four pesticides, which he believed caused cancer and birth defects. As part of that effort, the United Farm Workers labor union also started a grape boycott to force the growers to agree to their demands. The hunger strike brought the McFarland problem to national attention and attracted presidential candidate Jesse Jackson and other celebrities to McFarland.

Another case involves international commercial crops such as bananas or soybeans, which also carry rucksacks of pesticides and illnesses. Banana plantations export large amounts of the potassium (K) in bananas, which does not come back to the fields, creating a metabolic gap; they also "virtually" export the large amounts of water used to grow bananas (rather than local crops). Growing bananas also requires the use of pesticides, including the soil fumigant dibromochloropropane (DBCP), which have caused health problems in thousands of workers and their families (Navas 2022). In Central America, Ecuador, and the Philippines, the herbicide glyphosate has become a household name. Large quantities of glyphosate are used in aerial crop spraying on GMO soybean plantations in Argentina and elsewhere, mobilizing local groups try to get it banned, often with the support of health professionals. The Mothers of Ituzaingó in Cordoba, Argentina, were in the vanguard of this movement, together with the network of Pueblos Fumigados (literally, "fumigated towns").

The high prevalence of chronic kidney disease (CKD) has become an environmental health issue of national concern in Sri Lanka. Hypertension and diabetes are known to be the main causes of renal failure, but in areas with high CKD prevalence, the majority of patients do not show any identifiable cause. Endemic kidney disease was recognized in the 1990s in Sri Lanka's North Central Province and North Western Province. More recently, this epidemic was found in the Southern Province near Hambantota as well. The affected area covered approximately 17,000 square kilometers (more than 6,500 square miles), with a population of about 2.5 million, more than 95 percent of whom live in rural areas. The widespread use of agrochemicals and high fluoride levels and the presence of the heavy metals cadmium, lead and arsenic, and uranium in the soil and water are postulated as contributory factors. The highest prevalence of CKD is found among paddy farmers and agricultural laborers. Many of these farmers die simply because they cannot afford the cost of treatment. Apart from the cost, the lack of dialysis facilities in nearby hospitals makes it extremely difficult for the poor to avail themselves of treatment. In most cases, people find out they are sick at a very late stage, so that it is not possible to reverse the disease—again, the "silent killers" and "slow murder." The Centre for Environmental Justice in Sri Lanka and other EJOs have launched campaigns to increase awareness of the problem, which we know is not confined to Sri Lanka.

In El Salvador, Nicaragua, and other Central American countries, cases of CKD have been reported on agricultural plantations, affecting tens of thousands of workers. In the community of Chichigalpa, on Nicaragua's Pacific coast, there is an epidemic of chronic renal failure (CKD). This disease mainly affects young men who work on the sugarcane plantations (although children and women have also been found to be ill). The emergency situation led the communities to form organizations, such as the Chichigalpa Association for Life, made up of former workers and the widows of former workers at the San Antonio sugar mill. The mill, founded in 1890, is today owned by the Pella Group, producers of the famous Flor de Caña rum and ethanol. The affected communities held several demonstrations against the sugar mill asking for compensation and help to buy medicines and treatments for the sick (which are not economically accessible). According to the communities, the demonstrations were repressed. In January 2014, the national police killed Juan de Dios Cortés, forty-eight years old, while he was demonstrating, demanding compensation for his illness.

Carbon Capture in Uganda

Local peoples have often defended forests against capitalist or state logging, and they continue to do so. Famous cases that coincided with the awareness of the environmentalism of the poor in the 1970s and 1980s include the Chipko movement in Uttarakhand in the Himalayas and Chico Mendes's defence of rubber trees as part of the forest in Acre, Brazil (for which he paid with his life). What we discuss here is different. The excessive production of carbon dioxide from the burning of fossil fuels has caused different types of land conflicts. On one hand are the attempts to "capture" CO_2 in tree plantations (in Reducing emissions from deforestation and forest degradation in developing countries (REDD) schemes, which have had well-known social and political failures in Uganda, Ecuador, and elsewhere). On the other is the growth in the use of windmills and solar panels as substitutes for fossil fuels, which is causing a new "plague" of land grabbing (and of mining, for rare earth minerals, conflicts over lithium and cobalt mining, besides the old conflicts over copper and nickel mining at the extraction frontiers).

Here I give examples from Uganda of carbon capture in tree plantations,. The FACE Foundation (Forests Absorbing Carbon Dioxide Emission) was created in 1990, an initiative of the four major Dutch electricity companies of the Dutch Electricity Generating Board. FACE began controversial pine-tree-planting projects in the highlands of Ecuador and in Uganda, in the west of the country at the Kibale National Park, and in the east at Mount Elgon National Park. Some of the foundation's Uganda projects have had turbulent histories, including human rights abuses. The Mount Elgon project involved the planting of twenty native tree species over a total area of 27,000 hectares, sequestering 700,000 tons of CO_2 over its seventeen-year tenure. In 1992 and 1993, forest dwellers and peasants were evicted under the World Bank's Uganda Forestry Rehabilitation Project, cofinanced by the European Union; these evictions were followed by more in 2002.

The performance in 1999 of Green Resources, a Norwegian company with plantations in Mozambique, Tanzania, and Uganda, totaling 45,000 hectares of land, appears to have been even worse. The company acquired a fifty-year license to 2,670 hectares of land in the government-owned Kachung Central Forest Reserve in Northern Uganda. The plantations were registered under the Clean Development Mechanism, and the company sold carbon credits generated from its plantation operations. Green Resources converted grassland, savanna, and small-scale cultivated land into nonnative tree plantations, violently forcing local inhabitants off their land or them denying them access to land to grow food, graze animals, and engage in cultural practices. Land pollution from the use of agrochemicals on the plantations was reported. Finally, on November 3, 2015, the Swedish Energy Agency announced that it was freezing future payments to Green Resources, after an episode aired on Sweden's TV4 program *Kalla Fakta* about the problems that the plantations were causing for local communities. The episode focused on conflicts over land rights. Uncertainties remain about the potential of tree plantations to really sequester carbon (Figure 13.2).

FIGURE 13.2. Uganda: Carbon offsets. Source: Oakland Institute.

Tree Plantations Are Not Forests

Of course, tree plantations are much older than REDD schemes—one of the main reasons for their existence is the appetite for wood of the pulp and paper industries, but there are also rubber plantations and many other types of tree plantations, as well as those for wood. The plantations are land extensions devoted to growing one or a few tree species, geared to the international market. They very often exclude local populations. A great book by Ricardo Carrere and Larry Lohmann (1996) introduced the slogan "Plantations are not true forests." The issue of carbon absorption arose around that time. Tree plantations are a typical extractivist industry; there are hundreds of cases of conflict (many of them documented by the World Rainforest Movement (WRM) network). I shall describe a few of them, starting with eucalyptus plantations Aracruz in Brazil and the resistance to them, and others in India (Figure 13.3). But first, a brief introduction.

With Julien-Francois Gerber and Sandra Veuthey, the author published one of the first articles linking political ecology to ecological economics in tree-plantation conflicts. We focused on Cameroon and Ecuador (*Ecological Economics*, 68, 2009). The EJAtlas was not yet available to study tree-plantation conflicts with a methodology of comparative, statistical political ecology, and so we compared only two case studies.[1]

Today, one of the most (in)famous cases of industrial tree plantations' generating conflict involved the pulp and paper manufacturer Aracruz Celulose, located in the town of Barra do Ribeiro, in the state of Rio Grande do Sul, Brazil. Women played a particular role in this conflict, organizing an action whose name in Portuguese was Mulheres Em Ação, Eucalipto No Chão! (Women in action to cut down the eucalyptus!). On International Women's Rights Day on March 8, 2006, around three thousand women

FIGURE 13.3. Women against the expansion of Eucalyptus. Source: EJAtlas. (Grettel Navas)

from the Via Campesina occupied Aracruz Celulose's eucalyptus nurseries. Just two months earlier, Aracruz Celulose, with the assistance of the federal police, had forced the eviction of Indigenous people in the state of Espírito Santo. The occupation in Barra do Ribeiro was both an expression of solidarity with the evicted Indigenous people in Espirito Santo, and a protest against the "green deserts" in Rio Grande do Sul. The organized women were reported to have destroyed more than five million eucalyptus seedlings to denounce the social and environmental consequences of the advancing eucalyptus monoculture and condemn what they called the "green latifundia" or "green deserts." Women from the Via Campesina, jointly with the Landless Workers' Movement, protested against this monoculture because of the land grabbing it entailed, the large amounts of water it required, and the use of chlorine in the bleaching process for the eucalyptus pulp, which might cause several health problems.

Eucalyptus trees have come to be seen as an invasive species in Portugal and Spain, where they take up water and facilitate fires. "Despite being the wettest region in Spain, Galicia has turned into a wildfire hotspot in recent years; nearly 40 percent of fires in the country between 2001 and 2015 broke out here. Experts have pointed to the increased presence of eucalyptus in the region as one of the causes. The area covered by eucalyptus jumped from 28,000 hectares (69,190 acres) in 1973 to more than 300,000 hectares (741,300 acres) in 2018—more than a tenfold increase in 45 years."[2]

India has been the site of two emblematic cases of anti-eucalyptus-plantation and anti-land-grab conflicts. The first one took place in West Bengal, where Indigenous villagers chopped down around 6,600 young eucalypts on a 6-hectare state forest department plantation. The residents claimed that the land was theirs and they wanted it back. The villagers of Khorikashuli, West Medinipur district, comprising mostly Lodha tribals, used to grow multiple crops on this land, which, they say, provided them with enough food for at least six months a year. One activist said: "In 2001, officials asked for land along the fringes of our fields. Then they took our thumb impressions on some papers and by 2004 they took over all our land." The eucalypt plantation started in 2004 as a fake Joint Forest Management scheme funded by the Union Ministry of Environment and Forests. Under the scheme, after ten years, every family in the village was to receive 25 percent of the cash earned from selling the harvested trees. But the villagers said that they could not afford to wait that long: "Eucalypt doesn't give us food." The Indigenous peoples were thus reclaiming the land under the provisions of the Scheduled Tribes and Other Traditional Forest Dwellers (Recognition of Forest Rights) Act, 2006. The land in question was originally a mahal forest owned by rich landowners or local royalty. The West Bengal Private Forests Act, of 1948, which was the state's first attempt to assert control over the south Bengal forests, stipulated that the rights of the forest dwellers should be recorded and settled by specially appointed forest settlement officers. However, after 1953 no survey was ever conducted.

The second conflict in India, known as the KPL conflict, took place in the 1980s in the state of Karnataka. On November 14, 1984, the government of Karnataka made an agreement with Harihar Polyfibres, a rayon-producing company owned by the Birla family, to form a new company, Karnataka Pulpwood Limited (KPL), owned 51 percent by the government and 49 percent by Birla. The KPL eucalyptus plantation would occupy almost 30,000 hectares in the northern part of Karnataka. The plan ignored the customary land claims of the local villagers, who depended on these lands to meet their basic needs. The move sparked widespread protest by the local villagers and several EJOs. The Samaj Parivartana Samudaya, a Dharward-based NGO, with the support of other organizations and such notable personalities as Shivaram Karanth (a famous writer in Kannada language), Justice D. M. Chandrashekhar, and Kadilal Manjappa, led the Save the Common Lands Movement to reclaim their people's lands and rights. Initially, the campaigners sent petitions to local government officials and met with the chief minister to a plead with him to cancel the KPL agreement. When these efforts did not yield the desired results, the affected people held a series of protest meetings and demonstrations in several places on November 14, 1986, the two-year anniversary of the setting up of the KPL.

In December 1986, a public interest lawsuit was filed in the Supreme Court by Shivaram Karanth, Anil Agarwal (of the Centre for Science and Environment), and others. The Supreme Court issued a stay order on March 24, 1987, maintaining the status quo with regard to the possession of land. However, the KPL continued its operations. Meanwhile, the local people launched a satyagraha on November 14, 1987, now popularly known as the Kunsur satyagraha, with a novel form of protest termed the Kitikho-Hachiko (pluck and plant) satyagraha. Led by drummers and waving banners and shouting slogans, the protesters uprooted eucalyptus seedlings and planted in their place tree species that would be useful for fruit or fodder. In a sustained struggle lasting over seven years, seventy-two legislators from various political parties put effective pressure on the government to close the KPL. On October 3, 1991, the government wound down the KPL. There was a connection to the Chipko movement in the Himalayas of the 1970s: in 1990, on India's Independence Day, August 15, the respected Chipko leader Chandri Prasad Bhatt had led a pluck-and-plant satyagraha in Hirekerur taluka of Dharwad, in northwest Karnataka.

Similarly, the EJAtlas has recorded nearly a hundred conflict cases on oil palm plantations. Where to start? We can do comparative case studies using the EJAtlas (Dell'Angelo et al. 2021). There have been many oil palm plantation conflicts in Southeast Asia, as well as in the Gulf of Guinea and tropical America. In Palawan, a valuable island of the Philippines, for example, Indigenous people and traditional farmers formed the Coalition Against Land Grabbing, which has been very active. In 2014 the coalition submitted a petition calling for a moratorium on oil palm expansion that was signed by more than 4,200 farmers and Indigenous people. Indonesia has had many palm oil conflicts as well. Palm oil companies have engaged in international efforts to "green" their image through the Roundtable on Sustainable Palm Oil, whose goal is to create a "sustainable" palm oil industry, as they continue their expansion.

Fighting against Deforestation in Brazil and Peru

The resistance to illegal logging and land grabbing has led to hundreds of deaths in the state of Pará, Brazil. Among them are the deaths of José Cláudio Ribeiro da Silva, who was known by the nickame "Zé Claudio," and his wife, Maria do Espírito Santo da Silva. The couple had been leading the Praia Alta conservationist group Piranheira Extractive Reserve Project, which had been working to stop land grabbing by outsiders, until they were ambushed near their home and killed, on May 24, 2011. As Felipe Milanez has noted in his doctoral thesis at Coimbra University and in blog entries for the news magazine *Carta Capital* (https://www.cartacapital.com.br/author/felipe-milanez/), one glint of hope in Zé Claudio and Maria's case for justice to be made was the fact that they were murdered the same morning as important revisions to Brazil's Forest Code were voted on in Congress. Their deaths were announced to the country from the floor of the Congress in Brasilia. The killings took place against a background of ongoing campaigns to silence land rights defenders in Brazil. The couple left behind a powerful legacy, but it has not been enough to stop the relentless deforestation of the Amazon. And unlike the rubber tappers of Acre at the time of Chico Mendes's assassination in 1988, they were not defending *seringais* (rubber plantations) but *castanhais*. They considered themselves to be "sustainable extractivists," opposed to the false production, "unsustainable extraction," of timber, cattle, and soybeans. They were local leaders in this alternative vision, and because of it they were killed.

As in Brazil, the Amazon territory in Peru is subject to deforestation. The Melka Group, led by the Czech American businessman Dennis Melka, owns twenty-six companies in Peru, all dedicated to cocoa and oil palm plantations. The Romero Group is another powerful Peruvian conglomerate that since 1979 has invested heavily in oil palm plantations in Amazonia, causing deforestation.

The Melka Group uses various methods, ranging from corruption, fraud, land grabbing from settlers to the purchase of land by settlers and even false settlers to later reacquiring these lands, in violation of national environmental legislation. It has no environmental certification. Thus, deforestation in the Amazon continues and conflicts among populations, the authorities, and the Melka Group multiply. It is estimated that some 13,000 hectares of land has already been deforested. The regional governments have been complicit, providing Melka with information about land to be acquired. The regional governments must carry out the "land classification" and determine the areas to be exploited and those to be protected. In 2013, Indigenous and international organizations filed complaints against the company, including the Indigenous community of Santa Clara de Uchunya (Ucayali), home to more than 760 Shipibo-Conibo people, who saw more than 5,000 hectares of their land sold by the Regional Government of Ucayali. In the hamlet of Bajo Rayal, in the district of Nueva Requena (Ucayali), company workers slashed and burned nearly a thousand hectares of primary forests, pastures, and farmers' crops. Despite the fact that in 2015 the Ministry of Agriculture (MINAGRI) ordered the Melka Group to halt its activities, it continues to operate, and not even anyone in the Public Prosecutor's Office has been able to enter the group's land to enforce the halt.

In May 2016, the 9th Constitutional Court ordered a precautionary measure against MINAGRI and the Regional Government of Loreto in response to a lawsuit filed by the NGO Kene to stop Cacao del Peru Norte, a subsidiary of United Cocoa. In May 2016, protest marches were held to prevent the company from being favored by the court. In October 2016, the company Plantaciones de Pucallpa withdrew from the Roundtable on Sustainable Palm Oil and decided to abandon oil palm production. This followed a complaint filed by the Shipibo community of Santa Clara de Uchunya together with Feconau with others accusing the company of deforestation and land usurpation.

In the lawsuit against Cacao del Perú Norte SAC (now Tamshi SAC), the court ruled against the company; it fined a group of directors 15 million Peruvian soles and sentenced them to eight years in prison for trafficking and deforestation. The decision was not ratified, but the state subsequently appealed the nonratification. The case remains open. Then, in May 2020, Tamshi SAC accused environmental defender and forestry engineer Lucila Pautrat of defamation. In March 2021, the Criminal Court of Lima sentenced her to two years in prison (suspended for one year, and a fine of 50 thousand soles). The Tamshi suit is what is internationally called a SLAPP (strategic lawsuit against public participation), intended to censor, intimidate, and silence critics by burdening them with the costs of a legal defense until they abandon their criticism or opposition.

Wind Energy, Water, and Mining Conflicts That Imply Land Conflicts

We could bring in here other land conflicts, for instance, in coastal areas over the destruction of mangroves by shrimp farming or other encroachments, or, indeed, conflicts that are not about land use but the use of the seas, such as those in Kerala between artisanal fisheries and industrial fisheries that became famous in the 1980s and implied the defense of the commons (see Ertör 2021).

Other land conflicts arise, not from issues of agriculture and plantation forestry (or deforestation), but indirectly, from the land requirements for open-cast coal and metal mining, oil and gas pipelines, windmills and solar panels, and urban sprawl, as well as other types of land grabbing, for instance, by the military. But I want to focus here on the land requirements for wind energy, as seen in a typical conflict with pastoralists in Gujarat.

The EJAtlas records about forty windmill conflicts around the world (Avila 2018). Consider the Suzlon Energy wind farms in Kutch District—a large-scale wind power farm of the Suzlon company has deployed on the coast and wetlands of Kutch, Gujarat, displacing pastoralist peoples and threatening wildlife. India kicked off its energy diversification into wind energy in the 1980s when the Government of India set up the Commission for Additional Sources of Energy (CASE). India is said to have the potential to harness 48,500 megawatts of wind energy at a 50-meter height and 102,788 megawatts at an 80-meter height from wind projects. Gujarat has the greatest potential to generate energy from wind: 10,609 megawatts at a 50-meter height and 35,071 megawatts at an 80-meter height. We know that India is in a transition to coal and to more gas and oil, and that at the same time, it is increasing renewable sources of energy. Hydroelectricity causes very grave conflicts in the Himalayas and elsewhere. The number of windmills is also increasing as is the use of photovoltaic energy. Everything grows, except for *Jatropha*, which proved to be rather a failure.[3]

From the year 2001 onward, the Gujarat state government implemented a special road map of local area development for the Kutch district by integrating it into the global economy. Since then, vast tracts of wasteland, coastline, and grassland areas in Kutch have been allotted to Indian and foreign corporations to establish various industries, including for wind energy and solar energy projects. The area affected by windmills belongs to the coastal villages and the villages surrounding the Little Rann of Kutch. The barricading of the land by massive industrial units and the development of infrastructure road-building projects have blocked the traditional migration routes used by the pastoralists and their herds. This has resulted in the increased marginalization of all the traditional communities—the "ecosystem peoples"—having natural-resource-based economies. This, in turn, has increased social unrest and violence in the region.

Companies such as Suzlon, Vestas, and NEPC have established hundreds of wind power production units across the Little Rann of Kutch, a wild life sanctuary for the wild ass. Suzlon is building a huge wind farm that includes a cluster of windmills surrounding the Little Rann. The first turbine of the Suzlon wind farm was commissioned at the village of Lathedi in December 2005. By 2014, the company had completed the installation of windmills capable of generating 1,100 megawatts of wind power at this wind park. The Suzlon Group is planning to complete a 2,000-megawatt Kutch wind park. Once it is finished, it will become the world's largest wind farm at a single location or belt, capable of producing power equivalent to two large coal-fired or nuclear energy plants. It is easy to be enthusiastic about it, disregarding the ample land requirements not only for the windmills themselves but also for the building and maintenance of roads and the electricity transmission towers and lines.

The authorities have been trying for several years to ban the entry of other migrating cattle herds and salt-panning activities at the Little Rann of Kutch, triggering strong social resistance by the marginalized local salt farmers, cattle breeders, and fishermen. Wind energy companies like Suzlon are allotted land to set up wind farms, at the cost of dispossessing Indigenous people from their common lands. Large-scale wind farms pose a danger to India's grasslands and scrublands, which are officially considered "waste" lands. These areas have little, if any, legal protection against land grabs or environmental degradation. The farms also threaten birdlife, and in windmill conflicts we often see alliances between the local inhabitants, who need land that is now occupied by wind energy parks, and conservationists, who are worried about birds—that is, alliances between "the cult of wilderness" organizations and the local environmentalism of the poor and Indigenous, pastoralists in this case.

India's Ministry of Environment, Forest and Climate Change assumed that, because wind farms produce renewable energy, no environmental impact assessment (EIA) was required for these projects. However, windmills have several socio-environmental impacts. The Centre for Science and Environment and several other organizations lobbied the Indian government to bring wind power projects under the EIA mandate. The most visible impact of windmills on the natural world is their effect on birds and bats. Rich in marine life, the Gulf of Kutch is the breeding ground for endemic prawn species. Many migratory birds come to this wetland, and flamingos congregate in two or three sites. Windmills and the transmission lines pose a risk not only to critically endangered birds, such as the great Indian bustard, but to other species as well, including vultures.

Wind turbines require regular maintenance, but this is done by highly skilled engineers from outside the communities. At most, the wind farms generate a few security jobs for local villagers to guard the windmills. But these are low-wage jobs, because they are outsourced to private security agencies.

Finally, I want to mention the conflicts over the land and water requirements of hydroelectricity, in particular, one in Honduras that resulted in the murder of the environmental activist Berta Cáceres, who was one of several mortal victims in a group that was fighting against a small hydropower project. Land and water was of great cultural and livelihood importance for the Lenca people and the case became memorable for the global movement for environmental justice.

It is obvious that almost all dam projects involve the taking up of land and water and the displacement of people. This requires force and sometimes open violence (Del Bene et al. 2018). Per megawatt of electricity, hydropower is often more land-intensive than nuclear power and even Carbon Free Power Project (CFPP), which, in turn, require coal mining and transport. Biomass energy in the form of ethanol or agro-diesel would be even more land intensive, as noted earlier.

Very big dams are being planned and built all the time, occupying large spaces, for instance, in the Amazon basin, but also in China, the Republic of the Congo, and Ethiopia. Jawaharlal Nehru praised the diversion of land and water for dams as a necessary sacrifice to build these "temples" of modern India, although we do not know what he how he would have responded to the complaints by the Narmada Bachao Andolan.

The Agua Zarca project in Honduras was a small hydropower project in a small country that is marginal in world politics and run by a small military dictatorship at present. The opposition to this project led to the killing of Berta Cáceres (1971–2016) and other environmentalists. The commodities in question were Water, Land, Electricity, and, in this case, impudently, Carbon Offsets. And the keywords are "Indigenous territory," "sacred site," "hydropower," "CDM (Clean Development Mechanism)," the "ILO (International Labour Organization) convention 169," and the

FIGURE 13.4. Berta Cáceres. COPINH is the Consejo Cívico de Organizaciones Populares e Indígenas de Honduras.

"criminalization and murder of activists." They all intersect with the Agrarian Question and Environmentalism and with WED (women environmental defenders) and Indigenous peoples. Berta Cáceres was a leader of peasant, Indigenous, and environmentalist movements. (Figure 13.4) Her death resonated globally, partly because she had recently been awarded a Goldman Prize. In Latin America she has become known as the Chico Mendes of the early twenty-first century. The financing of the Agua Zarca dam by European banks was eventually withdrawn.

Conclusion: The Cornering of Communal Land and Water for Biomass and Energy Production and the Resistance to It

In the past, generally speaking, agrarian studies did not really focus on environmental issues, separating issues that are economic and social (such as land reform or land redistribution or rural labor exploitation and migration) from those of human ecology and the study of social metabolism. This started to change in the 1970 and 1980s with some economic anthropologists and ethnoecologists, with Victor Toledo's (1990) work on "the ecological rationality of peasant production," and with the political ecology of Blaikie and Brookfield (1987), among other contributions. Socio-environmental conflicts are not extraterrestrial, although some geoengineering experiments might take place in the upper atmosphere trying to stop incoming solar radiation to compensate for the enhanced greenhouse effect. There are also plans to travel to the moon for new materials. Leaving this aside, environmental conflicts imply disputes on access to land, water, and breathable air on planet Earth. But such disputes are the effects, whereas the causes are growth and the changes in the social metabolism and the technologies used to expand or deepen the commodity extraction frontiers to get energy and materials. To get more biomass production, you have to get land, water for irrigation, and pesticides to eliminate competitors. To get more fish, you need bigger boats and more energy, and that eventually will eliminate some fisheries. To get land for cattle farming or export crops, you deforest, and eventually, you replace true forests with uniform tree plantations and get carbon credits.

Leaving anecdotal evidence aside, one would like to ask and get answers to these questions:

1. Who are the main protagonists in such conflicts, on both sides? National public or private companies or transnational companies? The police and the military? Farmers, peasants, and pastoralists representing the environmentalism of the poor and the Indigenous, sometimes belonging to groups affiliated to Via Campesina but certainly not always? The activists that appear in conflicts in this chapter sometimes belong to organizations that are also members of Friends of the Earth International—but this is not the rule. Sometimes the activists belong to religious groups or are professionals (such as Dr. Carrasco and Dr. Medardo Avila in the Madres de Ituzaingó conflict over glyphosate in Argentina). Often they are WEDs, women environmental defenders. Some might even be awarded a Goldman Prize and become well known—though this might not always stop the violence against them.
2. Which repertoires of contention are displayed in such struggles? For instance, direct action blockades but also simple letter writing, judicial activism, public consultations? And what forms of violence are used against socio-environmental activists and local inhabitants—not only open violence, not only "slapping" threats, but also racist violence and the "slow violence" of toxins (Navas et al. 2018)?
3. What are the outcomes? How often are investment projects that take land, water, and air away from communal use for commercial use stopped by local socio-environmental activists? Social movements need some successes from time to time to keep going, and the world movements for environmental justice are no exception to this rule.
4. Which social values are displayed, such as, for instance, livelihood values, sacredness, ecological values, archaeological and other cultural values? How often is money compensation offered, and it is really equivalent to other values which are sacrificed?

Notes

1. J.-F. Gerber, one of the main contributors to EJAtlas, also wrote the first statistical article on the political ecology of tree plantations, based on a large sample of conflicts. See Julien-François Gerber (2011), "Conflicts over Industrial Tree Plantations in the South: Who, How and Why?," *Global Environmental Change* 21 (1): 165–176.
2. CNN. https://cyclejackson.com/2021/08/23/spanish-volunteers-remove-eucalyptus-in-bid-to-prevent-wildfires/.
3. Pere Ariza-Montobbio, Sharachchandra Lele, Giorgos Kallis, and Joan Martinez-Alier (2010), "The Political Ecology of Jatropha Plantations for Biodiesel in Tamil Nadu, India," *Journal of Peasant Studies* 37 (4): 875–897.

References

Avila, S. 2018. "Environmental Justice and the Expanding Geography of Wind Power Conflicts." *Sustainability Science* 13 (3): 599–616.

Blaikie P., and H. Brookfield, eds. 1987. *Land Degradation and Society*. London and New York: Methuen.

Carrere, Ricardo, and Larry Lohmann. 1996. *Pulping the South: Industrial Tree Plantations and the World Paper Economy*. London: Zed Books.

Del Bene, Daniela, Arnim Scheidel, and Leah Temper. 2018. "More Dams, More Violence? A Global Analysis on Resistances and Repression around Conflictive Dams through Co-produced Knowledge." *Sustainability Science* 13 (3): 617–633.

Dell'Angelo, Jampel, G. Navas, M. Witteman, G. D'Alisa, A. Scheidel, and L. Temper. 2021. "Commons Grabbing and Agribusiness: Violence, Resistance and Social Mobilization." *Ecological Economics* 184. https://doi.org/10.1016/j.ecolecon.2021.107004.

Ertör, Irmak. 2021. "'We Are the Oceans, We Are the People!': Fisher People's Struggles for Blue Justice." *Journal of Peasant Studies* 50 (3): 1157–1186. https://doi.org/10.1080/03066150.2021.1999932.

Franco, Marco Vianna. 2019. "Essays on the History and Philosophy of Ecological Economic Thought." PhD diss. Belo Horizonte, Brazil: Universidade Federal de Minas Gerias (UFMG). Belo Horizonte, Brazil: Universidade Federal de Minas Gerais (UFMG)

Foster, John Bellamy. 2000. *Marx's Ecology: Materialism and Nature*. New York: Monthly Review Press.

Georgescu-Roegen, Nicholas. 1971. *The Entropy and the Economic Process*. Cambridge, MA: Harvard University Press.

Gerber, J. F., Veuthey, S., and Martínez-Alier, J. (2009). Linking political ecology with ecological economics in tree plantation conflicts in Cameroon and Ecuador. *Ecological Economics* 68 (12): 2885–2889.

Giampietro, Mario, and Kozo Mayumi. 2009. *The Biofuel Delusion: The Fallacy of Large Scale Agro-Biofuels Production*. London: Routledge.

Gómez-Baggethun, Erik. 2020. "More Is More: Scaling Political Ecology within Limits to Growth." *Political Geography* 76 (January): Article 102095. https://doi.org/10.1016/j.polgeo.2019.102095.

González de Molina, Manuel, and Víctor M. Toledo. 2014. *The Social Metabolism: A Socio-ecological Theory of Historical Change*. Cham: Springer.

Hall, Charles, and Cutler Cleveland. 1981. "Petroleum Drilling and Production in the United States: Yield per Effort and Net Energy Analysis." *Science* 211 (4482): 576–579.
Hall, Charles, Cutler Cleveland, and Robert Kaufmann. 1986. *Energy and Resource Quality: The Ecology of the Economic Process*. New York: Wiley.
Martinez-Alier, Joan. 1990. *Ecological Economics: Energy, Environment and Society*. Oxford: Blackwell.
Martinez-Alier, Joan. 1995. "In Praise of Smallholders." *Journal of Peasant Studies* 25: 140–148.
Martinez-Alier, Joan. 2011. "The EROI of Agriculture and Its Use by the Via Campesina." *Journal of Peasant Studies* 38 (1): 145–160.
Martinez-Alier, Joan. 2021. "Mapping Ecological Distribution Conflicts: The EJAtlas." *Extractive Industries and Society* 8 (4): Article 10083. https://doi.org/10.1016/j.exis.2021. 02.003.
McMichael, Philip. 2013. *Food Regimes and Agrarian Questions*. Halifax, NS, Canada: Fernwood Press.
Navas, Grettel, et al. 2018. "Violence in Environmental Conflicts: The Need for a Multidimensional Approach." *Sustainability Science* 13 (3): 649–660.
Navas, Grettel. 2022. "If There's No Evidence, There's No Victim': Undone Science and Political Organisation in Marginalising Women as Victims of DBCP in Nicaragua." *Journal of Peasant Studies*. Online, March 6. https://doi.org/10.1080/03066150.2021.2024517.
Odum, H. T. 1971. *Environment, Power, and Society*. New York: Wiley-Interscience.
Pimentel, David, L. E. Hurd, A. C. Bellotti, M. J. Forster, I. N. Oka, O. D. Sholes, et al. 1973. "Food Production and the Energy Crisis." *Science* 182: 443–449.
Robbins, Paul. 2019. "Is Less More . . . or Is More Less? Scaling the Political Ecologies of the Future." *Political Geography* 76: Article 10218. https://doi.org/10.1016/j.polgeo.2019.04.010.
Temper, Leah 2016. "Who Gets the HANPP (Human Appropriation of Net Primary Production)? Biomass Distribution and the Bio-economy in the Tana Delta, Kenya." *Journal of Political Ecology* 23 (1): 410–433.
Temper, Leah, Sofia Avila, Daniela Del Bene, Jennifer Gobby, Nicolas Kosoy, Philippe Le Billon, et al. 2020. "Movements Shaping Climate Futures: A Systematic Mapping of Protests against Fossil Fuel and Low-Carbon Energy Projects." *Environmental Research Letters* 15 (12): Article 123004.
Toledo, Víctor M. 1990. "The Ecological Rationality of Peasant Production." In *Agroecology and Small Farm Development*, edited by M. Altieri and S. B. Hecht, Boca Raton, FL: CRC Press.
Vernadsky, V. I. 1924. *La Géochimie*. Paris: Alcan.
"The CAFO-like 'Farm of a Thousand Cows,' France." (Gabriel Weber, J. Martínez-Alier). https://ejatlas.org/conflict/the-farm-of-a-thousand-cows.
"CAFO Pollution in Lenawee County, Michigan." (Dalena Tran). https://bit.ly/324ydZ8.
"Pesticides and Childhood Cancer, California, USA." (Sara Orvis, University of Michigan). https://ejatlas.org/conflict/pesticides-and-childhood-cancer.
"Agrochemical Pesticides and Kidney-Related Diseases, Sri Lanka." (CEJ Sri Lanka and Paula Camisani). https://bit.ly/3wP1YYN.
"Epidemia de insuficiencia renal crónica (IRC) en las plantaciones de caña, Nicaragua." (Grettel Navas). https://bit.ly/3tioVkT.
"FACE Project: Rehabilitation of Mt. Elgon and Kibale National Park, Uganda." (Patrick Bond). https://bit.ly/3wX7Lve.
"Forest Plantation by Green Resources in Kachung, Uganda." (EJAtlas Team). https://bit.ly/32emeVA.
"West Bengal Eucalyptus Conflict, India." (J.-F. Gerber). https://bit.ly/3s6QcsP.

"KPL conflict, Karnataka, India." (J.-F. Gerber). https://bit.ly/3J4y499.
"Illegal Logging, Land Grabbing and Deaths of Zé Claudio and Maria do Espirito Santo, Pará, Brazil." (J. Martínez-Alier). https://bit.ly/3teucd8.
"Deforestación en Loreto y Ucayali por Grupo Melka, Perú." (Raquel Neyra). https://bit.ly/3sg58Bm.
"Deforestation by Grupo Romero in Amazonia with Oil Palm Plantations, Peru." (Raquel Neyra). https://ejatlas.org/conflict/deforestacion-en-selva-peruana-por-cultivo-de-palma-de-aceite-peru.
"Santa Clara de Uchunya against Palm Oil Plantation, Peru." (Thomas Younger).
"Suzlon Energy Wind Farms in Kutch District, India." (Sofía Ávila and J. Martínez-Alier). https://bit.ly/2RA9OFv.
"Proyecto Hidroeléctrico Agua Zarca, Honduras." (Grettel Navas and Daniela Del Bene). https://bit.ly/3tkziVp.

CHAPTER 14

SOCIOECOLOGICAL RELATIONS IN LAND POLITICS

An Assemblage Perspective

MARVIN JOSEPH F. MONTEFRIO

LAND'S SOCIOECOLOGICAL RELATIONS

AN immersion into the study of land politics compels us to first ask, What is land? Li (2014) answers this question by framing land as having plural social and material dimensions. It has multiple beings, affordances, uses, and meanings, depending on how, where, and when the question is asked and to whom it is addressed. Common in the conception of land, though, is its treatment as an ecological resource that either structures the existence of the social world or is subject to exploitation and change by human activities.[1]

From a scholarly perspective, the ways in which we have thought about the social and material dimensions of land and their relations with each other are diverse. The natural sciences, for example, have focused on understanding the workings of land's biophysical dimensions, and some scholars have drawn from sociobiology (Wilson 1975) and evolutionary psychology (Kurzban 2012) to explain the biological basis and Darwinian evolution of social behaviors. Responding to the growing need to address environmental problems in the mid-twentieth century, the environmental sciences have focused on the impacts of human populations on the biotic and abiotic elements of land. On the integrative social science side, cultural ecologists have examined how humans adapt to diverse environments and the social practices, systems of meanings, and technologies they have created to respond flexibly to environmental change and stresses (Steward 1955; Rappaport 1979; Harrison 1993). Political ecology has critiqued the political ambivalence of cultural ecology and environmental science, asserting that adaptation and environmental change should be situated vis-à-vis broader structural forces. Rather than just accept a narrative of (mal)adaptation to environmental change that risks blaming peasants and smallholder farmers, political ecologists have sought to link socioecological relations observed on the ground to multiscalar political economic forces, such as colonialism and the regional and international dynamics of capitalist accumulation (Watts 1983, 2000; Blaikie and Brookfield 1987; Peet and Watts 1996). Political ecology has also complicated the tendency to represent agrarian communities as unitary, cohesive wholes by framing socioecological relations as land politics depicting power differentials and struggles across social hierarchies within and beyond localities (Watts 2004; Mosse 2010).[2]

As political ecology gains traction in the study of land politics and its socioecological relations (Walker 2005), it continues to negotiate the balance between the social (political) and the ecological. Vayda and Walters (1999), for example, critique the propensity of political ecology to have a priori theories that place importance on political factors in explaining environmental change.[3] Within political ecology, scholars have asked how sufficiently ecological and political the field is, can, and should be. The field does have roots in cultural ecology and environmental science, and many of the books and papers published in the 1980s and 1990s contain detailed ecological analysis. (See Bunker 1984 on the use of flows of energy and matter in his world systems analysis; Hecht 1985 on the analysis of biogeochemical quality of Amazon soils in the political economy context of ranching subsidies; and Turner 1998 on the impacts of grazing on the spatial distribution of plant nutrients, to name a few.) Peter Walker (2005) contends that the accusation that political ecology is becoming a study of "politics without ecology" is exaggerated. But with the poststructuralist turn in political ecology, he urges political ecologists to reflect on to what extent the field should remain inclusive of the biophysical and ecological sciences.

Meanwhile, social science disciplines that contribute to political ecology have gone through a "material turn" or "ontological turn" that began the 1990s (Coole and Frost 2010). Part of this wave of scholarship conceives of our world as complex webs of human and nonhuman relations that are contingent, processual, plural, and emergent, challenging essential and enduring identities in social theorizing (Coole and Frost 2010, 27–28; Escobar 2007).[4] Various concepts and theories have emerged with the material and ontological turn, including those that examine sociomaterial relations as *assemblages* (Fletcher 2023; Fox and Alldred 2015).[5] Many of these theories have been adopted in disciplines such as sociology, geography, and anthropology, including integrative critical social science fields such as political ecology. The material and ontological turn has, then, furthered the scholarship on land as studied by critical integrative fields such as political ecology, development studies, environmental studies, and food and agrarian studies, raising promising intellectual trajectories but also sparking debates.

In this chapter I discuss the emergence, current developments in, and the potential trajectories of studying the socioecological dimensions of land politics, specifically through the joint lens of assemblage scholarship and political economy and political ecology (see Gutiérrez-Escobar on poststructuralism and the more-than-human in this volume). I argue that this approach captures the conception of land as having multiple social and material dimensions that often play out in land politics. The merits of adding an assemblage perspective in studying the political economy/ecology of land are its ability to add layers of explanation and nuance to the dynamics of land politics and power, as well as to reveal emergent relations that expose fissures in structures of dominance. A meaningful analysis can be achieved by striking a balance between the propensity of the assemblage perspective to complexify power and the emphasis in political economy/ecology to interrogate structures of dominance. I then illustrate the value of an assemblage perspective by providing a socioecological analysis of two case studies of plantation politics in the Philippines.

Multiple Conceptions of Assemblages

There are several conceptions of assemblages as relational views of sociomaterial realities. One is actor-network theory (ANT), associated with Bruno Latour, Michel Callon, and John Law. Another version is taken from Gilles Deleuze and Félix Guattari's *A Thousand Plateaus: Capitalism and Schizophrenia* (1987), which draws from dynamical systems theory, a body of scholarship that explores complex co-evolutions, chaos, self-organization, and emergence. Manuel DeLanda, in his book *A New Philosophy of Society* (2006), further developed Deleuze and Guattari's version to propose an assemblage theory. I will refer to the versions of Deleuze, Guattari, and DeLanda collectively as *assemblage thinking*. There are those who have combined these two threads of scholarship in their theorizing of sociomaterial relations (see Bennett 2010; Müller and Schurr 2016); others have proposed a similar concept that uses the term "assemblage" but without heavily referencing ANT and assemblage thinking (see, for example, Tsing 2015).

There are notable differences among the various conceptions of assemblage, but almost all the conceptions depict the world as made up of complex and *emergent* associations of humans and nonhumans. Both ANT and assemblage thinking examine the coming together of human and more-than-human actants (or entities playing an active role) in the formation and dissolution of sociomaterial relations. ANT has a more established set of theories that examine these formations in depth. For example, its concept of *translation* depicts how human and nonhuman entities (such as smallholder farmers, state and nonstate institutions, farming technologies, animals, plants, soil, and synthetic pesticides in the agrarian and environmental context) are transformed and enrolled to fit within a socioecological network (e.g., the high-input industrial agri-food system). This process of translation can reinforce itself to eventually result in the stabilization of the network, the durability of which is enabled by the continual interaction of the actants involved (Callon 1990).

A useful concept in ANT is "action at a distance," which explains how networks are formed and sustained across far spatial distances, as in the case of the globalization of the agri-food system. According to Latour (1987), technologies of communication, transport, and inscription allow the centers of networks (often the "West" or the "Global North" in the context of agri-food systems) to "act at a distance" to transform worlds in their own image. An example is the transfer of scientific facts through food-certification standards and agriscientific practices, which may fail to respect the complexities of local food systems (Kloppenburg 1991; Campbell and Stuart 2005; Yates-Doerr 2012) and result in adverse agrarian and environmental change, as is typically seen in the establishment of monocrop plantations. In an assemblage perspective, however, the effects of "action at a distance" may not necessarily be linear and predictable. ANT scholars suggest that some level of flexibility in knowledge and material flows can take place. In the process of translation, knowledge and materials moving across geographies can be distorted, albeit not completely deviating from the original source (Latour 1983, 1987, 2005). Hence, "action at a distance" may not redefine worlds to the *exact* images of the centers of networks, because distortions can take place (see, for example, Montefrio 2020; Montefrio et al. 2020).

Although ANT has the theoretical tools to describe the formation and stability of networks, assemblage thinking reminds us that these networks (sociomaterial relations) cannot just remain stable or change incrementally. In assemblage thinking, an assemblage (*agencement* in French) denotes an arrangement and/or fitting together of two or more parts (or actants; Phillips 2006), just as ANT depicts. However, assemblage thinking puts more emphasis on the plurality and uncertain trajectory of assemblages, because these sociomaterial relations are perpetually in flux (Deleuze and Guattari 1987; Deleuze and Parnet 1987). Hence, one cannot presume that an assemblage has achieved a final essence or that it has completed its process of becoming (Nail 2017). Furthermore, the coming together of various parts to form assemblages may result in the creation of something entirely new (DeLanda 2006). This is referred to as *emergence*, a concept borrowed from ecological systems dynamics, which allows for the possibility of unpredictability and surprise. Finally, assemblages are not always coherent wholes; they can be incongruous, disconnected, tense, and laden with contradictions (Anderson and McFarlane 2011; Allen 2011). Tsing's (2015) variant captures this, describing assemblages as polyphonic—that is, with multiple harmonious and dissonant rhythms and trajectories from which unintentional coordination could develop. These characteristics will become more comprehensible later when I illustrate how the coming together of elite institutions, capital, technoscientific agricultural knowledge, smallholder farmers, and more-than-human entities inhabiting lands may not always result in the dominance of industrial agriculture over smallholder systems.

The fluidity of assemblages as depicted by Deleuze, Guattari, and DeLanda can be described by the interplay of two processes: *(de)territorialization* and *(de)coding*. Territorialization is the process of consolidation, stabilization, and homogenization of an assemblage's identity (similar to ANT's network stabilization), which can be achieved by solidifying spatial boundaries and excluding certain human and nonhuman actants. One can imagine, for example, the consolidation of industrial agriculture. Conversely, deterritorialization is a process of destabilization, heterogeneity, and the erosion of the consistency of an assemblage's identity. Coding is the process by which particular discourses are used to facilitate the stabilization and homogenization of an assemblage's identity. On the other hand, decoding is the process of using discourses that disrupt or destabilize an assemblage's identity (Deleuze and Guattari 1987; DeLanda 2006, 2016; Dovey 2010). The combined processes of (de)territorialization and (de)coding, then, produce various types of assemblage trajectories (Nail 2017): *relative negative*, or the reproduction of an established territorial, statist, or capitalist assemblage (e.g., the co-optation of alternative food movements into the hegemonic industrial food regime); *absolute positive*, or the creation of an entirely new assemblage that escapes the capture of established territorial, statist, or capitalist assemblages (e.g., the emergence of successful agrarian alternatives); *relative positive*, or the process of change that is ambiguously located between a new assemblage or a co-opted one; and *absolute negative*, or the rejection of any form of organized assemblage. Based on this typology, not all assemblage formations then result in emergence or the formation of something novel.

Many scholars have since built on one or more of these conceptions of assemblage, adopting them in various sociomaterial contexts, including land politics in the context of food, agrarian, and environmental studies.

Assemblages and Land Politics

The introduction of assemblage perspective in agriculture and food studies—bodies of scholarship that tackle various facets of land politics—goes back to the late 1990s as part of the material and ontological turn in the social sciences. Scholars who study the political economy of the industrial agri-food system, the globalization of food, and the emergence of alternative food movements have advocated for the adoption of ANT in an attempt to bridge the seeming ontological divide between humans and nonhumans in the study of food and agriculture (Busch and Juska 1997; Whatmore and Thorne 1997; de Sowa and Busch 1998; Goodman 1999; Guthman 2002; Raynolds 2002). Assemblage thinking, on the other hand, has also been increasingly adopted in critical food, agrarian, rural, and environmental studies, with varying attention to the more-than-human in sociomaterial relations relevant to land politics (see, for example, Li 2007; Le Velly and Dufeu 2016; Guthman 2019; Montefrio 2020; Montefrio et al. 2020; Wang 2021). Some of these studies directly contribute to debates in critical agrarian studies, such as de- or re-agrarianization and the future of family and smallholder farming (see Dressler, Smith, and Montefrio 2018; Hebinck 2018; Hebinck, Mtati, and Shackleton 2018; van den Berg et al. 2018) and processes of inclusion and exclusion (Astuti and McGregor 2017).

Assemblages can add layers of explanation to our understanding of socioecological phenomena that appear to be path dependent, where past decisions and outcomes constrain later events that result in an almost predictable trajectory. In her exploration of California's strawberry industry, Guthman (2019) asserts, "Assemblage thinking enriches the explanation about how the strawberry industry came to rely on fumigants, as well as how this same reliance ultimately undermined the conditions of strawberry production, leading to iatrogenic harm" (17). While the pesticide treadmill is a well-documented phenomenon, Guthman's use of assemblage thinking uncovered the complex relations among material things (plants, pathogens, fumigants etc.), environments (soils and climate), and social forces (policies, land rents etc.) that are entangled in the strawberry industry. Her socioecological analysis goes beyond just narrating the emergence of novel pathogens and iatrogenic harm; it also uncovers how these problems reverberate throughout the strawberry assemblage and to other assemblages that have emerged from it, such as the network of institutions and technologies that develop and administer the repair. As Adam Romero noted, Guthman's analysis makes us realize that the solution cannot be simple, such as finding an alternative to chemical fumigants, as the problem is so much more complex and entrenched in multiple layers within and beyond the agri-industrial strawberry assemblage (Lave et al. 2021, 45–46).

The analytical power of an assemblage perspective, however, lies not just in adding layers to our understanding of the political economy of land politics. Its openness to emergence leaves room for unpredictable and surprising outcomes in seemingly familiar narratives. From a political economy perspective, a preliminary examination of a situation of land politics may immediately invite the usual hypotheses. For example, an industrial agricultural system may trigger the commodification of land and its resources, which may lead to accumulation through the dispossession and exclusion of smallholder farmers, resulting in the erosion of peasant and Indigenous moral economies and the homogenization of market values in the locality of concern. An assemblage perspective may uncover fissures in this narrative. Instead of seeing the situation as deterministically leading to the reproduction of an established capitalist assemblage (relative negative trajectory), the *possibility* of a new one may emerge (i.e., an absolute positive trajectory). The case studies I discuss below illustrate this kind of emergence.

In most circumstances, however, an assemblage lens would uncover ambiguous trajectories that are contradictory (i.e., a relative positive trajectory). For example, Legun (2015) shows how technologies can reproduce entrenched power structures in food systems, while at the same time providing openings for alternative forms of assemblage. As she shows with the case of the apple industry in the Midwest United States, dwarfing rootstock technologies appear to perpetuate a neoliberal ethic and greater integration with market governance. Yet they also facilitate experimentation with diverse market strategies that move away from large-scale commodity production. Moreover, when analyzed temporally, assemblages in land politics often exhibit fluidity and instability over time (see, for example, Wang 2021 on translocal organic food markets in East Asia; and Santo and Moragues-Faus 2019 on the unstable, transitory, and place-contingent nature of local policy groups and their role in shaping the assemblage of translocal agri-food governance).

There is potential in incorporating an assemblage perspective in the critical study of land politics. Although this analytical approach has gained traction in critical food, agriculture, rural, and environmental studies, there remains a vibrant debate over whether or not it can interface with critical scholarship that interrogates and challenges uneven power dynamics in land politics.

Assemblages and Power

Throughout history, land politics has been rife with uneven power dynamics involving colonial, imperial, statist, patriarchal, capitalist, and neoliberal forces. This reality has urged critical studies on land politics, such as from a political economy/ecology perspective, to focus on comprehending structures of dominance and their impacts on societies and environments across geographies and time (in this volume, see McMichael on food regimes, Patel on the world-ecology perspective, Ribot on access, and Bernstein on Marxism). And because the impacts are disconcertingly pervasive, many of these studies have also carried a normative approach, finding not just explanations of problems but also solutions to address the social inequalities and environmental harms wrought by uneven power dynamics (see, for example, Vandermeer and Perfecto on agroecology, and Holleman on ecosocialism, this volume). How, then, does an assemblage lens fit this scholarly tradition?

An assemblage perspective complicates our understanding of power. Rather than being something that is possessed, accumulated, and used by human entities within assemblages, power is conceived of as an emergent outcome of human and nonhuman associations within socioecological networks. Because of the emergent nature of power, some assemblage scholars, particularly from the ANT tradition, urge analysts of sociomaterial relations to have no a priori assumptions about how power operates in any given system (Callon and Law 1995; Latour 2005). Many scholars who identify with assemblage thinking also caution against an overemphasis on hegemonic power structures, but they do not abandon the possibility of unequal power relations (Anderson and McFarlane 2011). Thus power dynamics can be as fluid and messy as the assemblages themselves. It is the complexifying of power vis-à-vis the commitment to challenge dualities and categories that faces skepticism.

Several scholars are critical of assemblage scholarship, based on the view that certain conceptions of assemblage tend to accord symmetric treatment to humans and nonhumans and to flatten power dynamics in their analysis. For example, Lave's (2015) sharp critique of ANT asserts that "a Latour-inspired analysis of a development project would focus on the construction and extent of the network supporting the project, not on the legacies of colonialism, global political economy, racism, and sexism that shape who is enrolled and what level of influence they are accorded within that network" (218; see also Fine 2005). Similarly, McCall Howard (2018) points out that the emphasis on the diversity of more-than-human actors has resulted in a decentering of our understanding of the political-economic forces shaping land and land politics. She sees this as problematic, as it steers our attention away from the social inequalities that capitalist relations bring about. To confront the ecological crises we face, especially at the global level, it is, then, crucial that we continue understanding the dynamics of capitalist-driven social inequalities. McCall Howard adds, "What is actually needed is an identification, analysis, and sharp critique of the human activities that have brought the planet to the present crisis, and which can potentially assist with action to change the systems responsible" (76; see also Hartwick 2000).

Other scholars recognize the value of an assemblage perspective (and the ontological turn, in general), but express concerns about the development of the scholarship. Kinkaid (2020) acknowledges that assemblage thinking might be able to provide a more nuanced understanding of the (re)production of social inequalities, but cautions that "in disavowing social categories [race, gender, sexuality etc.], assemblage thinking may further obscure the operations of power and inequality" (469; see also Davis et al. 2019 on how assemblages potentially obscure racial violence). Todd (2015) likewise recognizes the promise of assemblages and the ontological turn in decolonizing knowledge, but she also admits that the epistemes behind these bodies of scholarship remain Euro-American-centric (Todd 2016; see also Sundberg 2013). By neglecting important epistemes in academic discourse—such as Indigenous knowledge—assemblage scholarship not only may obscure dominant powers in its analysis but also perpetuate the legacies of colonialism and imperialism by continuing the dominance of the Euro-American academy.

A significant question in the debate is whether critical scholarship that challenges structures of dominance, such as political economy/ecology, should incorporate assemblage concepts in its analysis. Such concern stems from the growing number of critical scholars who engage the assemblage scholarship, many of whom study issues related to land politics, as I illustrated earlier. ANT is particularly contentious. Several critical scholars who are strongly associated with the political economy tradition, such as Swyngedouw (2009) and Robbins (2007), readily incorporate ANT concepts into political ecology and critical socioecological analysis. Their levels of engagement vary, some being more circumspect than others, such as Whatmore (1999), who *cautiously* promotes ANT. Others, however, strongly advise against such incorporation, arguing that incompatible theories should not be put together in the first place (Fine 2005; Lave 2015). Castree (2002) recognizes ANT's incompatibilities with political economy/ecology, but still argues that reconciliation is possible with weaker versions of ANT. A weaker ANT analysis would mean recognizing power asymmetries and the role of structures of dominance, while simultaneously recognizing that neoliberal and capitalist structures are nontotalizing, that power may not necessarily be concentrated, and that agency can exist in sociomaterial relations (135).

Meanwhile, political economy studies that draw on the variant described by Deleuze, Guattari, and DeLanda seem to comfortably fit an assemblage perspective into their analysis. The critical food, agrarian, and environmental studies employing assemblage thinking that I mentioned earlier (e.g., Li 2007; Astuti and McGregor 2017; Dressler, Smith, and Montefrio 2018; Hebinck 2018; Hebinck, Mtati, and Shackleton 2018; van den Berg et al. 2018; Guthman 2019; Montefrio 2020; Wang 2021) did not shy away from a political economic lens that continued to critique structures of dominance. Kinkaid

(2020) also provides examples of assemblage thinking that continues to confront the power differentials of social categories, such as Weheliye's (2014) *Habeas Viscus*, which brings together assemblage thinking and feminist and antiracist analytics. Perhaps these scholarly trends are unsurprising, as assemblage thinking recognizes that the power dynamics within a particular assemblage can be contingent on the larger, systemic assemblages where it is nested (Collier 2006; DeLanda 2006). What this means is that power relations in assemblages should not always be flattened, as human and nonhuman relations may generate varying kinds and degrees of power depending on the particular context in which they are situated (Bennett 2010). In the context of land politics, the assemblages being examined are often, if not always nested, in already established territorial, statist, and capitalist assemblages. Hence, it would be exceptionally challenging to take "the view from nowhere," where a priori assumptions of power are nonexistent.

My standpoint in this debate is that an assemblage perspective should be allowed to find its way into the theoretical and methodological toolkits of political economy/ecology, even if it means diluting the former. As a systems scholar and a methodological pluralist following Norgaard (1989), I believe there is merit in borrowing concepts from other disciplines and epistemes, even at the risk of ending up with weaker or diluted versions of these concepts. Allowing the cross-fertilization of ideas across theories and methodologies could result in emergent ways of knowing and doing that could be meaningful for both the positive and normative commitments of studying land politics. Some of these emergent ways may provide a more nuanced and complete picture of land politics and its power dynamics, as the case studies that follow will illustrate. When navigating the cross-fertilization of knowledge, I echo Kinkaid's (2020, 467–468) call for assemblage scholarship to adopt feminist ethical principles by engaging in questions of *positionality* (i.e., attending to "how the subjective positions we inhabit inform the knowledge we produce") and *reflexivity* (i.e., committing to "interrogating one's epistemological limitations and potential complicity in relations of dominance"). Doing so would help strike a balance between openness to the emergent possibilities of more-than-human relations and continued attention to uneven power dynamics and structures of dominance.

Two Illustrative Cases in the Philippines

The Philippines is a geography that has a long history of uneven land politics, from the Spanish (1565–1898) and American (1898–1946) colonizations to the postcolonial struggles of state formation and the country's engagements with neoliberal capitalism. Much of the rural land in the archipelago is captured by the state, business entities, and elite families, which has left many of the marginalized populations—peasants, small fisherfolk, and Indigenous smallholders—struggling to secure access to land and resources. In the hinterlands, development aggression ensues in the form of traditional resource extraction (e.g., plantation development and mining) and newer variants couched in the language of sustainable and inclusive development. Meanwhile, climate change becomes an ever greater threat as the magnitude and frequency of extreme weather events intensify and the sea level rises. A political ecology analysis imbued with an assemblage perspective is, then, apt for the kinds of social and environmental circumstances that characterize the uneven land politics in the Philippines.

Plantation Assemblages in Palawan

Plantations producing cash crops such as sugarcane, cacao, pineapples, bananas, rubber, and oil palm abound in the Philippine hinterlands. These plantation regimes are often characterized by elite capture, land control and exclusion, exploitative labor conditions and contracts, environmental degradation, and violence. Since 2008, plantations have found their way onto the ecological frontiers of the province of Palawan, where "green economy" cash crops such as oil palm, jatropha, and rubber have been grown in ancestral lands (Montefrio, Sonnenfeld, and Luzadis 2015; Montefrio 2016, 2017; Montefrio and Dressler 2016).

The development and entrenchment of cash-crop plantations in Palawan and the uneven land politics are best analyzed with a political ecology lens but also supported by an assemblage perspective. Oil palm plantations in Indigenous Pala'wan lands can be described as an assemblage of competing environmental discourses, land accumulation by oil palm companies, declining fallow lands, eroding swidden fields, and intimate exclusions.[6] During my field research, the oil palm company and the state were framing Indigenous swidden cultivation practices as "destructive"; swidden fields and second-growth forests as "idle lands"; and oil palm as a harbinger of green growth and "inclusive" rural development. If these institutions were implicated in the overt territorialization of ancestral lands, they also created conditions for class differentiation and intimate forms of exclusion, as exercised by non-Indigenous smallholders, to the detriment of the Indigenous Pala'wan swidden cultivators. By being attentive to the materialities of oil palm and the socioecological transformations of swidden agriculture, I was able to discern feedback mechanisms that seem to point to the further exclusion of Indigenous Pala'wan smallholders. The combined processes of fallow-land conversion, soil degradation, and the erosion of systems of borrowing and renting fallow land owing to the intensification of capitalist relations led to the decline of smallholder benefits from integral swidden. This, in turn, resulted in the intensification and abandonment of swidden cultivation, which then risked reinforcing the antiswidden discourses that fuel fallow-land conversion to oil palm plantations (see Montefrio 2017 for more discussion of this sociomaterial dynamic).

In another part of the province, where rubber was grown, I documented a kind of land politics involving another group of Indigenous Pala'wan that did not parallel the logics of the oil palm plantations. Instead of seeing expansive monocrop plantations of rubber,

I was surprised to find a patchwork landscape of rubber trees, swidden fields, and old and second-growth forests, despite the aggressive campaigns that had been waged to promote the cash crop in the ancestral domain (Montefrio 2016).

My analysis entailed studying the materialities of rubber and the sociomaterial relations between humans (the Indigenous Pala'wan, migrant smallholder farmers, and rubber-plantation laborers and managers) and nonhumans (rubber trees, forests, swidden fields, and forest spirits). This approach compelled me to comprehend the nuances of land politics and decision-making involving the Indigenous peoples engaged in rubber production in southern Palawan. The proponents of growing commercial rubber did not anticipate the difficulty of establishing rubber plantations on Indigenous Pala'wan lands, notwithstanding the promise of favorable returns from the marketing of the cash crop and the Pala'wan smallholders' openness to growing rubber in their swidden fields. According to the Pala'wan smallholders, young rubber trees could still be intercropped with other subsistence and commercial crops they were growing in their swidden fields. The linchpin of the narrative was the existence of malevolent spirits in "sacred" or "taboo" forests. When there were rumors of laborers getting ill after the commercial rubber plantations began encroaching on "sacred" forests, many Pala'wan smallholders quit laboring for the rubber company, and the Indigenous elders resisted the expansion of the plantations. The rubber plantation developers complied, yielding to the warnings of the Pala'wan elders and the *belian* (medicine woman) to take the threats of forest spirits seriously (Montefrio 2016; see also Theriault 2017 on ontological multiplicity and how invisible forest beings have complicated environmental governance in Palawan).

An attention to the materiality of oil palm and rubber allowed me to comprehend the varied ways in which the plantations encroached on Indigenous swidden cultivation lands, while an appreciation of more-than-human relations (as in the case of forest spirits) opened new understandings of how unexpected land politics can transpire on the ground (see Dressler, Smith, and Montefrio 2018 on other cases of assemblage analysis that challenge the narrative of de-agrarianization in Palawan).

Decolonial Experimental Assemblage in Mindanao

A recognition of sociomaterial relations likewise complicates the narrative of the seeming dominance of plantation regimes in the large-scale agri-industrial production zones of Minadanao. We turn to the case of the commercial Cavendish banana sector, one of the most lucrative export-driven agri-industries in the Philippines. The sector is dominated by multinational corporations and local landed elites that have control of, not only expansive production lands, but also the agricultural labor and inputs needed to sustain the plantations and the commodity output markets. Both groups have exercised power to cease and control vast tracts of land and found ways to evade and maneuver their way around land-redistribution policies (Borras and Franco 2005).

Although the commercial banana industry in the Philippines appears to be a durable force of domination, its monocrop plantations have been threatened by crop diseases: one is the more manageable black sigatoka caused by the ascomycete fungus Mycosphaerella fijiensis; and another is the seemingly "incurable" Fusarium Wilt Tropical Race Four (popularly known as Panama disease), the latest race of the fungus Fusraium oxysporum f.sp. cubense. The industry has responded by carrying out intensive spraying of a cocktail of fungicides, many of which the Pesticide Action Network has identified as toxic (Paredes 2020). Although the emergence of banana-crop pathogens and the industry's responses are interesting to examine using an assemblage perspective, in the way that Julie Guthman studied the California strawberry industry, Alyssa Paredes focused on the emergence of an unlikely assemblage.

Paredes's (2023) research documented the emergence of "science-in-vivo"—a decolonial assemblage of human, nonhuman, and extrahuman forces born out of secular and nonsecular experimentations—that attempted to offer a solution to the Fusarium Wilt Tropical Race Four disease.[7] Her analysis involved following the story of the Crop Vaccine, a biological concoction "developed" by a citizen scientist—a farmer, self-made agricultural entrepreneur, and devout Christian committed to teaching organic agriculture in poor communities. The citizen scientist claimed that his "discovery" was a collaborative effort between God and the forest, a process that was largely inspired by visions in his dreams and involved his wandering in neighboring forests and exposing petri dishes to microorganisms that eventually served as the experimental ingredients for making the concoction. The science-in-vivo that created the Crop Vaccine did not take place in sophisticated laboratories, where standard in-vitro Fusarium biocontrol research is typically conducted. Yet the struggling banana industry eventually adopted the Crop Vaccine.

The case of the science-in-vivo assemblage enriches our understanding of plantation politics and resistance. According to Paredes (2023), science-in-vivo "has marked a break in the plantation's epistemic imperialism and become a source of unexpected counter-plantation politics" (858). Desperate to address its own environmental contradictions, the banana industry had no choice but to accommodate a solution that deviated from its technoscientific episteme. The willingness of the citizen scientist to share his Crop Vaccine with the industry and the industry's adoption of this unorthodox solution did not represent co-optation. Paredes interprets it instead as an expansion of the strategies of resisting plantation logics that are perceived by many to be rigid and uncompromising. As she eloquently writes, "Because the remedies it offers are relational in nature, science-in-vivo does not resuscitate the industrial agriculture unconditionally, but instead challenges the conventions at its very heart. The plantation it hopes to return, then, is no longer the plantation as we knew it" (858). Paredes clarifies that Crop Vaccine is not an agrarian solution that brings land back to the peasantry. However, the industry's adoption of this biocontrol necessitated that it "make many changes to their management protocol, like decreasing the reliance on weeding and the application of other synthetic pesticides and fertilisers. This is the only way that Crop Vaccine works . . . nothing else has convinced Big Ag to make these changes—not even decades of mobilisation and campaigning" (pers. comm., February 15, 2004).

An assemblage interpretation of the two Philippine cases can reinforce a political economy analysis of plantation politics in several ways. A keen understanding of the sociomaterial relations surrounding oil palm plantations and swidden agriculture, for example, can help further explain the nuances of the dynamics by which Indigenous smallholders are excluded from access to land. Social and material processes can reinforce each other to create feedback mechanisms that potentially lead to path-dependent outcomes. The value of an assemblage perspective, however, goes beyond merely reinforcing familiar hypotheses in political economy. In the two cases described here, assemblage thinking helps us recognize that plantation politics does not always result in a relative negative trajectory toward further territorialization of statist or capitalist assemblages. Rather, what we see are relative positive trajectories—messy and still evolving land politics full of tensions and contradictions—but with the potential for absolute positive deterritorialization. Tensions may come in the form of counterplantation politics and modes of resistance beyond what we typically encounter in a human-centered agrarian political economy—that is, land reform, insurgency, and social mobilization. Some of the entities easily left out of the narrative—such as forest microbes and spirits—can be crucial elements in emancipatory land politics.

Conclusion

Land politics have multiple material and social dimensions, requiring a type of analysis that examines socioecological (sociomaterial) relations. A political economy/ecology approach has been central in exposing the uneven social relations in land politics, but it could potentially benefit by giving more attention to human and nonhuman relationalities. Incorporating an assemblage perspective could provide the following advantages: First, it can add layers of explanation and nuance to the dynamics of land politics, which typically involve the agrarian political economic processes of commodification, capital accumulation, adverse incorporation, dispossession, exclusion, social differentiation, de-agrarianization, depeasantization, migration, resistance, among others. The cases described here already illustrate how attention to socioecological relations enriches our understanding of several of these dynamics.

Second, an assemblage perspective can reveal emergent properties in sociomaterial relations that expose fissures in the structures of dominance. Assemblage thinking (and poststructuralist political economy) reminds us that the forces of the state and capitalism are nonuniversalizing and nontotalizing, and that sociomaterial relations may be able to open opportunities for resistance. We saw these opportunities in the two cases from the Philippines, where the assemblages of science-in-vivo in Mindanao and the extrahuman forces of the forests in Palawan influenced the trajectories of plantation regimes. And since assemblages are always in flux, even a relative positive deterritorialization opens possibilities (and hope) for an absolute positive deterritorialization. Tensions and contradictions in assemblages do not always result in co-optation. In systems theory, one may be able to influence the direction of assemblages by taking advantage of leverage points—places of possible intervention in the system—which one can learn by closely understanding socioecological relations (Meadows 1999). For example, identifying feedback loops early could prevent path-dependent outcomes. Care must be taken, though, not to treat these interventions as deterministic solutions and to always be mindful of the emergent consequences of interventions. More subtly, just being cognizant of the possibilities of emergences in assemblages could help us (re)imagine and reinvigorate desires for emancipatory land politics.

I would like to conclude by offering an important caveat. An overreliance on more-than-human analysis that flattens power may be counterproductive to the positive and normative scholarly goals of studying land politics. Of course, one is always free to engage in a horizontal power analysis of sociomaterial relations; I believe such an analysis would still yield useful insights on land politics. However, the scholarship on land politics, broadly, *should not* undermine its political economic roots. Land politics, after all, will always involve political economic structures of dominance. So while an assemblage perspective accords a glimpse of an emergent emancipatory land politics, the machinations of territorial, statist, and neoliberal capitalist assemblages will always exert influence, shifting a relative positive deterritorialization toward a relative negative trajectory. An assemblage perspective, then, should encourage its observers to be reflexive, learning to turn the critical lens onto their own analysis.

NOTES

1. This characterization of land is common in encyclopedic and textbook entries, as well as international governance discourse.
2. I use *sociomaterial* and *socioecological* interchangeably, with the latter referring more to the environmental context.
3. Several scholars have responded to Vayda and Walters in support of political ecology, including Michael Watts, who defended the poststructuralist turn in the field (Walker 2005).
4. Boellstorff (2016) describes the ontological turn as having two recursive emphases: one on perspectives and representation, as represented by scholars like Viveiros de Castro (1998); and the other on relations, which is the focus of this chapter. Escobar (2007) also refers to assemblage scholarship as part of a broad trend in social theorizing, which he refers to as "flat alternatives" or "flat ontologies."
5. The other concept is "entanglements" (Giraud 2019).
6. Intimate exclusions are forms of land control exercised by covillagers and kin—smallholder farmers themselves—through enclosures, price control, credit-debt obligations, among others (Hall, Hirsch, and Li 2011).
7. The term *science-in-vivo* was coined by Paredes (2023), referring to a practice describing the discovery of Crop Vaccine that involves "drawing meaningful patterns out of bits and pieces" and necessitating "a tendency to operate in and out of scientific conventions" (847). *In vivo* (meaning "inside a living body") connotes an endeavor of discovery by "working with the complexities and dynamisms of life, rather than against it" (847).

References

Allen, John. 2011. "Powerful Assemblages?" *Area* 43 (2): 154–157.

Anderson, Ben, and Colin McFarlane. 2011. "Assemblage and Geography." *Area* 43 (2): 124–127.

Astuti, Rini, and Andrew McGregor. 2017. "Indigenous Land Claims or Green Grabs? Inclusions and Exclusions within Forest Carbon Politics in Indonesia." *Journal of Peasant Studies* 44 (2): 445–466.

Bennett, Jane. 2010. *Vibrant Matter: A Political Ecology of Things*. Durham, NC: Duke University Press.

Blaikie, Piers M., and Harold C. Brookfield. 1987. *Land Degradation and Society*. London: Methuen.

Boellstorff, Tom. 2016. "For Whom the Ontology Turns: Theorizing the Digital Real." *Current Anthropology* 57 (4): 387–407.

Borras, Saturnino M., Jr., and Jennifer C. Franco. 2005. "Struggles for Land and Livelihood: Redistributive Reform in Agribusiness Plantations in the Philippines." *Critical Asian Studies* 37 (3): 331–361.

Bunker, Stephen G. 1984. "Modes of Extraction, Unequal Exchange and the Progressive Underdevelopment of the Extreme Periphery: The Brazilian Amazon, 1600–1980." *American Journal of Sociology* 89: 1017–1064.

Busch, Lawrence, and Arunas Juska. 1997. "Beyond Political Economy: Actor-Networks and the Globalization of Agriculture." *Review of International Political Economy* 4 (4): 668–708.

Callon, Michel. 1990. "Techno-economic Networks and Irreversibility." *Sociological Review* 38 (S1): 132–161.

Callon, Michel, and John Law. 1995. "Agency and the Hybrid Collectif." *South Atlantic Quarterly* 94 (2): 481–507.

Campbell, Hugh, and Annie Stuart. 2005. "Disciplining the Organic Commodity." In *Agricultural Governance: Globalization and the New Politics of Regulation*, edited by Vaughan Higgins and Geoffrey Lawrence, 84–97. New York: Routledge.

Castree, Noel. 2002. "False Antitheses? Marxism, Nature and Actor-Networks." *Antipode* 34: 111–146.

Collier, Stephen J. 2006. "Global Assemblages." *Theory, Culture, & Society* 23 (2–3): 399–401.

Coole, Diana H., and Samantha Frost, eds. 2010. *New Materialisms: Ontology, Agency, and Politics*. Durham, NC: Duke University Press.

Davis, Janae, Alex A. Moulton, Levi Van Sant, and Brian Williams. 2019. "Anthropocene, Capitalocene, . . . Plantationocene?: A Manifesto for Ecological Crisis in an Age of Global Crisis." *Geography Compass* 13: Article e12438.

DeLanda, Manuel. 2006. *A New Philosophy of Society: Assemblage Theory and Social Complexity*. New York: Continuum.

DeLanda, Manuel. 2016. *Assemblage Theory*. Edinburgh, UK: University of Edinburgh Press.

Deleuze, Gilles, and Felix Guattari. 1987. *A Thousand Plateaus: Capitalism and Schizophrenia*. Minneapolis: University of Minnesota Press.

Deleuze, Gilles, and Claire Parnet. 1987. *Dialogues II*. New York: Columbia University Press.

de Sowa, Ivan Sergio Freire, and Lawrence Busch. 1998. "Networks and Agricultural Development: The Case of Soybean Production and Consumption in Brazil." *Rural Sociology* 63 (3): 349–371.

Dovey, Kim. 2010. *Becoming Places: Urbanism/Architecture/Identity/Power*. London, UK: Routledge.

Dressler, Wolfram, Will Smith, and Marvin Joseph F. Montefrio. 2018. "Ungovernable? The Vital Natures of Swidden Assemblages in an Upland Frontier." *Journal of Rural Studies* 61:343–354.

Escobar, Arturo. 2007. "The 'Ontological Turn' in Social Theory: A Commentary on 'Human Geography without Scale,' by Sallie Marston, John Paul Jones II and Keith Woodward." *Transactions of the Institute of British Geographers* 32 (1): 106–111.

Fine, Ben. 2005. "From Actor-Network Theory to Political Economy." *Capitalism, Nature, Socialism* 16 (4): 91–108.

Fletcher, James R. 2023. "An Ontological Turn in the Sociology of Personal Life: Tracing Facet Methodology's Connective Ontology." *Sociological Review*. https://doi.org/10.1177/00380261231212099.

Fox, Nick J., and Pam Alldred. 2015. "New Materialist Social Inquiry: Designs, Methods and the Research-Assemblage." *International Journal of Social Science Research Methodology* 18 (4): 399–414.

Giraud, Eva Haifa. 2019. *What Comes after Entanglement? Activism, Anthropocentrism, and an Ethics of Exclusion*. Durham, NC: Duke University Press.

Goodman, David. 1999. "Agro-food Studies in the 'Age of Ecology': Nature, Corporeality, Biopolitics." *Sociologia Ruralis* 39 (1): 17–38.

Guthman, Julie. 2002. "Commodified Meanings, Meaningful Commodities: Re-thinking Production-Consumption Links through the Organic System of Provision." *Sociologia Ruralis* 42 (4): 295–311.

Guthman, Julie. 2019. *Wilted: Pathogens, Chemicals, and the Fragile Future of the Strawberry Industry*. Oakland: University of California Press.

Hall, Derek, Philip Hirsch, and Tania Murray Li. 2011. *Powers of Exclusion: Land Dilemmas in Southeast Asia*. Singapore: NUS Press.

Harrison, G. A., ed. 1993. *Human Adaptation*. Oxford: Oxford University Press.

Hartwick, Elaine. 2000. "Towards a Geographical Politics of Consumption." *Environment and Planning A* 32:117–192.

Hebinck, Paul. 2018. "De-/re-agrarianisation: Global Perspectives." *Journal of Rural Studies* 61: 227–235.

Hebinck, Paul, Nosiseko Mtati, and Charlie Shackleton. 2018. "More Than Just Fields: Reframing Deagrarianisation in Landscapes and Livelihoods." *Journal of Rural Studies* 61:323–334.

Hecht, Susanna B. 1985. "Environment, Development, and Politics: Capital Accumulation and the Livestock Sector in Eastern Amazonia." *World Development* 13: 663–684.

Kinkaid, Eden. 2020. "Can Assemblage Think Difference? A Feminist Critique of Assemblage Geographies." *Progress in Human Geography* 44 (3): 457–472.

Kloppenburg, Jack. 1991. "Social Theory and the De/reconstruction of Agricultural Science: Local Knowledge for an Alternative Agriculture." *Rural Sociology* 56 (4): 519–548.

Kurzban, Robert. 2012. "Evolutionary Psychology." In *Encyclopedia of Human Behavior*, 2nd ed., edited by V. S. Ramachandran, 118–124. Netherlands: Elsevier.

Latour, Bruno. 1983. "Give Me a Laboratory and I Will Raise the World." In *The Science Studies Reader*, edited by Mario Biagioli, 258–275. London: Routledge.

Latour, Bruno. 1987. *Science in Action: How to Follow Scientists and Engineers through Society*. Cambridge, MA: Harvard University Press.

Latour, Bruno. 2005. *Reassembling the Social: An Introduction to Actor-Network Theory*. New York: Oxford University Press.

Lave, Rebecca. 2015. "Reassembling the Structural: Political Ecology and Actor-Network Theory." In *The Routledge Handbook of Political Ecology*, edited by Tom Perrault, Gavin Bridge, and John McCarthy, 213–223. New York: Routledge.
Lave, Rebecca, Adam Romero, Christine Biermann, Alyssa Paredes, Megan Betz, and Julie Guthman. 2021. "Wilted: Pathogens, Chemicals, and the Fragile Future of the Strawberry Industry." *AAG Review of Books* 9 (1): 44–52.
Legun, Katherine. 2015. "Tiny Trees for Trendy Produce: Dwarfing Technologies as Assemblage Actors in Orchard Economies." *Geoforum* 65: 314–322.
Le Velly, Ronan, and Ivan Dufeu. 2016. "Alternative Food Networks as 'Market *Agencements*': Exploring Their Multiple Hybridities." *Journal of Rural Studies* 43: 173–182.
Li, Tania Murray. 2007. "Practices of Assemblage and Community Forest Management." *Economy and Society* 36 (2): 263–293.
Li, Tania Murray. 2014. "What Is Land? Assembling a Resource for Global Investment." *Transactions of the Institute of British Geographers* 39 (4): 589–602.
McCall Howard, Penny. 2018. "The Anthropology of Human-Environment Relations: Materialism with and without Marxism:" *Focaal* 82: 64–79.
Meadows, Donella H. 1999. "Leverage Points: Places to Intervene in a System." The Sustainability Institute. https://1aoc26.p3cdn2.secureserver.net/wp-content/userfiles/Leverage_Points.pdf.
Montefrio, Marvin Joseph F. 2016. "Cooperation and Resistance: Negotiating Rubber in Upland Philippines." *Journal of Rural Studies* 46: 111–120.
Montefrio, Marvin Joseph F. 2017. "Land Control Dynamics and Social-Ecological Transformations in Upland Philippines." *Journal of Peasant Studies* 44 (4): 796–816.
Montefrio, Marvin Joseph F. 2020. "The 'Queen of Greens' Comes to the Tropics: (De) territorialization of Kale's Socio-material Relations in the Philippines." *Geoforum* 116: 24–32.
Montefrio, Marvin Joseph F., Jeremy C. De Chavez, Antonio Contreras, and Dennis Erasga. 2020. "Hybridities and Awkward Constructions in Philippine Locavorism: Reframing Global-Local Dynamics through Assemblage Thinking." *Food, Culture & Society* 23 (2): 102–116.
Montefrio, Marvin Joseph F., and Wolfram H. Dressler. 2016. "The Green Economy and Constructions of the 'Idle' and 'Unproductive' Uplands in the Philippines." *World Development* 79: 114–126.
Montefrio, Marvin Joseph F., David A. Sonnenfeld, and Valerie A. Luzadis. 2015. "Social Construction of the Environment and Farmer Intentions to Cooperate in Biofuels and Rubber Production in Upland Palawan, the Philippines." *Ecological Economics* 116: 70–77.
Mosse, David. 2010. "A Relational Approach to Durable Poverty, Inequality and Power." *Journal of Development Studies* 46 (7): 1156–1178.
Müller, Martin, and Carolin Schurr. 2016. "Assemblage Thinking and Actor-Network Theory: Conjunctions, Disjunctions, Cross-Fertilisations." *Transactions of the Institute of British Geographers* 41: 217–229.
Nail, Thomas. 2017. "What Is an Assemblage?" *SubStance* 46 (1): 21–37.
Norgaard, Richard B. 1989. "The Case for Methodological Pluralism." *Ecological Economics* 1 (1): 37–57.
Paredes, Alyssa. 2020. "Chemical Cocktails Defy Pathogens and Regulatory Paradigms." In *Feral Atlas: The More-Than-Human Anthropocene*, edited by Anna L. Tsing, Jennifer Deger, Alder Keleman-Saxena, and Feifei Zhou. Stanford University Press digital monograph.

https://feralatlas.supdigital.org/poster/chemical-cocktails-defy-pathogens-and-regulatory-paradigms.
Paredes, Alyssa. 2023. "Experimental Science for the 'Bananapocalypse': Counter Politics in the Plantationocene." *Ethnos* 88 (4): 837–863.
Peet, Richard, and Michael Watts. 1996. *Liberation Ecologies: Environment, Development, Social Movements*. New York: Routledge.
Phillips, John W. P. 2006. "Agencement/Assemblage." *Theory, Culture & Society* 23 (2–3): 108–109.
Rappaport, Roy A. 1979. *Ecology, Meaning, and Religion*. Richmond, CA: North Atlantic Books.
Raynolds, Laura T. 2002. "Consumer/Producer Links in Fair Trade Coffee Networks." *Sociologia Ruralis* 42 (4): 404–424.
Robbins, Paul. 2007. *Lawn People: How Grasses, Weeds, and Chemicals Make Us Who We Are*. Philadelphia, PA: Temple University Press.
Santo, Raychel, and Ana Moragues-Faus. 2019. "Towards a Trans-local Food Governance: Exploring the Transformative Capacity of Food Policy Assemblages in the US and UK." *Geoforum* 98: 75–87.
Steward, Julian. 1955. *Theory of Culture Change: The Methodology of Multilinear Evolution*. Champaign: University of Illinois Press.
Sundberg, Juanita. 2013. "Decolonizing Posthumanist Geographies." *Cultural Geographies* 21 (11): 33–47.
Swyngedouw, Eric. 2009. "The Political Economy and Political Ecology of the Hydro-social Cycle." *Journal of Contemporary Water Research & Education* 142: 56–60.
Theriault, Noah. 2017. "A Forest of Dreams: Ontological Multiplicity and the Fantasies of Environmental Government in the Philippines." *Political Geography* 58: 114–127.
Todd, Zoe. 2015. "Indigenizing the Anthropocene." In *Art in the Anthropocene: Encounters among Aesthetics, Politics, Environment and Epistemology*, edited by Heather Davis and Etienne Turpin, 241–254. Open Humanities Press.
Todd, Zoe. 2016. "An Indigenous Feminist's Take on the Ontological Turn: 'Ontology' Is Just Another Word for Colonialism." *Journal of Historical Sociology* 29 (1): 5–22.
Tsing, Anna L. 2015. *The Mushroom at the End of the World: On the Possibility of Life in Capitalist Ruins*. Princeton, NJ: Princeton University Press.
Turner, Matthew D. 1998. "Long-Term Effects of Daily Grazing Orbits on Nutrient Availability in Sahelian West Africa: 1. Gradients in the Chemical Composition of Rangeland Soils and Vegetation." *Journal of Biogeography* 25: 669–682.
van den Berg, Leonardo, Dirk Roep, Paul Hebinck, and Heitor Mancini Teixeira. 2018. "'Reassembling Nature and Culture' Resourceful Farming in Araponga, Brazil." *Journal of Rural Studies* 61: 314–322.
Vayda, Andrew P., and Bradley B. Walters. 1999. "Against Political Ecology." *Human Ecology* 27 (1): 167–179.
Viveiros de Castro, Eduardo. 1998. "Cosmological Deixis and Amerindian Perspectivism." *Journal of the Royal Anthropological Institute* 4 (3): 469–488.
Walker, Peter A. 2005. "Political Ecology: Where Is the Ecology?" *Progress in Human Geography* 29 (1): 73–82.
Wang, Chi-Mao. 2021. "Performing and Counter-Performing Organic Food Markets in East Asia: The Role of Ahimsa, Scientific Knowledge and Faith Groups." *Geographical Journal* 187 (4): 361–372.

Watts, Michael. 1983. *Silent Violence: Food, Famine and Peasantry in Northern Nigeria.* Berkeley: University of California Press.
Watts, Michael. 2000. "Political Ecology." In *Companion to Economic Geography*, edited by Eric Sheppard and Trevor Barnes, 257–275. Oxford: Blackwell.
Watts, Michael. 2004. "Antinomies of Community: Some Thoughts on Geography, Resources and Empire." *Transactions of the Institute of British Geographers* 29 (2): 195–216.
Weheliye, Alexander. 2014. *Habeas Viscus: Racializing Assemblages, Biopolitics, and Black Feminist Theories of the Human.* Durham, NC: Duke University Press.
Whatmore, Sarah. 1999. "Hybrid Geographies: Rethinking the 'Human' in Human Geography." In *Human Geography Today*, edited by Doreen Massey, John Allen, and Phil Sarre, 22–39. Cambridge, UK: Polity Press.
Whatmore, Sarah, and Lorraine Thorne. 1997. "Nourishing Networks: Alternative Geographies of Food." In *Globalising Food: Agrarian Questions and Global Restructuring*, edited by David Goodman and Michael Watts, 287–304. London: Routledge.
Wilson, Edward O. 1975. *Sociobiology: The New Synthesis.* Cambridge, MA: Harvard University Press.
Yates-Doerr, Emily. 2012. "The Opacity of Reduction." *Food, Culture & Society* 15 (2): 293–313.

CHAPTER 15

LAND, INDUSTRIAL LIVESTOCK, AND INTERSPECIES RELATIONS

The Pursuit of Scale and the Deceits of Productivity

TONY WEIS

Introduction: The Rising Scale of Livestock Production and Consumption

On a world scale, human societies devote far more land to raising livestock than to any other activity, and the trajectory of livestock production and consumption bears heavily on climate change, biodiversity loss, and a range of other urgent social and environmental problems (Xu et al. 2021; IPCC 2019; Willett et al. 2019; Springmann et al. 2018, 2016; Godfray et al. 2018; Poore and Nemecek 2018; Crist, Mora, and Engelman 2017; Machovina, Feeley, and Ripple 2015; Ripple et al. 2014; Lymbery 2014; Weis 2013; Cederberg et al. 2013; Vermeulen, Campbell, and Ingram 2012; Imhoff 2011). One clear illustration of this bearing lies in weight: a handful of livestock species now constitute over 70 percent of all bird biomass and around 60 percent of all mammalian biomass (with humans, another 36 percent and wild mammalian species, just 4 percent; Bar-On, Phillips, and Milo 2018; Smil 2013). In contrast, wild animals everywhere are being pushed into small fragments of their former habitats, which are simultaneously being destabilized by climate change (Lees et al. 2022; WWF 2020; Ceballos, Ehrlich, and Dirzo 2017; Ripple 2016; Ripple et al. 2015; Dirzo et al. 2014).

The scale of both industrial monocultures and livestock production has grown dramatically over the past century, and industrial livestock operations now command close to one-third of all the world's cropland, and much larger shares of the best land in temperate regions (IPCC 2019; Springmann et al. 2018; Ramankutty et al. 2008; Steinfeld et al. 2006). The combination of industrial monocultures and livestock operations lie at the heart of the massive increases in livestock production since the middle of the twentieth century and the accompanying meatification of diets, which describes the movement of animal flesh from the periphery of human diets, where it was for most of the history of agriculture, toward the center (Weis 2013). Between 1961 and 2021, per capita meat consumption nearly doubled on a world scale, increasing from 23 to 45 kilograms per year, and total annual meat consumption rose fivefold, increasing from 71 to 357 million tonnes, as the human population rose from roughly 3 to 8 billion. This global picture conceals vast disparities in per capita consumption between high- and low-income countries, while both per capita and total growth have been heavily concentrated in middle-income countries since the late twentieth century.[1]

Rising per capita meat consumption pivots on poultry birds and pigs. The combined global annual production of poultry and pigs rose nearly eightfold between 1961 and 2021, from 34 to 258 million tonnes, now accounting for 72 percent of the annual global volume of meat produced (FAOSTATS 2023). It is also important to appreciate this growth in terms of animal populations. In 1961, the global livestock population topped 7 billion, and roughly 8 billion animals were killed for food. In 2021, the global livestock population topped 33 billion livestock animals, and roughly 83 billion animals were killed for food—the latter representing a tenfold increase in just sixty years, driven principally by chickens (see Figure 15.1). Far more animals are now killed every year than exist at any one point in time, because of the accelerating life cycles from birth to slaughter in industrial systems, which should be understood to amplify the dramatic disparity in biomass between livestock and wild birds and mammals noted earlier. By 2050, on the current course, global per capita meat consumption will surpass 50 kilograms/year in a world with close to 10 billion people (provided demographic projections are not subverted by additional devastating pandemics, worsening climate impacts, or intensifying conflicts), with further growth dominated by industrial poultry and pig production.

It is clear that industrial livestock production has succeeded in generating relatively cheap and abundant commodities, achieving tremendous cost savings through the displacement of labor, acceleration of reproduction and genetic change, and confinement of animal bodies in densely packed enclosures. However, the great gains in volume, labor productivity, and yield should not be confused with efficiency. On the contrary, the industrialization of livestock constitutes a highly inefficient way of organizing land to produce food, and why contesting it is so crucial to the prospects for a healthier planet. To begin to grasp how the soaring scale and changing nature of livestock production relates to land and environmental change, it helps to first consider the key biological and physical compulsions, or organizing imperatives, that prevailed in mixed farming and herding over the long course of agrarian history.

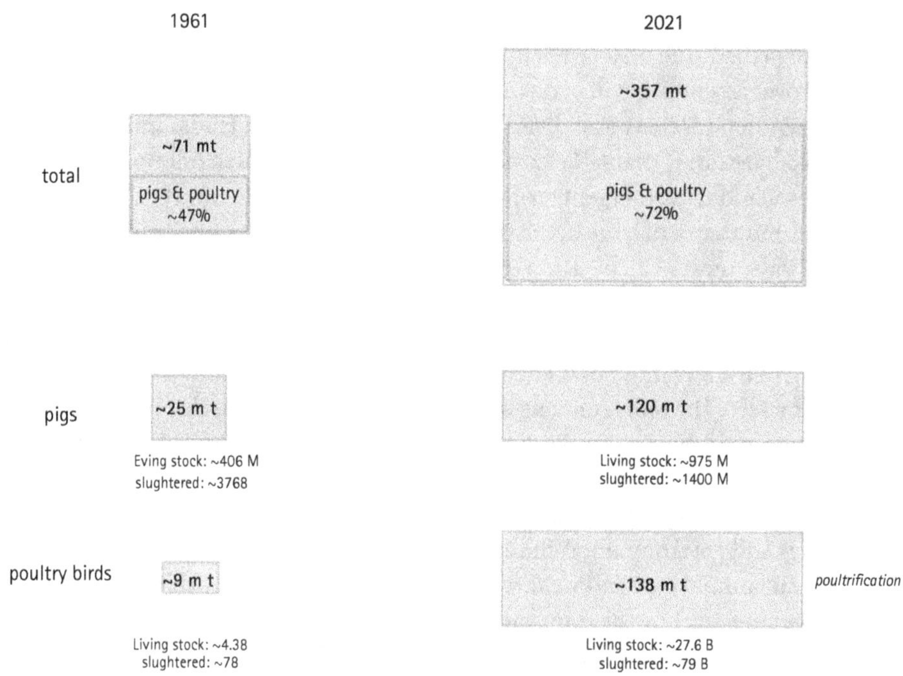

FIGURE 15.1. Snapshots of global meat production, 1961 and 2021.

Source: Data from FAOSTATS (2023).

Land and Livestock in Mixed Farming and Herding

The domestication of livestock revolutionized human relationships to animals and land. As with the earlier domestication of dogs,[2] the process of artificial selection that transfigured wild mammalian and bird species into living stock involved favoring docile individuals and killing more obstinate ones, which made handling easier over the long term. Unlike the domestication of dogs, where there was a high degree of mutualism, and selection for behavioral traits drove the physiological changes, the driving motivation in breeding livestock species was to enhance various bodily outputs (flesh, milk, eggs, and fibers) for human use, and the combination of physiological and behavioral changes steadily diminished capacities to respond to predators and hence to survive beyond human-managed landscapes. The prospects for domesticating livestock were uneven on a planetary scale; Eurasia was endowed with by far the most good candidates—namely, large grazing herbivores that live in herds—and the course of domestication played a crucial part in different civilizational trajectories (Fagan 2015; Nibert 2013; Zeder 2012; Sale 2006; Diamond 2002).

The domestication of livestock can also be understood to have revolutionized how energy was marshalled. The first part of this energy revolution involved the increasing control exerted over assemblages of plants and animals, which in a general sense reduced the total photosynthetic activity and diversity of animals in a given landscape.[3] The second part involved harnessing plant-fueled animal muscle power, which followed rather than drove domestication, as emergent farming and herding cultures came to realize that the strength and endurance of large herbivorous mammals could be mobilized in highly advantageous ways, most of all by using their muscle power on farms and for transporting people and goods.[4] The desire to enhance certain laboring characteristics shaped selective breeding in some large-bodied mammalians species, and was accompanied by the development of training methods, coercive techniques, and technologies such as whips, bits, and harnesses. The more humans were able to harness the muscle power of animals, the faster they could alter natural ecosystems and to make land suitable for cultivation and better for grazing (Fagan 2015; Nibert 2013; Montgomery 2007; Rifkin 1992).

Although a wide range of animal husbandry approaches developed in relation to different species and environmental conditions, along with varying cultural and religious attitudes about animal care and welfare, it is nevertheless possible to identify important common elements in how peasants and pastoralists organized animals in relation to land. Most peasant cultures outside the Americas (which had far fewer animal options) tended to rear a small range of livestock species at relatively low densities, without explicitly dedicating much cropland to feeding them. This involved feeding animals with some combination of the plants used to reinvigorate fallowed fields (e.g., alfalfa and clover),[5] crop stubble left following harvests, household food wastes, and various plants found on common lands that were kept in grasses or in managed forests. The protein obtained from animal milk, eggs, and flesh augmented human diets, and animal manure came to had an important role fertilizing agricultural land (Fagan 2015; Fairlee 2010; Lappe 1991; Bayless-Smith 1982).[6] The degree to which animal muscle power was utilized on farms varied greatly, depending on factors like topography, climate, and the available species.

In contrast to mixed farming systems, pastoralists have generally focused on a single mammalian species, and compelled small herds to move with seasonal changes in search of more plentiful plant productivity, moisture, and comfortable temperatures. Some seasonal movements involved modest distances, such as in alpine regions, where significant bioclimatic differences could be found by moving up and down in elevation. In other cases, such as in drylands with extreme moisture variability, herders have had to undertake long migrations contingent on seasonal rains that allowed drought-adapted grasses to spring back to life. Over long periods of time, herding cultures alter the distributions of plants and animals in the landscapes they move across, affecting the array of species to a far lesser degree than do sedentary agriculturists while acting on far greater total land area (Scoones 2021; Reid, Fernández-Giménez, and Galvin 2014; Galvin 2009).[7]

There are some obvious reasons why both peasants and pastoralists would have wanted to increase livestock populations, given the various uses derived from livestock and the fact that animal ownership was an important source of wealth, power, and food security (helping store some fodder "on the hoof") for much of agrarian history. The general thrust of these motivations is also abundantly clear in the long-term growth of livestock populations, the development of new breeds based on the desire for particular characteristics, the geographic diffusion of various species and breeds, and the fact that the expansion of cultivation and pasture has been by far the leading force in reducing and fragmenting natural grasslands, forests, and wetlands over time. This long-term diffusion of different livestock species and breeds and the growth in their populations was dialectically related to the growth of human populations and the advance of civilizations, playing pivotal roles in increasing food surpluses and in conveying the animal muscle power that helped to till soils and forge transportation and trade networks, cities, irrigation systems, and modes of warfare (Scott 2017; Fagan 2015; Nibert 2013; Montgomery 2007; Williams 2006; Sale 2006; Rifkin 1992).[8]

Yet as central as livestock have been to the reconfiguration of landscapes over time, it is also important to recognize that until very recently there were significant barriers limiting the extent to which animal reproduction could be accelerated and the density of livestock populations increased. That is, though farming and herding cultures could enhance the carrying capacity of land through trial and error and the long-term accumulation of knowledge, they would, at some point, inevitably maximize the amount of useable photosynthetic activity relative to the nutritional needs of humans and animals, given the extent of their knowledge and the available labor at the time. Once the carrying capacity of land was well understood, relatively stable livestock densities formed a key aspect of both the socioecological balances established in durable farming cultures and the ability to respond to environmental variability that is a core feature of durable herding cultures (Scoones 2021; Reid, Fernández-Giménez, and Galvin 2014; Galvin 2009; Bayless-Smith 1982). But when excessive livestock densities were maintained for protracted periods, overgrazing and overtilling frequently proved destructive, driving the colonization of new frontiers and factoring heavily in many instances of soil degradation, agrarian decline, and state collapse (Scott 2017; Montgomery 2007; Rifkin 1992; Worster 1990).

Another prevailing consideration in rearing livestock throughout history was the fact that there was typically much more value bound up in living animals (i.e., muscle power, milk, eggs, fibers, fertilization, fuel, reproducing offspring) than in killing and consuming flesh. This gave farmers and herders a vested interest in sustaining healthy and relatively long-lived individuals and meant that flesh tended not to be at the center of food consumption patterns in agrarian societies (Fairlee 2010; Mintz and Schlettwein-Gsell 2001; Lappe 1991).[9] The generalized interest in animal longevity, together with the limits on density, meant that peasants and pastoralists knew the animals they reared as individual beings and had to be attentive to their injuries, localized infections, and diseases, at the same time as the conditions of animal life tended to foster the development of robust immune systems. Some of the key conditions supporting animal health included being reared in multigenerational groups, where infants were nurtured with maternal care (including, for mammals, being nursed and weaned on their own timelines); having social interactions with fellow members of their species, with an ability to give and receive affection; having diverse diets and regular exercise; breathing fresh air; and being exposed to the sun's rays. But interest in animal health and the conditions that created robust immune systems could do nothing to inhibit the heightened risks of zoonotic disease that resulted from the far greater levels of sustained contact between humans and mammal and bird populations, and many of the infectious diseases that have haunted human societies since the Neolithic Revolution are known or strongly suspected to have spilled over from livestock (Scott 2017; Nibert 2013; Diamond 2002).

In transforming ecosystems, the slow advance of cultivation, pasture, and livestock populations can also be understood to have cut into the habitats and distributions of an array of wild animal species. The loss and fragmentation of habitat was generally the most damaging for large-bodied species that live at low densities and range across the most land, and for large predators the effects of habitat loss were often compounded by hunting, trapping, and poisoning intended to reduce the threat they posed to livestock. However, prior to the rise of European imperialism, the encroachment of livestock into the habitats of wild animals was mostly limited to Eurasia and Africa, where all major livestock species were domesticated, and only involved the extirpations of some species from parts of their former ranges, without driving any extinctions. The introduction of cattle, pigs, sheep, goats, horses, donkeys, and chickens played an important part in European imperialism in the Americas and Australasia, and their populations and geographic extent grew quickly and dramatically. Livestock had a critical role in sweeping enclosures of land and the interrelated advance of settler-colonial agricultures, dispossessions of Indigenous peoples, and declines in wild animal habitats and populations, and in enabling resource extraction more generally, as key sources of food, materials, and muscle power that were crucial to the growth of mining and forestry sectors. Some species also moved beyond European-controlled landscapes, especially cattle and pigs, altering environments and acting as a sort of vanguard for settler-colonial migration, farms, and ranches (Weis 2021; Nibert 2013; Anderson 2006; Rifkin 1992; Crosby 1986, 1972; see Patel, this volume, on the importance of commodity frontiers in the development of global capitalism; and McMichael, this volume, on the centrality of enclosures to the rise of a global food regime).

The rapid enclosures and proliferation of new farms and ranches in the US Midwest in the nineteenth century contributed to momentous industrial innovations that greatly increased the productivity of grain farming, livestock rearing, and slaughter and processing and, ultimately, caused radical transformation in the relations between humans, land, and livestock (Rifkin 1992; Cronon 1991; Worster 1990).

The Industrialization of Agriculture and the Separation of Livestock from Land

Livestock populations in the United States, especially of cattle and pigs, initially burgeoned across the natural prairie grasslands in the vacuum created by the dispossession of Indigenous peoples and the decimation of large herbivores and predators. However, as settler-colonial farmers poured westward, they began converting the grasslands to expansive grain monocultures at a breakneck pace, and animal muscle power, paired with the development of the steel plow, played a crucial part tearing up the thick-rooted grasses. As extensive monocultures boomed upon the rich soil frontier, livestock were increasingly corralled away from planted fields and fed some of the surplus of cultivated grains, especially corn (Cronon 1991; Worster 1990). Fast-rising populations of pigs, cattle, and sheep fueled the development of industrial slaughter and disassembly lines, most dramatically in Chicago's famed Union Stockyards, which marked a profound shift: it was the first time in world history that animals were systematically moved great distances from the land where they had been reared to the spaces where they were slaughtered and butchered, and some of the ensuing commodities moved farther still, to the eastern seaboard of the United States and across the Atlantic to Europe. The rising distance and scale of animal slaughter and meatpacking (and development of a new industry rendering nonedible body parts) was entwined with the sudden emergence of a new set of large corporations, and the equally sudden erosion of knowledge about the nature of animal lives and deaths among large segments of consumers (Pacyga 2015; Cronon 1991).

There are many reasons why consumer demand for meat and other animal foods has marched in step with increasing productive capacity. Although there are undoubtedly those who are inclined to view this as a relatively straightforward matter of palate pleasure, taste cannot be reduced to physiological impulses, because food-getting and culinary practices have varied greatly over human history, and modern corporations have shown great ability to affect dietary aspirations (Moss 2013; Nestle 2013; Mintz and Schelettwein-Gsell 2001). In modern times, powerful interests in livestock-related industries have successfully stoked consumer demand for animal-based foods in a range of ways, including marketing campaigns that have foregrounded them in all meals; processing and retail innovations, including the rise and spread of fast food; and lobbying to influence national dietary guides (Howard 2016; Moss 2013; Nestle 2013). Such efforts have tended to play upon and benefit from certain cultural associations (e.g., periodic celebrations and displays of masculinity) and ideas about nutrition and the superiority of animal protein that were formed over long periods of time when the consumption of animal foods, especially flesh, was much rarer (Adams 2010; Fiddes 1992; Rifkin 1992; Harris 1974).

Along with opening a large new realm of accumulation in itself, the industrialization of livestock slaughter, processing, and rendering also had the compelling effect of greatly expanding the scope of accumulation in grain production. Because the commodities derived from animal bodies can earn relatively higher prices than the cost of the feed going into them, this quickly became a durable way to profitably absorb the grain surpluses that would have otherwise undermined prices and the basic impulse for growth. From the mid-twentieth century onward, the surplus absorption capacity of animal feed was the primary reason for the explosive growth of oilseeds, primarily soybeans, and secondarily, canola (Weis 2013; Winders and Nibert 2004; Berlan 1991).

Livestock remained critical to the functioning of large monocultures throughout the nineteenth century, as animal muscle power was still needed for tillage and transport, as well as in harvesting and milling certain crops, and manure continued to be valued on fallowed or recently harvested land. However, in the early twentieth century, rapidly improving combustion-powered tractors and combine harvesters began to displace animal muscle power on a rising scale,[10] and the boom in mined and manufactured fertilizers undercut the need for manure and the practice of fallowing (Erisman et al. 2008; Fitzgerald 2003; Smil 2001). Thus, though there had been a range of preindustrial examples of monocultures, the industrialization of cultivation greatly intensified the separation of livestock from land. The speed and functionality of farm machinery also increased the pressure to biologically simplify and standardize agricultural landscapes, as advantages hinge on planting and harvesting the same crop at the same time and treating them the same way, and the ability to rationalize operational costs increases with scale. This trajectory has been interwoven with the development of high-yielding seed varieties, the shrinking crop diversity, and varieties planted across large areas, the weaving together of seed and pesticide development, and the narrowing control over the associated intellectual property rights (IPES-Food 2017; Howard 2016).

As the multifunctionality of livestock in mixed farming landscapes was being outmoded, the value of rearing animals came to center entirely on the production of their flesh, eggs, and milk (complemented by the rendering of nonedible body parts) and a new function, that of profitably absorbing the rising surpluses from high-yielding monocultures (Weis 2013; Winders and Nibert 2004; Berlan 1991). Taken together, both developments substantially heightened the motivation to rear animals in large densities and to accelerate how fast they reproduced, gained weight, and generated reproductive outputs; objectives that all had preindustrial antecedents but took on a wholly different intensity in the twentieth century, starting with the development of chicken sheds in the 1920s (Davis 2009; Boyd 2001). One of the basic economic advantages of densifying animal populations and moving them indoors was that it greatly reduced the labor time required per animal, to an extent that outweighed the expanded fixed and operational expenses associated with enclosures; and these efficiencies increased farther as more tasks were automated over time. Besides vastly reducing labor, density also reduces various operational expenses per animal, including feed, electricity, and seasonal heating, as controlled temperatures and bodily confinement limit the energy that animals would otherwise expend on nonproductive metabolic processes; that is, doing anything other than putting on flesh (and other saleable byproducts) and turning out eggs and milk (Blanchette 2020; Gillespie 2018; Lymbery 2014; Weis 2013; Imhoff 2011; Davis 2009; Striffler 2007; Boyd 2001).[11]

Technoscientific innovations in reproduction and animal genetics have also played a crucial part in the industrialization of livestock production. The development of instruments and techniques to extract semen from males and artificially inseminate females has enabled the dramatic acceleration of reproduction on an ongoing basis and quickened the pace of genetic selection, and together these have resulted in greatly increased rates of weight-gain, egg-laying, and lactation. Chickens were at the forefront of modern genetic changes, starting with their specialization for either rapid weight gain (broilers) or egg production (layers). In industrial systems, the acceleration of weight gain is such that broilers grow from hatch to slaughter in just six weeks; while layer hens can now produce roughly three hundred eggs per year, or almost an egg a day (Davis 2009; Boyd 2001).[12] Accelerated growth in pigs means that they can be raised from birth to slaughter in just six months, and beef cattle accelerated on feedlots can now reach slaughter weight at between one and two years of age (Blanchette 2020; Gillespie 2018; Schneider 2018).

The physiological superiority of poultry birds and pigs over ruminants in converting feed inputs to food outputs, and their greater malleability within industrial systems, are fundamental reasons why they—and chickens especially—have been at the forefront of global production increases and the meatification of diets, augmented by rising health advocacy about the negative impacts of red meat. From 1961 to 2021, the annual global volume of poultry produced rose by a factor of 15, surging from 13 to 39 percent of global meat production (FAOSTATS 2023), abetted by a range of processing and retail innovations, such as the popularization of chicken wings, nuggets, balls, fingers, dumplings, and fried breasts. One well-publicized indication of the "poultrification" of global meat supply and demand is that the magnitude of chicken bones produced annually is "likely to leave a widespread and distinctive biostratigraphic signal in the sedimentary record, as a key fossil index taxon of the Anthropocene" (Bennett et al. 2018, 8).

As with seeds, the creation of new, high-yielding livestock breeds is enmeshed with the assertion of intellectual property rights over the altered genetics, which a handful of corporations have come to dominate (IPES-Food 2017; Howard 2016). Reliance on artificial insemination and ownership of altered and patented animal genes have led to the increasing specialization of breeding sites and subpopulations, whose lives are dedicated to turning out scores of new generations. With breeding males and females held in separate spaces and newborn animals swiftly shipped off to other enclosures and deprived of maternal care, there is a total negation of intimacy and familial relations.

Overriding Barriers to Scale in Industrial Livestock Production

As with all industrial production, the pursuit of economies of scale in agriculture is rooted in the competitive discipline of markets and the pressure to develop technologies that reduce the relative cost of labor. Innovation in genetics is an important part of this in both industrial monocultures and livestock operations. Although farmers and herders have always selected for yields to some degree, among other valued traits, the quest for yield gains in crops and livestock species intensified under industrial capitalism because the development of higher-yielding organisms effectively amplifies the labor investment per plant or animal. The phenomenal increases in labor productivity and plant and animal yields achieved over the past century form the basis of the competitive triumph of industrial agriculture, and help to explain why it has steadily advanced on a world scale and generated such great volumes of comparatively cheap animal flesh, eggs, and milk (Benton et al. 2021; Sage 2012; Weis 2010; Worster 1990). But none of this should imply that these systems are an efficient way to use land.

While the pursuit of scale has clearly been successful in certain terms, productivity gains are mired in contradictions and, however robust they may appear, increasingly precarious. As we have seen, the pursuit of scale pivots on the biological simplification and standardization of productive environments as a basic condition that enables an array of labor-substituting technologies. But organizing land this way also establishes or exacerbates a series of biological and physical problems that can collectively be understood as biophysical barriers to scale, which can never be fully resolved and are, instead, overridden—for an indefinite period of time—through the use of various external inputs, or "biophysical overrides." The trouble with these overrides is twofold: first, they entail an array of resource budgets and pollution loads; and second, while the immediate problems are masked, the long-term risks keep increasing (Weis 2013, 2010).

In industrial monocultures, key biophysical barriers to scale include worsening soil fertility due to the exposure of more bare ground and the use of large machinery; heightened threats from insects, weeds, and fungus when large areas are devoted to a single crop; the insufficiency of soil moisture and rainfall relative to the water demands of high-yielding seed varieties; and, for some crops, the insufficiency or decline of local pollinator populations. The primary ways these barriers are overridden are by manufacturing and applying huge volumes of fertilizers and pesticides, diverting countless lakes and rivers, pumping underground aquifers, developing genetically modified seeds, and trucking bee colonies over long distances (Benton et al. 2021; Ellis et al. 2020; Sage 2012; Weis 2010). The biophysical overrides in industrial monocultures entail a large fossil-fuel budget and the attendant CO_2 emissions (e.g., from manufacturing fertilizers and pesticides; running irrigation pumps; moving fertilizers, pesticides, seeds, and bees farther across space as landscapes are increasingly specialized, etc.) that adds to the increased energy and CO_2 emissions from powering farm machinery. The reliance on overrides exacerbates biophysical problems within farming landscapes, such as when pesticides further harm soil organisms and pollinator species and excessive irrigation results in the salinization of soils. In addition to the CO_2 emissions, it is also implicated in a range of other biophysical problems far beyond farming landscapes, such as the damaging accumulation of nutrient loads from fertilizers and persistent toxins from pesticides; nitrous oxide emissions associated with the use of nitrogen fertilizer; the depletion of aquifers; and decline of free-flowing rivers (Benton et al. 2021; Bijay-Singh and Craswell. 2021; Famiglietti 2014; Sage 2012; Weis 2010).

The displacement of labor is more complicated in industrial livestock production than it is with monocultures, because there are not only forbidding biophysical barriers to scale but additional problems posed by the physiology, behavioral repertoires, and desires of animals. The barriers to scale in the industrialization of animal production start with the normal rhythms of copulation and gestation. As noted, artificial insemination is crucial to the acceleration of animal reproduction and genetic changes, and the shortness of animal lives in industrial systems makes it a practical necessity as well, since the vast majority of animals are killed as juveniles before reaching sexual maturity, and since some bodies have been so altered that copulation would not be possible even if maturation were permitted. Although insemination remains a relatively labor intensive part of breeding operations, requiring human dexterity to perform the invasive and disturbing tasks (Gillespie 2018; Davis 2017), it nevertheless substantially reduces the amount of labor time that would otherwise be needed to move animals around and manage copulation, and allows the physical space in growing operations to be further simplified. Another task that still requires human dexterity and cognition is to sex layer chicks, sorting the females for production and the males for disposal.[13]

A sizable barrier to scale in livestock production is the ineffable suffering that stems from the combination of intense crowding, immobility, monotony, stench, and noise. Some animals become dejected and lethargic, but others respond by harming themselves or attacking their neighbors. For instance, chickens living in small flocks establish a social hierarchy, which can involve tussles that typically end in submissive individuals' moving away without injury. But in dense enclosures with thousands of individuals, where birds lack the ability to move away, pecking at neighbors—whether out of confusion, anger, or fear—can cause injuries, deaths, and costly losses for operators (Davis 2009; Boyd 2001). Distressed pigs similarly pose risks to their neighbors, commonly chewing on tails or ears that are within reach. One of the principal ways these damaging behaviors get overridden is through blunt force: systematically mutilating bodies, typically without anesthetic. Most intensively reared chickens have their beaks lopped off shortly after birth in a rapid-fire process (another grim and relatively labor-intensive task at breeding sites), and other routine mutilations include needle-teeth clipping, tail-docking, dehorning, and castration (Blanchette 2020; Gillespie 2018; Genoways 2014; Lymbery 2014; Weis 2013; Imhoff 2011).

Although the acceleration of breeding and genetic changes have significantly improved feed conversion ratios, much of the nutrition contained in crops is still invariably burned in nonproductive metabolic processes. Massive aggregations of feces and urine are a stark manifestation of this structural wastage, as well as another barrier to scale in maintaining great densities of animal populations. Overriding this biowaste problem requires large volumes of water to regularly flush out enclosures, along with varying combinations of disinfectants, insecticides, and rodenticides. The resulting slurry contains residues from these chemicals along with residues of the pesticides used on feed crops, and frequently dangerous concentrations of infectious bacteria such as *Escherichia coli* (*E. coli*) and *Salmonella*. Some of the slurry from industrial livestock enclosures is treated and sprayed, but the volumes are too great to be consistently absorbed on nearby cropland (especially given the clustering of livestock facilities in particular regions), necessitating the construction of what are euphemistically called "lagoons" or holding "ponds," which dot the landscapes. In short, not only is there a quantitative difference in the volume of animal biowastes, but also a qualitative change from the fertilization role that livestock manure had over millennia (Neubert 2020; Blanchette 2020, 2019; Levitt 2019; Mallin and Cahoon 2003).

Industrialization eradicates all the historic conditions of husbandry that tended to foster relatively hardy animals, and the great gains in rates of weight gain, laying, and lactation bely the frailty of the animals every any respect other than yield. Instead, a series of interconnected barriers to health are established: extreme immobility and lack of exercise; chronic pain from weak bones and joints;[14] cardiovascular problems; stressful, inescapable crowding; the homogenization of diets; and bad air (Davis 2020; Wallace 2016; Lymbery 2014; Reichert et al. 2011; Imhoff 2011; Pew Commission 2008). Bad air is one of the most elemental contradictions of rearing large densities of animals indoors, because the level of respiration generates intolerably high CO_2 concentrations, compounded by the noxious gases and particulate matter emanating from the aggregations of feces and urine, and powerful ventilation systems are needed to make the ambient conditions livable (Sinel and Weis, forthcoming).

Industrial livestock operations are also extremely vulnerable to the spread, evolution, and periodic eruptions of communicable diseases. Innovations in antibiotics and vaccines are the central means to override the risks from infectious pathogens (Mulchandani et al. 2023; Davis 2020; Wallace 2016), and the reliance on antibiotics deepened with the recognition that subtherapeutic applications (essentially, use at levels that mask general ill-health rather than treat a particular illness) had the side benefits of enhancing feed conversion ratios and making stressed animals somewhat more lethargic. The use of antibiotics at sub-therapeutic levels remains common in many parts of the world, despite the repeated scientific warnings that it is heightening the risk of antibiotic-resistant strains of bacteria emerging (Mulchandani et al. 2023; Morehead and Scarbrough 2018; O'Neill 2016; Ventola 2015; Economou and Gousia 2015).[15]

One striking indication of generalized ill-health and chronic risks of infectious disease is that an expectation of premature mortality has given rise to a subindustry manufacturing incinerators geared to large-scale operations, mainly in broiler chicken production. The basic assumption is that a small percentage of the many thousands of birds in each six-week growing cycle will die before being shipped off to slaughter, becoming an anticipated expense to be written off that is outweighed by the economic advantages of scale (Davis 2009). Industrial livestock operations also increasingly deploy sophisticated monitoring and surveillance systems and hazmat suits and decontamination showers for workers, in an attempt to physically limit the potential for pathogens to either slip into or out of the large sheds. Such interventions are increasingly described in terms of biosecuritization, and the practices and associated rationality contributes to the further consolidation of production by simultaneously stigmatizing small-scale husbandry (and livestock populations raised outside rather than inside) as the locus of greatest risks, exaggerating the degree to which the movement of dangerous microbes can ever be contained, and distracting from the dangers of disease evolution with which industrial production is laden (Blanchette 2020, 2015; Davis 2020; Wallace 2016; Allen and Lavau 2015; Dixon 2015).

Most of the time, the circulation of infectious diseases is conceived as a slow-burning challenge for industrial livestock production, which can be managed at an acceptable level of premature mortality through the combination of pharmaceuticals, incineration, and biosecurity precautions. But this slow burn carries the omnipresent risk of periodic eruptions, when more virulent or transmissible new variants spread like wildfire through dense animal populations (Sinel and Weis, forthcoming; Davis 2020; Wallace 2016). There is also a cauldron-like character to the system as a whole, because not only is there a risk of new variants entering sheds (which biosecurity measures might reduce but can never eliminate), but the nature of production amplifies the risk that dangerous new variants will evolve. That is, the pursuit of scale and the ways that biophysical problems are overridden increases the number of mutations that are bound to occur among viruses, bacteria, and other microbes when endemic diseases circulate through larger and denser flocks and herds of young, genetically similar animals with weak immune systems that are being fed unnatural diets (and frequently a lot of antibiotics)—a combination of dynamics that increase the chances infectious pathogens could acquire greater virulence, transmissibility, or both (Marchese and Hovorka 2022; Davis 2020; Wallace 2016). In short, the challenge of overriding disease is never a fixed target, but rather, perpetually sows further risks, with operational challenges and costs that extend far beyond industrial livestock operations, reaching the level of the national and international institutional infrastructures involved in disease surveillance and response (e.g., US Centers for Disease Control and the World Health Organization). This institutional infrastructure plays a crucial part in identifying dangerous new variants of infectious diseases and assessing the threats they pose to either production or of spillover into human or other animal populations. When a specific threat is deemed to be sufficiently high, the response is to swiftly kill all herds and flocks within a specified radius (discussed further below; Sinel and Weis, forthcoming; Davis 2020; Wallace 2016).[16]

As indicated in the previous section, animal slaughter and packing began to be industrialized well before the breeding and growing of animals, but in general, there are much greater barriers to substituting technology for labor at this point in the production process. Because animals tend to writhe, kick, and try to escape when they sense peril, human dexterity and reflexes are needed to respond to this unpredictability as soon as the trucks are unloaded, with the pursuit of speed balanced against the goal of preventing damage to the end products. Engineers have succeeding in automating some parts of fast-moving lines, like stunning and slicing the throats of birds—mechanizing the act of killing billions annually—but many difficult tasks requiring human labor persist, such as offloading animals from transport trucks; shackling them to slaughter lines; firing stun-guns; and slicing mammalian throats. There are also limits to how much packing lines can be mechanized, as workers are needed for tasks like deskinning, deboning, eviscerating, and sectioning carcasses. Thus, while on one level there is something very familiar about the reduction of work to a series of repetitive, mind-numbing tasks, each constituting a fragment of the overall production process, there is also something very particular to the physical risks and psycho-social impacts for those working in these industrial environments (Blanchette 2020; Genoways 2014; Pachirat 2011; Striffler 2007; Eisnitz 2006).

Finally, though the pursuit of scale offers economic advantages in each of the specialized breeding facilities, growing operations, and slaughter-packing plants, at a system level, these industrial innovations—and the tendency toward fewer and larger sites of breeding, growing, and slaughter—serve to extend the distance that animals, feed, and other inputs must be shipped over land, along with the distance that the final commodities have to move. This barrier to scale is overridden with transport trucks, logistics systems, and fossil fuels, and the demand for energy increases as a result of the greater relative refrigeration demands of animal-based foods, something that is evident in modern supermarkets, where animal flesh, dairy, and eggs occupy a disproportionate share of refrigerated units. China's well-publicized "Hog Hotels'" provide a new model that eliminates the distance animals move in industrial life cycles by integrating specialized breeding, intensive growing, and slaughter and packing operations within multistory buildings that can produce an astonishing one million pigs per year. While this integration obviously reduces the energy and emissions associated with shipping live animals over land, the scale heightens various the other biophysical challenges that have been discussed in this section, such as managing even greater aggregations of feces, urine, corporal wastes, cleaning agents, slurries, wastewater, noxious gases, and particulate matter (*The Guardian* 2020; Patton 2018).

Illusory Cheapness: Discounted Costs and Risks

If a certain economic efficiency and rationality is at work in industrial livestock production, there is also deep inefficiency and irrationality in biophysical terms, together with immeasurable interspecies violence. The preceding section outlined key problems that are exacerbated or established in the course of achieving great increases in labor productivity and animal yields, and how these are never resolved but instead overridden in a range ways. Appreciating this dialectic relation between barriers to scale and the ways they are overridden provides a basis for unpacking the mounting costs and risks associated with industrial livestock, which effectively subsidize the productivity gains and ensuing abundance of relatively cheap commodities (Weis 2013, 2010).

As emphasized, the disarticulation of animals from land and into dense enclosures is an elemental aspect of the pursuit of scale, binding livestock to crop production in a fundamentally new way, and much of the world's livestock population now relies on concentrated feed derived from industrial grain and oilseed monocultures. This command of cropland represents one of the chief environmental burdens of industrial livestock production, because, though breeding and confinement have increased animal yields, much of the useable nutrition contained in this feed is still burned in nonproductive metabolic processes (Springmann et al. 2018; Lymbery 2014; Weis 2013; Foley et al. 2011; Ramankutty et al. 2008; Lappe 1991). The structural wastage of using grains and oilseeds this way increases the amount of land needed for agriculture, along with the resource budgets and pollution loads from the associated farm machinery and input use (e.g., fertilizers, pesticides, irrigation), and amplifies the myriad long-term problems posed by monoculture production: erosion and the loss of soil biodiversity, the bioaccumulation of persistent toxins, damage to pollinator populations, heightened risks of pesticide resistance, pressure on freshwater ecosystems, the overpumping of groundwater; and the salinization of arid and semiarid lands (Sage 2012; Weis 2010). Along with the direct climatic burden of using more fossil fuels and increasing greenhouse gas emissions, the inflated amount of land in cultivation represents foregone potential for ecological restoration and enhanced carbon sequestration. This amounts to a calamitous opportunity cost in light of the urgent need to respond to the crises of climate change and biodiversity loss, which is cast onto those on the frontlines of the climate emergency, future generations, and other species. Large-bodied animal species are disproportionately vulnerable to habitat loss and fragmentation, and roughly 60 percent of all top predator and large herbivore species now face proximate extinction risks (WWF 2020; Ripple 2016; Ripple et al. 2015). The role of expanding industrial monoculture in the loss of biodiversity also implicates it in heightened zoonotic disease risks, as further encroachment into forests and wetlands increases the opportunities for dangerous new diseases or variants to either spillover from their reservoir host species into human populations or jump to an amplifier host species that is in more regular contact with humans, and these risks are compounded by the surge in poaching and trade of wild animals and the novel cross-species encounters this is engendering (Akram-Lodhi 2021; WWF 2020; Wallace 2016).

The rising scale and specialization of breeding, growing, and slaughter-packing operations can be understood to form a series of spatially disaggregated conveyor belts, which involve resource- and pollution-intensive spaces and flows. As with monocultures, part of this stems from the production and movement of various inputs, including pharmaceuticals, pesticides, chemical disinfectants, and feed. Among these inputs, the fossil fuel consumption and CO_2 emissions associated with transport are highest with feed because of its bulkiness combined with the increased reliance on long-distance shipments within and between countries, such as the large volumes of corn inports flowing to Europe and soybean imports flowing to China (Oliveira and

Schneider 2016; Schneider and Sharma 2014). Further energy use and emissions result from the trucking of animals between specialized breeding facilities, growing operations, and slaughter-packing plants and the powering of various building operations (e.g., incubators, automated feeding systems, fans, lighting, air quality and security monitors, seasonal heating in certain climates, slaughter and disassembly lines, scalding tanks, and refrigeration units). The energy and emissions intensity of any one facility is contingent on a range of factors, including the distance animals are moving, the nature of the electricity grid, climate-related heating or cooling requirements, and the physiology of different species (ruminants tend to have far greater atmospheric impacts than monogastric species owing to worse feed conversion ratios and the methane generated by enteric fermentation) (Hayek and Miller 2021; Herrero et al. 2013).

Industrial livestock operations also generate more localized pollution burdens. The massive aggregations of biowastes in cesspools and feedlots and the ventilation from sheds result in airborne particulates (e.g., desiccated fecal dust) and gases (e.g., ammonia, hydrogen sulfide) that often carry a fierce stench and have been empirically linked to disproportionate levels of headaches and respiratory health problems in nearby communities (Neubert 2020; Blanchette 2019; Mallin and Cahoon 2003). Large cesspools and feedlots pose both chronic and periodic risks of water pollution. Variable standards govern how cesspools are lined, sometimes with only clay beds, which translates to variable risks of seepage and occasional rupture, though more durable foundations can also fail or spill over when triggered by heavy rainfall. The risks of sudden failure are intensifying with climate change, especially in tropical and subtropical regions facing intensifying storm surges.[17] Seepage and runoff from cesspools adds to the excess nutrient loads from synthetic fertilizers, and applications of treated slurries contribute to destructive nutrient loading that is affecting dead zones in both freshwater ecosystems and nearshore marine environments around the world. The water-pollution burden increases as a result of the heavy demand for water in slaughter and packing plants, the associated cleaning solvents, and disposal of blood and corporeal wastes (Neubert 2020; Blanchette 2020; Mallin and Cahoon 2003).

Efforts to contain infectious diseases obviously involve some direct costs for producers, mostly through the pharmaceutical override, but other costs are transferred to states, multilateral organizations, and populations at large—along with the incalculable long-term risks of the accelerated evolution of pathogens, or what was referred to above as the "cauldron effect" of industrial livestock (Marchese and Hovorka 2022; Davis 2020; Wallace 2016). One underappreciated way that the costs of infectious disease get passed on to consumers relates to the bacteria, such as *Salmonella* and *E. coli*, contained in various livestock products. These are often present at low concentrations and do little harm, or may cause diarrhea, cramps, and nausea that passes quickly and goes undiagnosed and untreated, but sometimes dangerous concentrations reverberate in public and private health costs and necessitate widespread product recalls. Much greater costs are associated with the emergence of dangerous new variants, both in terms of the perpetual monitoring activities of the national and international institutions (e.g., the costs of field and laboratory scientists) and in the emergency responses to wildfires, which involve state supports for mass killing and disposal of infected populations and compensation to producers (Sinel and Weis, forthcoming; Davis 2020; Wallace 2016). The calamitous scale of African Swine Fever in 2019–20 in China and other parts of Asia highlights this wildfire risk clearly (Kassam 2022). The rapid spread of this viral disease increased mortality rates and drew a mass killing response that led to a sharp fall in the annual volume of China's pig production, from 55 million tonnes in 2018 to an average 43 million tonnes in 2019–2020, and a brief decline in the annual volume of global meat production FAOSTATS 2023). The wildfire risks are also evident in mass killing events aimed at containing outbreaks of dangerous variants of avian and swine flu, which have occurred in many countries since the 1990s. With diseases like influenza, where there is a rare but always looming possibility that a more virulent and transmissible variant will at some point emerge, spillover into a human body, and become transmissible in human-to-human contact, the scope of the unaccounted costs associated with the cauldron effect of industrial livestock production are difficult to fathom, especially since it is quite plausible this could be the source of the next pandemic(Marchese and Hovorka 2022; Davis 2020; Wallace 2016).

Another undercounted cost in industrial livestock production relates to the nature of work. As discussed, while a pivotal organizing imperative is to replace labor with technology, there are a number of miserable and violent tasks that cannot yet be automated, from artificial insemination to bodily mutilations, shackling live bodies to dismembering carcasses. Large-scale slaughter and packing plants are still labor-intensive spaces despite their greatly increased labor productivity relative to that of small-scale butchers. Of course, these jobs do register as operational costs, but there is an exploitation that goes beyond the extraction of surplus value, where the labor processes center on the routinized painful or deathly acts or dismembering recently killed bodies. This burden is undoubtedly greatest on fast-moving kill floors, where workers encounter large numbers of writhing animals and are immersed in spaces filled with agonized cries and bloodshed. Demand for labor remains highest on fast-moving disassembly lines, where tasks center on quick and repeated cuts, which results in high rates of accidents, injuries, repetitive stress disorders, and job turnover (Blanchette 2020; Pachirat 2011; Striffler 2007; Eisnitz 2006).

Considering how fast artificial intelligence is advancing, it is highly possible that some of these tasks may soon be displaced by robots capable of quicker adjustments, moving even more of the interspecies violence from physical to intellectual labor and farther into the realm of science, engineering, and computer programing. But regardless of the extent of further mechanization, the design of the spaces of industrial livestock production relates to a final set of unaccounted, and incalculable costs: how it bears on anguishing conditions of life for a large and growing share of the world's mammals and birds.

Conclusions

Rising livestock populations have always played an important part in environmental change through the slow but steady advance of agricultural frontiers over millennia. While a great range of husbandry practices developed over long periods of time under diverse biophysical conditions, in general, the interspecies relations between peasants and pastoralists and their livestock were influenced by the fact that animals had an array of functions or use values and could only be reared at relatively low densities. This involved some restrictions to movement, interventions in reproduction, and, for certain large mammalian species, compelled muscle power. With respect to land, it is crucial to remember that animal-based foods and various functionalities were typically generated without the need to dedicate large amounts of cultivation to livestock. Key aspects of these relations continue to endure and evolve in the modern world among small mixed farms and pastoralists, though often in the context of highly unequal distributions of land, as small farmers have been widely pushed toward lower-quality agricultural land and herders face heightened barriers to movement. The resilience of both small farming and pastoralism is also increasingly strained by climatic changes, including rising average temperatures and rates of evapotranspiration, intensifying heat waves, and changing rainfall patterns.[18]

A range of important environmental problems are related to extensive grazing, the world's largest use of land. These includes the disastrous role of pasture in Amazonian deforestation; the methane emissions from large populations of ruminants; the role overgrazing plays in desertification; and the foregone potential for ecological restoration and carbon sequestration (Benton et al. 2021; Hayek and Miller 2021; IPCC 2019; Phillips et al. 2019; Machovina, Feeley, and Ripple 2015; Ripple et al. 2014; Gerber et al. 2013; Hedenus, Wirsenius, and Johansson 2014; Hecht and Cockburn 2010; Geist and Lambin 2004). Animals, especially in the arid and semiarid tropics, face increasing physiological strain from climate change, along with a range of other welfare concerns (Temple and Manteca 2020). The problems associated with extensive grazing have led some to insist that industrial livestock production, principally of poultry birds (given the superior feed conversion relative to mammalian livestock), represents a more climate-friendly way to meet the present and future demand for meat. This perspective can also be found in certain conceptions of "sustainable intensification" that prioritize the maximization of yields as the primary basis for reducing the total amount of land devoted to agriculture (Zampiga, Calini, and Sirri 2021; Grossi et al. 2019; Gerber et al. 2013; Hedenus, Wirsenius, and Johansson 2014; Thornton and Herrero 2010).

Although the contest to define sustainable intensification is beyond the scope of the discussion here, there is an unassailable tenet at its center: human nutritional needs can be met using far less land than is used at present, and doing so is crucial to prospects of mitigating the extent of climate change and increasing the space available for biodiversity, by releasing (or "sparing") land and restoring more forests, grasslands, and wetlands

(Pretty et al. 2018; Crist, Mora, and Engelman 2017; Tilman et al. 2011). What should be clear is that any attempt to fold industrial livestock production into conceptions of sustainable intensification must be fiercely contested. Instead of considering how best to meet both present and projected future demands for meat, any rational conception of sustainable intensification and land sparing must acknowledge, as a fundamental premise, the need to urgently reduce the consumption of animal-based foods and to dismantle industrial livestock operations. There is overwhelming scientific evidence that cycling grains and oilseeds through animals to produce food is an inefficient way to meet nutritional needs, and that livestock-heavy diets tend to command far more land, water, and other resources, and generate far more greenhouse gas emissions than diets that derive a comparable level of nutrition mainly or entirely from plant-based sources (Xu et al. 2021; IPCC 2019; Willett et al. 2019; Springmann et al. 2018, 2016; Poore and Nemecek 2018; Crist, Mora, and Engelman 2017; Machovina, Feeley, and Ripple 2015; Tilman and Clark 2014; Cederberg et al. 2013; Vermeulen, Campbell, and Ingram 2012; Mekonnen and Hoekstra 2012; Ramankutty et al. 2008; Gerbens-Leenes and Nonhebel 2002). It is also abundantly clear that the spaces of industrial livestock production carry highly unpredictable but immense risks of disease evolution (Marchese and Hovorka 2022; Davis 2020; Wallace 2016).

Finally, it is vitally important to understand how the compulsions of industrial capitalism have reconfigured the relations between humans, land, and livestock so radically from the sorts of relations, premised on multifunctionality, that were forged by diverse farming and herding cultures in the past and that still prevail on agroecological farms and among surviving herding cultures, which, however marginalized, constitute enduring and evolving alternatives to mechanized, input-intensive production (Scoones 2021; see Vandermeer and Perfecto, this volume, for a discussion of the material and ontological alternatives represented by agroecology). The great productivity increases achieved through industrialization in terms of labor and yields must not be conflated with efficiency gains. To appreciate the nature of this industrial revolution—its economic logic, biophysical illogic, and moral obliviousness to how animal lives are conceived and organized—this chapter examined the key steps in the disarticulation of livestock from land and the confinement of animals in densely-populated islands, including the outmoding of animal muscle power and the growing reliance on feed grains, a significant aspect of which was the role concentrated animals played in profitably absorbing grain and later oilseed surpluses. It then focused on the functioning of specialized breeding sites, growing operations, and slaughter and packing plants, which resemble spatially disaggregated conveyor belts that now dot and rely upon large areas of the world's highest quality agricultural land. The technological assemblages that underpin great productivity gains include proprietary breeding stock, instruments for artificial insemination and bodily mutilations, incubators, concentrated feed and automated feeders, pharmaceuticals, ventilation systems, high pressure sprayers, cesspools and slurry processing equipment, incinerators, decontamination showers, trucking operations, and whirring slaughter and packing lines. These systems subject billions of animals to lives of unfathomable pain and suffering, while establishing great spatial and cognitive distance between production and consumption (Weis 2016). The prevailing unconsciousness about the conditions of animal life is another of the great deceits of industrial livestock production, and efforts to illuminate and contest this interspecies violence have an important part to play in struggles to build more just, sustainable, and humane relations to land.

Acknowledgments

The author is sincerely grateful to Jun Borras, Jennifer Franco, Phil McMichael, and Jostein Jakobsen for their constructive input that helped in revising this chapter, and to Jun and Jennifer their patience and encouragement throughout. Any shortcomings remain mine alone.

Notes

1. For instance, the average person in the United States consumes about 120 kg of meat per year; whereas the average person in Africa consumes less than 20 kg of meat per year; and the average person in South Asia, well under 10 kg/year. Per capita consumption in China was well below the world average in 1980, around 20 kg/year, but today it is well above it, over 60 kg/year, and China is by far the world's leader in total meat production and consumption and home to roughly half the world's pigs (FAOSTATS 2023; Schneider 2018; Schneider and Sharma 2014).
2. Recent research now places the period of the first domestication of dogs much farther before the Neolithic than previously thought. Dogs simultaneously enhanced human hunting capacity and protection from other predators, and they had important roles supporting livestock husbandry, helping to herd, warn, and guard other animals.
3. Even at low densities and with limited technologies, humans managed landscapes and affected considerable ecological changes, using fire to augment the extent of grasslands, arrest forest succession, and enhance the distributions of large mammalian prey species (Pyne 2001; Flannery 2001). Human hunting prowess exerted a great deal of pressure on large animal species, especially as humans moved into new environments, to an extent that contributed (along with climatic pressures) to the extinction of many large mammalian species (Dawson 2016; Flannery 2001). With the rise of agriculture and herding, human groups began to manipulate the dynamics of ecosystems in far more calculated and spatially expansive ways.
4. Even the species used to quantify animal muscle power, the horse, was first domesticated for food rather than for transport or tillage.
5. The use of nitrogen-enhancing plants in fallowed fields was widely practiced without understanding the science of nitrogen fixation and its importance in soil fertility. The product of fallowed land could also be used in preparing hay and silage, which was needed in some climates to help sustain animals through hard winter conditions.
6. This was especially important where farming patterns did not include good plant-based sources of protein such as beans, peas, and nuts.
7. The big difference in the degrees of environmental management is reflected in the fuzziness about the total extent of extensive rangelands, with estimates ranging from 25 to 40 percent of all land in the modern world (Scoones 2021; Steinfeld et al. 2006).

8. Scott (2017) discusses the important role that livestock rearing played in relation to the expansion of cereal cultivation and the earliest state formations in the Fertile Crescent, while also emphasizing the considerable time lag between the initial period of crop and livestock domestication and the first states. That is, rather than quickly giving rise to marked social hierarchies, as some outdated narratives claim, farmers and herders continued to live in small groups far beyond the Neolithic Revolution, relying on foraging, fishing, and hunting to varying degrees, and it took many millennia before new classes and forms of surplus extraction eventually emerged.
9. This does not entail a tolerance for geriatric animals and natural lifespans, as at some point, waning utility typically led to slaughter for flesh.
10. Although animal muscle power involves some "free" elements (i.e., the unaccounted toil of animals), it also involves considerable human labor and time in tending, training, and compelling animals, and the opportunity cost of the land used to feed them. Early farm machinery tended to be more expensive to buy and operate than the labor and land associated with marshaling animal muscle power (Fitzgerald 2003).
11. One aspect of the electricity demand is that additional light was found to significantly enhance the bodily productivity of layer hens and dairy cows.
12. As a result of this specialization, male layer chicks—which have inferior flesh and grow slower than broilers—are uneconomical to raise, with the result that they began to be conceived as a waste product to be disposed of upon hatching, with variously techniques developed for killing and disposing infant birds. It is only within the past decade that some legal protections have begun to regulate these practices, and only in a handful of countries (Rutt and Jakobsen 2022).
13. Scientists are presently at work on a new mode of potentially overriding this task through biotechnology, which would reducing the time and cost associated with the waste disposal (Rutt and Jakobsen 2022).
14. This results from a combination of immobility and genetic changes, as accelerated rates of growth outpace skeletal development, most dramatically with modern chicken breeds, and accelerated rates of laying and lactation placing a great bodily strain on producing females.
15. For instance, in the United States, livestock consume over three-quarters of all antibiotics by volume, and most of this is administered at sub-therapeutic levels where it has been identified as a major public health concern (Hollis and Ahmed 2013).
16. When serious disease outbreaks have occurred, powerful interests advancing industrial livestock production have regularly sought to cast blame on small-scale husbandry (Allen and Lavau 2015; Dixon 2015). One glaring example occurred in Southeast Asia in the early 2000s, when leading corporations (most of all, Charoen Pokphand) pushed for a sweeping destruction of backyard poultry flocks in response to the emergence of a dangerous variant of avian flu (Davis 2020).
17. The state of North Carolina illustrates these risks dramatically. North Carolina has the second largest pig population in the United States, and one of the greatest densities of pigs of anywhere in the world, and it has been hit with multiple hurricanes in the recent decades. When Hurricane Floyd, in 1999, and Hurricane Florence, in 2018, tore through the big pig belt in North Carolina, they induced heavy flooding that sent huge volumes of untreated wastes into streams and rivers, causing two of the biggest freshwater pollution events in US history and devastating fish mortality—in addition to drowning many pigs and chickens.

18. Scoones (2021) provides an excellent detailed discussion of the socioecological diversity of pastoralism, and the resilience of herding cultures in the modern world in the face myriad challenges.

References

Adams, Carol J. 2010. *The Sexual Politics of Meat: A Feminist-Vegetarian Critical Theory*. 2nd ed. London: Bloomsbury.

Akram-Lodhi, Haroon. 2021. "Contemporary Pathogens and the Capitalist World Food System." *Canadian Journal of Development studies* 42 (1–2): 18–27.

Allen, John, and Stephanie Lavau. 2015. "'Just-in-Time' Disease: Biosecurity, Poultry and Power." *Journal of Cultural Economy* 8 (3): 342–360.

Anderson, Virginia D. 2006. *Creatures of Empire: How Domestic Animals Transformed Early America*. New York: Oxford University Press.

Bar-On, Yinon M., Rob Phillips, and Ron Milo. 2018. "The Biomass Distribution on Earth." *Proceedings of the National Academy of Sciences* 115 (25): 6506–6511.

Bayless-Smith, Timothy P. 1982. *The Ecology of Agricultural Systems*. Cambridge, UK: Cambridge University Press.

Bennett, Carys E., Richard Thomas, Mark Williams, Jan Zalasiewicz, Matt Edgeworth, Holly Miller, et al. 2018. "The Broiler Chicken as a Signal of a Human Reconfigured Biosphere." *Royal Society Open Science* 5. https://doi.org/10.1098/rsos.180325.

Benton, Tim, Carling Bieg, Helen Harwatt, Roshan Pudasaini, and Laura Wellesley. 2021. *Food System Impacts on Biodiversity Loss: Three Levers for Food System Transformation in Support of Nature*. London: Chatham House.

Berlan, Jean-Pierre. 1991. "The Historical Roots of the Present Agricultural Crisis." In *Toward a New Political Economy of Agriculture*, edited by William H. Friedland, Lawrence Busch, Frederick H. Buttel, and Alan P. Rudy, 115–136. Boulder, CO: Westview Press.

Bijay-Singh, and Eric Craswell. 2021. "Fertilizers and Nitrate Pollution of Surface and Ground Water: An Increasingly Pervasive Global Problem." *SN Applied Sciences* 3 (518): doi:10.1007/s42452-021-04521-8. https://link.springer.com/article/10.1007/s42452-021-04521-8.

Blanchette, Alex. 2015. "Herding Species: Biosecurity, Posthuman Labour, and the American Industrial Pig." *Cultural Anthropology* 30 (4): 640–669.

Blanchette, Alex. 2019. "Living Waste and the Labor of Toxic Health on American Factory Farms." *Medical Anthropology Quarterly* 33 (1): 80–100.

Blanchette, Alex. 2020. *Porkopolis American Animality, Standardized Life, and the Factory Farm*. Durham, NC: Duke University Press.

Boyd, William. 2001. "Making Meat: Science, Technology, and American Poultry Production." *Technology and Culture* 42 (4): 631–664.

Ceballos, Gerardo, Paul R. Ehrlich, and Rodolfo Dirzo. 2017. "Biological Annihilation via the Ongoing Sixth Mass Extinction Signaled by Vertebrate Population Losses and Declines." *Proceedings of the National Academy of Sciences* 114 (30): E6089–E6096.

Cederberg, Christel, Fredrik Hedenus, Stefan Wirsenius, and Ulf Sonesson. 2013. "Trends in Greenhouse Gas Emissions from Consumption and Production of Animal Food Products—Implications for Long-Term Climate Targets." *Animal* 7 (2): 330–340.

Crist, Eileen, Camila Mora, and Robert Engelman. 2017. "The Interaction of Human Population, Food Production, and Biodiversity Protection." *Science* 356 (6335): 260–264.

Cronon, William. 1991. *Nature's Metropolis: Chicago and the Great West.* New York: W. W. Norton.
Crosby, Alfred W. 1986. *Ecological Imperialism: The Biological Expansion of Europe, 900–1900.* Cambridge, UK: Cambridge University Press.
Crosby, Alfred W. 1972. *The Colombian Exchange: Biological and Cultural Consequences of 1492.* Westport, CT: Greenwood Press.
Dawson, Ashley. 2016. *Extinction: A Radical History.* New York: OR Books.
Davis, Karen. 2017. "Interspecies Sexual Assault: A Moral Perspective." *Animal Liberation Currents,* July 12. https://www.animalliberationcurrents.com/interspecies-sexual-assault/.
Davis, Karen. 2009. *Prisoned Chickens, Poisoned Eggs: An Inside Look at the Modern Poultry Industry.* 2nd ed, Summertown, TN: Book Publishing Company.
Davis, Mike. 2020. *The Monster Enters: Covid-19, Avian Flu, and the Plagues of Capitalism.* New York: OR Books.
Diamond, Jared. 2002. "Evolution, Consequences and Future of Plant and Animal Domestication." *Nature* 418 (6898): 700–707.
Dixon, Marion W. 2015. "Biosecurity and the Multiplication of Crises in the Egyptian Agri-food Industry." *Geoforum* 61 (5): 90–100.
Dirzo, Rodolpho, Hillary S. Young, Mauro Galetti, Gerardo Ceballos, Nick J. B. Isaac, and Ben Collen. 2014. "Defaunation in the Anthropocene." *Science* 345 (6195): 401–406.
Economou, Vangelis, and Panagiota Gousia. 2015. "Agriculture and Food Animals as a Source of Antimicrobial-Resistant Bacteria." *Infection and Drug Resistance* 8:49–61.
Ellis, Rebecca E., Tony Weis, Sainath Suryanarayanan, and Kata Beilin. 2020. "From a Free Gift of Nature to a Precarious Commodity: Bees, Pollination Services, and Industrial Agriculture." *Journal of Agrarian Change* 20 (3): 437–459.
Eisnitz, Gail A. 2006. *Slaughterhouse: The Shocking Story of Greed, Neglect, and Inhuman Treatment inside the US Meat Industry.* 2nd ed. Amherst, NY: Prometheus.
Erisman, Jan Willem, Mark A. Sutton, James Galloway, Zbigniew Klimont, and Wilfried Winiwarter. 2008. "How a Century of Ammonia Synthesis Changed the World." *Nature Geoscience* 1 (10): 636–639.
Fairlie, Simon. 2010. *Meat: A Benign Extravagance.* White River Junction, VT: Chelsea Green.
Fagan, Brian. 2015. *The Intimate Bond: How Animals Shaped Human History.* New York: Bloomsbury.
Famiglietti, Jay S. 2014. "The Global Groundwater Crisis." *Nature Climate Change* 4 (11): 945–948.
Fiddes, Nick. 1992. *Meat as a Natural Symbol.* London: Routledge.
Fitzgerald, Deborah. 2003. *Every Farm a Factory: The Industrial Ideal in Agriculture.* New Haven, CT: Yale University Press.
Flannery, Tim. 2001. *The Eternal Frontier: An Ecological History of North America.* New York: Grove Press.
Foley, Jonathan A., Navin Ramankutty, Kate A. Brauman, Emily S. Cassidy, James S. Gerber, Matt Johnston, et al. 2011. "Solutions for a Cultivated Planet." *Nature* 478 (7369): 337–342.
FAOSTATS. 2023. *Production & Resource STAT Calculators.* Rome: Food and Agriculture Organization of the United Nations, Statistics Division. http://www.fao.org/faostat/en/.
Galvin, Kathleen A. 2009. "Transitions: Pastoralists Living with Change." *Annual Review of Anthropology* 38: 185–198.
Geist, Helmut J., and Eric F. Lambin. 2004. "Dynamic Causal Patterns of Desertification." *BioScience* 54 (9): 817–829.

Genoways, Ted. 2014. *The Chain: Farm, Factory, and the Fate of Our Food*. New York: HarperCollins.

Gerbens-Leenes, P. Winnie, and Sanderine Nonhebel. 2002. "Consumption Patterns and Their Effects on Land Required for Food." *Ecological Economics* 42 (1–2): 185–199.

Gerber, PierreJ., Henning Steinfeld, Benjamin Henderson, Anne Mottet, Carolyn Opio, Jeroen Dijkman, et al. 2013. *Tackling Climate Change through Livestock—A Global Assessment of Emissions and Mitigation Opportunities*. Rome: Food and Agriculture Organization of the United Nations.

Gillespie, Kathryn. 2018. *The Cow with Ear Tag #1389*. Chicago: University of Chicago Press.

Godfray, H. Charles, Paul Aveyard, Tara Garnett, Jim W. Hall, Timothy J. Key, Jamie Lorimer, et al. 2018. "Meat Consumption, Health, and the Environment." *Science* 361 (6399). doi:10.1126/science.aam5324.

Grossi, Giampiero, Pietro Goglio, Andrea Vitali, and Adrian G. Williams. 2019. "Livestock and Climate Change: Impact of Livestock on Climate and Mitigation Strategies." *Animal Frontiers* 9 (1): 69–76.

The Guardian. 2020. "China's 26-Story Pig Skyscraper Ready to Slaughter 1 Million Pigs a Year." *The Guardian*, November 25. https://www.theguardian.com/environment/2022/nov/25/chinas-26-storey-pig-skyscraper-ready-to-produce-1-million-pigs-a-year.

Harris, Marvin. 1974. *Cows, Pigs, Wars, and Witches: The Riddles of Culture*. New York: Vintage.

Hayek, Matthew N., and Scot M. Miller. 2021. "Underestimates of Methane from Intensively Raised Animals Could Undermine Goals of Sustainable Development." *Environmental Research Letters* 16 (6): Article 063006.

Hecht, Susanna B., and Alexander Cockburn. 2010. *The Fate of the Forest: Developers, Destroyers and Defenders of the Amazon*. 2nd ed. Chicago: University of Chicago Press.

Hedenus, Fredrik, Stefan Wirsenius, and Daniel J. A. Johansson. 2014. "The Importance of Reduced Meat and Dairy Consumption for Meeting Stringent Climate Change Targets." *Climatic Change* 124:79–91.

Herrero, Mario, Petr Havlik, Hugo Valin, An Notenbaert, Mariana C. Rufino, Philip K. Thornton, et al. 2013. "Biomass Use, Production, Feed Efficiencies and Greenhouse Gas Emissions from Global Livestock Systems." *Proceedings of the National Academy of Sciences* 110 (52): 20888–20893.

Hollis, Aidan, and Ziana Ahmed. 2013. "Preserving Antibiotics, Rationally." *New England Journal of Medicine* 26 (369): 2474–2476.

Howard, Philip H. 2016. *Concentration and Power in the Food System*. New York: Bloomsbury.

Imhoff, Daniel, ed. 2011. *The CAFO Reader: The Tragedy of Industrial Animal Factories*. Berkeley: University of California Press.

IPES-Food. 2017. *Too Big to Feed: Exploring the impacts of mega-mergers, consolidation and concentration of power in the agri-food sector*. Report of the International Panel of Experts on Sustainable Food Systems and the ETC Group. https://www.ipes-food.org/_img/upload/files/Concentration_FullReport.pdf.

IPCC. 2019. *Special Report on Climate Change, Desertification, Land Degradation, Sustainable Land Management, Food Security, and Greenhouse Gas Fluxes in terrestrial Ecosystems*. Intergovernmental Panel on Climate Change, Geneva. https://www.ipcc.ch/site/assets/uploads/sites/4/2022/11/SRCCL_Full_Report.pdf.

Kassam, Ashifa. 2022. "Scientists Rush to Create Vaccine for World's Biggest Animal Disease Outbreak." *The Guardian*, October 20. https://www.theguardian.com/environment/2022/oct/20/scientists-rush-to-create-vaccine-for-worlds-biggest-animal-disease-outbreak.

Lappé, Frances M. 1991. *Diet for a Small Planet*. 3rd ed. New York: Ballantine.

Lees, Alexander C., Lucy Haskell, Tris Allinson, Simeon B. Bezeng, Ian J. Burfield, Luis Miguel Renjiet, et al. 2022. "State of the World's Birds." *Annual Review of Environment and Resources* 47 (1): 233–260.

Levitt, Tom. 2019. "The Smell, the Noise, the Dust: My Neighbour, the Factory Farm." *The Guardian*, July 24. https://www.theguardian.com/environment/2019/jul/24/the-smell-the-noise-the-dust-my-neighbour-the-factory-farm.

Lymbery, Philip. 2014. *Farmageddon: The True Cost of Cheap Meat*. New York: Bloomsbury.

Machovina, Brian, Kenneth J. Feeley, and William J. Ripple. 2015. "Biodiversity Conservation: The Key Is Reducing Meat Consumption." *Science of the Total Environment* 536:419–431.

Marchese, Alyssa, and Alice Hovorka. 2022. "Zoonoses Transfer, Factory Farms and Unsustainable Human-Animal Relations." *Sustainability* 14 (19): Article: 12806. doi.org/10.3390/ su141912806. https://www.mdpi.com/2071-1050/14/19/12806.

Mallin, Michael, and Lawrence B. Cahoon. 2003. "Industrialized Animal Production: A Major Source of Nutrient and Microbial Pollution to Aquatic Ecosystems." *Population and Environment* 24 (5): 369–385.

Mekonnen, Mesfin M., and Arjen Y. Hoekstra. 2012. "A Global Assessment of the Water Footprint of Farm Animal Products." *Ecosystems* 15 (3): 401–415.

Mintz, Sidney W., and Daniela Schlettwein-Gsell. 2001. "Food Patterns in Agrarian Societies: The 'Core-Fringe-Legume Hypothesis.'" *Gastronomica* 1 (3): 40–52.

Montgomery, David R. 2007. *Dirt: The Erosion of Civilizations*. Berkeley: University of California Press.

Morehead, Martha S., and Catherine Scarbrough. 2018. "Emergence of Global Antibiotic Resistance." *Primary Care* 45 (3): 467–484.

Moss, Michael. 2013. *Salt, Sugar, Fat: How the Food Giants Hooked Us*. Toronto: McClelland and Stewart.

Mulchandani, Ranya, Yu Wang, Marius Gilbert, and Thomas P. Van Boeckel. 2023. "Global Trends in Antimicrobial Use in food-Producing Animals: 2020 to 2030." *PLOS Global Public Health* 3: article e0001305.

Nestle, Marion. 2013. *Food Politics: How the Food Industry Influences Nutrition, and Health*. 3rd ed. Berkeley: University of California Press.

Neubert, Christopher. 2020. "The Anthropocene Stinks! Odor, Affect, and the Entangled Politics of Livestock Waste in a Rural Iowa Watershed." *Society and Space* 38 (4): 736–752.

Nibert, David A. 2013. *Animal Oppression and Human Violence: Domesecration, Capitalism, and Global Conflict*. New York: Columbia University Press.

Oliveira, Gustavo de L. T., and Mindi Schneider. 2016. "The Politics of Flexing Soybeans: China, Brazil and Global Agroindustrial Restructuring." *Journal of Peasant Studies* 43 (1): 167–194.

O'Neill, Jim. 2016. *Tackling Drug-Resistant Infections Globally: Final Report and Recommendations*. London: Review on Antimicrobial Resistance.

Pachirat, Timothy. 2011. *Every Twelve Seconds: Industrialized Slaughter and the Politics of Sight*. New Haven, CT: Yale University Press.

Pacyga, Dominic A. 2015. *Slaughterhouse: Chicago's Union Stock Yard and the World It Made*. Chicago: University of Chicago Press.

Patton, Dominique. 2018. "China's Multistory Hog Hotels Elevate Industrial Farms to New Levels." Reuters, May 10. https://www.reuters.com/article/us-china-pigs-hotels-insight-idUSKBN1IB362.

Pew Commission. 2008. *Putting Meat on the Table: Industrial Farm Animal Production in America*. Report. Washington, DC: Pew Charitable Trusts and Johns Hopkins Bloomberg School of Public Health.

Pretty, Jules, Tim G. Benton, Zareen Pervez Bharucha, Lynn V. Dicks, Cornelia Butler Flora, H. Charles Godfray, et al. 2018. "Global assessment of agricultural system redesign for sustainable intensification." *Nature Sustainability* 1 (8): 441–446.

Poore, Joseph, and Thomas Nemecek. 2018. "Reducing Food's Environmental Impacts through Producers and Consumers." *Science* 360 (6392): 987–992.

Phillips, Dom, Daniel Camargos, Andre Campos, Andrew Wasley, and Alexandra Heal. 2019. "Revealed: Rampant Deforestation of Amazon Driven by Global Greed for Meat." *The Guardian*, July 2. http://www.theguardian.com/environment/2019/jul/02/revealed-amazon-deforestation-driven-global-greed-meat-brazil.

Pyne, Stephen J. 2001. *Fire: A Brief History*. Seattle: University of Washington Press.

Ramankutty, Navin, Amato T. Evan, Chad Monfreda, and Jonathan A. Foley. 2008. "Farming the Planet: 1. Geographic Distribution of Global Agricultural Lands in the Year 2000." *Global Biogeochemical Cycles* 22 (1): Article GB1003.

Reichert, Joshua S., Karen Steuer, Velma Smith, Robert Martin, Julie Janovsky, and Micaela Fischer. 2011. *Big Chicken: Pollution and Industrial Poultry Production in America*. Washington, DC: PEW Environmental Group.

Reid, Robin S., María E. Fernández-Giménez, and Kathleen A. Galvin. 2014. "Dynamics and Resilience of Rangelands and Pastoral Peoples around the Globe." *Annual Review of Environment and Resources* 39:217–242.

Rifkin, Jeremy. 1992. *Beyond Beef: The Rise and Fall of the Cattle Culture*. New York: Dutton.

Ripple, William J. 2016. "Saving the World's Terrestrial Megafauna." *BioScience* 66 (10): 807–812.

Ripple, William J., Thomas M. Newsome, Christopher Wolf, Rodolfo Dirzo, Kristoffer T. Everatt, Mauro Galetti, et al. 2015. "Collapse of the World's Largest Herbivores." *Science Advances* 1: Article e1400103.

Ripple, William J., Pete Smith, Helmut Haberl, Stephen A. Montzka, Clive McAlpine, and Douglas H. Boucher. 2014. "Ruminants, Climate Change, and Climate Policy." *Nature Climate Change* 4 (1): 2–5.

Rutt, Rebecca L., and Jostein Jakobsen. 2022. "The 'Brother Layer Problem': Routine Killing, Biotechnology and the Pursuit of 'Ethical Sustainability' in Industrial Poultry." *Environment and Planning E: Nature and Space* 6 (3): 1785–1803.

Sage, Colin. 2012. *Environment and Food*. London: Routledge.

Sale, Kirkpatrick. 2006. *After Eden: The Evolution of Human Domination*. Durham, NC: Duke University Press.

Schneider, Mindi. 2018. "Reforming the Humble Pig: Pigs, Pork, and Contemporary China." In *Animals through Chinese History*, edited by Roel Sterckx, Martina Siebert, and Dagmar Schafer, 233–243. Cambridge, UK: Cambridge University Press.

Schneider, Mindi, and Shefali Sharma. 2014. *China's Pork Miracle? Agribusiness and Development in China's Pork Industry*. Washington, DC: Institute for Agriculture and Trade Policy.

Scoones, Ian. 2021. "Pastoralists and Peasants: Perspectives on Agrarian Change." *Journal of Peasant Studies* 48 (1): 1–47.

Scott, James C. 2017. *Against the Grain: A Deep History of the Earliest States*. New Haven, CT: Yale University Press.

Sinel, Martin, and Tony Weis. Forthcoming. "Ventilation Shutdown and the Breath-Taking Violence of Infectious Disease Emergency Management in Industrial Livestock Production." *Environment and Planning E: Nature and Space.*

Smil, Vaclav. 2001. *Enriching the Earth: Fritz Haber, Carl Bosch, and the Transformation of Food Production.* Cambridge, MA: MIT Press.

Smil, Vaclav. 2013. *Harvesting the Biosphere: What We Have Taken from Nature.* Cambridge, MA: MIT Press.

Springmann, Marco, Michael Clark, Daniel Mason-D'Croz, Keith Wiebe, Benjamin Leon Bodirsky, Luis Lassaletta, et al. 2018. "Options for Keeping the Food System within Environmental Limits." *Nature* 562:519–525.

Springmann, Marco, H. Charles Godfray, Mike Rayner, and Peter Scarborough. 2016. "Analysis and Valuation of the Health and Climate Cobenefits of Dietary Change." *Proceedings of the National Academy of Sciences* 113 (15): 4146–4151.

Steinfeld, Henning, Pierre Gerber, Tom Wassenaar, Vincent Castel, Mauricio Rosales, and Cees de Haan. 2006. *Livestock's Long Shadow: Environmental Issues and Options.* Rome: Food and Agriculture Organization of the United Nations.

Striffler, Steve. 2007. *Chicken: The Dangerous Transformation of America's Favorite Food.* New Haven, CT: Yale University Press.

Temple, Deborah, and Xavier Manteca. 2020. "Animal Welfare in Extensive Production Systems Is Still an Area of Concern." *Frontiers in Sustainable Food Systems* 4: Article 545902.

Thornton, Philip K., and Mario Herrero. 2010. "Potential for Reduced Methane and Carbon Dioxide Emissions from Livestock and Pasture Management in the Tropics." *Proceedings of the National Academy of Sciences* 107 (46): 19667–19672.

Tilman, David, and Michael Clark. 2014. "Global Diets Link Environmental Sustainability and Human Health." *Nature* 515 (7528): 518–522.

Tilman, David, Christian Balzer, Jason Hill, and Belinda L. Befort. 2011. "Global Food Demand and the Sustainable Intensification of Agriculture." *Proceedings of the National Academy of Sciences* 108 (50): 20260–20264.

Ventola, C. Lee. 2015. "The Antibiotic Resistance Crisis. Part 1: Causes and Threats." *Pharmacy and Therapeutics* 40 (4): 277–283.

Vermeulen, Sonja J., Bruce M. Campbell, and John S. I. Ingram. 2012. "Climate Change and Food Systems." *Annual Review of Environment and Resources* 37:195–222.

Wallace, Rob. 2016. *Big Farms Make Big Flu: Dispatches on Infectious Disease, Agribusiness, and the Nature of Science.* New York: Monthly Review.

Weis, Tony. 2010. "The Accelerating Biophysical Contradictions of Industrial Capitalist Agriculture." *Journal of Agrarian Change* 10 (3): 315–341.

Weis, Tony. 2013. *The Ecological Hoofprint: The Global Burden of Industrial Livestock.* London: Zed.

Weis, Tony. 2016. "Toward 120 Billion: Dietary Change and Animal Lives." *Radical Philosophy* 199 (5): 8–13.

Weis, Tony. 2021. "Animals as and on Resource Frontiers." *Commodity Frontiers* 3:1–13.

Willett, Walter, Johan Rockstrom, Brent Loken, Marco Springmann, Tim Lang, Sonja Vermeulen, et al. 2019. "Food in the Anthropocene: The EAT-*Lancet* Commission on Healthy Diets from Sustainable Food Systems." *The Lancet* 393 (10170): 447–492.

Williams, Michael. 2006. *Deforesting the Earth: From Prehistory to Global Crisis.* Chicago: University of Chicago.

Winders, Bill, and David Nibert. 2004. "Consuming the Surplus: Expanding 'Meat' Consumption and Animal Oppression." *International Journal of Sociology and Social Policy* 24 (9): 76–96.

Worster, Donald. 1990. "Transformations of the Earth: Toward an Agroecological Perspective in History." *Journal of American History* 76 (4): 1087–1106.

WWF. 2020. *Living Planet Report 2020: Bending the Curve of Biodiversity Loss*. Gland, Switzerland: World Wide Fund for Nature.

Xu, Xiaoming, Prateek Sharma, Shijie Shu, Tzu-Shun Lin, Philippe Ciais, Francesco N. Tubiello, et al. 2021. "Global Greenhouse Gas Emissions from Animal-Based Foods Are Twice Those of Plant-Based Foods." *Nature Food* 2:724–732.

Zampiga, Marco, Franco Calini, and Federico Sirri. 2021. "Importance of Feed Efficiency for Sustainable Intensification of Chicken Meat Production: Implications and Role for Amino Acids, Feed Enzymes and Organic Trace Minerals." *World's Poultry Science Journal* 77 (3): 639–659.

Zeder, Melinda A. 2012. "The Domestication of Animals." *Journal of Anthropological Research* 68 (2): 161–190.

CHAPTER 16

LAND AND AGROECOLOGY

Interpenetrating Theses

JOHN VANDERMEER AND IVETTE PERFECTO

Contrasting Narratives about the Origins of Agriculture

There is a standard story about how we, as a species, have related to land. For most of our existence, the story goes, our species has engaged in a style of food acquisition and territory recognition (land from which the food can be extracted) called "hunting and gathering," sometimes referred to simply as "foraging." Small groups of, usually related, people wandered the ecosystem gathering fruits, nuts, and tubers and hunting animals. For some scholars, this way of life was the original Hobbesian nightmare; to others, it was a Rousseauian paradise (Lee and Daly 1999). Recent archeological work rejects both the nightmare and paradise scenarios, and suggests that foragers in the past varied enormously, as do those who remain in today's world (Graeber and Wengrow 2021).

The standard story continues with what is considered almost the antithesis of the foraging lifestyle—agriculture. Agriculture, it is said, created a tipping point, where abundant food suddenly became available to human groups and the narratives regarding land and territory changed accordingly. On the one hand, people no longer had to go hungry; on the other hand, a surplus could be stolen and, therefore, needed to be protected. Speculation is easy in search of essentialist details—since we no longer need to spend all our time gathering food, we can make art. Or, since we have plenty of food stored, we need to organize an army to protect it. The empirical reality is considerably more complicated than most of the proffered generalizations (Graeber and Wengrow 2021) suggest. However, one generalization seems to outweigh others in historical importance and extends to how we understand the current situation of the relationship between land and agriculture, and especially of agroecology and its potential. Marx, among others, proposed that the ecological niche currently occupied by more than half of the human population, the "city," became a possibility because of the surplus food produced by the new technology of agriculture (Schwartz 1985; Harari 2014). Earlier bands of foragers, constrained to wander the environment looking for food to harvest and game to hunt, were unable to settle down to form what would become cities. But some authors argue that the current understanding of archaeological evidence suggests that the story may have been almost the reverse (Hodder 2020). The emergence of the "city" was first, and its very existence required developing the technology called agriculture. The association with land, its use value, and, eventually, its exchange value are part and parcel of this narrative, wherein the land value of a rural farm is valued by square hectare, while the land value of an urban garden is valued by square meter.

Not Completely Clear What Constitutes Agriculture, in the First Place

A rich panoply of analytical framings characterizes the question of what agriculture is, which began well before the recent emergence of agroecology as a dynamic intellectual and political framing.

Perhaps the particularities of the Huaorani, a people living in the upper Amazon of today's Ecuador, as reported extensively by Laura Rival (2002), offer clues to how to think expansively about the nature of agriculture and its traditional relationship to land and territory. The Huaorani are considered hunter-gatherers. They hunt and gather in the rainforest where they live, establishing temporary campsites that may last for several years. Although they are classified as a nonagricultural group, the Huaorani nevertheless cultivate some domesticated plants, in particular, the peach palm (*Bactris gasipaes*) and cassava (*Manihot esculenta*). The peach palm tree bears a nutritious fruit. The Huaorani typically gather all sorts of fruit from the forest, and so the fact that they feed on the fruit of a particular species of palm tree is not necessarily noteworthy. Yet they plant the palms quite purposefully to produce fruit for the future. As Huaorani people move from campsite to campsite, they remember where the palm groves are, which means they remember something of their ancestry through planting trees. Is this agriculture? A domesticated plant, the peach palm, is planted and later harvested, sometimes by future generations, activities that can be thought of as agriculture, yet most anthropologists insist that the Huaorani people are a hunter-gatherer society.

Furthermore, they also plant domesticated cassava (*Manihot esculenta*), mainly in natural light gaps in the forest. Culturally, the planted cassava is not so much used for food but for making a fermented drink used in ritualized drinking ceremonies. Cultivating cassava requires no plowing, minimal land clearing, and little, if any, maintenance, which could be the reason the Huaoranis are considered foragers rather than agriculturalists. But perhaps most telling is Rival's description of trekking with Huaorani and how they interact with the forest:

> People regularly leave their longhouses for hunting and foraging trips and move through vast territories in such a way that distinguishing between "extracting" and "management" becomes almost impossible. Wherever a Huaorani finds herself in the forest, she chances upon needed plants. She is particularly vague on whether these strategic and handy resources were planted by someone or just happened to grow there. She is even vaguer on *when* it was that people lived in the area marked by human activities. What matters to her is that the occurrence of useful plants can be related either to individuals or to house groups, or even to indeterminate users of a particular area.

She goes on to note that

> people engage in various daily activities (planting, selecting, transplanting, protecting, using, and discarding) that have a direct or indirect effect on the distribution of species. (2002, 80)

Rival (2002) argues that the Huaorani "procure" rather than "produce" their food, making a useful general distinction between the gatherer mode and the agriculturist mode. Yet the Huaorani challenge the idea of what the technology called *agriculture* is actually about, when they "plant, select, transplant, protect, use and discard" plants, yet are not regarded as agriculturalists. Furthermore, the "land" on which the Huaorani forage seems to share a philosophical kinship with the idea of a "built environment" (Horgan and Dimitrijević 2020) in that the land contains the consequences of humans constructing the nature it contains. If land is "the space where solar energy and soil fertility are converted, through human labor, into food and other agricultural products" (see van der Ploeg, this volume), it is clear that the Huaorani people, to some extent, engage in a relationship to land that is similar to that of many agriculturalist societies, of which many well-known examples could be cited from both post- and preagricultural time frames.

Going back even further, it seems probable that *Homo erectus*, having tamed fire, would have used that fire, perhaps to encourage the growth of particular plants or groups of plants and discourage others, or to attract prey to hunt, or to scare away predators who viewed them as prey. Perhaps more important are the ecosystem engineering effects the control of fire would have permitted. In other words, going back more than a million years, the ability of *Homo erectus* to control fire was, perhaps, the first major land modification caused directly by our ancestors, and it set the stage for our future relationship with land. This relationship persisted for millennia, changing gradually with the proliferation of fully agricultural societies and then dramatically over the last century as we will discuss in the next section (see "Setting the Stage: The Industrial Agricultural System").

In recent decades, anthropologists have come to view hunter-gatherer cultures as active participants in the process of ecosystem engineering, using such practices as "prescribed burning, tillage, pruning, seed broadcasting, transplanting, mulching/

fertilizing, weeding, and irrigating, as well as the tending of clam beds and fish eggs" (Lightfoot et al. 2013). These practices, when engaged in by what are basically foraging cultures, are referred to as "traditional resource and environmental management" (Fowler and Lepofsky 2011). Recently, Ellis and colleagues (2021) provided empirical analysis demonstrating that most of what we today call "wild nature" is, in fact, a complicated product of these sorts of traditional management and agriculture styles. Indeed, this kind of human relationship to the land has shaped terrestrial ecosystems in the biosphere for more than 12,000 years, and arguably been less destructive of biodiversity and normal ecosystem function than the modern counterparts (Ellis et al. 2021).

Land Ownership?

Mark Twain's fanciful story about a farm that slid down a mountain, brings up certain essential absurdities about land and agriculture (see Steinberg 1995). The buildings, stables, farmhouse, topsoil, and more, of one farm slide down the side of the mountain, which has been eroded by rainfall, onto land owned by a farmer in the valley. The question then arises, Who "owns" the farm now that it is on a different piece of land? In the story, the wisdom of the judge holds that the "owner" of the original land is entitled to dig out his original farm, but the Lord chose to slide the farm down the mountain, and who are we to question the wisdom of the almighty?

Land ownership, assumed to be almost a human right, inevitably bends to the will of human political necessity, and from the English enclosures of the seventeenth century to the US-influenced enclosures of the Mexican ejidos in preparation for NAFTA toward the end of the twentieth century, it has been understood that fences shall surround private land to distinguish private property and permit its selling to the highest bidder. Under capitalism, this seemingly divine ordination is as foundational as the atomic theory of matter or the germ theory of disease. The Enclosure Act 1773 in Great Britain set in motion a series of political maneuvers to restrict access to common land that by 1883 had culminated in 46 distinct pieces of legislation. The effect of this movement, recognizable today in the massive land grabbing that continues around the world (Borras et al. 2011), was to provide the dual platforms of the capitalist agricultural system—dispossession of the actual tillers of the land and the creation of the needed industrial reserve army for the emerging capitalist system, with its basic social construction of land as either rural or urban. The modern industrial agricultural system is ultimately dependent on both the early version of land grabbing and the parallels we see today.

Bringing the "Factories into the Fields"

In Samuel Copland's (1866) mighty tome *Agriculture, Ancient and Modern*, there is a drawing that illustrates how those who thought about agriculture in the nineteenth century envisioned the future. The scene is inside a barn, or what looks like a barn. But then you notice that it is filled with all the new mechanical inventions that were transforming agriculture at that point—corn huskers, seed grinders, seed sorters—an impressive array of newfangled machines. All of them are connected to belts, which are connected to a central rod, high up near the ceiling, which is, in turn, connected to a stationary steam engine. At first glance, you would not be faulted for thinking you were looking into a small factory in the nineteenth century. And, of course, that was the point. The "farmer" was not wearing overalls, but a vest, and he held in his hand, not a hoe, but an oil can, looking just like a factory worker. This was the image of visionary analysts in the nineteenth century. The farm was to follow everything else, and wind up housing a factory full of workers dutifully operating machines. It would be another triumph of the Industrial Revolution.

Things did not work out as Copland envisioned, and nature seems to have resented being packed up and stuffed into a container. But the underlying logic won out in the end, even if the initial vision turned out to be silly. As the title of a much later (1935) book, *Factories in the Fields*, suggests, rather than bringing a recalcitrant nature into the factory, the factories were brought into the fields (McWilliams 2000). Industrial capitalism penetrated agriculture, but not with the presumed inevitable inertia that Samuel Copland's vision suggested. Indeed, the capture of agriculture by industrial capitalism happened slowly. It was not really until the two great world wars of the twentieth century that the full vision was realized.

The Chemicalization of Agriculture

The wars stimulated major breakthroughs in chemistry. German chemists were able to mimic what nature had been doing through biological nitrogen fixation and took nitrogen out of the air and, with a lot of energy, made ammonia, which was easily converted to nitrate (Kumar and Elias 2019), a major component of the explosives and munitions used during World War I. The explosive power of ammonium nitrate may have killed many soldiers on the battlefield, but after the war, its provisioning of nitrogen in the fields enabled nitrogen depleted land to be productive again.

A second major push to the industrial system came in the wake of World War II and, again, involved major inputs from the science of chemistry. Pests, which is to say, organisms that either eat the food we produce or interfere with our ability to get that food, have been the bane of food acquisition since well before agriculture. Attempts to control them are recorded in ancient records from Egypt (Evans and Weinstein 2021) to China (Chengxiang, 1988). Those efforts were revolutionized by events that played out while the Allies were fighting the Fascists in Germany and Japan, especially in the aftermath of that war (Russell 2001). As in all previous wars, soldiers during World War II had to contend with horrible extra-battle conditions, from low food supplies to sleeping in muddy fox holes and, especially, coming down with diseases transmitted by insect vectors, like mosquitoes, killing more soldiers than were killed in battle. In 1939, an inventive Swiss chemist realized that the chemical dichlorodiphenyltrichloroethane

(DDT) was a poison that effectively killed insects. Eliminating the mosquitos that carried the diseases that killed soldiers was a major benefit that the science of chemistry provided.

The main problem emerged after the war. Yes, the pesticides did kill the mosquitoes and probably saved many lives during the war, but it was the prospect of peace that troubled those who manufactured the chemicals. Various chemical companies had been producing vast quantities of DDT and other chemicals for the war effort. As the war was winding down, rational planners expected an "underconsumption crisis." With all the manufacturing capacity having been lavishly funded by vast militaries from several countries (both winners and losers), a way for utilizing the enormous wartime capacity was desperately needed as the war ended. Agriculture, with its long history of dealing with insect pests, was the obvious solution. The problem was that farmers did not easily accept the idea of poisoning their farms. To convince farmers that DDT could solve their traditional problems with pests, pesticide manufacturers (especially in the United States) came up with the idea for a major propaganda campaign (Russell 2001). So much support had been generated for the war effort, that anything associated with winning the war against fascism was golden. The companies leveraged this patriotic feeling to create a parallel between the armaments that helped win the war (DDT and other pesticides) and the "war" against insect pests the farmers already knew was ongoing in their fields. Advertisements, mainly in farming magazines, pictured farmers holding pesticide spray cans in positions reminiscent of soldiers with machine guns. Cannons that looked like spray nozzles attacked bugs with the heads of Hitler and Mussolini. Gradually, the prewar narrative of the farmer as a wise nurturer of a piece of land in harmony with nature was replaced by the narrative of the farmer as a soldier fighting battles against an unscrupulous enemy—that is, from health caretaker who keeps the patient healthy and prevents disease, to warrior who dominates and extirpates the enemy. One way of looking at it, contrary to the popular triumphalist story, is as the transformation of agriculture from a system of land management to a system of land domination.

The nitrogen originally used to make wartime explosives, the pesticides originally used to free soldiers from diseases, and the machines Copland had envisioned in 1866 all combined to give us the modern system that burdens us today. Bringing the large machines into the fields made sense only if the fields themselves were large, so those infamous land enclosures ensured that ownership would become excessively concentrated. Killing pests with poisons also killed many of the predators of those pests and of other herbivores (i.e., potential pests) in the system, ironically causing more insects to become pests as their original predators were killed—thus more demand for pesticides was created by the pesticides themselves, which was good for the companies. Saturating the soil with nitrogen solved the problem of supplying this essential nutrient to the crops, even though much of it ran off the land in solution with the water that ran off into the streams and rivers, and perhaps even more got converted to nitrous oxide, contributing in a major way to the problem of global warming.

The Green Revolution as an Ideological Revolution

This new system was eagerly embraced mainly in the United States and in Europe and some of its former colonies, the so-called First World, in the postwar frenzy to capture the world political and economic leadership. The Soviet Union had lost 27 million citizens in the war and had roundly defeated the fascists throughout eastern Europe, consolidating a "Second World," thus initiating a Cold War terminology—the Soviet Union as the "East" in contrast to the United States and England as the "West," both engorged from the fortunes of war on a very large scale. Here were two worlds, the capitalist world (creatively called the "free" world) and the socialist/communist world. But looming in the center of the fight was most of the world's population, who lived neither in the first nor the second world, but sort of in limbo, a "third" world. This Third World, it was called, would eventually be transformed into a communist utopia (according to some) or a capitalist utopia (according to others).

Although there were enormous ideological differences between the two purported utopias, when it came to the agricultural land of the times, the ideological narrative was only marginally different. Both saw the small-scale farmer of the Third World, the global South, as a backward peasant who had to be saved by modern agriculture; and both capitalists and socialists had the same technological vision of how to do that—big machines, lots of pesticides, lots of chemical fertilizers, monocultures, concentrated land (held by the prosperous under capitalism, and by the state under socialism). The difference between the visions had to do with how to get there and who owns the land. Both agreed that the modern industrial system should and would be the result.

The capitalist world acknowledged the ideological attractiveness of the socialist/communist narrative, especially from the point of view of the world's poor. Since the majority of the world's poor lived in the global South, and most were peasant farmers, delivering on the promises of the modern agricultural system became central to the political strategies of both sides in the Cold War. As the Red Revolution seemed to be spreading around the world, and revolutionary movements began gaining strength in the Americas, South Asia, and Africa, the narrative on the capitalist side was that poor people could easily be victims of communist propaganda—someone telling poor people that their condition stems from inherent contradictions in the capitalist system is dangerous when you're fighting a war to claim it's not. The fact that the world's poor were mainly farmers suggested that the main problem was the poverty that stems from poor production technology. In avowed contradiction to the Red Revolution, US policy counterposed the "Green Revolution" explicitly to counter this seemingly convincing narrative. The Green Revolution would bring machinery, pesticides, fertilizers, high-yielding hybrid seeds, irrigation, and the like, to those poor peasants, helping them to resist the temptations of the propaganda of the Red Revolution. It must be understood from the beginning the worldwide expansion of the industrial capitalist system had this very political logic, having only marginally to do with "feeding the world" and more to do with winning the Cold War (Patel 2013). Ironically, in Latin America, the Green

Revolution and the rural development programs used to promote it left out the one component that may have succeeded in capturing the hearts and minds of the peasant farmers in the global South—land reform. Consequently, only landed mid- and large-scale farmers benefited from those programs (Escobar 2011).

Consequences of the Intensification

If the publication of Copland's book in 1866 was a landmark event at the beginning of the modern industrial agricultural system, the publication of Rachel Carson's *Silent Spring* in 1962 represents a milestone signaling the beginning of its end. Carson's book is sometimes heralded as the midwife of the modern environmental movement. It deserves that honor, but let us remember that it was about agriculture, specifically the malignant growth of that industrial system that resulted in superfund sites, dead waterways, ocean dead zones, and, only recently understood, global climate change. In citing that work as a milestone, we are attempting to close the book on sensible evaluation. The modern industrial agricultural system has been evaluated and found wanting—perhaps not merely wanting, but, figuratively and literally, poisonous and destructive. We may disagree on just what needs to be promoted to replace it, but we need no longer argue about the need to close the book on it.

The shift from an agricultural system where farmers depended on the resource base provided mostly by the land to a system where most inputs were bought into the market from outside the farm, had obvious consequences for how farmers care for their land. In the former, farmers needed to constantly rebuild their resource base, which required taking care of their land, recycling nutrients, diversifying crops to reduce pest problems, saving water, and so on—in other words, focusing on the long-term sustainability of the land. In the latter, the farmer's relationship with land became extractive and exploitative, resulting ultimately in the degradation of the land.

The Transformative Potential of Agroecology

On most of what we regard as agricultural land, a system of large-scale industrial agriculture, unique in history, still dominates. Yet across the world, most of the people we regard as farmers do not grow crops this way—the average small-scale producer uses a variety of more traditional methods, usually not in a monoculture and usually not heavily dependent on external and expensive inputs like pesticides and chemical fertilizers. So if a majority of farmland is currently devoted to the industrial system, most farmers are not. And though a majority of that industrial farmland produces animal feed, industrial feedstocks, ethanol, and additives for the food processing industry, most farmers produce food (Altieri 2009; Rosset 2000; Perfecto et al. 2019; Perfecto and Vandermeer 2010; Rosset and Altieri 2017; Vandermeer et al. 2018).

Small and medium-scale farmers, recognizing that the industrial agricultural system does not improve their livelihoods, are turning to agroecology, which, though it contains elements of the science of ecology, its etymological parent, is much more than science. Traditional knowledge, gathered from those who have been farming in a traditional manner for generations, has become an essential feature of agroecology. Many peasant farmers have almost completely rejected the ideology of complete domination over nature in favor of using nature's architecture as a blueprint for design. Furthermore, the political actions of peasant farmers, broadly conceived, have come front and center, from the rebellions against historical land enclosures to the current rallying cry for "food sovereignty" (Wazel et al. 2009; Rosset and Martínez-Torres 2012; Toledo and Barrera-Bassols 2017).

Today, agroecology has come to signify a radical departure from the post–World War II industrial agricultural consensus, in both the global North and the global South. It is a powerful movement, with expansive expectations for "regime change." As with other potentially transformative movements (e.g., socialism, democracy), its precise meaning is inevitably vague, typically taking on the specific meaning any practitioner deems correct, or at least convenient. Yet it clearly reflects a kind of "ideal" that has made its entrance in diverse forums, ranging from the Food and Agriculture Organization of the United Nations (FAO; Giraldo and Rosset 2018; Loconto and Fouilleux 2019) to the Zapatista revolutionaries of southern Mexico (Gahman 2017; Hernández et al. 2020).

So, what, indeed, is agroecology, and what is its relationship to land? Agroecology has developed over the past few decades into a complicated topic. In our interpretation, agroecology as it is currently envisioned by most of the interested parties is a platform for research, practice, and political action that promotes small-scale (or peasant) agriculture, and strongly rejects the well-known harmful and exploitative practices of industrial capitalist agriculture. It is a platform that can be visualized as resting on four pillars; science, traditional knowledge, nature, and political action, all tightly related to land.

The Four Pillars of Agroecology

Western science has been simultaneously demonized and worshiped, frequently depending on the milieu in which it is situated. Applying science to agriculture has two recent histories. There is a science that emerged from the post-WWII conventional consensus, with its extreme form of reductionist thinking—effectively confusing the question, What is it? with the question, What is it made of?—and adherence to the institutionalized structure of publishing, grant-getting, and influencing. The other science admits that science itself is an evolving tradition. As Levins (1981) noted, the actual practice of science and philosophy of science in the Western tradition are flexible and changing, depending on where you are in time and space.

Applied to the question of land restoration, a most inspirational twentieth-century practitioner was George Washington Carver in the United States. From an active concern with the real problems faced by the small-scale Black farmers dealing with nutrient-depleted soils, Carver not only did scientific research on the role of legumes, such as peanuts and cowpeas, in restoring nutrients, but based his science on the needs of the community he sought to serve. His program might be likened to the general idea of "science for the people" in that his focus was on improving the practice of agriculture through crop diversification and careful soil management, and he brought that knowledge directly to the poor Black farmers of the southern United States. But most importantly, he recognized the importance of applying scientific knowledge to rational land usage (Hersey 2011).

The second pillar of agroecology is traditional knowledge. The natural world surrounds "traditional" people with a profound classroom, sometimes only personally experienced, but sometimes with a long list of remembrances from generations past. Indeed, most knowledge is Indigenous knowledge. Embedded in every culture is knowledge not only about the culture itself but also about how that culture intersects with the natural world. This evident fact becomes especially important in agriculture.

It is important to acknowledge that traditional knowledge is not ipso facto truth or necessarily beneficial or sustainable (Krech 1999), and the tendency to romanticize it remains a barrier to legitimate acknowledgment. The immense variety of knowledge systems known to exist in human societies over at least the past ten millennia (Greaber and Wengrow 2021) provide enormous evidence of both the laudable and the ludicrous. Rather than an automatic acceptance (or rejection) of traditional knowledge systems, agroecology urges a respectful attempt to understand each one in its local (both in time and space) contexts, promoting a *diálogo de saberes*—a dialogue among types of knowledge and ways of knowing (Martínez-Torres and Rosset 2014).

The third pillar of agroecology is nature itself. Much as traditional knowledge frequently claims, the structure of the natural world provides us with insight about how our agriculture works. Rachel Carson is an inspirational figure on this front, and not just for her pioneering *Silent Spring*. Two of her previous books, *The Sea Around Us* and *At the Edge of the Sea*, published in the early 1950s, present the natural world as wondrous, but also complex. She never said anything about using nature as a template for agriculture, but she certainly saw the intricate structure of the natural world that was being harmed by the agrochemicals that were then being increasingly used in agriculture.

The fourth pillar of agriculture stems from a social structure that has existed for centuries, if not millennia—political struggle. For example, in seventeenth-century England, the True Levelers, or, as they became known, the Diggers, were peasant farmers who were especially concerned with land rights. They collectively challenged the restrictions placed on them for the use of natural areas owned by royalty. Taking collective political action for land and other rights on behalf of those who provide food to the people, symbolized here by the Diggers, is part and parcel of agroecology. A contemporary example is the Movement of Landless Workers (MST) in Brazil (Robles 2001; Stedile 2008; Wolford 2010) and La Via Campesina, a global organization of rural political organizations (Rosset 2013). However, revolts and social movements by peasants go back as far as recorded history, and undoubtedly formed part of the fabric of how societies evolve. And that power dynamic frequently is contained in the contradiction between the rural and the urban, a powerful foundation from which class structure can emerge or be exaggerated.

So, in summary, we view the agroecological platform as sitting on four pillars: *science*, especially the science of ecology; *traditional knowledge* as a major spark for developing agroecological processes, *nature* as a template for agricultural design, and *political action*, as the means for transforming agriculture. Yet it is not the case that we see these as four distinct subjects. Agroecology, as properly conceived, is the intersection of all of these, and at the center of this intersection is land. The science of ecology gives us insights about how to strengthen the resource base of farming lands and territories so that production and the livelihoods of peasants may be improved and sustained. Traditional knowledge emerged from the interactions of Indigenous peoples with the land from generation to generation. Nature represents the natural state of the land. And political action revolves around the issue of access to land and support for agroecology. Although some thinkers and actors emphasize one or the other of these, the proper philosophical position is that the intersection of these pillars is the most important nourishment that brings forth a true agroecology. Science is strongly influenced by traditional knowledge, much of which comes from a deep and abiding appreciation of the natural world, which is frequently conditioned by the political actions of peasants seeking to redress grievances.

Land, Territory, and Dignity: From the Diggers to La Via Campesina

From the cries of the Diggers and others in the seventeenth century to the demands for agrarian reform that fueled much of the revolutionary activity throughout Latin America in the 1970s and 1980s, to the struggles of peasant farmers against the massive land grabbing of today, political struggles animate a deep and complicated analysis of the meaning of land and territory. "Land to the tiller" may have been a slogan for the early land reform activists, but, especially through the continued international analysis of La Via Campesina, the question of land and territory has become far more sophisticated and nuanced today; and its connection to political action and agroecology, more complicated.

Rosset (2013) provides a useful recent history. Partly in response to international adjustments that followed on the heels of the fall of the Soviet bloc, a group of peasant leaders from Central America, the Caribbean, North America, and Europe met in Managua, Nicaragua, in 1996 to discuss the plight of peasant farmers and farmworkers in the neoliberal world. Following up on that meeting, farmer and farmworker leaders met a year later in Mons, Belgium, to form La Via Campesina. The revolutionary activities of the 1980s had been strongly influenced by the demand for land reform among the peasantry and by the assault on peasant agriculture by neoliberal policies. The international capitalist movement embodied by the World Bank, the International Monetary Fund, and the Washington Consensus moved in quickly after the Soviet defeat and the end of the Cold War. Chief among their goals was to eliminate agrarian reform as a political project through the creation (or re-creation) of markets in land, thought to be necessary to attract investment into rural areas. The protests at the 1999 World Trade Organization conference in Washington State, the so-called Battle of Seattle, marked a turning point in that the militant international nature of the struggle had to be recognized by agencies such as the World Bank. Soon after, La Via Campesina created the Global Campaign for Agrarian Reform, which began re-examining the central tenets of agrarian reform. Taking on the contradictions between classic notions of agrarian reform and the neoliberal policies promoted by the World Bank, the Campaign centered its analysis on the right to food and the issue of women in agriculture.

In 2000, the Third International Assembly of La Via Campesina was held in Bangalore, India, and it was there that the initial ideas about food sovereignty were formed, and the basics of agrarian reform reanalyzed. At this point, it was evident that land titling offered titleholders nothing more than a legal document and was a less-than-ideal approach to reform. There was agreement that agrarian reform should be concerned with more than the legalities of land ownership and should include the right to instruments of production, such as seeds, water, implements, and others, beyond the land itself. "In strategic terms, land reform was pitched not as an exclusive struggle of peasants, but rather as a solution to many of the larger problems of society." (Rosset, 2013: pg. 724).

In 2006, La Via Campesina helped to organize the "Forum on Land, Territory, and Dignity" in Porto Alegre, Brazil. In this forum the larger issues concerning the rights of other occupants of land and territories, such as fishers, herders, and forest dwellers, came to the fore, resulting in a broader conceptualization of agrarian reform, including the central role of women and opposition to land grabbing. Thus, this process of international cooperation in political analysis and developing strategy enriched the very idea of what land and territory mean to the peasant movement, and by implication, to agroecology. The analysis began with the objective of gaining title to a piece of land, but through analyses by peasant organizations interacting in various fora organized by La Via Campesina, developed into a "genuine, integral agrarian reform in which access to land was to be accompanied by policies and programs supportive of peasant agriculture" (Rosset 2013), integrating agrarian reform seamlessly with the emergence of food sovereignty and agroecology.

In all of this is the important the concept of "territory" as a focus of analysis emerged, as eloquently expressed by agrarian leader Faustino Torrez:

> Territory expresses the identity of people, it is where the ancestors lived and where they still reside, it means knowledge and ways of knowing, historical memory, and the right of usufruct of the communal resources which properly speaking belong to the Mother Earth.
>
> (quoted in Rosset 2013, 726)

Which brings up the important question, "Land and territory for what?" And it is in this final question that agroecology enters. The intersection between land/territory and the transformation of industrial, or conventional, agriculture to agroecology cements an essential connection between the political action pillar of the agroecology movement and the analysis of land and territory. Ultimately, the dialectics of land and territory are clearly related to most of the structural complications currently facing rural society, specifically, and food and agriculture, more generally.

The Agroecological Territory: The Example of Coffee Rust

Coffee rust disease is one of many possible examples that bring agroecology and land ownership into a dialectical whole. Wind-borne coffee rust spores can travel very long distances (one suggestion is that spores traveled from Africa to the Americas on wind currents in the stratosphere; McCook and Vandermeer 2015). The traditional mode of coffee production took advantage of coffee's natural propensity to be an understory plant growing in the shade of overstory trees. Those overstory trees also act as a windbreak, reducing the wind currents that can carry spores to the coffee bushes. Thus the disease dynamics partly involve activities occurring in the broader landscape. The surrounding vegetation can either promote or disrupt the wind currents. A forest that surrounds the farm will act as a windbreak, slowing the entrance of spores into the farm (Avelino et al. 2012). Deforestation, of both the coffee farms (a "modernization" effort that encouraged eliminating shade trees) and the surrounding natural forest, has a positive effect on the incidence of the coffee rust disease (less surrounding vegetation cover, as in pastures, for example, means more wind and more disease). Thus, more deforestation, or less tree cover, generally results in more coffee rust disease locally.

If the deforestation of neighboring land creates more disease on our "land," our "territory" must also include that neighboring land. There is a generalization here. If we seek agroecological management of coffee rust, we must incorporate a broader area than only the land on which the farm is located. The disease (and by implication other ecological management issues of the farm) itself knows nothing of borders and land titles. All the recipes and traditions that focus on a local response (on a particular farm)—special mixtures of natural fungicides, unique interplants, or traditional soil-management techniques—will not help if the surrounding land is open pasture or soybean fields saturated with inoculating spores of the disease brought to the farm with the unbroken winds that sweep across such open landscapes. The relevant territory, that in which the reality of the disease lives, is the *agroecological territory*, and it includes all the land on which the ecological dynamics of the disease occurs. The agroecological territory, and by implication, the collective action of the farmers within that territory, acknowledges the reality of both traditional land use and the ecological forces operative within the traditional system. Since agroecological management relies on biodiversity and the interactions among the many organisms that live in an agroecosystem, and since those organisms do not respect the legal property boundaries, the concept of land,

and, especially, private ownership of land, is inconsistent with a true agroecology. The concept of the "agricultural landscape" addresses the ecological concerns but does not capture the sociopolitical and cultural factors that necessarily play a role in collective planning. The concept of "agroecological territory" reflects a more integrated and realistic approach.

From Traditional Ecosystem Management to the Agroecological Territory

Looking to the future, as technological developments outside agriculture advance, ecologically destructive activities such as deforestation may continue and political action against them will likewise continue. Yet other, less direct technological developments will continue their own independent evolution. For example, as with paved roads, motorized transport, digital communication, and other developments in the continually evolving modern condition, it is hard to imagine conceptualizations of land and territory remaining constant. The consequences when son or daughter left the farm for the city in 1950 are certainly different from what those consequences would be today. Hecht's (2010) notion of the "new rurality" acknowledges this recent development as communication, both physical and remote, between families split between city and countryside continues.

Reflecting on the general political and ecological forces operative in the adjudication of land and territory, whether the old rurality or the new, agroecology comes to play a major role. We have argued that traditional visions of the landscape, both in the present and the past, effectively acknowledged both the role of nature and the ability of humans to modify that nature. The use of fire, perhaps the oldest tool of ecosystem management, is an obvious example. However, many more examples of formal and informal land management support the basic conclusion that humans have been managing their ecosystems for a long time, and that agriculture, however defined, is just a more (sometimes very much more) intensive way of engaging in that management. The excessive deviation toward land degradation, realized mostly in the industrial capitalist mode of agricultural production, is from this point of view, a very recent and likely temporary deviation from a long history of ecosystem management based on ecological principles and traditional knowledge.

Such reflections bring into focus some obvious contradictions that cement the idea of agroecology to other issues, most notably, to the very question of what agriculture is in the first place. Traditional societies routinely modify their local environments to promote better, or more convenient, access to food. Sometimes that means clearing a piece of land so that a tuber crop can be grown, or doing controlled burning to attract particular species of animal to be hunted, or planting a tree, and sometimes it means a dramatic modification of soils and a strong preference for a single crop (usually a cereal). Traditional societies also frequently know to practice agriculture, but choose not to do so, from the traditional hunter-gatherers to current factory workers. Sometimes interchange with spatially proximate agricultural cultures is common, along with the adoption of some forms of agriculture, only to be discarded later. What seems clear is the general tendency, reflected in the attitude of the Huaorani, that nature is there for the taking, but is also there to nurture through wise management. It is difficult to imagine such a society actively and knowingly extracting to the point of destroying.

Agroecology fits into all of this as a key variable, both in its implied broad operation in preindustrial times and in its current expansion as an alternative to the industrial system. The science of ecology has made considerable progress since agroecology became popular, and popular notions, such as the "balance of nature," and "equilibrium," have been largely abandoned as more sophisticated ideas, such as long-term persistence, chaotic populations, critical transitions, and similar topics, have been adopted and become central to the science. Traditional knowledge, likewise, has come into its own, not, of course, among small and Indigenous farmers, for whom it has always been the basic framework for practice, but in a broader context of international recognition across broad sectors of world society. The appreciation of nature has also become a clear and acceptable element of general accounting, and its evident architectures are being incorporated into actual operations. Finally, with the growth of social movements, especially the rapid expansion of La Via Campesina and other, more regionally focused, ideologically committed groups like the Zapatistas and the Rojavanians, grassroots-level political action on agrarian issues has grown rapidly (Vergara-Camus 2009; Giraldo and McCunne 2019; Hernandez et al. 2020; Pimbert 2021). All these components of agroecology contain their own elements of land and territory, indicating the importance of agroecology, with its four pillars individually and collectively interpenetrating with all aspects of the contemporary dynamics of land and agrarian change (Perfecto et al. 2019).

References

Altieri, Miguel A. 2009. "Agroecology, Small Farms, and Food Sovereignty." *Monthly Review* 61 (3): 102–113.

Avelino, Jacques, Alí Romero-Gurdián, Héctor F. Cruz-Cuellar, and Fabrice A. J. Declerck. 2012. "Landscape Context and Scale Differentially Impact Coffee Leaf Rust, Coffee Berry Borer, and Coffee Root-Knot Nematodes." *Ecological Applications* 22 (2): 584–596.

Borras, Saturnino M., Jr., Ruth Hall, Ian Scoones, Ben White, and Wendy Wolford. 2011. "Towards a Better Understanding of Global Land Grabbing: An Editorial Introduction." *Journal of Peasant Studies* 38 (2): 209–216.

Carson, Rachel. 1962. *Silent Spring*. Boston: Houghton Mifflin.

Chengxiang, Pan. 1988. "The Development of Integrated Pest Control in China." *Agricultural History* 62 (1): 1–12.

Copland, Samuel. 1866. *Agriculture, Ancient and Modern: A Historical Account of Its Principles and Practice, Exemplified in Their Rise, Progress, and Development*. London: Virtue and Co.

Ellis, Erle C., Nicolas Gauthier, Kees Klein Goldewijk, Rebecca Bliege Bird, Nicole Boivin, Sandra Díaz, et al. 2021. "People Have Shaped Most of Terrestrial Nature for at Least 12,000 Years." *Proceedings of the National Academy of Sciences* 118 (17): Article e2023483118.

Escobar, Arturo. 2011. *Encountering Development: The Making and Unmaking of the Third World*. Vol. 1. Princeton, NJ: Princeton University Press.

Evans, Linda, and Philip Weinstein. 2021. "Begone from Me, O Crooked-Lips! Integrated Pest Management in Ancient Egypt." *American Entomologist* 67 (1): 46–53.

Fowler, Catherine S., and Dana Lepofsky. 2011. "Traditional Resource and Environmental Management." *Ethnobiology*, 2011: 285–304.

Gahman, Levi. 2017. "Building 'a World Where Many Worlds Fit': Indigenous Autonomy, Mutual Aid, and an (Anti-capitalist) Moral Economy of the (Rebel) Peasant." In *Sustainable Food Futures*, edited by Jessica Duncan and Megan Bailey, 103–116, London: Routledge.

Giraldo, Omar Felipe, and Nils McCune. 2019. "Can the State Take Agroecology to Scale? Public Policy Experiences in Agroecological Territorialization from Latin America." *Agroecology and Sustainable Food Systems* 43 (7–8): 785–809.

Giraldo, Omar Felipe, and Peter M. Rosset. 2018. "Agroecology as a Territory in Dispute: Between Institutionality and Social Movements." *Journal of Peasant Studies* 45 (3): 545–564.

Graeber, David, and David Wengrow. 2021. *The Dawn of Everything: A New History of Humanity*. Lendon: Penguin.

Harari, Y. N. 2014. *Sapiens: A Brief History of Humankind*. New York: Random House.

Hecht, Susanna. 2010. "The New Rurality: Globalization, Peasants and the Paradoxes of Landscapes." *Land Use Policy* 27 (2): 161–169.

Hernández, Carol, Hugo Perales, and Daniel Jaffee. 2020. "'Without Food There Is No Resistance': The Impact of the Zapatista Conflict on Agrobiodiversity and Seed Sovereignty in Chiapas, Mexico." *Geoforum* 128: 236–250.

Hersey, M. D. 2011. *My Work Is That of Conservation: An Environmental Biography of George Washington Carver*. Athens: University of Georgia Press.

Hodder, Ian, ed. 2020. *Consciousness, Creativity, and Self at the Dawn of Settled Life*. Cambridge, UK: Cambridge University Press.

Horgan, Donagh, and Branka Dimitrijević. 2020. "Social Innovation in the Built Environment: the Challenges Presented by the Politics of Space." *Urban Science* 5 (1): 1.

Krech, Shepard. 1999. *The Ecological Indian: Myth and History*. New York: W. W. Norton.

Kumar, Dheeraj, and Anil J. Elias. 2019. "The Explosive Chemistry of Nitrogen: A Fascinating Journey from 9th Century to the Present." *Resonance: Journal of Science Education* 24 (11): 1–20.

Lee, Richard, and Richard Daly. 1999. "Introduction: Foragers and Others." In *The Cambridge Encyclopedia of Hunters and Gatherers*, edited by Richard Lee and Richard Daly, 1–20. Cambridge: Cambridge University Press, 1999.

Levins, Richard. 1981. "Class, Science and Scientific Truth." In *Working Papers on Marxism and Science*, vol. 1: 1–15. New York: New York Marxist School.

Lightfoot, Kent G., Rob Q. Cuthrell, Chuck J. Striplen, and Mark G. Hylkema. 2013. "Rethinking the Study of Landscape Management Practices among Hunter-Gatherers in North America." *American Antiquity* 78 (2): 285–301.

Loconto, Allison Marie, and Eve Fouilleux. 2019. "Defining Agroecology: Exploring the Circulation of Knowledge in FAO's Global Dialogue." *International Journal of Sociology of Agriculture and Food* 25 (2): 116–137.

Martínez-Torres, María Elena, and Peter M. Rosset. 2014. "*Diálogo de saberes* in La Vía Campesina: Food Sovereignty and Agroecology." *Journal of Peasant Studies* 41 (6): 979–997.

McCook, Stuart, and John Vandermeer. 2015. "The Big Rust and the Red Queen: Long-Term Perspectives on Coffee Rust Research." *Phytopathology* 105 (9): 1164–1173.

McWilliams, Carey. 2000. *Factories in the Field: The Story of Migratory Farm Labor in California*. Berkeley: University of California Press.

Patel, Raj. 2013. "The Long Green Revolution." *Journal of Peasant Studies* 40 (1): 1–63.

Perfecto, Ivette, and John Vandermeer. 2010. "The Agroecological Matrix as Alternative to the Land-Sparing/Agriculture Intensification Model." *Proceedings of the National Academy of Sciences* 107 (13): 5786–5791.

Perfecto, Ivette, John Vandermeer, and Angus Wright. 2019. *Nature's Matrix: Linking Agriculture, Biodiversity Conservation and Food Sovereignty*. Oxfordshire, UK: Routledge.

Pimbert, Michel P. 2021. "Regenerating Kurdish Ecologies through Food Sovereignty, Agroecology, and Economies of Care." In *Ecological Solidarity in the Kurdish Freedom Movement: Thought, Practice, Challenges, and Opportunities*, edited by Steven Hunt, 115–132. London: Lexington Books.

Rival, Laura. 2002. "Trekking through History", New York: Columbia University Press.

Robles, Wilder. 2001. "The Landless Rural Workers Movement (MST) in Brazil." *Journal of Peasant Studies* 28 (2): 146–161.

Rosset, Peter. 2000. "The Multiple Functions and Benefits of Small Farm Agriculture in the Context of Global Trade Negotiations." *Development* 43 (2): 77–82.

Rosset, Peter. 2013. "Re-thinking Agrarian Reform, Land and Territory in La Via Campesina." *Journal of Peasant Studies* 40 (4): 721–775.

Rosset, Peter M., and Miguel A. Altieri. 2017. *Agroecology: Science and Politics*. Warwickshire, UK: Practical Action.

Rosset, Peter M., and Maria Elena Martínez-Torres. 2012. "Rural Social Movements and Agroecology: Context, Theory, and Process." *Ecology and Society* 17 (3): 1–28.

Russell, Edmund. 2001. *War and Nature: Fighting Humans and Insects with Chemicals from World War I to "Silent Spring."* Cambridge, UK: Cambridge University Press.

Schwartz, Nancy L. 1985. "Communitarian Citizenship: Marx and Weber on the City." *Polity* 17 (3): 530–548.

Stedile, João Pedro. 2008. "The Class Struggles in Brazil: The Perspective of the MST." *Socialist Register* 44: 193–216.

Steinberg, Theodore. 1995. *Slide Mountain, or, The Folly of Owning Nature*. Berkeley: University of California Press.

Toledo, Víctor M., and Narciso Barrera-Bassols. 2017. "Political Agroecology in Mexico: A Path toward Sustainability." *Sustainability* 9 (2): 268.

Vandermeer, John, Aniket Aga, Jake Allgeier, Catherine Badgley, Regina Baucom, Jennifer Blesh, et al. 2018. "Feeding Prometheus: an Interdisciplinary Approach for Solving the Global Food Crisis." *Frontiers in Sustainable Food Systems* (2): 39.

Vergara-Camus, Leandro. 2009. "The MST and the EZLN Struggle for Land: New Forms of Peasant Rebellions." *Journal of Agrarian Change* 9 (3): 365–391.
Wezel, Alexander, Stéphane Bellon, Thierry Doré, Charles Francis, Dominique Vallod, and Christophe David. 2009. "Agroecology as a Science, a Movement and a Practice: A Review." *Agronomy for Sustainable Development* 29 (4): 503–515.
Wolford, Wendy. 2010. *This Land Is Ours Now*. Durham, NC: Duke University Press.

CHAPTER 17

BEYOND LAND AS PROPERTY

A Feminist Perspective

DIANA OJEDA

Introduction

In the face of unevenly distributed dispossession and devastation, land remains at the center of political mobilizations, strategies of emancipation, demands for justice and reparation, aspirations to autonomy, and everyday disputes. The last two decades, since the early 2000s, marked by growing inequalities, sustained land grabbing, and acute environmental crises, all laid bare by the Covid-19 pandemic, have created a sense of urgency that has translated into important reflections on the ongoing struggles around the meaning, use, and control of land. The renewed relevance of the old question posed by critical agrarian studies—what is the relation between land and power?—has gained importance in current historical, anthropological, geographical, sociological, and other academic conversations that are exploring this question, as well as in public discourse.

In this chapter, I contribute to this conversation by paying close attention to the processes through which land is turned into property. This entails questioning what Emel et al. (1992) refer as "the ideologies of property"—that is, the hegemonic, commonsensical character of private property—when trying to understand access to land, water, and other life-affording elements. Using a feminist lens, I look at the relation between land as property and state-making, pointing to the gendered exclusions that result from it. I highlight current work that, in my view, allows for more complex views of land. I then explain my understanding of land, property, and state power and how they are all traversed by gender, and then point to important aspects of the entangled history of land property and dispossession, including its profound and long-lasting exclusions based on class, race, and gender. Finally, I provide a brief overview of the agrarian history of the Montes de María region of the Colombian Caribbean since the 1960s through three key moments of reconfiguration of landed property: the agrarian reform policies of the 1960s, neoliberal multicultural policies of the 1990s, and the efforts at land restitution and transition to postconflict in the 2010s. I argue that these three formations of land as property help us to identify historically and geographically situated processes of state-making and reveal the inequality and violence they engender. I am interested in how this inequality and violence is profoundly shaped by gender, while also resulting in gendered access to land and control over it. In the conclusion, I suggest the need to further study the relation between land and power beyond what property relations make legible.

Complicating the Question of Land

Hardly a static entity, land is better understood as a complex web of relationships that are at once social and biological, symbolic and material, and technological and organic. These relationships are shaped by the long histories of violence and resistance that land materializes. Beyond land as a piece of ground or a plot, various authors have paid attention to its different dimensions, pointing to the mutual constitution of land and people. As Haroon Akram-Lodhi (2021) put it, "While land is something that is constructed by humans over their daily lives, both physically and symbolically, by being invested with meaning, memory, and value, land is also something that constructs humans as social beings" (73).

The mutual constitution of land and people has been shaped throughout history by violent relations of differentiation, exclusion, and subordination. Reflecting on the African American diaspora, scholar and activist Monica White suggests understanding land as both "a scene of a crime and a strategy of freedom" (quoted in Hennessy 2019, 3). Her work resonates with a growing body of literature on racial capitalism that critically analyzes processes of differentiation through racialization and sustained colonial domination, their relation to land theft and control, and how they enable capitalist accumulation (Bhattacharyya 2018; Gilmore 2020). Priscilla McCutcheon's (2019) proposal for a "Black agrarian geography" situates the agrarian question on the scale of the body, the field or farm, and the landscape, challenging the invisibility of Black women and their knowledge in both the agrarian and the Black radical food movements. She posits that "land has historically been a fraught space for Black people in the rural South. It is simultaneously the site of struggle, oppression, liberation and ideally autonomy" (207), noting that "ownership of land is not the end goal," but a means toward justice.

Indigenous scholars have extensively pointed out that land is both "home" and a living being, bringing attention to the interdependence and mutual responsibility that land embodies (Daigle 2016; Liboiron 2021; Tuck and McKenzie 2015). For example, Indigenous water defender Winona LaDuke (1999) insists on the notion "the land of the people," which suggests that land does not belong *to* human beings but that we belong on the land. In the context of invigorated opposition to extractivism, Latin American popular and communitarian feminisms have considered land in its central role in sustaining life and enacting more viable forms of existing in relationship with others. This perspective centers on the inseparability of land and body, insisting on the violence that patriarchal domination and capitalism inflicts on both (Cabnal 2015; Cruz 2016; Guzmán 2019).

Other relevant work on the different aspects of the relations that constitute land has included detailed analyses of disputed processes of land commodification (Li 2014); transnational relations between land, authority, and identity (Hall 2013); the state's role in land grabbing (Wolford et al. 2013), the multifaceted legal disputes that are involved in peasants' claims to land (Hetherington 2011), how law and land property are constituted through violence (Correia 2013); mobilization of social movements for land (Wolford 2010); and the inseparability of land and water (Camargo, 2022).

In trying to better understand land in its complexity, I have found Tania Murray Li's (2014) conceptualization particularly useful: land as a "provisional assemblage of heterogeneous elements including material substances, technologies, discourses and practices" (589). Following her argument, land's assemblage is an unfinished and contested process, one that involves economic, political, and cultural conditions that are always in dispute. A key part of this process is the simplification of *land as property*, which does not operate as an automatic or direct abstraction. On the contrary, in tandem with land as parcel, resource, or commodity, land as property must be analyzed as a nonlinear organization of relationships among people (Blomley 2003 and of people with the materiality of nature (Olarte-Olarte, 2019). State authority and legal intervention are generally invoked in this process (Latorre 2015). But state authority, as different authors have noted, does not precede property; rather, state authority is constituted by land (Sikor and Lund 2009; Lund 2016), and as such, processes of land-making and state-making should be understood relationally (Sud, this volume).

Land, Property, and State Power

Through the configuration of land as property, *what land is*, *who owns it*, and *what for* are simultaneously defined (Valverde, 2009; Humphrey and Verdery, 2004) and always in tension with other ways of thinking about land. Although there are different forms of property, including public property and common property, I pay closer attention to modern configurations of private property that, coming from the liberal tradition, depend on the separation of subject and object. In general terms, Western property is based on three elements: possession, exclusion, and state authority. As Carol Rose (1985) asserts, the explicit intention to possess is what underlies property arrangements. And correspondingly, "private property" describes the exclusive use of land by one individual or group of people. Lastly, property requires an authority to enforce it. This authority is not always that of the state; nonetheless, property is a constitutive aspect of state power and citizenship.

Examining specific assemblages of *land as property* allows us to learn about the political lives and sedimented histories of land. I am concerned with the ways historic and geographically specific configurations of land as property entail different forms of gendered inequality and violence. Land property contributes to localized state formations through which the definitions of *who* owns land and *what is it for* serve different forms of dispossession that are not equally distributed along gender lines. I came to this interest through my work on land grabbing in the Colombian Caribbean, where I discovered a jarring contradiction: women have a disproportionate responsibility in working, caring for, and defending and reclaiming the land, but they have little power to make decisions about it. Despite what public policy and development interventions have long predicted, property did not seem to solve this contradiction.

Land has been extensively analyzed as a powerful locus of state power, especially in relation to how the determination of the exclusive use, possession, or management of land by a person or group contributes to the constitution of state authority and, in the process, results in the production of particular spaces and subjects. Lund (2016) asserts: "The ability to entitle and disenfranchise people with regard to property, to establish the conditions under which they hold that property . . . is constitutive of state power" (1200–1201). In relation to this, Hall, Hirsch, and Li (2011) have examined the processes of land allocation and how the definition of property rights is inevitably linked to processes of exclusion that demand a closer look into how this process of definition works within spaces, such as those of community and kin.

I suggest that we think of the processes of turning land into property as powerful acts of state-making through which, at the same time, the production of subjects and natures, including of land itself, occurs. The ethnographic research of Margarita Serje (2001), Tania Murray Li (2007 (see also Li and Semedi 2021), Andrés León Araya (forthcoming), and others has shown that state-making practices in, respectively, Colombia, Indonesia, and Honduras in involve the disciplining of peasants and landscapes in ways that are often at odds with guaranteeing the livelihoods and autonomy of rural communities. Their work gives us a better understanding of how land is, in part, assembled through the disputes about who owns which pieces of land and for what use. It also shows that one key land-grabbing mechanism is making a determination about who is likely to put the land to good use. Narratives of empty or idle lands, as well as underused lands, have been historically effective in processes of dispossession.

Land as Property, Dispossession, and Violence

The birth of the modern liberal state was bound up with the making of rights-bearing individuals. One of these rights was the right to own property. Land ownership became a prerequisite of citizenship, a status reserved for White male adults (Wallerstein 2003, 653–656). As Lund (this volume) puts it, "Historically, virtually all societies have treated large portions of their members as legal minors with less than full rights, inferior status, and reduced capacity to own land and participate in political life." This has entailed the exclusion of women, children, and migrants, as well as racialized and impoverished populations, who are often not considered full subjects. This is evidenced by the fact that, even though women in many countries in Latin America gained a legal right to own property in the 1930s, today women are only 18 percent of landowners in the region (FAO, 2018; see also Deere and León, 2001).

This masculine attribute of property, in particular land property, has roots in a hegemonic masculinity that has historically been predicated on men's sense of women and children, as well as nature, as property, as many ecofeminist thinkers have pointed out (d'Eaubonne [1974] 2000; Plumwood 1993; Shiva 1988). The process of turning land into property created the landowner as a rational subject holding possession, the right of exclusion, and authority and simultaneously made land a static, exploitable, and available object. Land as property seals the production of land as feminine and the concomitant construction of the liberal subject as always already masculine, an issue feminist thought questions as part of the phallogocentric idea of the universal subject (Butler and Scott 1992; Rivera Cusicanqui 1997). Caballero and Gago (2020) have referred to the need for a "renewed battle for property," one that recognizes that property is itself a gender relation. According to the authors, all property comes already paired up with a gendered division of labor and household debt expands the frontiers of capitalist accumulation, which largely relies on women's unpaid labor. They thus turn the attention to social reproduction as "the strategic sphere on which neoliberal dispossession and household debt stand" (n.p.; my translation).

To be sure, because property is itself a negotiation over who has the right to own, and thus who has the right to exclude, it is inextricably linked with power, and its history is one of violence. If we look at the history of colonial domination, we see that theft of land and its reduction to property have been at the heart of a long and ongoing history of dispossession dating back at least five centuries. This "colonial horizon of long duration," as Silvia Rivera Cusicanqui (2010) defines it, consists of a matrix of domination that constantly recreates dispossession, exclusion, and discipline. In her work, Rivera Cusicanqui explains how the imposition of a masculine and lettered order under the Spanish colonial rule translated into a relationship to land based on boundaries, property, and parental authority, which had dire consequences for Indigenous populations and women. The transition from land ownership by the Crown to land ownership by states and individuals brought more continuities than ruptures because *cédulas reales* (royal charters) were conferred on White male Americans descended from the Spaniards. In the case of Bolivia that Rivera Cusicanqui (1997) analyzes, as in the rest of Latin America and the Caribbean, inheritance and property rights, particularly those related to land, have historically worked as an efficient form of the naturalized inequality that was imposed by colonizers and then consolidated by the institutions of the republican state (see also Coronil 2000; Wynter 1995).

The violence of property regimes is made evident in Cheryl Harris's (1993) analysis of property and whiteness as two prominent forms of the right to exclude. Harris has traced the role of slavery and conquest in the definition of "racially contingent" property and property rights in the United States. Slavery, she reminds us, was a property regime based on the idea that White people held the exclusive right to property, a category that included Black people. Within them, Black women were both a form of property and in charge of reproducing it. Stolen land and stolen life became inextricably linked, and remain so today (Roy 2021), because racialized and gendered privilege was institutionalized by law. According to Harris, "Whiteness as property has taken on more subtle forms, but retains its core characteristic—the legal legitimation of expectations of power and control that enshrine the status quo as a neutral baseline, while masking the maintenance of white privilege and domination" (Harris 1993, 1715).

The establishment of capitalism relied heavily on private property, stolen land, and violence. Processes of primitive accumulation that took place in England between the sixteenth and eighteenth centuries were fueled by the enclosure of the commons and the impoverishment of rural populations, as Marx (*Capital*, vol. 1, chap. 27) analyzed at length. The separation of workers from the means of production through plunder forced them into new labor conditions and made them dependent on wages for their subsistence (Marx, *Capital*, vol. 1, pt. 3). This separation was reproduced by the individual property regime. Controlling land made possible the capture and exploitation of labor that, in turn, enabled profit and capitalist accumulation. There was an assertion that private property was a necessary element in the correct functioning of society: "The scarcity paradigm of Thomas Malthus, the utilitarianism of James and John Stuart Mill and Jeremy Bentham, John Locke's sacralization of private property and Adam Smith's and David Ricardo's analysis of the mutual benefits from free exchanges in unencumbered markets: these, and many others, served to reify the role of and benefits from the private property owner in capitalist societies" (Akram-Lodhi 2021, 76).

The imposition of private property was at the center of the critique of Pierre-Joseph Proudhon ([1840] 1993) and other nineteenth-century anarchists. In *What Is Property? Or, an Inquiry into the Principle of Right and of Government*, Proudhon famously declared, "Property is theft!" As Robert Nichols (2018) points out in his analysis of the genealogy of dispossession, this critique meant that "modern property was per se illegitimate, since other inequalities in ownership were derivative of the originary seizure of communal land" (7). Marx did not completely agree, believing that the notion of "expropriation" implied an already existing possession. As noted, for him, alienation, rather than property, was at the center of dispossession (see Nichols 2018).

A key point here, as Silvia Federici (2004) and other Marxist feminists have shown, is that the story of capitalism is incomplete when it does not take into account the subordination of and violence against women it has historically entailed. At the same time, far from being a finished process, the enclosure of the commons (including riverbanks, waterholes, forests, and wildlands) continues to shape capitalist accumulation—and subsistence efforts—around the globe, particularly in the global South (Menéndez and Garcia 2021; Mies 1999).

How is it that despite this sustained history of violence, liberal forms of citizenship and state-making are almost unthinkable without the security that property is predicated on? These "ideologies of property," as conceptualized by Emel et al. (1992), then, reduce land to property rights. Accordingly, public policy and development interventions have assumed that the fixation and titling of land are necessary to ensure land access and control, and even as a way out of poverty (de Soto 2000), minimizing that titling has in different contexts been a land-grabbing strategy, as work in Latin America has shown (Grajales 2011; Hetherington, 2009; Rocheleau and Edmunds 1997; Ybarra 2009).

Given women's exclusion of property regimes, many efforts of public policy and development interventions have deemed landed property as a way of achieving more equitable gender relations. Since the 1970s or so, many studies have given preeminence to the expansion and definition of property rights as a strategy for guaranteeing land access and control, paying growing attention to women's ownership (e.g., Agarwal 2003). In this hegemonic view, property is understood as a way of securing use, access, and control. It is seen as part of a set order, which can be disrupted by intrusion, invasion, and theft. But as we have seen, property and theft are not antagonistic practices. In fact, we should consider violence to be inherent to the definition and establishment of property (Blomley 2003; Mansfield 2007; Correia 2013) and a way of rendering theft invisible. As such, it is worth questioning the institutionalization of property, including its dependence on gendered logics (Roy 2021). To do so, I point to three moments in Montes de María, a region in the Colombian Caribbean, when specific assemblages of land as property laid out state-sanctioned exclusion and dispossession, and how these processes were shaped by gender.

Gendered Exclusions in the Assembling of Land as Property

Montes de María is in the Colombian Caribbean, in the northern part of the country. The region is well known for land conflicts between peasant organizations and the landowning elites, who are invested in cattle ranching, growing and harvesting rice, and palm-oil plantations. A site of both land recuperations and anarchist associations, the longstanding conflict in Montes de María is testimony to a strong political mobilization for land access. At the same time, its recent history has been marked by the deadly incursion of paramilitary forces, the ensuing reconfiguration of land ownership, and the expansion of plantations in ongoing processes of dispossession. This exclusionary system remains in place today despite land restitution efforts and the transitional justice apparatus established in the peace accords between the FARC-EP guerrilla group and the Colombian state in 2016. Although one can read this history as one of failed or weak state power, it attests to how land property is at the core of state-making practices, which often entail both direct and structural forms of violence.

"La Tierra para el que la Trabaja": Masculinist Notions of Work and Property

Throughout Latin America, the 1960s brought different state-led agrarian reforms. Strategies to delimit individual land ownership and register official titles were rooted in seemingly contradictory efforts to guarantee the social function of land property and to quell the Cold War anxieties of the peasants, which were seen as a breeding ground for communism, subversion, and guerrillas, framed within US president John F. Kennedy's Alliance for Progress. In the nineteenth century, rural change in Colombia was marked by the expansion of the agrarian frontier and the coercive appropriation of more land by the landowning elites (LeGrand 1986). The deeply uneven access to land led to conflicts that intensified in the 1920s and 1950s and that the agrarian reform of 1968 sought to ameliorate. Among these efforts, the state incentivized the creation of the Asociación Nacional de Usuarios Campesinos (National Association of Peasant Users), bringing together plantation-workers' unions, cooperatives, and smaller organizations, thought by the government to be suitable to become individual owners of plots of land. The association initially was a means for the state to identify who to issue land titles; however, it became an important space of peasant mobilization and land struggle in Montes de María, in part because of peasants' efforts to distance themselves from the state (Rivera Cusicanqui 1982; Zamosc 1987). Nonetheless, the agrarian reform efforts mostly amounted to strategies of directed colonization that relied on state lands and left private property untouched. Nothing that was done changed the fact that land for the most part remained in the hands of few landowners. As Maite Yie (2015) showed in her analysis of agrarian reform in Colombia, access to property translated into the promise of effective citizenship but did little to transform the place the peasants occupied within a deeply uneven social structure.

Moreover, Carmen Diana Deere and Magdalena León (2001) have shown that agrarian reform efforts in Colombia were based on a masculinist definition of who should own land. Reforms were based on a family-centered vision and the idea that peasant households were represented by men, and so they benefited the husband as the head of the household and subordinated women by reducing them to the role of helpers rather than workers of the land. Widows could sometimes access land property, but typically, their sons had priority. In this sense, the well-known saying "la tierra para el que la trabaja" (land to the tiller or for the one who works the land) did not seem to include women or feminized forms of labor more easily identified as "care," such as weeding, planting trees, picking fruit and gathering mushrooms, and tending to gardens. This is in line with how acts of possession by women and other feminized subjects such as children and Indigenous populations are rarely recognized as a basis of property ownership. This is related to the fact that social reproduction as "the intersecting complex of political-economic, sociocultural, and material-environmental processes required to maintain everyday life and to sustain human cultures and communities on a daily basis and Intergenerationally" (Di Chiro 2008, 281) has been for the most part considered as extra-economic activities, as some Marxist Feminists have shown (Federici 2004; Fraser 2014; Pérez Orozco 2019).

For the few women who were included in agrarian reform, despite land adjudications and land titles, land ownership did not immediately translate into the ability to make decisions about their plots or put them in a better position to negotiate their social standing. As Fernandez, Gopal, and Ruthven (2016) and Mollet (2010) have shown for India and Honduras, respectively, titling does not immediately mean securing land rights for women. Their gendered position, together with the factors of class, age, caste, race, and origin, more often than not required constant "patriarchal bargaining" within their households and communities.

Alianzas Productivas: Debt and Neoliberal Ransacking

The 1990s brought about a modification of agrarian law in most Latin American countries. While this included making it possible for women to hold land titles, the access to landed property was shaped by the concomitant processes of neoliberalization and the institutionalization of official multiculturalism (Ojeda and González 2018). The need to define land titles was championed by multilateral organizations such as the World Bank and the United Nations, informing state efforts to establish property outside consuetudinary arrangements and privileging individual and exclusionary property rights. The gender issue thus arrived on the scene at the same time processes of privatization, deregulation, and the erosion of labor rights were advancing, with disproportionate negative consequences for women.

In Montes de María, the late 1990s and the beginning of the 2000s were also marked by the violent incursion of paramilitary forces sanctioned by the state that sometimes even acted side-by-side with the police and the army. Between 1996 and 2005, 56 massacres, 6,000 selective murders, 215,000 cases of forced displacement, and 82,000 hectares of stolen and abandoned lands were registered (Agencia Presidencial para la Acción Social y la Cooperación Internacional 2010; Centro Nacional de Memoria Histórica 2010). These grabbed lands were quickly legalized and bought by individual landowners and corporations (Bargent 2011; Instituto Latinoamericano por una Sociedad y un Derecho Alternativos [ILSA] 2012; Verdad Abierta 2018). The violent expropriation was complemented by state mechanisms that included both the militarization of the region and the allocation of direct subsidies to landowners (Grajales 2011; ILSA 2012; Molano, 2011; Verdad Abierta 2012). One of these mechanisms was *alianzas productivas* (productive alliances) between peasants and palm barons. A development instrument that was a response to persistent narratives of the yield gap, the *alianzas productivas* pushed peasants to devote their land and labor to palm oil production. In exchange, the palm barons would provide the capital and buy the harvest, which allowed them to set the conditions of production as well as the price. Not surprisingly, *alianzas productivas* gave rise to complicated forms of contract farming that resulted in insurmountable debt for the peasants, and many ended up losing their land (Ojeda et al. 2015). In this way, in the context of the neoliberal assemblage of land as property in Montes de María, land titles, which were the prerequisite for entering the alliance and getting backing for credit, were not only insufficient to secure land ownership but ultimately became a link in the chain of dispossession because they disadvantaged the peasants they claimed to be helping.

Both the rampant dispossession caused by the paramilitary attacks and the sustained dispossession brought on by the establishment and expansion of oil palm plantations revealed the little power land titles had in this context. Forced to sell through direct violence, threats, or debt, many peasants, who decades before had been able to access plots because of the agrarian reform, were now landless. Those who were able to keep the land faced other forms of dispossession related to the privatization of water and the expansion of plantations through land leasing. Debt, and the ways in which it opened the door to renewed forms of dispossession, was not evenly distributed along gender lines. The heightened uncertainty and income volatility pushed women—historically assigned to be primary caretakers—to double their efforts to provide food and water for themselves and their families (Ojeda, 2021). In this context of what Cindi Katz (2001) calls "the neoliberal attack" on social reproduction (see Caballero and Gago, 2020, as well), it was evident that, in Montes de María, gendered roles, expectations, and responsibilities were central in defining who gets to decide what land means, what is it for, and what to do with it, as has been documented in León Araya's (2017) work on Honduras and in Erika Sebastián Aguilar's (2019) work on Mexico.

Failed Restitution

The 2010s in Colombia were marked by land-restitution policies and the signing of the peace accord between the FARC-EP guerrillas and the Colombian government in 2016. Postconflict transition efforts concentrated on the need to restitute lands that had been violently taken or forcibly abandoned in the context of war. These, however, coincided with global land-grabbing dynamics associated with the financial crisis of 2008 and an increased demand for food (Borras et al. 2011), unleashing a new wave of dispossession in Colombia, while the state's efforts were directed at redistributing confiscated and public lands (ILSA 2012).

At the same time, though the national land-restitution policies made it possible for women to have land titles, either individually or in dual (spousal) titling, women's access to land is still mediated largely by men, either their partners or male relatives. As Donny Meertens (2017) showed, decisions about what to produce and how are still largely made by men, and women's economic and social contributions remain unrecognized. Despite important legal changes, landownership is still seen as a male prerogative. Meertens suggests that judges are reluctant to recognize feminized work as property practices. And even when women do receive titles, their position remains vulnerable, which can push them to sell their land, usually at a below the market price. In this assemblage of land as property associated with peacebuilding and the incorporation of a gender-sensitive approach, women's formal land ownership does not directly translate into a greater capacity to make decisions about the land. Even if access to land property is necessary in contexts of heightened dispossession, it does not seem sufficient, as the experience of peasant women in Montes de María suggests.

Conclusion

The ways in which we understand and relate to land are complex and multidimensional, but hegemonic conceptualizations of land tend to reduce it to property. To better account for the political lives and sedimented histories of land, I suggest that we analyze specific assemblages of land and the ways in which they turn land into property. In examining land as property from a feminist perspective, we gain insight into how landed property works as a powerful mechanism of state-making, one made possible through gendered exclusions. At the same time, by tracing the inherent violence of land as property, we can question the generalized view of property as the solution to conflicts over access to and control over land, and of the state as guarantor.

Even if struggles over the property of land are an important strategy for mobilizations toward subsistence, justice, reparation, and autonomy, they constitute a limited political horizon, one that often fails to halt dispossession, mounting inequalities, and sustained land-grabbing. State-centric strategies of land redistribution or market-led agrarian reforms, for example, limited to formal property regimes, stand at risk of overlooking structural forms of violence that are not accidental but constitutive of landed property. On the contrary, a feminist perspective on property complicates this vision of land and power, not only by including women and other feminized subjects, but also by taking seriously the realm of social reproduction and other forms of relationality between people and land.

Acknowledgments

I thank two anonymous reviewers and the editors Jun Borras and Jennifer Franco for their on-point questions and suggestions. I also thank Andrés León Araya for his comments on a previous draft. The initial idea for this article was discussed in the writing group some women colleagues and I formed in 2021, amid mounting labor and care responsibilities due to the Covid-19 pandemic and the misogynist responses to it. I want to thank all its members, particularly Tatiana Acevedo and Claudia Rivera Amarillo, for their observations and support.

References

Agarwal, Bina. 2003. "Gender and Land Rights Revisited: Exploring New Prospects via the State, Family and Market." *Journal of Agrarian Change* 3 (1–2): 184–224.

Agencia Presidencial para la Acción Social y la Cooperación Internacional. 2010. "Unidades agrícolas familiares, tenencia y abandono forzado de tierras en Colombia." Bogotá: República de Colombia.

Akram-Lodhi, Haroon. 2021. "Land." In *Handbook of Critical Agrarian Studies*, edited by Haroon Akram-Lodhi, Kristina Dietz, Bettina Engels, and Ben McKay, 72–79. Northampton, MA: Edward Elgar.

Bargent, James. 2011. "Montes de María: Quién heredó la riqueza manchada de sangre de las AUC?" *Kavilando* 3 (2): 85–89.

Bhattacharyya, Gargi. 2018. *Rethinking racial capitalism: Questions of reproduction and survival.* Washington, DC: Rowman & Littlefield.

Blomley, Nicholas. 2003. "Law, Property, and the Geography of Violence: The Frontier, the Survey, and the Grid." *Annals, Association of American Geographers* 93 (1): 121–141.

Borras, Saturnino, Ruth Hall, Ian Scoones, Ben White, and Wendy Wolford. 2011. "Towards a Better Understanding of Global Land Grabbing: An Editorial Introduction." *Journal of Peasant Studies* 38 (2): 209–216.

Butler, Judith, and Joan W. Scott. (Eds). 1992. *Feminists Theorize the Political,* 239–340. New York: Routledge.

Caballero, Luci, and Verónica Gago. 2020. "La batalla por la propiedad en clave feminista." Elsaltodiario.com, June 26. https://www.elsaltodiario.com/el-rumor-de-las-multitudes/la-batalla-por-la-propiedad-en-clave-feminista.

Cabnal, Lorena. 2015. "Sin ser consultadas: La mercantilización de nuestro territorio cuerpo-tierra." In *Mujeres defendiendo el territorio: Experiencias de participación en América Latina,* edited by Christina Papadopoulou and Laura María Carvajal, 41–55. Bogotá: Fondo de Acción Urgente.

Camargo, Alejandro. 2022. "Land Born of Water: Property, Stasis, and Motion in the Floodplains of Northern Colombia." *Geoforum* 131: 223–231.

Centro Nacional de Memoria Histórica. 2010. *Memorias de despojo y resistencia campesina en la costa Caribe (1960–2010).* Bogotá: Ediciones Semana.

Coronil, Fernando. 2000. "Naturaleza del poscolonialismo: Del eurocentrismo al globocentrismo." In *La colonialidad del saber: Eurocentrismo y Ciencias sociales: Perspectivas Latinoamericanas,* edited by Edgardo Lander, 53–67. Buenos Aires: CLACSO, Consejo Latinoamericano de Ciencias Sociale.

Correia, David. 2013. *Properties of Violence: Law and Land Grant Struggle in Northern New Mexico.* Athens: University of Georgia Press.

Cruz, Delmy Tania. (2016). "Una mirada muy otra a los territorios-cuerpos femeninos." *Solar* 12 (1): 35–46.

Daigle, Michelle. 2016. "*Awawanenitakik*: The Spatial Politics of Recognition and Relational Geographies of Indigenous Self-Determination." *Canadian Geographer* 60 (2): 259–269.

Deere, Carmen Diana, and Magdalena León. 2001. "Who Owns the Land? Gender and Land-Titling Programmes in Latin America." *Journal of Agrarian Change* 1 (3): 440–467.

Di Chiro, Giovanna. 2008. "Living environmentalisms: coalition politics, social reproduction, and environmental justice." *Environmental Politics* 17(2): 276–298.

d'Eaubonne, Francoise. [1974] 2020. *Feminism or Death.* London: Verso.

Emel, Jody, Rebecca Roberts, and David Sauri. 1992. "Ideology, Property, and Groundwater Resources." *Political Geography* 11: 37–54.

FAO. 2018. *The Gender Gap in Land Rights.* https://www.fao.org/family-farming/detail/es/c/1119178/.

Federici, Silvia. 2004. *Caliban and the Witch: Women, the Body and Primitive Accumulation.* Brooklyn: Autonomedia.

Fernandez, Bina, Meena Gopal, and Orlanda Ruthven. 2016. Introduction to *Land, Labour and Livelihoods: Indian Women's Perspectives,* edited by Bina Fernandez, Meena Gopal, and Orlanda Ruthven, 1–27. London: Palgrave Macmillan.

Fraser, Nancy. 2014. "Behind Marx's Hidden Abode." *New Left Review* 86: 55–72.

Gilmore, Ruth. 2020. *Geographies of Racial Capitalism.* Film. Directed by Kenton Card. Antipode Foundation. https://www.youtube.com/watch?v=2CS627aKrJI.

Grajales, Jacobo. 2011. "The Rifle and the Title: Paramilitary Violence, Land Grab and Land control in Colombia." *Journal of Peasant Studies* 38 (4): 771–792.

Guzmán, Adriana. 2019. *Descolonizar la memoria, descolonizar los feminismos.* La Paz, Bolivia: Redición Llojeta.

Hall, Derek. 2013. *Land.* New York: Polity Press.

Hall, Derek, Philip Hirsch, and Tania Li. 2011. *Powers of Exclusion: Land Dilemmas in Southeast Asia.* Honolulu: University of Hawai'i Press.

Harris, Cheryl. 1993. "Whiteness as Property." *Harvard Law Review* 106 (8): 1710–1791.

Hennessy, Elizabeth. 2019. "What Is Land? A Conversation with Tania Murray Li, Rafael Marquese, and Monica White." Edge Effects, December 17. https://tspace.library.utoronto.ca/bitstream/1807/103868/2/What%20is%20Land_TSpace.pdf

Hetherington, Kregg. 2009. "Privatizing the Private in Rural Paraguay: Precarious Lots and the Materiality of Rights." *American Ethnologist* 36 (2): 224–241.

Hetherington, Kregg. 2011. *Guerrilla Auditors: Transparency, Democracy and Rural Politics in Paraguay.* Durham, NC: Duke University Press.

Humphrey, Caroline and Katherine Verdery. 2004. *Property in Question: Value Transformation in the Global Economy.* London: Routledge.

Instituto Latinoamericano por una Sociedad y un Derecho Alternativos. 2012. *Primer informe Montes de María: Entre la consolidación del territorio y el acaparamiento de tierras, aproximación a la situación de derechos humanos y del DIH en la región (2006–2012).* Bogotá: ILSA.

Katz, Cindi. 2001. "Vagabond Capitalism and the Necessity of Social Reproduction." *Antipode* 33 (4): 709–728.

LaDuke, Winona. 1999. *All Our Relations: Native Struggles for Land and Life.* Cambridge, MA: South End Press.

Latorre, Sergio. 2015. "The Making of Land Ownership: Land Titling in Rural Colombia—a Reply to Hernando de Soto." *Third World Quarterly* 36 (8): 1546–1569.

LeGrand, Catherine. 1986. *Frontier Expansion and Peasant Protest in Colombia, 1830–1936.* Albuquerque: University of New Mexico Press.

León Araya, Andrés. 2017. "Domesticando el despojo: Palma africana, acaparamiento de tierras y género en el Bajo Aguán, Honduras." *Revista Colombiana de Antropología* 53 (1): 151–185.

León Araya, Andrés. Forthcoming. *The Coup and the Palm Trees.* Athens: University of Georgia Press.

Li, Tania. 2007. *The Will to Improve: Governmentality, Development, and the Practice of Politics.* Durham, NC: Duke University Press.

Li, Tania. 2014. "What Is land? Assembling a Resource for Global Investment." *Transactions of the Institute of British Geographers* 39 (4): 589–602.

Li, Tania, and Semedi Pujo. 2021. *Plantation Life: Corporate Occupation in Indonesia's Oil Palm Zone.* Durham, NC: Duke University Press.

Liboiron, Max. 2021. *Pollution Is Colonialism.* Durham, NC: Duke University Press.

Lund, Christian. 2016. "Rule and Rupture: State Formation through the Production of Property and Citizenship." *Development and Change* 47 (6): 1199–1228.

Mansfield, Becky. 2007. "Privatization: Property and the Remaking of Nature-Society Relations: Introduction to the Special Issue." *Antipode* 39 (3): 393–405.

McCutcheon, Priscilla. 2019. "Fannie Lou Hamer's Freedom Farms and Black Agrarian Geographies." *Antipode* 51 (1): 207–224.

Meertens, Donny. 2017. "Restitución de Tierras, Justicia de Género y Paz. Reflexiones sobre el potencial transformador de la política rural en Colombia." *Papeles de Paz y Derechos Humanos* 1. Bogotá: Instituto de Derechos Humanos y Construcción de Paz Alfredo Vázquez Carrizosa, Pontificia Universidad Javeriana.

Menéndez, Mariana, and Mariana García, comps. 2021. *La vida en el centro: Feminismos, reproducción y tramas comunitarias*. Mexico City: Minervas Ediciones and Bajo Tierra Ediciones.

Mies, Maria. 1999. *Patriarchy and Accumulation on a World Scale*. London: Zed Books.

Molano, Alfredo. 2011. *Del otro lado*. Bogotá: El Áncora Editores.

Mollett, Sharlene. 2010. "*Está listo* (Are you ready)? Gender, Race and Land Registration in the Río Plántano Biosphere Reserve." *Gender, Place and Culture* 17 (3): 357–375.

Nichols, Robert. 2018. "Theft is property! The recursive logic of dispossession." *Political Theory* 46 (1): 3–28.

Ojeda, Diana. 2021. "Social Reproduction, Dispossession, and the Gendered Workings of Agrarian Extractivism in Colombia." In *Agrarian Extractivism in Latin America*, edited by Ben M. McKay, Alberto Alfonso-Fradejas, and Arturo Ezquerro-Cañete, 85–98. New York: Routledge.

Ojeda, Diana, and María Camila González. 2018. "Elusive Space: Peasants and Resource Politics in the Colombian Caribbean." In *Land Rights, Biodiversity Conservation and Justice: Rethinking Parks and People*, edited by Sharlene Mollet and Thembela Kepe, 89–106. London: Routledge.

Ojeda, Diana, Jennifer Petzl, Catalina Quiroga, Ana Catalina Rodríguez, and Juan Guillermo Rojas. 2015. "Paisajes del despojo cotidiano: Acaparamiento de tierra y agua en Montes de María, Colombia." *Revista de Estudios Sociales* 54: 107–119.

Olarte-Olarte, María Carolina. 2019. "From territorial peace to territorial pacification: Anti-riot police powers and socio-environmental dissent in the implementation of Colombia's peace agreement." *Revista de Estudios Sociales* 67: 26–39.

Pérez Orozco, Amaia. 2019. *Subversión Feminista de La Economía. Aportes Para Un Debate Sobre El Conflicto Capital-Vida*. Madrid: Traficantes de Sueños.

Plumwood, Val. 1993. *Feminism and the Mastery of Nature*. London: Routledge.

Proudhon, Pierre-Joseph. (1840) 1993. *What Is Property?* Cambridge, UK: Cambridge University Press.

Rivera Cusicanqui, Silvia. 1982. *Política e ideología en el movimiento campesino: el caso de la ANUC (As. Nacional de Usuarios Campesinos)*. Bogotá: CINEP.

Rivera Cusicanqui, Silvia. 1997. "La noción de "derecho" o las paradojas de la modernindad postcolonial: Indígenas y mujeres en Bolivia." *Temas Sociales* 19: 27–52.

Rivera Cusicanqui, Silvia. 2010. *Violencias (Re) Encubiertas En Bolivia*. La Paz: Editorial Piedra Rota.

Rocheleau, Dianne, and David Edmunds. 1997. "Women, Men and Trees: Gender, Power and Property in Forest and Agrarian Landscapes." *World Development* 25 (8): 1351–1371.

Rose, Carol. 1985. "Possession as the Origin of Property." *University of Chicago Law Review* 52 (1): 73–88.

Roy, Ananya. 2021. "Undoing Property: Feminist Struggle in the Time of Abolition." Society+Space, May 3. https://www.societyandspace.org/articles/undoing-property-feminist-struggle-in-the-time-of-abolition.

Sebastián Aguilar, Erika. 2019. "Mujeres me'phaa, resistencia y sentido del lugar ante los despojos del extractivismo y el narcotráfico." *Iconos* 64: 69–88.

Serje, Margarita. 2001. *El revés de la nación: Territorios salvajes, fronteras y tierras de nadie.* Bogotá: Universidad de los Andes.

Shiva, Vandana. 1988. *Staying Alive: Women, Ecology and Development.* London: Zed Books.

Sikor, T., and Christian Lund. 2009. "Access and Property: A Question of Power and Authority." *Development & Change* 40 (1): 1–22.

Soto, Hernando de. 2000. *The Mystery of Capital: Why Capitalism Triumphs in the West and Fails Everywhere Else.* New York: Basic Books.

Tuck, Eve, and Marcia McKenzie. 2015. *Place in Research: Theory, Methodology, and Methods.* New York: Routledge.

Valverde, Mariana. 2009. "Jurisdiction and Scale: Legal 'Technicalities' as Resources for Theory." *Social & Legal Studies* 18 (2): 139–157.

Verdad Abierta. 2012. "La tierra y el conflicto en los Montes de María." December 1, 2012. Verdadabierta.com. https://verdadabierta.com/la-tierra-y-el-conflicto-en-los-montes-de-maria.

Verdad Abierta. 2018, April 30. "Los acuatenientes: La historia del agua, la tierra y la agroindustria de la palma de aceite en María La Baja, Bolívar." https://verdadabierta.com/especiales-v/2018/acuatenientes/#contenido.

Wallerstein, Immanuel. 2003. "Citizens All? Citizens Some! The Making of the Citizen." *Comparative Studies in Society and History* 45(4): 650–679.

Wolford, Wendy. 2010. *This Land Is Ours Now: Social Mobilization and the Meaning of Land in Brazil.* Durham, NC: Duke University Press.

Wolford, Wendy, Saturnino Borras, Ruth Hall, Ian Scoones, and Ben White. 2013. "Governing Global Land Deals: The Role of the State in the Rush for Land." *Development & Change* 44 (2): 189–210.

Wynter, Silvia. 1995. "The Pope Must Have Been Drunk, the King of Castile a Madman: Culture as Actuality, and the Caribbean Rethinking Modernity." In *The Reordering of Culture: Latin America, the Caribbean and Canada in the Hood*, edited by Alvina Ruprecht, 17–41. Montreal: McGill-Queen's University Press.

Ybarra, Megan. 2009. "Violent Visions of an Ownership Society: The Land Administration Project in Peten, Guatemala." *Land Use Policy* 26 (1): 44–54.

Yie, Maite. 2015. *Del patrón-Estado al Estado patrón: La agencia campesina en las narrativas de la Reforma Agraria en Nariño.* Bogotá: Pontificia Universidad Javeriana and Universidad Nacional de Colombia.

Zamosc, León. 1987. *La cuestión agraria y el movimiento campesino en Colombia: Luchas de la Asociación Nacional de Usuarios Campesinos (ANUC), 1967–1981.* Bogotá: Instituto de Investigaciones de las Naciones Unidas para el Desarrollo Social.

CHAPTER 18

LAND, SOCIAL REPRODUCTION, AND AGRARIAN CHANGE

BEN COUSINS

Introduction

RAPID and ongoing processes of urbanization mean that most of the world's population today is located in urban areas, but rural areas remain important. Around 45 percent of the world's 7.7 billion people continue to reside in rural settlements, mainly in the global South and in low- and middle-income countries.[1] A recent study shows that around a third of the world's food is produced on farms less than 2 hectares in size (Lowder et al. 2021). However, fewer rural dwellers than ever before depend wholly on land and agriculture, and farming on a small scale is increasingly but one component of wider sets of livelihood strategies that include both nonfarm and nonlocal sources (Bernstein 2010, 110). Nonetheless, land and agriculture remain significant and play vital roles in the life and livelihoods of many rural households, as well as of migrants who leave rural areas, either temporarily or permanently, to seek employment in urban areas (or other countries) but retain close ties to their places of origin. Thus land and agriculture continue to play key roles in both productive and social reproductive activities engaged in by large numbers of people in the world today.

"Social reproduction" refers to "the activities and attitudes, behaviours and emotions directly involved in the maintenance of life on a daily basis and intergenerationally.... [It includes] how food, clothing and shelter are made available for immediate consumption, the ways in which the care and socialization of children are provided, the care of the infirm and the elderly, and the social organization of sexuality" (Laslett and Brenner 1989, 382).

The term "social reproduction" has a particular analytical provenance located within Marxist and feminist analyses of capitalism and is not synonymous with notions of "livelihoods" or the "care economy." Social reproduction features prominently in critiques by Marxist feminists of the neglect of gender relations by mainstream Marxism. In a lively literature, debates initiated in the 1960s and 1970s have recently been renewed and extended. As argued by many scholars, including Mariarosa Della Costa, Silvia Federici, Heidi Hartmann, Maxine Molyneaux, Wally Seccombe, Selma James, Maria Mies, Lisa Vogel, Eli Zyretsky, Johanna Brenner, Isabella Bakker and Meg Luxton (see Bhattacharya 2017b; and Ferguson et al. 2016 for overviews), the gendered and generational character of social reproduction is critically important. It is deeply shaped and conditioned by class relations but, in turn, powerfully conditions those relations.

One key insight is that the primary logic of capitalism, the appropriation of surplus value from workers in the process of production as a basis for the accumulation of capital, is itself dependent on processes in which the workers themselves are produced. This is social reproduction, secured partly by the consumption of commodities but also by unpaid labor within households, kin-based units, communities, and a wide range of other institutions and activities, including those focused on socialization, education, and health. This means that the relations of social reproduction are as central as relations of production to the understanding of capitalism, as well as to struggles within and against the capitalist system (Bhattacharya 2017a).

In rural settings in the global South, both daily and intergenerational reproduction are often supported and enabled by access to land, even when other sources of livelihood (including migrant labor) become as or more important than land. Land looms large in "customary" norms and values, which often continue to underpin kinship and familial relations and structures of rural authority. Of course, rural areas today are subject to rapid processes of social, cultural, economic, political, and ecological change—as Marx and Engels (1967) remarked, under capitalism "everything that is solid melts into air" (16). But at the same time, it is rarely the case that the social and cultural aspects of life entirely disappear.[2] The question then becomes: How are the processes of social reproduction in rural contexts changing, and in what ways do they in turn influence the course of social change, including processes of capitalist accumulation? What forms of politics emerge from these linked dynamics, and do they contribute to the formation of contemporary social movements engaged in struggles over land?

The issues brought into view through the lens of social reproduction are vitally important for understanding the dynamics of change in contemporary rural social formations. Here I argue that although social reproduction "shapes" social change in critically important ways, the dominant logic of accumulation "pushes" ongoing social transformation. This is important when one is reflecting on the potential contributions of a politics of rural social reproduction to anticapitalist struggles more broadly.

Social Reproduction Theories and Debates

Originally, social reproduction theory developed as an effort to make sense of aspects of life under capitalism that are not commodified, such as relationships and labor processes in the domestic sphere (for example, cooking, housework, and care of children and the elderly, which are in most cases undertaken by women), as well as in healthcare and education services that are provided at low or no cost by the state. Theorists in the 1960s and 1970s asked how the commodified and noncommodified aspects of life under capitalism are connected and about the role of noncommodified dimensions of existence in the workings of the capitalist system as a whole.

The manner in which the capitalist system reproduces itself over time was a central issue for Marx, who argued that it is the capitalist production process that "produces and reproduces the capital-relation itself: on the one hand the capitalist, on the other the wage-labourer" (Marx 1976, 724). On the labor side, wages are converted into "means of subsistence which have to be consumed to reproduce the muscles, nerves, bones and brains of existing workers, and to bring forth new workers into existence." Marx went on to argue that "the maintenance and reproduction of the working class remains a necessary condition for the reproduction of capital. But the capitalist may safely leave this to the worker's drives for self-preservation and propagation" (717–778).

From the vantage point of capital, then, how workers reproduce themselves outside the "cost" of their wages is their own business. Marx does not pursue the issue in any depth, noting merely that the "production of labour-power consists in his reproduction of himself or his maintenance" (Marx 1976, 274), and that "the number and extent of his so-called necessary requirements, as also the manner in which they are satisfied, are themselves the product of history," thus "the determination of the value of labour-power contains a historical and moral element" (275).

There is clearly much more than this to be said about social reproduction. From the 1960s, Marxist and feminist scholars began to explore the issue in depth, initiating fierce debates on the role of domestic labor under capitalism. Theorists argued that although wages are necessary for the purchase of commodities by workers, the social reproduction of labor relies on institutions, such as marriage, the household, and the state, to regulate the unpaid labor of women, which often takes place under oppressive conditions (Molyneaux 1979). In poor countries, social reproduction includes the labor expended in subsistence farming, which can provide a hidden subsidy to capitalist employers who able to pay wages below the cost of reproducing the worker (Meillassoux 1972; Wolpe 1972).

Marxist feminists tend to see social reproduction not as a separate or autonomous domain but as an integral feature of capitalism. Katz (2001), for example, defines social reproduction as a "set of structured practices that unfold in dialectical relation with production, with which it is mutually constitutive and in tension" (711). Bhattacharya (2017b) argues that social reproduction theory is not premised on the existence of "two separate spaces and two separate processes of production, the economic and the social" (59). Rather, capitalism is understood as a complex totality in which "the economic impulse of capitalist production conditions the so-called noneconomic" but does not determine it.

Some theorists, such as Picchio (1992), emphasize that capitalism both requires a sphere of noncommoditized social reproduction and tends to erode the relations that constitute it. Similarly, Fraser (2016, 103) argues that capitalism depends on several background conditions that it tends to bring into crisis, one being noncommodified processes of social reproduction. In today's era of financialized and neoliberal capitalism, the tensions and contradictions between accumulation and state-supported forms of social reproduction were exacerbated by the period of stagnation initiated by the global financial crisis of 2007–2008 and the austerity policies many governments enacted in response. They have also been starkly revealed in the Covid-19 pandemic (Stevano et al. 2021). The tensions have given rise to new forms of struggle that are contributing to a revitalization of anticapitalist politics (Bhattacharya 2017a).

Current debates within social reproduction theory focus on a wide range of issues and questions, and only a few can be sketched here. One focuses on the scope of the term: Does it refer to the production and reproduction of labor power as a commodity, to the reproduction of the total workforce of a capitalist economy, thus involving generational reproduction, immigration, colonization, and enslavement, or to the reproduction of the capitalist system as a whole (sometimes equated with "societal reproduction")? Or, perhaps, all of these?

A second debate more closely examines the relationship between production and reproduction. Many theorists argue that a sole focus on the appropriation of surplus value in workplaces where wages are paid, as in so-called "productivist" forms of Marxist theory, is narrow and misleading. Other theorists suggest that a broader conception of social reproduction as itself "value-producing" is needed. This can shed light on how reproductive realms shape and condition the appropriation of surplus value, for example, by reinforcing patterns of labor control in capitalist workplaces; by absorbing the costs of reproduction; and in the "formal subsumption" of (outsourced) production processes, where labor is unwaged. These are all common in societies in the global South (Mezzadri 2019). In this view, productive labor and socially reproductive labor are distinct but inseparable within capitalism. For O'Laughlin (2021) any conception of social reproduction as a "separate sphere" should be jettisoned. It is the "everyday struggles of living labor that determine its reproduction . . . not just in the kin-based family but in overlapping, shifting spaces and processes, including struggles for better wages and working conditions in capitalist firms" (17).

A third key debate focuses on the relationship between different forms of oppression in a capitalist society (class, race, gender, sexual orientation, etc.) beyond the gender–class binary (Ferguson 2016; McNally 2017). This has implications for how to theorize social reproduction and its connections with workplace exploitation. Some Marxist feminists see class and other forms of oppression and exploitation as mutually constitutive within processes that are "internally relational" and "dialectical" in character (Ferguson 2016, 43). In this view, the structural connections between different forms of oppression under capitalism serve to highlight the interdependence of production and social reproduction, with key implications for politics.

A fourth debate is centered on oft-neglected connections between social reproduction and *ecological* reproduction, sometimes theorized as two key forms of "unpaid work" that furnish essential preconditions for the exploitation of labor in capitalist production processes, but that also tend to be undermined or destroyed as accumulation proceeds. Mies ([1986] 2014) provides an influential formulation, asserting that "the unpaid work of women, nature and colonies" is essential for capitalism but lies outside the circuits of capital itself. Moore (2017) argues that unpaid work by human and extrahuman energies is "appropriated" by capital and that this complements workplace exploitation within a wider framework in which value is "co-produced" (7).

The Role of Land and Agriculture in Production and Social Reproduction

This section discusses the variable and changing contributions of land and agriculture to production and social reproduction, focusing mainly on the global South. It also assesses the roles played by social reproduction and accumulation in processes of agrarian change.

The Role of Crises of Social Reproduction in Class Differentiation

The social reproduction of labor and life takes particular forms in the rural areas of the global South. It can include the use of crop and livestock production for both domestic consumption and cash income, and the gathering of natural resources, such as wild foods, fuelwood, timber, and other materials, for own use, sale, and craft production. Many natural resources are found on commons, held "collectively" by a range of social units. All these activities are structured by distinctions of age, gender, ethnicity, and so on, with women assuming major roles in the so-called "subsistence economy," which includes small-scale food production; fuel and water collection; domestic labor; and the care of young children, the frail elderly, and the sick (Razavi 2009, 206).

Production and reproduction through both noncommodified and commodified relations are as dynamically intertwined in agrarian societies as in industrial economies, but in distinctive ways (Chung 2017). Access to and control over land and natural resources, in conjunction with the labor required for production and gathering, are key for household subsistence in many contexts (Naidu and Ossome 2016, 61). However, given the general tendency under capitalism for all aspects of existence to be commodified, cash income is increasingly required for many items of subsistence. Employment for wages, in cash or in kind, locally or farther afield, is necessary to ensure the social reproduction of increasing numbers of rural households; and employment and levels of remuneration are always gendered and often highly unequal. Employment can both constrain production for own use (e.g., by drawing away labor or resources) and support it (e.g., by providing cash for purchasing crop inputs).

Pressures on the social reproduction of rural households arise from class dynamics both in the wider economy and in small-scale farming itself. As Bernstein (2010) argues, small-scale farmers should be conceived of as "petty commodity producers," who concentrate two contradictory imperatives under capitalism: to secure their social reproduction and to surmount competitive market pressures. These imperatives involve meeting the demands of four competing "funds": a *consumption fund* for food, clothing, shelter etc., including for household members too young or unfit to work; a *replacement fund* for productive capital (e.g., seed, tools, draught animals)—but also for labor, through generational reproduction in childbearing and raising, as well as care of the old and unfit; a *ceremonial fund*, for activities that "create and recreate the cultures and social relations of farming communities, such as rituals and festivities" (20); and a *fund of rent*, where farmers make payments to others such as landlords, moneylenders, or states.

It is difficult for small-scale producers to meet all these demands simultaneously, creating a built-in tendency toward class differentiation. Some agricultural producers successfully reproduce themselves as both capital and labor, maintaining similar scales of production and consumption over time, and are sometimes characterized as "middle peasants" (Bernstein 2010, 104). Others ("poor peasants") are unable to reproduce their farms and themselves from their own production alone as a result of, for example, drought, crop losses, or the death of a productive adult. These events can permanently undermine their productive capacity. To survive, they become dependent on the sale of their labor, on other forms of petty enterprise, or on receiving external assistance from family members or the state. However, access to at least some land and natural resources often continues to underpin their survivalist strategies, as in the case of rural workers who are employed by local farmers or as cross-region or cross-border migrant workers (Borras et al. 2021; Shah and Lerche 2020).

In contrast, some agricultural petty-commodity producers make use of opportunities to produce a substantial surplus over and above the amount needed to secure their simple reproduction and are able to reinvest all or part of this surplus in extending the material base of a production unit. Such producers move beyond the *simple reproduction* of their farms into *expanded reproduction*, hiring in wage labor as they do so.[3] Often, hired-in labor is supplied by poor households from the immediate locale or farther afield.

Class differentiation in the contemporary world is clearly identifiable, but it involves complex and variable combinations of livelihood strategies, locales, and class "places" rather than linear processes that reduce class identities to those of "capitalists," "petty bourgeoisie," and "proletariat." Thus Bernstein (2010, 111) suggests that "classes of labour" are increasingly "fragmented"; and similarly, Shivji (2017) argues that the composite term "working people" is often more appropriate than the simple distinction between "peasants" and "workers."

Case studies from across the global South illustrate these processes. Li's (2014) study of a frontier zone in Indonesia reveals how the embrace of a boom crop, cacao, by small-scale producers resulted in the deepening of capitalist relations. This saw successful accumulation by a minority and loss of access to land by many others, who were plunged into poverty and a "crisis of social reproduction." In rural Zimbabwe, similar class dynamics have been described both in densely settled "communal areas" and on land redistributed through the occupations movement ("fast-track land reform") after 2000 (Cousins et al. 1992; Moyo 2011; Scoones et al. 2012).

Zhang's (2015) analysis of rural class differentiation in contemporary China emphasizes three key dynamics: accumulation of capital, commodification of subsistence, and state interventions. He identifies five emerging agrarian class categories: capitalists, petty commodity producers, dual-employment households, wage workers, and subsistence peasants. Dual-employment households are the largest group in rural China today (359), most of their wage work takes place in urban areas, and their wage income helps to capitalize agricultural petty commodity production. Household divisions of labor are gendered, with men migrating to jobs elsewhere and women engaged in farming and care work and local waged work. A key factor in households' deciding to continue to invest in farms, "often at great cost to their family lives and subjective well-being" (359–360), is the lower financial cost of social reproduction that this affords, as well as the degree of security against the precarity of wage work it provides.

The role of land and agriculture in social reproduction thus varies greatly by class location and by the degree of dependence on land versus other sources of livelihoods, within combined, complex, and diverse strategies of survival, often across different locales. Class relations and dynamics in both rural production and social reproduction are closely intertwined, analytically distinct but inseparable, and subject to more or less rapid change over time.

Land, Social Reproduction, and Migration

A common theme in the recent literature on social reproduction in the global South is the large-scale movement of migrants from rural areas to both urban areas and other countries in search of waged employment, some maintaining their membership in a rural home or strong connections to a rural base (e.g., Locke et al. 2013). Migration is the result of a variety of processes that both "push" people out of the countryside and "pull" them into zones of urban employment. Migration can be prompted by the contradictions of petty commodity production (see above), and by state policies that seek to promote capitalist farming. The latter often involve small-scale producers' losing their land to large-scale enterprises. It can also be deliberately engineered by policies designed to pull rural labor into urban and industrial settings, often for extremely low wage rates, as in contemporary China and in the past in Southern Africa.

The enclosure of common lands, the consequent immiseration of rural populations, and a shift to wage employment in urban industry played key roles in the original transition from feudalism to capitalism in England (Marx 1976). In colonial settings, the cheap wages paid to migrant workers were often "subsidized" by productive and reproductive labor undertaken in rural homesteads. In the present, massively increased rates of both intra- and international migration are now observed across the contemporary world, and many rural families have effectively become “translocal” or “multilocational” in character. Land and natural resources can provide a key anchor for families or households that engage in a range of complex and diverse social reproduction strategies across the rural-urban divide. Land also offers opportunities for rural accumulation, in some cases funded in part by urban earnings.

Recent scholarship on translocality and social reproduction explores the variable significance of the rural base, for example, in China (Jacka 2018; Nguyen and Locke 2014; Zhao and Scully 2018), Thailand (Coyle and Kwong 2000), Vietnam (Nguyen and Locke 2014), India (Gidwani and Ramamurthy 2018; Lerche and Shah 2018; Shah and Lerche 2020); Mynamar (Borras et al 2021); Mexico (Kunz 2010), and South Africa (Cousins et al. 2018).

Despite much variation, some common features emerge from these studies. Firstly, the absence of migrating adult males and/or females (the latter now becoming more common) often reorganizes gendered and generational relations and divisions of labor within rural families and communities. Jacka (2018) suggests that in rural China “recent changes in family reproduction are associated with tremendous fluidity and flux in intrafamily relations.” Women are often forced to take responsibility for farming, even in previously male-dominated domains such as rice or livestock production, but this “feminization of agriculture” can give way over time to the “ageing of agriculture,” as adult women also begin to migrate in search of wage income (1351). The division of care labor is also subject to change, and many studies have described an increased role for elderly or retired family members, as Nguyen and Locke (2014) did in their analysis of rural Vietnam and China.

Secondly, the significance of rural land varies greatly between families, with class being one key differentiator, as in China (Jacka 2018; Zhang 2015), though class often combines with other forms of oppression, such as caste in India (Gidwani and Ramamurthy 2018; Lerche and Shah 2018).

Thirdly, even when land loses its significance as a means of agricultural production or for the harvesting of natural resources, it can continue to shape the dynamics of social reproduction. In Southern Africa, “land” is often a key pivot for such dynamics, offering a place to properly bury the dead; bury the umbilical cords of children; provide a place of connection and return for migrant kin; establish continuity with the past (including the ancestors); shore up control of women by men; underpin the powers of traditional authorities; and symbolize collective identity and belonging (Ferguson 2013, 168). Borras et al. (2021) refer to the significance of land with multiple meanings for cross-border migrants from Myanmar, for whom a range of forms of access to land is “key to keeping their rootedness to their community, now and in the future, where social care can be coordinated and carried out” (10).

Gidwani and Ramamurthy (2018) show how “middle migrants” in India (those of rural origin, now urban dwellers and earning relatively good incomes), can nevertheless retain their orientation to the agrarian, “the point from which the world unfolds” (1002). Their life histories show how systems of kinship, marriage, and patriarchy continue to shape the life course of female middle migrants.

The Role of Land in Structuring Social Relations and Identities

Social reproduction in agrarian contexts involves the reproduction of social and cultural relations and identities in specific social formations and contexts, as well as reproduction of the capital-labor relation. In the global South, therefore, the scope of societal reproduction (reproducing the social) includes the institutions and practices of kinship, marriage, family and the constitution of households, underpinned by culturally inflected systems of belief (Borras et al. 2021; Cousins et al. 2018; Gidwani and Ramamurthy 2018; Peters, 2022).

Land often plays a key role in the constitution of rural households, which can be seen as a node embedded within a complex web of social networks structured by notions and practices of kinship, ethnicity, religion and "community." Borras et al. (2021) argue that for cross-border migrant agricultural workers from Myanmar, "land access conjures and concretizes a place to satisfy one's feeling and sense of longing and belonging. Land access allows for the reproduction of people as a distinct social group based on race or ethnicity" (16).

In South Africa, the significance of rural land as a means of production has greatly declined (Cousins et al. 2018; Ferguson 2013). Nevertheless, cultural norms involving patrilineal descent, the constitution of a "homestead" with differentiated and unequal gendered roles, remain powerfully resonant. These are invoked within a ceremonial economy in which communication with ancestral spirits occurs through the sacrifice of livestock at a homestead (Hornby and Cousins 2019). The form and expense of ceremonies and the significance of land in circuits of distribution, vary along lines of class, gender, and generation and are often fraught with tension.

These examples illustrate the interdependence of the relations of production and social reproduction. The core relations of capitalism are reproduced on a daily basis, but so are a complex web of noncommodified norms, institutions, roles, practices, and forms of labor that are deeply interwoven with class realities. In rural social formations, land remains central to both social reproduction and production, even as its significance is fundamentally altered by the impacts of accumulation and class formation more broadly, producing socially differentiated forms of land-based social reproduction.

The Significance of Property Rights over Land and Natural Resources

Given the centrality of land and natural resources in rural social formations, access to and control over these resources is a key aspect of social reproduction. These are structured by regimes of property rights. In precapitalist societies land and natural resources were held in a wide variety of ways, from relatively egalitarian distributions of resources in decentralized systems to systems in which class power was rooted in unequal ownership and control of land, as in feudalism. Land could belong to communities, clans, or families or to overlords, aristocrats, and elites in an array of complex and context-specific arrangements. Land and resources such as forests, grazing areas, and fisheries often had the status of commons, where recognized users in a collective entity had agreed rights and obligations (Federici 2011).

Today, capitalist property regimes based on private ownership are dominant throughout the world. Older and more "socially embedded" forms of property have given way to individual private property, or its near equivalents, in many contexts, including in relation to land, through contemporary versions of the "enclosure of the commons" (Mies 2014). These processes have underwritten massive concentrations of ownership of the means of production in the hands of capitalist classes, including land.[4] Enclosures continue in the global South today, mainly in the form of corporate land grabs (Borras et al. 2011), understood by some as part of a wider dynamic of "accumulation by dispossession" (Harvey 2005). Nevertheless, older systems of property often survive, including customary land tenure and common property regimes (Cousins 2000; Wily 2011). This means that core features of social reproduction in many societies with large rural and agrarian populations are property regimes that are distinct from private and individualized forms.

Transformations of property rights in Africa are examined by Peters (2004), who describes a "socio-cultural dynamic of differentiation" emerging in Africa, with "group boundaries [becoming] more exclusively defined" (302). However, as Mathieu et al. (2002,). emphasized, the continuing social and political embeddedness of land rights means that these kinds of changes are not "linear or automatic," the process being "totally embedded in social relationships" and hence "contradictory, complex and ambiguous," since past meanings of land "retain their significance in the local social reality" (126–127).

Of course, property regimes that originated in the precapitalist era can involve highly unequal social relations, especially in relation to the "invisible work" of women (Ossome and Naidu 2021), but they can also be relatively egalitarian. Some struggles over property rights are defensive in character, seeking to prevent large-scale dispossession. Others are more assertive, attempting to broaden the social base of land ownership and to strengthen the rights of vulnerable groups, including women (Walker 2009). To date, the gains have been few and far between (Naidu and Ossome 2016; Jacobs 2013), but a key motivation is that stronger land rights can be crucial for ameliorating the precarity of social reproduction.

The Role of Social Reproduction Dynamics in Trajectories of Agrarian Change

How do the contradictory dynamics of social reproduction influence trajectories of agrarian transformation? How determinative are they within processes of social change?

A case study from India sheds light on the central importance of accumulation. Fernandez (2018) analyzes social reproduction as a key aspect of the land-based livelihoods of thousands of families in the Little Ran of Kutch in Gujarat. Major sources of household income are prawn harvesting and artisanal salt production, complemented by small-scale agriculture; other income sources include wage labor and microenterprises. Land-based livelihoods are currently under threat from dispossession, including attempts to enforce the exclusion of salt collectors from a designated conservation area and encroachment by large salt companies. Other threats involve violent incursions by outsiders seeking to enter the increasingly lucrative prawn export industry, as well as the "neo-bondage" of harvesters by agents of export companies (150). Class formation within the ranks of the poor is another key factor; a small number of prawn-harvesting households are engaged in accumulation while the majority wage a desperate struggle for survival (154). Fernandez describes the crucial work performed by the female members of poor households and shows how the social reproduction capacities of women are being rapidly depleted, as is evident in poor health and low levels of well-being, with likely effects on their capacity for biological reproduction (158). As a consequence, dependence on wage labor (proletarianization) is increasing.

This case suggests that the most powerful agents of agrarian change in this part of Gujarat are the prawn exporters, salt companies, and local accumulators, which are all favored and supported by the state. Poor households, especially the female members responsible for social reproductive labor, are systematically marginalized in these processes of accumulation. Given the subordinate role of social reproduction within households, as well as within capitalist relations more broadly, this is not surprising.

Other cases cited in this chapter also suggest that the primary drivers of agrarian change tend to be processes of capital accumulation. However, it should be noted that social reproduction concerns continue to shape the strategies of accumulating households and thus influence the outcomes of change. In the analyses of emerging class and other forms of differentiation in rural China provided by Zhang (2015) and Jacka (2018), how successfully households secure, arrange, and organize the labor and resources required for social reproduction, most often by reallocating responsibilities by gender, generation, and location, does make a difference to their class trajectory. This suggests that the character of social reproduction *shapes* change, but that change is mostly *driven* by the restless and relentless forces of capital in one guise or another.

State policies are also important, as shown Nguyen and Locke (2014) show for China and Vietnam. Forms of politics centered on social reproduction can result in state support for improved social services and forms of social protection, more secure land rights, or the redistribution of land to poor rural households. But these kinds of interventions tend to ameliorate the consequences of change, instead of acting as their determinants.

The Role of Social Reproduction in Struggles over Land and Natural Resources

Social reproduction, in particular the contradictions and tensions that arise from its subordination to the imperatives of capital, may play a more central role in the politics of land, agriculture, and natural resources than is generally acknowledged. Given the tendency for corporate agribusiness and capital-intensive capitalist farming and fishing enterprises to marginalize small-scale producers and natural-resource users, the pressures on the survival and reproduction of agricultural and rural households across the world are immense (Bernstein 2010, 85–88). In addition, the exclusion from land as a result of mining, construction of large dams, imposition of conservation policies and programs, or designation of special economic zones or other forms of land use also threaten the livelihoods of many rural households. Growing food insecurity is one result, among a range of kinds of vulnerability.[5] This helps account for the *defensive* character of much rural mobilization.

Of course, mobilization also involves positive demands, such as calls for enhanced state support to small-scale producers to help them to expand levels of production and increase farm income, for land redistribution to the poor, for policies that promote "food sovereignty," and so on (Borras et al. 2015). In some contexts, these demands are combined with struggles to improve the wages and work conditions of farm workers, including casual and seasonal workers, and to advance a right to security of tenure (see Hall et al. 2013 for the South African case). However, many analysts note the tensions between the agendas pursued by diverging class forces within these rural social movements (Edelman and Borras 2016). The livelihoods of poor farmers, "perhaps the most numerous type of farmer in the world today" (43–44), are often highly precarious; they often work small pieces of poor-quality land, relying household labor, and, unable to survive on agriculture alone, are forced to sell their labor or engage in other survival strategies. The policies that rural social movements propose often reflect a heterogeneity of class positions, as well as other, non-class interests (gender, race, ethnicity, caste), or may embody the interests of one dominant grouping within a movement (43–44).

Given their poverty and precarity, as well as their numerical majority, it is likely that the interests of poor rural households are the key focus of much mobilization and struggle in relation to land. Women play key roles in poor farming households, in relation to both production and reproduction, and their concerns include household food security, land tenure security, and access to resources on commons. Strategically, the availability of livelihood strategies that enable women to flexibly combine different roles and responsibilities, such as small-scale agriculture, the harvesting of natural resources, and petty trade, can be crucial. Land struggles are thus often highly gendered (Levien 2017).

But the politics of social reproduction in the lives of (rural) "classes of labor" does not focus only on securing land rights. The focus of mobilization may be quite different in contexts where large-scale capitalist agricultural enterprises dominate or are strongly promoted by state policies. Here, the struggles often focus on wages or conditions of labor, or combine these concerns with contestations around access to land, livestock, or natural resources (Hall et al 2013). In addition, tensions and conflicts between men and women, youth and the older generation, or groups with different social identities (e.g., of caste or ethnicity) may have their roots in the contradictions of social reproduction. In contexts where integration into the capitalist economy takes the form of seasonal labor migration, there can be a "shift in focus away from single location struggles to their spatial and temporal fragmentation, allowing for fluid, episodic, and multi-sited forms" (Shah and Lerche 2020, 11).

Unsurprisingly, "social reproduction" as such is rarely named as the key focus of rural political mobilization. This does not mean, however, that it is not an appropriate way to understand the core concerns of many rural struggles. In some cases, for example, the Adivasis of rural India, such struggles even suggest the potential for a "counter-politics," based on egalitarian values, that proposes alternatives to capitalism (Shah and Lerche 2020, 11). However, as Levien et al. (2018) point out, land struggles are also "inextricably bound up with nonclass forms of power and domination, whether patriarchy, racism, casteism, or anti-immigrant nativism" (876), and their anticapitalist character is not guaranteed.

The Contributions of Land-Based Struggles to Wider Mobilizations against Capitalism

Contemporary capitalism shows symptoms of a gathering systemic crisis in many dimensions. Economic problems are evident in the slowing rates of profit in previously dominant Western economies from declining industrial bases, heightened financialization, periods of global financial turmoil, and challenges to the global hegemony of the United States and its partners from China (Fine and Saad-Filho 2016). Enormous numbers of people across the globe are unable to secure adequately paid employment or self-employment (Davis 2006).

Deep-seated social and political crises accompany these economic ills, expressed in part in massive dislocations and movements of populations from the global South who are seek entry into wealthy countries in the wake of the dysfunction or collapse of their own economies, often generating a politically charged backlash (Cross 2020). Crises of social reproduction are another result, exacerbated by the austerity measures adopted by many governments and the impacts of the Covid-19 pandemic (Stevano et. al. 2021). Political systems across the world are also in disarray, given the ascendancy of capital and the erosion of systems of public provision. The claims of political parties to represent citizens in both liberal forms of democracy and the increasingly prevalent forms of authoritarian nationalism or right-wing populism, are being called into doubt (Panitch and Albo 2017). Politics in many countries is thus much more fluid and uncertain now than was the case in preceding decades, posing challenges to agrarian social movements that embrace "progressive" forms of populism (Borras 2020).

In addition, a global ecological catastrophe now looms, the result of both global warming and the material impacts of capitalist systems of production and consumption (and their infrastructures) on ecosystems (Hickel 2020). Industrialized forms of large-scale agricultural production, distribution, and consumption are deeply implicated in climate change, and droughts, floods and other environmental disasters are contributing to social and political upheavals (Moore 2017).

How are the different components of these crises connected, and what might the political implications be? If the capitalist system is beginning to be understood as being at the root of these crises, what are the prospects for anticapitalist struggles?

Nancy Fraser's recent writings (e.g., Fraser 2016, 2017, 2020) explore these connections and suggest that they have their origin in the nature of capitalism as such, inflected by its globalized and financialized character at present. She suggests that capitalism's economic subsystem depends on several noneconomic "background conditions" but at the same time tends to bring these into crisis. These include the exploitation of the natural world as a source of materials and as a sink for waste (the ecological crisis), the exercise of legitimate public power to govern social life, and processes of social reproduction. If these are threatened, the effect over time will be that "capitalism's accumulation dynamic effectively eats its own tail" (Fraser 2016, 103).

Fraser argues that the capitalist economy, social reproduction, politics, and ecological relations constitute distinct ontological and normative domains, interrelated in the overarching institutional order of capitalism (Fraser 2017, 152–154). The boundaries between these domains often become foci of conflict, or what she terms "boundary struggles," which are themselves constitutive in character. Each of these normative orders, as well as struggles over their boundaries with each other, are "pregnant with critical-political possibility," thus considerably broadening the scope of anticapitalist struggle, to include "multiple sets of actors" and "vectors of struggle" (158). Critics argue that Fraser's revisionism fails to appreciate many of Marx's key insights, instead "splitting his totalizing analysis into a plurality of subordinate fields of life and action" (Sandemose 2016, 196; see also O'Kane 2021). They may be right. But Fraser's attempt to "join the dots" at the present moment of crisis is usefully provocative in its scope and ambitions and resonates strongly with debates in critical agrarian studies.

Borras (2020, 16), for example, argues that rural activists across the world are actively exploring potential links between agrarian, environmental, climate justice, and food sovereignty movements (16). He calls for "an enriched and reinvigorated left-wing populism, that is anti-capitalist in character, socialist in orientation, pluralist in ideological orientation, heterogeneous in institutional platforms, and fundamentally founded on an alliance between the classes of labor or working people" (26).

If many agrarian struggles are indeed motivated by crises of social reproduction, perhaps understood to be the core of an "agrarian question of labor" (Bernstein 2010), then they have the potential to connect directly with worker's struggles within capitalist production, as well as other forms of mobilization. Efforts by small-scale food producers to counter their marginalization could motivate their participation in cross-class alliances that focus on postcapitalist systems of food provisioning (Selwyn 2021). Growing awareness of the need to radically reconfigure systems of food production and distribution as a key component of actions to head off ecological disaster (IPCC 2021) suggests that the time is ripe for this kind of cross-fertilization.

Conclusion

Social reproduction and its complex relationship with production are being energetically theorized and debated at present, and the literature is beginning to explore the realities in contexts outside the global North. This chapter has focused on rural contexts in which land, agriculture, and natural resources remain key for both production and reproduction. There is much evidence of their rapid reconfiguration within processes of social change, due primarily to class and other forms of social differentiation, "from below," "from above," and "from outside" (i.e., wrought by powerful external forces). The migration of family members to urban contexts and other countries means that many households are now translocal in character, which often changes the significance of land and farming. The central role of female labor in both social reproduction and production, often differentiated by race, ethnicity, caste, and other forms of oppression, is beginning to be widely acknowledged, and is increasingly the focus of political mobilization. A key issue is thus how to directly connect different social and political struggles. As the gathering ecological crisis begins to make itself felt, at the same time as massive inequalities within and between nation-states become ever more visible, making these connections is now an urgent task.

Acknowledgments

Many thanks to Jun Borras, Jenny Franco, Pauline Peters, Henry Bernstein, and Jens Lerche for their useful comments and suggestions on an earlier draft.

Notes

1. Data for 2019 from World Bank (https://data.worldbank.org/indicator/SP.RUR.TOTL.ZS).
2. I am grateful to Pauline Peters for this point.
3. Note that the terms "simple reproduction" and "expanded reproduction" refer here to the dynamics of capitalist enterprises, not to social reproduction, which refers to the life processes of a class or classes outside the relations of production.
4. In some capitalist countries, aspects of the highly skewed patterns of land ownership derived from precapitalist social formations have been reinforced under capitalism rather than replaced, as in the UK (Shrubsole 2019).
5. McMichael is one of the few scholars of rural struggles to identify social reproduction as a motivating force, but he tends to equate it with food security alone (McMichael 2012).

References

Bernstein, Henry. 2010. *Class Dynamics of Agrarian Change*. Halifax, CAN: Fernwood Press.

Bhattacharya, Tithi. 2017a. "How Not to Skip Class: Social Reproduction of Labor and the Global Working Class." In *Social Reproduction Theory: Remapping Class, Recentering Oppression*, edited by Tithi Bhattacharya, 55–72. London: Pluto Press.

Bhattacharya, Tithi, ed. 2017b. *Social Reproduction Theory: Remapping Class, Recentering Oppression*. London: Pluto Press.

Borras, Saturnino M., Jr., Ruth Hall, Ian Scoones, Ben White, and Wendy Wolford. 2011. "Towards a Better Understanding of Global Land Grabbing: An Editorial Introduction." *Journal of Peasant Studies* 38 (2): 209–216.

Borras, Saturnino M., Jr., Jennifer C. Franco, and Sofia Monsalves Suárez. 2015. "Land and Food Sovereignty." *Third World Quarterly* 36 (3): 600–617.

Borras, Saturnino M., Jr., Jennifer C. Franco, Doi Ra, Tom Kramer, Mi Kamoon, Phwe Phyu, et al. 2021. "Rurally Rooted Cross-Border Migrant Workers from Myanmar, Covid-19, and Agrarian Movements." *Agriculture and Human Values* 39 (1): 315–338. doi.org/10.1007/s10460-021-10262-6.

Borras, Saturnino M., Jr. 2020. "Agrarian Social Movements: The Absurdly Difficult but Not Impossible Agenda of Defeating Right-Wing Populism and Exploring a Socialist Future." *Journal of Agrarian Change* 20 (1): 3–36.

Chung, Youjin B. 2017. "Engendering the New Enclosures: Development, Involuntary Resettlement and the Struggles for Social Reproduction in Coastal Tanzania." *Development and Change* 48 (1): 98–120.

Cousins, Ben. 2000. "Tenure and Common Property Resources in Africa." In *Evolving Land Rights, Policy and Tenure in Africa*, edited by Camilla Toulmin and Julian Quan, 151–179. London: Department for International Development, International Institute for Environment and Development and Natural Resources Institute.

Cousins, Ben, Alex Dubb, Donna Hornby, and Farai Mtero. 2018. "Social Reproduction of 'Classes of Labour' in the Rural Areas of South Africa: Contradictions and Contestations." *Journal of Peasant Studies* 45 (5–6): 1060–1085.

Cousins, Ben, Dan Weiner, and Nick Amin. 1992. "Social Differentiation in the Communal Lands of Zimbabwe." *Review of African Political Economy* 19 (53): 5–24.

Coyle, Saolawee, and Julia Kwong. 2000. "Women's Work and Social Reproduction in Thailand." *Journal of Contemporary Asia* 30 (4): 492–506.

Cross, Hannah. 2020. *Migration beyond Capitalism*. Oxford: John Wiley & Sons.

Davis, Mike. 2006. *Planet of Slums*. London: Verso.

Edelman, Mark, and Saturnino M. Borras Jr. 2016. *Political Dynamics of Transnational Agrarian Social Movements*. Halifax, CAN: Fernwood Press.

Federici, Silvia. 2011. "Women, Land Struggles, and the Reconstruction of the Commons." *Working USA* 14 (1): 41–56.

Ferguson, James. 2013. "How to Do Things with Land: A Distributive Perspective on Rural Livelihoods in Southern Africa." *Journal of Agrarian Change* 13 (1): 166–174.

Ferguson, Susan. 2016. "Intersectionality and Social-Reproduction Feminisms." *Historical Materialism* 24 (2): 38–60.

Ferguson, Susan, Genevieve LeBaron, Angeliki Dimitrikaki, and Sara Farris. 2016. "Special Issue on Social Reproduction: Introduction." *Historical Materialism* 24 (2): 25–37.

Fernandez, Bina. 2018. "Dispossession and the Depletion of Social Reproduction." *Antipode* 50 (1): 142–163.

Fine, Ben, and Alfredo Saad-Filho. 2016. *Marx's Capital*. London: Pluto Press.

Fraser, Nancy. 2016. "Contradictions of Capital and Care." *New Left Review* 100: 99–117.

Fraser, Nancy. 2017. "Behind Marx's Hidden Abode: For an Expanded Conception of Capitalism." In *Critical Theory in Critical Times*, edited by Penelope Deutscher and Cristina Lafont, 141–159. New York: Columbia University Press.

Fraser, Nancy. 2020. "What Should Socialism Mean in the Twenty-First Century?" *Beyond Market Dystopia: New Ways of Living; Socialist Register 56, 2020*, edited by Greg Albo and Leo Panitch, 282–295. New York: New York University Press.
Gidwani, Vinay, and Priti Ramamurthy. 2018. "Agrarian Questions of Labour in Urban India: Middle Migrants, Translocal Householding and the Intersectional Politics of Social Reproduction." *Journal of Peasant Studies* 45 (5–7): 994–1017.
Hall, Ruth, Poul Wisborg, Shirhami Shirinda, and Phillan Zamchiya. 2013. "Farm Workers and Farm Dwellers in Limpopo Province, South Africa." *Journal of Agrarian Change* 13 (1): 47–70.
Harvey, David. 2005. *The New Imperialism*. Oxford: Oxford University Press.
Hickel, Jason. 2020. "What Does Degrowth Mean? A Few Points of Clarification." *Globalizations* 18 (7): 1105–1111. https://doi.org/10.1080/14747731.2020.1812222.
Hornby, Donna, and Ben Cousins. 2019. "'Reproducing the Social': Contradictory Interconnections between Land, Cattle Production and Household Relations in the Besters Land Reform Project, South Africa." *Anthropology Southern Africa* 42 (3): 202–216.
International Panel on Climate Change. 2021. *Climate Change 2021: The Physical Science Basis; Contribution of Working Group I to the Sixth Assessment Report of the Intergovernmental Panel on Climate Change*, edited by V. Masson-Delmotte, P. Zhai, A. Pirani, S. L. Connors, C. Péan, S. Berger, et al. Cambridge, MA: Cambridge University Press.
Jacka, Tamara. 2018. "Translocal Family Reproduction and Agrarian Change in China: A New Analytical Framework." *Journal of Peasant Studies* 45 (7): 1341–1359.
Jacobs, Susie. 2013. *Gender and Agrarian Reforms*. London: Routledge.
Katz, Cindi. 2001. "Vagabond Capitalism and the Necessity of Social Reproduction." *Antipode* 33 (4): 708–727.
Kunz, Rahel. 2010. "The Crisis of Social Reproduction in Rural Mexico: Challenging the 'Re-privatization of Social Reproduction' Thesis." *Review of International Political Economy* 17 (5): 913–945.
Laslett, Barbara, and Johanna Brenner. 1989. "Gender and Social Reproduction: Historical Perspectives." *Annual Review of Sociology* 15 (1): 381–404.
Lerche, Jens, and Alpa Shah. 2018. "Conjugated Oppression within Contemporary Capitalism: Class, Caste, Tribe and Agrarian Change in India." *Journal of Peasant Studies* 45 (5–6): 927–949.
Levien, Michael. 2017. "Gender and Land Dispossession: A Comparative Analysis." *Journal of Peasant Studies* 44 (6): 1111–1134.
Levien, Michael, Michael Watts, and Yan Hairong. 2018. "Agrarian Marxism." *Journal of Peasant Studies* 45 (5–6): 853–883.
Li, Tania Murray. 2014. *Land's End*. Durham, NC: Duke University Press.
Locke, Catherine, Janet Seeley, and Nitja Rao. 2013. "Migration and Social Reproduction at Critical Junctures in Family Life Course." *Third World Quarterly* 34 (10): 1881–1895.
Lowder, Sarah K., Marco V. Sanchez, and Raffaele Bertini. 2021. "Which Farms Feed the World and Has Farmland Become More Concentrated?" *World Development* 142: 105455. doi.org/10.1016/j.worlddev.2021.105455.
Mathieu, Paul, Mahamadou Zongo, and Lacinan Paré. 2002. "Monetary Land Transactions in Western Burkina Faso: Commoditisation, Papers and Ambiguities." *European Journal of Development Research* 14 (2): 109–128.
Marx, Karl. (1867) 1976. *Capital*. Vol. 1. Harmondsworth, UK: Penguin.
Marx, Karl, and Friedrich Engels. (1848) 1967. *The Communist Manifesto*. London: Penguin.

McMichael, Philip. 2012. "Food Sovereignty, Social Reproduction and the Agrarian Question." In *Peasants and Globalization*, edited by Haroon Akram-Lodhi and Cristóbal Kay, 300–324. London: Routledge.

McNally, David. 2017. "Intersections and Dialectics: Critical Reconstructions in Social Reproduction Theory." In Bhattacharya, *Social Reproduction Theory*, 72–83. London: Pluto.

Meillassoux, Claude. 1972. "From Reproduction to Production: A Marxist Approach to Economic Anthropology." *Economy and Society* 1 (1): 93–105.

Mezzadri, Alessandra. 2019. "On the Value of Social Reproduction: Informal Labour, the Majority World and the Need for Inclusive Theories and Politics." *Radical Philosophy* 2 (4): 33–41.

Mies, Maria, 2014. *Patriarchy and Accumulation on a World Scale: Women in the International Division of Labour*. London: Bloomsbury Publishing.

Molyneux, Maxine. 1979. "Beyond the Domestic Labour Debate." *New Left Review* 116 (3): 27.

Moore, Jason W. 2017. "The Capitalocene. Part I: On the Nature and Origins of Our Ecological Crisis." *Journal of Peasant Studies* 44 (3): 594–630.

Moyo, Sam. 2011. "Changing Agrarian Relations after Redistributive Land Reform in Zimbabwe." *Journal of Peasant Studies* 38 (5): 939–966.

Naidu, Sirisha C., and Lyn Ossome. 2016. "Social Reproduction and the Agrarian Question of Women's Labour in India." *Agrarian South: Journal of Political Economy* 5 (1): 50–76.

Nguyen, Minh T., and Catherine Locke. 2014. "Rural-Urban Migration in Vietnam and China: Gendered Householding, Production of Space and the State." *Journal of Peasant Studies* 41 (5): 855–876.

O'Kane, Chris. 2021. "Critical Theory and the Critique of Capitalism: An Immanent Critique of Nancy Fraser's 'Systematic' 'Crisis-Critique' of Capitalism as an 'Institutionalized Social Order.'" *Science & Society* 85 (2): 207–235.

O'Laughlin, Bridget. 2021. "No Separate Spheres: The Contingent Reproduction of Living Labour in Southern Africa." *Review of International Political Economy* https://doi.org/10.1080/09692290.2021.1950025.

Ossome, Lyn, and Sirisha C. Naidu. 2021. "The Agrarian Question of Gendered Labour." In *Labour Questions in the Global South*, edited by Praveen Jha, Walter Chambati, and Lyn Ossome, 63–86. Singapore: Palgrave Macmillan.

Panitch, Leo, and Greg Albo, eds. 2017. *Rethinking Democracy: Socialist Register 2018*. New York: New York University Press.

Peters, Pauline. 2004. "Inequality and Social Conflict over Land in Africa." *Journal of Agrarian Change* 4 (3): 269–314.

Peters, Pauline. 2022. "Kinship." In *The Edward Elgar Handbook of Critical Agrarian Studies*, edited by Haroon Akram-Lodhi, Kristina Dietz, Bettina Engels, and Ben McKay, 139–149. Cheltenham, UK: Edward Elgar.

Picchio, Antonella. 1992. *Social Reproduction: The Political Economy of the Labour Market*. Cambridge, MA: Cambridge University Press.

Razavi, Shahra. 2009. "Engendering the Political Economy of Agrarian Change." *Journal of Peasant Studies* 36 (1): 197–226.

Sandemose, Jorgen. 2016. "Nancy Fraser: Revolutionary Empiricism?" *Journal of Social Science Studies* 3 (1): 196–212.

Scoones, Ian, Nelson Marongwe, Blasios Mavedzenge, Felix Murimbarimba, Joseph Mahenehene, and Crispen Sukume. 2012. "Livelihoods after Land Reform in Zimbabwe:

Understanding Processes of Rural Differentiation." *Journal of Agrarian Change* 12 (4): 503–527.

Selwyn, Ben. 2021. "Community Restaurants: Decommodifying Food as Socialist Strategy." In *Beyond Digital Capitalism: New Ways of Living, Socialist Register 57*, edited by Leo Panitch and Greg Albo. London: Merlin Press.

Shah, Alpa, and Jens Lerche. 2020. "Migration and the Invisible Economies of Care: Production, Social Reproduction and Seasonal Migrant Labour in India." *Transactions of the Institute of British Geographers* 45: 719–734.

Shivji, Issa. G. 2017. "The Concept of 'Working People.'" *Agrarian South: Journal of Political Economy* 6 (1): 1–13.

Shrubsole, Guy. 2019. *Who Owns England? How We Lost Our Green and Pleasant Land and How to Take It Back*. London: William Collins.

Stevano, Sara, Rosimina Ali, and Merle Jamieson. 2021. "Essential for What? A Global Social Reproduction View on the Re-organisation of Work during the COVID-19 Pandemic." *Canadian Journal of Development Studies/Revue canadienne d'études du développement* 42 (1–2): 178–199.

Walker, Cherryl. 2009. "Elusive Equality: Women, Property Rights and Land Reform in South Africa." *South African Journal on Human Rights* 25 (3): 467–490.

Wily, Liz Alden. 2011. "'The Law Is to Blame': The Vulnerable Status of Common Property Rights in Sub-Saharan Africa." *Development and Change* 42 (3): 733–757.

Wolpe, Harold. 1972. "Capitalism and Cheap Labour Power: From Segregation to Apartheid." *Economy and Society* 1 (4): 425–456.

Zhan, Shaohua, and Ben Scully. 2018. "From South Africa to China: Land, Migrant Labour and the Semi-proletarian Thesis Revisited." *Journal of Peasant Studies* 45 (5–6): 1018–1038.

Zhang, Forrest Q. 2015. "Class Differentiation in Rural China: Dynamics of Accumulation, Commodification and State Intervention." *Journal of Agrarian Change* 15 (3): 338–365.

CHAPTER 19

LAND ALIENATION, PROLETARIANIZATION, AND CHANGING LABOR MARKET REGIMES IN SOUTHERN AFRICA

WALTER CHAMBATI

INTRODUCTION

A long-standing, unresolved question in contemporary sub-Saharan Africa's predominantly agrarian economies, which since the colonial period have been unevenly integrated into global capitalism (Amin 1972), concerns the extent and nature of rural proletarianization in which peasants, who are disproportionately dispossessed of their land, are compelled into wage labor and the question of whether farm and nonfarm labor activities constitute a continuum of the labor processes of the peasantry. This chapter analyzes the different trajectories of rural labor under dynamic economic conditions and land access patterns, which have been characterized as constituting processes of proletarianization, semi-proletarianization, de-agrarianization, and repeasantization in (Southern) Africa. Access to land, which is modified by pressures from "above" to concentrate land in the minority that are largely driven by the state and pressures from "below" to redistribute land to the majority that are advanced mainly by movements of landless workers and land-short peasants, is seen as central in shaping the trajectories of labor relations. Although access to land is not the only determining factor, it is crucial in affecting who sells or hires labor (Cousins 2009; O'Laughlin 2002; Moyo 2011). Other resources, such as financing, seeds, fertilizers, and machinery, are required to make land productive and thus possible to make a living from (Cousins 2009). Since differentiated and uneven access to land prevails under capitalist social relations, those lacking access to this important means of production are therefore forced into wage labor for their social reproduction (Cousins 2009; Moyo 2011). The research will demonstrate that the peasantry has persisted in the countryside, representing the *dominant* agrarian labor relation in rural Africa, based on the "ownership" and utilization of small plots of land mainly by self-employed family labor in various agricultural and nonfarm production and exchange activities. These tendencies prevail despite the crises rooted in the neoliberal reforms that have undermined peasant agricultural production over the last four decades.

Taking this stand, the chapter challenges the dominant perspectives that generally perceive a post-peasant society evolving from colonial and postcolonial land alienation and adverse agrarian conditions. Neoclassical economic theories reflected such perspectives because they argued that urban industrial growth will reduce the importance of agriculture and absorb the peasantry into wage employment (Lewis 1954). Similar outcomes were also foreseen by the full "proletarianization" thesis, which postulated the conversion of the peasantry dispossessed of their land during the colonization period into wage employees in the capitalist sectors (Arrighi 1970). This chapter also contests recent narratives that the proliferation of nonfarm rural labor activities among the peasantry induced by the economic crises associated with structural adjustment programs is unraveling a de-agrarianization process (Bryceson 2000, 2002; Bryceson, Kay, and Mooij 2000; Rigg 2006). Together with livelihood studies that consider agriculture as but one of many activities for which household labor resources are utilized in the construction of people's livelihoods (Scoones 2015; Niehof 2004), such perspectives undervalue the significance of land and (self-employed) agricultural labor in the survival of (rural) people.

Peasant farm labor diversification strategies in the postindependence period will be depicted here, not only as inevitable, but also as risk aversion in the context of the land alienation and economic crises intensified by structural adjustment programs (see Moyo and Yeros 2005b). Semi-proletarianization, which maintains the importance of land and recognizes the unevenness of colonial land dispossession and access to land, is therefore seen to appropriately capture the diversity of agrarian labor relations in the process of social reproduction.

Moreover, de-agrarianization will be shown to be, not permanent, but amenable to reversals and part of the dynamism of the peasantry's labor process in relation to shifting socioeconomic conditions between town and country. Because (urban) wage incomes are currently facing threats, repeasantization is a conduit for rebuilding social reproduction.

To analyze the trajectories of rural labor, the chapter draws from secondary literature and primary data mobilized in 2017 in Goromonzi and Kwekwe, two Zimbabwean rural districts with contrasting socioeconomic and agroecological characteristics. The primary data mainly entailed randomized household surveys of land-reform beneficiaries and Communal Areas. A separate purposive survey was also conducted with former and new farmworker households.[1] The surveys elicited information on a broad range of issues, including respondents' socioeconomic backgrounds, land access, land use and agricultural production, labor utilization, and nonfarm sources of income. A total of 228 households were sampled in Goromonzi; of these, 76 were from A1; 74, from A2; and 78 were Communal Areas. In Kwekwe, respectively 194, 63, and 85 A1, A2, and Communal Area households were interviewed.[2] The farmworker survey encompassed 199 households in Goromonzi and 208 in Kwekwe.

The next section, "Evolution of Land and Labor Relations since the Colonial Era," examines the implications of colonial land alienation on the proletarianization of rural labor. The chapter then proceeds to analyze the resilience of peasant forms of production, notwithstanding the labor diversification linked to the structural adjustment programs that have instigated economic crises. Using the recent Zimbabwean land reforms as a case study, the research exposes how the peasantry with enlarged land access are reconstituted through repeasantization and semi-proletarianization processes. Finally, the conclusion summarizes the study's findings and draws out their theoretical significance.

Evolution of Land and Labor Relations since the Colonial Era

The agrarian labor relations in African countries can be broadly differentiated according to the varying degrees of land alienation and extra-economic coercion the peasantry faced under colonialism (Mafeje 2003; Neocosmos 1993), with relatively distinct landholding patterns emerging in settler and non-settler Africa (Amin 1972).

In settler Southern Africa, uneven land dispossession resulted in dual agrarian structures composed of large-scale commercial farms existing alongside a differentiated peasantry (Bush and Cliffe 1984; Clarke 1977; Neocosmos 1993). These studies show that the peasantry were generally subordinated to the wage labor markets in the large-scale commercial farms and beyond, while also farming small plots to meet their costs of social reproduction.

Under "indirect mode of colonial rule" in non-settler Africa (e.g., Ghana, Nigeria, Ivory Coast), where land was not expropriated from the peasantry and remained under customary tenure except for few agricultural plantations and mining extraction enclaves (Amanor 2001; Mamdani 1996), peasant labor was not directly incorporated into the labor markets. Rather, such labor was systematically exploited through the extraction of surpluses by the state, markets, and indirect taxation of production, and compulsion into export/cash crops (Amanor 2001). Over time, a differentiated peasantry also evolved there.

These broad agrarian structures that emerged from colonialism have, however, been dynamic, shaped in some instances by the extensive redistribution of large-scale commercial farms in some of the former settler economies in Southern Africa, such as Zimbabwe (Moyo and Yeros 2005b), while the demand for this has been escalating in South Africa (Jacobs 2018; Zhan and Scully 2018).

Land concentration has also been underway during the 2000s in much of non-settler Africa through the acquisition of peasant-owned lands by both domestic and foreign capital and the subsequent development of these lands into middle- to large-scale capitalist farms (Hall et al. 2017; Moyo, Jha, and Yeros 2019). Therefore, the agrarian structures in most African countries can be characterized as predominantly comprised of the peasantry and a rise in small and medium- to large-scale capitalist farms, as well as a few agroindustrial estates that have been established since colonial times (Moyo 2014, 2011). Within such agrarian structures are landless and land-short people who sell their labor to others. The farm classes differ in terms of the land sizes accessed, land tenure relations, commercial orientation of production, and the extent of their use of wage labor (Moyo 2011; Hall, Scoones, and Tsikata 2017).

Various theorists have predicted an evolution to a post-peasant society due to the absorption of peasant labor into wage labor in the industrial sector and to the recent transition to multiple nonagricultural activities in the process of social reproduction. Economic transformation is said to reduce the importance of land and agriculture in national output because it shifts economic activity to the modern or urban industrial capitalist sector. Based on the "unlimited labor supplies model," it was predicted that labor would be transferred from the peasantry, who constitute reservoirs of surplus labor and scarce capital, to the expanding modern capitalist sector, which is endowed with abundant capital but labor short (Lewis 1954), and thus would resolve the inequities in the factors of production between the two sectors (Todaro 1989). This view remains influential in multilateral institutions such as the World Bank that continue to view economic development as the transfer of labor from rural areas to the industrial sectors (World Bank 2013).

Colonial land dispossession and the accompanying extra-economic measures in settler Southern Africa were also argued to have destroyed the peasantry (Arrighi 1970). These analysts postulated a "linear process of proletarianization" of the peasantry in the capitalist sector, arguing that land alienation had irreversibly dented the capacity of the peasantry to survive based only on farming. Proletarianization implies the conversion of self-employed forms of (farm) labor into wage labor in the capitalist sector (Arrighi 1970). Indeed, petty-commodity production on land that remained under peasants' control, if any, had become insignificant for their sustenance, and a continuing trajectory of proletarianization in expanding capitalist sectors was inevitable (Arrighi 1970).

Due to the persistence of self-employed peasant family laborers engaging in petty-commodity production in the Communal Areas, others analysts considered the incomplete and uneven land dispossession to have created "worker-peasants" (Bush and Cliffe 1984, 77), in a process that has been defined as a systemic twentieth-century trajectory of "semi-proletarianization" (Moyo and Yeros 2005b, 26). During the colonial and postindependence period, semi-proletariats were seen as subsidizing capital because they received low wages that were inadequate to meet their costs of social reproduction, hence their supplementation by farming on small pieces of land (Scully 2012; Moyo and Yeros 2005b; Bush and Cliffe 1984). At any rate, the industrialization process in (settler Southern) Africa stalled, and then was unable to absorb the expanding labor force from the peasantry, so that chronic unemployment and underemployment endure in many countries (ILO 2015). Unstable semi-proletarianization therefore represents the dominant labor relation that emerged from land alienation.

However, semi-proletarianization is not only *contingent* on limited land access evoked by (colonial) dispossession; even those endowed with land enter the wage economy for various reasons, including to harness resources for farming, spread their risks, and meet other household needs that are not easily met by farming under the current neoliberal economic conditions (O'Laughlin 2002; Moyo and Yeros 2005a; Shivji 2017).

Persistent Peasantries and Repeasantization: Diverse Agrarian Labor Relations

The peasantry has thus persisted in the countryside, representing the dominant agrarian labor relation in rural Africa, centered as it is on the "ownership" and the utilization of small plots of land mainly by self-employed family labor in various agricultural and nonfarm production and exchange activities[3] (Moyo 2014; Moyo and Yeros 2005b). The labor relations of the peasantry are to a large extent shaped by their degree of access to land and thus are modified by the processes of land alienation or the extension of access through land redistribution. Rather than being "backward" or "traditional," peasants are, in fact, modern, "producing for own consumption" and being integrated into markets for surplus sales and the acquisition of modern farm inputs (Mafeje 2003; Petras and Veltmeyer 2001).

Differentiation tendencies are inherent among peasants owing to the uneven dispersal of capital and labor within and across peasant households (Moyo and Yeros 2005b; Moyo 2014). Men are the heads of most peasant households and control the organization of production and labor, but female-headed households in sub-Saharan Africa have also been growing (O'Laughlin 1998).

Across settler Southern Africa, in numerical terms the peasantry represents the dominant form of organization of production and labor despite colonial land alienation, and in non-settler Africa, they are not only the majority producers but also hold most of the land. At independence in 1980, Zimbabwean peasants controlled 16.4 million hectares, at an average size of 2 hectares of arable land per household, and were engaged mostly in food production, alongside the 5,400 export-oriented large-scale commercial farms (UNDP 1999, 24). These commercial farms held about 15.5 million hectares, with farm sizes averaging over 2,000 hectares (Moyo 2011, 512). Moreover, in the 1990s, semi-proletarianization was perceptible in about 75 percent of the mostly male and urban industrial workers (Peta et al. 1991, 99) and in about half of those employed part-time on the large-scale commercial farms as they straddled between wage labor and petty-commodity production in the Communal Areas (Amanor-Wilks 1995).

In South Africa, the most industrialized country in sub-Saharan Africa, 12.7 million people (representing 31.4 percent of the population) were domiciled in the former homelands around 1997 (Statistics South Africa 1999 n.p.). These peasants accessed about 17 million hectares, compared to the more than 102 million hectares owned by approximately 55,000 large-scale commercial farms (Sihlongonyane 2005, 146). Subsistence agriculture on arable land of less than one hectare was predominant, but 6 percent of the households also produced surpluses for sale (Statistics South Africa 1999 n.p.). Most migrants remain on the outskirts of the formal economy, residing in city slums, and continue to be connected to agricultural production activities in the rural areas of origin (Jacobs 2018; Zhan and Scully 2018).

Namibia was no different. About 70 percent of the Black population, five years after democratic dispensation, subsisted in the Communal Areas on approximately 48 percent of the total agricultural land (33.5 million hectares); they coexisted with approximately 4,200 large-scale farmers on 36.2 million hectares (GoN 1995, 1–2).

As before, farming on small plots remains omnipresent in the countryside in nonsettler countries in Southern Africa (Moyo 2014, 2008). In Malawi, for instance, 2.2 million rural households, owning on average 1.2 hectares of land per household, produce most of the food crops; and about 30,000 middle- to large-size farms, ranging from 10 to 500 hectares, specialize in export production (Zuka 2013, 155). In Mozambique, 90 percent of the rural households (translating to about 80 percent of the national population) practice farming on arable plots of less than 2 hectares (Mucavele n.d.). Small-scale producers in Zambia account for 76 percent of the estimated 600,000 farming households, and agriculture is the largest income contributor for 97.4 percent of the rural households (approximately 45 percent of the population; Mucavele n.d., 4).

More recently, the increases in the peasantry's participation in nonfarm labor activities over the last three decades since the structural adjustment programs were implemented in Africa have been said to portend the "end of the peasantry" or to be proof that a process of "de-agrarianization" or "depeasantization" is underway in the countryside (Bernstein 2014; Bryceson 2000, 2002; Bryceson et al. 2000). De-agrarianization implies a "permanent" shift from "agricultural based modes of livelihoods" in the countryside to more nonfarm activities (including migration to towns) that results from the crisis in agriculture induced by the structural adjustment programs (Bryceson 1999, 192–193).[4] Others go even further to claim that "an increasing number of rural households have no commitment to farming whatsoever" (Rigg 2006, 181–182).

Livelihood approaches also underemphasize the significance of agricultural labor, in both its wage and nonwage variants, to the social reproduction of rural dwellers because they conceptualize labor as one of the resources at the household's disposal that could be diversified in different agricultural and nonagricultural livelihood portfolios (Niehof 2004) rather than being crucial for the social reproduction of the peasants. The centrality of land to peasants is overlooked because land is perceived "as just one among several different assets/capitals required to make a living" (Chimhowu and Hulme 2006, 729–730), notwithstanding that land has multiple social, economic, political, and cultural functions that are critical to the sustenance of households (Moyo 1995). By analyzing land and labor as separate entities, livelihood approaches disguise how land access can increase self-employment in agriculture or compel the landless into wage labor (Amanor 2001; Tsikata 2015).

These perspectives are akin to Bernstein's (2014, S97–S98) argument that since "petty commodity production" is not viable across most of Africa, due to the limited access to finance for even those who hold land, rural households pursue their reproduction through "various and complex *combinations* of employment and self-employment" in small-scale farming and nonfarm activities across rural and urban spaces. There are "infinitely diverse combinations of elements of this or that type of labor" (Bernstein 2014, S99–S100), rendering the "identities" of "worker," "peasant," "trader," "urban," "rural," "employed," and "self-employed" (Bernstein 2014, S98) inadequate in analyzing agrarian labor relations. For the latter, the countryside is instead permeated by "fragmented classes of labor" that are differentiated by resource inequalities, gender, and kinship.

However, nonfarm activities historically were combined with farming by peasants in the process of social reproduction, long before the onset of structural adjustment programs. Peasants in Southern Africa have, since the colonial period, benefited from the natural resources on lands they accessed through direct consumption and selling in the markets (Moyo 1995; Shackleton, Shackleton, and Cousins 2001).

Furthermore, the seasonal nature of dry-land agricultural production in sub-Saharan Africa and elsewhere also opens possibilities of selling labor in the broader labor markets (Shivji 2017). Yet this has not translated to full wage employment outside agriculture. Peasants should thus not be viewed only as agriculturalists because this creates a false dichotomy between farming and nonfarm labor activities, which are interdependent in the process of social reproduction (Gibbon et al. 1993).

Van der Ploeg (2013) also argued that the peasantry enter into nonfarm activities (including wage labor) not only to augment their social reproduction, but also to raise their incomes, which are reinvested into petty-commodity production. Actually, wage-labor remittances to peasant households in Southern Africa in the 1980s partially influenced the advancing rural social differentiation (O'Laughlin 1998; Potts 2000).

Moyo and Yeros (2005b) further argue that these peasant farm labor diversification strategies in the postindependence period represent a spreading of risk into various economic spheres in the context of the land alienation and economic crises intensified by the structural adjustment programs.[5] The risks and opportunities of peasant production present themselves in the forms of land control, integration into various markets, linkages to large landowners and agrarian capital, external shocks (droughts and disease), and the dynamic agricultural and economic policies (Cousins 2009; Mamdani 1996).

Therefore, the concept of "semi-proletarianization" (Moyo and Yeros 2005b; Neocosmos 1993), including its variant labels, such as "worker-peasant" (Bush and Cliffe 1984; Potts 2000), better captures the diversity of agrarian labor relations in the process of social reproduction, not only in former settler colonies such as Zimbabwe, but also elsewhere.

Notwithstanding the decline in farm incomes since the 1990s, the number of people involved in farming in sub-Saharan Africa grew from 316.21 million in 1988 to 432.49 million in 2007 (IFAD 2011, 247–248). Such findings are not surprising in the context of the decrease in manufacturing jobs propelled by deindustrialization, as well as of the pervasive precarity of urban jobs, which many are leaving for farming (ILO 2015). Another survey in the nine countries where 51 percent of sub-Saharan Africa's population live also discovered that 92 percent of rural households were in involved in independent farming, which contributed about 69 percent of the total household income (Davis, Di Giuseppe, and Zezza 2017, 169).[6] This points to the continued importance of agriculture to the sustenance of rural households, as does the growing demand for land for farming small plots that is manifest in the comeback of land repossession movements in many of the rural areas of the global South (van der Berg et al. 2018; Edelman and Borras 2016; Moyo, Jha, and Yeros 2019). The post-peasant society envisioned by some scholars is therefore yet to arrive (Bryceson 2000; Rigg 2006). Instead, the peasantry is being resuscitated, and such a process is expressed in the concept of "repeasantization."

Repeasantization is a process where former proletariats and semi-proletariats take up farming as a major component of their social reproduction (Bernstein 2010, 128; van der Berg, Hebinck, and Roep 2018, 4). It epitomizes the reorientation away from non-agricultural-based social reproduction strategies toward those that are dominated by farming and require access to land.

Ownership of land is central because it provides autonomy for social reproduction and reduces dependency on exploitative labor markets (van der Ploeg 2013; Moyo et al. 2019). Economic crises caused by massive formal urban unemployment, poor wages and deindustrialization, food shortages, and energy crises are accelerating repeasantization in the global South (van der Berg et al. 2018; Moyo, Jha, and Yeros 2019).[7] Consequently, farming in rural areas is increasingly being seen as an option to rebuild livelihoods (Moyo et al. 2019).

Prior to the recent land reforms in Zimbabwe, the return to the countryside by retrenched mine-, industrial-, and farmworkers due to structural adjustment program–induced economic deprivation represent forms of repeasantization or re-agrarianization (Moyo and Yeros 2005a). Retrenched copper-mine and urban industrial workers in Zambia in the 1990s, during the era of structural adjustment programs, also retraced their roots back to the land (Ferguson 1999). Ncapayi (2005) and Fay (2015) also observed a trend of migrants abandoning town jobs to establish themselves in farming in the economically distressed rural areas in the Eastern Cape Province in South Africa. Additionally, not only do some of the rural migrants in cities, such as Cape Town, display "peasant characteristics" in the towns, they continue to invest in land in rural areas in the hopes of returning one day (Jacobs 2018). In Malawi, nonfarm businesses are paving way for diversified farming as peasants respond to producer incentives via state-subsidized inputs (Djurfeldt et al. 2018).

Zimbabwe's Land Reforms: Repeasantization and Perpetual Semi-Proletarianization

Whereas the transformation of Zimbabwe's agrarian labor relations has been ongoing since colonization in the 1890s (Arrighi 1970; Rutherford 2001; Moyo and Yeros 2005a), the initiation of the "fast track" land reform program in 2000 dramatically altered the labor regime. Up to 1999, the minimalist land redistribution meant that the labor reserve system generated by land dispossession during the colonial era (Moyo 2011) had influenced agrarian labor relations as peasants from the Communal Areas with limited access to land were compelled to sell their labor in the mines, industries and to the minority 4,000 large-scale commercial farms which owned most of the agricultural land (Bush and Cliffe 1984). Since only 3.7 million hectares were redistributed to 75,697 households between 1980 and 1999, the dual agrarian structure was only marginally changed (Moyo 2011, 498).

Agrarian wage laborers on the large-scale commercial farms, the largest section of the formal workforce nationally, however, earned the lowest incomes compared to other segments of formally employed workers, and they also worked under various exploitative practices (Amanor-Wilks 1995; Moyo et al. 2000; Kanyenze 2001; Rutherford 2001). However, peasants from the Communal Areas had only limited opportunities to earn incomes adequate for social reproduction through self-employment as independent agricultural producers, largely because of their marginalization in land access (Rukuni 1994). So semi-proletarianization was a pervasive social reproduction strategy in the countryside.

As poverty levels rose and massive urban job retrenchments ensued following the implementation of the Economic Structural Adjustment Programme since 1991, the state succumbed to increased demands for land redistribution by a national land movement that was led by veterans of the liberation struggle but also involved peasants, farmworkers, and urban working classes (Yeros 2013; Sadomba 2011). The Government of Zimbabwe (GoZ) thus formally initiated the fast-track land reform program in 2001, compulsorily acquiring and redistributing mostly White-owned large-scale commercial farms.

Over 90 percent of the 11.8 million hectares formerly held by White-owned large-scale commercial farms were transferred to a diverse range of smaller-scale farmer beneficiaries, dominated by the peasantry (Matondi 2012, 56). The A1 and A2 settlement schemes promoted by the fast-track land reform program generated, respectively, about 145,775 and 22,896 new farm units (Moyo 2011, 498). In the districts studied, land allocations to A1 beneficiaries were also emphasized, but they received smaller shares of land in Goromonzi because of the overwhelming demand for A2 lands near Harare by urban professionals (Chambati 2013). The peasantry, comprising Communal Areas, Old Resettlement land, and A1 resettlement land are now the dominant force numerically and in terms of land area held (Moyo 2013, 2011). The small to medium and large capitalist farms, encompassing the new A2 farms, small-scale commercial farms, and remaining large-scale commercial farms, who produce mainly for the market and depend on hired farm labour are the other constituents of the new agrarian structure.

The land tenure relations were also substantially changed when the acquired freehold large-scale commercial farms were nationalized (GoZ 2001) to secure the rights of new landholders, while partially protecting former farmworkers' land rights.

This process altered the unequal landownership in the agrarian structure and changed key agrarian relations, production relations, market structures, and labor relations that had existed before 2000 (Moyo and Yeros 2005a; Moyo 2013). The structure of agricultural production has shifted from the production of export commodities, such as horticulture and tobacco, toward the predominant production of staple food crops, such as maize, for own consumption, while over 300,000 of Zimbabwe's 1.4 million peasants produce, on small-scale land units, cash and export crops, including surplus maize, for sale in domestic markets (World Bank 2012, 44). However, land utilization is based on lower levels of productivity while replicating aspects of the large-scale commercial farm export agricultural model (World Bank 2006; Moyo et al. 2009; Scoones et al. 2010; Matondi 2012).

The fast-track land reform program also coincided with a changing policy context characterized by a macroeconomic crisis between 2002 and 2008 (World Bank 2006; Moyo et al. 2009; Scoones et al. 2010). Then from 2009 onward, economic stabilization efforts were underway after the demonetization of the Zimbabwe dollar and the adoption of multiple foreign currencies and reliberalization of the economy (World Bank 2012). Postsettlement support and economic, agricultural, social, and labor policies thus also combined with land redistribution to affect labor relations. Labor relations were also shaped by capitalist transformation processes entailing the incorporation of peasants into global agricultural output and input markets, such as contract farming and outgrower schemes (see Chambati 2019).[8]

But what is the precise nature and trajectory of the changes in agrarian labor relations that have emerged out of these new patterns of access to land and tenure relations, shifting agricultural production systems, and the transforming agrarian labor and socioeconomic policies? The sections that follow articulate how the enlarged land access via the fast-track land reform program reconstituted the peasantry through the processes of semi-proletarianization and repeasantization within the context of an enduring economic crisis.

Land Reform and Repeasantization

The land allocations of the fast-track land reform program attracted a diverse set of beneficiaries beyond the main targets of resettlement—the land-short and landless peasants from the Communal Areas (GoZ 2001), across the two districts studied. An interesting feature in both of the resettlement models is related to the sizeable proportions of land claimants who originated from the urban areas, whose livelihoods are mainly associated with wage incomes (Table 19.1). Nor were these patterns unique to these two districts; they were pervasive in many other places throughout the country (Moyo et al. 2009; Scoones et al. 2010). However, the overwhelming majority of the resettled households had a rural background from the Communal Areas, Old Resettlement Areas, and large-scale commercial farms; the exception was in the A2 scheme of Goromonzi, where there was intense competition for land among urbanites due to its close proximity to the capital city, Harare (Chambati 2013).

The ownership of land by women in their own right was advanced by the fast-track land reform program because women accounted for 12 percent and 18 percent of the beneficiaries in the A1 and A2 schemes, respectively (Moyo et al. 2009), compared to less than 5 percent in the Communal Areas, Old Resettlement Areas, and former large-scale commercial farms (Gaidzanwa 1995). However, the regressive patriarchal practices that impede women's effective control of land and the distribution to women of benefits from the land were not entirely reversed (Chingarande 2008).

Many land beneficiaries have established permanent residential homes on the farms they received during the land reform, where they stay with their families. In fact, over 80 percent of the members of resettled households were full-time residents there, and were thus in effect the family labour pool, whose labor was extracted to organize agricultural production, especially in the small-scale A1 farms. Recruitment of hired labor was present in both resettlement schemes, but in the A1 farms up to 60 percent of the work was undertaken by unpaid family laborers, compared to less than 20 percent in the market-oriented A2 farms.

Wage employment in the towns and cities was differentiated among the beneficiaries. It was most common among the A2 landholders, who also held qualitatively better managerial jobs in the private and public sectors, with higher wages and benefits, than the A1 landholders. The majority of the A1 landholders were on the lower rung of the employment ladder as junior workers in the civil and private sectors, or as regular commissioned members of the uniformed forces (police or army). The disparities in formal employment patterns between male and female landholders in the resettled areas were miniscule. In fact, adult women accounted for 52.2 percent and 34 percent of the wage employees counted in Goromonzi and Kwekwe, respectively. This upset past trends of male-dominated migration to urban employment (O'Laughlin 1998; Potts 2000) as women combined their efforts with those of men to meet income needs for education and health and acquiring expensive agricultural inputs, which were marketized after the economic structural adjustment (Mkandawire and Soludo 1999) in a context of poor returns on agricultural production (World Bank 2012). State employment policies, which entail freedom of movement, no longer restrict rural women to working in the countryside, as was the case during the colonial era, when it was mostly men who were allowed to migrate for work (O'Laughlin 1998).

Table 19.1 Origins of Fast-Track Land Reform Program Land Beneficiaries (%)

	Goromonzi			Kwekwe		
Origin	A1	A2	Total	A1	A2	Total
Communal Area	57.9	16.2	37.3	54.9	50.8	53.9
Large-scale commercial farms	3.9	1.4	2.7	8.3	4.8	7.4
Urban	36.8	79.7	58	35.2	38.1	35.9
Other*	1.3	2.7	2	1.5	6.4	2.8
Total	100	100	100	100	100	100
N	76	74	150	193	63	256

* Mining centers and rural growth points

Beneath the flows of urbanites to rural areas (Table 19.1), the data revealed interesting patterns of delinking from the labor markets by some landholders after getting access to land during the fast-track land reform program, akin to the process of "re-peasantization" (Moyo and Yeros 2005a; Moyo 2011; Moyo et al. 2019; van der Ploeg 2013; van den Berg et al. 2018). This was more widely recognized among the Kwekwe A1 landholders. Of the 86 landholders who were formally employed by the year 2000, 79 subsequently left their jobs after receiving land allocation. On a reduced scale, 22 of the 44 A1 landholders in Goromonzi followed suit. The A2 landholders exited the formal labor markets in a similar fashion—enumerated in 29 of the 51 Kwekwe landholders and 28 of the 59 Goromonzi landholders. Considering that the average age of the landholders was around 55 years, most of them were below the retirement age of 65 years in most occupations. Since over 17 years had lapsed since the fast-track land reform program unraveled, many land beneficiaries would have received land when they were in their early forties and thus had at least 20 years of work life left in them.

Even within the Communal Areas, as the economic decline proceeded apace, 23 of the 28 landholders in Goromonzi had also discontinued their employment, and 6 of the 20 landholders in Kwekwe did the same. These patterns were, of course, influenced by the hyperinflation that by 2008 had made wages worthless, as well as by retrenchments that had surfaced in the 1990s and persisted in the 2000s as institutions wavered under the weight of economic decline (Yeros 2013).

The dynamic relationships that landholders had with the labor markets challenge the widely held assumption about the tendency of labor to *permanently* divest away from farming toward other, nonfarm based activities, including wage employment, espoused in the de-agrarianization thesis (Bryceson 2000; Rigg 2006). Instead of the movement of labor from "farm to factory" as the only route perceived by studies drawing on Lewisian dual models of economic transformation (see also World Bank 2013), the data demonstrated that the reverse is equally true: when urban labor markets become unstable, access to land provides an escape route. Contrary to being "permanent" or causing a total severing of links with the countryside (Petras and Veltmeyer 2001), rural-to-urban migration can, indeed, be overturned.

Repeasantization tendencies were also manifest in the bidding for land by former farmworkers or semi-proletariats previously employed by the large-scale commercial farms. Despite the perception of farmworkers as passive victims of the land reform (Ridderbos 2009), they were actively immersed in the land struggles during the fast-track land reform program.

As was the case before 2000 (Rutherford 2001; Moyo et al. 2000), many farmworkers still desire to be landowners or to delink from the farm labor markets by venturing into independent nonfarm businesses. These aspirations were manifest in their involvement in land occupations and when they officially applied for land allocations with government officials (Moyo 2001; Moyo et al. 2000; Sadomba 2011). Like their counterparts from the Communal Areas, farmworkers were land short and poor, and thus they were on board with the land occupation movement's agenda to redress the inequitable land distribution. Race and class grievances thus converged in the land occupation movement, which encompassed peasants, farmworkers, and others (Moyo 2011). Not all farmworkers who wanted fast-track land reform program land allocations succeeded in getting them, for various reasons, and less than 10 percent of them were beneficiaries.[9] So other informal routes to gain land were pursued, including in Communal Areas and negotiating leases with A1 farmers.

Disengaging from the farm labor markets is thus a key marker of the struggles of farm laborers as they seek autonomous land-based social reproduction. This disengagement should be seen in different light from the thesis advanced by Bernstein (2014), which reduced peasants to "fragmented classes of labour" presumably preoccupied with the struggles to improve their conditions as workers. Yet the evidence presented here suggests that both the land question and the labor question remain key in rural areas of Africa.

Beyond repeasantization, the application for land by urban professionals employed in relatively secure and well-paid civil service and private sector jobs during the fast-track land reform program, especially in the A2 scheme, also reflected a trend noticeable across many parts of sub-Saharan Africa. Specifically, this has been evident in the rise of investments in commercial farming, mainly on the basis of urban wage income, to widen sources of accumulation (Hall et al. 2017).

Land Access and Perpetual Semi-Proletarianization

Zimbabwean resettled households behaved no differently from rural households elsewhere in terms of the allocation of their family labor beyond farming (Yeros 2013; Scoones et al 2011). The fast-track land reform program also increased access to other, related natural resources previously monopolized by the large-scale commercial farms, and these were being traded by land recipients and farmworkers (Mkodzongi 2013).

Moreover, the state tenures enable the free movement of people, unlike in the past, when trespass laws were strictly enforced by the freehold large-scale commercial farms (Kanyenze 2001; Amanor-Wilks 1995), and this has permitted land beneficiaries and others to engage in variegated trading of goods and services. Natural resource trading continues to contribute to rural livelihoods in Communal Areas.

In more than two-thirds of the households, agricultural-based social reproduction was thus combined with either urban/rural (formal) wage employment or nonfarm rural-based income-earning activities, such as natural resource trading, as well as other entrepreneurial activities. In districts, such as Kwekwe, endowed with gold resources, artisanal mining was also frequently done alongside farming.[10] Cumulatively, these processes were akin to the semi-proletarianization of rural labor (Moyo and Yeros 2005b; Moyo 2011), which has continued even after land reform. But not all the households exhibited this semi-proletarian character; at least 22 percent of households in all the settlements allocated family labor to farming alone.

It is, however, not true that the diversification of family labor resources into nonfarm income-earning activities by these households has led to the total displacement of self-employed labor farming activities, as the de-agrarianization thesis holds (Bryceson 2002, 2000; Rigg 2006). A larger number of household members was allocated to farming activities instead of nonfarm activities, and in effect, they provided their labor supplies in both activities, forming a continuum in the social reproduction of the rural households.

Semi-proletarianization served both survival and accumulation needs in the rural areas. Nonfarm incomes occupied a significant share of total household income, particularly for the peasants in A1 scheme and the Communal Areas.[11] Yet this has not reversed the ubiquity of the continued application of unpaid family farm labor on the small peasant plots in the A1 and Communal Areas even in a low potential agroecological district such as Kwekwe. There, food production took place every season despite the low returns and high probabilities of crop failure. The poor peasants in the A1 and Communal Areas, who coincidentally failed to achieve adequate financial returns from farming, also had the largest share of households among the nonfarm income participants in natural resource trading. These findings imply that agrarian distress and/or risk aversion was a major driver of diversification of labor resources in the rural areas, especially for the small farmers (see Shivji 2017; Moyo and Yeros 2005b). Similarly, for survival other semi-proletariats supplement low farm income with low farm wages earned on the remaining large and the new smaller-scale capitalist farms, or from joint-venture farming agreements involving former large farmers and the new landholders.[12] In contrast, semi-proletarianization for capitalist farmers in the A2 sector entailed combining professional wage employment with farming and venturing into capital, demanding activities such as transport provision to augment accumulation.

While integration in the agricultural output markets was concentrated in the capitalist farms in the A2 sector, for many peasants in the A1 and Communal Areas, application of family labor in own production was key for auto-consumption. These trends also suggest that the classification of rural areas in Africa as littered with "fragmented classes of labour" who are "directly or indirectly" dependent on the wage economy for their sustenance (Bernstein 2014, S97–S98) is not plausible, because self-employed family labor and/or land access remains key for organizing social reproduction. Consequently, the conclusion that the rural households are still "*primarily* agriculturalists," despite the diversified labor activities seen today (Shackleton et al. 2001, 34) can hardly be escaped.

Slack time between agricultural seasons also created opportunities for the sampled households to enter nonfarm labor markets, beyond the structural-adjustment-program-engendered economic crises emphasized by the de-agrarianization theorists. That nonfarm rural activities attracted a substantial section of the households in the dry season should therefore not be unexpected.

Conclusion

The chapter has demonstrated how the trajectories of rural labor in Southern Africa are to a large extent shaped by the degree of access to land, and are thus altered by processes of land alienation or extension of access through land redistribution. Notwithstanding the colonial land alienation and economic crises prompted by structural adjustment programs in the postindependence period, peasant forms of production have remained resilient in the countryside. They are based on the ownership and cultivation of small pieces of land for auto-consumption and for surplus sales in domestic markets, and integrated into various nonfarm exchange activities based on mobilized family labor. Certainly, viewing peasants as only agriculturalists creates a false dichotomy between farming activities and nonfarm activities, which are interdependent for their sustenance. The trajectories of peasant labor cannot be foreclosed (O'Laughlin 2002), and subsequently, suggestion by the de-agrarianization and full proletarianization theorists of a *permanent* reorientation of self-employed family labor away from farming due to adverse agrarian conditions seems misplaced.

Instead, proletarianization, semi-proletarianization, de-agrarianization, and repeasantization are constituent of the dynamism of the peasantry's labor process and are, in fact amenable to *reversals*. They are influenced by the transformations of the agrarian structures that are underway in the countryside, including through land reforms and the wider shifts in the economic conditions. As such, it is quite possible for people to alternate between proletarianization in the rural/urban labor markets and peasant production as the socioeconomic conditions in both town and country transition. During land reforms, semi-proletarianization and repeasantization can therefore take place concurrently (Moyo and Yeros 2005a).

The disengagement from the labor markets by Zimbabwean land reform beneficiaries suggests that repeasantization is more than a struggle to reclaim dispossessed land. It can also be seen as a type of labor resistance or "resistance to proletarianization" by former proletariats and semi-proletariats against the exploitation in wage labor markets in favor of self-employment on the (newly) acquired lands. The evidence from land reform beneficiaries also points to the metamorphoses of the process of semi-proletarianization. Instead of only supplementing inadequate land-based social reproduction arising from colonial dispossession, the semi-proletarian strategy among capitalist farms provided an important conduit for mobilizing resources to invest in farming. Poor peasants perpetuate semi-proletarianization to augment their low farm incomes, but with relative autonomy provided by enhanced land access. A more stable semi-proletarianization process is thus an outcome of wider access to land.

Today, when urban-based social reproduction strategies are faltering under the weight of economic crises in Southern Africa and elsewhere on the continent, evident in deindustrialization and rising unemployment, repeasantization and semi-proletarianization, which maintain the importance of land, are the *overarching* tendencies that evolve, side by side, from the socioeconomic conditions the peasantry in the rural areas face. In spite of the so-called labor diversification, struggles in the countryside are explicitly informed by both the land and labor questions.

Acknowledgments

I would like to thank the editors and anonymous reviewers for their comments on an earlier draft of this chapter. The research assistance received from Steven Mberi is also gratefully acknowledged.

Notes

1. *Farmworkers* is a term historically used to denote the full- and part-time employees of large-scale commercial farms since the colonial period (Amanor-Wilks 1995; Moyo et al. 2000; Rutherford 2001). Post-2000, its use has been extended to refer both to those previously employed in the large-scale commercial farms and to the new workers who now constitute the employ of the new landholders and remaining large-scale commercial farms (Chambati 2019; Scoones et al. 2019).
2. A bifurcated approach was adopted to redistribute the large-scale commercial farms acquired during the fast-track land reform program through the A1 and A2 models/schemes. The peasantry sector, which already incorporated the Communal and Old Resettlement Areas, was aimed for extension by the A1 model. The A2 model was conceptualized as the commercial farming scheme. On average, A1 beneficiaries received between 5 and 7 hectares of arable land and 15 hectares of shared grazing land (GoZ 2001). The A2 beneficiaries were targeted to receive larger land sizes than those in the A1 settlement, ranging from 20 to 2000 hectares and also contingent upon the agroecological location (Moyo et al. 2009).
3. These activities include natural resources extraction (e.g., firewood collection, fruits, medicine, minerals etc.), petty-commodity trading, rural artisans, and the processing of farm and nonfarm produce (Moyo 1995).
4. Rural-to-urban migration takes place simultaneously with urban-to-rural migration when those who are retrenched from urban jobs during structural adjustment programs also seek refuge in the countryside (Moyo and Yeros 2005a, 2005b).

5. The structural adjustment programs in Africa rolled back state support to rural, agricultural, and social development, and entrenched the economic distress and impoverishment of the peasantry (Mkandawire and Soludo, 1999; Mamdani 1996). The drastic reduction of agricultural input subsidies, for instance, worsened the poor peasants' access to critical productivity-enhancing inputs and their ability to survive on petty commodity production on their small plots (Mafeje 2003; Moyo & Yeros 2005b; Shivji 2017).
6. The nine countries studied were Ethiopia, Ghana, Kenya, Madagascar, Malawi, Niger, Nigeria, Tanzania, and Uganda.
7. The quality of employment is also a major challenge, as 80 percent of the people employed in sub-Saharan Africa are in vulnerable employment. Vulnerable employment includes workers who earn less than US $2 per day (ILO 2015, 54, 43).
8. Space does not allow for a substantial discussion of these policy intersections here, but see Chambati (2019) for a detailed discussion.
9. For a detailed expose of the factors that hamstrung farm workers' quest for land, see Chambati (2011, 2013).
10. About 39.2 percent and 31.6 percent of the A1 and A2 households, respectively, surveyed in Kwekwe combined farming with artisanal gold mining.
11. Up to 43 percent of the household income of the peasants in the A1 and Communal Areas originated from nonfarm activities, compared to less than 7 percent in the capitalist farms in the A2 scheme.
12. Farmworker trade unions were weak, and the balance of power that tilted in favor of the agricultural employers kept the wages negotiated during collective bargaining low, as did the limited enforcement of labor rights by the state's national employment council.

References

Amanor, Kojo Sebastian. 2001. *Land, Labour and the Family in Southern Ghana: A Critique of Land Policy under Neoliberalisation*. Research Report No. 116. Nordiska Afrikainstitutet, Uppsala.

Amanor-Wilks, Dede. 1995. *In Search of Hope for Zimbabwe's Farm Workers*. Harare, Zimbabwe: Dateline Southern Africa and Panos Institute.

Amin, Samir. 1972. "Underdevelopment and Dependence in Black Africa: Origins and Contemporary Forms." *Journal of Modern African Studies* 10 (4): 503–524.

Arrighi, Giovanni. 1970. "Labor Supplies in Historical Perspective: A Study of Proletarianziation of the African Peasantry in Rhodesia." *Journal of Development Studies* 6 (3): 197–234.

Bernstein, Henry. 2010. *Class Dynamics of Agrarian Change*. Nova Scotia: Fernwood Publishing.

Bernstein, Henry. 2014. "African Peasants and Revolution Revisited." *Review of African Political Economy* 41 (1): S95–S107.

Bryceson, Deborah. 1999. "African Rural Labour, Income Diversification and Livelihood Approaches: A Long-Term Development Perspective." *Review of African Political Economy* 26 (80): 171–189.

Bryceson, Deborah. 2000. "Peasant Theories and Smallholder Policies: Past and Present." In *Disappearing Peasantries?Rural Labour in Africa, Asia and Latin America*, edited by Deborah Bryceson, Cristóbal Kay, and Jos Mooij, 1–36. London: Intermediate Technology Publishing.

Bryceson, Deborah, Cristóbal Kay, and Jos Mooij, eds. 2000. *Disappearing Peasantries? Rural Labour in Africa, Asia and Latin America*. London: Intermediate Technology Publishing.
Bryceson, Deborah. 2002. "Multiplex Livelihoods in Rural Africa: Recasting the Terms and Conditions of Gainful Employment." *Journal of Modern African Studies* 44 (2): 173–202.
Bush, Ray., and Lionel. Cliffe. 1984. "Agrarian Policy in Migrant Labour Societies: Reform or Transformation in Zimbabwe?" *Review of African Political Economy* 11 (29): 77–94.
Chambati, Walter. 2011. "Restructuring of Agrarian Labour Relations after Fast Track Land Reform in Zimbabwe. *Journal of Peasant Studies* 38 (5): 1047–1068.
Chambati, Walter. 2013. "The Political Economy of Agrarian Labour Relations in Zimbabwe after Redistributive Land Reform." *Agrarian South: Journal of Political Economy* 2 (2): 189–211.
Chambati, Walter. 2019. "Changing Agrarian Labour Relations in Zimbabwe in the Context of the Fast Track Land Reform." PhD diss., University of South Africa.
Chimhowu, Admos., and David. Hulme. 2006. "Livelihood Dynamics in Planned and Spontaneous Resettlement in Zimbabwe: Converging and Vulnerable." *World Development* 34 (4): 728–750.
Chingarande, Sungurai D. 2008. "Gender and the Struggle for Land Equity." In *Contested Terrain: Land Reform and Civil Society in Contemporary Zimbabwe*, edited by Sam Moyo, Kirk Helliker, and Tendai Murisa, 275–304. Pietmaritzburg, South Africa: S&S Publishers.
Clarke, Duncan G. 1977. *Agricultural and Plantation Workers in Rhodesia*. Gwelo, Rhodesia: Mambo Press.
Cousins, Ben. 2009. "Capitalism Obscured: The Limits of Law and Rights-Based Approaches to Poverty Reduction and Development." *Journal of Peasant Studies* 36 (4): 893–908.
Davis, Benjamin, Stefania Di Giuseppe, and Alberto Zezza. 2017. "Are African Households (Not) Leaving Agriculture? Patterns of Households' Income Sources in Rural Sub-Saharan Africa." *Food Policy* 67 (2017): 153–174.
Djurfeldt, Agnes Andersson, Göran Djurfeldt, Ola Hall, and Maria Francisca A. Bustos. 2018. "Agrarian Change and Structural Transformation: Drivers and Distributional Outcomes." In *Agriculture, Diversification, and Gender in Rural Africa: Longitudinal Perspectives from Six Countries*, edited by Agnes Andersson Djurfeldt, Fred Mawunyo Dzanku, and Aida Cuthbert Isinika, chap. 5. Oxford Scholarship Online. doi:10.1093/oso/9780198799283.003.0005.
Edelman, Marc., and Saturnino M. Borras Jr. 2016. *Political Dynamics of Transnational Movements*. Nova Scotia: Fernwood Publishing.
Fay, Derick. 2015. "Keeping Land for Their Children: Generation, Migration and Land in South Africa's Transkei." *Journal of Southern African Studies* 41 (5): 1083–1097.
Ferguson, James. 1999. *Expectations of Modernity: Myths and Meanings of Urban Life on the Zambian Copperbelt*. Berkeley: University of California Press.
Gaidzanwa, Rudo. 1995. "Land and the Economic Empowerment of Women: A Gendered Analysis." *Southern Africa Feminist Review: The Gendered Politics of Land* 1 (1): 1–2.
Gibbon, Peter, Kjell Havnevik, and Kenneth Hermele. 1993. *A Blighted Harvest: The World Bank and African Agriculture in the 1980s*. Trenton, NJ: Africa World Press.
GoN (Government of Namibia). 1995. "The National Agricultural Policy." Ministry of Agriculture, Water and Rural Development. Republic of Namibia. Accessed July 24, 2015. https://www.atf.org.na/cms_documents/8f7-nationalagriculturalpolicy1995.pdf.

GoZ (Government of Zimbabwe). 2001. *Fast Track Land Reform Programme*. Harare: Government Printers.

Hall, Ruth, Ian Scoones, and Dzodzi Tsikata. 2017. "Plantations, Outgrowers and Commercial Farming in Africa: Agricultural Commercialisation and Implications for Agrarian Change." *Journal of Peasant Studies* 44 (3): 515–537.

IFAD (International Fund for Agricultural Development). 2011. *Rural Poverty Report 2011: New Realities, New Challenges: New Opportunities for Tomorrow's Generations*. Rome: IFAD.

ILO (International Labour Office). 2015. *World Employment and Social Outlook: The Changing Nature of Jobs*. Geneva: ILO.

Jacobs, Ricardo. 2018. "An Urban Proletariat with Peasant Characteristics: Land Occupations and Livestock Raising in South Africa." *Journal of Peasant Studies* 45 (5–6): 884–903.

Kanyenze, Godfrey. 2001. "Zimbabwe's Labour Relations Policies and the Implications for Farm Workers." In *Zimbabwe's Farm Workers: Policy Dimension*, edited by Dede Amanor-Wilks, 86–113. Lusaka: Panos Southern Africa.

Lewis, William Arthur. 1954. "Economic Development with Unlimited Supplies of Labour." *Manchester School* 22: 139–191.

Mafeje, Archie. 2003. *The Agrarian Question, Access to Land, and Peasant Responses in Sub-Saharan Africa*. Research Report. Geneva: United Nations Research Institute for Social Development.

Mamdani, Mahmood. 1996. *Citizen and Subject: Contemporary Africa and Legacy of Late Colonialism*. Cape Town: David Phillip.

Matondi, Prosper. 2012. *Zimbabwe's Fast Track Land Reform*. London: Zed Books.

Mkandawire, Thandika, and Charles C. Soludo. 1999. *Our Continent, Our Future: African Perspectives on Structural Adjustment*. Trenton, New Jersey: Africa World Press.

Mkodzongi, Grasian. 2013. "New People, New Land and New Livelihoods: A Micro-Study of Zimbabwe's Fast Track Land Reform." *Agrarian South: Journal of Political Economy* 2 (3): 345–366.

Moyo, Sam. 1995. *The Land Question in Zimbabwe*. Harare, Zimbabwe: SAPES Books.

Moyo, Sam. 2001. "The Land Occupation Movement and Democratization in Zimbabwe: Contradictions of Neoliberalism." *Millennium: Journal of International Studies* 30 (2): 311–330.

Moyo, Sam. 2008. *African Land Questions, Agrarian Transitions and the State: Contradictions of Neoliberal Land Reforms*. Dakar, Senegal: CODESRIA.

Moyo, Sam. 2011. "Three Decades of Agrarian Reform in Zimbabwe." *Journal of Peasant Studies* 38 (3): 493–531.

Moyo, Sam. 2013. "Land Reform and Redistribution in Zimbabwe since 1980." In *Land and Agrarian Reform in Zimbabwe: Beyond White Settler Capitalism*, edited by Sam Moyo and Walter Chambati, 29–78. Dakar, Senegal: CODESRIA.

Moyo, Sam. 2014. "Family Farming in Sub-Saharan Africa." In *Deep Roots*, edited by Jacqui Griffiths, 17–21. Rome: Food and Agriculture Organisation of the United Nations.

Moyo, Sam, Walter Chambati, Tendai Murisa, Dumisani Siziba, Charity Dangwa, Kingstone Mujeyi, and Ndabezinhle Nyoni. 2009. *Fast Track Land Reform Baseline Survey in Zimbabwe: Trends and Tendencies, 2005/06*. AIAS Monograph. Harare, Zimbabwe: African Institute for Agrarian Studies.

Moyo, Sam, Praveen Jha, and Paris Yeros. 2019. "Introduction: The Scramble for Land and Natural Resources in Africa." In *Reclaiming Africa: Scramble and Resistance in the 21st Century*, edited by Sam Moyo, Praveen Jha, and Paris Yeros, 3–30. Singapore: Springer.

Moyo, Sam, Blair Rutherford, and Dede Amanor-Wilks. 2000. "Land Reform and Changing Social Relations for Farm Workers in Zimbabwe." *Review of African Political Economy* 27 (84): 181–202.

Moyo, Sam, and Paris Yeros. 2005a. "Land Occupations and Land Reform in Zimbabwe: Towards the National Democratic Revolution." In *Reclaiming the Land: The Resurgence of Rural Movements in Africa, Asia and Latin America*, edited by Sam Moyo and Paris Yeros, 165–208. London and New York: Zed Books.

Moyo, Sam, and Paris Yeros. 2005b. "The Resurgence of Rural Movements under Neoliberalism." In Moyo and Yeros, *Reclaiming the Land*, 8–66.

Mucavele, Firmino. n.d. "True Contribution of Agriculture to Economic Growth and Poverty Reduction: Malawi, Mozambique and Zambia Synthesis Report." 9th Annual Food Agriculture and Natural Resources Policy Analysis Network (FARNPAN) Policy Dialogue, August 31 to September 4, 2009. Maputo, Mozambique.

Ncapayi, Fani. 2005. "Land Demand and Rural Struggles in Xhalanga, Eastern Cape: Who Wants Land and for What?" Master's thesis, University of the Western Cape.

Neocosmos, Michael. 1993. *The Agrarian Question in Southern Africa and "Accumulation from Below": Economics and Politics in the Struggle for Democracy*. Research Report 93. Uppsala: Scandinavian Institute of African Studies.

Niehof, Anke. 2004. "The Significance of Diversification for Rural Livelihood Systems." *Food Policy* 29: 321–338.

O' Laughlin, Bridget. 1998. "Missing Men? The Debate over Rural Poverty and Women Headed Households in Southern Africa." *Journal of Peasant Studies* 25 (2): 1–48.

O' Laughlin, Bridget. 2002. "Proletarianisation, Agency and Changing Rural Livelihoods: Forced Labour and Resistance in Colonial Mozambique." *Journal of Southern African Studies* 28 (3): 511–530.

Peta, Gregory, Gift Chibatwa, Etwell Whanya, Trust Ngirandi, and Douglas Phiri. 1991. *An Organisational Study of Five Trade Unions in Zimbabwe: An Interim Report*. Harare, Zimbabwe: Friedrich Ebert Foundation.

Petras, James and Henry Veltmeyer. 2001. "Are Latin American Peasant Movements Still a Force for Change? Some New Paradigms Revisited." *Journal of Peasant Studies* 28 (2): 83–118.

Potts, Deborah. 2000. "Worker-Peasants and Farmer-Housewives in Africa: The Debate about 'Committed' Farmers, Access to Land and Agricultural Production." *Journal of Southern African Studies* 26 (4): 807–832.

Ridderbos, Katinka. 2009. "Stateless Former Farm Workers in Zimbabwe." *Forced Migration Review* 32: 73.

Rigg, Jonathan. 2006. "Land, Farming, Livelihoods and Poverty: Rethinking the Links in the Rural South." *Journal of World Development* 34 (1): 180–202.

Rukuni, Mandivamba. 1994. "The Evolution of Agricultural Policy: 1890–1990." In *Zimbabwe's Agricultural Revolution*, edited by Mandivamba Rukuni and Carl K. Eicher, 14–39. Harare: University of Zimbabwe Publications.

Rutherford, Blair. 2001. *Working on the Margins: Black Workers, White Farmers in Post-colonial Zimbabwe*. London: Zed Books.

Sadomba, Wilbert Zvakanyorwa. 2011. *War Veterans in Zimbabwe's Revolution: Challenging Neo-colonialism and Settler and International Capital*. Suffolk, UK, and Harare, Zimbabwe: James Currey and Weaver Press.

Scoones, Ian. 2015. *Sustainable Livelihoods and Rural Development*. Rugby, UK: Practical Action Publishing.

Scoones, Ian, Nelson Marongwe, Blasio Mavedzenge, Jacob Mahenehene, Felix Murimbarimba, and Chrispen Sukume. 2010. *Zimbabwe's Land Reform: Myths and Realities*. Harare, Zimbabwe: Jacana Media and Weaver Press.
Scoones, Ian, Nelson Marongwe, Blasio Mavedzenge, Jacob Mahenehene, Felix Murimbarimba, and Chrispen Sukume. 2011. "Zimbabwe's Land Reform: Challenging the Myths." *Journal of Peasant Studies* 38 (5): 967–993.
Scully, Ben. 2012. "Land, Livelihoods, and the Decline of Work: South African Lessons for Current Debates. *Journal of World Systems Research* 28 (1): 90–102.
Shackleton, Charlie. M., Sheona. E. Shackleton, and Ben Cousins. 2001. "The Role of Land-Based Strategies in Rural Livelihoods: The Contribution of Arable Production, Animal Husbandry and Natural Resource Harvesting in Communal Areas in South Africa." *Development Southern Africa* 18 (5): 581–604.
Shivji, Issa. 2017. "The Concept of 'Working People.'" *Agrarian South: Journal of Political Economy* 6 (1): 1–13.
Sihlongonyane, Mfaniseni Fana. 2005. "Land Occupations in South Africa." In Moyo and Yeros, *Reclaiming the Land*, 142–164.
Statistics South Africa. 1999. "Statistical Release P0360, Rural Survey 1997." Pretoria, South Africa. Accessed July 3, 2015. https://www.statssa.gov.za/publications/P0360/P0360June1999.pdf
Todaro, Michael. 1989. *Economic Development in the Third World*. 4th ed. New York: Longman. (Original work published in 1977).
Tsikata, Dzodzi. 2015. "The Social Relations of Agrarian Change." IIED Working Paper. Institute of Environment and Development. London. https://pubs.iied.org/17278IIED.
UNDP (United Nations Development Programme). 1999. *Zimbabwe Human Development Report 1999*. Harare, Zimbabwe: UNDP.
van der Berg, Leonardo, Paul Hebinck, and Dirk Roep. 2018. "'We Go Back to the Land': Processes of Re-peasantisation in Araponga, Brazil." *Journal of Peasant Studies* 45 (3): 653–675.
van der Ploeg, Jan Douwe. 2013. *Peasants and the Art of Farming: A Chayanovian Manifesto*. Winnipeg, CAN: Fernwood.
World Bank. 2006. *Agricultural Growth and Land Reform in Zimbabwe: Assessment and Recovery Options*. Report No. 31699-ZW. Harare, Zimbabwe.
World Bank. 2012. *Zimbabwe: From Economic Rebound to Sustained Growth: Growth Recovery Notes*. Harare, Zimbabwe: World Bank.
World Bank. 2013. *World Development Report 2013: Jobs*. Washington, DC: World Bank. https://siteresources.worldbank.org/EXTNWDR2013/Resources/8258024-1320950747192/8260293-1322665883147/WDR_2013_Report.pdf.
Yeros, Paris. 2013. "The Rise and Fall of Trade Unionism in Zimbabwe. Part I: 1990–1995." *Review of African Political Economy* 40 (136): 219–232.
Zhan, Shaohua and Ben Scully. 2018. "From South Africa to China: Land, Migrant Labor and the Semi-Proletarian Thesis Revisited." *Journal of Peasant Studies* 45 (5–6): 1018–1038.
Zuka, Sane Pashane. 2013. "Butterfly Land Policy Reform Initiatives in Southern Africa: Any Promise from Malawi's New Land Act". *Research Journal of Agricultural and Environmental Management* 2 (6): 154–163.

CHAPTER 20

LAND POLITICS AND HUMAN MOBILITIES

The Land-Mobility Nexus as an Analytical Lens

KEI OTSUKI AND ANNELIES ZOOMERS

Introduction

Land politics and human mobilities—various forms of migration—increasingly influence each other, and therefore the land-mobility nexus needs to be established as a proper analytical lens in the studies of land politics and on migration. A study by Zoomers, Leung, and van Westen (2016) has shown that opportunities for local development are significantly shaped by actors' positionality with respect to two dominant types of global flows—of international migration and financial capital. On the one hand, recognition of the global flow of financial capital into land has led to lively debates on land grabs in the field of agrarian and development studies. The land grab debates have problematized various forms of dispossession and displacement, especially like those small-scale farmers in the Global South have experienced since the mid-2000s (Cotula et al. 2009; Borras et al. 2011). On the other hand, "migration and development" became a hotly debated topic among migration scholars, because the intensifying flows of migrants led to remittances, which began to be recognized as a potential driver for economic development in migrants' areas of origin (de Haas 2008; Bastia and Skeldon 2020). At the same time, in the destination areas, migration came to be seen as a "security threat," and this view resulted in anti-immigration policies and investments aimed at controlling and keeping out "the others" (Bello 2022).

At a macro level, these two flows initially seemed to reflect the North–South relations: Southern countries receive capital flows from the North, and the Northern countries host migrants from the South. However, emerging case studies show that the flows of capital and people are multidirectional and multiscaler. For example, domestic investment flows affect land use and ownership. The majority of migrants stay close to their homelands in the North and in the South, and the South–South migration is in fact much greater in scale than South–North migration (Shewel and Debray 2023). The multidirectional mobilities of people, goods, technologies, and ideas shape land politics and establish various settlements and cities, and displacements and migrant inflows often happen in the same area (Carmody and Owusu 2016; Zoomers et al. 2017).

Today, we need to acknowledge that the financial capital and migrant flows form the land-mobility nexus, which transforms land and the built and natural environments in and across contemporary "translocal geographies" (Datta and Brickel 2011). Translocal kinship and various forms of business relations in multiple localities across the globe can both enable and impede people's further investing in or moving to snf from places of their choice to build their livelihoods (Zoomers et al. 2021). Yet the scholarly and policy discussions on the implications of land grabs and migration for people's well-being continue developing separately. Moreover, each tends to focus on how to fix people to land by securing tenure or how to protect a territory by integrating migrants or by keeping them out. In studies on the increasing incidence of climate-induced disasters, discussions about fixing people to land and a territory are used to justify planned displacement and resettlement (de Sherbinin et al. 2011). But efforts to plan mobilities to control movements of people fail to acknowledge the wider effects of spontaneous human mobilities, which influence land and migration politics and governance over time and in multiple locations.

We aim to deepen engagement with the land-mobility nexus by asking: How are land politics and human mobilities related, and how do we systematically approach this relationship? We address these questions by looking into three aspects of the nexus. First, we look at how land investment causes human mobility, especially when the investment is in agribusiness and infrastructure development, urbanization, and extractivism, which attract newcomers and expand settlement areas (Mkodzongi and Spiegel 2020; Beier et al. 2022) but also induce displacement and resettlement (Rogers and Wilmsen 2020). Second, we examine how migration itself leads to land investments and human mobilities. Because migration studies are less prominent in discussions of land relations compared to studies on how land politics affects human mobilities, we look extensively into how and why migration politics and policies affect land politics, as for example, when land is acquired to (temporarily) settle migrants and refugees in camps and new settlements (Islam et al. 2023). Further, we identify two patterns in land investment dynamics: on the one hand, in migrant receiving areas such as the European Union (EU), migrants are encouraged to settle and revitalize the host countries' shrinking economies (Moralli, Pachocka, and Leung 2023). On the other hand, migrants, including the highly skilled, often invest in land in their homelands, causing new enclosures and displacements (Kaag and Steel 2019). These dynamics affect the well-being of people in the sending communities and in the receiving communities and have implications for the environmental and socioeconomic sustainability of both the invested lands and the new settlements, including refugee and labor camps and the surrounding areas.

Third, the land-mobility nexus is increasingly affected by the politics of climate change (Borras et al. 2020), as well as the actual impacts of climate change itself (Sliuzas

2023). Climate change politics and climate disasters work to encourage planners and decision-makers to categorize places where particular groups of people can and should live. Planned mobilities in this context may further marginalize some groups and influence the ways that people move or invest in making and developing livelihoods in their new places.

We explore these three aspects of the land-mobility nexus through a review of publications from the academic and policy literature and draw from our own past and ongoing research projects. We then discuss how using the land-mobility nexus as an analytical lens should help us understand the different, and crucial, roles that migrants and nonmigrants alike play in triggering or reconfiguring land investments. Refugees and migrant workers, in particular, deserve more attention, not only as victims, but also as agents who are creating landscapes (Mitchell 1996) and shaping multilocal livelihoods that are connected at multiple temporary and spatial scales (Datta and Brickell 2011). They constitute a vital part of what seems to be a *local* development process or a *local* community, because they use mobilities as a part of their core livelihood strategies (Zoomers and Otsuki 2017). We advocate this translocal approach to the land-mobility nexus, because it allows us to move beyond the current focus on fixing people to land and a territory and thus pay more concrete attention to the multidirectional and long-term effects of land investment and migration.

Land Politics Leading to Human Mobilities

Studies on land investment causing land grabs conventionally problematize enclosure and the displacement of people living on the invested land. These displacement effects were observed initially in relation to agribusiness and nature conservation, and later on, the discussion was extended to include various forms of dispossession in urban contexts (Zoomers et al. 2017; Otsuki et al. 2023). In particular, it was recognized that the transformation of land markets in cities induced violent evictions globally (Sassen 2014; Shaw 2019). More recent studies have shown a resurgence of large-scale infrastructure development on both rural land and urban land in the name of enhancing climate resilience or promoting climate mitigation (Otsuki, Steel, Panquene 2022). As we showed in a series of research projects in Mozambique,[1] land investments associated with the so-called sustainable infrastructure development to control periodic flooding in coastal cities such as Beira have induced the physical and economic displacement of the city's low-income dwellers (Shannon 2021). In Cabo Delgado, natural gas and new mineral extraction in the context of international and national investments in energy transition projects has meant the physical displacement or enclosure of the local communities surrounding the extraction sites and resulted in violent contestations underpinned by the land conflicts, as well as in extensive land use and tenure change (Namaganda, Otsuki, and Steel 2023).

At the same time, land investments attract newcomers, and urbanization ensues. When investments are made into land and real estate, and infrastructure development or neighborhood upgrading, they expand the "frontiers of land commodification" (Kelly and Peluso 2015) and create private properties. The commodification eliminates customary access to "common" land and livelihoods for small farmers in rural areas and to informal settlements for urban dwellers, especially in the Global South context (Otsuki 2019). Commodification does not always specifically intend to displace low-income citizens; however, it gradually displaces an informal neighborhood, which is likely to be replaced by formal settlements and inflows of new residents (Shih 2017). The displacement induced by the land commodification thus creates various fluxes of actors, such as real estate companies, construction workers, local authorities, registration offices, and incoming residents, blurring the "structure of responsibility" for the well-being of the displaced people (Ferguson 2012).

Consequently, a planned resettlement often takes place, because the investor or the government plans the mobility of the people displaced by the land investment (Rogers and Wilmsen 2020). Across rural and urban land investments, resettlements are seen as a the possible solutions to unplanned displacement and to the promotion of more responsible investments (Beier et al. 2022). Although the proponents of resettlement, following international guidelines, often promise livelihood improvements for the displaced people, actual experience shows that such resettlements are often contested, primarily because no long-term visions for sustainable development are made available to resettled communities (Cernea and Maldonado 2018). A consequence of the contestations is the migration of resettled people seeking better livelihood opportunities, as has been observed in connection with the large-scale resettlement program at Limpopo National Park, on the Mozambique–South Africa border (Salomão 2020; Otsuki 2021), and in a resettlement village built near a large-scale hydroelectric dam in Vietnam, where the displaced people further migrated to urban areas (Pham Huu 2015).

Land investments and the subsequent human mobilities will increase as more infrastructure and energy projects are undertaken, especially in the context of promoting a transition to sustainability and climate investments. Land investments will also spontaneously increase because of ongoing processes of urbanization, and precarious labor conditions are expected to proliferate in cities (Otsuki 2019). In the rural sphere, migrant rural workers have constituted fragmented agrarian classes of labor (Bernstein 2011), and their well-being is constantly in question because they remain largely invisible in both the theory and practice of rural development (Borras et al. 2022). It is therefore vital to be vigilant and constantly look at whether land investments lead to the planned or unplanned (or "intended or unintended") human mobilities and how the well-being of migrants is related to our understanding of the "impacts" of land investments (Zoomers and Otsuki 2017).

By the same token, the politics of migration is currently geared toward "orderly, safe, regular and responsible migration and mobility of people, including through the implementation of planned and well-managed migration policies" (International Labour Organization, 2024). Ensuring the well-managed mobility of people is increasingly important, including in the context of climate-related disasters, as is the promotion of orderly resettlement, which requires more land acquisition and investments.

Migration Politics: Shaping Landscapes and Land Investments

In migration politics and policies there is increasingly recognition of the need to invest in land for the purpose of managing migration, primarily to keep people out or in place. According to the International Organization for Migration (IOM), the so-called migration crisis that has erupted in EU since 2015 needs to be addressed "in an integral manner" (International Organization for Migration 2023). One of the necessary elements of this is the protection of land and property to prevent forced migration and to facilitate the return and reintegration of migrants into their societies of origin (International Organization for Migration 2023). In addition, European Commission launched EU-Turkey joint action plan in October 2015, to introduce a migration partnership framework ("migration deals") with the countries of origin and transit (European Commission, 2015).[2] The migration deals provide that these countries receive large sums of money for stopping or taking back illegal migrants, enabling migrants and refugees to stay closer to home and helping the migrant sending countries to work on preventing outmigration.

Such policies, reaffirmed in 2023 as a part of the New Pact on Migration and Asylum (European Commission, 2023), support large-scale land investments, not only to establish refugee camps and detention centers in these countries, but also to develop projects aimed at improving local land situations, which would presumably help people to stay on their land (Zoomers, Van Noorloos, and Van Liempt 2018). Similar deals have been made between the United States and Mexico, Australia and Nauru, and the United Kingdom and Rwanda. To different degrees, all these deals externalize migration border control, involving land acquisition for building walls or detention centers and expanding refugee camps and for projects to reduce land conflicts by securing land tenure for particular groups.

One of the consequences of the blocking of migrants in the transit countries is the expanding, prolonged presence of refugee camps, especially in Africa, the Middle East, and Asia, as well as in Europe. Since 2015, scholars have studied how the refugee camps and concentrations of migrants with liminal status have shaped new urban centers and hubs of new urban land investments (Sanyal 2015; Jansen 2016). As Islam et al. (2023)

recently showed, refugee camps can be closely linked to the rise of new land use within and surrounding the camps, especially leading to urbanization, putting an extra pressure on existing land and water conflicts and accelerating deforestation and environmental degeneration. In rural areas in Europe, refugees often become "illegal" rural workers, and land is acquired to build labor camps to house them, as Perrota and Raeymaekers (2022) observed on tomato farms in southern Italy.

The land-change dynamics triggered by policy efforts to contain large groups of forced migrants receive relatively little attention from scholars of land or migration politics. This disarticulation between land and migration scholarship has led to the neglect of a fundamental question: What kind of investments serve both the host communities and forced migrants themselves? Instead of trying to block and expulse migrants, or consigning them to perpetual liminal citizenship status in camps, solutions might be found in directing and encouraging decision-makers to plan pathways toward "emplacement" and create opportunities for everyone (Zoomers 2023). This attention to emplacement also applies to the ongoing discussions on how to reintegrate migrants into their places of origin when they return, not only from the richer parts of the world but also from their seasonal or internal migrations. Many smallholder farmers in semi-arid areas migrate seasonally, traveling to more humid areas during dry season to work as farm laborers or to extraction sites and cities to work as casual laborers. They regularly return to their homeland to continue developing or reinvesting in their own land-based livelihoods (Otsuki, Jasaw, and Lolig 2018). Migrant rural workers are also increasingly recognized as an integral part of agrarian struggles (Borras et al. 2022).

Recognizing the roles migrant workers play in creating and shaping landscapes over time (e.g., Mitchell 1996), we wish to further highlight two investment flows that migrants themselves can generate, both in the receiving and sending areas.

Migrant Workers and Investments in Shrinking Areas

Within the EU and other migrant "receiving" areas, there is an increasing awareness of the need to "welcome" migrants into the process of local economic development (Moralli, Pachocka, and Leung 2023).[3] In countries such as Italy or Spain, where rural areas are experiencing depopulation, ageing, and divestments, migrants are increasingly seen as a "solution" to revitalizing the so-called shrinking—often remote and marginalized—rural areas (Zoomers 2023). The welcomed migrants have the potential to invest in land and property to improve their livelihoods if opportunities are there and the institutional environments allow. So far, however, as has long been observed in the United States, migrant workers are always a vital part of large-scale corporate agribusiness development, yet are treated as disposable laborers (Mitchell 1996; Rothenburg 2000; see also Perrota and Raeymaekers (2022) for a recent study in the EU). The rural areas in the Global North could thrive on land concentration and corporate agriculture despite depopulation because of the availability of migrant laborers, who accept cheap wages (Ploeg, Franco, and Borras 2015). We now need to ask the question of how the quality of labor can be enhanced by migrant policies and the process of integration.

The EU's experiment with creating "welcoming spaces" envisions alternative ways to develop marginalized rural areas by integrating migrants into, for example, the organic farming sector or the rural tourism sector (Moralli, Pachocka, and Leung 2023). This experiment shows that it is not necessary to make a sharp distinction between migrants and local populations or to put an overt emphasis on integration. It promotes the emplacement as a collective imagination about what sustainable rural development looks like in places where new land use and labor arrangements take place among both migrants and nonmigrants (Zoomers 2023). This means that visions for social-cultural benefit-sharing must be in place, in addition to the economic incentives.

Diasporas Investing in Their Homelands

Diaspora populations, which often include successful or highly skilled migrants, are investing in land in their areas of origin, by purchasing agricultural plots or houses as insurance, for example, often with the intention to return after retirement. Government policies often encourage such investments. In Mexico's "Programa 3x1 para Migrantes," for example, the government provides three pesos to a family sending migrants for every one peso of remittance received from the migrants in order to fund basic infrastructure, community services, and agricultural development and to encourage the migrants to return or their families to reinvest the received remittances in productive activities (Government of Mexico 2017). These investments generally require land acquisitions in the migrant sending areas. Studies in other Central American countries have shown that small farmers who receive remittances do invest in more land to increase the amount of land they own, though the ways that the land is used hardly change (Davis and Lopez-Carr 2014). There is thus a possibility that use of remittances for land investments recreates the conditions of land concentration and inequalities that caused outmigration in the first place.

Another example of diasporas making land investments is a seen in Khartoum, the capital of Sudan. Kaag and Steel (2019) show that investors from Saudi Arabia and other Gulf States heavily invest in land and real estate markets by teaming up with national counterparts on commercial and residential development projects (Crombé 2009; Choplin and Franck 2014). The investors include Sudanese diaspora working in the Gulf States who anticipate returning to their homeland in the future (Klaufus et al. 2017). By circulating advertisements at Sudanese embassies and on social media platforms used by members of the Sudanese diaspora, the Khartoum state government is actively recruiting potential buyers for the so-called empty lands on the outskirts of the city (Kaag and Steel 2019). Similarly, the Diaspora Investment in Agriculture initiative of International Fund for Agricultural Development, encourages widely dispersed diasporas from the conflict areas to return and/or invest in land for food production in their home countries. In the case of Khartoum, it is known that the urban farmers, internally displaced people, and other migrant populations who customarily lived on such "empty lands" without formal agreement have been pushed out of these previsioned and materialized investment sites (Three City Land Nexus Research Team 2020).[4]

In all cases of land investments by migrants, opportunities to revitalize marginalized areas and risks of further displacements coexist. However, migrants will continue making land investments in various sending countries, with the expected ripple effects for land change and mobilities (Mack et al. 2023). The question of how this will lead to more sustainable development in both migrant receiving and sending areas requires further examination.

Climate Change and the Land-Mobility Nexus

From the examples presented here, the land-mobility nexus emerges as an analytical lens to understand the impact of land investments on human mobilities and of migration politics on land investments. This nexus is additionally influenced by climate change. As we have discussed elsewhere, climate change politics setting various global goals and agreements for transitioning to sustainability mobilizes more investments, which will affect the ways that land is acquired for climate mitigation and adaptation purposes (Otsuki, Steel, and Panquene 2022). Extracting energy-transition minerals, building new energy parks and hydroelectric dams, establishing conservation and reforestation areas for carbon businesses, and developing infrastructure to connect these project sites requires large tracts of land. The recent climate agreement at COP28, for example, established a loss and damage fund for areas hit by disasters to be able to better adapt to climate change effects. Whereas these funds are desired by low income countries and meant to enhance the resilience of vulnerable communities, these can also lead to more infrastructure construction, such as seawalls or dikes for flood prevention, and land acquisition for resettlement. Consequently, such development might allow governments and investors to use climate change as a pretext to further displace certain groups of people from the "hazardous areas," undermining their existing practices of adaptation (Borras et al. 2020; Shannon 2021).

In addition to politically influenced mobilities, climate change itself is causing displacement and migration (de Sherbinin et al. 2011). The numbers of climate migrants are on a steep rise, with implications for the home and destination areas (UNHCR, the UN Refugee Agency 2023). Land access and tenure security are often described as preconditions for increasing the climate resilience of communities, and the importance of orderly resettlements with compensation based on the value of the land assets is discussed both in policy and scholarly circles (Hino, Field, and Mach 2017). Community members who are facing climate change hazards—or those who become climate migrants—are expected to make land investments in order to recover from disasters and reconstruct and develop their livelihoods. Land and property are also meant to make it possible for climate migrants to return after displacement or to prosper in the resettlement. However, climate-related disasters are increasingly making land unusable, even with tenure security (Sliuzas 2023).

Many coastal communities in the Pacific Islands, for example, have lost land because of the rising sea level (McEvoy, Mitchell, and Trundle 2020). This phenomenon is expected to become more common in the coming decades. These island states are also major migrant sending and remittance-dependent countries, whose migrants now have fewer prospects of returning and reinvesting in their land-based livelihood activities. Similarly, desertification, severe land degradation, and land subsidence may render much land unusable, irrespective of the land tenure situation. Land useability will thus further determine whether people wish to stay in their homeland or decide to migrate. Because the useability of land, and of related resources such as water, is likely to influence land conflicts, land and migration politics—and the land-mobility nexus—need to explicitly consider the effects of climate change and its impact on land and human mobilities.

We can, at least, anticipate more resettlement projects and different types of planned and unplanned human mobilities that may further drive land-use change and labor mobility in multiple directions. The question is how to establish a long-term vision about investments in redeveloping places affected by climate change—both sending and receiving areas—by engaging, for example, often highly skilled diaspora (International Organization for Migration 2016) and migrants themselves. If disasters such as floods or droughts hit the agricultural areas, investments could be made in new ways of intensifying farming to add value to crops or in developing the capacities of people to create new business opportunities, also by engaging with the existing translocal livelihoods. Otherwise, the very structure that had pushed people to migrate will be reproduced, even though the expansion of properties, real estate, or resettlement projects is envisioned as a way of enhancing the climate resilience of vulnerable populations.

The Land-Mobility Nexus, People's Agency, and the Structure of Responsibility

The land-mobility nexus established thus far allows us to look beyond the present to the future of land and migration politics in two main ways. First, it illuminates the importance of recognizing people's agency—that is, the capacity of migrants and nonmigrants alike to make differences by reworking the structural conditions. People's actions create "chains" of development beyond what is planned and implemented, and ripple effects of those actions are expected *after* a particular piece of land is invested or people are resettled (Zoomers and Van Westen 2011; Mack et al. 2023). Therefore, as Richter, Derkzen, and Zoomers (2020) write: "Land governance needs to explicitly consider people, who are 'out of place' in land regimes, which too often hinge on who was there first, who has a customary claim, and/or who holds paper titles, instead of who is there now and who needs the land most for purposes of livelihood and communal lives." The people who are out of place change over time, and it is important that migration policies constantly provide newcomers with opportunities to settle, stay, invest, or move again if they wish. Our examples have also shown that when migrants invest in their new countries or in their original homelands, the investments change the social and cultural dynamics. Migrants can revitalize depopulating and shrinking areas with new initiatives, and they can also reproduce inequalities and induce displacements. When investment in rural areas leads to urbanization, farmers' livelihoods and land prices change, and people are expected to adapt, not only to the new livelihoods, but also to new ways of living in relation to various social groups. We need to understand how these unfolding dynamics work and benefit all the actors involved in land investments and migration.

Secondly, the land-mobility nexus allows us to take a closer look at who is actually responsible for managing land investment *and* human mobilities. Land investors are indeed responsible for the well-being of displaced populations if their investments cause enclosure and displacement, but the land-mobility nexus adds a temporal element to this responsibility. For how long should investors and governments guarantee and enhance the livelihoods of people? Or, when migrants invest in their homelands, land prices could rise, and this might lead to further migration. Who should be in charge of ensuring the well-being of migrants as agents and of the nonmigrants whom they impact through their movements and investments? If migration intensifies due to climate change, are the current climate agreements and mechanisms for addressing climate justice sufficient to deal with the future effects of migration and the associated land investments?

These questions are partly addressed through the promotion of the so-called participatory planning. However, when planners define "beneficiaries," their focus tends to be on members of the existing community and how to regulate the presence of settled people; they hardly pay attention to people who are on the move or the fact that land and landscapes are being transformed due to people moving in and out (Richter, Derkzen, and Zoomers 2020; Zoomers, Leung, and van Westen 2016). Ultimately, we need to rethink current land and migration policies and scholarship that sharply distinguish migrants, including people who have been resettled because of land-investment-induced displacements, from the receiving local or host populations. In reality, communities are increasingly diverse and often fluid—and it has become commonplace for people to have translocal relationships and livelihood activities that span multiple localities. Land and migration policies and governance need to operate in continuity and in close collaboration, extending beyond administrative boundaries or targeted project areas.

Conclusions

This chapter has drawn on the scholarly and policy recognition of the fact that land politics and human mobilities are intricately related, and that the land-human mobility nexus is therefore a useful analytical lens through which to study the impact of both land and migration politics. We have reviewed cases that show how land investments cause human mobilities, as well as cases of migration that induces land acquisitions and new investments. Such cases are likely to proliferate due to climate change and its politics, mobilizing land investment in climate-mitigation and adaptation projects. The land-mobility nexus allows us to be more sensitive to impact of mobility on land politics, of land investment on migration politics, and to the political and physical effects of climate change on land transformation and human mobilities.

Given that there are a variety of mobilities and effects on land, we need to firmly focus our analysis on the ways that people—both migrants and nonmigrants—exercise their agency and take action. Up until now, providing apparently settled *local* people with secure and equal access to land has been seen as an important solution to the problem of evictions and displacements. In cases of resettlement, the principles of free, prior, and informed consent are followed to ensure that the people targeted for displacement to receive compensation. The land titles are the prerequisite for people to receive such compensation and, more broadly, to defend their rights to belong to a place and develop their land-based livelihoods. However, if we look at people as agents, we can also understand why people use the land titles to sell their land and migrate or how the migration further mobilizes new investments in rural and urban lands, and changing the dynamics of land development by creating absentee owners and new settlements and neighborhood development.

In the context of climate change, people's investments and mobilities are likely to be geared toward safer ground and the shaping of translocal livelihoods, because there is no guarantee that the people will be able to return to their land. The livelihoods need to be more diversified across multiple locations, because all these combined dynamics of the land investments, human mobilities, and climate change effects are largely unpredictable, requiring various measures to address risks of impoverishment and a worsening of vulnerabilities. By taking a translocal approach to the dynamics, we could at least observe the various patterns and experiences of land investment and human mobility, which are reported as separate case studies in the fields of land politics, migration studies, or climate science. The land-mobility nexus allows us to make connections and establish synergies between these separate cases. From these connections, we could infer possibilities to direct land, migration, and climate politics toward supporting people's actions and practices of sustainable land use and translocal livelihood development.

Notes

1. The projects include Diamonds in Delta in the case of Beira, Inside Investment Frontiers of Sustainability Transitions (InFront) in the case of energy projects, and the Limpopo National Park resettlement program referred to in this section.
2. These countries include Jordan, Lebanon, Niger, Nigeria, Senegal, Mali, Ethiopia, Tunisia, Libya, Morocco, Algeria, Iran, Egypt, Afghanistan, Pakistan, and Bangladesh.
3. This paragraph draws from an EU Horizon research project Welcoming Spaces.
4. The Khartoum case is also discussed in Otsuki et al. (2023).

References

Bastia, Tanja, and Ronald Skeldon. 2020. *Routledge Handbook of Migration and Development*. Abingdon, UK: Routledge.

Beier, Raffael, Amandine Spire, and Marie Bridonneau. 2022. *Urban Resettlements in the Global South: Lived Experiences of Housing and Infrastructure between Displacement and Relocation*. Abingdon, UK: Routledge.

Bello, Valeria. 2022. "The Spiralling of the Securitisation of Migration in the EU: From the Management of a 'Crisis' to a Governance of Human Mobility?" *Journal of Ethnic and Migration Studies* 48 (6): 1327–1344.

Bernstein, Henry. 2011. "Is There an Agrarian Question in the 21st Century?" *Canadian Journal of Development Studies* 27 (4): 449–460.

Borras, Saturnino M., Jr., Jennifer Franco, and Zau Nam. 2020. "Climate Change and Land: Insights from Myanmar." *World Development* 129: 104864.

Borras, Saturnino M., Jr., Jennifer C. Franco, Doi Ra, Tom Kramer, Mi Kamoon, Phwe Phyu, et al. 2022. "Rurally Rooted Cross-Border Migrant Workers from Myanmar, Covid-19, and Agrarian Movements." *Agriculture and Human Values* 39:315–338.

Borras, Saturnino M., Jr., Ruth Hall, Ian Scoones, Ben White, and Wendy Wolford. 2011. "Towards a Better Understanding of Global Land Grabbing: An Editorial Introduction." *Journal of Peasant Studies* 38 (2): 209–216.

Carmody, Padraig, and Francis Owusu. 2016. "Neoliberalism, Urbanization and Change in Africa: The Political Economy of Heterotopias." *Journal of African Development* 18:61–73.

Cernea, Michael M., and Julie K. Maldonado. 2018. "Challenging the prevailing paradigm of displacement and resettlement". In *Challenging the Prevailing Paradigm of Displacement and Resettlement: Risks, Impoverishment, Legacies, Solutions*, edited by Michael M. Cernea and Julie K. Maldonado, 1–42. Abingdon and New York: Routledge.

Choplin, Armelle, and Alice Franck. 2014. "Seeing Dubai in Khartoum and Nouakchott: 'Gulfication' on the Margins of the Arab World." In *Under Construction: Logics of Urbanism in the Gulf Region*, edited by Steffen Wippel, Katrin Bromber, Christian Steiner, and Birgit Krawietz, 271–284. Farnham, UK: Ashgate.

Cotula, Lorenzo, Sonja Vermeulen, Rebeca Leonard, and James Keeley. 2009. *Land Grab or Development Opportunity? Agricultural Investment and International Land Deals in Africa*. Report. International Institute for Environment and Development, Food and Agriculture Organization of the United Nations, International Fund for Agricultural Development, London and Rome.

Crombé, Laure. 2009. "Building Khartoum's Future?" EspacesTemps.net. 27 May. https://www.espacestemps.net/en/articles/building-khartoum-future/.
Datta, Ayona, and Katherine Brickel. 2011. *Translocal Geographies: Spaces, Places, Connections*. Abingdon, UK: Routledge.
Davis, Jason, and David Lopez-Carr. 2014. "Migration, Remittances and Smallholder Decision-Making: Implications for Land Use and Livelihood Change in Central America." *Land Use Policy* 36: 319–329.
De Haas, Hein. 2008. "The Myth of Invasion: The Inconvenient Realities of African Migration to Europe." *Third World Quarterly* 29 (7): 1305–1322.
de Sherbinin A., M. Castro, F. Gememme, M. Cernea, S. Adamo, P. M. Fearnside, et al. 2011. "Preparing for Resettlement Associated with Climate Change." *Science* 334: 456–457.
European Commission. 2015. EU-Turkey Joint Action Plan. https://ec.europa.eu/commission/presscorner/detail/en/MEMO_15_5860.
European Commission. 2023. New Pact on Migration and Asylum. https://commission.europa.eu/strategy-and-policy/priorities-2019-2024/promoting-our-european-way-life/migration-and-asylum/new-pact-migration-and-asylum_en.
Ferguson, James. 2012. "Structures of Responsibility." *Ethnography* 13 (4): 558–562.
Government of Mexico. 2017. Programa 3x1 para migrantes. https://www.gob.mx/bienestar/acciones-y-programas/programa-3x1-para-migrantes.
Hino, Miyuki, Christopher B. Field, and Katharine J. Mach. 2017. "Managed Retreat as a Response to Natural Hazard Risk." *Nature Climate Change* 7: 364–370.
International Labour Organization. 2024. "Goals 10: Reduce Inequality within and among Countries – Targets Linked to SDG10 and Related Thematic Areas." https://www.ilo.org/global/topics/dw4sd/theme-by-sdg-targets/WCMS_558134/lang--en/index.htm#T10.7.
International Organization for Migration. 2016. "IOM Supports Diaspora Engagement Initiative in Mozambique." IOM (online), July 19. https://www.iom.int/news/iom-supports-diaspora-engagement-initiative-mozambique.
International Organization for Migration. 2023. "Migration, Sustainable Development and the 2030 Agenda." IOM (online). https://www.iom.int/migration-sustainable-development-and-2030-agenda.
Islam, Md. Tariqul, Sujit Kumar Sikder, Mark Charlesworth, and Atta Rabbi. 2023. "Spatial Transition Dynamics of Urbanization and Rohingya Refugees' Settlements in Bangladesh." *Land Use Policy* 133:106874.
Jansen, Bram J. 2016. "The Protracted Refugee Camp and the Consolidation of a 'Humanitarian Urbanism.'" "Web Content." "Spotlight on the Urban Refugee 'Crisis': Reflections on Cities, Citizenship, and the Displaced." *International Journal of Urban and Regional Research*. https://www.ijurr.org/spotlight-on/the-urban-refugee-crisis-reflections-on-cities-citizenship-and-the-displaced/the-protracted-refugee-camp-and-the-consolidation-of-a-humanitarian-urbanism/.
Kaag, Mayke, and Griet Steel. 2019. "Transnational Migrants, Land and New Investment Hubs in African Cities." *Built Environment* 44 (4): 477–492.
Kelly, Alice, and Nancy Peluso. 2015. "Frontiers of Commodification: State Lands and Their Formalization." *Society and Natural Resources* 28 (5): 473–495.
Klaufus, Christien, Paul van Lindert, Femke van Noorloos, and Griet Steel. 2017. "All-Inclusiveness versus Exclusion: Urban Project Development in Latin America and Africa." *Sustainability* 9: 2038.

Mack, Elizabeth A., Laura Aileen Saules, Brad D. Jakisch, Kersten Nolte, Birgit Schmook, Yifan He, et al. 2023. "Remittances and Land Change: A Systematic Overview." *World Development* 168: 106251.

McEvoy, Darryn, David P. Mitchell, and Alexei Trundle. 2020. "Land Tenure and Urban Climate Resilience in the South Pacific." *Climate and Development* 12 (1): 1–11.

Mitchell, Don. 1996. *The Lie of the Land: Migrant Workers and the California Landscape.* Minneapolis: University of Minnesota Press.

Mkodzongi, Grasian, and Samual J. Spiegel. 2020. "Mobility, Temporary Migration, and Changing Livelihoods in Zimbabwe's Artisanal Mining Sector." *Extractive Industries and Society* 7 (3): 994–1001.

Moralli, Melissa, Marta Pachocka, and Maggi W.H. Leung. 2023. "'Welcoming Spaces': Migration and New Communities in Marginalised Regions." *Journal of International Migration and Integration* 24: 823–838. https://link.springer.com/article/10.1007/s12134-023-01092-y.

Namaganda, Emilinah, Kei Otsuki, and Griet Steel. 2023. "Understanding Cumulative Socioenvironmental Impacts of Energy Transition-Induced Extractivism in Mozambique: The Role of Mixed Methods." *Journal of Environmental Management* 338: 117811.

Pham Huu, Ty. 2015. "Dilemmas of Hydropower Development in Vietnam: Between Dam-Induced Displacement and Sustainable Development." PhD thesis, Utrecht University.

Otsuki, Kei. 2019. "Who Is in the "Public"? Infrastructures of Displacement and Urban Resettlement in Mozambique." *Built Environment* 44 (4): 493–508.

Otsuki, Kei. 2021. "Making Justice the Subject of Resettlement Planning." *Antipode* 53 (6): 1745–1766.

Otsuki, Kei, Godfred Jasaw, and Victor Lolig. 2018. "Linking Individual and Collective Agency to Enhance Community Resilience." *Society and Natural Resources* 31 (2): 151–165.

Otsuki, Kei, Murtah Shannon, Griet Steel, and Femke van Noorloos. 2023. "Urban Land Grabs: An Overview of Issues." In *Routledge Handbook of Global Land and Resource Grabbing*, edited by A. Neef, C. Ngin, T. Moreda, and S. Mollett, 375–385. Abingdon, UK: Routledge.

Otsuki, Kei, Griet Steel, and Celio Panquene. 2022. "Exploring Synergies between the 2030 Agenda for Sustainable Development and Involuntary Resettlement Guidelines: The Case of Mozambique's Natural Gas Project." *Sustainability Science* 17 (4): 1663–1676.

Perrota, Domenico, and Timothy Raeymaekers. 2022. "Caporalato Capitalism, Labor Brokerage, and Agrarian Change in a Mediterranean Society." *Journal of Peasant Studies* 50 (5): 2002–2023.

Ploeg, Jan Douwe van der, Jennifer Franco, and Saturnino M. Borras Jr. 2015. "Land Concentration and Land Grabbing in Europe: A Preliminary Analysis." *Canadian Journal of Development Studies* 36 (2): 147–162.

Richter, Christine M., Marthe Derkzen, and Annelies Zoomers. 2020. "Land Governance from a Mobilities Perspective." *Land* 9 (2): 32.

Rogers, Sarah, and Brooke Wilmsen. 2020. "Towards a Critical Geography of Resettlement." *Progress in Human Geography* 44 (2): 256–275.

Rothenburg, Daniel. 2000. *With These Hands: The Hidden World of Migrant Workers Today.* Berkeley: University of California Press.

Salomão, Alda. 2020. "Land Based Investment in Mozambique: Challenges in Community Rights Protection, Participation and Benefit Sharing." PhD thesis, Utrecht University.

Sanyal, Romola. 2015. "Refugees and the City: An Urban Discussion." *Geography Compass* 6 (11): 633–644.

Sassen, Saskia. 2014. *Expulsions: Brutality and Complexity in the Global Economy*. Cambridge, MA: Harvard University Press.

Shannon, Murtah. 2021. "Urban Infrastructure and Displacement: Two Sides of the Sustainability Coin." In *Handbook on Translocal Development and Global Mobilities*, edited by Annelies Zoomers, M. Leung, Kei Otsuki, and G. van Westen, 216–229. Cheltenham, UK: Edward Elgar.

Shaw, Ian G. R. 2019. "Worlding Austerity: The Spatial Violence of Poverty." *Environment and Planning D: Society and Space* 37 (6): 971–989.

Shih, Mi. 2017. "Rethinking Displacement in Peri-urban Transformation in China." *Environment and Planning A* 49 (2): 389–406.

Shewel, Kerilyn, and Alix Debray. 2023. "Global Trends in South-South Migration." In *The Palgrave Handbook of South-South Migration and Inequality*, edited by Heaven Crawley and Joseph Kofi Teye, 153–181. Cham, Switzerland: Palgrave Macmillan.

Sliuzas, Richard. 2023. *Land Governance for Climate Resilience: A Review and Case Studies from Land-at-Scale Projects*. Climate Scoping Study. Utrecht: LANDac.

Three City Land Nexus Research Team. 2020. *Examining the Urban Land Nexus and Inclusive Urbanization in Dar es Salaam, Mwanza and Khartoum*. Synthesis Report. Institute of Development Studies (IDS) and East African Research Fund (EARF), Brighton, UK. https://assets.publishing.service.gov.uk/media/5e5783bed3bf7f0700fef995/Urban_Land_Nexus_-_Synthesis_Report.pdf.

UNHCR, the UN Refugee Agency. 2023. "Climate Change and Disaster Displacement." https://www.unhcr.org/what-we-do/build-better-futures/environment-disasters-and-climate-change/climate-change-and.

Zoomers, Annelies. 2023. "Epilogue: Chicken or Egg? The Role of Newcomer Migrants in the Revitalization of 'Left-Behind' Areas." *Journal of International Migration and Integration* 24: 1001–1011. Open access: https://link.springer.com/article/10.1007/s12134-023-01084-y.

Zoomers, Annelies, Maggi Leung, Kei Otsuki, and Guus van Westen, eds. 2021. *Handbook on Translocal Development and Global Mobilities*. Cheltenham, UK: Edward Elgar.

Zoomers, Annelies, Maggi Leung, and Guus van Westen. 2016. "Local Development in the Context of Global Migration and the Global Land Rush: The Need for a Conceptual Update." *Geography Compass* 10 (2): 56–66.

Zoomers, Annelies, and Kei Otsuki. 2017. "Addressing the Impacts of Large-Scale Land Investments: Re-engaging with Livelihood Research." *Geoforum* 83:164–171.

Zoomers, Annelies, Femke van Noorloos, Kei Otsuki, Griet Steel, and Guus van Westen. 2017. "The Rush for Land in an Urbanizing World: From Land Grabbing toward Developing Safe, Resilient, and Sustainable Cities and Landscapes." *World Development* 92: 242–252.

Zoomers, Annelies, Femke van Noorloos, and Isle van Liempt. 2018. "Between Sticks and Carrots: The Future of EU Migration Deals." *Clingendael Spectator* 4. https://spectator.clingendael.org/pub/2018/4/_/pdf/CS-2018-4-zoomers-van-noorloos-van-liempt.pdf.

Zoomers, Annelies, and Guus van Westen. 2011. "Introduction: Translocal Development, Development Corridors and Development Chains." *International Development Planning Review* 33 (4): 377–388.

CHAPTER 21

LAND FOR LIVELIHOODS

Urban Agriculture and the Agrarian Question in the Twenty-First Century

RICARDO JACOBS

INTRODUCTION

LAND remains a central focus of a new wave of urban struggles that are contesting capitalist urbanization in the twenty-first century. Twenty-first century urbanization is embedded in multifactorial crises of capitalism, combining as ecological, profitability, and legitimacy crises, configuring a historically specific process of capitalist urbanization (Karatasli 2022; Silver 2019; Soriano 2018). The rapid process of urbanization and the ever-expanding surplus populations are rooted in the tendency of global capitalism to destroy established livelihoods faster than it creates new ones. The result is a growing relative surplus population, which is often differentiated along racial, gender, and citizenship lines. Relatedly, there has been an explosion of urban land struggles for agricultural livelihoods, putting both anti-neoliberal and anticapitalist alternatives on the horizon.

Although not all forms of spatial contestations for agricultural livelihoods are sites of social struggles, one form does take is land occupations for urban agricultural communes that engage in both crop and livestock production. The protagonists of these land occupations are a combination of new entrants and long-term urban residents, who range from being gainfully employed to underemployed and unemployed (Jacobs 2021). The most dramatic expression of these urban spatial struggles in the twenty-first century are those that took place in the city of Harare (Zimbabwe) in the early 2000s. In the case of Harare, land was occupied, on both state- and privately owned land, for a combination of agricultural livelihoods, housing, and small-scale enterprises (Sadomba 2013, 103). Similarly, in many other African cities, and in India and the global South more broadly, rural peasants who were dispossessed from their land "either through the erosion of communal tenure or market forces," among other things, engage in direct land occupations for crop production and animal husbandry (Gillespie 2016, 68; Owens 2016; Gururani 2020). These urban households are occupying land for urban farming and livestock raising, not as a transitional activity in which recent "rural peasant migrants adapt to urban life," but as an integral and stable part of the urban class structure and urban built environment (Guendel 2002; Jacobs 2018). This phenomenon is not limited to cities in the global South. In the cities of Detroit (United States) and Vancouver (Canada), for example, urban households are engaging in livestock keeping and crop farming (White 2018; McClintock 2018), resembling the land occupiers of the global South. The Cooperation Jackson municipal project in Jackson, Mississippi, is also centering land for agriculture communes in building municipal anticapitalist alternatives (Akuno 2023).

Land occupation for livelihoods, and for urban agriculture specifically, raises several important questions and confounds existing perspectives on urbanization, class formation, dispossession, and the agrarian question. One, why and how are dispossessed (agrarian and urban) in urban spaces, resisting and contesting capitalist urbanization? Two, what type of urban politics emerges and how does it reconfigure urban space? Three, how do these new urban struggles for land shape our understandings—including the spatial parameters—of the agrarian question and food production in the twenty-first century and how we think about the alternatives beyond capitalism?

This chapter draws on examples from the secondary literature on urban spaces and on my own ethnographic research on land occupations in Cape Town (South Africa). It argues that sections of the dispossessed rural classes are reproducing themselves in urban spaces and converging with different strata of wage laborers to eke out an agricultural livelihood by returning some means of production to subaltern groups and establishing urban agricultural communes. This places urban agriculture and food production as an important arena of land struggles and a livelihood option for sections of both the old and the newly made urban classes. It is thus one of the key pillars of the urban dimension of the agrarian question and anticapitalist agrarian struggles in the twenty-first century.

In the existing literature, global capitalism is seen as having torn asunder the rural-urban divide (Brenner 2019), subsuming peasants into generalized commodity production (Bernstein 2009; Araghi 2000). Cities are often ascribed a class structure, where class and space map neatly onto each other; that is, the countryside is synonymous with peasants, and urban spaces with wage laborers (proletarians). Moreover, these urban proletarians are seen as surviving through a combination of wage labor and a growing mass of informal labor and self-employment that is taking place in urban slums (Davis 2004 Petras and Veltmeyer 2014; Portes and Hoffman 2003). Urbanization is seen as a reflection of a fundamental underlying transformation in which the historical class categories (peasant, proletariat, or semi-proletariat) have been rendered irrelevant, replaced by informal workers who are surviving by "the sale of their labor power for their own reproduction." According to this literature, what we are witnessing today is a twin process of depeasantization and deagrarianization, which has led to fragmented classes of labor that have been dislodged from their historical agency and have "little access to the culture of collective labor and large-scale class struggle" (Davis 2004, 28).

By emphasizing only the economic structures of capitalism, this literature fails to apprehend that urbanization does not proceed in a linear fashion whereby dispossessed agrarian classes lose interest in access to land for agricultural production or cultural practices. The approach put forward here emphasizes that, instead of disappearing, the peasantry (or agrarian classes) has been relocated and reconstituted in the cities. This is leading to what I call the *agrarian in the urban*,[1] a process that is unfolding in varied forms across the cities of the global South and the global North. If the existing scholarship focuses on rapid urbanization and the creation of the best global cities, my research has uncovered a simultaneous process of the "agrarian in the urban" that is an integral part of capitalist modernity. This is because urbanization in the cities of the global South is shaped by their own historically specific reality, as classes from a noncapitalist formation persist in the new urban environments. As capitalist agriculture and extractivism continue to displace people from the countryside, the urban centers are unable to absorb them into wage employment. Urban agriculture is both a means of survival and resistance against the effect of neoliberal global capitalism.

Instead of being resolved, the land and agrarian question is in part being shifted spatially to urban areas, giving rise to new social struggles (Jacobs 2018; Harriss-White 2021; Ghosh and Meer 2021; Batubara and Rachman 2022). The self-activity of the urban and rural classes is often dismissed as a form of agrarian populism, rather than understood as a central component of both contemporary agrarian and urban struggles. Urban land occupations that are specifically for agricultural livelihoods indicate that, despite the monumental transformations that have taken place in the countryside, the land and agrarian question has not vanished from the global arena. Instead of the agrarian class structure dissolving, it is mapped onto urban spaces. These land struggles are shaping in consequential ways the urbanization process, transforming socioecological relations and landscapes in the city. It further opens "new analytical horizons" that are consequential for exploring the agrarian question and the accompanying alternatives, a question that is undoubtedly political and social. This requires rethinking the agrarian question beyond its overdetermined and mechanistic conceptualization as a transition to capitalism. In short, we can detect an important urban dimension to the land and agrarian question in the early twenty-first century.

Historicizing Urbanization and the Role of Land in Urban Class Formation

Neil Brenner's (2019) concept of "planetary urbanization," or generalized urbanization, provides us with an important "meta theoretical exercise" to describe the monumental transitions being driven by twenty-first-century capitalist urbanization. The specificity of planetary urbanization is not the generalization of the city, but rather, the intensified subordination of hinterlands (nonurban spaces) on a world scale in the service of accelerated city-building. This represents an important break with views that the urban is a "fixed, bounded and universally generalizable settlement type" (Brenner and Schmid 2015).

Mike Davis, in his seminal article "Planet of Slums," systematically uncovers a process of urbanization in which deindustrialization and declining agricultural productivity in rural areas are the main forces of underdevelopment in Africa and the global South more broadly. For Davis, this has important implications for the processes of class formation and agency, leading to the proliferation of slums populated by an informal working class, detached from historical agency, or what Henry Bernstein (drawing theoretical inspiration from Davis's analysis) calls "fragmented classes of labor" (Bernstein 2009, 251). As Davis (2004) puts it, slums are "settlements [where] uprooted rural migrants and informal workers have been largely dispossessed of fungible labour-power or reduced to domestic service in the houses of the rich, [and] have little access to the culture of collective labour or large-scale class struggle" (28).

Although Davis and Brenner open up the analytical horizons for critical agrarian studies, their analysis continues to veer toward a unidirectional view of these monumental processes of global change. To move toward a less linear view of these processes, it is necessary to historicize "planet of slums," planetary urbanization, and class formation. Examining urban agriculture and urban occupations for agricultural livelihoods today shifts our attention away from "naturalizing dispossession," urbanization, and class formation and toward an approach that sees history and the present as a process of tensions, conflict, disruption, and contestations.

Capitalism and urbanization, particularly in the global South, "cannot be presumed to manifest itself or be transformed in an identical manner everywhere" (Mafeje 1973, 30). Likewise, cities and rural areas are not just physical spaces but also have their own historically specific social relations. The "rural in the urban" (Mamdani 1996) has been an enduring feature in the formation of many African cities, and consequential in configuring the social relations and landscapes in urban areas. In contrast, the concept of planetary urbanization often obscures the lived experience of real people by erasing traditionally understood boundaries of urban and rural (Schindler 2017, 47–48), while this meta theory ignores or wishes away the agency of classes from different temporal formations. Likewise, Davis's monolithic class subject has never existed properly in Africa; nor does the current configuration of class formation suggest a "working class entirely dislodged from its historical agency" (Dwyer and Zeilig 2012, 46).

To be sure, in many cities today we can see the forces of combined and uneven development that Davis so eloquently describes in "Planet of the Slums." It takes the form of an urban core characterized by a "small island of modern industrial, financial and commercial enterprises—often multinational—surrounded by a sea of the poor, composed of street vendors, prostitutes, unemployed workers, rubbish collectors and small-time drug dealers" (Löwy 2010, 147).

Nevertheless, we should not assume that informal settlements or slums are just containers of surplus populations and an informal proletariat; they are also containers of formal wage laborers and, in some instances, self-employed middle classes (Hendricks et al. 2013, 4). The employed and unemployed coexist in the same informal settlements (and often even in the same households), living intertwined in spaces in which the divide between workers and nonworkers is blurred (Benya 2015). Today, in the cities of Accra in Ghana and Dar es Salaam in Tanzania, rural peasants who have been dispossessed from their land engage in direct land occupations for crop production and animal husbandry (Gillespie 2016, 68; Owens 2016). Similarly, in the urban periphery of Morelia in Mexico, peasant holdings, commercial agriculture, gated communities, and informal settlements coexist and compete over land, natural resources, and infrastructure (Napoletano et al. 2019, 48). The unilinear conception of urban space "obscures the way in which space is constituted through social relations and material practices just as much as social relations are spatially constructed" (Makki 2014, 93). This new form of combined and uneven development in cities generates and heightens existing, already "explosive tensions" and occasional rebellions.

Dispossession past and present engenders a particular process of urban class formation that is the outcome of class struggles with uneven results. While urban agriculture often has multiple logics, ranging from neoliberal to reformist, radical, and emancipatory, for a critical mass it is also an important terrain of class struggle in the sphere of social reproduction for resisting capitalist urbanization and forging alternatives (McClintock 2018; White 2018). The agency and self-activity of the dispossessed in urban spaces can either contest, constrain, or enable capitalist urbanization. As Traverso (2016) argues, "Classes are not abstract sociological categories but living subjects—subjects that forge themselves in the frame of social relations" (216). It is as living historical subjects that they contest the past and the present (Arruza and King 2020; Bensaïd 2002). In this view, classes only become conceivable and exist within the "dialectic of class struggle" and antagonism. While dispossession is the dominant ongoing temporality within capitalism, tensions emerge between different temporal and social strata. In urban spaces different temporal layers are present and deactivated at various historical periods

Moreover, as sociologist William Martin has pointed out in Southern Africa, increasing proletarianization on one end required that there be "stable forms of partial dispossession elsewhere," suggesting that capital accumulation is hinged on "spatially divergent forms of partial dispossession" (Martin 2013, 174–175). A nonlinear approach to dispossession provides an important lens through which to analyze processes of urban class formation and class struggle.

The specificity of how these processes manifests itself in the "hidden abode of everyday life" (Arrighi et al. 1989), and its "non correspondence to political economy and politics" (Neocosmos 2016) in regions like Southern Africa or the global South more broadly is not always sufficiently theorized or empirically investigated. Arrighi and Piselli (1987), in "Capitalist Development in Hostile Environments," departed from a linear reading of class formation. In so doing, they make the important observation that selling labor power for a wage cannot be taken a priori as an expression of proletarianization. Likewise, urbanization should not be taken a priori as an expression of proletarianization or modernization. Wage labor can be an expression of either proletarianization or semi-proletarianization, or even of petty accumulation. Arrighi and Piselli illustrate that there is both an objective and a subjective component to ongoing primitive accumulation, dispossession, and class formation. For example, they found that participation in wage labor through seasonal and long-distance migration by the peasants of Consentino, in the Calabria region of southern Italy, was motivated by the goal to earn cash destined for investment in land and the reproduction of peasant households engaged primarily in subsistence production. It was therefore an expression, not of proletarianization, but of the "non-proletarian condition" in a context of what the authors term "extreme peripheralization" (Arrighi and Pisseli 1987, 693). In South Africa, for example, some urban land occupiers engage in wage labor, not in order to be permanently embedded in the city as urban workers, but to reinvest in livestock raising and agrarian activities, both in urban spaces and in communal areas in the countryside (Jacobs 2021)

Arrighi and Piselli's framework enables us to grasp both what the sale of wage labor and agricultural production represents and what it is an expression of in different historical periods and contexts. They allow us to re-examine contemporary class struggles, urbanization, and the agrarian question beyond the assumed capital and wage labor relationship, and to interrogate the important element of worker subjectivity, particularly the identification of multiple expressions embodied in the same worker. Moreover, this perspective departs from an overly economic deterministic approach that views economic conditions as outside the conscious control of classes, denying the role of human agency and the subjective role of class. The Arrighi-Piselli approach recasts processes of class formation and class struggles in a different light and foregrounds ongoing struggles of different scales and intensities, again underlining that class has both a subjective and an objective factor. This is consequential for how we understand the general process of urbanization and dispossession on a world scale.

In *The Condition of the Working Class in England*, Frederick Engels ([1845] 2009) detailed the horrific emergence of filthy slums, disease, poverty, surplus populations, and immigrant labor as a result of dispossession and then the concentration of the dispossessed in the cities of England. Here is where the life of the workers is undermined, and ecological landscapes destroyed, but also where new forms of agency and organization emerge. Slums are not unique to late capitalism, but they take on a particular and a more generalized form globally.

Historically, the dispossession of producers from the means of production set in motion a "spatial rift" (Saito 2022), seen in the antithesis between town and country. The "spatial rift" leads to a massive process of depeasantization and the concentration of working people in dense urban spaces. In this realm, the process transforms and undermines the independent "mode of social reproduction" (Sevilla-Buitrago 2015) in the countryside, which also extends to the newly formed urban spaces. Dispossessed classes are pushed into the cities and cut off from autonomous managed access to food and housing, resulting in a general impoverishment of their living conditions, destroying the physical health of the newly formed urban workers (Saito 2022), and creating generalized artificial scarcity. The basis of the social reproduction of the urban classes is inevitably more dependent on commodities provided by capital, where "capitalist use values" (Tomba 2013) become the dominant form of use value on a global scale.

Capitalist use values determine access to healthy, safe, and nutritionally sufficient food, precisely because access to food is based on the ability to pay. Urban food security is socially constructed and historically determined. According to *State of Food Security and Nutrition in the World 2022*, approximately 3.1 billion people were unable to afford a healthy diet (FAO et al. 2022, 1). Both rural and urban areas are experiencing what scientists describe as the *double burden of malnutrition*, defined as the coexistence of undernutrition and obesity/overweight (Popkin, Corvalan, and Grummer-Strawn 2020; Ruel, Garrett and Yosef 2017). The social questions arising in urban areas are directly tied to the intensity, scale, and pace of agrarian change. It is in this sense that the rural coproduces the urban, linking agrarian change to the contemporary process of urbanization (Gururani 2020, 984).

The agency and resistance of the dispossessed producers against immiseration and the proletarian condition gives rise to the state-capital expropriation and reclamation by the dispossessed that is intrinsic to historical capitalism. This often-overlooked expropriation-reclamation interconnection occurs when dispossession takes place in one locale, such as in rural areas, but gives rise to land repossession in another locale, for example, in urban spaces. This expropriation-reclamation process could also take place in the reverse direction, such as when an urban crisis engenders a movement toward the countryside.[2] Urban-to-rural movement became a common feature of countries in Africa and other parts of the global South during the height of the COVID-19 crisis (Ossome 2021). More importantly, the agency and resistance of dispossessed producers, based on multiple determinations, generates a nonlinear process of urban class formation and the reconfiguration of urban space.

The Agrarian in the Urban

The remapping of urban space by dispossessed classes opens "new analytical horizons" (to use Brenner's [2016, 124] phrase). Although there is a meteoric tendency toward planetary urbanization (Brenner and Schmid 2015) or a planet of urban slums (Davis 2004), because of insurgent self-activity from below, there is a simultaneous tendency toward the "agrarian in urban space." The planetary logic of capital accumulation has to confront "resistance, frictions and interruptions across different places, territory and scales" (Mezzadra and Neilson 2019, 3). Urban land occupations are part of a broader process of the agrarian in urban space that is currently unfolding throughout the global South; it is a general process with its own historical specificity and contradictory logics at each site.

In many cities across the African continent and the global South, these newly forming urban land occupations and urban agriculture have a multilayered class character that includes peasants. However, there is also an important *within country* variation among the different land occupation sites, and protagonists are emerging from different social formations, past and present. In the current period of capitalist crisis and transformation, rapid urbanization with deindustrialization, rural dispossession and displacement, and the massive expansion of surplus populations are propelling subaltern actors toward agrarian livelihoods in urban spaces. Notwithstanding the push provided by the effects of the crisis of capitalism and capitalist development in general, the existence of land occupations for agricultural livelihoods cannot just be understood as a response to the crisis of social reproduction. Land occupation for urban agriculture should be conceived as an urban practice and an important aspect of everyday urban life, and not restricted to newly emerging classes who have been displaced from the countryside or as a temporary survival strategy by long-term urban residents. Urban agriculture in African cities such as Dar Es Salaam (Owens 2016; McLees 2011) and in the Congolese and Zambian Copperbelt (Peša 2020) was historically (and continues to be) a constitutive part in the formation of urban space (Siebert 2020). My own research shows that dispossessed agrarian classes have been reproducing their agrarian activities in the city of Cape Town since the 1950s, despite their being deeply embedded in the city. For example, one of the protagonists of a land occupation in Cape Town, who was born the city in 1952, remembers that when his parents came from the rural communal areas in KwaZulu Natal province, they acquired enough land for housing and to farm with thirty cattle and then sold milk to surrounding urban residents. In the 1960s the apartheid municipality forced them to discontinue farming and to sell their cattle cheaply to a White farmer (Jacobs 2021).

We can observe analogous processes in cities in the global North, where sociologists and geographers have identified similar long-term trends.[3] In the US Midwest, Detroit is a city where Black urban households are engaging in urban agriculture. The collapse of the auto industry, combined with the effects of Detroit being a "predatory city", that is "urban areas where public officials systematically take property from residents and transfer it to public coffers, intentionally or unintentionally violating domestic laws or basic human rights" (Atuahene 2020, 107), has led to mass unemployment, depopulation, and foreclosures that are disproportionately affect working-class African Americans. But while a crisis of social reproduction (including deep-seated hunger and food insecurity) is certainly driving the Black urban residents of Detroit, for them urban agriculture is also a form of resistance against racism. Thus urban agriculture and the creation of a community-based food system are both strategies of survival and forms of resistance rooted in a philosophy of antiracism and anticapitalism and a quest for self-determination (White 2018, 118–120; Safransky 2017). Detroit's urban Black farmers are the descendants of sharecroppers, tenant farmers, domestic workers, and farm laborers who migrated from the South to work in the automobile sector. In this way, the politics of the Detroit urban land movement has strong analogies with the urban repossession in Cape Town (Jacobs 2018). This resistance is most often against what scholars and activists refer to as a "food apartheid" or "food deserts" that are spatially restricted to Black or low-income neighborhoods (Gripper et al. 2022; Gripper 2020).

During the fast-track land occupation movement in Zimbabwe in 2000, the emergence of autonomist communing also spread to the urban landless and unemployed. Here, the urban landless occupied land for agriculture and urban housing. Both municipal and privately owned White farms were targeted for what local scholars refer to as their "indigenous industrialization." A key feature of the occupation was the establishment of housing cooperatives, leading to the construction of more than 10,000 houses without state support (Sadomba 2013, 90; Helliker et al. 2021). Despite being illegal, urban agriculture is continuing apace in the cities of Zimbabwe in the current period. Urban agriculture takes three forms: open-space crop farming around towns and cities; backyard farming, where residents engage in crop production and farm with broilers, rabbits, and turkeys, among other things, in backyards and in formally designated plots, of usually around six hectares, around the periphery of towns and cities (Scoones 2022). Studies have also found that the recent pandemic and economic crisis engulfing Zimbabwe also precipitated a shift toward urban farming.

The "agrarian in urban space" is where historical, social, economic, and political factors intersect, where subaltern actors contest urban space, shaping the urban morphology with uneven outcomes. The class, race, and gender basis of this politics is markedly diverse across different spatial locales. For example, in Dar Es Salaam "open space farming" is driven by the "middle classes,"[4] such as civil servants, among others. Whereas in West African cities like Accra, Ghana (Gillespie 2016), and Lagos, Nigeria (Omobowale and Adeyanyu 2017), land occupations are driven by dispossessed peasants from Nigeria and immigrants from countries in West Africa who have been unable to find gainful employment. In the city of Nairobi, Kenya, it is estimated that in 2013 the livestock population was approximately 1.3 million (Alarcon et al. 2017). Similarly, in shack or informal settlements such as Nkaneng, near Marikana in South Africa, are also engaging in livestock farming (Ngwane 2021, 110). I have argued that these land occupations are sites where the employed, unemployed, middle class, and poor converge in a single space, contesting for hegemony. These diverse socioeconomic class actors are contesting urban space and engaging in a form of *anti-neoliberal urban planning from below* in the twenty-first century.

Capitalism is a social relation, or a "nexus of complex relations" (Callinicos 2014; Ollman and Smith 2008), instead of a structural whole. As such, urbanization is better conceived as a nexus of complex relations, shaped by its own specific internal (and certainly external) relations, and structuring the morphology of cities across space and time. These include ecological relations, or "humans' metabolic relations to nature" (Foster and Clark 2020). With the "agrarian in urban space," insurgent protagonists—whether intentionally or unintentionally—are deeply engaged in the restoration of the urban social metabolism, directing us to future possibilities. Amid an unfolding ecological crisis, the class protagonists in these spaces are important ecological actors, confronting the assumptive logic of capitalist urbanization. This independent "practical agency" from below combines a struggle for survival with struggles for redistribution and environmental justice. This independent practical agency, or the self-activity of subaltern classes, is the missing element in otherwise seminal sociological studies of global urban transformations in the twenty-first century, including those by Neil Brenner (2019) and Mike Davis (2004). These struggles from below will likely be at the forefront in challenging the ways in which capitalist urbanization is undermining the ecological basis for life, and in developing alternative forms of livelihood beyond capitalism.

The Urban Agrarian Question and Anticapitalist Agrarian Change

The analysis of the "agrarian in urban space" put forward here allows us to expand the spatial and research horizon of the agrarian question. Moreover, it can also help navigate the "transition problematic" that has long gripped the scholarly debates and reached what some suggest is an impasse (Levien et al. 2018). The "over-determined category of transition" (Harootunian 2015) has captured academic attention for over a century, leading to a sharply polarized debate. But if the transition problematic has reached a cul-de-sac (Levien et al. 2018), its underlying theoretical lineages and (Eurocentric) assumptions are still deeply embedded in linear thinking. In contrast to this linear approach, we should conceive of (agrarian) transitions as permanent and ongoing processes with temporal and spatial unevenness.

In critical agrarian studies, the transition problematic is framed as the "Bernstein-Byres debate" (Oya 2013; Byres 2016). The Bernstein-Byres (transition) debate, as Giovanni Arrighi argued in a different context, lends itself to all the features of a "non-debate": "The real, though generally undeclared purpose of such non-debates is not so much the shedding of light on their alleged subject matter as establishing or undermining the legitimacy of a particular research program—that is, what subject matter is worth investigating and how it should be investigated" (Arrighi 1998, 113). There appears to be a real disconnect between (transition problematic) theory and concrete reality for many countries in the global South. As Mafeje (1973, 39) noted, "All theories receive a certain measure of confirmation on practice, but all theories are not valid." My research on land occupations in the City of Cape Town, as well as South African historiography, contradicts the central assumptions of the transition problematic—a problematic that has by now transformed itself into a nondebate—albeit an influential nondebate.

This current "transition debate" revolves around the extent to which agrarian transitions are incomplete or whether agrarian transitions in the global South are blocked. Henry Bernstein, one of the key protagonists in this "debate," contends that complete agrarian transitions are impossible because commodity relations have been fully achieved everywhere through the juggernaut of neoliberal capitalist globalization, signaling the final completion of capitalist domination of everyday life (Bernstein 2009).

In this perspective, the relative weight of income derived from wage labor is consequential in understanding class formation. The absence of a theory of mediation between class as an objective and a subjective factor "reduce[s] all social relations to mere quantities" (Mafeje 1985, 1981). Class is both a socioeconomic concept and a political category and mediating these is critical to understanding the noncorrespondence between political economy and politics (Neocosmos 2016). This one-sided conception reduces the agrarian transition to a "structural issue of political economy," where neoliberal capitalist globalization completed capitalist transitions on a world scale. In a structuralist fashion, capitalism's unevenness is made linear, and the present is separated from the past. Yet, despite capitalist relations in agriculture in Zimbabwe in the twenty-first century, we have witnessed a successful mass movement of land occupations (in both rural and urban areas) and repeasantization that a linear conceptualization cannot account for (Moyo and Yeros 2005; Neocosmos 2016). Nor does it account for the insurgent movement of class-differentiated Indigenous "peasants" in Chiapas, Mexico, in 1994 against the North Atlantic Free Trade Agreement (Anderson [1995] 2022, 48). In essence, the transition problematic and scholarship on the agrarian question has unevenly focused on how ecological transformation, urbanization, racialization, and colonization configure the agrarian question and contemporary struggles.

What escapes this notion of "universal history" or "historic-philosophical theory" is that there is a "heterogeneous mix of temporalities rather than the destruction of one made by another" (Harootunian 2015, 206). These heterogeneous temporalities unfold where the noncapitalist or "archaic coexist and overlap with new forms, [which] gives rise to social and political conflict, whose outcomes are not predetermined by any law of history" (Tomba 2019, 6). The co-presence of different temporal formations in urban spaces is a core feature of capitalist urbanization. Instead of linear transitions we are confronted with uncertain outcomes as a result of political struggles, creating the possibilities for what Tomba (2019) calls "new historical trajectories." The self-activity and independent self-organization are at the forefront of creating these new historical possibilities. A nonlinear approach to the "transition problematic" suggests that we have multiple, ongoing agrarian transitions across time and space, whose political consequences are important for understanding anticapitalist agrarian change.

In academic settings the agrarian question is the subject of ongoing fierce scholarly "debates" (Bernstein 2006; Moyo and Yeros 2005; Akram-Lodhi and Kay 2016).[5] Linear and mechanical stageist thinking still permeates much of the theory and practice on the agrarian question and critical agrarian studies. Nevertheless, as Vergara-Camus correctly notes, "The core of the dispute around the agrarian question remains the same [as it was in the twentieth century], namely: who will control and how will they control the resources necessary to sustain life" (Vergara-Camus 2012, 1134; Vergara-Camus 2014).

The process of global agrarian change, planetary urbanization, and the real movement of subaltern classes has shifted the spatial parameters of the scholarly debates on the agrarian question, variously characterized as the extended urban agrarian question or urban agrarianism (Jacobs 2018; Gururani 2020; Ghosh and Meer 2021; Bowness and Wittman 2021; Harriss-White 2021). What this scholarship highlights is that the agrarian question has always been tied to processes of urbanization (Jacobs 2021; Sivaramakrishnan 2021; Balakrishnan and Gururani 2021; Akram-Lodhi et al. 2021). Rural and urban spaces are always interconnected and mutually constitutive, whose spatial form and outcome is historically determined by the outcome of class struggles. The capitalist mode of production is transfiguring and disrupting the metabolism between humans and nature, making the agrarian question a critical form of the ecological and social question (Sumida 2021). An existential question of life or death for most of the working people and humanity in general is at the heart of the contemporary agrarian question.

Some of the contemporary critical interventions, attentive to these changes, reproduce the old linear and Eurocentric approaches to the transition debate and agrarian question, entangling contemporary discussions of the urban dimension of the agrarian question with a similar approach (Ghosh and Meer 2020; Ghosh 2022). The continuation of this form of stageist and linear thinking can be attributed to the dominant Kautskyian approach to the peasantry or the agrarian question (Anderson 2022) and critical agrarian studies. The Kautskyian approach to the agrarian question can be broadly summarized as follows:

1. Capitalist agriculture takes hold of small-scale producers and transforms the basis of production. The agrarian question in this view is essentially restricted to the transition problematic.
2. Peasants are a backward social force incapable of revolutionary consciousness. Even newly dispossessed peasants entering the working class are backward in their consciousness and yearning for an idyllic rural past.
3. Peasants are essentially a dying social class and their ruin is inevitable. They can coexist with capitalist agriculture, though subject to "adverse incorporation." However, their continued existence is based on a "self-exploitation" and the acceptance of a "subhuman level of existence."

As stated earlier, a major blind spot in discussions on the agrarian question is how the real movement of Indigenous people, peasants, the racialized, and the dispossessed is "denaturalizing" dispossession, transition, and the agrarian question. On a global scale, landless peasants, Indigenous people, farmers, and agricultural workers are at the forefront of struggles to protect the environment, over climate breakdown, and against a new wave of dispossession by extractive capital. It is the real movement of these social categories in their quest for emancipation that has placed questions of ecology, the agrarian question, and alternatives to capitalism as new social questions for our time. Arguably, it is within these struggles that eco-socialist thinking as a concrete alternative emerged, and women often play a leading role. Capitalist social relations do not resolve or render the agrarian question obsolete, because its basis is also beyond the ambit of political economy (Neocosmos 2016). Oppression, patriarchy, racism, (settler) colonialism, expropriation, exploitation, planetary destruction of the environment—the "wicked ways of the structure of capitalism" (Linebaugh 2023)—are all consequential in rethinking the agrarian question, its urban dimensions, and the alternatives beyond capitalism.

A focus on the real movement of people and the planetary ecological crisis is increasingly compelling scholars and agrarian social movement activists to call into question the prospects for successful land and agrarian transformation within a neoliberal capitalist framework. What these scholars and activists propose is an anticapitalist agrarian-change framework that at a minimum should be based on "human needs, social equity and participatory democracy" (Jacobs 2012, 178). At the heart of the agrarian question is the political question of class struggle (Shivji 2009) for anticapitalist agrarian change by working people and oppressed groups. This question has, with a few notable exceptions (Xu 2018; Borras 2020; Shivji 2009; Moyo and Yeros 2005; Moyo, Jha, and Yeros 2015), received scant attention from academics, if not taken entirely off their research agenda. Most academic scholarship has reduced the agrarian question to an analysis of the structures of political economy, capitalist relations in agriculture, and class differentiation, paying little attention to the political consequences of their approaches and entirely avoiding alternatives to capitalism. As Harriet Friedmann so eloquently put it, scholarship on the agrarian question has simply been reduced to the sociology of capitalist transition, whose political implication is simply that a "capitalist future is better than barbarism" (Friedmann 2016, 678).

The findings of this chapter recast the agrarian question centrally as a political, social, and ecological question for anticapitalist social change, consisting of

- the expropriation, exploitation and oppression of rural and urban classes,
- the democratization of rural and urban social relations,
- the nature and form of the multiple transitions within and beyond capitalism,
- the classes or social forces emerging out of these ongoing transitions—the class composition of the countryside and cities, the role of the different classes in the struggles within and beyond capitalism;
- the material-ecological basis for noncapitalist alternative futures that will restore a sustainable metabolism and the type of state (democratic self-governance) and forms of social organization that are required; and
- the struggles (real movement of people) to return common resources to collective ownership (associations) and the movement toward the abolishing labor (value production) as a transitional basis for alternatives to capitalism (Jacobs 2019, personal communication; Neocosmos 2016; Shivji 2009).

This provides us with a more productive theoretical framework to examine the agrarian question as both an urban and a rural "question" and their mutual interactions. It raises a further question—that is, who are the agents of social change in the twenty-first century? Issa Shivji (2009) implores us to get back to basics, or the agrarian question proper: "Agrarian questions need to be addressed, analysed, and understood so as to discover the agency for social change and transformation in Africa" (86) and beyond.

In relation to urban areas with rapid urbanization and deindustrialization, my research is pointing to the potential social forces for anticapitalist agrarian change in both rural areas and urban areas. The political salience of the "unresolved agrarian question" (Neocosmos 2016, 296) remains an important arc of struggle for large sections of the rural and urban populations, Indigenous people, and other oppressed racialized social groups. Capitalist social relations in the countryside and cities do not resolve the agrarian question, but they do alter its contours. "Peasants" and "workers" remain central to the agrarian question, but in the twenty-first century they are often embodied within the same laboring class, household, and/or individual in urban (but also rural) areas. Moreover, the agrarian question is both an urban question and rural question; it is shaped by relationships between the urban and the rural. Historically, we saw the importance of these rural-urban linkages, which described the role played by rural landless people in radicalizing the urban occupiers. The urban component is becoming an important part of the rural-urban agrarian struggles.

Eric Wolf (1987) identified the middle-peasant and the migrant labor with ties to the countryside and cities as the most radical and revolutionary forces in the twentieth-century peasant rebellions (see also Drew 1996; Löwy 2010). In South Africa, for example, circular peasant migrants played a seminal role in the countryside peasant revolts in the 1960s and in labor-community struggles in the city. Today, however, I find that it is the poorer section of urban labor, those with dual proletariat and peasant social characteristics, and the stagnant surplus population, particularly women, who are at the forefront of urban agrarian struggles and a politics of repossession. To be sure, the middle layer of the latter class was instrumental in leading the initial occupations of land at my fieldwork sites in Cape Town, subsequently drawing broader layers of the laboring classes into the occupation landscape. In the twenty-first century, we are seeing that the social agents of anticapitalist agrarian change in both urban and rural areas include the semi-proletarian, nonproletarian, and relative surplus populations, Indigenous, racialized, and oppressed groups. In this urban context the urban dimension of the agrarian question has to incorporate the issue of land for housing, which appears to be intractable across the global South and North. Land for housing and land for agricultural livelihoods are not mutually exclusive (Araghi 2000), often, these demands are found in the same space or next to each other. The massive ongoing wave of rural-to-urban migration, as well as migration of the rural poor to towns in rural areas, is further combining the land question (housing and agriculture) in these spaces in interesting ways.

By reclaiming part of the city for agricultural livelihoods, the land occupiers are breaking down the boundaries between rural and urban and the sphere of production and social reproduction. The real existing struggles of the land occupiers open up new fields of possibilities and point us to alternative trajectories of agrarian transformation beyond capitalism.

Rethinking Emancipatory Alternatives to Capitalism

Rethinking emancipatory alternatives beyond capitalism is another component that receives limited focus within critical agrarian studies. Emancipatory alternatives in this context entail the historical investigation of noncapitalist agrarian communal forms and contemporary communal social experiments that resist capitalist globalization. A new body of scholarship attentive to an open Marxism highlights Marx's studious investigation of noncapitalist agrarian communal social forms, such as the Russian mir, the Indigenous societies of the Americas, the Kabyile revolt (communal property) in Algeria, North Africa, and the urban Paris Commune, as the real movement resisting capital and producing alternatives to capitalism (Tomba 2019; Linebaugh 2023; Hudis 2023; Jeong 2016; Sumida 2021). Contemporary urban land occupations, Indigenous struggles against environmental destruction at Standing Rock, and urban agricultural communal social experiments allow us to examine and "grasp the anticipatory character of these struggles within capitalism and the possibility of transcending it (Basso 2015). By occupying land for food production and housing, the occupiers call into question the sanctity of existing private property based on labor commodity production, instead point to the importance of noncapitalist use values. "Social property as a practice and the democratic use of common resources" through communal holding based on use rights, as well as the obligations of users to the land through labor, is brought to the forefront (Tomba 2023, 80; Otani 2018).

Through their independent self-organization land occupiers are making an important paradigmatic shift, moving toward the social property from below, where use rights are transferred in some instances by democratically elected self-governing bodies. Policymakers and agrarian movements could learn from the paradigmatic shift visible in the daily practice of these land occupations and social experiments. Though the abolition of private property is a necessary but not sufficient basis to transcend capitalism, it remains an important step in a context where gendered, class-based, racialized environments and spaces of domination are continually reproduced by the logic of capitalism.

A massive redistribution of land will immediately transform the racialized and class power relations in the countryside and urban areas, as the case of Zimbabwe demonstrates. This "land redistribution from below" path has strong political salience, especially in the context of continuing entrenched racialized and class power structures, at both the national and global levels. In relation to the return of the means of production, Marx wrote, in the preamble for the program of the French Parti Ouvrier, or Workers' Party: "The productive class will emancipate all human beings without distinction of sex or race. They can be free only by possessing the means of production collectively. This must be accomplished by revolutionary action which may include universal suffrage as an instrument of emancipation rather than deception. The aim is he political and economic expropriation of the capitalist class and the return to community of all the means of production" (quoted in Linebaugh 2023, 91).

As capitalist globalization continues to deepen the metabolic rift between humans and nature, the commune as a political form, whether urban or rural, becomes as strong point of resistance against the power of capital. Agrarian reconfiguration in urban spaces gives rise to an *urban ecological politics and the creation of an urban agrarian ecological commons* that are consequential in the restoration of the urban social metabolism. In an embryonic mold, this presents us with *a transitional form with progressive possibilities*, particularly by providing "equal access to the means of (re) production," and serves as a starting point for configuring new social relations based on nonalienated labor as an alternative form (Hudis 2023). Despite the vast changes in the communal form wrought by capitalist globalization, the co-presence of different temporal forms is important for understanding the form of class struggle in the current conjuncture. As the Japanese Marxist Ryuji Sasaki (2021a) cautions: "No matter how far the power of capital penetrates society it is not able to eliminate local communities, traditional cultures, and ecological practices that people have built up over long period of time. In this sense, today's social movements still have lessons to learn from Marx's view of the power of premodern elements to resist capital" (167).

However, we need to be attentive to the extent to which this communal social form is an inclusive form of democracy with a much more expansive conception of class and class struggle. At a bare minimum, it should include the different forms and expressions of the peasantry, surplus populations, women, Indigenous communities, racialized social categories, and sexual minorities, the so called "non-class elements" (Sasaki 2021b) that constitute the basis of class and class struggle today. Within the currents of intellectual and academic Marxism, the form in which class struggle is expressed is often mistakenly categorized as identity politics, or pejoratively, as agrarian populism. In the countryside this should also include farm workers, who are often neglected in discussions on agrarian transformation (a key weakness in the Zimbabwean land occupation movement, as noted by Walter Chambati [2013]). The unprecedented 2012 farm-worker strike in South Africa (Wilderman 2015) further shows that the land and agrarian question is more than just a "peasant" question; it is an important part of labor and agrarian struggles in the twenty-first century. Urban land occupations for agricultural livelihoods and the urban agrarian commune as a political form are essential signposts indicating the way toward alternative trajectories beyond capitalism.

Conclusion

The chapter has attempted to uncover the processes of urbanization, class formation, and agrarian change, particularly the co-presence of classes from different temporal social formations in urban spaces. In the twenty-first century, amid an intensified ongoing wave of rural and urban land dispossession, urbanization without industrialization, and the massive expansion of surplus populations, we should also expect a new wave of urban and rural "land wars" or rebellions.

This new wave of urban and rural "land wars," however, will have a markedly different class character and focus than the twentieth-century peasant wars described by Eric Wolf (1969). Multilayered urban classes—including what I have called an "urban proletariat with peasant characteristics" (Jacobs 2018), or what Moyo and Yeros (2005) and Yeros 2023 called a generalized semi-proletariat will be an important part of these rebellions. This requires a new comparative research agenda whose goal is to construct a "historically specific totality" that incorporates into the analysis an understanding of both the general processes of capitalist development and historical specificity, along with a research agenda that is grounded in agency from below and that takes seriously the self-activity and independent self-organization of subaltern classes.

The analysis of the urban land occupations for agricultural livelihoods and urban agrarian communes as a political form to resist the power of capital lays the groundwork for further comparative research on the "agrarian in urban space" across the global South. Methodologically, it calls for research that is attentive to constructing comparisons in ways that are sensitive to historical specificity and are "open-ended," or to what Kevin B Anderson calls a "universality with contradiction" (Anderson 2018). Along these same lines, it calls for research that is attentive to *within* site differences, as the dislocations and disruptions of daily life and livelihoods caused by capitalist development fall with differential weight and effect according to race, class, ethnicity, sexuality, and gender. To arrive at a truly "universal" picture, or a theoretical framework with universal ambitions, requires a theory of mediation between what Mafeje (1973) characterized as the "historical specific totality" and the "historical general totality." This provides us with a rigorous tool for studying the unfolding national, regional, and global patterns of the agrarian in urban space and urban agriculture as direct and indirect resistance to capitalist globalization, as well as tools to transform the world. As Daniel Bensaïd (2021, 56) puts it, paraphrasing Marx, we need to "change the world before it crushes us," aptly capturing the stakes involved in the twenty-first century.

Notes

1. Mamdani (1996) in *Citizen and Subject* calls it the "rural in the urban," referring to migrant labor in South African cities.
2. In volume one of *Capital*, Karl Marx, referring to a crisis in Italian urban centers toward the end of the fifteenth century, states: "The urban workers were driven en-masse into the countryside, and gave a previously unheard-of impulse to small-scale cultivation, carried on in the form of market gardening." Today examples would be the MST (Landless Workers' Movement) in Brazil or the land occupation movement in Zimbabwe.
3. See McClintock and Simpson (2014) for a survey of urban agriculture in the US and Canada; and Bowness and Wittman (2021) for a discussion of Canada.

4. Albeit, middle classes that are unable to survive on their salary and resorting to farming to supplement their income.
5. For an excellent survey of the agrarian debate see, Akram-Lodhi and Kay 2010 (part 1) and Akram-Lodhi and Kay 2010 (part 2).

References

Akram-Lodhi, A. Haroon, and Cristóbal Kay. 2016. "Back to the Future? Marx, Modes of Production and the Agrarian Question." In *Critical Perspectives on Agrarian Transition: India in the Global Debate*, edited by B. B. Mohanty, 43–66. New York: Routledge.

Akram Lodhi A. Haroon and Kay, Cristóbal. 2010. "Surveying the agrarian question (part 1): unearthing foundations, exploring diversity." *The Journal of Peasant Studies* 37 (1): 177–202. doi: 10.1080/03066150903498838.

Akram Lodhi, A Haroon, Dietz, Kristina, Engels, Bettina, and MacKay Ben M (eds). 2021. *Handbook of Critical Agrarian Studies*. Edward Elgar Publishing. https://doi.org/10.4337/9781788972468.

Akuno, Kali. 2023. "Build and Fight: The Program and Strategy of Cooperation Jackson." In *Jackson Rising Redux: Lessons on Building the Future in the Present*, edited by Kali Akuno and Matt Meyer, 12–55. Oakland: PM Press.

Alarcon, P., Eric M. Fèvre, P. Muinde, M. K. Murungi, S. Kiambi, J. Akoko et al. 2017. "Urban Livestock Keeping in the City of Nairobi: Diversity and Production Systems, Supply Chains, and Their Disease Management and Risk." *Frontiers in Veterinary Science* 4:171.

Anderson, Kevin B. (1995) 2022. *Lenin, Hegel and Western Marxism: A Critical Study*. Leiden: Brill.

Anderson, Kevin. 2018. "Marx at 200: Beyond Capital and Class Alone." *Economic and Political Weekly* 53, no. 40 (October): 33–39.

Araghi, Farshad. 2000. The great global enclosure of our times: Peasants and the agrarian question at the end of the twentieth century. In *Hungry for Profit: The Agribusiness Threat to Farmers, Food, and the Environment*, edited by Magdoff Fred, Buttel Frederick H, and Foster John Bellamy, 145–160. New York: Monthly Review Press.

Arrighi, Giovanni. 1998. "Capitalism and the Modern World-System: Rethinking the Nondebates of the 1970's." *Review (Fernand Braudel Center)* 21 (1): 113–129.

Arrighi, Giovanni, Terence K. Hopkins, and Immanuel Wallerstein. 1989. *Anti-systemic Movements*. London: Verso.

Arrighi, Giovanni, and F. Piselli. 1987. "Capitalist Development in Hostile Environments: Feuds, Class Struggles, and Migrations in a Peripheral Region of Southern Italy." *Review (Fernand Braudel Center)* 104 (4): 649–751.

Arruza, Cinzia, and Patrick King. 2020. '"Class Struggle Is Not a Game': Daniel Bensaïd's Relational Conception of Class." *Século XXI* 10 (1): 21–44.

Atuahene, Bernadette. 2020. "Predatory City." *California Law Review* 108 (107): 107–182. https://doi.org/10.15779/Z38NS0KZ30.

Balakrishnan, Sai and Gururani, Shubhra. 2021. "New Terrains of Agrarian–Urban Studies: Limits and Possibilities." *Urbanisation* 6 (1): 7–15. https://doi.org/10.1177/24557471211020849.

Basso, Luca. 2015. *Marx and the Common: From "Capital" to the Late Writings*. Leiden: Brill.

Benya, Asanda. 2015. "The Invisible Hands: Women in Marikana." *Review of African Political Economy* 42 (146): 545–560.

Batubara, Bosman, and Rachman, Noer Fauzi. 2022. "Extended Agrarian Question in Concessionary Capitalism: The Jakarta's Kaum Miskin Kota." *Agrarian South: Journal of Political Economy*, 11 (2): 232–255. https://doi.org/10.1177/22779760221095121.

Bensaïd, Daniel. 2002 [1995]. *Marx for Our Times. Adventures and Misadventures of a Critique*. London and New York: Verso.

Bensaïd, Daniel. 2021. *The Dispossessed: Karl Marx's Debates on Wood Theft and the Right of the Poor*. Minnesota: University of Minnesota Press.

Bernstein, Henry. 2006. "Is There an Agrarian Question in the 21st Century?" *Canadian Journal of Development Studies* 27 (4): 449–460.

Bernstein, Henry. 2009. "Agrarian Questions from Transitions to Globalization." In *Peasants and Globalization: Political Economy, Rural Transformation and the Agrarian Question*, edited by A. Haroon Akram-Lodhi and Cristóbal Kay, 239–261. London: Routledge.

Borras, Saturnino M., Jr. 2020. "Agrarian Social Movements: The Absurdly Difficult but Not Impossible Agenda of Defeating Right-Wing Populism and Exploring a Socialist Future." *Journal of Agrarian Change* 20 (1): 3–36.

Bowness, Evan and Wittman, Hannah. 2021. Bringing the city to the country? Responsibility, privilege and urban agrarianism in Metro Vancouver. *The Journal of Peasant Studies* 48 (6): 1141–1166. doi: 10.1080/03066150.2020.1803842.

Brenner, Neil. 2016. "The Hinterland, Urbanized?" *AD / Architectural Design*, July–August, 118–127.

Brenner, Neil. 2019. *New Urban Spaces: Urban Theory and the Scale Question*. New York: Oxford University Press.

Brenner, Neil, and Christian Schmid. 2015. "Towards a New Epistemology of the Urban?" *City* 19 (2–3): 151–182. doi:10.1080/13604813.2015.1014712.

Byres, Terence. J. 2016. "In Pursuit of Capitalist Agrarian Transition." *Journal of Agrarian Change* 16 (3) (July): 432–451.

Callinicos, Alex. 2014. *Deciphering Capital: Marx's Capital and Its Destiny*. London: Bookmark.

Chambati, Walter. 2013. "The Political Economy of Agrarian Labour Relations in Zimbabwe after Redistributive Land Reform." *Agrarian South: Journal of Political Economy* 2 (2): 189–211.

Davis, Mike. 2004. "Planet of Slums: Urban Involution and the Informal Proletariat." *New Left Review* 26 (March–April): 5–34.

Drew, Allison. 1996. "The Theory and Practice of the Agrarian Question in South African Socialism, 1928–60." *The Journal of Peasant Studies*, 23 (2–3): 53–92. doi: 10.1080/03066159608438608.

Dwyer, Peter, and Leo Zeilig. 2012."Social Movements and the Working Class in Africa." In *African Struggles Today: Social Movements since Independence*, edited by Peter Dwyer and Leo Zeilig, 18–49. Chicago: Haymarket Books.

Engels, Frederick. 2009 [1845]. *The Condition of the Working Class in England*. Oxford World Classics. Oxford University Press.

FAO, IFAD, UNICEF, WFP, and WHO. 2022. *The State of Food Security and Nutrition in the World 2022: Repurposing Food and Agricultural Policies to Make Healthy Diets More Affordable*. Rome: FAO. https://doi.org/10.4060/cc0639en.

Foster, John Bellamy, and Bret Clark. 2020. *Capitalism and the Ecological Rift: The Robbery of Nature*. New York: Monthly Review Press.

Friedmann, Harriet. 2016. "Commentary: Food Regime Analysis and Agrarian Questions: Widening the Conversation." *Journal of Peasant Studies* 43 (3): 671–692. doi:10.1080/03066150.2016.1146254.

Ghosh, Swarnabh, and Ayan Meer 2021. "Extended Urbanisation and the Agrarian Question: Convergences, Divergences and Openings." *Urban Studies* 58 (6): 1097–1119. doi:10.1177/0042098020943758.

Ghosh, Swarnabh. 2022. "In what sense ruralization?" *Dialogues in Human Geography* 12 (2): 208–212. https://doi.org/10.1177/20438206221102947.

Gillespie, Tom. 2016. "Accumulation by Urban Dispossession: Struggles over Urban Space in Accra, Ghana." *Transactions of the Institute of British Geographers* 41: 66–77.

Gripper, Ashley B., Rachel Nethery, Tori L. Cowger, Monica White, Ichiro Kawachi, and Gary Adamkiewicz. 2022. "Community solutions to food apartheid: A spatial analysis of community food-growing spaces and neighborhood demographics in Philadelphia." *Social Science & Medicine* 310 (115221): 1–9.

Gripper, Ashley B. 2020. We don't farm because it's trendy; we farm as resistance, for healing and sovereignty: Farming is not new to Black people. https://www.ehn.org/black-farming-food-sovereignty-2645479216.html.

Guendel, Sabine, co-ord. 2002. *Peri-urban and Urban Livestock Keeping in East Africa: A Coping Strategy for the Poor?* Scoping study. Commissioned by the Livestock Production Programme (LPP). UK Department for International Development (DFID), London.

Gururani, Shubhra. 2020. "Cities in a world of villages: agrarian urbanism and the making of India's urbanizing frontiers." *Urban Geography* 41 (7): 971–989. https://doi.org/10.1080/02723638.2019.1670569.

Harootunioan, Harry. 2015. *Marx after Marx: History and Time in the Expansion of Capitalism*. New York: Columbia University Press.

Harriss-White, Barbara. 2021. "India's Non-metropolitan Agrarian Urbanisation and Urban Agrarianisation." *Urbanisation* 6 (1): 104–112. doi:10.1177/24557471211019863.

Helliker, Kirk, Bhatasara, Sandra, Chiweshe, and Manase Kudzai. 2021. *Fast Track Land Occupations in Zimbabwe: In the Context of the Zvimurenga*. Cham: Springer.

Hendricks, Fred, Lungisile Ntsebeza, and Kirk Helliker. 2013. Land Questions in South Africa. In *The Promise of Land: Undoing a Century of Dispossession in South Africa*, edited by F. Hendricks, L., Ntsebeza, and K. Helliker, 1–23. Jacana Media.

Hudis, Peter. 2023. Introduction. In Critique of the Gotha Program, by Karl Marx, with a new introduction by Peter Hudis, Translated by Kevin B. Anderson and Karel Ludenhoff, 1–40. Spectre Classics. Oakland, CA: PM Press.

Jacobs, Peter. 2012. "Whither Agrarian Reform in South Africa?" *Review of African Political Economy* 39 (131): 171–180. doi:10.1080/03056244.2012.658720.

Jacobs, Ricardo. 2018. "An Urban Proletariat with Peasant Characteristics: Land Occupations and Livestock Raising in South Africa." *Journal of Peasant Studies* 45 (5–6): 884–903.

Jacobs, Peter T. 2019 (Personal Communication, May, 20, 2019)

Jacobs, Ricardo. 2021. "Insurgent Working Class Self-Organization outside the Wage Labour Relation: Land and Livestock in the City." In *Labour Questions in the Global South*, edited by Praveen Jha, Walter Chambati, and Lyn Ossome, 387–411. Cham, Switzerland: Palgrave Macmillan.

Jeong, Sheongjin. 2016. Marx's Communism as Associations of Free Individuals: A Reappraisal. *Marx-Engels Jahrbuch* 2015 (1): 115–134. https://doi.org/10.1515/mejb-2016-0108.

Karatasli, Şahan Savaş. 2022. "Surplus Populations, Working-Class Struggles and Crises of Capitalism: A World-Historical Materialist Reconceptualization." In *Marxism, Social Movements and Collective Action*, edited by Adrian Piva and Agustin Santella, 207–250. Cham, Switzerland: Palgrave Macmillan.

Levien, Michael., Michael Watts, and Yan Hairong. 2018. "Agrarian Marxism." *Journal of Peasant Studies* (5–6): 853–883. doi:10.1080/03066150.2018.1534101.
Linebaugh, Peter. 2023. "Afterward: The Alternative to Capitalism in Marx's Critique of the Gotha Program." In *Critique of the Gotha Program*, by Karl Marx, with a new introduction by Peter Hudis, translated by Kevin B. Anderson and Karel Ludenhoff, 79–93. Spectre Classics, Oakland, CA: PM Press.
Löwy, Michael. 2010 [1981]. *The Politics of Combined and Uneven Development: The Theory of Permanent Revolution*. Chicago: Haymarket Books.
Mafeje, Archie. 1973. "The Fallacy of Dual Economies Revisited." In *Dualism and Rural Development in East Africa*, edited by R. Leys, 27–52. Institute for Development Research.
Mafeje, Archie. 1981. "On the Articulation of Modes of Production: Review Article. In "Anthropology and History." Special issue. *Journal of Southern African Studies* 8 (1) (October): 123–138.
Mafeje, Archie. 1985. "Peasants in Sub Saharan Africa." *Africa Development* 10 (3): 29–38.
Makki, Fuad. M. 2014. "Development by Dispossession: Terra Nullius and the Social Ecology of New Enclosures in Ethiopia." *Rural Sociology* 79:79–103.
Mamdani, Mahmood. 1996. *Citizen and Subject: Contemporary Africa and the Legacy of Late Colonialism*. Princeton, NJ: Princeton University Press.
Martin, Bill. 2013. "Living in a Theoretical Interregnum: Capital Lessons from Southern African Rural History." In *The Promise of Land: Undoing a Century of Dispossession in South Africa*, edited by Fred Hendricks, Lungisile Ntsebeza, and Kirk Helliker, 159–184. Auckland Park, South Africa: Jacana Media.
McClintock, Nathan. 2018. "Urban Agriculture, Racial Capitalism, and Resistance in the Settler-Colonial City." *Geography Compass* 12 (6): Article 12:e12373. https://doi.org/10.1111/gec3.12373.
McClintock, Nathan, and Mike Simpson. 2014. "A Survey of Urban Agriculture Organizations and Businesses in the US and Canada: Preliminary Results." Working paper. Portland State University, Toulan School of Urban Studies and Planning, Portland, OR. https://web.pdx.edu/~ncm3/files/PSU_UA_Survey.pdf.
McLees, Leslie. 2011. "Access to Land for Urban Farming in Dar es Salaam, Tanzania: Histories, Benefits and Insecure Tenure." *Journal of Modern African Studies* 49 (4): 601–624. doi:10.1017/S0022278X11000498.
Mezzadra, Sandro, and Brett Neilson. 2019. *The Politics of Operations: Excavating Contemporary Capitalism*. Durham, NC: Duke University Press.
Moyo, Sam, Praveen Jha, and Paris Yeros. 2015. "The Agrarian Question in the 21st Century." *Economic and Political Weekly* 1 (37) (September): 35–41.
Moyo, Sam, and Paris Yeros, eds. 2005. *Reclaiming the Land: The Resurgence of Rural Social Movements in Africa, Asia and Latin America*. London: Zed Books.
Napoletano, Brian. M., Jaime. Paneque-Galvez, Yadira. Mendez-Lemus, and Antonio. Vieyra. 2019. "Geographic Rift in the Urban Periphery, and Its Concrete Manifestations in Morelia, Mexico." *Journal of Latin American Geography* 18 (1): 38–64. https://link.gale.com/apps/doc/A581621771/AONE?u=googlescholar&sid=bookmark-AONE&xid=6d18078c.
Neocosmos, Michael. 2016. *Thinking Freedom in Africa: Towards a Theory of Emancipatory Politics*. Johannesburg: Wits University Press.
Ngwane, Trevor. 2021. *Amakomito: Grassroots Democracy in South African Shack Settlements*. London: Pluto Press.

Ollman Bertell, and Tony Smith, eds. 2008. *Dialectics for the New Century*. New York: Palgrave Macmillan.

Omobowale, Ayokunle Olumuyiwa, and Adefemi Abdulmojeed Adeyanyu. 2017. "Makoko Slum Settlement: Migrant Peasants on the Lagos Lagoon, Nigeria." In *Urban Revolt: State Power and the Rise of People's Movements in the Global South*, edited by Trevor Ngwane, Luke Sinwell, and Immanuel Ness, 51–66. Chicago: Haymarket Books.

Ossome, Lyn. 2021. "The Care Economy and the State in Africa's Covid-19 Responses." *Canadian Journal of Development Studies / Revue canadienne d'études du développement* 42 (1–2): 68–78. doi:10.1080/02255189.2020.1831448.

Otani, Teinosuke. 2018. *A Guide to Marxian Political Economy: What Kind of a Social System Is Capitalism?* Cham, Switzerland: Springer International.

Owens, Geoffrey Ross. 2016. "'We Are Not Farmers': Dilemmas and Prospects of Residential Suburban Cultivators in Contemporary Dar es Salaam, Tanzania." *Journal of Modern African Studies* 54 (3): 443–467.

Oya, Carlos. 2013. "The Land Rush and Classic Agrarian Questions of Capital and Labour: A Systematic Scoping Review of the Socioeconomic Impact of Land Grabs in Africa." *Third World Quarterly* 34 (9): 1532–1557.

Peša, Iva. 2020. "Crops and Copper: Agriculture and Urbanism on the Central African Copperbelt, 1950–2000." *Journal of Southern African Studies* 46 (3): 527–545. doi:10.1080/03057070.2020.1750872.

Petras, James, and Henry Veltmeyer. 2014. *Extractive Imperialism in the Americas: Capitalism's New Frontier*. Leiden: Brill.

Popkin, Barry M., Camila Corvalan, and Laurence M. Grummer-Strawn. 2020. "Dynamics of the Double Burden of Malnutrition and the Changing Nutrition Reality." *The Lancet* 395 (10217): 65–74. https://doi.org/10.1016/S0140-6736(19)32497-3.

Portes, Alejandro, and Kelly Hoffman. 2003. "Latin American Class Structures: Their Composition and Change during the Neoliberal Era." *Latin American Review* 38 (1): 41–82.

Ruel, Marie T., James L. Garrett, and Sivan Yosef. 2017. "Food Security and Nutrition: Growing Cities, New Challenges." In *2017 Global Food Policy Report*, 24–33. Washington, DC: International Food Policy Research Institute (IFPRI). https://doi.org/10.2499/9780896292529_03.

Sadomba, Zvakanyorwa Wilbert. 2013. "A Decade of Zimbabwe's Land Revolution: The Politics of War Veteran Vanguard." In *Land and Agrarian in Zimbabwe: Beyond White Settler Capitalism*, edited by Sam Moyo and Walter Chambati, 79–121. Dakar: CODESRIA and AIAS. https://publication.codesria.org/index.php/pub/catalog/book/74.

Safransky, Sara. 2017. "Rethinking Land Struggle in the Post Industrial City." *Antipode* 49 (4): 1079–1100.

Saito, Kohei. 2022. *Marx in the Anthropocene: Towards the Idea of Degrowth Communism*. Cambridge, UK: Cambridge University Press.

Sasaki, Ryuji. 2021a. *A New Introduction to Karl Marx: New Materialism, Critique of Political Economy, and the Concept of Metabolism*. Cham, Switzerland: Palgrave Macmillan.

Sasaki, Ryuji. 2021b. "The Theory of Class Struggle in *the Peasant War in Germany*." In *Reexamining Engel's Legacy in the Twenty-First Century*, edited by Kohei Saito, 25–44. Cham, Switzerland: Palgrave Macmillan.

Schindler, Seth. 2017. "Towards a Paradigm of Southern Urbanism." *City* 21 (1): 47–64.

Scoones, Ian. 2022. "The growth of urban agriculture in Zimbabwe". https://zimbabweland.wordpress.com/2022/06/27/the-growth-of-urban-agriculture-in-zimbabwe/.

Sevilla-Buitrago, A. 2015. "Capitalist Formations of Enclosure: Space and the Extinction of the Commons." *Antipode* 47 (4): 999–1020.

Shivji, Issa. G. 2009. *Accumulation in an African Periphery: A Theoretical Framework*. Dar Es Salaam: Mkuki na Nyota.

Siebert, Anne. 2020. "Transforming urban food systems in South Africa: unfolding food sovereignty in the city." *The Journal of Peasant Studies* 47 (2): 401–419. doi: 10.1080/03066150.2018.1543275.

Silver, Beverly J. 2019. "'Plunges into Utter Destruction' and the Limits of Historical Capitalism." In *Capitalism in Transformation*, edited by R. Atzmüller, B. Aulenbacher, U. Brand, F. Décieux, K. Fischer, and B. Sauer, 35–45. Cheltenham, UK: Edward Elgar Publishing. https://doi.org/10.4337/9781788974240.00008.

Sivaramakrishnan, Kalyanakrishnan. 2021. "Social Structures and Spatial Alignments of Agrarian Urbanisation." *Urbanisation* 6 (1): 113–122. https://doi.org/10.1177/2455747121 1016597.

Soriano, Carles. 2018. "The Anthropocene and the production and reproduction of capital." *The Anthropocene Review* 5 (2): 202–213. https://doi.org/10.1177/2053019617749260.

Sumida, Soichiro. 2021. "Engels and the Irish Question: Rethinking the Relationship between Peasants and Socialism." In *Reexamining Engel's Legacy in the Twenty-First Century*, edited by Kohei Saito, 215–236. Cham, Switzerland: Palgrave Macmillan.

Tomba, Massimilliano. 2013. *Marx's Temporalities*. Chicago: Haymarket Books.

Tomba, Massimiliano. 2023. "Social Property in the Cochabamba Water War, Bolivia 2000." *Angelaki, Journal of Theoretical Humanities* 28 (1): 73–86. https://doi.org/10.1080/09697 25X.2023.2167785.

Tomba, Massimiliano. 2019. *Insurgent Universality: An Alternative Legacy of Modernity*. New York: Oxford University Press.

Traverso, E. 2016. *Left-Wing Melancholia: Marxism, History, and Memory*. New York: University of Colombia Press.

Vergara-Camus, L. 2014. *Land and Freedom: The MST, the Zapatistas and Peasant Alternatives to Neoliberalism*. London: Zed Books.

Vergara-Camus, Leandro. 2012. "The legacy of social conflicts over property rights in rural Brazil and Mexico: Current land struggles in historical perspective." *The Journal of Peasant Studies* 39 (5): 1133–1158. doi: 10.1080/03066150.2011.653345.

White, Monic. M. 2018. *Freedom Fighters: Agricultural Resistance and the Black Freedom Movement*. Chapel Hill: University of North Carolina Press.

Wilderman, Jesse. 2015. "From Flexible Work to Mass Uprising: The Western Cape Farm Workers' Struggle." Working paper 4. SWOP, Society, Work and Development Institute, Johannesburg, South Africa, April. https://2b912727-9f2a-44dd-9a10-190714b850bf.filesusr.com/ugd/4e496b_4672cd0a5f0c4e549a5e091ba35d5771.pdf.

Wolf, Eric. R. 1987. "On Peasant Rebellions." In *Peasants and Peasant Societies*, 2nd ed., edited by Teodor Shanin, 367–374. Oxford, UK: Basil Blackwell.

Wolf, Eric. (1969) 1999. *Peasant Wars of the Twentieth Century*. Norman: University of Oklahoma Press.

Xu, Zhun. 2018. *From Commune to Capitalism: How China's Peasants Lost Collective Farming and Gained Urban Poverty*. New York: Monthly Review Press.

Yeros, Paris. 2023. "Generalized Semiproletarianization in Africa." *Indian Economic Journal* 71 (1): 162–186. https://doi.org/10.1177/00194662221146.

CHAPTER 22

CONTRACT FARMING, AGRIBUSINESS, AND LAND IN AFRICA

Empowering Farmers or Appropriating Resources and Value?

KOJO S. AMANOR

Introduction

Contract farming is usually defined as an arrangement between companies and farmers in which the farmer undertakes to produce a given volume and quality of a crop, and the buyer commits to purchase it at an agreed price. The buyer usually provides other services to the farmer as well, which may include the upfront delivery of inputs, seeds, mechanized services, credit, extension and training, and transport, among others. Contract farming is closely associated with the expansion of global agribusiness and the emergence of the vertical integration of production with processing and input industries (Lewontin 2000; Watts 1994; McMichael 2000). Contract farming is frequently part of a process of food governance whereby lead firms gain the ability to control, direct, and supervise the production of farmers. It often develops in the context of joint ventures and partnerships and the relations between the producers, processors, merchandizers, and input suppliers in a commodity chain. Contract farming arises out of both attempts to modernize peasant agriculture and the expansion of international agrarian capital into rural markets.

Contract farming is related to the land question in three distinct ways. Firstly, contract farming enables agribusiness corporations to engage in production without undergoing the complex procedures of acquiring and registering land in compliance with national legislation and restrictions on foreign ownership (Dinham and Hines 1983). This has recently led to the framing of contract farming as a potentially more inclusive way of transforming agriculture that does not involve marginalizing and dispossessing small farmers (Vermeulen and Cotula 2010). Secondly, contract farming is embedded in the wider structural relations of the commodification of land and productive resources and social differentiation (Watts 1994; Hall, Scoones, and Tsikata 2017). Although contract farming seeks to gain control over farmers' production without the alienation of their land, the organization of a competitive infrastructure frequently leads corporations to establish their own nucleus plantations, which alienates significant areas of land from smallholders. The promotion of agricultural commercialization by agribusiness also gives rise to medium-scale farmers, increased land purchases, and competitiveness, which often results in increasing the land pressures on smallholder farmers, more social differentiation, and a rise of farm debt, and pressures smallholders to exit from agriculture. Thirdly, contract farming results in the increasing capitalization of agriculture and puts pressures on farmers to invest in new costly input technologies. This results in the need for access to finances and collateral and creates pressure for more pervasive forms of land titling and the land titling of customary land, which also encourages the commodification of land and the rise of land markets and distress sales.

In recent years, venture capital has made large inroads into Africa, and microfinance is rapidly extending into rural farming areas and smallholder agriculture. As a consequence, new institutional arrangements are being created for farm credit, involving digital currencies and farmer and community organizations; these are being integrated with contract farming into new frameworks for agribusiness, which may be creating new forms of digital property. Combinations of approaches linking community participation and social capital, digital currencies, the digital surveillance of farmers, and microfinance are significantly redefining contractual relations between farmers and agribusiness. These are resulting in new and complex institutional arrangements. These developments also draw from approaches to community-based natural resource management and the contractual relations within the forestry sector, which include timber contracts, benefit sharing in environmental service provisioning, and corporate social responsibility. Although these new arrangements often go well beyond the confines of a formal written contract, the contract continues to be embodied in them, expressing a relationship between farmers, land, inputs, credit, standardization, processing, and market control. Many new actors are entering into agribusiness contracting, including nongovernmental organizations (NGOs), microfinance corporations, development banks, venture capitalists, and a host of intermediary agricultural traders and service providers. This has resulted in new alliances between transnational agribusiness, financial capital, and the state.

Contract farming is characterized by fluidity and transformation. To understand the transformations, it is useful to examine the history of contract farming, tracing the logic of its evolution. This is the approach adopted in this chapter, which traces the various elements of the organization of colonial commercial agriculture and international agribusiness that came together in the 1960s to define contract farming in Africa, and the subsequent development of agribusiness, contract farming, and food-chain governance following structural adjustment and market liberal reforms. The first section of the chapter summarizes recent debates on contract farming, focusing on the relationship between contracts, inequality, and access to land. The following section traces the colonial footprints on contract farming schemes within Africa and their transformation after independence as US multinational corporations began to make inroads into the African continent, reorganizing and privatizing input supplies and agriprocessing. This is followed by an analysis of the contribution of the forestry sector and community-based natural resources management in embedding contracts in a framework of community institutions, social participation, social capital, and civil society. The chapter then examines the impact of structural adjustment, the privatization of agricultural service provisions, and the rise of venture capital and microfinance on the recent development of contracts and its implications for land relations.

Contract Farming, Inequality, Benefit Sharing, and Access to Land

Contract farming is usually embedded in highly unequal relations between farmers and corporations, characterized by very high rates of extraction of value by corporations and control over the farming undertaken by family farms, smallholders, and medium-scale farmers (Lewontin and Berlan 1986; Clapp 1988; Watts 1994; Cohen, Vicol, and Pol 2022). Lewontin and Berlan (1986) estimate that agribusiness corporations gain about 40 percent of the value of agriculture through the provision of inputs to farmers, and 50 percent of the value through processing and marketing, leaving farmers with around 10 percent of the value of agriculture. Although farmers may maintain legal title to their land and other means of production under a contract farming arrangement, they lose control over the product of their labor and the means to determine their own production strategies. Thus, the appropriation of surplus value by corporations and inequality are central to contract farming.

Cohen, Vicol, and Pol (2022) argue that recent policy-oriented approaches are transforming the issue of inequality in contract farming. Originally, inequality in contract farming was seen as a deeply embedded problem. Currently, contracts are seen as solving the poverty of farmers by integrating them into "inclusive" markets. Contract farming has been proposed as a possible solution to land grabbing that will enable peasant farming to modernize and be incorporated into agribusiness, without the appropriation of their land by large-sale agricultural estates (Vermeulen and Cotula 2010). This position is usually accompanied by a new vision of contracting that embraces community participation, benefit sharing, and corporate social responsibility (Vermeulen and Cotula 2010; Djiré, Keita, and Diawara 2012). This is usually derived from models of community participation and civil society integration based on new institutional economics (Oya 2012; Ostrom 1990), inclusive participatory governance (Hickey and

Mohan 2004; Gaventa 2004), and community-based natural resource management (Brockington, Duffy, and Igoe 2008).

Benefit-sharing approaches assume that land grabbing is a recent phenomenon in Africa. In reality, there was considerable appropriation of land during the colonial period, particularly in southern, central, and east Africa; and international capital and corporations have a long history of involvement in African agriculture. Large-scale farm ventures and agricultural processing industries were well established by the 1950s and 1960s, involving both state and international agribusiness capital (Dinham and Hines 1983). Many of the early contract farming initiatives were based on the creation of large nucleus plantations surrounded by outgrowers, which resulted in significant appropriation of farmlands (Watts 1994). Nucleus plantations continue to be important in contract farming, undermining the claim that contract farming provides a radical alternative to land grabbing. Apart from directly appropriating land from specific farmers, nucleus estates also intensify land pressures on the remaining landowning farmers, because the dispossessed farmers look to purchase or rent land. Increasing pressures on land can also result in declining fertility, greater use of fertilizer and other inputs by farmers to compensate for the loss of fallow land, leading to debt and the further erosion of farmers' autonomy. Contract farming has been depicted as resulting in the proletarianization of farmers (Watts 1994; Clapp 1988; Lewontin 2000) in the sense that contracts and capital loans make farmers dependent on the directives of agribusiness. However, the high costs of inputs may also limit the abilities of smallholders to participate. This encourages the development of an entrepreneurial class of contract farmers made up of those who are able to invest heavily in new technologies and in land and create some economies of scale and increase their turnover to be more competitive. This also increases the pressures on small farmers, as land becomes increasingly transacted and rented out to medium-scale farmers and enterprises (Hall, Scoones, and Tsikata 2017; Isager, Fold, and Mwakibete 2022; Shonhe and Scoones 2022). The result is the increasing capitalization of agriculture on a technology treadmill, the taking on of more farm debt by small farmers, the exit of smallholders from agriculture, and the increasing domination of contract farming by wealthy entrepreneurial farmers with the capital to invest in inputs, seeds, and machinery, to the detriment of smallholders (Röling, 2008). Thus contract farming may be increasingly transformed into an activity for entrepreneurial rather than smallholder farmers.

Contract farming frequently facilitates the expansion of an entrepreneurial class of wealthy and medium-scale farmers and facilitates their investments in commercial agriculture. This includes an urban-based class that looks to accumulate the capital that often arises from savings within the trading and professional sectors (Oya 2012). Veldwisch and Woodhouse (2022) note the existence of many informal contracts between traders and farmers on irrigated plots in Mozambique. Entrepreneurial farmers and agricultural traders do not invest only in crop production; they also invest in an array of other services, including the provision of inputs, storage warehouses for farmers, and tractor services, among others. This has given rise to a wide range of intermediaries that provide these agribusiness services to farmers and integrate farmers into the agribusiness markets. These intermediaries are often linked into chains of capital that are ultimately derived from investments by transnational corporations and finance capital, and from attempts by these interest groups to kick-start commercial agriculture. Spadotto et al. (2021) have shown how various intermediaries in Brazil operate at the behest of international agribusiness to develop financial, input, processing, and land markets. The intermediaries facilitate the appropriation of land, establish national front companies for the international agribusiness, and create the political linkages to erode peasant farmers' customary rights to land and natural resources. These networks extend to multilateral financial institutions, including the World Bank and state organizations, all working together to gain control over agricultural production. It is therefore important to follow the linkages of contract farming from the rural localities into the international agribusiness circuits. In recent reflections on the development of the literature on contract farming, Little and Watts (2022) noted the recent proliferation of detailed case studies of contract farmers contextualized within state-farmer relations but also the lack of studies that place contract farming within the wider picture of the expansion of transnational agribusiness. Hence, it is important to explore the recent developments in contract farming in the context of the changing relations between transnational agribusiness, financial capital, and the state, rather than attribute patterns of social differentiation largely to elitist state policies and the rise of medium-scale farmers.

The growth of wealthy contract farmers has led Oya (2012) to question the viability of contract farming as an alternative to large-scale commercial farming for smallholder farmers. He argues that there is very little evidence that smallholders have been able to upgrade their production through contract farming; most of the significant accumulation by rising medium-scale farmers has taken place outside agricultural production—in trade and the savings of urban civil servants. Oya (2012) contends that the rise of agribusiness, supermarket chains, and agri-food chains (with the attendant quality controls, certification and grading systems, vertical integration, and just-in-time marketing) has raised the barriers to entry for smallholder farmers in contract farming, resulting in a declining in their participation in commercial outgrower linkages. However, Poulton, Dorward, and Kydd (2010) caution that the scale of supermarket expansion in Africa and its displacement of production by smallholder farmers should not be exaggerated; many export crop sectors, such as cotton, cocoa, tea, and coffee, which often involve outgrower relations, continue to be dominated by smallholders. Hall, Scoones, and Tsikata (2017) have also argued that contract farming occurs in a wide variety of conditions, where wealthy farmers dominate more capital intensive sectors, and poor smallholders who lack financial means depend upon loans provided in contract farming arrangements in less capital intensive sectors. Although there may be a decline in direct farming contracts between smallholder farmers and lead agribusiness corporations as suggested by Oya (2012), this reflects the huge expansion of agribusiness corporations into global concerns that operate with many levels of subsidiary companies. Contractual relations are managed by these intermediary organizations involved in service provisions, which closely monitor farmers' production and ensure that this meets the standards and regulations set by the lead corporations. Aside from regulating production and integrating farmers into commercial markets these intermediaries may also own large agricultural estates. Thus the structure of acquisitions of subsidiary companies and sub-contracting of food-chain governance to intermediary entities hides the prevalence of contract-farming and large-scale land acquisitions within the commodity chains of lead agribusiness corporations.

The increasing capitalization of farming also has ramifications for landownership. It has led to efforts at tenure reform that seek to facilitate and streamline land titling as a means of providing collateral for farm investment and security for corporations that advance capital to farmers. Many of the land tenure reforms of the last twenty years are concerned with extending land titling to customary land (Amanor 2019b; see Peters, this volume) and with facilitating land and rental markets to enable the redistribution of land from less efficient to more efficient farmers (World Bank 2008). Borras and Franco (2012) argue that recent changes in land use and property relations are grounded in market liberal models of governance, which reject social distribution and redistributive land reforms and favor the reconcentration of wealth. In the 1980s, the original debates underpinning administrative land reform that were taking place at the World Bank and other international institutions arose out of a concern with creating stable property rights that would facilitate foreign investors to acquire land and property rights. They were also concerned with enabling farmers to acquire collateral to invest in farm production and purchase commercial inputs (Bruce 1993; Bruce, Migot-Adholla, and Atherton 1993). In the context of contract farming, the commodification of land, and farmers' access to land titles and collateral create a greater scope for corporations to legally enforce contracts. Interest in secure land rights and contract farming did not emerge out of concerns for equality.

The Origins and Development of Contract Farming in Africa

Contract farming relations in Africa originated in the dynamics of integrating peasant farmers into export-crop production under colonialism via large state development schemes. However, contract farming also emerged in Africa as a part of a particular coherent set of relations worked out by US agribusiness, which was exported abroad from the 1950s onward. In contrast with the earlier forms of contract farming in Africa, which developed in the context of state-led development, the US variants were private sector agribusiness initiatives that sought to build networks of commercial agricultural service providers that were interested in expanding their markets. This eventually gave rise to the notion of the value chain as an instrument of food governance, replacing state regulation. A third major influence on outgrower relations arose in the forestry sector, which has been important in embedding contractual relations within frameworks of community participation. This section explores the development of outgrower relations in these three sectors and the ways in which these have given rise to a sphere of community participation that is increasingly shaped by liberal market governance reforms.

Evolution of Contract Farming within the African Agricultural Sector

Colonial indirect rule or *association* (in Francophone territories) created an independent peasantry involved in the production of cash crops. This peasantry was, however, subject to corvée labor, taxation, and economic coercion to cultivate export crops (Amin 1972; Suret-Canale 1971). This resulted in an alliance between colonial authorities and traditional authorities that constituted the bedrock of colonial indirect rule, resulting in a political structure that Mamdani (1996) characterizes as "decentralised despotism." Coercion was justified as arising out of custom and the rights of traditional rulers to service from their subjects. Colonial agriculture policies were concerned with maintaining peasant export production as the most viable means of supplying European markets with cheap staple commodities, at minimum cost to the colonial administration. This came to be seen as a more viable and cost effective solution to export-crop production than supporting settler Europeans and their need for wage labor and expropriated land (Cowen and Shenton 1996).

Although independent African smallholder cultivation became the dominant form of export-crop production, the colonial regimes expressed much concern about the backwardness of Africa's agriculture and the need for modernization in the areas under indirect rule (Phillips 1989). This led to the eventual development, in the late 1920s, of large state-agricultural schemes directed by the colonial administrations, including the Gezira Scheme in British Sudan and the Office du Niger in French West Africa. These laid the foundations for the emergence of the large state- and quasi-state-controlled agricultural schemes of the 1950s, particularly those of the British Colonial Development Corporation, which attempted to build linkages between modern mechanized agriculture and community-based production and began exploring contractual relations with farmers (Cowen 1984; Cowen and Shenton 1996).

Following independence, the long history of accumulation by colonial agricultural corporations and the desire of the newly independent African states to develop agricultural modernization projects resulted in joint ventures in which contract farming arrangements became significant (Dinham and Hines 1983). International agricultural corporations provided contractual services to governments to modernize their agricultural infrastructure, and governments provided services to farmers in exchange for the right to market their crops and determine their production strategies. For instance, international corporations have developed irrigation infrastructure on land that governments had expropriated for national development, and the governments released this land back to farmers provided they agreed to cultivate particular crops and sell them to the project-marketing agency (Watts 1994; Botchway 1993). This built upon the traditions of modernizing agriculture created by the large colonial development schemes of the late 1930s to 1950s. Alternatively, where governments sought to limit the land acquisitions and operations of the multinational corporations or to nationalize foreign acquisitions from the colonial period, the multinational corporations became hesitant to invest in large estates, fearing state nationalization of their assets. This also resulted in the expansion of contract farming and joint ventures to reduce the insecurity and uncertainty of direct investment in land (Dinham and Hines 1983). During the early independence period, contract farming became important in the context of states' promotion of agricultural modernization through programs that continued to develop the mantle of the Office du Niger and the Gezira project and to rely on Western expertise. The Commonwealth Development Corporation—formerly the Colonial Development Corporation—played a significant role in promoting the expansion of contract farming in Africa after independence (Glover and Kusterer 1990).

In the early independence period contract farming and the enticements of loans and access to inputs and land were used by the state to encourage farmers to adopt the state's vision of agricultural modernization and its control over agricultural markets. However, there have been problems with implementing and enforcing contracts. This has been reflected in *side selling*—the diversion of crops away from the contracting agency when its prices are lower than in other markets—and in the diversion of inputs from contracted crops to other food crops (Poulton, Dorward, and Kydd 2010). There have also been problems in recruiting household labor for contract farming and with gender tensions arising when women have not been involved in the drawing up of the contract but are expected to work on their husbands' plots. Thus women have often voiced opposition to contract farming (Carney 1988; Botchway 1993).

By the 1980s, with the introduction of structural adjustment, many African states were pressured by international financial institutions to privatize state agricultural enterprises, resulting in a significant shift in contract farming to private sector initiatives, and the expansion of international agribusiness into African markets. This has resulted in the development of new models of contract farming that are rooted in the expansion of US agribusiness into global markets and the rise of market reforms in Africa.

US Agribusiness and the Technology Treadmill

The second important influence in the development of contract farming originates in the expansion of US agribusiness into a global system. Lewontin (2000) argues that the most significant transition in US agriculture in the twentieth century has been the rise of the agri-food system and the movement of capital from farm production to control over the supply of inputs, seeds, and machinery to farmers and over the processing and retailing of food. As a consequence, the value of farm production within the food system has declined from around 40 percent of total agricultural value at the beginning of the twentieth century to around 10 percent at the end of the century. Contracts became important in enabling farmers to purchase expensive machinery and inputs (in relation to the value of their outputs) and in developing the vertical integration of the input and output market components of the food system. Lewontin (2000) argues that contract farming redefined the position of the farmer within the agri-food system to that of provider of labor and land, while the corporations provided capital inputs. In effect, this allowed the corporations to take control of the decision-making process in farming and establish governance over food production.

These developments result in a *technology treadmill* (Cochrane 1979; Lewontin 2000; Röling 2008)—when farmers expend increasing resources on acquiring new technology, but the increases in productivity are accompanied by falling prices and profits. The increased competitiveness of agricultural markets and price squeezes force farmers to adopt new technology or exit agriculture. Those who continue to farm do so in an increasingly competitive environment with falling profit margins (Halweil 2002).

As US agribusiness expanded throughout the world, US farmers were forced to compete with new production zones in developing countries. This has led to a series of farm crises in the United States, beginning in the 1970s, in which thousands of farmers have been forced out of agriculture (Vogeler 1981; Buttel 1989), resulting in serious rural stagnation. According to the US Census Bureau, over fifty million Americans in rural areas are caught in a cycle of increasing stagnation characterized by high poverty, dwindling economic opportunities, persistent population decline, and falling migration to urban areas or other sectors (Partridge 2020). Thus, the agribusiness technology treadmill results in a worldwide problem of impoverishment among growing numbers of rural people and an exit from agriculture, including in the global centers of capitalist agriculture.

Contract farming facilitates the participation of farmers in the treadmill by advancing them capital to purchase inputs. But it also results in the increasing absorption of surplus value by agribusiness. One of the major concerns in expanding contract farming in developing countries is that it will replicate the technology treadmill and promote the uptake of inputs by more farmers (Röling 2008). The expansion of US agribusiness into a global system has effectively embedded contract farming in a system of mergers and takeovers and acquisitions. Because large transnational corporations have expanded their operations throughout the world, they no longer directly engage in either large estate production or contract farming; they do both through subsidiaries and platforms that contract many aspects of production out to third parties. This frequently links financial services with the provision of inputs and market services in African rural settings, within the framework of building value chains and more effectively capturing markets.

Contracts and Community Participation in Forestry

A third important influence in contract farming has emerged from the promotion of community forestry in natural resource management. Community forestry originated under colonial indirect rule, which empowered Africa's traditional rulers to gazetteer forest reserves, gain royalties from forest products, and enact environmental bylaws. The *taungya* system was also introduced into many African colonies as a contractual relation between their Forestry Department and land-hungry farmers in the vicinity of forest reserves, whereby the farmers were provided access to land for food crop cultivation in exchange for their labor in planting and managing timber trees among their crops. By the 1970s, commercial timber corporations and some large agricultural estates in southern Africa had begun investing in timber plantations and developing outgrower schemes with landowners to cultivate timber. The companies provide the farmers with technical assistance and upfront loans taken out against the future value of the timber (Chamshama et al. 2009). There was a major expansion of capital investments into timber plantations, wildlife, and ecotourism beginning in the 1980s, as under market liberalization, governments sought to open up state forests and wildlife parks to international capital (Benjaminsen and Bryceson 2012; Moyo 1994). The infusion of international capital into these sectors also resulted in attempts to incorporate smallholders into the arrangements. For instance, in Zimbabwe, the Communal Areas Management Programme for Indigenous Resources (CAMPFIRE) promoted the commercial use of woodlands in communal areas. It expanded the terrain of commoditized natural resources by building contractual linkages with the tourism and wildlife industries, embracing NGOS, international capital, White commercial farmers, and small Black businesses (Moyo 1994).

A variety of contractual forms between corporations, intermediaries, and farmers have developed in the forestry sector. In some instances, corporations contract and support individual outgrowers and community associations to plant and supply them with timber in the future. A second variation involves landowners leasing their own land to a timber corporation for timber production, which may involve land-lease payments or a share of the profits. A third form involves a community leasing its land to a corporation in a benefit-sharing arrangement, usually a very small portion of corporate profits. A fourth form involves contracts between community groups and timber corporations and the environmental certification of a community group or association by an internationally accredited third party. A fifth variant involves communities providing environmental services, including biodiversity conservation, watershed protection, or carbon storage for which they receive payments from the government and conservation organizations. A sixth arrangement involves corporate social responsibility, where a corporation provides social welfare and infrastructure projects in return for access to the resources of a community. And a seventh form involves joint ventures and partnerships between state agencies, communities, and the private sector in which communities provide land and labor, and the corporations provide capital, with equity sharing arrangements (Chamshama et al. 2009; Mayers and Vermeulen 2002), including modern variants of *taungya* system (Acheampong et al. 2016).

Natural resource management projects have expanded notions of contractual relations with farming groups into broader frameworks of community participation. In francophone West Africa during the economic recession of the 1980s, the *gestion de terroir* approach to natural resource management gained prominence. It sought to fill the gaps left by the declining reach of the state in a period of economic crisis by providing rural development initiatives and environmental services. It recruited villagers to manage their lands by formally recognizing the legal rights of a community to manage its territory, by mapping out village lands, and creating management contracts in which producers provided environmental services in return for the recognition of these rights. A team of technical officers from various state departments was responsible for mobilizing the villagers and devising a management contract for the village group to implement. However, the process could also lead to the marginalization and denial of the rights of groups outside of the management contract, such as pastoralists and migrant settler farmers (Guèye and Laban 1992; de Haan 1998).

Many of these community natural resource management projects involve embedding the recognition of rights in land and resources in a complex framework of contractual obligations, which can be coercive and exploitative. For instance, Fay (2008) characterizes the restitution of the Dwesa-Cweba forest reserve in South Africa to its original owners as a form of "civil subjugation." This contract provided nominal rents to the communities, enabled tourism and wildlife corporations to commercially exploit the forest resources, and prevented the "owners" from farming, collecting forest products, and establishing residential properties on their land. Benjaminsen and Bryceson (2012) analyze similar developments in Tanzania, which they depict as "green grabbing," a form of dispossession in which rural community members continue to hold rights in land, while the benefits from the land and natural resources are privatized and controlled by large corporations. Brockington, Duffy, and Igoe (2008), Southgate (2006), and Homewood, Trench, and Brockington (2013) report similar developments in other parts of East Africa. In the West African Sahel, Ribot (1999) argues that community participation has devolved a limited set of rights to communities that are associated with the planting of trees, while ensuring that an overwhelming proportion of the surplus value created in the villages is absorbed by a handful of urban merchants, who, through a state licensing system, are able to control the trade in charcoal. The licenses effectively exclude smallholder farmers from trading in charcoal beyond the village. Chiefs who had been co-opted by urban traders into their commodity chains of charcoal delivery were selected by the state to represent the communities, resulting in participation without genuine representation (Ribot 1999). In Cameroon, community forestry has resulted in negligible gains for community members who were recruited into community groups, and most of the value is absorbed by forestry corporations and the chiefly and elite interests that dominate and control the process of formation of community groups (Brown 1999; Kenfack Essougong, Foundjem-Tita, and Minang 2019).

Natural resource management projects have been important in embedding benefit-sharing and contractual arrangements within notions of community development and participation (World Bank 2016). However, this notion of community obfuscates processes of social differentiation and conflicting interests in rural areas, and the inclusive business models often appropriate control over particular resources that are alienated from community use without dispossessing communities of their claims to land title. These inclusive business models are often embedded in complex contractual and institutional arrangements, governance reforms, and civil society initiatives that create new opportunities for private investment in rural markets.

Contract Farming and Market Liberalization

The introduction of market liberal reforms and opening up of national markets to foreign investment that began the 1980s led to both the rapid expansion of agribusiness throughout the world and the growth of civil society initiatives. The rapid expansion of agribusiness was achieved through mergers and acquisitions. Agribusiness corporations moved into new sectors and gained access to new technology and monopoly control over markets through the acquisitions of companies rather than acquisitions of land and plantations. Perhaps the most spectacular instance of this in Africa was the aggressive takeover of the Ivorian cocoa industry by Cargill, Barry Callebaut, and Archer Daniels Midland (ADM) in the 1990s, which gave them control of over 60 percent of global cocoa processing because Côte d'Ivoire then produced around 50 percent of total world production (Losch 2002; Amanor 2020). Nevertheless, agribusiness has been selective in its investments, focusing on the most promising national sectors and states that are willing to invest in infrastructure and create the most favorable market opportunities for agribusiness (World Bank 2008). This intensifies the technology treadmill and tends to erode farmers' profit margins.

Since the 1990s donors have funded NGOs that provide agricultural services in sectors where the private sector has been reluctant to invest, to enable the process of economic liberalization of state enterprises to maintain momentum. For instance, the removal of agricultural subsidies resulted in higher prices for inputs that were prohibitive, resulting in a decline in the use of fertilizers and certified seeds by farmers. In several African countries the NGO Global 2000, an initiative of the Jimmy Carter and Sasakawa Foundations, began distributing subsidized input packages and loans to farmers to try to stimulate the uptake of inputs by farmers (Plucknett 2004). Selective agribusiness investments in only the most profitable sectors have also enabled African states to continue to intervene in the agricultural sector. However, given the limited access to international finances for state enterprises and donor pressure to roll back the state sector, state enterprises have been reconstituted as autonomous and semiautonomous corporations with commercial mandates. State agencies have also developed joint partnerships with local businesses and international corporations to gain control over smallholder production and interventions into input supplies and processing.

Many public-private partnerships build upon the outgrower relations that were established by state enterprises during the 1970s, extending them into networks of commercially oriented service providers that are intent upon extracting profits from the reorganization of food commodity chains. They include input suppliers, food processors and distributors, and banks. For instance, in Ghana, networks that were involved in the state's provisioning of inputs during the 1970s, reconstituted themselves as a private corporation, Wienco, which in the 1990s emerged as the largest input supplier (Amanor 2019a). As the commercial rice sector collapsed in the 1980s, a new relationship developed between the Ghana Irrigation Development Corporation, Wienco, private rice processing and distribution corporations, and the Ghana Agricultural Development Bank (ADB). ADB financed the provision of inputs to farmers; private rice distributors entered into contractual relations with farmers to provide loans for the purchase of inputs that were distributed by Wienco; and ADB provided the capital for the loans and paid farmers for the rice they delivered to the rice distributors after deducting the cost of the loans (Dannson et al. 2004). Thus, contract farming was adapted and embedded within the new networks arising out of the processes of economic liberalization.

A second type of arrangement involved the reconstitution of state corporations as semiautonomous commercial institutions and the development of partnerships with international financial organizations. For instance, in Kenya in 2009, the Kenyan Tea Development Agency reconstituted its outgrower sector as Greenland Fedha Limited, a semiautonomous microfinance institution mandated to work with smallholder farmers and train them in modern "sustainable" methods of tea production and "financial literacy." Greenland Fedha has provided more than 105,000 farmers, cultivating over 100,000 hectares of tea, with loans. It is supported by IDH (the Sustainable Trade Initiative), a Dutch development foundation; the Dutch development bank FMO (Entrepreneurial Development Bank); and Unilever and works with the Rainforest Alliance to gain international certification.[1]

Similar linkages also occur between the state, private corporations, and NGOs. The NGOs become directly responsible for the provision of marketing services by linking farmers and corporations through outgrower contracts (Kindness and Gordon 2001). They also assume the responsibility for training farmers to honor their contractual obligations in "business relations" and "financial services," and frequently create farmer associations and market linkages with private corporations For instance, in Uganda, the Agribusiness Development Centre (an NGO) established a bean outgrower scheme with the Uganda National Farmers Association and the Buganzi Export Commodities Limited. The procured beans were sold to a Kampala-based exporter (Kindness and Gordon 2001).

These types of relationships also exist between large transnational corporations and international NGOs, with the NGOs providing training and extension in agricultural production, organizational support, and business and financial-management training. Other components related to sustainable development, gender equality, quality control, and certification may be added. For instance, CARE International works with both Cargill, on their Cocoa Promise program, and with Mondelez International, on their Cocoa Life program, in Cote D'Ivoire and Ghana to mobilize communities for improved cocoa production. Their interventions are concerned with providing better access to agricultural inputs, encouraging adoption of good farming practice through better extension, strengthen farmer organizations, and increase access to financial loans and financial services.[2] In Kenya and Uganda the NGO Technoserve works with Coca Cola and the Gates Foundation to strengthen farmers' agricultural and business skills (Jenkins and Fries 2013). The US NGO ACDI/VOCA (American Co-operative Development Initiative and Volunteers in Co-operative Assistance) also specializes in linking farmers with large agribusiness corporations, as in its Smallholder Agribusiness Development Project in Malawi, which builds farmer associations and links them with commercial credit providers, inputs providers, and processors (Kindness and Gordon 2001). In Ghana ACDI/VOCA promotes the uptake of Dupont Pioneer seeds by farmers, with funding from USAID (Guyver and MacCarthy 2011). These initiatives often work with variants of contract farming involving advanced loans of inputs and control over the marketing of produce.

A recent development involves the embedding of outgrower contracts within the warehouse receipt system, a form of inventory credit. This involves a tripartite agreement between a bank, a trader, and a warehouse operator. The trader uses an existing stock of food crop stored in a warehouse as collateral for a bank loan. The crop must meet certain verifiable criteria related to quality, grades, and standards (often verified by a third party). The trader uses the loan to acquire additional stocks of food crop and must settle all the warehouse costs before the grain is removed (Kindness and Gordon 2001).

The warehouse receipt system works through digital receipts of stocks of food stored in a warehouse, which can be used by both the warehouse owner and the farmer as collateral for loans. These stocks of food are graded and subjected to price differentials and certification by a third-party certification. This encourages farmers to increase their quality of production and storage, and may also be used to influence the particular crop varieties planted and the cultural practices of production. The warehouse receipt system uses electronic transactions through mobile phones, which enable individual farmers to be tracked through their mobile footprints. It has enabled collateral to be established as digital receipts, representing the value of stocks of food stored in a warehouse that can be presented to banks for loans (Brand 2017). It facilitates loans to farmers for improved production that are recorded in mobile phone transactions and automatically deducted from the value of farmers' food stocks. The warehouse receipt system is often conceptualized within an outgrower business model; the warehouse functions as an outgrower warehouse, supplying farmers with inputs, seeds, tractor ploughing services, grading and assuring quality control of produce; engaging in forward buying contract relations with buying firms, and capitalizing warehouse receipts with financial service providers to develop contracts with farmers (Kolavalli, Mensah-Bonsu, and Zaman 2015; Brand 2017; Kindness and Gordon 2001). The warehouse receipt system has become significant in both Ghana and Kenya, and linkages between NGOs, agribusiness, inputs suppliers, and farmers are increasingly becoming embedded within inventory credit. In both countries, Grain Councils, rooted in civil society governance structures, certify warehouses, introduce regulations, facilitate the dissemination of information, and encourage increased use of commercial seeds and inputs production (Kolavalli, Mensah-Bonsu, and Zaman 2015; Brand 2017; Bashuna 2020). Thus, the warehouse receipts system transforms contract farming by embedding it within digital currencies and electronic collateral and a formal institutional governance structure based on linkages between the state, civil society, and commerce.

Financial Services and Downstream Linkages

Financial services have become increasingly involved in contract farming in recent years. Their function has been to facilitate the incorporation of contract farming into supply chains involving lead firms, input suppliers and processors. The results is that microfinance companies play a significant role in the food supply chain, supervising contract farming arrangements alongside NGOs, and undertaking farmer training and institutional development. This has enabled the expansion of downstream linkages, pushing commercial food chains deeper into rural communities through networks of input dealers, agricultural service providers, and large farm estates, all of which receive financial support to become the hubs of outgrower schemes and commercial agricultural supply chains.

KfW (the German Development Bank) plays a significant role in kick-starting new agribusiness ventures with outgrower relations. In Ghana it has funded private commercial corporations to develop outgrower relations with surrounding communities. One of its most interesting investments has been with the Global Agri-Development Company (GADCO), an international rice-growing corporation that acquired a 5,000-hectare concession and a processing mill in the Volta Region of Ghana. GADCO has been praised for developing a highly refined form of community participation, based on gender sensitivity and inclusive business models. GADCO entered into agreements with communities to provide them with 2.5 percent of corporate profits and forty-five irrigated outgrower plots of land for community members. However, Lanz, Prügl, and Gerber (2020) argue that, far from being an exemplary model of equitable development, the GADCO initiative has undermined the economic interests of the rural poor. Community participation was largely limited to the chiefs as the representatives of the community, and gender participation was with women of the noble lineage. The appropriation of land for the project "was not originally planned but was realized gradually as the company and chiefs advanced their own narrow interests without consultation of affected populations" (Lanz, Prügl, and Gerber 2020, 536). Most of the land allocated to the company by the chiefs was agricultural land that was used by migrant communities and common land used mainly by women. Neither group received any compensation for their loss of land. After the irrigation infrastructure was completed, the irrigated plots were allocated to members of the chiefly lineage, effectively resulting in the appropriation of the land of the marginalized within the community. Having established a nucleus estate and a rice-processing mill, GADCO expanded its outgrower schemes, developing an alliance with Wienco to expand into other areas of the Volta Region in which Wienco provided inputs to farmers and GADCO controlled their rice outputs. Subsequently, RMG Concept, an African subsidiary of Syngenta, one of the largest transnational agribusiness corporations in the world, has acquired both GADCO and the agrochemical division of Wienco, which includes farmer associations that Wienco originally set up with Yara, the second-largest fertilizer producer in the world (Amanor 2019a). Thus, the development of downstream linkages, community participation, and "ethical" land transaction has effectively resulted in the appropriation of the land of the rural poor by agribusiness.

Similarly, in the Ashanti Region of Ghana, the World Bank has provided loans to the paramount chief of Juaben (*Juabenhene*) to establish a large oil palm plantation, with a mill and outgrower relations. During the 1980s the *Juabenhene* acquired a divested state oil palm mill with his own private capital and also invested in a rural bank. His creation of the outgrower scheme has placed many of his subjects in an uneasy position. They feel compelled and coerced into participating as outgrowers (Berry 2013; Arhin Brempong and Pavanello 2006), because the National Constitution of Ghana recognizes the chiefs as allodial owners of the land and vests only user rights in the farmers.

Conclusion

Contract farming in Africa occurs alongside the expansion of international agribusiness. It is frequently associated with rising inequality and social differentiation. This inequality is intrinsic to agribusiness: it should not be seen as arising solely from internal factors and elitist state policies that are corrupting and deflecting the lofty ideals and exemplary business practices of Western corporations. The fact that growing inequality, impoverishment, and stagnation are endemic in rural areas of the United States shows that they are a both a global trend and a product of the competitive environment of agribusiness.

Contract farming relations continue to be important among African smallholders and central to the development of agricultural input supply chains. However, these contracts are often mediated by NGOs, microfinance companies, venture capitalists, warehouses, input distributors, medium-scale commercial farmers, commercial farming companies, tractor service providers, wholesale food traders and processors, state organizations, and farmer associations, all recruited by lead firms and international financial corporations. The lead firms "dictate the terms of participation to their immediate suppliers" and "make them the gatekeepers to participation in the value chain" (Kolavalli, Mensah-Bonsu, and Zaman 2015, 1). The lead firms determine the distribution of value among the networks of service providers and farmers. The lead agribusiness corporations are no longer concerned with the appropriation of agricultural estates, because they have gained control of entire food sectors through takeovers and mergers of state and private corporations, which include the agricultural estates created by the historical appropriation of land. Since the process of market liberal reforms has rejected any social redistribution of land in favor of market-based reforms (Borras and Franco 2012), the privatization of state agricultural assets has tended to reallocate and concentrate them in commercial circuits under the control of international agribusiness rather than address historical inequalities. The increasing involvement of medium-scale farmers and smaller corporations in the expansion of agribusiness networks into rural hinterlands has deep and long-term implications for land appropriations, particularly when these agents are deeply involved in land acquisition and asset accumulation.

Contemporary acquisitions of land are increasingly subtle and veiled; the transnational corporations frequently appropriate resources and the control of resources, while leaving formal ownership in the hands of communities (Benjaminsen and Bryceson 2012). They often achieve this under the guise of community participation, particularly where customary authorities have been co-opted into the process of capturing resources from the rural poor, and in the name of sustainable development. Hence, notions of community-based land administration, corporate social responsibility, and progressive benefit-sharing—which have become entangled in the lexicon of contract farming relations—need to be subjected to critical analysis and unpacked, as Lanz, Prügl, and Gerber (2020) have deftly done in the case of GADCO. The claims of communities and individuals to formal ownership do not necessarily amount to much, since the recognition of ownership can lead to "civic subjugation" (Fay 2008) or the impoverishment of large numbers of farmers as large transnational corporations gain multibillion-dollar turnovers of profits. Ultimately, the relationship between contract farming, agriculture, and landownership must be analyzed in the context of the distribution and control of value in the various food chain networks operating under the lead agribusiness firms.

Acknowledgments

I would like to thank the editors and anonymous reviewers for their very useful comments on an earlier draft.

Notes

1. See FMO Website Project Details. Greenland Fedha Limited. Status: Approved Investment. https://www.fmo.nl/project-detail/53705. Accessed April 20, 2023.
2. See Cocoa Life's Partners. https://www.cocoalife.org/the-program/partners. Accessed April 20, 2023.

References

Acheampong, Emmanuel, Thomas F. G. Insaidoo, and Mirjam A. F. Ros-Tonen. 2016. "Management of Ghana's Modified Taungya System: Challenges and Strategies for Improvement." *Agroforest Systems* 90: 659–674.

Amanor, Kojo S. 2019a. "Global Value Chains and Agribusiness in Africa: Upgrading or Capturing Smallholder Production." *Agrarian South: Journal of Political Economy* 8 (1–2): 30–63.

Amanor, Kojo S. 2019b. "Land Reform: Strengthening Customary Rights under Community Management." In *From Divided Pasts to Cohesive Futures: Reflections on Africa*, edited by Hiroyuki Hino, Arnim Langer, John Lonsdale, and Frances Stewart, 246–299. Cambridge, UK: Cambridge University Press.

Amanor, Kojo S. 2020. "Transnational Corporations, Financialization and Community Development in West African Cocoa." *Community Development Journal* 56 (1): 59–78.

Amin, Samir. 1972. "Underdevelopment and Dependence in Black Africa: Origins and Contemporary Forms." *Journal of Modern African Studies* 10 (4): 503–524.

Arhin Brempong, Kwame, and Mariano Pavanello. 2006. *Chiefs in Development in Ghana: Interview with Four Paramount Chiefs in Ghana*. Legon: Institute of African Studies.

Bashuna, Sabdiyo Dido. 2020. *Grain Hub Project: Enhancing Structured Grain Trade for Smallholder Farmers in Eastern Africa*. Completion report project no. 1381018 of the Eastern Africa Grain Council. Technical Centre for Agriculture and Rural Cooperation (CTA), Wageningen, The Netherlands.

Benjaminsen, Tor A., and Ian Bryceson. 2012. "Conservation, Green-Blue Grabbing and Accumulation by Dispossession in Tanzania." *Journal of Peasant Studies* 39 (2): 335–355.

Berry, Sara. 2013. "Questions of Ownership: Proprietorship and Control in a Changing Rural Terrain—A Case Study from Ghana." *Africa* 85 (1): 36–56.

Borras, Santurino M., Jr., and Jennifer C. Franco. 2012. "Global Land Grabbing and Trajectories of Agrarian Change: A Preliminary Analysis." *Journal of Agrarian Change* 12 (1): 34–59.

Botchway, Jack. 1993. "Implications of Farming and Household Strategies for the Organization of a Development Project." In *Cultivating Knowledge: Genetic Diversity, Farmer Experimentation and Crops Research*, edited by Walter de Boef, Kojo Amanor, Kate Wellard, with Anthony Bebbington, 27–34. London: Intermediate Technology Publications.

Brand, Nicole. 2017. *Using Digital Tools to Support Ghana's Smallholder Farmers: A Case Study of ADVANCE II*. Washington, DC: United States Agency for International Development. https://www.usaid.gov/sites/default/files/2022-05/ADVANCE_II_Case_Study_2.pdf Accessed April 15 2023.

Brown, David. 1999. "Principles and Practice of Forest Co-management: Evidence from West-Central Africa." European Union Tropical Forestry Paper 2. Overseas Development Institute, London. https://cdn.odi.org/media/documents/5688.pdf. Accessed July 5, 2022.

Brockington, Dan, Rosaleen Duffy, and Jim Igoe. 2008. *Nature Unbound: Conservation, Capitalism and the Future of Protected Areas*. London: Earthscan.

Bruce, John W. 1993. "Do Indigenous Tenure Systems Constrain Agricultural Development?" In *Land in African Agrarian Systems*, edited by Thomas J. Basset and Donald E. Crummey, 35–56. Madison: University of Wisconsin Press.

Bruce, John W., Shem E. Migot-Adholla, and Joan Atherton. 1993. "The Findings and Their Policy Implications: Institutional Adaptation or Replacement." In *Searching for Land Tenure*

Security in Africa, edited by John W. Bruce and Shem E. Migot-Adholla, 251–266. Dubuque, IA: Kendall/Hunt.

Buttel, Frederick H. 1989. "The US Farm Crisis and the Restructuring of America Agriculture: Domestic and International Dimensions." In *The International Farm Crisis*, edited by David Goodman and Michael Redclift, 48–83. London: Palgrave Macmillan.

Carney, Judith. 1988. "Struggles over Crop Rights and Labour within Contract Farming Households in a Gambian Irrigated Rice Project." *Journal of Peasant Studies* 15 (3): 334–349.

Chamshama, Shabani A. O., Francis O. C. Nwonwu, B. Lundgren, and Godwin S. Kowero. 2009. "Plantation Forestry in Sub Saharan Africa: Silvicultural, Ecological and Economic Aspects." *Discovery Innovation* 21 (3) Special Edition 1: 42–49.

Clapp, Roger. 1988. "Representing Reciprocity, Reproducing Domination: Ideology and the Labour Process in Latin American Contract Farming." *Journal of Peasant Studies* 16 (1): 5–39.

Cochrane, Willard W. 1979. *The Development of American Agriculture*. Minneapolis: University of Minnesota Press.

Cohen, Amy J., Mark Vicol, and Ganesh Pol. 2022. "Living under Value Chains: The New Distributive Contract and Arguments about Unequal Bargaining Power." *Journal of Agrarian Change* 22 (1): 179–196.

Cowen, Mike. 1984. "Early Years of the Colonial Development Corporation: British State Enterprise Overseas during Late Colonialism." *African Affairs* 83 (330): 63–75.

Cowen, Mike P., and Robert W. Shenton. 1996. *Doctrines of Development*. London: Routledge.

De Haan, Leo. 1998. "Gestion de Terroir at the Frontier: Village Land Management Including Both Peasants and Pastoralists in Benin." In *The Arid Frontier: Interactive Management of Environment and Development*, edited by Hendrik J. Bruins and Harvey Lithwick, 209–277. Boston: Kluwer Academic.

Dannson, Angela, Chuma Ezedinma, Tom R. Wambua, Bernard B. Bashasha, Johann Kirsten, and Kurt Satorius. 2004. *Strengthening Farm-Agribusiness Linkages in Africa*. Rome: Food and Agricultural Organization of the United Nations.

Dinham, Barbara, and Colin Hines. 1983. *Agribusiness in Africa: A Study of the Impact of Big Business on Africa's Food and Agricultural Production*. London: Earth Resources Research Publication.

Djiré, Moussa, Amadou Keita, and Alfousseyni Diawara. 2012. *Agricultural Investments and Land Acquisitions in Mali: Context, Trends and Case Studies*. London: International Institute for Environment and Development.

Fay, Derick. 2008. "Property, Subjection and Protected Areas: The 'Restitution' of Dwesa-Cwebe Nature Reserve, South Africa." In *The Rights and Wrongs of Land Restitution: "Restoring What Was Ours'*, edited by Derick Fay and Deborah James, 25–42. Abington, UK: Routledge-Cavendish.

Gaventa, John. 2004. "Towards Participatory Governance: Assessing the Transformative Possibilities." In *Participation: From Tyranny to Transformation? Exploring New Approaches to Participation in Development*, edited by S. Hickey and G. Mohan, 25–41. London: Zed Books.

Glover, David, and Ken Kusterer. 1990. *Small Farmer, Big Business: Contract Farming and Rural Development*. Basingstoke, UK: Macmillan Press.

Guèye, Ibrahima, and Peter Laban. 1992. "From Woodlots to Village Land Management in the Sahel." Dryland Networks Programme. Issue Paper No. 35. International Institute for Environment and Development, London.

Guyver, Patrick, and Mavis MacCarthy. 2011. "The Ghana Grains Partnership." *International Journal of Agricultural Sustainability* 9 (1): 35–41.

Hall, Ruth, Ian Scoones, and Dzodzi Tsikata. 2017. "Plantations, Outgrowers and Commercial Farming in Africa: Agricultural Commercialisation and Implications for Agrarian Change." *Journal of Peasant Studies* 44 (3): 515–537.

Halweil, Brian. 2002. "Farming in the Public Interest." In *State of the World 2002*, edited by Christopher Flavin, Hilary French, and Gary Garner, 51–74. New York: W. W. Norton.

Hickey, Samuel, and Giles Mohan. 2004. "Towards Participation as Transformation: Critical Themes and Challenges." In *Participation: From Tyranny to Transformation? Exploring New Approaches to Participation in Development*, edited by Samuel Hickey and Giles Mohan, 3–24. London: Zed Books.

Homewood, Katherine, Pippa C. Trench, and Dan Brockington. 2013. "Pastoralism and Conservation – Who Benefits?". In *Biodiversity Conservation and Poverty Alleviation: Exploring the Evidence for a Link*, edited by Dilys Roe, Joanna Elliott, Chris Sandbrook and Matt Walpole, 239–252. Chichester: John Wiley & Sons.

Isager, Lotte, Niels Fold, and Anne Mwakibete. 2022. "Land and Contract Farming: Changes in the Distribution and Meanings of Land in Kilombero, Tanzania." *Journal of Agrarian Change* 22 (1): 36–57.

Jenkins, Beth, and Lorin Fries. 2013. *Project Nurture: Partnering for Business Opportunity and Development Impact*. Cambridge, MA: The CSR Initiative at the Harvard Kennedy School.

Kenfack Essougong, Urcil P., Divine Foundjem-Tita, and Peter A. Minang. 2019. "Addressing Equity in Community Forestry: Lessons from 20 Years of Implementation in Cameroon." *Ecology and Society* 24 (1): 9. https://doi.org/10.5751/ES-10656-240109. Accessed July 5, 2022.

Kindness, Heather, and Ann Gordon. 2001. *Agricultural Markets in Developing Countries: The Role of NGOS and CBOs*. London: Natural Resource Institute, University of Greenwich.

Kolavalli, Shashidhara, Akwesi Mensah-Bonsu, and Saima Zaman. 2015. "Agricultural Value Chain Development in Practice: Private Sector-Led Smallholder Development." IFPRI Discussion Paper 1460. Washington, DC: International Food Policy Research Institute.

Lanz, Kristina, Elisabeth Prügl, and Jean-David Gerber. 2020. "The Poverty of Neoliberalized Feminism: Gender Equality, in a 'Best Practice' Large-Scale Land Investment in Ghana." *Journal of Peasant Studies* 47 (3): 525–543.

Lewontin, Richard C. 2000. "The Maturing of Capitalist Agriculture: Farmer as Proletarian." In *Hungry for Profits: The Agribusiness Threat to Farmers, Food, and the Environment*, edited by Fred Magdoff, John Bellamy Foster, and Frederick H. Buttel, 93–106. New York: Monthly Review Press.

Lewontin, Richard C., and Jean-Pierre Berlan. 1986. "Technology, Research and the Penetration of Capital: The Case of US Agriculture." *Monthly Review* 38 (3): 21–34.

Little, Peter D., and Michael Watts. 2022. "The Afterlife of Living under Contract, an Epilogue." *Journal of Agrarian Change* 22 (1): 197–206.

Losch, Bruno. 2002. "Global Restructuring and Liberalization: Côte d'Ivoire and the End of the Cocoa Market?" *Journal of Agrarian Change* 2 (2): 206–227.

Mamdani, Mahmood. 1996. *Citizen and Subject: Contemporary Africa and the Legacy of Colonialism*. Princeton, NJ: Princeton University Press.

Mayers, James, and Sonja Vermeulen. 2002. *Company Community Forestry Partnerships: From Raw Deals to Mutual Gains*. London: International Institute for Environment and Development.

McMichael, Philip M. 2000. "Global Food Politics." In *Hungry for Profits: The Agribusiness Threat to Farmers, Food, and the Environment*, edited by Fred Magdoff, John Bellamy Foster, and Frederick H. Buttel, 125–144. New York: Monthly Review Press.

Moyo, Sam. 1994. *Land Reform under Structural Adjustment in Zimbabwe*. Uppsala: Scandinavian African Institute.

Ostrom, Elinor. 1990. *Governing the Commons: The Evolution of Institutions for Collective Action*. Cambridge, UK: Cambridge University Press.

Oya, Carlos. 2012. "Contract Farming in Africa: A Survey of Approaches, Debates and Issues." *Journal of Agrarian Change* 12 (1): 1–33.

Partridge, Mark D. 2020. *Rural America's Stagnant Economic Performance: What's the Role of Declining Dynamism?* Report. American Enterprise Institute, Washington, DC. https://www.aei.org/research-products/report/rural-americas-stagnant-economic-performance-what-is-the-role-of-declining-dynamism/. Accessed April 3, 2022.

Phillips, Anne. 1989. *The Enigma of Colonialism: British Policy in West Africa*. London: James Currey.

Poulton, Colin, Andrew Dorward, and Jonathan Kydd. 2010. "The Future of Small Farms: New Directions for Services, Institutions, and Intermediation." *World Development* 38 (100): 1413–1428.

Plucknett, Donald L. 2004. "Africa: Global 2000 Extension Efforts in Africa." In *Revitalization within Public Sector Services: Case Studies of International Initiatives, Volume 4* , edited by William Rivera and Gary Alex, 34–41. Agricultural and Rural Discussion Paper 11. Washington, DC: World Bank Group.

Ribot, Jesse. 1999. "Decentralisation, Participation and Accountability in Sahelian Forestry: Legal Instrument of Political-Administrative Control." *Africa* 69 (1): 23–65.

Röling, Neils. 2008. "Conceptual and Methodological Developments in Innovation." In *Innovation in Africa: Enriching Farmers' Livelihoods*, edited by Pascal C. Sanginga, Ann Waters-Bayer, Susan Kaaria, Jemimah Njuki, and Chesha Wettasinha, 9–34. London: Earthscan.

Shonhe, Toendepi, and Ian Scoones. 2022. "Private and State-Led Contract Farming in Zimbabwe: Accumulation, Social Differentiation and Rural Politics." *Journal of Agrarian Change* 22 (1): 118–138.

Southgate, Christopher R. J. 2006. "Ecotourism in Kenya: The Vulnerability of Communities." *Journal of Ecotourism* 5 (1–2): 80–96.

Spadotto, Bruno R., Yuri M. Saweljew, Samuel Frederico, and Fábio T. Pitta. 2021. "Unpacking the Finance-Farmland Nexus: Circles of Cooperation and Intermediaries in Brazil." *Globalizations* 18 (3): 461–481.

Suret-Canale, Jean. 1971. *French Colonialism in Tropical Africa 1900–1945*. London: C. Hirst and Company.

Vermeulen, Sonja, and Lorenzo Cotula. 2010. *Making the Most of Agricultural Investment: A Survey of Business Models That Provide Opportunities for Smallholders*. London: International Institute for Environment and Development.

Veldwisch, Gert J., and Philip Woodhouse. 2022. "Formal and Informal Contract Farming in Mozambique: Socially Embedded Relations of Agricultural Intensification." *Journal of Agrarian Change* 22 (1): 162–178.

Vogeler, Ingolf. 1981. *The Myth of the Family Farm: Agribusiness Dominance in US Agriculture*. Boulder, CO: Westview Press.

Watts, Michael. J. 1994. "Life under Contract: Contract Farming, Agrarian Restructuring, and Flexible Accumulation." In *Life under Contract: Contract Farming and Agrarian Transformation in Sub-Saharan Africa*, edited by Peter D. Little and Michael J. Watts, 21–77. Madison: Wisconsin University Press.

World Bank. 2008. *World Development Report 2008: Agriculture and Development*. Washington, DC: World Bank.

World Bank. 2016. *World Bank Group Forest Action Plan FY16–20: The WBG Contribution to the Forest Agenda*. Washington, DC: World Bank. http://pubdocs. worldbank.org/en/190381459984535520/WBG-Forest-Action-Plan-FY16-6apr16-CODE.pdf. Accessed July 5, 2022.

CHAPTER 23

PUBLIC AUTHORITY, PROPERTY, AND CITIZENSHIP

What We Talk about When We Talk about Land

CHRISTIAN LUND

A Sense of Land

When we talk about land, there is tension between perspectives. From one vantage point, land breeds a range of affective connotations: home, sense of being, and the soil from which we are issued and to which we belong. From more singular and analytical perspectives, we could focus on how land is linked to production and the agrarian question (Akram-Lodhi and Kay 2010a,b; Peters 2004), or we could investigate the importance of land for consumption and distribution (Du Toit 2018; Ferguson 2013). This article discusses land as the fulcrum of the *institutions* that make up society's essential contract of rights and authority, property, citizenship, and rule. It investigates institutional perspectives on state and citizenship mediated by land. "Institutions" is not a discipline; it is a concept with wanderlust. It strides through economics, sociology, and political science, as well as anthropology, history, geography, and legal scholarship. The concept takes its hue from the discipline in which it is used. Yet there is a broad understanding that institutions are about rules and their organization, and about how these rules come about, reproduce, and change.

In advance of the analytical discussion of institutions, it is, nonetheless, useful to recapture the urgency and magnitude of the question of access to land on which the lives and livelihoods of so many people depend. Paradoxically, fictional accounts often provide the truest and most compelling descriptions of the complexity of land questions and their manifold implications. From the most intimate to the ambit of nations, land, and place animate emotions. The feelings of attachment and dejection caused by eviction are difficult to capture in the relatively impoverished language and syntax of scholarship. Literature, on the other hand, can capture the complexity and contrasts between life worlds and their destruction in change, between intimate relations and the greater powers of politics, struggle, and dramatic transformation of society. Books like *Things Fall Apart* (Achebe 2001), *Grapes of Wrath* (Steinbeck 1962), *Growth of the Soil* (Hamsun 2007), and *This Earth of Mankind* (Toer 1990), all show how life worlds and the connection between self and land are first strained and then shattered in the encounter with the juggernauts of colonialism, capitalism, and modernity. Labor and land become commodities; and alienation, the order of the day. This is not to romanticize the past or turn this text into a literary critique of any currency, but simply to introduce the following institutional analysis by reminding ourselves that when we talk about land, we do so in a contexture where even the most abstract notion of space, right, and governance has emotional, visceral, and sometimes subliminal, counterpoints in the hearts and guts of the people whose land—whose *ideas* of land—are at stake. It may be abstract, but it is also palpable; it may be theoretical, but it is also real.

Public Authority, Property, and Citizenship

Moving to institutional perspectives on land, it is productive to first establish how to understand the fundamental dynamics among public authority, property, and citizenship, and subsequently, to review some literature from each perspective in turn.[1] Treating public authority, property, and citizenship as finished product gets in the way of understanding them. They are always in the making. Moreover, they come about *through* each other; they are linked in ways where one always invokes the others. Hence, we need to know not just what they are, but also how they come about in conjunction. This is especially relevant in agrarian societies where the political authority and the status of individuals and groups are mediated by land. The political power to rule and access to livelihoods go through land control. Thus, the institutional relations between authority, property, and citizenship—in a broad sense and at all scales—are central to societal dynamics.

Property and citizenship are intimately related in their constitution. The core element of both is recognition. What is yours can only be yours as property through the presence—the existence—of others and their recognition of it as yours. Hence, property is different from mere access or possession by the recognition of powerful and credible institutions.[2] Similarly, social and political identity only exists through recognition by others. Hence, citizenship (and other degrees of status) is different from mere existence by the recognition of powerful and credible institutions. Thus, both property and citizenship are profoundly related to institutions for recognition.

However, no single institution defines and enforces rights and exercises public authority as such. Moreover, governance is not reserved for statutory institutions alone. The ability to govern can reside in institutions other than formal government. Statutory institutions (legislative, judiciary, and executive) may effectively govern, but it is more appropriate to treat this as an empirical question than a pre-established fact, and more productive to identify the *actual* authorities in semi-autonomous social fields of property and citizenship (Benda-Beckmann 1981; Moore 1978). Government institutions are not the only source of state effects, as it were.

Rights and authority are dialectically connected. The processes of recognizing claims to land and other resources as property and political identity as belonging work simultaneously to invest the institution that provides such recognition with the legitimation and recognition of its authority to do so. That is to say, the act of authorizing recursively authorizes the authorizer. These are the "contracts," so to speak, that link property and citizenship to political authority in society. Consequently, struggles over property and citizenship are as much about the scope and constitution of authority as about access to resources and membership in society (Lund 2016). To grasp the dialectics of rights and authority, we need to dispense with simple assumptions that political authority exists prior to rights of property and citizenship. Claims to rights are ways to invoke public authority and governing capacity in different institutions and prompt their exercise of authority, be they statutory or not. And conversely, a categorization of property and citizenship is a way to acquire and exercise public authority. Rights and public authority are contemporaneous, and the control exercised by institutions over resources and political subjectivities does not merely *represent* a preexisting authority; they also reproduce it.

In addition to their similar co-constitution with public authority, property in land and citizenship are often connected, one facilitating the other. To be a legal subject—to be visible to the law as a person with legal standing and rights—may seem self-evident to the well-endowed. However, historically, virtually all societies have treated large portions of their members as legal minors, with less than full rights, inferior status, and reduced capacity to own land and participate in political life. Women, serfs, "coloreds," children, immigrants, and the poor are just the beginning of a long line of human beings for whom the concern of legal standing is far from redundant, and "attributes such as gender, race, and caste, as well as class, creed, and conviction . . . allow . . . for more or less punch in a property claim" (Lund 2020, 8; see also Harris 1993; Pottage 2004; and Strathern 1999, who points out how the social productions or "persons" and "things" intertwine, and can become one another).

Let us move on to discuss some of the tensions and contrasts in each of these dimensions. A variety of works will bring out different facets of what we talk about when we talk about land.

Public Authority: Recognizing Claims as Rights

Institutions compete to control categorical distinctions. Hence *what* institution supports *which* claims as rights and, especially, *how* it does so—combine to constitute significant points of struggle. This becomes complicated when several competing normative and legal orders legitimize competing claims, and several groups and institutions compete over which of them has jurisdiction to settle disputes and establish norms. Often in such situations, therefore, public authority is challenged or completely fragmented by uneven interdependence, antagonistic collaboration, and fickle alliances between institutions. Statutory institutions compete among themselves and with institutions ranging from churches and associations to gangs and development projects that are all effectively trying to authorize and certify who has what right to what resource. This creates different opportunities for both the powerful and the powerless to seize. It is anything but a level field with certain outcomes.[3] In light of the huge variation in rules and institutions, it is all the more remarkable how relatively uniform the languages of law and bureaucracy are. Legalization and documents are therefore the starting points of this discussion.

Legalization

Just as public authority is not reserved for statutory institutions, so, too, is law not exclusively produced by official legislatures. However, law, as an institutionalized medium, a language, and a field of meaning, is coveted by people who are engaged in a struggle over land, and the desire to speak *in the name of law* seems ubiquitous among the motley crew of institutions engaged in land questions.

There are two main reasons for this. Law pledges to "secure state power backing for a claim in order to solidify it as a right that forces competing claims to dissolve. When a claim becomes a right, in theory, the cost and responsibility of its protection and enforcement shifts from the landholder to the state and its institutions" (Lund 2020, 4). Such a shift of responsibility allows landholders to redirect the resources and efforts of protecting land to other activities. This is attractive to companies and peasants alike. However, legalization holds a second attraction. Law *promises* some enduring predictability. This is especially attractive in situations of regime change when the established structures are challenged. Consequently, most landholders try to legitimate and legalize possessions as property by locking settlements into relatively tough and durable structures of recognition through legalization and reference to law. Indeed, law promises to take land claims safely through times of changing political fortunes as *rights* (Lund 2020, 4, 2022).

In this article, the term "legalization" broadly encompasses processes whereby particular rules, claims, or administrative operations are legitimated through reference to law as people understand it, regardless of whether a genuine correspondence between them and statutory law exists. The affinity between statutory law and legalization is often assumed and asserted but is not necessarily juridically accurate. The presumption of the legality of statutory law is often used to bestow an *air of legality* on a rule or claim. The legalization of property, therefore, is a successful persuasion that a claim to land and other resources is legal. Consequently, a rule's quality as law is not intrinsic to the rule itself but is something attributed to it in social and political interaction. This means that what effectively becomes law are the rules that are effectively sanctioned and justified by various authorities or communities *in the name of law* (Lund 2020, 6).

This makes spectacles of law and legalization central. And they tend to follow a script. To be sure, there are regional and other variations, but they can be seen as improvisations on the same theme: legitimation by reference to law and legalization by reference to the state. The most interesting literature often does not have a singular focus on law or land. Instead, it combines and embeds these questions in issues of the popular understanding of justice, imaginaries of state, bureaucratic practice, and ideas about the inevitability of private property and rule of law.[4]

Government Sign Language

The representations of land rights and citizen rights vary. However, official documents, including deeds; permits; ledgers; tax receipts; planning documents; maps of plot allocations and land use; certificates; contracts with paper stamps, letterheads, and signatures; and so on, constitute important props for state recognition and the representation of a right.

Ordinary people who find the proper legal and administrative avenues to be inaccessible often pursue varying forms of legalization through the production of counterfeit documents that have the appearance of genuine permits, deeds, and lease agreements. Such documents constitute a particular language of legal posturing, letting people and other actors enter the orbit of certain governing institutions and establish a potential "contract" of mutual recognition. Lease contracts, tax receipts, residence permits, construction permits, receipts for payment of public utilities—authentic, doctored, or outright fabricated—together with court rulings, political announcements, road signs, inaugurations attended by public officials, and even having the street names of your informal settlement appear on Google Maps, can all be mobilized as suggestive inferences of rights because they combine to make reference to the powers, imaginary or real, of the state (see Baitenmann 2005; Campbell 2015; Correia 2013; Feldman 2008; Ferrier 2012; Graeber 2015; Hetherington 2011; Hull 2012; Latour 2010; Mathur 2016; Nugent 2010; Sadiq 2009; Winichakul 1994). Even if the actual governing institutions are weak, such as starved statutory land offices or inexperienced movements occupying land, the representation of state recognition projects the idea of powerful durable definitude. Registration of citizens and their rights would seem to be a generalized feature of modernity (Breckenridge and Szreter 2010; Clanchy 2013; Dalberto and Banégas 2021; Mitchell 2000; Scott et al. 2002)—long in the making but persevering.

Let us now move on to what rights are established, legalized, and represented and how. We start with property in land.

Land Rights: Property

Property is profoundly relational. Let us look at the relations by briefly canvassing the substance of land rights, and the ways to represent them or make them visible. This will lead to the question of who is a legal subject.

Substance—Rights to What?

In legal scholarship there is a classical division between *ownership* of a resource and *rights* to it (Singer 2000; Praduroux 2017; Robilant 2013; Underkuffler 2003). Ownership, or freehold, is often regarded as having all the powers over a particular resource. The powers to use it, to exclude from it, and to transfer it at will without any interference from relatives, neighbors, or government, are firmly in the hands of the owner. There is, at the base of "ownership," a rather absolutist assumption of the sovereign *concentration* of powers, and a presumption about their *clear simplicity*.

In an alternative view to ownership, the totality of rights constitutes a proverbial "bundle," and each stick in the bundle represents a particular distinguishable right, so to say. In different societies, these elements are conceived differently according to cultural norms, institutional history, and production systems. But the metaphor is useful, for quite often, no single person controls all the rights in the bundle. For example, some may have a right to farm the land, but others hold a right to graze it or glean from it after harvest. In addition to different access rights, there are often different and variable rights to transact them. Some people may, for example, have a right to farm the land but are not free to transact this right outside of their kin group. The metaphor of separate rights in a bundle allows us to inquire whether the grazing rights are as strong as the farming rights, for example, or is the momentary right of gleaning as secure as the more enduring right of farming? Does the *certainty* of a right correspond to its *extent* and its *duration*, so to say? Such perceptions of how (much) something belongs to somebody are not merely academic (Hall 2013; Shipton and Goheen 1992). They are at odds in real life, and the tension manifests itself in many daily situations. There is therefore a tug-of-war between one understanding of land ownership that presumes to concentrate most sticks of the bundle in the tight grip of the owner, and another understanding that separates out different rights among different land rights claimants.

Land itself is not property. Even if we often refer to land as the "thing," which is inherited, bought, owned, mortgaged, bequeathed, sold, or lost, it is not the land itself that is being transacted, but a set of rights to it (Gluckman 1965; Hohfeld 1913; MacPherson 1978; Rose 1994). What is transacted, is, therefore, quite often not the full totality of rights but a selection of them, even if there is a popular understanding that what changes hands is *all of it*. Most often what is sold is an *incomplete* bundle of rights. A seller sells the imperfect rights s/he has, and the new landholder or house owner will hold the land and house under similar conditions of legal imperfection and possible uncertainty and contention (Lund 2020, 129). Yet, it is tempting to conflate the palpable earthy space with the idea of a full entitlement. Typically, we talk about land ownership or property as if it covers all possible rights to the material space, and property and space become the same thing. There is often a reification where the property right becomes identified with the material thing in which rights are held (Strathern and Hirsch 2004). "This is my property," sounds simple but is, in fact, an obfuscation. "Freehold" and "bundles of rights" are therefore eloquent metaphors, but both sound clearer than they are (Robilant 2013). Freehold, unfettered and unencumbered by social obligations, is a fiction, almost an oxymoron. For freehold (or "any-hold") to work in a social context, it must be recognized by an authority or society, and the political and contingent nature of any such political authority is easy to overlook if we are blinkered by the "free" in hold (Rose 1998, 601). Similarly, the bundle metaphor can also lead us astray in our understanding of property. The notion of a bundle may give the impression that we are dealing with multiple equal rights. That is likely to be the exception, however. More often, some of the "sticks" in the bundle will be mere slivers, others slender staves, and others yet will be massive beams. They are neither equal in reach, duration, or recognition, nor are they always stable, equally certain, or neatly separable. Such reification—and commodification (Polanyi 1944)—of rights can be subtle and inadvertent, or quite deliberate. The outcome, however, is that the identification of the rights with the "thing" moves the understanding of *how* something belongs to someone, in the direction of ownership of a commodity: the idea of a distinct and integral thing, and an undivided, unfettered, integral right seem to correspond. While deceptive and inaccurate, this idea feeds popular understandings of property and its transaction. The point to be made at this stage is that these conceptions of entitlement are not simply more or less adequate analytical descriptions of reality; they are also forward-looking, proleptic, designs for claims to be hammered out in the process, in real time, with real consequences.

There has been a historical tendency for states and the powerful in society to promote the totalizing ownership model over a more distributed set of rights. A classic example is the enclosure of the commons between the 16th and 18th centuries in England described by Marx (1978: Ch. 27) and E. P. Thompson (1975). The landed classes enclosed and privatized large areas of common land. This land, which had served poor families for grazing and collection of firewood, was taken by the landed classes through manipulation of the law, by deception, and by force. Land was concentrated on fewer hands, and the peasantry was dispossessed.

Similar dynamics of concentration have occurred at all scales, from colonial policies of declaring all land in the colony for "property of the state," to much more recent land reforms in Africa in the late 20th century, for example. While these reforms aimed at securing property rights for the poor, they often assigned ownership to the male head of the household effectively dispossessing wives and children in the process (Bruce and Migot-Adholla 1994; Bryceson 1995).

The push for "clear" and "concentrated" rights still has its champions. De Soto (2000) identifies a range of real frustrations among landholders who hold land with the uncertainty of inadequate recognition and all the perils this entails. De Soto proposes that the solution is to *own outright*, but he mistakes the exclusivity of rights for the certainty of them. The extent and the certainty of rights are not the same. However, there is often a political and ideological move toward increased simplicity and exclusivity—from sticks toward ownership, as it were. Hence, people may be tempted to buy land from people who are not fully entitled to sell the full set of integral rights to it. The buyer may claim to buy more than the seller can legally or legitimately sell, and, sometimes, buyers are surprised once secondary right holders begin to appear. This is likely to precipitate a conflict of interpretation of the significance of the transaction, over how many "sticks" were actually sold, and what elements of the property are now in new hands; all of them or a single twig. Secondary right holders, thus categorized by culture, politics, or law, often lose out in this process. Even time-honored rights are, therefore, at risk especially if held by politically weaker groups.

In this ongoing struggle to convince the relevant public and authority of the rightfulness of a claim, people rely on representations of rights.

Representations—Making Land Rights Visible

Rights are immaterial; they are social, political, and legal conventions. Consequently, they depend on representations to be seen. Deeds, permits, contracts, surveys, maps, and other documents are used to record events, transactions, and rights. Documents are important reference points for state recognition of a variety of claims. In addition, outside of the document repertoire, physical markers in the landscape (hedges, fences, trees, ancestral graves, and so on) and performative acts (such as marches, inaugurations, festivals, and so on) also serve to document or commemorate historical use and future rights.

Many of the representations of rights are produced or validated by government and statutory institutions. Deeds, permits, and certificates are, ideally, issued by government institutions. But as pointed out by de Soto (2000), in many poorer societies, it is simply not happening, especially not for the poorer classes. Even if society has a constitution and laws that protect land rights, access to law and legal instruments may be reserved for the very few. In their work on law and society, Nonet and Selznick (2009) show how the legal infrastructure can be captured by an autocratic elite in society (see also Balibar 2007; Heyman 1999; and Nader 2009). Political control over legal institutions and rampant official discretion places the legal system outside the reach of the citizenry. Similarly, Holston (1991, 2008) shows how government institutions manipulate the law, while ordinary people are forced to create legality for themselves. This will resonate with many societies where the separation of powers exists on paper only. Consequently, people run the risk of being invisible to the law and deprived of rightful means of claiming their rights. Therefore, many revert to other arrangements. Not to act in illegality, but, on the contrary, to access what they believe is legally theirs. Briefly, we encounter several forms of improvisation, namely counterfeit, imitation, and indirect forms of recognition.

The option of counterfeit is generally the illegal production of deeds, contracts, and so on. In his work on the colonization of the Amazon, Campbell (2015) offers a very vivid example of how people made documents of land transactions, official deeds, government approvals, and maps, and how they cured and aged them. Once the forged land deeds were placed in a box with crickets, the insects would over time "chew about the edges of the falsified title and defecate on the papers, lending them an antique look" (62). Over time, the function of such documents can outweigh their fraudulence.

Similarly, there are many examples of people recording land transactions and transfers in the absence of government. Official language and crests are imitated to give credence to the document.[5] These imitations often represent actual facts, only they are not recorded by statutory authorities, leaving it to people themselves to register events (Lavigne Delville 2003).

If neither government, counterfeit, nor imitated recognition is within reach, people can resort to indirect recognition. In everyday situations, indirect recognition can perform important legal and political work. If people are unable to have land claims recognized, other claims may effectively perform the work. People improvise to present themselves and their claims in ways that are visible and meaningful to the appropriate institution of authority, as well as to a public for more general support. And sometimes such visibility can indirectly support a land claim. Maps, surveys, regulations, and written settlements (customary as well as statutory), memos, tax receipts, fines, permissions, and authorizations all form traces of decisions peppering the political field as actual and potential reference points for land claims. Hence, if people are recognized as residents through a census, or have acquired fiscal visibility by paying taxes, they may, sometimes, have acquired the second-best thing to land rights. Villages situated in national parks, or informal urban settlements may be visible in planning, infrastructure, health, schooling, or other kinds of government activities. This does not provide formal land rights, but it does represent a government acknowledgment of presence and land use. These fragments of recognition may have been insignificant and had no effective meaning at one point in time, but later, in a new political context, they become potent "proof" of the rightfulness of claims. In Indonesia, for example, many smallholders received residence certificates during the Sukarno era in the 1950s. During the Suharto years from the 1960s, these documents were declared null and void because they were considered issued by "Communists." After Suharto's fall in 1998, the same certificates regained a new potential validity as land right documents and were dug out from family chests anew. Indirect recognition may not stand up in court, but people live most of their lives outside the courtroom, and in everyday situations, indirect recognition can deliver certain rewards of legalization. Such visibility—fiscal, cultural, political, economic, and so on—may be the first step to recognition as a legal subject with legalized claims. Undoubtedly, these are often weak protections of rights, but often, the realistic alternative is not strong rights, but none at all.

The paradox of these representations of rights and of rendering recognition visible is that in all their technical illegality and imperfection, they do not undermine the ideas of the state, law, and rights. On the contrary, they underpin them.

Legal Subjects: Citizenship

Just as it is a question what specific rights (or sticks) include, there is an equivalent question of who holds what sticks when and how. Some rights are held by individual persons, but many more are held by consortia of different stripes. Just think of couples, households, families, clans, lineages, village communities, companies, and so on.

To engage such complexity, it its useful to be able to see right holders from without and from within. Seen from the "outside," a household or a family, or even a village community can be seen as an economic actor and a legal subject with specific land rights. Seen from within, however, all consortia raise questions of governance and representation (Agarwal 1994; Bryceson 1995; Moore 1988). No doubt, Ostrom's (1990) work on the commons is among the most influential. Her work shows how conflict and dialogue over management rules and access rights are inherent to any consortium of land rights. While illuminating, Ostrom's focus on the commons can make us forget the profound structural inequalities within households, families, villages and so on (Le Roy et al. 1996). This takes us to citizenship and political subjectivity, and the fundamental issue raised by Arendt (1979) about the right to have rights.

Legal standing and political subjectivity are fundamental when we talk about land. Who is visible to authorities and can act to acquire rights? *The American Declaration of Independence* is a beautiful document as it states, "We hold these truths to be self-evident, that all men are created equal, that they are endowed by their Creator with certain unalienable Rights, that among these are Life, Liberty and the pursuit of Happiness" (*United States Declaration of Independence 1776*). Slave trade, colonialism, genocide, and totalitarianism (and let me throw in patriarchy, for good measure) induced Arendt to adjust the statement from the aspirational to something more operational: "Equality, in contrast to all that is involved in mere existence, is not given to us, but is the result of human organization insofar as it is guided by the principle of justice. We are not born equal; we become equal as members of a group on the strength of our decision to guarantee ourselves mutually equal rights" (Arendt 1979, 301). The strength of this decision varies, and legal visibility and subjectivity is a political struggle. Citizenship can be defined as a meaningful membership of an organized political body. Struggles for citizenship are, generally, struggles for the recognition of the very right to have rights in a body politic (Arendt 1979; Lund 2011; Somers 2008). Formal national citizenship is just one of several configurations of socially constructed collective subjectivities. In many places, land is a resource to which access is ensured not merely through the market or by membership of a national community—local citizenship and status are often just as important. For most people, several political bodies are relevant for different aspects of life (Benda-Beckmann 1997; van Klinken 2007). We can, therefore, see citizenship as a shorthand for people's agency and recognized political subjectivity. It makes up their political "visibility" and denotes the political institution through which a person derives rights of membership to that community. There is little doubt that land rights are contingent on citizenship in a broad sense. Political subjectivity, in all its shades, inflects how land is accessed and held. It is, therefore, useful to explore how people enact this subjectivity and make claims to citizenship heard and seen. Let us briefly look at what are legal subjects and how do they form in struggles between self-professed claims to citizenship and the trammeling of society's subordinates.

Legal Subjects

Let us start with colonialism. Colonial power worked through "difference" and the reproduction of the "self" and the "other" (Brown 1970; Engerman and Metzer 2004; Galeano 2009; Guha 1997; Mamdani 2012, 2020; Mitchell 1988; Peluso 1992). Colonization describes the most dramatic and violent rupture and reordering of property and political subjectivity in human history; the mother of all land-grabs, to be sure.

Western ideas of the "oriental" justified a template of domination and confiscation of land along the lines of race, color, culture and so on (Said 1978). Race was a fundamental instrument in this operation. Hussain (2019) argues that "race is the source of the differentiation that structures a grand evolutionary narrative of civilization – the idea that some races need help evolving toward a civilized rule of law facilitates the tutelary justification of colonial rule" (136). Colonial agents—governments and private companies in various combinations—dispossessed colonial subjects and established new property regimes new subject categories and degrees of (dis)enfranchisement of the people in their new dominions. The colonial administration produced these new identities and categories of property by exercising their everyday power to categorize, regulate, and exclude. The capacity to form and reproduce categorical distinctions as principles for recognizing or dismissing claims—for granting or denying rights to property and political participation for entire groups—was key in the colonial enterprise, as it is in state formation more generally. Racial difference has been associated with the capacity to own, or govern, land, and was enshrined in law in colonies in general.[6] It found some of its most egregious forms in settler-colonies.[7]

Processes of "othering" continue to be fundamental to modern society. The end of colonialism, of socialism, of liberalism, of authoritarianism, and of different conflicts have marked ruptures and "new beginnings" in many places—just as their advents had marked earlier ruptures. As colonial possessions were challenged, property structures were reworked; socialized property was undone in different ways, and land concentrations amassed during authoritarian rule were called into question. Likewise, racialized categories of colonial citizenship, and various categories of "patriots" and "enemies of the state" have been reshuffled in moments of rupture. All the same, it is striking how the pattern of graded citizenship continues to this day in a multitude of forms. We see it from paternalist acquisition of stewardship of nature by an elite, to much more violent exclusion of people labeled primitive, migrants, foreigners, and so on.

Not all legal subjects are citizens. Families, lineages, enterprises, towns, municipalities, and the state are all composite legal subjects. Big reforms such as socialist nationalizations and post-socialist de-collectivization of land and property have had dramatic effects on how persons, or consortia of people, enjoy rights to land (Harms 2016; Ho 2005; Hsing 2010; Kerkvliet 2005; Sikor et al. 2017; Verdery 1996). When the nature of the legal subject changes, the compositions of "sticks"—of rights to land—have usually also changed. The change in legal subjects is not only the result of socialist regime change, back and forth. Liberalization of land markets has also often opened the field for new legal subjects (Borras and Franco 2010; Borras et al 2011; Cotula 2012, 2013; Fairbairn 2020; Levien 2018; Li 2014; Sauer and Pereira Leite 2012). International land transactions have, thus, partly been enabled by changes in legislation allowing non-nationals and companies to own or control land in different countries where this was not as easy previously.

Claiming Subjectivity—Making Citizenship Visible

The demand to have citizenship or political subjectivity count as a legitimate way to have land rights is articulated in many ways. Sometimes, rights are hard-fought and result of collective action and collective identity. At other times, they are the result of more subtle everyday maneuvers designed to accommodate what people expect that government expects of them. Let is briefly look at the movements first.

Unfair land distribution and the desire for land rights have often prompted significant changes in the rights and capacities of citizens and other legal subjects in relation to land (Wolf 1971). Collective action, often organized in social movements, claims land by virtue of particular identities. Landless peasants and indigenous people are labels to represent subjectivity and justify claims by staging and developing a narrative of injustice. The context and timing are crucial for the success of any such narrative, but clear and single messages are not always easy to establish. In Indonesia, for example, several competing or intersecting narratives can be at odds. An evicted indigenous community claims ancestral land, whereas a dispossessed or impoverished peasantry claim means of production or fair markets, yet both fight against industrial logging and for more sustainable land use. No doubt, any concrete claimant could be both, but the claim, the narrative, and the argument differ whether propelled as a culture, a class, or a socio-environmental issue (Li 2000; Peluso et al. 2008, see also Apostolopoulou and Cortes-Vasquez 2018; Carruthers 2008; Latta and Wittman 2010). The political spaces in which indigeneity, class and the environment play out are also vastly different; they overlap, but they are not the same (Tsing 2005). Some of the more radical positions were coined by Indigenous groups in Indonesia at the turn of the millennium: "If the state will not recognize us, we will not recognize the state." This was the slogan of 400 indigenous leaders forming the congress of the Indigenous Peoples' Alliance of the Archipelago in March 1999. It is radical because it talks about the state as optional. By that very token, however, the statement also invokes the contractual nature of recognition.

Many such movements have not only struggled to find their own policies and right label; they have been branded and persecuted by governments and the landed classes. Bandits, communists, immigrants, pirates, poachers, rebels, redskins, separatists, *talibans*, terrorists, and thieves, are only some of the derogatory garlands adorning the necks of protesters just afore the noose. Again, there is no need to romanticize agrarian struggle and conflict or identify absolute heroes; it is a bloody business and human casualties speckle history all around.[8]

Subtler ways of claiming citizenship and land rights involve the language of government in a different way. Subtle forms of protest and resistance also make up civil disobedience (Scott 1985; see also Kerkvliet 2005). There is a short distance from such forms of resistance to instrumental compliance and using the opportunities within the power structure to be heard and seen (O'Brien and Li 2006; for lampooning power by ostentatious excessive compliance, see Monroe 2005). There are many examples of how ordinary people attempt to become visible to the relevant authorities to which they would otherwise be invisible. Just as people try to make their possessions visible as property, they try themselves to become visible as legal subjects and citizens. Agrawal's (2001, 2005) work on community forestry in India demonstrates how organization in village committees rendered communities visible to government and "compatible" with its policies. People act in the anticipation of government regulation long before any is adopted. This way, property and its regulation are conjured up by popular state practices in a supposedly ungoverned space. Das (2011), De Boeck (2011), Körling (2011), Nielsen (2011), and Winayanti (2010) show how residents of informal urban settlements in Delhi, Kinshasa, Niamey, Maputo, and Jakarta have—to some degree—organized their settlement in conformity with the formal technical norms (such as street width or the numbering of houses). By forming "societies" or "associations" with "*présidents de secteurs*" people may resist and avert eviction and ensure access to public utilities; established presence may enable people to acquire identity cards (or proxies such as voting cards, or cards of membership of political or cultural associations); paying for utilities provides customers with receipts documenting and legitimizing residence; and people's possession of land—plus the fact that government institutions ignore or tolerate a land market—allows for the gradual build-up of expectations of recognition. Citizens enter the orbit of certain governing institutions and conjure up the exercise of authority and recognition by anticipating the "contract." In order to establish a "contract" of mutual recognition, the inhabitants may be able to act and organize as they anticipate the government would expect proper citizens to act. Such efforts at legal visibility are not without obstacles. Processes of rightlessness are equally at play. For example, when government and companies in the Indonesian palm oil sector collude to ignore existing entitlements, improvise expeditious self-seeking rules, twist provisions, delay public hearings, and act *as if* proper procedures are followed, formal rights to land can be rendered ineffectual and meaningless (Berenschot and Dhiaulhaq, forthcoming).[9] This way, rights can be eviscerated, and their subjects dispossessed. So, just like property, citizenship is a claim to be actively pursued. Rights are not simply bestowed on people by benevolent authority; they are wrested from power by claims, performance, and determination. It is hard work, and success is never guaranteed.

What We Talk about . . .

Institutional perspectives on land are eminently relational. Actors engage in claims for recognition, and institutions compete to control categorical distinctions. This is always in the making through spectacles of recognition by legalization and reference to law as people understand it. Who has what rights to a particular piece of land, and how they are worked out and institutionalized, is, in a nutshell, what we talk about when we talk about land.

Acknowledgments

The text has benefitted from generous comments from Bernardo Ribeiro de Almeida, Mattias Borg Rasmussen, Pauline Peters, Ruth Hall, and the Handbook's editors, Jun Borras and Jenny Franco. Remaining infelicities are mine alone.

Notes

1. This article is based on earlier work in Lund (2006, 2008, 2019, 2011, 2016, 2020, 2022, and 2023); Lund and Boone (2013); Rasmussen and Lund (2018); and Sikor and Lund (2009). Elements of these earlier publications appear in the present text as inspiration, and also, in places, as turns of phrases, paraphrasing, and entire paragraphs.
2. You can make the cut between "property" and "access and possession" in different ways (Praduroux 2017); the point in the present text is that one claim to resources is *institutionally recognized*, and the other is not. This also means that "property" is not simply "private property" but a range of institutionally recognized resource claims. Right of way, right to settle, to graze or farm, rights to extract, and the rights to transact any or all such rights, and so on, fall under the broad category of property rights. The devil in the detail is that there is always more than one powerful and credible institution about, ready to back competing claims. The institutional recognition of claims is therefore more or less certain, effective, and durable depending on a great number of things.
3. See, e.g., Bakker 2015; Bakker and Moniaga 2010; Berry 1993, 2002, 2009; Boone 2003, 2014; Fitzpatrick 2006; Hadiz 2010; Hansen and Stepputat 2001, 2006; Jacob and Le Meur 2010; Joiremann 2011; Lentz 2013; Lev 1985; Lund 2006; Moore 1986; Peters 2009; Rasmussen 2015; Tilly 1985; Ubink 2008a, 2008b; Ubink et al. 2009; Wilson 2015.
4. See, especially, Aspinall and van Klinken 2011; Bakker 2015; Benton 2002; Comaroff and Comaroff 2006; Das 2007; Guha 1996; Hansen and Stepputat 2001, 2006; Hoffmann and Kirk 2013; Mathur 2016; Mitchell 2002; Moore 1986; Onoma 2010; Sundar 2011.
5. I once met a professional typist and letter writer who was working on his orange Olivetti by the stairs of the post office in Dori, Burkina Faso. He would type contracts, declarations, deeds, and so on, at very reasonable rates.
6. Benton 2002; Breman 1983, 2015; Chanock 1998; Chatterjee 2004; Guha 1997; Herzog 2015; Hussain 2019; James 1963; Stoler 1995.
7. See, e.g., Bhandar 2018; Comaroff and Comaroff 2006, 2009; Fanon 2021; Mamdani 1996 2020; Mbembe 2001; Merry 2000; Oomen 2005; Simpson 2014. Stoler 1995.
8. Some of the most dramatic confrontations are analyzed in Baczko 2016; Ballvé 2020; Bhandar 2018; Borras 2009; Brown 1970; Colloredo-Mansfeld 2009; Grajales 2016; Grajales and Le Cour Grandmaison 2019; Hetherington 2020; Hobsbawm 1981; Joseph and Nugent 1994; Kikon 2019; Lucas and Warren 2013; N'gweno 2007; Nuijten 2003; Onghokham 2003;

Sen 2020; Sundar 2016; Taussig 2005; Thompson 1993; Watts 2004, 2018; Wolford 2010; Woods and Naimark 2020.

9. For variations over this theme, see Almeida 2020; Gündoğdu 2014; Hall et al. 2011; Hall et al. 2015; Kouwagam 2020; Levien 2018; Lund 2020; Ribot and Peluso 2003.

References

Achebe, Chinua. (1958) 2001. *Things Fall Apart*. London: Penguin.

Agarwal, Bina. 1994. *A Field of One's Own*. Cambridge, UK: Cambridge University Press.

Agrawal, Arun. 2001. "State Formation in Community Spaces? Decentralization of Control over Forests in the Kumaon Himalaya, India." *Journal of Asian Studies* 60 (1): 9–40.

Agrawal, Arun. 2005. *Environmentality: Technologies of Government and the Making of Subjects*. Durham, NC: Duke University Press.

Akram-Lodhi, A. Haroon, and Cristóbal Kay. 2010a. "Surveying the Agrarian Question (Part 1): Unearthing Foundations, Exploring Diversity." *Journal of Peasant Studies* 37 (1): 177–202.

Akram-Lodhi, A. Haroon, and Cristóbal Kay. 2010b. "Surveying the Agrarian Question (Part 2): Current Debates and Beyond." *Journal of Peasant Studies* 37 (2): 255–284.

Almeida, Bernardo. 2020. "Building Land Tenure Systems: The Political, Legal, and Institutional Struggles of Timor-Leste." PhD diss. Leiden: Leiden University.

Apostolopoulou, Elia, and Jose A. Cortes-Vasquez, eds. 2018. *The Right to Nature: Social Movements, Environmental Justice, and Neoliberal Natures*. London: Routledge.

Arendt, Hannah. (1948) 1979. *The Origins of Totalitarianism*. New York: Harvest.

Aspinall, Edward, and Gerry van Klinken, eds. 2011. *The State and Illegality in Indonesia*. Leiden: KITLV Press.

Baczko, Adam. 2016. "Legal Rule and Tribal Politics: The US Army and the Taliban in Afghanistan (2001–13)." *Development and Change* 47 (6): 1412–1433.

Baitenmann, Helga. 2005. "Counting on State Subjects. State Formation and Citizenship in Twentieth-Century Mexico." In *State Formation: Anthropological Perspectives*, edited by C. Krohn-Hansen and G. Nustad, 171–194. London: Pluto Press.

Bakker, Laurens. 2015. "Illegality for the General Good? Vigilantism and Social Responsibility in Contemporary Indonesia." *Critique of Anthropology* 35 (1): 78–93.

Bakker, Laurens, and Sandra Moniaga. 2010. "The Space Between: Land Claims and the Law in Indonesia." *Asian Journal of Social Science* 38: 187–201.

Balibar, Étienne. 2007. "(De)constructing the Human as Human Institution: A Reflection on the Coherence of Hannah Arendt's Practical Philosophy." *Social Research* 74 (3): 727–738.

Ballvé, Teo. 2020. *The Frontier Effect: State Formation and Violence in Colombia*. Ithaca, NY: Cornell University Press.

von Benda-Beckmann, Franz. 1997. "Citizens, Strangers and Indigenous Peoples: Conceptual Politics and Legal Pluralism." *Law and Anthropology* 9: 1–42.

von Benda-Beckmann, Keebet. 1981. "Forum Shopping and Shopping Forums, Dispute Processing in a Minangkabau Village in West Sumatra." *Journal of Legal Pluralism* 19: 117–162.

Benton, Lauren. 2002. *Law and Colonial Cultures: Legal Regimes in World History, 1400–1900*. Cambridge, UK: Cambridge University Press.

Berenschot, Ward, and Ahmad Dhiaulhaq. Forthcoming. "The Production of Rightlessness: Dispossession, land Conflict, and Palm Oil Expansion in Indonesia."

Berry, Sara. 1993. *No Condition Is Permanent: The Social Dynamics of Agrarian Change in Sub-Saharan Africa*. Madison: University of Wisconsin Press.
Berry, Sara. 2002. "Debating the Land Questions." *Comparative Studies in Society and History* 44 (4): 638–668.
Berry, Sara. 2009. "Property, Authority and Citizenship: Land Claims, Politics and the Dynamics of Social Division in West Africa." In *Politics of Possession*, edited by T. Sikor and Christian Lund, 23–45. London: Blackwell.
Bhandar, Brenna. 2018. *Colonial Lives of Property: Law, Land, and Racial Regimes of Ownership*. Durham, NC: Duke University Press.
Boone, Catherine. 2003. *Political Topographies of the African State: Territorial Authority and Institutional Choice*. Cambridge, UK: Cambridge University Press.
Boone, Catherine. 2014. *Property and Political Order in Africa, Land Rights and the Structure of Politics*. Cambridge, UK: Cambridge University Press.
Borras, Saturnino M., Jr. 2009. *Competing Views and Strategies on Agrarian Reform*. 2 vols. Manila: Ateneo de Manila University Press.
Borras, Saturnino M., Jr., and Jennifer Franco. 2010. "Towards a Broader View of the Politics of Global Land Grab: Rethinking Land Issues, Reframing Resistance." Working Paper Series No. 001. Transnational Institute, Initiatives in Critical Agrarian Studies.
Borras, Saturnino M., Jr., Ruth Hall, Ian Scoones, Ben White, and Wendy Wolford. 2011. "Towards a Better Understanding of Global Land Grabbing." *Journal of Peasant Studies* 38 (2): 209–216.
Breckenridge, Keith, and Simon Szreter, eds. 2010. *Registration and Recognition: Documenting the Person in World History*. Oxford: Oxford University Press.
Breman, Jan. 1983. *Control of Land and Labour in Colonial Java*. Leiden: Foris.
Breman, Jan. 2015. *Mobilizing Labour for the Global Coffee Market: Profits from an Unfree Work Regime in Colonial Java*. Amsterdam: Amsterdam University Press.
Brown, Dee. 1970. *Bury My Heart at Wounded Knee: An Indian History of the American West*. New York: Holt, Rinehart & Winston.
Bruce, John, and Shem E. Migot-Adholla, eds. 1994. *Searching for Land Tenure Security in Africa*. Dubuque, IA: Kendall/Hunt.
Bryceson, Deborah F., ed. 1995. *Women Wielding the Hoe: Lessons from Rural Africa for Feminist Theory and Development Practice*. New York: Berg.
Campbell, Jeremy. M. 2015. *Conjuring Property: Speculation and Environmental Futures in the Brazilian Amazon*. Seattle: University of Washington Press.
Carruthers, David. V. 2008. *Environmental Justice in Latin America: Problems, Promise, and Practice*. Cambridge, MA: MIT Press.
Chanock, Martin. 1998. *Law, Custom and Social Order: The Colonial Experience in Malawi and Zambia*. Portsmouth, NH: Heinemann.
Chatterjee, Partha. 2004. *The Politics of the Governed: Reflections of Popular Politics in Most of the World*. New Delhi: Permanent Black.
Clanchy, Michael. T. 2013. *From Memory to Written Record: England 1066–1307*. 3rd ed. London: Wiley-Blackwell.
Colloredo-Mansfeld, Rudi. 2009. *Fighting like a Community: Andean Civil Society in an Era of Indian Uprisings*. Chicago: University of Chicago Press.
Comaroff, Jean, and John Comaroff. 2009. "Reflexions on the Anthropology of Law, Governance and Sovereignty." In *Rules of Law and Laws of Ruling*, edited by Franz von Benda-Beckmann, Keebet von Benda-Beckmann, and Julia Eckert, 31–60. London: Ashgate.

Comaroff, Jean, and John Comaroff, eds. 2006. *Law and Order in the Postcolony*. Chicago: University of Chicago Press.
Correia, David. 2013. *Properties of Violence: Law and Land Grant Struggle in Northern New Mexico*. Athens: University of Georgia Press.
Cotula, Lorenzo. 2012. *Human Rights, Natural Resource and Investment Law in a Globalised World: Shades of Grey in the Shadow of Law*. London: Routledge.
Cotula, Lorenzo. 2013. *The Great African Land Grab*. London: Zed Books.
Dalberto, Séverine A., and Richard Banégas, eds. 2021. *Identification and Citizenship in Africa: Biometrics, the Documentary State, and Bureaucratic Writings of the Self*. London: Routledge.
Das, Veena. 2007. *Life and Words: Violence and the Descent into the Ordinary*. Berkeley: University of California Press.
Das, Veena. 2011. "State, Citizenship, and the Urban Poor." *Citizenship Studies* 15 (3–4): 319–333.
De Boeck, Filip. 2011. "Inhabiting the Ocular Ground: Kinshasa's Future in the Light of Congo's Spectral Urban Politics." *Cultural Anthropology* 26 (2): 266–286.
de Soto, Hernando. 2000. *The Mystery of Capital: Why Capitalism Triumphs in the West and Fails Everywhere Else*. New York: Basic Books.
Du Toit, Andries. 2018. "Without the Blanket of the Land: Agrarian Change and Biopolitics in Post–Apartheid South Africa." *Journal of Peasant Studies* 45 (5–6): 1086–1107.
Engeman, Stanley L., and John Metzer, eds. 2004. *Land Rights, Ethno-nationality, and Sovereignty in History*. London: Routledge.
Fairbairn, Madeleine. 2020. *Fields of Gold: Financing the Global Land Rush*. Ithaca, NY: Cornell University Press.
Fanon, Frantz. (1952) 2021. *Black Skin, White Masks*. London: Penguin.
Feldman, Ilana. 2008. *Governing Gaza: Bureaucracy, Authority, and the Work of Rule, 1917–1967*. Durham, NC: Duke University Press.
Ferguson, James. 2013. "How to Do Things with Land: A Distributive Perspective on Rural Livelihoods in Southern Africa." *Journal of Agrarian Change* 13 (1): 166–174.
Ferrier, Myriam. 2012. "Securing Property in Informal Neighbourhoods in Damascus through Tax Payments." In *Popular Housing and Urban Land Tenure in the Middle East: Case Studies from Egypt, Syria, Jordan, Lebanon and Turkey*, edited by Myriam Ababsa, Baudoin Dupret, and Eric Dennis, 67–91. Cairo: American University in Cairo Press.
Fitzpatrick, Daniel. 2006. "Private Law and Public Power: Tangled Threads in Indonesian Land Regulation." In *Indonesian Transitions*, edited by H. Schulte Nordholt and I. Hoogenboom, 75–113. Yogyakarta: Pustaka Pelajar.
Galeano, Eduardo. 2009. *Open Veins of Latin America: Five Centuries of the Pillage of a Continent*. London: Serpent's Tail.
Gluckman, Max. 1965. *Politics, Law, and Ritual in Tribal Society*. Oxford: Blackwell.
Grajales, Jacobo. 2016. *Gouverner dans la violence: Le paramilitarisme en Colombie*. Paris: Karthala.
Grajales, Jacobo, and Romain Le Cour Grandmaison, eds. 2019. *L'État malgré tout: Produire l'autorité dans la violence*. Paris: Karthala.
Graeber, David. 2015. *The Utopia of Rules: On Technology, Stupidity and the Secret Joys of Bureaucracy*. Brooklyn, NY: Melville House.
Guha, Ranajit. 1996. *A Rule of Property for Bengal: An Essay on the Idea of Permanent Settlement*. Durham, NC: Duke University Press.
Guha, Ranajit. 1997. *Dominance without Hegemony: History and Power in Colonial India*. Cambridge, MA: Harvard University Press.

Gündoğdu, Ayten. 2014. *Rightlessness in an Age of Rights: Hannah Arendt and the Contemporary Struggles of Migrants*. Oxford: Oxford University Press.

Hadiz, Vedi R. 2010. *Localizing Power in Post-authoritarian Indonesia: A Southeast Asia Perspective*. Stanford, CA Stanford University Press.

Hall, Derek. 2013. *Land*. London: Polity.

Hall, Derek, Philip Hirsch, and Tania Li. 2011. *Powers of Exclusion: Land Dilemmas in Southeast Asia*. Singapore: National University of Singapore Press.

Hall, Ruth, Marc Edelman, Saturnino M. Borras, Jr., Ian Scoones, Ben White, and Wendy Wolford. 2015. "Resistance, Acquiescence or Incorporation? An Introduction to Land Grabbing and Political Reactions 'from Below.'" *Journal of Peasant Studies* 42 (3–4): 467–488.

Hamsun, Knut. (1917) 2007. *Growth of the Soil* [*Markens grøde*]. London: Penguin Classics.

Hansen, Thomas B., and Finn Stepputat, eds. 2001. *States of Imagination: Ethnographic Explorations of the Postcolonial State*. Durham, NC: Duke University Press.

Hansen, Thomas B., and Finn Stepputat. 2006. "Sovereignty Revisited." *Annual Review of Anthropology* 35: 295–331.

Harms, Erik. 2016. *Luxury and Rubble: Civility and Dispossession in the New Saigon*. Oakland: University of California Press.

Harris, Cheryl I. 1993. "Whiteness as Property." *Harvard Law Review* 106 (8): 1707–1791.

Herzog, Tamar. 2015. *Frontiers of Possession: Spain and Portugal in Europe and the Americas*. Cambridge, MA: Harvard University Press.

Hetherington, Kregg. 2011. *Guerrilla Auditors: The Politics of Transparency in Neoliberal Paraguay*. Durham, NC: Duke University Press.

Hetherington, Kregg. 2020. *The Government of Beans: Regulating Life in the Age of Monocrops*. Durham, NC: Duke University Press.

Heyman, Josiah M., ed. 1999. *States and Illegal Practices*. Oxford: Berg.

Ho, Peter. 2005. *Institutions in Transition: Land Ownership, Property Rights, and Social Conflict in China; Studies on Contemporary China*. Oxford: Oxford University Press.

Hobsbawm, Eric. (1969) 1981. *Bandits*. New York: Pantheon Books.

Hoffmann, Kasper, and Tom Kirk. 2013. "Public Authority and the Provision of Public Goods in Conflict-Affected and Transitioning Regions." JSRP paper 7. Justice and Security Research Programme, London School of Economics.

Hohfeld, Wesley Newcomb. 1913. "Some Fundamental Legal Conceptions as Applied in Judicial Reasoning." *Yale Law Review* 23: 16–59.

Holston, James. 1991. "The Misrule of Law: Land and Usurpation in Brazil." *Comparative Studies in Society and History* 33 (4): 695–725.

Holston, James. 2008. *Insurgent Citizenship: Disjunctions of Democracy and Modernity in Brazil*. Princeton, NJ: Princeton University Press.

Hsing, You-tien. 2010. *The Great Urban Transformation: Politics of Land and Property in China*. Oxford: Oxford University Press.

Hull, Matthew S. 2012. *Government of Paper: The Materiality of Bureaucracy in Urban Pakistan*. Berkeley: University of California Press.

Hussain, Nasser. 2019. *The Jurisprudence of Emergency: Colonialism and the Rule of Law*. Ann Arbor: University of Michigan Press.

Jacob, Jean-Pierre, and Pierre-Yves Le Meur, eds. 2010. *Politique de la terre et de l'appartenance: Droits fonciers et citoyenneté locale dans les sociétés du Sud*. Paris: Karthala.

James, Cyril Lionel Robert. 1963. *The Black Jacobins: Toussaint L'Ouverture and the San Domingo Revolution*. New York: Vintage Books.

Joireman, Sandra. 2011. *Where There Is No Government: Enforcing Property Rights in Common Law Africa*. Oxford: Oxford University Press.
Joseph, Gilbert, and Daniel Nugent, eds. 1994. *Everyday Forms of State Formation: Revolution and the Negotiation of Rule in Modern Mexico*. Durham, NC: Duke University Press.
Kerkvliet, Ben. 2005. *Power of Everyday Politics: How Vietnamese Peasants Transformed National Policy*. Ithaca, NY: Cornell University Press.
Kikon, Dolly. 2019. *Living with Oil and Coal: Resource Politics and Militarization in Northeast India*. Seattle: Washington University Press.
Körling, Gabriella. 2011. *In the Search of the State: An Ethnography of Public Service Provision in Urban Niger*. Uppsala: Uppsala University.
Kouwagam, Santy U. 2020. "How Lawyers Win Land Conflicts for Corporations: Legal Strategy and Its Influence on the Rule of Law in Indonesia." PhD diss. Leiden: Leiden University.
Latour, Bruno. 2010. *The Making of Law: An Ethnography of the Conseil d'Etat*. Cambridge, UK: Polity.
Latta, Alex., and Hannah Wittman. 2010. "Environment and Citizenship in Latin America: A New Paradigm for Theory and Practice." *European Review of Latin American and Caribbean Studies* 89: 107–116.
Lavigne-Delville, Phillippe. 2003. "When Farmers Use 'Pieces of Paper' to Record Their Land Transactions in Francophone rural Africa: Insights into Institutional Innovation." In *Securing Land Rights in Africa*, edited by T. Benjaminsen and Christian Lund, 89–108. London: Frank Cass.
Le Roy, Étienne, Alain Karsenty, and Alain Bertrand. 1996. *La sécurisation foncière en Afrique*. Paris: Karthala.
Lentz, Carola. 2013. *Land, Mobility, and Belonging in West Africa*. Bloomington: Indiana University Press.
Lev, Daniel. 1985. "Colonial Law and the Genesis of the Indonesian State." *Indonesia* 40: 57–74.
Levien, Michael. 2018. *Dispossession without Development: Land Grabs in Neoliberal India*. Oxford: Oxford University Press.
Li, Tania M. 2000. "Articulating Indigenous Identity in Indonesia: Resource Politics and the Tribal Slot." *Comparative Studies in Society and History* 4 (1): 149–179.
Li, Tania M. 2014. "What Is Land? Assembling a Resource for Global Investment." *Transaction of the Institute of British Geographers* 39: 589–602.
Lucas, Anton, and Carol Warren, eds. 2013. *Land for the People: The State and Agrarian Conflict in Indonesia*. Columbus: Ohio University Press.
Lund, Christian. 2006. "Twilight Institutions: Public Authority and Local Politics in Africa." *Development and Change* 37 (4): 685–705.
Lund, Christian. 2008. *Local Politics and the Dynamics of Property in Africa*. Cambridge, UK: Cambridge University Press.
Lund, Christian. 2011. "Property and Citizenship: Conceptually Connecting Land Rights and Belonging in Africa." *Africa Spectrum* 46 (3): 71–75.
Lund, Christian. 2016. "Rule and Rupture: State Formation through the Production of Property and Citizenship." *Development and Change* 47 (6): 1199–1228.
Lund, Christian. 2019. "Urban Frontiers: A Review Essay on Political Power, Violence, and Paperwork." *Antipode*. https://antipodeonline.org/2019/07/06/luxury-and-rubble-civility-and-dispossession-in-the-new-saigon/.
Lund, Christian. 2020. *Nine-Tenths of the Law: Enduring Dispossession in Indonesia*. New Haven, CT: Yale University Press.

Lund, Christian. 2022. "An Air of Legality: Legalization under Conditions of Rightlessness in Indonesia." *Journal of Peasant Studies* 49: 1–22.

Lund, Christian. 2023. "Who Belongs Where, and What Belongs to Whom? An Epilogue." In *This Land Is Not For Sale*, edited by L. Meinert and S. Reynolds Whyte, 250–255. New York: Berghahn Books.

Lund, Christian, and C. Boone. 2013. "Land Politics in Africa: Constituting Authority over Territory, Property, and Persons." *Africa* 83 (1): 1–13.

MacPherson, Crawford Brough. 1978. *Property: Mainstream and Critical Positions*. Oxford: Basil Blackwell.

Mamdani, Mahmood. 1996. *Citizen and Subject: Contemporary Africa and the Legacy of Late Colonialism*. London: James Currey.

Mamdani, Mahmood. 2012. *Define and Rule: Native as Political Identity*. Cambridge, MA: Harvard University Press.

Mamdani, Mahmood. 2020. *Neither Settler nor Native: The Making and Unmaking of Permanent Minorities*. Cambridge, MA: Belknap Press of Harvard University Press.

Marx, Karl. (1867) 1978. *Capital*. Vol. 1. Moscow: Progress Publishers.

Mathur, Nayanika. 2016. *Paper Tiger: Law, Bureaucracy, and the Developmental State in Himalayan India*. Cambridge, UK: Cambridge University Press.

Mbembe, Achille. 2001. *On the Postcolony*. Berkeley: University of California Press.

Merry, Sally Engle. 2000. *Colonizing Hawai'i: The Cultural Power of Law*. Princeton, NJ: Princeton University Press.

Mitchell, Timothy. 1988. *Colonizing Egypt*. Berkeley: University of California Press.

Mitchell, Timothy. 2000. "The Stage of Modernity." In *Questions of Modernity*, edited by T. Mitchell, 1–34. Minneapolis: University of Minnesota Press.

Mitchell, Timothy. 2002. *Rule of Experts: Egypt, Techno-Politics, Modernity*. Berkeley: University of California Press.

Monroe, Alexei. 2005. *Interrogation Machine: Leibach and NSK*. Cambridge, MA: MIT Press.

Moore, Henrietta. 1988. *Feminism and Anthropology*. London: Polity.

Moore, Sally Falk. 1978. *Law as Process*. London: Routledge and Kegan Paul.

Moore, Sally Falk. 1986. *Social Facts and Fabrications: "Customary" Law on Kilimanjaro 1880–1980*. Cambridge, UK: Cambridge University Press.

Nader, Laura. 2009. "Law and the Frontiers of Illegalities." In *The Power of Law in a Transnational World*, edited by Franz von Benda-Beckmann, Keebet von Benda-Beckmann, and A. Griffiths, 54–73. New York: Berghahn Books.

Ng'weno, Bettina. 2007. *Turf Wars: Territory and Citizenship in the Contemporary State*. Stanford, CA: Stanford University Press.

Nielsen, Morten. 2011. "Inverse Governmentality: The Paradoxical Production of Peri-Urban Planning in Maputo, Mozambique." *Critique of Anthropology* 31 (4): 329–358.

Nonet, Philippe, and Philip Selznick. (1978) 2009. *Law and Society in Transition: Toward Responsive Law*. New Brunswick, NJ: Transaction.

Nugent, Paul. 2010. "States and Social Contracts in Africa." *New Left Review* 63: 35–68.

Nuijten, Monique. 2003. *Power, Community, and the State: The Political Anthropology of Organisation in Mexico*. London: Pluto Press.

O'Brien, Kevin, and Lianjiang Li. 2006. *Rightful Resistance in Rural China*. Cambridge, UK: Cambridge University Press.

Onghokham. 2003. *The Thugs, the Curtain Thief, and the Sugar Lord: Power, Politics and Culture in Colonial Java*. Jakarta: Metaphor Publishing.

Onoma, Ato Kwamena. 2010. *The Politics of Property Rights Institutions in Africa*. New York: Cambridge University Press.
Oomen, Barbara. 2005. *Chiefs in South Africa: Law, Power and Culture in the Post-Apartheid Era*. Oxford: James Currey.
Ostrom, Elinor. 1990. *Governing the Commons: The Evolution of Institutions for Collective Action*. Cambridge, UK: Cambridge University Press.
Peluso, Nancy. 1992. *Rich Forests, Poor People: Resource Control and Resistance in Java*. Berkeley: University of California Press.
Peluso, Nancy, Suraya Afiff, and Noer Fauzi Rachman. 2008. "Claiming the Grounds for Reform: Agrarian and Environmental Movements in Indonesia." *Journal of Agrarian Change* 8 (2–3): 377–407.
Peters, Pauline. 2004. "Inequality and Social Conflict over Land in Africa." *Journal of Agrarian Change* 4 (3): 269–314.
Peters, Pauline. 2009. "Challenges in Land Tenure and Land Reform in Africa: Anthropological Perspectives." *World Development* 37 (8): 1317–1325.
Polanyi, Karl. 1944. *The Great Transformation: Economic and Political Origins of Our Time*. New York: Farrar and Rinehart.
Pottage, Alain. 2004. "The Fabrication of Persons and Things." In *Law, Anthropology, and the Constitution of the Social: Making Persons and Things*, edited by A. Pottage and M. Mundy, 1–39. Cambridge, UK: Cambridge University Press.
Praduroux, Sabrina. 2017. "Objects of Property Rights: Old and New." In *Comparative Property Law: Global Perspectives*, edited by M. Graziadei and L. Smith, 51–70. London: Edward Elgar.
Rasmussen, Mattias Borg. 2015. *Andean Waterways: Resource Politics in Highland Peru*. Seattle: Washington University Press.
Rasmussen, Mattias Borg, and Christian Lund. 2018. "Reconfiguring Frontier Spaces: The Territoriality of Resource Control." *World Development* 101: 388–399.
Ribot, Jesse, and Nancy Peluso. 2003. "A Theory of Access." *Rural Sociology* 68 (2): 153–181.
Di Robilant, Anna. 2013. "Property: A Bundle of Sticks or a Tree?" *Vanderbilt Law Review* 66 (3): 879–932.
Rose, Carol. 1994. *Property and Persuasion: Essays on the History, Theory and Rhetoric of Ownership*. Boulder, CO: Westview Press.
Rose, Carol. 1998. "Canons of Property Talk; or Blackstone's Anxiety." *Yale Law Journal* 108 (3): 601–632.
Sadiq, Kamal. 2009. *Paper Citizens: How Illegal Immigrants Acquire Citizenship in Developing Countries*. Oxford: Oxford University Press.
Said, Edward. 1978. *Orientalism*. New York: Vintage Books.
Sauer, Sérgio, and Sergio Pereira Leite. 2012. "Agrarian Structure, Foreign Investment in Land, and Land Prices in Brazil." *Journal of Peasant Studies* 39 (3–4): 873–898.
Scott, James. 1985. *Weapons of the Weak: Everyday Forms of Peasant Resistance*. New Haven, CT: Yale University Press.
Scott, James, John Theranian, and Jeremy Mathias. 2002. "The Production of Legal Identities Proper to States: The Case of Permanent Family Surnames." *Comparative Studies in Society and History* 44 (1): 4–44.
Sen, Somdeep. 2020. *Decolonizing Palestine: Hamas between the Anticolonial and the Postcolonial*. Ithaca, NY: Cornell University Press.
Shipton, Parker, and Mitzi Goheen. 1992. "Understanding African Land Holding: Power, Wealth, and Meaning." *Africa* 63 (3): 307–325.

Sikor, Thomas, Stefan Dorondel, Johannes Stahl, and P. X. To. 2017. *When Things Become Property: Land Reform, Authority and Value in Postsocialist Europe and Asia*. New York: Berghahn.

Sikor, Thomas, and Christian Lund. 2009. "Access and Property: A Question of Power and Authority." *Development and Change* 40 (1): 1–22.

Simpson, Audra. 2014. *Mohawk Interruptus: Political Life Across the Border of Settler States*. Durham, NC: Duke University Press.

Singer, Joseph. 2000. *Entitlement: The Paradoxes of Property*. New Haven, CT: Yale University Press.

Somers, Margaret. 2008. *Genealogies of Citizenship: Markets, Statelessness, and the Right to have Rights*. Cambridge, UK: Cambridge University Press.

Steinbeck, John. [1939] 1962. *The Grapes of Wrath*. London: Penguin Modern Classics.

Stoler, Ann Laura. 1995. *Race and the Education of Desire: Foucault's "History of Sexuality" and the Colonial Order of Things*. Durham, NC: Duke University Press.

Strathern, Marilyn. 1999. *Property, Substance and Effect: Anthropological Essays on Persons and Things*. London: Athlone Press.

Strathern, Marilyn, and Eric Hirsch. 2004. "Transactions and Creations." In *Transactions and Creations: Property Debates and the Stimulus of Melanesia*, edited by Eric Hirsch and Marilyn Strathern, 1–18. New York: Berghahn Books.

Sundar, Nandini. 2011. "The Rule of Law and Citizenship in Central India: Post-colonial Dilemmas." *Citizenship Studies* 15 (3-4): 419–432.

Sundar, Nandini. 2016. *The Burning Forest: India's War in Bastar*. Delhi: Juggernaut.

Taussig, Michael. 2005. *Law in a Lawless Land: Diary of a* Limpieza *in Colombia*. Chicago: University of Chicago Press.

Thompson, E. P. 1975. *Whigs and Hunters: The Origin of the Black Act*. New York. Pantheon.

Thompson, E. P. 1993. *Customs in Common*. London: Penguin.

Tilly, Charles. 1985. "War Making and State Making as Organized Crime." In *Bringing the State Back In*, edited by P. Evans, D. Rueschemeyer, and T. Skocpol, 169–191. Cambridge, UK: Cambridge University Press.

Toer, Pramoedya Ananta. 1990. *This Earth of Mankind (The Buri Quartet)*. London: Penguin.

Tsing, Anna. 2005. *Friction: An Ethnography of Global Connection*. Princeton, NJ: Princeton University Press.

Ubink, Janine. 2008a. *In the Land of the Chiefs: Customary Law, Land Conflicts, and the Role of the State in Peri-urban Ghana*. Leiden: Leiden University Press.

Ubink, Janine. 2008b. *Traditional Authorities in Africa: Resurgence in an Era of Democratisation*. Leiden: Leiden University Press.

Ubink, Janine, André J. Hoekema, and Willem J. Assies, eds. 2009. *Legalising Land Rights: Local Practices, State Responses and Tenure Security in Africa, Asia and Latin America*. Leiden: Leiden University Press.

Underkuffler, Laura. 2003. *The Idea of Property: Its Meaning and Power*. Oxford: Oxford University Press.

van Klinken, Gerry. 2007. *Communal Violence and Democratization in Indonesia: Small Town Wars*. London: Routledge.

Verdery, Katherine. 1996. *What Was Socialism, and What Comes Next?* Princeton, NJ: Princeton University Press.

Watts, Michael. 2004. "Resource Curse? Governmentality, Oil and Power in the Niger Delta, Nigeria." *Geopolitics* 9 (1): 50–80.

Watts, Michael. 2018. "Frontiers: Authority, Precarity and Insurgency at the Edge of the State." *World Development* 101: 477–488.

Wilson, Ian. 2015. *The Politics of Protection Rackets in Post–New Order Indonesia: Coercive Capital, Authority and Street Politics*. London: Routledge.

Winayanti, Lana. 2010. *Community Struggles for Land in Jakarta: A Case Study of Kampung Community Struggle to Obtain Security of Tenure*. Saarbrücken, GE: Lambert Academic Publishing.

Winichakul, Thongchai. 1994. *Siam Mapped: A History of the Geo-Body of a Nation*. Honolulu: University of Hawai'i Press.

Wolf, Eric. 1971. *Peasant Wars in the Twentieth Century*. London: Faber and Faber.

Wolford, Wendy. 2010. *This Land Is Ours Now: Social Mobilization and the Meaning of Land in Brazil*. Durham, NC: Duke University Press.

Woods, Kevin, and Jared Naimark. 2020. "Conservation as Counterinsurgency: A Case of Ceasefire in a Rebel Forest in Southeast Myanmar." *Political Geography* 83: 1–11.

CHAPTER 24

LAND-MAKING AS STATE-MAKING

NIKITA SUD

THE history of human civilization has centered around settling, governing, and seeking to control our surroundings, especially the land. Land in this case is hardly the solid and dry crust of the earth. This chapter takes a relational view in which the social interacts with the natural to mutual effect. In a relational perspective, land is the surface of the earth and what lies below it, plus us. 'Us' refers to a multitude of socialities that interact with and shape land, though my focus is on the land-state relationship. This is because in modern times, the state has been the key authority governing land.

The modern state has continually acted upon land and impacted its contours. In that sense, the modern state is a land-making state. Land can be read multi-dimensionally as (a) the state's institutional *authority* invested in space; (b) *property*, where the state decrees the right to own and use land to private individuals in exchange for their loyalty and tax revenue; and (c) *territory*, or a technology of rule that ordains insiders and outsiders via practices of bordering, migration control, and more (Elden 2010). Territory applies not just to international borders, but is also socially produced in the everyday. Further, land is (d) *enlivened* with history, memory, identity, and sacrality (Ulloa 2005), wherein humans and their institutions, such as states, infuse land with enlivenment, and anchor their politics and social selves within this.[1] In the sections that follow, I will analyze land through this multi-dimensional reading, across time and space.

The state's engagement with multi-dimensional land is an exercise in order-making. *Order* is a systematization based on regularities (Foucault 1966, 2002; Graeber 2015); it determines how things get done around a place. Tracing the making of order allows us to delineate power traversing through a system. In other words, the state's making of land as authority, property, territory, and enlivened allows for an exercise of power over land and the peoples that live off it. Following through on the relational argument, land that is in the making via the workings of the state, opens up a window into the ongoing processes of state-making. Ordering land produces order and authority for the state. It makes the state.

The following pages trace the land-making practices of the colonial state, which produced legitimacy and control. Next, I explore the transition to the postcolonial period. I argue that the postcolonial state showed much continuity with its colonial counterpart. Barring some exceptions, the state did not overturn the iniquitous landed order of colonialism. A major break in this order was propelled by the turn to the market in the late twentieth century. This happened in much of the world. States reinvented their role as more or less successful creators of growth and development, to facilitators of private firms that increasingly took over the latter tasks. With the liberalization of the market came the liberalization of land, and the opening up of this land to capital, sometimes on a grand scale. The order of business-friendly states' channeling land to the select few is currently dominant. However, it is not absolute. A final section looks at the land-state relationship as it plays out at the frontiers of global capitalism. Chinks in the dominant order of land-making and state-making, made ethnographically visible by the actions of a range of stakeholders, especially middlemen in land deals, allow us to see transgressions in how things are. Land, the state, and their respective boundaries, remain unfixed and dynamic.

The chapter draws on examples from the global South. Here, land-making and state-making have been changeable, contested, and intimately linked to the course of history in what constitutes much of the world. The final section is based on primary, ethnographic research on middlemen in land in India. It was conducted for a book project for which qualitative research was carried out in multiple field locations between 2008 and 2016 (see Sud 2021). In its discussion of land-state relations in a range of Southern countries, the chapter does not attempt cross-country comparison or systematization. Instead, it offers extensive examples to demonstrate some trends across time. More micro and empirically grounded studies would no doubt add depth and nuance to the analytical breadth that is attempted here.

Overall, this is an argument about variegated land-making that reveals the state across space, scales, and time, as the colonial and civilizing state, the postcolonial developmental state, and the open-for-business globalizing state, as well as the porous, everyday, informalized state. I argue for a co-productive view of land and the state or, more broadly, of nature and human society and institutions. The era of colonial and postcolonial modernity has conditioned us to see development as the institutional control of land, and nature. The era of climate change demands a rethinking of these relationships. The chapter thus contributes to fresh perspectives on socio-natures. Here, land-making and state-making are mutually reinforcing, rather than a one-way street. Land-making is state-making, and vice versa.

Colonial Land-Making as State-Making

Colonialism was an audacious project, with a handful of states ruling continents over several centuries. Colonial states had to build legitimacy for their rule. A claim to superior knowledge and productivity was one of the routes to legitimacy (Locke 1960). Colonial states supposedly "discovered" vast empty spaces, or *terra nullius*, and forged these into lands of plenty via their values of enlightenment and enterprise. Savage lands were apparently transformed by modern, civilizing states (Mill 1836).

The twin projects of land-making and state-making implicate the inhabitants of the land. The latter were fashioned as populations—the masses who lived on and worked the land, and subjects—who owed allegiance to the state as sovereign on this land, particularly through their inclusion in codes of law and governance (Mamdani 2018). Technologies of surveying, mapping, and the census were modes of knowing, and eventually subjectifying, the colonized populace (Appadurai 1993; Cohn 2002). Those who resisted the regimes of knowledge and control, and lands that could not be mapped and enumerated, were deemed wild and waste. These lands were typically inhabited by indigenous and itinerant populations, and other such groups that live off the commons and forests. They bear the stamp of the deviant till date (Makki 2014).

Just as the colonial state conducted rule by land-based authority, it perpetuated rule by property. This state succeeded what it saw as despotic rulers who had practiced unquestioned control over land. Instead, in a bid to herald a "universal" rule of law and rationality, colonial states awarded property rights to those whose labor or enterprise they considered the most productive and profitable for that land. In the process, they looked to cultivate a class of loyalist landholders who would help in revenue collection, and keep restive populations in check. The making of land as property strengthened the position of the colonial state. However, it also flattened out a complex system of land rights and land use that had been built over centuries. In contexts ranging from Egypt (Mitchell 2002) to India (Habib 2013; Chatterjee 2020), we know that pre-colonial sovereign control over land was not unqualified. Instead, a layered system of use and rights incorporated tillers, grazers, those with access to the produce of the land and the waterbodies on it, and those with the ability to collect taxes. By imposing rule by property, the colonial state strengthened its position in the name of rationality, law, and order. It also set in motion a break with land-based relationships for millions, with repercussions on livelihoods, food, income, and climate security that carry on to this day. This is not to suggest that some sort of pre-colonial utopia was unsettled by colonial land ordering. Rulers across time have exercised power via inclusions and exclusions from the land. Colonialism further distilled this order.

The Postcolonial State Takes Over from Where the Colonial State Left Off

Newly independent states inherited the modalities of the colonial state. In South Asia for instance, India and Pakistan were created at independence from British rule in 1947. British colonial territory was rather arbitrarily divided into Hindu-majority India and

Muslim-majority Pakistan. Testimony to the bizarreness of territory-making is the fact that East Pakistan, which became independent Bangladesh in 1971, was separated from West Pakistan by 1,600 kilometers of Indian space. Till today, fantastical feats of territorial (b)ordering and control are attempted to maintain the demarcation between Pakistan and India. This includes stationing soldiers at an elevation of 6700 meters, in minus 50 degrees Celsius temperatures, on the Siachen Glacier in the Karakoram mountain range.

Similarly, well before Donald Trump conjured up a wall to keep Central and South American migrants out of the USA, India was fencing its border with Bangladesh to exclude "infiltrators." India was instrumental in Bangladesh's "war of liberation" from Pakistan in 1971, and has long designated Bangladesh a 'friendly neighbour' (Chowdhury 2020). This is in stark contrast to its overtly tense and aggressive relationship with Pakistan. Yet belligerent patrolling and "shoot to kill" orders are in place to curb Bangladeshi "infiltration." This is for a border that is well recognized as porous, where labor, trade, and familial interactions across territorial boundaries are routine (Basu Ray Chaudhury and Ghosh 2021).

Just as land-making in the form of territorial (b)ordering has entrenched state authority across time, land-making has also been used by states to embed regimes of property, as also regimes of development more broadly. Of course, the state is not a monolith, unchanging over centuries. Successful independence struggles across the colonial world brought into play postcolonial governments that pledged a radical break with the old order. States did try to incorporate the aspirations of newly independent citizens in the governance of land. Asset redistribution was often a promise held out to struggling populations. We see this prominently in Zimbabwe, the former Rhodesia, where redistribution of land from White settlers to Black native populations was a promise that came alongside a hard-fought independence from the British in 1980 (Alexander 2006). Yet in practice, redistribution has been deeply political and unequal, its processes appropriated by ruling party elites, military strongmen from the liberation war, and other social and political institutional authorities (Chamunogwa 2019).

In Pakistan, overthrown Prime Minister Zulfiqar Ali Bhutto was assassinated in 1979 by the army, backed by landed elites. Among other transgressions, Bhutto had announced higher taxation of the landed rich, the takeover of over a million acres of land for redistribution to the landless under the slogan "land to the tiller," and ceiling limits on the property of large landowners (Ahmed 1980). Where land reform happened, say, in South Korea in 1949–50, it was enabled by a very particular set of factors. In this case, approximately 18 percent of land was released from Japanese settler occupation to South Korean tenants and tillers. This amounted to 663,950 acres. Although the end of Japanese colonial rule was a key factor, so was the growing threat of communism, including in North Korea which carried out a far more extensive redistribution of land. South Korea's American allies encouraged land reform in this context, even though property redistribution would have been a no-go area in the United States itself. Importantly, as in Southern Africa or South Asia, in South Korea too the land of Korean landowners remained unaffected by the reform (Kim 2016).

Communist states such as Cuba and Vietnam are an exception to the general rule of unaccomplished land reform seen in much of the postcolonial world. Communist North Vietnam under Ho Chi Minh, for instance, was guided by the principle of "land to the tiller." After Vietnam gained its independence from France in 1954, land was redistributed from large French plantations and Vietnamese landlords to small farmers. Soon after, following the nationalization of farmland, and the spur to collectivized farming in China and the USSR, Vietnam also undertook collectivization. However, food shortages and resistance from Vietnamese farmers led to a reversal of this system in the 1980s. Since the 1990s, land has been equally distributed among households on long term leases, of twenty years for annual crops and fifty years for perennial crops. By 2013, all land in Vietnam could be leased for fifty years (To, Mahanty and Wells-Dang 2019). This land can be exchanged, willed, transferred, leased, and mortgaged. The right to land has been acknowledged as taking millions out of poverty and ensuring food sovereignty (Do and Iyer 2008). Alongside the benefits to individuals, a state that has faced high-stakes wars with powers such as the French and the Americans has used land to build its legitimacy among the population, and to keep up their morale through political upheaval. Lease rights in land have territorially and politically secured the state.

Despite notable outliers, most postcolonial states veered in the direction of reproducing the property-based inequalities of colonial regimes. The equitable intentions of some within new governments did not quite translate to radical land reform. The rule of property, and of the propertied, reflected where power in the state was located. As an apparatus of rule, the state has for long been termed a "capitalist state" (Poulantzas 1973). This is a state in (and shaped by) a capitalist society (Miliband 1969), and a state of the dominant proprietary classes (Bardhan 1998). The discussion above etches how this state was forged in a regime of land as property. Here the state was decreeing, through its actions and inaction, which of its allied groups had the right to control land and which groups did not.

Even as most postcolonial states ensured that land remained in the hands of the few rather than the many, in a parallel action, they took land away from largely disenfranchised groups in the name of development. The mid-twentieth century was the Age of Development, with the developmental state as its champion and chief architect. Development, though, was not conjured out of thin air. The large infrastructure and heavy industry that was synonymous with development at the time required vast amounts of land. The authority of the state was once again deployed to shape land allocation. Land reflected state authority, and state authority was forged in the administering of the land. It is in this context that the Indian state displaced over 18.5 million people in the name of development between 1950 and 1990 (Lama 2000). This included 200,000 people, mostly indigenous Adivasis, who were made to leave their fields, forests, and homes so that a series of dams could be built on the Narmada River. The dams' reservoirs have submerged approximately 37,000 hectares of forest and agricultural land. The canals, waterways, and field channels that take Narmada water farther afield for drinking, irrigation, and industry have submerged another 152,000 hectares (Parasuraman 1999). Although development projects have tended to promise rehabilitation, and replacement plots of land for the displaced, this promise has rarely been delivered (Dungdung 2019).

As with India, in China too, the depredations of development disproportionately affect the rural populace, and those in internal, disenfranchised, and ethnic minority areas. Xinjiang, with its Muslim minority Uyghurs, has long been China's main site for testing its nuclear arsenal. It is also a key mining field for oil and gas, and for the extraction of uranium, which fuels China's nuclear program (Alexis-Martin 2019). Like earlier colonial states, China treats the western minority province, and its population, as a space of extraction. This is a land considered waste and unsettled. It is therefore easily deployed in the service of the larger nation. More recently, as China has tried to mainstream Xinjiang via its Go West policy, it has encouraged ethnic majority Han Chinese to settle there. Simultaneously, Uyghurs seen as dissidents have been imprisoned in "re-education" camps (Maizland 2021). Vast infrastructure projects like highways and railway lines, with their familiar story of accompanying displacement, synonymize "development."

As the state has written its authority into the land, and its peoples via regimes of territory, property, extraction, and development, its story is not linear. While I have argued for more continuity than change in the transition from colonialism to the postcolonial, there have been points in time when the state's connection with land has been significantly amended. From the close of the twentieth century, the shift to the market in much of the global South has precipitated a re-constitution of the relationship between land, state, and people.

Liberalizing land

States have embraced market liberalization in the twenty-first century. This includes the liberalization of land markets, which has entailed opening up to the forces of capital, particularly sought-after foreign capital (Deininger 2003; Sud 2007, 2009; Fairbairn 2020). In many cases in Central and South America, Africa, and Asia, this opening up to the market has been further compelled by debt servicing conditions imposed by International Financial Institutions such as the International Monetary Fund. Southern countries have been most vulnerable to the process that a vast literature recognizes as large-scale land deals, and even "land grab." This is the at times coercive takeover of substantial tracts of land, usually over 200 hectares, by regional and international capital, often facilitated by the state (Borras and Franco 2012). By one estimate, international investors have acquired 64.6 million hectares of land in the last twenty years (Land Matrix 2022). This land can be used for corporate farming, biofuel production, industrial manufacturing, tourism, logging, privatized infrastructure such as ports, export-promotion zones, and more. Even when the land lies unused, non-operational land deals become instruments of dispossession, affecting land-owning farmers and farm labor, as well as fishworkers, forest produce pickers, pastoralists, and other users of common land. Operational and non-operational land deals serve the current and future interests of capital (Borras et al 2022). Land, and what is built on it, remains flexible and expandable, and often defies categorization as infrastructure, real estate, or climate mitigation projects, etc. (Sud 2020a). Invariably, through all this contortion and expropriation, humans and nature are disrupted for globalized private investment.

Market reform via the liberalization of land holdings has raised questions about state authority and territorial sovereignty (Zoomers 2010). This is particularly pertinent in large, privatized infrastructure zones that have been propped up across the world to encourage manufacturing and global trade. Variously termed Special Economic Zones (SEZs), Special Infrastructure Zones, Trade Promotion Zones, Infrastructure Corridors, Economic Corridors, and the like, they can be privately owned or deploy some form of Public Private Partnership. In the case of the China–Pakistan Economic Corridor (CPEC), for instance, concerns have been raised that Pakistan could become a "satellite state" of China. China has invested $62 billion in CPEC, which is integral to its vast Belt and Road Initiative that spans Asia and Europe and is key to its global ambitions. In return, according to the CPEC Master Plan prepared by China, Pakistan has leased swaths of its land to China; allowed the establishment of a monitoring and surveillance system in key locations; agreed to deepen Chinese market presence in sectors ranging from electronics to agricultural technologies; and agreed to non-reciprocal visa-free travel for Chinese nationals, including personnel deployed to work for, and manage, CPEC (Qaiser 2018).

In contrast to concerns about the whittling away of state sovereignty in the garb of market liberalization, a robust literature points to the continued importance of the state in the regime of the market (Evans 1995, Sud 2009, Kohli 2012). This is even the case in debt-exposed countries like Pakistan. While China's geo-strategic presence is undeniable, scholars have also pointed to the room for maneuver that the construction and operation of CPEC has provided to the Pakistani military (Hameed 2018). Relations between Pakistan's powerful military and civilian governments have typically been tense. Increased security concerns around CPEC have given the military more say in internal strategic matters. The fact that CPEC incorporates the sensitive border province of Balochistan has led to accusations that the military is using the infrastructure project to increase control over the region, further tap into its mineral resources, clamp down on dissent, and mainstream Balochistan to the detriment of its peoples, who seek autonomy (Ahmad and Mehmood 2017; Virk 2020). Thus, even at a time when its territorial sovereignty is being unsettled, elements of Pakistan's state have used the moment to reassert their territorial authority on a troubled frontier.

Now as before, the state is central to the making of land—as property, as authority, and as territory. The state has had to work with a range of actors in these processes of land-making, be they colonial comprador elites, postcolonial landlords, farmers who had to be brought on board amid the threat of revolution, industrialists seeking land for "national" progress, or, increasingly, transnational capital. As the state has channeled land for various projects over time, it has been made in turn: as promoting the rule of property, as constituting territorial order, as frontier authority, and as a facilitator of development and market-driven globalization. The making of land has thus allowed the state to don the garb of the colonial and civilizing state, the postcolonial developmental state, or the open-for-business globalizing state. Through all of this, generally speaking, land for the many has continued being channeled to the few. Even in communist states such as Vietnam, which I presented as an exception in the era of failed land reform, recent governments have encouraged a "land concentration" policy. This policy favors private infrastructure and industry. It has given rise to the fear of a "new landlordism" in the name of market efficiency and productivity (To, Mahanty and Wells-Dang 2019).

In this context, how has the state managed to maintain its hold over both land and people? States have periodically faced unrest over land and agrarian issues in the periods covered in this paper. Recently, there have been protests and even violent resistance to land grab by big companies, often aimed at the role of the state in this process. There have been agitations against private ports, SEZs, Special Industrial Regions in India (Sud 2020a; Akhtar 2020); biofuel plantations in Tanzania (Makoye 2013); urban gentrification in Brazil (Perry 2013); corporate land concessions in Cambodia (Mi Young Park 2019); and in a host of other contexts across the world (Hall et al 2015). The state has used persuasion, incorporation of key actors and consequent de-politicization of their agitational causes, and even coercion and violence to control land-based protest. In this way, it has re-asserted its authority when this may have been called into question on account of partisan governance. At the same time, the control of protest against largescale corporate land transfers cannot be a substantive solution to a restive and asset-poor population. It is here that the state as idea (Abrams 1988), as imagination (Hansen and Stepputat 2001), or even as a brand (Kaur 2020) must step in.

States have routinely conjured dreams around land, well beyond what they can fulfill in practice. The old slogan of "land to the tiller" was a rallying cry for newly independent nations. It energized the populace, even if it could not meet the hunger for land and livelihoods. More recently, the state has once again animated populations around the idea of land. However, now it hardly ever promises land to the tiller. Instead, the state is peddling pride in the land or, rather, in the motherland. Here, the territorial identity and integrity of the nation, invested in a defined piece of land, becomes the totemic object around which increasingly unequal nations (Sanchez-Ancochea 2020) are asked to cohere. We see such politics centering on blood and soil, which "others" at will. This othering could include real or imagined terrorists, international aggressors, and migrants at the borders. It may also single out refugees, migrants, and ethnic minorities within countries, in a range of Northern and Southern contexts.

In the South, we are witnessing this phenomenon in Modi's India which is being construed as "one nation, one culture, one people" despite being an extremely diverse, multi-cultural and multi-religious society. Now every resident must put "India First," or be labelled an "anti-national terrorist." Allegiance to Bharat Mata, or Mother India is repeatedly demanded in a charged context, where the soil and the country's borders are becoming increasingly fetishized. Dramatically professing allegiance to the soil, say, by putting it symbolically on one's forehead as a mark of respect and loyalty, is routinely expected of Modi-supporting "sons of the soil." Similarly in Brazil, the ultra-right-wing authoritarian Jair Bolsonaro came to power in 2018 vowing to defend national sovereignty. He immediately withdrew Brazil from a UN-led global compact on safe and orderly migration (behaving much as Trump did in the United States). He and his Cabinet have regularly portrayed migrants as threatening the security, order, and culture of the nation (Filomeno and Vicino 2021). Those who argue for more welcoming borders are branded "enemies of the nation." This rhetoric justifies an aggressive, securitized state, and strongmen, nativist authoritarians standing guard over a supposedly threatened land. The land itself is invested with the aspirations of a homogenized nation. It is enlivened with sacrality, identity, and notions of grandeur. Enlivened land protected by the authoritarian state overlaps with liberalized land channeled to the market via a business-friendly state. Despite many twists and turns, the state by and large remains the force juggling the competing demands of politics, society, and the economy as they intertwine with multi-dimensional land. The state continues to govern the land and being made and re-made in the process.

While the state etches order through its governing of land, it would be analytically flawed to portray it as a unitary entity perpetually and tightly in control. A fine-grained study can unpick the chinks in the ordering logic of the land-making state, and in the make-up of this state as well. Now we turn to such scenes of seeming dis-order, which stretch what we know about both land and the state.

Everyday transgressions as land-making and state-making

A vibrant literature in anthropology and cognate disciplines takes us past the unitary state that rules from above via grand policies and headline practice. Instead, it highlights an everyday state (Fuller and Benei 2001) that is a set of ideas, practices, and politics that need not cohere (Abrams 1988; Sud 2009). This state is a porous hybrid of official and unofficial actors (Jaffe 2013), which stretch its boundaries (Sud 2020b). This stretched-out state, which regularly exceeds its legally mandated duties, is also a shadowy state at the margins (Das and Poole 2004). Ultimately, the shadows and stretched-out porosity of the state are routinized. They become the state. This snapshot of the everyday state is critical to understanding everyday land-making on the ground. For this exercise, I take the reader to one of my field sites in Kachchh, coastal western India. The everyday state and everyday land-making practices are best studied through a micro, high-definition lens, departing from the wider angle of the previous sections.

Kachchh is a vast semi-arid region on the sensitive border with Pakistan. An earthquake in 2001, followed by then Chief Minister Narendra Modi's push to modernize the region's economy, has led to a proliferation of enterprise in Kachchh. This drive has been spearheaded by big capital from India and beyond. It has resulted in manufacturing units, private ports and jetties for facilitating export, massive infrastructure zones, and energy hubs in the form of thermal power plants and, more recently, wind and solar farms (Sud 2020a). Kachchh's land has been fundamental to its ongoing transformation. In the reading of senior state actors that I interviewed, as well as the emissaries of large firms, this land is "waste." It is mere desert, and unproductive marshy coastland. It will be turned into something of value via capitalist enterprise, facilitated by a business-friendly state (Sud 2009, 2020a). Such rhetoric is starkly reminiscent of the colonial *terra nullius* trope I discussed earlier.

Moving away from *terra nullius*, and arguing along the analytical lines I have already sketched here, the story of contemporary Kachcch could be written via the making and re-making of its land. This story would highlight (a) the state's regulatory authority, which decrees how land is to be used and by whom; (b) the use of laws like India's Land Acquisition Act, as well as persuasion and coercion to transfer commons and private agricultural land to big capital in an increasing commodification and "propertyfication"; (c) nationalist rhetoric around the territorially sensitive borderland of Kachchh that must be protected through a proliferation of productivity and enterprise, as opposed to shady activities carried out by itinerant coastal fishworkers and desert pastoralists; (d) the enlivenment of Kachchhi space as a sacred, Hindu motherland needing protection from the Muslim and Pakistani "other," which is then manifested in renewed temple-building activity that also harks back to real or imagined glorious pasts (see Sud 2021, 2022). The federal state, and the national state, are currently deeply involved in the multi-dimensional making and re-making of Kachchhi land as authority, property, territory and enlivened. In the process, the state is reinvigorated as pro-business, enterprising, decisive, strong, and steeped in Hindu nationalist values.

The preceding argument follows the established analytical arch of this chapter. Now, I argue that the story of Kachchh's land can be pushed further by exploring around the edges of both land and the state. I do this through the figure of the middleman. My field research in Kachchh at a large SEZ and surrounding manufacturing facilities brought me into contact with many intermediaries in land. They were locals, often well connected via networks of caste and community, and eager to get a share of the development pie. Some ran shops; others were small-time political workers; and several had some family land to leverage in their pursuit of bigger aspirations. As capital started to filter into their area, these local men made it their business to be involved in mushrooming land transactions. They became carriers of information, negotiators of deals, bargaining hubs for buyers and sellers, settlers, and, at times, starters of conflict, as well as hangers on in government offices to gather key information, peddle bribes, and befriend relevant officials. While some on this spectrum of middlemen engaged the upper end of the land market, others were local rowdies, deployed to nudge recalcitrant land users and owners. I have elaborated elsewhere on the chain of land middlemen, from the large land aggregators to the local errand boys and musclemen (Sud 2014). Regardless of the part of the chain they occupy, these land middlemen can be defined as go-betweens. They are facilitative and/or obstructive agents in a process that may contain seemingly apparent start and end points. The latter could be sale and purchase of land, confirmation of property status, or even distortion of property status or of state regulatory authority over land.

A middleman interviewee in Kachchh described his land work this way:

> Whatever [property] title we can get on the land is good. And sometimes if there is very *seedha sadhaa* [straightforward] title, we can also spoil it. Power is in *kabza* [access via possession]. You [the farmer seeking to sell land to a Company via a middleman] don't sleep in the *khet* [field] do you? No, you don't. I will just send five men; they will go and sit in your *khet* at night. Next morning, they will put [a] fence on your *khet*. Now will you want to fight me in court or just settle with money? If you go to court, you will be dead before anything comes out. *Litigation mein toh zindagi nikal jayegi*. If you take possession your position becomes strong, because everybody is scared of Court *chakkar* [rounds of the Courts].
>
> — Interviewed, Village Lahiyaria, August 12, 2015, my translation from the Hindi

This man, let us call him JB, lives in one of the villages bordering the SEZ. He is a former village headman and is affiliated to the ruling Bharatiya Janata Party (BJP). In this quotation, JB is asserting his authority over land. He derives this authority from the lingering influence of his official position in the village and from his social and political standing. In addition to bringing our attention to land as a crucible of authority—not just of the state, but also of local strongmen—JB is pointing to another dimension of land that we have overlooked so far. This is land as *access* and *exclusion*. Here, beyond the right to own and exchange property, is the ability to derive benefit from it (Ribot and Peluso 2003). Similarly, non-state actors may territorialize and enliven land. JB's collaborator, MB, for instance, proudly told me about the socially etched borders in their rapidly changing village.

> We have *soch* [thinking] that we will not keep non-Gujaratis in this *gaon* [village]... We have a high Rajput [upper caste] culture, which we don't want spoiled by others. You will see there is no non-veg [food] in this village. Our women vomit at just the thought of it.
>
> —Interview, Village Lahiyaria, August 22, 2015, my translation from the Hindi

MB, supported by his upper-caste Hindu neighbors, is highlighting a territorial distinction between the "original" and pure (apparently vegetarian) village, and the supposedly polluted peripheries occupied by the migrant laborers who now work in the factories and zones of his homeland. Women, as enforced bearers of purity, and Mother India more symbolically must be protected from the defiled "other." Clearly, along with powers of making land as access, territory, and enlivened, come coterminous powers of exclusion, that is, to exclude others from benefiting from the different dimensions of land (Hall, Hirsch and Li 2011).

By inserting themselves into ongoing land deals and the larger politics of land, middlemen like JB further prize open the state that is multi-dimensional and dynamic.

The middlemen's wheeling and dealing around land invariably involves the state, which is brought in for dispute resolution or persuaded to look away. A state that looks away is not inefficient or lacking in capacity. On the contrary, it is fortifying the business-friendly, neoliberal form that its overt alignment with contemporary capitalism demands. This state of commission, or omission, is acknowledging and facilitating extra-economic means for the eventual transfer of land in the service of capital.

At the same time, by working with the state while land is, say, transitioned from property to disputed access, to formalized property once again, middlemen are able to push at where the boundaries of the state lie. In my field research in Kachchh, I observed influential middlemen hang out with ground-level state officials at tea shops. They also had opportunities to visit the houses of officials or other notables to discuss land deals. This blurring of the boundaries (Gupta 1995) of state work chips away at an otherwise overbearing and inaccessible state, whose sights are set on global investment and big business. The everyday actors of my ethnography stretch the state into some diluted and mediated version of access. That is, this everyday, porous state is made somewhat more accessible to a populace that can now approach it through well-connected middlemen. Of course, even this access is via the caveats of class, caste, gender, or other social characteristics. The state, on high or on the ground, is never equally accessible to all. Importantly, in the process of bargaining and mediation, middlemen find themselves associated with power and stateness, which further elevates their ability to intervene in land matters.

In my field site, middlemen use their power and proximity to the state to align with capitalist projects in the making. MB, for instance, is involved in transport, labor, and materials contracting for a factory that supplies the SEZ that now dominates the landscape. At the same time, the factory management and the SEZ personnel try to keep individuals like JB and MB on their side. They are aware that "it takes very little" for these local strongmen to incite a dispute, challenge a particular land deal, or generally "make life difficult."[2] Confirming this, JB recounts showing personnel from a well-known beverages company around, when they expressed an interest in setting up a bottling plant in the area. JB offered to work for them as a land broker, even extracting a cash advance for himself and his hangers on. Yet, he was fully aware that given the brackishness of water in the region, and the rapidly falling water table, the Company was not likely to get far in its quest for a factory-site.[3]

In a context where big capital works closely with state elites to dominate an area, the stories of middlemen and the porous state they tap into, show us land-state-people relationships at the edges of land governance. At the same time, these relationships constitute the very heart of global capitalism, in that they embed capital via its spatial, locational fix (Harvey 2005). Importantly, relations between a porous, land-making state, and aspirational societal actors in land that is undergoing capitalist transition show us a picture of land-making and state-making that is a little beyond the dominant story.[4]

It is this variegated picture that other stakeholders in my field locations tap into to question the state-business hegemony around land. The SEZ discussed here has been a site of protest and litigation for decades. Local fishworkers, pastoralists, and farmers who have lost land to it have consistently questioned its making in regulatory terms, in its land use, as well as its environmental credentials (see Sud 2021). A wide-ranging literature tells us that challenging contemporary capitalist land-making and related state intervention is an uphill battle globally (Perry 2013; Yaro and Tsikata 2013; Hall et al. 2015; Nielsen 2018; Joshi 2020). But that such protest is undertaken again and again points to spaces believed to have some give. Understanding land, the state, and the structures they work with and enable relationally allows us to see this give. This is alongside an acute recognition of the dominant, ordering patterns of land-making and state-making highlighted throughout this chapter (see also Cousins, this volume).

Conclusion

This chapter has analyzed land-making as state-making, and vice versa. It followed a relational perspective that appreciates the intertwinement of the social and the natural worlds. Here, land is not fixed or inert. It is continually made and re-made along socially-infused dimensions. These reveal land multi-dimensionally as authority, property, territory, enlivened, and as access and exclusion. Although different social entities can act on land, my focus was on the state as a preeminent actor in the many lives of land.

Through much of its trajectory, the state has made and re-made land. It has exercised its authority over land via policy, practice, and politics. It has ordered and controlled land as territory, thereby also controlling who can be on the land and who is to be kept out. It has designated a class of collaborators by decreeing a right to private property. Simultaneously, the state has engaged with land as enlivened, harking to a politics of sacrality, memory, and identity to reach larger portions of the populace. Finally, the state that is hardly unitary has also been stretched into shadows and porosity by claims around land-making from aspirational populations. Using the example of local middlemen, I showed land being accessed beyond its formal, state-assigned dimensions based on the ability rather than right to derive benefit from it. Powers of access and exclusion are routinely exercised over land, with the state as a party via omission or commission. In the process, the porosity of the state is routinized. The making of land as state-designated order, but also disorder, becomes the multiplicity through which land and the state are made and re-made in the everyday. This is, as the title of the chapter suggests, land-making as state-making.

The chapter demonstrated processes of land-making as state-making over an expanse of time, with a spatial focus on the global South, and across scales from the continental to the national and local. It showed colonial states instituting regimes of property and territory, which then spilled over into postcolonial land-making and state-making. Although there were exceptions, say, in Communist states, most newly independent states of the South carried on with narrow regimes of property, further constricted by the march of modernizing development. This demanded that forest, field, and common be converted into heavy-industry, infrastructure, and urban space. A state comprising dominant groups, and working on their behalf, has been further narrowed in its agendas as Southern countries have moved to market-oriented economies from the late twentieth century. With the liberalization of land markets, swaths of land have been channeled to private corporations, triggering fears of a land grab. Added to this are concerns of the "foreignization of space" (Zoomers 2010) as international companies, banks, and governments invest in land, infrastructure, and production across the globe, especially in countries with high indebtedness and weak regulatory checks and balances.

Reading the state and land multi-dimensionally allows us to appreciate the doubling down of the state, not just its hollowing out in the age of global capital. Today, a renewed politics of territorial security and migration control exists alongside the enlivened rhetoric of blood and soil. There are proliferating examples of strong states standing tall to protect endangered motherlands, often with authoritarians at the helm. Even as strong states assert control over land to keep territory and populations in check, they enter into shadowy arrangements, with elements of the population acting on land as socialized territory, identity, memory, access, exclusion, and more. This partial sharing of power over land is a mechanism of societal appeasement in an age of global capital, but also of wider social control.

Overall, the picture the chapter presents is of state power exercised through the making and re-making of land, along with influential sections of society and the economy. This includes property-owning colonized natives and landlords, regional and international capital, and socially and politically connected intermediaries. Throughout the argument, the relationship between land, state, and people has been far from one-way or constant. This compels us to keep an eye on the changing big picture of both land-making and state-making.

As a final point, it is worth underlining the contribution of this chapter to the handbook it is part of. The introduction by the handbook's editors sets out a provocation to understand "change in continuity" in land and commodity frontier-making. Here, powerful global forces are overlapping, materially and discursively, with classic agrarian issues of environmental crises, the scope and forms of extractivism, land and commodity frontier-making, and their exhaustion (see also chapter by Peters, this volume). This chapter demonstrates change in continuity in land and commodity frontier-making by historicizing the material and discursive processes of extraction and state-making in the first half of the argument, and moving on to the more contemporary forms of the same in the second half. Future work may want to take up these themes more fully, and for different parts of the world.[5]

Acknowledgments

Very many thanks to the reviewers: Mihika Chatterjee and Sango Mahanty, who provided careful and detailed feedback on an initial draft. Their suggestions are reflected at several points in the finalized chapter. I also acknowledge the editors of this volume: Jun Borras and Jenny Franco, who invited me to contribute a chapter, read a draft, and provided helpful and encouraging comments at various stages of writing.

Notes

1. See Ojeda (this volume) for a feminist perspective on land beyond property.
2. SEZ manager, interviewed on site, December 22, 2008.
3. Former village headman and land broker JB, interview with the author, Village Lahiyaria, August 12, 2015.
4. A rich literature on borderlands points to contingent state sovereignty in these frontier regions (Mahanty 2018). While Kachchh is indeed a border region, in larger writing on different parts of India, I show similar contestations and transgressions around the everyday state and multi-dimensional land (Sud 2021). Borderlands might reveal these processes in heightened form.
5. Thanks to Dr Mihika Chatterjee for insisting on, and framing, this last point.

References

Abrams, P. 1988. "Notes on the Difficulty of Studying the State." *Journal of Historical Sociology* 1(1): 58–89.

Ahmad, M and R. Mehmood 2017. "Surveillance, Authoritarianism and 'Imperial Effects' in Pakistan." *Surveillance and Society* 15 (3/4): 506–513.

Ahmed, M. 1980 *Contemporary Pakistan: Politics, Economy, and Society*. Durham, NC: Carolina Academic Press.

Akhtar, R. 2020. "Neoliberalism and Hindutva in the Actually Existing State: The case of Dholera Smart City." Unpublished DPhil thesis, University of Oxford.

Alexander, J. 2006. *The Unsettled Land: State-making and the Politics of Land in Zimbabwe 1893–2003*. Oxford: James Currey.

Alexis-Martin, B. 2019. "The Nuclear Imperialism-Necropolitics Nexus: Contextualizing Chinese-Uyghur Oppression in Our Nuclear Age." *Eurasian Geography and Economics* 60 (2): 152–176.

Appadurai, A. 1993. "Number in the Colonial Imagination." In *Orientalism and the Postcolonial Predicament: Perspectives on South Asia*, edited by C. A. Breckenridge and P. Van der Veer, 314–339. Philadelphia: University of Pennsylvania Press.

Bardhan, P. 1998. *The Political Economy of Development in India*. Oxford: Basil Blackwell.

Basu Ray Chaudhury, A. and A. K. Ghosh 2021. "Trans-Border Migration: Bridging the Gap between State and Human Security." *ORF Occasional Paper* No. 311, April, Observer Research Foundation. https://www.orfonline.org/wp-content/uploads/2021/04/ORF_OccasionalPaper_311_Migration_26April.pdf.

Borras, S. M. Jr. and J. Franco 2012. "Global Land Grabbing and Trajectories of Agrarian Change: A Preliminary Analysis." *Journal of Agrarian Change* 12(1): 34–59.

Borras, S. M. Jr., J. C. Franco, T. Moreda, Y. Xu, N. Bruna, and B. A. Demena 2022. "The Value of so-called 'Failed' Large-scale Land Acquisitions." *Land Use Policy* 119: 106199.

Chamunogwa, A. 2019. Power at the margins of post-colonial states in Africa: Remaking authority on fast track resettlement farms in Zimbabwe. Unpublished DPhil Thesis, University of Oxford.

Chatterjee, N. 2020. *Negotiating Mughal Law: A Family of Landlords across Three Indian Empires*. Cambridge: Cambridge University Press.

Chowdhury, S. M. 2020. "Bangladesh-India Relations: History and the Way Forward." *Indian Foreign Affairs Journal* 15(3): 191–198.

Cohn, B. S. 2002. *Colonialism and Its Forms of Knowledge. The British in India*. New Delhi: Oxford University Press.

Cousins, B. (forthcoming). "Land, Social Reproduction and Agrarian Change." In *Oxford Handbook of Land Politics*, edited by S. Borras and J. Franco, 385–403. Oxford: Oxford University Press.

Das, V. and D. Poole (eds.) 2004. *Anthropology in the Margins of the State: Comparative Ethnographies*. Oxford: James Currey Ltd.

Deininger, K. 2003. "Land Markets in Developing and Transition Economies: Impact of Liberalization and Implications for Future Reform." *American Journal of Agricultural Economics* 85(5): 1217–22.

Do, Q.-T. and L. Iyer 2008. "Land Titling and Rural Transition in Vietnam." *Economic Development and Cultural Change* 56(3): 531–579.

Dungdung, G. 2019. "Development over Deadbodies." Adivasi Hunkar: Amplifying the Voice of the Indigenous Peoples of India, https://adivasihunkar.wordpress.com/2019/01/08/development-over-deadbodies/.

Elden, S. 2010. "Land, Terrain, Territory." *Progress in Human Geography* 34(6): 799–817.

Evans, P. 1995. *Embedded Autonomy. States and Industrial Transformation*. Princeton, NJ: Princeton University.

Fairbairn, M. 2020. *Fields of Gold: Financing the Global Land Rush*. Ithaca, NY: Cornell University Press.

Filomeno, F. A. and T. J. Vicino 2021. "The Evolution of Authoritarianism and Restrictionism in Brazilian Immigration Policy: Jair Bolsonaro in Historical Perspective." *Bulletin of Latin American Research* 40(4): 598–612.

Foucault, M. 1966, 2002. *The Order of Things: An Archaeology of the Human Sciences*. London: Routledge.

Fuller, C. J. and V. Benei (eds.) 2001. *The Everyday State and Society in Modern India*. London: Hurst and Company.

Graeber, D. 2015. *The Utopia of Rules: On Technology, Stupidity and the Secret Joys of Bureaucracy*. London: Melville House Publishing.

Gupta, A. 1995. "Blurred Boundaries: The Discourse of Corruption, the Culture of Politics, and the Imagined State." *American Ethnologist* 22(2): 375–402.

Habib, I. 2013. *The Agrarian System of Mughal India: 1556–1707*, 3rd edn. New Delhi: Oxford University Press.

Hall, D., P. Hirsch, and T. M. Li 2011. *Powers of Exclusion: Land Dilemmas in Southeast Asia*. Honolulu: University of Hawai'i Press.

Hall, R. et al. 2015. "Resistance, Acquiescence or Incorporation? An Introduction to Land Grabbing and Political Reactions 'from below'." *Journal of Peasant Studies* 42(3–4): 467–488.

Hameed, M. 2018. "The Politics of the China-Pakistan Economic Corridor." *Nature: Humanities and Social Sciences Communications* 4: 64, https://doi.org/10.1057/s41599-018-0115-7.

Hansen, T. B. and F. Stepputat 2001. *States of Imagination: Ethnographic Explorations of the Postcolonial State*. Durham, NC: Duke University Press.

Harvey, D. 2005. *A Brief History of Neoliberalism*. Oxford: Oxford University Press.
Jaffe, R. 2013. "The Hybrid State: Crime and Citizenship in Urban Jamaica." *American Ethnologist* 40(4): 734–748.
Joshi, S. 2020. "Contesting Land Grabs, Negotiating Statehood: The Politics of International Accountability Mechanisms and Land Disputes in Rural Cambodia." *Third World Quarterly* 41(9): 1615–1633.
Kaur, R. 2020. *Brand New Nation: India in the Global Economy*. Stanford, CA: Stanford University Press.
Kohli, A. 2012. *Poverty Amid Plenty in the New India*. New York: Cambridge University Press.
Kim, I. 2016. "Land Reform in South Korea under the US Military Occupation, 1945–1948." *Journal of Cold War Studies* 18(2): 97–129.
Lama, M. P. 2000. "Internal Displacement in India: Causes, Protection and Dilemmas." *Forced Migration Review*, August: 24–26.
Land Matrix 2022. Global Observatory, https://landmatrix.org/map.
Locke, J. 1960. *Two Treatises of Government*, edited by P. Laslett. Cambridge: Cambridge University Press.
Mahanty, S. 2018. "Contingent Sovereignty: Cross-Border Rentals in the Cambodia-Vietnam Borderland." *Annals of the American Association of Geographers* 108(3): 829–844.
Makki, F. 2014. "Development by Dispossession: *Terra Nullius* and the Social-Ecology of New Enclosures in Ethiopia." *Rural Sociology* 79(1): 79–103.
Maizland, L. 2021. "China's Repression of Uyghurs in Xinjiang." *Council on Foreign Relations*, Backgrounder, https://www.cfr.org/backgrounder/chinas-repression-uyghurs-xinjiang.
Makoye, K. 2013. "Tanzania Farmers Accuse Biofuel Investors of Land Grab." Thomson Reuters Foundation, https://news.trust.org/item/20130718134927-q50zx.
Mamdani, M. 2018. *Citizen and Subject: Contemporary Africa and the Legacy of Late Colonialism*. Princeton, NJ: Princeton University Press.
Mi Young Park, C. 2019. "'Our Lands are Our Lives': Gendered Experiences of Resistance to Land Grabbing in Rural Cambodia." *Feminist Economics* 25(4): 21–44.
Miliband, R. 1969. *State in Capitalist Society*. London: Quartet Books.
Mill, J. S. 1836. "Civilization: Signs of the Times." In *The Collected Works of John Stuart Mill, Volume XVIII: Essays on Politics and Society, Part I*, edited by John M. Robson, 117–48. Toronto: University of Toronto Press.
Mitchell, T. 2002. *Rule of Experts: Egypt, Techno-Politics, Modernity*. Berkeley: University of California Press.
Nielsen, K. B. 2018. *Land Dispossession and Everyday Politics in Rural Eastern India*. London: Anthem Press.
Ojeda, D. (forthcoming). "Beyond Land as Property: A Feminist Perspective." In *Oxford Handbook of Land Politics*, edited by S. Borras and J. Franco. Oxford: Oxford University Press.
Parasuraman, S. 1999. *The Development Dilemma: Displacement in India*. London: Palgrave Macmillan.
Perry, K.-K. Y. 2013. *Black Women Against the Land Grab: The Fight for Racial Justice in Brazil*. Minneapolis: University of Minnesota Press.
Peters, P. (forthcoming). "Struggles over land under Customary Tenure in Contemporary Sub-Saharan Africa." In *Oxford Handbook of Land Politics*, edited by S. Borras and J. Franco. Oxford: Oxford University Press.
Poulantzas, N. 1973. *Political Power and Social Classes*. New York: Verso.

Qaiser, A. 2018. "CPEC: Pakistan's 'Chinaization' or Colonization?" *On Track: The Conference of Defence Associations Institute* 23(1): 12–21.
Ribot, J. C. and N. L. Peluso 2003. "A Theory of Access." *Rural Sociology* 68(2): 153–181.
Sanchez-Ancochea, D. 2020. *The Costs of Inequality in Latin America: Warnings and Lessons for the Rest of the World.* Cambridge: Cambridge University Press.
Sud, N. 2007. "From Land to the Tiller to Land Liberalisation: The Political Economy of Gujarat's Shifting Land Policy." *Modern Asian Studies* 41(3): 603–637.
Sud, N. 2009. "The Indian State in a Liberalizing Landscape." *Development and Change* 40(4), 645–665.
Sud, N. 2014. "The Men in the Middle: A Missing Dimension in Global Land Deals." *Journal of Peasant Studies* 41(4): 593–612.
Sud, N. 2020a. "Making the Political, and Doing Politics: Unfixed Land in an Amoebal Zone in India." *Journal of Peasant Studies* 47(6): 1348–1370.
Sud, N. 2020b. "The Unfixed State of Unfixed Land." *Development and Change* 51(5): 1175–1198.
Sud, N. 2022. "The Actual Gujarat Model: Authoritarianism, Capitalism, Hindu Nationalism and Populism in the Time of Modi." *Journal of Contemporary Asia* 52(1): 102–126.
Sud, N. 2021. *The Making of Land and The Making of India.* New Delhi: Oxford University Press.
To, P. X., S. Mahanty, and A. Wells-Dang 2019. "From 'Land to the Tiller' to the 'New Landlords'? The Debate over Vietnam's Latest Land Reforms." *Land* 8(8): 120, https://www.mdpi.com/2073-445X/8/8/120.
Ulloa, A. 2005. *The Ecological Native: Indigenous Peoples' Movements and Eco-governmentality In Colombia.* New York: Routledge.
Virk, H. F. 2020. "CPEC: A Discourse on Space, Security and Development in Balochistan." *Journal of Global Peace and Security Studies* 1(1): 47–69.
Yaro, J. A. and D. Tsikata 2013. "Savannah Fires and Local Resistance to Transnational Land Deals: The Case of Organic Mango Farming in Dipale, Northern Ghana." *African Geographical Review* 32(1): 72–87.
Zoomers, A. 2010. "Globalisation and the Foreignisation of Space: Seven Processes Driving the Current Global Land Grab." *Journal of Peasant Studies* 37(2): 429–447.

CHAPTER 25

STATE, LAND, AND CITIZENSHIP

ANDREW OFSTEHAGE AND WENDY WOLFORD

INTRODUCTION

THE modern state is fundamentally a territorial project (Elden 2010; Paquette 2019). Born in the so-called Age of Discovery (Seed 1995), refined through conquest, and increasingly measured by the well-being and productivity of its population, the modern state is co-constituted by the designation of a territory (the land) and a people (Fitzmaurice 2014).[1] As an ideology, form of power, and a set of political institutions (Mitchell 1991), the state defines and defends a group of citizens through their material, symbolic, and cultural relationship to the land (see Sud, this volume). The connection between national land (often referred to as "homeland," "fatherland," or "motherland") and citizenship is produced over time and across space through formal and informal means. Citizenship is formally conferred through birthright (i.e., by blood, *jus sanguinis*, or by soil, *jus soli*) and naturalization. It is recognized through a combination of legal rights conferring the right to settle on the land and participate in governance and elections.[2] Legal rights and citizenship, however, sit alongside everyday negotiations over descent, belonging, heritage, and territorial origin (Berry 2009). Informal means of conferring citizenship and the shaping of partial or full enjoyment of its rights and responsibilities turn on norms that define good groups and bad groups or good or bad behavior, access to state provisioning and public policies, and symbolic inclusion and belonging.[3] Charles Tilly famously said, paraphrasing Max Weber, that "war made the state and the state made war" (1975, 42). An origin in armed revolution or conquest produces particular notions of citizenship and of citizens in both the courtroom and on the land.

Given the nature of the state as an often-violent claim to territory and population, it is no wonder that challenges to political authority and reach play out in relation to who has access to, belongs on, and can use the land. For centuries, state-building has generated passionate opposition that has taken myriad forms, from peasant revolutions to organized social movements to the formation of maroon communities and areas "outside" state control, where alternatives flourish. These struggles over land include fights over physical territory, but also over counterhegemonic memories and relations on the land. James C. Scott documents how intertwined these struggles really are. Avoiding the state for many highland communities of Southeast Asia is made possible by the cultivation of "escape crops" (those that are easily planted and can be left alone until harvest) and by terrain that is inhospitable to both soldiers and bureaucrats (Scott 2009). History suggests that revolution and rebellions seeking to establish alternative ways of living on the land are often put down with more force than is seemingly warranted, because the state is responding to the challenge to its authority rather than to the threat itself (Thompson 1993).

In this chapter, we discuss the various academic fields that focus on the relationship between land, citizenship, and the state. We highlight the key themes that run through the contemporary literature and suggest important directions for future research. Our focus is on the themes of state formation and property; soil, science, and settlement; political mobilization and resistance; and frontiers and alternative possibilities. Each of these themes speaks to the ways states and subjects make land and are made by land—sometimes in conjunction with one another, other times in competition; sometimes making the land a material thing and, at other times, a collective symbol, and so on.

A Brief History of the Co-Constitution of Land, States, and Citizenship

Many different areas of scholarship analyze the relationship between the land, states, and citizenship. Early theories of the state, particularly those building on Marxist political economy, did not focus on land, in part because of a preoccupation with the development of markets and the material conditions of industrial production. Vladimir Lenin's analysis of the various paths of capitalist development stands out as an analysis of the relationship between state formation and landed classes. In conversation with multiple scholars, Lenin's debate with Karl Kautsky and Alexander Chayanov generated the so-called agrarian question and laid the basis for the long-standing field of agrarian studies (Chayanov 1966; Kautsky 1988; Lenin 1964). Kautsky had initially framed the agrarian question to investigate the ways in which capitalism (does or does not) penetrate peasant society, revisiting the earlier "peasant question," which had focused on aligning the peasantry in a class struggle and on their potential for revolutionary thought and action (Marx 1926; Engels 1976).

Since the original formulation of the agrarian question, scholars have wrestled with the incorporation and exclusion of landed and landless groups (e.g., property holders, peasants, and laborers) into national and colonial societies (Gramsci 2005; Daniel, Bernstein, and Brass 1992). Many subsequent theories of citizenship and the national imaginary neglected the role of the land because of a widespread conviction that rural societies were undergoing a transition to urban industrial societies (e.g., Benedict Anderson [2016], whose analysis of nationalism followed the cultural markers most associated with urban settlement, including the circulation of print media and establishment of a unifying language). In the 1960s, historical sociologists developed an analysis of state formation, focusing on the relationship between landed classes and the formation of particular states (Moore 1993; Polanyi 1957; Sewell 1992; Skocpol 1979). World systems theorists (Arrighi 1994; Wallerstein 1979) drew on the broad historical sociology tradition, focusing on the relations between nation-states in the development of a world-historical geo-polity and "geo-culture" organized around a global market; this global market consisted of core nations and peripheries that had begun as colonies and then transitioned to third world countries after World War II. World systems analyses, from those of Immanuel Wallerstein to Jason Moore, allow us to see national territories as mutually competitive but connected to a global whole, such that one nation's quest for resources pushes it deeper into a frontier seen as "empty," cheap, and there for the taking (Moore 2015). Philip McMichael's (1990) notion of "incorporated comparison" highlights the ways in which national ambitions are connected not only in space but also in time, where one nation's strategies for territorial conquest or development are shaped by the strategies deployed by those who came before, whether the ruling class within its borders or other nation states.

Scholarship on citizenship and land complicates the subjectivity of landholders and land users as more than state subjects. As Christian Lund notes in this volume, both formal national citizenship and other collective subjectivities (for example, membership in a community) are subject to political wrangling in which groups and individuals struggle for rights and protections. Political democratization without the extension of citizenship rights can result in mass exclusion (Fox 1994). In the last thirty years, the emergence of new social movements and new forms of citizenship, particularly in Latin America, have complicated and challenged structural and simplified notions of state-subject relationships (Wolford 2016; Wolford and French 2016). These political struggles include the fight for the protections afforded by already established rights, as well as the fight to establish new sets of rights, such as that engaged in by Indigenous communities from Peru to Mexico (Yashar 1998) to challenge states to recognize Indigenous territory and authority (Galeana 2022). The struggles over collective rights can be uneven; they are full of hope, resistance, and aspirations, as well as internal factionalism and violence, that together change citizens' rights, sense of belonging, and political possibilities (Harvey 1998).

Political geographers such as Stuart Elden (2010) have developed theories of territory (land as a geo-body) and territorialization (the locally specific drive to create new territories in a particular image) in which both are constituted by land and subjects. Meanwhile, scholars working within or positioned from postcolonial locations (Berry 1992; Mamdani 2018; Benton 2012; Quijano 2000) question the linear relationships between the state, land, and citizens and reject Eurocentric notions of the commons, property, rights, and community, by asking how rural people *engage* with colonial and state institutions.

What all of these studies have in common is the belief that land is fundamental to the formation of the modern state, and that the modern state, in turn, establishes the rules for land use, ownership, and access that define citizenship. State actors—authoritarian, democratic, postcolonial, or otherwise—legislate and normalize exclusion from and inclusion on the land, even as these dictates are countered and opposed in practice (Peluso and Lund 2011; Wolford and French 2016).

In the social sciences, life on the land is generally viewed through disciplinary lenses, as property, commodity, field, forest, and infrastructure (Nadasdy 2017). These ideas run throughout many fields, as historians, anthropologists, geographers, and economists all highlight the importance of locating the relationships between classes, genders, generations, and ethnic groups in the dynamics of colonization and resistance. In Brazil, for example, in-depth studies have focused on the role of land maldistribution in creating a political elite oriented toward extracting natural resources and exporting raw materials, where citizenship rights and privileges accrues preferentially to landowners, and vice versa (de Souza Martins 2000). Land was first formally given to colonial landholders under the Lei das Sesmarias, and later taken control of and occupied by plantation owners and *bandeirantes*, who took possession of Indigenous land as property and Indigenous people as slaves (Evans and Dutra Silva 2017). Landowners who enjoy the fullest benefits of citizenship are lighter skinned than their poorer counterparts, many of whom share some lineage with the African slaves who were brought to Brazil to plant, harvest, and process the lucrative, but perilous sugar cane crop, one of the earliest engines of economic growth (Schwartz 1973). In Africa, colonial conquest generally meant that farming land went to a colonial elite and indigenous Africans were relocated through "villagization" efforts or campaigns. The colonial states claimed jurisdiction over the appropriation and settlement of national land for the benefit of elites and the metropole. The ongoing effects of these appropriations and exclusions can be seen everywhere today, perhaps nowhere more clearly than in transcontinental development projects that dispossess local residents in order to create land for large-scale investment (Wolford et al. 2013). One example is the ambitious ProSavana project, a trilateral collaboration between Mozambique, Japan, and Brazil designed to promote agricultural modernization in Mozambique, is intended to mimic an earlier project implemented in the Center-West of Brazil that promised development and modernity through establishing large-scale, agroindutrial soy production in the region (Wolford and Nehring 2015; Wolford 2021. This contextualization of nation-state political economies offers more than detail and nuance—it shows, through in-depth qualitative research, how different perspectives, interests, uses, and values on the land come to dominate or be excluded.

State Formation, Property, Titles

Agriculture is closely linked to the development of states and societies (Ofstehage 2020). In the Southern Moche state in the arid Moche Valley in Peru, agriculture depended heavily on irrigation systems, the control of which afforded a centralized, expansive state. The extensification (expansion of farmland area that is under cultivation) and intensification of agriculture in the Alps of Europe in AD 1000 required clearing forests to extend arable land and reducing the fallow period to intensify production. Both processes were directed by land-controlling elites, who used the profits from the increased production to consolidate their control of territory and people (Wolf 1982). Agriculture can increase the number of calories produced per person, making sedentary life more viable; it also enables the control of society by states (Scott 2017).

James C. Scott's (2017) work demonstrates the difficulties introduced by longterm cultivation of the land as opposed to hunter-gatherer societies, including nutritional stress, a higher incidence of infectious disease, increased physical stress for those doing difficult field labor, and greater control over people by the early states. Generally, "small, stratified, tax-collecting, walled states" (7) emerged from grain-producing societies. Population control in these early states met state demands that farmers produce in excess of subsistence needs.[4] The development of intensive agriculture and land use is connected to the formation of states and the mechanisms of state power, while the trajectories toward the rule of government were partially determined by the rise and fall of the peasantry and the bourgeoisie (Moore 1993).

Alongside establishing borders and bureaucracies to defend landed property, agricultural societies developed norms of good and proper behavior toward the land. Just as the rise of the territorial state had been preceded by imperial ambitions for land and political control, so too, the construction of land as a commodified object of individual ownership was not automatic or inevitable. Rather, it was a slow process nurtured by particular acts of enclosure and exclusion. In England, over a period of two hundred years, land enclosures upended the prevailing norms that regarded land as a natural resource, held in common, but dispensed by the king according to the doctrine of divine right. The norms that had defined the right distribution of resources, particularly land, were what E. P. Thompson (1971) referred as the basis of a moral economy—an "alternative economics" shaped by collective notions of fairness. Although life for peasants in feudal English society was hard, unequal, and unfair, collective notions about the importance of the commons and of giving aid to the poorest, who lived off the land, were at least minimally constituted through historically and culturally specific relations of production and social reproduction. Violating those principles—that is, dispossessing both the rural poor and the landed gentry (though more of the former, to be sure) in favor of productivity—incited riots, organized protests, and revolution but, eventually, private property in land was internalized as "common sense" (Thompson 1967). Land enclosures redistributed land to a capitalist class, redefined land as a commodity, and, most pertinently to our topic here, restricted access, making land available not to those who needed land, but to those who could afford land.

Today, states continue to use both land enclosure and land titling to enroll, exclude, and transform citizens and citizenship. Land enclosures have historically reoriented the idea of land as collective, multifunctional, and Indigenous territory to land as individualistic, capital-driven, and under property ownership (Chung 2019; Koch and Perreault 2019). This is the case even when the land remains in Indigenous control (Nadasdy 2017). Exclusion, which is often based on state power and coercion, legitimizes colonial logics, racial hierarchies, and dominance over the land (Rotz 2017). States' recognition of Indigenous land rights has increased since the 1990s, with the multicultural (Hale 1994), or neoliberal "territorial turn" (Bryan 2012; Wainwright 2008), particularly in Latin America, but land titling does not guarantee the title holder the entire set of rights that have long been assumed to apply to private property. Recent studies focusing on governance in communities after they have won title suggest that titling mainly serves to make Indigenous communities more legible to the state, and that any benefits may take decades to materialize (Anthias 2018; Galeana 2022). Indigenous peoples can either refuse to engage or choose to engage with land titling projects as a way of asserting self-determination or disrupting settler colonial articulations of recognition; yet such engagement often means recognizing state-appointed court jurisdiction over the land (Correia 2021; Povinelli 2002; Nadasdy 2017). Ultimately, land reform and land titling programs are often about making land accessible to some and inaccessible to others (Hall, Hirsch, and Li 2011). The dynamic of making land unavailable to some is not unique to state power or capitalist relations. Common-use agreements are about the collective "we," as well as the collective "them" and who is seen as having worked for the rights to the land (Wolford 2007). For Rignall (2021), land enclosure can be an essential part of communal governance and the fight for autonomy against intrusive state power. Forms of recognition, as Lund (2011b) writes, are not "set in stone" but can be adapted to include or exclude people. There is still a possibility that recognition of other knowledges (*saberes*) through emancipatory territorial claims can support alternative lifeworlds (Escobar 2008), but this depends on building productive relations with other communities on and off the land (Escobar 2007).

Although capital seems to have particular facility for enclosing land, it relies on states to make land "investible" through implementing land titling, providing judicial and police protection of property rights, and easing restrictions on foreign and domestic capital investment (Li 2014). Discourses, technologies, rules, and ecologies shape this creation of investible land, while other possibilities and alternatives are simultaneously unmade (Goldstein and Yates 2017). The state makes land for itself and for capital, creating, in the case of the Brazilian Cerrado, a land of capital, where production, trade, and labor itself are regarded solely in terms of their exchange value (Sauer 2012), becoming, in de Souza Martin's (1980) framing, a *terra de negocio*, a "land of business." In this way, the state makes landowners and the landless into citizens and partial citizens, respectively.

Soils, Science, and Settlement

Nation-states shape citizenship communities and rights through the treatment of soil, science, and settlement. For 12,000 years, humanity has gained sustenance through the intensification of land use. Today, humans have left their mark on between 75 percent and 95 percent of earth's arable land, producing food, fuel, and fiber—and contributing to biodiversity loss; greenhouse emissions; habitat conversion, fragmentation, and loss; species introductions and invasions; and soil and water pollution (Ellis 2021). The Paleolithic shift to the cultural practices of burning vegetation and planting favored seeds near homesites and, later, to the "tending, weeding, tillage, manuring, pruning, replanting, and transplanting of favored wild plant species and the protection, taming, and herding of favored wild animal prey" (Ellis 2021, 10) improved human carrying capacity but also led to increased sedentism as suggested in James Scott's work cited earlier. Not only did it become easier to stay put, but the continued cultivation of crops in place required it. Increased sedentism, in turn, facilitated the emergence of agricultural societies. People domesticated an ever-greater number of plants and animals, and the increasing human investment in plants and animals "incentivized social arrangements including private property and inequalities that further shaped landscapes, such as walled cities, fences, and borders, although the opposite pathway has also been proposed" (Ellis 2021, 11).

Soil is the biophysical basis of land, itself a site of state- and citizen-making: to wit, the symbolic imagery of kissing the soil or running one's hands through the soil to celebrate a return to one's national home. Soil is made to labor productively through advancements in soil science that increase crop yields and profits at the cost of the soil's ecological health. Even the conservation of land is a state-making process in its designation of certain land as off-limits, removal of prior inhabitants, and exclusion of all but those who can pay the gate price. Research on soils embeds notions of nationhood and citizenship in the land (Marchesi 2016), as scientists map a region's soils, cataloguing their properties according to state and national interests in production, crop exports, and improvement (Puig de la Bellacasa 2017; Lyons 2020; Van Sant 2021). The documentation, interpretation, and framing of soil as an agricultural asset enables soil transformation that, in turn, makes land suitable for large-scale commodity agriculture and, therefore, for financial investment (Goldstein 2016; Wolford et al. 2013). The idea that soil constitutes a factor of production, generating profits as long as it is in use, is one of the reasnos why swidden farmers have been long targeted by the state as inefficient and "lazy" (Yeh 2013; Wolford 2021). Framing soil as an asset ignores "traditional environmental knowledge" that classifies soil differently, enables alternative uses of soil, and reflects the memories, values, and lives of local Indigenous peoples (cf. Miller 2019). Governments' support for the industrial use of the soil and simultaneous abandonment or disavowal of nonindustrial farming, shapes the notions of who is a good farmer or who is a farmer at all (Pritchard, Wolf, and Wolford 2015). On the one hand, hegemonic and productivist evaluations of soil quality place value on soils that are useful for industrial agriculture; on the other hand, they devalue soils that are productive for other land uses (Ofstehage, forthcoming). At the same time, soil science's general focus on and preference for industrial agriculture validates industrial farmers as "proper" farmers and therefore worthy beneficiaries of state and market largesse, even as it excludes other farmers as outside the realm of proper farming. Defining soils as "marginal" and then categorizing the land as wasteland (or *terra nullius*, Fitzmaurice 2014) enables processes of privatization and land acquisition—in other words, state formation (Baka 2014).

India is just the latest country to embark on a program of converting wasteland to productive land through what Baka (2014) calls a "wasteland governmentality." Soil management and the transformation of "wastelands" for monocultural production create "authoritarian soils" and "soil-based authoritarian states" in which soils are mobilized to serve the priorities of authoritative regimes and made inaccessible for alternative uses (Biasillo and Silva 2021). Wastelands are created where "the huge untapped potential of idle lands, [await] . . . only technology and capital to make them productive" (Li 2014, 596). The creation-of-wasteland discourse makes processes otherwise labeled "deforestation" and "degradation" into processes of growth and renewal in which, supposedly, nothing is lost and much is gained (Ofstehage, forthcoming; Ofstehage and Nehring 2021). Following Craib (2004) and Scott (1999), Lyons argues that soil surveys are key to nation-state consolidation by documenting, classifying, and demarcating land and soil (Lyons 2020). States and development organizations give meaning to soil fertility in terms of promoting national vitality, encouraging labor exploitation, and enabling commodity production to create model farmer-citizens (Marchesi 2016). A Colombian soil management guide from the 1930s tells the farmer-reader:

> This earth that you cultivate, to which you are bound by need and by love—like an infant at its mother's breast—is tired; it is exhausted; it is dying in your hands, victim of an unrelenting enemy called erosion. And you aren't alone in depending on this land; we all depend on it. The soil is the most precious material resource of the nation, and you, *amigo campesino*, are its steward and guardian. The subsistence of you and your family depends on the fertility of the soil you cultivate, as does the prosperity of your country and the security of the nation.
>
> (quoted in Marchesi 2016, 736)

Here, the citizen, as amigo, campesino/a, and steward, is named as guardian of both the soil and the nation. Like a mother caring for her infant, so must the farmer-citizen care for the soil (and land) in order for the nation to thrive. Those who control the land often have power over, not only land use and access, but also over the narratives of land and of land management (Peluso and Lund 2011; Wolford 2010b).

Working with the soil literally feeds narratives of citizenship. Nikita Sud (2021) reminds us that states and subjects attempt to make land even as the land also remakes both state and subject. In many societies, working on the land indexes one's contribution to the society or community. In Bolivia, some Altiplano communities maintain collective land-use agreements, called *ayllus*, in which community belonging and land access are conferred on those who work their own land as well as that of their neighbors (Walsh-Dilley 2016). In Brazil and the United States, putting land to "good use" acts as an impetus to both land dispossession (at the hands of White settlers in the American West and by, first, *bandeirantes* and, later, agribusiness in Brazil) and to landless rural workers who want to put idle land to use (Wolford 2010b; Wolford 2007; Wright and Wolford 2003). Land is fundamental to the formation of states, and land-use rights that involve working the soil are a linchpin in recognizing or excluding state subjects from citizenship (understood as belonging, inclusion, and having access to property rights). States produce the soils within their boundaries discursively through scientific mapping, the creation of agroecological or pedological zones, the application of agronomic "fixes" for poor soils (understood as soils not conducive to large-scale cultivation), and through laws or regulations that promote specific kinds of land use in specific places, for the good of the whole.

Mobilization and Resistance

A long tradition that dates back to the early political economy suggests that privileging productivity will create "rational," profit-maximizing landowners who will efficiently dispose of land, as they would any other fungible commodity. Others argue that land can be possessed but not fully commodified—it is, if anything, a "fictitious commodity" because it is not produced for sale (Polanyi 1957), and the quality of being alive carries with it the capacity to produce (as well as embody) value (a lá Marx). The unique qualities of land are its relative fixity (notwithstanding the acres of "new land" created in central Brazil by the planting of new soybean varieties and massive additions of calcium to the soil), its multiple ecologies, its long memory, and the continual production and degradation of soil through natural and social processes. Land is not just capital or a means of production; for many is also a holder of seeds, a teacher, a relative, and a home (Kimmerer 2013).

The idea that land belongs to those who will work it has been used to displace Indigenous peoples and to disenfranchise the poor. It also has a subversive side, as the primary rallying cry of many, if not most, revolutionary or subaltern movements. The Zapatistas in early twentieth-century Mexico, the Russian Revolution, and the multiple Chinese revolutions were all motivated by the argument that land was being misused by the wealthy. More recently, the labor theory of property has upheld the neoliberal commitment to market-led agrarian reform (MLAR) and to massive titling projects even as the theory has also motivated populist landless movements from Brazil to South Africa and in India and the Philippines (Wolford 2007). For Brazilian peasants, struggles for land are struggles for the freedom to reproduce family and social values and to produce on the land (Sauer 2012). This is the double-edged sword of the labor theory of property that many people have noted: centering productivity in a legal claim of "proper work" means that one's use of the land is always open to surveillance and contestation.

The creation and governance of land by states can, as in the case of Brazil, respond to both grassroots demands for land reform and neoliberal market-based priorities to pacify rural populations while also satisfying elite landholders and capitalist interpretations of productivity and property rights (Wolford 2005). In Brazil, the inability of the state to handle land reform by itself means that the government depends on social movement actors and social movements, such as the MST (Movimento dos Trabalhadores Rurais Sem Terra) (Wright and Wolford 2003), leaving individuals who are landless but do not want to organize without a viable option for gaining land access, thus curtailing their possibilities (Wolford 2010a). Similarly, the "Leopard Skin" land reform[5] in Cambodia is held up by development practitioners as a model for rural reform, but fundamentally, it was aimed at securing rural voters, producing modern farmers, and wresting control over land distribution away from local officials. In effect, the reforms place rural people under strict state bureaucracies, make people and land more legible to the state, and extend formal property rights (Beban 2021). In Brazil and Cambodia, land reform is not only reforming access to land; it is re-forming land relations and human relations, creating more pliable, pacified, and legible citizens.

Resistance to state-led land governance is a fight for alternative uses and ownership of land, but also for different ways of being a citizen. Although the MST has created alliances with the Brazilian state and Brazilian elites, it has also simultaneously situated itself to advocate for substantive transformation, what Hannah Wittman calls "agrarian citizenship." This emergent subjectivity places importance on political participation, local food production, and environmental stewardship, while creating a common sense of values and practices (Wittman 2009). Carter (2010) argues that the MST is promoting democratic governance by redistributing resources, extending basic citizenship rights, and "fostering a sense of hope and utopia through the affirmation of ideals imbued in Brazil's long-term, complex, and open-ended democratization process." Grassroots and revolutionary movements struggle for access to the land access to live and work on, but also for land rights in the more complete sense of reproducing their own communities, values, and livelihoods on the land.

Recent work has focused on transnational organizing that "jumps scale" (Smith 1996) to seek rights in multilateral fora, such as the United Nations (Claeys and Edelman 2020) and umbrella movements, of which La Via Campesina is the most prominent (Desmarais 2008; Wittman 2011). Because these spaces are not connected to a concrete territory, it is not clear how effective they will be in mobilizing rights: states are reluctant to cede control over their physical or imagined territory. For transnational organizing to successfully re-shape the relationship between producers and the land, the very nature of the state may have to change.

Frontiers and Alternative Imaginaries

Frontiers have been treated with almost mythic reverence. There is a popular belief in the United States, for example, that colonizing the western frontier underwrote

American democracy as progressively more advanced forms of production tamed nature and spread civilization. In Mexico, a similar argument suggests that migration to the Lancandon jungle gave rise to a more collective frontier democracy and shaped the contemporary Zapatista uprising (Womack 1968). These frontier myths highlight narratives of legitimate conquest in ways that define both national character and citizenship rights. If land has memory, as legal scholar Eduardo Peñalver (2008) has suggested, then frontiers cast the longest shadows. As territorial entities from their birth, modern nation-states memorialize the frontier in ways that reflect deeply held narratives of national character. Frontiers have a way of changing, too, both as they further encroach upon Indigenous territory, and as national conditions and priorities abruptly change, when a frontier can quickly become a border (Grandin 2019). Through these mechanisms of property, territory, and frontier, states demarcate land and give shape and materiality to the state/nation itself.

A forest may contain thousands of species, impede easy travel, and have irregular and unclear borders. Comparing a forest to a tree plantation with its straight rows of a single tree species, wide lanes for travel, and cookie-cutter borders, as James C. Scott (1999) has done, we can see the utility of simplified landscapes for both capital production and state governance. States create territory out of land to better control (or at least document) the land and the people on it and to make it more productive for capital. The Amazon frontier, for example, has been the focus of Brazilian (Hecht and Cockburn 2011) and Bolivian (Hecht 2005) state interest as a dark corner on national maps. This dark corner is seen by Bolivian and Brazilian elites and governments as insufficiently Bolivian or Brazilian (respectively) and as insufficiently productive for their respective economies. The people, too, are imagined alternately as too few to matter or as subjects to be made into better citizens. For Garrett et al. (2021), deforestation in the Brazilian Amazon is the outcome of an "explicit federal project to occupy, integrate, and 'modernize' the region," including, of course, the people. State development programs incentivize the territorialization of this space, and the lack of regulation or the enforcement of regulation lowers the risk to ranchers, farmers, and loggers of converting this land to more productive use, while allowing a high-level risk of violence and dispossession for Indigenous and peasant communities. Territory is a map until land has been physically claimed. This territorialization and making of land is done through incentives, violence (Campbell 2015), and discourse (Yeh 2013). Land reform places landed property and landed people more squarely under control by government institutions and regulations and makes the state the arbiter of land conflicts and relations (Lund 2011a). This fundamentally erases other conceptions of the land that perhaps see it as a relation or a teacher (Kimmerer 2013; Nadasdy 2017).

Yet, if states create land and people in their image, so do sovereign ethnic territories. "Ethnic territories," for Anthias and Hoffmann (2021), "are created by diverse subjects engaged in situated struggles over categories, recognition and boundaries." Ethnic territorialization opposes nation-state power over land, but at the same time may "reproduce dominant ethno-territorial regimes of truth." For example, land titling in Southeastern Bolivia for Native Community Lands confers land rights and access but reinforces "colonial hierarchies of race and property" and provides access primarily to marginal, isolated, discontinuous fragments of land (Anthias 2021). Land reforms, Rasmussen (2021) writes, "produce people as either surplus, savage, or citizen," and conservation areas can leave prior settlers in livelihood and legal limbo (290). State recognition of Indigenous land rights and land titling comes without guarantees. The dynamic of inclusion or exclusion becomes a contradiction when state power supports capitalist production through land governance while alienating rural populations, and voters, through the same governance (Chung 2019).

In Brazil, Canada, and the United States, state-driven and frontiersman-driven processes of settler colonialism (Whyte 2018) were enacted to take land from Indigenous communities and provide it to White settlers. In Canada (and the United States), the celebrated family farm emerged from this process and is maintained via state protection of land ownership and support for settler logics of land domination (Rotz 2017). Settler logics can give meaning to land occupation, as in the case of the militia occupation of Malheur National Wildlife Refuge in the United States. Although the occupiers' motivations were mixed (among them White supremacy, their Mormon faith, and grievances with the Bureau of Land Management), they were unified by settler-colonial logics of race and class-based land rights (Gallaher 2016). Where land is made available to Indigenous people, it is with the understanding, or demand, that they will adopt the land-use practices of White settlers (Biolsi 2018).

Although land is made unavailable to certain racial, ethnic, and nationalist groups, foreign investors are often courted and given access to investible lands and given protections (Castro, Hershaw, and Sauer 2018; Fairbairn 2020; Ofstehage 2016, 2018a, 2018b), and in some cases, massive tracts of land are specifically demarcated for development by foreign investors and development agencies (Wolford and Nehring 2015). This foreignization of land highlights the limitations of citizenship in the face of capital. For a nation-state, advancing frontiers are a sign of progress and development, seemingly regardless of the nationality of the so-called pioneers.

Conclusion

Michel Foucault defined the transition from sovereign power to biopower as a move from control over territory to control over a population, and the two remain inseparable today. The intimate relationship between land and citizenship is now more evident than ever. The rise of authoritarian populists around the world, who equate belonging with defense of a primordial fatherland (Ofstehage, Wolford, and Borras 2022; Scoones et al. 2018), accentuates the relationship between national territory, belonging, and the state.

Through the operations of settlement, mobility, and resistance, land makes people, and people make land. Citizenship is bestowed, contested, and performed via these encounters with land and soil. Land is at the center of many contestations of citizenship, belonging, and even personhood.[6] Citizenship and land are deeply intertwined in material practices and policies, as well as more effervescent ideas of belonging in place. Making territory is a messy and complex process through which citizenship and resources (including land) are co-created (Byrne, Nightingale, and Korf 2016). One could say the same for counterhegemonic territory-making. These entangled landscapes define the relationship between land, state, and citizenship, where material realities and ideological notions shape one another and emerge together.

Acknowledgments

We thank the editors, Jun Borras and Jenny Franco for inviting us to write for this chapter and for their guidance throughout the process. We also thank Jonathon Fox and Christian Lund for their thoughtful feedback on earlier drafts.

Notes

1. Almost every national anthem in the world indexes the nation with references to the land, whether to specific topographic features or other physical characteristics or to a more abstract notion of "fatherland," or collective land.
2. When this naturalized connection is missing, loyalty to a fatherland is cultivated and measured by bureaucratic means (forms, tests, and achievements).
3. The literature here spans various disciplines and concerns. Scholars as diverse as Renato Rosaldo (2003) and David Harvey (2003) have illustrated the ways in which citizenship "rights" are withdrawn or mediated by social class and culture.
4. Anthropologist David Graeber adds that many early civilizations did not rule with a heavy hand (Graeber and Wengrow 2021).
5. The term Leopard Skin land reform refers to the practice of distributing small plots of land to smallholders in areas dominated by large, corporate land concessions (see Beban 2021).
6. In the United States there are several cases of this: (1) the intimidation and violence toward Black farmers in the post-Reconstruction South and later US Department of Agriculture discrimination against Black farmers applying for loans; (2) the forced removal of American Indians from their land and the destruction of their means of living on the land; and (3) the forced removal of Japanese farmland owners during the Japanese internment of the 1940s. In each of these cases, land is a weapon by which citizenship is not conferred, but violently taken away.

References

Anderson, Benedict R. 2016. *Imagined Communities: Reflections on the Origin and Spread of Nationalism*. London: Verso Books.

Anthias, Penelope. 2018. *Limits to Decolonization: Indigeneity, Territory, and Hydrocarbon Politics in the Bolivian Chaco*. Ithaca, NY: Cornell University Press.

Anthias, Penelope. 2021. "Rethinking Territory and Property in Indigenous Land Claims." *Geoforum* 119: 268–278.

Anthias, Penelope, and Kasper Hoffmann. 2021. "The Making of Ethnic Territories: Governmentality and Counter-Conducts." *Geoforum* 119: 218–226.

Arrighi, Giovanni. 1994. *The Long Twentieth Century: Money, Power, and the Origins of Our Times*. London: Verso.

Baka, Jennifer. 2014. "What Wastelands? A Critique of Biofuel Policy Discourse in South India." *Geoforum* 54: 315–323.

Beban, Alice. 2021. *Unwritten Rule: State-Making through Land Reform in Cambodia*. Ithaca, NY: Cornell University Press.

Benton, Lauren. 2012. "Possessing Empire: Iberian Claims and Interpolity Law." In *Native Claims: Indigenous Law against Empire, 1500–1920*, edited by Sahila Belmessous, 19–40. Oxford: Oxford University Press.

Berry, Sara. 1992. "Hegemony on a Shoestring: Indirect Rule and Access to Agricultural Land." *Africa: Journal of the International African Institute* 62 (3): 327–355.

Berry, Sara. 2009. "Property, Authority and Citizenship: Land Claims, Politics and the Dynamics of Social Division in West Africa." *Development and Change* 40 (1): 23–45.

Biasillo, Roberta, and Claiton Marcio da Silva. 2021. "The Very Grounds Underlying Twentieth-Century Authoritarian Regimes: Building Soil Fertility in Italian Libya and the Brazilian Cerrado." *Comparative Studies in Society and History* 63 (2): 366–399.

Biolsi, Thomas. 2018. *Power and Progress on the Prairie*. Minneapolis: University of Minnesota Press.

Bryan, Joseph. 2012. "Rethinking Territory: Social Justice and Neoliberalism in Latin America's Territorial Turn." *Geography Compass* 6 (4): 215–226.

Byrne, Sarah, Andrea J. Nightingale, and Benedikt Korf. 2016. "Making Territory: War, Post-war and the Entangled Scales of Contested Forest Governance in Mid-western Nepal." *Development and Change* 47 (6): 1269–1293.

Campbell, Jeremy M. 2015. *Conjuring Property: Speculation and Environmental Futures in the Brazilian Amazon*. Seattle: University of Washington Press.

Carter, Miguel. 2010. "The Landless Rural Workers Movement and Democracy in Brazil." *Latin American Research Review* 45: 186–217.

Castro, Luís Felipe Perdigão de, Eva Hershaw, and Sérgio Sauer. 2018. "Estrangeirização e internacionalização de terras no Brasil: Oportunidades para quem?" Estudos internacionais: Revista de relações internacionais da PUC. *Minas* 5 (2): 74–102.

Chayanov, Alexander. 1966. "On the Theory of Non-Capitalist Economic Systems." In *Peasant Livelihood: Studies in Economic Anthropology and Cultural Ecology*, edited by Rhoda Halperin, 257–268. New York: St. Martin's Press.

Chung, Youjin B. 2019. "The Grass Beneath: Conservation, Agro-industrialization, and Land–Water Enclosures in Postcolonial Tanzania." *Annals of the American Association of Geographers* 109 (1): 1–17.

Claeys, Priscilla, and Marc Edelman. 2020. "The United Nations Declaration on the Rights of Peasants and Other People Working in Rural Areas." *Journal of Peasant Studies* 47 (1): 1–68.

Correia, Joel E. 2021. "Reworking Recognition: Indigeneity, Land Rights, and the Dialectics of Disruption in Paraguay's Chaco." *Geoforum* 119:227–237.

Craib, Raymond B. 2004. *Cartographic Mexico: A History of State Fixations and Fugitive Landscapes*. Illustrated ed. Durham, NC: Duke University Press.

Daniel, E. Valentine, Henry Bernstein, and Tom Brass, eds. 1992. *Plantations, Proletarians, and Peasants in Colonial Asia*. Library of Peasant Studies 11. London: Frank Cass.

Desmarais, Annette A. 2008. "The Power of Peasants: Reflections on the Meanings of La Vía Campesina." *Journal of Rural Studies* 24 (2): 138–149.
de Souza Martins, José. 1980. "Terra de negócio e terra de trabalho: Contribuição para o estudo da questão agrária no Brasil." In *Expropriação and violência (a questão política no campo)*, edited by José de Souza Martins, 43–60. São Paulo, Brazil: Editora Hucitec.
de Souza Martins, José. 2000. *Reforma agrária: O impossível diálogo*. São Paulo: Edusp.
Elden, Stuart. 2010. "Land, Terrain, Territory." *Progress in Human Geography* 34 (6): 799–817.
Ellis, Erle C. 2021. "Land Use and Ecological Change: A 12,000-Year History." *Annual Review of Environment and Resources* 46 (1): 1–33.
Engels, Friedrich. 1976. *The Peasant Question in France and Germany*. Moscow: Progress Publishers.
Escobar, Arturo. 2007. "Worlds and Knowledges Otherwise." *Cultural Studies* 21 (2–3): 179–210.
Escobar, Arturo. 2008. *Territories of Difference: Place, Movements, Life, Redes*. Durham, NC: Duke University Press.
Evans, Sterling, and Sandro Dutra e Silva. 2017. "Crossing the Green Line: Frontier, environment and the role of bandeirantes in the conquering of Brazilian territory." *Fronteiras: Journal of Social, Technological and Environmental Science* 6 (1): 120–142.
Fairbairn, Madeleine. 2020. *Fields of Gold: Financing the Global Land Rush*. Ithaca, NY: Cornell University Press.
Fitzmaurice, Andrew. 2014. *Sovereignty, Property and Empire, 1500–2000*. Cambridge, UK: Cambridge University Press.
Fox, Jonathan. 1994. "The Difficult Transition from Clientelism to Citizenship: Lessons from Mexico." *World Politics* 46 (2): 151–184.
Galeana, Fernando R. 2022. "Vernacular Legibility in Counter-Mapping: Assembling the Geobody of an Indigenous Socio-territorial Movement in Honduras." *Geoforum* 128:158–167.
Gallaher, Carolyn. 2016. "Placing the Militia Occupation of the Malheur National Wildlife Refuge in Harney County, Oregon." *ACME: An International Journal for Critical Geographies* 15 (2): 293–308.
Garrett, Rachael D., Federico Cammelli, Joice Ferreira, Samuel A. Levy, Judson Valentim, and Ima Vieira. 2021. "Forests and Sustainable Development in the Brazilian Amazon: History, Trends, and Future Prospects." *Annual Review of Environment and Resources* 46 (1): 625–652.
Goldstein, Jennifer, E. 2016. "Knowing the Subterranean: Land Grabbing, Oil Palm, and Divergent Expertise in Indonesia's Peat Soil." *Environment and Planning A* 48 (4): 754–770.
Goldstein, Jennifer E., and Julian S. Yates. 2017. "Introduction: Rendering Land Investable." *Geoforum* 82:209–211.
Graeber, David, and David Wengrow. 2021. *The Dawn of Everything: A New History of Humanity*. New York: Farrar, Straus and Giroux.
Gramsci, Antonio. 2005. *The Southern Question*. Toronto, CAN: Guernica Editions.
Grandin, Greg. 2019. *The End of the Myth: From the Frontier to the Border Wall in the Mind of America*. New York: Metropolitan Books.
Hale, Charles R. 1994. *Resistance and Contradiction: Miskitu Indians and the Nicaraguan State*. Stanford, CA: Stanford University Press.
Hall, Derek, Philip Hirsch, and Tania Murray Li. 2011. Introduction to *Powers of Exclusion: Land Dilemmas in Southeast Asia*. Honolulu, HI: University of Hawaii Press.
Harvey, David. 2003. *The New Imperialism*. Oxford: Oxford University Press.

Harvey, Neil. 1998. *The Chiapas Rebellion: The Struggle for Land and Democracy*. Durham, NC: Duke University Press.
Hecht, Susanna B. 2005. "Soybeans, Development and Conservation on the Amazon Frontier." *Development and Change* 36 (2): 375–404.
Hecht, Susanna B., and Alexander Cockburn. 2011. *The Fate of the Forest: Developers, Destroyers, and Defenders of the Amazon*. Chicago: University of Chicago Press.
Kautsky, Karl. 1988. *The Agrarian Question*. Ann Arbor, MI: The University of Michigan.
Kimmerer, Robin Wall. 2013. *Braiding Sweetgrass: Indigenous Wisdom, Scientific Knowledge and the Teachings of Plants*. Minneapolis, MN: Milkweed Editions.
Koch, Natalie and Thomas Perreault. 2019. "Resource Nationalism." *Progress in Human Geography* 43 (4): 611–631.
Lenin, Vladimir I. 1964. *The Development of Capitalism in Russia*. Vol. 3. Moscow: Progress Publishers.
Li, Tania M. 2014. "What Is Land? Assembling a Resource for Global Investment." *Transactions of the Institute of British Geographers* 39 (4): 589–602.
Lund, Christian. 2011a. "Fragmented Sovereignty: Land Reform and Dispossession in Laos." *Journal of Peasant Studies* 38 (4): 885–905. https://doi.org/10.1080/03066150011.607709.
Lund, Christian. 2011b. "Property and Citizenship: Conceptually Connecting Land Rights and Belonging in Africa." *Africa Spectrum* 46 (3): 71–75.
Lyons, Kristina M. 2020. *Vital Decomposition: Soil Practitioners and Life Politics*. Durham, NC: Duke University Press.
Mamdani, Mahmood. 2018. *Citizen and Subject: Contemporary Africa and the Legacy of Late Colonialism*. Princeton, NJ: Princeton University Press.
Marchesi, Greta. 2016. "The Blood of Heroes: Nationalist Bodies, National Soils, and the Scientific Conservation of the Federation of Colombian Coffee-Growers (1927–1946)." *Environment and Planning A: Economy and Space* 48 (4): 736–753.
Marx, Karl. 1926. *The Eighteenth Brumaire of Louis Bonaparte*. New York: International Publishers.
McMichael, Philip. 1990. "Incorporating Comparison within a World-Historical Perspective: An Alternative Comparative Method." *American Sociological Review* 55 (3): 385–397.
Miller, Theresa L. 2019. *Plant Kin: A Multispecies Ethnography in Indigenous Brazil*. Austin: University of Texas Press.
Mitchell, Timothy. 1991. *Colonising Egypt*. Berkeley: University of California Press.
Moore, Barrington. 1993. *Social Origins of Dictatorship and Democracy: Lord and Peasant in the Making of the Modern World*. Boston: Beacon Press.
Moore, Jason. 2015. *Capitalism in the Web of Life: Ecology and the Accumulation of Capital*. New York: Verso Books.
Nadasdy, Paul. 2017. *Sovereignty's Entailments: First Nation State Formation in the Yukon*. Toronto: University of Toronto Press.
Ofstehage, Andrew. 2016. "Farming Is Easy, Becoming Brazilian Is Hard: North American Soy Farmers' Social Values of Production, Work and Land in Soylandia." *Journal of Peasant Studies* 43 (2): 442–460.
Ofstehage, Andrew. 2018a. "Farming Out of Place: Transnational Family Farmers, Flexible Farming, and the Rupture of Rural Life in Bahia, Brazil." *American Ethnologist* 45 (3): 317–329.
Ofstehage, Andrew. 2018b. "Financialization of Work, Value, and Social Organization among Transnational Soy Farmers in the Brazilian Cerrado." *Economic Anthropology* 5 (2): 274–285.

Ofstehage, Andrew. 2020. "Farming". In The Open Encyclopedia of Anthropology, edited by Felix Stein. Facsimile of the first edition in *The Cambridge Encyclopedia of Anthropology*. http://doi.org/10.29164/20farming.

Ofstehage, Andrew. forthcoming. "Wasteland and Oasis in the Brazilian Cerrado: The Socio-material Life of Land in Soylandia." In *The Social Lives of Land*, edited by M. Goldman, N. L. Peluso, and Wendy Wolford, 168–189. Ithaca, NY: Cornell University Press.

Ofstehage, Andrew, and Ryan Nehring. 2021. "No-Till Agriculture and the Deception of Sustainability in Brazil." *International Journal of Agricultural Sustainability* 19 (3–4): 335–348.

Ofstehage, Andrew, Wendy Wolford, and Saturnino M. Borras Jr. 2022. "Contemporary Populism and the Environment." *Annual Review of Environment and Resources* 47:671–696. https://doi.org/10.1146/annurev-environ-012220-124635.

Paquette, Gabriel B. 2019. *The European Seaborne Empires: From the Thirty Years' War to the Age of Revolutions*. New Haven, CT: Yale University Press.

Peluso, Nancy L., and Christian Lund. 2011. "New Frontiers of Land Control: Introduction." *Journal of Peasant Studies* 38 (4): 667–681.

Peñalver, Eduardo M. 2008. "Land Virtues." *Cornell Law Review* 94:821.

Polanyi, Karl. 1957. *The Great Transformation*. Boston: Beacon Press.

Povinelli, Elizabeth A. 2002. *The Cunning of Recognition*. Durham, NC: Duke University Press.

Pritchard, Sara, Steven Wolf, and Wendy Wolford. 2015. "Knowledge and the Politics of Land." *Environment and Planning A: Economy and Space* 48 (4): 616–625.

Puig de la Bellacasa, Maria. 2017. *Matters of Care*. Minneapolis: University of Minnesota Press.

Quijano, Anibal. 2000. "Coloniality of Power, Eurocentrism and Latin America." *Nepantla* 1 (3): 533–580.

Rasmussen, Mattias B. 2021. "Institutionalizing Precarity: Settler Identities, National Parks and the Containment of Political Spaces in Patagonia." *Geoforum* 119:289–297.

Rignall, Karen E. 2021. *An Elusive Common: Land, Politics, and Agrarian Rurality in a Moroccan Oasis*. Ithaca, NY: Cornell University Press.

Rosaldo, Renato, ed. 2003. *Cultural Citizenship in Island Southeast Asia: Nation and Belonging in the Hinterlands*. Berkeley: University of California Press.

Rotz, Sarah. 2017. "'They Took Our Beads, It Was a Fair Trade, Get Over It': Settler Colonial Logics, Racial Hierarchies and Material Dominance in Canadian Agriculture." *Geoforum* 82:158–169.

Sauer, Sérgio. 2012. "Land and Territory: Meanings of Land between Modernity and Tradition." *Agrarian South: Journal of Political Economy* 1 (1): 85–107.

Schwartz, Stuart B. 1973. *Sovereignty and Society in Colonial Brazil: The High Court of Bahia and Its Judges, 1609–1751*. Berkeley: University of California Press.

Scoones, Ian, Marc Edelman, Saturnino M. Borras Jr., Ruth Hall, Wendy Wolford, and Ben White. 2018. "Emancipatory Rural Politics: Confronting Authoritarian Populism." *Journal of Peasant Studies* 45 (1): 1–20.

Scott, James C. 1999. *Seeing like a State: How Certain Schemes to Improve the Human Condition Have Failed*. New Haven, CT: Yale University Press.

Scott, James C. 2009. *The Art of Not Being Governed*. New Haven, CT: Yale University Press.

Scott, James C. 2017. *Against the Grain: A Deep History of the Earliest States*. New Haven, CT: Yale University Press.

Seed, Patricia. 1995. *Ceremonies of Possession in Europe's Conquest of the New World, 1492–1640*. Cambridge, UK: Cambridge University Press.

Sewell, William H., Jr. 1992. "A Theory of Structure: Duality, Agency, and Transformation." *American Journal of Sociology* 98 (1): 1–29.
Skocpol, Theda. 1979. *States and Social Revolutions: A Comparative Analysis of France, Russia and China*. Cambridge, UK: Cambridge University Press.
Smith, Neil. 1996. "Spaces of Vulnerability: The Space of Flows and the Politics of Scale." *Critique of Anthropology* 16 (1): 63–77.
Sud, Nikita. 2021. *The Making of Land and the Making of India*. Oxford: Oxford University Press.
Thompson, E. P. 1967. "Time, Work-Discipline, and Industrial Capitalism." *Past and Present* 38:56–97.
Thompson, E. P. 1971. "The Moral Economy of the English Crowd in the Eighteenth Century." *Past and Present* 50:76–136.
Thompson, Edward P. 1993. *Customs in Common*. New York: New Press.
Tilly, Charles. 1975. "Reflections on the History of European State-Making." In *The Formation of National States in Western Europe*, 3–89. Princeton, NJ: Princeton University Press.
Van Sant, Levi. 2021. "'The Long-Time Requirements of the Nation': The US Cooperative Soil Survey and the Political Ecologies of Improvement." *Antipode* 53 (3): 686–704.
Wainwright, Joel. 2008. *Decolonizing Development: Colonial Power and the Maya*. Malden, MA: Wiley-Blackwell.
Wallerstein, Immanuel. 1979. *The Capitalist World-Economy*. Cambridge, UK: Cambridge University Press.
Walsh-Dilley, Marygold. 2016. "Tensions of Resilience: Collective Property, Individual Gain and the Emergent Conflicts of the Quinoa Boom." *Resilience* 4 (1): 30–43.
Whyte, Kyle. 2018. "Settler Colonialism, Ecology, and Environmental Injustice." *Environment and Society* 9 (1): 125–144.
Wittman, Hannah. 2009. "Reframing Agrarian Citizenship: Land, Life and Power in Brazil." *Journal of Rural Studies* 25 (1): 120–130.
Wittman, Hannah. 2011. "Food Sovereignty: A New Rights Framework for Food and Nature?" *Environment and Society* 2 (1): 87–105.
Wolf, Eric. 1982. *Europe and the People without History*. Berkeley: University of California Press.
Wolford, Wendy. 2005. "Agrarian Moral Economies and Neoliberalism in Brazil: Competing Worldviews and the State in the Struggle for Land." *Environment and Planning A: Economy and Space* 37 (2): 241–261.
Wolford, Wendy. 2007. "Land Reform in the Time of Neoliberalism: A Many-Splendored Thing." *Antipode* 39 (3): 550–570.
Wolford, Wendy. 2010a. "Participatory Democracy by Default: Land Reform, Social Movements and the State in Brazil." *Journal of Peasant Studies* 37 (1): 91–109.
Wolford, Wendy. 2010b. *This Land Is Ours Now: Social Mobilization and the Meanings of Land in Brazil*. Durham, NC: Duke University Press.
Wolford, Wendy. 2016. "State-Society Dynamics in Contemporary Brazilian Land Reform." *Latin American Perspectives* 43 (2): 77–95.
Wolford, Wendy, Saturnino M. Borras Jr., Ruth Hall, Ian Scoones, and Ben White. 2013. "Governing Global Land Deals: The Role of the State in the Rush for Land." *Development and Change* 44 (2): 189–210.
Wolford Wendy, and John D. French. 2016. "Deconstructing the Post-Neoliberal State: Intimate Perspectives on Contemporary Brazil." *Latin American Perspectives* 43 (2): 4–21.

Wolford, Wendy, and Ryan Nehring. 2015. "Constructing Parallels: Brazilian Expertise and the Commodification of Land, Labour and Money in Mozambique." *Canadian Journal of Development Studies/Revue Canadienne d'études du développement* 36 (2): 208–223.

Wolford, Wendy. 2021. "The colonial roots of agricultural modernization in Mozambique: the role of research from Portugal to ProSavana." *The Journal of Peasant Studies* 48 (2): 254–273.

Womack, John. 1968. *Zapata and the Mexican Revolution*. New York: Vintage Books

Wright, Angus, and Wendy Wolford. 2003. *To Inherit the Earth: The Landless Movement and the Struggle for a New Brazil*. Oakland, CA: Food First Books.

Yashar, Deborah. 1998. "Contesting Citizenship: Indigenous Movements and Democracy in Latin America." *Comparative Politics* 31 (1): 23–42.

Yeh, Emily T. 2013. *Taming Tibet: Landscape Transformation and the Gift of Chinese Development*. Ithaca, NY: Cornell University Press.

CHAPTER 26

LAND IN VIOLENT CONFLICT STUDIES

JACOBO GRAJALES AND JEAN-PIERRE CHAUVEAU

INTRODUCTION

THE aim of this chapter is to explore the multiple connections between land and violent conflict.[1] We argue that these connections cannot be reduced to simple forms of causality; instead, land access and exclusion must be viewed as entrenched in broader forms of political, economic, and social change. As such, the chapter presents three fundamental interconnections. First, it details the role of land tensions in the production of violent conflict. Civil wars and armed crises are often nurtured and made more complex by their connections to histories of land conflict, yet most empirical evidence shows that the variables of land scarcity or outright inequality alone are not sufficient to explain the origins of violent conflict and the ways in which it takes shape. More fundamentally, conflicts over land are embedded in deeper struggles over how—and by whom—authority over people and resources is organized and exercised. As such, studying the intersection between land and violent conflict comes down to analyzing how land tensions are magnified, politicized, and instrumentalized over the course of armed mobilization. Second, the chapter will explore the impact of violence on the political economy of rural land. Land tensions are shaped by the occurrence of armed conflict as political identities are transformed and clientelist networks are built or broken. This can have enduring effects on the ways in which political authority is produced and reproduced. War can weaken existing forms of rule and offer a favorable context for new actors to wield freshly acquired power to distribute land, thus transforming the scope of political authority. This, of course, is intertwined with deeper transformations in the agrarian political economy. Violent conflict is just one of the many factors that shape resource grabbing, control over labor, and, ultimately, participation in agrarian capitalism's (re)production. Third, the chapter will delve into the effects of conflict-resolution policies on the political economy of land. Over the last two decades, the governance of land and natural resources has become a persistent concern for those involved in peacebuilding efforts. However, multiple biases have undermined attempts to include it in the peacebuilding process: the depiction of land policies as mere technical challenges to overcome, the entrenched belief in the capacity of modern capitalist private property to pacify social relations, or the deliberate disregard shown for the multiple and complex ramifications of land conflicts in the organization of politics and economies. Overall, the chapter seeks to reinscribe land conflicts and violence in their social, political, and economic substrate and offer a better understanding of how land struggles and agrarian changes occur and are produced by violent means.

Land Tensions and the Mechanisms of Violent Conflict

Over the last two decades, interest in the relationship between armed violence and land tensions has grown substantially in the field of critical agrarian studies (see, for instance, the special issue of Journal of Agrarian Change edited by Cramer and Richards 2011). Important works of research have renewed our understanding of the connection between agrarian political economies and the way violent conflict unfolds. This, of course, is not a new concern for students of agrarian societies. However, recent studies have introduced a more nuanced view of causality and a more complex analysis of the ties between agrarian issues and the broader organization of the political sphere.

Land Grievances and War

Early research conducted at the intersection of agrarian studies and conflict studies focused on the hypothesis of a causal relationship between the structure of land tenure and the emergence of violent conflict. Classical works of comparative historical analysis, such as those of Theda Skocpol (1979), Barrington Moore (1973), and Eric Wolf (1999), shared a common concern for how revolutions reflected the characteristics of class relations, access to land ownership, and the exploitation of agrarian labor. Focused explicitly on agrarian relations of production, Jeffrey Paige's (1978) germinal book outlined a typology of agrarian conflicts, with the aim of establishing causal relationships between different agrarian economies and diverse patterns of political conflict.

In direct opposition to this view, an approach focused on "environmental security" emerged in the 1990s that sought to dissociate class relations from the causal relationship and to instead stress environmental factors as the primary variable determining the likelihood that land tensions would escalate into violent conflict. Homer-Dixon's (1999) neo-Malthusian work paved the way for this approach by contending that scarcity is the main explanatory factor for a violent escalation of land tensions. This approach, characterized by a focus on individualistic rational choice, has been discredited in scholarly analysis because of its deterministic view and failure to consider resource conflicts as the result of histories of political and social struggles (Le Billon 2001; Peluso and Watts 2001). However, this mechanistic view, which uncritically associates environmental factors with armed conflict, has lived on in two forms: the first consists of analyses of the climate crisis that obliterate history and politics because they draw simple causal relationships between climate change and violence. The second, which often overlaps with the first, echoes popular accounts of conflicts between herders and farmers that naturalize the perceived conflictual relationship between them. Both views have been widely criticized for their depoliticizing and resource-deterministic perspectives, which fail to consider that conflicts for land are embedded in histories of class relations, accumulation of wealth, and struggles for legitimate authority. However, the research community's scant esteem for these ideas is inversely proportional to their influence in policymaking circles, where such straightforward narratives legitimize technical (rather than political) approaches.

Contemporary scholarship on the relationship between land and violent conflict has turned its back on simple deterministic views and embraced a more wide-ranging approach that seeks to associate land tensions with the broader political economy by insisting on ties with historical transformations and macroprocesses, institutional transformations, and complex agency. These approaches share the view that land tensions alone cannot explain the escalation of violent conflict. They consider that land grievances are embedded in and connected to larger social struggles—in other words, they are never only about land. This adoption of a more expansive approach is influenced by the transformation of the conflict studies field itself, which has progressively moved away from identifying simple causal relations to tracing the ways in which armed action emerges and takes place. There are several reasons for this; first, more refined empirical analyses have shown that simple causal perspectives fail to account for one fundamental trait of armed conflicts: they continuously produce their own contexts as consequences turn into causes. Second, much closer attention has been paid to agency, considering that "war does not break out because conditions happen to be 'right,' but because it is organized" (Richards 2005a, 4).

Three important approaches exemplify contemporary discourse in this field: political ecology, legal anthropology, and micropolitical analysis (for a more detailed account, see Van Leeuwen and Van der Haar 2016). Political ecology studies have stressed that conflicts over land access and exclusion are embedded in the historical realities of exploitation; they are the result of what are often long-term struggles for the accumulation of land and labor. They are also shaped by global macroprocesses such as colonialism and globalization. This is well illustrated by the analysis of the impact of rising financial incentives for land ownership, coupled with more structural transformations, such as the globalization of value chains and the financialization of agriculture. In cases as varied as Guatemala (Ybarra 2012; Grandia 2013), Colombia (Ballvé 2020; Grajales 2021a), Ethiopia (Lavers 2012; Korf, Hagmann, and Emmenegger 2015), and Myanmar (Woods 2011), violent conflicts over land cannot be dissociated from the promotion of extraverted development models, often resulting in the dispossession of peasant communities to the benefit of large-scale agribusiness. These cases underscore the fact that one of the many purposes of armed violence is to provide security for extractivist ventures.

Political ecology also offers tools for understanding the ties between biological and climatic features (e.g., the life cycle of cash crops or the seasonality of rains); political and economic processes; and moral representations of hierarchy, belonging, and power. A good exemplification of this can be found in political ecologists' interpretation of farmer-herder conflicts, which is a far cry from the simplistic accounts offered by the environmental security school of thought. Political ecologists contend that rain scarcity and land degradation are insufficient (even flawed) explanatory factors for violence. In the Sahel, the promotion of agriculture by national development policies, establishment of commercial farms, and political marginalization of formerly prestigious lines of cattle breeders emerge as far more convincing factors in explaining the politicization of land tensions and the expression of grievances in the terms used by ethnic narratives (Turner 2004; Moritz 2006; Benjaminsen, Maganga, and Abdallah 2009; Benjaminsen and Ba 2019).

Studies in the field of legal anthropology are closely related to political ecology and share the view that land conflicts are less about the resource itself than about the legitimacy of the rules and the authorities responsible for their application (Leach, Mearns, and Scoones 1997; Peters 2004; Sikor and Lund 2009; Lund and Boone 2013; Lund 2016). Two major consequences arise from this observation. First, land conflicts, and the possibility that they might escalate into armed confrontations, are part and parcel of the processes that underlie state formation. As specific institutions (the central state, customary courts, militias, etc.) struggle against rival ones, they build their legitimacy on their capacity to sanction property rights (Sikor and Lund 2009; Lund, this volume). Consequently, land conflicts are often linked to larger confrontations between two (or more) antagonistic authorities who claim supremacy over the power to recognize property rights. Unruh (2016), for instance, explains how in Syria, the state and its paramilitary allies on one side, and insurgency groups on the other, both claimed the authority to recognize or deny people's property rights to farmland. This authority is "weaponized" in that it is used to favor people who are perceived to be loyal and to punish those seen as dissidents. Second, once it is understood that land tenure regimes are about not only land but also, more broadly, about governing people and territories, it follows that the characteristics of these regimes should shape the ways in which violent mobilization unfolds. This is the point made in Catherine Boone's (2014) important book in which she argues that variations between and among land institutions determine the patterns of politicization and nationalization of land conflicts.

Micropolitics: Locating Agency

Political ecology and legal anthropology have greatly contributed to the study of violent land conflicts by enabling us to see how land tensions are embedded in larger patterns of conflict, and how the escalation of these tensions often implies fundamental questions about political authority and identity. However, some authors argue that political ecology and legal anthropology perspectives are less useful when it comes to analyzing the specific processes through which violence is organized and exerted. As Van Leeuwen and Van der Haar (2016) put it, "Local insecurities and disputes about land do not simply 'add up' to produce large-scale violence, but the nexus between them remains undertheorized" (97). The methodological question then becomes, How do we articulate localized conflicts about land property and use to larger-scale political conflicts, often framed in more abstract terms (ideology, partisanship, ethnicity, religion, etc.)? Most of the available responses adopt a framework that draws from Kalyvas (2006), who argues that "individual and local communities involved in the war tend to take advantage of the prevailing situation to settle private and local conflicts whose relation to the grand causes of the war or the goals of the belligerents is often tenuous" (364–365). From that perspective, the key mechanism that ties a national "master cleavage" to local quarrels is an alliance between "supralocal and local actors, whereby the former supply the latter with external muscle" while the latter "are able to tap into local networks and generate mobilization" (383). This framework has two important implications. First, it makes manifest that political violence can spill over from a limited set of grievances and come to embrace a larger variety of social conflicts; in other words, it shows that existing conflicts are reconfigured by the occurrence of armed activity (Autesserre 2010, 126; Van Leeuwen and Van Der Haar 2016, 98). Second, it places agency at the junction of the master cleavages of civil war (ethnicity, partisanship, class, religion, etc.) and the everyday localized conflicts over resources; it stresses the fact that violence is jointly produced by political elites (the supralocal actors in Kalyvas's frame) and ordinary citizens (Korf 2005; Klaus 2020). According to various works in this vein, the articulation between local and supralocal actors requires the production of linkages to tie local grievances to the cleavages in the national conflict. Kathleen Klaus (2020) uses the concept of "land narratives" to describe this sort of "key device around which elites and citizens coordinate the use of violence." Such narratives can stress the injustice of arbitrary past land allocation or raise the specter of imminent threats to land tenure security (6, 39).

Although micropolitical perspectives can open fruitful avenues to help us understand the production of armed violence, it also leaves some blind spots that scholars should look at carefully and address. First, the micropolitical approach considers the existence of two separate spheres—a private sphere and a political sphere—which interact in the course of civil war (Kalyvas 2006, 382). The problems and discourses at work are intrinsically political or private, and the key methodological challenge is to trace their interactions. This approach risks conveying a static view of what is political and what is not and reifying the sphere of the political through ideological terms that correspond to the researcher's expectations. Yet the boundaries of what is political are constantly shifting and subject to struggles and negotiations. The second blind spot left by the micropolitical approach concerns the very process of politicization. Though Kalyvas and others insist on the joint production of violence, the idea of a "master cleavage" that is produced at the supralocal level before being tied into private quarrels at the local level reflects a division of labor between local and national political entrepreneurs. It is expected that ideology and friend-and-foe discourses will be produced nationally, while being translated in terms of material and territorial grievances locally. This conveys a simplistic view of how political discourses are built, particularly regarding land narratives.

The relationship between localized land conflicts and the broader political landscape is not binary. Rather, it can be found in multiple formal and informal arenas, where agents cannot be characterized unequivocally as "local" or "supralocal." These labels obscure the fact that individuals can play parallel roles in different arenas (the central committee of a political party, a village council, the parliament, etc.), adopting different discourses and using a diversity of resources in different situations (Bierschenk and Olivier de Sardan 1998). In addition, local government offices or village councils are not simply subordinate repositories of supralocal political influences, but instead serve as key places where land tensions are recast in terms of citizenship, belonging, and political affiliation. In Côte d'Ivoire, for instance, political discourses about citizenship and belonging and about land-registration policies and land conflicts were shaped by the breakdown of land tenure arrangements in areas that had experienced a recent expansion of the cash-crop economy. Land grievances came to be politicized in multiple and parallel arenas that, in and of themselves, are not necessarily "political" in nature, such as cocoa cooperatives, parent-teacher associations, and vigilante committees. Political cleavages were expressed both at the village level and in central arenas (also noted by Autesserre 2010, 142). "Land narratives" (Klaus 2020) were conveyed by actors that escape the binary categories of "local" and "national": partisan networks, ethnic associations, and urban migrant networks (Chauveau 2017). In short, the use of spatial metaphors, which can often serve as a convenient linguistic shorthand, should not obscure the fact that relationships between people and political arenas cannot be reduced to simple "local" and "national" labels, and are better understood in the terms of embedded, porous, and hybrid norms, institutions, and scales.

The Effects of Violence

Most of the works reviewed here are in accord that the relationship between land and violent conflict should not be reduced to a quest for the original causes of a confrontation; instead, they adopt a diachronic view of how land antagonisms unfold. This is because violence inherently creates its own context, redrawing political identities and transforming governance institutions. This observation remains valid even as countries transition out of war. Indeed, most studies of contemporary civil wars have shown that when a war ends, peace seldom ensues (Richards 2005b). Instead, the consequences of violence are perpetuated in the unequal access to land among different categories of people. Recent literature has strengthened our understanding of the effects of violence on land access. It is possible to identify three major perspectives in these works: those inquiring into the effects of hostilities on land conflicts and land struggles themselves, those focusing on land governance institutions, and those that center on the mechanisms of land accumulation and labor control.

A Reconfiguration of Land Conflicts

Civil wars offer favorable contexts for the escalation of land disputes into larger-scale conflicts. The literature on agency discussed above carefully disentangles the mechanisms of this escalation. However, in thinking about the effects of war on social struggles, it should be noted that violent conflict often results in transformations in the characteristics and the exercise of political authority. These transformations have distributional consequences, empowering some social groups and disempowering others. Disenfranchised groups might resort to violence to resist, whereas newly dominant ones will tend to use their recently acquired armed muscle to withstand opposition from below. This corresponds to Benedikt Korf's (2005) observations linking the production of violence in Sri Lanka to the effects of a clientelistic warfare[2] strategy, which produces antagonistic identities to spur violent mobilization:

> The political economy of war produces a self-sustaining logic of clientelism along the lines of perceived "friends" and "foes"; these dividing lines are not only produced by the logics of polarization and politicization of land grievances, but are also reproduced and reinforced by the fact that people depend on "political networks of survival." (202)

These clientelistic warfare strategies result in transformations in identity and belonging. Baczko and Dorronsoro (2017; 2022) use the notion of "identity capital" as a tool for analyzing the capacity to utilize one's identity as leverage to obtain access to political and economic resources. Typically, the value of identity capital in civil wars is highly volatile, owing to changes in political authority, fluid social orders, and the transnationalization of societies. Identity (ethnic, religious, partisan etc.) then becomes the rationale for being granted—or refused—access to property rights; this nurtures a self-sustaining process in which the use of identity capital is sustained by clientelistic networks of redistribution.

Another critical effect of violence is the massive displacement of rural inhabitants. Waves of forced displacement often spark mobilizations to define who has a right to settle where, often resulting in overlapping ownership claims. Autesserre (2010, 167) describes how local militias reacted to the resettlement of IDPs in eastern Democratic Republic of the Congo by mounting violent attacks against returnees. The fact that land transactions continue to happen, and can even be bolstered in conflict-ridden contexts, is a further source of violence. Chauveau and Colin (2014), as well as Toukpo (forthcoming), document how land was abundantly sold and purchased during the Ivorian civil war and its immediate and violent aftermath. In the west of the country, where most of the rural violence was concentrated, this created a volatile social climate that did not calm down with the official end of the war in 2011. Similarly, Counter (2019) and Tchatchoua-Djomo et al. (2018), working respectively on Colombia and Burundi, showed how war creates new identities to allow the recognition of land claims. Labels that are framed in ethnic terms or that rely on the state's recognition of "victims" restructure land conflicts even as they redistribute resources between the competing parties.

Land Governance in the Midst of War

Violence transforms the conditions in which struggles for land access occur, but it also fashions land governance institutions. Baczko (2016) shows how land conflicts in Afghanistan interact with the counterinsurgency strategy of the US army. The military's strategy of instrumentalizing local conflicts to create bonds with local auxiliaries puts their allies in a highly favorable position for excluding other groups from access to land. Examples of this kind of instrumentalization abound in the literature. The fundamental aspect for broader reflection on land and violent conflict is that repeated instrumentalization inexorably weakens institutions, because they can no longer aspire to appear as neutral arbitrators for competing claims. This is the key takeaway from Baczko's work, in which he demonstrates how the US military's divide-and-rule tactics hindered foreign donors' efforts to create a legitimate and respected Afghan judiciary (Baczko 2021).

Institutional weakening can also stem from the simple fact that authorities are under attack and that situations of forced displacement and mass murder give rise to far less rigid conditions for making land claims. This is one of the arguments Paul Richards put forth in his influential analysis of the war in Sierra Leone. Not only was the Revolutionary United Front's insurrection aimed at a local-level gerontocracy that used neo-customary rules to impose a system of forced labor on young men, but these "traditional" rules were also weakened by the disarticulation of rural communities (Richards 2005c; 2022). War's effects on institutional transformations are made even more acute by the consequences of rebel governance. As state or neo-customary authorities are contested and weakened, they are often replaced by rebel rule. Yet this armed social order is often enforced by people (generally men) with social profiles that are radically different from those of the prewar authorities. In short, land-allocation and conflict-resolution powers can end up in the hands of unseasoned young men, as Autesserre (2010) has documented in Congo. The efforts of these former rebel rulers to hold on to a portion of their power in transitional situations often defines the patterns and intensity of postwar violence and instability. Munive's work in Central Liberia exemplifies this; when former loyalist militiamen succeeded in keeping their grip on local institutions in the northern parts of Nimba County at the end of the war, the return of refugees from a different ethnic background (Mandingos) represented a risk, both for those who now occupied other people's lands and homes, and for the authorities that had claimed land allocation authority during the late stages of the war (Munive 2010).

Challenges posed to land allocation authorities do not stem solely from the direct effects of violence and armed governance; they can also result from the fact that forced migration and life in exile transform social hierarchies. The capacity of women and young men to become "clients" of humanitarian assistance agencies can provide them with the resources they need to demand a more significant role in decision-making at a community level. This point is made by Joireman and Yoder (2016, 569), who argue that "changing authority structures after conflict can have unexpected benefits to some individuals, such as empowering youth, women and others in a society who previously had no say, or limited voice, in community decisions."

Violence and Agrarian Change

A third perspective from which the effects of violence on land access and exclusion can be observed takes a broader view of historical processes of accumulation, class formation, and agrarian change. This is a much less explored perspective in the literature so far, and it is a particularly fruitful approach to analyzing the continuity between war and its aftermath. Adopting this broader frame of reference with regard to land and violence requires us to place land within the larger political economy of postwar transitions. In the past three decades (if not more), transitions out of war have also been characterized by the formal establishment of liberal democracy and market-compliant economic institutions (Ottaway 2002). The idea that political and economic (neo)liberalization are both equally essential to durable institutional consolidation is firmly entrenched in contemporary approaches to peacebuilding (Richmond 2012). As such, capitalism becomes the impassable horizon of out-of-war transitions. However, this entails considerable political implications, as equating the free market with the peace economy conceals the contribution of war and violence to enduring forms of accumulation and the continuity between wartime and peacetime accumulation.

The case of Mozambique is a good illustration of how transitions out of war are tied into processes of economic neoliberalization. Even before the peace accord between the Frelimo government and the Renamo insurgency was reached in 1992, an Economic Rehabilitation Programme was implemented with the aim of liberalizing the economy and attracting foreign investment, particularly in the agribusiness sector. West and Myers (1996, 29) report that, as of January 1994, just a little more than a year after the peace agreement was signed, over 20 million hectares of land had been granted in concession. However, the neoliberal transition that occurred did not result in a free-market environment, but rather led to rent capture by political elites and/or capitalist cronies. In reality, government officials and former soldiers massively benefited from the privatization of Mozambican state farms.

This example does not fundamentally differ from other cases of rapid neoliberalization. The key difference is that postconflict transition becomes a resource in the accelerated imposition of economic reforms. Under the guise of peace, peacebuilding, and postconflict development, land policies are depoliticized and defined as matters too urgent for deliberation (Grajales 2021b). In this respect, postwar capitalism does not differ much from what Naomi Klein calls "disaster capitalism," in which exceptional conjunctures characterized by a less rigid social order are employed as a window of opportunity to push through neoliberal reform (Klein 2008). Peace negotiations add another facet to this emergency climate. During these peace talks, rebels are often willing to sacrifice their demands for immediate economic reform to obtain concessions on political participation. This is the argument put forth by Elisabeth Wood (2000), in her comparative analysis of South Africa and El Salvador. In both cases, progressive revolutionary movements made significant compromises on their economic agenda in exchange for guarantees in the area of political participation. Economic reform was then defined as a longer-term perspective, while political participation became the keystone of transition. However, as analyzed by Binford with regard to El Salvador, the road to political moderation meant dispensing with agrarian justice as a common grammar for the revolutionary movement. As former guerrilla cadres came to condone structural adjustment policies in the countryside, rural movements ceased to be laboratories for political change (Binford 2010).

War and postwar contexts are also characterized by reconfigurations in the territorialization of agrarian capitalism. One of the best examples of this is the expansion of agrarian frontiers (Rasmussen and Lund 2018, 391). As relative stability is brought to rural areas, government officials and corporations see new business opportunities, depicting rural populations' activities as "archaic" and fostering the idea that rural territories are open for colonization. Colombia's Orinoco Savannah offers a good illustration of this. During the early 2000s, expanding military consolidation in the region was accompanied by new legislation on land use that empowered the government to allocate huge tracts of land to agribusiness corporations. Promoters of this legislation made the case that the region's marginality—which is a result of a long history of state neglect—precluded peasant agriculture. There were simply no roads to allow small farmers' products to reach the market. This legitimized the controversial idea that corporations alone were capable of pursuing capitalist development in such a marginal area (Grajales 2020).

One last important feature of transitions out of war is the transformation of wartime accumulation and exclusion. While postconflict contexts are often characterized by persistent levels of violence (Kurtenbach and Rettberg 2018), they also involve an expectation of de-escalation and the idea that armed violence should no longer be the primary vehicle for political action and economic accumulation (Suhrke and Berdal 2013). Studying the legacies of armed violence thus implies paying particular attention to how forms of power built or consolidated through violent means adapt to a new context (Cramer 2006). This consolidation can be read through the metaphor of "laundering," in which the violent origins of property are concealed by institutional and political devices (Ballvé 2013). Of course—as discussed in the next section—the law can play a critical role in this laundering mechanism. Other discourses, such as environmental conservation, can play a similar legitimizing role. In the case of Colombia, Diana Ojeda shows how supposedly environment- and community-friendly models of development such as ecotourism have contributed to consolidating the effects of wartime dispossession (Ojeda 2012). More broadly, one should note that the common perception of postwar states and societies as "clean slates" where everything remains to be done inevitably conceals the implications of reconstruction in terms of distributive justice. In other words, because war has winners and losers, it is essential to recognize the differential effects of postwar development on people and territories in the postconflict economic order. This is rarely the case. Jon Unruh offers one striking example of the economic effects of such a bias. In Syria—Unruh argues—scorched-earth military campaigns altogether drove the population out of some pre-existing informal settlements. These zones were then "offered to companies from the Gulf States, Europe and elsewhere for reconstruction investments" (Unruh 2022).

The above examples stress the importance of dispossession and restitution in the larger landscape of postwar land policies. As transnational policy communities have recognized, this is a critical aspect of transitions out of war. The following section deals with these policies.

Dealing with Violence and Land

The Emergence of a Global Agenda

Since the late 1990s, there has been renewed interest among development and humanitarian professionals, donors, and multilateral organizations in the kind of land policies promoted for postconflict societies. This stems from the conjunction of various processes. First, this novel preoccupation is the result of the increased scope and ambition of peacebuilding activities. Beginning in the second half of the 1990s, in the aftermath of the end of the Cold War, the Yugoslavian wars, and the Tutsi genocide in Rwanda, international organizations, national governments, and peacebuilding experts advocated for a comprehensive approach to peacebuilding (Richmond 2012). This pertained not just to issues directly linked to the war (such as security-sector reform or transitional justice), but also to more sweeping, fundamental reforms of social and political structures: the economy, the rule of law, gender equality, and even education suddenly became issues requiring intervention (Mac Ginty and Williams 2016). In many countries, land policies were an important topic in this expansive understanding of peacebuilding. For instance, peace talks in Burundi or Bosnia and Herzegovina recognized the importance of land issues to building a sustainable agreement (Takeuchi 2014).

This expansion of the peacebuilding field intersected with a growing focus among academics and practitioners on environmental and natural-resource conflicts. Concerns about the destabilizing effects of environmental degradation, mounting competition for scarce vital resources (land, water), and plunder-driven violence were brought together under an "environmental security" paradigm (see, among others, Unruh and Williams 2013; Young and Goldman 2015; Bruch, Muffett, and Nichols 2016). Land has become a major topic of concern for a transnational academic and policy network on "environmental peacebuilding," as is evidenced by a series of publications addressing the issue of land tenure rights and land law reforms in postconflict settings.

In parallel, transnational policy circles were approaching the issue of land from the point of view of forced displacement, dispossession, and asset restitution. The United Nations played a critical role in the emergence of the problem through the production of policy standards, but it was also joined by the determined action of advocacy groups such as the Brookings Institution, the International Peace Academy, and the Norwegian Refugee Council. This process resulted in the adoption, in 2005, of the Pinheiro Principles on Housing and Property Restitution for Refugees and Displaced Persons by the UN Sub-Commission on the Promotion and Protection of Human Rights. The Pinheiro Principles consist of a set of guidelines and standards intended to guide states, international organizations, and civil society institutions in designing and implementing asset-restitution policies (Smit 2013, 23–29).

Lastly, it should not be forgotten that these policy discussions all took place in a context of mounting interest in land and agriculture in development assistance circles, which, through an expanded focus on the generic challenges of economic development and poverty alleviation, went well beyond postconflict transition. During the 1990s, key development assistance actors such as the US government and the World Bank became interested in investing aid funds in agriculture and land tenure projects (Deininger and Binswanger 1999). This was the fruit of parallel transformations taking place in the dominant discourses on poverty alleviation, which stressed the need to push for endogenous development and small-scale economic entrepreneurship. The influence of the private-property rights approach, which considered individual land ownership rights to be the cornerstone of a pro-poor development strategy, attracted a great deal of donor attention to land tenure projects (Manji 2006; Musembi 2007; Colin, Le Meur, and Léonard 2009). In parallel, World Bank economists praised the inclusion of smallholders in the global commodity chain as instrumental for rural development and the modernization of agriculture (Amanor 2009). Fostering the security of land tenure, modernization, and globalization came to be seen as three complementary strategies for generating economic growth in rural areas of the global South. It goes without saying that these were promoted with particular emphasis in the postconflict contexts in Africa, Latin America, and Asia.

Postconflict Land Policy Instruments

Through these concurrent processes, land had become an integral facet of the discussion on postconflict stabilization and development by the first half of the 2000s. It was integrated into the strategies of various international organizations, each adopting its own sectoral prism. Despite the diversity of views, common standards emerged through subsequent intervention in such countries as Afghanistan, the Democratic Republic of the Congo, and Burundi. Through the transposition of models and discussions on "best practices," international development actors became involved in producing standardized policy instruments. Policy papers such as the Food and Agriculture Organization of the United Nations' report on tenure rights (FAO 2005) and the Organisation of Economic Cooperation and Development's working paper on land, violent conflict, and development (Pons-Vignon and Lecomte 2004) illustrate the global policy debate. Today, policy instruments can be broadly classified in three categories: land restitution, land formalization and conflict resolution, and land access policies for vulnerable populations.

Land restitution is probably the most formalized and standardized policy in the field. The production of international standards, the judicialization of transitional justice, and the existence of advocacy actors who invest substantial resources in researching and producing "best practices" explain this high degree of formalization. The problem most clearly associated with these policies concerns state capacity. Collecting evidence of land ownership and organizing the return of forcibly displaced people to the property being restored to them presents daunting logistical challenges, particularly when the state's administrative apparatus has been weakened by war (Pantuliano 2009). Very often, restitution operations have heavily relied—at least in their early phases—on the strong involvement of the international community. The case of Bosnia and Herzegovina, which marked an important milestone in the transnational policy discussion on restitution, exemplifies this (Williams 2006). Beyond the problem of cost and the inherent logistical challenges, restitution policies shine a spotlight on the contentious and chaotic history of property claims in many regions of the world. Efforts to implement these policies confront challenges such as overlapping property claims, the lack of recognized proof of ownership, and the absence of a state monopoly on the registration and recognition of property rights (Unruh 2014; Joireman and Yoder 2016; Tchatchoua-Djomo and Van Dijk 2022). Of course, these are not merely technical obstacles. They pose intrinsically political questions of land access and exclusion and of whose rights should ultimately be protected and whose claims are more legitimate. This entails complex trade-offs that go well beyond purely legal issues and imply political choices, such as when social groups perceived as "loyal" to the regime are favored, as in contemporary Syria (Stubblefield and Joireman 2019), or when the claims of large agribusiness corporations are deemed more legitimate than those of forcibly displaced peasants, as in Mozambique (Unruh 2005) or Colombia (Vargas Reina 2022). Similarly, the interests of restitution claimants can stand in opposition to large infrastructure development projects but also to conservation initiatives seeking to transform formerly inhabited areas into sanctuaries for endemic flora and fauna (Ybarra 2018). Lastly, as analyzed by Cherryl Walker (2008) in the case of South Africa, the limitations of restitution can also be seen in people's capacity and willingness—or lack thereof—to return to formerly dispossessed land. When and where a return to rural life is rendered cumbersome by economic deregulation and liberalization, as in contemporary South Africa, capacity and willingness should be understood in political terms as a product of agricultural, economic, and social policies.

How can one make sense of all these competing interests? To step back from the operational challenges and produce a more radical critique, a good place to start is by questioning the very effects of restitution policies on how agrarian justice problems are defined. In other words, it is important to recognize that land restitution frameworks determine the problems development practitioners and governments perceive as deserving of urgent attention and which issues are dismissed or postponed. We suggest two ways of identifying these effects (Grajales 2021a, 2021b). First, restitution schemes define war-related dispossession as the central concern for postconflict land policies. Indisputably, repairing the consequences of war can be a meaningful objective, yet returning to the status quo ante often means reinstating a deeply unjust social and economic order. Not only is transitional justice often incapable of dealing with the structural issues of agrarian justice, but implementing restitution programs also runs the risk of legitimizing existing inequalities; for as long as these inequalities do not directly result from violence and dispossession, they are presumed to be legitimate. Second, land restitution schemes are built on a clear-cut distinction between wartime and peacetime. Yet transitions out of war inevitably produce winners and losers, entailing new claims that are attached to the conditions under which the victor's peace is enforced or a peace deal is (or fails to be) implemented. Claims that originate from the postwar economic order rather than from the direct consequences of the war, however, are dismissed as irrelevant (Lai 2020). People who suffer from the effects of postwar capitalism do not qualify as victims of an armed conflict. They are simply subjects who are unsuited to the requirements of the market.

Land formalization is the next policy instrument that has gained international currency in the toolkit of peacebuilders. Land formalization has a long history in rural development, which goes well beyond postconflict transition. Beginning in the mid-1990s, donors and experts promoted land formalization as an essential element of rule-of-law reforms. They generally argued that formalization would stimulate investment and growth by recognizing property rights (Manji 2006; Musembi 2007; Dwyer 2015; Peters, this volume). In the specific field of peacebuilding policies, land formalization was praised as a way to reduce the risk of lingering conflicts and to promote much-needed postconflict development (Unruh and Shalaby 2012; Unruh and Williams 2013). Of course, these two objectives sometimes involve complicated trade-offs. Land formalization policies have assimilated conflict-resolution procedures with different degrees of institutionalization. They can rely on the judiciary but also on local assemblies and participatory procedures—and frequently on a combination of both. The debate on conflict resolution can be roughly described as structured by two competing viewpoints: one is a narrow approach that insists on security and stability and considers land conflicts fertile ground for the expression of underlying social discord; the other is a broader perspective that considers land conflicts to be fashioned by violence, but also by longer histories of exploitation, accumulation, and authority formation. If the second perspective is to be given credence, it follows that conflict resolution cannot be limited to dealing with the manifestations of conflict but should also confront the agrarian justice issues that shape and nurture violence (Van Leeuwen et al. 2022). Additionally, some researchers have noted the incapacity of conflict-resolution procedures to actually maintain stability. For instance, Tchatchoua-Djomo, Van Leeuwen, and Van der Haar (2020) insist that in Burundi, land certification and dispute resolution "can rekindle old and generate new disputes," by opening new venues for making land claims, generating competition among representatives of local institutions seeking to impose their authority, and providing opportunities for clientelistic capture and mobilization.

Other debates concern the degree of bureaucracy and formalism associated with land policies. In recent years, the dominant approach has moved away from an insistence on legal recognition (sometimes called "land legalization") toward more flexible approaches that account for local governance practices and norms. The rationale behind this movement toward "localization" has been that postconflict states often have neither the administrative capacity nor the legal institutions needed to implement large-scale land titling, and therefore should opt for less costly, bureaucratically demanding solutions (Murtazashvili and Murtazashvili 2021). In practice, these land formalization policies have delegated the power to recognize land rights to local authorities, who often enjoy the supposedly "traditional" legitimacy of neo-customary rulers. While these policies are certainly more flexible than centralized solutions, they carry a risk of creating new sources of conflict, particularly when one accounts for the fact that the legitimacy of so-called traditional authorities is often subject to violent contestation (as well as to capture and transformation) in wartime (Chauveau and Richards 2008; Autesserre 2010). In Afghanistan, in a case praised in the neo-institutional literature on customary rights recognition (Murtazashvili and Murtazashvili 2021), the United States Agency for International Development (USAID) supported land rights projects that delegated authority to local assemblies known as "jirgas" or "shuras." Although US officials praised the capacity of these "traditional" bodies to deal with land conflicts, but they had overlooked the fact that these institutions had been transformed by more than twenty years of civil war, in a typical process of "reinvention of tradition." As Baczko (2016; 2021) insightfully argued, representations of "traditional" legitimacy had much more to do with the "imaginary anthropology" of US bureaucrats and military forces than with the reality of these local assemblies. In practice, local strongmen often controlled these bodies and instrumentalized customary justice in the pursuit of patronage and territorial influence.

The third dimension of postconflict land policy—access and distribution—has been the most limited aspect of the policy debate. True, there is a broad consensus on integrating concerns for vulnerability in postconflict land policies, adopting differential approaches for women, young people, or ethnic minorities. However, these policy debates have been constrained by the requirement that policy instruments be both compatible and compliant with a market-led approach (Grajales 2021b). In a review of five peace agreements that integrated land policies into postconflict transition plans—El Salvador, Guatemala, Nepal, South Africa, and Colombia—García Trujillo (2020) shows that redistributive measures are mostly off the table, even when policy contexts seem favorable to ambitious land-reform policies. This, of course, is due to the enviable position enjoyed by landed elites in state institutions and the imposition of neoliberal economic policies that often accompanies postconflict transition processes. El Salvador's peace agreement and South Africa's post-apartheid transition, for example, feature compromises in which political reform is secured by providing guarantees to business elites about the stability of their property rights (Wood 2000). In consequence, whenever land access has been integrated into postconflict policy packages, it has been tied to market-driven approaches such as purchase subsidies or assisted land markets. This policy instrument choice is paradoxical at best, given the poor results delivered by these kinds of policies in the past (Borras 2003). A critical view would even suggest that these market-driven approaches function as a masquerade, concealing the sanctuarization of property rights even when evidence exists that they were consolidated through violent means (Grajales 2021a).

Conclusion

This chapter has endeavored to contextualize land and agrarian issues in the study of violent conflict. We began by considering that land tensions can affect the ways in which violent conflict unfolds. Although monocausal approaches seeking to determine the original causes of war are of little help in assessing the role of land in the production of violence, it is argued that land tensions must be studied in the context of changing institutions, transforming modes of production, and polarizing processes of political and violent mobilization. However, though land grievances can play an essential role in understanding armed conflict, this view is complemented by a reflection on the effects of violence on property relations. With due consideration for the idea that violence produces its own context, the chapter advocates in favor of a diachronic and process-centered view, which is deeply attentive to how violence transforms pre-existing struggles, fashions governance institutions, and alters the conditions of land accumulation and exploitation. Violence must therefore be fully integrated into the analysis of the political economy of land, not as an exogenous factor, but as an integral part of the historical transformations affecting modes of production. Lastly, this chapter tied these reflections into a critical appraisal of how the peacebuilding field has integrated land policies into a standardized package of postconflict transition measures. This is the result of a particular historical conjuncture that saw the emergence of parallel debates on transitional justice, rural development, and environmental security. Stemming from this are three main approaches seen in the practices of international organization and peacebuilding experts: land restitution, land formalization, and land access. By connecting these approaches to their underlying political choices, the chapter shows that they are not politically neutral; rather, they are molded by diverse interests, trajectories of accumulation, and the conditions of transition out of war.

This chapter is underpinned by a set of methodological and epistemological choices.[3] First, it aims to strike a balance between two extremes: neither seeing land tensions as a meta-cause that explains how violent conflict unfolds nor reducing it to a mere backdrop against which strategic choices are made. Second, it stresses continuity over rupture in the study of land and violent conflict. This complexifies simplistic representations that trace neat differences between times preceding armed confrontation, times in which armed confrontation occurs, and times often too rapidly considered as belonging to the postconflict transition category. Even if these categories can sometimes subsist for convenience's sake, it remains fundamentally important to reject the view that violence is a mere hiatus from normality, and to remain attentive to the connections between more extended transformations in the political economy of land and shorter-term variations in the intensity of the use of violence. Last, the chapter does not define land-related conflicts as a specific and distinct kind of conflict. Instead, it connects land tensions to larger structures of conflict dealing with class, identity, and the relationship between people and the state. This approach is at odds with the practical choices implemented by many aid agencies that try to insulate land tensions from other social conflicts. This invariably leads to critical contradictions in the implementation of land policies. Overcoming these contradictions is not only an operational challenge; it is a fundamental issue of agrarian justice.

Acknowledgments

The authors wish to thank Paul Richards, Jun Borras, and Jennifer Franco for their careful and considerate reading of a previous version of this chapter.

Notes

1. This chapter expands some of the ideas initially developed in Chauveau, Grajales, and Léonard (2020).
2. I borrow this expression from Francisco Gutiérrez's (2019) work on paramilitary militias in Colombia.
3. A similar perspective is developed in Jacob and Léonard, in collaboration with Chauveau (2022).

References

Amanor, Kojo Sebastian. 2009. "Global Food Chains, African Smallholders and World Bank Governance." *Journal of Agrarian Change* 9 (2): 247–262.

Autesserre, Séverine. 2010. *The Trouble with the Congo: Local Violence and the Failure of International Peacebuilding*. Cambridge, UK: Cambridge University Press.

Baczko, Adam. 2016. "Legal Rule and Tribal Politics: The US Army and the Taliban in Afghanistan (2001–13)." *Development and Change* 47 (6): 1412–1433.

Baczko, Adam. 2021. *La guerre par le droit: Les tribunaux Taliban en Afghanistan*. Paris: CNRS Editions.

Baczko, Adam, and Gilles Dorronsoro. 2017. "Pour une approche sociologique des guerres civiles." *Revue française de science politique* 67 (2): 309–327.

Baczko, Adam, and Gilles Dorronsoro. 2022. "Thinking about Civil Wars with and beyond Bourdieu: State, Capital and Habitus in Critical Contexts." *Journal of Classical Sociology* 22 (2): 199–221.

Ballvé, Teo. 2013. "Grassroots Masquerades: Development, Paramilitaries, and Land Laundering in Colombia." *Geoforum* 50 (December): 62–75.

Ballvé, Teo. 2020. *The Frontier Effect: State Formation and Violence in Colombia*. Ithaca, NY: Cornell University Press.

Benjaminsen, Tor A., and Boubacar Ba. 2019. "Why Do Pastoralists in Mali Join Jihadist Groups? A Political Ecological Explanation." *Journal of Peasant Studies* 46 (1): 1–20.

Benjaminsen, Tor A., Faustin P. Maganga, and Jumanne Moshi Abdallah. 2009. "The Kilosa Killings: Political Ecology of a Farmer-Herder Conflict in Tanzania." *Development and Change* 40 (3): 423–445.

Bierschenk, Thomas, and Jean-Pierre Olivier de Sardan. 1998. "Les arenes locales face à la décentralisation et à la démocratisation: Analyses comparatives en milieu rural béninois." In *Les pouvoirs au village: Le Bénin rural entre démocratisation et décentralisation*, 11–55. Paris: Karthala.

Binford, Leigh. 2010. "A Perfect Storm of Neglect and Failure: Postwar Capitalist Restoration in Northern Morazán, El Salvador." *Journal of Peasant Studies* 37 (3): 531–557.

Boone, Catherine. 2014. *Property and Political Order in Africa: Land Rights and the Structure of Politics*. New York: Cambridge University Press.

Borras, Saturnino M. 2003. "Questioning Market-Led Agrarian Reform: Experiences from Brazil, Colombia and South Africa." *Journal of Agrarian Change* 3 (3): 367–394.

Bruch, Carl, Carroll Muffett, and Sandra S. Nichols. 2016. *Governance, Natural Resources and Postconflict Peacebuilding*. London: Routledge.

Chauveau, Jean-Pierre. 2017. "Autochtonie nomade et État frontière: Conflit et post conflit en Côte d'Ivoire au prisme de la question agraire." Working paper. https://doi.org/10.13140/RG.2.2.28573.20964.

Chauveau, Jean-Pierre, and Jean-Philippe Colin. 2014. "La question foncière à l'épreuve de la reconstruction en Côte d'Ivoire: Promouvoir la propriété privée ou stabiliser la reconnaissance sociale des droits." *Les Cahiers du Pôle Foncier* 6.

Chauveau, Jean-Pierre, Jacobo Grajales, and Eric Léonard. 2020. "Foncier et violences politiques en Afrique: Pour une approche continuiste et processuelle." *Revue internationale d'études du développement* 3 (223): 7–35.

Chauveau, Jean-Pierre, and Paul Richards. 2008. "West African Insurgencies in Agrarian Perspective: Côte d'Ivoire and Sierra Leone Compared." *Journal of Agrarian Change* 8 (4): 515–552.

Colin, Jean-Philippe, Pierre-Yves Le Meur, and Eric Léonard, eds. 2009. *Les politiques d'enregistrement des droits fonciers: Du cadre légal aux pratiques locales*. Paris: Karthala.

Counter, Max. 2019. "In Good Faith: Land Grabbing, Legal Dispossession, and Land Restitution in Colombia." *Journal of Latin American Geography* 18 (1): 169–192.

Cramer, Christopher. 2006. *Civil War Is Not a Stupid Thing: Accounting for Violence in Developing Countries*. London: Hurst.

Cramer, Christopher, and Paul Richards. 2011. "Violence and War in Agrarian Perspective." In "The Agrarian Roots of Violent Conflict." Special issue. *Journal of Agrarian Change* 11 (3): 277–297.

Deininger, Klaus, and Hans Binswanger. 1999. "The Evolution of the World Bank's Land Policy: Principles, Experience, and Future Challenges." *World Bank Research Observer* 14 (2): 247–276.

Dwyer, Michael B. 2015. "The Formalization Fix? Land Titling, Land Concessions and the Politics of Spatial Transparency in Cambodia." *Journal of Peasant Studies* 42 (5): 903–928.

FAO. 2005. *Access to Rural Land and Land Administration after Violent Conflicts.* FAO Land Tenure Studies 8. Rome: Food and Agriculture Organization of the United Nations.

García Trujillo, Andrés. 2020. *Peace and Rural Development in Colombia: The Window for Distributive Change in Negotiated Transitions.* London: Routledge.

Grajales, Jacobo. 2020. "A Land Full of Opportunities? Agrarian Frontiers, Policy Narratives and the Political Economy of Peace in Colombia." *Third World Quarterly* 47 (7): 1141–1160.

Grajales, Jacobo. 2021a. *Agrarian Capitalism, War and Peace in Colombia: Beyond Dispossession.* London: Routledge.

Grajales, Jacobo. 2021b. "Losing Land in Times of Peace: Postwar Agrarian Capitalism in Colombia and Côte d'Ivoire." *Journal of Peasant Studies* 48 (5): 1054–1074.

Grandia, Liza. 2013. "Road Mapping: Megaprojects and Land Grabs in the Northern Guatemalan Lowlands." *Development and Change* 44 (2): 233–259.

Gutiérrez, Francisco. 2019. *Clientelistic Warfare: Paramilitaries and the State in Colombia.* Oxford: Peter Lang.

Homer-Dixon, Thomas F. 1999. *Environment, Scarcity, and Violence.* Princeton, NJ: Princeton University Press.

Jacob, Jean-Pierre, and Eric Léonard, in collaboration with Jean-Pierre Chauveau. 2022. "Les conflits pour la terre: Configurations et trajectoires." In *Le foncier rural dans les pays du Sud: Enjeux et clés d'analyse*, edited by Jean-Philippe Colin, Philippe Lavigne-Delville, and Eric Léonard, 541–631. Marseille: IRD Editions/QUAE.

Joireman, Sandra F., and Laura S. Meitzner Yoder. 2016. "A Long Time Gone: Postconflict Rural Property Restitution under Customary Law." *Development and Change* 47 (3): 563–585.

Kalyvas, Stathis. 2006. *The Logic of Violence in Civil War.* New York: Cambridge University Press.

Klaus, Kathleen. 2020. *Political Violence in Kenya: Land, Elections, and Claim-Making.* Cambridge, UK: Cambridge University Press.

Klein, Naomi. 2008. *The Shock Doctrine: The Rise of Disaster Capitalism.* London: Penguin Press.

Korf, Benedikt. 2005. "Rethinking the Greed-Grievance Nexus: Property Rights and the Political Economy of War in Sri Lanka." *Journal of Peace Research* 42 (2): 201–217.

Korf, Benedikt, Tobias Hagmann, and Rony Emmenegger. 2015. "Re-spacing African Drylands: Territorialization, Sedentarization and Indigenous Commodification in the Ethiopian Pastoral Frontier." *Journal of Peasant Studies* 42 (5): 881–901.

Kurtenbach, Sabine, and Angelika Rettberg. 2018. "Understanding the Relation between War Economies and Postwar Crime." Third World Thematics: *A TWQ Journal* 3 (1): 1–8.

Lai, Daniela. 2020. *Socioeconomic Justice: International Intervention and Transition in Postwar Bosnia and Herzegovina.* Cambridge, UK: Cambridge University Press.

Lavers, Tom. 2012. "'Land Grab' as Development Strategy? The Political Economy of Agricultural Investment in Ethiopia." *Journal of Peasant Studies* 39 (1): 105–132.

Le Billon, Philippe. 2001. "The Political Ecology of War: Natural Resources and Armed Conflicts." *Political Geography* 20 (5): 561–584.

Leach, Melissa, Robin Mearns, and Ian Scoones. 1997. "Institutions, Consensus and Conflict: Implications for Policy and Practice." *IDS Bulletin* 28 (4): 90–95.

Lund, Christian. 2016. "Rule and Rupture: State Formation through the Production of Property and Citizenship." *Development and Change* 47 (6): 1199–1228. https://doi.org/10.1111/dech.12274.

Lund, Christian, and Catherine Boone. 2013. "Introduction: Land Politics in Africa – Constituting Authority over Territory, Property and Persons." *Africa* 83 (1): 1–13. https://doi.org/10.1017/S000197201200068X.

Mac Ginty, Roger, and Andrew Williams. 2016. *Conflict and Development*. London: Routledge.

Manji, Ambreena. 2006. *The Politics of Land Reform in Africa: From Communal Tenure to Free Markets*. London: Zed Books.

Moore, Barrington. 1973. *Social Origins of Dictatorship and Democracy: Lord and Peasant in the Making of the Modern World*. London: Penguin Books.

Moritz, Mark. 2006. "Changing Contexts and Dynamics of Farmer-Herder Conflicts across West Africa." *Canadian Journal of African Studies / Revue Canadienne Des Études Africaines* 40 (1): 1–40.

Munive, Jairo. 2010. "Ex-combatants, Returnees, Land and Conflict in Liberia." DIIS Working Paper 2010:05. Danish Institute for International Studies, Copenhagen. https://www.econstor.eu/handle/10419/44706.

Murtazashvili, Jennifer Brick, and Ilia Murtazashvili. 2021. *Land, the State, and War: Property Institutions and Political Order in Afghanistan*. Cambridge, UK: Cambridge University Press.

Musembi, Celestine Nyamu. 2007. "De Soto and Land Relations in Rural Africa: Breathing Life into Dead Theories about Property Rights." *Third World Quarterly* 28 (8): 1457–1478.

Ojeda, Diana. 2012. "Green Pretexts: Ecotourism, Neoliberal Conservation and Land Grabbing in Tayrona National Natural Park, Colombia." *Journal of Peasant Studies* 39 (2): 357–375.

Ottaway, Marina. 2002. "Rebuilding State Institutions in Collapsed States." *Development and Change* 33 (5): 1001–1023.

Paige, Jeffrey M. 1978. *Agrarian Revolution*. New York: Free Press.

Pantuliano, Sara, ed. 2009. *Uncharted Territory: Land, Conflict and Humanitarian Action*. Rugby, UK: Practical Action Publishing.

Peluso, Nancy Lee, and Michael Watts, eds. 2001. *Violent Environments*. Ithaca, NY: Cornell University Press.

Peters, Pauline E. 2004. "Inequality and Social Conflict over Land in Africa." *Journal of Agrarian Change* 4 (3): 269–314.

Pons-Vignon, Nicolas, and Henri-Bernard Solignac Lecomte. 2004. "Land, Violent Conflict and Development." Working Paper No. 233. OECD Development Centre, Paris.

Rasmussen, Mattias Borg, and Christian Lund. 2018. "Reconfiguring Frontier Spaces: The Territorialization of Resource Control." *World Development* 101 (January): 388–399.

Richards, Paul. 2005a. "New War: An Ethnographic Approach." In *No Peace, No War: An Anthropology of Contemporary Armed Conflicts*, edited by Paul Richards, 1–21. Oxford: James Currey.

Richards, Paul, ed. 2005b. *No Peace, No War: An Anthropology of Contemporary Armed Conflicts*. Oxford: James Currey.

Richards, Paul. 2005c. "To Fight or to Farm? Agrarian Dimensions of the Mano River Conflicts (Liberia and Sierra Leone)." *African Affairs* 104 (417): 571–590.

Richards, Paul. 2022. "The Moral Economy of Isolates: 'Escape Agriculture' and Warzone Public Authority." *Journal of Peasant Studies*, Early view, DOI: 10.1080/03066150.2022.2052279

Richmond, Oliver. 2012. *A Post-liberal Peace*. London: Routledge.

Sikor, Thomas, and Christian Lund. 2009. "Access and Property: A Question of Power and Authority." *Development and Change* 40 (1): 1–22.
Skocpol, Theda. 1979. *States and Social Revolutions: A Comparative Analysis of France, Russia and China*. Cambridge, UK: Cambridge University Press.
Smit, Anneke. 2013. *The Property Rights of Refugees and Internally Displaced Persons*. London: Routledge.
Stubblefield, Emily, and Sandra Joireman. 2019. "Law, Violence, and Property Expropriation in Syria: Impediments to Restitution and Return." *Land* 8 (11): 173.
Suhrke, Astri, and Mats Berdal, eds. 2013. *The Peace in Between: Postwar Violence and Peacebuilding*. London: Routledge.
Takeuchi, Shinichi, ed. 2014. *Confronting Land and Property Problems for Peace*. London: Routledge.
Tchatchoua-Djomo, Rosine, and Han van Dijk. 2022. "Ambiguous Outcomes of Returnees' Land Dispute Resolution and Restitution in War-Torn Burundi." *Land* 11 (2): 191.
Tchatchoua-Djomo, Rosine, Gemma van der Haar, Han van Dijk, and Mathijs van Leeuwen. 2018. "Intricate Links: Displacement, Ethno-political Conflict, and Claim-Making to Land in Burundi." *Geoforum* 109: 143–151.
Tchatchoua-Djomo, Rosine, Mathijs van Leeuwen, and Gemma van der Haar. 2020. "Defusing Land Disputes? The Politics of Land Certification and Dispute Resolution in Burundi." *Development and Change* 51 (6): 1454–1480.
Toukpo, Oscar. Forthcoming. *Le foncier rural en Côte d'Ivoire entre guerre et paix*. Abidjan: L'Harmattan.
Turner, Matthew D. 2004. "Political Ecology and the Moral Dimensions of 'Resource Conflicts': The Case of Farmer–Herder Conflicts in the Sahel." In "Ethics in Political Ecology." Special Issue, *Political Geography* 23 (7): 863–889.
Unruh, Jon D. 2005. "Property Restitution Laws in a Postwar Context: The Case of Mozambique." *African Journal of Legal Studies* 1 (3): 147–165.
Unruh, Jon D. 2014. "Evidencing the Restitution Landscape: Pre-emptive and Advance Techniques for War-Torn Land and Property Rights Reacquisition." *Land Use Policy* 38 (May): 111–122.
Unruh, Jon D. 2016. "Weaponization of the Land and Property Rights System in the Syrian Civil War: Facilitating Restitution?" *Journal of Intervention and Statebuilding* 10 (4): 453–471.
Unruh, Jon D. 2022. "Housing, Land and Property Rights as War-Financing Commodities: A Typology with Lessons from Darfur, Colombia and Syria." *Stability: International Journal of Security and Development* 10 (1): 1–19.
Unruh, Jon D., and Mourad Shalaby. 2012. "A Volatile Interaction between Peacebuilding Priorities: Road Infrastructure (Re)Construction and Land Rights in Afghanistan." *Progress in Development Studies* 12 (1): 47–61.
Unruh, Jon D., and Rhodri Williams. 2013. *Land and Postconflict Peacebuilding*. London: Routledge.
van Leeuwen, Mathijs, Gillian Mathys, Lotje de Vries, and Gemma van der Haar. 2022. "From Resolving Land Disputes to Agrarian Justice – Dealing with the Structural Crisis of Plantation Agriculture in Eastern DR Congo." *Journal of Peasant Studies* 49 (2): 309–334.
van Leeuwen, Mathijs, and Gemma van der Haar. 2016. "Theorizing the Land–Violent Conflict Nexus." *World Development* 78: 94–104.
Vargas Reina, Jenniffer. 2022. "Coalitions for Land Grabbing in Wartime: State, Paramilitaries and Elites in Colombia." *Journal of Peasant Studies* 49 (2): 288–308.

Walker, Cherryl. 2008. *Landmarked: Land Claims and Land Restitution in South Africa*. Athens: Ohio University Press.

West, Harry G., and Gregory W. Myers. 1996. "A Piece of Land in a Land of Peace? State Farm Divestiture in Mozambique." *Journal of Modern African Studies* 34 (1): 27–51.

Williams, Rhodri C. 2006. "The Significance of Property Restitution to Sustainable Return in Bosnia and Herzegovina." *International Migration* 44 (3): 40–61.

Wolf, Eric R. 1999. *Peasant Wars of the Twentieth Century*. Norman: University of Oklahoma Press.

Wood, Elisabeth Jean. 2000. *Forging Democracy from Below: Insurgent Transitions in South Africa and El Salvador*. Cambridge, UK: Cambridge University Press.

Woods, Kevin. 2011. "Ceasefire Capitalism: Military-Private Partnerships, Resource Concessions and Military-State Building in the Burma–China Borderlands." *Journal of Peasant Studies* 38 (4): 747–770.

Ybarra, Megan. 2012. "Taming the Jungle, Saving the Maya Forest: The Military's Role in Guatemalan Conservation." *Journal of Peasant Studies* 39 (2): 479–502.

Ybarra, Megan. 2018. *Green Wars: Conservation and Decolonization in the Maya Forest*. Oakland: University of California Press.

Young, Helen, and Lisa Goldman. 2015. *Livelihoods, Natural Resources, and Postconflict Peacebuilding*. London: Routledge.

CHAPTER 27

STRUGGLES OVER LAND UNDER CUSTOMARY TENURE IN CONTEMPORARY SUB-SAHARAN AFRICA

PAULINE E. PETERS

INTRODUCTION: THE PAST IN THE PRESENT

TODAY, customary modes of landholding are under considerable threat from the increasing acquisition of customary land by a range of agents, national and international, as well as from land policies and agricultural development programs that push privatization. Most of the useable land in African countries is under customary forms of tenure. The current struggles over its control are shaped by past patterns—before colonization, during colonial overrule, and since political independence—as well as by current circumstances. The term "customary" is tricky. It is commonly used to describe practices "as they've always been done," but in reality, what is done has been adapted over time. The result is different, often competing, interpretations of what "customary" means, requiring scrutiny of who is claiming "custom" in what circumstances, in the past as today.

British colonial officers described the body of law they set up in distinction from statutory law as "customary," including "customary tenure." Yet colonial "customary law" was not a preexisting oral system that was merely put into writing; it was produced out of political expedience and the need for accommodation between colonial and "traditional" leadership. It was less something that was "created" in the sense of a supposed absence of land management (the doctrine of terra nullius) than a negotiated outcome between the interests and (mis)representations of colonial officials and traditional leaders (Colson 1971; Snyder 1981; Chanock 1991a; Peters 1994). The two "limitations" imposed were that "the customary law did not expressly conflict with [other colonial] legislation" and "that it was not 'repugnant to justice, equity and good conscience'" (Allott 1984, 59). For the British (and other colonial powers), accusations of witchcraft and sorcery were "repugnant" and not understood in their specific contexts as part of a moral philosophy of good and evil. Today, such exclusions continue to cause dilemmas and ad hoc arrangements between state courts and the police, on one hand, and customary authorities and the wider population, on the other (see Kyed [2018] on Mozambique). The French colonial regime appropriated all land in the name of the state and did not set up a separate "customary" law (Coquery-Vidrovitch 1982). But like the British, "French colonial officials were [so] few and far between [that] in practice, they too left local land matters to customary authorities in what often amounted to indirect rule de facto" (Berry 2017, 107; cf. Spear 2003). The resultant mix of legal systems in African countries proved to be not a neat, parallel system but a sometimes complementary, sometimes contradictory blend—not "informal" or "traditional," clearly separate from "formal" law, but increasingly, over time, mutually imbricated (Moore 1978; Chanock 1985; Griffiths 1997; O'Laughlin 2000; Kuba and Lentz 2006; Ubink and Amanor 2008; Zenker and Hoehne 2018; Chimhowu 2019; Manji 2020).

The colonial static representation of customary tenure ignored the variation in landholding practices across the continental diversity in environmental, livelihood, and political conditions and the evidence of the land transfers, including rentals and sales, made over the previous centuries, particularly in West African regions of commercial agriculture and trade (Hill 1963; Mouser 1975; Amanor 2008; Kriger 2017). The unchanging image also obscured, sometimes to the advantage of the chiefs and male elders, more flexibility in gender-, age-, and seniority-based relations around land than the "rewriting" of custom allowed for (Pala 1980; Chanock 1991a; Mackenzie 1990; Mamdani 1996; Amanor 2008).

The colonial officials' notion of customary law as unchanging suited their concern with stable "law and order." It also enabled some African traditional leaders to use the added layer of authority in ways that inhibited the formerly available "exit option" that had allowed dissatisfied citizens to take advantage of abundant land and competing polities (Cooper 2014, 15). A static representation of land tenure, however, proved more problematic. It reflected long-held, prejudiced opinions that African agricultural and land-use practices were "backward." Missionaries in the nineteenth century had sought to modernize African agriculture in the British image of the "yeoman" farmer, a romanticized stereotype of the innovative farmer of the "agricultural revolution" (Comaroff and Comaroff 1997). The missionaries and other Europeans recognized the collective aspect of landholding practices but misinterpreted it as inimical to "healthy individualistic competition" (John Mackenzie, quoted in Dachs 1972) and, hence, to agricultural "improvement." Historians of the centuries-long process of enclosure and dissolution of commons and the common field system in Britain show the privileging of individualistic principles that are embedded in private property to be part of the growth of capitalism (Thompson 1993; Yerby 2016). This ideology, combined with the negative images of Africans as mired in "anachronistic and archaic" ways, prevented colonial regimes from recognizing the agricultural innovation shown, for example, in cocoa production in Nigeria, Ghana, and Côte d'Ivoire. "Africans were not only producing valuable crops, but they were doing so in their own flexible ways . . . that cannot be reduced to either 'peasant' or 'capitalist'" (Cooper 2014, 22–24). But opinions biased by European models shaped the legal and administrative approaches to land.

The improving individualist-farmer image resurfaced in the 1930s when some colonial agricultural officers became convinced that individual ownership of customary land was necessary for creating a yeoman class of progressive farmers to modernize agriculture, but they were overruled by their superior officers in the name of "law and order" (e.g., Galvan 2004; 114). However, when "development" (*mise en valeur*) became the aim of outgoing colonial regimes in the late 1940s and early 1950s, the imperative for "progressive" farmers and privatized landholding dominated (Cooper and Packard 1997). Nevertheless, except in Kenya, most privatization programs were short-lived and resisted by African cultivators, so that, in most countries, customary tenure in its various forms continued after political independence (Moore and Vaughan 1994; Peters 1997). As Sara Berry (2017) commented, "Many newly independent African governments left colonial land laws on the books, rewriting them when it seemed politically expedient rather than in pursuit of any consistent programme of land reform" (108; cf. Chanock 1991b). In countries such as Tanzania and Mozambique, which sought to abolish all customary institutions, these reappeared willy-nilly (Moore 1988) or were legislated back in.

Before this article considers the efforts to reform customary tenure through legislation, the general principles of landholding are briefly sketched. The typical basis of landholding across Sub-Saharan Africa was, and continues to be, through belonging to a localized descent group (a lineage or clan). Such groups are the main decision-makers in extending access to land to others, including migrants. This article concentrates on cultivated land, but the principle of collective holding applies to resources (woodlands, wetlands, rivers) now referred to as "commons," as well as to pastoralists' more extensive resource management. Such descent- and kinship-based groups are the main units of social and political formations, although networks and alliances through trade, territory, religion, and so forth, also link people and enable (various forms of) access to landed resources. The descent/kinship groups with authority over their own land are usually set within other administrative or residential units such as villages, and there is both upward and downward recognition of authority, obligation, and responsibility within and between such "nested" systems (Gluckman 1965; Hornby et al. 2017). Within each group, entitlements to land are extended to the constituent units—compounds, conjugal units, individuals.[1]

Patrilineal groups, which dominate in sub-Saharan Africa, limit the inheritance of land to male heirs (sons or brothers), but the use and cultivation rights are granted to adult sons and unmarried daughters while the father is living, and to the incoming wives of sons. In the less common matrilineal groups, nephews usually inherited land in virilocal groups, while only daughters inherited land in matrilineal matrilocal groups, and still do. Cultivation rights are granted to spouses in matrilineal societies—to wives in virilocal groups and to husbands in matrilocal groups—for the duration of the marriage, although they may be extended after death of the spouse in certain circumstances. Today, rights acquired this way are usually referred to as "secondary" rights, but this supposed inferiority is a product of the powerful discourse on, and direct attempts to define, individual property rights in land as the proper mode of land ownership.

Virtually all field studies of African landholding continue to show these described features, though, in many places, the definition of the descent group or entitled members (family) has narrowed over time (Marchal 1987; Peters 2002; Soro and Colin 2008; Bainville 2015) but also adapted, for example, through the extension of land rights to formerly excluded categories such as sisters and daughters in patrilineal groups (Claassens and Weeks 2009; Kingwill 2016; Munthali et al. 2017). The idiom of "guardianship" is found across the continent in relation to the senior authorities concerned with land, whether these are the elders of a lineage or clan, a smaller lineal or family segment, or specialized custodians of rain and land shrines (Schoffeleers 1978; Galvan 2004; Mandala 2005; Kuba and Lentz 2006; Lund 2008; Lavigne Delville 2014). Even in face of actions that are contrary to "guardianship," such as the illicit sale of land by chiefs, the idea that collective landholding is basic to material and spiritual life continues. For the Kenyan Luo, "a place on the landscape implied, and still does, a place in a kin group" (Shipton 2007, 51), with all that means for social reproduction (cf. Ossome [2021]) and "non-productionist" uses of land (Ferguson 2013). In the majority-Malawian matrilineal areas, where husbands move to their wives' villages (matrilocal residence), and where only daughters inherit land, the ritual detritus from the funerals of matrilineal members is buried at the boundaries (crossroads) of cultivated plots, a powerful symbol of belonging to each other and to the land. Ansoms and Hillhorst (2014, 18) describe how, throughout many waves of land appropriation via policies or violence, peasants in the Congo/DRC recreate group-based practices of land management and livelihood that entail "living together and cultural identity, which [are] at the heart of resilience [but] often invisible" to outsiders. Brockington et al. (2021) emphasize that for Tanzanians most "assets . . . land, houses, livestock . . . are effectively owned and managed by social units larger than individuals. Their benefits are experienced collectively (if rarely equally)" (160; cf. Hornby et al. 2017). Despite the wealth of such evidence, the failure to appreciate the social embeddedness of African land relations—the multiple and overlapping land entitlements that combine group and individual cultivation rights, facilitating flexibility in use and negotiated social and political economic outcomes—continues to prove a major problem in land legislation and policy.

Colonial customary law denied the status of property to customary landholdings by placing the land in the trust of "native" or "tribal" authorities, setting a path that has influenced subsequent patterns of holding, inheritance, and the transfer of land (Chanock 1991a, 1991b; Peters 2004; Alden Wily 2011, 2017), as well as of inequality and class (O'Laughlin 2000). Giving authority to traditional leaders, albeit subordinate to the colonial and postindependence states, also helped shape the politics of legitimate authority and the exercise of power over land and people. As with all social formations, fundamental principles of organization, such as the descent-based nested systems of land rights described, contain tensions that feed into actions and the ideas guiding them. Some members will seek greater benefit than their neighbors or kin. The colonial vesting of authority, though not ownership, in chiefs of various sorts provided some of them with the chance of treating their trusteeships as ownerships. Hence, the removal (destooling) of the many chiefs in Ghana who were found to be selling land in the 1930s (Balakrishnan 2020), or the way the Barolong senior chief hid land sales under the claim that the recipient was paying "tribute" (Comaroff 1982). Today, such maneuvers are common, and many chiefs, especially those at senior levels, are implicated in the land rush and the increasing vulnerability of customary landholders (Oomen 2005; Ubink and Amanor 2008; Lund and Boone 2013; Berry 2017; Comaroff and Comaroff 2018), along with other elite and politically influential nationals, as well as foreign agents.

Flawed Land "Reforms," Increased Land Appropriation, and Conflict, 1960s–1990s

The new African states wanted to increase agricultural output, and since most of that output came from "smallholders" on customary land, attention turned to agricultural and land policies. Customary land users produced considerable food, as well as cocoa, coffee, and oil palm exports from the 1940s into the late 1960s. But this did not continue. Marketing boards reduced smallholders' choices and rewards, and neglect of smallholder farming in favor of large-scale "modern" projects and disruptive land policies further inhibited expanded output. Up to the early 1970s, many African countries were achieving increases in the average life span, decreases in infant mortality, and rising literacy, but a worsening of these and other social indicators accelerated in the 1980s (Cooper 2014, 29) with the imposition of structural adjustment.

The land reforms of the 1960s and 1970s repeated the premises of those of the late colonial years in portraying customary tenure as inhibiting security and incentive and an obstacle to agricultural and economic development. Yet detailed research on the implementation of the reforms showed how mistaken those premises were and how few their positive outcomes. A narrow interpretation of the necessary superiority of individual property rights over land blinded policymakers, who saw "confused" and "fuzzy" rights and boundaries rather than the overlapping land entitlements. Customary tenure did not inhibit commercial farming but allowed adaptations to fluctuating markets; nor did it exclude the land management by individuals and small familial units having separable claims, rights, and responsibilities and who in many places are able to arrange land transfers, even though most land is vested in collectivities (Okoth-Ogendo 1989). In many regions, cultivated land has been passed on within kin segments in ways that more resemble "family" (properly lineal) property (Francis 1984; Peters 1997). Most titling programs failed to increase productivity or to improve the ability of small-scale producers to receive credit from banks (Haugerud 1983; Place and Hazell 1993; Bruce and Migot-Adholla 1994). Instead, they often increased tensions and competition and reduced the security of some categories of users, such as young people and wives (Pala 1980).

The obstacles to investment and productive use do not inhere in customary tenure (or in any tenure per se) but are found in political, social, and economic processes, such as poor agricultural research and extension programs; shifts in the markets for crops and inputs; increasing shortage and commodification of land; internal or cross-border migration (which is especially critical for West African countries); rural-urban linkages, and so forth. The oil price shocks of the 1970s; the related economic crises and rising indebtedness of African states; the effects of World Trade Organization (WTO) policies; the erosion of preferential trade agreements; and the donor shift during the 1980s and 1990s away from a sectoral approach, where agriculture was key, toward structural adjustment and liberalized markets, all combined to reduce the supports given to the majority of land users (Mkandawire and Soludo 1999; Bryceson 2000; Bernstein and Woodhouse 2001).

The intensification of competition and conflict over land resulted from a set of interacting processes: in face of economic decline and the loss of state supports, families sought to draw even more from their land, despite a declining supply of affordable inputs. Those forced out of state employment, from civil servants to laborers, turned to rural kin and customary land as a source of food and income, while some with urban wages or pensions acquired land as both "diversification of income" and investment (Downs and Reyna 1988, 9, 15). In addition, foreign companies, with the encouragement of African governments, sought sites for oil and mineral exploration, logging, and ecotourism and safari operations (Moore 2001; Reno 2001; Hardin 2002). Competition over land was not new, especially in the more densely populated regions of Africa, but it was occurring in more areas, accelerating, and becoming a major element in socioeconomic differentiation and inequality (Downs and Reyna 1988; Bassett and Crummey 1993). In areas where there was no serious land shortage, research showed considerable adaptation and innovation in use, such as the shifts in crops, in labor/machinery relations, and specialization in southern Nigeria between 1968 and 1988 (Guyer and Lambin 1993) or, in southeast Ivory Coast, the accommodation between migrant and autochthonous farmers, entailing considerable productive shifts in crops according to land type and markets for over more than thirty years (Colin 2017a, 2017b). But for most areas, the above-described trends increased the sense of insecurity among customary landholders, a turn to various forms of "informal formalization" (such as *petits papiers*), an upturn in sales of land and contestations over their validity and legality, and considerable contestation and conflict over land that sometimes led to civil violence (Kishindo 2004; Chauveau and Richards 2008; Berry 2009; Kanyinga 2009).

In turn, the documentation and debate led to a shift in the perception of customary landholding. Land researchers at the World Bank, the major advocate for land privatization, accepted some of the criticisms of land reforms and acknowledged that "community-based or customary [land] systems are dynamic and changing" (Ubink and Amanor 2008, 11; cf. Toulmin and Quan 2000). However, this acceptance remains within the context of an "evolutionary theory" of land change which holds that collective or customary forms inevitably evolve into individual property rights in response to economic change, an assumption that has shaped contemporary donor interpretation of what the "incorporation" of customary landholders entails. Other researchers and activists began to argue for legal "recognition" of existing entitlements and customary rights that did not require individual titling (Cousins 2007). Yet they recognize that land relations have become ever more politicized, caught up in local and national politics and decentralization programs, resulting in tensions among "traditional" authorities, representatives of various levels of state government, and sections of the populace. All this has caused more confusion and insecurity among customary landholders, leading some to engage in preemptive transfers of land when they fear appropriation by government or private agents (Chitonge et al. 2017); others seek to revoke earlier agreements with incoming migrants over entitlements to land (Chauveau and Colin 2010).

The Current State of Play, Late 1990s to 2021

The failures to achieve the desired ends of land privatization and overall economic growth through land reform based on an evolutionary theory of property rights, and then, through the "shock therapy" of market liberalization and structural adjustment, have led to a more aggressive wave of land-titling reforms. Although the premised need to convert customary tenure into private property to boost agricultural development remains, a significant change is replacing the state with private capital as the main agent of development. Donor emphasis is on liberalizing international trade in food and agricultural products; privatizing parastatals with minimal to no subsidies; producing exports as the "comparative advantage" for poorer countries; and formalizing informal and customary tenures by registering and titling, with a preference for private-sector economic agents, who sometimes act in "partnership" with the state. Multinational corporations, especially the major agrofood companies, also play a significant role in large-scale agricultural development and "green revolution" programs in Africa, which have pressed governments for legislation that will facilitate the privatization of land. Although current land reforms purport to benefit "smallholders"—that is, customary landholders—the goal of increased investment in land takes precedence, "freeing" land for private investment, especially in large-scale agriculture and contract farming. In a 2008 World Development Report emphasizing the importance of agricultural development, the stated aims included "better integrating smallholders into global agrofood commodity chains" through outgrower or contract farming (Akram-Lodhi 2008, 1148–1149), rather than supporting and encouraging relatively independent small-scale land use and the production of locally important crops as well as export crops. Because it has long been understood that only the more progressive smallholders would "transition" to such "integration," it was decidedly odd that the report made no mention of the current dearth of employment for those it assumed would "exit" agriculture (Oya 2009; Veltmeyer 2009; cf. Li 2009).

The Land Rush and Foreign Investors

The rise in world petroleum and food prices, especially the spike of 2007–2008, combined with the energy policies in Europe and the United States that were subsidizing the production of biofuels, generated an increased demand for land from rich and medium-income countries to grow food, biofuel, and "flex" crops (Borras et al. 2011; Cotula and Berger 2017; Giger et al. 2019). Countries, corporations, and private-equity funds also increasingly seek land deals for oil, minerals, timber, and rare earths (Le Billon and Sommerville 2017), as typified in the current scramble among national and international interests over coltan (Smith 2022).

In Africa, the most targeted region, large-scale land deals were made to acquire lands in tropical savannahs and forests, temperate zones, and along water sources in arid areas—which are the antithesis of the "waste" or "underutilized" lands portrayed in donor publications. Africa was described as having "large amounts of suitable but currently uncultivated land" (World Bank 2010), a portrayal that has consistently been challenged by research showing that most of the land acquired by both national and foreign agents is productive land already in use, either farm cultivation or woods, wetlands, and other common lands. The status of African customary lands as "nonproperty" accounts for land prices being so low and has made them extremely vulnerable to appropriation in legal and illicit ways, jeopardizing the livelihoods of the millions who live and depend on such lands. Consider the Brazilian investor who judged an offer by the Government of Mozambique of one US dollar per hectare as "too good to ignore," compared with the 2,000 to 15,000 US dollars per hectare in Brazil (Oxfam 2014, 17; cf. Alden Wily 2012, 769). Land tenure and policy reforms are also embraced by most African governments as a means of increasing national agricultural growth and for political interests and private benefit (Kanyinga 2017).

Research conducted on these large-scale land deals so far reveals fewer beneficial effects than overall negative effects on most local farming populations (Cotula 2013; Anseeuw 2013). Far fewer jobs were created than projected, and most were seasonal, temporary, and poorly paid, often at less than the going rates in the area; and the projects often led to the loss of water, farmlands, rangelands, and common resources (Hall et al. 2015; cf. German et al. 2013; Cotula et al. 2014; Moreda 2015: Yaro and Tsikata 2015; Schoneveld 2017; Sulle 2020).

Also problematic is the overly influential role private corporations play in land acquisitions, including in "public-private" partnerships. The "cooperation frameworks," such as the New Alliance for Food Security and Nutrition that the G8 countries set up with African countries, require governments to institute policies and land laws that make it easier for private companies to acquire land that invariably comes from customarily held land (Maganga et al. 2016, 7; cf. Sulle and Hall 2014). The World Economic Forum plays a central role in setting up public-private partnerships "with a heavy influence of large agro-processing or agro-supply corporations including Monsanto, DuPont, General Mills, Unilever, Yara and Syngenta" (Maganga et al. 2016, 8; cf. McMichael 2012). These (now partly merged) multinational corporations are also explicit "partners" of AGRA (Alliance for a Green Revolution in Africa), which receives major funding from the Gates and Rockefeller Foundations, and of the Millennium Challenge Account (MCA) projects. The MCA grants are awarded to eligible countries only if they agree to adapt their land and related policies to facilitate the acquisition of land, most of it from customary or "common" lands (Koopman 2012). Researchers tracking the New Alliance program in Malawi found a concentration on large-scale production, requiring "the appropriation of land from the very smallholders who were at the centre" of previously successful smallholder-focused programs (Chinsinga and Chasukwa 2015, 133).

Similarly, the International Finance Corporation (IFC), the private-sector arm of the World Bank, funds many foreign and national agencies' acquisitions of large areas of land for agriculture, mining, and logging. Much of this financing is handled through intermediaries, like private-equity funds and commercial banks, often with problematic results, including the displacement of local land users and pollution of water sources (Inclusive Development International 2017). The "huge support" given to private-equity funds becomes an inappropriate vehicle for development and poverty elimination when "fund managers have the mandate to invest in almost any asset class in any location provided the return potential makes investment sense" (Daniel 2012, 724; cf. Fairbairn 2014). Issues of rural development and socioeconomic benefit to national customary landholders, let alone environmental sustainability, are not their concerns.

In addition, studies in Ghana, Malawi, Mozambique, and Tanzania show that, besides the exposure to increased risk, "the outgrower model was found to have several weaknesses . . . contract rigidities that favour companies over outgrowers, lack of transparency in the weighing and measuring of products, the fixing of prices of inputs and products, harvesting delays, broken guarantees of a ready market for products, limited permanent employment, and the loss of time for growing food" (Hall et al. 2015, 15–16; cf. Little and Watts 1994; Richardson 2010; Little 2014; Chinsinga 2017; Adams et al. 2019). The contract farmers who do benefit are the minority of smallholders with larger amounts of land that enable them to maintain their own farming, especially of food crops (Hall et al. 2015, cf. Takane 2004; Victor 2007). Similarly, that a contract rice-farming scheme in Benin was found to benefit all contract farmers was apparently owing to rice being the staple food, high prices for rice, no land shortage, and contract farmers having more land than noncontract farmers (Maertens and Velde 2017).

The Land Rush and National Investors

Research from the 1960s to the 1990s period showed an accumulation of land by urban-based, salaried people, and by rural traders and business owners (Downs and Reyna 1988). Recent systematic research reveals an acceleration in this trend. Research in Ghana, Kenya, Tanzania, and Zambia documents an increase since the mid-1990s in land transfers away from smallholders (with less than 5 hectares of land) to medium-scale farms (5 to 100 hectares), acquired for cultivation or investment or both by urban professionals, those with pensions, or other better-off and influential rural people. Medium-scale farms now control roughly 20 percent of total farmland in Kenya, 32 percent in Ghana, 39 percent in Tanzania, and more than 50 percent in Zambia (Jayne et al. 2014a; Jayne et al. 2016; cf. Ansoms and Marysse 2011; Boamah 2014; Peters and Kambewa 2007; Ubink and Amanor 2008; Anseeuw et al. 2016; Colin and Tarrouth 2017).

Customary land is acquired through various means, in addition to (usually still illegal) sales. These include higher-income people giving loans to customary landholders against the "collateral" of their land and then, in the unfortunately common cases of default, acquiring the land. Some lenders provide loans in cash, others in staple food or other goods; others informally contract with a customary landholder to produce valuable crops on the landholder's own land but with inputs as well as food and/or cash given to the landholder. This can benefit some customary landholders, but, again, considering the commonly slim margins and everyday crises, as well as unfair dealing, this often ends with the "investor" acquiring the land. Where programs of titling or certification are in place, some appropriations take place through someone obtaining a document for a particular piece of land that was customarily held by someone else, and partly through illicit dealings with officials at several levels (Tchatchoua-Djomo et al. 2020).

Setting aside the shady or illegal aspects of these transfers, economists and others may welcome them if they result in a shift of land from less to more "efficient" users—an explicit aim of most land tenure reforms. However, if the land being acquired is not used more efficiently (however that is measured) or if it is merely being held as an asset and accumulating value, then the implications of this shift in "farm structure" become negative (Jayne et al. 2016). Many of the people acquiring customary land are urban-based: in Malawi and Zambia, between 25 percent and 40 percent of cultivated land is now owned by absentee urban landholders (Jayne et al. 2014a; Anseeuw et al. 2016; cf. Chitonge et al. 2017, 136, for Zambia). A study in the Ivory Coast found that very few titles were acquired between 2006 and 2017; but almost all of them were by outsiders—most were professionals, like engineers, doctors, civil servants, and military personnel, and "the vast majority of the home addresses provided by applicants were located in Abidjan [while] six declared their residence to be in Europe or North America" (Grajales 2020, 83).

It is possible, then, that "a sizeable proportion of revenue from agriculture, despite being generated in rural areas, is spent in urban areas," thus reducing the multiplier effects in rural areas (Jayne et al. 2016, 210). This contrasts with cases where significant increases in rural smallholder income are mostly spent locally, with clear positive results for the local markets for food, clothing (from tailors or the ubiquitous used-clothing dealers), bicycle and motorbike mechanics, pot- and basketmakers, and so on. The losses of this rural income and consumption exacerbate the problems of diminishing access to land for the remaining customary landholders, especially in many of the already land-short regions and countries. This lack of land is particularly critical in the context of a dearth of employment outside agriculture.

The implications for African rural and agricultural development are clear: "The creation of new jobs in the non-farm economy is unlikely to grow fast enough to absorb the rapidly growing young labour force. . . . [Hence] smallholder agriculture will remain a fundamental safety valve for absorbing much of the new labour force into gainful employment, at least [for] several decades" (Jayne et al. 2014b, 4; cf. Losch 2012). Unfortunately, despite a slight decline in large-scale land acquisitions over the past decade, the trends continue to be for the increased appropriation of Africa's customary and common lands by national medium-scale investors, the increasing value of land as an asset class for national and international agents, and the projected increase in global demand for agricultural commodities (Cotula and Berger 2017; cf. White et al. 2012).

In short, both global and national trends of capital mobility and accumulation look dire for customary landholders across Africa. Thus, "in spite of rhetorical support for small-scale farmers, there are increasing concerns that de facto agricultural and land policies . . . are continuing to encourage the transfer of land to large-scale foreign interests without due cognizance of how this is affecting land access by future generations of indigenous rural communities" (Jayne et al. 2014a, 13). The acquisition of land from smaller-scale customary landholders by largely urban investors with money and influence is likely to "exacerbate land scarcity in rural areas and constrain the rate of growth in the number of small-scale farm holdings" (Jayne et al. 2016, 197; cf. Anseeuw 2013). Since "medium-scale farmers tend to dominate farm lobby groups and influence agricultural policies and public expenditures to agriculture in their favor," this is also likely to exacerbate customary landholders' vulnerability to expropriation and to divert programs of agricultural research, extension, and support away from the latter (Jayne et al. 2016, 207). On the other hand, a recent study by some of the same authors concluded for Zambia that "on balance, the growth of medium-scale farms and large-scale traders seems to have positive spillover effects on nearby smallholder marketing options" (Burke et al. 2020, 517). But judging from other research, this refers mostly to the top stratum of smallholders, the same tiny minority who generally benefit from agricultural programs and contract farming.

Attempts to Protect Customary Land Rights and Mitigate Land Loss

The increasing appropriation of customary lands has led some governments to include varying degrees of protection of customary rights in constitutions or legislation. Alden Wily lists Botswana, Burkina Faso, Ghana, Morocco, Mozambique, Namibia, South Sudan, South Africa, Swaziland, Tanzania, The Gambia, and Uganda. However, "few have been more than moderately successful in applying the norms their laws provide for" (Alden Wily 2017, 472; cf. McAuslan 2013; Roudart and Guénard 2019). In Ghana, Uganda, and Mozambique, chiefs, the government, and party representatives exert considerable authority over land allocation, including illicit sales, which essentially subverts customary landholders' rights (Fairbairn 2013; van Leeuwen et al. 2014). Legislation in Mozambique, Benin, and Tanzania that provides (degrees of) legal recognition has not prevented appropriation (McAuslan 2013; Maganga et al. 2016; Lavigne Delville 2020). Collective ownership is either ignored or placed at very high levels of administration, such as the "tribe" in Botswana and Namibia or local government in Senegal, further reducing the customary land users' role in governance.

The complexity and specificity of landholding across and within countries reveal the problems of imposing a single mode of titling or certification (Nghitevelekwa 2020). In many areas, due to mobility, migration, and/or involuntary movements through policy or civil unrest, the layering of land entitlements often leads to competing claims of priority (Odgaard and Askew 2018). A review comparing "community" (customary) land formalization through certification with land acquisition by private companies found that the procedures for the companies were simpler and faster, often evaded social and environmental protections, and favored investors over communities (Notess et al. 2021). A study of "best practice legal protections" for customary landholders in Ghana, Mozambique, Tanzania, and Zambia concluded that, despite the laws, there were "egregious shortcomings in practice" resulting in vulnerability for "customary rights and rural livelihoods in the context of large-scale land acquisitions" (German, Schoneveld, and Mwangi, 2013, 15; cf. Ayano 2018). New statutory law and administrative procedures, in the context of unequal knowledge and authority and bureaucratic bungling and contradictory interests, often result in the less powerful losing land rights (Locher 2016; Greco 2015; van Leeuwen 2014). Even where legislation purports to protect customary rights, ongoing agricultural and other developmental plans, such as "development corridors," as well as conservation projects, often entail land loss and evictions, as in Tanzania (Laltaika and Askew 2018; Maganga et al. 2016; Alden Wily 2020).

In some places, customary landholders, including some peasant organizations, have some input to land and agricultural policies, but their more substantial concerns are ignored in key policies (see Peemans 2014 on the Congo/DRC). Protests by customary land users have sometimes managed to reduce or prevent a particular appropriation, as in Mozambique (Verhaegen and Kiala 2019); but many have been met with police or other violence, as in Malawi (Chinsinga and Wren-Lewis 2014) and Uganda (Martiniello 2015). Calls to establish "responsible" codes of conduct for the "investors" in land, whether national or foreign, or for public investment in infrastructure, research, and extension targeted to smallholders, are inadequate without a serious account of "power dynamics that render rural dwellers vulnerable to land grabbing" (van Leeuwen et al. 2014, 122). Some stress the need for political mobilization, to counter not only "elite power" but also of a lack of "political will" and the attachment of state governments to models of large-scale agriculture and private capital, but this is not easily achieved (cf. Li 2020 on Indonesia).

Alternatives to conventional land reforms have been proposed, one being the *plans fonciers ruraux*, or rural land maps, that enable customary landholders to identify local land rights and participate in new local administrative bodies to manage disputes. Lavigne Delville (2014) reported that these land maps "are a tool to formalize existing land rights, as they are in the field, with their specificities, without transforming them into private [and exclusionary] ownership" (7). However, the actual implementation of such methods in central Benin led to a less sanguine assessment: the realities of multiple varying rights in land ran against the notion of discrete plots with discrete "owners," even allowing for the interplay between collective (group) entitlements and individual entitlements, and the history of settlement, with its distinction between original (autochthonous) and incoming (migrant, stranger) groups, exacerbated tensions and disagreements about "ownership," as Lavigne Delville and Moalic (2019) observed. By the time of the latter paper, the program had come to a halt and the government was allowing only individual titles: thus, back to the conventional land reform "solution."

The main potential that can lead governments to recognize collective ownership appears to be in "common" lands such as woods, wetlands, grazing land, bush, and so forth (see discussions by Alden Wily 2017, 2020). But the degree of protection remains low in most places, given the political and private interests in maintaining the power basis in land ownership and control (Kanyinga 2017). There are almost no examples of the legal titling of customary descent groups (or similar units) that currently hold the vast majority of customary land, yet such group titling would allow them to continue their preferred means of land management while adapting to the inevitably changing contexts of land use. One rare case is in Madagascar, where local descent-based groups have been able to work closely with local state representatives to achieve legal recognition, a negotiated outcome that provides protection for their family (lineal) members yet does not inhibit land transfers (Tessyier et al. 2009; Di Roberto and Bouquet 2018; Di Roberto 2020).

Where legislation and other state policies mention "group" or "family" titling options, they either refer to conjugal groups or remain unspecified. The problem with conjugal-group ownership or titling is that it is entirely antithetic to the descent-group system in place in most of rural Sub-Saharan Africa. Most marriages in Africa are exogamous—that is, a spouse belongs to a different descent group. Thus, if an in-marrying spouse is given title to the plot from the other spouse's lineal land, this policy represents a direct threat to the majority principles and practices of landholding because it takes land away from the existing descent group. This applies to wives in patrilineal groups and to husbands in matrilineal-matrilocal groups. It is no wonder that there is widespread objection and resistance to conjugal-group titling for all but the tiny proportion of rich families and for some urban areas. Yet, in the name of discrimination against "women," the titling of the land rights of individual wives is a current element of land policies in the majority patrilineal areas. The comment of one Tanzanian man explains the problem: he worried that giving title/ownership to his wife meant "that the land would go to the family of the wife if he passed away first" (pers. comm., Howard Stein). In the majority matrilineal-matrilocal areas of Malawi, I was told repeatedly that "our daughters inherit our land, and our sons use their wives' fields" (Peters 2010; cf. Berge et al. 2014). The idea that husbands could become the owners of their wives' lineal land was inconceivable. The sisters of the husband feel the same way in their own lineal areas (see Peters 2018 for the profound difference between "women" as wives or widows compared with daughters and sisters). Although there are real concerns about gender-based inequalities, the adaptational changes in the land rights of sisters and daughters in the cases of South Africa and Malawi mentioned above indicate that these are best negotiated within the specific groups rather than imposed from above in a "one rule fits all" manner. That almost all current land policies ignore the dominant descent-based mode of landholding is a major contributor to dissension and insecurity, and a threat to a vital element in the entire system of material and cultural support systems.

Legal recognition that customary entitlements are a type of property would afford customary landholders the same kind of status provided by statutory property rights. This has been called "social tenure" (Hornby et al. 2017) or "community tenure" (Alden Wily 2020). In Madagascar, where it has been achieved, it is called *propriété privée non titrée*, "untitled private property" (Teyssier et al. 2009), and it recognizes and supports *both* the group or collective entitlements *and* the individual or personal entitlements, as these are conceptualized and practiced by the specific people in question. Only in this way might customary landholders be able to stem the current pervasive appropriation of their land, at a dangerously high cost to them, but at an extremely low or no cost to the appropriators. Such property rights would treat customary landholders as citizens rather than as "subjects" of trustees or "tenants" of the state (cf. Hann 1998).

Conclusion

Over a long historical period, customary modes of landholding have withstood "development" efforts to convert them to commodity systems, and they have proven to be effective vehicles for agricultural production and for supplying fundamental material and spiritual support to millions of African people. To try to erase customary forms of land tenure is to threaten the very foundations of life.[2] Extremely few countries in sub-Saharan Africa have effective social-welfare and support programs, let alone social insurance. People overwhelmingly depend on social relations for such support, especially those of descent, kinship, and residence, which are fundamentally tied to their relations to land. This is not to suggest that there is a completely harmonious solidarity. Intimate relationships, whether of kinship or other kinds, are disruptive as often they are as a source of solidarity. Kin relations produce both enormous support but also jealousy and disturbing witchcraft accusations (Marwick 1970; Geschiere 1997). But this does not gainsay the centrality of kin and descent relations in land governance and the entire structure of life and livelihood (cf. Spiegel 2018). The extension of kin status to close relations bred in work, religious organizations, or elsewhere (called "kinning" by some researchers) reinforces the significance of these ties.

What is required is a shift from policy insistence on individual ownership through titling to an embrace of the encompassing forms of local ownership that combine collective and individual rights. Actual land use is almost always in the hands of individual cultivators or of units such as "households," yet the larger units of "family" (properly lineage) continue to have considerable oversight for the purposes of having a meaningful, safe, social life. Crucially, lands are not to be seen as "held in trust" by the state or "traditional" authorities, or anyone other than the existing groups of landholders. Even in South Africa, where rural people have been subjected to the most oppressive land appropriations, the same mix of individual and collective rights and management holds (Cousins 2007, 2021; Kingwill 2016). Extending the legal protection to customary landholding as "property" should not strip it of its social management—the Madagascar case mentioned earlier is exemplary.

Finally, it would throw more light on the agents and processes driving the appropriation of customary land and its role in wider national and global processes if the now separate debates on rising national and global inequality, the growth and effect of financialized capital, the demise of redistribution as a policy goal, and the resurgence of research on class formation in Africa were to seriously engage more with each other and with the research that has been discussed here.

Acknowledgments

I am grateful for incisive comments on earlier drafts by Kojo Amanor, Jean-Philippe Colin, John Comaroff, Ben Cousins, Edge Kanyongolo, Elias Mandala, and Liz Wily, and by the editors of this Handbook and reviewers.

Notes

1. I do not address Islamic law in its interactions with customary principles and practices. For that, see, for example, Benjaminsen and Lund (2003); Blanchy (2019).
2. This is the danger of the 2020 version of the Malawi Land Law, which eliminates the legal category of "customary land" in favor of only two land types: public (including government) and private. Since only a miniscule number of customary landholders is likely to be able to convert their land into a private "customary estate," the vast majority will essentially become squatters on public/government land. Amendment bills to the Land Law discussed in 2022 reverse that decision and return to the three categories of land: customary, public, and private. The legal category of 'customary' land could be a basis for current customary landholders to maintain a form of lineal ownership.

References

Adams, Timothy, Jean-David Gerber, Michèle Amacker, and Tobias Haller. 2019. "Who Gains from Contract Farming? Dependencies, Power Relations, and Institutional Change." *Journal of Peasant Studies* 46 (7): 1435–1457.

Akram-Lodhi, A. Haroon. 2008. "(Re)imagining Agrarian Relations? The World Development Report 2008: Agriculture for Development." *Development and Change* 39 (6): 1145–1161.

Alden Wily, Liz. 2011. "'The Law Is to Blame': The Vulnerable Status of Common Property Rights in Sub-Saharan Africa." *Development and Change* 42 (3): 733–757.

Alden Wily, Liz. 2012. "Looking Back to See Forward: The Legal Niceties of Land Theft in Land Rushes." *Journal of Peasant Studies* 39 (3): 751–775.

Alden Wily, Liz. 2017. "Customary Tenure: Remaking Property for the 21st Century." In *Comparative Property Law: Global Perspectives*, edited by Michele Graziadei and Lionel Smith, 458–477. Northampton, MA: Edward Elgar.

Alden Wily, Liz. 2020. "Adjusting to New Era Agrarianism: Tackling the Troubled Interface of Public and Community Property." In *Rethinking Land Reform in Africa: New Ideas, Opportunities and Challenges*, edited by Cosmas Ochieng, 57–69. African Natural Resources Centre, African Development Bank.

Allott, Anthony N. 1984. "What Is to Be Done with African Customary Law? The Experience of Problems and Reforms in Anglophone Africa from 1950." *Journal of African Law* 28 (1–2): 56–71.

Amanor, Kojo S. 2008. "The Changing Face of Customary Tenure." In *Contesting Land and Custom in Ghana*, edited by Janine M. Ubink and Kojo S. Amanor, 55–80. Leiden: Leiden University Press.

Anseeuw, Ward. 2013. "The Rush for Land in Africa: Resource Grabbing or Green Revolution?" *Journal of South African Journal of International Affairs* 20 (1): 159–177.

Anseeuw, W., Thomas Jayne, Richard Kachule, and John Kotsopoulos. 2016. "The Quiet Rise of Medium-Scale Farms in Malawi." *Land* 5 (19): 1–22.

Ansoms, An, and Thea Hillhorst, eds. 2014. *Losing Your Land: Dispossession in the Great Lakes.* Woodbridge, UK: James Currey.

Ansoms, An, and Stefaan Marysse, eds. 2011. *Natural Resources and Local Livelihoods in the Great Lakes Region of Africa: A Political Economy Perspective.* Basingstoke, UK: Palgrave Macmillan.

Ayano, Mekonnen. 2018. "Rural Land Registration in Ethiopia: Myths and Realities." *Law & Society Review* 52 (4): 1060–1097.

Bainville, Sébastien. 2015. "De la grand à la petite famille au Burkina Faso." In *Diversité des agriculture familiales*, edited by P.-M. Bosc, J.-M. Sourisseau, P. Bonnal, P. Gasselin, E. Valette, and J.-F. Bélières, 251–261. Versailles: Éditions Quae.

Balakrishnan, Sarah M. 2020. "Anticolonial Public: From Slavery to Independence in Southern Ghana, c.1500–1957." PhD diss., Harvard University.

Bassett, Thomas J., and Donald E. Crummey, eds. 1993. *Land in African Agrarian Systems.* Madison: University of Wisconsin Press.

Benjaminsen, Tor A., and Christian Lund, C., eds. 2003. *Securing Land Rights in Africa.* London: Frank Cass.

Berge, Erling, Daimon Kambewa, Alister Munthali, Henrik Wiig. 2014. "Lineage and Land Reforms in Malawi: Do Matrilineal and Patrilineal Landholding Systems Represent a Problem for Land Reforms in Malawi?" *Land Use Policy* 41: 61–69.

Bernstein, Henry, and Philip Woodhouse. 2001. "Telling Environmental Change Like It Is? Reflections on a Study in Sub-Saharan Africa." *Journal of Agrarian Change* 1 (2): 283–324.

Berry, Sara. 2009. "Property, Authority and Citizenship: Land Claims, Politics and the Dynamics of Social Division in West Africa." *Development and Change* 40 (1): 23–45.

Berry, Sara. 2017. "Struggles over Land and Authority in Africa." *African Studies Review* 60 (3): 105–125.

Blanchy, Sophie. 2019. "A Matrilineal and Matrilocal Society in Flux: Negotiating Gender and Family Relations in the Comoros." *Africa* 89 (1): 21–39.

Boamah, Festus. 2014. "How and Why Chiefs Formalise Land Use in Recent Times: The Politics of Land Dispossession through Biofuels Investments in Ghana." *Review of African Political Economy* 41 (141): 406–423.

Borras, Saturnino, Ruth Hall, Ian Scoones, Ben White, and Wendy Wolford. 2011. "Towards a Better Understanding of Global Land Grabbing: An Editorial Introduction." *Journal of Peasant Studies* 38 (2): 209–216.

Brockington, Dan, Ernestina Coast, Anna Mdee, Olivia Howland, and Sara Randall. 2021. "Assets and Domestic Units: Methodological Challenges for Longitudinal Studies of Poverty Dynamics." *Journal of Peasant Studies* 48 (1): 159–179.

Bruce, John, and Shem E. Migot-Adholla. 1994. *Searching for Land Tenure Security in Africa.* Washington, DC: World Bank.

Bryceson, Deborah. 2000. "Peasant Theories and Smallholder Policies: Past and Present." In *Disappearing Peasantries? Rural Labour in Africa, Asia and Latin America*, edited by Deborah Bryceson, Cristobal Kay, and Jos Mooij, 1–36. London: Intermediate Technology Publications.

Burke, William J., Thomas S. Jayne, and Nicholas J. Sitko. 2020. "Do Medium-Scale Farms Improve Market Access Conditions for Zambian Smallholders?" *Journal of Agricultural Economics* 71 (2): 517–533.

Chanock, Martin. 1985. *Law, Custom and Social Order: The Colonial Experience in Malawi and Zambia.* Cambridge, UK: Cambridge University Press.

Chanock, Martin. 1991a. "Paradigms, Policies and Property: A Review of the Customary Law of Land Tenure." In *Law in Colonial Africa*, edited by K. Mann and R. Roberts, 61–86. Portsmouth, NH: Heinemann.

Chanock, Martin. 1991b. "A Peculiar Sharpness: An Essay on Property in the History of Customary Law in Colonial Africa." *Journal of African History* 32 (1): 65–88.

Chauveau, Jean.-Pierre., and Paul Richards. 2008. "West African Insurgencies in Agrarian Perspective: Côte d'Ivoire and Sierra Leone Compared." *Journal of Agrarian Change* 8 (4): 515–552.

Chauveau, Jean-Pierre., and Jean-Philippe Colin. 2010. "Customary Transfers and Land Sales in Côte d'Ivoire: Revisiting the Embeddedness Issue." *Africa* 80 (1): 81–103.

Chimhowu, Admos. 2019. "The 'New' African Customary Land Tenure: Characteristic Features and Policy Implications of a New Paradigm." *Land Use Policy* 81: 897–903.

Chinsinga, Blessings. 2017. "The Green Belt Initiative, Politics and Sugar Production in Malawi." *Journal of Southern African Studies* 43 (3): 501–515.

Chinsinga, Blessings, and Michael Chasukwa. 2015. "Trapped between the Farm Input Subsidy Programme and the Green Belt Initiative." In *Africa's Land Rush: Rural Livelihoods and Agrarian Change*, edited by Ruth Hall, Ian Scoones, and Dzodzi Tsikata, 132–149. Woodbridge, UK: James Currey.

Chinsinga, Blessings, and Liam Wren-Lewis. 2014. "Grabbing Land in Malawi." In *Corruption, Grabbing and Development: Real World Challenges*, edited by Tina Soreide and Aled Williams, 93–102. Edward Elgar.

Chitonge, Horman, Orleans Mfune, David Kafwamba, and Gear Kajoba. 2017. "Hybrid Land Markets: Monetarised Customary Land Transactions in Zambia." *Canadian Journal of African Studies* 51 (1): 123–143.

Claassens, Aninka, and Sindiso Weeks. 2009. "Rural Women Redefining Land Rights in the Context of Living Customary Law." *South African Journal of Human Rights* 25 (4): 491–516.

Colin Jean-Philippe. 2017a. "Contractual Practices and Land Conflicts: The 'Plant & Share' Arrangement in Côte d'Ivoire." *Journal of Agrarian Change* 17 (1): 144–165.

Colin, Jean-Philippe. 2017b. *Emergence et dynamique des marchés fonciers ruraux en Afrique sub-saharienne*. Les Cahiers du Pôle Foncier 18. Montpellier: Insitut de Recherche pour la Développement.

Colin, Jean-Philippe, and Gabin Tarrouth. 2017. "Les élites urbaines comme nouveaux acteurs du marché foncier en Côte d'Ivoire." *Géographie, Économie, Société* 19: 331–335.

Colson, Elizabeth. 1971. "The Impact of the Colonial Period on the Definition of Land Rights." In *Colonialism in Africa, 1870–1960*, edited by Victor Turner, 193–215. Cambridge, UK: Cambridge University Press.

Comaroff, John L. 1982. "Class and Culture in a Peasant Economy: The Transformation of Land Tenure in Barolong." In *Land Reform in the Making*, edited by R. P. Werbner, 85–113. London: Rex Collings.

Comaroff, John L., and Jean Comaroff. 1997. *Of Revelation and Revolution*. Vol. 2: *The Dialectics of Modernity on a South African Frontier*. Chicago: Chicago University Press.

Comaroff, John L., and Jean Comaroff, eds. 2018. *The Politics of Custom: Chiefship, Capital and the State in Contemporary Africa*. Chicago: Chicago University Press.

Coquery-Vidrovitch, Catherine. 1982. "Le régime foncier rural en Afrique noire." In *Enjeux fonciers en Afrique Noire*, edited by Émile. LeBris, Etienne LeRoi, and Francois Leimdorfer, 65–83. *Bondy*: Office de la Recherche Scientifique et Technique Outre-Mer. Paris: Karthala.

Cooper, Frederick. 2014. *Africa in the World: Capitalism, Empire, Nation-State*. Cambridge, MA: Harvard University Press.

Cooper, Frederick, and Randall Packard. 1997. *International Development and the Social Sciences: Essays on the History and Politics of Knowledge*. Berkeley: University of California Press.

Cotula, Lorenzo. 2013. *The Great African Land Grab? Agricultural Investments and the Global Food System*. London: Zed Books.

Cotula, Lorenzo, and Thierry Berger. 2017. *Trends in Global Land Use Investment: Implications for Legal Empowerment*. Research report. International Institute for Environment and Development, London.

Cotula, Lorenzo, Carlos Oya, Emmanuel A. Codjoe, Abdurehman Eid, Mark Kakraba-Ampeh, James Keeley, et al. 2014. "Testing Claims about Large Land Deals in Africa: Findings from a Multi-country Study." *Journal of Development Studies* 50 (7): 903–925.

Cousins, Ben. 2007. "More Than Socially Embedded: The Distinctive Character of 'Communal Tenure' Regimes in South Africa and Its Implications for Land Policy." *Journal of Agrarian Change* 7 (3): 281–315.

Cousins, Ben. 2021. "A Response to William Beinart and Peter Delius' Rejoinder to Ben Cousins' Review of Rights to Land." *South African Historical Journal*.

Dachs, Anthony. 1972. "Missionary Imperialism in the Case of Bechuanaland." *Journal of African History* 13: 647–658.

Daniel, Shepard. 2012. "Situating Private Equity Capital in the Land Grab Debate." *Journal of Peasant Studies* 39 (3–4): 703–729.

Di Roberto, Hadrien. 2020. "Le marché foncier, une affaire de famille? Une analyse institutionnelle des transactions de terres agricoles dans les Hautes Terres à Madagascar." Thesis. Université Montpellier.

Di Roberto, Hadrien, and Emmanuelle Bouquet. 2018. "Le rôle de la famille dans la régulation des marchés fonciers à Madagascar." *Économie Rurale* 366 81–96.

Downs, R. E., and Stephen P. Reyna, eds. 1988. *Land and Society in Contemporary Africa*. Hanover, NH: University Press of New England.

Fairbairn, Madeleine. 2013. "Indirect Dispossession: Domestic Power Imbalances and Foreign Access to Land in Mozambique." *Development and Change* 44 (2): 335–356.

Fairbairn, Madeleine. 2014. " 'Like Gold with Yield': Evolving Intersections between Farmland and Finance." *Journal of Peasant Studies* 41 (5): 777–795.

Ferguson, James. 2013. "How to Do Things with Land: A Distributive Perspective on Rural Livelihoods in Southern Africa." *Journal of Agrarian Change* 13 (1): 166–174.

Francis, Paul. 1984. " 'For the Use and Common Benefit of All Nigerians': Consequences of the 1978 Land Nationalization." *Africa* 54 (3): 5–28.

Galvan, Dennis C. 2004. *The State Must Be Our Master of Fire*. Berkeley: University of California Press.

German, Laura, G. Schoneveld, and Esther Mwangi. 2013. "Contemporary Processes of Large-Scale Land Acquisition in Sub-Saharan Africa: Legal Deficiency or Elite Capture of the Rule of law?" *World Development* 48 (1): 1–18.

Geschiere, Peter. 1997. *The Modernity of Witchcraft: Politics and the Occult in Post-colonial Africa*. Charlottesville: University of Virginia Press.

Giger, Markus, Kerstin Nolte, Ward Anseeuw, Thomas Breu, Wytske Chamberlain, Peter Messerli, et al. 2019. "Impacts of Large-Scale Land Acquisitions on Common-Pool Resources: Evidence from the Land Matrix." In *The Commons in a Glocal World: Global Connections and Local Responses*, edited by Tobias Haller, Thomas Breu, Tine De Moor, Christian Rohr, and Heinzpeter Znoj, 257–279. London: Routledge.

Gluckman, Max. 1965. *The Ideas in Barotse Jurisprudence*. Manchester, UK: Manchester University Press.

Grajales, Jacobo. 2020. "From War to Wealth? Land Policies and the Peace Economy in Côte d'Ivoire." *Review of African Political Economy* 47 (163): 78–94.

Greco, Elisa. 2015. "Landlords in the Making: Class Dynamics of the Land Grab in Mbarali, Tanzania." *Review of African Political Economy* 42 (144): 225–244.

Griffiths, Anne M. O. 1997. *In the Shadow of Marriage: Gender and Justice in an African Community*. Chicago: University of Chicago Press.

Guyer, Jane I., and Eric F. Lambin. 1993. "Land Use in an Urban Hinterland. Ethnography and Remote Sensing in the Study of African Intensification." *American Anthropologist* 95 (4): 839–859.

Hall, Ruth, Ian Scoones, and Dzodzi Tsikata, eds. 2015. *Africa's Land Rush: Rural Livelihoods and Agrarian Change*. Woodbridge, UK: James Currey.

Hann, Chris. 1998. *Property Relations: Renewing the Anthropological Tradition*. Cambridge: Cambridge University Press.

Hardin, Rebecca. 2002. "Concessionary Politics in the Western Congo Basin: History and Culture in Forest Use Practices." Working Paper No. 6, Environmental Governance in Africa Working Paper Series. World Resources Institute.

Haugerud, Angelique. 1983. "The Consequences of Land Tenure Reform among Smallholders in the Kenya Highlands." *Rural Africana* 15/16: 65–89.

Hill, Polly. 1963. *Migrant Cocoa Farmers of Southern Ghana: A Study in Rural Capitalism.* Cambridge, UK: Cambridge University Press.

Hornby, Donna, Rosalie Kingwill, Lauren Royston, and Ben Cousins. 2017. *Untitled: Securing Land Tenure in Urban and Rural South Africa*. Pietermaritzburg, South Africa: University of Kwazulu-Natal Press.

Inclusive Development International. 2017. *Unjust Enrichment: How the IFC Benefits from Land Grabbing in Africa.* Report. IDI and the Oakland Institute.

Jayne, Thomas S., Anthony Chapoto, Nicholas Sitko, Chewe Nkonde, Milu Muyanga, and Jordan Chamberlin. 2014a. "Is the Scramble for Land in Africa Foreclosing a Smallholder Agricultural Expansion Strategy?" *Journal of International Affairs* 67 (2): 35–53.

Jayne, Thomas S., Ferdinand Meyer, and Lulama Traub. 2014b. *Africa's Evolving Food Systems: Drivers of Change and the Scope for Influencing Them*. Working Paper. International Institute for Economic Development, London.

Jayne, Thomas S., Jordan Chamberlin, Lulama Traub, Nicholas Sitko, Milu Muyanga, Felix K. Yeboah, et al. 2016. "Africa's Changing Farm Size Distribution Patterns: The Rise of Medium-Scale Farms." *Agricultural Economics* 47 (S1): 197–214.

Kanyinga, Karuti. 2009. "The Legacy of the White Highlands: Land Rights, Ethnicity and the Post-2007 Election Violence in Kenya." *Journal of Contemporary African Studies* 27 (3): 325–344.

Kanyinga, Karuti 2017. "Demystifying the Politics of Land Tenure: Okoth-Ogendo and the Concept of Land in Africa." In *The Gallant Academic: Essays in Honour of HWO Okoth-Ogendo*, edited by Patricia Kameri-Mbote and Collins. Odote, 185–204. Nairobi: University School of Law.

Kingwill, Rosalie 2016. "Engendering the Norms of Customary Inheritance in Botswana and South Africa." *Journal of Legal Pluralism and Unofficial Law* 48 (2): 208–237.

Kishindo, Paul. 2004. "Customary Land Tenure and the New Land Policy in Malawi." *Journal of Contemporary African Studies* 22 (2): 213–225.

Koopman Jeanne 2012. "Land Grabs, Government, Peasant and Civil Society: Activism in the Senegal River Valley." *Review of African Political Economy* 39 (134): 500–511.

Kriger, Colleen E. 2017. *Making Money: Life, Death and Early Modern Trade on Africa's Guinea Coast*. Athens: Ohio University Press.

Kuba, Richard, and Carola Lentz, eds. 2006. *Land and the Politics of Belonging in West Africa.* Leiden: Brill.

Kyed, Helene M. 2018. "State Police and Tradition in Post-War Mozambique: The Dilemmas of Claiming Sovereignty in Legal Pluralistic Contexts." In *The State and the Paradox of Customary Law in Africa*, edited by Olaf Zenker and Markus V. Hoehne, 64–86. Abingdon, Oxon; New York, NY: Routledge.

Laltaika, Elifuraha, and Kelly Askew. 2018. "Modes of Dispossession of Indigenous Lands and Territories in Africa." Paper presented at United Nations Expert Group Meeting on Sustainable Development in Territories of Indigenous Peoples, New York.

Lavigne Delville, Philippe. 2014. *Competing Conceptions of Customary Land Rights Registration (Rural Land Maps—plans fonciers ruraux): Methodological, Policy and Polity Issues.* Les Cahiers du Pôle Foncier, No. 5. Montpellier: Insitut de Recherche pour la Développement.

Lavigne Delville, Philippe. 2020. "Analyzing the Benin Land Law: An Alternative Viewpoint of Progress." *Land Use Policy* 94.

Lavigne Delville, Philippe, and Anne-Claire Moalic. 2019. "Territorialities, Spatial Inequalities and the Formalization of Land Rights in Central Benin." *Africa* 89 (2): 329–352.

Le Billon, Phillipe, and Melanie P. Sommerville. 2017. "Landing Capital and Assembling 'Investable Land' in the Extractive and Agricultural Sectors." *Geoforum* 82: 212–224.
Li, Tania M. 2009. "To Make Live and Let Die? Rural Dispossession and the Protection of Surplus Populations." *Antipode* 41 (S1): 66–93.
Li, Tania M. 2020. "Epilogue: Customary Land Rights and Politics, 21 Years On." *Asia Pacific Journal of Anthropology* 21 (1): 77–84.
Little, Peter D. 2014. *Economic and Political Reform in Africa: Anthropological Perspectives.* Bloomington: Indiana University Press.
Little, Peter D., and Michael J. Watts, eds. 1994. *Living under Contract: Contract Farming and Agrarian Transformation in Sub-Saharan Africa.* Madison: University of Wisconsin Press.
Locher, Martina. 2016. "'How Come Others Are Selling Our Land?' Customary Land Rights and the Complex Process of Land Acquisition in Tanzania." *Journal of Eastern African Studies* 10 (3): 393–412.
Losch, Bruno. 2012. "Agriculture: The Key to the Employment Challenge." CIRAD Perspective no. 19, October. CIRAD.
Lund, Christian. 2008. *Local Politics and the Dynamics of Property in Africa.* Cambridge, UK: Cambridge University Press.
Lund, Christian, and Catherine Boone. 2013. "Introduction: Land and Politics in Africa—Constituting Authority over Territory, Property and Persons." *Africa* 83 (1): 1–13.
Mackenzie, Fiona. 1990. "Gender and Land Rights in Murang'a District, Kenya." *Journal of Peasant Studies* 17 (4): 609–643.
Maertens, Miet, and Katrien Van de Velde. 2017. "Contract-Farming in Staple Food Chains: The Case of Rice in Benin." *World Development* 95: 73–87.
Maganga, Faustin, Kelly Askew, Rie Odgaard, and Howard Stein. 2016. "Dispossession through Formalization: Tanzania and the G8 Land Agenda in Africa." *Asian Journal of African Studies* 40 (1): 3–49.
Mamdani, Mahmood. 1996. *Citizen and Subject: Contemporary Africa and the Legacy of Late Colonialism.* Princeton, NJ: Princeton University Press.
Mandala, Elias. 2005. *The End of Chidyerano: A History of Food and Everyday Life in Malawi, 1860–2004.* Portsmouth, NH: Heinemann.
Manji, Ambreena. 2020. *The Struggle for Land and Justice in Kenya.* Woodbridge, UK: James Currey.
Marchal, Jean-Yves. 1987. "En Afrique des savanes, le fractionnement des unités d'exploitation rurales ou le chacun pour soi: L'exemple des Moose du Burkina Faso." *Cahiers des Sciences Humaines* 23 (3–4): 445–454.
Martiniello, Giuliano. 2015. "Social Struggles in Uganda's Acholiland: Understanding Responses and Resistance to Amuru Sugar Works." *Journal of Peasant Studies* 42 (3–4): 653–669.
Marwick, Max, ed. 1970. *Witchcraft and Sorcery: Selected Readings.* Harmondsworth, UK: Penguin Books.
McAuslan, Patrick. 2013. *Land Law Reform in East Africa, Traditional or Transformative? A Critical Review of 50 Years of Land Law Reform in Eastern Africa, 1961–2011.* Abingdon, UK: Routledge.
McMichael, Philip. 2012. "The Land Grab and Corporate Food Regime Restructuring." *Journal of Peasant Studies* 39 (3–4): 681–701.
Mkandawire, Thandika, and Charles C. Soludo. 1999. *Our Continent, Our Future: African Perspectives on Structural Adjustment.* Trenton, NJ: Africa World Press.

Moore, David B. 2001. "Is the Land the Economy and the Economy the Land? Primitive Accumulation in Zimbabwe." *Journal of Contemporary African Studies* 19 (2): 253–266.

Moore, Henrietta L., and Megan Vaughan. 1994. *Cutting Down Trees: Gender, Nutrition, and Agricultural Change in the Northern Province of Zambia, 1890–1990*. Portsmouth, NH: Heinemann.

Moore, Sally F. 1978. *Law as Process: An Anthropological Approach*. London: Routledge and Kegan Paul.

Moore, Sally F. 1988. *Social Facts and Fabrications: 'Customary' Law on Kilimanjaro, 1880–1980*. Cambridge, UK: Cambridge University Press.

Moreda, Tesegaye. 2015. "Listening to Their Silence? The Political Reaction of Affected Communities to Large-Scale Land Acquisitions: Insights from Ethiopia." *Journal of Peasant Studies* 42 (3–4): 517–539.

Mouser, Bruce L. 1975. "Landlords-Strangers: A Process of Accommodation and Assimilation." *International Journal of African Historical Studies* 8 (3): 425–440.

Munthali, Alister, Erling Berge, Stanley Khaila, Daimon Kambewa, and Henrik Wiig. 2017. "Women in Power: Land Access and Inheritance and Emerging Village Headpersons." Unpublished manuscript.

Nghitevelekwa, Romie V. 2020. *Securing Land Rights: Communal Land Reform in Namibia*. Windhoek: University of Namibia Press.

Notess, Laura, Peter Veit, Iliana Monterroso, Andiko, Emmanuel Sulle, Anne. M. Larson, et al. 2021. "Community Land Formalization and Company Land Acquisition Procedures: A Review of 33 Procedures in 15 Countries." *Land Use Policy* 110: 1–11.

Odgaard, Rie, and Kelly Askew. 2018. "'Collective Land Rights' Reconsidered: Experiences from Tanzania." Paper presented at Max Planck Institute for Social Anthropology, Halle/Salle, May 23–25.

Okoth-Ogendo, Hastings W. O. 1989. "Some Issues of Theory in the Study of Tenure Relations in African Agriculture." *Africa*, 59 (1): 6–17.

O'Laughlin, Bridget. 2000. "Class and the Customary: The Ambiguous Legacy of the Indigenat in Mozambique." *African Affairs* 99: 5–42.

Oomen, Barbara. 2005. *Chiefs in South Africa: Law, Power and Culture in the Post-apartheid Era*. Woodbridge, UK: James Curry.

Ossome, Lyn. 2021. "Pedagogies of Feminist Resistance: Agrarian Movements in Africa." *Agrarian South* 10 (1): 41–58.

Oya, Carlos 2009. "The World Development Report 2008: Inconsistencies, Silences and the Myth of 'Win-Win' Scenarios." *Journal of Peasant Studies* 36 (3): 593–601.

Oxfam. 2014. "Moral Hazard? 'Mega' Public-Private Partnerships in African Agriculture." Briefing Paper, September. Oxfam, Oxford.

Pala, Achola. O. 1980. "The Joluo Equation: Land Reform = Lower Status for Women." *Ceres*, May–June: 37–42.

Peemans, Jean-Philippe. 2014. "Land-Grabbing and Development History: The Congolese Experience." In Ansoms and Hillhorst, *Losing Your Land*, 11–35.

Peters, Pauline E. 1994. *Dividing the Commons: Politics, Policy and Culture in Botswana*. Charlottesville: University of Virginia Press.

Peters, Pauline E. 1997. "Against the Odds: Matriliny, Land and Gender in the Shire Highlands of Malawi." *Critique of Anthropology* 17 (2): 189–210.

Peters, Pauline E. 2002. "Bewitching Land: The Role of Land Disputes in Converting Kin to Strangers and in Class Formation in Malawi." *Journal of Southern African Studies* 28 (1): 155–178.

Peters, Pauline E. 2004. "Inequality and Social Conflict over Land in Africa." *Journal of Agrarian Change* 4 (3): 269–314.
Peters, Pauline E. 2010. "'Our Daughters Inherit Our Land, but Our Sons Use Their Wives' Fields': Matrilineal-Matrilocal Land Tenure and the New Land Policy in Malawi." *Journal of Eastern African Studies* 4 (1): 179–199.
Peters, Pauline E. 2018. "Revisiting the Social Bedrock of Kinship and Descent in the Anthropology of Africa." In *Companion to the Anthropology of Africa*, edited by Roy Richard Grinker, Stephen C. Lubkemann, Christopher B. Steiner, and Euclides Gonçalves, 33–62. New York: Wiley.
Peters, Pauline E., and Daimon Kambewa. 2007. "Whose Security? Deepening Social Conflict over 'Customary' Land in the Shadow of Land Tenure Reform in Malawi." *Journal of Modern African Studies* 45 (3): 447–472.
Place, Frank, and Peter Hazell. 1993. "Productivity Effects of Indigenous Land Tenure Systems in Sub-Saharan Africa." *American Journal of Agricultural Economics* 75 (1): 10–19.
Reno, William. 2001. "How Sovereignty Matters: International Markets and the Political Economy of Local Politics in Weak States." In *Intervention and Transnationalism in Africa: Global-Local Networks of Power*, edited by Thomas Callaghy, Ronald Kassimir, and Robert Latham, 197–215. Cambridge, UK: Cambridge University Press.
Richardson, Ben. 2010. "Big Sugar in Southern Africa: Rural Development and the Perverted Potential of Sugar/Ethanol Exports." *Journal of Peasant Studies* 37 (4): 917–938.
Roudart, Laurence, and Charlotte Guénard. 2019. "Introduction: Dépossessions foncières en milieu rural." *Revue Internationale des Études du Développement* 238: 7–29.
Schoffeleers, Matthew, ed. 1978. *Guardians of the Land: Essays on Central African Territorial Cults*. Gwelo, Zimbabwe: Mambo.
Schoneveld, George C. 2017. "Host Country Governance and the African Land Rush: 7 Reasons Why Large-Scale Farmland Investments Fail to Contribute to Sustainable Development." *Geoforum* 83: 119–132.
Shipton, Parker. 2007. *The Nature of Entrustment: Intimacy, Exchange, and the Sacred in Africa*. New Haven, CT: Yale University Press.
Smith, James H. 2022. *The Eyes of the World: Mining the Digital Age in the Eastern DR Congo*. Chicago: Chicago University Press.
Snyder, Francis. 1981. "Colonialism and Legal Form: The Creation of 'Customary Law' in Senegal." *Journal of Legal Pluralism* 19: 49–90.
Soro, Debegnoun M., and Jean-Philippe Colin. 2008. "Marchandisation, individualisation et gestion intra-familiale des droits sur la terre en basse Côte d'Ivoire." *Economie Rurale* 303/305: 154–168.
Spear, Thomas. 2003. "Neo-traditionalism and the Limits of Invention in British Colonial Africa." *Journal of African History* 44 (1): 3–27.
Spiegel, Andrew D. 2018. "Reconfiguring the Culture of Kinship: Poor People's Tactics during South Africa's Transition from Apartheid." *Africa* 88 (S1): S90–S116.
Sulle, Emmanuel. 2020. "Bureaucrats, Investors and Smallholders: Contesting Land Rights and Agro-commercialisation in the Southern Agricultural Growth Corridor of Tanzania." *Journal of Eastern African Studies* 14 (2): 332–353.
Sulle Emmanuel, and Ruth Hall. 2014. *International and Regional Guidelines on Land Governance and Land-Based Investments: An Agenda for African States*. Policy Brief 77. Future Agricultures. Cape Town, South Africa.
Takane, Tsutomu. 2004. "Smallholders and Nontraditional Exports under Economic Liberalization: The Case of Pineapples in Ghana." *African Study Monographs* 25 (1): 29–43.

Tchatchoua-Djomo, Rosine, Mathijs van Leeuwen, and Gemma van der Haar. 2020. "Defusing Land Disputes? The Politics of Land Certification and Dispute Resolution in Burundi." *Development and Change* 51 (6): 1454–1480.

Teyssier, A., R. A. Ratsialonana, R. Razafindralambo, and Y. Razafindrakoto. 2009. "Décentralisation de la gestion des terres à Madagascar: Processus, enjeux et perspectives d'une nouvelle politique foncière." In *Les politiques d'enregistrement des droits fonciers*, edited by Jean-Philippe. Colin, P.ierre-Yves-. Le Meur, and Éric Léonard, 273–297. Paris: Karthala.

Thompson, Edward P. 1993. *Customs in Common*. London: Penguin.

Toulmin, Camilla, and Julian Quan, eds. 2000. *Evolving Land Rights, Policy and Tenure in Africa*. London: International Institute for Environment and Development.

Ubink, Janine M., and Kojo S. Amanor, eds. 2008. *Contesting Land and Custom in Ghana*. Leiden: Leiden University Press.

van Leeuwen, Mathijs. 2014. "Renegotiating Customary Tenure Reform: Land Governance Reform and Tenure Security in Uganda." *Land Use Policy* 39: 292–300.

van Leeuwen, Mathijs, Ilse Zeemeijer, Doreen Kobusingye, Charles Muchunguzi, Linda Haartsen, and Claudia Piacenza. 2014. "The Continuities in Contested Land Acquisition in Uganda." In *Losing Your Land*, edited by Ansoms and Hillhorst, 103–124.

Veltmeyer, Henry. 2009. "Commentary: The World Bank on 'Agriculture for Development': A Failure of Imagination or the Power of Ideology?" *Journal of Peasant Studies* 36 (2): 393–410.

Verhaegen, Etienne, and Sandra Kiala. 2019. "Réactions paysannes aux investissements étrangers." *Revue International des Études de Développement* 238: 89–114.

Victor, Afari-Sefa. 2007. "The Dynamics of Horticultural Export Value Chains on the Livelihood of Small Farm Households in Southern Ghana. *African Journal of Agricultural Research* 2 (9): 435–440.

White, Ben, Saturnino M. Borras Jr., Ruth Hall, Ian Scoones, and Wendy Wolford. 2012. "The New Enclosures: Critical Perspectives on Corporate Land Deals." *Journal of Peasant Studies* 39 (3–4): 619–647.

World Bank. 2010. *Rising Global Interest in Farmland: Can It Yield Sustainable and Equitable Benefits?* Washington, DC: World Bank.

Yaro, Joseph A., and Dzodzi Tsikata. 2015. "Recent Transnational Land Deals and the Local Agrarian Economy in Ghana." In Hall, Scoones, and Tsikata, *Africa's Land Rush*, 46–64.

Yerby, George. 2016. *The English Revolution and the Roots of Environmental Change: The Changing Concept of the Land in Early Modern England*. New York: Routledge.

Zenker, Olaf, and Markus V. Hoehne, eds. 2018. *The State and the Paradox of Customary Law in Africa*. London: Routledge.

CHAPTER 28

TOURISM TROUBLES

The Intimate and Embodied Geographies of Land Grabbing in Panama

SHARLENE MOLLETT

INTRODUCTION

LAND grabbing and domestic service are mutually embedded in tourism development in Panama. On the Panamanian Caribbean coast and within and the Bocas del Toro archipelago (pop. 18,000), Afro-Panamanian resident Angelo Martinez owns and manages a small marina on his family's private cay. Each Saturday, Angelo's marina is a site of Afro-Panamanian hospitality where Liala, Angelo's twenty-eight-year-old daughter, leads her family in hosting a long-running weekend barbeque, and where patrons enjoy grilled lobster, conch, octopus, and the beloved *patacones* (fried plantains). With Afro-Caribbean music bellowing across the calm waters of the Caribbean Sea, the Martinez's weekend barbeque attracts a largely affluent, White foreign community, many of whom own significant land, homes, and hotels throughout Bocas.

Foreign land ownership is legal in Panama (Spalding 2017). But over the last twenty years, domestic land control for many Indigenous, mestizo, and Black residents, whether statutory or customary, has been shrinking. Land access is profoundly insecure as domesticresidents are compelled to defend their place on the coast against foreign land developers, wealthy migrants-cum-residential tourists, and the state (Spalding 2011; Thampy 2013; Mollett 2016). As Liala explained, one year, a Canadian couple, returning marina tenants, insisted on borrowing land from her father so they could grow fruits and vegetables while they were living in their boat at the Martinez marina. Angelo lent them the parcel, and he and his sons prepared the soil for planting. But as the monthspassed, the couple increasingly asked Liala to plant and maintain the garden, despite their stated desire to grow a garden of their own. During the season, Liala not only managed the garden, but also regularly hand washed the couple's laundry. Although the couple paid Liala the standard three-dollar hourly wage for washing, they did not pay her for her work in the garden. Then, as the season was winding down, Angelo learned that the Canadians were attempting to claim his "borrowed" plot without his knowledge or benefit. Fearing that the couple would use the planted garden as proof of their claim to his land, he instructed Liala to remove the plants and terminated the Canadians' tenancy at the marina. Angelo was relieved that he was able to protect his family land "against gringo land invasions." But over the last two decades, many local *Bocatorenos*, particularly Indigenous Ngäbe and Afro-Panamanian residents, have not been so fortunate; they have lost hundreds of hectares of land to residential tourists from North America and Europe, who use a variety of legal and extralegal tactics to grab land and *settle*in Bocas (see also Mollett 2016; Prado 2011; Spalding 2011).

In Panama, tourism development is constitutive of and spurs land grabbing. The scholarship on land grabbing is vast; it is an arena where scholars write about disparate resource-grabbing scenarios, from mining to conservation (Borras and Franco 2012; Himley 2019; Lunstrum 2016; Ojeda 2012; Ybarra 2018), and Marx's theory of primitive accumulation is commonly used to conceptualize land grabbing in various contexts (Hall 2013). Indeed, as Mehta, Veldwisch, and Franco (2012) and Hall (2013) maintain, Marxian political economic analyses centering capitalist logics are important to scholarly understandings of land and resource grabbing and tie "today's 'new enclosures' to the land seizures crucial to centuries of imperialism and capitalist expansion" (Hall 2013, 1583). However, as I have argued elsewhere, land grabbing scholarship tends to overstate the central role that capitalist logics play in a variety of land dynamics, obscuring how land grabbing is "spatially contingent on enduring pejorative representations of [race]" that disparage and dismiss "Indigenous and Afro-descendant peoples' land use practices and customary and collective tenure arrangements." Such state and elite suppositions are "part of a long [Euro-American–centric] racial-cultural project with specific targets for change and in some cases erasure" (Mollett 2016, 4, 5) and fuel ongoing land grabbing.

Colonial projects of erasure are also gendered (Goeman 2009; McClintock 1995). As Maria Lugones's (2007, 2010) theoretical contributions on the "coloniality of gender power" illustrate, colonial land expansion is not underpinned only by a "coloniality of power," a concept that crystalizes how racial power threads through the quilt of land control, religious and racial social orders, and Black and Indigenous people's subjugation (Quijano 2007; see also Mollett 2021). Patriarchy and coloniality are *co*-constitutive, shaping gendered difference and fostering differentiation among women—namely, "humanizing white women, while simultaneously dehumanizing Black, Indigenous and poor women more generally" (Mollett 2023, 1575). Aligning with feminist political ecological demands to weave how race and gender complicate scholarly understandings of access to and control of natural resources, decolonial/postcolonial, Black and Indigenous feminist scholarly insights on coloniality, offer a "more rigorous treatment of the body as a material and political site" within political ecology (Doshi 2017, 2125). Such thinking advances research on land grabbing by expanding the notions of coloniality, conquest, and dispossession as material, intersectionally differentiated, and embodied

(De Leeuw 2016; Zaragocin 2019; Mollett 2023). I attempt to provide a messier and more grounded analysis of the sedimented forms of power that shape land grabbing. Such an analysis duly notes, following Beverley Mullings, that "frameworks that foreground capitalism—even if attentive to race, easily lose sight of the historical dispositions, conventions, relations and practices that mark racialized subjects as already more vulnerable to and intimately familiar with loss, risk, pain and death" (2022, 746).

Critical geographers maintain that in many locales, colonial logics of power underpin contemporary tourism development (Kothari 2015; Emard and Nelson 2021). These logics privilege affluent foreigners through incentivized land policies while disenfranchising domestic local populations from family lands and common resources (Devine 2017; Ojeda 2012; Kothari 2015; Emard and Nelson 2021; Loperena 2017). Residential tourism development is a case in point. In fact, the term *residential tourism*—namely, "a mix of permanent and temporary mobilities" (Van Noorloos 2013, 571)—describes a process whereby foreign migrants travel to places like Panama with the purpose of establishing permanent and supplementary homes and making real estate investments (Hayes 2015; Mollett 2016). This tourism model is sanctioned by global development organizations and presented as an effective way to attract foreign direct investment, spur land markets, and generate employment, often rhetorically pitched "in the name of the poor" (World Bank 2009; Gomez, Kandel, and Moran 2009). It is in this way, for Indigenous Ngäbe and Afro-Panamanian residents, *tourism troubles*.

Indeed, Latin American countries are settler colonial landscapes (Zaragocin 2019; Correia 2022; Mollett 2021; see also Speed 2017; Gott 2007). I understand *settler colonialism*, borrowing from Morgensen (2010), as "the social processes and narratives that displace Native people while granting settlers belonging to native land and settler society" (117). I am particularly interested in the "logic of elimination" posited as a central organizing principle in settler landscapes, which, according to the late Patrick Wolfe (2006), not only "strives for the dissolution of native societies" but "destroys to replace" (388). In Bocas, a logic of elimination works to displace both Indigenous Ngäbe and Afro-Panamanians; however, I focus on Afro-Panamanian women. I do so for two overlapping reasons: First, I seek to complicate the reproduction of settler-native binaries in geographic scholarship on settler landscapes (see Day 2015; King 2019; Pulido 2018). In so doing, I acknowledge Lowe's (2015) insistence that "the operations that pronounce colonial divisions of humanity—settler seizure and native removal, slavery and racial dispossession, and racialized expropriations of many kinds—are imbricated processes, not sequential events" (7). Second, following Indigenous, Black, and decolonial feminist scholars writing on the Americas, I want to highlight that "a logic of elimination" does not only play out on the land, but also on subaltern bodies, including Afro-Panamanian women (Goeman 2009; King 2019; Simpson 2016).

The chapter combines ethnographic data and material from semistructured interviews (collected from 2011 to 2013) with archival and historical data collection conducted in the Archive of the Indies in Seville, Spain; the Benson Bee Latin American Library at the University of Texas at Austin; and the Panamanian National Library in Panama City (collected from 2011 to 2017), and during supplementary travel to Panama in 2017. These findings are contextualized alongside Afro-Latin American historiographies, which help to reveal the ways in which colonial spatial relations are historically woven into the social fabric of Bocas. Reading ethnographic data alongside Afro-Latin American historiographies and archival data demonstrates that the weaving of past with the present punctuates the workings of what Stoler (2016) calls "recursive logics." By blending the two, I aim to illustrate how contemporary Bocas is shaped by a "sort of history [that] is marked by the uneven, unsettled, contingent quality of histories that *fold back on themselves* (orig. emphasis)" (Stoler 2016, 26), offering an optic of blurred temporalities. Such blurred temporalities defy seeing history as linear and may suggest that these racial, gendered, and carnal relations, though structural and persistent, are neither fixed nor settled. As historical geographers maintain, attention to histories of place effectively capture the "lingering effects of European expansion on environments and environmental epistemologies" as seen through "the continuity of material and discursive forms of resource control" (Offen 2004, 28; 2012). I wish to highlight the particular case of Afro-Panamanian women as domestic-service providers and demonstrate the co-constitutive ways in which antiblackness and patriarchy are intimately woven within the eliminatory processes of (settler) colonialism at work in residential tourism in Bocas, complicating the questions of where, how, and for whom settler colonial histories tell a story.

In Bocas, settler land grabs and the concomitant land displacement of Indigenous and Black residents are about, not simply land, but also, simultaneously, about people and their bodies (Mollett 2021; Zaragocin 2019). These land-body relations are infused with imaginaries that reflect conventional histories, which take for granted Black female servitude and Black peoples' landlessness. Such imaginaries yoke economically "poor" Afro-Panamanian women to particular kinds of work. To illustrate this, I entangle feminist political ecological assertions that struggles over nature are embodied struggles with intersectional and relational understandings of land and body (Doshi 2017; Sultana 2011; Mollett 2021). Drawing insights from a fusion of anticolonial, Indigenous, and Black feminist critiques of coloniality and settler colonialism (Simpson 2016; Zaragocin 2019; King 2016; Mollett 2017, 2021; Radcliffe 2015), I will show how a logic of elimination operates within the legal geographies of tourism development. Next, I highlight the ways in which Afro-Panamanian women are naturalized as *criadas* (maids), a process that accompanies land enclosure and illuminates Afro-Panamanian women's livelihood struggles through both their acquiescence and their resilience in the face of Bocas's anti-Black patriarchal coloniality. To demonstrate how land grabbing involves more than what happens to the land, I draw upon the concepts of postcolonial intersectionality and *cuerpo-territorio* to highlight the co-constitution of land and body within colonial imaginaries and the concomitant role that gender and race play in the extractive-development enclosures that shape life in Bocas. Finally, I argue that Afro-Panamanian women's desire for inclusion in Bocas' tourism enclave—a project that seeks to eliminate Indigenous and Black relations to coastal lands and to ensure their (domestic) servitude to foreign nationals—reflects Afro-Panamanians' enduring relations to the lands of the Bocas archipelago and their embodied struggles for the right to remain on the coast.

Feminist Fusions: Postcolonial Intersectionality

As noted, I situate this examination of Afro-Panamanian women's livelihood struggles at the entanglements of feminist political ecology and a fusion of anticolonial, Indigenous, and Black feminist thinking, woven within the concept of *postcolonial intersectionality* (Mollett 2017; 2021; Radcliffe 2015). Postcolonial intersectionality acknowledges the ways "patriarchy and racialized processes are consistently bound in a postcolonial genealogy that embeds race and gender ideologies within nation building and international development processes" (Mollett and Faria 2013, 120). My aim is to make visible multiple structures of power to show the myriad, and messy, forms of rule at work in the colonial spatial formations imbued in contemporary development practice (Christian and Namaganda 2018; Mollett and Faria 2013; Radcliffe 2015). Across the Americas, Indigenous feminist thought articulates Indigenous women's bodies as a collective site of settler colonial violence, both during and after conquest, and the scale upon which multiple forms of power sear (Simpson 2016; Goeman 2009; Women's Earth Alliance and Native Youth Sexual Health Network 2016). Maya-Xinka feminist Lorena Cabnal conceptualizes this entanglement as "cuerpo-territorio," an embodied ontology that centers people and territory as a single, unique, and mutually constituted subjectivity. *Cuerpo-territorio* challenges the ways both historical and contemporary forms of conquest are constitutive with extraction, to enclose and control women's bodies, like territory (Cabnal 2016; Zaragocin 2019).

Black feminist scholars also weave together bodies and colonial expansion (i.e., land) in scholarship on the transatlantic slave trade—a key temporal moment marking Black dehumanization. Indeed, the objectification of the captive Black body legitimated and sustained African slavery (Spillers 1987; McKittrick 2006; see also Ojeda, this volume). Moreover, "the black female body [acts] as a historical signifier" and is a symbolic site for slavery's reproduction (Santos de Araújo 2016, 150; Smith 2016; Morgan 2004; Hartman 2016). Such symbolism is exemplified in European male travel writing that depicts "black women as simultaneously unwomanly and marked by a reproductive value that was both dependent on their sex and evidence of their lack of femininity," a presupposition made ever more salient as European-American slave owners used Black women's bodies "to produce both crops and other laborers" (Morgan 2004, 14; see also Lugones 2007). These presuppositions fuel settler desires, making the "discovery of new lands . . . inextricable from the language of sexual conquest" (Morgan 2004, 17). In the face of such violence, and in spite of it, the Black female body also represents fugitivity and possibility, which collectively enables a "breach in the system to which Blacks [are] morally submitted," offering hope for freedom from an enduring colonial racist patriarchy (Nascimento 1985, cited quoted in Smith 2016, 84; McKittrick 2006, 2013). Hence, a focus on the entanglement of land and body helps demonstrate how settler land accumulation (i.e., land grabbing) structures Afro-Panamanian women's livelihood struggles and their concomitant resilience in the face of the racial, gendered, and carnal colonialities shaping both Black female subjectivities and access to land for *Bocatorenos*.

Historical Racial Geographies of Land Control in Bocas

Bocas' history is part of the contemporary fabric and allure of the archipelago. The website of region's largest resort, the Red Frog Beach Island Resort and Spa, invites tourists and prospective foreign residents to visit Bocas, just as Christopher Columbus did in 1502:

> Columbus an innovative explorer was immediately captivated by the beauty and abundance on Isla Bastimientos . . . . *Just as Columbus did* . . . discover a new world for yourself in Bocas del Toro. We consider it fortunate that the heritage, Caribbean lifestyle, enduring culture, and nature-given 'provisions' are *much like the same as several hundred years ago*.
>
> (my emphasis; http://www.RedFrogrealestate.com)

The invitation to "discover" Bocas through the spatial image of "several hundred years ago" is not benign. This historical-geographic representation remakes Bocas as *terra nullius*, imagined to be waiting for settler discovery and innovation, in a place seemingly stuck in time, where cultures and nature "are much like the same as several hundred years ago." Although this use of colonial history in tourism advertising suggests an availability of land and nature, even more salient are the constant and pervasive celebrations of the twentieth-century past as a United Fruit Company stronghold in Bocas.

Throughout the archipelago's main islands Colon and Bastimentos, many of the interior walls of hotels and restaurants feature photos depicting the "boom days" of the United Fruit Company's Bocas Division and plantations. The photos forward images of Afro-Caribbean harvesters and their deplorable housing, often in contrast to images of the UFC's White administrators and the fancy homes and lawns of the "White zone," a place that was off limits to Afro-Caribbean workers. As Philippe Bourgois (1989) wrote, "The luxury of the white zone contrasts violently with the squalor of the overcrowded barracks area, likewise the unpaved roads, and walkways are either covered with ankle-mud or engulfed by clouds of dust" (4). Such images of the past compiled in photographs, postcards, posters, pamphlets, and books celebrate the historical role of the UFC and the making of Bocas (Stephens 2008). Today, Bocas is a place filled with the embodied histories of Euro-American settlement and imperial desires, a place layered with histories of land dispossession and free and unfree labor that often culminate in a celebration of Panama's key infrastructural projects, The Canal, The Railroad, and in particular, the United Fruit Company (Lasso 2019; O'Reggio 2006).

Yet the images and the celebration of the UFC's "boom days" are more complicated for some *Bocatorenos*. US racial segregation under Jim Crow organized the life and labor of the UFC. From the late 1800s to the early 1930s, the company, under the auspices of the Chiriqui Land Company, shaped land, labor, and daily life along the Caribbean coast from Bocas del Toro, Panama, to Talamanca, Costa Rica (Bourgois 1989; O'Reggio 2006; Putnam 2002). While many different ethnic groups worked as laborers for the UFC, including Guna and Ngäbe Indigenous peoples, in the early years, a disproportionate number of those working as harvesters were Afro-Caribbean migrants (Bourgois 1989; O'Reggio 2006). In the mid-nineteenth century, impoverishment and ongoing anti-Black discrimination followed the decline of the sugar trade and the abolition of slavery in the former British and Spanish colonies. The well-publicized labor shortages facing the UFC targeted and attracted primarily Black men from Jamaica, Barbados, and, later, from Martinique to the Isthmus (Newton 1984). As harvesters, Black men cleared swampland and snakes, faced plagues of mosquitos and experienced debilitating, often fatal disease (Stephens 1997, 2008). According to Bourgois (1989), the Bocas division was "structured by a complicated and hierarchal productive process, subdivided into dozens of job categories involving different degrees of technological skill, as well as physical and mental stress," what he calls "a *de facto* apartheid occupational hierarchy" (331). In fact, though many Afro-Caribbean migrants were able to establish small family farms adjacent to the plantation and to sell bananas and cacao as independent producers, UFC administrators used their entrepreneurialism to justify paying them exploitatively low wages (Bourgois 1989).

In Central America, the UFC orchestrated an enormous land grabbing operation throughout the early twentieth century. Importantly, the materiality of such land accumulation was made possible by an embedded and embodied racialized labor operation. Company officials sought "suitable" laborers to fill the ranks. In Panama, the imperial desires of the UFC's American administrators meant carrying out very detailed search for the strongest and healthiest Afro-Caribbean (Black) men (Bourgois 1989; Stephens 1997). As Newton (1984) explains,

> As the men came up they were formed in a line around the wall . . . all those who looked too old, or too young, or too weakly, were picked out and sent away. Then [the doctor], he went over the whole line again for trachoma, rolling back their eyelids and looking for inflammation . . . Then he made them strip, and went over them round after round for tuberculosis, heart trouble and rupture. (76)

Afro-Caribbean men lived in the small, cramped UFC barracks. But a lack of formal work for women on the plantation often meant that the Afro-Caribbean women lived in the port towns. It was along the railroad lines that Black social reproduction stretched between the plantations and the port towns on both sides of the Panama–Costa Rica border (Putnam 2002; Bourgois 1989). The exclusionary logics of Latin American nationalist thinking under *mestizaje* and *blanqueamiento* that were imbued in the Panamanian nationalist movements reinforced US racial ideologies on the plantation

(Mollett 2016; Milazzo 2012). These narratives employed a variety of anti-Black policies that targeted Black people for deportation and subjugation in the early twentieth century and reified antiblackness by disavowing Black humanity in Panama (Watson 2012; Lasso 2019). These histories of labor and embodied dispossession are important to understanding how overlapping racial projects are threaded in the development of residential tourism in the present.

"Sustainable Tourism" and the Legal Geographies of Indigenous and Black Land Dispossession

Since the 1990s, successive state Master Tourism Plans have promoted tourism as a development strategy in Panama. These plans, particularly the emphasis on attracting foreign direct investment, are part of a global trend led by the United Nations World Tourism Organization (UNWTO) and the World Bank, which, along with numerous environmental and development NGOs, celebrate "sustainable tourism development" (World Tourism Organization 2018; International Finance Corporation 2017). This global tourism strategy argues that sustainable tourism is a vehicle for "poverty reduction," a "critical sector for women's economic and social advancement" and a tool for "inclusive growth" through "efficient and effective" job creation (World Tourism Organization 2018; International Finance Corporation 2017,19; Klytchnikova and Dorosh 2013). For the last twenty years, tourism has been one of the main drivers of exceptional growth, making Panama a regional leader in generating foreign direct investment (Benson 2013; Spalding 2011). Panama is an attractive place for visitors; its economy is dollarized, English is widely spoken, and political stability helps to bolster investment, most visibly in infrastructure, real estate, and large- and small-scale residential tourism development (Runk 2012; Spalding 2011). It is estimated that Panama receives approximately 2.3 million tourists annually, which accounts for 16.2 percent of the nation's GDP. Of that, beach and leisure tourism accounts for 70 percent of tourism receipts (World Travel and Tourism Council 2017). Additionally,the World Bank reports that in Panama "the tourism sector was found to have higher multipliers than any of the country's seven other principal sectors. With a multiplier of 2.87, tourism was more than twice that of textiles at 1.3 and maize at 1.4" (International Finance Corporation 2017, 16). Thus, tourism development is touted as benefiting large numbers of people through its multiplying power to produce employment. Nonetheless, the tourism benefits in Panama are unevenly distributed (Koehler-Geib et al. 2015; Gomez, Kandel, and Moran 2009).

Though the state relies on Afro-Panamanian and Indigenous cultures to "sell" cultural diversity and biodiversity, Panama's wealth from tourism is concentrated in elite enclaves and special economic zones in urban areas. Even when visitors travel to the culturally rich and biodiverse regions that are largely located in the rural parts of the country, tourism's benefits often bypass the places "where agriculture is the main source of livelihood" and where the economic situation is already dire—namely, Indigenous and Afro-Panamanian communities (Klytchnikova and Dorosh 2013, 4; Runk 2012; Guerrón Montero 2014). Indigenous Ngäbe peoples claim the lands of the Bocas del Toro archipelago as part the Ngäbe-Bugle homelands. For more than five hundred years, people of African descent have shared this coast with the Ngäbe and other Indigenous peoples (Bourgois 1989; Diez Castillo 1981; Reid 1983; Wickstrom 2003). However, the state's comarca system only partially acknowledges these histories, but for Indigenous peoples only (Herrera 2012; Jordan 2008). Black land and territorial rights, by contrast, enjoy no formal collective protections from the state at all. Furthermore, in the early 1990s, Panama formalized a business-oriented sustainable tourism model that continues to rely heavily on designing "ecologically balanced" accommodations and tourism amenities through foreign direct investment (Guerrón Montero 2005, 2014; Spalding 2011). For local *Bocatorenos*, this vision has materialized across a number of land grabs. In 1988, the Bastimentos Island National Marine Park, which is managed by the National Environmental Authority, enclosed a sizeable portion (13,360 hectares, 1630 acres of which are terrestrial and 11,730, marine) of island territory and marine resources (Spalding 2011). A consortium of state agencies, international and national NGOs, and settler residents (US American, European, and Canadian retirees and Latin American elites) spurred the park's creation, while excluding Afro-Panamanian and the Ngäbe peoples from the consultations (Guerrón Montero 2005).

Numerous laws exist to promote the state's vision for attracting foreign direct investment in tourism development. Established in 1994, Law 80, known colloquially as the "tourism law" offers foreign investors incentives (i.e., tax exemptions, residency). Law 80 also entrenches the state's tourism plan (World Bank 2009). Under the law, which emerged as part of the multimillion dollar World Bank–funded land regularization project PRONAT (Panama Land Administration Project, 2001–2009), foreign nationals hold the same rights to own island land as Panamanians, including Indigenous and Afro-Panamanian citizens. As a result, Law 80 intensifies domestic land dispossession and effectively reorders land access through multiple forms of enclosure (Spalding 2017; Thampy 2013; Mollett 2016). The legal geographies of tourism and shifting property rights disrupt customary forms of land tenure in Bocas. Throughout the archipelago, *Bocatorenos* rely upon a system of *derechos posesorios*, "rights of possession" (ROP). ROPs are a type of land holding, embedded in the country's first Civil Code in 1917, "which established a process through which individuals had the right to possess land as long as they could demonstrate 'use' and were not trying to claim rights over inalienable government land" (Spalding 2017, 547). Today, many ROPs remain unregistered, and so there exists no formal record of the holding or its holder, either in the local municipality or in the ANATI (National Authority of Land Administration) office in Panama City. While recent land regularization seemingly sought to make land holdings legible and bolster land markets, many Afro-Panamanian and Ngäbe residents find that their tenure security is eroded (author's fieldnotes, 2011–2013; Mollett 2017, 2016; World Bank 2009). Land formalization renders holders of customary ROPs vulnerable to land fraud when settlers make claims in legal and extralegal ways (Thampy 2013; see Mollett 2016). Recall the story of Angelo and Liala. The Canadians' attempt to steal Angelo's plot failed because Angelo is known in the community, and the cadastral office intervened on his behalf. Nevertheless, such extralegal moves, in the words of Angelo, make it likely that those who "have money to pay tax on the land to end up owning it" (interview with the author, Bocas, 2011). Indeed, part of a process to convert ROPs to land titles (under Law 80) requires payment of taxes on the market value of the land. For most local residents, the inability to afford the tax prohibits them from legally owning (fee simple) their customary held lands (author's fieldnotes, 2011, hereafter cited as "fieldnotes"). The Canadians likely assumed that Angelo's land tax was unpaid because this has been one of the extralegal ways that land theft occurs in Panama and throughout region (fieldnotes, 2011, Mollett 2016). The foreign enclosure of land throughout the archipelago means that access to land and other nature is dwindling, prompting many Afro-Panamanians residents to ask, What's in it for us? (fieldnotes, 2013).

Embodied Political Ecologies: In Search of "Dignity" and "Respect"

> It's not just our land that makes Basti our home. We are Afro-Caribbean and we are workers.... This is our place too.
> (Maxine Williams, resident of Old Bank, Bastimentos Island, 2011)

A report prepared by the regional project Afro-descendant Population of Latin America II of the United Nations Development Programme (UNDP) that focused on the perceptions of Black identity and development in Panama cited the need to protect Black land rights. Indeed, many Afro-Panamanians, in their struggles for land and housing, echo the sentiment (Swaby 2014; UNDP 2013). In Bocas, similarly, many Afro-Panamanians make claims to land based on their historical presence on the coast and familiar links to the early days of the UFC plantation. But for many, embedded within discursive claims to land are Afro-Panamanian collective histories of work and identities as "workers" (fieldnotes, 2011, 2012, 2013). These histories also punctuate Afro-Panamanian land claims (Prado 2011; UNDP 2013). Many Afro-Panamanians insist that they, too, not just their Indigenous neighbors, have intimate relations with nature in the archipelago, and it is as "workers" on its lands and waters that they seek commitments on the state's promise of employment as a "trade-off" for their increasing displacement from land and nature (fieldnotes, 2011, 2012, 2013). But it is what these trade-offs entail that reveals the multiple power relations embedded in tourism development. Afro-Panamanian women maintain that, despite state's promises of employment and its touting of the mutual benefits of tourism for developers and residents, the opportunities afforded to them lack "dignity." Although "grateful" for the income, they sought employment that comes with "respect" (author's interviews, 2012; hereafter cited as "interviews"). Undignified work conditions are a common target of scorn, particularly among Afro-Panamanian women working in domestic service (Mollett 2017). Afro-*Bocatorenas* reported that, despite possessing a secondary-level education, and even sometimes one to two years at university as well, the work opportunities beyond domestic service are severely limited (interviews, 2012). Kenya, a bartender at a local hotel, explains, "I went to Changuinola for Business school (2-year program). I wanted to work in hotel reception. But after I graduated, there were no jobs in Bocas so I moved to Panama City . . . I worked as a maid . . . it was like Bocas" (interview, Old Bank, Bastimentos Island, 2012). Many women were content just to have employment, however precarious. Indeed, work rooted them to a place on the coast (fieldnotes, 2012). Still, overwhelmingly, all participants (n = 30) argued that the work expectations placed on housekeepers are excessive (interviews, Bocas, 2012). I illustrate with ethnographic testimony from Simona.

Simona explains how her *limipiadora* (housekeeping) job "consumes her." At Palmas Property and Realty, a vacation home and property management company, a typical workday officially extends from seven o'clock in the morning to three o'clock in the afternoon, five days a week. However, because her boss requires that the all-women domestic staff perform "special" errands for guests, she sometimes works every day. Three months into their stay, one couple, asked Simona to help them prepare for their family's arrival from the United States. Her female employer (Daisy) needed her to cook the welcome dinner:

> Because [Daisy] wanted fresh, really fresh fish, the next day I woke up at 3 a.m. to go with my father. He is a fisherman, and I needed to catch a ride on his boat to the fish market in Almirante . . . I waited for two hours for the market to open and then another two hours before my father could come pick me up . . . I had to work in Bocas Town . . . They were happy with what I provided for the dinner: lobsters, crabs, beautiful fish and conch. So a few days later, [Daisy] asked me to help with a farewell dinner . . . . so I once again woke up at 3 a.m. to catch a ride from my father.

According to Simona, after that, there was always extra work. Although Simona was remunerated for all these chores, including her "regular job," she was never paid for the extra travel time to obtain the fish or for her father's labor and connections. Simona said that Daisy treated her "like a machine some days and the rest like an animal." When she finally found the courage to ask the property manager if he could assign her to a different house, he refused and told her "extra work is expected and *you* come with the house" (Bocas Town interviews 2011, 2012).

Servicing Desire in Plantation Landscapes

Afro-Panamanian women insist that there is an "attitude" among tourists and settlers (often perpetuated by national elites) that underpins the material relations of service between locals and foreigners (fieldnotes, 2012). The opining of an American restaurateur I witnessed at the opening ceremony of a new hotel and restaurant on Colon Island serves as an example:

> What we are doing is good for the people of Bocas. Bocatorenos have jobs because we [foreigners] are here building homes, hotels, doing business, eating in restaurants, starting schools . . . We fund conservation; we raise money for poor Indian kids, and drive the sustainable tourism economy. Without us, without us, Bocas would be a dead zone, we don't just bring the jobs . . . we bring [cultural] sophistication and a global awareness of modern life.
>
> (fieldnotes, Bocas Town, Colon Island, 2017)

Such presuppositions do not only fuel land enclosure; it seems that settler land control comes with affordances that extend not just over the land but over local people and their bodies. For Afro-Panamanian women, being a *criada* is "dirty" work, but not just because they spend all day cleaning up after strangers. Every single participant (n = 30) reported experiencing some form of sexual abuse or harassment while working as a housekeeper (interviews 2012, 2013; see also Mollett 2017). I illustrate with ethnographic testimony from Dixa.

Dixa is a thirty-two-year-old woman from Old Bank, Bastimentos Island. When she was younger, she worked at a popular bar in Carenero (an island in the archipelago). The money was great, and she and her boyfriend were able to build a two-room house on his family's property. After a few years, Dixa took time off from her job to have the couple's baby. When her son was about four months old, Dixa approached her former boss about how soon she could go back to work,. To her surprise, he claimed that the only position available for her was as a *criada* (maid) in his hostel business in town. According to Dixa, "He said I was too fat to be behind the bar, that I'm not sexy . . . not youthful anymore." Dixa, insulted that he thought she was only fit to be a *criada*, insisted "I am a great bartender, I speak English [in addition to Spanish and Creole], and tourists love me . . . They really do, when I go by them on the street they say, Dixa, Dixa, Are you working tonight? I deserve a better job. I am more than a maid!" Determined, Dixa found a job as a personal assistant in an American woman's clothing store in Bocas Town, earning no more than three dollars an hour. Dixa recounted that "at the beginning I unpacked the new merchandise, helped customers and kept the inventory organized." But soon, her duties increased. One day, "Miss Kathy" [her boss] offered her $50 extra to spend the afternoon cleaning her home and doing laundry because their regular "girl" was sick. Dixa insisted that she was *always* paid for the extra chores, but said that eventually she was doing "everything, everything." After Dixa had worked there for about a about a year, as business was slowing for the low season Kathy told Dixa that she could no longer offer her full-time work at the store, but if she wanted to clean her house and help Mr. Tim [Kathy's husband], she could be their maid. Dixa agreed to the work, she said, because Mr. Tim is nice to her: "I also cook lunch for the couple and sometimes give Mr. Tim massages. When Miss Kathy goes to David or Panama City to buy merchandise for the store, I go with her to help carry things and to speak Spanish to the wholesalers who do not speak good English . . . When Miss Kathy visits the US, she pays me extra to stay at the house to help Mr. Tim. [When asked, *What do you do? Where do you sleep when Mrs. Kathy is away?* she answers after a pause] "Sometimes, I sleep with Mr. Tim." Dixa explained that Mr. Tim is "always kind" "respectful" and that sharing his bed, "it's just part of [her] job" (interview, 2012). Incredibly, such expectations are normalized in Bocas. Settlers, however, often shrug off these instances—as well as *Bocatoreno* complaints of land theft and fraud—often using the same expression, "This is Bocas." The ubiquitousness of this and similar phrases (e.g., "This is Panama") suggests that the limited employment opportunities, a lack of dignified work and the grabbing of land and bodies by foreign nationals are "just how it is" on the archipelago.

Histories in the Making of Place in the Present

In Bocas, the taken for grantedness of land grabbing and Black women's servitude has a history. The stories of Liala, Simona, and Dixa illustrate how colonial logics of race, gender, and sexuality structure space in Bocas. Black feminist scholar Saidiya Hartman, in theorizing Black women in the "afterlife" of the transatlantic slave trade, explains that "the fungibility of the commodity makes the captive body an abstract and empty vessel vulnerable to the projection of others' feelings, ideas, desires and values" (Hartman 1997, 6, 21). Similarly, Tiffany King, in contextualizing Black women in settler landscapes, argues that blackness, "as expansion and spatial possibility, becomes a constituting feature of the spatial imagination of the conquistador/settler rather than just another human laborer exploited as a mere technology to produce space" (King 2016, 1023). To be clear, I am not equating contemporary livelihood struggles to slave life. However, Bocas's history on the Caribbean re-emerges in the contemporary as partial and incomplete legacies, rewritings, and discontinuities from the past (Stoler 2016). I wish to reiterate that while Liala, Simona, and Dixa were paid for their assigned tasks, they were not remunerated for the *time* that it took *to do* many of the other tasks; weeding gardens, traveling by boat to buy fish, using family labor, biking to deliver parcels, giving massages and companionship, and more. Embodied labor and familial connections were taken for granted, and it would seem from the settler comments above, their labor (body) is perceived to come with the marina rental/house/land! The repetitive and fungible way Black women serve as *criadas* (maids) in the homes and businesses of foreign settlers and elites embodies a collective geographic imaginary that not only assumes that specific kinds of labor are meant to be done by particular people, but that some of their labor must go unpaid. Still, and perhaps counterintuitively for some, for Afro-Panamanian women, such unequal power dynamics inform their collective imaginaries, as they see (and hope) that their work makes legible their place on the coast, even when their embodied histories of survival and resilience seem not to reverse impending settler land grabs.

Final Thoughts

In this chapter, I configure complexity into land grabbing debates in an attempt to demonstrate how land dispossession via grabbing is not only about the land itself, but about people, land, and their bodies. Building upon the insights from a fusion of feminist thought and, in particular, the concepts of postcolonial intersectionality and *cuerpo-territorio*, reveals that land grabbing as it unfolds in the Bocas Archipelago is a material and embodied process. I illustrate these racial regimes of land control through ethnographic testimonies blended with Afro-Latin American historiographies to disclose the naturalization and devaluation of Black women as *criadas*, in a context where, simultaneously, Indigenous and Black lands and territories and women's bodies seem therefor settler exploitation.

Returning to the women of Bocas, Simona no longer works for Palmas Property. She now sells fish caught by her father and other fishers to small hotels and restaurants throughout the archipelago, and life seems better. To cope with less income she eats once a day, grows more food in her garden, and when there is no food, she drinks coffee to suppress her appetite. Dixa has also changed jobs. She left "the store" and works as a part-time teacher in a small private school run by a settler. Liala and her family raised the rent on the marina slips, began charging double for the barbeque and, it would seem, no longer allow foreigners to "borrow" family land (fieldnotes, 2013, 2017). Disclosing the ways in which a logic of elimination unfolds in Bocas through settler land grabbing, Indigenous and Black land enclosure, and Black women's servitude-as-subjugation not only questions tourism as a development strategy, but challenges scholars of land grabbing to complicate how land grabs are operationalized beyond capitalist accumulation acknowledging the ways in which other forms of power are embedded in the processes of resource- grabbing-induced dispossession. Lastly, attending to how blurred temporalities inform tourism development, how a particular moment in the past continues to inform the present in the name of the future, at once *troubles* the assumptions embedded in sustainable tourism and punctuates how land grabbing is not simply about capitalist-induced land dispossession. Indeed, histories of race, gender, and sexuality continue to structure place in embodied ways, across time and space.

Acknowledgments

This chapter is a partial reproduction of my article, "Swiss Human Geographies Lecture 2019 Tourism Troubles: Feminist Political Ecologies of Land and Body in Panama." *Geographica Helvetica* 77, no. 3 (2022): 327–340.

References

Benson, Michaela Caroline. 2013. "Postcoloniality and Privilege in New Lifestyle Flows: The Case of North Americans in Panama." *Mobilities* 8 (3): 313–330.

Borras, Saturnino M., Jr., and Jennifer C. Franco. 2012. "Global Land Grabbing and Trajectories of Agrarian Change: A Preliminary Analysis." *Journal of Agrarian Change* 12 (1): 34–59.

Bourgois, Philippe. 1989. *Ethnicity at Work: Divided Labor on a Central American Banana Plantation*. Baltimore, MD: John Hopkins University Press.

Cabnal, Lorena. 2016. "De las opresiones a las emancipaciones: Mujeres indígenas en defensa del territorio cuerpo-tierra" [From oppression to emancipation: Indigenous women in defense of their body-land territory]. *Biodiversidadla*. Accessed January 29, 2024. https://www.biodiversidadla.org/Documentos/De_las_opresiones_a_las_emancipaciones_Mujeres_indigenas_en_defensa_del_territorio_cuerpo-tierra.

Christian, Michelle, and Assumpta Namaganda. 2018. "Transnational Intersectionality and Domestic Work: The Production of Ugandan Intersectional Racialized and Gendered Domestic Worker Regimes." *International Sociology* 33 (3): 315–336.

Correia, Joel E. 2022. "Between Flood and Drought: Environmental Racism, Settler Waterscapes, and Indigenous Water Justice in South America's Chaco." *Annals of the American Association of Geographers* 112 (7): 1–21.

Day, Iyko. 2015. "Being or Nothingness: Indigeneity, Antiblackness, and Settler Colonial Critique." *Critical Ethnic Studies* 1 (2): 102–121. https://doi.org/10.5749/jcritethnstud.1.2.0102.

De Leeuw, Sarah. 2016. "Tender Grounds: Intimate Visceral Violence and British Columbia's Colonial Geographies." *Political Geography* 52:14–23.

Diez Castillo, Luis. 1981. *Los Cimarrones y Los Negros Antillanos en Panama* [Maroons and Black Antillians in Panama] 2nd ed. Panama: Julio Mercado Rudas.

Devine, Jennifer A. 2017. "Colonizing Space and Commodifying Place: Tourism's Violent Geographies." *Journal of Sustainable Tourism* 25 (5): 634–650.

Doshi, Sapana. 2017. "Embodied Urban Political Ecology: Five Propositions." *Area* 49:125–128.

Emard, Kelsey, and Lise Nelson. 2021. "Geographies of Global Lifestyle Migration: Towards an Anticolonial Approach." *Progress in Human Geography* 45 (5): 1040–1060.

Goeman, Mishuna. 2009. "Notes toward a Native Feminism's Spatial Practice." *Wicazo Sa Review* 24 (2): 169–187.

Gomez, Ileana, Susan Kandel, and Wilfredo Moran. 2009. "Conflictos y respuestas territoriales frente al auge inmobiliario del turismo: El caso del Archipiélago de Bocas del Toro" [Conflicts and territorial responses to the tourism-generated real estate boom: The case of Bocas del Toro Archipelago], PRISMA, San Salvador." San Salvador: PRISMA. http://www.prisma.org.sv/index.php.

Gott, Richard. 2007. "Latin America as a White Settler Society." *Bulletin of Latin American Research* 26 (2): 269–289.

Guerrón Montero, Carla. 2005. "Marine Protected Areas in Panama: Grassroots Activism and Advocacy." *Human Organization* 64 (4): 360–373. https://doi.org/10.17730/humo.64.4.2mx2j6qdoxyg1rqv.

Guerrón Montero, Carla. 2014. "Multicultural Tourism, Demilitarization, and the Process of Peace Building in Panama." *Journal of Latin American and Caribbean Anthropology* 19 (3): 418–440.

Hall, Derek. 2013. "Primitive Accumulation, Accumulation by Dispossession and the Global Land Grab." *Third World Quarterly* 34 (9): 1582–1604.

Hartman, Saidiya. 1997. *Scenes of Subjection: Terror, Slavery, and Self-Making in Nineteenth-Century America*. New York: Oxford University Press.

Hartman, Saidiya. 2016. "The Belly of the World: A Note on Black Women's Labors." *Souls* 18 (1): 166–173. https://doi.org/10.1080/10999949.2016.1162596.

Hayes, Matthew. 2015. "Introduction: The Emerging Lifestyle Migration Industry and Geographies of Transnationalism, Mobility and Displacement in Latin America." *Journal of Latin American Geography* 14 (1): 7–18.

Herrera, Francisco. 2012. "La evolución de las demandas indígenas sobre la tierra y las respuestas del Estado en Panamá" [The evolution of Indigenous demands for land and responses from the Panamanian State]. *Quaderns-e de l'Institut Català d'Antropologia* 17 (1): 44–59.

Himley, Matthew. 2019. "Extractivist Geographies: Mining and Development in Late-Nineteenth and Early-Twentieth-Century Peru." *Latin American Perspectives* 46 (2): 27–46.

International Finance Corporation. 2017. *Twenty Reasons Sustainable Tourism Counts for Development*. Washington, DC: World Bank. Accessed December 30, 2021. https://openknowledge.worldbank.org/handle/10986/28388.

Jordan, Osvaldo. 2008. "I Entered during the Day, and Came Out during the Night: Power, Environment, and Indigenous Peoples in a Globalizing Panama." *Tennessee Journal of Law and Policy* 4:467.

King, Tiffany L. 2016. "The Labor of (Re)reading Plantation Landscapes Fungible(ly): Fungibility." *Antipode* 48 (4): 1022–1039. https://doi.org/10.1111/anti.12227.

King, Tiffany L. 2019. *The Black Shoals: Offshore Formations of Black and Native Studies*. Durham, NC: Duke University Press.

Klytchnikova, Irina, and Paul Dorosh. 2013. "Tourism Sector in Panama: Regional Economic Impacts and the Potential to Benefit the Poor." *Natural Resources Forum* 37 (2): 70–79.

Koehler-Geib, Friederike, Kinnon Scott, Ayat Soliman, and Humberto Lopez. 2015. "Panama: Locking in Success." World Bank eLibrary. https://elibrary.worldbank.org/doi/epdf/10.1596/K8332.

Kothari, Uma. 2015. "Reworking Colonial Imaginaries in Post-colonial Tourist Enclaves." *Tourist Studies* 15 (3): 248–266.

Lasso, Marixa. 2019. *Erased: The Untold Story of the Panama Canal*. Cambridge, MA: Harvard University Press.

Loperena, Christopher A. 2017. "Settler Violence? Race and Emergent Frontiers of Progress in Honduras." *American Quarterly* 69 (4): 801–807.

Lowe, Lisa. 2015. *The Intimacies of Four Continents*. Durham, NC: Duke University Press.

Lugones, Maria. 2007. "Heterosexualism and the Colonial / Modern Gender System." *Hypatia* 22 (1): 186–209. https://doi.org/10.1111/j.1527-2001.2007.tb01156.x.

Lugones, María. 2010. "Toward a Decolonial Feminism." *Hypatia* 25 (4): 742–759.

Lunstrum, Elizabeth. 2016. "Green Grabs, Land Grabs and the Spatiality of Displacement: Eviction from Mozambique's Limpopo National Park." *Area* 48 (2): 142–152.

McClintock, Anne. 1995. *Imperial Leather: Race, Gender, and Sexuality in the Colonial Contest.* New York: Routledge.

McKittrick, Katherine. 2006. *Demonic Grounds: Black Women and the Cartographies of Struggle.* Minneapolis: University of Minnesota Press.

McKittrick, Katherine. 2013. "Plantation Futures." *Small Axe: A Caribbean Journal of Criticism* 17:1–15. https://doi.org/10.1215/07990537-2378892.

Mehta, Lyla, Gert Jan Veldwisch, and Jennifer Franco. 2012. "Introduction to the Special Issue: Water Grabbing? Focus on the (Re)appropriation of Finite water Resources." *Water Alternatives* 5 (2): 193–207.

Milazzo, Marzia. 2012. "White Supremacy, White Knowledge, and Anti–West Indian Discourse in Panama: Olmedo Alfaro's *El peligro antillano en la América Central*." *Global South* 6 (2): 65–86.

Mollett, Sharlene. 2016. "The Power to Plunder: Rethinking Land Grabbing in Latin America." *Antipode* 48 (2): 412–432. https://doi.org/10.1111/anti.12190.

Mollett, Sharlene. 2017. "Irreconcilable Differences? A Postcolonial Intersectional Reading of Gender, Development and Human Rights in Latin America." *Gender Place and Culture* 24 (1): 1–17. https://doi.org/10.1080/0966369X.2017.1277292. https://doi.org/10.1177/2514848620907470.

Mollett, Sharlene. 2021. "Hemispheric, Relational, and Intersectional Political Ecologies of Race: Centring Land-Body Entanglements in the Americas." *Antipode* 53 (3): 810–830, https://doi.org/10.1111/anti.12696.

Mollett, Sharlene. 2023. "Racial Geographies of Land and Domestic Service in Panama." *Annals of the American Association of Geographers* 113 (7): 1573–1588.

Mollett, Sharlene, and Caroline Faria. 2013. "Messing with Gender in Feminist Political Ecology." *Geoforum* 45:116–125. https://doi.org/10.1016/j.geoforum.2012.10.009.

Morgan, Jennifer. 2004. *Laboring Women: Reproduction and Gender in New World Slavery.* University of Pennsylvania Press.

Morgensen, Scott Lauria. 2010. "Settler Homonationalism: Theorizing Settler Colonialism within Queer Modernities." *GLQ: A Journal of Lesbian and Gay Studies* 16 (1–2): 105–131. https://doi.org/10.1215/10642684-2009-015.

Mullings, Beverley. 2022. "Racial Capitalism, Coloniality and the Financialization of Caribbean Remittances." *Environment and Planning A: Economy and Space* 54 (4): 744–760.

Nascimento, Maria Beatriz. 1985. «O Conceito de Quilombola ea Resistencia Afro-Brasileira.» *Afrodiaspora* 6–7: 41–49.

Newton, Velma. (1984). *The Silver Men: West Indian Labour Migration to Panama, 1850–1914.* Kingston, Jamaica: Ian Randle Publishers.

Offen, Karl. 2004. "Historical Political Ecology: An Introduction." *Historical Geography* 32: 19–42.

Offen, Karl. 2012. "Historical Geography I: Vital Traditions." *Progress in Human Geography* 36 (4): 527–540.

Ojeda, Diana. 2012. "Green Pretexts: Ecotourism, Neoliberal Conservation and Land Grabbing in Tayrona National Natural Park, Colombia." *The Journal of Peasant Studies* 39 (2): 357–375.

O'Reggio, Trevor. 2006. *Between Alienation and Citizenship: The Evolution of Black West Indian Society in Panama 1914–1964.* Lanham, MD: University Press of America.

Prado, Anayasi, dir. 2011. *Paraiso for Sale*. Documentary film. Impacto Films. Available on Kanopy. https://www.kanopy.com/en/product/paraiso-sale-growing-migration-panama. Accessed July 19, 2022.

Pulido, Laura. 2018. "Geographies of Race and Ethnicity III: Settler Colonialism and Nonnative People of Color." *Progress in Human Geography* 42 (2): 309–318.

Putnam, Lara. 2002. *The Company They Kept: Migrants and the Politics of Gender in Caribbean Costa Rica, 1870–1960*. Chapel Hill: University of North Carolina Press.

Quijano, Aníbal. 2007. "Coloniality and Modernity/Rationality." *Cultural Studies* 21 (2–3): 168–178.

Radcliffe, Sarah A. 2015. *Dilemmas of Difference: Indigenous Women and the Limits of Postcolonial Development Policy*. Durham, NC: Duke University Press.

Red Frog Beach Island Resort and Spa. Columbus Discovery of Bocas Del Toro. Accessed June 23, 2018. https://web.archive.org/web/20180922165614/http:/redfrogrealestate.com/columbus-discovery-of-bocas-del-toro/.

Reid, Charles. 1983. "Folkloric History of Bocas del Toro. Book 2, Bocas Town, Colon Island." Unpublished manuscript. Bocas Public Library.

Runk, Julie Velásquez. 2012. "Indigenous Land and Environmental Conflicts in Panama: Neoliberal Multiculturalism, Changing Legislation, and Human Rights." *Journal of Latin American Geography* 11 (2): 21–47. https://doi.org/10.1353/lag.2012.0036.

Santos de Araújo, Flávia. 2016. "Beyond the Flesh: Contemporary Representations of the Black Female Body in Afro-Brazilian Literature." *Meridians* 14 (1): 148–176. https://doi.org/10.2979/meridians.14.1.10.

Simpson, Audra. 2016. "The State Is a Man: Theresa Spence, Loretta Saunders and the Gender of Settler Sovereignty." *Theory & Event* 19 (4). https://www.muse.jhu.edu/article/633280.

Smith, Christen Anne. 2016. "Towards a Black Feminist Model of Black Atlantic Liberation: Remembering Beatriz Nascimento." *Meridians* 14 (2): 71–87. https://doi.org/10.2979/meridians.14.2.06.

Spalding, Ana K. 2011. "Re-making Lives Abroad: Lifestyle Migration and Socio-Environmental Change in Bocas Del Toro, Panama." PhD diss., University of California, Santa Cruz.

Spalding, Ana. K. 2017. "Exploring the Evolution of Land Tenure and land Use Change in Panama: Linking Land Policy with Development Outcomes." *Land Use Policy* 61:543–552. https://doi.org/10.1016/j.landusepol.2016.11.023.

Speed, Shannon. 2017. "Structures of Settler Capitalism in Abya Yala." *American Quarterly* 69 (4): 783–790.

Spillers, H. J. 1987. "Mama's Baby, Papa's Maybe: An American Grammar Book." *Diacritics* 17 (2): 65–81.

Stephens, Clyde. 2008. *Outline of History of the Province of Bocas del Toro, Panama*. Eutis, FL: SPS Publications.

Stephens, Clyde. 1997. *History of Hospital Point, Pioneer Medical Centre, 1899–1920*. Bocas del Toro, Panama: Banana Book Company.

Stoler, Ann Laura. 2016. *Duress: Imperial Durabilities in Our Times*. Durham, NC: Duke University Press.

Sultana, Farhana. 2011. "Suffering *for* Water, Suffering *from* Water: Emotional Geographies of Resource Access, Control and Conflict." *Geoforum* 42 (2): 163–172. https://doi.org/10.1016/j.geoforum.2010.12.002.

Swaby, Aliyya. 2014. "Is Racism Behind the Panama's Canal Zone Land Grabs?" *Equal Times*. Accessed December, 30, 2014. https://www.equaltimes.org/is-racism-behind-panama-s-canal#.YcznZmjMKUk.

Thampy, Gayatri. 2013. "Indigenous Contestations of Shifting Property Regimes: Land Conflicts and the Ngobe in Bocas del Toro, Panama." PhD diss., Ohio State University.

United Nations Development Program (UNDP). 2013. *Percepción y autopercepción de la población afropanameña*. Accessed July 19, 2022. https://www.undp.org/es/panama/publications/percepci%C3%B3n-y-autopercepci%C3%B3n-de-la-poblaci%C3%B3n-afropaname%C3%B1a.

van Noorloos, Femke. 2013. "Residential Tourism and Multiple Mobilities: Local Citizenship and Community Fragmentation in Costa Rica." *Sustainability-Basel* 5 (2): 570–589. https://doi.org/10.3390/su5020570.

Watson, Sonja Stephenson. 2012. "Poetic Negrism and the National Sentiment of Anti-West Indianism and Anti-Imperialism in Panamanian Literature." *Callaloo* 35 (2): 459–474. https://doi.org/10.1353/cal.2012.0067.

Wickstrom, Stefanie. 2003. "The Politics of Development in Indigenous Panama." *Latin American Perspectives* 30 (4): 43–68.

Wolfe, Patrick. 2006. "Settler Colonialism and the Elimination of the Native." *Journal of Genocide Research* 8 (4): 387–409. https://doi.org/10.1080/14623520601056240.

Women's Earth Alliance and Native Youth Sexual Health Network. 2016. *Violence on the Land, Violence on our Bodies: Building an Indigenous Response to Environmental Violence*. Report. Berkeley, CA, and Toronto: WEA and NYSHN. http://landbodydefense.org/uploads/files/VLVBReportToolkit2016.pdf?.

World Bank. 2009. "Panama Land Administration Project: *Inspection Panel Investigation Report (Loan No. 7045-PAN)*. Last Accessed January 29, 2024. https://documents.worldbank.org/en/publication/documents-reports/documentdetail/699921468331799752/panama-land-administration-project-inspection-panel-investigation-report.

World Tourism Organization. 2018. *Tourism for Development*. Vol. 1: *Key Areas for Action*. Madrid: United Nations World Tourism Organization. https://www.e-unwto.org/doi/book/10.18111/9789284419722.

World Travel and Tourism Council (WTTC). 2017. *Travel and Tourism: Economic Impact 2017 Panama*. London: World Travel and Tourism Council.

Ybarra, Megan. 2018. *Green Wars: Conservation and Decolonization in the Maya Forest*. Oakland: University of California Press.

Zaragocin, Sofia. 2019. "Gendered Geographies of Elimination: Decolonial Feminist Geographies in Latin American Settler Contexts." *Antipode* 51 (1): 373–392. https://doi.org/10.1111/anti.12454.

CHAPTER 29

ETHNIC POLITICS AND LAND GRABBING

TSEGAYE MOREDA

Introduction

This chapter argues that the contemporary global land rush has impacted the social relations that regulate land access and livelihoods, which, in turn, contribute to the heightening of existing interethnic tensions and conflicts. Since recent large-scale land acquisitions have almost always targeted the productive land and other landed resources of poor rural people, they constitute a direct threat to not only the reproduction of the social and economic lives of rural populations, but also their identities (Borras et al. 2011; Wolford et al. 2024; Neef et al. 2023). Across Africa, access to and control over land resources often reflect and are shaped by ethnically stratified citizenship and belonging (Mamdani 2001). This has become particularly evident during the most recent phenomenon of global land grabbing. As Catherine Boone (2015) rightly noted, "Changes in the political-economic context over the course of the last few decades, especially rising pressure on the land and heightening tensions between commercial investors and smallholders, are fueling a new era of land politics and land-related conflict" (173). Yet the ethnic dimension of the political conflict over land is currently underexplored. Initial studies show that ethnicity-based tensions around land grabs may be more widespread than has previously been assumed. A recent study examining the effects of large-scale land acquisitions on ethnic grievances and conflicts, based on data for 133 countries collected from 2000 to 2012, shows that large-scale land acquisitions are associated with a higher risk of ethnic tension and conflict (Krieger and Meierrieks 2016). The study emphasized that this may be due to increased land scarcity and the patterns of competition this engenders, environmental degradation, increased food insecurity, and the evictions of existing land users that are associated with land grabs. That is, ethnic tensions and conflicts may result from diminishing land resources and the reduced opportunities for social and economic reproduction for poor people that land grabbing causes or aggravates. This is certainly true in many ways, but these issues are also rooted in the wider political economy.

In contemporary Ethiopia, as embodied in its current constitution, ethnicity has been a key element of social differentiation and a source of political power and privilege. This has profound implications for land, and shapes how land rights are defined, distributed, and claimed among social groups. Although the law in Ethiopia guarantees the right to a piece of land to all citizens living in rural areas who aspire to engage in farming, in practice, land access is tightly bound up with ethnicity, and groups who are not indigenous to a particular ethnic homeland may face exclusion or constrained access rights. For example, in the Oromia region, being an Oromo or Amhara makes a difference in terms of getting priority and opportunity to access land. The region is identified as a homeland for the Oromo ethnic group, and the Amhara and others who reside in this region but are not ethnically Oromo are viewed as non-Indigenous ethnic minorities and can be disenfranchised. Similarly, members of the Oromo ethnic group who reside outside the homeland are identified as minorities in those places and may face disenfranchisement.

In many African countries, as Boone (2007) argues, "Today's land questions also lie at the core of a complex bundle of constitutional issues," emphasizing the need to pay "much attention to the constitutional aspects of land politics" (557–558). The 1994 Constitution of Ethiopia reorganized the country into a federation of nine ethnically defined regional states and two federally administered city-states. The constitution also demands that each ethnicity has its own regional state/homeland. This means that the number of ethnically defined regional states will continue to grow, as the recent creation of the Sidama region, the Southwest Ethiopia region, the South Ethiopia region, and the Central Ethiopia region illustrates. These four new regions were carved out of the Southern Nations, Nationalities, and Peoples Region (SNNPR) between 2018 and 2023. And the process involves the redrawing of more internal administrative boundaries. Unsurprisingly, a significant number of other ethnic groups are currently also demanding the right to form their own regional states. The critical problem is that as the number of regional states expands, the number of ethnicized minorities—and thus the number of political minorities with second-class citizenship or who are considered marginal subjects in each regional state—proliferates. For example, when the Sidama region was created from the multi-ethnic SNNPR as a homeland for the Sidama ethnic group, members of all other ethnic groups residing in the territory that makes up the new region, which includes Hawassa, which was the capital of the then SNNPR, emerged as new minorities in the region. The constitution defines ethnicity as the basis of rights: that is, rights to land, political rights, political justice, political representations, government jobs, and so on, is based on being considered ethnically indigenous (indigeneity) to a particular regional ethnic state rather than on Ethiopian citizenship. Under this system of ethnic federalism, political identities are defined first and foremost in relation to ethnicity. These identities "shape our relationship to the state and to one another through the state," and they "need to be understood as specifically a consequence of the history of state formation" (Mamdani 2001, 662–663). As Mahmood Mamdani put it, "The politicization of ethnicity create[s] an enfranchised majority alongside disenfranchised minorities in each [regional ethnic states]" (Mamdani [1996] 2018, xviii; 2001). The implication of this for land politics is profound.

Mamdani's *Citizen and Subject* ([1996] 2018) remains a powerful theoretical handle for understanding the current dynamics of ethnic politics and interethnic conflict over land and power. In much of Africa, the politicization of ethnicity is linked to the legacy of British colonial rule. The colonial powers established "indirect rule" as a mechanism for fragmenting the colonized population (and the capacity for resistance) into many minorities, whereby internally partitioned territories/land and ethnic groups were created and turned into local administrative units. Indirect rule fragmented entire colonies into various ethnically demarcated homelands where authority based on customary law was enforced, which conferred such privileges as access to land and other rights on the members of the ethnic group deemed indigenous to that homeland, at the expense of non-Indigenous ethnic minorities. Members of the "official" Indigenous groups who moved out of their ethnic homelands were not considered indigenous to other homelands and risked being disenfranchised in their new lands. The issue was that ethnic groups did not necessarily live and work only in their homelands but were dispersed across the country for different reasons including to find work, which meant they would be subordinates whenever they moved to live and work outside their homeland. Because most African countries are multi-ethnic, this system endlessly creates ethnic minorities and perpetuates fragmentations based on ethnicity in each country. As Mamdani ([1996] 2018) argued, "The latest development along these lines has been the introduction of 'ethnic federalism' in Ethiopia" (xii). Although Ethiopia has never been colonized, by introducing ethnic federalism, it has, in a way, replicated the British colonial system of indirect rule (Mamdani 2019). As a consequence, every part of the country is now divided into the ethnic homelands or regions of particular ethnic groups, creating a majority and minorities in each homeland/region. This has profound implications for the land rights of minorities (see Lavers 2018). Note that the reason for establishing a decentralized federal system in Ethiopia may have been entirely understandable and appropriate as a way to reverse a century-old trend of the centralization of state power; the problem lies in the choice to create a federal system based on ethnic constituencies that has bred competitive ethnic politics (Markakis 2011, Mamdani [1996] 2018). The goal may have been to address ethnic marginalization and promote equality; however, this system has actually generated the inequality that has become a source of ethnic tension and conflict. In this context, the impacts of land grabs are usually unevenly distributed among ethnic groups. Land grabs can generate new patterns of inequality that become sources of interethnic competitions and conflicts or heighten existing ones.

Still, though ethnicity is a key determining factor in land access and control and conflict dynamics in Ethiopia, it is not the only one. In the contemporary context of increased demand for land across the country, access to land is increasingly mediated through intertwined and constitutive relationships of ethnicity, class, generation, and gender that unfold within state-society interactions. In fact, ethnicity gets activated and manipulated through these co-constitutive interactions. It was in contexts shaped by these constitutive relationships around land that the contemporary land rush started to unfold in Ethiopia more than a decade ago, leading in many parts of the country to land grabbing on an unprecedented scale (Rahmato 2011; Lavers 2012). It is therefore crucial to investigate structural, institutional, and political changes that may have been accelerated, caused, or unleashed by the contemporary land rush over the last decades, and to examine the related political consequences, including the recasting of interethnic relations, conflicts, and citizenship rights (Borras and Franco 2024). Explicitly, it is imperative to investigate not only how the contemporary land rush and the ensuing and continuing land grabbing affect land access, food security, and livelihoods through the specter of displacement and dispossession, but also how they may reshape the character and nature of ethnic conflicts over land and create new "subjects."

This chapter argues that the tensions and conflicts we see today across much of Ethiopia have been generated by ethnic competition and rivalries over the control of land and power enabled and reinforced by the ethnic federal system. At the same time, these conflicts are increasingly intertwined with, and cannot be separated from, national and global dynamics and trajectories of capitalist development that are engendering commodification and large-scale acquisitions of land and resources by the state and capital. Such large-scale land acquisitions lead to displacements, dispossessions, and widespread rights violations that, in turn, produce and intensify the land struggles, tensions, social exclusions, and insecurity that lead to interethnic conflict and violence.

Interethnic Competition and Conflict over Land in Ethiopia

Conflict over land resources in Ethiopia is not a new phenomenon. A large body of literature documents widespread conflict in Ethiopia over land resources within and between ethnic groups, farmers and pastoralists/agro-pastoralists, rural households, genders, generations, and urban and peri-urban land users and state authorities, and contestations between state authorities at various levels, investors, and local land users, and so on (see Abbink 2006; Tafesse 2007; Yusuf 2019; Barata 2019; Lavers 2018; Cochrane and Legault 2020; Moreda 2023; Rahmato 2011). Abbink (2006), for example, found that most of the conflicts in Ethiopia have been land and border disputes between territorialized ethnic groups on either side of the ethnically delineated regional states. In the wake of recent state-facilitated land grabs, these land-related conflicts appear to be intensifying, and land-related conflict, violence, and displacement have occurred on an unprecedented scale. Many of these conflicts and the violence and ensuing displacements that continue to make headlines often have an ethnic character and are ethnic conflicts over land and power (Yusuf 2019; Lavers 2018). They have generated staggering numbers of internally displaced people (IDPs) in the last few years and continue to cause forced expulsions. For example, although the causes of the recent catastrophic civil war in the Tigray region, which claimed the lives of hundreds of thousands of people, are multifaceted and conjunctural (especially the fallout between the regional government and the federal government), the conflict ultimately boiled down to the question of land, and specifically to the long-running claims and disputes between the Tigray and the Amhara regional states over the agriculturally fertile areas of the Wolkayit, Tsegede, and Raya districts. The two-year civil war ended with a peace agreement, signed in November 2022, between the Tigray regional administration and the federal government, but the land question in these highly contested areas between the Amhara and Tigray regions has not yet been resolved. The potential for conflict to break out again remains a major concern.

There were over 4.5 million IDPs in Ethiopia at the end of 2022, with conflict and violence accounting for over 3.8 million of these. In 2022 alone, over two million internal displacements due to conflict and violence were recorded in Ethiopia (Internal Displacement Monitoring Centre 2023, 137). This figure is likely to rise due to the ongoing conflict within the Amhara and Oromia regions. Aside from the violent civil war in the Tigray region, other widespread violent conflicts and displacements have occurred across several regional states, including the Oromia, Amhara, Benishangul-Gumuz, Gambella, Somali, Afar, and regions carved out of the then SNNPR. Although these conflicts have an ethnic dimension and manifest as such, the underlying causes run deeper and include the firm entrenchment of "exclusivist and authoritarian political institutions" (Yusuf 2019; see also Abbink 2006). Indeed, interethnic conflict and violence are not uncommon in post-1991 Ethiopia (Berhane and Tefera 2018; Beyene 2017; Tache and Oba 2016; Adugna 2011; Aalen 2011; Kefale 2010; Abbink 2006), where the issue of access to and control of land resources is linked to broader social, political, and economic relations and processes on multiple levels.

As already noted, the pressure on land resources in Ethiopia is increasing because of the high demand for access to farmland and pasture required for social reproduction and the growing demand for urbanization, industrial projects, mining, conservation, large-scale agricultural projects, and infrastructure projects. Since 2007 in particular, a surge in demand for land is associated with the global land rush. Contestations over land in varied forms and involving various actors proliferate as land values rise and patterns of land access become increasingly commercialized. Land claims and contestations are then framed or articulated and manifest along social fault lines, which are often characterized by the dynamics of social division, inclusion, and exclusion. The issue is, in fact, more than just about the expanding demand for land. Ethiopia is "a multi-ethnic and multi-nation state where nationality and culture are intimately tied to place" (wa Githinji and Mersha 2007, 310). Questions of land are intimately linked to ethnicity, citizenship, and the state and are therefore complex and often historically, socially, and politically embedded. As discussed earlier, ethnic groups often have distinct claims over territory and recognition. Their claims for territorial rights are shaped by and, in turn, shape the character and trajectory of state-citizen relations and citizenship rights. Land conflicts are structured by institutions and occur within given territorial jurisdictions; thus they involve political actors (Lund 2016). As such, the question of land is perhaps the single most crucial and highly contested arena where conflicts over political power and the legitimacy of complex layers of competing claims to authority are played out, and where state-society interaction is restructured.

However, if conflicts over land resources are often framed and fought over as ethnic conflicts, overemphasizing their ethnic character conceals the multiple complex and intersecting processes that also underlie land conflicts in Ethiopia. I argue that it is precisely the interaction of the co-constitutive variables of ethnicity, class, and generational issues with the dynamics of land grabbing and linkage to political elites and (trans)national capital that is producing ethnic and class-based rent-seeking and new patterns of social differentiation, marginalization, and displacement that are leading to conflicts over land.

Recent studies from many parts of Africa have revealed the role of land grabbing by varied actors (domestic and foreign investors, the state, etc.) in heightening social conflicts over land in many rural and peri-urban areas since the late 2000s (Abebe 2020; Tufa, Amsalu, and Zoomers 2018; Lavers 2018; Martiniello 2019; Bukari and Kuusaana 2018; Ndi and Batterbury 2017; Askew, Maganga, and Odgaard 2013; Peters 2013). Land grabs resulting from the recent land rush not only cause displacement and the loss of valuable resources for existing land users, but also result in conflict that, in turn, "produces stricter definitions of those with legitimate claims to resources, that is, group boundaries become more exclusively defined" (Peters 2013, 11). Land issues have always been highly contested in Africa. However, since the 2000s increased land commodification, the widespread land and land-based resources grab, and intensified contestations over land that are "sometimes violent and exclusionary" have become key "forces that are accelerating changes in state-society relations" across much of the continent (Boone 2013, 199). Similarly, recent studies of the dynamics of land grabbing in Ethiopia reveal that land grabs by state and corporate actors have displaced people, undermined local people's ability to obtain a livelihood from land resources, and caused or unleashed conflicts between and among social groups (Bekele et al. 2022; Wondimu and Gebresenbet 2018; Wayessa 2020; Moreda 2015; Shete and Rutten 2015; Rahmato 2011). Wondimu and Gebresenbet (2018), for example, highlight how land deals have fed into and exacerbated existing interethnic tensions and conflict between the Suri and Dizi people of Southern Ethiopia. In 2012, a violent clash between these two neighboring ethnic groups, which claimed many lives, was triggered when local authorities tried to demarcate a contested piece of borderland for a Malaysian-company-owned plantation (see also Wagstaff 2015 and Abbink 1993 for background on the long-running interethnic conflict between the Dizi and Suri people).

Similarly, though the largest ethnic groups in Gambella regional state, the Anywa and the Nuer, have fought violent and protracted conflicts over land resources in the past, the recent expansion of large-scale land acquisitions in the region have contributed to intensifying such conflicts and triggered new conflict dynamics involving other actors, such as investors and migrant farmworkers from other parts of the country (Ojulu 2013). The expansion of state-facilitated large-scale agricultural investments in the region, which often prioritizes the interests of outside investors, has undermined the land rights of Indigenous ethnic groups. The threat of interethnic conflict associated with these dynamics is therefore ongoing in the region.

A similar dynamic has also been documented in the Benishangul-Gumuz regional state, where the grabbing of land claimed by Indigenous ethnic groups has been facilitated by federal and regional state authorities and has become a flashpoint for conflicts between these groups and the state and outside actors, including investors and seasonal migrant farmworkers, particularly over land and access to employment and state politics (Moreda 2015). Recent expansions of commercial farms have resulted in a large influx of seasonal agricultural wage laborers' migrating from the central highlands of the Amhara region, causing tensions with the local Indigenous ethnic groups that at times escalate into violent confrontations and clashes. In this regard, the proliferation of large-scale land investments in Benishangul-Gumuz, which has been one of the main areas for land investment in Ethiopia, has led to opportunistic efforts by seasonal migrant farmworkers to acquire land in the areas where they go to seek wage work. These migrant workers not only work as seasonal agricultural laborers; they also take the opportunity to squat in those areas as a strategy to lay claim to the communal lands, including the forestlands, of the local Indigenous communities. The creation of these "illegal" squatter settlements has generated bitter resentment and conflict with the local communities, particularly with the Gumuz ethnic groups, who see their communal land resources diminishing and fear that they will not have much land left for their children. The seasonal migrant farmworkers turned "illegal settlers" mainly belong to the Amhara ethnic group, and they hope to lay claim to permanent access and control of the land they are on once they have occupied and farmed it for a few years. This has led to several instances of violent attacks and killings. The Gumuz have resisted the influx of migrant workers, and not just to prevent their encroachment on local land resources, but also to undermine land investment projects by denying the investors access to labor. The local authorities consider the "illegal settlements" to be major challenges to the peace and security of the area (Moreda 2015). In fact, the Benishangul-Gumuz region has a history of interethnic tensions and conflicts. This can be partly attributed to the central state's resettlement schemes in the 1980s that moved tens of thousands of people from other parts of the country into the region and resulted in competition and conflict centered on land and resources (Abbute 2002; Yntiso 2001). Current contestations around land grabs often turn to these historical precedents and trajectories as important factors shaping the contemporary processes and struggles. In this sense, it is critical, as Berry (2002) noted, "to emphasize the importance of situating land struggles in specific historical contexts, taking account of the way multiple interests and categories of people come into play, and impinge on one another, as people seek to acquire, defend, and exercise claims on land" (640).

Ethnic Conflicts Centered on the Conversion of Farmland for Urban Land Use

It should be noted that land conflicts are not always centered on land for commercial agricultural purposes. Another aspect central to conflict over land involves the conversion of farmland for urban land uses, particularly urban expansion that entails the appropriation of peri-urban and rural land. A case in point is the recent conflict and large-scale political mobilization that was sparked by the unveiling, in 2014, of the Addis Ababa Master Plan, which sought to extend the territory of the capital city into the surrounding areas in the Oromia regional state. This would have resulted in complex and competing claims to land and authority. The Oromo resented the plan, particularly the young people, who viewed it as a further attempt to expropriate their land and territory. Although the Master Plan was eventually dropped, the protests and ethnic mobilizations it had sparked did not stop; instead, they spread to other regions, mainly to the Amhara region, where people mobilized, partly in solidarity with the Oromo protests, but also over their own historical claims to disputed areas on the border of the Amhara region and the Tigray regional state (that is, the Wolkayit and Tsegede area and Raya). During the Oromo protests, residents belonging to non-Indigenous ethnic groups in the Oromia region were attacked and displaced in certain parts of the regional state.[1] The attacks on and displacement of non-Indigenous minority ethnic groups in the Oromia region took the form of politicized ethnic-based land-related violence, pitting members of the Oromo ethnic group against members of the non-Indigenous minority ethnic groups, although all were Ethiopian citizens. It showed the reality of citizenship hierarchies in which those not indigenous to a given officially recognized ethnic homeland/ethnic region have second-class status, lacking not only the economic but also the political rights enjoyed by members of the Indigenous ethnic group. This dynamic has played out in various conflicts in which the ethnic outsiders were the targeted group. Further, this ethnic conflict and violence is taking place in the context of rising pressure on land caused by land acquisitions by large-scale commercial investors, with the result that investment projects and properties are also attacked and vandalized. The attacks targeting the land investment projects themselves demonstrate that land acquisition by commercial investors has not only created ethnic tensions and conflicts but also resulted in class conflict.

Similar dynamics have been documented in the Benishangul-Gumuz region, where, in reaction to large-scale land acquisitions that led to dispossession and displacement, the affected Indigenous ethnic groups targeted the investors by destroying the their field crops and farm machinery and encroached on land the investors had already acquired (Moreda 2015; see Rahmato 2014 for cases in Oromia and Gambella regions). These instances further reveal that land-related conflicts and grievances occur not only along ethnic lines but also along class cleavages. As Lavers (2018) rightly noted, the land conflicts and grievances seen in recent years in much of Ethiopia boil down to "questions of land and territory under ethnic federalism, both in terms of the delineation of ethnoregional borders and the relative prioritization of land access for the indigenous population and outside investors" (464). Although the conflicts and political mobilizations were triggered by threats to land rights and displacements, they were as much about political power, historical marginalization, the legitimacy of overlapping and competing claims to authority, issues of governance and accountability politics, and the high rate of youth unemployment and landlessness as they were about loss of local land rights and livelihoods and the distribution of resources (see Yusuf 2019; Abebe 2020; Abate 2019; Moreda 2018).

Although land in Ethiopia has been under state ownership since 1975, Lavers (2018) pointed out the ambiguities in the land-tenure institutions that remain, particularly regarding the authority of various state and nonstate actors and the continuing influence of the neocustomary land-tenure systems, which still influence land issues in many parts of the country. He argues that the continuing relevance of different land-tenure institutions has implications for questions of citizenship, and that this has partly to do with the ethnic federalism that links ethnicity with territory, which, in turn, has direct implications for the land rights of various ethnic groups and the land conflicts among them. Consequently, ethnic minorities living outside their "home" region are particularly vulnerable in terms of their land rights, and their economic and political rights are also limited. There are numerous and growing cases of the large-scale dispossession and displacement of non-Indigenous ethnic minority groups in Oromia, SNNPR, the Benishangul-Gumuz region, along the Oromia-Somali border area, and in the Amhara-Tigray boundary areas (Yusuf 2019). It should be stressed that the displacements and attacks on the Amhara communities living in the rural parts of the Oromia region, particularly in Wollega, have become widespread. The considerable loss of human life and the large-scale displacement of ethnic minorities across the area have been extensively documented by the Ethiopian Human Rights Council and the Ethiopian Human Rights Commission.

The state's response to the land conflicts that result in the displacement of non-Indigenous ethnic minorities and general uncertainty about their land rights has been to either turn a blind eye or to facilitate their evictions by returning or relocating them to their home regions. This happens despite the ownership of land by the state, which should protect the land rights of ethnic minorities uniformly across the country (Lavers 2018). Boone (2015), explaining a Tanzanian case, notes that local land politics are linked and embedded in national-level institutions and processes under a national statist land regime: "And under the statist land regime, ethnic identities have little salience in making land claims; national identities are mobilised to claim land rights" (185). Of course, the character and underlying causes of ethnic conflict are largely constituted by the state itself, and the state is usually directly implicated in such conflicts. Regardless of its action or inaction in relation to land-related ethnic conflicts and violence, the state is a key actor that contributes to and shapes the course of such conflicts. Evidently, given the existing ethnic-based federalism, ethnic claims, demands, and justifications are constituted in the state structure.

Land-Related Conflicts Surrounding Conservation Projects

Green grabbing—appropriating land and land-based resources for environmental purposes—is a key component of contemporary global land and resource grabbing (Fairhead, Leach, and Scoones 2012). This has consequences for rural people, undermining local livelihoods, violating their rights, reinforcing inequities and social exclusions, and causing land-related conflicts across the global South (Hunsberger et al., 2017; Corbera, Hunsberger, and Vaddhanaphuti 2017). For instance, a study by Bergius et al. (2020) shows how environmental conservation initiatives in Tanzania resulted in the violent eviction of pastoralists that, in turn, led to a spillover of pastoralists into other areas, which then created new farmer-herder and conservation conflicts. Changing land-use patterns, such as the expansions of cash cropping, conservation frontiers, and large-scale commercial agriculture, are increasingly becoming a source of conflict between farmers and pastoralists as they compete over the diminishing land resources produced by these processes (Soeters, Weesie, and Zoomers 2017; Lind, Okenwa, and Scoones 2020). Yet these farmer-pastoralist conflicts are, in a way, also ethnic-group conflicts since being a farmer or a pastoralist in much of Africa is typically tied to ethnic identity, though this is not a rigid pattern (Egwu 1998). In a different context, a study in Cambodia shows how climate change responses are deeply entangled with conflicts over resources: climate change mitigation strategies alter the patterns of access to land and water resources, resulting in insecurity and conflict (Hunsberger, Work, and Herre 2018). Such conflicts are centered on conservation and the associated enclosure of common property resources, as well as a loss of cultivable and grazing land. As Peters (2004) noted, "In light of the intensifying competition over land and landed resources across Africa, it is not surprising that new schemes to promote environmental protection along with benefits to locals have themselves become new resources over which groups compete" (300).

In Ethiopia, initiatives and programs aimed at natural resource conservation, predominantly influenced by "state environmentalism," have been implemented at various levels, mainly since the second half of the 1970s (Admassie 2000; Rahmato 2003; Campbell 1991). More recently, since 2011, the Ethiopian government, as part of its Climate Resilient Green Economy strategy, has been implementing forest conservation and sustainable land-use programs, including those linked to environmental services and climate change mitigation objectives (Federal Democratic Republic of Ethiopia 2011). These primarily include community-based rehabilitation of degraded ecosystems and community-based carbon sequestration projects. Such projects provide means through which Ethiopia in general and local communities in particular can participate in and benefit from global climate finance opportunities, including those linked to clean development mechanisms (CDMs) and Reducing Emissions from Deforestation and Degradation (REDD+; Federal Democratic Republic of Ethiopia 2011). As a result, millions of hectares of land throughout the country have been put under enclosure for rehabilitation since 2011. One government report indicated that by 2014–2015, about 10.9 million hectares of land had been enclosed and rehabilitated, compared to the 3.2 million hectares enclosed in 2009–2010 (National Planning Commission 2016). Certainly, conservation projects, such as community-based watershed development and agroforestry, can positively affect local social groups through benefit-sharing, an overall improvement to ecosystems (e.g., improved soil, water, and forest resources), and enhanced carbon sequestration. Nevertheless, some recent land enclosures and other conservation projects that are underpinned by market mechanisms designed to address global climate change are becoming an arena of contestation and are fueling conflict within and between different groups who may have competing interests and claims to land and forests (Kemerink-Seyoum et al. 2018; Ango 2018). A recent study, for example, suggests that some climate-financed forest conservation projects in Ethiopia may have been "aggravating conflicts over resources as a result of social exclusion, elite capture and even state-sanctioned land grab" (Kemerink-Seyoum et al. 2018, 271). Other studies have also shown how fortress conservation in the Nechisar National Park in Southern Ethiopia has produced conflicts (Nishizaki 2014). Recently, it was reported that the Swiss-based multinational ASC Impact may have acquired an estimated 22,000 hectares of land in the Gambella regional state for large-scale tree plantations, carbon credits, and agriculture. There is concern that the project may already be generating tensions and conflicts (Anywaa Survival Organization 2024).

Overall, the recent land rush has unleashed land grabbing for various purposes, frequently resulting in the displacement and dispossession of local land users, disrupting social relations and social life in general, and often culminating in social conflicts over land. However, the conflicts and contestations that result from the recasting of land use and land-based social relations triggered by the recent land rush should be seen within the context of ongoing broader struggles over social identities (ethnic, gendered, generational, class identities) and the dynamics of the production of subjects and citizens (e.g., Peluso and Lund 2011; Mamdani [1996] 2018). As Boone (2013) argues, it is important to link land conflicts with the role and location of land politics in national political trajectories and to an analysis of the state. It is thus crucial to understand how the dynamics of generation, gender, class, and ethnic relations intersect and overlap with the dynamics of land grabbing to produce dynamics of differentiation, exclusion, marginalization, and displacement that may, in turn, shape land-related conflicts and the character and trajectory of state-citizen relations. In the context of the recent global land rush, as Peters (2013, 20) so nicely put it, "any attempt to understand 'the question of land' in contemporary Africa has to grapple even more than in the past with the dynamics of social transformation at multiple levels—global, regional, national, subnational—that are reshaping not merely access to land itself but the very bases of authority, livelihood, ownership and citizenship."

Conclusion

The recent central-state-facilitated transfer of vast tracts of land to state and private capital (leading to a dramatic increase in the value of land, the pervasive commoditization of communal land, and a reduction in the amount of land available to poor rural people), has profoundly impacted the social relations around land access and land use, with direct implications for the land rights and livelihoods of socially differentiated poor rural people. In many multi-ethnic settings, the ensuing processes of dispossession and displacement have made land an issue of heightening interethnic conflict and violence. These interethnic conflicts and grievances are the result of land use changes and patterns of competition over dwindling resources (especially land) created by these processes. The patterns of land use change are, in turn, partly a reflection of the balance of social forces within the state and society based on ethnicity and class. It should be stressed that although the pressure on land from the state and capital is increasingly prevalent and constitutes a major source of the economic and social grievances that have led to or exacerbated the ethnic tension and conflict, this should not obscure the fact that grievances, conflicts, and protests have also been directed against capitalist classes, the state, and the political elite. The well-documented political reactions and resistance of affected communities against state and foreign and domestic investors in many of the areas affected by land grabs illustrate this (Hall et al. 2015; Borras and Franco 2013; Gerber 2011).

The urgent political and analytical task now is to identify and tackle the mechanisms by which class and political elites' interests use ethnic politics as the most effective mechanism for advancing their own narrow political and economic agenda through demagoguery and by sowing ethnic tension and fragmentation. It is crucial to explore how genuine ethnic grievances, mobilizations, and struggles that may in fact call for far-reaching changes in state policies do not end up as conflicts and violence along ethnic lines, pitting poor people against poor people. More critical investigation is needed to explain how, why, and where struggles over land tend to result in ethnic tensions and conflicts rather than in class conflicts that directly challenge the state and those who benefit from land grabbing.

The consequences of large-scale land and land-based resource acquisitions in recasting social relations and existing patterns of land use, and the role of such acquisitions in engendering ethnic conflicts and fragmentation are certainly profound. Yet they must necessarily be situated and understood in the broader political-economic context of deep-seated resentments around uneven development, access to resources and state power, historical land claims, structural inequalities and marginalizations, and broader questions of democratization. Only then can we understand the complexity and multilayered nature of land-related conflicts that are prevalent today in Ethiopia and much of Africa.

Acknowledgments

I would like to thank Jun Borras and the reviewers for the constructive comments and suggestions on the previous version of this chapter.

Note

1. It is important to note that interethnic relations are not always conflict-based. As we see here, the Oromo protests that were triggered by the plans to expand Addis Ababa into the surrounding Oromo lands ushered in collaborations between the Oromo and the Amhara.

The protests spread to the Amhara region, where the Amhara joined forces, partly in solidarity, mobilizing in mass protests to demand land rights, equal political representation, and an end to rights abuses. This collaboration, which finally forced Ethiopia's then prime minister to resign and brought in a new leadership under the current prime minister, Abiy Ahmed, was named the "Oro-Amhara alliance" by political observers and analysts of Ethiopian politics.

References

Aalen, Lovise. 2011. *The Politics of Ethnicity in Ethiopia: Actors, Power and Mobilisation under Ethnic Federalism*. African Social Studies Series 25. Leiden: Brill.

Abate, Abebe Gizachew. 2019. "The Effects of Land Grabs on Peasant Households: The Case of the Floriculture Sector in Oromia, Ethiopia." *African Affairs* 119 (1): 90–114.

Abbink, Jan. 1993. "Ethnic Conflict in the 'Tribal Zone': The Dizi and Suri in Southern Ethiopia." *Journal of Modern African Studies* 31 (4): 675–682.

Abbink, Jan. 2006. "Ethnicity and Conflict Generation in Ethiopia: Some Problems and Prospects of Ethno-regional Federalism." *Journal of Contemporary African Studies* 24 (3): 389–413.

Abbute, Wolde-Selassie. 2002. "Gumuz and Highland Resettlers: Differing Strategies of Livelihood and Ethnic Relations in Metekel, Northwestern Ethiopia." PhD thesis, University of Göttingen.

Abebe, Tatek. 2020. "Lost Futures? Educated Youth Precarity and Protests in the Oromia Region, Ethiopia." *Children's Geographies* 18 (6): 584–600.

Admassie, Yeraswork. 2000. *Twenty Years to Nowhere: Property Rights, Land Management and Conservation in Ethiopia*. Lawrenceville, NJ: Red Sea Press.

Adugna, Fekadu. 2011. "Overlapping Nationalist Projects and Contested Spaces: The Oromo–Somali Borderlands in Southern Ethiopia." *Journal of Eastern African Studies* 5 (4): 773–787.

Ango, Tola Gemechu. 2018. "'Medium-Scale' Forestland Grabbing in the Southwestern Highlands of Ethiopia: Impacts on Local Livelihoods and Forest Conservation." *Land* 7 (24): 1–20.

Anywaa Survival Organization. 2024. "Indigenous Community Alarmed over a Swiss Company's Large Land Deal for Carbon Plantations in Gambela, Ethiopia." farmlandgrab.org. February 16, 2024. https://farmlandgrab.org/post/32017-indigenous-community-alarmed-over-a-swiss-company-s-large-land-deal-for-carbon-plantations-in-gambela-ethiopia.

Askew, Kelly, Faustin Maganga, and Rie Odgaard. 2013. "Of land and Legitimacy: A Tale of Two Lawsuits." *Africa* 83 (1): 120–141.

Barata, Data D. 2019. *Contesting Inequalities, Identities and Rights in Ethiopia*. New York: Routledge.

Bekele, Adugna Eneyew, Dusan Drabik, Liesbeth Dries, and Wim Heijman. 2022. "Large-Scale Land Investments and Land-Use Conflicts in the Agro-Pastoral Areas of Ethiopia." *Land Use Policy* 119: 106166. https://doi.org/10.1016/j.landusepol.2022.106166.

Bergius, Mikael, Tor A. Benjaminsen, Faustin Maganga, and Halvard Buhaug. 2020. "Green Economy, Degradation Narratives, and Land-Use Conflicts in Tanzania." *World Development* 129: 104850.

Berhane, Zerihun, and Samuel Tefera. 2018. "Does Federalism Reduce Ethnic Conflict? Evidence from the Ethiopian Experience." *Ethiopian Journal of the Social Sciences and Humanities* 14 (1): 105–131.

Berry, Sara. 2002. "Debating the Land Question in Africa." *Comparative Studies in Society and History* 44 (4): 638–668.

Beyene, Fekadu. 2017. "Natural Resource Conflict Analysis among Pastoralists in Southern Ethiopia." *Journal of Peacebuilding & Development* 12 (1): 19–33.

Boone, Catherine. 2007. "Property and Constitutional Order: Land Tenure Reform and the Future of the African State." *African Affairs* 106 (425): 557–586.

Boone, Catherine. 2013. "Land Regimes and the Structure of Politics: Patterns of Land-Related Conflict." *Africa* 83 (1): 188–203.

Boone, Catherine. 2015. "Land Tenure Regimes and State Structure in Rural Africa: Implications for Forms of Resistance to Large-Scale Land Acquisitions by Outsiders." *Journal of Contemporary African Studies* 33 (2): 171–190.

Borras, Saturnino M., Jr., and Jennifer C. Franco. 2013. "Global Land Grabbing and Political Reactions 'from Below.'" *Third World Quarterly* 34 (9): 1723–1747.

Borras, Saturnino M., Jr., and Jennifer C. Franco. 2024. "Land Rush." *Journal of Peasant Studies*. https://doi.org/10.1080/03066150.2024.2317961.

Borras, Saturnino M., Jr., Ruth Hall, Ian Scoones, Ben White, and Wendy Wolford. 2011. "Towards a Better Understanding of Global Land Grabbing: An Editorial Introduction." *Journal of Peasant Studies* 38 (2): 209–216.

Bukari, Kaderi Noagah, and Elias Danyi Kuusaana. 2018. "Impacts of Large-Scale Land Holdings on Fulani Pastoralists' in the Agogo Traditional Area of Ghana." *Land Use Policy* 79: 748–758.

Campbell, John. 1991. "Land or Peasants? The Dilemma Confronting Ethiopian Resource Conservation." *African Affairs* 90 (358): 5–21.

Cochrane, Logan, and Danielle D. Legault. 2020. "The Rush for Land and Agricultural Investment in Ethiopia: What We Know and What We Are Missing." *Land* 9 (167): 1–13. doi:10.3390/land9050167.

Corbera, Esteve, Carol Hunsberger, and Chayan Vaddhanaphuti. 2017. "Climate Change Policies, Land Grabbing and Conflict: Perspectives from Southeast Asia." *Canadian Journal of Development Studies* 38 (3): 297–304.

Egwu, Samuel G. 1998. *Structural Adjustment, Agrarian Change and Rural Ethnicity in Nigeria*. Research Report No. 103. Uppsala: Nordiska Afrikainstitutet.

Fairhead, James, Melissa Leach, and Ian Scoones. 2012. "Green Grabbing: A New Appropriation of Nature?" *Journal of Peasant Studies* 39 (2): 237–261.

Federal Democratic Republic of Ethiopia. 2011. *Ethiopia's Climate-Resilient Green Economy (CRGE) Strategy*. https://www.mofed.gov.et/media/filer_public/9e/23/9e23b2bc-0f3f-4035-ac8a-f0009b5b704a/crge_strategy.pdf. Accessed June 18, 2024.

Gerber, Julien-Francois. 2011. "Conflicts over Industrial Tree Plantations in the South: Who, How and Why?" *Global Environmental Change* 21 (1): 165–176.

Hall, Ruth, Marc Edelman, Saturnino M. Borras Jr., Ian Scoones, Ben White, and Wendy Wolford. 2015. "Resistance, Acquiescence or Incorporation? An Introduction to Land Grabbing and Political Reactions 'from Below.'" *Journal of Peasant Studies* 42 (3–4): 467–488.

Hunsberger, Carol, Esteve Corbera, Saturnino M. Borras Jr., Jennifer C. Franco, Kevin Woods, Courtney Work, et al. 2017. "Climate Change Mitigation, Land Grabbing and Conflict: Towards a Landscape-Based and Collaborative Action Research Agenda." *Canadian Journal of Development Studies* 38 (3): 305–324.

Hunsberger, Carol, Courtney Work, and Roman Herre. 2018. "Linking Climate Change Strategies and Land Conflicts in Cambodia: Evidence from the Greater Aural Region." *World Development* 108:309–320.

Internal Displacement Monitoring Centre. 2023. *Global Report on Internal Displacement 2023: Internal Displacement and Food Security*. Geneva, Switzerland.

Kefale, Asnake. 2010. "Federal Restructuring in Ethiopia: Renegotiating Identity and Borders along the Oromo–Somali Ethnic Frontiers." *Development and Change* 41 (4): 615–635.

Kemerink-Seyoum, J. S., T. M. Tadesse, W. K. Mersha, A. E. C. Duker, and C. De Fraiture. 2018. "Sharing Benefits or Fueling Conflicts? The Elusive Quest for Organizational Blue-Prints in Climate Financed Forestry Projects in Ethiopia." *Global Environmental Change* 53 (1): 265–272.

Krieger, Tim, and Daniel Meierrieks. 2016. "Land Grabbing and Ethnic Conflict." *Journal of Behavioral and Institutional Economics* 33 (3): 243–260.

Lavers, Tom. 2012. "'Land Grab' as Development Strategy? The Political Economy of Agricultural Investment in Ethiopia." *Journal of Peasant Studies* 39 (1): 105–132.

Lavers, Tom. 2018. "Responding to Land-Based Conflict in Ethiopia: The Land Rights of Ethnic Minorities under Federalism." *African Affairs* 117 (468): 462–484.

Lind, Jeremy, Doris Okenwa, and Ian Scoones, eds. 2020. *Land, Investment and Politics: Reconfiguring Eastern Africa's Drylands*. Woodbridge, UK: James Currey.

Lund, Christian. 2016. "Rule and Rupture: State Formation through the Production of Property and Citizenship." *Development and Change* 47 (6): 1199–1228.

Mamdani, Mahmood. 2001. "Beyond Settler and Native as Political Identities: Overcoming the Political Legacy of Colonialism." *Comparative Studies in Society and History* 43 (4): 651–664.

Mamdani, Mahmood. [1996] 2018. *Citizen and Subject: Contemporary Africa and the Legacy of Late Colonialism*. Princeton, NJ: Princeton University Press.

Mamdani, Mahmood. 2019. "The Trouble with Ethiopia's Ethnic Federalism." *New York Times*. January 3, 2019. https://www.nytimes.com/2019/01/03/opinion/ethiopia-abiy-ahmed-reforms-ethnic-conflict-ethnic-federalism.html.

Markakis, John. 2011. *Ethiopia: The Last Two Frontiers*. London: James Currey.

Martiniello, Giuliano. 2019. "Social Conflict and Agrarian Change in Uganda's Countryside." *Journal of Agrarian Change* 19 (1): 550–568.

Moreda, Tsegaye. 2015. "Listening to Their Silence? The Political Reaction of Affected Communities to Large-Scale Land Acquisitions: Insights from Ethiopia." *Journal of Peasant Studies* 42 (3–4): 517–539.

Moreda, Tsegaye. 2018. "The Right to Food in the Context of Large-Scale Land Investment in Ethiopia." *Third World Quarterly* 39 (7): 1326–1347.

Moreda, Tsegaye. 2023. "Beyond Land Rights Registration: Understanding the Mundane Elements of Land Conflicts in Ethiopia." *Journal of Peasant Studies* 50 (5): 1791–1819.

Ndi, Frankline A., and Simon Batterbury. 2017. "Land Grabbing and the Axis of Political Conflicts: Insights from Southwest Cameroon." *Africa Spectrum* 1: 33–63.

Neef, Andreas, Chanrith Ngin, Tsegaye Moreda, and Sharlene Mollett, eds. 2023. *Routledge Handbook of Global Land and Resource Grabbing*. London: Routledge.

Nishizaki, Nobuko. 2014. "'Neoliberal Conservation' in Ethiopia: An Analysis of Current Conflicts in and around Protected Areas and Their Resolution." *African Study Monographs* 50: 191–205.

National Planning Commission. 2016. *Growth and Transformation Plan II (GTP II), 2015/16–2019/20*. National Planning Commission report, May 2016. Federal Democratic Republic of Ethiopia, Addis Ababa.

Ojulu, Ojot Miru. 2013. "Large-Scale Land Acquisitions and Minorities/Indigenous Peoples' Rights under Ethnic Federalism in Ethiopia: A Case Study of Gambella Regional State." PhD thesis, University of Bradford.

Peluso, Nancy Lee, and Christian Lund. 2011. "New Frontiers of Land Control: Introduction." *Journal of Peasant Studies* 38 (4): 667–681.

Peters, Pauline E. 2004. "Inequality and Social Conflict over Land in Africa." *Journal of Agrarian Change* 4 (3): 269–314.

Peters, Pauline E. 2013. "Conflicts over Land and Threats to Customary Tenure in Africa." *African Affairs* 112 (449): 543–562.

Rahmato, Dessalegn. 2003. "Littering the Landscape: Environmental Policy in Northern Ethiopia." In *African Savannas: Global Narratives and Local Knowledge of Environmental Change*, edited by Thomas J. Bassett and Donald Crummey, 205–224. London: James Curry.

Rahmato, Dessalegn. 2011. *Land to Investors: Large-Scale Land Transfers in Ethiopia*. FSS Policy Debates Series No. 1. Addis Ababa: Forum for Social Studies.

Rahmato, Dessalegn. 2014. "The Perils of Development from Above: Land Deals in Ethiopia." *African Identities* 12 (1): 26–44.

Shete, Maru, and Marcel Rutten. 2015. "Impacts of Large-Scale Farming on Local Communities' Food Security and Income Levels: Empirical Evidence from Oromia Region, Ethiopia." *Land Use Policy* 47: 282–292.

Soeters, Sebastiaan, Ruben Weesie, and Annelies Zoomers. 2017. "Agricultural Investments and Farmer-Fulani Pastoralist Conflict in West African Drylands: A Northern Ghanaian Case Study." *Sustainability* 9 (11): 1–19.

Tache, Boku, and Gufu Oba. 2016. "Policy-Driven Inter-ethnic Conflicts in Southern Ethiopia." *Review of African Political Economy* 36 (121): 409–426.

Tafesse, Tesfaye. 2007. *The Migration, Environment and Conflict Nexus in Ethiopia: A Case Study of Amhara Migrant-Settlers in East Wollega Zone*. Addis Ababa: Organization for Social Science Research in Eastern and Southern Africa (OSSREA).

Tufa, Fekadu A., Aklilu Amsalu, and E. B. Zoomers. 2018. "Failed Promises: Governance Regimes and Conflict Transformation Related to Jatropha Cultivation in Ethiopia." *Ecology and Society* 23 (4): 26.

wa Githinji, Mwangi, and Gebru Mersha. 2007. "Untying the Gordian Knot: The Question of Land Reform in Ethiopia." In *Land, Poverty and Livelihoods in an Era of Globalization*, edited by A. Haroon Akram-Lodhi, Saturnino M. Borras Jr., and Cristóbal Kay, 310–343. London: Routledge.

Wagstaff, Quincey A. 2015. "Development, Cultural Hegemonism and Conflict Generation in Southwest Ethiopia: Agro-Pastoralists in Trouble." *Note* 13, Observatoir des Enjeux Politiques et Securitaires dans la Corne de L'Afrique. December 2015.

Wayessa, Gutu Olana. 2020. "Impacts of Land Leases In Oromia, Ethiopia: Changes in Access to Livelihood Resources for Local People." *Land Use Policy* 97: 1–11. https://doi.org/10.1016/j.landusepol.2020.104713.

Wolford, Wendy, Ben White, Ian Scoones, Ruth Hall, Marc Edelman, and Saturnino M. Borras Jr. 2024. "Global Land Deals: What Has Been Done, What Has Changed, and What's Next?" *Journal of Peasant Studies*: 1–38. doi:10.1080/03066150.2024.2325685.

Wondimu, Tagel, and Fana Gebresenbet. 2018. "Resourcing Land, Dynamics of Exclusion and Conflict in the Maji Area, Ethiopia." *Conflict, Security and Development* 18 (6): 547–570.

Yntiso, Deko Gebre. 2001. "Population Displacement and Food Insecurity in Ethiopia: Resettlement, Settlers and Hosts." PhD thesis, University of Florida.

Yusuf, Semir. 2019. "Drivers of Ethnic Conflict in Contemporary Ethiopia." *Institute for Security Studies Monographs* 202: 1–46.

CHAPTER 30

ETHNIC POLITICS AND LAND

BAO-NGUYET DANG, DOI RA, LORENZA ARANGO, MOGES BELAY, SAI SAM KHAM, AND ZEYNEP CEREN EREN BENLISOY

Introduction

LAND and ethnic politics are closely interlinked. For ethnic-based groups, land is a defining aspect of their identity and a social and material basis of their lives. Consequently, the specific location of the lands they are in and the conditions under which land access and control are procured have direct effects on the life trajectory of different ethnic groups. Across the global South, in particular, the rapid transformation of rural landscapes, and of rural land-tenure patterns, has resulted in the dispossession of countless ethnic communities, with serious consequences for their livelihoods. These changing relations around land have, in turn, changed the character of their labor conditions.

This chapter uses an intersectionality approach to ethnicity and class (Bhattacharya 2017; Fraser 2008) to better understand the politics around the land-labor nexus. It elaborates on the interconnectedness of land and labor, as means of both production and social reproduction, while articulating the issue of ethnicity and class in an analysis of emerging patterns of informal wage labor. Building on Mamdani (1996b, 2005), we understand *ethnicity* (generally defined as the quality of a group of people who share a common cultural background) as a "political identity" that can be used simultaneously as an instrument to exercise control over certain peoples and as a mechanism for their emancipation. We argue that contestations and struggles with respect to land are never *only* about land. On the contrary, claims over land access and control are permanently traversed by concerns around ethnicity, race, citizenship rights, and class relations.

We develop our argument in three parts. First, we see claims around ethnicity as deepening and accelerating ongoing inequalities and differentiations associated with the changing land-labor regimes. This is not to say that ethnicity and identity claims are necessarily a problem. However, whenever these claims are subject to politicization and are invoked to justify excluding, marginalizing, and discriminating against, ethnicity gains a new salience. The chapter aims to provide a nuanced understanding of such ethnic-based discrimination, subject-making, "the making and unmaking of permanent minorities" (Mamdani 2020), and the connections to land and labor in different agrarian settings in the global South.

Next, we look at the ways in which land grabs of various forms are contributing to the increasing prominence of ethnicity (see Mollett 2016). The struggles for land and other natural resources (e.g., water, forests, communal pathways) have exacerbated interethnic conflicts. Furthermore, faced with outright dispossession or restrictions imposed by new landowners (or both), ethnic-based groups have been forced to become migrant wage laborers to make ends meet, working under particularly harsh conditions.

Third, we focus on the role of the state and how it has (re)shaped the dynamics and relations in the land-labor nexus. We present specific cases that draw attention to different ways the states have used ethnicity for their own projects of state-making, further deepening ethnic-based injustices and inequalities and impacting the land-labor markets across rural areas in the global South. At the same time, we see ethnic groups invoking ethnicity in their claims for specific rights (around land control and citizenship) and autonomy, precisely in order to counteract discrimination and marginalization. To make sense of these seeming contradictions, we build from key analytical tools, to which we now turn.

Land and Ethnic Politics: Some Key Conceptual Tools

This section discusses key theoretical concepts relevant to understanding the connections between land, labor, and ethnic politics. In particular, it builds on two complementary subthemes. First, we look at the significance of land for production and social reproduction and the particular ways in which access to land is key to the social reproduction of ethnic communities as a distinctive groups. Second, we examine the role of the state and the practices of territorialization as they affect land and labor politics. We also bring in the politics of recognition and redistribution in relation to ethnicity and class, as dimensions of social justice.

Land is a crucial means of production but not the only one. In the global South, access to land is essential so that working people can meet their basic survival needs, such as food, shelter, clothing, and care, at the lowest possible cost. This is necessary if they are to remain competitive in the labor market or as petty commodity producers (Fraser 2016; Katz 2001). For working people who are forced to migrate from rural areas to urban areas or to another country, access to land similarly remains essential for their sustenance (Borras et al. 2021; see also Cousins, this volume). According to Shah and

Lerche (2020), in cases of labor migration, the social reproduction of working people increasingly occurs in both the destination areas of migrant workers and in their original home regions, and land is indispensable in both sites.

And yet land is not only important for the reproduction of people as labor power. Land is also crucial for the social reproduction of people as members of a distinct community, often marked by ethnicity or race. Ossome (2021, 558), for instance, has emphasized the broader meanings attributed to land beyond its purely productive dimension. She stresses the relevance of land as a sociocultural symbol that gives sense and meaning to different communities. Similarly, Silvia Federici (2004) highlights the importance of land, forests, and waters for the material and social aspects of social reproduction. She argues that land expropriation and the increasing deterioration of the commons challenge the reproduction of agrarian societies worldwide. Cousins (this volume) emphasizes the role of land in shaping social relations and identities and highlights the importance of paying attention to the reproduction of the "social." We emphasize that the conditions of political economy influence how ethnic identities are actively maintained and negotiated in society over time and space as Mamdani (2020) also suggested.

As we will see, having little or no access to land has forced many Indigenous peoples and peasants from particular ethnic groups to become informal wage laborers under acute or "hyperprecarity" conditions. This has put the ability of ethnic working people to reproduce, not only as labor power, but also as a distinctive ethnic community, at serious risk. As their access to land and livelihoods is increasingly threatened, new forms of struggles and confrontations have emerged. These conflicts have been occasionally labeled as *interethnic* or *intercommunal*, but their causes stem from deeper "strands of injustice and irrationality" (Fraser 2021).

This brings us to the central role of the state, which has dual, contradictory functions: to facilitate capital accumulation while trying to maintain a minimum level of political legitimacy (O'Connor 1973). In performing these functions, the state is not a neutral actor; it is a powerful one shaping the amount of access to and control of land will be available to different social classes and ethnic groups, often through the enactment of various inscription devices and performances. These contribute to the making of four components: territory, sovereignty, authority, and subjects and subjectivities; these elements aid in conceptualizing and justifying processes of dispossession, appropriation, and extraction (Wolford et al. 2013, 192–193). Politics within and among these components give shape to the broader political processes that make up the thing called the "state"—a historical construct forged by class and other social relationships (Abrams 1988).

The state creates and regulates governance instruments, such as homogenized codes, identities, statistics, regulations, and measures for shaping land property relations, which it then imposes on local customary systems (Scott 1976, 1999; Borras and Franco 2018; Borras et al. 2013). Yet it is important to note that the state is not a single, unified actor (Wolford et al. 2013). There are various actors and powers within the state, each attempting to maneuver through political spaces and to handle "the contradictory tasks of accumulation and legitimation, and the trade-offs involved" (Fox 1993, 31). One can comprehend state action as a consequence of power relations and frictions within and between both the state and civil society, as in the "interactive approach" developed by Fox (1993, 22). Another conceptual handle on the role of the state, called "regime of dispossession" by Levien (2013, 383), points to "socially and historically specific constellations of state structures, economic logics tied to particular class interests, and ideological justifications" to understand the patterns of land dispossession. Brenna Bhandar's work on property ownership is a good illustration. According to Bhandar (2018), modern property laws have deep roots in colonialism and are crucial mechanisms of the appropriation of land and capital accumulation. Within the "racial regimes of ownership" in settler colonialism, "property laws and racial subjectivity developed in relation to one another," and state-regulated formal property ownership, such as land title, was determined by racial identity and gender.

In relation to subjects and subjectivities, we draw attention to Mahmood Mamdani's two key concepts: "regime of tolerance" and the "two modes of rule" (Mamdani 1996a, 2020). *Regime of tolerance* refers to a contradictory foundation: the Westphalian nation-state-building model being reproduced in the settler colonial states by the colonial powers, where the majority, or the colonial power, "tolerates" minorities, or the "natives," and in return, the minorities give up the (struggle for) "sovereignty." Thus, a regime of tolerance casts the political identity of a permanent majority and a minority. The "two modes of rule" is manifested in direct and indirect rules. After direct rule, or the colonial nation-building project, fails, indirect rule is applied. In an indirect-rule model, the colonial powers demarcate or fix "tribal/indigenous homelands" using their own perceived "customary authority" to assist the colonial administration and "extraction." The concept of "indigeneity" has become a ground for privileging natives over nonnatives in terms of entitlement to land and other resources, and a powerful group of natives with a distinct religious or ethnic identity is being co-opted and often pitted against other minorities (Mamdani 2001a, 2020). In his 2001b article, Mamdani presented the case of how "indigeneity" allowed independent Congolese state to continue its colonial legacy. Specifically, it allows the state to give privilege to the indigenous (i.e., the Banyarutshuru) over the non-Indigenous (the Banyamasisi or the minority labor migrants who moved to Congo only in the colonial period) and to gain mass support for its hegemonic power; the former was reinforced by the country's 1991 law that defines a Congolese as anyone with an ancestor then living in the territory demarcated by Belgians as the colony of Congo. The actual result of this—according to Mamdani (2001b, 658)—is the native sat on the top of the political world designed by the settler. Mamdani (2001b) termed this particular relationship between the native and the settler as "the native-settler dialectic." At the microlevel or the level of the native authority, this dialectic relationship played out in ethnic clashes over rights, particularly the rights to land, for instance, in the case of Kivu in eastern Congo and the Rift Valley in Kenya. The "define and rule" method applied by the colonizers politicized the perceived (ethnic) differences into rigid and inviolable legal boundaries, such as "customary law" or ethnic categorization. Therefore, the right to have rights as a subject or citizen is determined by membership in an ethnic group or based on standards of cultural authenticity recognized by the state (Mamdani 2001a). Even after the colonial powers left, many countries continued to adopt and reproduce these two hegemonic colonial legacies.

The politics of recognition based on ethnicity intersects with the politics of redistribution based on class (Fraser 2008). Class injustice endemic to an unequal economic structure hides behind ethnicity. This is reflected in E. P. Thompson's framing of class as a social and cultural formation (Thompson 1963). As a result, ethnicity can "color a person's experience of class" (Becker 2006, 473). At the same time, the misrecognition of ethnicity through the erasure of a group's rights of self-determination and the creation of exploitative land and labor regimes lead to maldistribution. Hence, both ethnicity and class injustices need to be addressed separately and intersectionally (Bhattacharya 2017; Fraser 2008).

The Role of Land for Ethnic Minorities: Accounts from the Global South

Land is central to rural communities across the world. Let us look at this interplay by briefly considering different case studies from the global south.

Land, Ethnicity, and Competing Claims

Part one surveys the role of land for rural communities in Turkey, Ethiopia, and Myanmar, and some of the competing claims around it.

Syrian Refugees in Turkish Countryside

Today, as in the past, the sustainability of Turkey's agricultural production relies heavily on seasonal agricultural labor. However, there was a major shift in the Turkish countryside when the Syrian Civil War in 2011 caused millions of Syrians to flee to Turkey. Agriculture, with its high informality and abundance of jobs, has been an entry point for Syrians from the beginning (Dedeoglu 2022). This is particularly true in the Mediterranean region, which historically played and continues to play a leading role in agricultural production, particularly because of Turkey's expansion of export-oriented agriculture of fresh fruits and vegetables. Not only do the multiple harvests in a year-round growing season provide sustained employment for workers, but the expansion of greenhouse production, packaging, and processing facilities have been another source of livelihood for different groups of workers. Seasonal agricultural laborers are currently composed of two main groups: Kurdish/Arab IDPs and Syrian refugees.

Kurdish IDPs became the dominant agricultural labor force in Turkey in the 1990s. They came mainly from rural areas, East and Southeastern Turkey, and either had small landholdings or were landless. The civil war between the Turkish state and the Kurdistan Workers' Party's played out in rural areas in the late 1980s and 1990s, and as a result, the Kurdish agricultural workers suffered both forced displacement and dispossession. Keyder and Yenal (2011) have conceptualized this process as "proletarianization with forced dispossession." The precarious working and living conditions of Kurdish/Arabic IDPs have been frequently addressed in the literature (Kavak 2016; Pelek 2018, 2022).

The presence of Syrians in the Turkish countryside in the first years after the start of the Syrian war led to a harsh confrontation with other groups of workers in the agricultural sector and, consequently, to a reconstruction of refugee-host relations, daily encounters, and social differentiation in the rural areas. For several years after the Syrians' entry into agricultural work in the region, daily wages for agricultural workers tended to stagnate or did not increase as expected. The UN's Food and Agricultural Organization (FAO 2023) found that the decline in real wages after the arrival of Syrians was between 20 and 50 percent. The Syrian presence had already led to a massive replacement of Kurdish/Arab IDP workers with Syrians, who simultaneously became the "preferred" source of labor of the producers and employers in the region. Producers' "informed stereotypes" (Scott and Rye 2021) based on "racialized and gendered assumptions" (King et al. 2021), as well as the discriminatory attitudes and practices of other groups of workers, have further accelerated the processes of polarization and crystallization of identities in the region. This has also led to a strengthening of the "dynamics in the construction of discriminated migrant identities" (Bosc et al. 2022, 73). Syrians, who had previously been viewed as "victims of the war," began to be seen as (socioeconomic) "burdens" and "thieves and traitors" by the locals and other ethnic labor groups.

Ethiopia

As elsewhere in Africa, land in Ethiopia is more than an economic matter; it has cultural dimensions when people establish emotional attachment to and derive a sense of identity from the land they claim to own. It is also a source of the state's political power (Rahmato 2009; Lavers 2012; Moreda 2015). Ethiopia is an ethnically diverse nation, whose multiple ethnic groups identify with a specific area of land. The current system of ethnic federalism has increased the significance of this ethnicization of land. What is still up for debate under Ethiopia's current system of ethnic federalism is whether all citizens should have the right to use the land where they live, as is provided in the existing constitution, or whether the rights of an area's Indigenous ethnic group should take precedence (Lavers 2018). In essence, ethnic federalism entails the physical allocation to distinct territories with certain ethnic groups. This basically provides that every Indigenous ethnic group shall have its own homeland, thereby diminishing any claims to that land by the non-Indigenous ethnic minorities living there.

Ethnic federalism has in this way (re)produced non-Indigenous groups as ethnic minorities in areas where they live outside their constitutionally designated regions. For example, even when members of dominant ethnic groups, such as the Amhara and Oromo, live outside their designated homeland regions, they are treated as ethnic minorities and are targeted by the Indigenous groups, who assert that all the land in that region belongs to them. Consequently, hundreds of thousands of Tigrians and Amharas have been forced to leave Wollega and other parts of the Oromia region since 2000. Before the lack of land and ethnic federalism made things worse, the Tigrians and Amharas had moved into the region and coexisted amicably with the native Oromos for several decades (Lavers 2018; Tafesse 2007; Abbink 2006). Likewise, the Guji, an Oromo ethnic group that previously inhabited areas that are now included in the Southern Nations Nationalities People (SNNP) region, was threatened with forced relocation to the Oromia region when their territory was made part of the Nechi-Sar National Park administered by the SNNP region (Lavers 2018). So even though the Ethiopian government adopted ethnic federalism as a means of addressing ethnic disappointments, power imbalances, and tyranny, the system has, regrettably, created other issues that threaten national cohesion. The excessive emphasis on ethnicity has caused a shift in loyalty from the nation to one's ethnic group, and ethnic citizenship has become a key tool for obtaining socioeconomic and political advantages, such as access to land and positions of political power.

Myanmar

In Myanmar, the postcolonial state expanded upon the broad race-ethnicity categorization imposed by British colonizers by establishing fixed ethnic categories. The Bamar ethnic group was designated as the majority, along with seven other ethnic groups, which were further subdivided into 135 categories. Ethnicity was linked to indigeneity status and the allocation of citizenship rights, which provided access to land for production and social reproduction. The central state, controlled by the Bamar group, equated being Bamar with a privileged identity associated with material and ideological wages to compensate for social exploitation. The use of the word "wage" discouraged solidarity between poor Bamars and the workers and peasants of other ethnicities, perpetuating the latter's oppression. This interconnection between race and class has played a central role in the formation of racial capitalism in Myanmar (Campbell and Prasse-Freeman 2021).

In addition to the politics of Bamar and non-Bamar identities, a politics of "otherness" can be observed in the interaction between land claims of different scales and uses and social identities, such as ethnicity and class. Ethnic peasants, facing mounting pressure to relinquish control of their land following large-scale land enclosures by powerful local and nonlocal elites, felt compelled to protect what remained from outsiders, who often included other ethnicities, such as migrants from other regions. These actions and reactions are shaped by historically specific expectations, aspirations, and traditions of struggle (Hall et al. 2015). Alongside the struggle by armed ethnic groups for territorial control, there is a tense competition among working people for small-scale land enclosures. This competition is rooted in deeper dynamics of exploitation and dispossession, and may appear to outsiders as a simple case of interethnic tensions over land.

Production and Social Reproduction: Land, Displacement, and Migrant Labor

Part two looks at the ways in which the nexus between production, social reproduction, and land manifests at the ground level, taking into account cases from Colombia, Myanmar, Vietnam, and Ethiopia. A particular emphasis is given to the issue of labor migration and how it plays out within the nexus.

Indigenous Migrant Laborers in Colombia

For Indigenous peoples in Colombia "land is life." The Indigenous conceive of land as a source of their material reproduction, where they can practice different life-affording activities such as hunting, foraging, and shifting agriculture (Arango 2022). At the same time, land gives them reassurance and a sense of belonging in the place where they were born, which also comprises areas considered as sacred in their worldview. Land is therefore both a space for production and for the material and symbolic reproduction of Indigenous peoples.

The eastern Altillanura (high plains) region of Colombia is home to numerous Indigenous communities (e.g., Sikuani, Salliba, Cuiba, Amorúa), most of whom were nomadic or seminomadic (Calle 2017; Gómez 1998). Under Spanish colonial rule, these communities were relocated to defined areas known as Indigenous land reserves (*resguardos*), arguably as a means to satisfy increasing labor demand (Bohorquez 2002; Machado 2009). After independence, legislation was passed that strengthened the category of *resguardos* and granted official land titles to different Indigenous communities. Some of the *resguardos* in the eastern plains are quite large, exceeding the several thousands of hectares. At first glance, granting titles to large areas of land may seem like an important step in the preservation and well-being of Indigenous peoples, precisely because of the importance of land as a source of production and reproduction, materially and symbolically.

Nevertheless, many Indigenous people who hold titles to their land reserves are increasingly turning into informal migrant wageworkers. The *resguardos* tend to be located in distant and isolated areas with poor or nonexistent road infrastructure. Meanwhile, on their own land and in surroundings areas, the private landowning classes and corporations—which have taken control of vast amounts of land in the region, especially in the context of the contemporary global land rush, are gradually regulating access to water sources, communal forests, open savannas for hunting and foraging, and rural paths for transiting. In real terms, then, despite the existence of formal property rights, many of the *resguardos* are unable to meet the production and reproduction demands of the Indigenous, who have been forced to look for jobs outside their land, on nearby plots of private land owned by domestic and foreign businesspeople. At these sites, they are generally hired for short periods, two to three months at a time, to perform different tasks—for example, preparing the soil, cultivating it, and harvesting the crops.

Other Indigenous groups—also with titles to official land reserves—have had no choice but to move to small towns to be closer to other sources of wage work (e.g., palm oil and rubber plantations, oil extraction and construction sites). They also take jobs as waiters or cleaning staff at restaurants and in private households or become street vendors. The living conditions in these small towns are no less difficult than those on their official land reserves, but at least they have slightly better access to wage work and to basic infrastructure to cover their "material" reproduction (food, clothing, and shelter)—according to their testimonies (personal interviews). As long as the state does not guarantee different people, such as those in these informal settlements, meaningful access to land, the existence of Indigenous peoples remains under serious threat. Land lies at the heart of their subsistence and existence (Arango 2022). Land is everything to them.

Displaced Ethnic Kachin Peasants in Myanmar

The biggest land rush in the history of Kachin State in Myanmar occurred during a time of relative peace that followed the signing of a ceasefire agreement between the Kachin Independence Organization/Army (KIO/A) and the state military in 1994. It put a pause on the armed revolt against the central state over ethnicity- and religion-based grievances, which from 1962 had mainly been controlled by the ethnic Bamar Buddhist majority. In 2011, the ceasefire between the two sides broke, generating further massive waves of displacement in Kachin state, including in Waingmaw township. By 2013, the number of IDPs in Waingmaw township had reached over 6,000 (UNOCHA 2013). Many took shelter within a day's travel from their villages, so they were able to check their houses, properties, and the lands whenever the armed clashes ceased momentarily. They also attempted to grow crops on their *taungyar* lands (upland) in the forest, whenever there was some level of stability in the area, but frequently got stuck when the war intensified unexpectedly. Land is important for them for self-subsistence.

In 2006, tissue-cultured bananas were introduced into the township as part of China's opium substitution program. In reality, the majority of peasants affected did not grow opium, and this development had a significant impact on the area's agricultural landscape (Woods and Kramer 2012). One key enabler of the change in land control was the Vacant, Fallow, and Virgin (VFV) Land law (originating in the British colonial era), which legalized the theft of lands under customary tenure system majorly practiced by ethnic peasants. As of 2024, approximately 31 percent of the country's land has been classified as VFV land, 70 percent of which is located in ethnic territories. The law designates all lands and territories without a formal land title to be vacant, fallow, or virgin land. The underlying logic of the law remained consistent throughout different Myanmar's state regimes which have used similar legal instrument that involved classifying lands without land titles as "unoccupied" or "unused" and allocated the lands to the state, military, businesses, and powerful actors (LIOH and MATA, 2018). The law allowed the state to "legally" take away lands from people who had been practicing customary tenure across generations. Most of the IDPs in Waingmaw township have lost between one and five acres of farmland, *taungyar* (upland), and other types of land that had been managed traditionally for several generations. Facing such threats, combined with precarious sociopolitical conditions, the villagers were compelled to rent out their lands to Chinese investors through middle brokers from another ethnic group. But renting out land does not provide them with the sufficient means to reinvest in other productive activities, because of renters' irregular payments, nonpayment, low payments, or various deductions.

As a result, IDPs are forced to sell their labor to the rapidly growing agricultural industry being developed right on the very landscape within the township or to migrate to other extractive hotspots inside Kachin state. Another option is to migrate across the border into Yunnan province to work for different on-and-off farm sectors (Hayward et al. 2020). And the terms for selling their labor as migrant workers inside China are starkly different from those enjoyed by Chinese investors inside Kachin state. Another factor driving young people away from the villages to become migrant wage laborers is to their avoid recruitment, either by the KIO/A as soldiers to fight against the military for territorial control or by the state military to work as hard manual laborers during their military operations. Despite the grievances aired by the local ethnic peasants, the banana fields are kept going strong by a constant, ready labor supply from other regions of the country. As one village leader lamented: "Myanmar laborers are cheap, so we couldn't get any jobs. We need to create job opportunities for our people. We need to stand on our own feet" (Waingmaw villagers, pers. comm., February 2022). These past and present processes that continue to alienate people and their labor from the land weaken and erase the cultural meanings and purposes associated with their work, which are integral to the reproduction of labor power for survival and as a distinct ethnic community.

Cross-Border Agricultural Wage Workers in Vietnam

"C" (a pseudonym) is a Tay rice farmer from Dong Phuc commune in Ba Be district, Bac Kan province, Vietnam. He vividly remembers his initial journeys to Sung Cho to harvest sugarcane, which began in October 2014 and continued the next year. Sung Cho, or "Chong Zuo" in Chinese, is a township in Guangxi province, in the south of China. C's first trip in 2014 spanned thirty days; and in 2015, more than forty days. To reach his destination, C would leave his home at nightfall, navigating the marked trails and using various modes of transportation, including moto taxis and buses coordinated by local Chinese guides, ensuring his arrival at the worksite by the next evening so that he can begin to work in the sugarcane fields around 6 am the following day. From 2010 until the global outbreak of Covid-19 pandemic in early 2020, cross-borders farmwork wage labor was adopted by many rice farmers in Dong Phuc. To avoid being captured by the frontier police of both the Vietnam and China sides, those like C and his fellow villagers came up with various means to sneak in their worksites inside China using the unofficial border; this included paying a Chinese local guide so that their journey to their workplaces became shorter and easier. For C and many of his fellow Tay villagers in Dong Phuc commune, the substantial earnings from a month or two of sugarcane cutting in southern China are crucial to fulfill their families' financial needs (particularly of cash money) for Tet—the Vietnamese New Year.

Since 2010, a progressive decline in the fertility of the paddy fields in Na Hai valley has led to a reduction of cultivable land and shifted the crop cycle from a two crop to a single-crop cycle. This has prevented C and other rice farmers from planting their regular winter crops, leaving them with surplus labor between October and the next April, and diminishing an essential source of family income. Among other factors, the construction of the 4.5 MW Ta Lang hydropower plant and the 1.2-kilometer water irrigation scheme introduced between 2009 and 2010 have significantly influenced these shifts in labor and land dynamics within the Dong Phuc commune. The hydropower plant was constructed in 2009; it received its investment permit in accordance with Vietnam's participation in the United Nations' Clean Development Mechanism, a framework for mitigating climate change. The plant is situated on the upstream of the Ta Loong River on the land of Na Thau village. The river is an ancient watercourse that provides water to the 20-hectare Na Hai valley—the primary paddy rice production area for five of the commune's thirteen villages. The establishment of the plant necessitated the appropriation of 1.6 hectares of paddy rice land from five households, which represented 10 percent of Na Thau village's total paddy rice land area (16.4 hectares). An additional 3.3 hectares of state-owned protected forest land were also acquired for the project.

Although the appropriation of land for the construction of the hydropower plant did not significantly impact the farmers at the outset, the plant's daily operations have since profoundly and irreversibly altered the land access for 1,332 Tay paddy rice-farmers who have long cultivated in Na Hai valley; this number accounts for 45 percent of the commune's total population in 2019 (2,926 people). The situation escalated in 2010 when a new 1.2-kilometer state-led irrigation tunnel was constructed under the framework of Program 135—a social-economic development program targeting ethnic minority communities in remote, mountainous regions of Vietnam—using a preferential loan from the World Bank. This has effectively severed the natural water flow from the river to the hydropower plant, which only releases water twice daily to cover the farmers' agricultural and daily water needs. More seriously, the inappropriate design of the irrigation scheme, which branches out and abruptly narrows at the source, has resulted in reduced water pressure, preventing water from flowing downstream to the lower areas. For other downstream villages, the further away they are from the irrigation scheme, the more severe the water scarcity they have been experiencing.

Over a period of thirteen years, these operational patterns resulted in the conversion of 11 of the 20 hectares of two-crop paddy fields in Na Hai valley into single-crop fields. Moreover, the erratic water supply has turned 3.5 hectares of fertile land in the valley's western part (the Bản Lừu areas) into barren terrain. Meanwhile, excessive water in the eastern and central sections (originally, the Pá Ổ areas) has permanently swamped the land, so that rice farmers can no longer transplant their favorite local sticky rice needed for the most important traditional holidays in Vietnamese and Tay culture (Tet and Thanh Minh). The period of water scarcity becomes particularly severe during the dry months, coinciding with the annual winter-spring crop season (from November to March of the lunar calendar). In essence, the shift in land access did not alter the rice farmers' legal ownership of the land, and it did not result in forced evictions or resettlement. However, it has stripped land-poor farmers of their ability to cultivate the land to which they are legally entitled, and undermined their agricultural productivity and livelihoods.

Rohingya in Myanmar

In 2017, nearly one million Rohingya people from Rakhine state in the western part of Myanmar were violently expelled from their towns and villages. The pattern of violent mass expulsion, repatriation, return, and resettlement has been recurring ever since Myanmar military launched the first campaign in 1959, called Operation Shwe Kyi, (Habiburahman and Ansel 2019). This phenomenon was conceptualized as a "slow burning genocide" (Zarni and Cowley 2014), and the UN fact finding mission confirmed "On reasonable grounds, that the factors allowing the inference of genocidal intent are present" (UN IIFFM 2018), as the land and property of the Rohingyas were destroyed or confiscated. The Rohingya people are an ethnic group who practice Islam. They are primarily peasant communities and make important contributions to food production, particularly in the rice paddies and through artisanal fishery. They were being targeted for the ethnic and religious differences from the ruling Bamar Buddhist national majority and the dominant Rakhine Buddhist local majority. For several decades, the national and local majorities perceived them as an undesirable rival competing over control of land as a mean of production and a territory to socially reproduce as a people. The state's motivation for the violent expulsion of the Muslim Rohingyas could be based on the ethno-nationalist ideal of building a "pure blooded" state dominated by the Bamar Buddhist, or on what Zarni and Brinham (2017) conceptualize as "a continuum of racist strategic choices."

Other important factors, including the state's desire for legitimation and to exert territorial control, as well as to take over important means of production, such as agricultural land and coastal fisheries, could not be dismissed. Simply put, land plays a central role in the Rohingya crisis although majority of the academic literatures, news articles, and human rights reports focus on the debates around (legal interpretation of) genocide, (international) accountability, humanitarian needs, and refugee repatriation. To produce the state's "extreme nation building violence" (Mamdani 2020) and cataclysmic land dispossession, while making such atrocious crimes palatable and normal to the public, both coercion and consensus are needed. Coercion includes the passing of discriminatory laws, such as the Burma Citizenship Act of 1982 (commonly referred to as the1982 citizenship law), which tied ethnic categorization to citizenship rights, and issuing local instructions to control/limit Rohingya's mobility, marriage, and reproduction, and access to essential services (UN IIFFM 2018). The citizenship law's revocation of the Rohingyas' citizenship status affected their ability to access land and own property and was a crucial institutional tool of the "regime of dispossession" (Levien 2015). Consensus-making included turning public opinion against the Rohingyas by spreading lies and disinformation about them through state-owned media, rejecting the Rohingyas' ethnic identity and collective rights, and labeling them illegal "Bengali" interlopers or Muslim terrorists (UN IIFFM 2018). Myanmar's electoral competition during the transition to democracy, between 2010 and 2020, and the subsequent regime changes represent another important conjuncture. In order to compete with the extremely popular NLD party and the local Rakhine nationalist parties, the military-backed Union Solidarity and Development Party (USDP) needed Rohingya votes, so they allowed selective Rohingya leaders to compete in the election representing the USDP party. The USDP handed out hundreds of thousands of temporary citizenship cards so the Rohingyas could vote, but later nullified all these ID cards (Ibrahim 2016; Wade 2017; Smith 2019). Democratic transition and electoral competition created an environment where Rohingya's identity and citizenship were used, abused, conveniently discarded, erased, or being used as a political scapegoat by different factions, worsening their vulnerability. Although the Rohingya exodus continued after the violent mass expulsion following the events on August 25, 2017, Maungdaw town which is at the heart of the violent event was announced as Maungdaw Economic Zone, on September 13, 2017 (San 2017). Around October 2017, over 71,500 acres of ripe rice paddy fields of the Rohingya were left unharvested, according to Kyaw Lwin, the then Rakhine state minister of agriculture (Lewis et al. 2017). Later, the Rakhine state administration asked companies to take over and cultivate the "ownerless Bangali land" (Lewis et al. 2017). In January 2018, the Union Enterprise for Humanitarian Assistance, Resettlement and Development (UEHRD), a state entity chaired by Aung San Suu Kyi, ordered bulldozers to raze several villages to open up land for "reconstruction and development." Subsequently, Human Rights Watch warned that destroying evidence of grave crimes, such as an ethnic cleansing, is an "obstruction of justice" (Human Rights Watch 2008).

On February 23, 2019, the Rakhine Investment Forum was organized by the NLD government, with major support from the Japanese government (Lwin 2019), at which Myanmar's de facto leader Aung San Suu Kyi, eager to attract foreign investment, laid out the "sectors that offer great potential for investors," including agriculture, livestock, aquaculture, forestry, manufacturing, textiles and garments, power generation, infrastructure, and real estate (Kyi 2019). Investment in all of these areas would require a large areas of land. The cataclysmic dispossession of Rohingyas is a flagship example of "extreme nation building violence" (Mamdani 2020). It shows a culpable link between ethno-cultural identity-related violent land dispossession and state's accumulation projects. The pattern of violent land dispossession and state's capital extraction repeats in other parts of Myanmar, among other ethnic groups. The impact of the genocide spilled into southeast Asia when Bangladesh, India, and Malaysia took in large numbers of Rohingya refugees. Later, when some of the host communities began experiencing serious shortfalls of labor, these precarious Rohingya refugees become a source of cheap labor, actively engaging in farming wage work on the palm oil and rubber plantations, and taking construction and other "3D"—dirty, difficult, and dangerous—jobs (Putri and Gabiella 2022).

Migrant Farmworkers in Ethiopia

Ethiopia has attracted foreign investors from over forty countries who have responded to the government's aggressive campaign offering the resources of land and cheap labor (Teklemariam et al. 2017). In the context of the global land rush, which gained momentum around 2008, about 3.5 million hectares of land in Ethiopia have been transferred to domestic and international investors (Rahmato 2011). Although displacement and migration in the country have historically been linked to instances of conflict, natural calamities, hunger, and state-orchestrated persecution, the deterioration of rural economies in recent years, primarily because of landlessness, has sparked the phenomenon. These combined factors have contributed to Ethiopia's emergence as one of the Horn of Africa nations that is witnessing a substantial influx of both internal and international migrants. Dispossession entails not only the confiscation of land but also the deprivation of labor (Li 2011), where farmers who were formerly self-sufficient on their land are now either considered surplus or are forced to work for firms in jobs that do not provide their basic needs for survival (Tesema 2022).

A case study conducted in the upper Awash valley in Oromia region showed that the large and medium-scale land investment projects have had a considerable impact on the local population, resulting in the displacement of the local people from their land without offering them sufficient employment prospects or alternative means of sustaining their livelihoods. International corporations have undertaken several investment projects, including massive flower farms, sugarcane plantations, and large farms growing fruits for export, such as grapes and strawberries. Alongside the substantial land investments by foreign capital, there has been a notable expansion of small and medium-sized commercial farms in the region. This has had equally major effects on the local population's access to land and their labor conditions. After the land for these projects was transferred, the locals experienced a significant change in their economic activities, transitioning from being mostly self-reliant, small-scale agricultural producers to being wage laborers on farms owned by investors or migrating to neighboring urban areas to find work in other sectors. The scarcity of land available for younger generations to inherit, coupled with the dearth of job prospects, has compelled young males, in particular, to migrate away from their communities in pursuit of employment. The jobs that were pledged from these investments turned out to be fewer in number and less stable than was anticipated.

Despite the requirement that investors in Oromia give priority to employ unskilled workers from the local population, investors have expressed dissatisfaction with the local workforce, purportedly because of lack of interest and high salary demands. The outflow of local labor has resulted in a labor gap for large and medium-scale land investments in the community, which has necessitated the recruitment of cheap labor from immigrants of other ethnicities. As a result, the land investment projects in upper Awash Valley have simultaneously caused the outmigration of impacted locals and the immigration of farm laborers from other ethnic groups, such as Sidama and Wolayta from SNNP. Both groups have moved across regional territories in search of relatively better employment opportunities to earn the necessary income to meet the social reproduction tasks of their families back at home.

Ethnic Minorities, Land, and State-Society Relations

Through the implementation of various rural development policies and land laws, the state in the global south has a central role in shaping access to and control of land for different social classes and ethnic groups. The discussion that follows, focusing on Vietnam and Ethiopia, reveals that indigenous ethnic minorities, mainly located at the peripheries, have been targeted as frontiers of land-based development where non-participatory and inappropriate state policies have been implemented despite the resistance from the local communities. Such poorly designed state policies have led to various forms of social and ecological crises, aggravating the ethnic-based exclusion in land access.

Land and Political Regimes in Ethiopia

In the political history of Ethiopia, the state under different regimes has always been the sole owner of key resources, including land. Land has significantly influenced the political economy of the country, and it has been a contentious issue and topic of political discourse. The three regimes, the Imperial, the Derg, and the Ethiopian People's Revolutionary Democratic Front (EPRDF), share common characteristics in terms of their mechanisms of capital accumulation and building power. As rightly argued by Levien (2013), the nature and consequences of dispossession vary significantly, both spatially and temporarily, when different historical and political factors, not just economic ones, form different regimes of dispossession. Governments in Ethiopia use two contradictory approaches to ensure full control over the rural economy. On the one hand, they try to build legitimacy by designing development policies and establishing legal structures for law enforcement. On the other hand, they apply coercive power to suppress resistance in rural areas, which also significantly damages their economy and livelihood bases, weakening their ability to resist (Clapham 1988). The power relations between the Ethiopian state and its population have always been underpinned by land rights that took different forms during different political regimes and were supported with different justifications (Rahmato 2011). Subsequent governments endeavored to advance Ethiopia's development by expanding industries, commercial agriculture, and megadevelopment projects like the hydroelectric dams, which resulted in the dispossession of land, the displacement of thousands of people, and environmental degradation. Poorly planned development initiatives frequently resulted in social crises and landlessness, which disrupted the livelihoods of rural agrarian and pastoral communities. These communities were therefore compelled to migrate from their lands in search of livelihood options somewhere else.

Since the overthrow of the emperor in the 1974 revolution by the Derg regime, which also destroyed the long-established the landlord-tenant relationship in the country, different land laws and land-use policies have been developed and implemented. However, common to all these legal frameworks is that land remains the property of the state while giving different land-use rights to users under different arrangements. After the EPRDF took power in 1991, it constitutionalized state ownership of land in the 1995 constitution and granted peasants use rights that can be revoked at any moment if the land is needed for large-scale investment or any other public purpose. the state has often prioritized outsiders over Indigenous ethnic groups, which has eroded the land rights of the local people. This is particularly evident in the state's commitment to the large agricultural investments that have invaded community lands, displacing local smallholders. The administrative borders of Ethiopia, which adhere to an ethno-federalist structure, provide insight into the central government's land-leasing decisions regarding large-scale land investments. The regions politically referred to as "emerging regions" or "minority ethnic groups," such as Benishangul Gumuz and Gambella, have experienced substantial adverse consequences since their land was transferred to foreign and domestic investors (Moreda 2015; Gebresenbet 2016). Moreover, community people in these regions have been deliberately relocated to facilitate the acquisition of land by these investors (Cochrane and Skjerdal 2015).

Vietnam

For the Tay ethnic minority rice farmers in the Dong Phuc commune in Vietnam, the construction of a hydropower plant and establishment of an irrigation scheme have irreversibly transformed their access to and control over land, with profound implications for their lives and livelihoods. Despite their persistent efforts to raise their concerns over the past thirteen years, it has become evident that their local provincial government has not been responsive. And like their own local communal government, the grassroots Tay communities, who are the primary targets of state-led development initiatives, have not had a role in the decision-making processes that affect their development.

In Vietnam, development strategies aimed at ethnic minorities in remote, mountainous areas are often shaped by a persistent upland-lowland dichotomy (Sikor 2011, 1–2). This mindset, which is prevalent among the majority Kinh politicians and decision-makers, views ethnic minorities as "others," distinct from the Kinh majority residing in the lowlands. The upland regions are perceived as isolated, underdeveloped, and in need of modernization (Sikor 2011, 1–2; Sowerwine 2011, 51). At the policymaking level, this perspective has been manifested in various state projects designed to narrow the development gap between ethnic minorities and the majority population. However, these projects frequently adopt a one-size-fits-all approach, imposing Kinh-centric developmental criteria that often lack relevance to the contexts of ethnic minorities.

At the level of policy implementation, the execution of these state projects has largely depended on external actors, which has created opportunities for local elite capture. This reliance on outside agents, combined with the imposition of irrelevant development models, has served to exacerbate the existing inequalities between Vietnamese ethnic minorities and the majority Kinh population.

Conclusion

Land and labor issues are central to ethnic communities in the global South. This chapter has examined different rural areas in Myanmar, Vietnam, Turkey, Ethiopia, and Colombia in which land is key for both production and the social reproduction of ethnic populations, and how these dynamics play out in the face of land grabbing, dispossession, and increasing waves of rural to rural, as well as rural to urban labor migration, domestic and cross-border. The rapid changes in these areas, in turn, have exacerbated existing conflicts or created new ones among socially differentiated groups marked by ethnicity, and class relations, with serious implications for land and labor. States, for their part, have significantly shaped the character of such interactions around land and labor, often instrumentalizing ethnicity for their own state-projects. At the same time, however, ethnicity is permanently invoked by ethnic groups seeking reclaim distinct land and citizenship rights against social injustices and marginalization. These contradictions are part and parcel of the politics around ethnicity and land.

Acknowledgments

We would like to thank the editors and anonymous reviewers for their valuable comments and suggestions on earlier drafts of this chapter. Remaining inconsistencies are our responsibility alone.

References

Abbink, Jon. 2006. "Ethnicity and Conflict Generation in Ethiopia: Some Problems and Prospects of Ethno-regional Federalism." *Journal of Contemporary African Studies* 24 (3): 389–413.

Abrams, Philip. 1988. "Notes on the Difficulty of Studying the State (1977)." *Journal of Historical Sociology* 1 (1): 58–89. https://doi.org/10.1111/j.1467-6443.1988.tb00004.x.

Arango, Lorenza. 2022. "'Land Is Everything': Reclaiming Grabbed Indigenous Land in Colombia." August 2022. *Land and Life Stories Series*. RRUSHES-5 Project. https://www.iss.nl/en/media/2022-08-land-everythinglorenza-aranga-vasquezenglisho.

Becker, Marc. 2006. "Mariátegui, the Comintern, and the Indigenous Question in Latin America." *Science and Society* 70 (4): 450–479. http://www.jstor.org/stable/40404343.

Bhandar, Brenna. 2018. *Colonial Lives of Property: Law, Land, and Racial Regimes of Ownership*. Durham, NC: Duke University Press.

Bhattacharya, Tithi. 2017. "How Not to Skip Class: Social Reproduction of Labor and the Global Working Class." In *Social Reproduction Theory: Remapping Class, Recentering Oppression*, edited by Tithi Bhattacharya, 68–93. London: Pluto Press.

Bohórquez, Carmen L. 2002. "Resguardos y Derechos Humanos." *Procesos Históricos I* (2). https://www.redalyc.org/articulo.oa?id=20000203.

Borras, Saturnino M., and Jennifer C. Franco. 2018. "The Challenge of Locating Land-Based Climate Change Mitigation and Adaptation Politics within a Social Justice Perspective: Towards an Idea of Agrarian Climate Justice." *Third World Quarterly* 39 (7): 1308–1325. https://doi.org/10.1080/01436597.2018.1460592.

Borras, Saturnino M., Jr., Jennifer C. Franco, Doi Ra, T. Kramer, M. Kamoon, P. Phyu, et al. 2021. "Rurally Rooted Cross-Border Migrant Workers from Myanmar, Covid-19, and Agrarian Movements." *Agriculture and Human Values* 39 (1): 315–338. doi:10.1007/s10460-021-10262-6.

Borras, Saturnino M., Jr., Jennifer C. Franco, and Chunyu Wang. 2013. "The Challenge of Global Governance of Land Grabbing: Changing International Agricultural Context and Competing Political Views and Strategies." *Globalizations* 10 (1): 161–179. https://doi.org/10.1080/14747731.2013.764152.

Bosc, Igor, Jens Lerche, Alpa Shah, Miranda Fajerman, and Neha Wadhawan. 2022. *Understanding Patterns of Structural Discrimination of Migrant and Other Workers in Some Countries of South and West Asia.* Geneva: International Labour Organization. http://www.ilo.org/wcmsp5/groups/public/---dgreports/---dcomm/---publ/documents/publication/wcms_844072.pdf.

Calle, Laura. 2017. "Entre la violencia, la colonización y la adjudicación de reservas: Relatos sikuanis sobre el abandono, el despojo y la recuperación del territorio. *Revista Colombiana de Antropología* 53 (1): Article 1. https://doi.org/10.22380/2539472X.4.

Campbell, Stephen, and Elliot Prasse-Freeman. 2021. "Revisiting the Wages of Burman-Ness: Contradictions of Privilege in Myanmar." *Journal of Contemporary Asia* 52 (2): 175–199. doi:10.1080/00472336.2021.1962390.

Clapham, Christopher. 1988. *Transformation and Continuity in Revolutionary Ethiopia.* Cambridge, UK: Cambridge University Press.

Cochrane, Logan, and Terje Skjerdal. 2015. "Reading the Narratives: Resettlement, Investment and Development in Ethiopia." *Forum for Development Studies* 42 (3): 467–487.

Dedeoglu, Saniye. 2022. *Syrian Refugees and Agriculture in Turkey: Work, Precarity, Survival.* London: I. B. Tauris.

FAO. 2023. *An Overall Assessment of Challenges Faced by Seasonal Agricultural Workers from Syrians under Temporary Protection and Host Communities.* Food and Agriculture Organization of the United Nations, Ankara. https://doi.org/10.4060/cc5137en.

Federici, Silvia. 2004. "Women, Land-Struggles and Globalization: An International Perspective." *Journal of Asian and African Studies* 39 (1–2): 47–62. https://doi.org/10.1177/0021909604048250.

Fox, Jonathan. 1993. "State-Society Interaction and Distributive Reform in Mexico." In *The Politics of Food in Mexico: State Power and Social Mobilization, Food Systems and Agrarian Change*, edited by Frederick H. Buttel, Billie R. DeWalt, and Per Pinstrup-Andersen, 9–40. Ithaca, NY: Cornell University Press.

Fraser, Nancy. 2008. "From Redistribution to Recognition? Dilemmas of Justice in a 'Postsocialist' Age." In *The New Social Theory Reader*, edited by Jeffrey C. Alexander and Steven Seidman, 188–196. New York: Routledge.

Fraser, Nancy. 2016. "Contradictions of Capital and Care." *New Left Review* 100: 99–117.

Fraser, Nancy. 2021. "Climates of Capital." *New Left Review* 127:94–127.

Gebresenbet, Fana. 2016. "Land Acquisitions, the Politics of Dispossession, and State-Remaking in Gambella, Western Ethiopia." *Africa Spectrum* 51 (1): 5–28.

Gómez, Augusto Javier. 1998. "La guerra de exterminio contra los grupos indígenas cazadores-recolectores de los llanos orientales (siglo XIX y XX)." *Anuario Colombiano de Historia Social y de la Cultura* 25: Article 25.

Habiburahman and Sophie Ansel. 2019. *First, They Erased Our Name: A Rohingya Speaks*. Translated by Andrea Reece. Scribe Publications.

Hall, Ruth, Marc Edelman, Saturnino M. Borras Jr., Ian Scoones, Ben White, and Wendy Wolford. 2015. "Resistance, Acquiescence or Incorporation? An Introduction to Land Grabbing and Political Reactions 'from Below.'" *Journal of Peasant Studies* 42 (3–4): 467–488. https://doi.org/10.1080/03066150.2015.1036746.

Hayward, Daniel, Ko Lwin, Yang Bin, and Htet Kyu. 2020. *Chinese Investment into Tissue-Culture Banana Plantations in Kachin State, Myanmar*. MRLG Case Study Series, no. 4. Mekong Region Land Governance. https://www.mrlg.org/publications/publication-title-chinese-investment-into-tissue-culture-banana-plantations-in-kachin-state-myanmar/.

Human Rights Watch. 2018. "Burma: Scores of Rohingya Villages Bulldozed." Posted February 23, 2018. https://www.hrw.org/news/2018/02/23/burma-scores-rohingya-villages-bulldozed. Accessed April 11, 2024.

Ibrahim, Azeem. 2016. *The Rohingyas: Inside Myanmar's Hidden Genocide*. London: Hurst and Company.

Katz, Cindy. 2001. "Vagabond Capitalism and the Necessity of Social Reproduction." *Antipode* 33 (4): 709–728. https://doi.org/10.1111/1467-8330.00207.

Kavak, Sinem. 2016. "Syrian Refugees in Seasonal Agricultural Work: A Case of Adverse Incorporation in Turkey." *New Perspectives on Turkey* 54: 33–53. doi: 10.1017/npt.2016.7

Keyder, Çağlar, and Zafer Yenal. 2011. "Agrarian Change under Globalization: Markets and Insecurity in Turkish Agriculture." *Journal of Agrarian Change* 11 (1): 60–86.

King, Russell, Aija Lulle, and Emilia Melossi. 2021. "New Perspectives on the Agriculture–Migration Nexus." *Journal of Rural Studies* 85:52–58. https://doi.org/10.1016/j.jrurstud.2021.05.004.

Kyi, Aung San Suu. 2019. "Key Note Speech Delivered by State Counsellor Daw Aung San Suu Kyi at the Opening Ceremony of Rakhine State Investment Fair on 22 February 2019." February 22, 2019. https://www.google.com/url?sa=t&source=web&rct=j&opi=89978449&url=https://www.myanmarcgla.org/images/pdf/key-note-speech-delivered-by-state-counsellor-daw-aung-san-suu-kyi-english.pdf&ved=2ahUKEwj7mdKllPSHAxUrRUEAHZEmN2gQFnoECBsQAQ&usg=AOvVaw14DZYNf4-GoFud1t7niJik.

Lewis, Simon, Thu Thu Aung, and Kyaw Soe Oo. 2017. "Exclusive: Returning Rohingya May Lose Land, Crops under Myanmar Plans." *Reuters*, October 22. https://www.reuters.com/article/us-myanmar-rohingya-repatriation-exclusi-idUSKBN1CR0AS.

Lavers, Tom. 2012. "'Land Grab' as Development Strategy? The Political Economy of Agricultural Investment in Ethiopia." *Journal of Peasant Studies* 39 (1): 105–132.

Lavers, Tom. 2018. "Responding to Land-Based Conflict in Ethiopia: The Land Rights of Ethnic Minorities under Federalism." *African Affairs* 117 (468): 462–484.

Levien, Michael. 2013. "Regimes of Dispossession: From Steel Towns to Special Economic Zones." *Development and Change* 44 (2): 381–407.

Levien, Michael. 2015. "From Primitive Accumulation to Regimes of Dispossession: Six Theses on India's Land Question." *Economic and Political Weekly* 50, no. 22 (May): 146–157.

Li, Tania Murray. 2011. "Centering Labor in the Land Grab Debate." *Journal of Peasant Studies* 38 (2): 281–298.

LIOH and MATA. 2018. "Civil Society Organizations' Statement on the Vacant, Fallow & Virgin Land Management 2018 and Related Announcement." https://lioh.org/wp-content/uploads/2018/11/LIOH_MATA_Statement_20181116.pdf.

Lwin, Nan. 2019. "Japan to Take Leading Role in Pushing FDI in Rakhine." *The Irawaddy*, February 8. https://www.irrawaddy.com/news/japan-take-leading-role-pushing-fdi-rakhine.html.

Machado, Absalón. 2009. *Ensayos para la Historia de la Política de Tierras en Colombia*. Bogota: Universidad Nacional de Colombia.

Mamdani, Mahmood. 1996a. *Citizen and Subject: Contemporary Africa and the Legacy of Late Colonialism*. Princeton, NJ: Princeton University Press.

Mamdani, Mahmood. 1996b. "Indirect Rule, Civil Society, and Ethnicity: The African Dilemma." *Social Justice* 23, nos. 1–2 (63–64): 145–150. http://www.jstor.org/stable/29766931.

Mamdani, Mahmood. 2001a. *When Victims Become Killers: Colonialism, Nativism, and the Genocide in Rwanda*. Princeton, NJ: Princeton University Press.

Mamdani, Mahmood. 2001b. "Beyond Settler and Native as Political Identities: Overcoming the Political Legacy of Colonialism." *Comparative Studies in Society and History* 43 (4): 651–644. https://www.jstor.org/stable/2696665.

Mamdani, Mahmood. 2005. "Race and Ethnicity in the African Context." *Actuel Marx* 38:65–73. https://doi-org.eur.idm.oclc.org/10.3917/amx.038.0065.

Mamdani, Mahmood. 2020. *Neither Settler nor Native: The Making and Unmaking of Permanent Minorities*. Cambridge, MA: The Belknap Press of Harvard University Press.

Mollett, Sharlene. 2016. "The Power to Plunder: Rethinking Land Grabbing in Latin America." *Antipode* 48 (2): 412–432. doi:10.1111/anti.12190.

Moreda, Tsegaye. 2015. "Listening to Their Silence? The Political Reaction of Affected Communities to Large-Scale Land Acquisitions: Insights from Ethiopia." *Journal of Peasant Studies* 42 (3–4): 517–539.

O'Connor, James. 1973. *The Fiscal Crisis of the State*. New York: St. Martin's Press.

Ossome, Lyn. 2021. "Land in Transition: From Social Reproduction of Labour Power to Social Reproduction of Power." *Journal of Contemporary African Studies* 39 (4): 550–564. https://doi.org/10.1080/02589001.2021.1895431.

Pelek, Deniz. 2018. "Syrian Refugees as Seasonal Migrant Workers: Re-construction of Unequal Power Relations in Turkish Agriculture." *Journal of Refugee Studies* 32 (4): 605–629. doi:10.1093/jrs/fey050.

Pelek, Deniz. 2022. "Ethnic Residential Segregation among Seasonal Migrant Workers: From Temporary Tents to New Rural Ghettos in Southern Turkey." *Journal of Peasant Studies* 49 (1): 54–77. doi:10.1080/03066150.2020.1767077.

Putri, Ratu Ayu Asih Kusuma, and Dennyza Gabiella. 2022. "The Organisational Pattern of Rohingya Refugee Community in Malaysia: Structural Opportunities, Constraints, and Intra-community Dynamics." *Refugee Survey Quarterly* 41: 673–699. https://doi.org/10.1093/rsq/hdac010.

Rahmato, Dessalegn. 2009. *The Peasant and the State: Studies in Agrarian Change in Ethiopia, 1950s–2000s*. Addis Ababa, Ethiopia: AAU Press.

Rahmato, Dessalegn. 2011. *Land to Investors: Large-Scale Land Transfers in Ethiopia*. Addis Ababa, Ethiopia: Forum for Social Studies.

San, Myo Pa Pa. 2017. "Rakhine Govt Forges on with Maungdaw Economic Zone." *The Irawaddy*. September 13. https://www.irrawaddy.com/news/burma/rakhine-govt-forges-maungdaw-economic-zone.html.
Scott, James C. 1976. *The Moral Economy of the Peasant: Rebellion and Subsistence in Southeast Asia*. New Haven, CT: Yale University Press.
Scott, James C. 1999. *Seeing like a State: How Certain Schemes to Improve the Human Condition Have Failed*. New Haven, CT: Yale University Press.
Scott, Sam, and Johan Fredrik Rye. 2021. "Praised, Prized, yet Penalised: A Critical Examination of Low-Wage Hiring Queues in the Global Strawberry Industry." *Journal of Rural Studies* 88 (2): 473–481. https://doi.org/10.1016/j.jrurstud.2021.04.014
Shah, Alpa, and Jens Lerche. 2020. "Migration and the Invisible Economies of Care: Production, Social Reproduction and Seasonal Migrant Labour in India." *Transactions of the Institute of British Geographers* 45 (4): 719–734. https://doi.org/10.1111/tran.12401.
Sikor, Thomas. 2011. "Introduction: Opening Boundaries." In *Upland Transformations in Vietnam*, edited by Thomas Sikor, Nghiem Phuong Tuyen, Jennifer Sowerwine, and Jeff Romm, 1–24. Singapore: National University of Singapore Press.
Smith, Martin. 2019. *Arakan (Rakhine State): A Land in Conflict on Myanmar's Western Frontier*. Report. Amsterdam: Transnational Institute.
Sowerwine, Jennifer. 2011. "The Politics of Highland Landscapes in Vietnam Statecraft: (Re)framing the Dominant Environmental Imaginary." In *Upland Transformations in Vietnam*, edited by Thomas Sikor, Nghiem Phuong Tuyen, Jennifer Sowerwine, and Jeff Romm, 51–72. Singapore: National University of Singapore Press.
Tafesse, Tesfaye. 2007. *The Migration, Environment and Conflict Nexus in Ethiopia: A Case Study of Amhara Migrant-Settlers in East Wollega Zone*. Addis Ababa, Ethiopia: Organization for Social Science Research in Eastern and Southern Africa (OSSREA).
Teklemariam, Dereje, Hossein Azadi, Jan Nyssen, Sil Lanckriet, Tesfaalem Ghebreyohannes Asfaha, Mitiku Haile, Fatemeh Taheri, and Frank Witlox. 2017. "Dynamics of the North–South Capital Flows or Rise of South–South Land Deals? Features of Land Acquisition in Ethiopia." *Land Degradation and Development* 28 (8): 2389–2407.
Tesema, Yonas. 2022. "Interrogating Dispossession for Development in Ethiopia." *Forum for Development Studies* 49 (1): 53–76. doi:10.1080/08039410.2021.1984305.
Thompson, Edward Palmer. 1963. *The Making of the English Working Class*. New York: Vintage Books.
UN IIFFM. 2018. *Report of the Detailed Findings of the Independent International Fact-Finding Mission on Myanmar, September*. A/HRC/39/CRP.2. Report of the Independent International Fact-Finding Mission on Myanmar to the Human Rights Council, 39th session, September 17, 2018.
UNOCHA. 2013. "Reported IDP Figures, Kachin, Status 30 May 2013, Various Sources." UNOCHA. http://themimu.info/sites/themimu.info/files/documents/Infographic_IDP_Kachin_Reported%20IDP%20Figures_OCHA_30May13_A4.pdf.
Wade, Francis. 2017. *Myanmar's Enemy Within: Buddhist Violence and the Making of a Muslim 'Other'*. London: Zed Books.
Wolford, Wendy, Saturnino M. Borras, Jr., Ruth Hall, Ian Scoones, and Ben White. 2013. "Governing Global Land Deals: The Role of the State in the Rush for Land. *Development and Change* 44 (2): 189–210. https://doi.org/10.1111/dech.12017.

Woods, Kevin, and Tom Kramer. 2012. *Financing Dispossession: China's Opium Substitution Programme in Northern Burma*. Transnational Institute. https://www.tni.org/en/publication/financing-dispossession.

Zarni, Maung, and Natalie Brinham. 2017. "Reworking the Colonial-Era Indian Peril: Myanmar's State-Directed Persecution of Rohingyas and Other Muslims." *Brown Journal of World Affairs* 24 (1): 24.

Zarni, Maung, and Alice Cowley. 2014. "The Slow-Burning Genocide of Myanmar's Rohingya." *Pacific Rim Law & Policy Journal* 23 (3): 683.

CHAPTER 31

LAND AND NATIONAL DEVELOPMENT STRATEGIES IN THE COLD WAR ERA

CRISTÓBAL KAY

Introduction

Ownership of land or control over it is a source of wealth and power for landlords and capitalist farmers, but for the peasantry it is a source of livelihood, often of a precarious kind (see Cousins, in this volume). There have been revolutions, rebellions, and protests by peasants and rural workers over lack of access to land and exploitative relations in the countryside (see Grajales and Chauveau, this volume). The struggle over land determined the fate of landlords and peasants, as well as the development path of the countries. In this chapter I will discuss how countries in the global South have tackled the land issue and the extent to which this was central to their national development strategy during the Cold War period by comparing the experience of Latin America with South Korea and Taiwan during the same period. Hence, the analysis starts with the aftermath of World War II (henceforth, WWII) and, roughly, ends with the fall of the Berlin Wall, the break-up of the Soviet Union, and the demise of communism in Eastern Europe at the end of the 1980s and the early 1990s.

I will argue that countries that implement a radical redistributivist land reform before or concurrently with their industrialization process within a "synergetic development strategy" (SGDS), on which more later, are more likely to achieve a sustainable and equitable development process that raises living standards and drastically reduces poverty. South Korea and Taiwan were able to set on this course, whereas Latin America failed to do so and even relatively regressed during the second half of the twentieth century. Although the gross domestic product (GDP) per capita of South Korea and Taiwan was roughly only a tenth of that of the United States in 1960, the gap narrowed spectacularly, reaching respectively 42% and 55% of the US GDP per capita in 2000. In comparison, in

Argentina and Uruguay, the countries that have the smallest GDP per capita gap with the United States in Latin America, their GDP per capita, respectively 60% and 46% compared to that of the United States in 1960, the gap widened, reaching 33% and 29% of the US' GDP, respectively, in 2000. In brief, South Korea and Taiwan, which started in 1950 at a much lower GDP per capita compared to Argentina and Uruguay, had by 2000 achieved a much higher GDP per capita (Khan and Blankenburg 2009). Argentina and Uruguay were no exception since, in all Latin American countries, the gap with the United States widened. Furthermore, the income distribution is far better in South Korea and Taiwan, and poverty is much lower as compared to Latin America; for further economic comparative data, see Elson (2006) and Siddiqui (2022). How did this dramatic turnaround in favor of South Korea and Taiwan come about?

In each of the following sections I am going to compare South Korea and Taiwan, one of the most successful East Asian countries, and Latin America. I will start by discussing the role of the state in the development process. The question to explore is the degree of autonomy and capacity to design and implement development strategies in a coherent, flexible, and sustained manner over time. Thereafter, I will analyze whether the countries implemented a land reform, to what degree, and in what sequence regarding the process of industrialization. Above all, I am interested in discovering what particular policies the state pursued regarding agriculture's contributions to industrialization, and what linkages, if any, it created between the sectors that might have unleashed synergies between them and throughout the economy that lead to higher and more sustained productivity increases in the economy that otherwise would not have materialized. I will then continue to analyze the different phases of the industrialization process, the extent to which these were related to the performance of agriculture, and the role of the state in all these phases and interactions. I will throughout this comparative analysis note the different contexts facing the countries concerned. In the conclusion, I will attempt to draw some relevant lessons for contemporary discussions on land and strategies of development.

National Development Strategies

Soon after the end of WWII, the war time alliance of the Allied powers broke down and the Cold War between the "Western powers" and the communist countries began to dominate world politics. With the demise of the empires after WWII and the process of decolonization, the main geopolitical strategic goal of the developed countries, under the new hegemonic power of the United States, became the containment and eventual defeat of communism throughout the world. Once the colonial countries achieved independence in Africa and Asia, their former rulers and other Western countries tried to influence their development strategies with a variety of aid and investment projects, trade deals, military support, and technical and economic assistance programmes so as to bind these countries to the capitalist world system. The expectation was that this would prevent those newly independent countries to fall under the influence of the Soviet Union and China. But if these containment policies did not work, they often did not shy away from supporting counterrevolutionary forces, or intervening more directly, to prevent the rise of communist regimes in the South (Blum 2014; Bello 2019).

To gain a proper understanding of the land question and national developmental strategies during the Cold War period it is imperative to frame them within the uneven dynamics of the world system (see McMichael, this volume). I will explore whether and to what extent land reforms were implemented, their character and timing, the relationships between agriculture and industry, and the type and sequence of the industrialization process. All of this will be framed within what I refer to as a "synergetic development strategy" (SGDS), which is anchored in a comprehensive redistribution of land that includes a dynamic agrarian policy that leads to the widespread adoption of productivity-enhancing technologies. Concomitantly, this dirigiste strategy crafts key energetic linkages between agriculture and industry; these create the conditions for an increasing web of forward and backward linkages throughout the economy and beyond that unleash a dynamic of rising value added throughout the system and result in higher living standards. It is remarkable that Chayanov, already in 1917, had outlined some elements of an SGDS, see Van der Ploeg, this handbook.

Orthodox economists argued at the time that developing countries should continue to develop their agricultural and natural resources because they were their comparative advantage in the world market. However, Raúl Prebisch (1950), who was leading the United Nations Economic Commission for Latin America (ECLA), argued that the South should shift from an "outward-oriented" to an "inward-oriented" development strategy by promoting industrialization. The reasoning for this recommendation was as follows: he, together with the development economist Hans Singer, discovered that the trend of the terms of trade of the South (the ratio of prices of primary commodities, i.e. natural resource products, they exported to the North and the prices of the manufactured goods they imported from the North) had been deteriorating since the 1880s. Without going into details of why this had happened, it meant that the South had to export an increasing quantity of primary commodities over time to the North to obtain the same amount of industrial products from the North. Because technical progress grew faster in industry as compared to the production of primary commodities, all the opposite should have happened in a competitive market. Thus the South benefited only partially, if at all, from those productivity increases, which were largely retained by the North. And the opposite happened with the increases in productivity by the South, which were largely captured by the North. In short, there was an unequal exchange in the trade between the South and the North. This finding went against the predictions of orthodox international trade theory (Samuelson 1948), and it became known as the *Prebisch-Singer thesis* of the deterioration of the terms of trade. Hence Prebisch (1950) proposed an import-substitution industrialization (ISI) strategy as an alternative development strategy to the primary commodity exporting strategy, as well as a new international economic order (Kay 1989; FitzGerald 2000; and Toye and Toye 2003).

Prebisch (1950) also gave an additional reason for promoting industrialization that is related to the existence of surplus labor in the periphery countries, which led to low wages and hence, contributed to the undervaluation of those primary commodity exports. It was expected that industrialization would reduce this surplus labor, leading sooner or later to higher wages for agricultural workers and ameliorating the deterioration of the terms of trade because primary commodities would become more expensive. A few years later, Arthur Lewis (1954: 146) published his seminal article "Economic Development with Unlimited Supplies of Labour'" in which he characterized developing countries as having surplus labor in what he called the "subsistence sector" but more commonly referred to as the "traditional sector". He argued that shifting this low-productivity labor to the "capitalist sector" (i.e. "modern sector") would result in higher rates of capital accumulation and thus economic growth. The productivity of this labor in the modern sector was much higher, but workers' wages remained low, albeit slightly higher than in the traditional sector, leading to higher profits, investment, and economic growth. This became known as the Lewis model. It was widely used in the development literature and interpreted as meaning the transfer of redundant and low productive labor from the agriculture sector (mainly subsistence peasant households) to the industrial sector. But this is not completely accurate because the modern and traditional sectors can coexist in the agricultural sector, as well as in the industrial sector. The arguments by Prebisch and Lewis influenced the development strategies of several countries of the global South.

The arguments of Prebisch and his ECLA team, who later became known in development economics as the structuralist school, gave some scientific legitimacy to their pursuit of such an industrialization development strategy. As we will see, not all of those attempts succeeded, or if they had any success, it was to a far lesser extent than had been expected, due to the lack or late implementation of land reform, premature industrialization, and failure to move to an export-oriented industrialization (EOI). What is striking is the lack of proper attention to agricultural development received from several theorists and, especially, policymakers. There are, of course, notable exceptions, as we will see.

With the emergence of the so-called four tigers—Hong Kong, Taiwan, Singapore, and South Korea—during the late 1970s and 1980s, the attention of analysts shifted to those countries. In this Cold War period, no other developing countries had yet been able to achieve such consistently high rates of economic growth and at the same time improve the distribution of income and drastically reduce poverty as these four. As a wave of researchers tried to understand the reasons for their success, different interpretations were put forth, and debates ensued. With the rise of neoliberalism in the 1980s and 1990s, proponents used the success of these newly industrializing countries to validate their view that free markets were superior to state intervention. But this idea was challenged by the development experts Alice Amsden (1989), Robert Wade (1990), Dani Rodrik (1995), and Ha-Joon Chang (2003), among others, who demonstrated that the state had played a key role in this achievement.

My argument is that the policymakers in South Korea and Taiwan—by design, the force of circumstances, coincidences, trial and error, a certain path dependence, doing the right thing at the right moment, learning from mistakes, grasping opportunities, sheer luck, or any other yet unknown factors—ended up transforming themselves from poor, underdeveloped countries at the end of the WWII to the two highest ranked formerly developing countries, which have even joined the ranks of the developed world. In my assessment, they achieved this because they pursued what I call an SGDS after they had gained independence at the end of the war. At the start of their development process, they probably did not yet think in those terms, and it is possible they still do not, even today. Their policies evolved over time and were influenced by international and internal factors to different and changing degrees in their interactions over time. This idea of an SGDS helps me to explore the manifold linkages, articulations, and relations between the various economic sectors and their varying dynamics as the development process proceeds and they encounter new challenges and opportunities for the state, its policymakers, and other social actors.

The State and Class in the Development Process

The actions of the state are pivotal in determining what kind of development strategies and land reforms, if any, are pursued. It has been observed that developing countries wishing to speed up development needed to strengthen the capacity of the state to implement a development strategy for achieving this goal. It should not be forgotten that in the aftermath of WWII, the circumstances were relatively propitious for this task. After all, the war effort had involved a massive exercise in economic planning and state intervention in society.

Although the communist countries in the global South, such as North Korea, North Vietnam, China, and Cuba, followed variations of the Soviet model in their development strategies, most other countries in the global South pursued a capitalist strategy, with different degrees of planning and market intervention by the state. The development record in the global South varied greatly, and most of the initial expectations of catching up with the North, or even reducing the income per capita gap between the South and the North, remained unfulfilled. Only a handful of countries managed to do so and South Korea and Taiwan are particular relevant to study as they were able to build a developmental state that pursued an SGDS. How did they manage it, and what characteristics did this developmental state have?

After WWII, when South Korea and Taiwan gained independence with the defeat of Japan, both countries were faced with the urgent task of rebuilding their economies. South Korea was under US military occupation from 1945 to 1948 and, thereafter, was ruled by a succession of authoritarian governments until a process of democratization began in 1988. Meanwhile, Taiwan was under the control of Chiang Kai-shek, the leader of the nationalist party in China, who after his defeat by the communist forces under Mao Zedong, set up a government in exile in Taiwan, which he controlled until his death in 1975. The new rulers strengthened their domination over society by authoritarian means, but also implemented reformist measures, such as land reform, so as to gain legitimacy in society. Because those countries faced the communist regimes of North Korea and China, respectively, they received assistance from the United States in the form of economic aid, private investment directed by the state, and favorable trade relations. This gave each state more room to maneuver in relation to its domestic dominant classes, especially since they had been weakened during the colonial Japanese occupation, and the remaining communist organizations and supporters were persecuted and defeated.

In short, civil society was weak and the state was strong in South Korea and Taiwan thereby allowing the governments of both countries to achieve a degree of autonomy from the social forces. Davis (2004) refers to the "disciplinary capacity" of the state, "disciplinary regimes," the "disciplinary ethos," and "disciplinary development." In her view, these various situations are propelled by the rural and urban middle classes, who are imbued with these disciplinary values. However, although middle classes have played a progressive role in history, they also have been counterrevolutionary forces when they have felt threatened by the working classes (Bello 2019). Indeed, the developmental state in South Korea and Taiwan was partly staffed by middle-class employees and was able to dominate the lower classes; it was also able to exercise significant control over the upper classes, though this weakened in later decades (Teichman 2015). Although Davis's assertion is worthy of examination, her notion it was the middle classes who created the foundations for prosperity in East Asia is controversial. In my view, Davis projects a US-centric perspective of the progressive role of middle class onto developing countries.

Although South Korea and Taiwan managed to construct a powerful and effective "developmental state," the Latin American countries largely failed to do so, although some did attempt it (Ricz and Benczes 2020). Their efforts were thwarted by the opposition of the landlord and capitalist classes. Notable exceptions are Cuba, which established a communist regime a couple of years after the 1959 revolution, and Chile during the brief years of the socialist government of president Salvador Allende (1970–1973), which was overthrown by the military with the encouragement and support of the upper classes and sectors of the middle classes, as well as the US government. Some Latin American states retained some oligarchical features from before WWII; others had embarked on efforts to expand democratic rights to the middle classes and, to some extent, to urban workers, but peasants and rural workers continued to be excluded. A few countries had also begun to industrialize, especially after the 1930 economic crisis, and governments started to set up institutions to promote industrialization and to develop the required infrastructure. These measures were intensified after WWII, when a process of ISI took off.

Thus, glimpses of a developmental state began to emerge, but that state could not be fully established to the extent of being able to implement a development strategy with consistent high rates of growth over a longer period, and which was inclusionary and equitable. Although the middle classes gained political influence over the state, particularly over the administration of the state apparatus, it was limited in realizing its reformist intent due to the economic and political power of the upper class, which at times reversed the reforms. It also happened that middle classes themselves dared not to continue with the reform process after it unleashed mobilizations of the industrial working class, the peasantry, and rural workers, who were demanding further rights and reforms, as was the case with the military overthrow of the governments of Jacobo Árbenz in Guatemala 1954, João Goulart in Brazil in 1964, Juan José Torres in Bolivia in 1971, and Allende in 1973 in Chile, among others. It is significant that these governments were overthrown because they had started a process of land reform or intended to do so. There were also progressive military governments, as in Peru, when General Juan Velasco Alvarado overthrew the government of Fernando Belaúnde Terry in 1968 and undertook a radical land reform. The middle classes were not always involved in these military interventions, but history has shown their ambivalent and shifting interventions in politics.

In sum, even in developmental states, the autonomy of the state is only relative because in capitalist countries the state ultimately acts in the interests of the capitalist class. When conflicts arise in society, a "smart" state tries to defuse them by conceding some of the demands of the laboring classes that neither imperil the stability of the system nor the long-term goals of development. Where this is not possible, the state does not shy away from using force, as has happened in South Korea, Taiwan, and, to a far greater extent, in Latin America, as mentioned. In South Korea and Taiwan, the upper classes had been much weakened, and so were more willing to accept reforms of the state that affected their interests, such as the radical land reform; they were facing the communist threat, which would have eliminated them as a class. South Korea and Taiwan also experienced fewer mobilizations, protests, and uprisings from below compared to Latin America. Furthermore, by implementing a thoroughgoing land reform and improving living standards, they were able to take the wind out of the sails of the protest movements, mitigate class conflict, and gain some legitimacy (Leftwich 1995). The South Korean and Taiwanese states to a large extent also created an industrial bourgeoisie that they could mold to function according to the aims of their state development strategies. Hence, in South Korea and Taiwan, the state had a greater degree of autonomy than did the states in Latin America, and also had the advantage of creating a developmental state from the start of their new nations (Evans 1987).

Meanwhile, the communist threat was more remote in Latin America, which had been in the "sphere of influence" of the United States since the 1920s. This changed with the Cuban revolution in 1959, which the United States perceived as a threat to its regional hegemony, especially when Cuba aligned with the Soviet Union and became an inspiration to several other insurrectional movements in the region. The US response was to support counterinsurgency measures taken by the Latin American governments, whatever their democratic credentials, but also to encourage those governments to deal with some of the issues that had provoked the insurrections, such as the lack of access to land for rural people (Kay 2001), as we will see. In Latin America, the state was "captured" by the dominant classes and, in some cases, retained their oligarchic traits even after WWII, until the sugar barons, tobacco lords, the tin king Patiño in Bolivia, and other owners of the continent's natural resources were expropriated or split up and sold to various new owners. Foreign capital also controlled several of these resources and was able to influence government policy to a far greater extent than in South Korea and Taiwan. Landlords, merchants, bankers, and the nascent industrialists understood that to keep their wealth and power they had to form alliances. Indeed, a fused or coalesced bourgeoisie emerged through various means, including marriage between factions of the upper class, which solidified those ties (Zeitlin and Ratcliff 1988). Thus, miners also became landlords, while landlords, in turn, also became bankers, and merchants also became industrialists, and so on. Due to this partial or complete fusion of their economic interests the possible conflicts arising, for example, regarding price policy were ameliorated or vanished, as industrialists want cheap food so as to keep their workers' wages low and profitable prices for their industrial commodities, while landlords want profitable prices for their produce and low prices for their industrial inputs. Hence reformist forces in society found it difficult to split and weaken the upper classes enough to establish a developmental state able to undertake the reforms required to create a process of sustainable and equitable development.

Land Reform and Development

This section highlights the importance of land reform in countries in the global South for boosting agricultural development, as well as for achieving industrial development through a variety of linkages established through an SGDS. Such state policies are particularly important for countries with a significantly unequal land tenure structure. Land reforms can be pursued for economic or sociopolitical reasons, or both, but with different emphases. They can arise from below as a consequence of revolution and peasant revolts or from above by the state wishing to modernize agriculture or forestall possible peasant upheavals. The former tend to result in more radical land reforms than the latter. Hybrid situations also occur, and the state is involved to greater or lesser extent in all of them.

The land reform in South Korea and Taiwan was mainly undertaken for sociopolitical reasons given the geopolitical situation they were facing, externally, the communist threat from North Korea and China, respectively, and internally, the threat of peasant uprisings. In South Korea, where land ownership was very unequal, with 4% of landowners owning 50% of the land, this pushed the US military government forces to start a limited land redistribution. They confiscated the Japanese farms, which constituted 18% of the country's farmland, and distributed them to the tenants (Kim 2016). But they did not dare to expropriate the farms owned by the Korean landlords, whose support they needed. When the new South Korean republic took over the government in late 1948, it prioritized the redistribution of land to tenants. Expropriated landlords received compensation, and the former tenants, now owners of the land, had to pay for it in installments over a period of years. Before the land reform bill was promulgated in 1950, landlords managed to sell almost half of all the tenanted lands. In the end, only about 10% of the land remained under tenancy (Kim 2016, 126). In this way, the radical nature of the land reform resulted in quite an egalitarian agrarian system as only 6.7% of the land was cultivated in farms larger than 2 hectares (Griffin, Khan, and Ickowitz 2002, 305).

The situation in Taiwan was similar to the one in South Korea. The tenancy system also predominated there, and 20% of the cultivated land, which had belonged to the Japanese, was confiscated in 1948 and sold by the government to tenants and landless peasants in parcels averaging almost one hectare. Taiwanese landlords were later also expropriated, but with compensation, and they were allowed to retain less than 3 hectares of land. In the end, almost half of the peasant households received land at favorable installment payments, and tenancy declined to only 17%, and rental payments were lower than before the land reform. In short, the land tenure system became far more egalitarian (Griffin, Khan, and Ickowitz 2002, 304–305).

Latin America had a different agrarian system than the one in East Asia, which was, and still is despite several land reforms, the most unequal in the world. It was dominated by the latifundia, or large landed-estate, system, which in Latin America refers to haciendas, estancias, and plantations. The latifundia system was established during the colonial period and expanded in the years after independence in the nineteenth century, with the continuing incursion into the lands of Indigenous communities. It is estimated that by the late 1950s and early 1960s, the large landowners (*latifundistas*) owned about 80% of the land, comprising only 5% of all farms, while for the smallholders (*minifundistas*) the situation was reversed: they owned only 5% of the land, but were 80% of all farm units. The middle-sized farm sector was relatively minor, except in Argentina and Costa Rica, which pointedly did not undertake land reform (Barraclough 1973).

This latifundia system was first challenged by peasants demanding "land and liberty" during the Mexican Revolution of 1910–1920, which enacted the first land reform policy in Latin America; but it was only during the presidency of Lázaro Cárdenas (1934–1940) that most of the landlords lost their land, which the government transferred to peasants organized into *ejidos*, a communal system in which members (*ejidatarios*) retain rights to a parcel of land for their own subsistence cultivation. In the Cold War period, the nationalist Bolivian Revolution in 1952 expropriated the mining elite, as well as most of the latifundia in the highlands. But with the colonization of Bolivia's vast lowlands, a powerful capitalist landed class emerged that prospered with the boom in soybean production; whereas in the post-land-reform years, the indigenous peasant farmers in the highlands were neglected (Kay and Urioste 2007).

After the government of Jacobo Árbenz in Guatemala introduced a land reform program in 1952 and started to expropriate the large banana plantation owned by the United Fruit Company, it was overthrown by the military in 1954, unleashing a wave of violent confrontations. The US government and the US Central Intelligence Agency

(CIA) were involved in the coup d'état, fearing that the communist organizations would become more influential with Árbenz as president and wanting to protect the US economic interests in the country. No sooner was he overthrown than the land reform law was rescinded.

The Cuban Revolution of 1959 was a game changer. Not only did it establish, after a brief a transitional period, a communist regime headed by Fidel Castro, but it also expropriated the island's large US-owned sugar and tobacco plantations and other assets of US companies. In 1961, Cuban exiles, financed and supported by the US government and the CIA, launched an invasion of Cuba with the aim of overthrowing the Castro government. This time, they were quickly defeated; Cuba then further embraced the Soviet Union, leading to the famous missile crisis in 1962, which almost unleashed a nuclear war, and was the most dangerous incident of the Cold War. The Cuban agrarian reform was the most radical ever to be implemented in Latin America. State farms became dominant in the countryside, but they were not successful and, in later decades, were reformed several times but in the end broken up and turned into peasant cooperatives or leased directly to peasant farmers (Kay 1988).While these reforms went in the right direction, farmers were still unable to achieve their full potential due to the rigid and all-embracing state planning system that determines the supply of inputs, marketing, and so forth. Hence Cuba continues its historical dependence on food imports, even though it largely has the potential to be self-sufficient.

To counteract the influence of Cuban Revolution in the region, the US government in 1961, during the presidency of Jack Kennedy, launched the Alliance for Progress, which encouraged the Latin American governments that had not yet undertaken land reforms to do so by offering them aid and technical assistance, in cooperation with various inter-American and international organizations. The aim was to modernize an agrarian system considered inefficient, exclusionary, and unable to overcome rural poverty in order to forestall further revolutions and other communist regimes (de Janvry 1981). During the 1960s, the governments in Colombia, Ecuador, Chile, Peru, Honduras, and the Dominican Republic subsequently did pursue land reforms. During the 1970s and 1980s, due to insurrections and revolutions, and under the shadow of the Cold War, land reforms were enacted in Nicaragua and El Salvador (Browning 1983; Pelupessy 1993). But if the Alliance for Progress helped to legitimize land reforms, it was not the main factor in their implementation. Though the intention of the land reform of the military government of Velasco Alvarado (1969–1975) was the same as that of the US government—to forestall revolution and a communist regime—Alvarado's collectivist and statist land reform was certainly not what the United States had in mind (Kay 1982).

The land reform in Chile undertaken by the middle-class government of Eduardo Frei Sr. (1964–1970) probably came closest to what the United States intended, but it took on a dynamic of its own when the peasants, who had been left out, demanded a more radical reform. Instead of the sought-for political stability via social incorporation, the land reform led to more conflicts, mass mobilizations, and instability. This was encouraged by the left-wing parties, which had increased support among rural workers, and helped Salvador Allende to become president in late 1970. Allende's government was alliance of various parties, which included the socialists and communists. The reform process intensified, with the expropriation of the remaining two-thirds of the latifundia, as did the class conflict, not only in the rural areas but in the country at large (Kay 1975). On September 11, 1973, the Allende government was overthrown by the military, which ruled Chile until 1989. The gains of the land reform were essentially reversed, and Chile became a pioneering model of neoliberal economics (Kay 2004).

In Nicaragua, the Sandinista revolution overturned, in 1979, the authoritarian government of Anastasio Somoza, the latest member of a family dynasty that had ruled the country since 1937 and was supported by the US government. The Sandinistas were a coalition of left-wing parties, and their government soon became embroiled in Cold War politics. The latifundia were expropriated, and most became state and collective farms. Soon after the triumph of the revolution, the counterrevolutionary forces tried to overthrow the new government. They were referred to as the "Contras" (short for counterrevolutionaries), and the fiercely anticommunist Reagan administration supported them financially, including supplying military equipment, training, intelligence, and so on. Except for the traditional elites, who were associated with the Somoza dynasty, the middle class, and disgruntled peasant farmers tended to support the Contras, and some even joined them. The Sandinista government started to transform some of the state and collective farms into peasant cooperatives, and in those that remained state farms, the government gave the workers access to individual plots of land. It hoped that acceding to their demands for ownership or access to individual plots of land might undercut their support for the Contras (Baumeister 2019). The Sandinistas also received some limited support from the Soviet Union, but by this time the Cold War was beginning to unwind. In 1989, the warring forces signed a peace agreement and elections were held in 1990, which the Sandinistas lost.

In Brazil, strong opposition from landlords stalled any significant agrarian reform, as mentioned earlier with reference to the military overthrow of the Goulart government. Instead, governments used programs to colonize the vast Amazon region to try to reduce the pressure for land and to pursue geopolitical goals regarding neighboring countries. It was only after the restoration of democratic rule in the mid-1980s that some redistribution begun to take place. But it was only in 1995 that the land reform began gaining significance, under the governments of Fernando H. Cardoso (1995–2002) and Luiz Inácio Lula da Silva (2003–2010), but to analyze this is beyond the scope of this chapter—for a review, see Robles (2018).

What was the outcome of the Cold War reforms in Latin America? The centuries-old latifundia system as such largely disappeared. Those latifundia that were not expropriated, or that were able to recover all or part of their former estates with the unraveling of the land reforms, were transformed into modernizing capitalist farms. The peasant beneficiaries who had been able to retain access to land in the neoliberal turn at the end of the Cold War now faced major challenges to their survival because much of the former state support was withdrawn, and they were exposed to the rigors of the world market. The ongoing process of socioeconomic differentiation gained a new impetus. Although some peasant farmers were able to prosper, most had to find wage employment either temporarily or permanently, becoming semi- or fully proletarianized. By the early 1990s, an incredible 90% of the total arable land in Latin America are in large farms, accounting for only 26% of all farms; the 50% smallest farms, which are subsistence farms, only had 2% of the land. Moreover, "55% of rural households suffer from poverty, 60% of which are in extreme poverty" (de Janvry, Sadoulet, and Wolford 1998, 1–2). Land reforms, by shaking up property rights to land, prepared the terrain for land markets, which during the neoliberal turn intensified, opening the doors for a new process of concentration, not just of land but, more importantly, of capital (Kay 2016).

To summarize: Land reforms have complex and interrelated international and domestic causes of the economic, social, and political kind, but are ultimately the consequence of a country's class struggle, though geopolitical factors, especially during the Cold War, had a major bearing. Whereas it can be argued that land reform in South Korea and Taiwan largely fulfilled its promises, in Latin America those promises were largely broken (Thiesenhusen 1995). In South Korea and Taiwan, the landlord class disappeared, morphing into an industrial, commercial, and financial bourgeoisie. In Latin America, an industrial bourgeoisie had already emerged before the Cold War and coalesced with the landlords. In a way, industry took over agriculture with the development of agro-industry, which through the creation of commodity chains fuses agricultural, industrial, commercial and financial capital leading to new forms of concentration, domination, and rent capture (Vergara-Camus and Kay 2017).

Agrarian Linkages and Agrarian Questions

As we saw in the previous section the land reform in South Korea and Taiwan was far more radical in terms of land expropriated and rural beneficiaries relative to their total land and peasant population compared to Latin America's land reform. Furthermore, South Korea's and Taiwan's land reforms were redistributivist, whereas in Latin America they were mainly collectivist, though with the pressure from beneficiaries for individual land titles, its unraveling, and the counterreforms the collective character largely disappeared (Kay 1998). So far, I have only mentioned that the land reforms in South Korea and Taiwan preceded or were concurrent with their industrialization, while in most Latin American countries it was the opposite, as they happened several decades after industrialization had started. In this section I will examine the significance of this difference in timing had on the linkages between both sectors and, generally, on the outcome of the development process.

Capital Linkages and the Agrarian Question of Capital

An often-cited definition of the agrarian question of capital is that given by Karl Kautsky over a century ago, in 1899, who defined it as being "whether, and how, capital is seizing hold of agriculture, revolutionising it, making old forms of production and property untenable and creating the necessity for new ones" (Kautsky 1988, 12, cited in Akram-Lodhi and Kay 2010a, 179). Terence J. Byres (1996, 26), following Kautsky, linked it explicitly to industrialization, having in mind developing countries, by defining it as "the continued existence in the countryside, in a substantive sense, of obstacles to an unleashing of accumulation in both the countryside itself and more generally—in particular, the accumulation associated with capitalist industrialization" (see also Bernstein, this volume). Thus, the question is: To what extent was the agrarian question of capital tackled, if not resolved, in South Korea, Taiwan, and Latin America? Certainly, land reform in South Korea and Taiwan had radically transformed the old oppressive property relations in the countryside, but did this unleash a process of capital accumulation in agriculture and, above all, in industry? The short answer to both aspects of the question is yes.

This was achieved by the formulation and application of a synergetic development strategy (SGDS). In both countries, governments actively, if not forcefully, diffused the green revolution technologies to the peasant farmers, who were organized into cooperatives, irrigation associations, and other kinds of associations to facilitate the task of transferring the technical knowledge and ensuring its widespread usage. The high-yielding variety (HYV) seeds, such as rice, are input intensive, meaning that they require the proper treatment to ensure the expected substantial increase in yields, which sometimes even make it possible to harvest two or more crops in a year, instead of the usual single crop, thereby substantially increasing output. Hence this is a "land augmenting" technology and is particularly suitable for countries with a high labor-to-land ratio. And this technology is divisible because the amounts of seeds, fertilizers, and pesticides can be adjusted to the size of the farm, unlike, for example, with a tractor or harvest-combine. However, it requires also adequate irrigation, and in both countries, the government renewed and extended the irrigation system, supporting the wider use of the HYV seeds.

The dirigiste and authoritarian state captured a significant proportion of the increased agricultural surplus by a variety of means (Apthorpe 1979). The peasant farmers were forced to accept adverse terms of trade. They had to deliver a certain quota of rice, the main staple product, to the state procurement agency at a price fixed below the market rate, but were also being obliged to purchase the required inputs from state agencies at a mark-up price. In addition, farmers had to pay a land tax to the state, which was lower than the rent they had previously had to pay to the landlord. Similar measures were applied for other agricultural crops, such as sugar in the case of Taiwan. All these measures still left peasants with a portion of their increased output, which they had achieved by increasing the productivity of their farms (Karshenas 2004). Thus they still had a sufficient incentive to continue applying the green revolution package. But the state captured most of the increased agricultural surplus, which it partly used to finance the industrialization process.

In Latin America, the agrarian question of capital had been tackled in only a limited way before the Cold War. In many countries, the latifundia system relied on a precapitalist relation of production. Production was increased by expanding the area cultivated on the large estate, a sort of "internal colonization," and by moving into the country's land frontier, the "external colonization." Thus increases in productivity were limited and erratic. But a group of landlords gradually emerged who started to mechanize their estates, using chemical fertilizers, introducing irrigation, and so on, and thereby expanded production via increases in productivity. Landlords hardly paid any land tax on their vast estates, but agricultural exports were taxed. Industrialization had started in most countries of the region before the Cold War, as mentioned earlier. This early incipient industrialization was largely financed by private capital obtained from owners of the mineral resources, which were often foreign owned, as well as from landlords, and merchants. However, some countries, such as Argentina, Brazil, Chile, and Mexico, in the 1930s had already set up state agencies to support industrialization by supplying credit and developing the required infrastructure and some protective measures.

After WWII the incipient developmental state expanded its intervention in the economy by pursuing an ISI strategy that included a whole set of protective measures, such as tariff barriers, manipulation of the foreign exchange rate, import quotas, and so on. The aim was to provide security and incentives to capitalists who wished to set up industries but who were not yet able to compete with industrial imports from developed countries. The state had to ensure a sufficient supply of cheap food for the rapidly rising urban population to avoid possible food riots, and to garner their political support, but above all, to ensure that industrialists could keep wages to their workers as low as possible. Governments introduced price controls for some key staple foods, such as wheat, turning the internal terms of trade against agriculture. To indirectly subsidize industry, the state also imported cheap food from the United States and the European Union, which were subsidizing food exports to support their own farmers. This is considered unfair competition. The state also turned the external term of trade against agriculture by manipulating the exchange rate to overvalue the national currency. This meant that farmers received a smaller amount in local currency for their exports than they would have received with the equilibrium exchange rate; hence, they were indirectly or implicitly taxed, which may have come on top of the traditional export tax. In addition, the overvaluation of the domestic currency also meant that food imports put a downward pressure on domestic food prices. In short, the agricultural sector was partially squeezed (Schiff and Valdés 1992), more so in countries which did not possess a significant mining sector.

But this is not the full story. The question has to be asked: Who bore the burden of this squeeze in the countryside? In answering this question, it has to be considered that landlords captured the lion's share of the government's cheap credit and received most, if not all, of the subsidized fertilizer. Furthermore, landlords were the main importers of farm machinery and equipment and thus benefited from the overvaluation of the local currency because it cheapened imports. Sometimes, governments also subsidized key staple foods, thereby avoiding penalizing domestic food producers. Thus what the government took with one hand from agriculture, it returned to landlords with the other. More significantly, landlords were for centuries able to resist land reform, got away with exploiting their tenants and workers, and blocked trade-union legislation for agricultural workers. They thus also benefited from the high rents paid by their tenants and the low wages they paid to their workers. As mentioned earlier, land reforms came late, were limited in scope, and were partially reversed or unraveled. Hence, it was the peasants and agricultural workers who bore the brunt of the squeeze.

In conclusion, the industrial bourgeoisie and the emerging middle class failed to confront the landlord class to radically reform the land-tenure system and unleash the capitalist modernization of agriculture. But the land reforms, though limited in scope, did open the gates for the development of land markets, which, with the demise of the Cold War, the subsequent neoliberal reforms, and the opening to world markets, did capitalize agriculture, develop the productive forces, and change the social relations of production. (To analyze this new phase in the agrarian history of Latin America is beyond the remit of this chapter but I have done so in Kay 2015 and 2016). Thus the agrarian question of capital was not really resolved but bypassed as the capitalist class opened its doors to investors from all over the world. Following Bernstein (1996, 2006), neoliberal globalization in a way made redundant the agrarian question of capital; and the agrarian question of our times is the agrarian question of labor, as mentioned next. (For discussion of this topic, see Byres 2016; and Watts (2021.)

Labor Linkages and the Agrarian Question of Labor

To establish itself, industrialization needs not only capital but also an abundant supply of labor from the agricultural sector which needs to increase its output so as to keep up with the growing demand for food as labour migrates from the rural to the urban sector. The land reform in South Korea and Taiwan, by expropriating landlords, eliminated the control over their subordinated laborers that had restricted their mobility thereby releasing labor for industry. As tenants became proprietors, they were keen to improve the education of their children by sending them to school because they now had the means to do so. Industry benefited from this better educated labor force. In Latin America, minifundia peasants had a surplus of labor, which migrated to the urban areas in search of work, and with the rising rate of population growth after WW II industry faced no shortage of workers. Shanty towns began to sprout on the margins of the larger cities because of the increasing rural outmigration as a consequence of the gradual mechanization of the latifundia, and as rural laborers were also attracted to the better paid jobs in industry. However, only a small proportion found jobs in industry and most were occupied in the urban informal sector. Hence, the problem was initially one of unemployment and underemployment in the rural areas, but with the increasing outmigration these soon also became a major problem in the urban areas. This kept a downward pressure on wages, although some trade unions managed to negotiate higher wages for their members.

The surplus labor problem in Latin America became so acute that people trying to escape poverty, initially from Mexico but later from other countries in the region, migrated to North America, sending remittances to their families back home. Meanwhile, the peasant agrarian system in South Korea and Taiwan was far more labor intensive, especially after the diffusion of the green revolution, than the Latin American latifundia system was, and the first stage of South Korean and Taiwanese industrialization was of a more labor intensive kind, about which more later on.

Thus, the abundant supply of rural labor facilitated industrial development in both East Asia and Latin America. But, whereas the problem of surplus labor did not arise in South Korea and Taiwan, in Latin America the agrarian question of labor morphed into the problem of redundant surplus labor, and the lack of employment opportunities intensified the crises of livelihood and social reproduction, forcing labor to migrate abroad constituting a global reserve army of labor (Akram-Lodhi and Kay 2010b; see Cousins, this volume).

Agricultural and Industrial Linkages

Industrialization in South Korea and Taiwan developed within the framework of the SGDS that included a long-term industrial policy having due regard to the various phases of an optimal industrialization sequence. Thus the ISI policy operated under a time-limited protective shield that aimed at creating a competitive industry able to venture into the world market. Thus the state, while supporting the emergent industrial bourgeoisie, at the same time disciplined them.

As the South Korean and Taiwanese states advanced in implementing the SGDS they managed to unleash dynamic, multilayered, and mutually reinforcing linkages between the agricultural and industrial sectors that also increasingly involved the service sector. A distinction can be made between production linkages and consumption linkages (Hart 1998). As for the production linkages, because of the comprehensive land reform in South Korea and Taiwan and the widespread usage of the green revolution by peasant farmers, their demand for inputs stimulated, via backward linkages, the local fertilizer, pesticide, chemical, and seed industries and the metal mechanic industries for the production of agricultural tools, equipment, and machinery for ploughing, irrigation, harvesting, transportation, and so on. The forward linkages lead to the development of the food-processing industry and other industries that required domestically produced inputs.

As for the consumption linkages, as peasant farmers' incomes increased over time, and after they had covered their reproduction needs, they gradually spent a rising proportion of their income on industrial consumer goods such as clothing, shoes and radios. Because most of the population at the time was engaged in agriculture, this provided the impetus and solid foundation for the creation of a domestic consumer goods industry, also referred to as a "primary" industry, which are easier to start and more suitable in the initial phase of industrialization because of their relative labor intensity and lower capital and foreign exchange requirements.

This broad-based consumer goods industry, in turn, stimulated the establishment and growth of intermediate goods industries, which produce the required inputs for it, such as textiles, wood, and electronic components. As these industries grow, there comes a point where it becomes feasible and economical to set up a capital goods industry. The capital good industries create products that produce other products without being consumed in the process; they only depreciate, such as the machines for manufacturing tractors. These are the "secondary" industries, which are more capital intensive and whose operation requires a higher technological capability. A lot of foreign exchange is required to set these secondary industries up, because they have to be imported, at least in the initial phase. Because South Korea and Taiwan had limited supply of the natural resources needed to proceed to this next stage of the industrialization process, they had to shift from their primary ISI to a primary EOI (export-oriented industrialization); in short, they had to venture into the world market to gain the required foreign exchange, at the same time enabling them to fully reap economies of scale (Rodrik 1995). It is only then that they moved to a secondary ISI phase, also supported by foreign capital that flowed into these countries but under conditions made clear in their SGDS. Thereafter, they ventured into secondary EOI (Gereffi 1989). Following this sequence made it possible for South Korea and Taiwan to move up the ladder into industries that in each upward step generate more value added because of their higher capital intensity and technological sophistication, which was supported by a major investment in research and development. In the next higher step the development of human-capital-intensive modern sector services becomes important (Grabowski 2015).

In the Latin American case, the linkages between agriculture and industry failed to achieve the dynamic and positive impact because of the late implementation and unraveling of the land reforms, which perpetuated the high degree of inequality in the countryside (though a few countries experienced some improvements, which sometimes turned out to be temporary). This is in sharp contrast with South Korea and Taiwan, which had achieved an exceptional high degree of equity in the countryside. In Latin America, the lack of a mass consumer market in rural areas both hampered and distorted the industrialization effort. When the consumer goods industry started, it catered predominantly to the upper- and middle classes, who had the purchasing power, while workers and, especially, the peasants lived in poverty. The industrial structure was therefore slanted toward the consumer durables such as refrigerators and cars, whose production is more capital intensive so that they can only achieve economies of scale at high-volume outputs as their imported technology evolved to suit conditions in the rich countries (Kay 1989).

These industries often belonged to foreign transnational companies or had license agreements with them. There was limited technological transfer, if any, and the Latin American countries also failed to make major investments in research and development, unlike what happened in South Korea and Taiwan. Thus these industries wasted capital by operating well below their productive capacity. The inefficiency prevented them from moving into the primary EOI. In short, the industrial bourgeoisie choose the easy path by seeking increasing protectionism from a state that was unable to discipline them, if it ever intended to do so. Brazil was an exception; at various times, it tried to create a developmentalist state but never managed to do it consistently and comprehensively because it had failed to implement a major land reform at an early stage. Nevertheless, when late in the day countries like Argentina and Brazil tried to promote industrial exports to the United States, they came up against protectionist measures. This was something South Korea and Taiwan never had to face because the United States and other developed countries had granted them a special status during the Cold War, which facilitated their entry into those large, rich markets (Hart-Landsberg, Jeong, and Westra 2017).

This primary ISI phase, which was characterized as "easy ISI," began to run out of steam, or "exhausted" itself, because the growth of primary commodity exports was insufficient to cover the increasing demand for imports required for the functioning of industries, such as spare parts, chemicals, and machinery. This so-called external "strangulation," or throttling, of industry due to lack of foreign exchange was aggravated when the larger countries of the region moved into the secondary phase of the ISI process because these intermediate and capital goods industries were even more capital intensive and required even more foreign exchange (Kay 1989). By neglecting agriculture, some countries even had to increase food imports, further aggravating the foreign exchange problem. Countries increasingly went into debt to access foreign exchange, and it comes as no surprise that during the mid-1960s some Latin American countries started to implement land reform and to form regional common markets in the hope of widening the internal market for industry to achieve economies scale.

In sum, the failure of Latin American countries to design and implement an SGDS, which would have created a more egalitarian agrarian structure through comprehensive land reform and tackled the agrarian question of capital, explains the divergent performance of the East Asian and Latin American cases. Instead of forging "enhancing dynamic linkages" in the region, Latin American countries often ended up with "rentier exclusionary linkages." While the capitalist class in Latin America by abusing their state power was "rent-seeking," relying on their natural-resource-based comparative advantages that in South Korea and Taiwan was disciplined by the state to be "efficiency-seeking" by developing *competitive* advantages in the world market. But underlying this divergence is the international context of the Cold War, which the South Korea and Taiwan developmental states were able to steer in their favor. Latin America, by contrast, faced greater domestic challenges and the US government's interventions against their own progressive governments when they challenged the interests of the dominant classes, part of its efforts to ensure that the region remained within the US "sphere of influence." In addition, South Korea and Taiwan received billions of dollars in military and economic aid from the United States.

Conclusion

What lessons can be derived from this comparative study? For a start, it has to be born in mind that I have been discussing events in the Cold War period, which has been followed by neoliberal globalization that today is in crisis. Focusing on the land question, the neoliberal policy of a market-led land reform, in contrast to the state-led land reform of the Cold War period, has proved to be unable to deal with the persistent inequality in access to land, and may have even facilitated further land concentration through the operation of a more fluid land market (Borras, Kay, and Akram-Lodhi 2007; Borras, Kay, and Lahiff 2008). The challenges of undertaking land reforms are greater today because in many countries of the South, the state has been weakened by the neoliberal reforms, and the developmental state has been partly or completely dismantled. Although there was a resurgence of rural movements for land during the neoliberal period, in only a few countries were they able to reclaim the promised land (Moyo and Yeros 2005; Rosset Patel, and Courville 2006). Agribusiness and financial capital have directly or indirectly taken control of the land, even engaging in land grabbing fueled by the North's and China's extractivist demands for raw materials and agricultural commodities (Borras and Franco 2012; Borras et al. 2012).

In today's fundamentally different world context, one key lesson is not to follow mechanically in the footsteps of the South Korea and Taiwan; this is either impossible or would not achieve the desired results. For me, the key lesson is to seek to use and develop the incipient analytical framework of the synergetic development strategy I have sketched out and used to explain the success or failure of a country's development process. It is a framework that is adaptable to different contexts, stages, and paths of development, and that focuses on the creation and promotion of synergies throughout a country's economy, as well as in its linkages with the world system—that is, synergies promoted by the state that enhance the productive forces of the whole system through the making of intersectoral, intrasectoral, interenterprise and intraenterprise linkages, and linkages that maximize the value added in the web of linkages, which can at the same time ensure that the fruits of the productivity increases are distributed fairly across the system.

This is a big challenge, but with the emergence of a new Cold War and the climate change crisis it is imperative to bring such an SGDS about in as many countries as feasibly possible. Many linkages already exist; but they need to be abolished or reformed because they are controlled by agribusiness, corporate capital, and transnational companies that use them, such as in the case of commodity or value chains and contract farming, to extract exploitative rents and surplus value from peasants and workers. And new linkages will have to be formed as development requirements and priorities change. It is also possible to prioritize certain sectoral and enterprise linkages, but within a certain adaptable development sequence. And there are other ways to enhance the feasibility of an SGDS because it is not necessary to have a complete blueprint ready;

I doubt that policymakers even in South Korea and Taiwan had one, but they laid the foundations for an SGDS and had the determination to pursue it. Development policies and strategies have to be flexible and adaptable, but knowing what key goals one tries to reach is necessary.

Given the urgency of the global climate crisis, it follows that states have to prioritize in their development strategy policies that begin to tackle it, and this will also require new state interventions in the economy and society. Such a shift in and expansion of the state's role the offers opportunities for such an ecological SGDS. Undoubtedly, the contemporary agrarian question is ecological (Rosset and Altieri 2017; Watts 2021, 63; and Holleman, this volume) and it needs to be resolved through an agroecological agrarian transition, which family farmers are well suited to spearhead in the North and in the South (Akram-Lodhi 2021; Van der Ploeg 2008, and this volume). But such a transition will require a major transfer of resources to agriculture, particularly to peasant farmers, and this time, the resources will have to come from the natural resource extractivist rentier sector and from the rents captured by some companies in the service and industry sectors. This should provide a new impetus for land reform but of a fundamentally different type as it will have to be driven by ecological concerns and embedded in an ecological SGDS. Such an SGDS and ecological land reform may not seem feasible at present, but researchers need to prioritize these issues so that policymakers can benefit from their findings and social movements can garner support for an ecological transformation in society.

Acknowledgments

I am most grateful for the guidance, comments, and support I received from Saturnino Borras Jr. and Jenny Franco. They are, of course, not responsible for the remaining shortcomings of this final version of my text.

References

Akram-Lodhi, A. Haroon. 2021. "The Ties That Bind? Agroecology and the Agrarian Question in the Twenty-First Century." *Journal of Peasant Studies* 48 (4): 687–714.

Akram-Lodhi, A. Haroon, and Cristóbal Kay. 2010a. "Surveying the Agrarian Question (Part 1): Unearthing Foundations, Exploring Diversity." *Journal of Peasant Studies* 37 (1): 177–202.

Akram-Lodhi, A. Haroon, and Cristóbal Kay. 2010b. "Surveying the Agrarian Question (Part 2): Current Debates and Beyond." *Journal of Peasant Studies* 37 (2): 255–284.

Amsden, Alice H. 1989. *Asia's Next Giant: South Korea and Late Industrialisation*. New York: Oxford University Press.

Apthorpe, R. 1979. "The Burden of Land Reform in Taiwan: An Asian Model Land Reform Re-analysed." *World Development* 7 (4–5): 519–530.

Barraclough, Solon. 1973. *Agrarian Structure in Latin America*. Lexington, MA: D.C. Heath.

Baumeister, E. 2019. "Agrarian Reform." In *Revolution and Counterrevolution in Nicaragua*, edited by T. W. Walker, 229–426. London: Routledge.

Bello, W. 2019. *Counterrevolution: The Global Rise of the Far Right*. Rugby: Practical Action Publishing.

Bernstein, H. 1996. "Agrarian Questions Then and Now." *Journal of Peasant Studies* 24 (1/2): 22–59.

Bernstein, H. 2006. "Is There an Agrarian Question in the 21st Century?" *Canadian Journal of Development Studies* 27 (4): 449–460.

Blum, W. 2014. *Killing Hope: US Military and CIA Interventions Since World War II*. London: Zed Books.

Borras, Saturnino M., Jr., Cristóbal Kay, and A. Haroon Akram-Lodhi. 2007. "Agrarian Reform and Rural Development: Historical Overview and Current Issues." In *Land, Poverty and Livelihoods in an Era of Globalization: Perspectives from Developing and Transition Countries*, edited by A. Haroon Akram-Lodhi, Saturnino M. Borras Jr. and Cristóbal Kay, 1–40. London: Routledge.

Borras, Saturnino M., Jr., Cristóbal Kay, and E. Lahiff, eds. 2008. *Market-Led Agrarian Reform: Critical Perspectives on Neoliberal Land Policies and the Rural Poor*. London: Routledge.

Borras, Saturnino M., Jr., and Jennifer C. Franco 2012. "Global Land Grabbing and Trajectories of Agrarian Change." *Journal of Agrarian Change* 12 (1): 34–59.

Borras, Saturnino M., Jr., Cristóbal Kay, S. Gómez, and J. Wilkinson. 2012. "Land Grabbing and Global Capitalist Accumulation: Key Features in Latin America." *Canadian Journal of Development Studies* 33 (4): 402–416.

Browning, D. 1983. "Agrarian Reform in El Salvador." *Journal of Latin American Studies* 15 (2): 399–426.

Byres, Terence J. 1996. *Capitalism from Above and Capitalism from Below: An Essay in Comparative Political Economy*. London: Macmillan.

Byres, Terence J. 2016. "In Pursuit of Capitalist Agrarian Transition." *Journal of Agrarian Change* 16 (3): 432–451.

Chang Ha-Joon. 2003. "The East Asian Development Experience." In *Rethinking Development Economics*, edited by Chang Ha-Joon, 107–124. London: Anthem Press.

Davis, Diane E. 2004. *Discipline and Development: Middle Classes and Prosperity in East Asia and Latin America*. Cambridge, UK: Cambridge University Press.

de Janvry, Alain. 1981. *The Agrarian Question and Reformism in Latin America*. Baltimore, MD: Johns Hopkins University Press.

de Janvry, Alain, Elisabeth Sadoulet, and Wendy Wolford. 1998. "The Changing Role of the State in Latin American Land Reforms." Working Paper No. 852. Department of Agricultural and Resource Economics, University of California at Berkeley.

Elson, A. 2006. "The Economic Growth of East Asia and Latin America in Comparative Perspective: Lessons for Development Policy." *World Economics* 7 (2): 97–114.

Evans, P. 1987. "Class, State and Dependence in East Asia: Lessons for Latin Americanists." In *The Political Economy of New Asian Industrialism*, edited by F. C. Deyo, 203–226. Ithaca, NY: Cornell University Press.

FitzGerald, E. V. K. 2000. "ECLA and the Theory of Import Substituting Industrialization in Latin America." In *Industrialization and the State in Latin America: The Post-war Years*, edited by E. Cárdenas, J. A. Ocampo, and R. Thorp, 58–97. London: Macmillan.

Gereffi, G. 1989. "Rethinking Development Theory: Insights from East Asia and Latin America." *Sociological Forum* 4 (4): 505–533.

Grabowski, Richard. 2015. "Economic Strategy and Agricultural Productivity." *Journal of Social and Economic Development* 17 (2): 167–183.

Griffin, K., A. R. Khan, and A. Ickowitz. 2002. "Poverty and the Distribution of Land." *Journal of Agrarian Change* 2 (3): 279–330.

Hart, G. 1998. "Regional Linkages in the Era of Liberalization: A Critique of the New Agrarian Optimism." *Development and Change* 29 (1): 27–54.

Hart-Landsberg, M., S. Jeong, and R. Westra, eds. 2017. *Marxist Perspectives on South Korea in the Global Economy*. London: Routledge.

Karshenas, M. 2004. "Urban Bias, Intersectoral Resource Flows and the Macroeconomic Implications of Agrarian Relations: The Historical Experience of Japan and Taiwan." *Journal of Agrarian Change* 4 (1–2): 170–189.

Kautsky, Karl. 1988. *The Agrarian Question*. Vol. 1. London: Zwan Publications. (Original work published in German in 1899).

Kay, Cristóbal. 1975. "Agrarian Reform and the Transition to Socialism in Chile, 1970–1973." *Journal of Peasant Studies* 2 (4): 418–445.

Kay, Cristóbal. 1982. "Achievements and Contradictions of the Peruvian Agrarian Reform." *Journal of Development Studies* 18 (2): 141–170.

Kay, Cristóbal. 1988. "Economic Reforms and Collectivisation in Cuban Agriculture." *Third World Quarterly* 10 (3): 1239–1266.

Kay, Cristóbal. 1989. *Latin American Theories of Development and Underdevelopment*. London: Routledge.

Kay, Cristóbal. 1998. "Latin America's Agrarian Reform: Lights and Shadows." *Land Reform Settlement and Cooperatives*, 2, 8–31.

Kay, Cristóbal. 2001. "Reflections on Rural Violence in Latin America." *Third World Quarterly* 22 (5): 741–775.

Kay, Cristóbal. 2004. "Chile's Neoliberal Agrarian Transformation and the Peasantry." *Journal of Agrarian Change* 2 (4): 464–501.

Kay, Cristóbal. 2015. "The Agrarian Question and the Neoliberal Rural Transformation in Latin America." *European Review of Latin American and Caribbean Studies* No. 100: 73–83.

Kay, Cristóbal. 2016. "Neoliberalism and Rural Change: Land and Capital Concentration, and the Precariousness of Labour." In *The Handbook of Neoliberalism*, edited by Simon Springer, Kean Birch, and Julie MacLeavy, 398–409. London: Routledge.

Kay, Cristóbal, and M. Urioste. 2007. "Bolivia's Unfinished Agrarian Reform: Rural Poverty and Development Policies." In *Land, Poverty and Livelihoods in an Era of Globalization: Perspectives from Developing and Transition Countries*, edited by A. H. Akram-Lodhi, S. Borras, and Cristóbal Kay, 41–79. London: Routledge.

Khan, Mushtaq H., and Stephanie Blankenburg. 2009. "The Political Economy of Industrial Policy in Asia and Latin America." In *The Political Economy of Industrial Policy in Asia and Latin America*, edited by Mario Cimoli, Giovanni Dosi, and Joseph E. Stiglitz. Oxford Scholarship Online.

Kim, I. 2016. "Land Reform in South Korea under the U.S. Military Occupation, 1945–1948." *Journal of Cold War Studies* 18 (2): 97–129.

Leftwich, A. 1995. "Bringing Politics Back In: Towards a Model of the Developmental State." *Journal of Development Studies* 31 (3): 400–427.

Lewis, W. A. 1954. "Economic Development with Unlimited Supplies of Labour." *Manchester School of Economic and Social Studies* 22 (2): 139–191.

Moyo, S., and P. Yeros, eds. 2005. *Reclaiming the Land: The Resurgence of Rural Movements in Africa, Asia and Latin America*. London: Zed Books.

Pelupessy, W. 1993. "Agrarian Reform and Anti-Reform in El Salvador." In *Economic Maladjustment in Central America*, edited by W. Pelupessy and J. Weeks, 164–184. London: Palgrave Macmillan.

Prebisch, R. 1950. *The Economic Development of Latin America and Its Principal Problems.* Economic Commission for Latin America report. Lake Success, NY: United Nations Department of Economic Affairs.

Ricz, Judit, and István Benczes. 2020. "Comparative Analysis of the Historical Statist Development Models of East Asia and Latin America." POPREBEL Working Paper series No. 8.

Robles, W. 2018. "Revisiting Agrarian Reform in Brazil, 1985–2016." *Journal of Developing Societies* 34 (1): 1–34.

Rodrik, Dani. 1995. "Getting Interventions Right: How South Korea and Taiwan Grew Rich." *Economic Policy* 10 (20): 53–107.

Rosset, P., and M. Altieri. 2017. *Agroecology: Science and Politics*. Black Point, CAN: Fernwood Publishing.

Rosset, P. M., R. Patel, and M. Courville, eds. 2006. *Promised Land: Competing Visions of Agrarian Reform*. Oakland, CA: Food First Books.

Samuelson, P. 1948. "International Trade and the Equalisation of Factor Prices." *Economic Journal* 58 (230): 163–184.

Schiff, M., and A. Valdés. 1992. *The Plundering of Agriculture in Developing Countries.* Washington, DC: World Bank.

Siddiqui, K. 2022. "Comparing the East Asian and Latin American Countries: The Role of Agricultural Reforms in the Economic Transformation." *The World Financial Review.* Downloaded from https://worldfinancialreview.com/comparing-the-east-asian-and-latin-american-countries-the-role-of-agricultural-reforms-in-the-economic-transformation/

Teichman, J. 2015. "The Role of the Middle Class in Distributional Outcomes: Chile and South Korea." *Studies in Comparative International Development* 50 (1): 1–21.

Thiesenhusen, W. C. 1995. *Broken Promises. Agrarian Reform and the Latin American Campesino*. Boulder, CO: Westview Press.

Toye, J., and R. Toye. 2003. "The Origins and Interpretation of the Prebisch-Singer Thesis." *History of Political Economy* 35 (3): 437–467.

Van der Ploeg, J. D. 2008. *The New Peasantries: Struggles for Autonomy and Sustainability in an Era of Empire and Globalization*. London: Earthscan.

Vergara-Camus, L., and Cristóbal Kay. 2017. "The Agrarian Political Economy of Left-Wing Governments in Latin America: Agribusiness, Peasants and the Limits of Neo-developmentalism." *Journal of Agrarian Change* 17 (2): 415–437.

Wade, Robert. 1990. *Governing the Market: Economic Theory and the Role of Government in East Asian Industrialization*. Princeton, NJ: Princeton University Press.

Watts, M. 2021. "The Agrarian Question." In *Handbook of Critical Agrarian Studies*, edited by A. Haroon Akram-Lodhi, K. Dietz, B. Engels, and B. M. McKay, 53–66. Cheltenham, UK: Edward Elgar.

Zeitlin, M., and R. E. Ratcliff. 1988. *Landlords and Capitalists: The Dominant Class of Chile.* Princeton, NJ: Princeton University Press.

CHAPTER 32

LAND AND GEOPOLITICS

MICHAEL B. DWYER

INTRODUCTION

NORTHERN Laos, 2007. A provincial official with whom my colleagues and I were speaking had a complaint about the land deals that his superiors, as well as provincial officials elsewhere across the north, had been signing with Chinese rubber companies over the last few years. Although often glossed as "contract farming" projects, "there is a problem with [them]," he told us. "It's like a concession to a company: a big area. The companies say it's contract farming, but it's not actually contract farming."[1]

Over the last decade and a half, the proliferation of transnational land deals has become increasingly recognized as a coherent, if complex and frequently opaque, phenomenon. Sometimes termed a new "global land grab"—or more properly if less captivatingly, a global land *rush* (since only some of the land targeted has actually been acquired)—the linking of individual land deals to a larger pattern of transnational land access entered public consciousness around the time of the 2008 global financial crisis (Arezki, Deininger, Harris Selod 2011; Borras et al. 2012; Li 2011). Embodying a more explicitly interventionist, state-managed model of international cooperation, transnational land deals have generated concerns about land dispossession and foreign land access across the global South, as well as more specific questions about the changing politics of development aid and infrastructure investment exemplified by China's rise (Muldavin 2013; Nyíri 2009). As these concerns have remained current in the post-2008 landscape, they have helped to recenter attention to *geopolitics* in the sense discussed by critical geographers and other scholars: as the politics of not just geostrategic relations among states, but also of the social relations that surround land and, in doing so, shape political space both sub- and trans-nationally (see e.g., De Koninck 2006; Sassen 2013; Scurrah and Hirsch 2022).

On one level, the details of the land deal gestured to above—about crop (rubber), timing (middle-late 2000s), location (northwestern Laos, near the Chinese border) and nationalities (Lao officials, Chinese investors)—place it squarely within the global land rush. As I elaborate below, this boom in transnational land deals was recognized in the late 2000s, but it frequently concerned deals signed earlier in the decade as well. On another level, however, the precise issue that my provincial informant flagged—whether the deal in question was targeting state-owned land that could be legally conceded to investors, or whether it was a contract-farming scheme involving farmers' ongoing use of their own land—pointed to legal and bureaucratic questions of property and legibility that long preceded the land rush itself. My informant's complaint highlighted a key fact about the rubber plantation schemes that, as my use of scare quotes around the term "contract farming" indicates, were hardly the outgrower arrangements between companies and smallholders usually implied by this term: They were hybrid projects that contained both concessions to Chinese companies (in some areas) and outgrower arrangements with those same companies (in others)—a bit like the "nucleus-plasma" schemes described by Julia and White (2012, 999) in Indonesia's palm-oil sector, but much heavier on the concession side. The contract-farming label, in other words, provided political cover by shielding the deals from being labeled as concessions, which provincial authorities had officially banned in late 2005.

My informant's complaint thus pointed in two directions at once: first, and more obviously, toward the political work that labeling can do in a context where signing land away to foreign companies has become "sensitive" or controversial; second, and more subtly, toward the bureaucratic and legal difficulty of differentiating state-owned land from private land in many parts of upland Laos (and, I suggest, more broadly across the global South). In doing so, the complaint pointed to the complex political and temporal nature of the recent land rush, which was realized through deals signed under the boom conditions of the 2000s, when sovereign wealth was increasingly venturing abroad, but which took root in structural conditions—in particular, uncertainty around property—established over multiple decades prior, often from a mix of distinct processes.

In this chapter, I elaborate a critical approach to the geopolitics of land that uses the land-deal boom of the 2000s as an entry point into questions of why, when, and where "land" becomes a geopolitical issue at all—that is, the conditions under which questions of property, access, and enclosure become linked as political questions to issues of national development, vulnerability, and security. Land may be inherently geopolitical in a literal, trivial sense; but to take it as always-already geopoliticized risks losing this more specific and important meaning of how, when, and why domestic land access becomes explicitly embroiled in international affairs. Crucial, I suggest, is the social distribution of enclosure. Enclosure is an enduring feature of capitalist development, yet the differential aspects of enclosure processes—some areas and some populations endure far more than others—are inevitably a function of the interplay of historical and emergent geographies. Consideration of local, place-based histories, rather than international relations per se, is essential when analyzing the geopolitical dimensions of transnational land deals.

Drawing on my work in Laos, the chapter outlines what I describe as a conjunctural approach to land and geopolitics as a way to explain and understand this unevenness. My approach draws on the geographer Gillian Hart's blending of critical historical and geographical traditions to ask "how diverse forces come together" in space and time to create the "political terrain" where development occurs (Hart 2002, 27). I thus begin by describing how the global land rush opened a conversation about land and geopolitics, centering on the proliferation of transnational land deals during the boom decade of the 2000s. I then use what I see as the shortcomings of a particular way of talking about these geopolitics (through the use of what I call "authority gap" narratives) to introduce a more practically adequate approach, which I explain in terms of the need to examine both the "macro" and "micro" geopolitics surrounding land deals. I illustrate this approach using the case of northwestern Laos's rubber sector, drawing on my recent book *Upland Geopolitics: Postwar Laos and the Global Land Rush*. I conclude by arguing that the land-geopolitics nexus is best investigated as the governing of enclosure in contexts beset by multiple legacies of geopolitical struggle.

"A Neocolonial Pact"? Geopoliticizing Transnational Land Access

In the first decade of the 2000s, the economic and institutional linkages between agriculture, property, and finance deepened as sovereign and private wealth increasingly entered the global agribusiness arena (Fairbairn 2020). This coincided and overlapped with the emergence of more explicitly state-managed approaches to development, taking different forms in different contexts but, in general, reacting to the social instability created by the dominant market-fundamentalist (or neoliberal) approach of the preceding decades. China figured centrally here, having embraced a more regulated form of state capitalism in the 1980s and 1990s, and with the turn of the millennium, having begun to mobilize its substantial economic power into state-backed foreign investment and development cooperation abroad (Lee 2014; Oliveira 2019). This all came together in the buildup to the 2008 financial crisis, as private investors increasingly diversified into commodities as a way to hedge against stock market volatility, and a number of countries—worried about the effects of this hedging on their own commodity imports (both food and otherwise)—began to pursue direct land access abroad (Holt-Giménez and Patel 2009; Fairbairn 2020). GRAIN, an organization allied with the global peasant movement La Via Campesina, helped break the "global land grab" story in late 2008 (Grain 2008a).

Much of the initial urgency came from a public intervention by the then director-general of the UN Food and Agriculture Organization (FAO), Jacques Diouf, in late 2008. A few months earlier, the FAO had hosted a Conference on World Food Security in Rome addressing the recent spike in global food prices and the associated wave of unrest across the global South (Lacey 2008; Holt-Giménez and Patel 2009). At the conference, Diouf had called for "innovative new solutions" to the chronic problem of agricultural underinvestment in the global South, including "partnership or joint-venture agreements" between, "on the one hand, those countries that have the financial resources and on the other, those that possess land, water and human resources" (Diouf 2008, 8). Summer 2008 had seen the announcement of numerous transnational farmland deals across sub-Saharan Africa and Central, South, and Southeast Asia, mostly involving state-linked companies from across Asia, and often in the tens to hundreds of thousands of hectares each (Grain 2008b). Later that year, in a widely quoted article, "The Food Crisis and the Wrong Solutions," Diouf used some very blunt language to clarify his earlier remarks. Criticizing these new land deals as "unequal international relations and short-term mercantilist agriculture," he worried publicly about the creation of "a neocolonial pact" for the provision of raw materials to the rest of the world (Diouf 2008, 8).

Diouf's comments circulated widely. It was one thing for the head of the FAO to advocate increased investment in agricultural development, and quite another to warn of an emerging neocolonial pact targeting poor countries across the global South. Lending official legitimacy to what might otherwise have been dismissed as activist concerns, his comments also helped cement an explicitly geopolitical framing onto the new land rush. Exemplified by headlines invoking "the farms race" (*Toronto Globe and Mail*), "agricultural imperialism" (*New York Times Magazine*), and a "great land grab to safeguard [rich countries'] food supply" (the *Guardian*), this discourse reflected the resonance of the new land deals with the land grabs of the late colonial era (Borger 2008; Reguly 2009; Rice 2009). Decrying a new scramble for Africa and beyond (e.g., MacKinnon 2008), many Western observers were particularly worried about the global rise of China and other emerging economies like India and Brazil; more than a few preferred to focus their concerns here rather than on the linkages to Wall Street and the 2008 financial crisis, which also figured centrally in GRAIN's initial missive. The *Economist*, for instance, published a piece on "outsourcing's third wave" that wondered whether farmland might be the next logical step in globalization via comparative advantage. But in the same breath—and highlighting the tension between optimism and concern that characterized much of the mainstream reporting—the magazine readily rolled the land deals into what it criticized as "Chinese neocolonialism" in Africa, described in a pointed example as "going down well with Mozambique's elite" (Economist 2009).

Laos, where transnational land deals had already been underway for a few years (Dwyer 2007; Schönweger et al. 2012), became caught up directly in this discourse. Barely a month after the GRAIN report and Diouf's article, the *Guardian* published a multipart feature, with the headline quoted above about a "great land grab." It included a map based on GRAIN's data (Figure 32.1) that purported to show over 7.5 million hectares that had been purchased by governments and private companies from South Korea (which had allegedly bought 2.3 million ha), China (2.1 million ha), Saudi Arabia (1.6 million ha), the United Arab Emirates (1.3 million ha), and Japan (0.3 million ha). The locations of this "world land grab" included Indonesia (1.6 million ha), Madagascar (1.3 million ha), the Philippines (1.24 million m ha), Sudan (1.1 million ha), Pakistan

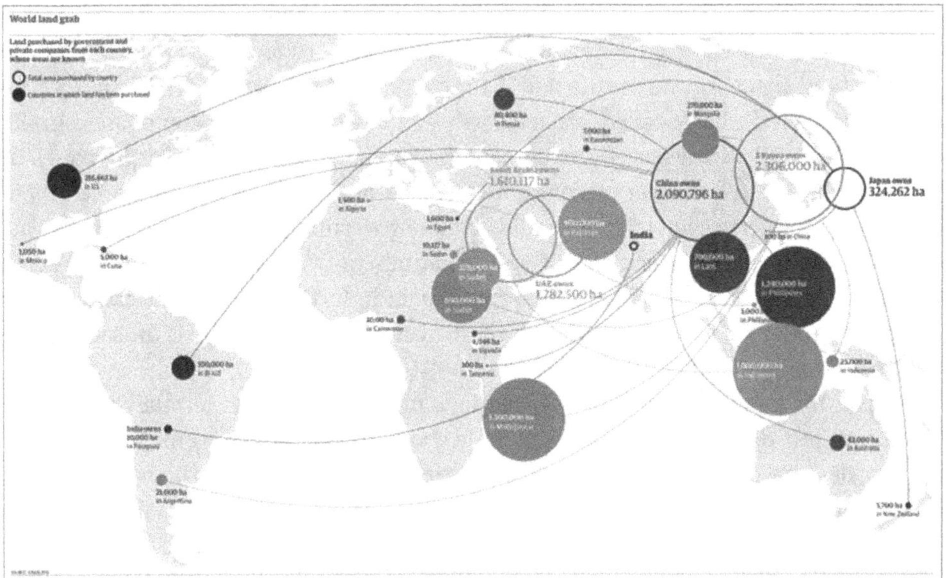

FIGURE 32.1. Geopoliticizing transnational land access ("World Land Grab").
Source: http://image.guardian.co.uk/sysfiles/Guardian/documents/2008/11/21/LANDGRAB.pdf (accessed 25 Sept. 2009).

(900,000 ha), Laos (700,000 ha), and Mongolia (270,000 ha); Laos's numbers, given its relatively small size, made it the most "grabbed" country shown.

The *Guardian* spread also included a feature story from Laos, which was arguably the most important piece of the set since it helped ground the almost unbelievably large numbers shown on the map (MacKinnon 2008). Echoing the *Economist*'s concern about national elites benefiting from foreign land deals at the expense of local citizens, the *Guardian* story implied that Lao officials had abdicated their public duties and were instead giving away land to line their own pockets. "The situation is completely out of control," it quoted one foreign adviser in the Lao capital, Vientiane, as saying. "It's a fire sale. People in power are just desperate to get their hands on the money so they don't miss out. For the companies coming in it's a massive land grab" (MacKinnon 2008). The feature also quoted a prominent historian of modern Laos, who described the situation as "simply a matter of greed. Officials are grabbing what they can. Companies need land and are prepared to pay well. It all goes under the table" (Martin Stuart-Fox, quoted in MacKinnon 2008).

These passages exemplify a common way of talking about transnational land deals that, while flagging them as geopolitical, also manifests a relatively thin notion of geopolitics itself. Using what I call an "authority gap" narrative, passages like the ones quoted above examine the interests and motivations of governments and firms that seek land abroad, but focus exclusively on corruption and elite self-interest when trying to explain the actions of host states. The phrase "authority gap" itself comes from a 2010 story on Asia Times Online (https://asiatimes.com/), a widely read English-language media outlet in Southeast Asia, decrying what it termed "Chinese expansionism" across northern Laos—in special economic zones, corporate rubber plantations, and the growing (and allegedly underestimated) Chinese population in northern Lao cities. The article bemoaned what it called "the authority gap in a growing number of areas in the country where Vientiane has effectively ceded sovereignty to Beijing" (Crispin 2010). In this narrative, as in the other pieces quoted above, local elites and corrupt officials are the ones in charge: foreign land deals and actually governing are framed as mutually incompatible. The authority-gap narrative has a number of variants, including references to "weak governance"—a staple of the development industry—or, in some cases, "anarchic" or "frontier" development.[2] Whatever the language, the message is the same: "The situation is completely out of control."

Despite their popularity, these explanations miss a lot. First of all, they ignore the significant role of host states in creating both the legal and the economic feasibility for large-scale land deals. By conjuring a weak or absent state, the authority-gap frame ignores the history of progressively stronger formal state ownership of rural hinterlands, first during the colonial era and, more recently, by newly independent countries of the global South, whose nationalization of untitled lands during the 1950s, '60s, and '70s reflected both elite self-interest and the prevailing socialist winds of Third World nationalism (Alden Wily 2012, 763). Authority-gap narratives likewise miss the more recent policy changes, often from the 1990s, that have drastically lowered taxation rates (on land, profits, and commodity exports) and altered national land laws in a bid to attract greater foreign investment to poor countries (Alden Wily 2012, 764–766; also see Dwyer and Nanhthavong 2023). Although these adjustments are often implemented by Southern governments under pressure from Northern lenders—whether as part of structural adjustment packages or more "voluntary" alternatives—they imply strategic state action under conditions of structural duress, not the absence of governing per se (cf. Ong 2000).

Authority-gap narratives also ignore the sociospatial unevenness that transnational land deals invariably manifest. Because they are negative descriptions—accounts of what is missing rather than what is actually going on—authority-gap narratives have little to say about why foreign land deals have been targeted into certain regions with good farmland but not others, or why they achieve large-scale enclosures in some places yet run up against prohibitively strong resistance elsewhere (see, e.g., Borras, Fig, and Monsalve Suárez 2011; Lavers 2012). As researchers have studied the global land rush over the last decade-plus, they have become increasingly convinced that, as one senior scholar put it, "an accelerated process of dispossession is clearly in motion" (Edelman 2013, 485). Yet as agriculture, energy, and finance merge, and as sovereign wealth becomes an increasingly global force (Cotula et al. 2009; Fairbairn 2020; Wolford et al. 2013), questions of *how* and *where* this "accelerated dispossession" is taking place have become increasingly intertwined. If accelerated dispossession is "clearly in motion," what enables that motion to gain traction in some places, but not others? Put another way, what turns a general land *rush* into a specific (and highly uneven) geography of land *grabs*?

Geopolitical Struggles over Land and Property: A Conjunctural Approach

In the boom years of the early and mid-2000s, Lao smallholders were confronted with a paradoxical situation when officials and investors began targeting their land for rubber plantations and other agribusiness schemes. Despite their long-standing use of those lands and, moreover, their having participated in a formal process of mapping of the village-territory boundaries within which those uses occurred (Lestrelin, Castella, and Bourgoin 2012), their claims to those lands were increasingly being questioned by state authorities due to a putative "lack of title" (Dwyer 2013, 2017; see also Vandergeest 2003). On the one hand, this shift in the meaning and the associated availability to outsiders of village lands had local and regional roots. Since colonial times, development planners have pointed to Laos's (and Cambodia's, and Sumatra's, etc.) substantial natural resources and relatively low population density as comparative advantages whose mobilization through external investment should fuel development. On the other hand, the meaningfulness of "lack of title" reflected a distinctly global dimension, one that Laos shared with a number of other countries across the global South: the arrival of land titling by registration. With this came, not just title documents themselves, but a shift in legal norms of ownership that, paradoxically, facilitated the creation of external access to land, all in the name of creating tenure security.

Property scholars have highlighted a long-standing and ongoing struggle, especially in colonial and postcolonial landscapes, between occupancy/use versus registration/formalization as competing bases for legitimate landownership (Bhandar 2015, 2018; Guldi 2021). Focusing on periods that long predate the recent land rush, this work has added much to the understanding of the geopolitics of contemporary land access. Not only does it illustrate and highlight the conjunctural nature of land access by linking colonial and postcolonial regimes and the associated struggles over what constitute "modern" forms of property. It also points squarely toward a pervasive, if often unrecognized, *geopolitical* dimension of land politics today: the shift toward legally abstract notions of landownership that are rooted in the European experience, often in specifically colonial contexts that favored easy land commodification. Ultimately, an adequate understanding of the geopolitics of land requires a conjunctural approach that accounts for multiply scaled spatiotemporal processes, from broad framings of landownership to the more localized social relations of property elaborated below using the concept of *micro-geopolitics*.

Framing Landownership

Struggles over property itself are nicely illustrated through the contrasting, but ultimately complementary, recent work of scholars Brenna Bhandar (2015, 2018) and Jo

Guldi (2021). A number of excellent scholars (e.g., Ong 2000; Nyíri 2009; Alden Wily 2012) have noted the colonial underpinnings of land law across the global South, along with its transmission into postcolonial regimes during the middle and late twentieth century (also see Kay, this volume). Bhandar's and Guldi's work adds both specificity and tension to this history, flagging the important and fundamental shift colonial legal regimes brought to Indigenous norms about land, as well as the importance of Indigenous critiques of this shift for subsequent political change.

In her history of Torrens titling—which, not coincidentally, has provided the model for land titling that has been financed in recent years by the World Bank and other Western donors across the global South—Bhandar (2015) writes that "the drive to render land as fungible as possible" (254) was operationalized in colonial Australia by the shift from deed-based legal norms grounded in "conveyance" practices to legal bureaucracies based on registration. This allowed a series of often-fraught questions (Who owned the land originally? By what means had it been "conveyed" from that owner to the next?) to be sidestepped in favor of a simpler one: To whom is the land currently registered? The rationale of this approach was explained by the colonial governor of South Australia, Robert Richard Torrens, after whom title by registration is often named. Writing in 1859, Torrens emphasized plainly the need to make colonial rule more expedient by abandoning certain legal niceties that had been developed in England to make sure that the rule of law was applied with adequate deliberation: "In playing out the game of life in this work-a-day part of the globe, we require something less costly, something less artificial, something which we may handle with more *freedom* and rapidity" (quoted in Bhandar 2015, 254). In England, property law had traditionally functioned in a Polanyian (1944) mode of social protection (albeit usually of the propertied), weighing down land transactions under a mass of bureaucratic procedure, legal principle, and potential uncertainty. As Bhandar describes, the replacement of conveyance with registration as the basis for legal ownership in the colonies lifted these protections significantly.

Torrens-style titling fit the belief, imported with the English into Australia and elsewhere across their empire and beyond (Vandergeest and Peluso 1995: 403), that "land was . . . a commodity without any [native] owners, to be claimed, partitioned, securitized, and cultivated. . . . Echoing earlier movements of enclosure in England and Wales, title by registration function[ed] during the nineteenth century as a technique of dispossession in the settler colony" (Bhandar 2015, 256). Lockean notions of improvement, Bhandar explains, conjoined ideas about physical mobility and racial inferiority, using fixity-in-place as a sign of civilization (Bhandar 2018, 182). Although her discussion is largely confined to settler-colonial contexts, her analysis applies far more broadly to state-territorial ones, both colonial and otherwise (e.g., across much of Southeast Asia or sub-Saharan Africa), where governments used mobility to define a class of nonowners of land (often, Indigenous shifting cultivators and/or pastoralists) against whose uses legitimate property could be contrasted. In such a context, state landownership became the default; and registration-based title, the parcel-by-parcel exception. Bhandar narrates this as a process of abstraction, a shift from land as a complex social relation (e.g., subject to multiple competing—or identity-dependent or spatially overlapping or temporally variable, etc.—sets of claims; see e.g., Peluso 1995) to land as a more singular and abstract "modern form of property" (Bhandar 2015, 256), exemplified by the official cadaster. In practical terms, despite the significant variety of landownership regimes that remained, this ushered in an increasingly general shift from *title* as a debated abstraction to titles (plural) as *documents*; if being "untitled" became a sufficient reason to lose one's land, the introduction of land registration was a key step in that justification's pre-history.

Jo Guldi's recent work, in contrast, takes up the postcolonial period to show just how contested and discontinuous this history has been. Echoing Bhandar's insistence that meaningful change "requires perspectives from the margins—those of the evicted, propertyless, impoverished"—to redefine legitimate ownership after decades or centuries of dispossession (Bhandar 2018, 185), Guldi's account focuses on struggles for landownership norms based on *occupancy*, rather than on registration or de facto state ownership. Guldi stresses what she calls "theory built on history"—specifically, theories of legitimate ownership that emerge from colonial experiences of dispossession, and that often emphasize processes of land redistribution, smallholder viability, and the avoidance of debt. Her account of the ascendence of occupancy-based landownership norms in the mid-twentieth century offers more than a glimpse of how collective experiences of dispossession helped forge a counternarrative about landownership that, for much of the 1950s and '60s, threatened to become globally mainstream (Guldi 2021). If this movement was ultimately limited by the neoliberal turn of the 1980s and '90s—which, again not coincidentally, helped usher in the title-by-registration boom popularized by the World Bank and Western donors—its articulation, first in late-colonial Ireland and India and then, increasingly, across much of the global South and, in 1950s, in the halls of the FAO, showed that understandings of property itself have long remained open for debate.

Across much of the global South today, these earlier struggles continue to resonate in the policy debates and social struggles over, among other things, competing forms of land titling: collective versus individual, rural versus urban, zoning-based versus standalone (see e.g., Peluso 1995; Bryan 2012). Amid these debates and, crucially, the ongoing unevenness of property formalization they both reflect and produce (Dwyer 2015), land deals such as the one with which I began the chapter have increasingly targeted rural hinterlands across the global South. In these landscapes it is often useful to consider, not just the uneven bureaucratic politics of property itself, but a range of other, often highly localized social and historical relations as well. Uneven dispossession, in short, emerges in the conjunctures.

Micro-Geopolitics

Development projects traffic in the complex and inevitably negotiated politics of force and consent, and transnational land deals, in particular, incite struggles over enclosure, dispossession, and compensation that wrestle as much with questions of sociopolitical legitimacy as with those of formal law and policy. The terms of engagement for all of these turn on citizenship in practice: the ability to choose a livelihood, to select between competing risks, to have a voice in defining what improvement itself looks like. Property is always a social relation, and, especially in legal-pluralist contexts, where multiple factors shape the control over land, land conflicts are never solely about land; the ability to resist or negotiate the terms of development often depends on the capacity—whether individual or collective—to articulate one's role as a worthy citizen (Berry 2009; Lund 2012; Moore 1999). Conversely, when nationalist-tinged aspersions articulate with long-standing prejudices against certain forms of land use, the enclosure process can operate that much more easily.

Attention to this sort of historically sedimented, place-based "micro-geopolitics" has begun to emerge in recent scholarship, but it remains in short supply (see, e.g., Ballvé 2012; Diepart and Sem 2016; Dwyer 2014; Hirsch et al. 2022; Woods 2011). As a work in the global-ethnographic tradition, my book *Upland Geopolitics: Postwar Laos and the Global Land Rush* (Dwyer 2022) adds an extended case to the literature, attempting to help move both popular and scholarly understandings of transnational land politics beyond such negative explanations as the "authority gap" (or a common variant, "weak governance"), as well as beyond the national-level explanations of authoritarian governments or (post)socialist property systems. Developing the concept of *micro-geopolitics*, I point to the ways that contemporary processes of enclosure have become grounded in and shaped by earlier geopolitical conflicts, as manifested in the effects of the Cold War on mainland Southeast Asia's "upland" landscapes and populations.

My approach is broadly inspired by Michael Perelman's (2007) work on the history of enclosure, albeit with adjustments inspired by additional scholarship in the Marxian and Foucaultian traditions (e.g., Robinson 1983; Peluso 1995; Ong 2000). Perelman examined the logic and tactics of those he called the "primitive accumulationists"—plantation managers, colonial officials, and others who worked at the nexus of state and corporate power—to understand how enclosure practices became "calibrated" to particular historical situations. This is important because dispossession and displacement are often partial or incomplete, especially in contexts where land deals are intended (at least by some of their proponents—see the next section, "Where the Rubber Meets the Road") to fulfill local social objectives. But if Perelman's work focuses on the rationalities of those he studied, my interest is more in the emergent forms of territorial power that developed as multiple rationalities collided, competed, and combined (cf. Watts 2004). In the case I describe below from northwestern Laos, this multiplicity is important: enclosure processes there involved multiple sets of actors—state authorities, rubber companies, development agencies, and upland residents themselves—each of whom had their own powers and liabilities, as well as their own internal differences.

In such a context, some plans come to naught; others are twisted into almost unrecognizable shapes as they move from theory into practice. Enclosure is always a struggle—a process—and although it would be foolish to ignore plans and intentions completely, it is the outcomes that ultimately matter. Foucault's concept of *micropolitics* is the obvious referent in the concept of micro-geopolitics. Echoing Marx's critique of the "commodity fetish," Foucault advised against thinking of power as a simple object that can be passed from person to person. Power is a social relation and needs to be studied in its native habitat, so to speak, from the ground up. This "ascending" approach to power, Foucault emphasized, differs markedly from a top-down approach that is focused on "who has power" (Foucault 2004, 28, 30), which often, in my experience, leads to variants on what I called the "authority gap" narrative. If one begins only with plans, laws, and regulations, complexity on the ground all too often looks like implementation failure, illegality, even anarchy—terms that appear with some regularity in development discourse (Rigg 2005). On the other hand, studying power's "infinitesimal mechanisms," each with "their own history, their own trajectory, their own techniques and tactics"—and examining how these get "invested, colonized, used, . . . extended, and so on by increasingly general mechanisms" of control (Foucault 2004, 30)—offers an approach that, though hardly simple, is at least adequate to the complexity at hand.

Where the Rubber Meets the Road: Geopolitical Conjuncture in Northwestern Laos

Rubber is a relative newcomer to montane Southeast Asia, especially to northern Laos. In the early twentieth century, French-colonial planters introduced the crop in the southern part of the country via their development of large plantation complexes in Cambodia and southern Vietnam. But the French-imported rubber varieties, brought from the Brazilian Amazon via British Malaya and London's Kew Gardens (Dean 1987), were adapted to the humid tropics. The cold-adapted varieties found today in the mountainous uplands of southern Yunnan, northern Laos, and northern Myanmar were developed much later by Chinese agronomists during the Korean War, when China faced a Western blockade that cut off its rubber supplies of Malaya, Thailand, and Indonesia. The lower rates of production of Chinese varieties made them uncompetitive for export, but they served important domestic purposes, helping to create self-sufficiency and aiding Chinese officials in their efforts to "modernize" the uplands of southern Yunnan (Xu 2006). With the various displacements and refugee movements across the Lao, China, Thai, and Burmese borders amid the upheavals of the 1960s, '70s, and early '80s, the Cold War also helped bring Chinese rubber varieties to northern Laos (Chanthavong et al. 2009; Sturgeon et al. 2013).

For Lao officials, rubber fit the governmental ideal of "permanent livelihoods" (*asiip thavon* or *asiip kong thi*). This concept drew on both Indigenous and imported notions of proper settlement and economy. Generalizing the ideal of flooded-paddy rice production long practiced in the lowland parts of mainland Southeast Asia, it exemplified the legible farmer: fixed in space, market-integrated, and taxable by the state (Scott 2009).

The concept of permanent livelihoods echoed colonial-era anxieties about shifting cultivation, which at the time was by far the dominant form of upland farming. French-colonial foresters thus echoed their British and Dutch colleagues across the region in calling Indigenous shifting cultivators *mangeurs du bois* (wood eaters), and subsequent generations of officials and bureaucrats from India to Indonesia inherited the tradition of trying to "stabilize" shifting cultivation in favor of more commercially oriented and spatially fixed forms of agrarian production (Bryant 1997; Lu 2017). That said, with the cost of establishing rubber plantations estimated at a few hundred dollars per hectare, the cost of financing rubber at the scale desired for an agrarian transition in Laos's northern uplands was widely seen as prohibitive—not just for farmers, but for the Lao state as well.

In November 2000, the state visit of China's president Jiang Zemin offered Lao officials a chance to address this via a joint declaration on development cooperation, as well as in a series of bilateral economic and trade agreements that included agricultural production. This diplomatic push helped usher in the northern Lao rubber boom of the mid-2000s. Widely framed as a win-win-win for Lao farmers, Lao officials, and Chinese companies, bilateral rubber cooperation blossomed at a time when governments from North America to Europe to East Asia were widely embracing regional connectivity in the name of economic prosperity. Northwestern Laos thus became progressively enrolled in regional imaginaries, such as like the Golden Quadrangle, the Greater Mekong Subregion (GMS), and (later) China's Belt and Road Initiative (BRI). In the process, once "isolated" and "remote" borderlands were reimagined as "natural economic areas" that had earlier "thrived" as part of the ancient silk route between Sichuan and Assam (Asian Development Bank 1997, 1, 2); these lands were then *actually* connected by new road infrastructure brokered by the Asian Development Bank as part of the GMS initiative. Framed as an "initializing project" that would "serve as a 'locomotive' for subregional economic development . . . along the [GMS's] north-south axis" (Asian Development Bank 1997, 8–9), the so-called Northern Economic Corridor (NEC) was built between roughly 2002 and 2006, connecting China's Yunnan and Thailand's Chiang Rai provinces via the interior of northwestern Laos. The rubber deals referenced by my provincial informant took advantage of this newly opened hinterland, often targeting the "lower uplands" below 800 meters above sea level (Figure 32.2).

The Enclosure Question

In early 2001, as the NEC agreement was being finalized, and in the wake of Jiang Zemin's state visit to Laos, provincial officials in northwestern Laos outlined a plan to develop 10,000 hectares of new rubber plantations in cooperation with a Chinese rubber company with which they had been in discussions since the previous year.[3] Their plan, summarized here as an excerpt from their instructions to provincial- and district-level government agricultural extension agents, outlined the respective roles of the initiative's two "sides" in a way that clearly describes a contract-farming-based business model:

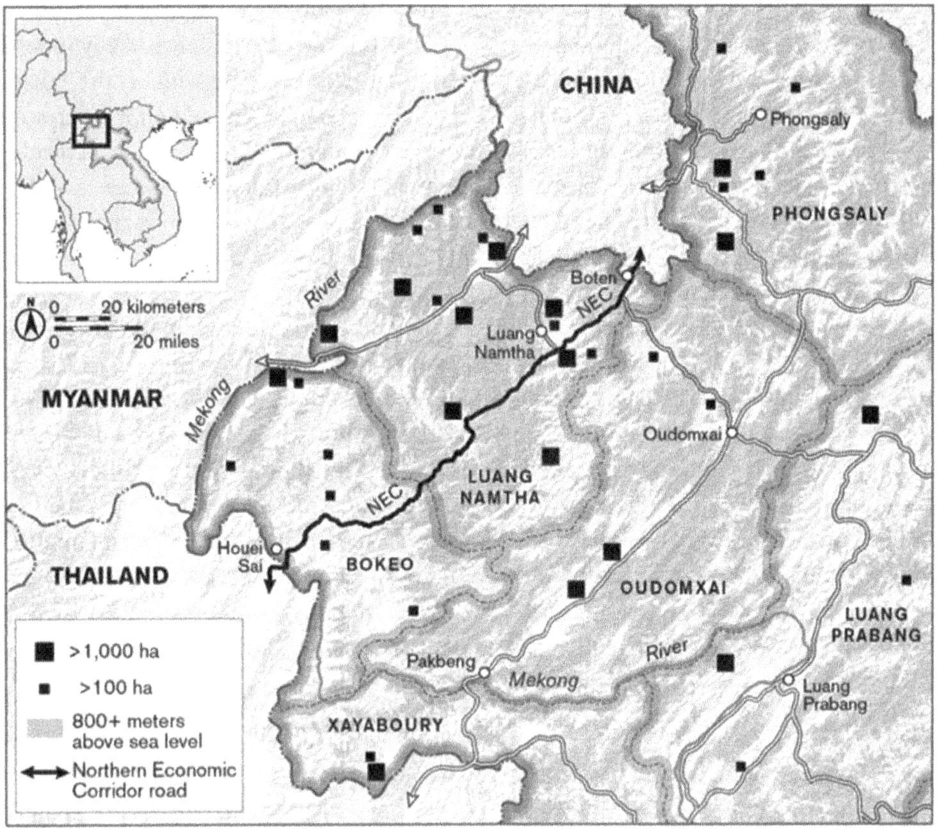

FIGURE 32.2. "Not actually contract farming" projects. Large Chinese rubber plantations in northern Laos. Map by Ben Pease.

Source: Dwyer (2022, 46). Reproduced with permission.

> The province . . . agrees to facilitate rubber planting and factory construction by convincing upland farmers to give up shifting cultivation-based livelihoods and plant rubber; to assign government staff from the relevant offices in order to coordinate with the Chinese investor side; and to implement rules, laws, etc. in order to assist the Chinese investor side in working in accordance with the policies of the exporting country [i.e., Laos]. The Chinese investor side will be solely responsible for investing in the building of the rubber-processing factory, contributing the relevant technical inputs, and providing the market for [the province's] upland farmers by buying their rubber and processing it for export.[4]

Contract farming, however, was not the form of bilateral cooperation that many Chinese companies had in mind. The half-decade from 2001 to 2005 thus marked a key period of regulatory struggle over the question of concessions versus contract farming among Chinese companies, Lao authorities, and, to a lesser but still significant extent, Lao villagers. Some of this took place in policy- and project-level negotiations among company and provincial representatives, but much of it took place out "in the field," so to speak: first, among district officials, who weighed the advantages and disadvantages of each business model to their own governmental needs, and second, at the village level, where district, village, and company representatives negotiated (not always on equal terms) over specific modalities of investment "cooperation" and, more specifically, questions of land availability. Companies pressed for large-scale land concessions, but provincial officials formalized a policy model in late 2005 that sought to make contract farming the norm, albeit with the significant caveat of it being conducted "in accordance with state land management."[5]

This gave rise to two processes that operated in parallel, at times articulating with each other, but often being in conflict in ways gestured to by my provincial informant's complaint. The first was the proliferation of a discourse of bilateral rubber cooperation based on "contract farming," "extension" or "promotion" (*songserm* in Lao), and a confusing and ambiguous terminology of "3 + 2" and "4 + 1" that allegedly referred to the various inputs required to bring a rubber crop to market (land, labor, financing, a market, and technical knowledge). The second was a series of on-the-ground rubber-plantation arrangements involving Chinese companies, many of which involved the use of coercive state zoning to produce enclosures for large-scale company plantations. In the district where I focused my research, some of the highest density of these enclosures occurred in a place called Khet Nam Fa.

Khet Nam Fa

Combining an abundance of land under 800 meters above sea level with a proximity to the NEC via the presence of newly built feeder roads, Khet Nam Fa's location made it a good candidate for a large-scale rubber operation whose eventual output was destined for overland export to China. The area thus exemplified the geography of the newly opened hinterland, described above, facilitated by regional integration, in general, and the GMS, in particular. As one of the new investment projects catalyzed by the NEC road upgrade, the operation—by a Chinese company that I will call Bolisat Ltd.—exemplified the "subregional economic development" that regional boosters were hoping for.

For local officials, a key dimension of Khet Nam Fa's appeal was its taxation potential. Local tax officials divided the district's villages into those that possessed village-level finance committees capable of calculating and collecting land taxes on an area basis and those that did not. Khet Nam Fa's villages all fell into the latter category. Contrary to assertions that upland areas in Laos are completely untaxed, this meant that Khet Nam Fa's agricultural lands were taxed indirectly by counting adults of working age, whom tax officials considered a reasonable proxy for upland fields that were too difficult to locate, map, and measure.[6] So, while it was not entirely untaxed, the land base of villages like those in Khet Nam Fa was seen as underproductive when it came to taxation; residents were among the poorest in the district, and the per-head tax rate was indeed quite low.[7] Large-scale rubber plantations offered the opposite, in the form of both a fixed, legible crop and a producer with the capacity to pay much more. In December 2006, the local provincial governor issued a rubber-tax policy that aimed to capitalize on precisely this: upon coming into production, rubber plantations over five hectares in size would be taxed six renminbi per tree per year; smaller plantations would be taxed less (Shi 2008, 14). During my fieldwork in 2006–2008, Bolisat Ltd.'s plantations in Khet Nam Fa already numbered at least a few hundred hectares, and they continued to grow through the end of the decade.[8] With their multiple hundreds of rubber trees per hectare, these plantations offered a potential tax windfall in the hundreds of thousands of dollars—far more than anything that had ever come off this land.

Still, Khet Nam Fa was hardly the only part of the district with these characteristics. A third and final piece of its "suitability" thus came via the relationship between citizenship and property that emerged from the micro-geopolitics of the area. Since the 1990s, state reorganization of the Lao uplands in general, and involuntary village resettlement and consolidation in particular, have drawn increasing and often critical attention from scholars and at least some development professionals (e.g., Vandergeest 2003). As numerous studies have shown, bringing remote villages closer to infrastructure and rural services, often apparently with a goal of freeing up hinterland forests for state use, has had major negative impacts, from the health consequences of moving highland villages down into warmer malarial zones to the consolidation-driven land loss and associated "new poverty" that geographer Jonathan Rigg (2005, 126) has aptly called a "policy-induced Malthusian squeeze." There has been more to this than the simple corralling of upland populations and the primitive accumulation of forestland—space that is "uninhabited, covered by forest, and administered by state agencies," as geographer Peter Vandergeest (2003, 52) put it in a thoughtful, early critique. Combining politico-military and economic rationales, the micro-geopolitics of population-management dynamics have been complex. As some upland groups were cleared out, others were left in place or even brought in (cf. Hardy 2003; De Koninck 2006).

Khet Nam Fa's residents had been resettled into the area in the late 1990s and early 2000s, putatively because of the development opportunities associated with fixed settlement closer to roads, but also reflecting a darker history of "security concerns." Northwestern Laos had been a hotspot of Cold War violence, bringing together both the east-west geography of national (Royalist vs. communist) struggle within Laos and the wider geopolitical conflicts of the Golden Triangle region, which also spilled much farther north into the borderlands of Burma and China (McCoy 2003). In 1962, the US Central Intelligence Agency had established a base in the area that recruited local upland population groups as part of the so-called secret war efforts conducted by the United States and its allies throughout the 1960s and early '70s (Warner 1996). Khet Nam Fa was the location of a focal site that was established in the 1990s, in part as a destination for the upland communities that had remained in remote areas or had deserted earlier, unsuccessful relocation efforts.

Bolisat Ltd.'s efforts thus fit, at least initially, within the district government's efforts to keep Khet Nam Fa's residents anchored in place with a mix of wage work, the provision of rubber seedlings, and—initially—a plan to eventually allocate to them 30 percent (by area) of the company's plantation lands under the so-called 4 + 1 policy model. This mix of land partition and wage work exemplified the concession-like nature of the scheme, contrasting with the province's main (3 + 2) rubber-cooperation model in ways that exemplified my provincial informant's concern that the plantations being developed there (and elsewhere) were "not actually contract farming." But "4 + 1" also differed slightly—at least in theory—from a concession, occupying an intermediate position on the enclosure spectrum between contract farming and concessions because of the planned land partition. This partial enclosure was a key reason Lao authorities throughout the northwest found the model attractive: like a land concession, it enticed companies to invest and provided wage work to poor communities in the short term; but it also offered the promise of a transition to a smallholder contract-farming model once the land partition took place.

When I returned to Khet Nam Fa in 2018, it did not take long to see that although the scheme had succeeded in creating available land for Bolisat Ltd., it had not forged the working partnership between the company and villagers that had been conjured a decade earlier. The enclosures begun more than a decade earlier had indeed expanded, and what had previously been a few hundred hectares had perhaps doubled. Yet the "permanent livelihoods" aspect of the project had essentially failed. Although the land itself had been transitioned from upland rice to a rubber plantation, the putative targets of the scheme—Khet Nam Fa's residents—had been excluded from this transition rather than brought along with it. The partitions that had figured so centrally in the narration of the scheme a decade earlier were nowhere to be found in the accounts of Bolisat Ltd. I collected in 2018. Instead, the local narratives had shifted from the nuance of a workable, best-of-both-worlds hybrid of concessions and contract farming to a simple binary of the two. District staff people I spoke with described Bolisat Ltd.'s overall operation as "concession and promotion" (*sampathan kap songserm*) and clarified that Khet Nam Fa was "entirely concession" (*sampathan leui*). Similarly, one of the village officials I spoke with in Khet Nam Fa ignored the partition plans of old and, instead, lamented the loss of land to the company. Another village official, interestingly, reinterpreted the company's distribution of rubber seedlings a decade earlier to residents who promised to stay in the village. Rather than describe this in the terms recounted above (wage labor in the short term, plantation partition and smallholder production in the medium to long term), he recounted Bolisat Ltd.'s plantation as the result of a simple land sale (of 70-plus hectares—a gross underestimate) that had been paid for solely with rubber seedlings.[9]

Conclusion: Governing (Enclosure) under Duress

Given this trajectory, it is essential to view Bolisat Ltd.'s activities in Khet Nam Fa, not only within the state-territorial logic of trying to secure a precarious villagization, but also within the (in this case, ultimately competing) economic logic of trying to develop a viable rubber-plantation business. Although the process was hardly straightforward, Bolisat Ltd. managed to address the land-access challenges that confronted Chinese companies more broadly across northwestern Laos and elsewhere (Lu and Schönweger 2019; also see Kenney-Lazar 2018; Oliveira, McKay, and Liu 2021). In large part, this success was achieved by capitalizing on a form of social land availability that sat at the conjuncture of both a general policy preference to "stabilize" upland shifting cultivation using fixed plantation crops like rubber and, as my account here emphasizes, a specific history of localized, postwar state territorialization. The regulatory pushback against Chinese rubber concessions that the official policy commitment to contract farming represented meant that, however tempting it may be to see the end result of company-owned plantations as simply the outcome of some initial plan, the history of actual events tells a more complex and dynamic story. Rather, the case of Bolisat Ltd. illustrates how micro-geopolitics helped create an important subsidy: cheap land.

I have used a conjunctural approach to examine the historical terrain on which citizenship is created and negotiated as a way to understand uneven enclosure. While mainland Southeast Asia's economic integration has been famously described as "turning battlefields into marketplaces," this phrase is usually interpreted both regionally and metaphorically by critics and proponents alike (Glassman 2010; Hirsch 2001). Here, I show the necessity of taking this phrase more literally, by examining Southeast Asia, not just as a Cold War landscape in a general sense, but also as an interlinked network of actual, local landscapes where Cold War conflict took place on the ground, and where place-specific struggles over land access continue today (see also Hirsch et al. 2022). It is in these groundings that we see how the slippages from protective efforts like "3 + 2," a regulatory pushback against the large-scale land concessions to Chinese rubber companies, came about and how the quasi-concessions of "4 + 1" became targeted into particular communities and landscapes. This was a far cry from the authority gap of a missing state. It was, by contrast, the governing of enclosure by a variety of state officials and institutions, using a whole set of tactics that spanned the realm of the discursive to the intimately material. Examining the "global" land rush in the landscapes and communities of northwestern Laos thus does not only illustrate the mechanics of land grabbing. It also shows the ways in which legacies of geopolitical conflict can linger on the ground, animating the micropolitics of land access for far longer than they have any right to.

Notes

1. This chapter draws heavily on ideas and text excerpted from my recent book *Upland Geopolitics: Postwar Laos and the Global Land Rush* (Dwyer 2022). The passages that appear below are taken largely from the book's introduction, chapter 1, and chapter 4, and are reproduced with permission of the University of Washington Press. This opening anecdote comes from chapter 1 (p. 45).

2. I qualify the reference here to "frontier-type" development to exclude the excellent explanatory work that uses the concept of the "frontier| (e.g., Barney 2009; Laungaramsri 2012; Padwe 2020; Patel and Moore 2018; Tsing 2005). Also see Dwyer (2022, chap. 4).
3. Author's data; for details on notes 3–7, see Dwyer (2022, chaps 1 and 4).
4. Author's data (project document, 2001).
5. Author's data (meeting minutes, 2005).
6. Fieldwork interviews, June 2007 and December 2007. On the narrative that the uplands are untaxed, see Dwyer (2013, 314–321).
7. Fieldwork interviews, June 2007 and December 2007.
8. On the difficulties with plantation area statistics, see Dwyer (2022, chap. 5).
9. Author interviews, July 2018.

References

Alden Wily, Liz. 2012. "Looking Back to See Forward: The Legal Niceties of Land Theft in Land Rushes." *Journal of Peasant Studies* 39 (3–4): 751–775.

Arezki, Rabah, Klaus Deininger, and Harris Selod. 2011. "What Drives the Global Land Rush?" IMF Working Paper WP/11/251. Washington, DC: International Monetary Fund.

Asian Development Bank. 1997. *Technical Assistance for the Chiang Rai-Kunming Road Improvement via Lao PDR Project. Report TAR: STU 30004*. Manila: Asian Development Bank. https://www.adb.org/sites/default/files/project-document/72434/30004-stu-tar.pdf.

Ballvé, Teo. 2012. "Everyday State Formation: Territory, Decentralization, and the Narco Landgrab in Colombia." *Environment and Planning D: Society and Space* 30 (4): 603–622.

Barney, Keith. 2009. "Laos and the Making of a 'Relational' Resource Frontier." *Geographical Journal* 175 (2): 146–159.

Berry, Sara. 2009. "Property, Authority and Citizenship: Land Claims, Politics and the Dynamics of Social Division in West Africa." *Development and Change* 40 (1): 23–45.

Bhandar, Brenna. 2015. "Title by Registration: Instituting Modern Property Law and Creating Racial Value in the Settler Colony." *Journal of Law and Society* 42 (2): 253–282.

Bhandar, Brenna. 2018. *Colonial Lives of Property: Law, Land, and Racial Regimes of Ownership*. Durham, NC: Duke University Press.

Borger, Julian. 2008. "Rich Countries Launch Great Land Grab to Safeguard Food Supply." *Guardian*, November 22.

Borras, Saturnino M., Jr., David Fig, and Sofía Monsalve Suárez. 2011. "The Politics of Agrofuels and Mega-Land and Water Deals: Insights from the ProCana Case, Mozambique." *Review of African Political Economy* 38 (128): 215–234.

Borras, Saturnino M., Jr., Jennifer C. Franco, Sergio Gómez, Cristóbal Kay, and Max Spoor. 2012. "Land Grabbing in Latin America and the Caribbean." *Journal of Peasant Studies* 39 (3–4): 845–872.

Bryan, Joe. 2012. "Rethinking Territory: Social Justice and Neoliberalism in Latin America's Territorial Turn." *Geography Compass* 6 (4): 215–226.

Bryant, Raymond L. 1997. *The Political Ecology of Forestry in Burma, 1824–1994*. Honolulu: University of Hawai'i Press.

Chanthavong, Nitkham, Khamsing Xayleuxong, Somneuk Chitpanya, Nathan Badenoch, and Thongsavanh Keonakhone. 2009. *Rubber Institutions in Ban Hat Nyao: Managing Trees, Markets and Producers*. UNDRP field report 0903. Upland Research and Capacity

Development Programme. Vientiane: Lao National Agriculture and Forestry Research Institute (NAFRI).

Cotula, Lorenzo, Sonja Vermeulen, Rebecca Leonard, and James Keeley. 2009. *Land Grab or Development Opportunity? Agricultural Investment and International Land Deals in Africa.* London and Rome: IIED, FAO and IFAD.

Crispin, Shawn. 2010. "The Limits of Chinese Expansionism." Asia Times Online, December 23. http://www.atimes.com/atimes/Southeast_Asia/LL23Ae01.html.

Dean, Warren. 1987. *Brazil and the Struggle for Rubber: A Study in Environmental History.* Cambridge, UK: Cambridge University Press.

De Koninck, Rodolphe. 2006. "On the Geopolitics of Land Colonization: Order and Disorder on the Frontiers of Vietnam and Indonesia." *Moussons* 9–10:33–59.

Diepart, Jean-Christophe, and Thol Sem. 2016. "Fragmented Territories: Incomplete Enclosures and Agrarian Change on the Agricultural Frontier of Samlaut District, North-West Cambodia." *Journal of Agrarian Change* 18 (1): 156–177.

Diouf, Jacques. 2008. "The Food Crisis and the Wrong Solutions." *Kommunikation Global/ Global Perspectives: Bumpy Road to Accra.* October 8.

Dwyer, Michael B. 2007. *Turning Land into Capital: A Review of Recent Research on Land Concessions for Investment in Lao PDR.* Working Group on Land Issues Report. Vientiane: Land Issues Working Group.

Dwyer, Michael B. 2013. "Building the Politics Machine: Tools for 'Resolving' the Global Land Grab." *Development and Change* 44 (2): 309–333.

Dwyer, Michael B. 2014. "Micro-Geopolitics: Capitalising Security in Laos's Golden Quadrangle." *Geopolitics* 19 (2): 377–405.

Dwyer, Michael B. 2015. "The Formalization Fix? Land Titling, Land Concessions and the Politics of Spatial Transparency in Cambodia." *Journal of Peasant Studies* 42 (5): 903–928.

Dwyer, Michael B. 2017. "Land and Forest Tenure in Laos: Baseline Overview 2016 with Options for Community Participation in Forest Management." UN-REDD Programme (FAO, UNDP, and UNEP).

Dwyer, Michael B. 2022. *Upland Geopolitics: Postwar Laos and the Global Land Rush.* Seattle: University of Washington Press.

Dwyer, Michael B., and Vong Nanhthavong. 2023. "Making Concessions Pay? Historical vs. Potential Tax Revenues from Laos's Rubber Sector." *World Development* 172: Article 106359.

Economist. 2009. "Outsourcing's Third Wave." *Economist*, May 21.

Edelman, Marc. 2013. "Messy Hectares: Questions about the Epistemology of Land Grabbing Data." *Journal of Peasant Studies* 40 (3): 485–501.

Fairbairn, Madeleine. 2020. *Fields of Gold: Financing the Global Land Rush.* Ithaca and London: Cornell University Press.

Foucault, Michel. 2004. *"Society Must Be Defended": Lectures at the College de France 1975–76.* London: Penguin Books.

Glassman, Jim. 2010. *Bounding the Mekong: The Asian Development Bank, China, and Thailand.* Honolulu: University of Hawai'i Press.

Grain. 2008a. "Seized! The 2008 Land Grab for Food and Financial Security." Grain (website). October 24, 2008. https://grain.org/article/entries/93-seized-the-2008-landgrab-for-food-and-financial-security.

Grain. 2008b. "Seized! The 2008 Land Grab for Food and Financial Security Annex." GRAIN Briefing Annex. Grain (website). October 2008. https://grain.org/media/BAhbBlsHOgZm

SSI3MjAxMS8wNi8zMC8xNl8wMV8zNF8oMTNfbGFuZGdyYWJfMjAwOF9lbl9hbm5leC5wZGYGOgZFVA/landgrab-2008-en-annex.pdf.

Guldi, Jo. 2021. *The Long Land War: The Global Struggle for Occupancy Rights*. New Haven, CT: Yale University Press.

Hardy, Andrew. 2003. *Red Hills: Migrants and the State in the Highlands of Vietnam*. Honolulu: University of Hawai'i Press.

Hart, Gillian Patricia. 2002. *Disabling Globalization: Places of Power in Post-Apartheid South Africa*. Pietermaritzburg, South Africa: University of Natal Press.

Hirsch, Philip. 2001. "Globalisation, Regionalisation and Local Voices: The Asian Development Bank and Rescaled Politics of Environment in the Mekong Region." *Singapore Journal of Tropical Geography* 22 (3): 237–251.

Hirsch, Philip, Kevin Woods, Natalia Scurrah, and Michael B. Dwyer, eds. 2022. *Turning Land into Capital: Development and Dispossession in the Mekong Region*. Seattle: University of Washington Press.

Holt-Giménez, Eric, and Raj Patel. 2009. *Food Rebellions! Crisis and the Hunger for Justice*. With Annie Shattuck. Cape Town, South Africa; Oakland, CA; Boston, MA: Pambazuka Press, Food First Books, Grassroots International.

Julia, and Ben White. 2012. "Gendered Experiences of Dispossession: Oil Palm Expansion in a Dayak Hibun Community in West Kalimantan." *Journal of Peasant Studies* 39 (3–4): 995–1016.

Kenney-Lazar, Miles. 2018. "Governing Dispossession: Relational Land Grabbing in Laos." *Annals of the American Association of Geographers* 108 (3): 679–694.

Lacey, Marc. 2008. "Across Globe, Empty Bellies Bring Rising Anger." *New York Times*, April 18.

Laungaramsri, Pinkaew. 2012. "Frontier Capitalism and the Expansion of Rubber Plantations in Southern Laos." *Journal of Southeast Asian Studies* 43 (3): 463–477.

Lavers, Tom. 2012. "'Land Grab' as Development Strategy? The Political Economy of Agricultural Investment in Ethiopia." *Journal of Peasant Studies* 39 (1): 105–132.

Lee, Ching Kwan. 2014. "The Spectre of Global China." *New Left Review* 89 (Sept/Oct): 28–65.

Lestrelin, Guillaume, Jean-Christophe Castella, and Jeremy Bourgoin. 2012. "Territorialising Sustainable Development: The Politics of Land-Use Planning in Laos." *Journal of Contemporary Asia* 42 (4): 581–602.

Li, Tania Murray. 2011. "Centering Labor in the Land Grab Debate." *Journal of Peasant Studies* 38 (2): 281–298.

Lu, Juliet N. 2017. "Tapping into Rubber: China's Opium Replacement Program and Rubber Production in Laos." *Journal of Peasant Studies* 44 (4): 726–747.

Lu, Juliet, and Oliver Schönweger. 2019. "Great Expectations: Chinese Investment in Laos and the Myth of Empty Land." *Territory, Politics, Governance* 7 (1): 61–78.

Lund, Christian. 2012. "Property and Citizenship: Conceptually Connecting Land Rights and Belonging in Africa." *Africa Spectrum* 46 (3): 71–75.

MacKinnon, Ian. 2008. "The Resentment Rises as Villagers Are Stripped of Holdings and Livelihood." *Guardian*, November 22.

McCoy, Alfred W. 2003. *The Politics of Heroin: CIA Complicity in the Global Drug Trade: Afghanistan, Southeast Asia, Central America, Colombia*. Chicago: Lawrence Hill Books.

Moore, Donald S. 1999. "The Crucible of Cultural Politics: Reworking 'Development' in Zimbabwe's Eastern Highlands." *American Ethnologist* 26 (3): 654–689.

Muldavin, Joshua. 2013. "From Rural Transformation to Global Integration: Comparative Analyses of the Environmental Dimensions of China's Rise." *Eurasian Geography and Economics* 54 (3): 259–279.

Nyíri, Pál. 2009. "Extraterritoriality: Foreign Concessions: The Past and Future of a Form of Shared Sovereignty. Inaugural Oration at Amsterdam's Free University." https://www.espacestemps.net/en/articles/extraterritoriality-pal-nyiri/.

Oliveira, Gustavo de L. T. 2019. "Boosters, Brokers, Bureaucrats and Businessmen: Assembling Chinese Capital with Brazilian Agribusiness." *Territory, Politics, Governance* 7 (1): 22–41.

Oliveira, Gustavo de L. T., Ben M. McKay, and Juan Liu. 2021. "Beyond Land Grabs: New Insights on Land Struggles and Global Agrarian Change." *Globalizations* 18 (3): 321–338.

Ong, Aihwa. 2000. "Graduated Sovereignty in South-East Asia." *Theory, Culture and Society* 17 (4): 55–75.

Padwe, Jonathan. 2020. *Disturbed Forests, Fragmented Memories: Jarai and Other Lives in the Cambodian Highlands*. Seattle: University of Washington Press.

Patel, Raj, and Jason W. Moore. 2018. *A History of the World in Seven Cheap Things: A Guide to Capitalism, Nature, and the Future of the Planet*. Berkeley: University of California Press.

Peluso, Nancy Lee. 1995. "Whose Woods Are These? Counter-Mapping Forest Territories in Kalimantan, Indonesia." *Antipode* 27 (4): 383–406.

Perelman, Michael. 2007. "Primitive Accumulation from Feudalism to Neoliberalism." *Capitalism Nature Socialism* 18 (2): 44–61.

Polanyi, Karl. 1944. *The Great Transformation: The Political and Economic Origins of Our Time*. Boston, MA: Beacon Press.

Rigg, Jonathan. 2005. *Living with Transition in Laos: Market Integration in Southeast Asia*. London: Routledge.

Robinson, Cedric J. 1983. *Black Marxism, Revised and Updated Third Edition: The Making of the Black Radical Tradition*. Chapel Hill: University of North Carolina Press.

Reguly, Eric. 2009. "The Farms Race." *Globe and Mail*, January 30.

Rice, Andrew. 2009. "Is There Such a Thing as Agro-Imperialism?" *New York Times Magazine*, November 16.

Sassen, Saskia. 2013. "Land Grabs Today: Feeding the Disassembling of National Territory." *Globalizations* 10 (1): 25–46.

Schönweger, Oliver, Andreas Heinimann, Michael Epprecht, Juliet Lu, and Palikone Thalongsengchanh. 2012. *Concessions and Leases in the Lao PDR: Taking Stock of Land Investments*. Bern, Switzerland: Geographica Bernensia.

Scott, James C. 2009. *The Art of Not Being Governed: An Anarchist History of Upland Southeast Asia*. New Haven, CT: Yale University Press.

Scurrah, Natalia, and Philip Hirsch. 2022. "Land and Capital across Borders: A Regional Geopolitics." In *Turning Land into Capital: Development and Dispossession in the Mekong Region*, edited by Philip Hirsch, Kevin Woods, Natalia Scurrah, and Michael B. Dwyer, 3–28. Seattle: University of Washington Press.

Shi, Weiyi. 2008. *Rubber Boom in Luang Namtha: A Transnational Perspective*. Report. Vientiane, Laos: German Technical Cooperation (GTZ).

Sturgeon, Janet C., Nicholas K. Menzies, Yayoi Fujita Lagerqvist, David Thomas, Benchaphun Ekasingh, Louis Lebel, et al. 2013. "Enclosing Ethnic Minorities and Forests in the Golden Economic Quadrangle." *Development and Change* 44 (1): 53–79.

Tsing, Anna Lowenhaupt. 2005. *Friction: An Ethnography of Global Connection*. Princeton, NJ: Princeton University Press.

Vandergeest, Peter. 2003. "Land to Some Tillers: Development-Induced Displacement in Laos." *International Social Science Journal* 55 (175): 47–56.

Vandergeest, Peter, and Nancy Lee Peluso. 1995. "Territorialization and State Power in Thailand." *Theory and Society* 24 (3): 385–426.

Warner, Roger. 1996. *Shooting at the Moon: The Story of America' Clandestine War in Laos.* South Royalton, VT: Steerforth Press.

Watts, Michael. 2004. "Resource Curse? Governmentality, Oil and Power in the Niger Delta, Nigeria." *Geopolitics* 9 (1): 50–80.

Wolford, Wendy, Saturnino M. Borras Jr., Ruth Hall, Ian Scoones, and Ben White. 2013. "Governing Global Land Deals: The Role of the State in the Rush for Land." *Development and Change* 44 (2): 189–210.

Woods, Kevin. 2011. "Ceasefire Capitalism: Military-Private Partnerships, Resource Concessions and Military-State Building in the Burma-China Borderlands." *Journal of Peasant Studies* 38 (4): 747–770.

Xu, Jianchu. 2006. "The Political, Social, and Ecological Transformation of a Landscape." *Mountain Research and Development* 26 (3): 254–262.

CHAPTER 33

LAND INSTITUTIONS AND AGRICULTURAL MODERNIZATION IN CHINA

JINGZHONG YE

Introduction

Agriculture, the countryside, and the peasantry have been priority concerns of the Chinese government, land and agriculture being the most crucial. With a growing population, less arable land, and often relatively low-quality land, Chinese peasant agriculture has been undergoing a form of modernization. In both policy documents and mainstream academic discourses, land transfer is seen as the prerequisite for the development of modern agriculture, or scaled-up agriculture, to improve efficiency, ensure food security, and promote labor migration and the local employment of rural labor (Ye et al. 2016). Since modern agriculture normally must be practiced at a certain scale, it is considered imperative that the tiny land plots contracted for by individual peasants should be transferred to larger "modern" farms (Yuan and Lin 2013).

However, beyond economic development functions, land bears extensive responsibilities in rural China, including alleviating employment pressure, providing subsistence security, and ensuring the food supply, and it also carries other functions such as social security, and social stability (Peng and Xiong 2006). In most rural areas, these unproductive functions of land far outweigh the productive ones (Liu 2013). Land is still the basis of most farmers' livelihoods, their basic source of survival and development (Han 2014), and an important factor in maintaining social stability. Particularly, land has the function of employment by absorbing peasants working on it, which will contribute to prevent unemployment in rural areas from causing social unrest (Yao 2000). At the same time, for farmers, farming the land is not only a means of livelihood but also a way of life (Zhang 2002).

China's current large-scale land transfers and the resultant scaled-up modern agriculture not only counter a long history of peasant farming practices (Jiang and An 2003; Pan 2012), but also have serious implications for the livelihoods of millions of peasant households, as well as national policies and development strategies. To understand the current features of land and agriculture in China, one has to study the wider and historical contexts, particularly the institutional and policy changes in agricultural production and land-tenure arrangements that reveal certain trends in the country's development trajectory.

Historical Changes in Land Institutions in China

Specific land-tenure patterns and institutions always have direct implications for agricultural production. Major changes in land policy are closely connected with key institutional changes related to agricultural production (Yuan and Lin 2013) and directly correspond to the official narratives at different times. This is because different modes of agricultural production are generally the result of the specific land-tenure systems and institutional arrangements that are in place at a given time. More than most other countries, China has experienced dramatic institutional changes in both domains. Since the Communist Party took power in 1949, land institutions in China have evolved through three major stages—confiscation and privatization, from 1949 to 1953; collectivization, from 1953 to 1978; and decollectivization and the household responsibility system (HRS), from 1978 to the present.

Land Reform and Family-Based Peasant Farming, 1949–1953

Before the Communists came to power in 1949, China had private ownership of property, and there were large disparities in people's living standards and access to resources, especially in rural areas (Zhang 2003). China was a largely agrarian country, with 90 percent of the population living in the countryside, and Chinese peasants had strong grievances about the existing land-tenure policies, under which landlords and rich peasants, who accounted for only 10 percent of the population, owned from 70 percent to 80 percent of the rural land; whereas poor peasants, tenants, and farm laborers, who made up 90 percent of the population, owned only from 20 percent to 30 percent (Ma 1999; Wu 2009). Shortly after the Communists came to power, they carried out a radical land reform that gave land ownership to poor tenant farmers (Wu 2009). This land reform eliminated the landlord system in the countryside, equalized land ownership within villages, broke the domination of the landlord-gentry class, and transferred power for the first time to poor peasants and tenants (Gurley 1975; Kerkvliet and Selden 1998).

It should be noted that, though land reform redistributed land and power, it did not change the principle of private land ownership. Instead, it shifted from a system of private ownership by landowners to one of private ownership by peasants (Stavis 1974; Qian 2000). Agriculture was thus transformed from the landlord-owned farms, worked by tenants and hired laborers, to smallholder family-based peasant farming. The peasantry had direct control over their own means of agricultural production. This kindled peasants' enthusiasm for farming, accelerated production, and resulted in a remarkable increase in grain output and productivity and the development of the rural economy (Chen 2002; Wu 2009).

Agricultural Collectivization, 1953–1978

In the course of more land reform in the early 1950s, land began to be distributed on a per capita basis, which resulted in inefficiencies and other problems for farming and management (Stavis 1974; Qian 2000). From 1953 onward, agriculture in China underwent a process of collectivization, or socialist transformation, from small private holdings to large-scale communes. The Communist leadership advocated and encouraged the formation of "mutual aid teams," lower-level agricultural-producer cooperatives (Lower APCs) and higher-level agricultural-producer cooperatives (Higher APCs) in succession, which gradually transferred the ownership of land, tools, and other means of production from the peasants to the collective, pooling peasants' resources to accelerate production (Stavis 1974; Gurley 1975; Wu 2009).

After the formation of the Higher APCs, there was a further enlargement of the scale of rural organization to better coordinate rural construction projects and provide an even larger economic base for financing rural development (Stavis 1974). In 1958, the Chinese central government instituted an economic and social plan known as the Great Leap Forward, which aimed to rapidly industrialize China through agricultural collectivization. People's communes (*renmin gongshe*) were established and immediately spread to all parts of the country, representing the final step in China's advancement to socialist agriculture. By the end of 1958, rural China was almost fully "communized" (Ma 1999; Wu 2009). The former Higher APCs became *production brigades* within the communes, and the former Lower APCs became *production teams*. The commune also became the basic unit of government; the communes ran factories, schools, and banks and controlled their own media (Gurley 1975).

In the early 1960s, the Great Leap Forward set unrealistic agricultural production goals that, coupled with natural disasters, brought about a devastating famine that resulted in the loss of many lives (Ma 1999; Wu 2009). After that, a three-level system consisting of the commune, the brigade, and the team was established, in which the production team was the basic unit of everyday production and management, and joint ownership was shared by the commune, brigade, and production team (*sanji suoyou duiwei jichu*; Stavis 1974; Ma 1999; Wu 2009). China's rural collectives were based on this system for the next two decades (Kerkvliet and Selden 1998).

Several authors lauded the achievements and performance of Chinese agricultural collectivization, believing that the centrally planned command economy played an important role in the increase in food production during this period (Stavis 1974; Kerkvliet and Selden 1998; Li and Wang 2011). However, it was also widely recognized that the state's program of low consumption and extracting agricultural surpluses had resulted in a stagnation of rural incomes during the two decades of the collective era (Kerkvliet and Selden 1998). Collectivization gradually reduced the peasants' enthusiasm for agricultural production, as they received almost the same income whether they worked hard or not, and were assigned work points (*gongfen*) based on tasks that were difficult to monitor (Huang, Otsuka, and Rozelle 2008; Li and Wang 2011). What little agricultural growth there was came mainly from increased inputs and the enormous investments made by central and local government funds. The rigidity of the system inhibited institutional innovation and the organization of production; and the pricing system and marketing institutions provided no incentives (Wen 1993).

On the positive side, a lot of large-scale rural infrastructure, particularly related to irrigation and soil improvement, was constructed during the collectivization period that continues to benefit agricultural production to this day. In the late 1970s, high-yield seeds and the use of chemicals were introduced. During this period, the industrial and infrastructure foundations were also, to some extent, laid down, and became the base for the country's development in the next period (Stavis 1974; Gurley 1975; Kerkvliet and Selden 1998; Ma 1999). The collective system had successfully achieved capital accumulation from agriculture, which was critical for the national industrialization strategy (Ma 1999). It was estimated that between 1953 and 1978, the state siphoned from 600 to 900 billion yuan from agriculture and the countryside through the "price scissors" mechanism, which was the main source for the primitive accumulation capital for industrial development (Wang and Zhang 1993; Zhang 1993; Wen 2000).

The Cultural Revolution from 1966 to 1976 created massive sociopolitical upheaval and led to the collapse of social order. The ensuing chaos made it difficult for peasants to maintain their normal production levels and social order, negatively impacting their livelihoods. The tensions created by the constant instability in the countryside and the peasants' opposition to collectivization came to a head in the late 1970s, when the peasants pressed the government to expand the role of the household and the market, which opened the way to change (Gurley 1975; Zhang, Li, and Shao 2006).

Decollectivization and the Household Responsibility System, 1978–Present

The collective system was broken up in 1978, becoming a milestone in China's rural reform and opening up (Ma 1999; Liu and Cheng 2007). The Household Production Contract (*baochan daohu*), or Household Responsibility System ([HRS]; *fentian daohu*) was established. Although farmland remained under the ownership of the rural collective, the HRS allowed peasant households to contract for land and manage their own agricultural production. The system granted peasants long-term land-use contracts and allowed them keep their produce after paying taxes. Accordingly, agriculture returned to a system of individual farming, which again kindled the peasantry's enthusiasm for production. The HRS reform shifted the Chinese economy from a planned system to a market-oriented system and toward a more open economy (Zhang 2003), and agriculture from a collective system to a family-based system (Brandt et al. 2002). Rural households emerged as the primary locus of agricultural production and many other economic activities, and farmers could exercise free decision-making about what to grow on their farmland (Kerkvliet and Selden 1998).

The HRS land redistribution began in 1978 and was completed by 1984 (Giles and Mu 2014). The initial land contracts were for fifteen years. Although the contract starting years may differ by several years between provinces, for most of the areas, the contracts started in 1983 and ended in 1997. During this period, despite the central government's mandate that rural households be given a fifteen-year tenure on the contracted land, in practice, the collective authorities often reallocated land in limited scale to restore equitable land distribution (Brandt et al. 2002; Zhang, Ma, and Xu 2004). Then, as 1993 approached and the first-round contracts for some areas were due to expire, the state proclaimed that they should be extended, unchanged. The 1993 No. 1 Policy Document[1] of the Central Committee of the Communist Party of China (CCCPC) and the State Council, *Policy Measures on Agriculture and Rural Economic Development*, and the Third Plenary Session of the 15th CPC Congress in October 1998 officially declared that the second-round of land contracts was to be prolonged thirty years, i.e., for most areas from 1998 to 2027. *Opinions on Keeping the Land Contracting Relationship Stable and Unchanged on a Long-Term Basis,* issued by CCCPC and the State Council in 2019, stated that the second-round of contracts would be extended for another thirty years upon expiration (i.e., from 2028 to 2057 for most areas), for the purposes of protecting the farmers' rights and interests in land contracting, further improving the rural land contracting management system, and advancing the implementation of the rural revitalization strategy.

Under the HRS, each household taking responsibility for a field also inherited a tax burden: a portion of the quota of grain sales the former team owed to the state, at a price fixed by the government (Kung and Liu 1997). As such, the HRS was perceived by the peasants as a shift of responsibility from the collectives to individual households—"paying enough to the state, saving enough for the collective and all that's left is ours" (Zhang, Liu, and Wang 2002a). Nonetheless, the HRS proved to be considerably more efficient than the commune system in many ways (Wen 1993; Yang and Wang 2002), though it benefited from the technological, industrial, and infrastructure foundations established in the commune period. Agricultural policy after the reform was complemented with a package of market-oriented reforms involving pricing, the reorganization of production, marketing, investments, technology and trade, and shifts from heavy industry to light industry and from infrastructure to consumer products

(Lin 1992; Huang, Otsuka, and Rozelle 2008). The numbers of China's rural poor (as officially defined) decreased dramatically after the reform, and peasants' consumption also increased due to their higher incomes after the reform (Kueh 1988; Zhang 2003).

Challenges and Innovations under HRS

In the early stage of the HRS, there was a clear division of three types of land rights—ownership, contract, and use—in which the collective has the land ownership rights, and both the land contract rights and use rights are with the peasants. This arrangement is referred to as the "splitting/division of land ownership, and land use rights and land contract rights," and it is considered the great pioneering achievement of the Chinese peasantry and rural reform since 1978 (Christiansen 1986). Nonetheless, many challenges related to farmland and agricultural production have emerged under the HRS. Different innovations in tenure arrangements and land management responding to these challenges have been tried. However, none of the trials and practices have challenged the collective ownership of farmland.

Land Fragmentation and Innovative Tenure Experiments

The egalitarian land distribution that occurred under the HRS led to a tremendous fragmentation of farmland. In theory, land distribution in a village entailed first classifying its arable land into different categories based on its fertility and productivity. Land in the different categories was to be evenly distributed to households according to the number of family members in each. In practice, the village's arable land was typically dispersed in several big plots that were located in different places. Each plots had different physical conditions such as soil fertility, access to irrigation etc. Although sometimes the differences were not significant, each household would want to get a share of the better plots. Thus, following such a way of rural land distribution, household landholdings in many villages are very small (e.g., 0.2–0.6 hectares), and the average number of plots held by one household is from five to ten, with an average plot size of about 0.3 to 1.0 *mu*.[2] And again, many of these household plots are dispersed in different locations and are often at some distance from one another (Kong 1993; Ye 2002).

Land fragmentation has led to a serious decline in land investment and acted as a constraint on land-use efficiency and the development of large- and medium-scale farms (Qian 2000). Some of the land-tenure trials that emerged to address these problems were aimed at enlarging the scale of land operations by transferring land to other entities or back to the collective, or by developing a land market. I will now outline some of the main types of trials.

First, there is the Two-Field System (*liangtian zhi*); this refers to a popular practice that combines grain-ration land (*kouliang tian*) and responsibility land (*zeren tian*).

Grain ration land is typically allocated based on household size to ensure that each household can produce enough for its own consumption needs. *Responsibility land* is allocated to households so that they can engage in agricultural production. There may be restrictions on how the household can use this land, and there is always a possibility that some of it may be taken away by the collective and allocated to another household (Brandt et al. 2002; Zhang, Liu, and Wang 2002a; Zhang 2003). Second, there is what is known as Scaled-Up Operation (*guimo jingying*), which has been practiced in some counties (such as Shunyi County in Beijing Municipality) since 1987. Under this system, plots were taken away from peasants before their land contracts expired and reassigned to fewer peasant households to increase the scale of that household's operations (Zhang, Liu, and Wang 2002a; Zhang 2003). Third, there is the Reverse Renting and Subcontracting (*fanzu daobao*) system under which the village authorities rent land back from the peasants (who originally contracted for it from the village collective), and then subcontract it out to a third entity. This practice was found mainly in the southeast coastal provinces (Zhang, Liu, and Wang 2002b; Zhang, Ma, and Xu 2004). A fourth form is the Land Trust (*tudi xintuo*), an innovation aimed at developing a local land market, whereby villagers can "deposit" the land rights of their contracted land, and the trust then acts as a broker, actively matching supply with demand, which could come from outside agribusinesses. This practice was first tried in Shaoxing County in Zhejiang Province in 2001 (Zhang, Ma, and Xu 2004). A fifth approach is the Four Wastelands Auction (*sihuang paimai*), a practice that started in the late 1980s in Lvliang Prefecture in Shanxi province. This was a new path designed to tackle soil erosion on the barren mountains of the Loess Plateau. Instead of wasteland being allocated to peasants on the basis of household size, wasteland-use rights were put up for open auction. There were four types of wasteland: waste mountains, waste gullies, waste hills, and waste river banks (Zhang, Liu, and Wang 2002a, 2002b; Ho 2005).

Land Appropriation and the Protection of Farmland

After the implementation of the HRS land redistribution, peasants enjoyed quite a few years of relatively stable use of land for farming, especially in the villages that are distant from urban centers and not covered by a national or local infrastructure development plan. However, in the past twenty-five years, the government has increasingly appropriated land for urban expansion and infrastructure construction, a process that has mainly affected peri-urban villages and those covered by an infrastructure development plan. As mentioned earlier, since the 1980s, China has shied away from the previously favored centrally planned system of socialist primitive accumulation and, instead, undertaken state-led development and state-directed accumulation strategies (Sargeson 2013). As a result, a considerable share of China's continuous economic growth has come from land-based development activities—mostly urban expansion and infrastructure construction. In particular, peri-urban land expropriation has offset the revenue shortfalls of local government, propelled urban-based capital accumulation, and contributed to meeting economic growth targets; it has thus been warmly embraced by local governments (Lin and Ho 2005; Lai et al. 2014). Land commodification has now become a major source of municipal finance, estimated to account for more than 30 percent of total municipal budgetary revenue and nearly 40 percent of the funding for urban maintenance and construction (Lin and Zhang 2014). At the same time, it has meant countless home demolitions and the resettlement of peasants, and created mass landlessness (Sargeson 2013). This has given rise to serious social conflict—land skirmishes have accounted for the majority of the mass rural conflicts—which has undermined the country's social stability and economic development.

Land-based development has also led to a serious decrease in the amount of national farmland. In 2006, the Chinese central government set a strict farmland protection objective aimed at ensuring that the amount of national farmland does not fall below a "red line" of 1.8 billion *mu*; however, by 2008 the amount had already dropped to just 1.82574 billion *mu*. This leaves little room for any further loss of farmland, which may be problematic, as the trends of urbanization and industrialization show no signs of abating (Long et al. 2012). Moreover, the central government sees urbanization as a long-term development strategy necessary to maintaining economic growth. This poses a challenge of where to find land for urban expansion, especially when the peri-urban areas are often high-quality farmland. In this regard, a land-use policy known as "Balanced Increase and Decrease of Farmland" (*zengjian guagou*) came into force in 2006, which has tackled this challenge by reclaiming farmland from rural villages in an amount equal to the amount of peri-urban farmland due to be appropriated for urban expansion (Ye and Meng 2012). The reclamation in rural areas entails demolishing peasant homesteads, converting the land, and obliging the peasants to resettle in high-rise buildings. This policy was piloted in five provinces in 2006 and extended to nineteen provinces in 2008–2009. It has been approved by the state central government with the narrative of active response to the overall trend of hollowing out and vanishing of rural communities. However, media reports have shown that most peasants are unwilling to move from their homesteads into crowded high-rise buildings, and some social research has concluded that this developmentalist policy has squeezed the space of peasants' everyday life and agricultural production (Ye and Meng 2012).

Rural-Urban Migration and the Feminization and Greying of Agriculture

Labor migration is often accompanied by land-system reform, which has posed new challenges to the HRS. With the increasing burden of heavy taxes and levies imposed on peasants in the 1990s by tax reforms between 1994 and 2002, as well as the increased pressure on peasant families to earn cash in the face of the commodification of subsistence, a massive and ongoing rural-urban migration in China began in the 1990s, and since then, significant numbers of Chinese peasants have turned into "peasant workers" (*nongmingong*), supporting the processes of industrialization and urbanization. In addition, with the widening gap between urban and rural areas, more and more young people are choosing to move to cities to seek out job opportunities and enjoy the urban life. By the end of 2021, there were 171 million peasant migrant workers (National Bureau of Statistics 2022). Because of the institutional segregation of the rural areas and urban areas (such as the household registration system – *hukou*), their own economic constraints, and the absence or curtailment of their "citizenship" rights (Wang 2009), migrant workers usually cannot move their families to the cities. This has created numerous split families—"left-behind households." Migrants have no choice but to leave some of their family members in the village, and a unique left-behind population has emerged in rural areas.

In some places, the rural demographic of China comprises left-behind children (*liushou ertong*), left-behind women (*liushou funv*), and left-behind elderly (*liushou laoren*; Du 2004). According to China's seventh national census, China had a total population of 1.412 billion in 2020, with 901.99 million living in urban areas and 509.79 million staying in rural areas, while the size of the floating population reached 376 million (National Bureau of Statistics 2021). It has been estimated that in the early twenty-first century, China once had approximately 61 million left-behind children (All-China Women's Federation 2013), 47 million left-behind women (Zhang and Zhang 2006), and 50 million left-behind elderly (Wu 2013) in China's rural communities.

As rural laborers continue migrating to the cities, farming is now mainly undertaken by the left-behind women and left-behind elderly, leading to the "feminization" and "greying" of agricultural production. As a result, the countryside is now has a shortage of laborers for small-scale family-based agricultural production. This has led to the extensification of land use, less multiple cropping, and land abandonment, all potential threats to food security in China. Today, the question being asked is, "Who will till the land?" (Mu and Walle 2011; Zhu and Yang 2011; Ye et al. 2013).

These challenges have led to initiatives for further splitting or dividing the land use/management rights from land contract rights, and to proposals for government intervention to increase the scale of farm operations (Wen 1993).

Land Transfer and "the Split or Division of Three Rights" on Rural Land

Apart from the foregoing challenges and innovations, another salient practice is land transfer, which has become one of the major driving forces of China's agricultural modernization. Starting from as early as the initial phase of the HRS, there has been a debate about the likely impact of small-scale individual landholdings and fragmented tiny land plots. Most commentators argued that both would have negative effects, including low land productivity, constraints on accumulation and capital investment, obstacles in the application of new technology and obtaining economies of scale, and hindrance of labor migration. Land transfers were recommended at the time as a way of tackling these problems (Yang 1985; Zhang 1988; Yuan and Lin 2013). After the first-round land contracts (1983–1997) and the second-round land contracts (1998–2027), some scholars delineate a third phase—that of land transfer and modern agriculture, termed "the rise of agrarian capitalism" (Jiang and An 2003; Zhang and Donaldson 2008, 2010). *Land transfer* here refers to the transfer of "land-use rights"—that is, when peasants who hold the land-contract rights (from the collective) transfer the land-use rights to other farmers or economic entities (Zhang 2001).

The Evolution of Policies on Land Transfer

Although land transfer has gradually been practiced since late 1980s, both the policy and the legal definition of the transfer of land-use rights were vague; the rules and procedures governing land-use rights transfers, and how to define and protect those rights had not been on anyone's agenda for a long time. Until 2013, "the split/division of three rights" (ownership, contract, and use) was the official policy. In general, land transfer policy evolved over time. When we review the official discourses and narratives on land transfer since the rural reform in early 1980s, we can observe an obvious shift from the strict prohibition of land transfers to a relaxation of that policy to the promotion of land transfers.

In early 1980s, land transfer was strictly forbidden. *The Regulations concerning Land Requisition for National Construction*, issued by the Standing Committee of the Fifth National People's Congress in 1982 stated: "Any entity is forbidden to purchase or rent land directly from rural communes, brigades and production teams or in any forms. Rural communes, brigades and production teams are forbidden to use land as shares for participating in any enterprise or business." Article 10 of the 1982 Constitution stipulated: "No organization or individual may appropriate, buy, sell or lease land, or unlawfully transfer land in other ways." The prohibition of land transfer was the legacy of the centrally planned economy during the people's commune period, and it went hand in hand with strict control of the countryside and rural production. Since the HRS came into effect, land-contract rights have been in the hands of individual peasants, and thus are potentially more flexible.

The central government's 1984 No. 1 Policy Document loosened the controls on land transfer, "encouraging the land to be concentrated in the master hands of farming," and stating that "peasants who ask to not contract farmland or to contract less farmland due to their inability to carry out farming or doing other business, can hand their land over to the collective for future arrangement or, by approval of the collective, transfer their land contracts to others." Yet despite this relaxation of land-transfer policy, land transfers rarely took place. In the early 1980s, this was because farmland was only newly distributed to peasants, and the peasants had much enthusiasm for working their plots of land. Rural–urban migration was still in its infancy, and most able-bodied peasants remained in rural communities and worked in agriculture (Shi and Yu 2001; Zhao 2007). However, in some of the southeastern coastal regions, the Township and Village Enterprises (TVEs) were already highly developed in the 1980s. Many local peasants worked in the TVEs, and thus they "left the land but not their home villages, [and] they entered factories but not the cities" (*litu bulixiang jinchang bujincheng*; Kerkvliet and Selden 1998; Ye, Rao, and Wu 2010). This posed a new challenge because some peasant households in these regions were no longer able to farm individually.

In response to this new challenge, the State Council in 1987 approved trials of concentrating the small-scale individual household landholdings into bigger farming plots in some coastal provinces and cities, which extended the transfer of land-use rights beyond farming units and individual households. This marked the start of the trial phase of land transfer. However, the state's industry-oriented and urban-biased development policy imposed increasingly heavy burdens on the peasants, especially after the tax reform of 1994.[3] This trial was therefore not extended nationally to the countryside as a whole, having been effectively suppressed by the heavy agricultural taxes and levies of that time. This resulted in land abandonment. Farming was not remunerative at this time and some peasants were even subcontracting their farmland to others by paying them some subsidies for keeping their land cultivated instead of claiming rent. Thus, land transfer did not become widespread scale in the 1990s (Zhang 2001).

In 1997, however, the Report to the 15th National Congress of the CPC highlighted the issue of agricultural modernization, and declared the importance of "promoting agricultural commoditization, specialization and modernization." In the Chinese context, agricultural modernization usually requires the scaling-up of farmland plots, and so this can be seen as an encouragement for land transfer (Liu and Yan 2012; Yuan and Lin 2013).

In the early twenty-first century, a series of policy documents and practical guidelines favoring land transfer were issued by different state bodies. These include the *Notice on the Transfer of Land Use Rights of Peasant Household Contracted Land* (issued by the CPC in 2001), *The Law of the People's Republic of China on Land Contract in Rural Areas* (by the National People's Congress in 2002), *Measures for the Administration of the Transfer of Land Management Rights of Peasant Household Contracted Land* (by the Ministry of Agriculture in 2005), *The Real Rights Law of the People's Republic of China* (by the National People's Congress in 2007), *The Decision on Major Issues concerning Rural Reform and Development* (by the Third Plenary Session of the 17th CPC Central Committee in 2008), and others (Zhang 2014). To facilitate land transfers in open market transactions, a movement calling for the certification and registration of land rights was established (Zhang and Chen 2013). The 2010 No. 1 Policy Document of the Central Government, *Suggestions on Enhancing the Concerted Urban and Rural Development and Strengthening the Development Foundation of Agriculture and the Countryside*, advocated "expediting the work of determining, registering and certifying the land rights for the collective ownership of land in villages, and the usufruct rights for rural house sites and collective construction land."

In 2013, "the split or division of three rights" (*sanquan fenzhi*) on rural land, as an institutional arrangement, was formalized and has since been further improved in China. The idea of dividing the land-use/management rights from land-contract rights was first advocated at the 2013 Central Rural Work Conference. Afterward, the CCCPC and the General Office of the State Council proposed a series of detailed guidelines for how the three types of land rights should be divided, including *Opinions on Guiding the Orderly Transfer of Rural Land Use Rights to Develop Moderate Scale Agricultural Operations* (2014), *Opinions on Improving the Separation of Rural Land Ownership and Contract Rights and Use Rights* (2016), and the yearly No. 1 Policy Documents (Li and Zhao 2020; Liu 2022). In December 2018, the rural-land-contract law of the People's Republic of China was amended to protect the transfer of land-use rights (Gong, Li, and Elahi 2022). Thus, the rural land institution in which collective ownership, the contractual rights of farmers, and land-use rights are separated in parallel, was essentially constructed (Liu 2022). It represents another institutional innovation in the rural land institution of China since the HRS and is an important foundation for the implementation of rural revitalization strategy (Han 2019).

The official narratives about land transfer can be traced back to the beginning of the HRS, later accompanied by policies for "agricultural modernization," "the construction of the new socialist countryside," "rural revitalization strategy," and others. Since the start of the new millennium these laws and policy documents have established a solid foundation for promoting and supporting land transfer in China's countryside. As such, the volume of land transfers has increased in recent years (see Table 33.1).

Table 33.1. Scale of land transfers in China, 2007–2017

Period	Areas of land transferred in rural China	Land transferred as a percentage of the total land contracted to peasant households
By 2007	64 million *mu*	5.2
By 2008	109 million *mu*	8.9
By 2009	150 million *mu*	12.0
By 2011	228 million *mu*	17.8
By 2012	278 million *mu*	21.2
By 2013	341 million *mu*	25.7
By 2014	403 million *mu*	30.3
By 2015	447 million *mu*	33.3
By 2016	479 million *mu*	35.1
By 2017	512 million mu	37.0

Source: Author's summary based on various reports (Editorial Board of China Agricultural Yearbook, 2012–2018; Chen 2010).

According to data from China Agriculture Yearbook (2018), by the end of 2017, the total amount of land transferred in rural China reached 512 million *mu*, which is eight times the amount that had been transferred by the end of 2007. This land accounted for around 37 percent of the total land contracted to peasant households. With the acceleration of the land-transfer process, land-transfer practice in rural China gradually matured into three modes—*rural collective-led* transfer, *capital-led* transfer, and *spontaneous between-farmer* transfer. Some innovative forms of land transfer such as Land Stock Cooperation[4] (*tudi gufen hezuo*) and Land Bank (*tudi yinhang*) also emerged (Luo 2019; Zeng and Zeng 2010). Since the reform and opening up, land transfer has, roughly, undergone a transition from a system of spontaneous transfer between farmers to one of rural collective-led transfer and capital-led transfer (Zhu 2020). The year 2012 witnessed big growth in the amount of the peasant household contracted land transferred to industrial and commercial enterprises/capital, showing a 34 percent increase from 2011 to 2012; whereas the figure in 2011 just showed a slight rise of 8.4 percent compared to 2010.

Potential Impacts on Peasants' Livelihood and Facilitation of Modern Agriculture

There have been a great number of media reports and academic papers on land transfers, particularly during the past two or three years. As more and more land is being transferred, and as policies supporting this are implemented, the debate over the issue among academics has grown. The different views on land transfer mainly reside in the different aspects and foci of the research, which largely result from different disciplines and their traditions. This debate also reflects a real-world trade-off between the social impacts and economic benefits of land transfer.

Many anthropologists and some sociologists focus their discussion on the impacts of land transfer on peasants' livelihoods and on rural society, and often the deleterious ones. They point out the problems and negative implications of growing land transfers and warn local governments about the dangers of allowing large capital investments in agriculture (Chen 2011). They argue that the big farms created by capital penetration into the countryside and land transfer are inappropriate for China's rural conditions, which are much better suited to small farms that bring greater economic and social benefits (He 2011). When land is freely transferred on the market, there is greater risk of land grabbing by capital and likelihood that peasants will be dispossessed (He 2013). Zhao and Tang (2011) argue that land transfers have harmed rather than improved the welfare of the peasantry. It is also argued that land transfers bring about changes in the income of peasant households, labor mobility, and rural societal structure, and thus disrupt the conventional village social order, differentiating the peasantry and intensifying conflicts within villages (Guan 2004; Wu 2009b). When land is transferred, peasants who do not have off-farm work lose their incomes, and the peasants temporarily working in the city and those living in the village but no longer relying on the land no longer have a safety net. In sum, it is argued that land transfers have negatively affected the livelihoods of most peasant households (Sun 2012). Some scholars argue that idle land should be concentrated in the hands of the village collectives, instead of being sold off to capital interests. The concentration of land in the hands of outside capital will hinder the future return of migrant peasants, potentially throwing them into crisis (Pan 2009).

Many economists and public policy specialists focus their discussion on advantages of facilitating land transfer for modern agriculture and economic efficiency. They believe that land transfer is an inevitable trend in economic development and an effective way of promoting rural modernization (Yu 2013; Dang 2014). They argue that it leads peasant households with low marginal outputs to contract their land to those with high marginal outputs, and that an increase in land transactions encourages capital investment in land and helps realize the land's value (Yao 2000). Both land and labor can be reallocated appropriately, and the utility of both the land suppliers and the land demanders is increased, bringing economic benefits to both (Cao, Wang, and Huang 2007). Land transfer also plays a major role in agricultural modernization and scaling-up (Ma and Cui 2002), and so is seen as a pivotal element of rural reform, enabling the effective flow and optimal allocation of resources and contributing to the growth of the rural economy (Xiao and Zhang 2002). Land transfers also ease the tension of a low land-tiller ratio, and encourage a well-organized transfer of labor. Land transfers can also allow a more scientific approach to agriculture, and the scaling-up of agriculture can enhance agricultural specialization and, thus, commoditization and efficiency. As the agricultural structure adjusts, it becomes possible to develop a more export-oriented agriculture (Yang 2009).

Under the thirty years of farmland contract law, peasants still firmly hold the land-contract rights, although the land-use/management rights are in some cases transferred to a third party (mostly agribusiness and commercial capital), believed to be capable of significantly increasing efficiency and productivity. Such practices, which respect both collective ownership and peasants' contract rights, are lauded by some scholars, who trust that agribusiness and commercial capital will increase agricultural production (and thereby drive modernization) without eliminating the benefits to hundreds of millions of peasants. They see it as a win-win situation that will allow the rise of agrarian capitalism in China to proceed without the mass displacement of peasants that has occurred in some other countries (Yao 2000; Zhang and Donaldson 2008; Zhang and Donaldson 2010).

Conclusion

Agricultural modernization has always been China's national development goal, and this primarily involves specialization, mechanization, scaling-up, and technocracy. The persistent pursuit of agricultural modernization is distinctively reflected in the government's official narratives and various land institution policies.

After 1949, Communist China mobilized peasants' mass power against their previous oppressors and quickly confiscated the land of the landlords and distributed it to the peasants. This land reform became the foundation for the subsequent collectivization: shortly after it had been carried out, individual small-scale, family-based landholdings were collectivized, and all land came to belong to the state, or to a vaguely defined local collective that in reality was an extension or incarnation of the state. During this collectivization period, a so-called Green Revolution involving the large-scale use of high-yield seeds, improved irrigation, and chemical fertilizers was launched (Kerkvliet and Selden 1998). It is obvious that the goal of the land reform and collectivization was the step-by-step nationalization of farmland, by first taking it away from the landlord owners, so that agricultural scaling-up operations could begin and new developments in the agricultural sciences and technologies could be applied. This was China's initial attempt at agricultural modernization, with the aim of contributing to primitive accumulation to advance the country's economic development and industrialization. Although these collectivization-era changes left the peasants relatively impoverished, the achievements of modernization in the agricultural and other sectors (e.g., the industrial and infrastructure base and agricultural technologies, particularly with respect to irrigation and soil improvements) had laid a solid foundation for the economic take-off and agricultural and rural development that has taken place under the HRS era since 1978. Without the former, the latter would not have succeeded to the degree it has.

Nonetheless, though the state approved the grassroots-led innovation of the HRS and returned agriculture to individual farming, the HRS left no room for private land ownership. Moreover, since the outset of the HRS, there has been support for land transfer, which has been always seen as a way of scaling up and promoting a technocratic, mechanized, specialized, and standardized agriculture. Peasants and peasant ways of farming have never been the goal of or seen as an ideal in the nation's modernization project; rather, they are more commonly seen as a way of life and of farming that should be abolished or transformed. So, if the HRS was the Chinese state's response to the problems and in the national economy and with peasants' livelihoods in the late 1970s, it has never suspended the pursuit of agricultural modernization. Hence, when challenges have emerged under the HRS, innovative practices have quickly been developed and trialed, many of these are further attempts to scale up and modernize agricultural operations. The serious fragmentation of farmland plots that made agriculture less or nonremunerative and hampered land and agricultural investments; the feminization and greying of agriculture that gave rise to the question, Who will till the land?; and the decrease in total farmland that has resulted from urban land development, have led to serious, urgent concerns about agricultural production and national food security. All these challenges have increased the pressure to have larger landholders, in order to attract capital investment and further modernize agriculture.

In China's pursuit of agricultural modernization, increasing productivity and efficiency to create the basis for capital accumulation has always been the focus of any changes within its land and agricultural institutions. Since 1949, there has been a clear drive for capital accumulation from the agricultural sector to finance China's industrialization and urbanization. During the first thirty years of the collectivization period, this took the form of socialist primitive accumulation and was based on the nationalization of the key factors of production, a centrally planned system, state-led development, and state-directed accumulation. In the subsequent thirty years of decollectivization, it was based on the commodification of the key factors of production and a decentralized market system (Sargeson 2013). According to Henry Bernstein (2010), the primitive accumulation in the commune period, though labeled "socialist," was typically "non-market" and "extra-economically coercive"; whereas in the HRS period, capital accumulation has been characterized by the market-derived compulsion of economic forces. The latter has led to a gradual process of (semi-)proletarianization. For instance, the relaxation of the household registration system and the promotion of rural–urban migration have greatly contributed to industrialization and urbanization. However, this has created millions of semi-proletarianized peasant workers (Pun and Lu 2010). In the wake of the recent land transfers and efforts at agricultural modernization, a second wave of semi-proletarianization has been taking place: the proletarianization of the left-behind women and the elderly, who were previously engaged in family-based individual farming and who have now become casual workers on land for which they have the contract rights but the land use rights have been transferred to external capital.

Today, land is still a critical issue in China. Capitalized development and the market system have triumphed in many sectors and areas of Chinese life, including agriculture and the countryside. However, it is precisely at this moment that we should pay heed to Karl Polanyi's warning that "leaving the fate of soil and people to the market would be tantamount to annihilating them" (Polanyi [1944] 1957). Based on the basic condition of "small peasants and huge country," how to deal with land issues remains a matter for the policy and academia, so as to serve the goal of rural revitalization and modernization.

Acknowledgments

This manuscript is an updated and shortened revision of the published article: Jingzhong Ye (2015), "Land Transfer and the Pursuit of Agricultural Modernization in China." *Journal of Agrarian Change* 15 (3): 314–337. I thank *Journal of Agrarian Change* and its publisher John Wiley and Sons for granting permission to include this version in the handbook.

Notes

1. No. 1 Policy Document refers to the first policy document promulgated by the CCCPC and the State Council every year. Since 1982, major agrarian reforms and policies have always been first introduced and elaborated in these documents, signifying the importance that the Communist Party and the central government attach to agrarian issues. From 1982 to 1986, five consecutive No. 1 Policy Documents mapped out rural reforms; from 2004 to 2023, twenty consecutive No. 1 Policy Documents underlined the importance of agrarian issues.

2. One *mu* is 1/15 of a hectare.
3. The central government's 1994 tax reform established a tax-sharing system with local governments. This strengthened the capacity of the national government to collect revenues from the local governments; but the center shifted the responsibility for some expenditures to the local governments and gave the lower levels of government more autonomy to levy local taxes and fees in order to make up the balance between central remittance and local expenditures. In 2000, a pilot reform policy on rural taxes and fees was started, and the agricultural taxes were fully abolished in 2006.
4. Land Stock Cooperation means that the land will be converted into shares and distributed to individual farmers, and the community will implement a unified plan for the development and utilization of the land.

References

All-China Women's Federation. 2013. *The Report on Situations of Chinese Left-Behind Children, Rural-Urban Migrant Children* [in Chinese]. Accessed March 20, 2023. https://news.12371.cn/2013/05/18/ARTI1368856796731481.shtml.

Bernstein, Henry. 2010. *Class Dynamics of Agrarian Change*. Halifax, CAN: Fernwood Publishing.

Brandt, Loren, Jikun Huang, Guo Li, and Scott Rozelle. 2002. "Land Rights in Rural China: Facts, Fictions and Issues." *China Journal* 47: 67–97.

Cao, Jianhua, Hongying Wang, and Xiaomei Huang. 2007. "Evaluation of the Supply and Demand and Efficiency of Rural Land Transfer" [in Chinese]. *Zhongguo tudi kexue* 5: 54–60.

Chen, Haiqiu. 2002. "On the Historical Changes of Rural Land System since the Founding of PRC" [in Chinese]. *Nandu xuetan (Humanities and Social Sciences)* 22 (5): 70–79.

Chen, Min. 2010. "Thoughts on Government Responsibility in Land Transfer" [in Chinese]. *Nongcun jingji* 8: 37–39.

Chen, Shuisheng. 2011. "The Study of the Performance and Constraints of Land Transfer Policy: Based on Comparative Analysis of Eastern, Central and Western Parts of China" [in Chinese]. *Shehui kexue* 5: 48–56.

Christiansen, Flemming. 1986. "An Analysis of Recent Developments in China's Land Legislation: Some New Trends in Chinese Land Ownership and Land Use." *China Information* 1 (3): 20–31.

Dang, Guoying. 2014. "Rural Land Transfer is Inevitable Trend" [in Chinese]. *Zhongguo nongcun keji* 9: 14.

Du, Peng. 2004. "Focus on '386199' Phenomenon and Care for Rural Left-Behind Families." *Renkou yanjiu* 28 (4): 25–36.

Editorial Board of China Agriculture Yearbook. 2018. *China Agriculture Yearbook* [in Chinese]. Beijing: China Agriculture Press.

Giles, John, and Ren Mu. 2014. "Village Political Economy, Land Tenure Insecurity, and the Rural to Urban Migration Decision: Evidence from China." Policy Research Working Paper 7080. World Bank.

Gong, Maogang, Hanjin Li, and Ehsan Elahi. 2022. "Three Rights Separation Reform and Its Impact over Farm's Productivity: A Case Study of China." *Land Use Policy* 122, 106393.

Guan, Bing. 2004. "Land Subcontract in Guanzhuang Village" [in Chinese]. *Shehuixue yanjiu* 1:99–106.

Gurley, John. G. 1975. "Rural Development in China 1949–72, and the Lessons to Be Learned from It." *World Development* 3 (7–8): 455–471.
Han, Changfu. 2019. "The Reform of China's Rural Land System" [in Chinese]. *Nongye jingji wenti* 1: 4–16.
Han, Jun. 2014. "Accurately Grasp the Basic Principles That Need to Be Adhered to in Land Transfer" [in Chinese]. *Shanxi nongjing* 3: 16–18.
He, Xuefeng. 2011. "On the Size of Farmland Management: Based on the Survey in Fanchang Municipality, Anhui Province" [in Chinese]. *Nanjing nongye daxue xuebao (Social Science Edition)* 11 (2): 6–14.
He, Xuefeng. 2013. "Reply to Professor Zhou Qiren on Logic of Land Ownership" [in Chinese]. *Huazhong nongye daxue xuebao (Social Science Edition)* 3: 1–9.
Ho, Peter. 2005. *Institutions in Transition: Land Ownership, Property Rights, and Social Conflict in China*. Oxford: Oxford University Press.
Huang, Jikun, Keijiro Otsuka, and Scott Rozelle. 2008. "Agriculture in China's Development: Past Disappointments, Recent Successes, and Future Challenges." In *China's Great Economic Transformation*, edited by Loren Brandt and Thomas G. Rawski, 467–505. Cambridge, UK: Cambridge University Press.
Jiang, Yongmu, and Yana An. 2003. "The Path Dependence and Innovations of Land Institutional Changes in Rural China" [in Chinese]. *Jingjixuejia* 3: 54–59.
Kerkvliet, Benedict J. Tria, and Mark Selden. 1998. "Agrarian Transformations in China and Vietnam." *China Journal* 40: 37–58.
Kong, Jingyuan. 1993. "Land Institutions in Rural China: Empirical Analysis of the Transformation Processes" [in Chinese]. *Jingji yanjiu* 2: 65–72.
Kueh, Y. Y. 1988. "Food Consumption and Peasant Incomes in the Post-Mao Era." *China Quarterly* 116: 634–670.
Kung, James Kai-sing, and Shouying Liu. 1997. "Farmers' Preferences Regarding Ownership and Land Tenure in Post-Mao China: Unexpected Evidence from Eight Counties." *The China Journal* 38: 33–63.
Lai, Yani, Yi Peng, Bin Li, and Yanliu Lin. 2014. "Industrial Land Development in Urban Villages in China: A Property Rights Perspective." *Habitat International* 41: 185–194.
Li, Junguo, and Xiaoqiang Zhao. 2020. "From 'Separation of Two Rights' to 'Separation of Ownership Rights, Contractor's Rights and Land Management Rights': Practice and Exploration of China's Land Transfer Policy since Reform and Opening Up" [in Chinese]. *Zhongguo jingji baogao* 3: 60–76.
Li, Xiubin, and Xiuhong Wang. 2011. "Changes in Agricultural Land Use in China: 1981–2000." *Asian Geographer* 22 (1–2): 27–42.
Lin, George CS, and Amy Y Zhang. 2014. "Emerging Spaces of Neoliberal Urbanism in China: Land Commodification, Municipal Finance and Local Economic Growth in Prefecture-Level Cities." *Urban Studies* 52 (15): 2774–2798.
Lin, Yifu. 1992. *Systems, Technology and China's Agricultural Development*. Shanghai: Sanlian and Shanghai People's Publishing House.
Liu, Guangdong, and Jiumiao Cheng. 2007. "Theories and Practices of Land Institutional Changes in Rural China since 1949" [in Chinese]. *Zhongguo nongcun guancha* 2: 70–80.
Liu, Jianping, and Ran Yan. 2012. "The Adaptability of Agricultural Land Institutional Changes to Modern Agriculture Development" [in Chinese]. *Nongcun jingji* 4: 27–31.
Liu, Lijun. 2013. "Domestic and Foreign Reviews on Rural Land Transfer" [in Chinese]. *Hunan keji daue xuebao (Social Science Edition)* 16 (1): 95–99.

Liu, Shouying. 2022. "The Reform of the Rural Land System: From the Household Contract Responsibility System to Three Rights Division" [in Chinese]. *Jingji yanju* 57 (2): 18–26.

Long, Hualou, Yurui Li, Yansui Liu, Michael Woods, and Jian Zou. 2012. "Accelerated Restructuring in Rural China Fueled by 'Increasing vs. Decreasing Balance' Land-/Use Policy for Dealing with Hollowed Villages." *Land Use Policy* 29: 11–22.

Luo, Yuhui. 2019. Research on the Current Situation, Problems and Countermeasures of Rural Land Transfer under the "Three Rights Division." *Lanzhou xuekan* 2: 166–180.

Ma, Xiaohe. 1999. "50 Years of Rural China: Agricultural Collectivization and Institutional Changes" [in Chinese]. *Dangdai zhongguoshi yanjiu* 5–6: 70–97.

Ma, Xiaohe, and Hongzhi Cui. 2002. "Establishing Land Transfer Institutions, Facilitating Regional Large-Scale Agricultural Production" [in Chinese]. *Guanli shijie* 11: 63–77.

Mu, Ren, and Dominique van de Walle. 2011. "Left Behind to Farm? Women's Labor Reallocation in Rural China." *Labour Economics* 18: 583–597.

National Bureau of Statistics of the People's Republic of China. 2021. *Communiqué of the Seventh National Population Census* [in Chinese]. Accessed March 20, 2023. http://www.gov.cn/guoqing/2021-05/13/content_5606149.htm.

National Bureau of Statistics of the People's Republic of China. 2022. *Report on Monitoring and Investigation of Migrant Workers in 2021* [in Chinese]. Accessed March 20, 2023. http://www.stats.gov.cn/sj/zxfb/202302/t20230203_1901452.html.

Pan, Lu. 2012. "Historical Review and Contemporary Debates on the Concept of 'Peasantry'" [in Chinese]. *Zhongguo nongye daxue xuebao (Social Science Edition)* 2: 34–48.

Pan, Wei. 2009. "Whom Should Agricultural Land Be Transferred and Concentrated To?" [in Chinese]. *Hongqi wengao* 5: 13–16.

Peng, Xiaobing, and Xiao Xiong. 2006. "The Reform of Farmland System and Social Security System in Urbanization" [in Chinese]. *Chongqing daxue xuebao (Social Science Edition)* 12 (6): 1–5.

Polanyi, Karl. (1944) 1957. *The Great Transformation: The Political and Economic Origins of Our Time*. Repr. Boston: Beacon Press.

Pun, Ngai, and Huilin Lu. 2010. "Unfinished Proletarianization: Self, Anger, and Class Action among the Second Generation of Peasant-Workers in Present-Day China." *Modern China* 36 (5): 493–519.

Qian, Zhonghao. 2000. "Economic Analysis of Historical Changes of Land Institutions in Rural China" [in Chinese]. *Jiangsu shehui kexue* 3: 74–85.

Sargeson, Sally. 2013. "Violence as Development: Land Expropriation and China's Urbanization." *Journal of Peasant Studies* 40 (6): 1063–1085.

Shi, Hongbin, and Yunfeng Yu. 2001. "Causes and Trends of Institutional Changes of Chinese Agriculture" [in Chinese]. *Zhonggong zhejiang shengwei dangxiao xuebao* 6: 25–29.

Stavis, Benedict. 1974. *People's Communes and Rural Development in China*. Rural Development Committee, Center for International Studies, Cornell University, Ithaca, NY.

Sun, Xinhua. 2012. "Land Transfer and Household Livelihood: Comparison of Two and Transfer Models Based on Empirical Studies in Village T in Jiangxi Province" [in Chinese]. *Guizhou shehui kexue* 4: 77–83.

Wang, Chunguang. 2009. "Positivist Analysis on the Semi-urbanization of Chinese Rural Urban Migrants" [in Chinese]. *Xuexi yu tansuo* 5: 94–103.

Wang, Gengjin, and Yisan Zhang, eds. 1993. *The Study on Chinese Agricultural Modernization and Accumulation*. Taiyuan: Shanxi Economic Publishing House.

Wen, Guanzhong James. 1993. "Total Factor Productivity Change in China's Farming Sector: 1952–1989." *Economic Development and Cultural Change* 42 (1): 1–41.

Wen, Tiejun. 2000. *The Study on Basic Economic Institutions of Rural China*. Beijing: China Economic Press.

Wu, Jian. 2009. "From a Legal Perspective to See the Evolution and Transformation of Land Tenure Institutions in China." *Frontiers of Law in China* 4 (4): 568–600.

Wu, Xiaoyan. 2009b. "The Transfer of Rural Land Use Rights and the Transformation of Village Governance" [in Chinese]. *Zhengzhixue yanjiu* 6: 45–53.

Wu, Yushao. 2013. *China Aging Development Report (2013)*. Beijing: Social Sciences Academic Press.

Xiao, Fei, and Guanghong Zhang. 2002. "Efficiency Analysis of Rural Land Use Rights Transfer" [in Chinese]. *Wuhan daxue xuebao (Social Science Edition)* 55 (5): 532–536.

Yang, Canming, and Sheng Wang. 2002. "Alternatives of Institutional Changes of Chinese Agriculture" [in Chinese]. *Caizheng yanjiu* 9: 12–22.

Yang, Jinglun. 1985. "The Overall Reform of Land Institutions in Rural China" [in Chinese]. *Nongye jingji congkan* 2: 12–15.

Yang, Xiaodong. 2009. "An Analysis on the Development and Performance of Agricultural Management Organizations in HRS: From Institutional Economic Perspective" [in Chinese]. *Noingye jingji wenti* 8: 38–44.

Yao, Yang. 2000. "Land System in Rural China: An Analytical Framework" [in Chinese]. *Zhongguo shehui kexue* 2: 54–65.

Ye, Jingzhong. 2002. "Processes of Enlightenment: Farmers' Initiatives in Rural Development in China." PhD diss., Wageningen University.

Ye, Jingzhong, and Yinghua Meng. 2012. "The Linking between Increase and Decrease of Land and Its Logic of Developmentalism" [in Chinese]. *Nongye jingji wenti* 10: 43–50.

Ye, Jingzhong, Jing Rao, and Huifang Wu. 2010. "'Crossing the River by Feeling the Stones': Rural Development in China." *Rivista di Economia Agraria* 65 (2): 261–294.

Ye, Jingzhong, Chunyu Wang, Huifang Wu, Congzhi He, and Juan Liu. 2013. "Internal Migration and Left-Behind Populations in China." *Journal of Peasant Studies* 40 (6): 1119–1146.

Ye, Jingzhong, Huifang Wu, Huijiao Xu, and Yan Jiang. 2016. "Myths and Realities of Land Transfer" [in Chinese]. *Kaifang shidai* 5: 76–91.

Yu, Aimin. 2013. "Several Major Issues of Land Transfer" [in Chinese]. *Zhengce* 11: 38–41.

Yuan, Guolong, and Jinzhong Lin. 2013. "The Impacts of Agricultural Land Institutional Changes on China's Agricultural Transformation" [in Chinese]. *Huanan nongye daxue xuebao (Social Science Edition)* 12 (2): 11–20.

Zeng Chaoqun, and Fusheng Zeng. 2010. "Analysis of the Dynamics and Patterns of Land Transfer" [in Chinese]. *Hunan shehui kexue* 2: 92–96.

Zhang, Hongyu. 2002. "Several Comments on Land Restructuring and Transfer of Use Rights in China" [in Chinese]. *Guanli shijie* 5: 76–87.

Zhang, Hongye, Xiaofeng Li, and Xiaomei Shao. 2006. "Impacts of China's Rural Land Policy and Administration on Rural Economy and Grain Production." *Review of Policy Research* 23 (2): 607–624.

Zhang, Haobo, and Chibo Chen. 2013. "Effects of Collective Land Rights Verification on Rural Land Transfer: Based on a Case Study of a County" [in Chinese]. *Jiangxi nongye daxue xuebao (Social Science Edition)* 12 (2): 166–169.

Zhang, Hongyu. 2001. "Political Economy Analysis of Land Institutional Changes in Rural China." PhD diss., Southwest University, Chongqing.

Zhang, Hongyu, Mei Liu, and Hui Wang. 2002a. "Land Use Institutional Changes in Rural China: Periodization, Diversification and Policy Adjustments" [in Chinese]. *Nongye jingji wenti* 2: 12–20.

Zhang, Hongyu, Mei Liu, and Hui Wang. 2002b. "Land Use Institutional Changes in Rural China: Periodization, Diversification and Policy Adjustments (second)" [in Chinese]. *Nongye jingji wenti* 3: 17–23.

Zhang, Jin. 2014. "The Narratives of Capital-Led Land Transfer: The Case of Ge Village in Sichuan Province." Master's thesis, China Agricultural University.

Zhang, Juncai, and Qian Zhang. 2006. "A Survey on the 50 Million Left-Behind Women's Abnormal Survival" [in Chinese]. *Zhongguo jingji zhoukan* 10: 14–19.

Zhang, Jinxuan. 2003. "Research of Chinese Agricultural Institutional Changes." PhD diss., Fudan University, Shanghai.

Zhang, Qian Forrest, and John A. Donaldson. 2008. "The Rise of Agrarian Capitalism with Chinese Characteristics: Agricultural Modernization, Agribusiness and Collective Land Rights." *China Journal* 60: 25–47.

Zhang, Qian Forrest, and John A. Donaldson. 2010. "From Peasants to Farmers: Peasant Differentiation, Labor Regimes, and Land-Rights Institutions in China's Agrarian Transition." *Politics & Society* 38 (4): 458–489.

Zhang, Qian Forrest, Qingguo Ma, and Xu Xu. 2004. "Development of Land Rental Markets in Rural Zhejiang: Growth of Off-Farm Jobs and Institution Building." *China Quarterly* 180: 1040–1062.

Zhang, Xiangshu. 1993. *Agricultural Dramatic Transformation and Strategic Choices in China*. Beijing: China Price Press.

Zhang, Zonglun. 1988. "Brief Analysis of the Establishment of Transfer Mechanism of Land Use Rights" [in Chinese]. *Nongcun jingji* 7: 28–29.

Zhao, Shuqin, and Shoupu Tang. 2011. "A Fuzzy Evaluation of Welfare Changes before and after Land Transfer Based on Sen's Theory" [in Chinese]. *Tongji yu juece* 11: 51–54.

Zhao, Yinglan. 2007. "Government Actions in the Processes of Agricultural Institutional Changes" [in Chinese]. *Shandong shifan daxue xuebao (Humanities and Social Sciences)* 52 (6): 145–150.

Zhu, Dongliang. 2020. "Farmers Are Getting Ever More Distant from the Land: Land Transfer and the 'Three Rights Separation' System" [in Chinese]. *Zhongguo shehui kexue* 7: 123–144.

Zhu, Qizhen, and Huiquan Yang. 2011. "Who Is Farming? Survey and Reflection on Rural Work Force" [in Chinese]. *Zhongguo nongye daxue xuebao (Social Sciences Edition)* 28 (1): 162–169.

CHAPTER 34

CHINA AND GLOBAL LAND USE CHANGE

YUNAN XU AND SATURNINO M. BORRAS JR.

Introduction

Recent changes to global land use have been rapid, extensive, and dramatic: natural forests converted to large-scale soya production, wetlands converted to industrial fishponds, rangeland converted to game parks, swidden landscape converted to sugarcane monoculture, and so on. The impacts of social relations and ecology, both human and nonhuman, on affected landscapes are far-reaching and often undermine the integrity of agroecological zones and their ability to sustain biodiverse life. The commodities produced from these transformed landscapes also impact the societies that receive them: soya imports facilitate large-scale industrial animal complexes (Weis, this volume); importation of cheap maize from elsewhere destroys local maize production, so that the lands used to grow maize are converted to other uses; the availability of a cheaper alternative vegetable oil like palm oil leads countries that were previously self-sufficient in canola oil production to repurpose land or crops in various ways. The spillover effects of global land use are multiple and wide-ranging.

The complexities of the global dynamics of land-use change have increased due to the convergence of food, energy, financial, and climate crises. According to the 2019 Intergovernmental Panel on Climate Change (IPCC) special report *Climate Change and Land* for (Shukla et al. 2019), "globally, cropland area changed by +15% and the area of permanent pastures by +8% since the early 1960s, with strong regional differences"; an "estimated 23% of total anthropogenic greenhouse gas emissions (2007–2016) derive from Agriculture, Forestry and Other Land Use (AFOLU)"; and "one-third of used land is associated with changed land cover" (pp. 82–86). Such land-use change has far-reaching consequences, given that land has multiple functions for both economic production and social reproduction. Looking at the broader context, it is clear that land is inseparable from water, forests, biodiversity, and minerals, and thus from agriculture and conservation (Swyngedouw 2004; Boelens 2016; Brockington and Duffy 2021). Specifically, current changes in global land use are significantly shaping global social life in various critical spheres, from food politics to climate change, labor, and livelihoods to environmental transformation and from finance to infrastructure, affecting humanity in urban and rural and global South and global North settings.

In this sense, the politics of global land-use change—Who gets to influence the character, extent, pace, and direction of change? How? For what purposes?—has become a compelling subject of debate in policy, political, and scientific communities in the face of a converging set of ongoing crises: the need to feed eight billion people, the quest for nature-and-land-based solutions to climate change, the search for and production of renewable energy, and the effects of expanding extractive industries and urban sprawl (Seto, Güneralp, and Hutyra 2012; Güneralp et al. 2020; Koroso, Zevenbergen, and Lengoiboni 2020). In the global land rush literature, there is much discussion about land and land-use change, but the dominant focus, plot by plot, case by case, is on corporate large-scale land acquisitions and the changes in land use that such cases entail (Zoomers 2010; Deininger and Byerlee 2011; Dell'Angelo et al. 2021; Liao et al. 2021). However, the dynamics of global land-use change are unfolding in more complicated ways: land-use change might not be an outcome of direct land acquisitions; the actors that control land-use change are not always visible and formal; internal transformations in a country investing in land play a role in its outward land initiatives. This implies a deficit in the current state of the art (see Meyfroidt et al. 2022 for a useful synthesis).

In this fluid and dynamic context of global land-use change, the role of China has captured much public attention, but in a relatively narrow sense. China is usually portrayed as a key land grabber in Africa, Southeast Asia, and Latin America, fueled by its demand for food and industrial raw materials. This public perception is reflected in newspaper reports with catchy titles, for example, "Chinese Companies Corralling Land Around World" (Chiba, Watanabe, and Nitta 2021) and "China Farms the World to Feed a Ravenous Economy" (Gray 2008). According to the Land Matrix, the largest database on contemporary land deals, China is one of the biggest land-investor countries worldwide, with total operational land acquisitions standing at 7.9 million hectares by December 2022. Some observers view this data as an overestimation of China's role in the global land rush, arguing that many of the land deals in which Chinese enterprises dominated were not actually pursued and were either blocked or canceled. To give an example, Beidahuang Group (a Chinese state-owned corporation) intended to acquire over 0.25 million hectares of land in Argentina's Rio Negro for food production, but withdrew as a result of political opposition from below (Mora 2022). It is in this context that a number of scholars argue that figures for China's land grabs are overestimated (Hofman and Ho 2012; Bräutigam and Zhang 2013; Oya 2013; Zoomers and Kaag 2014).

Looking at land politics through a different lens, we argue that the extent of China's involvement in driving land-use change in the world has actually been *under*estimated. This rereading expands the view of global land-use change to include cases in which China played a key role in causing, influencing, or directing the change to happen and to be sustained. In our analysis, the role of China in shaping global land-use change is both far more complicated and far more extensive than has previously been calculated. This also implies that related scientific research and global governance initiatives are missing the mark.

The argument proceeds as follows: the next section, "China and Nonoperational Land Deals," focuses on the relevance of nonoperational land deals in the part China plays in global land-use change. The section "Land-Use Change" then proposes a matrix to contribute to a better understanding of land-use-change politics that highlights the significance of indirect and informal forms of land-use change, as well as the internal transformation of China, and the interactions of those multiple variables within the matrix, followed by a concluding discussion.

China and Nonoperational Land Deals

As noted, many large-scale land deals involving Chinese actors eventually fell into the category of "nonoperational" land deals. According to the Land Matrix, China has, during the past decade or so, acquired 17 million hectares of land, but only 43 percent of those deals are operational. These nonoperational—also popularly referred as "failed"—land deals are not usually captured in databases and remain outside the media spotlight. There is a tendency in the literature to lose interest when a land deal has been stopped, canceled, or withdrawn—that is, considered failed or nonoperational. There seems to be no further appetite to investigate the impact of such land deals on the affected communities. We can surmise that a canceled land deal is generally assumed to have no impact on local communities (see the related discussion in Borras et al. 2022b).

We argue that nonoperational land deals have impact on society that warrants deeper investigation. Impact can be seen in two ways. First, we assume that operational land deals and nonoperational land deals are co-constitutive. Land deals in the context of a land boom or a land rush tend to be accompanied by or are outcomes (in part) of speculation and spectacularization. There is widespread speculation about the possible windfalls to be had from acquiring land, but no one really knows how much land, or in what location, is the optimum site for such investment. Similarly, no one really knows the optimum feasible level or type of investment. The inclination is to try to get ahead of other land prospectors (those seeking lands) and investment prospectors (those seeking investments). Under certain conditions, this can escalate into a land rush (Borras and Franco 2024), resulting in hyperbolic projections of amounts of land required and the size of investments expected. But once the frenzy dies down, the land and investment requirements start to settle, and the real level of operational—and nonoperational—land deals is revealed. Thus, the contemporary land rush produces operational and nonoperational land deals in a co-constitutive manner. In this sense, the operational land deals associated with Chinese investors have played an important role in the global land rush that has transformed agroecological zones or landscapes, as well as institutional landscapes, in terms of the thinking about and framing of land, land use, and land users.

Second, in many cases, land deals were concluded but the enterprises promised or expected either never got off the ground or were initiated but were later stopped or stalled. Despite the paucity of empirical studies on what happened on the ground in such cases, we argue that this category of nonoperational land deal can have important effects on the communities involved, legally, sociopolitically, economically, and environmentally. This is supported by the few studies that have begun to look into this question (Baird 2020; Borras et al. 2022b; Broegaard, Vongvisouk, and Mertz 2022; Cochrane et al. 2024). The case of the Chinese company Hengfu Sugar in Cambodia, where we carried out research in 2020–2024, is illustrative. There was a high-profile land deal with the government involving around 43,000 hectares of land. Indigenous communities protested against the land deal, claiming that the Cambodian government and the company had grabbed their ancestral lands. In 2016, the sugarcane company moved in. It built a state-of-the-art sugar mill with farm machinery intended for large-scale production. The Indigenous communities' land (second-growth forest and farmland) was cleared and planted to sugarcane, and operations began. In 2019, the operation of the sugar mill halted and the planting of sugarcane stopped; many of the Chinese expat workers left the site. But Hengfu Sugar did not return the land to the government and the Indigenous communities. Apparently managed by a skeleton staff, it started to lease small parcels of the land to Cambodian land entrepreneurs from nearby towns, who began producing commercial crops for market (rice, corn, and others). The land deal fit Land Matrix's profile of a failed or nonoperational land deal, but in fact, the deal was implemented and its impacts on the local communities were significant and are ongoing.

We therefore argue that failed land deals—including those associated with investors from China—tend to affect current and future land-use change in at least three ways: First is a change in land control; in many failed land deal cases, the land was accessed by investors before the stoppage, withdrawal, or scaling down of the land deal. Second are the ecological and socioeconomic impacts. Although they were stopped, the nonoperational land deals might have already resulted in land-use change (e.g., land preparation for infrastructure building, forest clear-cutting) or could cause land-use change going forward. Third are the institutional impacts, where changes in laws and policies could change land use. Given their large total size and their potentially significant impact, the failed land deals associated with investors from China, particularly the impact on land use, have been understudied. To reach a fuller understanding of China's role in shaping global land-use change, we need to study not only those operational large-scale land deals but also nonoperational deals and their impacts on the ground.

Land-Use Change

When capitalist investors take control of a plot of land, or a landscape, they may transform it in a number of different ways. One of the most visible effects of transformation is land-use change. When the physical constitution or purpose, or both, of a landscape is transformed, land-use or land cover change happens. An obvious example is a natural forest that is clear-cut and replaced by a monoculture crop, such as soya, sugarcane, maize, rubber, or oil palm or, indeed, another forest but of an industrial, single-species tree plantation, such as of eucalyptus or pine trees. Other examples include the clear-cutting of forest to replace it with cattle ranches, or even to leave it empty. Land-use change can also happen when land and crop use are repurposed, such as changing maize for use value in subsistence-oriented rural households to maize for exchange value in the form of feed for animals. Land-use change could result in property transformation, but not necessarily always and everywhere. Regardless of its impact on property relations (dispossession or not), land-use change is a key dimension of the politics of land and deserves specific attention.

The dominant land grab literature tackles the issue of land-use change through the lens of direct causality based on the demarcated space and temporality of a case. This is important. However, it is not the only way the owners of capital or the state can seize control of land and shift and repurpose its use. If we define land grabs along the lines of "control grabbing" (Peluso and Lund 2011; Borras et al. 2012; Wolford et al. 2024), then one way to determine whether a transaction is, in essence, a form of land control grabbing is to pay closer attention to the dynamics of land-use change. Our argument is that an entity, corporate or otherwise, may be able to take control of land and force a shift in its use and purpose without necessarily having to physically acquire the land by purchase, lease, forced occupation, or theft. We base this argument on an analytical mapping of possible types of land-use change. For example, land-use change can, and frequently does, unfold *indirectly*. Numerous forms of land deals are *informal* and not visible to formal monitoring mechanisms, such as the large-scale databanks on land deals. Finally, the focus on cross-border land deals de-emphasizes and tends to be blind to the societies where land grabbers originate. We propose to improve our understanding of China's role in shaping global land-use change by creating a matrix of multiple variables, including formal and informal, direct and indirect, and external and internal, as shown in Figure 34.1.

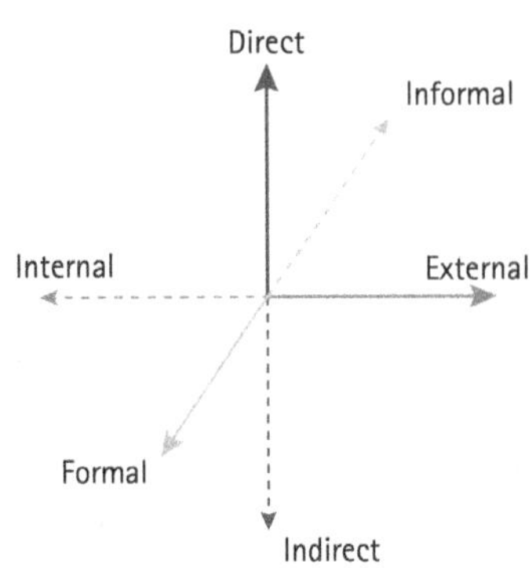

FIGURE 34.1. Analytical matrix re: China's role in global land-use change

Indirect Land-Use Change (ILUC)

We argue that indirect land-use change (ILUC) can have the same effect of land control grabbing as any direct land-use change caused by direct land grabs. The test for us is whether the villagers who previously had control of and access to the land or landscape could lose autonomy and control over their use of that plot of land or landscape, so that—even if they remain the nominal owners of the land—they do not in practice have any say about how it will be used and on what terms. They may continue to derive some benefits from having access, but it is the multiple actors in the global commodity chain of the commodity produced on the land that have the practical control over its use. A classic example of this is the monopoly capture of a commodity through all stages of the global commodity chain. For instance, if a global buyer controls the vast majority of the global supply trade of a particular commodity, that buyer is likely to be able to dictate the terms of trade, including the price of the commodity and other conditions of exchange. It becomes even more problematic when the buyer of the commodity is also the supplier of the inputs necessary to produce the commodity, such as fertilizers and pesticides.

Indirect land-use change is complex process and can involve long distances, making the connections from one point to another in the global commodity chain less apparent. It entails complicated interactions, where an action in one geographic space and time can trigger one or more processes at other sites and points in time. Some refer to this as *telecoupling*, defined as a framework that "integrates both socioeconomic and environmental interactions over distances as opposed to just socioeconomic or environmental interactions," and focuses on flows rather than geographic place (Liu et al. 2013, 8). We agree with discussion of "flows," and for us, these are deeply embedded in the combined political economy and political ecology of global land-use change. This builds on the notion of the combined and uneven development of capitalism as posited by O'Connor (1998) and Smith (2008), entangled in such processes as "metabolic rift" (Foster 1999; Moore 2011), and with broader implications for social relations and socioecological relations of global commodity chains. These issues are explored in Patel (2024, in this volume) and Holleman (2023, in this volume).

A political economy and political ecology notion of ILUC is encapsulated in China's control of the processing and trading of key commodities, such as soya and palm oil, in regions where it does not have significant direct land access. By controlling global trade to a quite significant extent, investors from China are able to enact and maintain far-reaching land-use change. In South America, industrial large-scale soya production is intertwined in forest-clearing processes, whether directly or indirectly (that is, by taking over former cattle ranches that were responsible for the original forest clearing). Converting the quantity of soya traded to China to its equivalence in land area, we estimate that China now has indirect control over 32 million hectares of soya cultivation overseas, mostly in South America. In this way, China, because it is the world's top buyer and consumer of commodities derived from cultivating the land, might have virtual control over at least 50 million hectares of land overseas. Using the same logic, we can track the actual geographic extent of the effective control in causing land-use change, for example, by the European Union or the United States.

ILUC can also be caused by (a) the domino effect, (b) the balloon effect, and (c) crop-use change. The *domino effect* occurs when a land-use change triggers knock-on effects within a land system. For example, in Laos, the shift from pasture to monoculture rubber tree plantations dominated by investors from China impacted the local ecological system. Rice production in the adjacent land plots has been adversely affected, and productivity reduced (Friis et al. 2016). Another domino effect is caused by infrastructure. As the major investor in the global infrastructure projects under the Belt and Road Initiative (BRI), China is shaping global land-use change both directly and indirectly. Infrastructure construction is a direct cause of land-use change and landscape transformation, while the infrastructure itself (physical, digital, financial) contributes in turn to the generalized commodification of land and labor, often paving the way for crop booms (Meyfroidt et al. 2014; Castella et al. 2023). BRI is indirectly shaping the direction of land-use change in the regions of the world where it is underway. This has happened countless times in history, such as with the construction of the railway from the east coast to the west coast of the United States.

The *balloon effect* refers to what happens when a balloon is squeezed in one place, which causes the latex to bulge outward somewhere else. ILUC can occur when a formal regulation related to land use is introduced in one region and leads to land-use change in another place, either within a nation-state or across borders. For instance, when the government of Laos placed restrictions on the expansion of banana plantations in northern Laos over environmental concerns, many investors, including many from China, moved their investments to Myanmar, Thailand, and Cambodia, causing land-use change there (Hayward et al. 2020). Calmon (2022) has observed a similar effect of regulations in the Amazon and the rise of Matopiba in the Cerrado as key sites of investments in Brazil.

Finally, in cases of *crop-use change*, "land cover" remains in the same category but the essence becomes radically different. An example is the conversion of natural forests to artificial monoculture forests. In Cambodia, a company got a concession license from the government to clear-cut a natural forest and replace it with a fast-growing, single-species monoculture tree plantation, ostensibly for the purpose of climate change mitigation and adaptation (Scheidel and Work 2018). On paper, the plot of land remains a forest, but in reality, it has a completely different land use and purpose. More common crop-use changes that have occurred during the past two decades include sugarcane crop use from sweetener to ethanol, sunflower crop use from cooking oil to biodiesel, and so on.

All these forms and flows of ILUC have become more complicated amid the rise of flex crops and commodities—crops and commodities that have multiple end uses, and can be easily and flexibly changed within the global commodity chain at commercial and industrial scale (Borras et al. 2016). Sugarcane, for example, can be used for sweeteners and alcohol and has many other commercial and industrial uses. Large tracts of land remain dedicated to sugarcane, as they have been for generations, and yet there is essentially a change of land use if the sugarcane is no longer intended to produce food (sweeteners), but rather to produce ethanol for fuel. Today, most sugar mills flexibly produce all types of products at one mill site. In some cases, there was no perceptible physical land-use change, but the outputs became involved in either real or anticipated flexing.

Informal Land-Use Change

The literature on contemporary global land grabbing has focused mainly on formal corporate land deals. Among these studies, only a few have looked at the impact on land-use change. Formal land deals are important, but they are not the only significant current in global land grabbing. *Pin-prick land grabs* are everyday land grabs, typically by noncorporate entities engaged in small-scale land grabbing or accumulation. The individual examples may be small-scale, but the in the aggregate, the total scope of these activities is a much larger in scale. For instance, a huge portion of Northern Shan State in Myanmar has been transformed from biodiverse swidden agriculture to monocultures of maize, rubber, and sugarcane. This was rarely accomplished through corporate land grabbing, but rather, through pin-prick land grabs. We might call it the death of agrarian societies by a thousand cuts (Borras and Franco 2024).

If large-scale overseas land-use changes dominated by investors from China have captured public attention, many informal land deals and land accumulations remain outside the glare of media and academic scrutiny. Some of these are large-scale land-use changes, driven by powerful individuals or informal groups, which proceed in informal ways to circumvent any involvement of the authorities in the host countries. They are usually assisted by local brokers or take advantage of loopholes in the local regulations, or both, often in partnership with actors in the host countries. Others are small-scale and widespread, as in the numerous cases of land-use change in the small-scale gold-mining sector dominated by Chinese operators in Ghana (Crawford and Botchwey 2017; Antwi-Boateng and Akudugu 2020), and cross-border farming practices around the China-Myanmar border (Woods 2020) and China-Russia border (Zhou 2016).

Although these informal land deals usually receive much less attention and are largely underexplored, they constitute a considerable share of the total land investments from China that cause extensive land-use change and landscape transformations. Investors from China are often individuals with money, who have organic links in the communities of the target land (Friis and Nielsen 2016; see also Dwyer 2022). For example, many Chinese entrepreneurs and villagers migrate across the border to set up and operate banana plantations in Myanmar. They often travel to Myanmar on tourist visas and usually access land with the assistance of local brokers and without formal registration. The size of a banana plantation run by Chinese entrepreneurs and villagers in Myanmar is typically less than 1,000 acres (405 ha). But the total area covered by such informal banana plantations in Kachin state in Myanmar is estimated to be around 170,000 hectares (Hayward et al. 2020).[1] Similarly, more than 50,000 Chinese individuals, usually from villages in Southern China, are estimated to be engaged in informal gold mining in Ghana (Antwi-Boateng and Akudugu 2020).

Transformation Internal to China

The attention on overseas land deals involving investors from China is clearly important, but it should not be at the expense of scrutinizing the dialectic between transformations that are internal and external to China. In the current world conjuncture, what happens inside China affects the world, and what happens in the world impacts China. We identify three main related social dynamics: (a) land-use change inside China, combined with the land system in rural China, is closely associated with Chinese overseas land investments; (b) labor shortages in rural China, caused by massive internal migration, have resulted in large-scale cross-boundary migration from countries such as Myanmar and Vietnam; this shapes land-use change both in China and in the home countries of the migrants; and (3) the dietary transition in China contributes to increased food and animal-feed commodity imports, which is related to land-use change in many countries and, at the same time, further shapes domestic land-use change inside China.

First, China carried out radical land reforms after 1949. In 1978, the government introduced the Household Responsibility System (HRS), which granted individual usufruct rights to households, ending the era of collective landholding. For the land reallocation to be democratic, land was roughly categorized into three types: best land (usually flat and irrigated or irrigable), good land (usually sloping lands), and rocky and hilly land that is not suitable for agriculture. Each household was allocated several plots of land from the different categories (Ye 2015). As agricultural productivity levels increased, and as demands for further productivity increases grew, the Chinese Communist Party (CCP) realized that fragmented land plots could become obstacles for mechanized farming and the installation of modern irrigation infrastructure, and so on. Frustration over the fragmented rural land regime was often one of the reasons for the national "going out" policy, to find cultivable lands outside China. The move toward land consolidation—whereby owners of plots are asked to exchange plots with others or to persuade villagers to lease their lands to farms to allow for consolidation into larger farm operations—is tightly linked to the investors' decisions to go outside China or not to expand production. This is true, for example, of sugarcane cultivation inside China and the border crossing to control lands in Myanmar, Laos, and Cambodia to produce sugarcane there (Borras et al. 2018; Xu 2020; Wang and Xu 2022). Combined with the national "going out" strategy, this agriculture-related demand for cross-border expansion contributes to the prevalence of overseas land investments of varying types, ranging from formal, large-scale, corporate-dominated investments to informal, small-scale individual-dominated arrangements (Hofman and Ho 2012; Woods 2020).

Second, exacerbated by the trend of massive rural–urban migration within China (Murphy 2002), there is a labor shortage in rural China. To fill this labor gap, large numbers of villagers from Myanmar and Vietnam have been recruited to cross the border into China to fill the vacuum left by the domestic Chinese labor force, which is now concentrated in the cities. Many of these migrants are involved in agricultural work, especially sugarcane cutting (Borras et al. 2022a; Wang and Xu 2022). It is the availability of this relatively cheap labor that enables many small plot owners and emerging capitalist agrarian entrepreneurs in China, to, respectively, hold on to their land or expand their operations, further shaping patterns of land-use change (Hua et al. 2019; Wang and Xu 2022). On the other side of the border, aligned with the "remittance effect" on land-use change posited by Lambin and Meyfroidt (2011), the migrant-sending households tend to make different livelihood choices at home, including expanding their land access, which usually means a shift from the previous use on those newly acquired land plots (Borras et al. 2022a).

Third, the changing food consumption pattern caused by the rise of the middle class, especially in areas undergoing rapid urban development in China, is leading to global changes to land-use, land control, and farming practices that favor chemical input-intensive and higher-value agroproducts, a trend described by Huang as a "hidden agricultural revolution" (Huang, Gao, and Peng 2012; Huang 2016). The dietary transition in China, particularly the increased consumption of meat, is linked to soaring soybean imports for animal feed (Oliveira and Schneider 2016; Lander, Schneider, and Brunson 2020). These soy imports not only contribute to the rise of soybean plantations in soy-exporting countries (especially in Latin America) but also cause a shift in the land-use and agrarian structure in China, as Chinese farmers struggle to compete in the market against cheap soy imports (Huang and Gao 2014; Yan, Chen, and Bun 2016).

Conclusion

China's role in shaping global patterns of land-use change and the extent of such change are far more extensive than previously thought. The complexity of this process makes it particularly challenging to govern transnationally. We have shown how investors from China play a significant part in bringing about landscape transformations in distant places. These forms of interaction need to be fully accounted for in studying the politics of land.

The dynamics described above (direct/indirect, formal/informal, and internal/external) are all important components of the political economy and political ecology of land-use change. However, the variables within this matrix are not independent or stand-alone but have blurred boundaries and mutually interact with one another. On the one hand, the variables are change over time. For example, the well-known formal Chinese investment in the Myitsone Dam project in Myanmar was suspended because of resistance from below (Lamb and Dao 2017). The site has now become the location of multiple small-scale gold-mining operations, with the informal involvement of Chinese entrepreneurs and villagers. This shows that the types of land-use change are not static but may shift over time within a certain landscape. On the other hand, there are close interactions between different matrix axes. For example, changes in the domestic diet in China are indirectly related to the expansion of soybean cultivation in Latin America (e.g., Brazil and Argentina). The shift from cattle ranching to soybean plantations in Brazil led cattle ranchers to clear-cut forests elsewhere in the Amazon (Novo et al. 2010; Franco and Borras 2019). This shows that one axis (internal/external) may closely interact with another axis (indirect/direct), and that they should be explored together rather than as multiple fragmented elements. Although it is, of course, possible to focus on only a single variable for the sake of academic inquiry, isolating one variable from the whole matrix hinders the possibility of fully understanding the dynamics at work, and is therefore problematic.

By drawing attention to the matrix of multiple variables around China's role in shaping global land-use change, we also want to highlight the importance of focusing on the social relations and socioecological relations around the land-use change process, rather than on the nationality of the land investors. On the one hand, an emphasis on the nationalities of land investors oversimplifies the complexity of the land-use change process and is thus misleading. Many different Chinese actors are involved, ranging from the Chinese state and state-owned companies to private companies and individual entrepreneurs. Different actors tend to have distinct goals and strategies in making land-based investments, which leads to different land-use-change trajectories. At the same time, we might ask why Chinese land investments have drawn so much public attention compared with their non-Chinese counterparts. Do Chinese investors conduct land deals and land-use change in a markedly different way, leading to more significant negative impacts on local communities than, say, European or American investors?

Note

1. Among these Chinese actors in Kachin State, Hayward et al. (2020) estimate that Chinese agribusiness companies (including Yunnan Yuanyuan Trading Company, Yunnan Kyushu Jinke Investment Company, and Yunnan Jinxin Agricultural Company) control around 50,000 acres of land for banana cultivation, some of which falls under the Opium Substitution Program.

References

Antwi-Boateng, Osman, and Mamudu Abunga Akudugu. 2020. "Golden Migrants: The Rise and Impact of Illegal Chinese Small-Scale Mining in Ghana." *Politics & Policy* 48 (1): 135–167. https://doi.org/10.1111/polp.12342.

Baird, Ian G. 2020. "Problems for the Plantations: Challenges for Large-Scale Land Concessions in Laos and Cambodia." *Journal of Agrarian Change* 20 (3): 387–407. https://doi.org/10.1111/joac.12355.

Boelens, Rutgerd. 2016. *Water, Power and Identity: The Cultural Politics of Water in the Andes*. London: Routledge.

Borras, Saturnino M., Jr., and Jennifer C. Franco. 2024. "Land Rush." *Journal of Peasant Studies* pp. 1–16. doi:10.1080/03066150.2024.2317961.

Borras, Saturnino M., Jr., Jennifer C. Franco, Sergio Gómez, Cristóbal Kay, and Max Spoor. 2012. "Land Grabbing in Latin America and the Caribbean." *Journal of Peasant Studies* 39 (3–4): 845–872. https://doi.org/10.1080/03066150.2012.679931.

Borras, Saturnino M., Jr., Jennifer C. Franco, S. Ryan Isakson, Les Levidow, and Pietje Vervest. 2016. "The Rise of Flex Crops and Commodities: Implications for Research." *Journal of Peasant Studies* 43 (1): 93–115. https://doi.org/10.1080/03066150.2015.1036417.

Borras, Saturnino M., Jr., Juan Liu, Zhen Hu, Hua Li, Chunyu Wang, Yunan Xu, et al. 2018. "Land Control and Crop Booms inside China: Implications for How We Think about the Global Land Rush." *Globalizations* 15 (1): 134–151. https://doi.org/10.1080/14747731.2017.1408287.

Borras, Saturnino M., Jr., Jennifer C. Franco, Doi Ra, Tom Kramer, Mi Kamoon, Phwe Phyu, Khu Khu Ju, et al. 2022a. "Rurally Rooted Cross-Border Migrant Workers from Myanmar, Covid-19, and Agrarian Movements." *Agriculture and Human Values* 39 (1): 315–338. https://doi.org/10.1007/s10460-021-10262-6.

Borras, Saturnino M., Jr., Jennifer C. Franco, Tsegaye Moreda, Yunan Xu, Natacha Bruna, and Binyam Afewerk Demena. 2022b. "The Value of So-Called 'Failed' Large-Scale Land Acquisitions." *Land Use Policy* 119 (August): Article 106199. https://doi.org/10.1016/j.landusepol.2022.106199.

Bräutigam, Deborah, and Haisen Zhang. 2013. "Green Dreams: Myth and Reality in China's Agricultural Investment in Africa." *Third World Quarterly* 34 (9): 1676–1696. https://doi.org/10.1080/01436597.2013.843846.

Brockington, Dan, and Rosaleen Duffy, eds. 2021. *Capitalism and Conservation.* Antipode Book Series. Chichester, UK: Wiley-Blackwell.

Broegaard, Rikke Brandt, Thoumthone Vongvisouk, and Ole Mertz. 2022. "The Impact of Unimplemented Large-Scale Land Development Deals." *Frontiers in Sustainable Food Systems* 6 (June 22). https://www.frontiersin.org/articles/10.3389/fsufs.2022.789809.

Calmon, Daniela. 2022. "Shifting Frontiers: The Making of Matopiba in Brazil and Global Redirected Land Use and Control Change." *Journal of Peasant Studies* 49 (2): 263–287. https://doi.org/10.1080/03066150.2020.1824183.

Castella, Jean-Christophe, Juliet Lu, Cecilie Friis, Thilde Bech Bruun, Robert Cole, Victoria Junquera, et al. 2023. "Beyond the Boom–Bust Cycle: An Interdisciplinary Framework for Analysing Crop Booms." *Global Environmental Change* 80 (May): 102651. https://doi.org/10.1016/j.gloenvcha.2023.102651.

Chiba, Daishi, Shin Watanabe, and Yuichi Nitta. 2021. "Chinese Companies Corralling Land around World." Nikkei Asia. https://asia.nikkei.com/Spotlight/Datawatch/Chinese-companies-corralling-land-around-world.

Cochrane, Logan, Eric P. H. Li, Melisew Dejene, and M. Mustahid Husain. 2024. "Why Foreign Agricultural Investment Fails? Five Lessons from Ethiopia." *Journal of International Development* 36 (1): 541–558. https://doi.org/10.1002/jid.3827.

Crawford, Gordon, and Gabriel Botchwey. 2017. "Conflict, Collusion and Corruption in Small-Scale Gold Mining: Chinese Miners and the State in Ghana." *Commonwealth & Comparative Politics* 55 (4): 444–470. https://doi.org/10.1080/14662043.2017.1283479.

Deininger, Klaus, and Derek Byerlee. 2011. *Rising Global Interest in Farmland: Can It Yield Sustainable and Equitable Benefits?* Washington, DC: World Bank Publications.

Dell'Angelo, Jampel, Grettel Navas, Marga Witteman, Giacomo D'Alisa, Arnim Scheidel, and Leah Temper. 2021. "Commons Grabbing and Agribusiness: Violence, Resistance and Social

Mobilization." *Ecological Economics* 184 (June): Article 107004. https://doi.org/10.1016/j.ecolecon.2021.107004.

Dwyer, Michael B. 2022. *Upland Geopolitics: Postwar Laos and the Global Land Rush*. Seattle: University of Washington Press.

Foster, John Bellamy. 1999. "Marx's Theory of Metabolic Rift: Classical Foundations for Environmental Sociology." *American Journal of Sociology* 105 (2): 366–405. https://doi.org/10.1086/210315.

Franco, Jennifer C., and Saturnino M. Borras Jr. 2019. "Grey Areas in Green Grabbing: Subtle and Indirect Interconnections between Climate Change Politics and Land Grabs and Their Implications for Research." *Land Use Policy* 84 (May): 192–199. https://doi.org/10.1016/j.landusepol.2019.03.013.

Friis, Cecilie, and Jonas Østergaard Nielsen. 2016. "Small-Scale Land Acquisitions, Large-Scale Implications: Exploring the Case of Chinese Banana Investments in Northern Laos." *Land Use Policy* 57 (November): 117–129. https://doi.org/10.1016/j.landusepol.2016.05.028.

Friis, Cecilie, Anette Reenberg, Andreas Heinimann, and Oliver Schönweger. 2016. "Changing Local Land Systems: Implications of a Chinese Rubber Plantation in Nambak District, Lao PDR." *Singapore Journal of Tropical Geography* 37 (1): 25–42. https://doi.org/10.1111/sjtg.12137.

Gray, Denis. 2008. "China Farms the World to Feed a Ravenous Economy." Fosters Daily Democrat (May 5). https://www.fosters.com/story/lifestyle/2008/05/05/china-farms-world-to-feed/52428617007/.

Güneralp, Burak, Meredith Reba, Billy U. Hales, Elizabeth A. Wentz, and Karen C. Seto. 2020. "Trends in Urban Land Expansion, Density, and Land Transitions from 1970 to 2010: A Global Synthesis." *Environmental Research Letters* 15 (4): Article 044015. https://doi.org/10.1088/1748-9326/ab6669.

Hayward, Daniel, U Ko Lwin, Yang Bin, and U Htet Kyu. 2020. "Chinese Investment into Tissue-Culture Banana Plantations in Kachin State, Myanmar." Mekong Region Land Governance Case Study. MRLG. https://www.mrlg.org/publications/publication-title-chinese-investment-into-tissue-culture-banana-plantations-in-kachin-state-myanmar/.

Hofman, Irna, and Peter Ho. 2012. "China's 'Developmental Outsourcing': A Critical Examination of Chinese Global 'Land Grabs' Discourse." *Journal of Peasant Studies* 39 (1): 1–48. https://doi.org/10.1080/03066150.2011.653109.

Holleman, Hannah. 2023. "Land and Ecosocialism: In Defense of the Commons." In *The Oxford Handbook of Land Politics*, edited by Saturnino M. Borras Jr. and Jennifer C. Franco, 1–13. Oxford: Oxford University Press. https://doi.org/10.1093/oxfordhb/9780197618646.013.28.

Hua, Xiaobo, Yasuyuki Kono, Le Zhang, Erqi Xu, and Renshan Luo. 2019. "How Transnational Labor Migration Affects Upland Land Use Practices in the Receiving Country: Findings from the China–Myanmar Borderland." *Land Use Policy* 84 (May): 163–76. https://doi.org/10.1016/j.landusepol.2019.03.012.

Huang, Philip C. C. 2016. "China's Hidden Agricultural Revolution, 1980–2010, in Historical and Comparative Perspective." *Modern China* 42 (4): 339–76. https://doi.org/10.1177/0097700415626137.

Huang, Philip C. C., and Yuan Gao. 2014. "大豆生产和进口的经济逻辑" [The economic logic behind soybean production and import]." 开放时代 [Open times] 1:176–188.

Huang, Philip C. C., Yuan Gao, and Yusheng Peng. 2012. "Capitalization without Proletarianization in China's Agricultural Development." *Modern China* 38 (2): 139–73. https://doi.org/10.1177/0097700411435620.

Koroso, Nesru H., Jaap A. Zevenbergen, and Monica Lengoiboni. 2020. "Urban Land Use Efficiency in Ethiopia: An Assessment of Urban Land Use Sustainability in Addis Ababa." *Land Use Policy* 99 (December): Article 105081. https://doi.org/10.1016/j.landusepol.2020.105081.

Lamb, Vanessa, and Nga Dao. 2017. "Perceptions and Practices of Investment: China's Hydropower Investments in Vietnam and Myanmar." *Canadian Journal of Development Studies / Revue Canadienne d'études Du Développement* 38 (3): 395–413. https://doi.org/10.1080/02255189.2017.1298519.

Lambin, Eric F., and Patrick Meyfroidt. 2011. "Global Land Use Change, Economic Globalization, and the Looming Land Scarcity." *Proceedings of the National Academy of Sciences* 108 (9): 3465–3472. https://doi.org/10.1073/pnas.1100480108.

Lander, Brian, Mindi Schneider, and Katherine Brunson. 2020. "A History of Pigs in China: From Curious Omnivores to Industrial Pork." *Journal of Asian Studies* 79 (4): 865–89. https://doi.org/10.1017/S0021911820000054.

Liao, Chuan, Kerstin Nolte, Jonathan A. Sullivan, Daniel G. Brown, Jann Lay, Christof Althoff, et al. 2021. "Carbon Emissions from the Global Land Rush and Potential Mitigation." *Nature Food* 2 (1): 15–18. https://doi.org/10.1038/s43016-020-00215-3.

Liu, Jianguo, Vanessa Hull, Mateus Batistella, Ruth DeFries, Thomas Dietz, Feng Fu, et al. 2013. "Framing Sustainability in a Telecoupled World." *Ecology and Society* 18 (2): 26. https://www.jstor.org/stable/26269331.

Meyfroidt, Patrick, Kimberly M. Carlson, Matthew E. Fagan, Victor H. Gutiérrez-Vélez, Marcia N. Macedo, Lisa M. Curran, et al. 2014. "Multiple Pathways of Commodity Crop Expansion in Tropical Forest Landscapes." *Environmental Research Letters* 9 (7): Article 074012. https://doi.org/10.1088/1748-9326/9/7/074012.

Meyfroidt, Patrick, Ariane de Bremond, Casey M. Ryan, Emma Archer, Richard Aspinall, Abha Chhabra, et al. 2022. "Ten Facts about Land Systems for Sustainability." *Proceedings of the National Academy of Sciences* 119 (7): Article e2109217118. https://doi.org/10.1073/pnas.2109217118.

Moore, Jason W. 2011. "Transcending the Metabolic Rift: A Theory of Crises in the Capitalist World-Ecology." *Journal of Peasant Studies* 38 (1): 1–46. https://doi.org/10.1080/03066150.2010.538579.

Mora, Sol. 2022. "Land Grabbing, Power Configurations and Trajectories of China's Investments in Argentina." *Globalizations* 19 (5): 696–710. https://doi.org/10.1080/14747731.2021.1920197.

Murphy, Rachel. 2002. *How Migrant Labor Is Changing Rural China*. Cambridge, UK: Cambridge University Press.

Novo, Andre, Kees Jansen, Maja Slingerland, and Ken Giller. 2010. "Biofuel, Dairy Production and Beef in Brazil: Competing Claims on Land Use in São Paulo State." *Journal of Peasant Studies* 37 (4): 769–792. https://doi.org/10.1080/03066150.2010.512458.

O'Connor, James R. 1998. *Natural Causes: Essays in Ecological Marxism*. New York: Guilford Press.

Oliveira, Gustavo de L. T., and Mindi Schneider. 2016. "The Politics of Flexing Soybeans: China, Brazil and Global Agroindustrial Restructuring." *Journal of Peasant Studies* 43 (1): 167–194. https://doi.org/10.1080/03066150.2014.993625.

Oya, Carlos. 2013. "Methodological Reflections on 'Land Grab' Databases and the 'Land Grab' Literature 'Rush.'" *Journal of Peasant Studies* 40 (3): 503–520. https://doi.org/10.1080/03066150.2013.799465.

Patel, Raj. 2024. "Land in World-Ecology Perspectives." In *The Oxford Handbook of Land Politics*, edited by Saturnino M. Borras Jr. and Jennifer C. Franco, 1–15. Oxford: Oxford University Press. https://doi.org/10.1093/oxfordhb/9780197618646.013.18.

Peluso, Nancy Lee, and Christian Lund. 2011. "New Frontiers of Land Control: Introduction." *Journal of Peasant Studies* 38 (4): 667–681. https://doi.org/10.1080/03066150.2011.607692.

Scheidel, Arnim, and Courtney Work. 2018. "Forest Plantations and Climate Change Discourses: New Powers of 'Green' Grabbing in Cambodia." *Land Use Policy* 77 (September): 9–18. https://doi.org/10.1016/j.landusepol.2018.04.057.

Seto, Karen C., Burak Güneralp, and Lucy R. Hutyra. 2012. "Global Forecasts of Urban Expansion to 2030 and Direct Impacts on Biodiversity and Carbon Pools." *Proceedings of the National Academy of Sciences* 109 (40): 16083–16088. https://doi.org/10.1073/pnas.121 1658109.

Shukla, P. R., J. Skeg, E. Calvo Buendia, V. Masson-Delmotte, H.-O. Pörtner, D. C. Roberts, et al. 2019. *Climate Change and Land: An IPCC Special Report on Climate Change, Desertification, Land Degradation, Sustainable Land Management, Food Security, and Greenhouse Gas Fluxes in Terrestrial Ecosystems*. Geneva: IPCC.

Smith, Neil. 2008. *Uneven Development: Nature, Capital, and the Production of Space*. 3rd ed. Athens: University of Georgia Press.

Swyngedouw, Erik. 2004. *Social Power and the Urbanization of Water: Flows of Power*. Oxford: Oxford University Press.

Wang, Chunyu, and Yunan Xu. 2022. "Reflecting on the Plantationocene: The Political Economy of Sugarcane Plantations in Guangxi, China." *Journal of Peasant Studies* (online), 1–22. https://doi.org/10.1080/03066150.2022.2087180.

Wolford, Wendy, Ben White, Ian Scoones, Ruth Hall, M. Edelman, and Jun Borras. 2024. "Global Land Deals: What Has Been Done, What Has Changed, and What's Next?" LDPI Working Paper Series 2024-001. Land Deal Politics Initiative. International Institute of Social Studies (ISS), The Hague.

Woods, Kevin M. 2020. "Smaller-Scale Land Grabs and Accumulation from below: Violence, Coercion and Consent in Spatially Uneven Agrarian Change in Shan State, Myanmar." *World Development* 127 (March): Article 104780. https://doi.org/10.1016/j.worlddev.2019.104780.

Xu Yunan. 2020. *Industrial Tree Plantations and the Land Rush in China: Implications for Global Land Grabbing*. New York: Routledge.

Yan, Hairong, Yiyuan Chen, and Ku Hok Bun. 2016. "China's Soybean Crisis: The Logic of Modernization and Its Discontents." *Journal of Peasant Studies* 43 (2): 373–395. https://doi.org/10.1080/03066150.2015.1132205.

Ye, Jingzhong. 2015. "Land Transfer and the Pursuit of Agricultural Modernization in China." *Journal of Agrarian Change* 15 (3): 314–337. https://doi.org/10.1111/joac.12117.

Zhou, Jiayi. 2016. "Chinese Agrarian Capitalism in the Russian Far East." *Third World Thematics: A TWQ Journal* 1 (5): 612–632. https://doi.org/10.1080/23802014.2016.1327795.

Zoomers, Annelies. 2010. "Globalisation and the Foreignisation of Space: Seven Processes Driving the Current Global Land Grab." *Journal of Peasant Studies* 37 (2): 429–447. https://doi.org/10.1080/03066151003595325.

Zoomers, Annelies, and Mayke Kaag. 2014. *The Global Land Grab: Beyond the Hype*. Illustrated ed. Halifax and London: Zed Books.

CHAPTER 35

CONSERVATION, LAND DISPOSSESSION, AND RESISTANCE IN AFRICA

CONNOR CAVANAGH AND TOR A. BENJAMINSEN

Introduction

The spatial ambition of the global conservation industry is once again resurgent. Between 2011 and 2020, the UN Convention on Biological Diversity (UNCBD) sought to coordinate multilateral cooperation on protected area governance through its *Strategic Plan for Biodiversity 2011 to 2020* and corresponding Aichi Biodiversity Targets. Aichi Target 11 aimed to achieve global protected area coverage of "at least 17 per cent of terrestrial and inland water, and 10 per cent of coastal and marine areas" by 2020 (UNCBD 2020). Although significant progress was made in relation to some of the targets—particularly those addressing protected area coverage—it is notable that none of the Aichi Biodiversity Targets were conclusively achieved throughout the now-concluded UN Decade on Biodiversity (2010–2020).

At the time of writing, negotiations concerning the UNCBD's "post-2020 framework for biodiversity" are still ongoing. Thus far, however, influential proposals for renewed protected area coverage targets reflect quite dramatic increases in spatial ambition. The appropriately named "High Ambition Coalition for Nature and People," for example, has proposed the much discussed "30 x 30" conservation target, which aims to achieve 30 percent global protected area coverage across both terrestrial and marine ecosystems by 2030. This would entail roughly a doubling of the existing terrestrial protected area estate, and a quadrupling of the marine protected area estate throughout the remaining years of this decade (UNEP-WCMC 2022). More ambitious still is the 50 percent global protected area coverage target emerging from the Half-Earth Project or the Nature Needs Half conservation movement, which is once again galvanizing considerable support in the wake of the 2022 passing of its founder, the influential Harvard biologist E. O. Wilson (see Wilson 2016).

Echoing these proposals, the recent IPCC Working Group II report on climate change "impacts, adaptation and vulnerability" recommends conservation of between 30 percent and 50 percent of the earth's land, freshwater, and ocean areas (International Panel on Climate Change 2022). This recommendation was, however, controversial throughout relevant IPCC assessment processes, as well as throughout broader academic and policymaking communities. Associated controversies stem not only from a hesitance to commit to expanding protected area coverage among various governments, but also from concerns about what will happen to people currently living in areas that may become subject to expanded conservation activities. Evoking the substance of earlier "back to the barriers" debates in conservation governance (e.g., Hutton, Adams, and Murombedzi 2005), important questions also arise about the exact institutional arrangements through which these targets are envisioned to be met. This is particularly the case with regard to whether 30 x 30 or Half-Earth targets are imagined to entail a dramatic upscaling of existing "fortress conservation" models (Brockington 2002), or an unprecedented rollout of new forms of "community-based conservation" (e.g., Dressler et al. 2010) across the fuller spectrum of the protected area management categories of the International Union for Conservation of Nature (IUCN).

Criticizing the Half-Earth proposal, for instance, Büscher et al. (2017) contend that the plan could have widespread negative consequences for rural populations, including increased injustice, inequality, and potentially also violent conflict. Empirically illustrating such concerns, a geospatial scenario analysis by Schleicher et al. (2019) finds that no fewer than one billion people live in regions that could be encompassed by protected areas if conservation initiatives are representatively expanded across all ecoregions in accordance with Half-Earth targets. It is thus not implausible that—as Büscher and Fletcher (2016) suggest—an "actually-existing" Half-Earth initiative "would entail forcibly herding a drastically reduced human population into increasingly crowded urban areas." In response to this critique, steadfast proponents of the Nature Needs Half campaign insist there is "a consensus among conservationists that local communities should be actively involved in conservation efforts," albeit with the caveat that "justice for people . . . should not come at the expense of interspecies justice" (Cafaro et al. 2017, 400). Similar concerns regarding interspecies justice are shared by a number of biocentric or "deep ecology"-inspired proponents of expansionary conservation (e.g., Kopnina 2019).

We examine this contested "dark side" of resurgent spatial ambition in conservation governance. Specifically, we assess risks that the rapid expansion of protected areas may result in the mounting dispossession of rural land users, including subsistence-oriented farmers and pastoralists. Indeed, it is important to note that increasingly ambitious protected area targets are now being proposed in the context of what has already been an extensive protected area expansion during the twentieth and early twenty-first centuries, entailing particularly substantial social and economic costs to local communities in the global South (West et al. 2006; Dowie 2009). From only a handful of protected areas in

1900, the global protected area estate has swiftly expanded to cover nearly 15 percent of terrestrial land area in 2022, amounting to approximately 20 million square kilometers (UNEP-WCMC 2022). To place this figure in context, the land area of the continent of South America is approximately 17.8 million square kilometers. Moreover, to meet emerging "30 x 30" targets, terrestrial protected areas would essentially need to encompass a total of roughly 40 million square kilometers of land area by 2030, expanding at an average rate of 2.5 million square kilometers annually between 2022 and 2030.

Considering this rapid rate of projected expansion, the chapter examines the risks and determinants of overt resistance arising in the aftermath of protected area establishment or expansion, as well as resulting displacement or dispossession. As numerous studies in political ecology have illuminated, the establishment of protected areas can in some cases result in forced migration or "internal displacement" to both urban areas and elsewhere (Brockington and Igoe 2006; Dowie 2009; Kabra 2009; Cavanagh 2018). In such cases, conservationists tend to perceive local populations as being "in the way" of protected area management, and thus as implicitly constituting a "surplus population" (Li 2009). In a conservation context, surplus populations are created when there is limited or no need for their labor in the new economic and institutional arrangements created through their dispossession (Kelly 2011). As such, the displacement of surplus populations may be spatial—unfolding through physical evictions of people and associated forced migration—but it may also occur in situ (Feldman et al. 2003), implying socioeconomic rather than spatial displacement (Ince 2014). That is to say, exclusionary forms of protected area establishment or expansion may amount to a form of "naturalization by dispossession" (Cavanagh and Benjaminsen 2014, 58) when conservation necessitates either the outright dispossession of de jure property rights or the curtailment of informal, customary, or other de facto forms of access to lands and natural resources (Ribot and Peluso 2003; see also Ojeda, this volume; Peters, this volume).

Aside from forced migration, protected area establishment—just like other forms of large-scale land and resource acquisition—can engender a range of local responses, including acquiescence, adaptation, circumvention, and negotiation (Hall et al. 2015a). Our focus, however, is primarily on the determinants of responses that can be accurately described with the term *resistance*, particularly those manifesting via instances of protest, opposition, or violent confrontation. The various forms of overt resistance to conservation tend to emerge from a general feeling of disempowerment and marginalization. Yet, as Brockington (2004) argues, these forms of resistance do not necessarily amount to an operational threat to conservation governance, given the widespread examples of conservation inequality or injustice simply being perpetuated with the backing of both state agencies and transnational financiers. Indeed, there is no necessary reason to assume that the mere presence of resistance to conservation will be "successful" in redressing the grievances of disaffected local populations. Conversely, overt resistance to protected area establishment or expansion may nonetheless precipitate manifold complications for the achievement of conservation objectives. Such complications can arise, for instance, via the deliberate slaughter of protected wildlife (Mariki, Svarstad, and Benjaminsen 2015), the reversal of restoration-associated forms of land cover change as a form of political protest (Grove 1997; Cavanagh and Benjaminsen 2014), or the recruitment of local people into poaching or illegal resource extraction networks (Hübschle 2017). Differently put, while there may be no necessary reason to expect resistance to conservation to effectively redress conservation injustices, such phenomena may nonetheless result in "lose-lose" outcomes for both conservation and local livelihoods rather than oft-promoted "win-win" outcomes for all concerned (Büscher 2014).

Examining the determinants of these variable manifestations of overt resistance, we aim to highlight how careful attention to associated empirical dynamics can enrich our understanding of factors that encourage conservation-affected populations to engage in specifically resistance-oriented responses to land dispossession, and with what implications. To fulfill this aim, we proceed as follows. First, we review both seminal and recent literatures on the livelihood impacts of protected area establishment across diverse historical and geographical contexts. Second, we revisit the implications of the latter dynamics for related scholarship on "resistance to conservation" (e.g., Brockington 2004; Holmes 2007; Cavanagh and Benjaminsen 2015). Third, we examine the extent to which recent developments in violent resistance, including the growth of jihadist groups, can be linked to the *expansion* of an environmental conservation agenda in rural Africa. Throughout, we suggest that mainstream conservation interventions, which tend to be implemented in top-down fashion, typically underestimate the risks of local resistance. Conversely, we note that ideology-focused explanations of violent extremism also tend to overlook the material determinants of violence and the associated grievances rooted in the loss of access to land, natural resources, and customary forms of livelihood. We conclude by illuminating how empirical studies of the latter factors—and particularly those which eschew single-factor determinism in favor of qualitative, multifactor explanation or contextualization—represent a promising new area for future research on resistance to conservation in political ecology, critical agrarian studies, and related fields.[1]

From Yellowstone to Green Militarization

The often-contested nature of protected area establishment and expansion is well known to political ecologists, environmental historians, and other critical scholars of conservation. Numerous studies, for instance, trace the "birth" of the modern protected area model of conservation governance to the contested establishment of Yellowstone National Park in the United States in 1872 (Spence 1999). In particular, Dowie (2009) notes the imbrication of protected area establishment at Yellowstone and Yosemite in the United States with broader processes of settler-colonial state formation, which

California's first governor—Peter Burnett—once described as a "war of extermination" against indigenous populations (in Dowie 2009, 1; see also Solnit 2014, 271).

As a substantial literature demonstrates, ensuing decades saw the associated "fences and fines" or "fortress conservation" model disseminated throughout (former) European colonies in Africa, Asia, and the Americas, as well as in European settler colonies such as Canada, Australia, and New Zealand (Brockington 2002; West, Igoe, and Brockington 2006; Brockington, Duffy, and Igoe 2012). An expansive case study literature from the Global South documents recurring instances of adverse livelihood impacts (Grove 1997; Neumann 1998; Adams and Hutton 2007; Holmes and Cavanagh 2016), as well as subsequent forms of resistance and various other "responses from below" (Hall et al. 2015a) to the imposition of conservation measures (e.g., Holmes 2007; Cavanagh and Benjaminsen 2015; Mariki, Svarstad, and Benjaminsen 2015). In contrast, throughout Europe, modern conservation has often included rather than excluded local livelihood practices and cultural perceptions of the rural landscape (Adams 2020), leading to a more complex range of outcomes in the contemporary era. Even within Europe, however—from a deeper historical perspective—it is notable that large-scale enclosures and associated land dispossession have also resulted in various forms of local resistance. This includes the forms of opposition that emerged in response to the creation of various royal hunting grounds, beginning in the thirteenth century (Grove 1997), as well as to the English enclosures and Scottish clearances throughout the eighteenth and nineteenth centuries (Marx [1867] 1995; see also Thompson 1975).

Despite these late nineteenth-century roots of modern fortress conservation, it was not until the "postwar conservation boom" in the 1950s—and the rise of aviation-fueled international (eco)tourism that drove it—that the global rate of protected area establishment began to increase more rapidly (Neumann 2002). Particularly from the 1980s onward, the governance of protected areas became subsumed within a broader "sustainable development" paradigm, which emphasized the potential for conservation to achieve "win-win" outcomes for both biodiversity and rural livelihoods (Adams et al. 2004). In this context, ecotourism began to be imagined as a key mechanism through which conservation would "pay its own way" (Eltringham 1994), and particularly so in recent years as part of a broader transition to a "green economy" (Cavanagh and Benjaminsen 2017). In this view, ecotourism and other income-generating ventures would potentially both defray the costs of protected area management and create employment opportunities or other benefits that could be shared with local populations. In response, a wide range of "collaborative" or "community conservation" project models emerged, which were intended to involve rural land users in conservation governance to varying degrees and to optimize the realization of associated benefits for livelihoods and protected species of flora and fauna alike (Hulme and Murphree 2001; Brockington 2004; Dressler et al. 2010).

As Adams and Hulme (2001) once asked, however, "If community conservation is the answer in Africa, what is the question?" Differently put, "win-win" conservation outcomes have often proved difficult to realize in many contexts, and particularly so throughout the African continent. As a result, recurring contestations have emerged regarding exactly which actors retain the authority to set conservation policy, acquire lands for conservation purposes, and determine the "acceptability" of trade-offs between conservation and livelihood objectives when they inevitably arise (Cavanagh, Sandbrook, and Tumusiime 2018). Indeed, these interrelations between authority and outcome "priority" are particularly important in conservation policy. As Murphree (2000, 12) once quipped regarding community-based conservation in the African context, in his view the approach has "not been tried and found wanting; it has been found difficult and rarely tried." This may still be the case today, more than twenty years later.

Interventions based on a fortress conservation approach clearly retain the potential to exclude or dispossess customary land and natural resource users. Yet initiatives labeled "community-based conservation" may—surprisingly to some—also have similar effects. For instance, Benjaminsen and Bryceson (2012) document how both community-based forms of wildlife and marine conservation in Tanzania dispossess villagers of benefits from village land. Similarly, Cavanagh, Weldemichel, and Benjaminsen (2020) highlight how the implementation of for-profit conservation models on privately owned and titled community lands in Kenya can result in the highly unequal distribution of profits and revenues to conservation or ecotourism investors rather than local landowners, leading to a proliferation of both intercommunity and intracommunity inequalities. In some cases, this process is gradual and piecemeal—perhaps amounting to a form of what Nixon (2011) terms "slow violence" (see also Cavanagh and Benjaminsen 2015; Weldemichel 2021). In other cases, it can entail the forthright use of violence to enforce conservation policy (Weldemichel 2020). In this way, the introduction of community-based conservation may in some cases function as a mechanism for capital accumulation by some actors or community strata (e.g., local elites, corrupt government officials, the tourist industry, and international conservation organizations that use the image of win-win conservation for fundraising), while allowing conservation a foothold on village land and establishing necessary preconditions for dispossession to take place.[2]

Although the achievement of win-win conservation outcomes via community-based conservation models is hypothetically possible, recent decades have also occasionally witnessed the outright abandonment of rhetorical pretenses regarding conservation's livelihood or socioeconomic benefits. Among certain communities of conservation biologists and policymakers, dissatisfaction with the empirical results of collaborative conservation models has in some cases resulted in a "back to the barriers" disposition (Hutton, Adams, and Murombedzi 2005). This advocates a return to stricter forms of exclusionary conservation, particularly so in ostensibly critical or "high value" ecosystems or landscapes. Though this trend was already well underway in the early twenty-first century (e.g., Wilshusen et al. 2002), it has been bolstered more recently by efforts to (re)frame conservation governance not only as a means of preserving biodiversity, but also as a mechanism for combating various forms of "threat finance" derived from the illegal exploitation of natural resources (Duffy 2014; Cavanagh, Vedeld, and Trædal 2015). In this regard, resurgent "back to the barriers" support for exclusionary conservation once again dovetails with the (re-)emergence of various types of "green militarization" (Lunstrum 2014) or the growing use of military, paramilitary, and law-enforcement agencies to bolster conservation governance and to enforce related protected area boundaries (see also Kelly and Ybarra 2016; Marijnen 2017; Adams 2020).

Resistance to Conservation in Africa

Amid this resurgence of support for exclusionary conservation—accompanied by varying degrees of militarization or securitization across diverse world regions—it is critical to revisit the risks and determinants of both "resistance" and various other forms of overt opposition to protected area expansion. Indeed, as Ybarra (2012) notes, the creeping securitization of conservation implies that such forms of "resistance" may be increasingly perceived through a broad "counterinsurgency" lens. Particularly in South(east) Asia, Africa, and the Americas, there is a long history of state counterinsurgency activity in forested protected areas and other landscapes thought to offer ostensibly "natural" forms of refuge for rebels, militias, or other armed groups (e.g., Peluso and Vandergeest 2011).

Such an incipient counterinsurgency paradigm contrasts rather sharply with long-standing conservationist perspectives on comparatively mundane forms of illicit resource use in rural areas. Typically perceived simply as a lamentable drain on the resources available to protected area managers (e.g., Himmelfarb and Cavanagh 2018), conservationists have often somewhat ambivalently viewed such illicit practices as being undertaken by rural populations who are trying to engage conservation governance to their "minimum disadvantage" (Hobsbawm 1973)—that is, in ways that minimize the everyday negative consequences of conservation policies for their livelihoods. It is not necessarily the case that such illicit resource access practices—which entail, inter alia, the unsanctioned collection of forest products or other protected resources, illegal grazing in protected areas, or the ostensible "poaching" of certain species for either subsistence or commercial purposes—constitute a form of "resistance," per se. As Fegan (1986) once put it in a critique of an earlier generation of literature on "everyday resistance" (e.g., Scott 1985), it is often difficult—if not simply impossible, without consulting the actors involved—to distinguish subtle acts of resistance from routine instances of petty criminality or economic opportunism. As Gupta (2001, 89) reminds us, the empirical substance of these practices has often been exaggerated by elites or state authorities precisely to justify the "routine repression" of various marginalized populations. Indeed, this insight seems to take on new importance vis-à-vis the recent rise of efforts to reframe illicit access to conserved resources as a potential source of financing for various groups of rebels, insurgents, militias, or even purported "terrorists" (Cavanagh, Vedeld, and Trædal 2015; Dutta 2020).

Accordingly, our intention here is not to "inflate" the concept of resistance to conservation such that it encompasses nearly every instance of allegedly illicit or illegal resource use occurring in the vicinity of protected areas. As Grove (1997) emphasizes, the history of these illicit practices is virtually as old as conservation itself, not only identifiable in case studies in the early European colonies (from the seventeenth century onward), but also within the "internal colonialisms" that precipitated the designation of game or forest reserves within Europe prior to the Industrial Revolution (from the thirteenth century onward). Particularly in contexts where rural land users face insurmountable risks or barriers to engaging in overt opposition to conservation, subtler forms of everyday resistance may be more commonly expressed via covert illicit practices (Holmes 2007; Mariki, Svarstad, and Benjaminsen 2015; Holmes 2016; Pas and Cavanagh 2022). This is especially so when overt forms of collective protest appear to entail an unacceptable degree of risk, or when avenues for "rightful resistance" (O'Brien 1996)—which enable grievances to be aired through legal or other institutional channels—are either unavailable, inaccessible, or ineffective.

While the latter manifestations of everyday resistance to conservation are important, here we are primarily interested in factors that lead conservation-affected populations to engage in more intentional—and perhaps more collectively "organized"—forms of overt resistance to conservation *as such* or in principle. To understand the conditions under which such forms of overt resistance to conservation may arise, it is useful to revisit the recurring grievances that have been shown to precipitate the recruitment of rural populations within various kinds of militias or other insurgent organizations throughout Sub-Saharan Africa more broadly. As Chauveau and Richards (2008) point out, the "agrarian" roots of grievance-based militias are particularly clear in several West African contexts. Through a comparative analysis of the recruitment of rural populations into armed groups in Sierra Leone and the Ivory Coast, for instance, the authors highlight the salience of both generational and socioeconomic factors in motivating young adults from historically lineage-based societies to participate in such mobilizations. Contrasting with neo-Malthusian conceptions of West African insurgencies as driven by the recruitment of youths dissatisfied with unsustainable *urbanization* and urban overpopulation (e.g., Kaplan 2001), surveys of former Sierra Leonean combatants—for instance—have found that roughly 85 percent of sampled respondents came from predominantly rural and agrarian backgrounds (Humphreys and Weinstein 2004).

Nonetheless, the extant literature illuminates diverse pathways to mobilization across historical and geographical contexts. Whereas Sierra Leonean and Liberian ex-combatants have often been found to harbor grievances *against* local authorities in the form of elders or chiefs—particularly when these authorities are perceived as preventing access to land, marriage, or other desirable positions in the local status hierarchy (e.g., Hoffman 2011; Mokuwa et al. 2011)—mobilization in the Ivory Coast has often occurred in *defense* of traditional authorities and in opposition to perceived incursions by "outsiders" (Chauveau and Richards 2008). In both cases, however, the dynamics of land availability and socioeconomic differentiation are particularly salient. Rural upward mobility for youths and other marginalized populations appears to be more likely in the context of relative land abundance and an open land frontier. In such instances, the value of available labor as a production factor in agriculture or other rural enterprises is comparatively high.

Not least, these dynamics highlight risks concerning the potential for protected area establishment or expansion to exacerbate existing tensions and grievances (Cavanagh 2018). In much of precolonial Africa, for instance, numerous customary systems developed in the context of relative land abundance and relative labor scarcity (Kopytoff 1987; see also Lonsdale 2015). In such contexts, patronage-based systems often developed to accumulate "wealth in people" rather than wealth in land or other natural resources per se (Peters 2013). This is often simply practicable, given that—in predominantly agrarian or agropastoral societies—land is of relatively little value or utility in the absence of sufficient volumes of labor for putting it to productive use. Throughout the late nineteenth and twentieth centuries, however, the gradual formation of colonial states under European rule—and later under postcolonial nationalist governance—precipitated the closure of land frontiers across much of the continent, albeit to varying degrees. Though much of the literature in eastern and southern Africa focuses on the role of European settler agriculture and the diffusion of cadastral property rights systems in gradually closing the land frontier (e.g., Moore 2005; Wily 2012; Capps 2016), protected areas have also played an important—if often overlooked—role in this process as well (Kelly 2011). This was known even to Marx himself, who noted the role of enclosures for forest reserves in the Scottish Highlands as a factor in the process that he termed "primitive accumulation." "Deer-forests and the people cannot co-exist," Marx ([1867] 1995, 509) wrote. "One or other of the two must yield. Let the forests be increased in number and extent during the next quarter of a century, as they have been in the last, and the Gaels will perish from their native soil."

Notably, conservation's revanchist ambitions now co-occur with a broader multidimensional land rush, involving acquisitions of land for agribusiness; extractive industry; and various kinds of energy, transportation, and development infrastructure (Rulli et al. 2013; Hall et al. 2015b). Across much of Sub-Saharan Africa, rural populations therefore increasingly find themselves trapped "between a rock and a green place" (Cavanagh 2018), in the sense that conservation-related displacements dovetail with both direct and indirect impacts of other land and resource acquisitions. Not unlike the West African examples mentioned earlier, the extent to which these acquisitions risk fueling the emergence of new—and the exacerbation of existing—conflicts will depend substantially upon the potential for displaced populations to be (re)incorporated into suitable livelihoods: either in situ or via numerous forms of migration to urban areas or other jurisdictions.

Indeed, as several critical scholars have highlighted, contemporary enclosures in Africa tend to produce "surplus populations." Today, however, surplus populations are increasingly created without associated opportunities for formal wage-based employment in cities, as envisaged by Marx in his description of primitive accumulation and its impacts of the Industrial Revolution in Europe (Peters 2013; Li 2017). Across much of the African continent, processes of "depeasantization" or de-agrarianization (e.g., Bryceson 2002) have often been paralleled by forms of "urbanization without industrialization" (e.g., Gollin, Jedwab, and Vollrath 2016), thus limiting the emergence of alterative livelihoods in nonagricultural sectors. In what follows, we draw on a range of

African examples to illuminate the empirical processes through which such dynamics may already have begun to unfold.

Conservation as a "Threat Multiplier"?

In recent decades, protected areas, and specifically transboundary protected areas, have increasingly been promoted as integral to peacebuilding initiatives both within and between African nations. These "peace parks" (e.g., Duffy 2001), which are sometimes incorporated into broader institutional frameworks for "environmental peacebuilding" (Ide 2020), have been touted as a means of producing "multiple win" outcomes. Such outcomes include, inter alia, improvements in livelihoods, biodiversity conservation, climate change mitigation, natural resource management, and security. Examples assessed in recent literature include the Great Limpopo Transfrontier Park, between South Africa, Zimbabwe, and Mozambique (Büscher and Ramutsindela 2016); the Gola Rainforest National Park, between Sierra Leone and Liberia (Cavanagh 2018); the Virunga transfrontier conservation area, among the Democratic Republic of the Congo, Rwanda, and Uganda (Marijnen 2017; Trogisch 2021; Trogisch and Fletcher 2022); as well as several protected areas on the transboundary Mount Elgon, straddling the border between Uganda and Kenya (Cavanagh and Benjaminsen 2015).

Several of the above contributions highlight a certain degree of irony implicit within these "conservation peacebuilding" efforts. Namely, the risk that resurgent state or military efforts to pursue security objectives via conservation governance may inadvertently result in mounting forms of *in*security instead (Büscher and Ramutsindela 2016; Trogisch and Fletcher 2022). In such cases, expanded conservation activities risk presenting as a "threat multiplier" rather than, necessarily, a contribution to multidimensional "environmental peacebuilding" efforts. That is, regardless of whether processes of protected area establishment or expansion *create* novel conflict risks, they may exacerbate existing tensions and conflicts to malign effect.

Here, a case in point is the emergence of ostensibly "jihadist" violent opposition to state institutions across the West African Sahel. Such insurgencies emerged first in northern Nigeria (from 2009 onward) and in northern Mali (from 2012), later spreading to several neighboring countries. As with the Sierra Leonean, Liberian, and Ivorian cases mentioned above, a robust understanding of the factors that lead rural populations to join apparently "jihadist" groups in such contexts needs to account for the political ecology of land and natural resource governance (Benjaminsen and Ba 2019, 2021).

Throughout the Sahel, rising support for jihadist groups is increasingly linked with anti-state, anti-elite, and pro-pastoral discourses. These discourses broadly lament state institutions that are perceived as being predatory, corrupt, or otherwise characterized by a "politics of the belly": a mode of government denoting the accumulation of wealth through holding political power (e.g., Bayart 2020). Jihadist leaders have demonstrated considerable skill in manipulating these grievances and feelings of resentment among rural populations. As a result, a growing number of young men, often from underprivileged social groups at the bottom of social hierarchies—and a large number of pastoralists—have joined various armed groups throughout the region. Yet such mobilization does not necessarily denote that recruits adhere to jihadist *ideologies*. In the context of widespread rent capture, corruption, and patronage-based informality, rural populations may simply come to perceive jihadist rule as "a lesser evil" that is preferable to the neopatrimonialist status quo (Benjaminsen and Ba 2019).

In the context of conservation and natural resource management, examples of the neopatrimonalist status quo include everyday instances of rent-seeking. This may entail, for instance, agents from the Forest Service in Mali engaging in predatory behavior by arbitrarily taxing or imprisoning female wood collectors or herders who are accused of causing desertification (Benjaminsen 1993, 1997, 2000). To understand such phenomena, one must consider how—particularly following structural adjustment agreements between Mali and the World Bank throughout the 1980s—both public spending and government employment were considerably downsized. Simultaneously, however, the state Forest Service increased in size and power as a direct response to the international attention to "desertification" as a global environmental threat. This attention led to a boost in funding to anti-desertification measures in the Sahel, which the Forest Service was mandated to implement and enforce. Simultaneously, forest legislation was strengthened, introducing extremely high fines compared with the income level in Mali (Benjaminsen 1993; Ribot 2001), This fueled perceptions that the Forest Service had become a key vehicle for "decentralised plunder" across the country (Poulton and Ag Youssouf 1998, 27), as state foresters were keeping a percentage of the fines collected, in addition to all the fines they collected informally without receipts, which further encouraged their rent-seeking behavior (Benjaminsen 2008).

These predatory practices of the Forest Service resulted in a number of attacks by rural people on state foresters during the period of state withdrawal in the transition from military rule to democracy in the early 1990s, and later by jihadists groups after 2012. Between 2012 and 2016, for example, at least ten state foresters were reported to have been killed in the Mopti region in central Mali. Jihadist leaders also target state foresters in their speeches, clearly knowing which "buttons to press" in order to garner local support for their cause among rural people (Benjaminsen and Ba 2019).

Likewise, in southeastern Africa, an armed insurgency in northern Mozambique has emerged since 2017 and has likewise been labeled "jihadist" in character by Western media outlets. The group is similarly composed of socially marginalized young people, precipitating debate about to the extent to which they are motivated by political and economic grievances related to land issues or by religious conviction (Morier-Genoud 2020).

Just across the Mozambique-Tanzania border, in the Rufiji district, there was also a similar "jihadist" revolt between 2015 and 2017, which led to the killing of more than thirty government officials and police before the government managed to curb the violence. There is hardly any information available in the media about these violent events in Rufiji. But in addition to the infiltration of radical Islamist ideas, the insurgency seems to have been influenced by perceptions of the government's unjust appropriation of forest products, the imposing of strict antipoaching policies, and what many people locally see as illegal transfers of agricultural land to local and foreign investors (Jingu 2018).

While these and similar mobilizations are often framed as being motivated by ostensibly "jihadist" ideology, it is notable that they are both influenced by and generative of implications for prevailing approaches to conservation and natural resource management throughout the African continent. Across the Sahel, for instance, ongoing insurgencies, political violence, and counterinsurgency operations have been blamed for slow progress in implementing the Great Green Wall (GGW) initiative. Originally planning to establish an 8,000-kilometer-long forest belt across eleven African countries by 2030, the GGW has been disrupted by recurring violence in, inter alia, Burkina Faso, Chad, Mali, Niger, and Nigeria. As a result, only approximately 4 percent of the original project area, amounting to a total of four million hectares, has been planted to date, and there is considerable uncertainty regarding the sustainability of established plantations (Benjaminsen, Svarstad, and Shaw of Tordarroch 2021; Kabukuru and Mednick 2022).

While the GGW is presented as a peacebuilding initiative (for instance, on its website https://www.greatgreenwall.org), this megaproject in practice represents a risk of the dispossession of pastoralists from large grazing areas if it is implemented as planned. This again may lead to increased rather than reduced recruitment to jihadist groups (Benjaminsen, Svarstad, and Shaw of Tordarroch 2021). In fact, such pastoral dispossession from grazing areas as a result of the project has already happened in Senegal, which is where most of the afforestation has taken place to date (Mugelé 2018, Magrin and Mugelé 2020).

Conclusion

In this chapter, we have sought to assess the extent to which recent developments in violent resistance, including the growth of jihadist groups, can be linked to the expansion of an environmental conservation agenda in rural Africa. Drawing on a range of case studies throughout Sub-Saharan Africa, we have suggested that large-scale conservation interventions generally underestimate the risks of local resistance. In addition, ideology-focused explanations of violent extremism risk overlooking the material determinants of violence and associated grievances rooted in the loss of access to land, natural resources, and customary forms of livelihood. As a result, empirical studies of the latter factors—and particularly those which eschew single-factor determinism in favor of qualitative, multifactor explanation or contextualization—represent a promising new area for future research on resistance to conservation in political ecology, critical agrarian studies, and related fields.

Among both conservation scientists and scholars specializing in violent extremism, the risks of violence related to top-down and/or large-scale environmental interventions in the global South are largely neglected. We conclude by highlighting three key knowledge gaps that—if addressed—would substantially improve the extant knowledge base in this regard. Firstly, further research is needed into the drivers and implications of rural socioeconomic differentiation across the African continent, and how these growing inequalities may influence recruitment into various insurgent groups. As highlighted above, large-scale acquisitions of land and resources for conservation will inevitably articulate with these ongoing processes of socioeconomic differentiation, and in some instances may exacerbate prevailing inequalities. Particularly where inequalities of wealth intersect with socioeconomic inequalities between generations, measures are urgently needed to ensure that conservation activities do not exacerbate grievances related to barriers in (inter)generational reproduction, or the ability of younger generations to establish locally meaningful livelihoods, relationships, and social functions. Notably, such barriers have repeatedly been found to influence recruitment into armed groups across a range of contexts throughout the African continent (e.g., Chauveau and Richards 2008).

Secondly, focused inquiries are needed into both direct and indirect implications of "jihadist" or other organized forms of insurgency for conservation activities. To date, most research in this domain has focused on existing forms of "threat finance," or the potential for armed groups to finance their activities through the illegal or illicit exploitation of natural resources (e.g., Cavanagh, Vedeld, Trædal 2015; Duffy 2014). Conversely, however, conservation itself may also function as a "threat multiplier" by activating socioeconomic mechanisms highlighted above, rather than—necessarily—as a means of bolstering processes of ostensible environmental peacebuilding. As a result, additional case studies are needed examining instances of both direct "resistance to conservation" involving organized violence, as well as indirect cases of mobilization into armed groups in ways that retain implications for conservation activities. As we note above, recruitment into such organizations does not necessarily imply that mobilization is *ideologically* motivated; rather, such groups may simply present as an accessible means of redressing material grievances related to the loss of lands, livelihoods, or incomes.

Thirdly, a new generation of empirical research is warranted examining possibilities for the effective (re)incorporation of relative surplus populations into either rural production systems, or into suitable livelihoods elsewhere. Across Sub-Saharan Africa, growing youthful populations understandably demand livelihood opportunities that are perceived to be both culturally appropriate, and accompanied by realistic prospects for upward mobility. In some cases, youths may envisage a future for themselves in rural production systems, and in other cases may aspire to educational advancement or non-agrarian livelihoods in urban areas. In both cases, researchers and policymakers must invest in identifying "bottom-up" approaches to navigating shifting livelihood conditions in the context of intensifying social, economic, and environmental change, rather than simply presuming to know and support the interests of various rural or other constituencies. Whether specific constituencies happen to desire broadly "rural" or "urban" futures for themselves and their families, poverty traps and "vicious cycles" characterized by downward mobility are of course universally feared and resented. This is the case regardless of whether such poverty traps manifest primarily in rural production systems, or in the context of transitions to rapidly urbanizing livelihoods. Further attempts to better understand effective means of avoiding such poverty traps—as well as the deleterious implications for "relative surplus populations" that they present—will be crucial in mitigating risks related to material grievances and armed mobilization throughout the (likely quite tumultuous) decades to come throughout the African continent.

Acknowledgments

We thank Jun Borras, Jennifer Franco, and George Holmes for helpful comments on previous versions of this chapter.

Notes

1. On "complex causality" and the need for multifactor explanations of violence in land politics more broadly, see also Grajales and Chauveau (this volume).
2. On the potential interactions between accumulation or dispossession "from above" and accumulation or dispossession "from below," see Bernstein (this volume). In a conservation context, processes of accumulation or dispossession "from above" are particularly evident in instances of "green grabbing" for fortress conservation, wherein both resources and rents are appropriated by state agencies, private firms, or other nonlocal actors. Conversely, however—and perhaps more subtly—some emerging forms of ostensibly "community-based" conservation can also entail processes of dispossession "from below." Such phenomena are perhaps especially evident within conservation programs that support the formalization of private land rights, thereby precipitating the risk of "dispossession via the market" (Fairhead et al. 2012) if newly titled lands or resources are sold or leased to nonlocal investors under exploitative conditions (see, especially, Cavanagh et al. 2020; Pas and Cavanagh 2022).

References

Adams, W. M., R. Aveling, Dan Brockington, B. Dickson, J. Elliott, J. Hutton, et al. 2004. "Biodiversity Conservation and the Eradication of Poverty." *Science* 306 (5699): 1146–1149.

Adams, W. M. 2020. "Geographies of Conservation III: Nature's Spaces." *Progress in Human Geography* 44 (4): 789–801.

Adams, W. M., and D. Hulme. 2001. "If Community Conservation Is the Answer in Africa, What Is the Question?" *Oryx* 35 (3): 193–200.

Adams, W. M., and J. Hutton. 2007. "People, Parks and Poverty: Political Ecology and Biodiversity Conservation." *Conservation and Society* 5 (2): 147–183.

Bayart, Jean-François. 2020. "Historical Regimes of Responsibility in 'the Politics of the Belly.'" In *Regimes of Responsibility in Africa: Genealogies, Rationalities and Conflicts*, edited by Benjamin Rubbers and Alessandro Jedlowski, 21–39. Oxford: Berghahn Books.

Benjaminsen, Tor A. 1993. "Fuelwood and Desertification: Sahel Orthodoxies Discussed on the Basis of Field Data from the Gourma Region in Mali." *Geoforum* 24 (4): 397–409.

Benjaminsen, Tor A. 1997. "Natural Resource Management, Paradigm Shifts and the Decentralization Reform in Mali." *Human Ecology* 25 (1): 121–143.

Benjaminsen, Tor A. 2000. "Conservation in the Sahel: Policies and People in Mali, 1900–1998." In *Producing Poverty and Nature in Africa*, edited by Vigdis Broch-Due and Richard A. Schroeder, 94–108. Uppsala: Nordic Africa Institute.

Benjaminsen, Tor A. 2008. "Does Supply-Induced Scarcity Drive Violent Conflicts in the African Sahel? The Case of the Tuareg Rebellion in Northern Mali." *Journal of Peace Research* 45 (6): 831–848.

Benjaminsen, Tor A., and I. Bryceson. 2012. "Conservation, Green/Blue Grabbing and Accumulation by Dispossession in Tanzania." *Journal of Peasant Studies* 39 (2): 335–355.

Benjaminsen, Tor A., and B. Ba. 2019. "Why Do Pastoralists in Mali Join Jihadist Groups? A Political Ecological Explanation." *Journal of Peasant Studies* 46 (1): 1–20.

Benjaminsen, Tor A., and B. Ba. 2021. "Fulani-Dogon Killings in Mali: Farmer-Herder Conflicts as Insurgency and Counterinsurgency." *African Security* 14 (1): 4–26.

Benjaminsen, Tor A., Hanne Svarstad, and Iselin Shaw of Tordarroch. 2021. "Recognising Recognition in Climate Justice." *IDS Bulletin*. Online first. DOI: 10.19088/1968-2021.127. https://opendocs.ids.ac.uk/opendocs/bitstream/handle/20.500.12413/16912/IDSBulletin_OnlineFirst_Benjaminsen_Svarstad_ShawofTordarroch.pdf?sequence=1&isAllowed=y.

Brockington, Dan. 2002. *Fortress Conservation: The Preservation of the Mkomazi Game Reserve, Tanzania*. Bloomington: Indiana University Press.

Brockington, Dan. 2004. "Community Conservation, Inequality and Injustice: Myths of Power in Protected Area Management." *Conservation and Society* 2 (2): 411–432.

Brockington, Dan, and Jim Igoe. 2006. "Eviction for Conservation: A Global Overview." *Conservation and Society* 4 (3): 424–470.

Brockington, Dan, Rosaleen Duffy, and Jim Igoe. 2012. *Nature Unbound: Conservation, Capitalism and the Future of Protected Areas*. New York and London: Routledge.

Bryceson, Deborah. F. 2002. "The Scramble in Africa: Reorienting Rural Livelihoods. *World Development* 30 (5): 725–739.

Büscher, Bram. 2014. "Selling Success: Constructing Value in Conservation and Development. *World Development* 57: 79–90.

Büscher, Bram, and Robert Fletcher. 2016. "Why E O Wilson Is Wrong about How to Save the Earth." Aeon. https://aeon.co/ideas/why-e-o-wilson-is-wrong-about-how-to-save-the-earth, accessed October 27, 2022.

Büscher, Bram, and Maano Ramutsindela. 2016. "Green Violence: Rhino Poaching and the War to Save Southern Africa's Peace Parks." *African Affairs* 115 (458): 1–22.

Büscher, Bram, Robert Fletcher, Dan Brockington, Chris Sandbrook, William M. Adams, Lisa Campbell, et al. 2017. "Half-Earth or Whole Earth? Radical Ideas for Conservation, and Their Implications." *Oryx* 51 (3): 407–410.

Cafaro, P., T. Butler, E. Crist, P. Cryer, E. Dinerstein, H. Kopnina, et al. 2017. "If We Want a Whole Earth, Nature Needs Half: A Response to Büscher et al." *Oryx* 51 (3): 400.

Capps, G. 2016. "Tribal-Landed Property: The Value of the Chieftaincy in Contemporary Africa. *Journal of Agrarian Change* 16 (3): 452–477.

Cavanagh, Connor J. 2018. "Enclosure, Dispossession, and the Green Economy: New Contours of Internal Displacement in Liberia and Sierra Leone?" *African Geographical Review* 37 (2): 120–133.

Cavanagh, Connor, and Tor A. Benjaminsen. 2014. "Virtual Nature, Violent Accumulation: The 'Spectacular Failure' of Carbon Offsetting at a Ugandan National Park." *Geoforum* 56: 55–65.

Cavanagh, Connor J., and Tor A. Benjaminsen. 2015. "Guerrilla Agriculture? A Biopolitical Guide to Illicit Cultivation within an IUCN Category II Protected Area." *Journal of Peasant Studies* 42 (3–4): 725–745.

Cavanagh, Connor J., and Tor A. Benjaminsen. 2017. "Political Ecology, Variegated Green Economies, and the Foreclosure of Alternative Sustainabilities." *Journal of Political Ecology* 24 (1): 200–216.

Cavanagh, Connor J., Chris Sandbrook, and David Tumusiime. 2018. "Introduction: Dynamics of Uneven Conservation and Development in Uganda." In *Conservation and Development in Uganda*, edited by Chris Sandbrook, and Connor J. Cavanagh, and D. Tumusiime, 3–15. London and New York: Routledge/Earthscan.

Cavanagh, Connor J., Pål O. Vedeld, and Leif Tore Trædal. 2015. "Securitizing REDD+ ? Problematizing the Emerging Illegal Timber Trade and Forest Carbon Interface in East Africa." *Geoforum* 60: 72–82.

Cavanagh, Connor J., Tekle Weldemichel, and Tor A. Benjaminsen. 2020. "Gentrifying the African Landscape: The Performance and Powers of For-Profit Conservation on Southern Kenya's Conservancy Frontier." *Annals of the American Association of Geographers* 110 (5): 1594–1612.

Chauveau, J. P., and P. Richards. 2008. "West African Insurgencies in Agrarian Perspective: Côte d'Ivoire and Sierra Leone Compared." *Journal of Agrarian Change* 8 (4): 515–552.

Dowie, Mark. 2009. *Conservation Refugees: The Hundred-Year Conflict between Global Conservation and Native Peoples*. Cambridge, MA: MIT Press.

Dressler, Wolfram, Bram Büscher, M. Schoon, Dan Brockington, T. Hayes, Christian A. Kull, et al. 2010. "From Hope to Crisis and Back Again? A Critical History of the Global CBNRM Narrative." *Environmental Conservation* 37 (1): 5–15.

Duffy, Rosaleen. 2001. "Peace Parks: The Paradox of Globalisation." *Geopolitics* 6 (2): 1–26.

Duffy, Rosaleen. 2014. "Waging a War to Save Biodiversity: The Rise of Militarized Conservation." *International Affairs* 90 (4): 819–834.

Dutta, Anwesha. 2020. "Forest becomes Frontline: Conservation and Counter-insurgency in a Space of Violent Conflict in Assam, Northeast India." *Political Geography* 77: 102117.

Eltringham, S. K. 1994. "Can Wildlife Pay Its Way?" *Oryx* 28 (3): 163–168.

Fairhead, James, Melissa Leach, and Ian Scoones. 2012. "Green Grabbing: A New Appropriation of Nature?" *Journal of Peasant Studies* 39 (2): 237–261.

Fegan, Brian. 1986. "Tenants' Non-violent Resistance to Landowner Claims in a Central Luzon Village." *Journal of Peasant Studies* 13 (2): 87–106.

Feldman S., G. Charles, and S. Louise. 2003. "Moving Targets: Displacement, Impoverishment, and Development." *International Social Science Journal* 55: 7–13.

Gollin, D., R. Jedwab, and D. Vollrath. 2016. "Urbanization with and without Industrialization." *Journal of Economic Growth* 21 (1): 35–70.

Grove, Richard. H. 1997. *Ecology, Climate and Empire: Colonialism and Global Environmental History, 1400–1940*. Cambridge, UK: White Horse Press.

Gupta, D. 2001. "Everyday Resistance or Routine Repression? Exaggeration as a Stratagem in Agrarian Conflict." *Journal of Peasant Studies* 29 (1): 89–108.

Hall, Ruth, Mark Edelman, Ian Scoones, Ben White, and Wendy Wolford. 2015a. "Resistance, Acquiescence or Incorporation?" *Journal of Peasant Studies* 42 (3–4): 467–488.

Hall, Ruth, Ian Scoones, and D. Tsikata. 2015b. "Introduction: The Contexts and Consequences of Africa's Land Rush." In *Africa's Land Rush: Rural Livelihoods and Agrarian Change*, edited by R. Hall, I. Scoones, and D. Tsikata, 1–29. Oxford: James Currey.

Himmelfarb, David, and Connor J. Cavanagh. 2018. "Managing the Contradictions: Conservation, Communitarian Rhetoric, and Conflict at Mount Elgon National Park." In *Conservation and Development in Uganda*, edited by Chris Sandbrook and Connor J. Cavanagh, and David Tumusiime, 85–103. London and New York: Routledge/Earthscan.

Hobsbawm, Eric J. 1973. "Peasants and Politics." *Journal of Peasant Studies* 1 (1): 3–22.

Hoffman, D. 2011. *The War Machines: Young Men and Violence in Sierra Leone and Liberia*. Durham, NC: Duke University Press.

Holmes, George. 2007. "Protection, Politics and Protest: Understanding Resistance to Conservation." *Conservation and Society* 5 (2): 184–201.

Holmes, George. 2016. "Conservation Crime as Political Protest." In *The Routledge International Handbook of Rural Criminology*, edited by J. F. Donnermeyer, 309–316. New York and London: Routledge.

Holmes, George, and Connor J. Cavanagh. 2016. "A Review of the Social Impacts of Neoliberal Conservation: Formations, Inequalities, Contestations." *Geoforum* 75: 199–209.

Hübschle, A. M. 2017. "The Social Economy of Rhino Poaching: Of Economic Freedom Fighters, Professional Hunters and Marginalized Local People." *Current Sociology* 65 (3): 427–447.

Hulme, D., and M. Murphree, eds. 2001. *African Wildlife and Livelihoods: The Promise and Performance of Community Conservation*. Oxford: James Currey.

Humphreys, M., and J. Weinstein. 2004. "What the Fighters Say: A Survey of Ex-combatants in Sierra Leone, June–August 2003." CGSD Working Paper No. 20. New York: Columbia University.

Hutton, Jon, William M. Adams, and J. C. Murombedzi. 2005. "Back to the Barriers? Changing Narratives in Biodiversity Conservation." *Forum for Development Studies* 32 (2): 341–370.

Ide, T. 2020. "The Dark Side of Environmental Peacebuilding." *World Development* 127: 104777.

Ince, O. U. 2014. "Primitive Accumulation, New Enclosures, and Global Land Grabs: A Theoretical Intervention." *Rural Sociology* 79 (1): 104–131.

International Panel on Climate Change. 2022. *Climate Change 2022: Impacts, Adaptation, and Vulnerability: Summary for Policymakers*. Contribution of Working Group II to the Sixth Assessment Report of the Intergovernmental Panel on Climate Change, edited by Hans-O. Pörtner et al. Cambridge, UK: Cambridge University Press. https://www.ipcc.ch/report/ar6/wg2/downloads/report/IPCC_AR6_WGII_SummaryForPolicymakers.pdf.

Jingu, J. K. 2018. "The Flurry of Crimes in Kibiti and Rufiji and the Quest for Effective Early Warning and Response Mechanism." *African Review* 45 (1): 93–109.

Kabra, Asmita. 2009. "Conservation-Induced Displacement: A Comparative Study of Two Indian Protected Areas." *Conservation and Society* 7 (4): 249–267.

Kabukuru, W., and S. Mednick. 2022. "Security Concerns, Lack of Support Stall Africa's Green Wall." *Associated Press*, May 23. https://apnews.com/article/climate-ouagadougou-politics-middle-east-57208ec04f9413fb06b181e9183d7cdd.

Kaplan, Robert. 2001. *The Coming Anarchy: Shattering the Dreams of the Post-Cold War*. New York: Random House.

Kelly, Alice B. 2011. "Conservation Practice as Primitive Accumulation." *Journal of Peasant Studies* 38 (4): 683–701.

Kelly, Alice B., and Megan Ybarra. 2016. Introduction to "Green Security in Protected Areas." Special issue, *Geoforum* 69: 171–175.

Kopnina, Helen. 2019. "Just Preservation and the Half-Earth View." *Animal Sentience* 4 (27): 10.

Kopytoff, Igor, ed. 1987. *The African Frontier: The Reproduction of Traditional African Societies*. Bloomington: Indiana University Press.

Li, Tania M. 2009. "To Make Live or Die? Rural Dispossession and the Protection of Surplus Populations." *Antipode* 41 (1): 66–93.

Li, Tania M. 2017. "After Development: Surplus Population and the Politics of Entitlement." *Development and Change* 48 (6): 1247–1261.

Lonsdale, Jon. 2015. "Have Tropical Africa's Nationalisms Continued Imperialism's World Revolution by Other Means?" *Nations and Nationalism* 21 (4): 609–629.

Lunstrum, Elizabeth. 2014. "Green Militarization: Anti-poaching Efforts and the Spatial Contours of Kruger National Park." *Annals of the Association of American Geographers* 104 (4): 816–832.

Magrin, Géraud, and Ronan Mugelé. 2020. "La boucle de l'Anthropocène au Sahel: Nature et sociétés face aux grands projets environnementaux (Grande Muraille Verte, Sauvegarde du lac Tchad)." *Belgeo* 2020 (3): 1–15.

Marijnen, Esther. 2017. "The 'Green Militarisation' of Development Aid: The European Commission and the Virunga National Park, DR Congo." *Third World Quarterly* 38 (7): 1566–1582.

Mariki, Sayuni B., Hanne Svarstad, and Tor A. Benjaminsen. 2015. "Elephants over the Cliff: Explaining Wildlife Killings in Tanzania." *Land Use Policy* 44: 19–30.

Marx, Karl. 1995 [1867]. *Capital: A Critique of Political Economy*. Volume 1. Moscow: Progress Publishers.

Mokuwa, Esther, M. Voors, E. Bulte, and P. Richards. 2011. "Peasant Grievance and Insurgency in Sierra Leone: Judicial Serfdom as a Driver of Conflict." *African Affairs* 110 (440): 339–366.

Moore, Donald. 2005. *Suffering for Territory: Race, Place, and Power in Zimbabwe*. Durham, NC: Duke University Press.

Morier-Genoud, E. 2020. "The Jihadi Insurgency in Mozambique: Origins, Nature and Beginning." *Journal of Eastern African Studies* 14 (3): 396–412.

Mugelé, Ronan. 2018. "La Grande muraille verte: Géographie d'une utopie environnementale au Sahel." PhD diss., Université Paris 1 Panthéon-Sorbonne.

Murphree, Marshall. 2000. "Community-based Conservation: Old Ways, New Myths and Enduring Challenges." In "Tanzania Wildlife Discussion Paper, No. 29," edited by Rolf D. Baldus and Ludwig Siege, 5–16. Dar er Salaam, Tanzania: Deutsche Gesellschaft für Technische Zusammenarbeit.

Neumann, Roderick P. 1998. *Imposing Wilderness: Struggles over Livelihood and Nature Preservation in Africa*. Berkeley: University of California Press.

Neumann, Roderick P. 2002. "The Postwar Conservation Boom in British Colonial Africa." *Environmental History* 7 (1): 22–47.

Nixon, Robert. 2011. *Slow Violence and the Environmentalism of the Poor*. Cambridge, MA: Harvard University Press.

O'Brien, K. J. 1996. "Rightful Resistance." *World Politics* 49 (1): 31–55.
Pas, Annemiek, and Connor Cavanagh. 2022. "Understanding 'Night Grazing': Conservation Governance, Rural Inequalities, and Shifting Responses 'from Above and Below' throughout the Nychthemeron in Laikipia, Kenya." *Geoforum* 134: 143–153.
Peluso, Nancy L., and Peter Vandergeest. 2011. "Political Ecologies of War and Forests: Counterinsurgencies and the Making of National Natures." *Annals of the Association of American Geographers* 101 (3): 587–608.
Peters, Pauline E. 2013. "Land Appropriation, Surplus People and a Battle over Visions of Agrarian Futures in Africa." *Journal of Peasant Studies* 40 (3): 537–562.
Poulton, R. E., and I. Ag Youssouf. 1998. *A Peace of Timbuktu: Democratic Governance, Development, and African Peacemaking*. New York and Geneva: UNIDIR.
Ribot, Jesse. 2001. "Science, Use Rights and Exclusion: A History of Forestry in Francophone West Africa." Paper. International Institute for Environment and Development, London.
Ribot, Jesse C., and N. L. Peluso. 2003. "A Theory of Access." *Rural Sociology* 68 (2): 153–181.
Rulli, M. C., Saviori, and P. D'Odorico. 2013. "Global Land and Water Grabbing." *Proceedings of the National Academy of Sciences* 110 (3): 892–897.
Schleicher, Judith, J. G. Zaehringer, C. Fastré, B. Vira, P. Visconti, and Chris Sandbrook. 2019. "Protecting Half of the Planet Could Directly Affect over One Billion People." *Nature Sustainability* 2 (12): 1094–1096.
Scott, James C. 1985. *Weapons of the Weak: Everyday Forms of Peasant Resistance*. New Haven, CT: Yale University Press.
Solnit, Rebecca. 2014. *Savage Dreams: A Journey into the Hidden Wars of the American West*. Berkeley: University of California Press.
Spence, M. D. 1999. *Dispossessing the Wilderness: Indian Removal and the Making of the National Parks*. Oxford: Oxford University Press.
Thompson, E. P. 1975. *Whigs and Hunters: The Origin of the Black Act*. New York: Pantheon.
Trogisch, L. 2021. "Geographies of Fear: The Everyday (Geo)Politics of 'Green' Violence and Militarization in the Virunga Conservation Area." *Geoforum* 122: 92–102.
Trogisch, L., and Robert Fletcher. 2022. "Fortress Tourism: Exploring Dynamics of Tourism, Security and Peace around the Virunga Transboundary Conservation Area." *Journal of Sustainable Tourism* 30 (2–3): 352–371.
UN Convention on Biological Diversity (UNCBD). 2020. Aichi Biodiversity Targets. https://www.cbd.int/sp/targets/, accessed April 20, 2022.
UNEP-WCMC. 2022. World Database on Protected Areas. https://www.protectedplanet.net/en, accessed April 20, 2022.
Weldemichel, Teklehaymanot G. 2020. "Othering Pastoralists, State Violence, and the Remaking of Boundaries in Tanzania's Militarised Wildlife Conservation Sector." *Antipode* 52 (5): 1496–1518.
Weldemichel, Teklehaymanot G. 2021. "Making land Grabbable: Stealthy Dispossessions by Conservation in Ngorongoro Conservation Area, Tanzania." *Environment and Planning E: Nature and Space*. Ahead-of print. https://doi.org/10.1177/25148486211052860.
West, Paige, James Igoe, and Dan Brockington. 2006. "Parks and Peoples: The Social Impact of Protected Areas." *Annual Review of Anthropology* 35: 251–277.
Wilshusen, Peter R., S. R. Brechin, C. L. Fortwangler, and Paige C. West. 2002. "Reinventing a Square Wheel: Critique of a Resurgent 'Protection Paradigm' in International Biodiversity Conservation." *Society & Natural Resources* 15 (1): 17–40.

Wilson, E. O. 2016. *Half-Earth: Our Planet's Fight for Life*. New York: W. W. Norton.
Wily, Liz A. 2012. "Looking Back to See Forward: The Legal Niceties of Land Theft in Land Rushes." *Journal of Peasant Studies* 39 (3–4): 751–775.
Ybarra, Megan. 2012. "Taming the Jungle, Saving the Maya Forest: Sedimented Counterinsurgency Practices in Contemporary Guatemalan Conservation." *Journal of Peasant Studies* 39 (2): 479–502.

CHAPTER 36

THE POLITICS OF RESISTANCE TO LAND ALIENATION

SHAPAN ADNAN

INTRODUCTION

THE literature on the politics of land grabs and the corresponding political responses is vast and continues to proliferate. Earlier stock-taking exercises noted that the initial phase of research had been concerned with "making sense" of the politics of land contestations and pointed out cutting-edge issues for further research (Borras et al. 2012; Edelman, Oya, and Borras 2013, 1518–1520; Oya 2013, 1535–1537). Since then, newer issues and debates have begun to animate the discourses on the politics of land dispossession and the struggles against it, modifying and innovating upon earlier scholarly contributions (Guha 1983; Scott 1985, 1986; Adas 1986; Turton 1986; Kerkvliet 1990, 2009). As a result, there is a need for a reframing of the analysis of the politics of land alienation and resistance to bring it up to date with current developments. To this end, the present chapter highlights a set of critical issues pertaining to dispossession and resistance to provide a signposted road map for concerned scholars, researchers, practitioners, and students. It also draws attention to research topics and questions that are likely to be of continuing significance in the future.

Among the diverse forms of land grabs, the present discussion focuses on *land alienation*—defined as the separation or expulsion of the preexisting holders from their lands. Correlatively, among the various possible political responses to land alienation, the analysis concentrates on resistance, as contrasted to compliance and collaboration. The discussion is centered on "struggles against expulsion," as contrasted to "struggles for incorporation" (Borras et al. 2012, 413; Edelman, Oya, and Borras 2013, 1523).

At the outset, reframing the politics of resistance to land alienation requires a reconsideration of a number of basic issues as posed in the following questions: First, in what ways can land alienation involving expulsion and separation from land be precisely delineated in relation to other kindred notions such as land grabs, land control, and land concentration? Second, how does resistance differ from other political responses to land alienation, such as compliance and demands for incorporation? Third, what is the difference between "resistance from below" and "resistance from above"? Do these necessarily correspond to the respective political responses of the "winners" and "losers" from land alienation? Fourth, what are the prevalent or emergent forms of resistance to land alienations, subsuming covert and overt and violent and nonviolent types, as well as intermediate ones, such as "rightful resistance"? Moreover, what are the "conditions of transformation" between these varied forms of struggle against land dispossession? Fifth, what features distinguish instances of land alienation mediating primitive and capitalist accumulation, and how do such differences shape the respective forms of resistance?

Clarifying these basic issues clears the ground for analyzing a number of critical questions concerning the interactive dynamics of the politics of land alienation and resistance. To what extent do the interactive struggles against expulsion lead to flexibility, adaptive change, and innovation in their respective strategies? What are the determinants of the outcomes of interactions between land alienation and resistance, inclusive of the balance of forces and the influence of exogenous factors? Can struggles against expulsion stop or change state policies of land acquisition aimed at facilitating accumulation by undermining their political legitimacy? Correlatively, what kinds of counterstrategies can be deployed to repress or co-opt the social groups involved in active struggles against land alienation or to pre-empt their potential resistance by foreclosing the possibility of collective action?

These issues are addressed here through arguments put forward in general terms and illustrated briefly with pertinent case-study evidence from countries of Asia, Africa, and Latin America. The core notions of land alienation and resistance, and the associated politics, are defined more precisely and situated in the context of the analytical framework specified in the next section. The subsequent sections deal with the politics of different forms of resistance and their transformation; interactions between the politics of land alienation and resistance, inclusive of adaptive change and innovation in their respective strategies; and pertinent research issues and questions for further investigation.

The Analytical Framework

The analysis draws on the pluralist tradition of critical agrarian studies (Borras 2023), making use of both Marxist and non-Marxist theoretical tools in the disciplinary fields of political economy and political sociology. It situates the issues pertaining to land dispossession and resistance in the context of contemporary neoliberal capitalism and the processes that propel its development. These include the distinct accumulative processes mediated by land alienation, namely: (a) ongoing primitive accumulation, (b) accumulation by dispossession (ABD), and (c) capitalist accumulation through the centralization of capital (Marx 1976; Kautsky 1988; Harvey 2005). The analysis also takes note of the ways in which struggles against expulsion are influenced by differences in the ethnic, racial, religious, and other aspects of the social and cultural identities of the concerned groups (Scott 1986; Li 2009).

The Notion of Land Alienation

Transfers of land from one agent to another have been loosely called *land grabs* or *land deals*, terms that lump together many different types of dispossession of land under diverse production relations (Hall 2013, 1596–1597). Among these diverse processes, the present discussion focuses on land alienation, defined as the separation or expulsion of the preexisting holders from their lands. In contrast to the broader category of land control, the notion of "alienation" excludes processes in which the incumbent holders are not expelled from their land, but incorporated into new production relations or supply chains, such as contract farming or "partnership arrangements" (Edelman, Oya, and Borras 2013, 1519–1522; Hall 2013, 1592; Borras and Franco 2018, 1315).

Land alienation involves the durable dispossession of land as *stock*, subsuming permanent transfers or long-term leases, while excluding short-term *flows* for current production, such as the seasonal leasing of operational rights. It is to be differentiated from the notion of "land concentration," which can be defined as a process that increases the skewness in the distribution of the historically accumulated stock of land among different holding size-groups (Edelman and León 2013, 1697; Edelman, Oya, and Borras 2013, 1523). It is in relation to this preexisting distribution that current acts of land alienation bring about incremental changes in the distribution of the aggregate stock of land, resulting in deconcentration or reconcentration at the margins.

The hierarchy of land rights varies in accordance with the distinctive systems of landed property in different countries. These can include instances of legal pluralism and multiple titling, such that two or more agencies hold distinct and layered rights on any given plot, as is seen, for example, in contemporary China (Walker 2008a). The notion of land alienation is defined broadly to subsume these wide-ranging variations in land rights, including the transfer of de jure or de facto rights of ownership, occupancy, possession, or usufruct, whether held by individuals or collectivities (cf. Lund, this volume).

In concrete cases of dispossession, these diverse types of land rights are found to be transferred through a wide variety of mechanisms, ranging from the use of (a) force or extra-economic coercion to (b) various noncoercive means, including fraud, material inducements, and/or market transactions, subject to varying degrees of constraint.[1] Because this conceptualization subsumes both forced and voluntary transfers of land rights, the terms *alienation* or *dispossession* are appropriate, in contrast to *grabs* or *seizures*, which have connotations of forcible capture alone.

The Politics of Land Alienation and Responses of the Dispossessed

In the context of struggles against expulsion from land, *politics* can be broadly defined as interactions based on relations of power and inequality between the concerned social agents. Its forms and modalities extend beyond the formal or official politics manifested in the activities of the state, government, and electoral processes to include informal, advocacy, and quotidian politics in arenas and institutions that are not conventionally regarded as political (Scott 1986, 28; Adas 1986, 69–72; Kerkvliet 2009, 228–240).

Moreover, political contestations involve elements of maneuver and manipulation among the protagonists, subsuming broad-based strategies and specific tactics to outwit or overwhelm opponents (Wolf 1959, 142; Mintz 1973, 97; Silverman 1979, 64). The politics of alienating land entails the use and manipulation of power relations, typically by the state, private corporations, social elites, the dominant classes, and other influential entities, to authorize, enforce, justify, and legitimize the dispossession of others from their lands. The specific forms of the politics of land alienation are shaped by the particular mechanisms of dispossession and the specific institutions through which these are implemented, for example, state acquisition or market purchase of land.

Correlatively, the political options of the dispossessed are critically influenced by their own capability in relation to the specific mechanisms and institutions deployed by the agencies taking over their lands. Faced with expulsion, the politics of the dispossessed are reactive and can take conciliatory, defensive, or counteroffensive forms. When existing holders transfer their lands willingly, as in voluntary market transactions, the question of resistance definitionally does not arise. However, when land alienation takes place under different degrees of constraint,[2] including outright coercion, the dispossessed groups need to use whatever countervailing and bargaining powers they have to pursue objectives ranging from negotiating for compensation to protecting or recovering their lands.

Range of Political Responses of Different Categories of the Dispossessed

The distributive impacts of land loss tend to impinge unevenly on the various sections and classes of the affected population—giving rise to distinct groups of "winners" and "losers" from land alienation (Oya 2013, 1537–1547). Moreover, the conditionalities imposed on the affected groups by expulsion or displacement can vary, resulting in significant differences in their political responses and subsequent trajectories (Borras and Franco 2013, 1732). The dispossessed groups may or may not be compensated for their loss of land with money, replacement plots, jobs, or other facilities (Vijayabaskar 2014, 316–320; Levien 2018, 83). They may or may not be resettled elsewhere or able to find employment in other sectors of the economy. Consequently, the differentiated outcomes of expulsion from land can lead to divergent—even diametrically opposed—political responses among dispossessed groups (Oya 2013, 1537–1547; Borras and Franco 2013, 1727–1728; Famerée 2016, 544).

Political responses to land alienation can also vary between dispossessed groups that are "poor and weak" and "wealthy and powerful," which can be differentiated as reactions from "below" and "above," respectively. However, the responses from above and below do not necessarily correspond with those of the winners and losers, respectively. Since the winners or losers can include both the "poor and weak" and the "wealthy and powerful," these two binaries are not necessarily convergent but can cross-cut each other.

Unlike the poor and weak groups, the wealthy and powerful ones are more likely to be in a position to manipulate the agencies and mechanisms of dispossession in ways that are advantageous to themselves. Political responses from above by dominant groups may enable them, not only to minimize loss, but also to make gains from the process of dispossession. For instance, in India "dominant castes . . . can find ways to gain by projects premised on their dispossession and often serve as brokers of this process . . . [Such] compliance from the better placed, diminish[es] the potency of resistance" (Andreas et al. 2020, 1121–1126). In China, the "wealthiest 'big households' often initiate land-taking projects to enlarge their own domains, or they sign on as key inside players in bigger schemes hatched by outsiders. Even if they are not involved in initiating a project, better-off, better-connected villagers can sometimes take advantage of it, while in other cases they can avoid being displaced or win better compensation" (1134).

In contrast, unorganized poor and weak groups do not usually have the capability to influence the process and agencies of dispossession to further their own interests. However, they may still have the option to respond politically in a number of different ways. In terms of broad responses from below, some may decide to resist outright, undertaking struggles against expulsion. Others may bargain for improved compensation or negotiate for incorporation into the production relations in operation following the loss of their lands (Borras et al. 2012, 412–413; Borras and Franco 2013, 1728).

It is evident that the political responses from below can take diverse and complex forms, displaying multiple variations "across space and time, along class and other social divides."[3] Resistance therefore cannot be presumed to be the only, or the "automatic," political response from below to dispossession. Nonetheless, it has been a major response to land alienation worldwide, subsuming different strategies and tactics (Li 2009, 78; Cousins, in this volume). Accordingly, the present analysis focuses on resistance from below in the sense of struggles against expulsion, while pointing out factors leading to switches between these and struggles for incorporation, wherever relevant.

When land is the object of contention, political contestations are concerned with not only its value as an economic asset but also its intangible and nonmaterial attributes, such as being the ancestral habitat or the current home of existing landholders, shaping their lives, livelihoods, status, and sense of belonging in terms of social and cultural identity (Adnan 2013, 93). Consequently, the politics of land cannot be reduced to interactions between agents that are dictated solely by their economic interests.

Differences in political responses can be further accentuated if the winners and losers from land alienation belong to distinct social groups distinguished by their ethnicity, race, religion, or other kinds of identity traits (Borras and Franco 2013, 1727). In such instances, the "differentiated impacts and variegated political reactions to land deals" are likely to include the additional dimension of identity politics, which would be superimposed on the differential responses of winners and losers engendered by the act of dispossession (Hall et al. 2015, 468–472). James Scott (1986, 14) has noted that the potential of collective action by dispossessed groups in response to land alienation can be seriously impeded by cleavages that cut across them in terms of ethnicity, race, religion, caste, class, and migration status, and so forth. Commenting on the eviction from land of ethnic minorities in Southeast Asia, Tania Li (2009, 76) points out: "Race is a crucial dimension of dispossession." Correlatively, there are also instances in which political innovation in the form of an appropriate "unifying frame" has brought disparate groups with different identities together in overarching coalitions under the banner of a common struggle against land alienation (Famerée 2016, 544–545; Adnan 2015, 38; Sampat 2015, 766–769).

The Aims, Forms, and Conditions of Transformation of Resistance

The objectives, forms, and conditions of transformation of resistance to land alienation can be broadly specified as follows: Insofar as resistance aims to prevent or stop the loss of existing lands to protect livelihoods and ensure social reproduction, it constitutes a *defensive* struggle (Cousins, this volume). When it attempts to regain or restitute former lands that others have captured, the nature of the struggle becomes *counteroffensive*.

Turton (1986, 39) contends: "There can be no adequate study of the forms of resistance without a prior and simultaneous study of forms of domination" (cf. Scott 1986, 28–29). A comparable relationship can be also postulated between the politics of land alienation and resistance, which are interdependent, and mutually shape each other (Adnan 2007a, 185). The dynamic interactions between them can potentially lead to flexibility, adaptive change, or innovation in the respective strategies of land alienation and resistance.

Struggles against expulsion from land can be broadly divided into *covert* and *overt* forms of resistance, as well as *intermediate* ones (see "Intermediate Forms: Working through the State Apparatus and 'Rightful Resistance'" below). Several kinds of transformation among these forms of resistance are of analytical interest: (a) shifts within forms of covert resistance or avoidance protest (Adas 1986); (b) the transformation of covert resistance into overt resistance, and vice versa; and (c) the transformation within overt resistance between nonviolent and violent forms (Adas 1986, 82–83).[4] These varied instances also raise the general question of why, and under what conditions, forms of resistance undergo transformation (Adnan 2007a, 185; Kerkvliet 2009, 235)

Both Scott (1986, 28) and Kerkvliet (2009, 235) note in general terms that "changing political circumstances" and critical shifts in the balance of forces between dominant and dominated groups can bring about the transformation of covert resistance into overt resistance, and vice versa. Michael Adas goes further, postulating the possible conditions of transformation to explain why existing strategies of domination and resistance can cease to be useful, while new ones are adopted because they are more effective. He shows based on historical evidence that shifts in the forms of resistance were brought about by critical changes in the social, political, and economic parameters that define the feasible options of avoidance protest, such as the advent of new technologies of communication, administration, logistics, and military repression, as well as changes in demographic composition and migratory flows (Adas 1986, 75–83; Scott 1986, 11).

Resistance to Land Alienation Mediating Capitalist and Primitive Accumulation

Forms of resistance to land alienation can be differentiated by the type of accumulative process they mediate. The expulsion of noncapitalist holders from their lands to create and renew the conditions of capitalist production corresponds to the historically ongoing process of primitive accumulation (Marx 1976, 873–895; Perelman 1984, 8–12; Harriss-White 2006, 1241–1246). Harvey (2005, 144–161) has "updated" and reconceptualized this notion as accumulation by dispossession (ABD) in the context of neoliberal globalization (Brenner 2006, 102; Ashman and Callinicos 2006, 115–117; Fine 2006, 143–144). Although there are conceptual differences between the notions of primitive accumulation and ABD, as well as specific limitations in their respective constructs, these are not pursued in detail here.[5] Instead, the present analysis regards ABD as the particular historical form of the generic category of primitive accumulation in the specific context of neoliberal globalization (Adnan 2013, 91–98, 122–123; 2016, paras 15–20; 2022, 178–209).

Land dispossession can also mediate capitalist accumulation through the processes of centralization or decentralization of capital. These involve the transfer of capital in the form of landed property from one capitalist agent to another.[6]

The politics associated with these distinct accumulative processes are qualitatively different, as are the respective political responses of the dispossessed. The discussion below addresses the politics of primitive accumulation and ABD through the alienation of the lands of noncapitalist landholders as well as the features of their resistance to dispossession. However, the politics of land alienation and resistance pertaining to the centralization of capital typically involves contestations among capitalist agents, such as corporations and financial institutions, which are not taken up in the present discussion (see Hall 2013, 1595; Fairbairn 2014; Daniel 2012).

Forms of Resistance and Processes of Transformation

The discussion in this section elaborates on the major forms of resistance to land alienation and the conditions of transformation between them, and also the distinctive features of resistance to primitive accumulation and ABD. The distinct traits characterizing and differentiating overt and covert resistance are specified. Intermediate forms of resistance that operate through the state apparatus are delineated, focusing on the notion of so-called "rightful resistance". The conditions of transformation between different forms of resistance are explored, including processes characterizing the microdynamics of transformation. The distinctive features of resistance to land alienation mediating primitive accumulation and ABD and their variable impacts on the pace and prospects of capitalist transformation are pointed out

Covert and Overt Resistance to Land Alienation

In reviewing struggles against land alienation it is useful to base the analysis on the classic distinction between (a) covert resistance (Scott 1985; 1986, 8–9) or avoidance protest (Adas 1986, 68–69)[7] and (b) overt resistance involving open confrontation.[8] Both these major forms of resistance can be characterized by the use of force in varying degrees or the absence of force altogether (Adas 1986, 68–78).

Covert resistance against powerful agencies can take the form of surreptitious sabotage or more violent actions, such as clandestine burning and destruction of their machinery and equipment.[9] The defining characteristics of covert resistance are its clandestine nature and the anonymity of those involved (Scott 1986, 10), which are typically made possible by a "complicity of silence" or "collective silence" among the entire social group to which the resisters belong (Scott 1986, 16; Chakma 2022, 19). Members of the group make a conscious choice not to divulge such information out of a sense of solidarity, which may be reinforced by the consideration that they all face the same common threat.

In contrast, overt resistance against land dispossession involves open protests that are public and visible. The participants do not have the protection of anonymity, since their identity cannot be kept hidden from those they resist, particularly the land-grabbing agencies and the private and security forces that support them. Overt resistance has both violent and nonviolent forms. The latter include procedural or ritual forms of protest that are usually constitutionally and legally permitted, such as street processions, demonstrations, and strikes. The violent forms can involve actions that are typically illegal, for example, the "calculated destruction of buildings, tools, live-stock, and crops" (Kerkvliet 1986, 78–80).

Evidence on actual struggles against expulsion from land indicates that the affected social groups might respond in a variety of ways, combining strands of covert and overt resistance. This was demonstrated by the multiple responses of the dispossessed to an instance of land alienation in rural Cambodia: "Villagers resisted. They started with combined covert and overt forms of resistance, including sabotage, arson, and stoning of bulldozers, but addressed their main demands to the Cambodian government" (Borras and Franco 2013, 1734).

Comparable patterns have been noted in struggles against expulsion from land in Africa. In a remote part of Uganda, the government attempted to provide land to a private corporate group for establishing a sugarcane plantation and processing factory. To protect their lands, the dispossessed groups mounted diverse forms of resistance through "the combined utilization of non-violent tactics (peaceful protests) and militant forms of struggle (permanent social mobilization of communities," inclusive of the proactive role of "peasant intellectuals . . . to articulate views and narratives that framed a common platform of multi-class interests" (Martiniello 2015, 660–665).

In Senegal, responses to land alienation for two investment projects involved both covert and overt resistance by the dispossessed groups. In one of these cases, involving an agroindustrial project, the affected peasant and pastoralist groups organized themselves into a collective that demanded the immediate termination of the project and called for "redistribution of the land to the local communities" (Prause and Le Billon 2021, 1110–1111). To this end, members of the collective undertook various forms of overt and covert protests that included an attempt "to block the clearing of the land by attacking workers and blocking and sabotaging the company's machines."

At the limit, overt resistance to land alienation can take the extreme form of armed struggle to stop further dispossession. This is illustrated by the attempts of the Pahari ethnic minorities (indigenous peoples) of the Chittagong Hill Tracts of Bangladesh to stop the ongoing alienation of their private and common lands by the state administration and security forces and to restitute their former holdings, which had been forcibly redistributed to in-migrating settlers.[10] These processes of mass dispossession and coercive land redistribution were critically shaped by identity politics, discriminatory practices, and *othering* based on ethnic and religious differences: the Pahari ethnic minorities were Buddhist, Christian, Hindu, or nature worshippers, whereas the security forces, civil administration, and settlers belonged mostly to the majority community of Bengali Muslims (Mohsin 1997; Adnan 2004, 26–31; 2007b). Although the leadership of the Pahari groups had appealed to the national government to protect their lands and distinct cultural traditions, these legal-procedural forms of resistance had proved futile, leaving them with little choice but to embark on an armed insurgency against the state and its security forces. The violent struggle lasted for around two decades, and eventually led to a peace accord, which resulted in only limited concessions regarding the political and land rights of the Pahari ethnic groups (Mohsin 1998, 106–107; Adnan 2007b; Adnan and Dastidar 2011). In this instance, the overt resistance of the Pahari peoples involved not only armed struggle but also social and cultural mobilization to counter the biopolitics of ethnoreligious discrimination and persecution (Foucault 2008; Li 2009, 66–80; Cavanagh and Benjaminsen 2015, 726), fostered by technologies of othering, and used to justify the forcible capture of their lands by the state and dominant Bengali interest groups (cf. Das 1998, 125; Mbembé 2003, 16–18; Cheesman 2017, 344–347).

Intermediate Forms: Working through the State Apparatus and "Rightful Resistance"

Turton (1986, 36) has postulated the existence of a "middle ground... [lying] in-between everyday and exceptional forms of resistance." Such intermediate categories can be identified within the broad spectrum formed by variations in the forms of covert and overt resistance.

One such intermediate form has been termed "rightful resistance," which pertains to engaging in struggles against the unjust actions of powerful officials and party cadres by working through the state apparatus rather than challenging it (O'Brien 2013, 1051–1053; Borras and Franco 2013, 1733). At work is the strategy of framing grievances against local government functionaries by claiming that they have contravened the policies of more powerful actors at higher levels of the state (Andreas et al. 2020, 1128). In the context of land alienation in post-socialist China, Chuang (2014) notes that it is "a strategy used by the aggrieved which exploits gaps between central state rights rhetoric and local state implementation to demand redress for unfulfilled rights. . . . [R]ightful resistance [provides] a way of seeking redress for collective grievances by drawing on the laws, policies, and rhetoric of the central state to 'hold the (local) state accountable' for rights and entitlements once promised" (650–651). Although it is a public, "noisy," and confrontational form of resistance, it is neither violent nor aimed at a revolutionary transformation of the existing order. On the contrary, "if rightful resistance performs as intended, it could help legitimate the current regime by proving to those perched on the verge of rebellion that the system works well enough . . . [In this sense], rightful resistance can be more effective than everyday resistance but safer than protest that edges toward rebellion" (O'Brien 2013, 1051, 1056–1058 fn 24).

Although the use of rightful resistance was initially noted in China, it has been also observed in other countries in Southeast Asia. For instance, in Laos, the struggle of an ethnic-minority Khmu community against the concession of its communal lands to a Chinese company for setting up a rubber plantation was based on the strategy of working through the state apparatus rather than challenging it (McAllister 2015, 829–831). The Khmu community invoked a state law which stipulated that "concession contracts are cancelled and assets are reclaimed by the state if the 'industrial farm' is not completed within seven years (McAllister 2015, 831)."[11] They also cited the Laotian state's earlier acknowledgments of their territorial rights as the "original owners of the land" and assiduously "framed their counter-claims to land by representing themselves as 'good,' 'deserving' and adequately 'developed' Lao citizens, mirroring various state ideologies and values for modernity." (McAllister 2015, 829).

Transformation in the Forms of Resistance

Evidence on the various types of transformation in the forms of resistance described here can be gleaned from case studies of struggles against land alienation. Dramatic transformation of covert to overt resistance has been witnessed in rural China, where, "since the mid-1980s rural collective protests and instances of outright insurgency have become commonplace . . . [i]nvolving tens of millions of participants" (Walker 2008a, 463). In the initial phases, acts of covert resistance "targeted tax collectors, corrupt village and township cadres, and the newly wealthy in the villages (often also cadres) by destroying their property, poisoning their livestock and poultry, and cutting down their trees. . . . [However, after the 1990s,] *land seizures* by local officials and cadres became the major focus of [overt] protest" (Walker 2008a, 467; emphasis added).

Responses to land alienation have also led to transformation in forms of overt resistance, from nonviolent and procedural actions to violent confrontations.[12] In India and Bangladesh, publicly visible resistance against land dispossession has typically begun with forms of procedural and ritual protest, such as street processions, petitions, appeals (*dharna*), and blockades (*gherao*), which are nonviolent and constitutionally permitted. However, when these peaceful demands have been met with repressive force, opposition to "displacement and dispossession from land-based livelihoods" has led to the taking up of armed resistance against the concerned security forces and vigilante groups.[13] In the Indian state of Chattisgarh, the government expelled the Indigenous peoples (*adivasi*) from their lands to grant mining concessions to domestic and foreign corporations. The peoples' efforts to contest their evictions through peaceful forms of protest were violently repressed by the paramilitary forces of the state and private vigilante groups (the Salwa Judum) hired by the mining corporations. Faced with combined state and corporate violence, the Indigenous peoples were compelled to engage in armed resistance to protect their lands by joining forces with the (Communist Party of India (Maoist) (Walker 2008b, 593–595; Adnan 2015, 31; Andreas et al. 2020, 1125–1127).

A case study of the shift from overt peaceful resistance to violent confrontation on a much smaller scale provides more detailed insights into the microdynamics of the process of transformation. In 2004, landless peasants in Bangladesh were undertaking peaceful protests against their forced eviction from state lands in their possession and the associated police harassment. However, when the police extracted bribes from the peasants but then reneged on the deal, it led to a violent clash during which several policemen were hurt, and some police uniforms and a rifle were snatched away by the angry peasants (Adnan 2013, 113). In this instance, the peaceful procedural protest turned into violent confrontation because of the illegal extortion and breach of agreement by the police, which aroused intense feelings of injustice and moral indignation among the affected group. The dynamics of the interaction led to the unintended consequence of triggering violent reactions by the peasantry, which were not preplanned and overrode their normally circumspect behavior towards the police to avoid possible reprisals.

In accordance with these examples, the interpersonal dynamics of the transformative process from covert to overt, and from nonviolent to violent, resistance can be postulated as follows: a critical requirement is the transmission of the "will to resist" among the members of the affected group, through which individuals decide to join the struggle only after seeing others in similar conditions doing the same. This process of *contagious defiance*, which can be also motivated by a shared sense of injustice, is what enables resisting individuals and groups to cross the threshold of fear when challenging more powerful groups and agencies (Guha 1983, 167; Adnan 2007a, 203–215; Walker 2008a, 469–471; Kerkvliet 2009, 234–235). In such circumstances, gathering the courage to display open defiance can result from the increasing strength in numbers and the corresponding rise in the collective bargaining power or retributive strength of the dispossessed. The microdynamics of such transformative processes involve an interactive growth of defiance among the individual agents of a collectivity until a critical mass is formed, leading to a tipping point at whichthe momentum for a switch in the form of collective action can no longer be held in check.[14]

Resistance to Land Alienation Mediating Primitive Accumulation and ABD

Struggles against land alienation mediating primitive accumulation or ABD, discussed above, have significant implications for the prospects of capitalist development. As has been observed in India and Bangladesh, whether resistance can stop, or slow down, land dispossession determines the pace of primitive accumulation or ABD (Adnan 2013, 119; 2015, 37–39). This, in turn, affects the possibility and prospects of capitalist transformation of the classes continuing to hold land under noncapitalist production relations.

In post-Mao China, peasants were evicted from their lands and livelihoods "within a web of growing state repression and the new levels of violence, brutality and human degradation generated by corruption and officially sanctioned crime, . . . [S]ince the late 1990s land struggles have surged ahead as the central grievance of the rural protests" (Walker 2008a, 474–475). These instances of alienating the land (use) rights of noncapitalist Chinese peasants or "petty commodity producers" (Andreas et al. 2020, 1123, 1128) correspond analytically to processes of ongoing primitive accumulation—admittedly, in a post-socialist context! However, the struggles by these peasants to oppose dispossession mediating primitive accumulation were typically crushed by the deployment of the state's paramilitary forces in combination with criminal gangs. For instance, the inhabitants of Sanchawang village in Shaanxi Province resisted the seizure of their lands for construction of a development zone for three years until they were overwhelmed by state repression (Walker 2008a, 474).

Exclusion of the preexisting landholders from "protected areas" for conservation projects under neoliberal auspices has been regarded as corresponding to ongoing primitive accumulation (Kelly 2011, 685–692; Corson and MacDonald 2012) or as ABD (Cavanagh and Benjaminsen 2015, 726). Faced with land alienation for a conservation project in Mount Elgon National Park in Uganda, the dispossessed social groups undertook various forms of overt resistance that made use of a range of "nonviolent, militant, discursive [and] formal-legal tactics." They also began illicit cultivation in parts of the park's protected area, termed "guerilla agriculture" (Cavanagh and Benjaminsen 2015, 727–741). These diverse but coordinated tactics constituted elements of an overall strategy of resistance to exclusion from land. It succeeded in slowing down the pace of primitive accumulation and ABD and capitalist transformation in the conservation area, and even reversed the process to some extent by reoccupying some of the alienated lands with "guerrilla agriculture."

Interactions between the Politics of Land Alienation and Resistance

The politics of land alienation and the struggles against them are interactive, mutually shaping each other in dynamic trajectories over time. The outcomes of these contestations are determined by the adoption of particular strategies by the protagonists and the changing balance of forces between them. On the one hand, broad-based and politically committed resistance can bring about changes in state policies of land acquisition. On the other hand, repression of resistance by the state and land alienating agencies can vary from discriminatory biopolitics to murderous violence and intimidation. Such interactive dynamics of land alienation and resistance can bring about adaptive changes and discrete innovation in their respective strategies. For example, novel strategies of land alienation have been designed with built-in mechanisms to pre-empt the very emergence of collective action.

Balance of Forces between Land Alienation and Resistance

The outcomes of interactions between the politics of land alienation and struggles against it depend on the balance of forces between them (Adnan 2013, 97; Famerée 2016, 549–550). The balance can vary between instances, as well as over time, due to political contestations and the influence of exogenous factors, such as the role of external allies and changes in official policy that affect the contested lands.

These propositions are illustrated by the contrasting outcomes of resistance against land acquisition by private companies in two regions of Peru (Famerée 2016, 546–551).

In one case (in the Alto Valley), the resistance of the dispossessed groups benefited from collaboration with the regional government, which was opposed to land deals promoted by the national government. Alliances with organizations supported by the Catholic Church, public officials, civil society organizations, and multisectoral protest groups put together a coalition of forces that created "a web of powerful and well-connected support." Mobilizing the struggle around a "unifying political frame" based on "the defense of land and the larger territory" succeeded in generating effective resistance against capture of the land by the private company (Famerée 2016, 544–550; cf. Alonso-Frajedas 2015, 499–500). Eventually, however, a "municipal order declaring the threatened lands an environmental protection area" undermined this unifying frame, generating heated political debates and creating confusion and division among the resisting groups. The resultant shift in the balance of forces led to the depoliticization and weakening of the struggle in its subsequent stages.

In the other case (the Bajo Valley), the struggle against land alienation by the company was less robust from the outset because of the differing views among the threatened groups about whether they should resist or compromise. Unlike the experience in Alto Valley, comparable support was not forthcoming from external allies such as state functionaries, the Church, and civil society organizations, which made the resistance in Bajo valley relatively weaker (Famerée 2016, 550–553). The cumulative impacts of these factors shifted the balance of forces against the movement, manifested in the gradual defection of individual members who began selling their land to the company. As the struggle against expulsion predictably collapsed, manipulation by the company diverted the dispossessed toward struggles over the terms of incorporation, which replaced their erstwhile collective resistance with individualized negotiations by each household to access services essential for survival.

Role of Resistance in Changing State Policies on Land Acquisition

The use of force by the state to acquire land, as well as to repress the ensuing resistance, can generate intense political contradictions that lead to significant policy changes (Scott 1986, 8). Borras and Franco (2013, 1729–1730) attribute the general basis of such contradictions to "Jonathan Fox's formulation of the two permanent contradictory tasks of the state, namely, to facilitate capital accumulation but at the same time to maintain a historically determined minimum level of political legitimacy" (Fox 1993; O'Connor 1973).

These political contradictions in the role of the state are evident in the experience of the "land wars" in India resulting from resistance to land alienation for special economic zones (SEZs) and stand-alone industrial and infrastructural projects driven by neoliberal policy imperatives (Adnan 2015, 30–31; 2016, para. 28; Andreas et al. 2020, 1124–1125). Mobilization of broad-based legal-procedural and ground-level struggles against such dispossession eventually led to the cancellation, postponement, or downsizing of significant numbers of these projects (Walker 2008b, 590; Levien 2012, 933–934). In the state of Goa, "mobilization by a cross-class, cross-society coalition led to the cancellation of 15 approved SEZs" and the discontinuation of the government policy of state acquisition of land for establishing such zones (Sampat 2015, 766–769; Hall et al. 2015, 476). Popular social movements against land acquisition for a car factory in Singur and an SEZ in Nandigram, in the state of West Bengal, were violently repressed by security forces with the support of ruling party cadres and criminal gangs. Nonetheless, continuation of these struggles by the affected social groups and allied political organizations eventually compelled the West Bengal government to cancel the projects—and to suspend its policy, by desisting from state acquisition of land for other SEZs (Nielsen 2010, 146; Banerjee 2014, 245–284; Adnan 2016, paras 64–66). The outcomes of these struggles in India are indicative of the critical role politically committed resistance can play in bringing about significant changes in the land acquisition policies of the regimes controlling state power.

Counterstrategies to Co-opt or Repress Active Resistance

When their efforts at land alienation are confronted by organized resistance, the concerned state and private corporations can take countermeasures to penalize, divide, co-opt, or crush the opposition. This kind of adaptive change in strategy to undermine resistance can be flexible and innovative. The repertoire of such strategies can range from the direct use of force and intimidation to noncoercive techniques of persuasion and the defusion of resistance, such as offering material inducements and making (deceptive) promises (Alonso-Frajedas 2015, 508–511).

A relatively straightforward example is provided by the measures taken to deal with resistance to the state acquisition of land for the Bibiyana gasfield in Bangladesh, which was operated by a transnational corporation (Gardner 2012, 87; Gardner et al. 2014, paras 5–7). Faced with the refusal by local landowners to cede the area that was needed for the mining site, the corporation decided to step in and offered them higher rates of compensation and development gifts including "promises of community development" and "contracts for the supply of labour and building materials" (Gardner 2012, 87–90; Ahasan and Gardner 2016, para 16; Adnan 2016, para. 61). The combination of material incentives and (eventually unfulfilled promises proved to be effective in defusing the landholders' opposition, enabling the state acquisition of their lands to proceed unhindered.

The private company in the Bajo Valley of Peru (see the section "Balance of Forces between Land Alienation and Resistance") deployed a much more elaborate array of countermeasures to appropriate lands for oil palm production. It pursued a comprehensive, multipronged strategy aimed at undermining both actual and potential opposition, mixing direct threats of force with noncoercive mechanisms of defusing the resistance through persuasion and material incentives. It applied numerous techniques aimed at co-opting and dividing the dispossessed and their leadership, including making unscrupulous offers of bribes, gifts, and donations to "buy" their compliance. In a strategic move, the company diverted the affected landowners' focus from the struggle against expulsion to the struggle for incorporation, by embroiling them in detailed negotiations on the terms and conditions involved (Famerée 2016, 550–555). The company also orchestrated the setting up of parallel associations among the landholders to create confusion among the resisters and break the unity of their movement. Not least, it used criminal forms of intimidation, in the form of death threats to the leaders of the resistance movement and threats of bodily harm to their family members. The complex and wide-ranging tactics deployed by this private company, with supporting interventions of the national and regional governments, constituted mutually reinforcing strands of an integrated strategy to undermine the resistance of the dispossessed against the alienation of their lands.

The experience of post-socialist China demonstrates the interactive dynamics of land alienation, overt resistance, and repressive countermeasures on a much vaster scale than in the instances described above. During the 1990s, repeated waves of land dispossession of the peasantry through state repression and violence were orchestrated by corrupt local-level functionaries operating in collusion with private gangs engaging in "officially sanctioned criminal violence". Since the loss of land drastically undermined the peasants' livelihoods and survival, it lay at the very heart of rural protest in China, generating an "escalating spiral of violence and resistance." When some of the dispossessed households attempted to recover their former lands, seized earlier, the concerned authorities deployed paramilitary troops and "helmeted thugs" to crush their efforts, resulting in death and injury among the resisting peasants (Walker 2008a, 473–475).

A limiting case of the use of violence to suppress resistance to land alienation is provided by the grim political contestations in the Aguan region of Honduras. Following the failure of agrarian reforms, the affected social groups attempted to resist the ongoing dispossession and to recover their previously expropriated lands. The response of the incumbent regime was to militarize the region and unleash brutal repression by the state's military and police operating in collusion with the landowners' private armies, which were given a free hand. "The result [w]as . . . a rising body count, with dozens assassinated and peasant activists suffering most of the casualties. The peasant organisations . . . faced a campaign of criminalisation," and hundreds of activists were charged with criminal offences (Edelman and León 2013, 1712). This instance epitomizes the crushing of resistance to land alienation by the state and dominant classes through sheer terror and intimidation. It signifies why, in limiting cases of land dispossession involving murderous violence, the political imperatives at work can go beyond discriminatory biopolitics (Foucault 2008; Li 2009; Cavanagh and Benjaminsen 2015, 726) toward the extreme form of "necropolitics," embodying "the subjugation of life to the power of death" (Mbembé 2003, 39–40).

Strategies Designed to Pre-empt Potential Resistance

A critical form of adaptive mutation noted in the recent politics of land alienation involves the designing of innovative strategies that have "built-in" mechanisms to pre-empt the very possibility of unified opposition. These manipulate the dispossessed to take part in individualized transactions that lead them on separate trajectories, foreclosing the potential for collective action. They include the following:

Market transactions, individualized compensation, and material incentives

Vijayabaskar has highlighted an innovative strategy designed "to curb resistance" to the procurement of land for SEZs, adopted by the government of the Indian state of Tamil Nadu as early as the 1990s. Instead of compulsory acquisition of land by the state, which could provoke organized resistance by the dispossessed, it promoted the use of "market mechanisms . . . [for] facilitating negotiations between landowners and private firms" that wanted to buy their lands (Vijayabaskar 2014, 305–306; Adnan 2016, paras 41–42). In 1995 a Government Order set up official committees that were authorized to negotiate land deals with individual landowners. Subsequently, a law was enacted to permit and streamline the purchase of land through market-based pricing systems.[15] In addition, substantial material incentives were offered by the Tamil Nadu state government to potential land sellers as part of an attractive package deal (Adnan 2016, para 42). Among the government's incentives were the provision of compensation plots in a "planned residential zone" and a job and the requisite skills training for one member of the selling household (Vijayabaskar 2014, 313–320). The result of this strategy of engaging landowners in voluntary transactions and tying the individually negotiated land prices to material incentives was that the government of Tamil Nadu's efforts to procure land for SEZs met with hardly any serious opposition, reflecting the success of what Vijayabaskar has termed "the politics of silence."

Levien documents a comparable but somewhat different strategy for the compulsory state acquisition of land for an SEZ in a village in the Indian state of Rajasthan. Dispossessed households holding officially recognized ownership rights were offered either a fixed cash compensation or a plot of "developed commercial-residential land adjacent to the SEZ" (Levien 2018, 83). The compensation plots could appreciate in value because of rising land prices following the establishment of the SEZ, potentially providing the recipients with coveted windfall gains from real estate speculation. The combined effects of dispossession, compensation, and speculation generated incremental differentiation among the dispossessed households, which were superimposed on their preexisting divisions based on caste, class, and social status and reflected in their divergent individual trajectories (Levien 2018, 105–126). Levien observes that there was no sustained collective resistance to land acquisition among the villagers, noting that most of the dispossessed households chose the compensation plot(s). This calculated gambit to co-opt the dispossessed households by offering them individualized compensation plots proved to "be a powerful mechanism for generating compliance" to dispossession while eroding the basis of collective opposition (Levien 2012, 953; 2018, 210).

Pre-emption of rightful resistance through change in residential status and associated land rights

Another innovative adaptation in the land alienation strategy designed to foreclose potential opposition has been noted in post-socialist China. Termed "bureaucratic absorption" by Julia Chuang (2014, 666), its objective is to undermine the basis of "rightful resistance." The political basis of the strategy was provided by the New Socialist Countryside Campaign (NSCC) by the Chinese central state (Liu 2022, 592; Chuang 2014, 649–652), which authorized local state officials to expropriate the lands used by farming households that had changed their registration (*hukou*) from the agricultural category to the nonagricultural category. The policy was implemented through the use of deceit and disinformation by county and township officials who initially provided gifts and financial rewards to farming households to encourage voluntary hukou transfers and only began to take over their lands after the transfer process had been completed. The overall framework of this elaborate process of dispossession through manipulation was set up by the NSCC which "recast land expropriation as a condition of 'rural-urban integration' purporting to 'let rural farmers upstairs' by incorporating them into urban citizenship and township residence. After evicting rural residents and resettling them in townships, officials convert[ed] [their former] rural land from collective to state ownership, then [resold their erstwhile] land-use contracts to developers via public auction" (Chuang 2014, 650-652). The net outcome of this complex, multistage process was that the farming households that changed their *hukou* status ended up losing their formally recognized entitlement to rural land and then were constrained to negotiate for urban accommodation and utility services through bureaucratic channels and individualized market transactions (Chuang 2014, 652).

A critical outcome of this elaborate strategy was to undercut the legal-institutional basis of "rightful resistance". By presenting the termination of the land-use rights of farming households that had changed their *hukou* status as authorized by the central state, local officials foreclosed any discursive space for (rightful) opposition based on invoking the gaps between central-government policy and local-government implementation (O'Brien 2013, 1051–1055; Chuang 2014, 658). At the same time, these farming households were manipulated into a position where they no longer had any recognized land rights that could provide the legal basis for reclaiming access to their former holdings.

Further Research

The preceding analysis has thrown into relief critical issues and questions that are of current concern and likely significance in the foreseeable future. Moreover, new issues can be expected to arise as the interactive politics of resistance to land alienation continue to evolve. It is therefore worthwhile to monitor ongoing trends, with an eye to identifying the new issues and innovative patterns, followed by analysis of their theoretical and political significance. The following themes and questions are put forward as suggestions for further research into the politics of resistance to land alienation.

First, specify the causal linkages between the outcomes of land alienation and the political responses of the dispossessed. This would involve identifying the processes through which the typically unequal distributive impacts of land alienation shape the political responses of the affected social groups, which can not only be different but also opposed to each other. The research would aim to provide more precise specification of the critical factors differentiating the winners and losers from land alienation and to delineate the feasible political options at their disposal, ranging from resistance to compliance and incorporation.

Second, explore the ways in which the politics of land alienation and resistance are shaped by differences in the social and cultural identities of the groups involved. This would involve identification of (a) evolving forms of politics, including biopolitics, of land alienation that are based on targeting and othering of particular groups in terms of their social and cultural identity, and (b) innovations in the cultural politics of resistance to counter these discriminatory practices. The research design should explicitly integrate the influences of ethnicity, race, religion, caste, age, gender, and other identity-based attributes on the outcomes of land alienation and the corresponding political responses. The pertinent research questions are, What novel forms of biopolitics and othering are being generated to justify land alienation, and are the corresponding forms of resistance forged along the same cleavages of identity-based discrimination, inverting the politics of persecution and othering used to justify dispossession?

Third, specify the conditions of transformation between different forms of resistance. This would involve detailed analysis of the transformative processes at work in the various forms of overt-covert and violent-nonviolent resistance in relation to the politics, including biopolitics, of land alienation. Research questions include, What are the critical factors and influential parametric shifts (e.g., technological and demographic changes) creating the conditions for different types of transformation in the forms of resistance to dispossession?

Fourth, trace the reciprocal and reiterative interactions between the strategies of land alienation and resistance. This would involve the identification of adaptative changes and innovation in evolving strategies of land alienation and resistance, specifying the ways in which interactions between them shape the dynamic trajectories of land contestations. The research design should ideally be longitudinal with provisions for repeat studies of cohorts. Research questions include, What new strategies of land alienation are emerging in response to evolving strategies of resistance, and vice versa? Are strategies of land alienation designed with built-in mechanisms to pre-empt and undermine collective resistance continuing to evolve? These considerations also underscore the urgency of identifying innovative strategies of resistance that can counter such anticipatory strategies of land alienation, based on concrete evidence from actual struggles against expulsion.

Fifth, highlight the differences between struggles against primitive and capitalist accumulation mediated by land alienation. This would require identification of the distinct features of the politics of resistance against evolving forms of land alienation mediating primitive accumulation or ABD. Of particular significance given its relative lack of coverage in the existing literature, would be the investigation of the politics of resistance to land alienation mediating capitalist accumulation through the centralization or decentralization of capital.These would involve contestations among capitalist corporations and agencies undertaking productive and speculative investments in farmland, inclusive of the financialization and securitization of land.

Acknowledgments

The research for this chapter was greatly facilitated by access to library resources of the London School of Economic and Political Science through a Visiting Professorship based in the Department of Geography and Environment. I am particularly indebted to Kasia Paprocki for her initiative in this matter. Comments and suggestions on the original draft of the paper by the editors of this volume and an anonymous reviewer helped to improve the contents and are greatly appreciated. I thank Jun Borras for his patience and understanding in the face of prolonged delays in the completion of the chapter.

Notes

1. See Walker (2008a, 463–464); Hall (2013, 1591–1594); Edelman and León (2013, 1706–1710); Edelman, Oya, and Borras (2013, 1519–1523); and Adnan (2013, 92–93; 2016, para. 40–45).
2. This would include "distress" sales such as surrender of mortgaged plots held as collateral to the lender to settle cumulative debts at accounting prices determined by the latter.
3. Borras and Franco (2013, 1724–1726); Oya (2013, 1547); Edelman, Oya, and Borras (2013, 1523); Hall et al. (2015, 467); and Famerée (2016, 541–542).
4. Transformation in the forms of resistance has been noted earlier in different contexts (Adnan 2013, 98 fn. 10), including specific instances in the Philippines (Kerkvliet 1990, 179–182), Bangladesh (Adnan 2007a), and China (Walker 2008a, 463).
5. In brief, primitive accumulation involves the dispossession of social groups from their means of production, for example, land, such that these resources and the labor of the dispossessed become available as commodities to be brought together in capitalist production. Marx (1976) innovated this concept to explain how the means of production and labor became available as separate commodities at the historical origin of capitalism and continued to be supplied during subsequent cycles of capitalist production. However, the mechanisms and agencies involved in primitive accumulation underwent significant change over the subsequent century, leading Harvey (2005) to put forward the notion of ABD to customize Marx's original concept to the drastically altered context of neoliberal globalization. Although the two concepts have functionally similar roles (Adnan 2013, 91–98, 122–123; 2022, 180–200), the notion of ABD is not aimed at explaining the availability

of resources at the origin of capitalism; but its conceptualization incorporates contemporary forms and mechanisms of dispossession that were not even conceivable at the time Marx formulated the notion of primitive accumulation.

6. Marx (1976, 777–779); Kautsky (1988, 146); Fine and Saad-Filho (2016); and Adnan (2022, 200–202; 2016, para. 11).
7. The notions of covert or "everyday" resistance and avoidance protest are similar but not identical (Scott 1985, 1986; Adas 1986; Kerkvliet 1986, 2009). The differences between these are not presently taken up.
8. Although the term "everyday resistance" (Scott 1985, 1986; Adas 1986, 69–72; Kerkvliet 1986, 2009) is often used as a synonym for covert resistance or avoidance protest, its meaning has become contested and ambiguous. For instance, in post-socialist China, the dominant form of "everyday" politics and resistance has been found to be overt collective action, often taking violent forms (Walker 2008a, 462–463).
9. Scott (1986, 8–9); Adas (1986, 78–79); Kerkvliet (1986, 109–117); Peluso (1992, 101); Guha (2000, 107–125); and Adnan (2013, 97).
10. R. D. Roy (1995, 67–73; 1997, 171); Mohsin (1997, 215–218); R. C. K. Roy (2000, 77–96); and Adnan (2004, 50–51; 2007b).
11. Government of Lao PDR. 2009. *Prime Minister's decree on state lease or concession. No. 135/PM, 25/05/2009*. Cited in McAllister (2015).
12. Comparable transformations of peaceful and procedural movements for agrarian reform into armed struggles and land invasions are noted in Colombia (Grajales 2011, 775–777).
13. Walker (2008b, 582–596); Harriss-White (2012, 142–143); Kunnath (2012, 104–107); and Adnan (2013, 97–98; 2015, 30–31).
14. Comparable processes have been noted by Ranajit Guha (1983, 167, 258) in the history of peasant insurgency in colonial India: "To rebel by seeing others engage in rebellion" (Adnan 2007a, 214–215nn.22, 25). Similar transmission of a growing will to resist among sharecroppers faced with the possibility of continuing encroachment on their land rights has been postulated by Hamza Alavi (1973, 37). Eric Hobsbawm (1959, 105–106) and George Rudé (1964, 249) have noted comparable processes of "rapid and contagious mobilization" in other historical contexts.
15. The Tamil Nadu Acquisition of Land for Industrial Purposes Act (TNALIPA) of 1999.

References

Adas, Michael. 1986. "From Footdragging to Flight: The Evasive History of Peasant Avoidance Protest in South and South-East Asia." *Journal of Peasant Studies* 13 (2): 64–86.

Adnan, Shapan. 2004. *Migration, Land Alienation and Ethnic Conflict: Causes of Poverty in the Chittagong Hill Tracts of Bangladesh*. Dhaka, Bangladesh: Research and Advisory Services.

Adnan, Shapan. 2007a. "Departures from Everyday Resistance and Flexible Strategies of Domination: The Making and Unmaking of a Poor Peasant Mobilization in Bangladesh." *Journal of Agrarian Change* 7 (2): 183–224.

Adnan, Shapan. 2007b. "Migration, Discrimination and Land Alienation: Social and Historical Perspectives on the Ethnic Conflict in the Chittagong Hill Tracts of Bangladesh. "*Contemporary Perspectives: History and Sociology of South Asia* 1 (2): 1–28.

Adnan, Shapan. 2013. "Land Grabs and Primitive Accumulation in Deltaic Bangladesh: Interactions between Neoliberal Globalization, State Interventions, Power Relations and Peasant Resistance." *Journal of Peasant Studies* 40 (1): 87–128.

Adnan, Shapan. 2015. "Primitive Accumulation and the 'Transition to Capitalism' in Neoliberal India: Mechanisms, Resistance, and the Persistence of Self-Employed Labour." In *Indian Capitalism in Development*, edited by Barbara Harriss-White and Judith Heyer, 23–45. London: Routledge.

Adnan, Shapan. 2016. "Alienation in Neoliberal India and Bangladesh: Diversity of Mechanisms and Theoretical Implications." *South Asia Multidisciplinary Academic Journal (SAMAJ)*. [Open Edition online], 13. https://journals.openedition.org/samaj/4130.

Adnan, Shapan. 2022. "The Contemporary Relevance of 'Primitive' Accumulation: A Comparative Review with Accumulation by Dispossession and Centralization of Capital." In *Badruddin Umarer Jiban o Kaj: Nibedito Probondhobali (The Life and Works of Badruddin Umar: Essays in Honour)*, edited by C. R. Abrar et al., 171–218. Dhaka, Bangladesh: Bangala Prokashona (chapter in English in the bilingual volume).

Adnan, Shapan, and Ranajit Dastidar. 2011. *Alienation of the Lands of Indigenous Peoples of the Chittagong Hill Tracts of Bangladesh*. Dhaka, Bangladesh, and Copenhagen: Chittagong Hill Tracts Commission and International Work Group for Indigenous Affairs (IWGIA). An electronic version is available on the University of Oxford South Asian Studies website. https://www.southasia.ox.ac.uk/sites/default/files/southasia/documents/media/oxford_university_csasp_-_work_in_progress_paper_15_adnan_dastidar_alienation_of.pdf.

Ahasan, Abu, and Katy Gardner. 2016. "Dispossession by 'Development': Corporations, Elites and NGOs in Bangladesh." *South Asia Multidisciplinary Academic Journal (SAMAJ)*. [Open Edition online], 13. http://journals.openedition.org/samaj/4136.

Alavi, Hamza. 1973. "Peasant Classes and Primordial Loyalties." *Journal of Peasant Studies* 1 (1): 23–62.

Alonso-Fradejas, Alberto. 2015. "Anything but a Story Foretold: Multiple Politics of Resistance to the Agrarian Extractivist Project in Guatemala." *Journal of Peasant Studies* 42 (3–4): 489–515.

Andreas, Joel, Sunila S. Kale, Michael Levien, and Qian Forrest Zhang. 2020. "Rural Land Dispossession in China and India." *Journal of Peasant Studies* 47 (6): 1109–1142.

Ashman, Sam, and Alex Callinicos. 2006. "Capital Accumulation and the State System: Assessing David Harvey's *The New Imperialism*." *Historical Materialism* 14 (4): 107–131.

Banerjee, Partha Sarathi. 2014. "Orissa and West Bengal: The SEZ Imbroglio." In *Power, Policy and Protest: The Politics of India's Special Economic Zones*, edited by Rob Jenkins, Loraine Kennedy, and Partha Mukhopadhyay, 273–304. New Delhi: Oxford University Press.

Borras, Saturnino M. 2023. "Politically Engaged, Pluralist and Internationalist: Critical Agrarian Studies Today." *Journal of Peasant Studies* 50 (2): 449–489.

Borras, Saturnino M., Jr., and Jennifer C. Franco. 2013. "Global Land Grabbing and Political Reactions 'from Below'." *Third World Quarterly* 34 (9): 1723–1747.

Borras, Saturnino M., Jr., and Jennifer C. Franco. 2018. "The Challenge of Locating Land-Based Climate Change Mitigation and Adaptation Politics within a Social Justice Perspective: Towards an Idea of Agrarian Climate Justice." *Third World Quarterly* 39 (7): 1308–1325.

Borras, Saturnino M., Jr., Cristóbal Kay, Sergio Gómez, and John Wilkinson. 2012. "Land Grabbing and Global Capitalist Accumulation: Key Features in Latin America." *Canadian Journal of Development Studies / Revue canadienne d'études du développement* 33 (4): 402–416.

Brenner, Robert. 2006. "What Is, and What Is Not, Imperialism?" *Historical Materialism* 14 (4): 79–105.

Cavanagh, Connor Joseph, and Tor A. Benjaminsen. 2015. "Guerrilla Agriculture? A Biopolitical Guide to Illicit Cultivation within an IUCN Category II Protected Area." *Journal of Peasant Studies* 42 (3–4): 725–745.

Chakma, Bablu. 2022. "Everyday Politics of Dadan Contracts in the Chittagong Hill Tracts, Bangladesh." *Development and Change* 54 (1): 143–167.

Cheesman, Nick. 2017. "Introduction: Interpreting Communal Violence in Myanmar." *Journal of Contemporary Asia* 47 (3): 335–352.

Chuang, Julia. 2014. "China's Rural Land Politics: Bureaucratic Absorption and the Muting of Rightful Resistance." *China Quarterly* 219 (September): 649–669.

Corson, Catherine, and Kenneth Iain MacDonald. 2012. "Enclosing the Global Commons: The Convention on Biological Diversity and Green Grabbing." *Journal of Peasant Studies* 39 (2): 263–283.

Daniel, Shepard. 2012. "Situating Private Equity Capital in the Land Grab Debate." *Journal of Peasant Studies* 39 (3–4): 703–729.

Das, Veena. 1998. "Specificities: Official Narratives, Rumour, and the Social Production of Hate." *Social Identities* 4 (1): 109–130.

Edelman, Marc, and Andrés León. 2013. "Cycles of Land Grabbing in Central America: An Argument for History and a Case Study in the Bajo Aguán, Honduras." *Third World Quarterly* 34 (9): 1697–1722.

Edelman, Marc, Carlos Oya, and Saturnino M. Borras Jr. 2013. "Global Land Grabs: Historical Processes, Theoretical and Methodological Implications and Current Trajectories." *Third World Quarterly* 34 (9): 1517–1531.

Fairbairn, Madeleine. 2014. "'Like Gold with Yield': Evolving Interactions between Farmland and Finance." *Journal of Peasant Studies* 41 (5): 777–795.

Famerée, Cécile. 2016. "Political Contestations around Land Deals: Insights from Peru." *Canadian Journal of Development Studies / Revue canadienne d'études du développement* 37 (4): 541–559.

Fine, Ben. 2006. "Debating the 'New' Imperialism." *Historical Materialism* 14 (4): 133–156.

Fine, Ben, and Alfredo Saad-Filho. 2016. *Marx's Capital*. 6th ed. London: Pluto Press.

Foucault, Michel. 2008. *The Birth of Biopolitics: Lectures at the Collège de France*, 1978–1979. New York: Palgrave Macmillan.

Fox, Jonathan. 1993. *Food Politics*. Ithaca, NY: Cornell University Press.

Gardner, Katy. 2012. *Discordant Development: Global Capitalism and the Struggle for Connection in Bangladesh*. London: Pluto Press.

Gardner, Katy, Zahir Ahmed, Mohammad Masud Rana, and Fatema Bashar. 2014. "Field of Dreams: Imagining Development and Un-Development at a Gas Field in Sylhet." *South Asia Multidisciplinary Academic Journal (SAMAJ)* [Open Edition online], 9. http://journals.openedition.org/samaj/3741.

Grajales, Jacobo. 2011. "The Rifle and the Title: Paramilitary Violence, Land Grab and Land Control in Colombia." *Journal of Peasant Studies* 38 (4): 771–792.

Guha, Ramachandra. 2000. *The Unquiet Woods: Ecological Change and Peasant Resistance in the Himalaya*. Expanded ed. Berkeley: University of California Press.

Guha, Ranajit. 1983. *Elementary Aspects of Peasant Insurgency in Colonial India*. Delhi: Oxford University Press.

Hall, Derek. 2013. "Primitive Accumulation, Accumulation by Dispossession and the Global Land Grab." *Third World Quarterly* 34 (9): 1582–1604.

Hall, Ruth, Marc Edelman, Saturnino M. Borras Jr., Ian Scoones, Ben White, and Wendy Wolford. 2015. "Resistance, Acquiescence or Incorporation? An Introduction to Land Grabbing and Political Reactions 'from Below.'" *Journal of Peasant Studies* 42 (3–4): 467–488.

Harriss-White, Barbara. 2006. "Poverty and Capitalism." *Economic and Political Weekly* 41 (13): 1241–1246.

Harriss-White, Barbara. 2012. "Capitalism and the Common Man: Peasants and Petty Production in Africa and South Asia." *Agrarian South: Journal of Political Economy* 1 (2): 109–160.

Harvey, David. 2005. *The New Imperialism*. Oxford: Oxford University Press.

Hobsbawm, Eric J. 1959. *Primitive Rebels. Studies in Archaic Forms of Social Movement in the 19th and 20th Centuries*. Manchester, UK: Manchester University Press.

Kautsky, Karl. 1988. *The Agrarian Question*. Vol. 1. Translated by Pete Burgess. Introduction by Hamza Alavi and Teodor Shanin. London: Zwan.

Kelly, Alice. 2011. "Conservation Practice as Primitive Accumulation." *Journal of Peasant Studies* 38 (4): 683–701.

Kerkvliet, Benedict J. Tria. 1986. "Everyday Resistance to Injustice in a Philippine Village." *Journal of Peasant Studies* 13 (2): 107–123.

Kerkvliet, Benedict J. Tria. 1990. *Everyday Politics in the Philippines: Class and Status Relations in a Central Luzon Village*. Berkeley: University of California Press.

Kerkvliet, B. J. Tria. 2009. "Everyday Politics in Peasant Societies (and Ours)." *Journal of Peasant Studies* 36 (1): 227–243.

Kunnath, George J. 2012. *Rebels from the Mud Houses: Dalits and the Making of the Maoist Revolution in Bihar*. New Delhi: Social Science Press.

Levien, Michael. 2012. "The Land Question: Special Economic Zones and the Political Economy of Dispossession in India." *Journal of Peasant Studies* 39 (3–4): 933–969.

Levien, Michael. 2018. *Dispossession without Development: Land Grabs in Neoliberal India*. New York: Oxford University Press.

Li, Tania M. 2009. "To Make Live or Let Die? Rural Dispossession and the Protection of Surplus Populations." *Antipode* 41 (S1): 66–93.

Liu, Jingping. 2022. "The Abolition of Agricultural Taxes and the Transformation of Clientelism in the Countryside of Post-Mao China." *Journal of Peasant Studies* 49 (3): 585–603.

Martiniello, Giuliano. 2015. "Social Struggles in Uganda's Acholiland: Understanding Responses and Resistance to Amuru Sugar Works." *Journal of Peasant Studies* 42 (3–4): 653–669.

Marx, Karl. 1976. *Capital: A Critique of Political Economy*. Vol. 1. London: Penguin.

Mbembé, J. A. 2003. "Necropolitics." *Public Culture* 15 (1): 11–40.

McAllister, Karen E. 2015. "Rubber, Rights and Resistance: The Evolution of Local Struggles against a Chinese Rubber Concession in Northern Laos." *Journal of Peasant Studies* 42 (3–4): 817–837.

Mohsin, Amena. 1997. *The Politics of Nationalism: The Case of the CHT, Bangladesh*. Dhaka, Bangladesh: University Press Limited.

Mohsin, Amena. 1998. "CHT Peace Accord: Looking Ahead." *Journal of Social Studies* 82 (August–October): 106–117.

Mintz, Sydney W. 1973. "A Note on the Definition of Peasantries." *Journal of Peasant Studies* 1 (1): 91–106.

O'Connor, James R. 1973. *The Fiscal Crisis of the State*. New York: St. Martin's Press.

Nielsen, Kenneth Bo. 2010. "Contesting India's Development? Industrialization, Land Acquisition and Protest in West Bengal." *Forum for Development Studies* 37 (2): 145–170.

O'Brien, Kevin J. 2013. "Rightful Resistance Revisited." *Journal of Peasant Studies* 40 (6): 1051–1062.

Oya, Carlos. 2013. "The Land Rush and Classic Agrarian Questions of Capital and Labour: A Systematic Scoping Review of the Socioeconomic Impact of Land Grabs in Africa." *Third World Quarterly* 34 (9): 1532–1557.

Peluso, Nancy Lee. 1992. *Rich Forests, Poor People: Resource Control and Resistance in Java*. Berkeley: University of California Press.

Perelman, Michael. 1984. *Classical Political Economy: Primitive Accumulation and the Social Division of Labor*. Totowa, NJ: Rowman & Allanheld.

Prause, Louisa, and Philippe Le Billon. 2021. "Struggles for Land: Comparing Resistance Movements against Agro-industrial and Mining Investment Projects." *Journal of Peasant Studies* 48 (5): 1100–1123.

Roy, Raja Devasish. 1995. "Land Rights, Land Use and Indigenous Peoples in the CHT." In *Bangladesh: Land, Forest and Forest People*, edited by Philip Gain, 49–100. Dhaka, Bangladesh: Society for Environment and Human Development (SEHD).

Roy, Raja Devasish. 1997. "The Population Transfer Programme of 1980s and the Land Rights of the Indigenous Peoples of the CHT." In *Living on the Edge: Essays on the CHT*, edited by S. Bhaumik, Meghna Guhathakurta, and S. B. Raychaudhury, 167–208. Kathmandu, Nepal: South Asia Forum for Human Rights.

Roy, Rajkumari Chandra Kalindi. 2000. *Land Rights of the Indigenous Peoples of the Chittagong Hill Tracts, Bangladesh*. IWGIA Document No. 99. Copenhagen: International Work Group for Indigenous Affairs (IWGIA). https://www.iwgia.org/images/publications/0128_Chittagong_hill_tracts.pdf.

Rudé, George. 1964. *The Crowd in History. A Study of Popular Disturbances in France and England 1730–1848*. New York: John Wiley & Sons.

Sampat, Preeti. 2015. "The 'Goan Impasse': Land Rights and Resistance to SEZs in Goa, India." *Journal of Peasant Studies* 42 (3–4): 765–790.

Scott, James C. 1985. *Weapons of the Weak: Everyday Forms of Peasant Resistance*. New Haven, CT: Yale University Press.

Scott, James C. 1986. "Everyday Forms of Peasant Resistance." *Journal of Peasant Studies* 13 (2): 5–35.

Silverman, Sydel. 1979. "The Peasant Concept in Anthropology." *Journal of Peasant Studies* 7 (1): 49–69.

Turton, Andrew. 1986. "Patrolling the Middle-Ground: Methodological Perspectives on "Everyday Peasant Resistance." *Journal of Peasant Studies* 13 (2): 36–48.

Vijayabaskar, M. 2014. "The Politics of Silence." In *Power, Policy and Protest: The Politics of India's Special Economic Zones*, edited by Rob Jenkins, Lorraine Kennedy, and Partha Mukhopadhyay, 305–330. New Delhi: Oxford University Press.

Walker, Kathy L. M. 2008a. "From Covert to Overt: Everyday Peasant Politics in China and the Implications for Transnational Agrarian Movements." *Journal of Agrarian Change* 8 (2–3): 462–488.

Walker, Kathy L. M. 2008b. "Neoliberalism on the Ground in Rural India: Predatory Growth, Agrarian Crisis, Internal Colonization, and the Intensification of Class Struggle." *Journal of Peasant Studies* 35 (4): 557–620.

Wolf, Eric R. 1959. *Sons of the Shaking Earth*. Chicago: University of Chicago Press.

CHAPTER 37

LAND IS A HUMAN RIGHT

PRISCILLA CLAEYS, LORENZO COTULA, JÉRÉMIE GILBERT, CHRISTOPHE GOLAY, MILOON KOTHARI, AND VERÓNICA TORRES-MARENCO

Introduction

The commodification of natural resources, and especially the conversion of land into a product that can be bought, sold, leased, or exchanged on markets, is one of the founding characteristics of capitalism (Bernstein 2010). Marx and Polanyi, for example, showed that the enclosure of land played a key role in the development of capitalism in England in the sixteenth and seventeenth centuries (Roudart and Mazoyer 2015; Vergara-Camus 2012). Today, an increasing proportion of the land and common resources on which rural communities depend is being commoditized. This historical process of commodification is far from complete, however. In many parts of the world, the establishment of private property rights on the land, enshrined in law and enforced by the state, is not yet a reality. It is challenged by social actors, particularly in the rural South but also in the North (Transnational Institute 2013).

The pressures on the land seem more numerous every day, as the result of urbanization, tourism, industrialization, financialization, mining, or conservation. Land has also been transformed into an opportunity for transnational investment, as shown by the growing number of large-scale land acquisitions, a phenomenon widely documented since the 2007–2008 food crisis and reinforced by the financialization of agriculture (Bourke Martignoni et al. 2022; Gironde, Golay, and Messerli 2015; Margulis, McKeon, and Borras 2013). States have played an active role in this process, often facilitating the appropriation of nature through legislative reforms to encourage companies, pension funds, and other states to invest in land (Künnemann and Monsalve Suárez 2013; Cotula 2020b).

The growing agrarian crisis fueled by the failure of land reform measures, corporate takeover of lands, privatization of basic services, increase in development-based displacement, and the dispossession of small-scale farmers has contributed to land issues becoming a central social justice and human rights problem (Gilbert 2013; De Schutter 2010). Over the last few decades, a growing range of actors have documented and denounced land issues from a human rights perspective (Golay and Biglino 2013). The climate crisis is compounding these trends: land degradation and soil erosion are leading to important changes in land use and land cover, adding to the well-documented impacts of extreme weather events such as droughts and floods, and threatening land-based livelihoods such as pastoralism and small-scale farming.

Responses to climate change are also exacerbating pressures on land, for example, in the form of renewable energy or carbon-credit projects. Many transnational corporations have made net-zero emissions pledges but remain embedded in the fossil fuel economy. To reach their zero targets, these companies are adopting so-called nature-based solutions—ranging from planting trees to increasing carbon storage in agricultural soils and closing off forests. These solutions ultimately seek to integrate the carbon-storage capacity of nature into corporate profit chains and turn nature and carbon into financial assets (Friends of the Earth International 2022). There is growing evidence that many land-based mitigation responses, such as afforestation or reforestation or carbon-offsetting projects, generate competition for land, and lead to land conversion and displacements of other land uses (IPCC 2019), threatening the human rights of those living on and off the land.

In response, a range of social movements, civil society organizations (CSOs), and scientists are pushing for sustainable land-management practices, agroecology, and the protection of the collective rights of local communities, highlighting the key roles these communities play for ecological restoration and stable and resilient carbon storing. Human rights have been central in these advocacy strategies.

This chapter explores and unpacks the land and human rights nexus from both a historical and a normative perspective. Its main argument is that the international human rights community has moved from exploring the articulation of land with a range of human rights (OHCHR 2015), to establishing and codifying land as an individual and collective human right. It looks at the development of key international instruments that have gradually led to the recognition of land as a new human right. The chapter presents some of the main dimensions of the human right to land and how it is protected in international human rights law, with a view to clarifying its normative content. It does not seek to be an exhaustive treatment of the topic but discusses what the protection of the right to land looks like for local communities. The term "local communities" refers to those whose livelihoods depend on land and related natural resources (UN Human Rights Council 2009; Clarke 2015; Kanosue 2015). It also points to future challenges for the realization and implementation of the right to land, with an emphasis on forced evictions and displacements, gender equality, and land investments and transnational corporations.

As scholars dedicated to the recognition, protection, and defense of the human right to land, we are committed to clearly distinguishing "land as a human right" from the broader term "land rights" that is often used by both state and non-state actors, in different policy and legal contexts and instruments. The term "land rights" encompasses all the specific rights related to land, such as ownership, tenancy, and usufruct, whether under national law or customary systems. An individual peasant or local community, for example, can have a range of important land rights, such as the right to own the land or the right to access a forest or grazing areas. It can also have certain protections (and obligations) as tenants. Land rights can provide an important avenue for protecting the connection between people and land, because they are usually embedded in legal and policy frameworks at national level, with their associated safeguards. Yet land rights constitute only some aspects of the human right to land, which comprises other elements and entitlements, as will be shown.

In our view, a human-rights-based approach to land brings other perspectives to the value of land, giving it social, cultural, and ethical dimensions and more importantly, recognition as a fundamental right. It takes the emphasis away from considering land as a commodity or an exclusively commercial good (Gilbert 2013) and insists on its social function (Cotula 2022). It affirms that land is not only a valuable economic asset but also a source of identity and culture. It promotes and protects the right of local people to use, own, and, most importantly, control the developments undertaken on their own lands (Gilbert 2013). It provides a powerful mobilizing frame for local, national, and transnational movements that are engaged in struggles to defend and control lands and territories (Claeys 2015). It is a tool for re-establishing a political limitation on "absolute private property" (Vergara-Camus 2012). As suggested by FIAN International, the explicit recognition of a human right to land also makes it possible to question the legal doctrines inherited from the colonial era (which grant states the almost absolute power to dispose of the soil and do not effectively protect informal or customary land rights), as well as to pursue political reforms aimed at promoting the privatization and commodification of the land such as titling programmes (FIAN International 2009). If the human right to land is well articulated at the international and regional levels and invoked by social actors in land-related struggles, then this right can influence land legislation and land reforms at the national level (Golay 2020b; Gilbert 2013; Cotula 2022).

For this reason, we will consistently refer to the human right to land here, to designate the bundle of individual and collective rights, freedoms and entitlements, and related state territorial and extraterritorial obligations that together give substance to land as human right. We will also refrain from using the term "rights to land," which tends to be used as an equivalent to land rights, creating further confusion.

The chapter is organized in three main sections: Part 1 discusses land and human rights from a historical perspective. Part 2 explores the emergence of the human right to land from below, leading to its recognition in various international instruments, with a focus on UN Declarations, Principles, and Guidelines. Part 3 points to some challenges for the realization of the human right to land.

Part 1: Land and Human Rights from a Historical Perspective

Even though there is no specific right to land enshrined in the International Bill of Human Rights (Universal Declaration of Human Rights, International Covenant on Civil and Political Rights, and International Covenant on Economic Social and Cultural Rights), several other rights have been interpreted to protect some of the main elements of the right to land. Based on positive interpretations of the rights to property, life, food, housing, water, culture, and health, international human rights bodies have developed a substantive jurisprudence that recognizes the importance of protecting land. Similarly, recognizing the indivisibility and interdependence of all human rights, international treaty-monitoring bodies have engaged in the discussion about land rights relying on civil and political rights, as well as economic, social, and cultural rights, which has also led to a rich and evolving jurisprudence. The prohibition of discrimination in access to property proclaimed under the International Convention on the Elimination of All Forms of Racial Discrimination (ICERD) has also been a strong anchor in efforts to protect and promote Indigenous Peoples' land rights. More recently, the Human Rights Committee protected peasants' land rights through a progressive interpretation of the right to be protected against the arbitrary or unlawful interference with their homes (as recognized in Art. 17 of the ICCPR). Furthermore, acknowledging the essential role land plays in the realization of a range of socioeconomic rights, the UN Committee on Economic, Social and Cultural Rights (CESCR) in 2022 adopted General Comment No. 26 to clarify the obligation of states with respect to land-related covenant rights (UN Committee on Economic, Social and Cultural Rights 2022). These normative developments have not happened in a vacuum. They have been shaped by transnational legal mobilizations—the use of the law "from below" by agrarian social movements, as Part 2 of the chapter highlights. These developments have also greatly benefited from the work of key special rapporteurs and UN committees within the UN human rights system. The continued work of the UN Independent Commissions of Inquiry, most recently, the Commission on South Sudan and the Commission on Palestine and Israel, is also important. At the regional level, the Inter-American Court of Human Rights has adopted several decisions on Indigenous Peoples' land rights based on their right to property, a recognition of the collective, cultural, and spiritual nature of land rights. Land has also been recognized as an important element in fulfilling the rights to housing and food and to practice religion, as adjudicated by the African Court on Human and Peoples' Rights. This section addresses some of these influential normative developments. It explores land in relation to the rights to food, housing, property, and economic, social, and cultural rights.

Land as a Component of the Right to Food

Access to land and security of tenure have long been described as key components of the right to food. In 2004, when states adopted the right to food guidelines at the Food and

Agriculture Organization of the United Nations, they recognized that the right to food protects the right of rural communities to access productive resources or the means of food production, including land (FAO 2004, guideline 8).

In two reports, presented in 2002 and 2010, the first two special rapporteurs on the right to food emphasized the need to guarantee access to land and security of tenure, including through agrarian reform, to ensure the right to food of rural communities (UN General Assembly 2002, 2010). Both reports underlined that access to land is essential for most of the people suffering from hunger, who often work as smallholder farmers or agricultural laborers, because the land they have is not sufficient or is otherwise inadequate. They also underlined that women and Indigenous Peoples enjoy special protections in international law. In March 2010, in response to a proliferation of large-scale land acquisitions, the special rapporteur on the right to food, Olivier De Schutter, submitted a report to the Human Rights Council in which he described the phenomenon and its causes and presented a set of human rights principles applicable to large-scale land acquisitions and leases (UN Human Rights Council 2009). In his 2010 report to the General Assembly, De Schutter recommended that international human rights bodies consolidate the right to land, and clarify "the issue of land as a human right." The special rapporteur also called on states to implement land redistribution programs in places with high concentrations of land ownership (UN General Assembly 2010).

Land as a Component of the Right to Housing

As noted by the first UN special rapporteur on the right to housing, land as an entitlement is often an essential element necessary to understand the degree of violation and the extent of the realization of the right to housing. In several reports and statements, the special rapporteur stressed that land is a critical element of the right to housing (Kothari 2020). Inadequate housing is often the consequence of being barred from access to land and common property resources. Inequitable land ownership patterns and landlessness give rise to interrelated problems ranging from inadequate housing, lack of livelihood options, poor health, hunger, and food insecurity to acute poverty. In several of these reports, the special rapporteur also stressed the need to recognize the link between the right to housing and women's rights to land, property, and inheritance (UN Commission on Human Rights 2001, 2002, 2005a, 2005b, 2006; UN Human Rights Council 2007).

International human rights instruments have made the link between the right to housing and land rights since 1991. The link has been established in General Comments from the CESCR on adequate housing and on forced evictions. The inseparable connection between the right to adequate housing and land is also reflected in "Basic Principles and Guidelines on Development-based Evictions and Displacement" (hereafter, the UN Evictions Guidelines) (UN Human Rights Council 2007, Annex 1) and in the "Guiding Principles on Security of Tenure for Urban Poor"—developed by the UN special rapporteurs on the right to housing (UN Human Rights Council 2013).

There is extensive recognition and substantiation, in the context of forced evictions and displacement, of the right to land in the UN Evictions Guidelines. In the section

"Implementation of State Obligations" (para. 16), the UN Evictions Guidelines stress the need for states to refrain from confiscating lands if doing so does not contribute to the enjoyment of the right to land, which can include implementing land reform or redistribution for the benefit of vulnerable persons, groups, or communities. Paragraph 25 of the UN Evictions Guidelines also urges states, in the context of providing legal protection against forced evictions, to take immediate measures to confer legal security of tenure on all those who do not have formal titles to home and land. The UN Evictions Guidelines (para. 26) stress, with the imperative of equal enjoyment of human rights, that such titles to housing and land are conferred on all women.

In the section of the UN Evictions Guidelines on the human rights safeguards required "Prior to Evictions" (para. 43), states are urged to ensure that evictions do not result in individuals becoming homeless. States must take all appropriate measures to ensure that alternative housing and access to productive land is made available to those evicted.

In the section "Compensation" (para. 60), the UN Evictions Guidelines stipulate that cash compensation should under no circumstances replace real compensation in the form of land and common property resources. The UN Evictions Guidelines state that in situations where land has been taken, the evicted should be compensated with land of commensurate quality, size, and value, or better. Paragraph 61 urges that compensation should accrue to all those who are evicted irrespective of whether they hold title to their property. Paragraph 63 urges states, in the context of estimating economic damage, to take into consideration the loss of land plots and the losses that would have accrued from lost wages and incomes. The UN Evictions Guidelines call for compensation to be disaggregated based on gender and on impact and loss assessment to account for the value of business losses, equipment and inventory, livestock, land, trees and crops, and lost or decreased wages or income.

Since being acknowledged by the UN Human Rights Council in 2007, the UN Evictions Guidelines have increasingly been used by a range of actors across the world. They have been relied on for continued human rights standard-setting based on the importance of the right to land. Some of the examples are included in the set of core principles put forward by the UN special rapporteur on the right to food regarding large-scale land acquisitions (UN Human Rights Council 2009), by the UN special rapporteur on the right to housing regarding security of tenure (UN Human Rights Council 2013), by the UN Committee on the Elimination of Discrimination against Women in its General Recommendation No. 34 articulating the rights of rural women to housing and land (CEDAW 2016), and, most recently, by the CESCR in its General Comment on land. The guidelines are also used extensively in manuals, handbooks, and technical- and human rights–education training material by numerous UN agencies, national and international civil society groups, and independent institutions (Kothari 2021).

The Right to Property as a Basis to Advance Land Rights

In several cases, the Inter-American Court on Human Rights has interpreted the right of Indigenous Peoples to property as implying the obligation of the state to recognize, delineate, and protect their land as collective property, especially so that they can continue to have access to their own means of subsistence (Golay and Cismas 2010; Mackay 2007).

In 2001, for example, in *Mayagna (Sumo) Awas Tingni Community v. Nicaragua*, the Court protected the access of some one hundred families of the Awas Tingni community to their ancestral lands, which were threatened by a concession the government of Nicaragua had awarded to a Korean company (Inter-American Court on Human Rights 2001). The Court ruled that the state must adopt positive legislative, administrative, or other measures, with the full participation of the community and in accordance with its values and customary law, to delineate, demarcate, and recognize the property titles of this community.

In 2006, the Court protected the right to property of the members of the Sawhoyamaxa Indigenous community against the lack of protective measures taken by the government of Paraguay (Inter-American Court on Human Rights 2006). The Court determined that the state must take legislative, administrative, and other necessary measures to ensure that the members of the community might enjoy, formally and physically, their ancestral lands.

This approach has also been adopted by both the African Commission and the African Court on Human and Peoples' Rights in two decisions concerning Indigenous Peoples in Kenya, where the court highlighted the connection between Indigenous peoples' right to property and their right to land (Gilbert 2017). This was first established in the case *Endorois Welfare Council v. Kenya* (2010), which took into account the jurisprudence of the Inter-American Court of Human Relations, including the Mayagna (Sumo) Awas Tingni Community case, referenced above. The case was important because it was the first time that the African Commission recognized Indigenous Peoples' rights to their ancestral lands under the African Human Rights System.

However, the very concept of property can contrast with Indigenous conceptions of the relationship between humans and nature (Gilbert 2022), and there are questions about whether, in the longer term, the property framing and court orders to the state to demarcate and title collective lands might ultimately compound the commodification of resources that human rights activists seek to resist (Cotula 2020a).

Land in Relation to Economic, Social, and Cultural Rights: General Comment No. 26

In December 2022, the CESCR adopted General Comment No. 26 on land and economic, social and cultural rights (GC26), following eight years of discussions. The

CESCR begins by highlighting the close relationship between various economic, social, and cultural rights and land, with a focus on the rights to food, housing, and water and to take part in cultural life. It further, for the first time in a general comment, links land to other rights of the Covenant such as the rights to health and to self-determination (paras 6–11). All these rights are now framed as "Covenant rights related to land" (paras 22, 26, 32) or "land-related rights of the Covenant" (para. 59).

Some of the elements inserted in the GC26 suggest an endorsement of a right to land by the CESCR, while putting more emphasis on a rights-based approach to land. First, the GC26 addresses the typology of state obligations to "respect, protect and fulfil" nationally and extraterritorially, as it ordinarily does in its general comments. On this occasion, though the GC26 does not explicitly refer to a particular right, it develops a framework of specific obligations of states parties' to the Covenant in a land-related context. One outstanding element is the obligation of states to respect, protect, and fulfill "access to, use of and control over land," when this is necessary to guarantee the aforementioned Covenant rights. These entitlements, especially the control over land, have been consistently endorsed by scholars and civil society organizations as a central element of a human right to land, and we welcome their inclusion in this general comment.

Second, the GC26 pays special attention to particularly affected and discriminated groups such as women, Indigenous Peoples, and peasants. Land is recognized to be a pivotal resource for women that allows them to meet their subsistence needs, access goods and services, engage in political participation, become more independent, and limit their exposure to violence. The central importance of land for the livelihoods of both Indigenous Peoples and peasants is also recognized and, deriving from this, their definition as holders of the right to land (paras 13–19). The GC26 also highlights the impact of forced evictions and displacement on the enjoyment of the land-related rights of the Covenant. In addition, it acknowledges the particular risk faced by human rights defenders, especially those engaged in land and environmental protection (paras 48–50, 54). The need to ensure that states effectively implement policy and legal frameworks related to land and Covenant rights, and that they provide effective remedies is considered crucial in this context (paras 59–61).

However, the GC26 fails to explicitly recognize the existence of the right to land as a stand-alone human right, which is a missed opportunity. We also regret the rather weak reference to the impact of climate change on access to land and rights holders, which could have gone further in addressing the links between land-based mitigation and adaptation and human rights. We further lament the lack of attention paid in the GC26 to urban land users, whose rights are not addressed, despite their being identified as one of the groups most impacted by long-term trends in high demand for land and urbanization, especially persons living in poverty in urban areas (para. 2). Despite these limitations, we hope that positive outcomes for the protection of the human right to land will nonetheless result from the adoption of GC26.

Part 2: The Recognition of the Human Right to Land

Over the last fifteen years, several important international human rights instruments have recognized the right to land as a stand-alone human right, giving it greater visibility and protection than could have been by simply highlighting the importance of access to land or land rights in the realization of other human rights, such as the rights to food, housing, or property. While these instruments have predominantly emanated from the human rights system in the form of UN Declarations, other UN bodies have contributed to the development of human- rights-based international norms relevant to the right to land, such as the UN Committee on World Food Security (CFS). As discussed below, the CFS makes global policy recommendations that are not legally binding but nevertheless have considerable impact thanks to the participatory way in which they are elaborated—notably, because the negotiation process involves representatives of affected constituencies and relies on consensus building among CFS participants (Claeys and Duncan 2019). This section discusses the relevance of the 2007 UN Declaration on the Rights of Indigenous Peoples (UNDRIP), the 2012 CFS Voluntary Guidelines on the Responsible Governance of Land, Fisheries and Forest (VGGT), and the 2018 UN Declaration on the Rights of Peasants. These instruments have contributed to the international recognition of the right to land as an individual and collective human right and to the rise of local communities as subjects of international law.

Conceptualization of the Right to Land "from below"

The normative developments of the right to land as described in detail here have been shaped by the progressive engagement of social movements with human rights as an emancipatory ideal. A distinctive aspect of the historical development of the human right to land is its emergence "from below" (Claeys 2015; Franco and Monsalve Suárez 2018; Cotula 2022): that is, rather than in a top-down diplomatic process, its normative content was directly shaped by the advocacy of peasants, migrants, women, Indigenous Peoples, and farmworkers. Transnational agrarian movements have insisted that international legal instruments should recognize that land is an essential part of the life, identity, and culture of rural communities and, as such, a foundational dimension of international human rights law.

The conceptualization "from below" is particularly evident in the case of the United Nations Declaration on the Rights of Peasants and Other People Working in Rural Areas (UNDROP), an international instrument directly championed by agrarian movements through local-to-global advocacy over several years (Claeys 2018). But "from below" also describes the long-standing engagement of civil society actors and social movements in international policy arenas where the right to land has been discussed, whether at the regional or global levels, such as the Civil Society and Indigenous Peoples Mechanism (CSIPM) of the CFS.

The dialogue between human rights experts, social movements, diplomats, and NGOs has helped to identify important limitations in the approach taken by UN human rights bodies to develop the right to land—that is, to see land, not as a stand-alone right, but as a key dimension of several internationally recognized human rights. For example, the right to property can protect peasants' land rights, including those based on customary systems, but landed elites have often invoked the same right when trying to prevent redistributive reforms. To address these limitations, organizations of peasants, Indigenous Peoples, and other people working in rural areas have long advocated for a more explicit and progressive recognition of the right to land. Their engagement has directly shaped the content of the right to land.

The Right to Land in the UN Declaration on the Rights of Indigenous Peoples (UNDRIP)

Coming from the most diverse places of the planet, Indigenous Peoples have approached international and regional human rights institutions to gain support for the recognition of their fundamental right to land and territories. Although Indigenous Peoples are among the world's most diverse populations, most Indigenous cultures share a similar deep-rooted relationship with their lands and ancestral territories. For Indigenous communities, the value of land often goes far beyond its economic value. Many have stressed that territories and lands are the basis not only of economic livelihoods but are also the source of spiritual, cultural, and social identity. Control of land and territories is one of the most pressing and significant issues for Indigenous communities, who are suffering from forced displacement, dispossession, and land encroachment. At the national level, there is a general lack of recognition of land rights for Indigenous Peoples, which has forced them to turn to international law to seek protection. International human rights law has therefore been an important legal framework to support Indigenous Peoples' fundamental right to their lands and territories.

In terms of the legal framework, one of the first challenges faced by Indigenous advocates has been the historical lack of recognition of the importance of their right to land under human rights law (Gilbert 2016). There is no specific right to land under the main human rights treaties, and as we have seen, land rights are barely mentioned in human rights norms and instruments. Although there is no specifically recognized universal human right to land, Indigenous rights activists and representatives have pushed the human rights system to change to integrate their fundamental rights to land and territory. This has materialized in two forms: first, by the positive interpretation of other relevant human rights, such as the rights to property, food, housing, and cultural rights (as discussed earlier); and second, through the development of a specialized body of norms concerning Indigenous Peoples' right to land.

The second approach emerged through the development of norms that are specifically recognizing and protecting Indigenous Peoples' right to land, notably UNDRIP, adopted in 2007 by the UN General Assembly. UNDRIP focuses a lot of its attention on the right to land of Indigenous Peoples, with more than half of its articles relating to this right. It notably affirms that "indigenous peoples have the right to own, use, develop and control the lands, territories and resources that they possess by reason of traditional ownership or other traditional occupation or use, as well as those which they have otherwise acquired" (art. 26). It also highlights that states shall give legal recognition and protection to these lands, territories, and resources, and recognize the customs, traditions, and land tenure systems of the Indigenous Peoples concerned. The significance of the right to land is embedded throughout UNDRIP; several articles highlighting its significance in terms of cultural rights, rights to the environment and spiritual and religious and cultural heritage. UNDRIP also puts great emphasis on the connection between land management and the rights of Indigenous Peoples, notably the right to free, prior, and informed consent.

The adoption of UNDRIP marks an important moment because it universally proclaims and recognizes the importance of the right to land for Indigenous Peoples. Although it is not strictly binding because it is a declaration, it reflects and integrates the evolution of the jurisprudence and customary norms developed under more general international human rights instruments. As such, it offers a comprehensive legal framework regarding Indigenous Peoples' right to land under international human rights law. There are, nonetheless, debates about the legal value of UNDRIP—over whether it is only "soft law" or more binding—as well as debates on whether it has reached the level of customary international law (Barelli 2009). Despite these debates, UNDRIP has been increasingly used in litigation and the jurisprudence of courts and human rights bodies (Allen and Xanthaki 2011). In terms of the contents of the right to land within UNDRIP, there is also an issue regarding its temporal application. Indeed, UNDRIP recognizes that for many Indigenous Peoples, the connection to land is ancestral and historical, opening the door to complex issues of restitution and reparations—an issue which is often very controversial with states, especially in former settler-colonized states (Lenzerini 2008).

The Right to Land in the Voluntary Guidelines on the Responsible Governance of Tenure of Land, Fisheries, and Forests (VGGT)

The Voluntary Guidelines on the Responsible Governance of Tenure of Land, Fisheries and Forests in the Context of National Food Security (VGGT) are the first global instrument to provide comprehensive guidance on land and resource governance. The CFS unanimously endorsed the guidelines on May 11, 2012, after two years of multistakeholder consultations and one year of intergovernmental negotiations (CFS 2012; Munro-Faure and Palmer 2012; Seufert 2013).

While the initiative to develop the VGGT was not intended to be a response to transnational land-based activities, its timing coincided with a global surge in large-scale land deals for agribusiness plantations, particularly around a spike in food prices spike in 2007–2008, which triggered widespread concerns about "land grabbing" and compounded public support for a new international instrument on land governance that would highlight the strong connections between land and human rights (Seufert 2013; Cotula 2017).

As highlighted above, the VGGT promote governance reform through multistakeholder dialogue and political consensus, rather than binding norms. But while the guidelines are not legally binding, they enjoy considerable legitimacy derived from the consultative process that led to their development and to subsequent expressions of high-level political support, including from the UN General Assembly and the G20. Some VGGT provisions—such as on gender equality and respect for human rights—reflect binding international law (CFS 2012; Cotula 2017).

As a negotiated text, the VGGT reflect diverse concerns ranging from social justice to land-market efficiency (Franco and Monsalve Suárez 2018). The VGGT take a holistic approach to the governance of natural resources, covering fisheries and forests, as well as land, and the guidelines explicitly link resource governance to realizing human rights and achieving food security. The VGGT call on states to recognize, respect, protect, promote, facilitate, and enforce all "legitimate tenure rights." This emphasis on legitimate tenure rights partly reflects the key demands of social movements during the negotiations (FIAN International 2011). It means that, alongside rights created or acquired through formal procedures ("legal" tenure rights), policy and practice should recognize and respect rights that have social legitimacy—for example, by virtue of customary use or the fairness of land acquisition. In line with this approach, the VGGT call on states to recognize, respect, and protect socially legitimate tenure rights "not currently protected by law" (CFS 2012, para. 4.4, see also paras 5.3, 7.1).

Even though the emphasis on legitimate tenure rights means that the VGGT are more relevant to land rights than to the human right to land per se, the guidelines do explicitly link land to human rights, and as such, they embody an important step forward to recognizing a right to land, while also providing insights, at least indirectly, about how to further clarify the normative content of that right. For example, various VGGT provisions relate the guidelines' overarching policy goal to the realization of the right to food; reiterate the human rights obligations of states and reaffirm the responsibility of businesses to respect human rights; and clarify the relationship between land and human rights in wide-ranging contexts, including private sector investment (see, e.g., CFS 2012, paras 1.1, 2.2, 3.2, 3B.1, 3B.4, 4.1, 4.3, 4.8, 4.9, 9.3, 12.4, 12.6, 12.8, 16.7, 16.9). In addition, the framing of the VGGT's guiding principles (sect. 3A) closely mirrors the human rights obligations to respect, protect, and fulfill. The VGGT's call for states to recognize, respect, and protect all legitimate tenure rights, including those that are not currently protected by law, resonates strongly with international human rights law, which protects Indigenous Peoples' right to their ancestral lands even in the absence of legal recognition under domestic law; while VGGT provisions on restitution and redistribution (CFS 2012, sects 14, 15) connect to the redistributive aspects of the right to land.

Although the notion of legitimate tenure rights provides a flexible concept that can cater to diverse land and resource claims, it is also vulnerable to abuse—for example, where public authorities do not recognize the legitimacy of certain forms of landholding or use, such as those of pastoralists or shifting cultivators (Touré 2018; Nguiffo, Kenfack, and Mballa 2009; Lavigne Delville et al. 2002). The VGGT call on states to identify the legitimate tenure rights in a given context through participatory processes (e.g., para. 4.4). They also explicitly discuss certain types of rights as legitimate tenure rights, including rights held by "indigenous peoples and other communities with customary tenure systems," women, pastoralists, and tenants (e.g., CFS 2012, para. 9.4).

Based on these foundational concepts, the VGGT provide more detailed guidance on specific issues such as land tenure reform, land restitution, land redistribution, land-based investments, and land administration. Regarding land-based investments, for example, the VGGT affirm the responsibilities of businesses to do no harm, to comply with national law and applicable international treaties, to respect human rights and legitimate tenure rights, to safeguard against environmental damage and tenure dispossession, to work in partnership with local tenure right holders, and to strive to contribute to policy objectives such as poverty eradication, food security, and sustainable resource use (CFS 2012, paras 3.2, 12.4, 12.12).

The VGGT guidelines have provided an international benchmark not only for states to reform their laws, policies, and institutions, but also for social movements to pioneer new rights-based approaches and hold governments accountable (Franco and Monsalve Suárez 2018; Sandwell et al. 2019). Monitoring these emerging and evolving practices over time can provide insights not only on the effectiveness of soft-law instruments in driving change but also on the place of rights constructs in land governance.

The Right to Land in the UN Declaration on the Rights of Peasants and Other People Working in Rural Areas (UNDROP)

The UN General Assembly adopted UNDROP in 2018, after almost twenty years of mobilization by the transnational agrarian movement La Via Campesina and its allies (Golay 2019). Peasant movements and organizations of other rural communities, including fishers, pastoralists, and agricultural workers, demanded that UNDROP be adopted to rebalance power relations in rural areas and to push states to respect, protect, and fulfill the human rights of peasants and other people working in rural areas (Golay 2020b). In its mission to strengthen these rights, which were only partially recognized in international human rights law before 2018, UNDROP addresses a number of fundamental questions, including the right to land, which is central for billions of people (Nyéléni Europe and Central Asia Platform for Food Sovereignty 2020). In endorsing a broad definition of rights-holders in its article 1, UNDROP recognizes that peasants and other people working in rural areas are made of socially differentiated classes and sectors that may in turn have differentiated access to land (Claeys and Edelman 2020).

UNDROP recognizes the right to land (and other natural resources, including water bodies, coastal seas, fisheries, pastures, and forests) for non-Indigenous Peoples and communities for the first time in international human rights law (CETIM 2014; FIAN International 2021; Golay 2020a, b). Its articles 5 and 17 provide that this right can be exercised individually and/or collectively, and that it includes freedoms and entitlements: freedom from discrimination; protection against forced eviction, displacement, and land exploitation; and entitlements to agrarian reform and to conservation and sustainable use of land and other natural resources (Golay 2020b, 2020a). These articles also provide that landless peasants, young people, small-scale fishers, and other rural workers should be given priority in the allocation of public lands, fisheries, and forests, and that the natural commons and their related systems of collective use and management shall be recognized and protected (Errico and Claeys 2019). Combined with article 4, these articles define important elements of the right to land of rural women, who shall be empowered and enjoy this right without discrimination (Golay 2020b).

UNDROP's article 17 provides that the right to land includes the right of peasants and other people working in rural areas to have access to, sustainably use, and manage land and other natural resources to achieve an adequate standard of living, to have a place to live in security, peace, and dignity and to develop their cultures.

UNDROP provides that all states, UN agencies, international and regional organizations shall contribute to its implementation. Civil society organizations and social movements, including peasant organizations, should also support UNDROP's implementation. Activities that these actors shall undertake to promote UNDROP and protect the right to land include raising awareness about UNDROP, fighting forced evictions and displacements, protecting land rights defenders, pushing for agrarian reform, pushing for the recognition of peasants and their communities as rights holders, pushing for the recognition of states and regional and international organizations as duty bearers, and calling for more accountability mechanisms while using existing ones (Golay 2020b).

In 2019, the UN Human Rights Committee was the first UN treaty body to refer to UNDROP in an individual case, in its decision in *Portillo Cáceres and Others v. Paraguay* (UN Human Rights Committee 2019; Golay 2020a, b, c). Portillo Cáceres and members of his family are peasants engaged in family farming in Paraguay. They live in a community that received land under the agrarian reform program in 1991. They sent a communication to the UN Human Rights Committee in 2016, claiming that the massive use of agrochemicals (pesticides and insecticides) in nearby large plantations had poisoned several of them, led to the death of their relative Ruben Portillo Cáceres, and polluted their land and other natural resources. In its decision, the UN Human Rights Committee found violations of Cáceres family members' rights to life, privacy, family, and home, and to an effective remedy. It explained that Portillo Cáceres and members of his family depend on their crops, fruit trees, livestock, fishing, and water resources for their livelihoods. It added that they have a special attachment to and dependency on the land, using the words of and referring to UNDROP's article 1. It concluded that these elements can be considered to fall under the scope of "home"—that is, the place where a person resides or carries out his or her usual occupation. Because the pollution has caused direct repercussions for the Cáceres family's crops, fruit trees, livestock, fishing, and water resources, their right to privacy, family, and home had been violated.

In December 2019, several UN human rights experts called the UN Human Rights Council to create a new special procedure to monitor UNDROP, and they committed to protect the rights enshrined in UNDROP, to integrate UNDROP's implementation in the exercise of their mandates, and to provide guidance to states on how they can implement UNDROP (UN Human Rights Independent Experts 2019). They also underlined that special measures shall be taken by states and other stakeholders to protect human rights defenders of the land, environment, and natural resources—who are the first victims of criminalization, intimidation, and attacks against their physical integrity and life—and that their safety must be prioritized and protected via all available mechanisms (UN Human Rights Independent Experts 2019).

Like UNDRIP, UNDROP offers a comprehensive legal framework regarding peasants' right to land under international human rights law that can be used by various actors at all levels. In the future, one of the challenges is going to be reconciling and ensuring synergies between UNDROP and UNDRIP, notably in situations involving potential clashes between peasants and Indigenous Peoples (Bessa and Gilbert 2022).

Part 3: Challenges for the Realization of the Right to Land

Despite important advances in the protection of the right to land through international instruments, local communities continue to face major challenges. Here we explore some of these challenges, with a focus on forced evictions and displacements, the gender dimensions of the right to land, and the impacts of corporate forms of land control led by transnational corporations.

The Right to Land and Forced Evictions and Displacements

The failure of many states to enshrine in law and policy the human rights to land, food, housing, and related rights at domestic level makes people and communities vulnerable to forced evictions and displacements. Globally, the trend to evict communities in the name of city beautification, urban renewal, industrialization, conservation, and development-based activities, including mining or the building of dams and other infrastructure, has been accelerating (Kothari 2015).

States continue to use their powers, often given to them by national law, of "eminent domain"—that is, the power to appropriate private property for public use, to force people to give up their lands and homes. The exercise of eminent domain and the cynical use of the doctrine of public purpose for private benefit has become common across the world. Formal laws that give states the power of eminent domain are also used to override claims to land and natural resources that are protected by the "customary rights" that, for example, Indigenous Peoples, claim (Ramanathan 2009). Groups that are not holders of legally recognized property rights are disproportionately impacted by evictions and displacements—Indigenous Peoples, peasants, pastoralists, fisher folk, nomads, and urban dwellers.

As we have seen, in the early 2000s, the UN special rapporteur on the right to housing led a process to draft the UN Evictions Guidelines (UN Human Rights Council 2007) to establish a universal standard that, by protecting rights to housing, land, and related rights, could put the brakes on the unfettered, speculative use of land and property. The UN Evictions Guidelines are today a key global operational tool to control and monitor the practice of forcibly evicting and displacing people from their homes and land. They protect people's and communities' human rights in the processes before, during, and after evictions, displacement, and resettlement, and the role of local governments is seen as critical in all three stages (before, during, and after evictions). The UN Evictions Guidelines also call on states to actively monitor and carry out evaluations to determine the consequences of evictions.

Yet fifteen years after the adoption of the guidelines, the continued implementation of neoliberal policies based on large-scale infrastructure projects in both urban and rural areas, the continued commodification and financialization of homes and land, and development- and conservation-based displacement continues across the world. The unwillingness to implement the human rights to housing and land, which could counter the neoliberal approach, further exacerbates the crisis and continues to take decision-making about what happens to land and land-based resources out of the hands of local people and communities.

The Right to Land from a Gender and Intersectional Perspective

Women have long been excluded from formal land rights and from participating in communal land governance (Razavi 2009). In response, feminist collectives within agrarian social movements have campaigned for the full integration of gender equality and women's rights into the policies and legal instruments designed to guarantee the human rights to food, land, work, and social security (Desmarais 2003). Despite important advances, there is still a long way to go. The UNDROP, for example, is an important achievement for rural people, because it explicitly recognizes the human rights to land, seeds, and food sovereignty. Yet, it fails to recognize a number of crucial issues for women and gender equality (Bourke Martignoni and Claeys 2022). First, UNDROP fails to recognize women's right to equality in marriage and family relations and women's sexual and reproductive health and rights. Second, UNDROP is silent on the disproportionate burden of unpaid reproductive and agricultural labor performed by women (Shah and Lerche 2020). Third, it does not recognize gender identity and sexual orientation as grounds for discrimination. And finally, it fails to acknowledge patriarchy as a source of violence and structural oppression against women and nature. The failure of UNDROP to directly address these issues robs this new international instrument of much of its political power.

Despite these shortcomings, UNDROP can be interpreted progressively, because it prohibits any kind of discrimination, including on the basis of sex and marital status (art. 3.1), and it provides that states "shall take appropriate measures to eliminate conditions that cause or help to perpetuate discrimination, including multiple and intersecting forms of discrimination, against peasants and other people working in rural areas" (art. 3.3). This explicit recognition of intersectionality is unique in an international human rights instrument.

Further, UNDROP article 4 reasserts the need to ensure women's substantive equality (art. 4). In that regard, it follows a similar approach to UNDRIP, which recognizes the rights of Indigenous women and children to "enjoy the full protection and guarantees against all forms of violence and discrimination" (art. 22.1). Although UNDRIP does not specifically mention the right of women to land, UNDROP emphasizes states' obligation to take "appropriate measures to remove and prohibit all forms of discrimination relating to the right to land" (art. 17.2). UNDROP also provides that states "shall ensure that peasant women and other women working in rural areas enjoy without discrimination all the human rights and fundamental freedoms set out in the present Declaration and in other international human rights instruments, including the rights: "[t]o equal access to, use of and management of land and natural resources, and to equal or priority treatment in land and agrarian reform and in land resettlement schemes" (art. 4.2(h)).

One promising avenue for a progressive interpretation of UNDROP is to build on CEDAW's interpretive General Recommendation (GR) no. 34 on the rights of rural women, which was elaborated in parallel to UNDROP and adopted in 2016 (CEDAW 2016).

GR no. 34 recognizes rural women's right to land as a fundamental human right, and it articulates several issues that are important to consider in promoting this human right (para. 56). First, it highlights the importance of identifying and redressing the "negative and differential impact" of trade liberalization, privatization, and the commodification of land and natural resources on rural women' rights. Second, it insists on the importance of enacting temporary special measures to achieve substantive gender equality in inheritance and user rights over land, including communal lands. Special measures can also be implemented to increase women's participation in political and public service. Guidance provided by the VGGT can also be useful in defending, promoting, and protecting women's right to inherit land. Indeed, guideline 4.6 highlights that states "should ensure equal tenure rights for women and men, including the right to inherit and bequeath these rights," which goes beyond UNDROP. Third, it points to the need to guarantee women's sexual and reproductive health and rights. Fourth, it recalls the obligations of states and other duty-bearers to redress the disproportionate burden of unpaid care and agricultural work performed by women. Fifth, in guideline 80, in the context of the need for strong measures to protect women against evictions from their homes and lands, it urges states to adopt measures that are in line with international standards, including the UN Evictions Guidelines.

GR no. 34 is more progressive than CEDAW (adopted in 1979), which advances women's rights within the confines of mainstream gender-equality policies and legal frameworks without advocating for radical or systemic change (Bourke Martignoni 2018). In contrast, GR no. 34 provides useful guidance for a feminist and progressive interpretation and implementation of UNDROP. Several transnational agrarian movements and human rights organizations, such as La Via Campesina and FIAN International, have developed training materials based on UNDROP and GR no. 34 (FIAN International 2020). In their publications, these organizations call for policies and legislation that acknowledge the intersection of patriarchy, race, social class, age, ability, and sexual orientation. Indeed, discrimination can affect all aspects of social and political identity (gender, race, class, sexuality, disability, age, etc.) and the way they overlap, or "intersect." Applying an intersectional approach is key to promoting and defending women's right to land, because this makes it possible to assess how multiple forms of oppression come together to create new types of discrimination and inequality and then take measures to address these. Applying an intersectional approach is also a powerful tool to address discrimination based on gender identity and sexual orientation (Gioia 2019).

The Right to Land and Transnational Corporations

Transnational corporations (TNCs) often lead and organize production and trade through global value chains (Gereffi, Humphrey, and Sturgeon 2005). Within these networks the TNCs select the types of business relationships that define the types of governance of the value chain and determine the level of control over the activities they exercise within the value chain. For this reason, it is important to consider, not only the direct land impact of foreign direct investment (FDI), but also the more indirect impacts arising from corporate-driven value chain relations and transformations, which make them one of the major drivers of violations of the right to land.

The kind of business relationships a TNC elects to engage in will vary depending on the business itself. In the case of land-related businesses, such as those in the extractive industry and agricultural production, TNCs have traditionally selected FDI relationships because they entail more direct control over land and subsoil resources.

However, TNCs have also engaged in other forms of land control besides FDI. These involve business relationships such as contract farming, where land control is realized through contractual arrangements that tie producers and production forms to specifications that are dictated by a lead firm (Borras et al. 2012) and, in a more sophisticated way, via arrangements governing control over technology and markets (Ribot and Peluso 2003). Through these processes, TNCs can control the value chain, including land, and therefore benefit from this resource (Torres-Marenco 2019).

Within this context, large-scale land-based investments for export-oriented activities can also be associated with food-crop importation (e.g., in the case of mining but also several cash crops); reduced support for locally grounded agriculture and increased land concentration; food insecurity; environmental contamination; land dispossession and displacement; harassment; impoverishment; and murders and forced disappearances.

Also impacting the right to land is the phenomenon known as the "financialization of land," which is especially linked to the corporate agriculture sector but also has growing relevance in the context of climate change adaptation and mitigation—notably, through "nature-based solutions" and carbon markets. This phenomenon consists of financial actors such as banks and investment funds taking ownership of land and companies throughout the agri-food sector, and prioritizing shareholder returns over agricultural production decisions linked to the land itself, their local environment, and their workers (Wegerif and Anseeuw 2020). This trend is changing the use of land as a productive resource to its use as a new asset class, where investors can diversify, protect, and increase their portfolios (Margulis et al. 2013; Wegerif and Anseeuw 2020; Clapp and Isakson 2018). Such a phenomenon is considered to have led to speculation on commodity prices, corporate concentration, land inequality and concentration, agricultural land grabbing, and insecurity over the long term about the social and ecological sustainability of food and agriculture (Bourke Martignoni et al. 2022; Anseeuw and Baldinelli 2020; Clapp and Isakson 2018; Clapp 2012).

This reality negatively impacts the right to land of local communities because they face not only issues of land deprivation, including changes in access to, use of, and control over land, but also wider issues concerning their human rights. These violations are even more concerning because the regulation of both processes—corporate-driven value chains and the financialization of land—is made more difficult by their complex structures and transnational character.

The adoption of human rights instruments addressing the activities of TNCs has remained on the international agenda since the 1970s. However, despite the magnitude of their impact on human rights, resistance to allocating human rights obligations to businesses has prevailed. For this reason, the approach to tackling human rights abuses in this context remains state-centric. This was reflected in the UN Guiding Principles on Business and Human Rights (UNGPs), a benchmark soft-law instrument endorsed in 2011 by the Human Rights Council, which developed the framework "protect, respect and remedy" and clarified distinct but complementary responsibilities: states have a duty to protect, and businesses have the responsibility to respect human rights. Access to effective remedy is primarily a duty of the state, which should provide both judicial and nonjudicial grievance mechanisms. Businesses should also establish operational-level grievance mechanisms for identifying adverse human rights impacts and facilitating early, direct remediation of those by the business entity. Access to an effective remedy is considered essential to ensure protection from human rights violations linked to businesses. However, this aspect of the UNGPs has faced some criticism and challenges, including a charge that the text gave preference to developing nonjudicial over judicial grievance mechanisms as it allocated major attention to the "effectiveness criteria" for the former (Deva and Bilchitz 2013); that there exist major barriers for victims wanting to access judicial mechanisms (Skinner et al. 2013); that there remains a lack of implementation of corporate grievance mechanisms, as well as any key criteria for their development (Martin and Bravo 2016); and that the UNGPs' effectiveness criterion is insufficient to measure an effective remedy (Wielga and Harrison 2021).

Since the endorsement of the UNGPs, the practice of human rights bodies has broadly followed the language of the framework "respect, protect and remedy" when discussing the human rights responsibilities of businesses; this is evidenced by CESCR General Comment No. 24 on States Obligations in the Context of Business Activities (UN Committee on Economic, Social and Cultural Rights 2017), the IACHR report on business and human rights (Inter-American Commission on Human Rights 2019), and the drafting of a Binding Treaty on Business and Human Rights (OEIGWG Third Revised Draft 2021). These address how states should domestically regulate the responsibility of businesses to respect human rights and the access to effective remedy based on the legally established general obligation to protect—including that of an extraterritorial nature—according to current human rights standards. And though all these instruments recognize that the impact of businesses often disproportionally affects local communities, none of them elaborate further on a right to land. Until recently, the CESCR General Comment No. 26 on Land and Economic, Social and Cultural Rights (2022) linked business activities to "land-related Covenant rights" by extending the standards of the CESCR General Comment No. 24 to this context (UN Committee on Economic, Social, and Cultural Rights 2022).

By clarifying the accountability of TNCs for human rights violations in their operations and supply chains, these instruments can address concerns linked to the right to land in the context of business activities. Measures taken to implement them could have a significant bearing on land issues. The range of relevant measures is broad and would include, for example, establishing effective human rights due-diligence legislation and accountability mechanisms that cover violations of the right to land in connection with the conduct of a given business or issues associated with its supply chain, both within and outside the jurisdiction of the relevant state (GC24 paras 32, 33; GC26 paras 30, 42). It would also include integrating a consideration of human rights, and specifically the right to land, into any support provided to business activities overseas, including, for example, in the form of development finance institutions; considering the right to land, the right to development and other human rights of the communities in decision-making related to negotiating international economic agreements (Inter-American Commission on Human Rights 2019, para. 45); abstaining from entering into trade or investment agreements that might affect the realization of human rights (GC24 paras 13,

29), for instance, ensuring they do not have an adverse impact on access to productive resources in other countries (GC26 para. 45); and paying special attention to the rights of land defenders and the serious risks they often face in advocating against violations of the right to land in the context of business activities.

In more systemic terms, the IACHR Report called on states to prevent land grabbing and situations of land concentration that would jeopardize the enjoyment of human rights; and the Commentary to the UNGPs recalled the need to clarify the governance of access, ownership, and use of land and to guide businesses on how to effectively consider issues of gender, vulnerability, and marginalization (at p. 3). Furthermore, General Comment No. 26 prescribes that states, in the context of land acquisitions, should ensure that the acquisition or lease of land by land investors does not violate international norms and guidelines or deprive local communities of access to the land they depend on for their livelihoods (GC26 para. 43). Several instruments call on states to ensure equitable access to productive resources (GC24, for example), while also preventing forced evictions (UNGPs, p. 12; GC24 paras 11–12; GC26 para. 27). International instruments also call on states to pay special attention to vulnerable groups such as Indigenous Peoples, Afro-descendant communities, peasants, and other people working in rural areas, including in the context of their participation, prior consultation, and free, prior, and informed consent to business-related processes.

The fact that none of the existing international instruments on business and human rights is legally binding hampers implementation and the ability to ensure effective remedies for violations. Social movements representing local communities in the Global South have strongly criticized the nonbinding character of the UNGPs and expressed disappointment over the progress and emerging outcomes in the negotiations on the Binding Treaty on Business and Human Rights, which have thus far failed to impose human rights obligations directly onto businesses (Campaña Global 2020). The proposed Binding Treaty on Business and Human Rights has been criticized in connection with its limited "legal teeth" and clarity about assuring accountability and remedies (López 2021). Further, it is not yet clear how the proposed treaty could meaningfully address issues related to the conduct of actors "upstream" of the business activities associated with human rights violations, such as lenders and investment funds. Additionally, regulating due diligence and the accountability of businesses along the value chain has proven inherently difficult owing to the complexity of these networks, as can be seen in the experience with the mandatory due-diligence norms adopted by European states (European Coalition for Corporate Justice 2021). All these factors represent critical challenges that would need to be met in order to address the drivers of violations of the right to land linked to business activities.

Concluding Remarks

The evolution of a human right to land, and the elements that encompass it, has historically been constructed from two complementary perspectives. The first conceptualizes land as a basis for the realization of other human rights, such as the right to food or housing. The second articulates a self-standing, more encompassing, human right to land that has ramifications affecting not only land relations but also the wider frameworks for addressing issues such as territorial control, climate change, and the regulation of business activities. This second perspective, which we support, sees the right to land as an individual and collective human right comprising the rights to access, use, manage, and control land and natural resources. It emphasizes the agency of Indigenous Peoples and local communities, such as peasants, pastoralists, and other small-scale food producers, which the right to land aims to protect. It sees the right to land as closely linked to cultural rights, cultural heritage, and spiritual and religious practices, as has been highlighted in many of the cases brought by Indigenous Peoples; and it argues that the right to land is central to the rights of future generations, as highlighted in the recently adopted Maastricht Principles on the Human Rights of Future Generations (Maastricht Principles, forthcoming).

The effective and progressive realization of the right to land faces many challenges, including the persistence of forced eviction and displacement, gender inequality and discrimination, and the need to redress the increasingly tight control over land by TNCs. In the future, additional research will be needed to document recent and emerging developments that may affect the right to land, and how we should conceptualize it. For example, the climate crisis highlights the need to conceptualize the right to land as a precondition for measures to address climate change and restore ecosystems, challenging the "technofixes" that fail to confront the deeper-level drivers of climate change or even masquerade land grabs as climate policies. Strengthening the right to land can provide a fundamental pillar supporting the rights of future generations by advancing equitable, sustainable, and localized responses to the social and environmental challenges associated with climate change. Another example is the spread of digital technologies in the land sphere—an area where real-life developments have vastly outpaced the elaboration of international guidance or regulations, particularly from a human rights perspective. Developing an understanding of the right to land that can do justice to all these complex challenges, while also providing practical guidance for implementation, will be key in realizing the right to land for both present and future generations.

Acknowledgments

All the authors have contributed equally to this manuscript.

References

Allen, Stephen, and Alexandra Xanthaki, eds. 2011. *Reflections on the UN Declaration on the Rights of Indigenous Peoples*. London: Bloomsbury.

Anseeuw, Ward, and Giulia Maria Baldinelli. 2020. "Uneven Ground: Land Inequality at the Heart of Unequal Societies." Research Findings from the Land Inequality Initiative. November. International Land Coalition. United form land rights, Oxfam.

Barelli, Mauro. 2009. "The Role of Soft Law in the International Legal System: The Case of the United Nations Declaration on the Rights of Indigenous Peoples." *International & Comparative Law Quarterly* 58 (4): 957–983.

Bernstein, Henry. 2010. *Class Dynamics of Agrarian Change*. Agrarian Change and Peasant Studies. Halifax, CAN, and Hartford, CT: Fernwood Publishing and Kumarian Press.

Bessa, Adriana, and Jérémie Gilbert. 2022. "Indigenous Peoples' Rights and the Declaration on the Rights of Peasants: Synergies and Challenges." In *The United Nations' Declaration on Peasants Rights*, edited by Mariagrazia Alabrese, Adriana Bessa, M. Brunori, and P. F. Giuggioli, 32–46. Abingdon, UK: Routledge.

Borras, Saturnino M., Jr., Jennifer C. Franco, Sergio Gómez, Cristóbal Kay, and Max Spoor, 2012. "Land Grabbing in Latin America and the Caribbean." *Journal of Peasant Studies* 39 (3–4): 845–872.

Bourke Martignoni, Joanna. 2018. "Engendering the Right to Food? International Human Rights Law, Food Security and the Rural Woman." *Transnational Legal Theory* 9 (3–4): 400–414. http://doi:10.1080/20414005.2018.1568789.

Bourke Martignoni, Joanna, and Priscilla Claeys. 2022. "Without Feminism There Is No Food Sovereignty? Negotiating Gender Equality in the United Nations Declaration on the Rights of Peasants and Other People Working in Rural Areas." In Alabrese et al., *United Nations' Declaration on Peasants' Rights*, 47–61.

Bourke Martignoni, Joanna, Christophe. Gironde, Christophe Golay, Elizabeth Prügl, and D. Tsikata, eds. 2022. *Agricultural Commercialization, Gender Equality and the Right to Food: Insights from Ghana and Cambodia*. London: Routledge.

Campaña Global. 2020. "Comentarios y modificaciones al segundo borrador revisado del instrumento jurídicamente vinculante sobre las corporaciones transnacionales y otras empresas comerciales en relación con los derechos humanos." https://www.stopcorporateimpunity.org/2do-borrador-revisado-del-tratado-vinculante-declaracion-de-la-campana-global/?lang=es.

CFS. 2012. Voluntary Guidelines on the Responsible Governance of Tenure of Land, Fisheries and Forests in the Context of National Food Security (VGGT). Adopted on 11 May 2012. Committee on World Food Security, Rome.

Claeys, Priscilla. 2015. "The Right to Land and Territory: New Human Right and Collective Action Frame." *Revue interdisciplinaire d'études juridiques* 73 (2): 115–137.

Claeys, Priscilla. 2018. "The Rise of New Rights for Peasants: From Reliance to NGO Intermediaries to Direct Representation." *Transnational Legal Theory* 9 (3–4): 394–397.

Claeys, Priscilla, and Jessica Duncan. 2019. "Food Sovereignty and Convergence Spaces." *Political Geography* 75: Article 102045.

Claeys, Priscilla, and Marc Edelman. 2020. "The United Nations Declaration on the Rights of Peasants and Other People Working in Rural Areas." *Journal of Peasant Studies* 47 (1): 1–68.

Clapp, Jennifer. 2012. *Food*. Cambridge, UK: Polity Press.

Clapp, Jennifer, and Isakson S. Ryan. 2018. "Risky Returns: The Implications of Financialization in the Food System." *Development and Change* 74 (2): 437–460.

Clarke, Alison. 2015. "Property, Human Rights and Communities." In *Property and Human Rights in the Global Context*, edited by T. Xu and J. Allain, 19–39. Oxford: Hart Publishing.

Cotula, Lorenzo. 2017. "International Soft-Law Instruments and Global Resource Governance: Reflections on the Voluntary Guidelines on the Responsible Governance of Tenure." *Law, Environment and Development Journal* 13 (2): 115–133. http://www.lead-journal.org/content/17115.pdf.

Cotula, Lorenzo. 2020a. "Between Hope and Critique: Human Rights, Social Justice and (Re) Imagining International Law from the Bottom Up." *Georgia Journal of International and Comparative Law* 48 (2): 473–521. https://digitalcommons.law.uga.edu/gjicl/vol48/iss2/5/.

Cotula, Lorenzo. 2020b. "(Dis)integration in Global Resource Governance: Extractivism, Human Rights, and Investment Treaties." *Journal of International Economic Law* 23 (2): 431–454. https://academic.oup.com/jiel/article/doi/10.1093/jiel/jgaa003/5875706.

Cotula, Lorenzo. 2022. "The Right to Land." In Alabrese et al., *United Nations' Declaration on Peasants' Rights*, 91–105.

CETIM. 2014. *The Right to Land and Other Natural Resources*. Geneva: CETIM.

De Schutter, Oliver. 2010. "The Emerging Human Right to Land." *International Community Law Review* 12 (3): 303–334.

Desmarais, Annette. 2003. "The Via Campesina: Peasant Women at the Frontiers of Food Sovereignty." *Canadian Women's Studies* 23: 140–145.

Deva, Surya, and Bilchitz, David eds. 2013. *Human Rights Obligations of Business: Beyond the Corporate Responsibility to Respect?* Cambridge, UK: Cambridge University Press.

Errico, Stefania, and Priscilla Claeys. 2019. "Human Rights and the Commons: Exploring Approaches to the Governance of Land and Natural Resources beyond Indigenous Peoples' Rights: The Case of Peasants." *International Journal on Minority and Group Rights* 27 (1) (Dec): 1–33.

European Coalition for Corporate Justice. 2021. "Corporate Due Diligence Laws and Legislative Proposals in Europe." Comparative Table, June 2021. https://corporatejustice.org/wp-content/uploads/2021/07/Corporate-due-diligence-laws-and-legislative-proposals-in-Europe-June-2021.pdf.

FAO. 2004. "Voluntary Guidelines to Support the Progressive Realization of the Right to Adequate Food in the Context of National Food Security (Right to Food Guidelines)." Adopted by the 127th Session of the FAO Council, November. Food and Agriculture Organization of the United Nations, Rome.

FIAN International. 2009. "Recognize Land as a Human Right. Sellout of Agricultural Lands Will Aggravate Food Crisis." Press release, December 10.

FIAN International. 2011. "Civil Society Organizations' Proposals for the FAO Guidelines on Responsible Governance of Land and Natural Resources Tenure." Heidelberg, Germany. https://www.fian.org/fileadmin/media/publications_2015/2011_3_CSOProposals_LandTenureGuidelines.pdf.

FIAN International. 2020. "Cooking up Political Agendas: A Feminist Guide on the Right to Food and Nutrition for Women in Rural Areas." Press release, September 6. https://www.fian.org/en/publication/article/cooking-up-political-agendas.

FIAN International. 2021. "The Right to Land and Other Natural Resources." Heidelberg, Germany: FIAN International.

Franco, Jennifer, and Sofía Monsalve Suárez. 2018. "Why Wait for the State? Using the CFS Tenure Guidelines to Recalibrate Political-Legal Struggles for Democratic Land Control." *Third World Quarterly* 39 (7): 1386–1402.

Friends of the Earth International. 2022. "Double Jeopardy: The Rising Threat to Food Sovereignty and Agroecology from False Climate Solutions." Friends of the Earth International report, November. https://www.foei.org/wp-content/uploads/2022/11/foei-double-jeopardy-full-report-EN-2.pdf.

Gereffi, Gary, Humphrey John, and Sturgeon Timothy. 2005. "The Governance of Global Value Chains." *Review of International Political Economy* 12 (1): 78–104.

Gilbert, Jérémie. 2013. "Land Rights as Human Rights: The Case for a Specific Right to Land." *SUR – International Journal on Human Rights* 10 (18): 115–136.

Gilbert, Jérémie. 2016. *Indigenous Peoples' Land Rights under International Law*. 2nd rev. ed. Leiden, NL; Boston: Brill Nijhoff.

Gilbert, Jérémie. 2017. "Litigating Indigenous Peoples' Rights in Africa: Prospects, Challenges and Limitations." *International & Comparative Law Quarterly* 66 (3): 657–686.
Gilbert, Jérémie. 2022. "The Rights of Nature, Indigenous Peoples and International Human Rights Law: From Dichotomies to Synergies." *Journal of Human Rights and the Environment* 13 (2): 399–415.
Gironde, Christophe, Christophe Golay, and Peter Messerli. 2015. "Large-Scale Land Acquisitions: Focus on South-East Asia." *International Development Policy* 6: 275–292.
Gioia, Paola. 2019. "Coming Out! Gender Diversity in the Food System." *The Right to Food and Nutrition Watch* (11): 6–15.
Golay, Christophe. 2019. *The Implementation of the United Nations Declaration on the Rights of Peasants and Other People Working in Rural Areas*. Geneva: Geneva Academy of International Humanitarian Law and Human Rights.
Golay, Christophe. 2020a. *The Right to Land and Other Natural Resources*. Geneva: Geneva Academy of International Humanitarian Law and Human Rights.
Golay, Christophe. 2020b. *The Right to Land and UNDROP. How Can We Use the United Nations Declaration on the Rights of Peasants and Other People Working in Rural Areas to Protect the Right to Land?*. Geneva and Rome: International Land Coalition and Geneva Academy of International Humanitarian Law and Human Rights.
Golay, Christophe. 2020c. The Role of Human Rights Mechanisms in Monitoring the United Nations Declaration on the Rights of Peasants. Geneva: Geneva Academy of International Humanitarian Law and Human Rights.
Golay, Christophe, and Irene Biglino. 2013. "Human Rights Responses to Land Grabbing: A Right to Food Perspective." *Third World Quarterly* 34:1630–1650.
Golay, Christophe, and Ioana Cismas. 2010. *Legal Opinion: The Right to Property from a Human Rights Perspective*. Geneva: Geneva Academy of International Humanitarian Law and Human Rights, Rights and Democracy.
Inter-American Commission on Human Rights 2019. *Business and Human Rights: Inter-American Standards*. IACHR Report. No. OEA/Ser.L/V/II CIDH/REDESCA/INF.1/19, November 1.
Inter-American Court on Human Rights (IACHR). 2001. *Mayagna (Sumo) Awas Tingni Community v. Nicaragua*. Judgment of August 31, 2001.
Inter-American Court on Human Rights (IACHR). 2006. *Sawhoyamaxa Indigenous Community v. Paraguay*. Judgment of March 29, 2006.
IPCC. 2019. "Summary for Policymakers." In *Climate Change and Land: An IPCC Special Report on Climate Change, Desertification, Land Degradation, Sustainable Land Management, Food Security, and Greenhouse Gas Fluxes in Terrestrial Ecosystems*, edited by P. R. Shukla, J. Skea, E. Calvo Buendia, V. Masson-Delmotte, H.-O. Pörtner, D. C. Roberts et al. https://doi.org/10.1017/9781009157988.001.
Kanosue, Yu. 2015. "When Land Is Taken Away: States Obligations under International Human Rights Law Concerning Large-Scale Projects Impacting Local Communities." *Human Rights Law Review* 15 (4): 643–667.
Kothari, Miloon. 2015. *The Global Crisis of Displacement and Evictions: A Housing and Land Rights Response*. New York: Rosa-Luxemburg Foundation.
Kothari, Miloon. 2020. "The Human Right to Adequate Housing and the New Human Right to Land: Congruent Entitlements." In *The Cambridge Handbook of New Human Rights: Recognition, Novelty, Rhetoric*, edited by Andreas von Arnauld, Kerstin von der Decken, and Mart Susi, 81–96. Cambridge, UK: Cambridge University Press.

Kothari, Miloon. 2021. "The Human Right to Adequate Housing and Land: Guaranteeing the Dignity to Dwell." In *Critical Issues in Human Rights and Development*, edited by Stephen P. Marks, François-Xavier Bagnoud, and Balakrishnan Rajagopal, 213–238. Cheltenham: Edward Elgar.

Künnemann, Rolf, and Sofía Monsalve Suárez. 2013. "International Human Rights and Governing Land Grabbing: A View from Global Society." *Globalizations* 10 (1): 123–139.

Lavigne Delville, Phillipe, Camilla Toulmin, Jean-Phillipe Colin, and Jean-Pierre Chauveau. 2002. *Negotiating Access to Land in West Africa: A Synthesis of Findings from Research on Derived Rights to Land*. London: International Institute for Environment and Development. https://pubs.iied.org/pdfs/9072IIED.pdf.

Lenzerini, Federico, ed. 2008. *Reparations for Indigenous Peoples: International and Comparative Perspectives*. Oxford: Oxford University Press.

Lopez, Carlos. 2021. "The Third Revised Draft of a Treaty on Business and Human Rights: Modest Steps Forward, but Much of the Same." September 3. http://opiniojuris.org/2021/09/03/the-third-revised-draft-of-a-treaty-on-business-and-human-rights-modest-steps-forward-but-much-of-the-same/.

Mackay, Fergus. 2007. "From 'Sacred Commitment' to Justiciable Norms: Indigenous Peoples' Rights in the Inter-American System." In *Casting the Net Wider: Human Rights, Development and New Duty-Bearers*, edited by M. E. Salomon, A. Tostensen, and W. Vandenhole, 371–394. Antwerp: Intersentia.

Margulis, Matias E., McKeon Nora, and Saturnino J. Borras. 2013. "Land Grabbing and Global Governance: Critical Perspectives." *Globalizations* 10 (1): 1–23.

Martin, Jena, and Karen E. Bravo. 2016. *The Business and Human Rights Landscape Moving Forward, Looking Back*. Cambridge, UK: Cambridge University Press.

Munro-Faure, Paul, and David Palmer. 2012. "An Overview of the Voluntary Guidelines on the Governance of Tenure." *Land Tenure Journal* 51 (12): 5–17.

Nguiffo, Samuel, Pierre Étienne Kenfack, and Nadine Mballa. 2009. *The Influence of Historical and Contemporary Land Laws on Indigenous Peoples' Land Rights in Cameroon*. Forest Peoples Programme report, January, Forest Peoples Programme, Moreton-in-Marsh, UK. https://www.forestpeoples.org/sites/default/files/publication/2010/05/cameroonlandrightsstudy09eng.pdf.

Nyéléni Europe and Central Asia Platform for Food Sovereignty. 2020. *Your Land, My Land, Our Land: Grassroots Strategies to Preserve Farmland and Access to Land for Peasant Farming and Agroecology*. Brussels: Nyéléni Europe and Central Asia Platform for Food Sovereignty.

OHCHR. 2015. Land and Human Rights: Standards and Applications. HR/PUB/15/5/Add.1. 2015. United Nations. https://www.ohchr.org/documents/publications/land_hr-standardsapplications.pdf.

OEIGWG (Open-Ended Intergovernmental Working Group) Chairmanship Third Revised Draft. 2021. "Legally Binding Instrument to Regulate, in International Human Rights Law, the Activities of Transnational Corporations and other Business Enterprises." https://www.ohchr.org/Documents/HRBodies/HRCouncil/WGTransCorp/Session6/LBI3rdDRAFT.pdf.

Ramanathan, Usha. 2009. "A Word on Eminent Domain." In *Displaced by Development: Confronting Marginalisation and Gender Injustice*, edited by Lyla Mehta, 133–145. New Delhi: SAGE.

Razavi, Shahra. 2009. "Engendering the Political Economy of Agrarian Change." *Journal of Peasant Studies* 36 (1): 197–226.

Ribot, Jesse, and Peluso Nancy. 2003. "A Theory of Access." *Rural Sociology* 68 (2): 153–181.

Roudart, Laurence, and Marcel Mazoyer. 2015. "Large-Scale Land Acquisitions: A Historical Perspective." *International Development Policy* 6:3–29. https://journals.openedition.org/poldev/2088.

Sandwell, Katie, Angelica Castañeda Flores, Lyda Fernando Forero, Jennifer Franco, Sofía Monsalve Suárez et al. 2019. *A View from the Countryside: Contesting and Constructing Human Rights in an Age of Converging Crises.* Report. Transnational Institute and FIAN International. https://www.tni.org/files/publication-downloads/web_countryside.pdf.

Seufert, Philip. 2013. "The FAO Voluntary Guidelines on the Responsible Governance of Tenure of Land, Fisheries and Forests." *Globalizations* 10 (1): 181–189.

Shah, Alpa, and Jens Lerche. 2020." Migration and the Invisible Economies of Care: Production, Social Reproduction and Seasonal Migrant Labour in India." *Transactions of the Institute of British Geographers* 45 (4): 705–951.

Skinner, Gwynne, Robert McCorquodale, Oliver De Schutter, and Andie Lambe. 2013. *The Third Pillar: Access to Judicial Remedies for Human Rights Violations by Transnational Business.* Report for International Corporate Accountability Roundtable (ICAR), CORE, and the European Coalition for Corporate Justice (ECCJ).

Suárez-Franco, Ana María, and Sandra Liebenberg. 2023. The Maastricht Principles on the Human Rights of Future Generations. In *Spotlight on Global Multilateralism. Perspectives on the future of international cooperation in times of multiple crises*, edited by Edgardo Bilsky et al., 59–63. Bonn/Geneva: Global Policy Forum Europe. https://www.globalpolicy.org/sites/default/files/Maastricht%20Principles_final.pdf

Torres-Marenco, Verónica. 2019. "A Human Right to Land for Local Communities: A Proposal in the Context of Transnational Corporations' Control of Land Use." PhD thesis, University of Greenwich, United Kingdom.

Touré, Oussouby. 2018. *Sécurisation du foncier pastoral en Afrique de l'Ouest: Des modèles divers et riches d'enseignements.* Report. International Institute for Environment and Development. https://www.iied.org/sites/default/files/pdfs/migrate/17634FIIED.pdf.

Transnational Institute. 2013. *Land Concentration, Land Grabbing and People's Struggles in Europe.* TNI Agrarian Justice Programme, June. Transnational Institute, Amsterdam.

UN Commission on Human Rights. 2001. Report of the Special Rapporteur on the Right to Housing, Mr. Miloon Kothari. UN Doc. E/CN.4/2001/51.

UN Commission on Human Rights. 2002. Report of the Special Rapporteur on the Right to Housing, Mr. Miloon Kothari. UN Doc. E/CN.4/2002/59.

UN Commission on Human Rights. 2005a. Report of the Special Rapporteur on the Right to Housing, Mr. Miloon Kothari. UN Doc. E/CN.4/2005/48.

UN Commission on Human Rights. 2005b. Report of the Special Rapporteur on the Right to Housing, Mr. Miloon Kothari. UN Doc. E/CN.4/2005/43.

UN Commission on Human Rights. 2006. Report of the Special Rapporteur on the Right to Housing Mr. Miloon Kothari. UN Doc. E/CN.4/2006/118.

UN Committee on the Elimination of Discrimination against Women (CEDAW). 2016. *General Recommendation No. 34 on the Rights of rural Women.* UN Doc. CEDAW/C/GC/34, March 4, para. 11.

UN Committee on Economic, Social and Cultural Rights. 2017. "General Comment No. 24 on State Obligations under the International Covenant on Economic, Social and Cultural Rights in the Context of Business Activities." E/C.12/GC/24, June 23.

UN Committee on Economic, Social and Cultural Rights. 2022. "General Comment No. 26 on Land and Economic, Social and Cultural Rights." E/C.12/GC/26, December 22.

UN General Assembly. 2010. Report of the Special Rapporteur on the Right to Food, Mr. Olivier De Schutter, UN Doc. A/65/281.

UN Geneva Assembly. 2002. Report of the Special Rapporteur on the Right to Food, Mr. Jean Ziegler. UN Doc. A/57/356.

UN Human Rights Committee. 2019. *Portillo Cáceres and Others v. Paraguay*. Decision of July 25. UN Doc. CCPR/C/126/D/2751/2016.

UN Human Rights Council. 2007. Report by the Special Rapporteur on the Right to Housing, Mr. Miloon Kothari, UN Doc. A/HRC/4/18.

UN Human Rights Council. 2009. Report of the Special Rapporteur on the Right to Food, Mr. Olivier De Schutter. UN Doc. A/HRC/13/33/Add.2.

UN Human Rights Council. 2013. Report of the Special Rapporteur on the Right to Housing, Ms. Raquel Rolnik. UN Doc. A/HRC/25/54.

UN Human Rights Independent Experts. 2019. "Statement at the Occasion of the First Anniversary of the Adoption of the UNDROP." December 19. Geneva: Office of the High Commissioner for Human Rights.

United Nations Office of the High Commissioner for Human Rights. 2011. Guiding Principles on Business and Human Rights: Implementing the United Nations "Protect, Respect and Remedy Framework." UN Doc. A/HRC/17/31. Geneva and New York. https://www.ohchr.org/sites/default/files/documents/publications/guidingprinciplesbusinesshr_en.pdf

Vergara-Camus, Leandro. 2012. "The Legacy of Social Conflicts over Property Rights in Rural Brazil and Mexico: Current Land Struggles in Historical Perspective." *Journal of Peasant Studies* 39 (5): 1133–1158.

Wegerif, Marc, and Ward Anseeuw. 2020 "Unearthing Less Visible Trends in Land Inequality." International Land Coalition, United for Land Rights, University of Pretoria.

Wielga, Marc, and Harrison James. 2021. "Assessing the Effectiveness of Non-state-based Grievance Mechanisms in Providing Access to Remedy for Rightsholders: A Case Study of the Roundtable on Sustainable Palm Oil." *Business and Human Rights Journal* 6 (1): 67–92.

CHAPTER 38

LAND STRUGGLES AND WORKING PEOPLE

JENNIFER C. FRANCO AND
SATURNINO M. BORRAS JR.

INTRODUCTION

> If there are agrarian questions of labour today, I believe that understanding and assessing them should be disciplined by some important qualifications, in contrast to more enthusiastic (triumphalist?) celebrations of popular struggles over land. First, such struggles do not have the same structural or world-historical significance as the agrarian question of capital, once central to conceptions of the transition to capitalism. Second, it is not helpful to regard land as the definitive political question and terrain of struggle of a (globalized) semi-proletariat, as some do . . . Third, it is even more misleading to regard popular struggles over land as a replay in contemporary conditions of the epic peasant movements and struggles of previous epochs, or as representing a dynamic of "re-peasantization" (other than in terms of an ideological yearning).
>
> —Henry Bernstein (2006, 456)

As land is grabbed for different forms of capital-intensive agriculture or for nonlabor absorbing industries, real estate or mining; divided up with each generation; or relinquished in the face of unfavorable agricultural policies in a globalized food system, increasing proletarianized or semiproletarianized agrarian populations can have decreasing faith that there will be buyers for their labor power. Struggles over means of both production and social reproduction remain as important as ever but are not playing out in remotely the same way as Marx predicted. Land remains an important focus of such struggles, even if its precise significance remains fiercely debated. Such struggles are also, Marxists increasingly

> recognize, inextricably bound up with non-class forms of power and domination, whether patriarchy, racism, casteism, or anti-immigrant nativism. Keeping in mind the extreme geographical variation in these trends, these are roughly the coordinates that define agrarian change and politics in the early twenty-first century.
>
> —Levien, Watts, and Yan (2018, 876)

Broad agrarian-ecological transformations are shaped by the politics of land in many ways, and vice versa. In the context of contemporary capitalism, such transformations are necessarily global. In critical agrarian studies (Edelman and Wolford 2017; Akram-Lodhi et al. 2021; Borras 2023), land politics has usually been considered within the context of agriculture's contribution to national development, which, in turn, is generally assumed to be industrial development in the context of capitalist development. This is the neoclassical economics assumption spelled out in the *World Development Report 2008: Agriculture for Development* (World Bank 2007). It is also the context of debates in Marxist agrarian political economy that underpin the overlapping but slightly different formulations by Bernstein and by Levien, Watts, and Yan in the opening quotations. In radical political economy (Marxist and the so-called agrarian populist, and hybrid versions of the two), one of the interesting areas of discussion concerns the fragmentation of classes. This is demonstrated by what we find in today's capitalist societies—namely, shrinking numbers of what we might call iconic full-time farmers or the industrial proletariat. In their place, we see households fighting for survival by combining different strategies and sources of livelihoods and increasing mobility in multiple sites of production and social reproduction along the rural-urban and agriculture-industry continuum, with some sites crossing national borders. These households face persistently precarious work and living conditions, most without healthcare and old-age pensions, and are frequently unable to secure the most basic level of care, such as food, clothing, and shelter/housing. Bernstein used the concept of "classes of labour," whereas Shivji uses a reconceptualized term *working people* to refer to this latest development among the working class and peasants in global capitalism (Bernstein 2006; Shivji 2017).

Generally subsumed in this way within the broader framing of agriculture's contribution to capitalist industrial development, land politics in classical agrarian studies was largely dealt with in the context of land in the sphere of production—that is, land for farmland, pasture, industrial forestry, and so on. Policy interventions were framed and pursued to make land serve its purpose in capitalist industrial development, and land policies usually took the form of "land reform" or "agrarian reform." Cristóbal Kay (this volume) has revisited this generation of land policymaking and the literature linked to it (see also Kay 2002). These policies have been significantly marginalized in the era of neoliberalism, which sees them as too state interventionist and coercive and advocates instead for voluntary, "willing seller–willing buyer" types of land reform (Deininger 1999). Nevertheless, there are still important currents among agrarian social movements that fight for classical redistributive land reform.

A consequence of this dominant perspective is that in agrarian studies land policy and politics have generally been framed in the context of agricultural rural land, and almost solely in the context of the Global South. Land struggles of the working class are thus interpreted as struggles, mainly by peasants, for land reform or agrarian reform (and, more recently, the struggles for ancestral land by Indigenous Peoples) in the Global South. The great peasant wars of the twentieth century as studied by Eric Wolf (1969) and Barrington Moore Jr. (1967) were generally located in this kind of framework. Agrarian struggles for land reform have persisted during the neoliberal era, but much reduced in extent and intensity and no longer taking place within a broader setting of armed revolutionary war. Nevertheless, there have been some dramatic national land movements and cases, such as the landless movement in Brazil (Wolford 2010) and the fast-track land reform of the 2000s in Zimbabwe (Moyo and Yeros 2005; Scoones 2010), as well as the less dramatic but still significant land reformism of the 1990s in the Philippines (Franco 2011).

The vast majority of land struggles today are quite different from the land struggles of the past, not only in terms of their intensity and breadth, but also in terms of the orientation and character of the social forces that support, or oppose, these struggles. In many ways, Bernstein's (2006) observation is correct—it is "misleading to regard popular struggles over land as a replay in contemporary conditions of the epic peasant movements and struggles of previous epochs" (456). We also agree with Bernstein that land is not the "definitive political question and terrain of struggle" for working people today (456).

Nevertheless, we would argue the following: (a) If we compare pockets of contemporary struggles for classical land reform in the Global South with the epic land struggles of the twentieth century or earlier, the current examples are indeed far less significant in character, intensity, and extent; and (b) struggles for land by working people today have become multisited and multiscalar, with a diverse character and an orientation that partly reflect the spatial characteristics of today's working people. Thus, important struggles are no longer restricted to agricultural land in the Global South but are far more diverse across the rural-urban, agricultural-nonagricultural continua. Classical formulations by rural land movements around agrarian reform remain important, but their overall share in global land struggles is less significant. Ultimately, we feel that the character, intensity, and extent of contemporary land struggles are not, and should not be, compared with or cast in the mold of the epic land struggles of the past, and that it is important to map, examine, and understand land struggles today as they unfold and to weigh the significance of each on its own terms.

The observation of Levien, Watts and Yan (2018) serves as an inspiration and guide for us: "Struggles over means of both production and social reproduction remain as important as ever, but are not playing out in remotely the same way as Marx predicted. Land remains an important focus of such struggles, even if its precise significance remains fiercely debated," they write, concluding, "Keeping in mind the extreme geographical variation in these trends, these are roughly the coordinates that define agrarian change and politics in the early twenty-first century" (876).

Context for Changing Land Issues

What is the overall shape of global land issues today, and what are the processes that have shaped it? Land has never left the agenda of mainstream economics. In fact, under neoliberalism, land has become an even more important focus of economic policy intervention, but in sharply contrasting ways to the conventional land-reform-centered framework discussed above and retraced by Kay (this volume). Neoclassical economists are preoccupied with how to transfer and transform land uses and land users from "less efficient" to "most efficient possible," ideally without much intervention from the state but, rather, through market mechanisms. Thus, the formalization of property rights has become a key pillar in the neoliberal push to transform land relations worldwide (Deininger and Binswanger 1999). This push was already underway when multiple crises in the world converged in the 2000s and pulled land back to center stage in development debates and policymaking in an era of global land grabbing (Zoomers 2010; Peluso and Lund 2011).

Crises around food prices, energy and fuel, climate, and finance have converged; debates on how to respond to them have erupted. One influential current coming from neoclassical economics, the corporate world, and central states is seen in the assumption or claim that part of the solution to these multiple crises lies in the existence of lands that are framed as marginal, under-utilized, empty, and available and in the notion that mobilizing these resources to address the crises can invigorate rural economies worldwide (Deininger 2011). The main idea is to respond to the crises more efficiently by using these lands to produce commodities (for example, food or biofuels) via climate-smart agriculture, and by demarcating and securing carbon sinks. This can, purportedly, be done without displacing local communities precisely because this land is assumed to be empty or under-utilized. This assumption, and the associated call to action, ushered in and provided the justification for the global land rush. Although the proponents of this mainstream approach acknowledge the many problems with large-scale land deals in terms of both processes and outcomes, they believe the problems can be managed by applying win-win ideas, fostering business and human rights and corporate social responsibility as middle-ground strategies to expand business while respecting human rights and promoting poor people's livelihoods. Hence, we have seen a proliferation of voluntary corporate self-regulating initiatives, including the Roundtable for Responsible Palm Oil and many others, and widespread manipulation of the spirit and intent of the Free, Prior and Informed Consent (FPIC) mechanism (Franco 2014). Such initiatives have partly legitimized ongoing corporate and nation-state land grabbing and opened the door for others to follow suit.

The land area targeted by this global land rush might have been in the past larger than most estimates suggest (Borras et al. 2022). It is also likely that elements of the land rush (land grabs, land enclosures, land deals, large-scale land investments, pin-prick land accumulation—see Borras and Franco forthcoming) will continue to gain momentum, now that land-oriented solutions to climate change have been popularly adopted in the Conference of the Parties processes of the United Nations Framework Convention on Climate Change (Franco and Borras 2021), among other drivers of the land boom.

Largely because of the global land rush, the wider politics of land is back in the global spotlight. The mainstream view that frames the current dynamics of global land grabbing builds on two mutually reinforcing narratives that are firmly anchored in both neoclassical economics and new institutional economics—namely, that particular types of agrarian production systems, land users, and land uses (peasant farming, especially swidden agriculture; mobile pastoralism; and artisanal fishing), many of which encompass customary tenure arrangements (Peters, this volume), are economically inefficient and ecologically destructive.

The first claim, that the institutions of access to and control over land and the orientation and organization of production in peasant and pastoralist societies are economically inefficient, has allowed the efficiency argument to become one of the most powerful narratives used to justify, implicitly or explicitly, the contemporary global resource rush. It suggests that though the peasant and pastoralist economy may be able to help poor rural villagers self-provision, it will not be able to feed a growing world population that has become largely urban. The second persistent claim maligns some rural production systems as ecologically destructive. In the past, mainstream conservation organizations and central states launched campaigns to delegitimize and illegalize traditional practices of mobile farming, livestock raising, artisanal fishing, and forest dwelling. They deployed schemes based on rehashed versions of sedentary farming and ranching, often promising to grant private land titles to entice communities to agree. Such campaigns have resulted in livelihood disruption and displacement in rural communities from Southeast Asia to sub-Saharan Africa to Latin America. But many farming and pastoralist communities have resisted and persisted. Today, in an effort to resurrect old tactics, the mainstream narrative has found a new justification in the climate change mitigation and adaptation discourse. Shifting cultivation, for example, is being framed as one of the causes of climate change and, therefore, as a production system that must be stopped.

The narratives that peasant and pastoralist production is economically inefficient or ecologically destructive are powerful. Increasingly, the two criticisms are becoming fused, justifying the claim that it is necessary to seize resources (land, water, forests) from poor rural communities (Franco and Borras 2019; Paprocki 2019). In the context of political claims about land, this recent development has altered the basis for redistributive land policies. Conventional land reform is based mainly on the redistribution of large, landed estates to previously landless or near-landless peasants to create a mass of small family farms or state farm collectives, or both, and it is largely framed as a question of economic and productive efficiency (Griffin, Khan, and Ickowitz 2002). The new context builds on conventional land reform but goes far beyond it, as we will now explore.

Although the land rush is largely focused on acquiring some form of land control, the logic that drives it now involves diverse institutional mechanisms that go beyond straightforward land grabbing through violent coercion to include such arrangements as joint ventures and contract farming (Oya 2012). Similarly, the current land rush is no longer only about land for agriculture, because the contested lands now include nonagricultural rural lands, such as Indigenous Peoples' territories and rural spaces. These lands are coveted for a variety of purposes, including as sites of housing and climate change mitigation and adaptation initiatives, such as hydropower dams, wind farms, and carbon sequestration, and to meet a surging interest in urban agriculture and community green spaces (Dunlap 2018; Torres Contreras 2021). Some frame this current agrarian transformation within the context of extractivism (McKay et al. 2021). We argue that many of the issues that arise are old issues taking place in new contexts, and others are new issues cast in old contexts.

Diversified Land Issues

The changed structure and institutions of the politics of land, as we have briefly described them here, require researchers to review and rethink the character of land issues and the struggles of working people. One outcome of the transformation of global land politics is that though the relevance of conventional land reform has been reaffirmed, its relative importance has diminished. Contemporary land issues can be clustered into four categories, of which conventional land reform, which might be expressed as *rural/agricultural in the South and North* is only one (type I). In academic agrarian studies research, this category demonstrates the relevance of political economy perspectives that focus on understanding dynamics of agrarian transformation that have been brought about by the penetration of capitalism into the countryside (see Bernstein, this volume).

The remaining categories (types II, III, and IV), which have arguably always existed but were never key themes in agrarian studies, have become more relevant and gained in relative importance. The category *rural/nonagricultural/South and North* (type II) has become, or should become, an equally compelling area for academic research and political action. The type II category is related to a wide array of climate change mitigation and adaptation initiatives and issues—notably, the dramatic expansion of nonagricultural neoliberal conservation and carbon-sequestration initiatives; the resurgence of hydropower projects and solar and wind farms; the massive expansion of "no dwelling zones" in areas deemed "fragile" due to climatic change; and land in the broader context of social reproduction, including land for home lots, home gardens, and so on (see Shah and Lerche 2020; Borras et al. 2022; Cousins, this volume). The sheer number of rural people directly affected by these policies and initiatives, and the logic that underpins them, demand the full incorporation of this category into critical agrarian studies.

The issue of rural-urban, agriculture-industry links (Kay 2009) has remained relevant; and recent developments have rendered it even more central in classical agrarian studies and critical agrarian studies (Borras 2023; Pattenden 2023), albeit in a significantly revised way. Recent demographic changes and patterns of capital accumulation have altered some of the traditional urban-rural links and flows, including those related to land, labor, dwelling, food, water, forests, the environment, and finance. The rural and urban categories have never been as blurred as they are now, and the same can be said about the politics around rural-urban links. Moreover, and even more importantly, the rural-urban corridor has become the key site of productive and social reproductive activities for many sections of the "classes of labor" or working people (Bernstein 2006; Shivji 2017; Borras et al. 2022; Pattenden 2023). The categories *urban/agricultural/South and North* (type III) and *urban/nonagricultural/South and North* (type IV) have thus become important in their own right, as capital attempts to seize as many resources and spaces and as much labor as it can to further the processes of accumulation, and as working people bring some aspects of agrarian practices into urban spaces (McClintock 2014; Jacobs 2018; Siebert 2020). Over the past two decades, we have seen an explosion of land conflicts worldwide that take place in urban and peri-urban areas, involving both agricultural and nonagricultural issues.

Traditionally, the main antagonism in the countryside, as framed in classical agrarian studies, existed between the peasants and the landowning classes (or the state, representing the landed interest) and was principally centered on agriculture and broader issues of national economic development. Today, antagonisms rooted in land are more plural and diverse. In many societies the landowning classes, including latifundistas and agribusiness plantation owners, remain entrenched and represent the key reactionary classes. But the current context has brought in other social forces that are equally, if not more, vicious. These include new corporate land grabbers, both transnational and domestic; cross-border noncorporate but pervasive individual land buyers, such as big farmers, brokers, renters, scammers, swindlers, and a "land mafia" (Sud 2014; Levien 2021); financial entities, including pension funds (Clapp 2014; Fairbairn 2014, 2020; Isakson 2014); the use of hypermodern digital technology in land and food systems (Fraser 2019); an array of nontraditional agricultural investors, ranging from auto companies to livestock processors; and big-time conservationists (Brockington and Duffy 2011; Arsel and Büscher 2012). Most of the targeted lands are being claimed by the central state, turning the state into a key land broker that enables and facilitates land grabs and often deploys extra-economic coercion (Wolford et al. 2013; Andreas et al. 2020).

In settings where the land is needed but the people are not, as framed by Tania Li (2011), villagers are likely to be expelled from their land. This is especially relevant amid the rise of contemporary plantations of various types (Hall, Scoones, and Tsikata 2017; Li and Semedi 2021), and has inspired a surge of multidisciplinary interest in plantation life, leading some to frame the issue from a "plantationocene" perspective (Wolford 2021). But capital is not committed to a particular mechanism or form of land control as long as a venture generates profit. Thus, land dispossessions may be caused by market relations, alongside a variety of other mechanisms for grabbing control that often involve extra-economic coercion (Grajales 2011; Levien 2018). For example, rural villagers may not be expelled from their land but may be subsumed in the emerging capitalist enterprises instead.

All of the foregoing dynamics have revived old and engendered new axes of political conflict, and generated a range of political reactions from below (Adnan 2013; Borras and Franco 2013; Hall et al. 2015). When land deals hit the ground, they impact already socially diverse and differentiated communities. They affect different social groups in different ways, provoking political reactions that have multiple complex, often contradictory dynamics in terms of class and co-constitutive axes of difference: race, ethnicity, caste, gender, generation, religion, and nationality (see, e.g., Gyapong 2019).

The political dynamics in the four categories we have just described are all fundamentally about the politics of land but cannot be subsumed in the conventional land politics narratives or political agitations of the past. Although the old ways of asking questions are still relevant, new ways are also required. Some have argued for broadening and deepening the thematic scope of critical agrarian studies to include fields that are not usually considered to be integral to it, such as pastoralism (Scoones 2021), migration and migrant farmworkers (Corrado, de Castro, and Perrotta 2016), labor (Oya 2013), and economic production and social reproduction (Shah and Lerche 2020; Pattenden 2023; Cousins, this volume). And though the classic tools of analysis remain relevant, tools that are yet to be imagined or created are urgently needed if we are to have a better understanding of the meanings and implications of what is happening on the global land front. The majority of progressive agrarian movements frame land struggles within the conventional struggles for "agrarian reform," with some additional stress on "territory" (Rosset 2013). This is of fundamental importance. But even the best-organized contemporary national movements remain largely focused on type I (rural/agricultural) issues.

Broadening the Fronts for Struggles for Land

The changing context of land politics has far-reaching implications for how we should frame the land issues and struggles of working people in contemporary global capitalism (Edelman 2024). As a result of the changed global context, social-justice movements that have an interest in land issues are no longer limited to those of farmers who are calling for agrarian reform in order to establish smallholder-based family farms. Rather, we are witnessing the emergence of social movements that reflect the changing character of the politics of land and social life. Capitalist penetration into the countryside takes diverse forms and uses new mechanisms, including those that are discursively linked to climate change imperatives, such as big-conservation initiatives; flex crops and commodities; and expansion of the urban and peri-urban sprawl for residential, commercial, and industrial real estate, tourism enclaves, and so on. This, in turn, has provoked reactions from a range of social groups and classes confronted by a variety of land issues, reactions that are in part manifested in the emerging political mobilizations and contentions around the *rural/agricultural*, *rural/nonagricultural*, *urban/agricultural*, and *urban/nonagricultural* themes in the Global South and Global North.

Rural Agricultural Land Struggles

Agrarian movements rooted in and oriented toward agriculture in the Global South and Global North remain a key type of rural social-justice movement today. As in the past, the mobilizations gravitate to contestations over property and issues of production, but contemporary agrarian movements that are heavily oriented to land reform struggles are comparatively few. There have been national agrarian movements that have had an important, even dramatic, impact in their own national contexts and generated varying degrees of international attention and inspiration (Moyo and Yeros 2005). Some of the coherently organized national land movements in this category include the Movement of Landless Workers of Brazil (Wolford 2010); several land movements in Indonesia (Bachriadi 2010; Lund 2021) and India (Levien 2018); organized and amorphous land claim-makers in Zimbabwe (Moyo 2011); and land movements using a range of claim-making strategies in the Philippines (Franco 2011). There are other countries, such as South Africa, Cambodia, and Ethiopia (Kepe and Hall 2018), where land has been highly contested, but the key protagonists are a combination of NGOs, development institutions, and radical academics rather than highly and coherently organized national peasant movements. There are also countries that do not fit into either of these groups, which have significant levels of participation by fledgling national land movements in political contestations around land but are not (yet) as organized and well-developed. This applies, for example, to Myanmar from 2010 until the military coup in February 2021 (Ra and Ju 2021).

Furthermore, the significant reconcentration of land in the North has triggered renewed interest and mobilizations by farmers there. In part, this is provoked by the skewed subsidies given to commercially powerful medium and large farms and the industrial food and agribusiness giants and the inability of young, aspiring farmers to get access to land or gain entry into the agricultural sector, a situation that was highlighted in a multicountry study by European Coordination Via Campesina and the Transnational Institute (Van der Ploeg, Franco, and Borras 2015). The specific context of ex-socialist countries in the North, meanwhile, has occasioned renewed debates about, and mobilizations around, land policies and agrarian movements, as described by Mamonova (2015) writing on Ukraine and Visser, Mamonova, and Spoor (2012) writing on Russia, but also in Western capitalist countries such as Canada, as studied by Magnan, Davidson, and Desmarais (2023).

Many contemporary agrarian movements have mobilized around production and trade-related issues, especially those having to do with genetically modified organisms (GMOs) and biotechnology, the corporate capture of agriculture, trade, the World Trade Organization, the construction of alternative agricultural and food systems, and food sovereignty. A few movements, like Brazil's Movement of Landless Workers, have managed to some extent to combine land-oriented mobilizations with productivist issues. North-based farmers' organizations have been particularly active on these issues. However, though mobilizations around international trade, biotechnology/GMOs, and the corporate capture of agriculture were particularly intense in the 1990s, and some movements were able to use these concerns to organize protests, in recent years, we have witnessed the relative waning of mass mobilizations and agitation over these matters. It remains to be seen whether the 2020–2021 farmers' protests in India will prove to have been outliers or a signal for a renewed focus on these issues (Baviskar and Levien 2021).

Further, some issues directly linked to agrarian matters should be part of agrarian movements' struggles but are not sufficiently and consistently addressed. The dominant framing of agrarian reform that movements inherited from the classical agrarian struggle is centrally about reforming farmland property relations—an "economic-production-centric" framework. We believe that this is a necessary but insufficient perspective in understanding land issues and land struggles today, because in many, if not most, societies land is also central to rural working people's social reproduction needs. In rural areas, besides access to farmland, land also means access to some or all of the following: home lots; kitchen gardens; community gardens; a community forest; river, lake, or spring water; a public playground for children; spiritual ground; a common grazing area; access routes for safer and shorter journeys; and so on. The lack, or the abrupt loss or diminution of, access to all or several of these have varying degrees of negative impact on a household's ability to reproduce their labor power and to secure the basic necessities of life: food, clothing, shelter, and care. If we take the view that the spheres of production and social reproduction are co-constitutive (Shah and Lerche 2020; Cousins, this volume), what happens to a household's degree of access to a range of land for social reproduction will impact its ability to perform or pursue tasks in the production sphere. If we draw a map of land access and the livelihoods of agrarian households from a production-centric perspective, using lines to show the access routes, we will get a minimalist view: a peasant home lot and farmland. If we draw a map of land access and livelihoods from a production and social reproduction perspective, we will see a complex, web-like picture that graphically shows the disastrous uprooting of agrarian livelihoods from their embeddedness in socio-agroecological zones. Viewing land from a combined production and social reproduction perspective entails understanding land access to mean "a range of access to a range of land" (Ribot and Peluso 2003; Borras et al. 2022).

In short, considering struggles for land from the economic-production-centric perspective reaffirms the importance of struggles for agrarian reform in the classical sense but, at the same time, shows that this framework is too narrow to capture the complexity of struggles for land in rural areas today. Far too many land issues in rural communities are not necessarily about, or not only about, farmland.

Rural Nonagricultural Land Struggles

The need for movements in the Global South and Global North that are rooted in the countryside but whose principal interests and demands are not agricultural is perhaps one of the most significant political developments on the rural front since the 1990s. This nonagricultural type of movement is likely to become even more important in the era of climate change, ongoing land grabs, and the large and growing size of the global relative surplus population. As capital widens its geographic target areas to secure cheap, if not free, natural resources and labor and to open new markets, it penetrates more spaces and integrates more people into capital accumulation processes. Nonagricultural forms and mechanisms of capitalist intrusion into the countryside have proliferated. The most prominent of these are big-conservation initiatives related to forest; fisheries; biodiversity and wildlife; and carbon-offsetting schemes, such as REDD+ (Reducing Emissions from Deforestation and Forest Degradation) and "blue carbon." These have been strengthened politically and logistically by mainstream climate change discourses and emerging mitigation and adaptation policies (Corbera 2012; Barbesgaard 2018). Many of these big-conservation projects are also heavily militarized (Verweijen and Marijnen 2018). Some conventional large-scale modernist development projects are being relabeled as climate change mitigation projects; they include hydropower mega projects, as well as the industrial tree plantations that have caused an unprecedented expansion in terms of forests cleared and areas planted since the 2000s (Hunsberger et al. 2017). There is a global trend of rezoning and reclassifying spaces, especially in areas deemed fragile due to climate change, and people are being either expelled from or refused access to such spaces, be they land, water, or forest.

These types of capitalist penetration into the countryside have triggered the recent rise of social-justice movements whose issues, demands, and struggles are not principally or strictly agricultural in character. For example, Indigenous Peoples mobilize to defend their territory; social-justice movements emerge out of anti-dam campaigns; mobilizations against industrial tree monocultures escalate; coastal communities fight enclosures being carried out in the name of climate change adaptation; and villagers establish movements to oppose various intrusive and extractive mining explorations in their communities. Mainstream climate change discourses continue to gain momentum (Ribot 2022), framing broad concepts such as "efficiency," "resilience" and "scarcity" from a neoclassical or new institutional economics perspective (Scoones et al. 2019). We are thus likely to witness more enclosures and expulsions, as well as political mobilizations and contentions, giving rise to increasing numbers of movements that encompass a variety of land struggles but are not strictly or classically agrarian in nature. The fusion of agrarian, environmental, and climate justice campaigns and movements is an outcome of these changes in the rural front (Yaşın 2022).

There are plenty more land issues in the countryside that are nonagricultural in character and not systematically addressed by contemporary agrarian movements, whether through direct organizing and mobilizing work or coalition work with other nonagrarian movements and political groups. These include land issues related to housing for many of the working classes living in village centers and small and medium-size towns, whose livelihoods are not directly linked to agrarian activities. These working classes include people who are often jobless, especially young people; street vendors; low-paid government employees, such as street cleaners; low-paid casual workers in the service sectors; artisans; artisanal miners; and mine and factory workers.

Many have houses or shanties installed in spaces where they have no security of tenure. These are the people included in Bernstein's definition of "classes of labour" and Shivji's "working people" (Bernstein 2006; Shivji 2017). Their access to a range of land is crucial for their social reproduction activities, and there is urgency to their need to struggle in an organized manner to secure or maintain access to the land they need. Many contemporary right-wing populists have taken up these issues and have gained support from rural communities as a result (Scoones et al. 2018; Edelman 2021). But these land issues are not agricultural in character, and they should not be subsumed into the agrarian movements' master frame of agrarian reform to build family farms. The numbers of the precarious working classes worldwide make clear that these issues are common and widespread; but in organized anticapitalist movements, they are also among the least attended to of all rural working people's issues. Contemporary agrarian movements have a role to play in terms of coalitional work with this sector, in addition to the other nonagricultural land struggles discussed earlier, such as environmental struggles.

Urban Agricultural Land Struggles

As urban and peri-urban sprawl has expanded exponentially, rural and urban issues have become ever more intertwined via agriculture and industry, labor flows, and food politics. And as that urban sprawl swallows up more agricultural lands, more rural and agricultural spaces are officially classified as urban (Jacobs 2018; Siebert 2020). The reverse also applies: urban populations spill over into the countryside, expanding suburban or peri-urban communities, such as Russian dachas (Mamonova and Sutherland 2015). As megacities become packed, we have seen unorganized, amorphous, self-provisioning initiatives by urban dwellers in cities in the Global South and Global North. They plant food crops in small patches of land wherever these can be found—on roadsides, along the edges of railways, in vacant lots—informally and often illegally. This runs parallel to, and at times overlaps with, more organized and consciously orchestrated types of urban agriculture, including those that are integrated in food sovereignty movements and other broad food-justice initiatives and alternative food networks (McClintock 2014). These emerging movements are small, scattered, often nebulous in form and spontaneous in character, but the initiatives themselves and the logic that has given birth to them are an interesting phenomenon that requires closer scholarly and political scrutiny, because it is possible that these groups will continue to grow, and that their political significance will increase. All of this has made the study of agrarian questions even more complex and, at the same time, the examination of the urban question more urgent.

Urban Nonagricultural Land Struggles

The final category is land-oriented urban mobilizations and movements that are not centered on agriculture. This type of struggle dates back to the emergence of mega cities.

Big capital and real estate companies, usually in collusion with governments, take over as much space as possible, displacing existing—usually working-class—neighborhoods in the process. Cities are often built with a history of class antagonism between capital and the working classes over the issue of space. As urban areas have expanded and the size of urban populations has overtaken that of rural populations on a global scale, struggles over urban land have become even more widespread. Neoliberal policies have privatized far more spaces than ever before, and land and nature that are important for their social reproduction needs—children's playgrounds, public parks, community forest, community gardens, access roads, and so on—have radically shrunk, taken over by big capital through various mechanisms, including abrupt and brutal coercive measures and the silent violence of gentrification. More recently, big capital and governments have also started to greenwash the urban spaces they take over, employing climate change narratives to justify their actions. For example, the urban coastal populations in many developing countries are either being expelled or threatened with expulsion from their communities by governments that use climate change adaptation discourses as a pretext. We have witnessed these trends worldwide, especially in recent decades, and we have also seen the rise of mobilizations by local communities fighting against such forms of enclosure.

These polarizing land issues are clearly widespread. They are quite different from the conventional notion in agrarian studies of the land question being resolved through agrarian reform (type I), but they are land questions, nevertheless. They have produced some of the fiercest class struggles by working people in urban communities.

In short, land politics has been transformed, and so have land struggles by working people. The old issues have persisted in new contexts, such as the ongoing land struggles in the context of agrarian reform centered on farmland in economic production, though these struggles are now fewer in number and politically weaker than their counterparts in the twentieth century. Meanwhile, new issues are framed in old contexts: for example, political contests around land-based climate change mitigation and adaptation measures are increasingly cast as land struggles that overlap with conventional agrarian struggles. Activists have struggled to find ideological and political routes to navigate the changes posing existential threats to the lives and livelihoods of working people, rural and urban, worldwide. But such transformations have also brought about unprecedented political opportunities for social-justice struggles.

Conclusion

The main message we wish to convey is that the land struggles of contemporary working people must be seen from a perspective that differs significantly from the classical view in agrarian studies based on debates around agriculture's contribution to capitalist industrial development. Working people today confront land questions around production and social reproduction, whether they are farmers doing part-time wage work or workers doing some farming or whether the main organization for this struggle is a workers' trade union, a farmers' movement, an urban-poor housing rights movement, an Indigenous People's community movement defending ancestral land, or a movement of urban gardeners demanding space. Inevitably, these struggles are dispersed and multisited, polycentric in political leadership and power, and multiscalar. Separately, few if any of these struggles (whether sectoral or spatial) are dramatic enough to represent a definitive political struggle of working people in general or any specific portion of the working class. Nevertheless, there is a potential for these disparate land struggles by various fractions of the working class to gain coherence at scale. If and when that potential is realized, even partially, this could become a significant social force and battlefront—not necessarily more dramatic or powerful than the twentieth-century peasant wars (here, we agree with Bernstein 2006), but just as profoundly important because of the global conjuncture it represents in history, as hinted at by Levien, Watts and Yan (2018). To reach this point, however, will be a serious challenge given the largely sectoral nature of many vibrant social-justice movement organizations today, the waning influence of the left-wing political parties that traditionally aggregated sectoral struggles into society-wide class struggles, and the intersectional character of antagonism around class and interlocking axes of social difference: race, ethnicity, caste, gender, generation, religion, and citizenship.

Acknowledgments

Significant parts of this chapter have been drawn from a chapter of our jointly authored book *Scholar-Activism and Land Struggles* (Borras and Franco 2023, chap. 2). JF received funding support from the Transnational Institute (TNI), Netherlands. JB received financial support from the Erasmus Professor Program of Erasmus University Rotterdam, Netherlands.

References

Adnan, Shapan. 2013. "Land Grabs and Primitive Accumulation in Deltaic Bangladesh: Interactions between Neoliberal Globalization, State Interventions, Power Relations and Peasant Resistance." *Journal of Peasant Studies* 40 (1): 87–128.

Akram-Lodhi, A. Haroon, Kristina Dietz, Bettina Engels, and Ben M. McKay. 2021. "An Introduction to the *Handbook of Critical Agrarian Studies*." In *Handbook of Critical Agrarian Studies*, edited by A. Haroon Akram-Lodhi, Kristina Dietz, Bettina Engels, and Ben M. McKay, 1–7. New York: Edward Elgar.

Andreas, Joel, Sunila S. Kale, Michael Levien, and Qian Forrest Zhang. 2020. "Rural Land Dispossession in China and India." *Journal of Peasant Studies* 47 (6): 1109–1142.

Arsel, Murat, and Bram Büscher. 2012. "Nature™ Inc.: Changes and Continuities in Neoliberal Conservation and Market-Based Environmental Policy." *Development and Change* 43 (1): 53–78.

Bachriadi, Dianto. 2010. "Between Discourse and Action: Agrarian Reform and Rural Social Movements in Indonesia Post-1965." PhD diss., University of Flinders.

Barbesgaard, Mads. 2018. "Blue Growth: Savior or Ocean Grabbing?" *Journal of Peasant Studies* 45 (1): 130–149.
Baviskar, Amita, and Michael Levien. 2021. "Farmers' Protests in India: Introduction to the JPS Forum." *Journal of Peasant Studies* 48 (7): 1341–1355.
Bernstein, Henry. 2006. "Is There an Agrarian Question in the 21st Century?" *Canadian Journal of Development Studies/Revue canadienne d'études du développement* 27 (4): 449–460.
Borras, Saturnino M. 2023. "Politically Engaged, Pluralist and Internationalist: Critical Agrarian Studies Today." *Journal of Peasant Studies* 50 (2): 449–489.
Borras, Saturnino M., Jr., and Jennifer C. Franco. 2013. "Global Land Grabbing and Political Reactions 'from Below.'" *Third World Quarterly* 34 (9): 1723–1747.
Borras, Saturnino M., and Jennifer C. Franco. 2023. *Scholar-Activism and Land Struggles.* Rugby, UK: Practical Action Publishing.
Borras, Saturnino M., Jr., Jennifer C. Franco, Doi Ra, T. Kramer, M. Kamoon, P. Phyu et al. 2022. "Rurally Rooted Cross-Border Migrant Workers from Myanmar, Covid-19, and Agrarian Movements." *Agriculture and Human Values* 39: 315–338.
Borras, Saturnino M., Jr., and Jennifer C. Franco. Forthcoming. "Land Rush." *Journal of Peasant Studies.* https://doi.org/10.1080/03066150.2024.2317961
Brockington, Dan, and Rosaleen Duffy, eds. 2011. *Capitalism and Conservation.* London: John Wiley & Sons.
Clapp, Jennifer. 2014. "Financialization, Distance and Global Food Politics." *Journal of Peasant Studies* 41 (5): 797–814.
Corbera, Esteve. 2012. "Problematizing REDD+ as an Experiment in Payments for Ecosystem Services." *Current Opinion in Environmental Sustainability* 4 (6): 612–619.
Corrado, Alessadra., Carlos de Castro, and Domenico Perrotta, eds. 2016. *Migration and Agriculture: Mobility and Change in the Mediterranean Area.* London: Routledge.
Deininger, Klaus. 1999. "Making Negotiated Land Reform Work: Initial Experience from Colombia, Brazil and South Africa." *World Development* 27 (4): 651–672.
Deininger, Klaus. 2011. "Challenges Posed by the New Wave of Farmland Investment." *Journal of Peasant Studies* 38 (2): 217–247.
Deininger, Klaus, and Hans Binswanger. 1999. "The Evolution of the World Bank's Land Policy: Principles, Experience, and Future Challenges." *World Bank Research Observer* 14 (2): 247–276.
Dunlap, Alexander. 2018. "Counterinsurgency for Wind Energy: The Bíi Hioxo Wind Park in Juchitán, Mexico." *Journal of Peasant Studies* 45 (3): 630–652.
Edelman, Marc. 2021. "Hollowed Out Heartland, USA: How Capital Sacrificed Communities and Paved the Way for Authoritarian Populism." *Journal of Rural Studies* 82: 505–517.
Edelman, Marc. 2024. *Peasant Politics of the Twenty-First Century.* Ithaca, NY: Cornell University Press.
Edelman, Marc, and Wendy Wolford. 2017. "Introduction: Critical Agrarian Studies in Theory and Practice." *Antipode* 49 (4): 959–976.
Fairbairn, Madeleine. 2014 "'Like Gold with Yield': Evolving Intersections between Farmland and Finance." *Journal of Peasant Studies* 41 (5): 777–795.
Fairbairn, Madeleine. 2020. *Fields of Gold: Financing the Global Land Rush.* Ithaca, NY: Cornell University Press.
Franco, Jennifer C. 2011. *Bound by Law: Filipino Rural Poor and the Search for Justice in a Plural-Legal Landscape.* Manila: Ateneo de Manila University Press.

Franco, Jennifer C. 2014. "Reclaiming Free Prior and Informed Consent (FPIC) in the Context of Global Land Grabs." Political brief. Amsterdam: Transnational Institute (TNI).

Franco, Jennifer C., and Saturnino M. Borras Jr. 2019. "Grey Areas in Green Grabbing: Subtle and Indirect Interconnections between Climate Change Politics and Land Grabs and Their Implications for Research." *Land Use Policy* 84: 192–199.

Franco, Jennifer C., and Saturnino M. Borras Jr. 2021. "The Global Climate of Land Politics." *Globalizations* 18 (7): 1277–1297.

Fraser, Alistair. 2019. "Land Grab/Data Grab: Precision Agriculture and Its New Horizons." *Journal of Peasant Studies* 46 (5): 893–912.

Grajales, Jacobo. 2011. "The Rifle and the Title: Paramilitary Violence, Land Grab and Land Control in Colombia." *Journal of Peasant Studies* 38 (4): 771–792.

Griffin, Keith, Azizur Rahman Khan, and Amy Ickowitz. 2002. "Poverty and Distribution of Land." *Journal of Agrarian Change* 2 (3): 279–330.

Gyapong, Adwoa Y. 2019. "Land Deals, Wage Labour, and Everyday Politics." *Land* 8 (6): 94.

Hall, Ruth, Marc Edelman, Saturnino M. Borras Jr., Ian Scoones, Ben White, and Wendy Wolford. 2015. "Resistance, Acquiescence or Incorporation? An Introduction to Land Grabbing and Political Reactions 'from Below.'" *Journal of Peasant Studies* 42 (3–4): 467–488.

Hall, Ruth, Ian Scoones, and Dzodzi Tsikata. 2017. "Plantations, Outgrowers and Commercial Farming in Africa: Agricultural Commercialisation and Implications for Agrarian Change." *Journal of Peasant Studies* 44 (3): 515–537.

Hunsberger, Carol, Esteve. Corbera, Saturnino M. Borras Jr., Jennifer C. Franco, Kevin Woods, CourtneyWork, et al. 2017. "Climate Change Mitigation, Land Grabbing and Conflict: Towards a Landscape-Based and Collaborative Action Research Agenda." *Canadian Journal of Development Studies/Revue canadienne d'études du développement* 38 (3): 305–324.

Isakson, S. Ryan. 2014. "Food and Finance: The Financial Transformation of Agro-Food Supply Chains." *Journal of Peasant Studies* 41 (5): 749–775.

Jacobs, R. 2018. "An Urban Proletariat with Peasant Characteristics: Land Occupations and Livestock Raising in South Africa." *Journal of Peasant Studies* 45 (5–6): 884–903.

Kay, Cristóbal. 2002. "Why East Asia Overtook Latin America: Agrarian Reform, Industrialization and Development." *Third World Quarterly* 23 (6): 1073–1102.

Kay, Cristóbal. 2009. "Development Strategies and Rural Development: Exploring Synergies, Eradicating Poverty." *Journal of Peasant Studies* 36 (1): 103–137.

Kepe, T., and Ruth Hall. 2018. "Land Redistribution in South Africa: Towards Decolonisation or Recolonisation?" *Politikon* 45 (1): 128–137.

Levien, Michael. 2018. *Dispossession without Development: Land Grabs in Neoliberal India.* New York: Oxford University Press.

Levien, Michael. 2021. "Coercive Rentier Networks: 'Land Mafias' in Neoliberal India." *Sociology of Development* 7 (2): 159–185.

Levien, Michael, Michael Watts, and Hairong Yan. 2018. "Agrarian Marxism." *Journal of Peasant Studies* 45 (5–6): 853–883.

Li, Tania. 2011. "Centering Labor in the Land Grab Debate." *Journal of Peasant Studies* 38 (2): 281–298.

Li, Tania M., and Pudjo Semedi. 2021. *Plantation Life: Corporate Occupation in Indonesia's Oil Palm Zone*. Durham, NC: Duke University Press.

Lund, Christian. 2021. *Nine-Tenths of the Law*. New Haven, CT: Yale University Press.

Magnan, André, Melissa Davidson, and Annette Aurélie Desmarais. 2023. "'They Call It Progress, but We Don't See It as Progress': Farm Consolidation and Land Concentration in Saskatchewan, Canada." *Agriculture and Human Values* 40 (1): 277–290.

Mamonova, Natalia. 2015. "Resistance or Adaptation? Ukrainian Peasants' Responses to Large-Scale Land Acquisitions." *Journal of Peasant Studies* 42 (3–4): 607–634.

Mamonova, Natalia, and Lee-Ann Sutherland. 2015. "Rural Gentrification in Russia: Renegotiating Identity, Alternative Food Production and Social Tensions in the Countryside." *Journal of Rural Studies* 42: 154–165.

McClintock, Nathan. 2014. "Radical, Reformist, and Garden-Variety Neoliberal: Coming to Terms with Urban Agriculture's Contradictions." *Local Environment* 19 (2): 147–171.

McKay, Ben M., Alberto Alonso-Fradejas, and Arturo Ezquerro-Cañete, eds. 2021. *Agrarian Extractivism in Latin America*. London: Routledge.

Moore, Barrington, Jr. 1967. *Social Origins of Dictatorship and Democracy: Lord and Peasant in the Modern World*. Harmondsworth, UK: Penguin.

Moyo, Sam 2011. "Three Decades of Agrarian Reform in Zimbabwe." *Journal of Peasant Studies* 38 (3): 493–531.

Moyo, Sam, and Paris Yeros, eds. 2005. *Reclaiming the Land: The Resurgence of Rural Movements in Africa, Asia and Latin America*. London: Zed.

Oya, Carlos. 2012. "Contract Farming in Sub-Saharan Africa: A Survey of Approaches, Debates and Issues." *Journal of Agrarian Change* 12 (1): 1–33.

Oya, Carlos. 2013. "The Land Rush and Classic Agrarian Questions of Capital and Labour: A Systematic Scoping Review of the Socioeconomic Impact of Land Grabs in Africa." *Third World Quarterly* 34 (9): 1532–1557.

Paprocki, Kasia. 2019. "All That Is Solid Melts into the Bay: Anticipatory Ruination and Climate Change Adaptation." *Antipode* 51 (1): 295–315.

Pattenden, Jonathan. 2023. "Progressive Politics and Populism: Classes of Labour and Rural–Urban Political Sociology—an Introduction to the Special Issue." In "Populism, Agrarian Movements, and Progressive Politics." Special issue, *Journal of Agrarian Change* 23 (1): 3–21.

Peluso, Nancy Lee, and Christian Lund. 2011. "New Frontiers of Land Control: Introduction." *Journal of Peasant Studies* 38 (4): 667–681.

Ra, Doi, and Khu Khu Ju. 2021. "'Nothing about Us, without Us': Reflections on the Challenges of Building Land in Our Hands, a National Land Network in Myanmar/Burma." *Journal of Peasant Studies* 48 (3): 497–516.

Ribot, Jesse. 2022. "Violent Silence: Framing out Social Causes of Climate-Related Crises." *Journal of Peasant Studies* 49 (4): 683–712.

Ribot, Jesse, and Nancy Peluso. 2003. "A Theory of Access." *Rural Sociology* 68 (2): 153–181.

Rosset, Peter. 2013. "Grassroots Voices: Re-thinking Agrarian Reform, Land and Territory in La Via Campesina." *Journal of Peasant Studies* 40 (4): 721–775.

Scoones, Ian, ed. 2010. *Zimbabwe's Land Reform: Myths and Realities*. London: James Currey.

Scoones, Ian. 2021. "Pastoralists and Peasants: Perspectives on Agrarian Change." *Journal of Peasant Studies* 48 (1): 1–47.

Scoones, Ian, Marc Edelman, Saturnino M. Borras Jr., Ruth Hall, Wendy Wolford, and Ben White. 2018. "Emancipatory Rural Politics: Confronting Authoritarian Populism." *Journal of Peasant Studies* 45 (1): 1–20.

Scoones, Ian, Rebecca Smalley, Ruth Hall, and Dzodzi Tsikata. 2019. "Narratives of Scarcity: Framing the Global Land Rush." *Geoforum* 101: 231–241.

Shah, Alpa, and Jens Lerche. 2020. "Migration and the Invisible Economies of Care: Production, Social Reproduction and Seasonal Migrant Labour in India." *Transactions of the Institute of British Geographers* 45 (4): 719–734.

Shivji, Issa. 2017. "The Concept of 'Working People.'" *Agrarian South: Journal of Political Economy* 6 (1): 1–13.

Siebert, Anne. 2020. "Transforming Urban Food Systems in South Africa: Unfolding Food Sovereignty in the City." *Journal of Peasant Studies* 47 (2): 401–419.

Sud, Nikita. 2014. "The Men in the Middle: A Missing Dimension in Global Land Deals." *Journal of Peasant Studies* 41 (4): 593–612.

Torres Contreras, Gerardo A. 2021. "Twenty-Five Years under the Wind Turbines in La Venta, Mexico: Social Difference, Land Control and Agrarian Change." *Journal of Peasant Studies* 49 (4): 865–883.

van der Ploeg, Jan Douwe, Jennifer C. Franco, and Saturnino M. Borras Jr. 2015. "Land Concentration and Land Grabbing in Europe: A Preliminary Analysis." *Canadian Journal of Development Studies* 36 (2): 147–162.

Verweijen, Judith, and Ester Marijnen. 2018. "The Counterinsurgency/Conservation Nexus: Guerrilla Livelihoods and the Dynamics of Conflict and Violence in the Virunga National Park, Democratic Republic of the Congo." *Journal of Peasant Studies* 45 (2): 300–320.

Visser, Oane, Natalia Mamonova, and Max Spoor. 2012. "Oligarchs, Megafarms and Land Reserves: Understanding Land Grabbing in Russia." *Journal of Peasant Studies* 39 (3–4): 899–931.

Wolf, Eric. 1969. *Peasant Wars of the Twentieth Century*. Norman: University of Oklahoma Press

Wolford, Wendy. 2010. *This Land Is Ours Now: Social Mobilization, and the Meanings of Land in Brazil*. Durham, NC: Duke University Press.

Wolford, Wendy. 2021. "The Plantationocene: A Lusotropical Contribution to the Theory." *Annals of the American Association of Geographers* 111 (6): 1622–1639.

Wolford, Wendy, Saturnino M. Borras Jr., Ruth Hall, Ian Scoones, and Ben White. 2013. "Governing Global Land Deals: The Role of the State in the Rush for Land." *Development and Change* 44 (2): 189–210.

World Bank. 2007. *World Development Report 2008: Agriculture for Development*. Washington, DC: World Bank.

Yaşın, Zehra Taşdemir. 2022. "The Environmentalization of the Agrarian Question and the Agrarianization of the Climate Justice Movement." *Journal of Peasant Studies* 49 (7): 1355–1386.

Zoomers, Annelies. 2010. "Globalisation and the Foreignisation of Space: Seven Processes Driving the Current Global Land Grab." *Journal of Peasant Studies* 37 (2): 429–447.

Index

For the benefit of digital users, indexed terms that span two pages (e.g., 52–53) may, on occasion, appear on only one of those pages.

Tables and figures are indicated by *t* and *f* following the page number